LIBERTY, EQUALITY, POWER

A HISTORY OF THE AMERICAN PEOPLE

Volume 1: To 1877

Enhanced Seventh Edition

John M. Murrin
Princeton University, Emeritus

Pekka Hämäläinen
University of Oxford

Paul E. Johnson
University of South Carolina, Emeritus

Denver Brunsman
George Washington University

James M. McPherson
Princeton University, Emeritus

Alice Fahs
University of California, Irvine, Emeritus

Gary Gerstle
University of Cambridge

Emily S. Rosenberg
University of California, Irvine, Emeritus

Norman L. Rosenberg
Macalester College, Emeritus

Australia • Brazil • Mexico • Singapore • United Kingdom • United States

Liberty, Equality, Power: A History of the American People, Volume 1: To 1877, **Enhanced Seventh Edition**

John M. Murrin, Pekka Hämäläinen, Paul E. Johnson, Denver Brunsman, James M. McPherson, Alice Fahs, Gary Gerstle, Emily S. Rosenberg, and Norman L. Rosenberg

Product Manager: Joseph Potvin

Product Assistant: Haley Gaudreau

Marketing Manager: Valerie Hartman

Content Manager: Claire Branman

Senior IP Analyst: Alexandra Ricciardi

IP Project Manager: Kelli Besse

Production Service/Compositor: SPi Global

Text Designer: Diane Beaseley

Cover Designer: Sarah Cole

Cover Image: Thomas Hart Benton, American (1889–1975). Palisades, ca. 1919-1924, series: American Historical Epic. Oil on canvas, mounted on aluminum honeycomb panel, 66 1/8 × 72 inches (168 × 182.9 cm). The Nelson-Atkins Museum of Art, Kansas City, Missouri. Bequest of the artist, F75-21/2. Photo courtesy Nelson-Atkins Media Services/Jamison Miller. Art © T.H. Benton and R.P. Benton Testamentary Trusts/UMB Bank Trustee/Licensed by VAGA, New York, NY

© 2020, 2016, 2012 Cengage Learning, Inc.

Unless otherwise noted, all content is © Cengage

ALL RIGHTS RESERVED. No part of this work covered by the copyright herein may be reproduced or distributed in any form or by any means, except as permitted by U.S. copyright law, without the prior written permission of the copyright owner.

For product information and technology assistance, contact us at **Cengage Customer & Sales Support, 1-800-354-9706** or **support.cengage.com**.

For permission to use material from this text or product, submit all requests online at **www.cengage.com/permissions**.

Library of Congress Control Number: 2018951021

Student Edition:
ISBN: 978-0-357-02231-3

Loose-leaf Edition:
ISBN: 978-0-357-02075-3

Cengage
20 Channel Center Street
Boston, MA 02210
USA

Cengage is a leading provider of customized learning solutions with employees residing in nearly 40 different countries and sales in more than 125 countries around the world. Find your local representative at **www.cengage.com**.

Cengage products are represented in Canada by Nelson Education, Ltd.

To learn more about Cengage platforms and services, register or access your online learning solution, or purchase materials for your course, visit **www.cengage.com**.

Printed in the United States of America
Print Number: 01   Print Year: 2018

About the Authors

JOHN M. MURRIN
Princeton University, Emeritus

John M. Murrin studies American colonial and revolutionary history and the early republic. He has edited one multivolume series and five books, including two essay collections, *Colonial America: Essays in Politics and Social Development*, Sixth Edition (2011), and *Saints and Revolutionaries: Essays in Early American History* (1984). His own essay topics range from ethnic tensions, the early history of trial by jury, the emergence of the legal profession, the Salem witch trials, and the political culture of the colonies and the new nation to the rise of professional baseball and college football in the 19th century. He served as president of the Society for Historians of the Early American Republic in 1998–1999.

PEKKA HÄMÄLÄINEN
University of Oxford

Pekka Hämäläinen is the Rhodes Professor of American History at the University of Oxford. A specialist in early American, Native American, borderlands, and environmental history, he is the author of *The Comanche Empire* (2008), which won multiple awards, including the Bancroft Prize, the Merle Curti Award, the Norris and Hundley Award, the William P. Clements Prize, and the Caughey Western History Association Prize. His writings have appeared in the *American Historical Review*; the *Journal of American History*; *History and Theory*; the *William and Mary Quarterly*; and the *Western Historical Quarterly*. He is currently working on a project on nomadic empires in world history, which is funded by the European Research Council. His new book, *Iktómi's People: The Lakota Age in America*, will be published by Yale University Press in 2019.

PAUL E. JOHNSON
University of South Carolina, Distinguished Professor Emeritus

A specialist in early national social and cultural history, Paul E. Johnson is the author of *The Early American Republic, 1789–1829* (2006); *Sam Patch, the Famous Jumper* (2003); and *A Shopkeeper's Millennium: Society and Revivals in Rochester, New York, 1815–1837*, 25th Anniversary Edition (2004). He is coauthor (with Sean Wilentz) of *The Kingdom of Matthias: Sex and Salvation in 19th-Century America* (1994) and editor of *African-American Christianity: Essays in History* (1994). He has been awarded the Merle Curti Award of the Organization of American Historians (1980), the Richard P. McCormick Prize of the New Jersey Historical Association (1989), and fellowships from the National Endowment for the Humanities (1985–1986), the John Simon Guggenheim Foundation (1995), the Gilder Lehrman Institute (2001), and the National Endowment for the Humanities (2006–2007).

DENVER BRUNSMAN
George Washington University

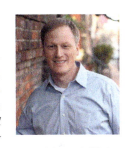

Denver Brunsman writes on the politics and social history of the American Revolution, the early American republic, and the British Atlantic world. His book, *The Evil Necessity: British Naval Impressment in the Eighteenth-Century Atlantic World* (2013), received the Walker Cowen Memorial Prize for an outstanding work in 18th-century studies in the Americas and Atlantic world. He is also a coauthor of *Leading Change: George Washington and Establishing the Presidency* (2017) and an editor of *The American Revolution Reader* (2013) and *Colonial America: Essays in Politics and Social Development*, Sixth Edition (2011), among other works. The recipient of numerous teaching awards, he was inducted into the George Washington University Academy of Distinguished Teachers in 2016.

JAMES M. MCPHERSON
Princeton University, Emeritus

James M. McPherson is a distinguished Civil War historian and was president of the American Historical Association in 2003. He won the 1989 Pulitzer Prize for his book *Battle Cry of Freedom: The Civil War Era*. His other publications include *Marching Toward Freedom: Blacks in the Civil War*, Second Edition (1991); *Ordeal by Fire: The Civil War and Reconstruction*, Third Edition (2001); *Abraham Lincoln and the Second American Revolution* (1991);

For Cause and Comrades: Why Men Fought in the Civil War which won the Lincoln Prize in 1998; *Crossroads of Freedom: Antietam* (2002); and *Tried by War: Abraham Lincoln as Commander in Chief* (2008), which won the Lincoln Prize for 2009.

ALICE FAHS
University of California, Irvine, Emeritus

Alice Fahs is a specialist in American cultural history of the 19th and 20th centuries. Her 2001 *The Imagined Civil War: Popular Literature of the North and South, 1861–1865* was a finalist in 2002 for the Lincoln Prize. Together with Joan Waugh, she published the edited collection *The Memory of the Civil War in American Culture* in 2004; she also edited Louisa May Alcott's *Hospital Sketches* (2004), an account of Alcott's nursing experiences during the Civil War first published in 1863. Her most recent book is *Out on Assignment: Newspaper Women and the Making of Modern Public Space* (2011). Her honors include an American Council of Learned Societies Fellowship and a Gilder Lehrman Fellowship, as well as fellowships from the American Antiquarian Society, the Newberry Library, and the Huntington Library.

GARY GERSTLE
University of Cambridge

Gary Gerstle is the Paul Mellon Professor of American History at the University of Cambridge. He previously taught at Princeton University, the Catholic University of America, the University of Maryland, and Vanderbilt University. A historian of the 20th-century United States, he is the author, coauthor, and coeditor of eight books and the author of nearly 40 articles. His books include *Working-Class Americanism: The Politics of Labor in a Textile City, 1914–1960* (1989); *American Crucible: Race and Nation in the Twentieth Century* (2001 winner of the Saloutos Prize for outstanding work in immigration and ethnic history (republished in 2017 with a new chapter on race and nation in the age of Obama); *The Rise and Fall of the New Deal Order, 1930–1980* (1989); *Ruling America: Wealth and Power in a Democracy* (2005); and *Liberty and Coercion: The Paradox of American Government from the Founding to the Present*, winner of the Organization of American Historians' Hawley Prize for the best book in American political history. He is the creator, writer, and narrator of a four-part radio series, "America: Laboratory of Democracy," that aired on BBC World Service in 2017 and on multiple National Public Radio stations in 2018. Gerstle has served on the board of editors of the *Journal of American History*, the *American Historical Review*, *Modern American History*, and *Past and Present*. He is a Fellow of the British Academy and a member of the Society of American Historians. Gerstle's other honors include a National Endowment for the Humanities Fellowship, a John Simon Guggenheim Memorial Fellowship, the Harmsworth Visiting Professorship of American History at the University of Oxford, and the 2013 Jeffrey Nordhaus Award for Excellence in Undergraduate Teaching at Vanderbilt University.

EMILY S. ROSENBERG
University of California, Irvine, Emeritus

Emily S. Rosenberg specializes in U.S. international relations in the 20th century and is the author of *Spreading the American Dream: American Economic and Cultural Expansion, 1890–1945* (1982); *Financial Missionaries to the World: The Politics and Culture of Dollar Diplomacy* (1999), which won the Ferrell Book Award; *A Date Which Will Live: Pearl Harbor in American Memory* (2004); and *Transnational Currents in a Shrinking World, 1870–1945* (2014). Her other publications include (with Norman L. Rosenberg) *In Our Times: America Since 1945*, Seventh Edition (2003), and numerous articles dealing with foreign relations in the context of international finance, American culture, and gender ideology. She has served on the board of the Organization of American Historians, on the board of editors of the *American Historical Review*, and as president of the Society for Historians of American Foreign Relations.

NORMAN L. ROSENBERG
Macalester College, Emeritus

Norman L. Rosenberg is DeWitt Wallace Professor of History and Legal Studies. His books include *Protecting the "Best Men": An Interpretive History of the Law of Libel* (1990) and (with Emily S. Rosenberg) *In Our Times: America Since 1945*, Seventh Edition (2003). He has published articles in the *Rutgers Law Review*, *UCLA Law Review*, *Constitutional Commentary*, *Law & History Review*, and many other journals and law-related anthologies.

Brief Contents

1. WHEN OLD WORLDS COLLIDE: ENCOUNTERS IN THE ATLANTIC WORLD TO 1600   2
2. COLONIZATION IN NORTH AMERICA, 1600–1680   36
3. EMPIRES, INDIANS, AND THE STRUGGLE FOR POWER IN NORTH AMERICA, 1670–1720   68
4. PROVINCIAL AMERICA AND THE STRUGGLE FOR A CONTINENT, 1720–1763   100
5. REFORM, RESISTANCE, REVOLUTION, 1763–1776   134
6. THE REVOLUTIONARY REPUBLIC, 1776–1789   166
7. COMPLETING THE REVOLUTION, 1789–1815   200
8. NORTHERN TRANSFORMATIONS, 1790–1850   230
9. THE OLD SOUTH, 1790–1850   254
10. TOWARD AN AMERICAN CULTURE, 1815–1850   278
11. WHIGS AND DEMOCRATS, 1815–1840   302
12. ANTEBELLUM REFORM, 1820–1860   330
13. MANIFEST DESTINY: AN EMPIRE FOR LIBERTY—OR SLAVERY? 1845–1860   352
14. THE GATHERING TEMPEST, 1853–1860   376
15. SECESSION AND CIVIL WAR, 1860–1862   406
16. A NEW BIRTH OF FREEDOM, 1862–1865   436
17. RECONSTRUCTION, 1863–1877   468

Contents in Detail

MAPS AND FEATURES — xvii

TO THE STUDENT — xxi

PREFACE — xxv

1 WHEN OLD WORLDS COLLIDE: ENCOUNTERS IN THE ATLANTIC WORLD TO 1600 — 2

1-1 Peoples in Motion 4
- 1-1a From Beringia to the Americas 4
- 1-1b The Great Extinction and the Rise of Agriculture 4

■ CHRONOLOGY 5

1-2 The Emergence of Complex Societies in the Americas 5
- 1-2a The Andes: Cycles of Complex Cultures 6
- 1-2b Inca Civilization 7
- 1-2c Mesoamerica: Cycles of Complex Cultures 7
- 1-2d The Aztecs and Tenochtitlán 10

1-3 Agricultural Take-Off in North America 10
- 1-3a Urban Cultures of the Southwest 11
- 1-3b North American Mound Builders 12
- 1-3c North America in 1491 14
- 1-3d The Norse Connection 15

1-4 Europe and the World by the 15th Century 15
- 1-4a China: The Rejection of Overseas Expansion 15
- 1-4b Christian Europe Challenges Islam 16
- 1-4c The Legacy of the Crusades 18
- 1-4d The Unlikely Pioneer: Portugal 18
- 1-4e Africa, Colonies, and the Slave Trade 19
- 1-4f Portugal's Asian Empire 21
- 1-4g Early Lessons 21

1-5 Spain, Columbus, and the Americas 22
- 1-5a Columbus 22
- 1-5b Spain and the Caribbean 23

■ INTERPRETING THE VISUAL PAST   How to Understand Columbus's Landing? 24

1-6 Conquest and Catastrophe 25
- 1-6a The Conquest of Mexico and Peru 25
- 1-6b North American Conquistadores and Missionaries 26
- 1-6c The Spanish Empire and Demographic Catastrophe 28

■ WHAT THEY SAID   Two Spanish Scholars Debate Indian Slavery 29

- 1-6d Brazil 31

1-7 Global Colossus, Global Economy 31

■ HISTORY THROUGH FILM   *Even the Rain* (2010) 32

1-8 Explanations: Patterns of Conquest, Submission, and Resistance 32

Conclusion 34

Chapter Review 34

2 COLONIZATION IN NORTH AMERICA, 1600–1680 — 36

2-1 The Protestant Reformation and the Challenge to Spain 38

2-2 New France and the Iroquois League 38
- 2-2a Early French Explorers 38
- 2-2b Missions and Furs 38

■ CHRONOLOGY 39

■ INTERPRETING THE VISUAL PAST   FRENCH-HURON ALLIANCE TAKES SHAPE 40

- 2-2c New France under Louis XIV 41

2-3 New Netherland 41
- 2-3a The East and West India Companies 42
- 2-3b New Netherland as a Pluralistic Society 42

■ HISTORY THROUGH FILM   *Black Robe* (1991) 43

- 2-3c English Encroachments 44

2-4 English Colonization Begins 44
- 2-4a The English Reformation 45
- 2-4b From Plundering to Colonization 45
- 2-4c The Swarming of the English 46

2-5 The Chesapeake and West Indian Colonies 46
- 2-5a The Jamestown Disaster 47
- 2-5b Reorganization, Reform, and Crisis 47
- 2-5c Tobacco, Servants, and Survival 48
- 2-5d The Collapse of Tsenacommacah 49
- 2-5e Maryland 49
- 2-5f Chesapeake Family Life 50
- 2-5g The West Indies and the Transition to Slavery 52
- 2-5h The Rise of Slavery in North America 53

2-6 The New England Colonies 54
- 2-6a The Pilgrims and Plymouth 54
- 2-6b Massachusetts Bay 54
- 2-6c Covenant Theology 54
- ■ WHAT THEY SAID   English Colonists and Huron Indians Enter New Worlds 55
- 2-6d Puritan Family Life 56
- 2-6e Conversion, Dissent, and Expansion 56
- 2-6f Puritan Indian Missions 57
- 2-6g Congregations, Towns, and Colony Governments 57
- 2-6h Infant Baptism and New Dissent 59

2-7 From Civil War to the First Restoration Colonies 59
- 2-7a Carolina, Harrington, and the Aristocratic Ideal 60
- 2-7b New York: An Experiment in Absolutism 61

2-8 Brotherly Love: The Quakers and America 61
- 2-8a Quaker Beliefs 62
- 2-8b Quaker Families 64
- 2-8c West New Jersey 64
- 2-8d Pennsylvania 65

Conclusion 66

Chapter Review 66

3 EMPIRES, INDIANS, AND THE STRUGGLE FOR POWER IN NORTH AMERICA, 1670–1720   68

3-1 Indians, Settlers, Upheaval: The Cataclysmic 1670s and 1680s 70
- ■ CHRONOLOGY 70
- 3-1a The Pueblo Revolt 71
- ■ WHAT THEY SAID   Why Did the Pueblo Indians Revolt against the Spaniards in 1680? 72
- 3-1b Metacom's War 73
- 3-1c Virginia's Indian War 74
- 3-1d Bacon's Rebellion 75
- 3-1e New France Besieged 76

3-2 Converging Empires: Spain and France in North America 78
- 3-2a Spanish New Mexico 78
- 3-2b French and Indians on the Middle Ground 78
- 3-2c French Canada in Transition 80
- 3-2d French Illinois, French Louisiana, and Spanish Texas 80

3-3 The Rise of England's Atlantic Empire 82
- 3-3a The Foundations of Empire: Mercantilism and the Navigation Acts 83
- 3-3b Crisis in England and the Expansion of Royal Authority 83
- 3-3c The Dominion of New England 84
- 3-3d The Glorious Revolution in England and America 85
- 3-3e The Salem Witch Trials 86
- 3-3f The New Imperial Order 87
- ■ HISTORY THROUGH FILM   Three Sovereigns for Sarah (1986) 88

3-4 An Empire of Settlement: The Growth of British America 88
- 3-4a The Atlantic Prism and the Spectrum of Settlement 89
- 3-4b The Engine of British Expansion: The Colonial Household 90
- 3-4c The Voluntaristic Ethic, Public Life, and War 93
- 3-4d Spanish and French Counterpoints 93
- 3-4e Queen Anne's War and the Yamasee War 93
- 3-4f The Colonial Rim and the Indigenous Interior 95
- ■ INTERPRETING THE VISUAL PAST   A Native American Representation of the Colonial Southeast 96

Conclusion 97

Chapter Review 98

4 PROVINCIAL AMERICA AND THE STRUGGLE FOR A CONTINENT, 1720–1763   100

4-1 Expansion versus Anglicization 102
- 4-1a Threats to Householder Autonomy 102
- ■ CHRONOLOGY 103
- 4-1b Anglicizing the Role of Women 103

4-2 Expansion, Immigration, and Regional Differentiation 104
- 4-2a Emergence of the Old South 104
- 4-2b The Mid-Atlantic Colonies: The "Best Poor Man's Country" 106
- 4-2c The Backcountry 107

4-2d New England: A Faltering Economy and Paper Money   107

4-3 Anglicizing Provincial America   108
4-3a The World of Print   108
4-3b The Enlightenment in America   109
4-3c Women and the Consumer Revolution   111
4-3d Georgia: The Failure of an Enlightenment Utopia   111

■ INTERPRETING THE VISUAL PAST   A Display of Consumer Goods   112

4-4 The Great Awakening   113
4-4a Origins of the Revivals   113
4-4b Whitefield Launches the Transatlantic Revival   113
4-4c Disruptions   114
4-4d Long-Term Consequences of the Revivals   114
4-4e New Colleges   115
4-4f The Denominational Realignment   115

■ WHAT THEY SAID   The Controversy over Religious Revivals   116

4-5 Political Culture in the Colonies   116
4-5a The Rise of the Assembly and the Governor   117
4-5b Court and Country Politics   117

4-6 The Renewal of Imperial Conflict   118
4-6a Challenges to French Power   118
4-6b The Danger of Slave Revolts and War with Spain   119
4-6c France versus Britain: King George's War   120
4-6d The Impending Storm   121

4-7 The War for North America   122
4-7a The Albany Congress and the Onset of War   123
4-7b Britain's Years of Defeat   124
4-7c A World War   125

■ HISTORY THROUGH FILM   *The War That Made America* (2006)   126

4-7d Imperial Tensions: From Loudoun to Pitt   127
4-7e The Years of British Victory   128
4-7f The Peace of Paris   130

Conclusion   130

Chapter Review   132

5 REFORM, RESISTANCE, REVOLUTION, 1763–1776   134

5-1 Imperial Reform   136
5-1a Impetus for Reform   136
5-1b Indian Policy and Pontiac's War   136

■ CHRONOLOGY   137

5-1c The Sugar Act   137
5-1d The Currency Act and the Quartering Act   139
5-1e The Stamp Act   139

5-2 The Stamp Act Crisis   140
5-2a Nullification   140
5-2b Repeal   141

5-3 The Townshend Crisis   143
5-3a The Townshend Program   143
5-3b Resistance: The Politics of Escalation   143

■ INTERPRETING THE VISUAL PAST   A British Cartoon of the Stamp Act Repeal   144

5-3c The Wilkes Crisis   145
5-3d The Boston Massacre   145

■ HISTORY THROUGH FILM   *John Adams* (2008)   147

5-3e Partial Repeal   148
5-3f Disaffection   148

5-4 Internal Cleavages: The Contagion of Liberty   149
5-4a Divided Loyalties   149
5-4b Urban and Rural Discontent   150
5-4c Slaves and Women   152

5-5 The Last Imperial Crisis   153
5-5a The Tea Crisis   153
5-5b Britain's Response: The Coercive Acts   155
5-5c The Radical Explosion   156
5-5d The First Continental Congress   157
5-5e Toward War   157

5-6 The Improvised War   158
5-6a The Second Continental Congress   159
5-6b War and Legitimacy, 1775–1776   160
5-6c Independence   160

■ WHAT THEY SAID   Contrasting Views of American Independence   162

Conclusion   163

Chapter Review   164

6 THE REVOLUTIONARY REPUBLIC, 1776–1789   166

6-1 Hearts and Minds: The Northern War, 1776–1777   168
6-1a The British Offensive   168

■ CHRONOLOGY   169

6-1b The Trenton-Princeton Campaign   169

6-2 The Campaigns of 1777 and Foreign Intervention   170
6-2a The Loss of Philadelphia   170
6-2b Saratoga   170
6-2c French Intervention   171
6-2d Spanish Expansion and Intervention   172

■ HISTORY THROUGH FILM   *Hamilton's America* (2016)   173

6-3 The Crisis of the Revolution, 1778–1783   173
6-3a Loyalists, Black and White   174

6-3b The Indian Struggle for Unity and Survival 175
6-3c Violence and Attrition 175
6-3d Mutiny and Reform 178

6-4 The British Offensive in the South 179
6-4a Britain's Southern Strategy 179
6-4b The Partisan War 180
6-4c From the Ravaging of Virginia to Yorktown and Peace 182

■ INTERPRETING THE VISUAL PAST A French View of Yorktown 183

6-5 A Revolutionary Society 185
6-5a Religious Transformations 185
6-5b The First Emancipation 186
6-5c The Challenge to Patriarchy 186
6-5d Western Expansion, Discontent, and Conflict with Indians 187
6-5e The Northwest Ordinance 189

6-6 American Constitutionalism 189
6-6a John Adams and the Separation of Powers 189
6-6b Early State Constitutions 190
6-6c Massachusetts Redefines Constitutionalism 190
6-6d Articles of Confederation 192

6-7 The Constitution: A More Perfect Union 192
6-7a Commerce, Debt, and Shays's Rebellion 192
6-7b Cosmopolitans versus Localists 193
6-7c The Philadelphia Convention 194

■ WHAT THEY SAID Virginians Debate the Constitution 195
6-7d Ratification 196

Conclusion 197
Chapter Review 197

---

7 COMPLETING THE REVOLUTION, 1789–1815 200

7-1 Establishing the National Government 202
7-1a The "Republican Court" 202
7-1b The First Congress 202

■ CHRONOLOGY 203

7-1c Hamiltonian Economics: The National Debt 203
7-1d Hamiltonian Economics: The Bank and the Excise 204
7-1e The Rise of Jeffersonian Opposition 204

■ WHAT THEY SAID Washington, Jefferson, and the Image of the President 205

7-2 The American Republic in a Changing World 206
7-2a New Spain and the Bourbon Reforms 206
7-2b Americans and the French Revolution 207
7-2c Citizen Genêt 208
7-2d Western Troubles 208
7-2e The Collapse of the Miami Confederacy 208
7-2f The Jay Treaty 209
7-2g The Election of 1796 211
7-2h Troubles with France, 1796–1800 211
7-2i The Crisis at Home, 1798–1800 212
7-2j The Election of 1800 213

7-3 The Jeffersonians in Power 213
7-3a The Republican Program 213
7-3b The Jeffersonians and the Courts 215
7-3c Justice Marshall's Court 216
7-3d Louisiana 216
7-3e Lewis and Clark 217

7-4 The Republic and the Napoleonic Wars, 1803–1815 218
7-4a The Dilemmas of Neutrality 219
7-4b Trouble on the High Seas 219
7-4c Embargo 219

■ INTERPRETING THE VISUAL PAST Capturing the World: The Illustrations of the Journals of Lewis and Clark 220

7-4d The Road to War 221
7-4e The War Hawk Congress, 1811–1812 221
7-4f American Strategy in 1812 222
7-4g The Rise of Tecumseh 222
7-4h The War with Canada, 1812–1813 223
7-4i Tecumseh's Last Stand 223
7-4j The British Offensive, 1814 223
7-4k The Hartford Convention 226
7-4l The Treaty of Ghent 226

■ HISTORY THROUGH FILM *Master and Commander: The Far Side of the World* (2003) 227

Conclusion 228
CHAPTER REVIEW 229

---

8 NORTHERN TRANSFORMATIONS, 1790–1850 230

8-1 Postcolonial Society, 1790–1815 232
8-1a Farms 232

■ CHRONOLOGY 233

8-1b Neighbors 233
8-1c Standards of Living 234
8-1d Inheritance 235
8-1e The Seaport Cities 235

■ HISTORY THROUGH FILM *A Midwife's Tale* (1998) 237

8-2 The Northwest: From Backcountry to Frontier 238
8-2a The Backcountry, 1790–1815 238
8-2b Settlement 238

8-3 Transportation Revolution, 1815–1850 239
8-3a Transportation in 1815 239
8-3b Internal Improvements 240
8-3c Time, Money, and New Markets 240

■ INTERPRETING THE VISUAL PAST Transportation before the Market Revolution 241

8-4 Northeastern Farms, 1815–1850   242
- 8-4a The New England Livestock Economy   242
- 8-4b New Farm Households   245
- 8-4c The Landscape of Privacy   246

8-5 The Northwest in Transition   247
- 8-5a Southern Settlers   247
- 8-5b Northern Farmers   247

8-6 The Beginnings of the Industrial Revolution   248
- 8-6a Factory Towns: The Rhode Island System   248
- 8-6b Factory Towns: The Waltham-Lowell System   249
- 8-6c Cities   249
- 8-6d Metropolitan Industrialization   250

■ WHAT THEY SAID   The Lowell Mill Girls   251

Conclusion   252

Chapter Review   253

9 THE OLD SOUTH, 1790–1850   254

9-1 Old Farms: The Southeast   256
- 9-1a The Chesapeake, 1790–1820   256
- CHRONOLOGY   257
- 9-1b Flirting with Emancipation   257
- 9-1c The Lowcountry, 1790–1820   257

9-2 New Farms: The Rise of the Deep South   258
- 9-2a Slavery and Capitalism   258
- 9-2b The Interstate Slave Trade   260
- 9-2c Cotton and Slave Labor   260
- 9-2d Mastery as a Way of Life   263

9-3 The Southern Yeomanry   264

■ INTERPRETING THE VISUAL PAST   A View of Slavery as Benevolent   265

- 9-3a Yeomen and Planters   265
- 9-3b Yeoman Neighborhoods   266

9-4 Slave Culture   267
- 9-4a Slave Families and the Slave Trade   267
- 9-4b Slave Theology   269

■ WHAT THEY SAID   The Treatment of Slave Families   270

- 9-4c Religion and Revolt   271
- 9-4d Gabriel's Rebellion   271
- 9-4e Denmark Vesey   272
- 9-4f Nat Turner   272

9-5 A Southern Market Revolution?   273

■ HISTORY THROUGH FILM   *12 Years a Slave* (2013)   274

Conclusion   275

Chapter Review   276

10 TOWARD AN AMERICAN CULTURE, 1815–1850   278

10-1 The Democratization of Culture   280
- 10-1a A Revolution in Print   280
- CHRONOLOGY   281

10-2 The Northern Middle Class   281
- 10-2a A New Middle Class   281
- 10-2b The Evangelical Base   281
- 10-2c Domesticity   282

10-3 The Plain People of the North   283
- 10-3a The Rise of Democratic Sects   284
- 10-3b The Providential Worldview   285
- 10-3c Family and Society   286
- 10-3d The Emergence of Mormonism   287

10-4 A New Popular Culture   287
- 10-4a Blood Sports   287

■ HISTORY THROUGH FILM   *Gangs of New York* (2002)   288

- 10-4b Boxing   289
- 10-4c An American Theater   289

■ WHAT THEY SAID   A Fatal Prizefight, 1842   290

- 10-4d Minstrelsy   291
- 10-4e Novels and the Penny Press   291

■ INTERPRETING THE VISUAL PAST   The Actors' War: Forrest and Macready   292

10-5 Family, Church, and Neighborhood: The White South   294
- 10-5a The Beginnings of the Bible Belt   294
- 10-5b Slavery and Southern Evangelicals   294
- 10-5c Gender, Power, and the Evangelicals   295
- 10-5d Religious Conservatism   295
- 10-5e Pro-Slavery Christianity   296
- 10-5f The Mission to the Slaves   296

10-6 Race   297
- 10-6a Free Blacks   297
- 10-6b The Beginnings of Modern Racism   298

10-7 Citizenship   299

Conclusion   300

Chapter Review   301

11 WHIGS AND DEMOCRATS, 1815–1840   302

11-1 The American System   304
- 11-1a National Republicans   304
- CHRONOLOGY   305
- 11-1b Commerce and the Law   306

11-2 1819   307
- 11-2a The Argument over Missouri   307
- 11-2b The Missouri Compromise   308
- 11-2c The Panic of 1819   309

11-3 Republican Revival 309
- 11-3a Martin Van Buren Leads the Way 309
- 11-3b The Election of 1824 310
- 11-3c "A Corrupt Bargain" 311
- 11-3d Jacksonian Melodrama 311

11-4 Adams versus Jackson 312
- 11-4a Nationalism in an International Arena 312
- 11-4b Nationalism at Home 312
- 11-4c The Birth of the Democratic Party 313
- 11-4d The Election of 1828 313
- 11-4e A People's Inauguration 314
- 11-4f The Spoils System 314

11-5 Jacksonian Democracy and the South 315
- 11-5a Southerners and Indians 315
- 11-5b Indian Removal 316
- ■ WHAT THEY SAID   President Andrew Jackson and the Cherokee Nation Debate Indian Removal 317
- 11-5c Southerners and the Tariff 318
- 11-5d Nullification 319
- 11-5e The "Petticoat Wars" 319
- 11-5f The Fall of Calhoun 320
- 11-5g Petitions, the Gag Rule, and the Southern Mails 320

11-6 Jacksonian Democracy and the Market Revolution 321
- 11-6a The Second Bank of the United States 321
- ■ HISTORY THROUGH FILM   *Amistad* (1997) 322
- 11-6b The Bank War 322
- 11-6c The Beginnings of the Whig Party 323
- ■ INTERPRETING THE VISUAL PAST   King Andrew the First 324

11-7 The Second American Party System 325
- 11-7a "Martin Van Ruin" 325
- 11-7b The Election of 1840 326

Conclusion 328

Chapter Review 328

---

12 ANTEBELLUM REFORM, 1820–1860 330

12-1 The Politics of Progress 332
- 12-1a Markets and Governments 332
- ■ CHRONOLOGY 333
- 12-1b Banks, Roads, Canals 333

12-2 The Politics of Social Reform: Schools and Asylums 334
- 12-2a Public Schools 334
- 12-2b Ethnicity, Religion, and the Schools 335
- 12-2c Prisons 335
- 12-2d Asylums 337

12-3 The Politics of Alcohol 337
- 12-3a The Alcoholic Republic 338
- 12-3b Temperance Movement 338
- 12-3c The Origins of Prohibition 340
- 12-3d The Washingtonians 340
- 12-3e Ethnicity and Alcohol 341
- 12-3f The South and Social Reform 341

12-4 The Politics of Slavery and Race 342
- 12-4a Democratic Racism 342
- 12-4b Antislavery before 1830 342
- 12-4c Abolitionists 343
- ■ INTERPRETING THE VISUAL PAST   An Abolitionist View of Southern Society 344
- 12-4d Agitation 345

12-5 The Politics of Gender and Sex 346
- 12-5a Moral Reform 346
- 12-5b Women's Rights 347
- ■ HISTORY THROUGH FILM   *Not for Ourselves Alone* (1999) 348
- ■ WHAT THEY SAID   Making Fun of Women's Rights 349

Conclusion 350

Chapter Review 350

---

13 MANIFEST DESTINY: AN EMPIRE FOR LIBERTY—OR SLAVERY? 1845–1860 352
- ■ CHRONOLOGY 354

13-1 Growth as the American Way 354
- 13-1a Manifest Destiny and Slavery 354
- 13-1b The Expansionist Impulse 354
- 13-1c New Mexico and California 355
- ■ INTERPRETING THE VISUAL PAST   Manifest Destiny 356
- 13-1d The Oregon and California Trails 356
- 13-1e The Mormon Migration 357
- 13-1f The Republic of Texas 358
- 13-1g The Annexation Controversy 358
- 13-1h Acquisition of Texas and Oregon 359
- ■ HISTORY THROUGH FILM   *The Alamo* (1960) 360

13-2 The Mexican War 360
- 13-2a Military Campaigns of 1846 361
- 13-2b Military Campaigns of 1847 361
- 13-2c Antiwar Sentiment 363
- 13-2d The Wilmot Proviso 363

13-3 The Election of 1848 364
- 13-3a The Free Soil Party 364
- 13-3b The Gold Rush and California Statehood 365

13-4 The Compromise of 1850 366
- 13-4a The Senate Debates 367
- 13-4b Passage of the Compromise 367
- 13-4c The Fugitive Slave Law 367
- ■ WHAT THEY SAID   The Senate Debates the Compromise of 1850 368
- 13-4d The Slave-Catchers 369
- 13-4e Uncle Tom's Cabin 370

13-5 Filibustering 371
   13-5a Cuba 371
   13-5b The Gray-Eyed Man of Destiny 373
Conclusion 373
Chapter Review 374

14 THE GATHERING TEMPEST, 1853–1860 376

■ CHRONOLOGY 378

14-1 Kansas and the Rise of the Republican Party 378
   14-1a The Kansas-Nebraska Act 378
   14-1b Death of the Whig Party 379

14-2 Immigration and Nativism 380
   14-2a Immigrants in Politics 381
   14-2b The Rise of the Know-Nothings 382
   14-2c The Decline of Nativism 382

14-3 Violent Conflict in the 1850s 383
   14-3a Bleeding Kansas 383
   14-3b The Caning of Sumner 384

14-4 The Election of 1856 385
■ INTERPRETING THE VISUAL PAST The Caning of Sumner 386
   14-4a The Dred Scott Case 387
   14-4b The Lecompton Constitution 387

14-5 The Economy in the 1850s 389
   14-5a "The American System of Manufactures" 389
   14-5b The Southern Economy 390
   14-5c The Sovereignty of King Cotton 393
   14-5d Labor Conditions in the North 393
   14-5e The Panic of 1857 394
   14-5f Sectionalism and the Panic 395
   14-5g Free-Labor Ideology 395
   14-5h The Impending Crisis 397
   14-5i Southern Nonslaveholders 398

14-6 The Lincoln-Douglas Debates 399
   14-6a The Freeport Doctrine 400
■ HISTORY THROUGH FILM *Abe Lincoln in Illinois* (1940) 401
   14-6b John Brown at Harpers Ferry 401
Conclusion 402
■ WHAT THEY SAID Reactions to John Brown 403
Chapter Review 404

15 SECESSION AND CIVIL WAR, 1860–1862 406

■ CHRONOLOGY 408

15-1 The Election of 1860 408
   15-1a The Republicans Nominate Lincoln 408
   15-1b Southern Fears 409

15-2 The Lower South Secedes 410
   15-2a Northerners Affirm the Union 411
   15-2b Compromise Proposals 411
   15-2c Establishment of the Confederacy 413

15-3 The Fort Sumter Issue 413
■ WHAT THEY SAID Cornerstone of the Confederacy 414

15-4 Choosing Sides 416
   15-4a The Border States 416
   15-4b The Creation of West Virginia 418
   15-4c Indian Territory and the Southwest 418

15-5 The Balance Sheet of War 418
■ HISTORY THROUGH FILM *Glory* (1989) 419
   15-5a Strategy and Morale 419
   15-5b Mobilizing for War 420
   15-5c Weapons and Tactics 420
■ INTERPRETING THE VISUAL PAST The Soldier's Dream of Home 422
   15-5d Logistics 422
   15-5e Financing the War 423

15-6 Navies, the Blockade, and Foreign Relations 424
   15-6a King Cotton Diplomacy 424
   15-6b The *Trent* Affair 425
   15-6c The Confederate Navy 425
   15-6d The *Monitor* and the *Virginia* 425

15-7 Campaigns and Battles, 1861–1862 427
   15-7a The Battle of Bull Run 427
   15-7b Naval Operations 427
   15-7c Fort Henry and Fort Donelson 429
   15-7d The Battle of Shiloh 430
   15-7e The Virginia Theater 430
   15-7f The Seven Days' Battles 431

15-8 Confederate Counteroffensives 432
   15-8a The Second Battle of Bull Run 434
Conclusion 434
Chapter Review 434

16 A NEW BIRTH OF FREEDOM, 1862–1865 436

16-1 Slavery and the War 438
   16-1a The "Contrabands" 438
   16-1b The Border States 438
■ CHRONOLOGY 439
   16-1c The Decision for Emancipation 439
   16-1d New Calls for Troops 440
   16-1e The Battle of Antietam 440
■ INTERPRETING THE VISUAL PAST Photographs of the Dead at Antietam 441
   16-1f The Emancipation Proclamation 442

16-2 A Winter of Discontent 443
- 16-2a The Rise of the Copperheads 444
- 16-2b Economic Problems in the South 444
- 16-2c The Wartime Draft and Class Tensions 445
- 16-2d A Poor Man's Fight? 446

16-3 Blueprint for Modern America 447
- 16-3a Women and the War 447
- 16-3b Women as Aid Workers and Nurses 447

16-4 The Confederate Tide Crests and Recedes 448
- 16-4a The Battle of Chancellorsville 448
- 16-4b The Gettysburg Campaign 449
- 16-4c The Vicksburg Campaign 451
- 16-4d Chickamauga and Chattanooga 451

16-5 Black Men in Blue 453
- 16-5a Black Soldiers in Combat 453
- 16-5b Emancipation Confirmed 454

16-6 The Year of Decision 454
- 16-6a Out of the Wilderness 454
- ■ HISTORY THROUGH FILM *Lincoln* (2012) 455
- 16-6b Spotsylvania and Cold Harbor 456
- 16-6c Stalemate in Virginia 457
- 16-6d The Atlanta Campaign 457
- 16-6e Peace Overtures 457
- 16-6f The Prisoner-Exchange Controversy 458
- 16-6g The Issue of Black Soldiers in the Confederate Army 460

16-7 Lincoln's Reelection and the End of the Confederacy 460
- 16-7a The Capture of Atlanta 461
- 16-7b The Shenandoah Valley 461
- 16-7c From Atlanta to the Sea 461
- ■ WHAT THEY SAID The Evacuation of Atlanta: General Hood versus General Sherman on the Laws of War 462
- 16-7d The Battles of Franklin and Nashville 463
- 16-7e Fort Fisher and Sherman's March through the Carolinas 464
- 16-7f The Road to Appomattox 465
- 16-7g The Assassination of Lincoln 465

Conclusion 466

Chapter Review 467

17 RECONSTRUCTION, 1863–1877 468

17-1 Wartime Reconstruction 470
- 17-1a Radical Republicans and Reconstruction 470

17-2 Andrew Johnson and Reconstruction 470
- ■ CHRONOLOGY 471
- 17-2a Johnson's Policy 471
- 17-2b Southern Defiance 471
- 17-2c The Black Codes 472
- 17-2d Land and Labor in the Postwar South 473
- 17-2e The Freedmen's Bureau 473
- 17-2f Land for the Landless 474
- 17-2g Churches and Schools 474

17-3 The Advent of Congressional Reconstruction 475
- 17-3a Schism between President and Congress 475
- 17-3b The Fourteenth Amendment 475
- 17-4c The 1866 Elections 475
- 17-3d The Reconstruction Acts of 1867 476
- ■ WHAT THEY SAID Black Codes versus Black Politics 477

17-4 The Impeachment of Andrew Johnson 478
- 17-4a The Completion of Formal Reconstruction 479
- ■ INTERPRETING THE VISUAL PAST An Unholy Alliance: "This Is a White Man's Government" 480
- 17-4b The Fifteenth Amendment 480
- 17-4c The Election of 1868 481

17-5 The Grant Administration 482
- 17-5a Civil Service Reform 482
- 17-5b Foreign Policy Issues 482
- 17-5c Reconstruction in the South 482
- 17-5d Blacks in Office 483
- 17-5e "Carpetbaggers" 483
- 17-5f "Scalawags" 485
- 17-5g The Ku Klux Klan 485
- 17-5h The Election of 1872 486
- 17-5i The Panic of 1873 487

17-6 The Retreat from Reconstruction 487
- 17-6a The Mississippi Election of 1875 487
- ■ HISTORY THROUGH FILM *The Birth of a Nation* (1915) 488
- 17-6b The Supreme Court and Reconstruction 489
- 17-6c The Election of 1876 490
- 17-6d Disputed Results 490
- 17-6e The Compromise of 1877 490
- 17-6f The End of Reconstruction 491

Conclusion 492

Chapter Review 492

APPENDIX A-1

GLOSSARY G-1

INDEX I-1

Maps and Features

MAPS

MAP 1.1	Indian Settlement of America 6	MAP 4.5	Conquest of Canada, 1758–1760 129
MAP 1.2	The Major Empires and Cities of the Andes and Mesoamerica from the 10th to the Early 15th Century 9	MAP 4.6	Growth of Population to 1760 131
MAP 1.3	Valley of Mexico, 1519 10	MAP 5.1	Pontiac's War and the Proclamation Line of 1763 138
MAP 1.4	Mogollon, Hohokam, and Anasazi Sites 13	MAP 5.2	Feudal Revival: Great Estates of Late Colonial America 151
MAP 1.5	Mound-Building Cultures of North America 16	MAP 5.3	Lexington, Concord, and Boston, 1775 161
MAP 1.6	Expansion of Islam 18	MAP 6.1	Revolutionary War in the Northern States 171
MAP 1.7	Africa and the Mediterranean in the 15th Century 20	MAP 6.2	War on the Frontier, 1777–1782 177
MAP 1.8	Columbus's First Voyage, 1492 25	MAP 6.3	War in the Lower South, 1780–1781 182
MAP 1.9	Principal Spanish Explorations of North America 27	MAP 6.4	Virginia and the Yorktown Campaign 184
MAP 1.10	Spanish Missions in Florida and New Mexico circa 1675 28	MAP 6.5	Western Land Claims during the Revolution 188
MAP 1.11	Spanish Empire and Global Labor System 33	MAP 6.6	Advance of Settlement to 1790 191
MAP 2.1	New France and the Jesuit Missions 42	MAP 7.1	The West, 1790–1796 210
MAP 2.2	Roanoke Colony, 1584–1590 46	MAP 7.2	Presidential Election, 1800 213
MAP 2.3	Virginia Company Charter, 1606 50	MAP 7.3	The Louisiana Purchase 218
MAP 2.4	Virginia and Maryland, circa 1675 51	MAP 7.4	War of 1812 224
MAP 2.5	Principal West Indian Colonies in the 17th Century 52	MAP 8.1	Population Density, 1790–1820 234
MAP 2.6	New England in the 1640s 58	MAP 8.2	Rivers, Roads, and Canals, 1825–1860 243
MAP 2.7	The Duke of York's Colonial Charter 62	MAP 8.3	Time Required to Travel from New York City, 1800 and 1830 244
MAP 3.1	Pueblo Rebellion, 1680 71	MAP 8.4	Railroads in the United States, 1840 and 1860 245
MAP 3.2	New England in Metacom's War, 1675–1676 74	MAP 9.1	Cotton Production, 1801 and 1859 259
MAP 3.3	Bacon's Rebellion in Virginia, 1676 77	MAP 9.2	Distribution of Slave Population, 1790, 1820, and 1860 261
MAP 3.4	French Middle Ground in North America, circa 1700 79	MAP 10.1	Growth of American Methodism, 1775–1850 285
MAP 3.5	French Louisiana and Spanish Texas in the 1720s 81	MAP 11.1	The Missouri Compromise, 1820 308
MAP 3.6	Government and Religion in the British Colonies, 1720 90	MAP 11.2	Presidential Election, 1824 311
MAP 3.7	Area of English Settlement by 1700 92	MAP 11.3	Presidential Election, 1828 314
MAP 3.8	Northeastern Theater of War, 1689–1713 94	MAP 11.4	Presidential Election, 1832 323
MAP 3.9	Southeastern Theater of War, 1702–1713 95	MAP 11.5	Presidential Election, 1836 325
MAP 4.1	Caribbean Theater of War, 1739–1742 120	MAP 11.6	Presidential Election, 1840 326
MAP 4.2	Southeastern Theater of War, 1739–1742 121	MAP 13.1	Free and Slave States and Territories, 1848 355
MAP 4.3	France versus Britain in North America by 1755 123	MAP 13.2	Overland Trails, 1846 357
MAP 4.4	British Offenses, 1755 125	MAP 13.3	Settlement of the Oregon Boundary Dispute, 1846 359
		MAP 13.4	Principal Campaigns of the Mexican War, 1846–1847 362
		MAP 14.1	Kansas-Nebraska and the Slavery Issue 385
		MAP 14.2	Counties Carried by Candidates in the 1856 Presidential Election 388

MAP 14.3 Main Transportation Routes in the 1850s 391
MAP 14.4 Slavery and Staple Crops in the South, 1860 396
MAP 15.1 Election of 1860 and Southern Secession 412
MAP 15.2 Principal Military Campaigns of the Civil War 417
MAP 15.3 Battle of Bull Run (Manassas), July 21, 1861 428
MAP 15.4 Kentucky–Tennessee Theater, Winter–Spring 1862 429
MAP 15.5 Battle of Shiloh, April 6–7, 1862 431
MAP 15.6 Peninsula Campaign, April–May 1862, and Seven Days' Battles, June 25–July 1, 1862 432
MAP 15.7 Second Battle of Manassas (Bull Run), August 29–30, 1862 433
MAP 16.1 Lee's Invasion of Maryland, 1862, and the Battle of Antietam, September 17, 1862 442
MAP 16.2 Battle of Chancellorsville, May 2–6, 1863 449
MAP 16.3 Battle of Gettysburg, July 1–3, 1863 450
MAP 16.4 Vicksburg Campaign, April–July 1863 451
MAP 16.5 Road to Chickamauga, June–September 1863 452
MAP 16.6 Battle of the Wilderness and Spotsylvania, May 5–12, 1864 456
MAP 16.7 Campaign for Atlanta, May–September 1864 459
MAP 16.8 Hood's Tennessee Campaign, October–November 1864, and Nashville, December 15–16, 1864 463
MAP 17.1 Black and White Participation in Constitutional Conventions, 1867–1868 479
MAP 17.2 Reconstruction in the South 483
MAP 17.3 Hayes-Tilden Disputed Election of 1876 491

FEATURES

History Through Film

Even the Rain (2010)   32
Black Robe (1991)   43
Three Sovereigns for Sarah (1986)   88
The War That Made America (2006)   126
John Adams (2008)   147
Hamilton's America (2016)   173
Master and Commander: The Far Side of the World (2003)   227
A Midwife's Tale (1998)   237
12 Years a Slave (2013)   274
Gangs of New York (2002)   288
Amistad (1997)   322
Not for Ourselves Alone (1999)   348
The Alamo (1960)   360
Abe Lincoln in Illinois (1940)   401
Glory (1989)   419
Lincoln (2012)   455
The Birth of a Nation (1915)   488

What They Said

Two Spanish Scholars Debate Indian Slavery   29
English Colonists and Huron Indians Enter New Worlds   55
Why Did the Pueblo Indians Revolt against the Spaniards in 1680?   72
The Controversy over Religious Revivals   116
Contrasting Views of American Independence   162
Virginians Debate the Constitution   195
Washington, Jefferson, and the Image of the President   205
The Lowell Mill Girls   251
The Treatment of Slave Families   270
A Fatal Prizefight, 1842   290
President Andrew Jackson and the Cherokee Nation Debate Indian Removal   317
Making Fun of Women's Rights   349
The Senate Debates the Compromise of 1850   368
Reactions to John Brown   403
Cornerstone of the Confederacy   414
The Evacuation of Atlanta: General Hood versus General Sherman on the Laws of War   463
Black Codes versus Black Politics   477

Interpreting the Visual Past

How to Understand Columbus's Landing?   24
French-Huron Alliance Takes Shape   40
A Native American Representation of the Colonial Southeast   96
A Display of Consumer Goods   112
A British Cartoon of the Stamp Act Repeal   144
A French View of Yorktown   183
Capturing the World: The Illustrations of the Journals of Lewis and Clark   220
Transportation before the Market Revolution   241
A View of Slavery as Benevolent   265
The Actors' War: Forrest and Macready   292
King Andrew the First   324
An Abolitionist View of Southern Society   344
Manifest Destiny   356
The Caning of Sumner   386
The Soldier's Dream of Home   422
Photographs of the Dead at Antietam   441
An Unholy Alliance: "This Is a White Man's Government"   480

To the Student

Why Study History?

Why take a course in American history? This is a question that many college and university students ask. In many respects, students today are like the generations of Americans who have gone before them: optimistic and forward looking, far more eager to imagine where we as a nation might be going than to reflect on where we have been. If anything, this tendency has become more pronounced in recent years, as the Internet revolution has accelerated the pace and excitement of change and made even the recent past seem at best quaint, at worst uninteresting and irrelevant.

But it is precisely in these moments of change that a sense of the past can be indispensable in terms of guiding our actions in the present and future. We can find in other periods of American history moments, like this one, of dizzying technological change, rapid alterations in the concentration of wealth and power, and basic changes in patterns of work, residence, and play. How did Americans at those times create, embrace, and resist these changes? In earlier periods of American history, the United States was home, as it is today, to a broad array of ethnic and racial groups. How did earlier generations of Americans respond to the cultural conflicts and misunderstandings that often arise from conditions of diversity? How did immigrants of the early 1900s perceive their new land? How and when did they integrate themselves into American society? To study how ordinary Americans of the past struggled with these issues is to gain perspective on the opportunities and problems that Americans face today.

History also provides an important guide to affairs of state. What role should America assume in world affairs? Should it participate in international bodies such as the United Nations, or insist on its ability to act autonomously and without the consent of other nations? What is the proper role of government in economic and social life? Should the government regulate the economy? To what extent should the government promote morality regarding religion, sexual practices, drinking and drugs, movies, TV, and other forms of mass culture? And what responsibilities do Americans as citizens owe to each other and to their nation? Americans of past generations debated these issues with verve and conviction. Learning about these debates and how they were resolved will strengthen our grasp of the policy possibilities for today and tomorrow.

History, finally, is about stories—stories that people tell about themselves; their families; their communities; their ethnicity, race, region, and religion; and their nation. They are stories of triumph and tragedy, of engagement and flight, and of high ideals and high comedy. When Americans tell these stories, "American history" may be the furthest thing from their minds. But, often, an implicit sense of the past informs what people say about grandparents who immigrated many years ago; the suburb in which they live; the church, synagogue, or mosque at which they worship; or the ethnic or racial group to which they belong. How well, we might ask, do we really understand these individuals, institutions, and groups? Do our stories about them capture their history and complexity? Or do our stories wittingly or unwittingly simplify or alter what these individuals and groups experienced? A study of American history helps us first to ask these questions and then to answer them. In the process, students can embark on a journey of intellectual and personal discovery and situate themselves more firmly than they had thought possible in relation to those who came before them. They can gain a firmer self-knowledge and a greater appreciation for the richness of the American nation and its history.

Analyzing Historical Sources

Astronomers investigate the universe through telescopes. Biologists study the natural world by collecting plants and animals in the field and then examining them with microscopes. Sociologists and psychologists study human behavior through observation and controlled laboratory experiments.

Historians study the past by examining historical "evidence" or "source" materials: government documents; the records of private institutions ranging from religious and charitable organizations to labor unions, corporations, and lobbying groups; letters, advertisements, paintings, music, literature, movies, and cartoons; buildings, clothing, farm implements, industrial machinery, and landscapes: anything and everything written or created by our ancestors that give clues about their lives and the times in which they lived.

Historians refer to written material as "documents." Excerpts of dozens of documents appear throughout the textbook. Each chapter also includes many visual representations of the American past as expressed in paintings, murals, cartoons, sculptures, photographs of buildings and individuals, and other kinds of historical evidence. The more you examine this "evidence," the more you will understand the main ideas of this book and of the U.S. history course you are taking. More generally, encounters with this evidence will enhance your ability to interpret the past.

Source Material Comes in Two Main Types: Primary and Secondary

"Primary" evidence is material that comes to us exactly as it was spoken, written, or drawn by the person who created it. The easiest way to locate examples of primary evidence in this textbook is to sample several *What They Said* features, each of which contains two or more primary documents. Each document introduces you to a point of view expressed by a past American in his or her own words, as he or she spoke them at the time. See, for example, "Virginians Debate the Constitution" in Chapter 6 (p. 195); "The Senate Debates the Compromise of 1850" in Chapter 13 (p. 368); "Differing Visions of Black Progress" in Chapter 18 (p. 515); or "Civil Liberties in Wartime" in Chapter 26 (p. 741).

"Secondary" evidence is an account constructed by an individual, usually a historian, about an event, organization, idea, or personality of historical significance. Stories about Abraham Lincoln recorded by his secretary of war would give us primary source information about Lincoln by someone who knew him. But imagine an account about Lincoln's performance as president written by someone who did not know Lincoln and who was born 50 or 100 years after Lincoln had lived. This individual would have to consult all the available primary sources he or she could find: Lincoln's own writings, letters, memos, and speeches; the accounts of Lincoln's presidency appearing in newspapers and magazines of the time; the writings and speeches of Lincoln's allies and enemies in civilian and military life; letters to Lincoln written by his supporters and opponents; documents pertaining to the performance of various government departments during Lincoln's presidency; and so on. Typically, someone studying Lincoln in such detail would do so with the ambition of writing a book about the man and his presidency. That book would be considered a secondary source of information about Lincoln.

In this textbook, we include lists of secondary sources at the end of each chapter under the heading, "Suggested Readings." These are books by historians pertinent to important issues discussed in that chapter. If you turn to the suggested readings for Chapter 17, for example, you will notice that two books listed there examine Reconstruction, the project begun during Lincoln's presidency to emancipate the slaves, establish racial equality in the South, and determine the circumstances under which the Confederate states would be readmitted to the Union. These books, Eric Foner, *Reconstruction: America's Unfinished Revolution, 1863–1877*, and Kenneth M. Stampp, *The Era of Reconstruction, 1865–1877*, are examples of secondary sources.

"Reading" and Studying Photographs, Artwork, and Movies

Your experience of this textbook will be enriched, we believe, if you take the time to study the artwork, photography, movies, and other forms of visual representation that are integral to it. For an example of what the textbook offers in its art program, and how you might study the art, consult the *Interpreting the Visual Past* feature in Chapter 23, "Turning the German Enemy into a Beast," (p. 640), reproduced below. This feature asks you, the student, to examine a U.S. Army recruiting poster from World War I that depicts the German enemy as a "mad brute" who must be destroyed. Take a close look at this poster. Among the questions you might ask about this poster are the following:

1. Why did the U.S. government choose to encourage support for the war by depicting the Germans as apes running amok in the land?
2. Why depict this beast as a sexual predator? Does the power of the poster stem in part from the contrast between the beast's dark brutishness and the light skin of the captive woman—a contrast that would have reminded early 20th century Americans of unresolved black–white tensions in their own society?
3. What do you think the consequences of representing Germans as beasts might have been for the millions of German immigrants and their descendants living in the United States?

23.9 Harry R. Hopps, *Destroy This Mad Brute, Enlist*, 1918.

Most of you will not be able to answer these questions simply by studying the poster. You will need to acquire knowledge of relevant historical background and context—knowledge that the pages that surround this poster provide. But a good part of historical understanding comes not simply from finding answers but from being able to ask the right questions. Examining a piece of artwork may lead you to ask a series of queries that are potentially full of insight and that otherwise might not have occurred to you. So, as you read through the chapters, please pause to study the posters, portraits, cartoons, and photographs that grace its pages. To facilitate such learning in this seventh enhanced edition, we have added questions to hundreds of images appearing throughout the book. Have a look at these questions, which can be found in the captions that appear underneath many images; pause to answer them, and to share answers with your professor or teacher and fellow students. Raise questions about the textbook images that we have not thought to ask. Questions of this sort—and the discussions that arise from them—spur the learning process.

Reading and Studying Maps

Historical events happen in specific places. It is important to learn all you can about those places, and good maps can help you do this.

Your textbook includes many different kinds of maps, including those that show political boundaries, election results, population, topography, military battles, and irrigation and transportation networks. To study maps effectively, you should first take the time to identify and study map labels. Take a look at the foldout insert inside the front cover, which includes territorial growth and elevation maps of the United States. These maps provide four kinds of basic labels. They do the following:

1. Identify the states within and the countries bordering the United States
2. Identify the state capitals and major cities
3. Identify the rivers, large lakes, major bays, gulfs, and oceans
4. Identify the mountain ranges, important individual mountains, plateaus, plains, and deserts

In addition, these maps contain a distance scale in miles and kilometers. The scales appear in the lower right-hand corner of each map. The scales permit a reader to determine the actual size of different parts of U.S. territory and the distances between them. These maps also contain insets to show parts of the United States that are either too far from the mainland to be drawn to scale (Alaska and Hawaii) or too small to show up clearly on the map (Puerto Rico and the Virgin Islands).

Many of the maps in this book contain legends that use colors and other forms of coding to convey important information without cluttering up the map with words. Most maps in this book also have captions written by the textbook authors. Each caption is meant to describe the basic purpose of the map and to draw readers' attention to particular details. For this edition, we have added critical thinking questions to each of the map captions.

Below are three examples of the kinds of historical information that maps can communicate.

Example #1: Using Maps to Study Geographic-Political Change Across the 240 years of U.S. history, the political boundaries of the country and the number of states belonging to the United States have changed a great deal. Maps can help us to see and study those changes. Compare these two maps: Map 3.7 (this notation refers to the seventh map in the third chapter, p. 92), which shows how small the area of English settlement was in 1700; and Map 6.5 (p. 188), which shows the original 13 states at the time of independence as well as their claims to western land. Can you identify which new states were added to the United States out of the western lands that the original 13 states ceded to the national government between 1784 and 1802?

Example #2: Using Maps to Study Battles Maps can convey a wealth of knowledge about military battles in a compressed and efficient way. Take a look at Map 16.2 (p. 449), which charts the progress of the Battle of Chancellorsville (and Fredericksburg) during the Civil War. The boxed legend defines the 10 different kinds of bars

▲ MAP 3.7

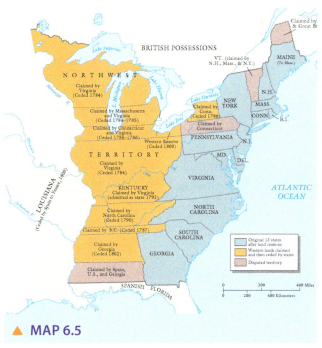

▲ MAP 6.5

and arrows that are used on the map to show the position of the Union and Confederate forces on the five different days of the battle and to demonstrate how the two armies conducted their advances and retreats. From studying the map itself, can you determine which side won the Battle of Chancellorsville? What information in the map led you to that conclusion?

Example #3: Using Maps to Study the American Economy   The most detailed legend in the book is attached to Map 19.1 (p. 525), which shows the distribution of industries across America in the years 1900–1920. Twenty-two industries are identified by icons in the legend, and those icons, in turn, demonstrate where those industries were concentrated in the 48 states. A second legend to the right of the first uses color coding to identify the scale of manufacturing (measured in the dollars of factory production generated in each state in 1919). After examining this map, answer these questions:

1. In what states were the meatpacking, textile, and petroleum-refining industries concentrated?
2. Which state had no significant industrial output of any sort?
3. Which seven states had the highest factory output, as measured in dollars? Which six states had the lowest factory output? Were the states with the highest and lowest factory outputs clustered in particular regions? If so, which ones? Do you think that the uneven distribution of industry in the United States shaped American politics and culture in the 20th century?

We invite you to explore the maps mentioned in this guide as well as the many others offered in the textbook.

Preface

We are pleased to present the Enhanced Seventh Edition of *Liberty, Equality, Power*. Like the previous seven editions, this one captures the drama and excitement of America's past, from the pre-Columbian era through our own time. It integrates social and cultural history into a political story that is organized around the themes of liberty, equality, and power, and synthesizes the finest historical scholarship to create a narrative that is balanced, lively, and accessible to a broad range of students.

The *Liberty, Equality, Power* Approach

In this book, we tell many small stories, and one large one: how America transformed itself, in a relatively brief period of world history, from a land inhabited by hunter–gatherer and agricultural Native American societies into the most powerful industrial nation on earth. This story has been told many times before, and those who have told it in the past have usually emphasized the political experiment in liberty and equality that took root in North America in the 18th century.

We, too, stress the extraordinary and transformative impact that the ideals of liberty and equality exerted on American politics, society, and economics during the American Revolution and after. We show how the creation of a free economic environment—one in which entrepreneurial spirit, technological innovation, and manufacturing have flourished—underpinned American industrial might. We have also emphasized the successful struggles for freedom that, over the course of the country's 240 plus years of existence, have brought rights and opportunities—first to all white men, then to men of color, then to women—that they had not previously known.

But we have also identified a third factor in this pantheon of American ideals—that of power. We examine power in many forms: the accumulation of vast economic fortunes and their influence on the economy and on politics; the dispossession of American Indians from land that they regarded as their home; the enslavement of millions of Africans and their African-American descendants for a period of almost 250 years; the relegation of women and of racial, ethnic, and religious minorities to subordinate places in American society; and the extension of American control over foreign peoples, such as Latin Americans and Filipinos, who would have preferred to have been free and self-governing. We do not mean to suggest that American power has always been turned to these negative purposes. Subordinate groups have also marshaled power to combat oppression, as in the abolitionist and civil rights crusades, the campaign for woman suffrage, and the labor movement. The government has at times used its power to moderate poverty and to manage the economy in the interests of general prosperity. And it has used its military power to defeat Nazi Germany, World War II Japan, the cold war Soviet Union, and other enemies of freedom.

The invocation of power as a variable in American history impels us to widen the lens through which we look at the past and to enrich the stories we tell. Ours has been a history of freedom and domination; of progress toward realizing a broadly democratic polity and of delays and reverses; of abundance and poverty; of wars for freedom and justice and for control of foreign markets. In complicating our master narrative in this way, we think we have rendered American history more exciting and intriguing. Progress has not been automatic, but the product of ongoing struggles.

In this book, we have tried to capture the diversity of the American past, both in terms of outcomes and in terms of the variety of groups who have participated in America's making. American Indians are not presented simply as the victims of European aggression but as peoples diverse in their own ranks, with a variety of systems of social organization and cultural expression. We give equal treatment to the industrial titans of American history—the likes of Andrew Carnegie and John D. Rockefeller—and to those, such as small farmers and ordinary workers, who resisted the corporate reorganization of economic life. We examine the major advances of 1863, when African Americans were freed from slavery, and of 1868, when they were made full citizens of the United States. But we also note how a majority of African Americans had to wait another 100 years, until the civil rights movement of the 1960s, to gain full access to American freedoms. We tell similarly complex stories about women, Latinos, and other groups of ethnic Americans.

Political issues are only part of America's story. Americans have always loved their leisure and have created the world's most vibrant popular culture. They have embraced technological innovations, especially those promising to make their lives easier and more fun. We have, therefore, devoted considerable space to a discussion of American popular culture, from the founding of the first newspapers in the 18th century and the rise of movies, jazz, and the comics in the early 20th century to the cable television and Internet revolutions in recent years. We have also analyzed how American industry has periodically altered home and personal life by making new products—such as clothing, cars, refrigerators, and computers—available to consumers. In such ways, we hope to give our readers a rich portrait of how Americans lived at various points in our history.

New to the Enhanced Seventh Edition

We wish to take note of two major changes to the last edition that are still heavily influencing this one: first, the addition of two new authors, Pekka Hämäläinen and Denver Brunsman, and, second, a dramatic expansion of our primary source program. Pekka and Denver, specialists in the history of early America and the early Republic, have enabled us to preserve our textbook's robust history of British America while also enhancing its coverage of Spanish America, French America, and Native America. Pekka and Denver have worked very closely with each other and the rest of the authors both to introduce new material and perspectives and to maintain the great strengths of earlier editions. They have enhanced the book's continental perspective, including far more on the early history of North American territory that would become California, New Mexico, and Texas. They have expanded significantly the attention to environmental history, and revised Chapters 4–10 to bring the latest scholarship to bear on these subjects: the role of women in 18th-century transatlantic consumer society; loyalists in the American revolutionary era; slavery and the Atlantic slave trade; the international threats faced by the United States in the early decades of the 19th century; and the relations among European empires, Native Americans, and the United States in the first half of the 19th century. We are delighted that Pekka and Denver have joined the *Liberty, Equality, Power* team.

We also chose to preserve in the enhanced seventh edition the major revision and expansion of the primary source program undertaken in the last edition. The most important change in that program was the introduction of a new feature, *What They Said*, which appears in every one of the textbook's 32 chapters. Each *What They Said* feature focuses on a controversial issue pertinent to the time period covered in that chapter and presents two or more sides of that issue in the words of individuals who were actual participants in the debates. The response to this feature has been very positive, which has impelled us to maintain it as a central feature of this new edition.

What They Said, in combination with two other primary document features, *Interpreting the Visual Past* and the much admired *History Through Film*, endow *Liberty, Equality, Power* with one of the most comprehensive, diverse, and intriguing programs of primary sources available in any U.S. history textbook. To keep our *History Through Film* series up-to-date, we have selected for this edition five new films to examine: *Even the Rain* (2010); *Hamilton's America* (2016); *Lincoln* (2012); *The Immigrant* (2013); and *Selma* (2014). We hope you will share our excitement about the inclusion of these new movies.

As in past editions, we have continued to make sure that the textbook's last chapter (Chapter 32) is up to date and gives adequate attention to the important developments in politics, economics, and culture of the 21st century. The revised Chapter 32 offers discussion of George W. Bush's victories in 2000 and 2004; the destruction of the World Trade Center towers on September 11, 2001; the resulting wars on terrorism and on Saddam Hussein in Iraq and the Taliban in Afghanistan; Barack Obama's victories in 2008 and 2012; the financial crash of 2008–2009; the passage of the Affordable Care Act and the rise of the Tea Party; and the 2016 election of Donald J. Trump.

In preparing for this revision, we solicited feedback from professors and scholars throughout the country, many of whom have used the seventh edition of *Liberty, Equality, Power* in their classrooms. Their comments proved most helpful, and many of their suggestions have been incorporated into this edition.

We have carried over and, in some cases, enhanced pedagogical changes that we made to earlier editions and that have proved popular with professors and students. Each chapter now begins with a set of **learning objectives**. **Chapter outlines** and **chronology boxes** continue to appear at the beginning of each chapter, and **focus questions** at the beginning of each major section and at each chapter's end, where they appear alongside *Critical Thinking* questions. We have updated our *Identifications* (boldfaced terms that appear throughout the text) and supply the definitions for these terms in a comprehensive *Glossary* appearing at the end of the book. Each map in our outstanding map program comes equipped with a brief caption instructing students about how to interpret the geographical and topographical data it contains. For the first time, we have inserted questions into each map caption to encourage students to engage with the material that the maps contain. For the first time as well, we have added student-focused questions to hundreds of images appearing throughout the text. In order to keep the art program fresh, we have replaced about 10 percent of the images. Finally, we have updated our *Suggested Readings* for each chapter while keeping the lists brief.

We believe that both instructors and students will find these aids to be useful and well-placed tools for reviewing what they have learned and for pushing outward the frontiers of their knowledge.

Finally, we have scrutinized each page of this textbook, making sure our prose is clear, the historical issues well presented, and the scholarship up to date and accurate.

Specific Revisions to Content and Coverage

Chapter 1   New History Through Film Feature, *Even the Rain* (2010).

Chapter 3   Expanded the discussion of the early 18th-century Indigenous Southwest as well as Indian women and gender dynamics.

Chapter 6   Updated material to highlight the role of loyalists and enslaved African Americans in the American Revolutionary War; added new section on "Violence and Attrition" that draws on growing scholarship that emphasizes the American Revolution as a violent event; new History Through Film feature, *Hamilton's America* (2016); streamlined discussion of state constitutions and American constitutionalism.

Chapter 9   Provided new section on "Slavery and Capitalism" and updated other sections to reflect emerging literature that links slavery to the development of American and global capitalism; consolidated content on southern families and the place of mastery and honor in southern culture.

Chapter 15   Updated History Through Film feature, *Glory* (1989).

Chapter 16   New History Through Film feature, *Lincoln* (2012).

Chapter 17   Updated "Education" section to "Churches and Schools" and provided additional information on the educational opportunities that were created for African American children by African Americans during Reconstruction. Revised "Blacks in Office" section to lend more focus to accomplishments of African Americans in this time.

Supplements

Instructor Resources

MindTap for *Liberty, Equality, Power: A History of the American People*, Enhanced Seventh Edition is a flexible online learning platform that provides students with a relevant and engaging learning experience that builds their critical thinking skills and fosters their argumentation and analysis skills. Through a carefully designed chapter-based learning path, MindTap supports students as they develop historical understanding, improve their reading and writing skills, and practice critical thinking by making connections between ideas.

Students read sections of the ebook and take Check Your Understanding quizzes that test their reading comprehension. They put higher-level critical thinking skills into practice to complete chapter tests. They also use these skills to analyze textual and visual primary sources in each chapter through an autograded image primary source activity and a manually graded short essay in which students write comparatively about multiple primary sources.

Beyond the chapter-level content, students can increase their comfort in analyzing primary sources through thematically-organized primary source autograded activities that span the text. They also practice synthesizing their knowledge and articulating what they have learned through responding to essay prompts that span broader themes in the book.

MindTap also allows instructors to customize their content, providing tools that seamlessly integrate YouTube clips, outside websites, and personal content directly into the learning path. Instructors can assign additional primary source content through the Instructor Resource Center and Questia, primary- and secondary-source databases located on the MindTap app dock that house thousands of peer-reviewed journals, newspapers, magazines, and books.

The additional content available in MindTap mirrors and complements the authors' narrative, but also includes primary-source content and assessments not found in the printed text. To learn more, ask your Cengage Learning sales representative to demo it for you—or go to www.cengage.com/mindtap.

Instructor's Companion Website The Instructor's Companion Website, accessed through the Instructor Resource Center (login.cengage.com), houses all of the supplemental materials you can use for your course. This includes a Test Bank, Instructor's Manual, and PowerPoint Lecture Presentations. The Test Bank contains multiple-choice and true-or-false questions for each chapter. The Instructor's Resource Manual includes chapter outlines, chronologies, thematic topics for enrichment, suggested essay topics, lecture outlines, and teaching resources. Finally, the PowerPoint Lectures are ADA-compliant slides that collate the key takeaways from the chapter in concise visual formats perfect for in-class presentations or student review.

Cengage.com/student Save your students time and money. Direct them to www.cengage.com/student for a choice in formats and savings and a better chance to succeed in your class. Cengage.com/student, Cengage Learning's online store, is a single destination for more than 10,000 new textbooks, ebooks, study tools, and audio supplements. Students have the freedom to purchase à la carte exactly what they need when they need it. Students can save up to 70% on the ebook electronic textbook.

CENGAGE UNLIMITED

The first-of-its-kind digital subscription designed specially to lower costs. Students get total access to everything Cengage has to offer on demand—in one place. That's 20,000 eBooks, 2,300 digital learning products, and dozens of study tools across 70 disciplines and over 675 courses. Currently available in select markets. Details at **www.cengage.com/unlimited**

Learn more at Cengage.com about books that build skills in doing history including:

- *Doing History: Research and Writing in the Digital Age*, 2e ISBN: 9781133587880 Prepared by Michael J. Galgano, J. Chris Arndt, and Raymond M. Hyser of James Madison University.
- *Writing for College History*, 1e ISBN: 9780618306039 Prepared by Robert M. Frakes of Clarion University.
- *The Modern Researcher*, 6e ISBN: 9780495318705 Prepared by Jacques Barzun and Henry F. Graff of Columbia University.

Reader Program. Cengage Learning publishes a number of readers. Some contain exclusively primary sources, others are devoted to essays and secondary sources, and still others provide a combination of primary and secondary sources. All of these readers are designed to guide students through the process of historical inquiry. Visit www.cengage.com/history for a complete list of readers.

Custom Options. Nobody knows your students like you, so why not give them a text that is tailor-fit to their needs? Cengage Learning offers custom solutions for your course—whether it's making a small modification to *Liberty, Equality, Power* Enhanced 7e, to match your syllabus or combining multiple sources to create something truly unique. Contact your Cengage Learning representative to explore custom solutions for your course.

Acknowledgments

We recognize the contributions of reviewers who read portions of the manuscript in various stages:

Sam Abrams, The Beacon School
William Allison, Weber State University
Angie Anderson, Southeastern Louisiana University
Kenneth G. Anthony, University of North Carolina, Greensboro
Rick Ascheman, Rochester Community and Technical College
Paul R. Beezley, Texas Tech University
David Bernstein, California State University at Long Beach
Sue Blanchette, Hillcrest High School
Jeff Bloodworth, Ohio University
Michael R. Bradley, Motlow College
Betty Brandon, University of South Alabama
Daniel Patrick Brown, Moorpark College
Ronald G. Brown, College of Southern Maryland
Susan Burch, Gallaudet University
Vanessa M. Camacho, El Paso Community College
Thomas M. Cangiano, The Lawrenceville School
Edward V. Carroll, Heartland Community College
Jeffrey W. Coker, Belmont University
Phil Crow, North Harris College
Lorenzo M. Crowell, Mississippi State University
Amy E. N. Darty, University of Central Florida
Thomas M. Deaton, Dalton State College
Norman C. Delaney, Del Mar College
Ted Delaney, Washington and Lee University
Andrew J. DeRoche, Front Range Community College
Rebecca de Schweinitz, Brigham Young University
Bruce Dierenfield, Canisius College
Brian R. Dirck, Anderson University
Maura Doherty, Illinois State University
R. Blake Dunnavent, Lubbock Christian University
Eileen Eagan, University of Southern Maine
Derek Elliott, Tennessee State University
B. Jane England, North Central Texas College
Joe Escobar, Lane Community College
William B. Feis, Buena Vista University
David J. Fitzpatrick, Washtenaw Community College
Van Forsyth, Clark College
Michael P. Gabriel, Kutztown University of Pennsylvania
Gary Gallagher, Pennsylvania State University
Kevin M. Gannon, Grand View University
Gerald Ghelfi, Santa Ana College
Michael Goldberg, University of Washington, Bothell
Kathleen Gorman, Minnesota State University, Mankato
David E. Hamilton, University of Kentucky
Michael J. Haridopolos, Brevard Community College
Mark Harvey, North Dakota State University
Brenda Hasterok, Spain Park High School
Kurt Hohenstein, Hampden Sydney College
Mark Huddle, University of Georgia
Samuel C. Hyde Jr., Southeastern Louisiana University
Thomas N. Ingersoll, Ohio State University
J. Michael Jeffries, Northeastern Technical College
Frank Karpiel, Ramapo College of New Jersey
Anthony E. Kaye, Pennsylvania State University
Michael Kazin, Georgetown University
Michael King, Moraine Valley Community College
Greg Kiser, Northwest Arkansas Community College
Michael Krenn, Appalachian State
Matthew Kruer, University of Oklahoma
Donna Kumler, Grayson College
Frank Lambert, Purdue University
Pat Ledbetter, North Central Texas College
Michelle LeMaster, Eastern Illinois University
Jan Leone, Middle Tennessee State University
Craig Livingston, Montgomery College
Robert F. Marcom, San Antonio College
Suzanne Marshall, Jacksonville State University
Brenda Taylor Matthews, Texas Wesleyan University
Joanne Maypole, Front Range Community College
Christopher McColm, Aims Community College
Jimmie McGee, South Plains College
Nora E. McMillan, San Antonio College
Jerry Mills, Midland College
Charlene Mires, Villanova University
Nancy Mitchell, North Carolina State University
Brock Mislan, Watchung Hills Regional High School
Rick Moniz, Chabot College
Rick Murray, Los Angeles Valley College
Caryn Neumann, Miami University of Ohio
James Nichols, Queensborough Community College
Michael R. Nichols, Tarrant County College, Northwest
Linda Noel, Morgan State University
Christy Olsen, Skyline High School
Richard B. Partain, Bakersfield College
William Pencak, Pennsylvania State University
Jaakko Puisto, Scottsdale Community College
Teresa Thomas Perrin, Austin Community College
David Poteet, New River Community College
Donald Rakestraw, Winthrop University
Howard Reed, University of Bridgeport
Jonathan Rees, Colorado State University–Pueblo
Thomas S. Reid, Valencia Community College
Anne Richardson, Texas Christian University
Lelia M. Roeckell, Molloy College
Thomas J. Rowland, University of Wisconsin, Oshkosh

Mark Sattler, Rockingham Community College
Roy Scott, Mississippi State University
Reynolds J. Scott-Childress, State University of New York at New Paltz
Katherine A. S. Sibley, St. Joseph's University
Herb Sloan, Barnard College
M. Todd Smallwood, Manatee Community College
John Smolenski, University of California, Davis
Steve Stein, University of Memphis
Michael J. Steiner, Northwest Missouri State University
Jennifer Stollman, University of Mississippi
Siegfried H. Sutterlin, Indian Hills Community College
Richard O. Swanson, Duxbury High School
John Wood Sweet, The University of North Carolina at Chapel Hill
Teresa Fava Thomas, Fitchburg State College
Xiansheng Tian, Metro State College of Denver
Jamie Underwood, Montana State University Northern
Juan Valenzuela, Kennesaw State University
Vincent Vinikas, University of Arkansas, Little Rock
Vernon Volpe, University of Nebraska
Harry L. Watson, The University of North Carolina at Chapel Hill
Thomas Weyant, University of Akron
William Benton Whisenhunt, College of DuPage
David K. White, McHenry County College
Laura Matysek Wood, Tarrant County College, Northwest

We wish to thank the members of the Cengage staff, many of them new to the project, for embracing our textbook wholeheartedly and for expertly guiding the production of this seventh enhanced edition. Special thanks to Joseph Potvin, Product Manager; Claire Branman and Erika Hayden, Content Managers; Kate MacLean, Learning Designer; and Hannah Whitcher, Project Manager at SPiGlobal. We wish to thank as well these members of the Cengage team: Sarah Cole, Senior Designer; Robert Alper, Senior In-House, SME; Valerie Hartman, Senior Marketing Manager; and Haley Gaudreau, Product Assistant. A big thanks, finally, to Cengage's marketing department and to the sales representatives who have worked hard and creatively to generate interest in our book among university, college, and high school teachers across America.

No project of this scope is completely error free. If you find any errors, please let us know what they are. Feel free as well to send queries and suggestions our way. The book will be enriched by such feedback. Please send comments to our product manager, Joseph Potvin at joseph.potvin@cengage.com.

Finally, each of us would like to offer particular thanks to those historians, friends, and family members who helped to bring this project to a successful conclusion.

Personal Acknowledgments

JOHN M. MURRIN Mary R. Murrin has provided the kind of moral and personal support that made completion of this project possible. James Axtell and Gregory Evans Dowd saved me from many mistakes, mostly about Indians. John E. Selby and Eugene R. Sheridan were particularly helpful on the Revolution. Fred Anderson and Virginia DeJohns Anderson offered acute suggestions. Several former colleagues and graduate students have also contributed in various ways, especially Stephen Aron, Andrew Isenberg, Ignacio Gallup-Diaz, Evan P. Haefeli, Beth Lewis-Pardoe, Geoffrey Plank, Nathaniel J. Sheidley, and Jeremy Stern.

PEKKA HÄMÄLÄINEN I would like to thank Gary Gerstle and the other authors for welcoming me so warmly to the team. Gary was an inexhaustible source of knowledge and guidance, and Denver Brunsman was an absolute delight to work with. I also want to express my gratitude to John Murrin and Paul Johnson for the opportunity to continue and build on their work. I am grateful to Margaret Beasley for her remarkable proficiency, support, and patience.

PAUL E. JOHNSON My greatest debt is to the community of scholars who write about the United States between the Revolution and the Civil War. Closer to home, I owe thanks to the other writers of this book, particularly to John Murrin. The Department of History at the University of South Carolina provided time to work, while my wife, Kasey Grier, and stray dogs named Lucy, Bill, Buddy, and Patty provided the right kinds of interruptions.

DENVER BRUNSMAN I thank my fellow authors, particularly Gary Gerstle for steering the good ship *LEP* into port. As always, it was a joy to collaborate with Pekka Hämäläinen. We all appreciate the editorial team at Cengage for their vision in committing to a new edition of the textbook in an industry experiencing massive changes. Without the dedicated work of countless scholars, a new edition would not be necessary. Moreover, without students, there would be no need for this book. At George Washington University, I am lucky to have the best students imaginable to help develop ideas and serve as my first test audience. Finally, I continue to draw on the boundless support and inspiration of my wife, Taryn, and our children, Gavin and Sanne, for this and all projects.

JAMES M. MCPHERSON My family provided an environment of affection and stability that contributed immeasurably to the writing of my chapters, while undergraduate students at Princeton University who have taken my courses over the years provided feedback, questions, and insights that helped me to understand what students know and don't know, and what they need to know.

ALICE FAHS Thanks are due to Gary Gerstle, whose keen editorial eye and judgment helped greatly with revisions of Chapter 19. Our "team leader" among the authors, Gary has given generously of his time to the rest of us, providing constant support. Margaret Beasley was a crucial resource of intelligence and good cheer during her years as development editor; we all know we are very lucky. I am grateful as well to

Ann West, our former editor at Cengage, for her exceptional leadership and commitment to excellence; and to James M. McPherson for the initial invitation to become part of *Liberty, Equality, Power*. At the University of California, Irvine, David Igler was an important resource for past revisions of Chapter 18. My students, both undergraduate and graduate, have continued to be a source of inspiration to me in conceptualizing this textbook. Finally, my family continues to listen patiently to history anecdotes over breakfasts, lunches, and dinners—whether in California or Texas. To Charlie and to Mimi, many thanks.

GARY GERSTLE A long time ago, Jerald Podair, Thomas Knock, and the late Roy Rosenzweig gave me exceptionally thorough, thoughtful, and insightful critiques on early drafts of my chapters. This textbook still benefits from their good and generous work. Former graduate students Kathleen Trainor, Reynolds Scott-Childress, Linda Noel, Kelly Ryan, Robert Chase, Marcy Wilson, Thomas Castillo, and Katarina Keane offered skillful research assistance on earlier editions. At Vanderbilt, research assistants Monte Holman and William Bishop made many indispensable and timely contributions to the sixth and seventh editions. My undergraduate students at the University of Maryland and at Vanderbilt University kept me young, and on my toes. Teaching modern American history abroad to Cambridge University undergraduates in the age of Brexit and Trump has been a privilege, and a source of new perspectives on my native land. A special thanks both to my original coauthors for their intelligence, wit, and deep commitment to this project, and to my new coauthors, who have helped me to imagine what a textbook for this new century ought to look like.

EMILY AND NORMAN ROSENBERG would like to thank our children—Sarah, Molly, Ruth, and Joe—for all of the wisdom and good cheer they provided while the six of us were moving through the period of history related in the final chapters of this book. Successive generations of students at Macalester College, some now academics themselves, offered pointed critiques of our classes, and these inspired (and provoked) us continually to revise our approach toward teaching and writing about the recent past. Our former colleagues at Macalester merit a similar kind of thanks. (Here, we note, with deep sadness and fond memories, the recent passing of one them, Jerry K. Fisher, a keen, inside observer of electronic and digital media as well as a professor who excelled in moving student learning beyond the classroom.) More recently, Emily Rosenberg's graduate students at the University of California, Irvine, helped clarify how our chapters might better reach out to students who may be using this enhanced seventh edition. We also thank the historians who offered both supportive and helpfully critical comments on earlier versions of *Liberty, Equality, Power*. We have not always followed their advice, but this enhanced seventh edition is much the better for their assistance.

John M. Murrin, Pekka Hämäläinen, Paul E. Johnson, Denver Brunsman, James M. McPherson, Alice Fahs, Gary Gerstle, Emily S. Rosenberg, Norman L. Rosenberg

1 When Old Worlds Collide: Encounters in the Atlantic World to 1600

1-1 Peoples in Motion
▶ *Learning Objective:* Describe how the extinction of megafauna shaped human history in the Americas.

From Beringia to the Americas
The Great Extinction and the Rise of Agriculture

1-2 The Emergence of Complex Societies in the Americas
▶ *Learning Objective:* Describe the major similarities and differences between the histories of the Andes and Mesoamerica during the first and early second millennia.

The Andes: Cycles of Complex Cultures
Inca Civilization
Mesoamerica: Cycles of Complex Cultures
The Aztecs and Tenochtitlán

1-3 Agricultural Take Off in North America
▶ *Learning Objective:* Trace how maize cultivation changed human history in North America.

Urban Cultures of the Southwest
North American Mound Builders
North America in 1491
The Norse Connection

1-4 Europe and the World by the 15th Century
▶ *Learning Objective:* Identify the factors that enabled relatively backward European societies to establish dominance over the oceans of the world.

China: The Rejection of Overseas Expansion
Christian Europe Challenges Islam
The Legacy of the Crusades
The Unlikely Pioneer: Portugal
Africa, Colonies, and the Slave Trade
Portugal's Asian Empire
Early Lessons

1-5 Spain, Columbus, and the Americas
▶ *Learning Objective:* Explain what kinds of different motives shaped early Spanish colonialism in the Americas.

Columbus
Spain and the Caribbean

1-6 Conquest and Catastrophe
▶ *Learning Objective:* Analyze what enabled relatively few Spanish conquerors to subjugate the powerful empires of the Aztecs and the Incas.

The Conquest of Mexico and Peru
North American Conquistadores and Missionaries
The Spanish Empire and Demographic Catastrophe
Brazil

1-7 Global Colossus, Global Economy
▶ *Learning Objective:* Describe the ways in which American silver both bolstered and weakened the Spanish Empire.

1-8 Explanations: Patterns of Conquest, Submission, and Resistance
▶ *Learning Objective:* Define the Columbian Exchange and describe how it has shaped world history.

1.1 **Sebastian Münster's Map of the New World, 1540** When overseas exploration brought the hemispheres together, Native Americans and European newcomers saw one another as strange and alien. Europeans struggled to make sense of the worlds they discovered, and Indians struggled to make sense of the motives and demands of the colonists. The encounters between natives and colonists in the Western Hemisphere resulted both in violent conquests and complex exchanges of technology, foods, pathogens, ideas, and styles. Indians and Europeans fought and killed one another, but, over time, they also found ways to cooperate and accommodate one another.

WHEN CHRISTOPHER COLUMBUS crossed the Atlantic, he did not know where he was going, and he died without realizing where he had been. Yet, he altered the history of the world. In two generations after 1492, European navigators mastered the oceans of the world, joining together societies that had lived in isolation for thousands of years. European invaders colonized the Americas, not just with sails, gunpowder, and steel, but also with their crops and livestock and, most of all, their diseases. They brought slavery with them as well. By 1600, they had created the first global economy in the history of humankind and had inflicted upon the native peoples of the Americas—unintentionally, for the most part—the greatest known catastrophe that human societies have ever experienced.

In the 15th century, when all of this started, the Americas were in some ways a more ancient world than Western Europe. For example, the Portuguese, Spanish, French, and English languages were only beginning to assume their modern forms during the century or two before and after Columbus's voyage. Centuries earlier, when Rome was falling into ruins and Paris and London were little more than hamlets, huge cities were thriving in the Andes and Mesoamerica (the area embracing Central America and southern and central Mexico). Which world was old and which was new is a matter of perspective. Each already had its own distinctive past. ■

1-1 Peoples in Motion

Q *How did the extinction of megafauna shape human history in the Americas?*

Like all other countries of North and South America, the United States is a nation of immigrants. Even the native peoples were once migrants who settled a strange new land.

Long before Europeans discovered and explored the wide world around them, many different peoples had migrated thousands of miles over thousands of years across oceans and continents. Before Christopher Columbus sailed west from Spain in 1492, several waves of immigrants had already swept over the Americas. The earliest came from Asia. The last, from northern Europe, did not stay.

1-1a *From Beringia to the Americas*

During the most recent Ice Age, glaciers covered huge portions of the Americas, Europe, and Asia. The ice captured so much of the world's water that sea level fell drastically and created a land bridge 600 miles wide across the Bering Strait between Siberia and Alaska. For thousands of years, this exposed area—Beringia—was dry land on which plants, animals, and humans could live. Starting about 15,000 years ago, people drifted in small bands from Asia to North America, probably following steppe bison, caribou, musk oxen, and other large prey animals (see Map 1.1). Slowly they moved southward, some following a narrow ice-free corridor that emerged on the eastern flank of the Rocky Mountains as the Ice Age drew to a close and the glaciers melted into oceans. Others may have moved down the Pacific coastline on small fishing vessels, subsisting on the rich sea life that flourished in an offshore kelp "forest" that stretched from Alaska to Baja California.

The numbers of these first Americans were, in all likelihood, quite small. They were distinctly healthy, for their long migrations across cold Beringia had destroyed many of the pathogens they might have carried. They were also highly mobile and their nomadic communities spread rapidly throughout the hemisphere. By 8000 BCE, they had reached all the way to Tierra del Fuego at the southern tip of South America. Near the eastern coast of North America, the Thunderbird dig in Virginia's Shenandoah Valley shows signs of continuous human occupation from before 9000 BCE until the arrival of Europeans.

Not everyone pushed to the south, however. The ancestors of the Inuits (called Eskimos by other Indians) crossed after 7000 BCE, when Beringia was again under water. Around 2000 BCE, these people began to migrate from the Aleutian Islands and Alaska to roughly their present sites in the Americas. Unlike their predecessors, they found the arctic environment to their liking and migrated across the northern rim of North America and then across the north Atlantic to Greenland.

1-1b *The Great Extinction and the Rise of Agriculture*

As the glaciers receded and the climate warmed, the people who had moved south and east found an attractive environment teeming with game. Imperial mammoths, huge mastodons, woolly rhinoceroses, a species of enormous bison, and giant ground sloths roamed the plains and forests, along with camels and herds of small horses, which could not be ridden and were valued only as food. These animals had thrived in a frigid climate but they had trouble adjusting to hot weather. They also had no instinctive fear of the two-legged intruders, who became ever more skillful at hunting them. A superior spear point, the fluted **Clovis tip**, appeared in the area of present-day New Mexico and Texas around 13,000 BCE, and its use spread rapidly throughout North and South America. As human families fanned out across the hemisphere, however, the big game began to disappear. Overhunting pushed the megafauna toward extinction, but the impact of human predation was vastly amplified by shifting environmental conditions. The warming climate reduced the available water and forage, debilitating the massive beasts. Most large animals of the Americas disappeared about 9,000 years ago.

Their passing left the hemisphere with a severely depleted number of animal species. Nothing as big as the elephant survived. The largest beasts left were bears, bison, and moose; the biggest cat was the jaguar. The extinction of these animal species probably led to a decline in human population as people struggled to cope with the diminished biodiversity and searched for new sources of food. Some Native Americans raised guinea pigs, turkeys, and ducks, but apart from dogs on both continents, they domesticated no large animals except in South America, where they used llamas to haul light loads in mountainous terrain and raised alpacas for wool. In Eurasia, with its numerous domesticated animals, the killer diseases such as smallpox and bubonic plague took hold first among domestic animals and then spread among humans. Disease by disease, over a long period of time, survivors developed some immunities. No comparable process occurred in the Americas, where few animals could be domesticated.

Some native peoples settled down without becoming farmers. Those in the Pacific Northwest sustained themselves through fishing, hunting, and the gathering of nuts, berries, and other edible plants. Men fished and hunted; women gathered. California peoples maintained some of the densest populations north of Mexico by collecting acorns and processing them into meal, which they baked into cakes. In the rain forests of Brazil, in south and central Florida, and in the cold woodlands of northern New England, hunter-gatherers also prospered without becoming farmers. In the Great Plains, the modern bison, a greatly dwarfed adaptation of the cold-climate bison, numbered in the millions, supporting numerous nomadic hunting societies for thousands of years.

CHRONOLOGY

30,000–13,000 BCE	Bering land bridge open • Migrations to the Americas begin
9000 BCE	Shenandoah Valley occupied
9000–7000 BCE	Most large American mammals become extinct
500 BCE–400 CE	Adena-Hopewell mound builders thrive in Ohio River valley
200–900	Mayan civilization flourishes in Mesoamerica
900–1250	Medieval Warm Period • Toltecs dominate the Valley of Mexico • Maize becomes a major food source in North America • Mogollon, Hohokam, and Anasazi cultures thrive in American Southwest • Cahokia becomes the largest Mississippian mound builders' city
1001–1014	Norse find Vinland on Newfoundland
1200s–1300s	Little Ice Age begins • Original inhabitants abandon Cahokia • Mogollon, Hohokam, and Anasazi cultures decline
1400s	Incas begin to dominate the Andes; Aztecs begin to dominate Mesoamerica (1400–1450) • Cheng Ho makes voyages of exploration for China (1405–1434) • Portuguese begin to master the Atlantic coast of Africa (1434) • First Portuguese slave factory established on African coast (1448) • Dias reaches Cape of Good Hope (1487) • Columbus reaches the Caribbean (1492) • Treaty of Tordesillas divides non-Christian world between Portugal and Spain (1494) • da Gama rounds Cape of Good Hope and reaches India (1497–1499)
1500s	Portuguese discover Brazil (1500) • Balboa crosses Isthmus of Panama to the Pacific (1513) • Magellan's fleet circumnavigates the globe; Cortés conquers the Aztec Empire (1519–1522) • de Vaca makes overland journey from Florida to Mexico (1528–1536) • Pizarro conquers the Inca Empire (1531–1532) • de Soto's expedition explores the American Southeast (1539–1543) • Coronado explores the American Southwest (1540–1542) • Jesuit mission established at Chesapeake Bay (1570–1571) • Philip II issues Royal Order for New Discoveries (1573) • Philip II unites Spanish and Portuguese empires (1580)

Most communities could not depend solely on hunting and gathering food, however. In a few places, some of them, almost certainly women, began to plant and harvest crops instead of simply gathering and eating what they found. In Asia and Africa, this practice—closely linked to the domestication of animals—happened quickly enough to be called the **Neolithic** (new or late Stone Age) revolution. But in the Americas the rise of farming had little to do with animals, occurred gradually, and might better be termed the Neolithic *evolution*. For millennia, farming supplemented diets that still depended mostly on fishing and hunting, now of smaller animals. In many regions, the main agricultural technique was the slash-and-burn system in which farmers cleared small patches of trees, burned away the underbrush, and planted seeds in an ashy soil that was rich with heat-released nutrients. Because this system gradually depleted the soil, communities had to move to new fields after a decade or two, often because accessible firewood had been exhausted. In this semisedentary way of life, few Indians acquired more personal property than the women could carry from one place to another, either during the annual hunt or when the whole community had to move. This limited interest in consumption would profoundly condition their response to capitalism after contact with Europeans.

Between 4000 and 1500 BCE, permanent farm villages developed in the Valley of Mexico, Central America, and the Andes. Their crops were different from those of the agricultural centers of Europe, the Middle East, and East Asia. The first American farmers grew manioc, chili peppers, pumpkins, potatoes, tomatoes, and several varieties of beans. Experimenting with different mutations of teosinte, a wild mountain grass, they transformed that modest plant into nutrient-rich maize, or Indian corn, which helped launch a population surge that was great enough to support cities.

1-2 The Emergence of Complex Societies in the Americas

 What were the major similarities and differences between the histories of the Andes and Mesoamerica during the first and early second millennia?

Despite their feats of plant manipulation and their soaring populations, even the most complex societies in the Americas faced daunting technological constraints. Indigenous Americans made use of metals, but more for decorative than practical purposes. Most metalworking skills originated in South America and spread to Mesoamerica during the early second millennium CE. Societies across the hemisphere fashioned copper into fishing tools and art objects, but they did not make bronze (a compound of copper and tin), nor did they find any use for iron. Nearly all of their tools were made of stone or bone, and their sharpest weapons were made from obsidian, a hard, glassy, volcanic rock. Some knew how to make a wheel—they had wheeled toys—but they did not seek practical purposes for this invention, apparently because North America had no draft animals, and South Americans used llamas mostly in steep, mountainous areas where wheeled vehicles would have been of no use.

▲ MAP 1.1 **Indian Settlement of America** The probable routes that people followed after they left Beringia and spread throughout the Americas.

Q Why did people follow several different routes into the Americas?

Q What factors may have encouraged people to stop and settle down?

1-2a The Andes: Cycles of Complex Cultures

Despite these technological limitations, indigenous Americans profoundly reshaped their worlds and built enduring civilizations. During the second millennium BCE, elaborate urban societies took shape in the Andes, where engineers devised highly productive agricultural systems at 12,000 feet above sea level, far above the altitude at which anyone else has ever been able to raise crops. In the 1980s, when archaeologists rebuilt part of the prehistoric Andean irrigation system according to ancient specifications, they discovered that it was far more productive than a system using modern fertilizers and machines. Some Andean peoples could produce 10 metric tons of potatoes per hectare (about 2.4 acres), as opposed to 1 to 4 tons on nearby modern fields. Lands using the Andean canal system never had to lie fallow.

This type of irrigation took hold around Lake Titicaca about 1000 BCE and spread throughout the Andes. Monumental architecture and urbanization appeared in the

1.2 Petroglyph Canyon, Valley of Fire, near Las Vegas, Nevada
People lived in the Valley of Fire since c. 2,000 BCE, recording important events and carving symbols into sandstone.

Q *What different meanings might the carvings have served and what different purposes might they have had?*

interior mountains and along the Peruvian coast. The coastal societies produced finely detailed pottery, much of it erotic, and built pyramids as centers of worship. In the highlands, people grew a great variety of food plants both tropical and temperate. Terraces, laid out at various altitudes on the mountainside, enabled communities to raise crops from different climatic zones, all a few hours distant from one another. At the lowest levels, they planted cotton in the hot, humid air. Farther up the mountain, they raised maize and other crops suitable to a temperate zone. At still higher elevations, they grew potatoes and grazed their alpacas and llamas. Taking advantage of the frost that formed most nights of the year, they invented freeze-dried food by carrying it far up the mountains. These classic Andean cultures collapsed by the 11th century, debilitated by prolonged droughts and intergroup rivalries. But the disruption that followed was temporary because new complex societies rose to reign over the region.

1-2b *Inca Civilization*

Around 1400 CE, the **Incas** emerged as the dominant imperial power in the Andes. They built their capital at Cuzco, high in the mountains. From that upland center, the Incas—the word applied both to the ruler and to the empire's dominant nation—forged an empire that eventually extended more than 2,000 miles from south to north. Narrow and long, the Inca Empire was the world's fastest-growing empire in the late 15th century. It was also one of the most ecologically diverse, covering steep mountains and deep valleys and extending from coastal lowlands to interior forests. The Incas bound their expanding realm together with an efficient network of roads and suspension bridges. Along these roads, the Incas maintained numerous storehouses for grain. They had no written language, but high-altitude runners, who memorized the Inca's oral commands, raced along the roads to relay their ruler's decrees over vast distances. They extracted resources from a variety of ecological niches, safeguarding themselves against climate shifts and crop failures, and they invented a decimal system that they used to keep records of the tribute they levied upon subject peoples. They used a device called a *quipu*, knotting variously colored strings in particular ways to encode information. By 1500, the Inca Empire ruled perhaps 8 to 12 million people. No other nonliterate culture has ever matched that feat.

1-2c *Mesoamerica: Cycles of Complex Cultures*

Mesoamerica experienced a similar cycle of change, but over a somewhat shorter period. Its successive cultures also comprised both upland and lowland societies. The **Olmecs**, who flourished in the hot and humid lowlands along the Gulf Coast between 1200 and 400 BCE, became the parent culture for the region. Theirs was the first urban culture in the Americas—it centered on three cities, San Lorenzo,

1.3 Terraces of Winay Wayna
Terraced agriculture was one of the most impressive achievements of pre-Columbian culture in the Andes. This terrace is located at the center of Inca power, near Cuzco and Machu Picchu.

Q *What were the advantages of terraced farming?*

1-2 The Emergence of Complex Societies in the Americas

Teotihuacan was already a city of 200,000 inhabitants, enormous temple pyramids, and brightly painted murals. Teotihuacan invested resources in comfortable apartment dwellings for ordinary people, not in monuments or inscriptions to rulers. It probably had a form of senate government, not a monarchy. The rapidly growing city extended its influence in all directions, founding new colonies across Mesoamerica to extract maize, beans, and other supplies. It remained a powerful force until its sudden destruction in the mid-8th century, apparently by conquest, because its shrines were toppled and the city was abandoned. Teotihuacan's growth may also have so depleted the resources of its core area that the city could not have sustained itself much longer.

In the tropical lowlands of Central America and the dry and hilly plateau of Yucatán, the **Mayan** culture went through a similar cycle from expansion to ecological crisis. It was also urban but less centralized than that of Teotihuacan, although some Mayan temples were just as monumental. For more than 1,000 years, Mayan culture rested on a network of competing city-states, which, as in ancient Greece, shared similar values. One of the largest Mayan cities, Tikal, arose on the plateau separating rivers flowing into the Caribbean from those emptying into the Gulf of Mexico. It controlled commerce with Teotihuacan and housed 100,000 people at its peak in the 8th century. Twenty other cities, most about one-fourth the size of Tikal, flourished throughout the region. Mayan engineers built canals to water the crops needed to support this urban system.

Mayans developed an expressive writing system that utilized stone carvings and they recorded their history in great detail. Scholars have deciphered most Mayan inscriptions, and Mayan texts are now studied much like those of Europe. Mayan art and writings reveal, for example, their preoccupation with astronomical computations, timekeeping, and a royal ritual of bloodletting, which facilitated communication with ancestors and gods. They also reveal the long reign of Pacal the Great, king (or "Great Sun") of the elegant city of Palenque, who was born on March 26, 603, and died on August 31, 683. His sarcophagus lists his ancestors through six generations. Other monuments tell of the Great Suns of other cities whom Pacal vanquished and sacrificed to the gods.

The classic Mayan civilization began to weaken after the fall of Teotihuacan, which disrupted Mayan trade with the Valley of Mexico. The crisis spread rapidly. Palenque, Tikal, and other prominent cities decayed in the 9th and 10th centuries when prolonged droughts destabilized their intensive farming system. The center of Mayan population and civilization shifted from the lowlands to the Yucatán plateau. Chichén Itzá, a city that had existed for centuries, preserved many distinctive Mayan traits but merged them with new influences from the Valley of Mexico, where the Toltecs had become dominant.

The Toltecs were a military society whose capital at Tula, with 40,000 people, was one-fifth the size of Teotihuacan at its peak. They prospered from the cocoa trade with tropical lowlands and extended their influence over surrounding societies. They controlled the Valley of Mexico until about 1200 CE, when they too declined. They left a legacy of conquest to later rulers in the valley, who all claimed descent from Toltec kings.

1.4 Olmec Stone Head This giant head is eight feet eight inches tall.

La Venta, and Tres Zapotes—which featured colossal stone heads that honored Olmec rulers. Aspects of Olmec culture became widely diffused throughout Mesoamerica. The Olmecs built the first pyramids and the first ballparks in the region. Their game, played with a heavy rubber ball, spread as far as what is now the southwestern United States. They developed a writing system and a dual calendar system that endured through the Aztec era. At the end of a 52-year cycle, the first day of the "short" calendar would again coincide with the first day of the "long" one. Olmecs faced the closing days of each cycle with dread, lest the gods allow the sun and all life on earth to be destroyed—something that, Olmecs warned, had already happened several times. They believed that the sacrifice of a god had been necessary to set the sun in motion in each new creation cycle and that only the blood of human sacrifice could placate the gods and keep the sun moving. These beliefs endured in Mesoamerica for millennia, regardless of the rise and fall of empires and cities. The arrival of the Spaniards in 1519 would create a religious as well as a political crisis, because that year marked the end of a 52-year cycle.

The Olmecs were succeeded by the city and empire of Teotihuacan, which emerged in the mountains not far from modern Mexico City (see Map 1.2). By the 4th century CE,

▲ **MAP 1.2 The Major Empires and Cities of the Andes and Mesoamerica from the 10th to the Early 15th Century** Both the Andes and Mesoamerica saw the rise and fall of numerous powerful regimes and cultural centers before the arrival of Europeans.

Q *Why did empires rise where they did between the 10th and early-15th centuries?*

Q *What were the main similarities and differences between the Aztec and Inca empires?*

1-2 The Emergence of Complex Societies in the Americas

1.5 *El Caracol*, **a Late Mayan Observatory at Chichén Itzá**
Astronomy was well developed in all of the pre-Columbian high cultures of Mesoamerica; however, if the Mayans used any specialized instruments to study the heavens, we do not know what they were.

1-2d The Aztecs and Tenochtitlán

By 1400, power in the Valley of Mexico was passing to the **Aztecs**, who had migrated from the north about two centuries earlier and had settled, with the bare sufferance of their neighbors, on the shore of Lake Texcoco. They built a great city, **Tenochtitlán**, out on the lake. Its only connection with the mainland was by several broad causeways. Lake Texcoco was 5,000 feet above sea level, and the lands around it were swampy, offering little cultivable soil. The Aztecs compensated by creating highly productive *chinampas*, floating gardens made of sediment and decaying vegetation, on swampy parts of the lake. Yet, their mounting population strained the food supply. In the 1450s, the threat of famine was severe (see Map 1.3).

Tenochtitlán, with a population exceeding 200,000, had forged an alliance with Texcoco and Tlacopan, two smaller lakeside cities. Together they dominated the area, but by the second quarter of the 15th century leadership was clearly passing to the Aztecs. As newcomers to the region, the Aztecs needed to prove themselves worthy heirs to Tula and Teotihuacan. They adopted the old religion and built and constantly rebuilt and enlarged their Great Pyramid of the Sun. They waged nearly constant wars to gain captives and to subdue bordering groups. Unlike the Incas, the Aztecs sought to extort rather than control others. By the late 15th century, Tenochtitlán held hundreds of tributary communities in its orbit, extracting massive amounts of maize, beans, cocoa, cotton, and luxuries from them. The Aztecs also acquired, through war and tribute, large numbers of captives, whose sacrifice they believed appeased the gods and empowered the empire.

Human sacrifice was an ancient ritual in Mesoamerica, but the Aztecs practiced it on an unprecedented scale. Although neighboring peoples shared the religious beliefs of the Aztecs, they nevertheless hated these conquerors from the north. After 1519, many Indians in Mesoamerica would help the Spaniards bring down the Aztecs. By contrast, the Spaniards would find few allies in the Andes, where resistance in the name of the Inca would persist for most of the 16th century and would even revive in the late 18th century—250 years after the conquest.

▲ **MAP 1.3 Valley of Mexico, 1519** Lake Texcoco and its principal cities, especially Tenochtitlán (built on the lake) and its allies, Tlacopan and Texcoco.

Q *Why did the Aztecs build their capital by Lake Texcoco?*
Q *How did the Aztecs transform the environment to meet their needs?*

1-3 Agricultural Take Off in North America

Q *How did maize cultivation change human history in North America?*

Mesoamerica was for North America what the Fertile Crescent was for Western Europe: a source of seeds and crops that would alter the parameters of human existence. The human-engineered maize was a life-transforming plant that could launch population explosions and prop up civilizations, but it was hard to transplant. A subtropical crop, it required warmth and long growing seasons, and it took centuries for people to develop new strains that could withstand the colder climates and drier soils in the north. Maize arrived in the semiarid highlands of the American Southwest around 2000 BCE, but it took several more centuries to turn it into a staple. Gradually, through trial and error, the region's farmers developed a new form of maize, *maiz de ocho*, a highly nutritious and adaptable eight-rowed flint corn that required a relatively short growing season. And when they began to plant squash and beans with maize, they produced a triad of crops that revolutionized food production in North America. Maize stalks provided structure for bean vines; beans restored nitrogen—which maize depleted—to the soil; and squash, spreading along the ground,

1.6 The Temple of the Sun at Teotihuacan The giant, stepped pyramid shown here is one of pre-Columbian America's most elegant pyramids.

Q Why did the Aztecs build their capital by Lake Texcoco?

Q How did the Aztecs transform the environment to meet their needs?

retained moisture in the soil and lessened weed growth. The three crops also complemented each other nutritionally. Maize is rich in carbohydrates, dried beans in protein, and together the three crops contain most essential vitamins and amino acids.

1-3a *Urban Cultures of the Southwest*

With the improved food production, complex societies emerged in the Southwest. The last century of the first millennium saw the onset of a warmer climate cycle—the Medieval Warm Period—which allowed the Mogollon and the Hohokam peoples to integrate farming firmly into their hunting and gathering economies. Both lived in villages and towns that featured multiroom adobe houses and public plazas, produced exquisitely painted pottery, and relied on canal irrigation farming. The Hohokams' irrigation system consisted of several hundred miles of canals and produced two harvests per year (see Map 1.4). They wove cotton cloth and traded with places as distant as California and Mesoamerica, circulating marine shells, turquoise, copper bells, and mirrors across vast distances. They imported a version of the Mesoamerican ball game and staged large public tournaments. Perhaps because of massive floods or because irrigation increased the salinity of the soil, their culture, after enduring for centuries, went into irreversible decline in the 14th century.

Even more tantalizing and mysterious is the brief flowering of the **Anasazi** (a Navajo word meaning "the ancient ones"), a cliff-dwelling people who have left behind some remarkable artifacts at Chaco Canyon in New Mexico,

1.7 Aztec Skull Rack Altar Displaying the skulls of sacrificial victims, such racks alienated native societies from the Aztecs and shocked the invading Spaniards.

Q What do skull racks tell us about the Aztec society and culture?

1-3 Agricultural Take Off in North America

1.8 Indian Women as Farmers
In this illustration, a French artist depicted 16th-century Indian women in southeastern North America.

at Mesa Verde in Colorado, and at other sites. In their caves and cliffs, they constructed apartment houses five stories high with hundreds of dwellings and with elegant and spacious kivas, meeting rooms for religious functions. The Anasazi were superb astronomers. Through an arrangement of rock slabs, open to the sun and moon at the mouth of a cave, and of spirals on the interior wall that plotted the movement of the sun and moon, they created a calendar that could track the summer and winter solstices and even the 19-year cycles of the moon, an astronomical refinement Europeans had not yet achieved. They traveled to their fields and brought in lumber and other distant supplies on a network of roads that ran for scores of miles in several directions. They achieved most of these feats over a period of about two centuries, although Anasazi pottery has been found that dates from much earlier times. In the late 13th century, apparently overwhelmed by a prolonged drought and by hostile invaders, they abandoned their principal sites. Pueblo architecture is a direct successor of that of the Anasazi, and the Pueblo Indians are descended from them.

1-3b North American Mound Builders

Another North American center of cultural innovation and social complexity emerged in the Eastern Woodlands, where distinct cultures of "mound builders" exerted a powerful influence over the interior. Named for the huge earthen mounds they erected, these cultures arose near the Mississippi and Ohio rivers and their tributaries. The earliest mound builders became semisedentary even before learning to grow crops. Fish, game, and the lush vegetation of the river valleys sustained them for most of the year and enabled them to erect permanent dwellings.

The first mound-building culture, the Adena-Hopewell, flourished between 500 BCE and 400 CE in the Ohio River valley (see Map 1.5). Its mounds were increasingly elaborate burial sites, suggesting belief in an afterlife and social stratification into elites and commoners. Mound-building communities participated in a commerce that spanned most of the continent between the Appalachians and the Rockies, the Great Lakes and the Gulf of Mexico. Obsidian from the Yellowstone Valley in the West, copper from the Great Lakes basin, and shells from the Gulf of Mexico have all been found buried in the Adena-Hopewell mounds. Both the mound building and the long-distance trade largely ceased after 400 CE, for reasons that remain unclear. Yet, the mounds were so impressive that when American settlers found them after the Revolution, they refused to believe that "savages" could have built them.

Adena-Hopewell culture had relied on casual cultivation of various crops. When the companion planting of squash, beans, and maiz de ocho spread into the Eastern Woodlands around 1000 CE, mound building revived, producing a dramatic epoch known as the Mississippian culture. This culture dominated the Mississippi River valley from modern St. Louis to Natchez, with the largest center at Cahokia in present-day Illinois. Ordinary people became "stinkards" in this culture, while some families had elite status. The "Great Sun" ruled with authority and was transported by litter from place to place. When he died, some of his wives, relatives, and retainers were sacrificed at his funeral to join him in the afterlife. Burial mounds thus became much grander in Mississippian communities. Atop the mounds in which their

CHAPTER 1 When Old Worlds Collide: Encounters in the Atlantic World to 1600

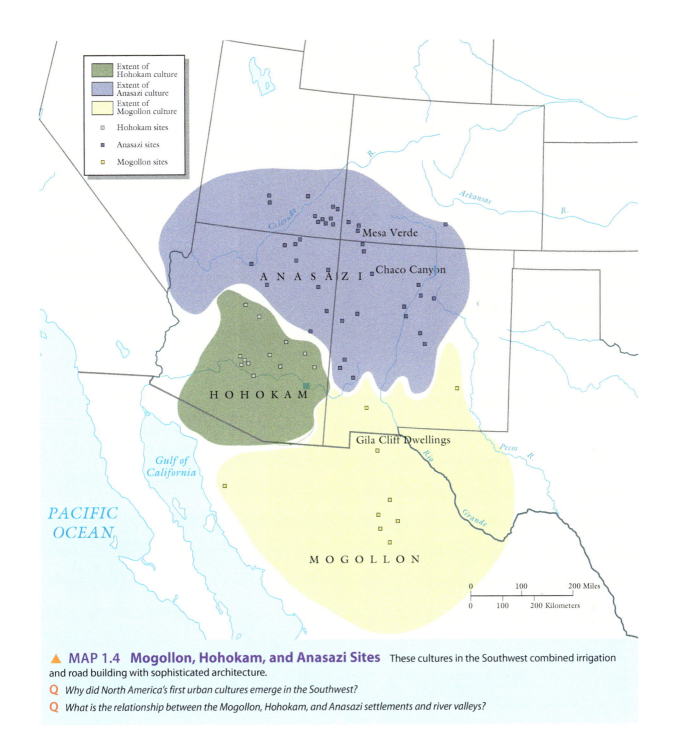

▲ **MAP 1.4 Mogollon, Hohokam, and Anasazi Sites** These cultures in the Southwest combined irrigation and road building with sophisticated architecture.

Q Why did North America's first urban cultures emerge in the Southwest?

Q What is the relationship between the Mogollon, Hohokam, and Anasazi settlements and river valleys?

rulers were interred, the Indians built elaborate places of worship and residences for the priests and Great Suns of their highly stratified society.

The city of **Cahokia**, near modern St. Louis, flourished from 900 to 1200 CE and may have had 20,000 or more residents at its peak, making it the largest city north of Mexico and half as populous as the contemporary Toltec capital at Tula. As was typical for many North American urban centers, a large portion of Cahokia's population consisted of captives and slaves, taken by war or via trade from other societies. Slaves added to Cahokia's labor force as well as its prestige. In North America control of people was more important than control of territory, and slaves were a tangible manifestation of Cahokia's power over others.

Sitting on the American Bottom, a broad floodplain at the juncture of the Mississippi and Missouri rivers, Cahokia was a bustling metropolis with an extensive hinterland. It had a grid pattern of rectangular plazas and platform mounds and it was surrounded by suburbs, auxiliary villages, and vast cornfields that stretched into the horizon. It was a center of continent-spanning trade networks and a seat of political power. Its enormous central mound, 100-foot-high Monks Mound, is the world's largest earthen work, and it speaks of the city's paramount status in the Mississippian world.

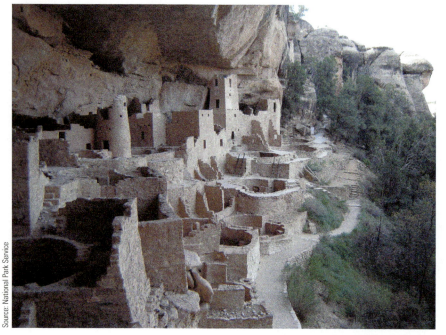

1.9 Anasazi Cliff Palace in Mesa Verde This building complex in what is today southern Colorado was a prominent Anasazi cliff dwelling that consisted of multistory stone rooms, towers, and underground kivas. It sat in a high alcove under a protruding cliff and was inhabited from the late 12th century until around 1300, when it was abandoned.

Q Why did the Anasazi build their houses on cliffs?

1-3c North America in 1491

Like the Hohokam and Anasazi cultures, Cahokia's preeminence did not last. Another climate shift, the onset of the Little Ice Age, together with soil depletion and enemy attacks brought down the great city by the 13th century. This sudden collapse of urban civilizations created a persisting caricature of North America as a somehow underdeveloped continent. Where European colonists encountered awe-inspiring indigenous empires in Mesoamerica and the Andes, in North America they found mere ruins, and came to see the continent as a vast wilderness world of savage natives and lost

1.10 The Great Serpent Mound Located near Chillicothe, Ohio, this mound is about 1,200 feet long and is one of the most spectacular mounds to survive from the Adena-Hopewell era.

1.11 Cahokia The largest Mississippian mound-building site was Cahokia, in Illinois, near St. Louis, Missouri. Depicted here is the city's sacred ceremonial center facing toward Monks Mound in the distance.

Q *How did Cahokia become so central and influential?*

cultural opportunities. Recent scholarship has overturned this image, showing how North America was culturally dynamic, covered with trade networks, and filled with people. In the late 15th century, North America was home to perhaps as many as 10 million people (the estimates for the entire hemisphere range from 50 million to more than 100 million) who spoke hundreds of languages, pursued diverse economic strategies, believed in numerous gods, and envisioned widely different ways of organizing the social worlds in which they lived. Some lived in locally oriented communities, while others—such as the Iroquois and the Hurons in the Northeast—formed powerful confederacies that dominated large areas. North America on the eve of European contact was an old and complex world in motion.

1-3d The Norse Connection

The Medieval Warm Period that had facilitated the agricultural take off and the rise of such urban centers as Chaco Canyon and Cahokia in North America also facilitated the movement of Europeans over long distances. The Norse, a Germanic people in Scandinavia, began to extend their excursions beyond the British Isles and France into the Atlantic. Challenging the contrary currents of the north Atlantic with their sleek, sail- and oar-powered longboats, Viking warriors occupied Iceland in the late 9th century; a century later they reached and settled in Greenland (then much greener than today), encountering the Inuits.

In 1001, Leif Ericsson sailed west from Greenland and began to explore the coast of North America. He made three more voyages and started a colony that he called "Vinland" on the northern coast of Newfoundland. The local Indians (called "Skrellings" by the Norse, which means "barbarians" or "weaklings") resisted vigorously, but the Norse soon quarreled among themselves and abandoned the colony by 1014. The Norse left Vinland, but they continued to visit North America for another century, probably to get wood. A 12th-century Norse coin, recovered from an Indian site in Maine, provides proof of their continuing contact with North America.

In the late 15th century, the Norse also lost Greenland. There, not long before Columbus sailed in 1492, the last Norse settler died a lonely death. In the chaos that followed the Black Death in Europe and Greenland after 1350 and the onset of the Little Ice Age, the colony suffered a severe population decline and slowly withered away. Despite their spectacular exploits, the Norse had no impact on the later course of American history. They had reached a dead end.

1-4 Europe and the World by the 15th Century

Q *What enabled relatively backward European societies to establish dominance over the oceans of the world?*

Nobody in the year 1400 could have foreseen the course of European expansion that was about to begin. Europe stood at the edge, not the center, of world commerce. It desired much that others possessed but made little that those others wished to acquire.

1-4a China: The Rejection of Overseas Expansion

By just about every standard, China under the Ming dynasty was the world's most complex culture. In the 15th century, the government of China, staffed by well-educated bureaucrats, ruled 100 million people, a total half again as large as the combined populations of all the European states west of Russia. The Chinese had invented the compass, gunpowder, and early forms of printing and paper money. Foreigners coveted the silks, teas, and other fine products available in China, but they had little to offer in exchange. China's capital

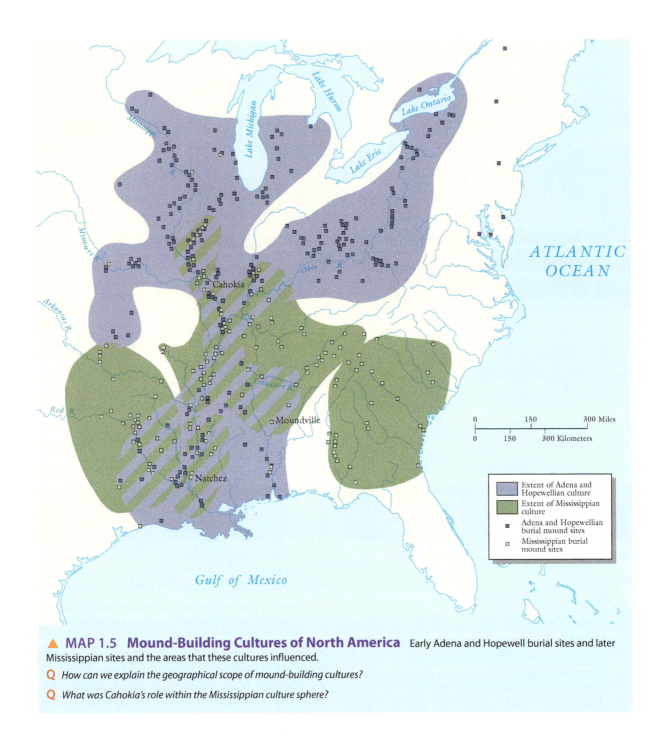

▲ MAP 1.5 **Mound-Building Cultures of North America** Early Adena and Hopewell burial sites and later Mississippian sites and the areas that these cultures influenced.

Q *How can we explain the geographical scope of mound-building cultures?*

Q *What was Cahokia's role within the Mississippian culture sphere?*

city (today's Beijing) was the world's largest and grandest, insisted the Venetian merchant-traveler Marco Polo; it received 1,000 cartloads of silk a day. China, he maintained, outshone Europe and all other cultures.

The Chinese agreed. Between 1405 and 1434, a royal eunuch, Cheng Ho, led six large fleets from China to the East Indies and the coast of East Africa, trading and exploring along the way. Had China thrown its resources and talents into overseas expansion, the subsequent history of the world would have been vastly different, but most of what the Chinese learned about the outside world merely confirmed their belief that other cultures had little to offer their Celestial Kingdom.

No one followed Cheng Ho's lead after he died. Instead, the emperor banned the construction of oceangoing ships and later forbade anyone to own a vessel with more than two masts. China turned inward.

1-4b Christian Europe Challenges Islam

Western Europe was, by global standards, a backward place in 1400. Compared with China or the Islamic world, it suffered severe disadvantages. Europeans desired China's

1.12a (top left), 1.12b (top right), and 1.12c (bottom left) Longhouse, Wigwam, and Tepee The longhouse (top left), made from bark or mats stretched over a wooden frame, was the standard communal dwelling of the Iroquois and Huron peoples. Most Algonquian peoples of the Eastern Woodlands lived in wigwams (top right) like this undated example. Wigwams were made by bending the boughs of trees into a frame to be covered with animal skins. West of the Mississippi, most Plains Indians lived in small but strong tepees (bottom left), which were usually made from poles covered with buffalo hides. All of these dwellings were constructed by women.

Q *Identify the similarities and differences among the three different dwelling styles. What might explain them?*

silks and coveted East Indian spices to enliven their food and help preserve it through long winters. But because Europeans produced little that Asians wished to buy, they had to pay for these imports with silver or gold, both of which were scarce. Moreover, Europe's location on the Atlantic rim of the Eurasian continent had always made access to Asian trade difficult and costly. Islamic societies controlled overland trade with Asia and the only known seaborne route to Asia through the Persian Gulf. As of 1400, Arab mariners were the world's best.

In fact, while Europe's sphere of influence was shrinking, and while China seemed content with what it already had, Islamic states embarked on another great phase of expansion. Europe's mounted knights in heavy armor failed to stop the Ottoman Turks, who took Constantinople in 1453, overran the Balkans by the 1520s, and even threatened Vienna. The Safavid Empire in Iran (Persia) rose to new splendor at the same time. Other Muslims carried the Koran to Indonesia and northern India, where they erected the powerful Mughal Empire (see Map 1.6).

Yet, Europe had its own advantages. Its economy had made impressive gains in the Middle Ages, primarily because of agricultural advances, such as improved plows and crop rotation, which fostered population growth. By 1300, more than 100 million people were living in Europe. Europe's farms could not sustain further growth, however. As the climate cooled, lean years and famines ensued, leaving people undernourished. In the late 1340s, the Black Death (bubonic plague) reduced the population by more than one-third. Recurring bouts of plague kept population low until about 1500, when vigorous growth resumed. The long decline during the 15th century had allowed overworked soils to regain their fertility, and per capita income rose dramatically among people who now had stronger immunities to disease.

By then, European metallurgy and architecture were quite advanced. The Renaissance, which revived interest in the literature and art of ancient Greece and Rome, also gave a new impetus to European culture, especially after Johannes Gutenberg invented the printing press and movable type in the 1430s. Soon information began to circulate more rapidly in Europe than anywhere else in the world. This revolution in communications permitted improvements in ship design and navigational techniques to become a self-reinforcing process. The Arabs, by contrast, borrowed block printing from China in the 10th century but gave it up by 1400.

Unlike China, none of Europe's kingdoms was a self-contained economy. All states had to trade with one another and with the non-Christian world. Although in 1400 this need was a handicap, it slowly became an asset. No single state had a monopoly on the manufacture of firearms or on the flow of capital, and European states began to compete with one another to gain access to these resources and master new maritime and military techniques. The ensuing rivalries and wars increased rather than undermined state power. States

1-4 Europe and the World by the 15th Century

▲ **MAP 1.6 Expansion of Islam** While Europeans were beginning to move overseas, Islam was also expanding into southeastern Europe, various parts of Africa, the Indian subcontinent, and the East Indies.

Q *What factors help explain the rapid expansion of Islam?*

Q *What advantages did European kingdoms have over Islamic states and empires?*

extracted the means of war—money, men, weapons—from their subjects, growing increasingly powerful in the process. European armies grew more formidable, and European fleets started to outsail and outfight their rivals.

1-4c The Legacy of the Crusades

Much earlier historical experiences helped turn Europe's growing power into overseas expansion. In the early second millennium, Europeans organized several crusades to conquer the Holy Land from Islam. Crusaders established their own Kingdom of Jerusalem, which survived for more than a century but was finally retaken in 1244. During the next 250 years, while a new wave of Islamic expansion seemed about to engulf much of the world, Christian Europe gained only a few Mediterranean and Atlantic islands but learned some important lessons in the process. To make Palestine profitable, the crusaders had taken over sugar plantations already there and had worked them with a combination of free and slave labor. After they were driven from the Holy Land, the crusaders retreated to the Mediterranean islands of Cyprus, Malta, Crete, and Rhodes, where they used slaves to raise sugar cane or grapevines.

Long before Columbus, these planters had created the economic components of overseas expansion. They assumed that colonies should produce a **staple crop**, at least partly through **slave labor**, for sale in Europe. The first slaves were Muslim captives. In the 14th and 15th centuries, planters turned to pagan Slavs (hence the word *slave*) from the Black Sea area and the Adriatic. Some black Africans were also acquired from Arab merchants who controlled the caravan trade across the Sahara Desert, but these early plantations did not exploit their laborers with the intensity that later became routine in the Americas.

1-4d The Unlikely Pioneer: Portugal

It seemed highly improbable in 1400 that Europe was standing on the threshold of a dramatic expansion. That Portugal would lead the way seemed even less likely. A small kingdom of fewer than a million people, Portugal had been united for less than a century. Lisbon, with 40,000 people, was the only city of any size. Portugal's maritime traditions lagged well behind those of the Italian states, France, and England. Its merchant class was tiny, and it had little capital.

But Portugal also had significant advantages. It enjoyed internal peace and an efficient government at a time when its neighbors were beset by war and internal upheaval. Moreover, its location at the intersection of the Mediterranean and

Atlantic worlds prompted its mariners to ask how they could transform the Atlantic from a barrier into a highway.

At first, the Portuguese were interested in short-term gains rather than in some all-water route to Asia. They knew that Arab caravans crossed the Sahara to bring gold, slaves, and ivory from black Africa to Europe, and they believed that an Atlantic voyage to coastal points south of the Sahara would undercut Arab traders and bring large profits. The greatest problem they faced in this quest was Cape Bojador, with its treacherous shallows, awesome waves, and strong northerly winds. Several bold captains had sailed around the cape, but none had returned. A member of the Portuguese royal family, Prince Henry, challenged this barrier by sponsoring several voyages along the African coast. In 1434, an expedition passed the cape, explored the coastline, and then sailed west into the Atlantic until it met favorable winds and currents that carried it back to Europe. Other expeditions followed, opening sea-lanes into the resource-rich West Africa below Sahara, where the Portuguese found the wealth they had been seeking—gold, ivory, and slaves.

During the following decades, Portugal vaulted past all rivals in two major areas—the ability to navigate the high seas beyond sight of land, and the capacity to defeat any non-European fleet on the world's oceans. Portuguese (and later Spanish) navigators mapped the prevailing winds and currents on the high seas over most of the globe. They collected geographic information from classical sources, foreigners, and modern navigators. They studied the superior designs of Arab vessels, copied them, and improved on them. They increased the ratio of length to beam (width at the broadest point of the hull) from 2:1 to 3:1, borrowed the lateen (triangular) sail from the Arabs, and combined it with square rigging in the right proportion to produce a superb oceangoing vessel, the caravel. A **caravel** could achieve speeds from 3 to 12 knots and could beat closer to a headwind than any other sailing ship. Portuguese captains also used the compass and adopted the Arabs' astrolabe, a device that permits accurate calculation of latitude, or distances north and south. (The calculation of longitude—distances east and west—is much more difficult and was not mastered until the 18th century.) As they skirted the African coast, these Portuguese sailors made precise charts and maps that later mariners could follow.

The Portuguese also learned how to mount heavy cannon on the decks of their ships—a formidable advantage in an age when others fought naval battles by grappling and boarding enemy vessels. Portuguese ships were able to stand farther off and literally blow their opponents out of the water. As the 15th century advanced, Portuguese mariners explored ever farther along the African coast, looking for wealth and eventually a direct, cheap route to Asia.

1-4e Africa, Colonies, and the Slave Trade

The mostly agricultural population that inhabited West Africa also included skilled craftsmen. West Africans probably learned how to use iron long before Europeans did, and they

1.13 *The Caravel:* A Swift Oceangoing Vessel This caravel is a modern reconstruction of the 15th-century *Niña*, which crossed the Atlantic with Columbus in 1492.

had been supplying Europe with most of its gold for hundreds of years through indirect trade across the desert. West Africa's political history had been marked by the rise and fall of a series of large inland states. The most recent of these, the empire of Mali, was already in decline by 1450. As the Portuguese advanced past the Sahara, their commerce began to pull trade away from the desert caravans, which further weakened Mali and other interior states. By 1550, the empire had fallen apart.

The Portuguese also founded offshore colonies along the way. They began to settle the uninhabited Madeira Islands in 1418, took possession of the Azores between 1427 and 1450, occupied the Cape Verde group in the 1450s, and took over São Tomé in 1470. Like exploration, colonization turned a profit. Lacking investment capital and experience in overseas settlement, the Portuguese drew on Italian merchants for both. In this way, the plantation complex of staple crops and slavery migrated from the Mediterranean to the Atlantic. Beginning in the 1440s, Portuguese island planters produced sugar or wine, increasingly with slave labor imported from nearby Africa. Some plantations, particularly on São Tomé, kept several hundred slaves at work growing and processing sugar (see Map 1.7).

At first, the Portuguese acquired their slaves by landing on the African coast, attacking agricultural villages, and carrying off everyone they could catch; but these raids enraged coastal peoples and made other forms of trade more difficult. In the decades after 1450, the slave trade assumed its classic form. The Portuguese established small posts, or **factories**, along the coast—or ideally, on small offshore islands, such as Arguin Island near Cape Blanco, where they built their first African fort in 1448. Operating out of these bases, traders would buy slaves from the local rulers, who usually acquired their victims by waging war. During the long history of the **Atlantic slave trade**, nearly every African shipped overseas had first been enslaved by other Africans.

Slavery had long existed in Africa. African societies raided their neighbors for slaves, which were a significant form of personal wealth, and Muslim traders may have transported more than 10 million people out of Africa between 750 and

▲ **MAP 1.7 Africa and the Mediterranean in the 15th Century** The Mediterranean islands held by Europeans in the late Middle Ages, the Atlantic islands colonized by Portugal and Spain in the 15th century, the part of West Africa from Cape Blanco to Angola that provided the main suppliers of the Atlantic slave trade, and the Portuguese all-water route to India after 1497.

Q *What factors explain the rapid rise of Portugal's empire?*
Q *Why did the Portuguese not build settler colonies in Africa and Asia?*

1500. Yet, the slavery that Europeans imposed marked a major departure. When the Atlantic slave trade began, no African middleman could have foreseen how the enslavement of Africans by Europeans would differ from the enslavement of Africans by Africans. In Africa, slaves were not forced to toil endlessly to produce staple crops, and their descendants often became fully assimilated into the captors' society. Slaves were not isolated as a separate caste. By the time African middlemen learned about the cruel conditions of slavery under European rule, the trade had become too lucrative to stop, although several African societies tried. They discovered, moreover, that those who refused to participate in the trade were likely

1.14 The Portuguese Slave-Trading Fortress of Elmina Located on the Gold Coast of West Africa, the fortress was built in 1481.

Q *How did slave-trading fortresses like Elmina shape world history?*

to become its victims. When the rulers of the Kongo embraced Catholicism in the 16th century, they protested against the Atlantic slave trade, only to see their own people become vulnerable to enslavement by others. The non-Christian kingdom of Benin learned the same lesson.

The Portuguese made the slave trade profitable by exploiting rivalries among the more than 200 small states of West and Central Africa, an area that was divided into more languages and small states than Europeans would find anywhere else in the world. Despite many cultural similarities among these groups, West Africans had never thought of themselves as a single people. Nor did they share a universal religion that might have restrained them from selling other Africans into slavery. Muslims believed it sinful to enslave a fellow believer. Western Europeans, although quite capable of waging destructive wars against one another, believed that enslaving fellow Christians was immoral. Enslaving pagan or Muslim Africans was another matter. Some Europeans even believed that they were doing these people a favor by making their souls eligible for salvation.

1-4f Portugal's Asian Empire

Portuguese exploration continued, paying for itself through gold, ivory, and slaves. The government finally decided to support the quest for an all-water route to Asia. In 1487, Bartolomeu Dias reached the Cape of Good Hope at the southern tip of Africa and headed east toward the Indian Ocean, but his crew rebelled in those stormy waters, and he turned back. Ten years later, Vasco da Gama led a small fleet around the Cape of Good Hope and sailed on to the southwestern coast of India. In a voyage that lasted more than two years (1497–1499), da Gama bargained and fought for spices that yielded a 20-to-1 profit.

Da Gama opened the way for Portugal's empire in the East. To secure their Asian trade, the Portuguese established a chain of naval bases that extended from East Africa to the mouth of the Persian Gulf, then to Goa on the west coast of India, and from there to the Moluccas, or East Indies. Portuguese missionaries penetrated Japan. The Moluccas became the Asian center of the Portuguese seaborne empire, with their spices yielding most of the wealth that Portugal extracted from its eastern holdings. In the early 16th century, African and Asian trade was providing two-thirds of Portugal's state revenues. Beyond ensuring its continued access to spices, Portugal made little effort to govern its holdings, and its eastern empire never became colonies of settlement. In all of their Asian outposts, the Portuguese remained heavily outnumbered by native peoples.

1-4g Early Lessons

As the Norse failure showed, the ability to navigate the high seas gave no guarantee of lasting success. Sustained expansion overseas required the support of a home government and ready access to what other states had learned. The Portuguese drew on Italian capital and maritime skills, as well as on Arab learning and technology, in launching their ventures. The Spaniards, in turn, would learn much from the Portuguese. The French, Dutch, and English would borrow from the Italians, Portuguese, and Spaniards.

The economic impulse behind colonization was thus in place long before Columbus sailed west. The desire for precious metals provided the initial stimulus, but staple crops and slavery kept that impetus alive. Before the 19th century, more than two-thirds of the people who crossed the Atlantic were slaves who were brought to America to grow sugar or other staples. The Atlantic slave trade was not some unfortunate exception to a larger story of liberty. For three and a half centuries, it was the norm.

1.15 The City of Benin (1668) By both European and African standards, Benin, a center of the slave trade, was a very large city in the 17th century.

1-5 Spain, Columbus, and the Americas

Q *What kinds of different motives shaped early Spanish colonialism in the Americas?*

While the Portuguese surged east, Spaniards more sluggishly moved west. Shortly after 1400, as Portugal gained experience by colonizing Madeira and the Azores, the Spanish kingdom of Castile sent its first settlers to the Canary Islands. The Spaniards spent the last third of the 15th century conquering the local inhabitants, the Guanches, who had left North Africa before the rise of Islam and had been living almost completely cut off from Africa and Europe for a thousand years. By the 1490s, the Spanish had all but exterminated them, the first people to face virtual extinction in the wake of European expansion.

Except for seizing the Canaries, the Spaniards devoted little attention to exploration or colonization. Instead, for most of the 15th century, the Iberian kingdoms of Aragon and Castile warred against other powers, quarreled with each other, or dealt with internal unrest. But in 1469 Prince Ferdinand of Aragon married Princess Isabella of Castile. They soon inherited their respective thrones to form the kingdom of Spain, which had a population of about 4.9 million by 1500. Together, Aragon and Castile formed a powerful, expansionist realm. Aragon, a Mediterranean society, had made good on an old claim to the Kingdom of Naples and Sicily and thus possessed an imperial bureaucracy with experience in administering overseas possessions. Castile had turned over much of its overseas trade to merchants and mariners from Genoa in northern Italy, who had settled in the port of Seville, imbuing the city with commercial ambition. Castilians had also taken the lead in expelling the Moors from the Iberian Peninsula, developing in the process a dynamic culture of expansion, violence, and fervent Catholicism.

In January 1492, Isabella and Ferdinand completed the reconquest of Spain by taking Granada, the last outpost of Islam on the Iberian Peninsula. Flush with victory, they gave unconverted Jews six months to become Christians or be expelled from Spain. More than half of Spain's 80,000 Jews fled. A decade later, Ferdinand and Isabella also evicted all unconverted Moors. Castile entered the 16th century as an expanding and fiercely Catholic society, and this attitude accompanied the Spanish overseas.

1-5a Columbus

A talented navigator from Genoa named Christopher Columbus sought to benefit from the victory at Granada. He had served the Portuguese Crown for several years, engaged in the slave trade between Africa and the Atlantic islands, married the daughter of a prominent Madeira planter, and may even have sailed to Iceland. He had been pleading for years with the courts of Portugal, England, France, and Spain to give him the ships and men to attempt an unprecedented feat: He planned to reach East Asia by sailing west across the Atlantic.

Columbus's proposed voyage was controversial, but not because he assumed the earth was round. Learned men agreed on that point, but they disagreed about the earth's size. Columbus put its circumference at only 16,000 miles. He proposed to reach Japan or China by sailing west a mere 3,000 miles. The Portuguese scoffed at his reasoning. They put the planet's circumference at about 26,000 miles, and they warned Columbus that he would perish on the vast ocean if he tried his mad scheme. Their calculations were, of course, far more accurate than those of Columbus; the circumference of the earth is about 25,000 miles at the equator. Even so, the fall of Granada gave Columbus another chance to plead his case. Isabella, who now had men and resources to spare, grew more receptive to his request. She put him in charge of a fleet of two caravels, the *Niña* and the *Pinta*, together with a larger, square-rigged vessel, the **Santa María**, which Columbus made his flagship.

Columbus's motives were both religious and practical. Like many contemporaries, he believed that the world was going to end soon but that God would make the Gospel available to all humankind before the last days. As the "Christ-bearer" (the literal meaning of his first name), Columbus was convinced that he had a role to play in bringing on the Millennium, the period at the end of history when Jesus would return and rule with his saints for 1,000 years; however, he was not at all averse to acquiring wealth and glory along the way.

Embarking in August 1492, Columbus headed south to the Canaries, picked up provisions, and sailed west across the Atlantic. He promised a prize to the first sailor to sight land. Despite his assurances that they had not sailed far, the crews grew restless in early October. Columbus pushed on. When land was spotted, on October 12, he claimed the prize for himself. He said he had seen a light in the distance the previous night (see Map 1.8).

The Spaniards splashed ashore on San Salvador, now Watling's Island in the Bahamas. Convinced that he was somewhere in the East Indies, near Japan or China, Columbus called the local inhabitants "Indians," a word that meant nothing to them but one that has endured. When the peaceful Tainos (or Arawaks) claimed that the Carib Indians on nearby islands were cannibals, Columbus interpreted their word for "Carib" to mean the great "Khan" or emperor of China, known to him through Marco Polo's account of his travels to China in the 1270s. Searching for the Caribs, Columbus poked about the coasts of Cuba and Hispaniola. Then, on Christmas, the *Santa María* ran onto rocks and had to be abandoned. A few weeks later, Columbus sailed for Spain on the *Niña*, leaving some of his crew to occupy Hispaniola. By then the Tainos had seen enough. Before Columbus returned on his second voyage in late 1493, they had killed all of them.

The voyage had immediate consequences. In 1493, Pope Alexander VI (a Spaniard) issued a bull, *Inter Caeteras*, which divided all non-Christian lands between Spain and Portugal. A year later, in the Treaty of Tordesillas, the two kingdoms adjusted the dividing line, with Spain eventually claiming most of the Western Hemisphere, plus the Philippines, and Portugal most of the Eastern Hemisphere, including the African coast, plus Brazil. As a result, Spain never acquired direct access to the African slave trade.

Columbus made three more voyages in quest of China and served as governor of the Spanish Indies. He made concerted efforts to plant colonies and Christianity in the new lands, but his efforts were frustrated by the kind of deep cultural misunderstandings that would complicate the relations between Europeans and Indians for centuries. On his second voyage, Columbus brought the first missionaries to the Americas. After one of them preached to a group of Tainos and presented them with some holy images, the Indians "left the chapel, … flung the images to the ground, covered them with a heap of earth, and pissed upon it." The governor, a brother of Columbus, had them burned alive. The Indians may have seen this punishment as a form of human sacrifice to a vengeful god. They had no context for understanding the Christian distinction between human sacrifice and punishment for desecration.

Columbus also faced resistance back in Spain. Castilians never really trusted this Genoese opportunist, who spoke their language with a foreign accent and was a weak and cruel administrator to boot. The colonists often defied him and in 1500, after his third voyage, they shipped him back to Spain in chains. Although later restored to royal favor, he died in 1506 a bitter, disappointed man.

1-5b Spain and the Caribbean

By then, overseas settlement had acquired a momentum of its own as thousands of ex-soldiers, frustrated hidalgos (minor nobles with little wealth), and assorted adventurers drifted across the Atlantic. They carried with them seeds for Europe's cereal crops and livestock, including horses, cows, sheep, goats, and pigs. On islands without fences, the animals roamed freely, eating everything in sight, and soon threatened the Tainos' food supply. Unconcerned, the Spaniards forced the increasingly malnourished Indians to work for them, mostly panning for gold. Under these pressures, the native population fell catastrophically throughout the Caribbean. By 1514, only 22,000 able-bodied adults remained on Hispaniola, from an initial population of perhaps 1 million. The native people died even more rapidly than the meager supply of placer gold disappeared. This story was soon repeated on Cuba, Jamaica, and other islands. A whole way of life all but vanished from the earth to be replaced by sugar, slaves, and livestock as the Spaniards despaired of finding other forms of wealth. African slaves, acquired from the Portuguese, soon arrived to replace the dead Indians as a labor force.

The Spaniards continued their New World explorations. Juan Ponce de León tramped through Florida in quest of a legendary fountain of youth, calculating that such an elixir would bring a handsome price in Europe. Vasco Núñez de Balboa became the first European to reach the Pacific Ocean after he crossed the Isthmus of Panama in 1513. Even so, a full generation after Columbus's first voyage, Spain had gained little wealth from these new possessions, whatever and wherever they turned out to be. One geographer concluded that Spain had found a whole new continent, which he named "America" in honor of his informant, the explorer Amerigo Vespucci. For those who doubted this claim, Ferdinand Magellan, a Portuguese mariner serving the king of Spain, settled the issue when his fleet sailed around the world between 1519 and 1522.

Interpreting the Visual Past

How to Understand Columbus's Landing?

When printed books became more affordable and common during the 16th century, Europeans increasingly learned about the Western Hemisphere—its indigenous habitants and its colonization—through images. One of the most prolific and influential illustrators of the age was Theodor de Bry, who produced several books based on firsthand observations by European explorers, each lavishly illustrated with engravings. This engraving, published in 1594, depicts Columbus's landing in San Salvador in 1492 and his first encounter with the Taino Indians. Produced and published more than a century after the actual event, de Bry's image captures how many Europeans had come to understand Columbus's landing and the subsequent colonization of the Americas. It is, therefore, both a portrayal and an interpretation of a seminal historical event. For historians, it is a value-laden document that invites critical scrutiny.

Q *By the late 16th century, the subjugation and enslavement of Native Americans had become an intensely debated question in Europe. How do you think images like this have shaped contemporary European understandings of New World encounters and the history of colonialism?*

Q *Consider how de Bry depicts different actors and the landscape. Does his image promote a particular political agenda? How do you think the advocates and opponents of Indian slavery might have reacted to the image?*

1.16 **Theodor de Bry, Christopher Columbus (1451–1506) Welcomed by the Natives, 1594.**

▲ **MAP 1.8 Columbus's First Voyage, 1492** The route taken by Columbus from Palos, Spain, to the Canary Islands, then to San Salvador or possibly Samana Cay (see inset map), and finally back to Europe.

Q *Compare this map with Map 1.7. Why did Portuguese and Spanish expansions unfold so differently?*

Q *What were the main differences between the Portuguese and Spanish empires?*

1-6 Conquest and Catastrophe

 What enabled relatively few Spanish conquerors to subjugate the powerful empires of the Aztecs and the Incas?

A generation after Columbus's landing on San Salvador, Spanish **conquistadores**, or conquerors, shifted their sights from the Caribbean islands to the American mainland. There, in the highlands of Mexico and Peru, they stumbled upon a different kind of Native America, one of ancient civilizations and vast empires. They found this Native America both daunting and irresistible.

1-6a *The Conquest of Mexico and Peru*

During the three years when Ferdinand Magellan's fleet was circumnavigating the globe, **Hernán Cortés** sailed from Cuba, invaded Mexico, and found the treasure that Spaniards had been seeking. In 1519, he landed at a place he named Veracruz (The True Cross), and over the next several months he succeeded in tracking down the fabulous empire of the Aztecs high in the Valley of Mexico. When his small army of 400 men first laid eyes on the Aztec capital of Tenochtitlán, they wondered if they were dreaming, but they marched on. Moctezuma (or Montezuma II), the Aztec "speaker," or ruler, sent rich presents to persuade the Spaniards to leave, but the gesture had the opposite effect. "They picked up the gold and fingered it like monkeys," an Aztec later recalled. "Their bodies swelled with greed, and their hunger was ravenous.... They snatched at the golden ensigns, waved them from side to side and examined every inch of them."

Ecstatic, Cortés led his army into Tenochtitlán and seized Moctezuma, the Aztec ruler, as prisoner and hostage. Although overwhelmingly outnumbered, Cortés and his men began to destroy Aztec religious objects, replacing them with images of the Virgin Mary or other Catholic saints. In response, while Cortés was away, the Aztecs rose against the intruders. Moctezuma was killed, and the Spaniards were driven out

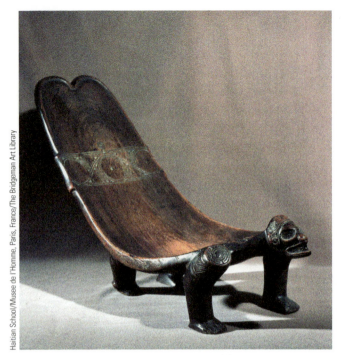

1.17 Wooden Stool (Duho) Inlaid with Gold From the late pre-Columbian era in the Caribbean, this stool probably honored the deities and ancestors of a chieftain.

with heavy losses. But then smallpox, which the Spaniards left behind, began killing Aztecs by the thousands. Cortés found refuge with the nearby Tlaxcalans, a proudly independent people who had never submitted to Aztec rule. With thousands of their warriors, he returned the next year, built several warships armed with cannons to dominate Lake Texcoco, and destroyed Tenochtitlán. He had hoped to leave the great city intact, not wreck it, but he and the Aztecs found no common understanding that would enable them to stop fighting before the city lay in ruins. With royal support from Spain, the conquistadores established themselves as new imperial rulers in Mesoamerica, looted all the silver and gold they could find, and built Mexico City on the ruins of Tenochtitlán.

Rumors abounded about an even richer civilization far to the south, and in 1531 and 1532 Francisco Pizarro finally located the Inca Empire high in the Andes. Smallpox had preceded him and killed the reigning Inca. In the civil war that followed, Atahualpa had defeated his brother to become the new Inca. Pizarro captured Atahualpa, held him hostage, and massacred many of his followers. Some of the Inca's recent enemies allied with Pizarro and the Spaniards. Atahualpa filled his throne room with precious metals as a truly royal ransom, but Pizarro had him strangled anyway. Tens of thousands of angry Indians besieged the Spaniards for months in Cuzco, the Inca capital, but Pizarro, although vastly outnumbered, managed to hold out and finally prevailed. After subduing the insurgents, the Spanish established a new capital at Lima on the coast.

In the course of a few years, some hundreds of Spanish soldiers with thousands of Indian allies had conquered two enormous empires with a combined population perhaps five times greater than that of all Spain. But only in the 1540s did the Spanish finally locate the bonanza they had been seeking. The fabulous silver mines at Potosí in present-day Bolivia and other smaller lodes in Mexico became the source of Spain's wealth and power for the next century. So wondrous did the exploits of the conquistadores seem by then that anything became believable, including rumors that cities of gold lay waiting in the interior of North America.

1-6b North American Conquistadores and Missionaries

Alvar Núñez Cabeza de Vaca was one of four survivors of a disastrous 1528 Spanish expedition to Florida (see Map 1.9). He made his way back to Mexico City in 1536 after an overland journey that took him from Florida through Texas and northern Mexico. In a published account of his adventures, he briefly mentioned Indian tales of great and populous cities to the north, and this reference soon became stories of "golden cities." An expedition led by Hernando de Soto landed in Florida in 1539 and raped and pillaged its way through much of the Southeast in quest of these treasures, leaving disease and mayhem in its wake. The expedition crossed the Mississippi in 1541, wandered through the Ozarks and eastern Oklahoma, and marched back to the great river. De Soto died there in 1542. His companions continued to explore for another year before returning to Spanish territory. Farther west, Francisco Vasquez de Coronado marched into New Mexico and Arizona, where he encountered several Pueblo towns but no golden cities. The expedition reached the Grand Canyon, then headed east into the Great Plains before returning to Mexico in 1542.

After the conquistadores departed, Spanish priests did their best to convert thousands of North American Indians to the Catholic faith. These efforts extended well north of New Spain (Mexico). In 1570, the Jesuits established a mission in what is now Virginia, but local Indians soon wiped it out. After the failure of the Jesuit mission, Spain tried to treat the Indians of Florida and New Mexico with decency and later came to rely on the missions to protect its holdings against English and French intruders. The Jesuits withdrew and Franciscans took their place. In 1573, King Philip II (1556–1598) issued the Royal Orders for New Discoveries, which prohibited the military conquest of the Indians and set limitations on labor coercion. Unarmed priests were to bring Indians together in missions and convert them into peaceful Catholic subjects of Spain. The Franciscans quickly discovered that, without military support, they were more likely to win martyrdom than converts. They reluctantly accepted military protection, but they tried, not always successfully, to make sure that none of the few soldiers who accompanied them behaved like conquistadores.

Franciscans built their missions within the permanent Indian villages of northern Florida and New Mexico's Pueblo communities along the upper Rio Grande Valley (see Map 1.10). The Spanish incursion into New Mexico began violently with the slaughter of some 800 Acoma Indian men, women, and children in 1599, and the imperial authorities in Mexico nearly aborted the project. New Mexico became a royal colony,

▲ **MAP 1.9 Principal Spanish Explorations of North America** Four Spanish expeditions marched through much of the interior of North America between 1513 and 1543.

Q What drew Spanish explorers to North America?

Q What factors encouraged Spanish exploration of North America?

and Franciscans continued to convert the Pueblos. By 1630, Pueblo Indian women, under the priests' supervision, had built more than 50 churches in New Mexico, and some 86,000 Pueblo, Apache, and Navajo Indians had accepted baptism. In Florida, 30 missions boasted about 26,000 baptized Indians by midcentury, covering an area that extended some 250 miles from the Atlantic coast of what is now Georgia westward into the Florida Panhandle.

The missions were not merely sites of religious conversion; they were also institutions of cultural modification. Many aspects of native social organization confounded the Europeans—that they were often **matrilineal**, tracing descent through the maternal line, and polygamous; that women did most of the farming, could own considerable property, and often had a say in such political matters as starting a war— and they tried to change them after their own image. The Franciscans pushed their converts to wear European clothing, give up their sacred dances and songs, abandon polygamy for monogamy, and provide labor for the missions. They also pressured the Indians to modify their labor and gender conventions to comply with European mores, forcing native men to take up such traditionally women's tasks as building construction and farming.

Many Indians converted to Christianity, but that did not necessarily mean that they became the kind of Christians the missionaries hoped for. Franciscan dreams of a spiritual paradise in the Americas remained elusive. Indians adopted the Christian doctrine selectively, mixing elements of it with their own religious traditions; often, Jesus, Mary, and various saints joined, rather than replaced, teeming indigenous pantheons. Native men refused to become farmers, protesting that it would turn them into women. A vast cultural gap between Europeans and Indians undermined the missionary work. Missionaries eagerly brought news of the Christ and of how he had died to save humankind from sin. Catholic worship, then as now, centered on the Mass and the Eucharist, in which a priest transforms bread and wine into the literal body and blood of Christ. To Indians, Christians seemed to be people

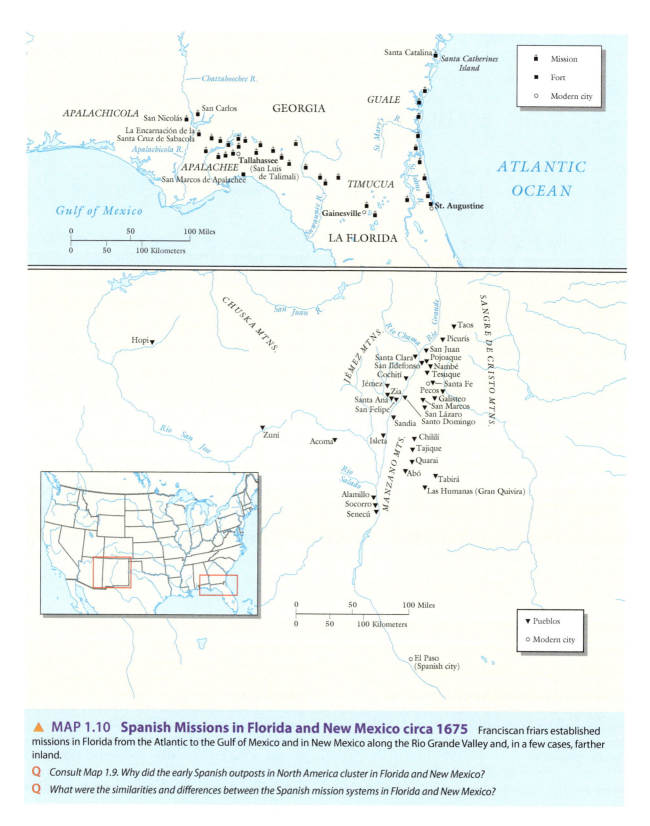

▲ **MAP 1.10 Spanish Missions in Florida and New Mexico circa 1675** Franciscan friars established missions in Florida from the Atlantic to the Gulf of Mexico and in New Mexico along the Rio Grande Valley and, in a few cases, farther inland.

Q Consult Map 1.9. Why did the early Spanish outposts in North America cluster in Florida and New Mexico?

Q What were the similarities and differences between the Spanish mission systems in Florida and New Mexico?

who ate their god but grew outraged at such lesser matters as serving multiple gods or having multiple wives. Neither side fully recognized such obstacles to mutual understanding. Although early missionaries converted thousands of Indians, the results were mixed at best. As Christianization and Hispanicization proceeded across the Americas, so too did indigenous resentment and resistance.

1-6c The Spanish Empire and Demographic Catastrophe

Spanish conquistadores had led small armies that rarely exceeded 1,000 men. Yet, because they were also able to raise large Indian armies as allies, they managed to subdue two indigenous empires much larger than Spain. Spain's core

What They Said

Two Spanish Scholars Debate Indian Slavery

Spanish colonization of the Americas became a highly charged, fiercely debated issue on both sides of the Atlantic. At the heart of the controversy was an uncertainty about the roles and rights the Indians would have in the emerging colonial societies. Was their subjugation and dispossession justified and, if so, on what grounds? In these selections from the mid-16th century, two Spanish scholars debate whether Indians were natural slaves.

▶ Juan Ginés de Sepúlveda

The man rules over the woman, the adult over the child, the father over his children. That is to say, the most powerful and most perfect rule over the weakest and most imperfect. This same relationship exists among men, there being some who by nature are masters and others who by nature are slaves. Those who surpass the rest in prudence and intelligence, although not in physical strength, are by nature the masters. On the other hand, those who are dim-witted and mentally lazy, although they may be physically strong enough to fulfill all the necessary tasks, are by nature slaves… . It will always be just and in conformity with natural law that such people submit to the rule of more cultured and humane princes and nations… .

These people [Indians] possess neither science nor even an alphabet, nor do they preserve any monuments of their history except for some obscure and vague reminiscences depicted in certain paintings, nor do they have written laws, but barbarous institutions and customs. In regard to their virtues, how much restraint or gentleness are you to expect of men who are devoted to all kinds of intemperate acts and abominable lewdness, including the eating of human flesh? And you must realize that prior to the arrival of the Christians, they did not live in that peaceful kingdom of Saturn that the poets imagine, but on the contrary they made war against one another continually and fiercely, with such fury that victory was of no meaning if they did not satiate their monstrous hunger with the flesh of their enemies… .

For numerous and grave reasons these barbarians are obligated to accept the rule of the Spaniards according to natural law. For them it ought to be even more advantageous than for the Spaniards, since virtue, humanity, and the true religion are more valuable than gold or silver.

▶ Bartolomé de las Casas

Let us now speak about the unbelievers who live in kingdoms ruled by non-Christians, such as the Moors of Africa, the Turks, the Scythians, the Persians, and those with whom the present controversy is concerned, the Indians. Surely, no matter how despicable the crimes they may commit against God, or even against religion among themselves or within their territories, neither the Church nor Christian rulers can take cognizance of them or punish them for these. For there is no jurisdiction, which is the necessary basis for all juridical acts, especially for punishing a person. Therefore, in this case, the emperor, the prince, or the king has no jurisdiction but is the same as a private citizen, and whatever he does has no force.

…this is proved, first, by the fact that unbelievers who have never accepted the faith of Christ are not actually subject to Christ and therefore not to the Church or its authority.

…Sepulveda claims that the Supreme Pontiff Alexander VI advised the kings of Castile to subjugate the Indians by war and that he condoned the war by which those peoples have been brought under our rule. This is absolutely false. The Pope granted the kings of Castile the right to set themselves over the Indian rulers whom they had converted to the faith of Christ and keep them as subjects under their protection and jurisdiction. But the Pope never commanded or permitted them to subjugate these rulers by war. For how would he permit something that conflicts with Christ's precept and instruction and produces hatred of the name of Christ in the hearts of unbelievers, and is utterly irreligious? For the will of a ruler is always judged to be in conformity with the law.

…the Pope praises the Kings and precisely because they wanted to seek new regions, unknown in former centuries, with the intention of spreading the Christian religion … [the kings] subjugate (that is, dispose) them [the Indians] for the faith in a way in which one should subjugate a most civilized, sincere, naked, docile, decent, and peaceful people who are very ready to serve, that is, mildly, in a Christian and humane way. As a result, after they first know the true God through belief in the gospel, they may at last freely subject themselves to the king of Castile (from whom they have received such a benefit) as to their supreme prince and emperor, while the rights of their natural lords are retained… .

Q *What are the key similarities and differences in these arguments? How do their notions of law, religion, and culture differ from each another? Which do you think was more successful in persuading the contemporary Spanish policymakers? How do you think contemporary Native Americans might have understood such a debate?*

Sources: (top) Juan Ginés de Sepúlveda speech from 1547 reprinted in John H. Parry and Robert G. Keith, eds. New Iberian World: A Documentary History of the Discovery and Settlement of Latin America to the Early 17th Century (New York: Times Books: Hector & Rose, 1984), 1: 324–26. (bottom) Bartolomé de Las Casas speech from 1547 reprinted in John H. Parry and Robert G. Keith, eds. New Iberian World: A Documentary History of the Discovery and Settlement of Latin America to the Early 17th Century (New York: Times Books: Hector & Rose, 1984), 1: 324–26.

1.18 The Ravages of Smallpox These drawings show the devastation of smallpox among the Aztecs, as depicted in the Aztec Codex, one of the few surviving collections of Aztec writing.

Q *What might the image reveal about how Native Americans understood the spread of such viral diseases like smallpox?*

American holdings in Peru and Mexico were protected by a strong defensive perimeter in the Caribbean and surrounded by a series of frontier missions, extending in the north into Florida and New Mexico. There, the Spaniards looked around for more worlds to conquer, but failed to replicate their triumphs in the south. The success of Spanish colonialism in the Americas depended on the exploitation and co-option of existing urban populations, agricultural economies, and social hierarchies. Beyond great indigenous empires, Spanish colonial expansion tended to slow down and falter.

By the late 16th century, the Spanish Empire had developed into a system of direct colonial rule in Mexico and Peru. Spanish conquistadores had targeted the largest and richest of the Americas' indigenous empires and placed themselves on top of them as masters. Leaving large parts of these empires' political and social structures intact, they took over their existing systems of tribute. The Spaniards also brought new systems of labor and new religious institutions to their overseas colonies, although in time both were altered by local conditions.

In the course of the 16th century, the Spanish Crown enacted a series of laws that specifically prohibited the buying, selling, and owning of Indian slaves. These laws were widely contested in the Americas, where the colonists employed other, formally legal methods of extracting and coercing native labor. For much of the 16th century, Spanish rulers in Mexico, Peru, and New Mexico relied on a form of labor tribute called **encomienda**. This system permitted the holder, or *encomendero*, to claim labor from an Indian district for a stated period of time. *Encomienda* worked because it resembled the way the Aztecs and the Incas had routinely levied labor for their own massive public buildings and irrigation projects. In time, the king intervened to correct abuses and limit labor tribute to Crown projects, such as mining and the construction of churches or other public buildings. Spanish settlers resisted the reforms at first but slowly shifted from demanding labor to claiming land. In the countryside, the **hacienda**, a large estate with its own crops and herds, became a familiar institution.

Although the Church never had enough clergy to meet its needs, it became a massive presence during the 16th century. Yet, America changed it, too. As missionaries acquired land and labor, they began to exhibit less zeal for Indian souls. The Franciscans—in Europe, the gentlest of Catholic religious orders—brutally and systematically tortured their Mayan converts in the 1560s whenever they caught them worshiping their old gods. To the Franciscans, the slightest lapse could signal a reversion to Satan worship, with human sacrifice a likely consequence. They did not dare to be kind.

Most important, the Spaniards brought deadly microbes with them. Smallpox, measles, typhus, cholera, and other crowd diseases, often spreading in successive pandemics, devastated the Indians. The reasons for the Indians' vulnerability to European diseases are not clear, but the evidence points to certain features in their immunological makeup. Having lived for millennia in relatively disease-free environments, the Indians, unlike the Europeans, may not have been genetically selected to resist infectious diseases. It is also possible that their immune systems were relatively homogenous—they had descended from a rather small sample of the total gene pool of Asia—making it easier for viruses to jump bodies. What is clear, however, is that the destructiveness of European diseases was greatly magnified by colonialism itself. The social turmoil, environmental stress, malnutrition, and psychological trauma caused by colonial expansion sapped the strength of indigenous societies, rendering them vulnerable to alien pathogens.

The result was an unprecedented population collapse. When Cortés arrived in 1519, the native population of Mexico probably exceeded 15 million. In the 1620s, after waves of killing epidemics, it bottomed out at 700,000 and did not regain its pre-Spanish level until the 1950s. Peru suffered nearly as horribly. Its population fell from about 10 million in 1525 to 600,000 a century later. For the hemisphere as a whole, any given region probably lost 90 to 95 percent of its population within a century of sustained contact with Europeans. Lowland tropical areas usually suffered the heaviest casualties; in some of these places, all of the Indians died. Highland areas and sparsely settled regions often fared better.

The Spanish Crown spent much of the 16th century trying to keep abreast of these changes, but eventually it imposed administrative order on the unruly conquistadores and brought peace to its colonies. At the center of the imperial bureaucracy, in Seville, stood the Council of the Indies. The council administered the three American viceroyalties of New Spain, Peru, and eventually New Granada, which were further subdivided into smaller *audiencias*, executive and judicial jurisdictions supervised by the viceroys. The Council of the Indies appointed the viceroys and other major officials, who ruled from the new cities that the Spaniards built with local labor at Havana, Mexico City, Lima, and elsewhere. Although centralized and autocratic in theory, the Spanish Empire allowed local officials a fair degree of initiative, if only because years could elapse in trying to communicate across its immense distances. "If death came from Spain," mused one official, "we should all live long lives."

1-6d *Brazil*

Pedro Álvares Cabral discovered Brazil for Portugal in 1500, when he was blown off course while trying to round the Cape of Good Hope. Like Spanish America, Portuguese Brazil became a colony with a strong autocratic streak, but it was divided into 14 "captaincies," or provinces, and so was far less centralized. The Portuguese invasion did not lead to direct rule over native societies but to their displacement or enslavement. After the colonists on the northeast coast turned to raising sugar in the late 16th century, Brazilian frontiersmen, or *bandeirantes*, foraged deep into the continent to enslave more Indians. They even raided remote Spanish Andean missions, rounded up the converts, and dragged them thousands of miles across mountains and through jungles to be worked to death on plantations. On several occasions, while Brazil was ruled by Spain (see below), missionaries persuaded the king to abolish slavery. Not even absolutism could achieve that goal. Slavery continued without pause, and Africans gradually replaced Indians as the dominant labor force. Brazil was the major market for African slaves until the 1640s, when Caribbean demand became even greater.

1-7 Global Colossus, Global Economy

Q *In what ways did American silver both bolster and weaken the Spanish Empire?*

American silver made the king of Spain the most powerful monarch in Christendom. Philip II commanded the largest army in Europe, held the Turks in check in the Mediterranean, and tried to crush the Protestant Reformation in northern Europe (see Chapter 2). In 1580, after the king of Portugal died with no direct heir, Philip claimed that throne, thus uniting under his own rule Portugal's Asian empire, Brazil, Spain's American possessions, and the Philippines. This colossus was the greatest empire the world had ever seen. It also sustained the first truly global economy, because the Portuguese used Spain's American silver to pay for the spices and silks they imported from Asia. The union of Spain and Portugal lasted until the 1640s, when Portugal revolted and regained its independence.

The Spanish colossus became part of an even broader economic pattern. **Serfdom**, which tied peasants to their lords and to the land, had been Europe's predominant labor system in the early Middle Ages. Although peasants could not move, neither could they be sold; they were not slaves. Serfdom had been declining in Western Europe since the 12th century and was nearly gone by 1500. A system of free labor gradually arose in its place, and overseas expansion strengthened that trend within Western Europe. Although free labor prevailed in the Western European homeland, unfree labor systems took root all around Europe's periphery, both overseas and in Eastern Europe, and the two systems were structurally linked. In general, free labor reigned where populations were dense and still growing. Large pools of labor kept wages low, but around the periphery of Western Europe, where land was cheap and labor expensive, coercive systems became the only efficient way for Europeans to extract from those areas the products they desired (see Map 1.11).

The forms of unfree labor varied greatly across space and time, from slavery to less brutal systems. In New Spain, as the native population dwindled, the practice of *encomienda* slowly yielded to debt peonage. Unpayable debts kept Indians tied to the **haciendas** of the countryside. The mining of precious metals, on the other hand, was so dangerous and unpleasant that it almost always required a large degree of physical coercion. In the Andes the Spaniards instituted a system of labor draft called *mita*, which forced communities to provide one-seventh of their male labor force for Spanish overlords. Similarly, any colonial region that devoted itself to the production of staple crops for sale in Europe also turned to unfree labor and eventually to overt slavery. Sugar production first reduced Indians to bondage in Brazil and the Caribbean and later, as they died off, led to the importation of African slaves by the millions. Other staples—tobacco, rice, coffee, cotton—later followed similar patterns. At first these crops were considered luxuries and commanded high prices, but as they became widely available on the world market, their prices fell steeply, profit margins contracted, and planters turned overwhelmingly to coerced labor. Even in Eastern Europe, which began to specialize in producing cereal crops for sale in the more diversified West, serfdom revived. In Russia, where the Orthodox Church never condemned the enslavement of fellow Christians, the condition of a serf came to resemble that of a slave in one of the Atlantic empires. Some serfs were even bought and sold.

Spain's rise had been spectacular, but its empire was vulnerable. Although silver from the Americas vastly enhanced the Crown's ability to wage war, the costs of continuous conflict, the inflation generated by a steady influx of silver, and

History Through Film: Even the Rain (2010)

Directed by Icíar Bollaín.
Starring Gael García Bernal (Sebastián), Luis Tosar (Costa), Juan Carlos Aduviri (Daniel), Karra Ejalade (Anton/Christopher Columbus).

Even the Rain opens in Cochabamba, the third largest city in Bolivia, in 2000. A movie crew has arrived to shoot a revisionist film about Christopher Columbus, and Cochabamba is to stand in for Hispaniola. Costa (Luis Tosar), the producer, has chosen Cochabamba less for authenticity than finances: The local Indians can be hired as manual laborers and extras for $2 per day. The pay is meager, but vast numbers line up for auditions; the queue of indigenous people vanishes into the horizon.

Things soon spin out of control. Pressured by the World Bank, the Bolivian government has sold the country's water rights to a multinational water consortium, which suddenly closes local wells, aiming to raise prices. Catching rainwater is about to become illegal; even the rain will belong to someone else. The poor, the country's vast majority, are in danger of being denied clean water. People start protesting, and the film crew finds itself in the midst of a populist uprising.

These real-life events are the setting for the director, Icíar Bollaín, to examine colonialism, imperialism, globalization, and exploitation over a long time span, from Columbus to the cusp of the 21st century. The film is steeped in irony. Costa and his idealistic director Sebastián (Gael García Bernal) want to make a film that exposes the brutality and callousness of European colonialism in the Americas, but end up, as embodiments of globalization, exploiting the Indians for their own purposes—not entirely unlike what Columbus did. Where Columbus was fixated on securing slaves, souls, and precious metals for the Spanish Crown, the filmmakers seem to have few scruples as they exploit the native people for their high-minded artistic ends. In keeping with true Hollywood mythology, Sebastián is an obsessive visionary determined to make the film he feels he needs to make.

Enter Daniel (Juan Carlos Aduviri), a passionate young Indian who not only is cast in the film's leading role but is also one of the leaders of the water-rights movement. Daniel's activism draws police attention to the film set, and the escalating unrest threatens to bring the production to a grinding halt. Confronted by the contemporary South American political struggles, the filmmakers find themselves grappling with the legacies of colonialism as they witness how their indigenous workers suffer under global inequalities. Daniel is the moral touchstone against which Costa and Sebastián must define their actions. They react in contrasting ways: Costa experiences an awakening of social conscience and seeks to help the protestors, while Sebastián remains committed only to his film, coldly ignoring the suffering around him.

Even the Rain is a highly self-conscious movie. It is a film within a film, and it pulls no punches in drawing parallels between 16th-century colonialism and modern-day globalization. The movie shifts from showing the film crew shooting scenes of Columbus burning Taino Indians alive; to Daniel being brutalized by the police; to the filmmakers inserting themselves into Bolivian politics; to Anton, a boozy actor playing Columbus (Karra Ejalade), reading Columbus's real letters to Ferdinand and Isabella. Fiction and reality and the past and present blur together, inviting the viewer to contemplate how oppression, exploitation, and inequality, in different forms, echo through the centuries. ■

1.19 Gael García Bernal (Sebastián) and Luis Tosar (Costa), play leading roles in *Even the Rain*.

---

the need to defend a much greater perimeter absorbed Spain's new resources and a great deal more. Between 1492 and 1580, Spain's population grew from 4.9 million to 8 million, but over the course of the following century, it fell by 20 percent, mostly because of the escalating costs, both financial and human, of Spain's wars. As population declined, taxes rose. Castile grew poorer, not richer, in its century and a half of imperial glory. Much of the wealth of the Indies went elsewhere to pay for goods or services that Spain failed to provide for itself: to merchants in Genoa, to manufacturers in Lombardy and the Low Countries, and to bankers in Augsburg.

1-8 Explanations: Patterns of Conquest, Submission, and Resistance

Q *What is the Columbian Exchange and how has it shaped world history?*

By the middle of the 18th century, Europeans who thought seriously about the discovery of America and its global implications generally agreed that the whole process had been

▲ **MAP 1.11 Spanish Empire and Global Labor System** While Western European states were becoming free-labor societies, they created or encouraged the establishment of societies built on or providing laborers for various unfree labor systems in the Americas, the Caribbean, Africa, and Eastern Europe.

Q *Why did slave societies emerge where they did?*
Q *How can the Columbian Exchange help explain the different patterns of colonial expansion in the two hemispheres?*

a moral outrage, possibly the worst in history. Conquest and settlement had killed millions of Indians, enslaved millions of Africans, and degraded Europeans. By comparison, the benefits to humanity seemed small even though economic gains by 1750 were large. If the cruelest of the conquerors had foreseen the results of this process, asked the Abbé Raynal, would he have proceeded? "Is it to be imagined that there exists a being infernal enough to answer this question in the affirmative?" The success of the American Revolution, with its message of freedom and human rights, quieted such thinking for a time, but the critique has revived in recent years, especially in the developing world.

Modern historians, less moralistic than Raynal, also realize that he considerably underestimated the death toll. Even so, they are more interested in asking how and why these things happened. One major reason is geographical. The Eurasian landmass, the world's largest, follows an east-west axis that permits life-forms and human inventions to travel immense distances without going through forbidding changes of climate. Domesticated plants and animals spread quickly from the Fertile Crescent across Eurasia in roughly similar climate zones. The intensifying food production fueled rapid population growth, which in turn stimulated rivalries and exchanges among societies. People learned from one another, and innovations moved from region to region. The use of iron spread gradually throughout most of Afro-Eurasia, and even though Europeans knew little about China, they slowly acquired Chinese inventions such as paper, the compass, and gunpowder.

Steel, far more than firearms or even horses, made European colonialism possible. Steel weapons became common in Europe in the early second millennium, giving its states a decisive technological edge. European armor stopped enemy spears and arrows, and European swords killed opponents swiftly without any need to reload. By contrast, the Americas lie along north-south axes, which frustrated intercultural exchanges and the spread of innovations. Separated by chasms of climate, human societies in the Americas remained more isolated than those in Eurasia and could not learn as easily from one another.

The biological consequences of isolation were even more momentous than the technological barriers. The devastation that European microbes inflicted upon the Indian population is the greatest tragedy in the history of humankind. European plants also thrived at the expense of native vegetation. For example, when British settlers first crossed the Appalachians, they marveled at the lush Kentucky bluegrass. They did not realize that they were looking at an accidental European import that had conquered the landscape even faster than they had. European animals also prevailed over potential American rivals. Horses spread north from Mexico with Spanish settlement, transforming the way of life of the Apaches, Comanches, and other Plains Indians. The lowly sparrow never had it so good until someone turned a few loose in North America. But other life-forms moved in the opposite direction, from the Americas to Europe, Asia, and Africa. Corn, potatoes, and tomatoes enriched the diets in Europe, supporting growing

1.20 Tribute Labor (*Mita*) in the Silver Mines
The silver mines of Potosí, in the Andes, are about two miles above sea level. The work, as depicted in this 1603 engraving by Theodor de Bry, was extremely onerous and often dangerous.

populations that could afford to send more and more of their numbers overseas. Historian Alfred W. Crosby has called this larger process the "**Columbian Exchange**." One of the most important historical transformations, it created a worldwide network of ecological exchanges, recast the biology of both hemispheres, bolstered and destabilized human societies, and paved the way for Europe's expansion into the Americas.

Conclusion

Americans like to believe that their history is a story of progress. They are right about its European phase. After its tragic beginnings in conquest, depopulation, and enslavement, some things finally did improve.

For thousands of years, the Americas had been cut off from the rest of the world. The major cultures of Eurasia and Africa had existed in relative isolation, engaging in direct contact with only their immediate neighbors. Islamic societies that shared borders with India, the East Indies, black Africa, and Europe had been the principal mediators among these cultures and, in that era, were more tolerant than most Christian societies.

In just 40 years, daring European navigators, supported by the crowns of Portugal and Spain, joined the world together and challenged Islam's mediating role in Afro-Eurasia. Between 1492 and 1532, Europe, Africa, Asia, the Spice Islands, the Philippines, the Caribbean, Aztec Mexico, Inca Peru, and other parts of the Americas came into intense and often violent contact with one another. The Atlantic Ocean transformed from a barrier into a communication conduit that linked together the continents around it. A few individuals gained much from these new connections, and Spain acquired a military advantage within Europe that endured into the 1640s. Nearly everybody else suffered, millions horribly, especially in the Americas and Africa. And Spain spent the rest of the 16th century trying to create an imperial system that could impose order on this turbulent reality. But Spain had many enemies. They too would find the lure of wealth and land overseas irresistible.

CHAPTER REVIEW

Review

1. How did the extinction of megafauna shape human history in the Americas?
2. What were the major similarities and differences between the histories of the Andes and Mesoamerica during the first and early second millennia?
3. How did maize cultivation change human history in North America?
4. What enabled relatively backward European societies to establish dominance over the oceans of the world?
5. What kinds of different motives shaped early Spanish colonialism in the Americas?

6. What enabled relatively few Spanish conquistadores to subjugate the powerful empires of the Aztecs and the Incas?
7. In what ways did American silver both bolster and weaken the Spanish Empire?
8. What is the Columbian Exchange and how has it shaped world history?

Critical Thinking

1. European expansion inflicted enormous destruction upon the peoples of sub-Saharan Africa and the Americas. Is there any way that this vast projection of European power overseas also contributed to an eventual expansion of liberty?
2. Why did the free-labor societies of Western Europe generate unfree labor systems in their colonies?

Identifications

Review your understanding of the following key terms, people, and events for this chapter (terms in bold in text are included in the Glossary).

Clovis tip, p. 4
Neolithic, p. 5
Incas, p. 7
Olmecs, p. 7
Mayan, p. 8
Aztecs, p. 10
Tenochtitlán, p. 10
Anasazi, p. 11
Cahokia, p. 13
staple crop, p. 18
slave labor, p. 18
caravel, p. 19
factories, p. 19
Atlantic slave trade, p. 19
Santa María, p. 23
conquistadores, p. 25
Hernán Cortés, p. 25
matrilineal, p. 27
encomienda, p. 30
hacienda, p. 30
serfdom, p. 31
Columbian Exchange, p. 34

Suggested Readings

Three recent general surveys of early American history provide excellent coverage up to U.S. independence: **Alan Taylor**, *American Colonies* (2001); **Richard Middleton**, *Colonial America: A History, 1565–1776*, 3rd ed. (2002); and **Daniel K. Richter**, *Before the Revolution: America's Ancient Pasts* (2011). For a useful collection of essays, see **Stanley N. Katz, John M. Murrin, Douglas Greenberg, Denver Brunsman, and David Silverman, eds.,** *Colonial America: Essays in Politics and Social Development*, 6th ed. (2010).

Brian M. Fagan, *The Great Journey: The Peopling of Ancient America* (1987) is a fine introduction to pre-Columbian America. See also **David Webster**, *The Fall of the Ancient Maya: Solving the Mystery of the Collapse* (2002). **Jared Diamond**, *Guns, Germs, and Steel: The Fates of Human Societies* (1997) is provocative and challenging in its global perspective. For the age of explorations, see **G. V. Scammell**, *The First Imperial Age: European Overseas Expansion c. 1400–1715* (1989); and **Alfred W. Crosby's** classic synthesis, *The Columbian Exchange: Biological and Cultural Consequences of 1492* (1972). **Charles C. Mann's** *1491: New Revelations of the Americas Before Columbus* (2005) and *1493: Uncovering the World Columbus Created* (2011) have helped popularize Crosby's work. For the slave trade, see **John Thornton,** *Africa and Africans in the Making of the Modern World, 1400–1800*, 2nd ed. (1998), which insists that Africans retained control of their affairs, including the slave trade, through the 17th century. For authoritative overviews of slavery in the Americas, see **David Brion Davis**, *Inhuman Bondage: The Rise and Fall of Slavery in the New World* (2006) and **Ira Berlin**, *Many Thousands Gone: The First Two Centuries of Slavery in North America* (1998). **Andres Reséndez's** *The Other Slavery: The Uncovered Story of Indian Enslavement in America* (2016) is an eye-opening study that reveals a long history of mass Indian enslavement in the Americas and argues that slavery was the key cause to indigenous depopulation.

James Lockhart and Stuart B. Schwartz, *Early Latin America: A History of Colonial Latin America and Brazil* (1983) is an outstanding introduction to the Iberian empires. **David J. Weber's**, *The Spanish Frontier in North America* (1992) is the best introduction to its subject. For Brazil, see **John Hemming**, *Red Gold: The Conquest of the Brazilian Indians, 1500–1760* (1978).

MINDTAP is a fully online personalized learning experience built upon Cengage Learning content. MindTap® combines student learning tools—readings, multimedia, activities, and assessments—into a singular Learning Path that guides students through the course and helps students develop the critical thinking, analysis, and communication skills that are essential to academic and professional success.

2 Colonization in North America, 1600–1680

2-1 The Protestant Reformation and the Challenge to Spain
▶ *Learning Objective:* Describe how Europe's political and religious landscape changed in the 16th century.

2-2 New France and the Iroquois League
▶ *Learning Objective:* Identify the main similarities and differences between French and Spanish colonial projects in North America.
Early French Explorers
Missions and Furs
New France under Louis XIV

2-3 New Netherland
▶ *Learning Objective:* Identify the key motivations that drove Dutch colonialism in North America.
The East and West India Companies
New Netherland as a Pluralistic Society
English Encroachments

2-4 English Colonization Begins
▶ *Learning Objective:* Trace what kinds of ambitions and historical developments committed England to overseas colonization.
The English Reformation
From Plundering to Colonization
The Swarming of the English

2-5 The Chesapeake and West Indian Colonies
▶ *Learning Objective:* Find out why the English, crossing the Atlantic at roughly the same time, created such radically different societies in the Chesapeake, the West Indies, and New England.
The Jamestown Disaster
Reorganization, Reform, and Crisis
Tobacco, Servants, and Survival
The Collapse of Tsenacommacah
Maryland
Chesapeake Family Life
The West Indies and the Transition to Slavery
The Rise of Slavery in North America

2-6 The New England Colonies
▶ *Learning Objective:* Describe how religious concerns shaped the colonization of New England.
The Pilgrims and Plymouth
Massachusetts Bay
Covenant Theology
Puritan Family Life
Conversion, Dissent, and Expansion
Puritan Indian Missions
Congregations, Towns, and Colony Governments
Infant Baptism and New Dissent

2-7 From Civil War to the First Restoration Colonies
▶ *Learning Objective:* Analyze in what ways the Restoration colonies differed from those founded in the Chesapeake and New England.
Carolina, Harrington, and the Aristocratic Ideal
New York: An Experiment in Absolutism

2-8 Brotherly Love: The Quakers and America
▶ *Learning Objective:* Specify how Pennsylvania's policy toward the Native Americans differed from the Indian policies of New England and the Chesapeake colonies and explain those differences.
Quaker Beliefs
Quaker Families
West New Jersey
Pennsylvania

2.1 **Working Beavers** Detail from Herman Moll, *A New Exact Map of the Dominions of the King of Great Britain* (1715). One of the earliest depictions of Niagara Falls consigns that site to the background, with beavers dominating the foreground. Although Europeans valued beavers primarily for their pelts and hunted them almost to extinction, they also admired their industry and their skill at building dams.

CATHOLIC FRANCE and two Protestant countries, the Dutch Republic and England, challenged Spanish power in Europe and overseas. None of them planted a permanent settlement in North America before 1600. In the quarter-century after 1600, they all did. Europeans, Indians, and Africans interacted in contrasting ways in this strange "New World." Spain's rivals created colonies of different kinds. Some, such as Virginia and Barbados, grew staple crops with indentured servants and African slaves. New France and New Netherland developed a prosperous trade with the Indians and forged close political ties with them. In New England, the Puritans relied on free labor provided mostly by family members. After 1660, England conquered New Netherland, and English Quakers created another free-labor society in the Delaware Valley. ■

2-1 The Protestant Reformation and the Challenge to Spain

Q *How did Europe's political and religious landscape change in the 16th century?*

By the time its enemies felt strong enough to challenge Spain overseas, the Protestant Reformation had shattered the religious unity of Europe. In November 1517, not long before Cortés landed in Mexico, Martin Luther nailed his 95 Theses to the cathedral door at Wittenberg in Saxony and touched off the Reformation. Salvation, he insisted, comes through faith alone, and God grants saving faith only to those who hear his Word preached to them, struggle to understand it, and admit that, without God's grace, they are damned. Within a generation, the states of northern Germany and Scandinavia had embraced Lutheranism.

John Calvin, a French Protestant, also embraced justification by faith alone and put his own militant principles into practice in the Swiss canton of Geneva. The Huguenot movement in France, the Dutch Reformed Church in the Netherlands, and the Presbyterian Kirk (or Church) of Scotland all embraced Calvin's principles. In England, the Anglican Church adopted Calvinist doctrines but kept much Catholic liturgy, a compromise that prompted the Puritan reform movement toward a more thoroughly Calvinist Church of England. After 1620, Puritans carried their religious vision across the Atlantic to New England.

Calvinists rejected the pope, all Catholic sacraments except baptism and the Lord's Supper, clerical celibacy, veneration of the saints, and the pious rituals by which Catholics strove to win salvation. They denounced these rites as "work righteousness." Calvin gave central importance to **predestination**. According to that doctrine, God has already decreed who will be saved and who will be damned. Christ died, not for all humankind, but only for God's elect. Because salvation and damnation were beyond human power to alter, Calvinists—especially English Puritans—felt a compelling need to find out whether they were saved. They struggled to recognize in themselves a conversion experience, the process by which God's elect discovered that they had received saving grace.

France, the Netherlands, and England, all with powerful Protestant movements, challenged Spanish power in Europe. Until 1559, France was the main threat, with Italy as the battleground, but Spain won that phase. In the 1560s, with France embroiled in its own Wars of Religion, a new challenge came from the 17 provinces of the Netherlands, which Spain ruled. The Dutch rebelled against the heavy taxes and severe Catholic orthodoxy imposed by Philip II. As Spanish armies put down the rebellion in the 10 southern provinces (modern Belgium), merchants and Protestants fled north. Many went to Amsterdam, which replaced Spanish-controlled Antwerp as the economic center of northern Europe. The seven northern provinces gradually took shape as the Dutch Republic, or the United Provinces of the Netherlands. The Dutch turned their resistance into a war for independence from Catholic Spain. The conflict lasted 80 years, drained Spanish resources, and spread to Asia, Africa, and America. England long remained on the edges of this struggle, only to emerge in the end as the biggest winner overseas.

2-2 New France and the Iroquois League

Q *What were the main similarities and differences between French and Spanish colonial projects in North America?*

In 1500, France had three times the population of Spain. The French made a few stabs at overseas expansion before 1600, but with little success.

2-2a Early French Explorers

In 1524, King Francis I sent Giovanni da Verrazano, an Italian, to America in search of a northwest passage to Asia. Verrazano explored the North American coast from the Carolinas to Nova Scotia and noted Manhattan's superb potential as a harbor but found no passage to Asia. Between 1534 and 1543, Jacques Cartier made three voyages to North America. He explored the St. Lawrence Valley without finding any fabulous wealth. Severe Canadian winters made him give up. For the rest of the century, the French ignored Canada, except for a few fur traders and for fishermen who descended on Newfoundland each year in growing numbers. By the 1580s, the Canadian fisheries rivaled New Spain in the volume of shipping they sustained.

After 1550, the French turned to warmer climates. **Huguenots** sacked Havana, prompting Spain to turn it into a fortified, year-round naval base under the command of Admiral **Pedro Menéndez de Avilés**. Others planted a settlement on the Atlantic coast of Florida. Menéndez attacked them in 1565, talked them into surrendering, and then executed adult males who refused to accept the Catholic faith.

France's Wars of Religion blocked further efforts for the rest of the 16th century. King Henry IV (1589–1610), a Protestant, converted to Catholicism and granted limited toleration to Huguenots through the Edict of Nantes in 1598, thus ending the civil wars for the rest of his reign. Henry was a *politique*; he insisted that the survival of the state take precedence over religious differences. Moreover, he believed in toleration for its own sake. Another *politique* was the Catholic soldier and explorer Samuel de Champlain.

2-2b Missions and Furs

Champlain believed that Catholics and Huguenots could work together, Europeanize the Indians, convert them, and even marry them. Before his death in 1635, he made 11 voyages to Canada. During his second trip (1604–1606), he planted a predominantly Huguenot settlement in Acadia (Nova Scotia). In 1608, he sailed up the St. Lawrence River, established friendly

CHRONOLOGY

1517	Luther begins the Protestant Reformation
1580s	Gilbert claims Newfoundland for England (1583) • Raleigh twice fails to colonize Roanoke Island (1585–1587) • England repels attack by the Spanish armada (1588)
1607	English settlement established at Jamestown
1608	Champlain founds Quebec
1609	Virginia receives sea-to-sea charter
1613–1614	Rolfe grows tobacco, marries Pocahontas
1619	First Africans arrive in Virginia • House of Burgesses and headright system created
1620s	Pilgrims adopt Mayflower Compact, land at Plymouth (1620) • Dutch West India Company chartered (1621) • Opechancanough launches war of extermination in Virginia (1622) • James I assumes direct control of Virginia (1624) • Minuit founds New Amsterdam (1626)
1630s	Puritans settle Massachusetts Bay (1630) • Maryland chartered (1632) • Williams founds Providence; Hooker founds Hartford (1636) • Anne Hutchinson banished to Rhode Island; Minuit founds New Sweden (1638) • New Haven Colony founded (1639)
1640s	Massachusetts "Body of Liberties" (1641) • English civil wars begin (1642) • Virginia subjugates Powhatans (1646) • Charles I beheaded (1649)
Mid-1650s	New Netherland conquers New Sweden • Quakers invade New England
1660s	Charles II restored to English throne (1660) • Puritans institute Half-Way Covenant (1662) • First Carolina charter granted (1663) • New France becomes Crown colony (1663) • New Netherland surrenders to the English (1664) • New Jersey becomes a separate colony (1665) • Carolina's Fundamental Constitutions proposed (1669) • Virginia laws stipulate that children of slaves inherit their mother's status
1670s	First permanent English settlement in South Carolina (1670) • Dutch retake New York (1673–1674)
1680s	Charleston founded (1680) • Pennsylvania charter granted (1681) • New York and Pennsylvania each adopt a Charter of Liberties (1683)
1662–1664	Charles II grants Rhode Island and Connecticut charters • England conquers New Netherland

2.2 Spaniards Torturing Indians, as Depicted by Theodor de Bry, Late 16th Century Among Protestants in northern Europe, images such as this one merged into a "black legend" of Spanish cruelty, which in turn helped justify their own challenge to Spanish power overseas. But in practice, the behavior of Protestant settlers toward Indians was often as harsh as anything the Spaniards had done.

relations with the Hurons, Montagnais, and Algonquins, and founded Quebec. "Our sons shall wed your daughters," he told them, "and we shall be one people." Many Frenchmen cohabited with Indian women, but only 15 formal marriages took place between them in the 17th century. Champlain's ties to the Indians of the St. Lawrence Valley also drew him into their wars against the Haudenosaunee, the five confederated Iroquois nations—Senecas, Cayugas, Onondagas, Oneidas, and Mohawks—who dominated the lands farther south. In the course of the 17th century, Iroquois power politics would almost destroy New France.

Champlain failed to unite Catholics and Protestants in mutual harmony. Huguenots in France were eager to trade with Canada, but few settled there. Their ministers showed no interest in converting the Indians, whereas Catholic priests became zealous missionaries. In 1625, the French Crown declared that only the Catholic faith could be practiced in New France, thus ending Champlain's dream of a colony that was more tolerant than France. Acadia soon became Catholic as well. As dreams of religious harmony faded, economic aspirations came to the fore. Itinerant traders, ***coureurs de bois*** (runners of the woods), pushed into the woodlands around the St. Lawrence Valley, where they traded metal utensils, beads, and brandy for beaver, otter, and other pelts with the Indians. The fur trade became New France's economic lifeline, providing exports that fetched high prices in Europe, where furbearing animals were becoming scarce.

But the fur trade also entangled New France in Indian politics. Champlain nurtured a close alliance with the Huron Confederacy, which competed with the powerful Iroquois Confederacy over hunting territories. Both confederacies were armed with European weapons—the Hurons by the French, the Iroquois by the Dutch—and both needed beaver pelts to fuel their arms trade. When beaver populations began to decline in their homelands in the 1640s, the Iroquois pushed to the north and the west, clashing with the Hurons and the French. In these attacks, they took large numbers of native captives whom they incorporated into their ranks to compensate for the losses they suffered to recurring outbreaks

Interpreting the Visual Past — French-Huron Alliance Takes Shape

The engraving below, "The Defeat of the Iroquois at Lake Champlain," depicts a battle that took place in 1609 between some 200 Mohawk Iroquois and 60 or so allied French, Hurons, Montagnais, and Algonquins. Fought near a Mohawk fort (depicted in the upper right corner), the battle marked a clash between Native American and European styles of warfare and it ended in a resounding defeat for the Mohawks. The battle helped solidify a long-lasting French-Huron alliance that contended with the Iroquois Confederacy for supremacy in the Northeast. The engraving is based on Samuel de Champlain's sketch that has been lost. The source and the key character of the image are therefore one and the same person, which makes it an interpretive challenge for historians.

Q Who do you think was the engraving's intended audience? What was its desired effect?

Q Historians have pointed out numerous factual inaccuracies in the engraving, including palm trees in Canada and Indian canoes that look like French ones. How do such inaccuracies affect the engraving's value as a historical source?

Q How does the engraving depict the relations between Champlain (at center, holding a costly arquebus and donning a high-crowned helmet usually worn by noblemen) and his Indian allies? Should we judge the image simply as Champlain's unabashed self-promotion or does it allow more nuanced interpretations?

Q Compare this engraving to the 1596 engraving of Columbus's landing in San Salvador in Chapter 1 (see page 24). What do the similarities and differences between the two images suggest about how the contemporaries understood Spanish and French colonial projects in the Americas?

2.3 **Engraving based on Samuel de Champlain's Original Drawing, The Defeat of the Iroquois at Lake Champlain, circa 1885**.

of smallpox and other diseases. The Iroquois wars were both "beaver wars" and "**mourning wars**." They were often initiated by grieving clan matriarchs who commanded warriors to go on raids and bring back enemy captives, who would be absorbed into Iroquois families. The captives took the social place of deceased loved ones, assuaging the emotional pain of loss and repairing fractured clans. By the mid-17th century, as much as one-half of the Iroquois population may have been captives.

While becoming embroiled with indigenous politics, the French worked to reshape Indian cultures. Jesuit missionaries made concerted efforts to bring Christ to the Indians. The Society of Jesus, or Jesuits, emerged in the 16th century as the Catholic Church's best-educated and most militant religious order. Uncompromising in their opposition to Protestants, Jesuits proved remarkably flexible in dealing with non-Christian peoples, from China to North America. Other missionaries insisted that Indians must be Europeanized before they could be converted, but the Jesuits were comfortable with a nation of Christians that retained most of its Indian culture.

The Jesuits mastered Indian languages, lived in Indian villages, accepted many Indian customs, and converted 10,000 Indians in 40 years, most of them members of the Huron Confederacy, but this success antagonized Indians who were still attached to their own rituals (see Map 2.1). When smallpox devastated the Hurons in the 1640s, Jesuits baptized hundreds

2.4 Iroquois Warriors Leading an Indian Prisoner into Captivity, 1660s Because Indian populations had been depleted by war and disease, the survival of the Iroquois became dependent on their ability to assimilate captives. This is a French copy of an Iroquois pictograph.

 What does this image reveal and perhaps miss about Iroquois slave raids and captivity?

of dying victims to ensure their salvation. The Hurons split into pro-French Catholics and those who rejected the Jesuits and their faith. Factionalized and weakened, the Huron Confederacy disintegrated under Iroquois attacks. Without it, New France sat exposed to Iroquois raids, which nearly wiped out the colony. By the 1660s, the Iroquois Confederacy was the dominant power in the northern woodlands. In an emergency measure, the French Crown assumed the control of the exposed and depleted New France.

2-2c New France under Louis XIV

Royal intervention transformed Canada. Louis XIV and his minister, Jean-Baptiste Colbert, took charge of the colony and tried to turn it into a model absolutist society—peaceful, orderly, and deferential. Government was in the hands of two appointive officials: a governor-general responsible for military and diplomatic affairs, and an **intendant** who administered affordable justice, partly by banning lawyers. The people paid few taxes, and the church tithe, or tax, was set at half its rate in France. The governor appointed all militia officers and granted promotion through merit, not by selling commissions.

Colbert also sent 774 young women to the St. Lawrence Valley, to provide brides for settlers and soldiers. He offered bonuses to couples that produced large families and fined fathers whose children failed to marry while still in their teens, and the colony's population began to grow. Between 1665 and 1667, New France negotiated peace treaties with the Five Nations, granting them trading privileges along the St. Lawrence Valley. The cessation of Iroquois attacks allowed cities to grow, and Quebec, Montreal, and Three Rivers started to instill New France with an urban flavor. Farming took hold in the St. Lawrence Valley, and by the 1690s Canada was growing enough wheat to feed itself and to provide its *habitants*, or settlers, a level of comfort about equal to that of contemporary New Englanders. A new class of *seigneurs*, or gentry, claimed most of the land between Quebec and Montreal, but they had few feudal privileges and never exercised the kind of power wielded by aristocrats in France. Yet, when the Church was also the *seigneur*, as often happened near Quebec and Montreal, the obligations imposed on farmers could be heavy.

But Canada did not long remain the center of French overseas activity. Most of the French who crossed the Atlantic preferred the warmer climes and greater economic prospects of the Caribbean. At first, the French in the West Indies joined with other enemies of Spain to prey upon Spanish colonies and ships, contributing the word "buccaneer" (*boucanier*) to the English language. Then they transformed the island colonies of Saint Domingue (modern Haiti), Guadeloupe, and Martinique into centers of sugar or coffee production, where a small planter class prospered from the labor of thousands of slaves. The sugar islands were worth far more than Canada. By the late 18th century, Saint Domingue was generating more wealth than any other colony in the world.

2-3 New Netherland

What key motivations drove Dutch colonialism in North America?

For most of the 17th century, the Dutch were more active overseas than the French. The Dutch Republic, whose 2 million people inhabited the most densely populated part of Europe, surpassed all rivals in finance, shipping, and trade. It offered an ideological as well as a political challenge to Spanish absolutism. In contrast to Spain, which stood for Catholic orthodoxy and the centralizing tendencies of Europe's "new monarchies," Dutch republicanism emphasized local liberties, prosperity, and, in major centers such as Amsterdam, religious toleration. Political power was decentralized to the cities and their wealthy merchants, who favored informal toleration, tried to keep trade as free as possible, and resisted the monarchical ambitions of the House of Orange. The Prince of Orange usually served as *stadholder* (captain general) of Holland, the richest province, and commanded its armies, and often those of other Dutch provinces as well.

The Dutch Republic—with Protestant dissenters from many countries, a sizable Jewish community, and a Catholic minority that exceeded 30 percent of the population—was

▲ **MAP 2.1 New France and the Jesuit Missions** The Jesuits established Indian missions near Montreal and far into the interior of North America, most of them well beyond the range of French military aid in an emergency.

Q What factors help explain the location of French missions?

Q Why did the French Jesuits keep pushing deeper and deeper to the interior?

actually a polyglot confederation. Amsterdam's merchant republicanism competed with the Calvinist Dutch Reformed Church for the allegiance of the people. The States General, to which each province sent representatives, became a weak central government for the republic. The broader public did not vote or participate actively in public life. The tension between tolerant merchant republicanism and Calvinist orthodoxy carried over into New Netherland.

2-3a The East and West India Companies

In 1602, the States General chartered the Dutch East India Company, the richest corporation the world had yet seen. It elbowed the Portuguese out of the Spice Islands and even out of Nagasaki in Japan, and the Dutch set up their own capital at Batavia (now Jakarta) on the island of Java. In the 17th century, Dutch merchants dominated Europe's trade in Asia.

The Atlantic and the Americas also attracted the Dutch. During their long wars with Spain, they forced the Spaniards to use expensive convoys to protect the silver fleets crossing the Atlantic, critically weakening their rival. In 1621, the States General chartered the Dutch West India Company and granted it jurisdiction over the African slave trade and commerce in the Americas. The company captured Portugal's slave-trading posts in West Africa and occupied the richest sugar-producing region of Brazil until the Portuguese took it back.

In 1609, Henry Hudson, an Englishman in Dutch service, sailed up what the Dutch called the North River (the English later renamed it the Hudson) and claimed the area for the Dutch Republic. The first permanent settlers arrived in 1624. Two years later, Deacon Pierre Minuit, leading a group of Protestant refugee families, bought, according to his own understanding, Manhattan Island from the Indians, and founded the port of New Amsterdam. The Dutch established Fort Orange (modern Albany) 150 miles upriver for trade with the Iroquois. Much like New France, New Netherland depended on the goodwill of nearby Indians, and the fur trade gave the colony a similar urban flavor. But unlike New France, few Dutchmen ventured into the deep woods. There were no *coureurs de bois* and hardly any missionary efforts. The Indians brought their furs to Fort Orange and exchanged them for firearms and other goods that the Dutch sold more cheaply than anyone else. The Dutch sold muskets to the Iroquois to win a larger share of the lucrative interior fur trade. By arming the Iroquois, they were effectively fighting the French by proxy, buttressing the military might of an indigenous confederacy that soon threatened the very existence of New France.

2-3b New Netherland as a Pluralistic Society

New Netherland became North America's first experiment in ethnic and religious pluralism. Primarily a commercial venture, the colony was ruled by autocratic governors. It

History Through Film — Black Robe (1991)

Directed by Bruce Beresford.
Starring Lothaire Bluteau (Father Laforgue), Aden Young (Daniel), Jean Brusseau (Samuel de Champlain), and Sandrine Holt (Annuka).

In *Black Robe*, director Bruce Beresford has given us the most believable film portrayal of 17th-century North America—both the landscape and its peoples—yet produced. This Canada–Australia co-production won six Genie Awards (Canada's equivalent of the Oscar), including best picture, best director, and best cinematography. The film is based on Brian Moore's novel of the same title, and Moore wrote the screenplay. It was filmed on location amid the spectacular scenery in the Lac St. Jean/ Saguenay region of Quebec.

In New France in the 1630s, Father Laforgue (Lothaire Bluteau), a young Jesuit, and Daniel (Aden Young), his teen-aged assistant and translator, leave on Laforgue's first mission assignment. Samuel de Champlain (Jean Brusseau), the governor of the colony, has persuaded the Algonquin tribe to convey the two to their mission site among the Hurons, far in the interior. Before long, Daniel falls in love with Annuka (Sandrine Holt), the beautiful daughter of Algonquin chief Chomina (August Schellenberg). When the priest inadvertently watches the young couple make love, he realizes that he has committed a mortal sin. From that point, his journey into the North American heartland almost becomes a descent into hell.

The Algonquins, guided by a dream quest, pursue a logic that makes no sense to the priest. Conversely, his religious message baffles them. Even so, when Chomina is wounded and Laforgue and Daniel are captured by the Iroquois, Annuka seduces the lone Iroquois guard, kills him, and enables all four of them to escape. Chomina dies of his wounds, politely but firmly rejecting baptism until the end. What Indian, he asks, would want to go to the Christian heaven, populated by many black robes but none of his own ancestors?

With the priest's approval, Daniel and Annuka go off by themselves. Laforgue reaches the mission, only to find many of the Indians dead or dying from some European disease. As the film closes, we learn that smallpox would devastate the mission in the following decade, and the Jesuits would abandon it in 1649.

Brian Moore's realism romanticizes nobody but treats both the Jesuits and the Algonquins with great respect. The screenplay drew criticism for its harsh depiction of the Iroquois, but it portrayed them through the eyes of the people they planned to torture. A smaller criticism is that Laforgue is the lone priest on the journey, during which he commits the sin of watching Daniel and Annuka make love. Jesuits, however, traveled in pairs precisely so they would always be accompanied by someone who could hear their confessions. Bruce Beresford, an Australian, directed *Breaker Morant* (1979), a highly acclaimed film set in the Boer War a century ago, and also *Driving Miss Daisy* (1989). ∎

2.5 *Black Robe*, based on Brian Moore's novel of the same title, is set in 17th-century North America.

2.6 New Amsterdam in 1660 This illustration, discovered in Florence about a century ago, is one of the finest city maps in all of early American history. It depicts 342 distinct structures, nearly all of them behind the wall that would later become Wall Street. At right angles to the wall, the broadest thoroughfare between it and the fort at the tip of Manhattan is what would later become Broadway. A census taken at the same time identifies the occupants of all 342 structures.

had no assembly and it attracted few immigrants. Only one settler, Killian Van Rensselaer, managed to build a thriving agricultural community on his gigantic personal estate, known as a **patroonship**, on the Hudson above and below Fort Orange.

But those who did immigrate to New Netherland were a diverse lot: Dutch-speaking Flemish and French-speaking Walloons from the Netherlands would intermingle with Danes, Swedes, Finns, Germans, and Scots. The government of the colony tried to utilize this diversity by drawing on two conflicting precedents from the Netherlands. On the one hand, it appealed to religious refugees by emphasizing the company's Protestant role in the struggle against Spain. On the other hand, the West India Company recognized that religious diversity could stimulate trade. After all, the pursuit of prosperity through toleration was the normal role of Amsterdam in Dutch politics.

Dutch toleration had its limits, though. In 1631, Pierre Minuit returned to Europe, where he organized another refugee project, this one for Flemings who had been uprooted by the war with Spain. When Dutch authorities refused to back him, he looked for support to the Lutheran kingdom of Sweden. Financed by private Dutch capital, he returned to America in 1638 with Flemish and Swedish settlers to found New Sweden, with its capital at Fort Christina (modern Wilmington) near the mouth of the Delaware River, on land claimed by New Netherland. Alarmed, Amsterdam sent troops to take over all of New Sweden, followed by settlers whose presence guaranteed Dutch control. Lutherans were persecuted in New Amsterdam, but they fared better in the Delaware Valley, where they became a majority.

2-3c *English Encroachments*

The English, already entrenched around Chesapeake Bay to the south and New England to the east (see the illustration of New Amsterdam in 1660), threatened to overwhelm the few thousand Dutch as they moved from New England onto Long Island. New Netherland welcomed them in the 1640s and gave them local privileges greater than those enjoyed by the Dutch, in the hope that their farms and herds would give the colony valuable exports. Governor Pieter Stuyvesant regarded these **Yankees** (a Dutch word that probably meant "land pirates") as good Calvinists, English-speaking equivalents of his Dutch Reformed settlers. They agitated for a more active role in government, but their loyalty was questionable. If England attacked the colony, would these Puritans side with the Dutch Calvinists or the Anglican invaders? Which ran deeper, their religious or their ethnic loyalties? Stuyvesant would learn the answer when England attacked him in 1664.

2-4 English Colonization Begins

Q *What kinds of ambitions and historical developments committed England to overseas colonization?*

England's interest in America emerged slowly. In 1497, Henry VII (1485–1509) sent Giovanni Cabato (John Cabot), an Italian mariner who had moved to Bristol, to search for a northwest passage to Asia. Cabot's two expeditions probably took him to Newfoundland, which he found teeming with cod. His report encouraged French, Spanish, and Portuguese fishermen to expand their operations on the north Atlantic coast. England itself would not develop interest in Newfoundland fisheries until the late 16th century, but Cabot's voyages did give it a vague claim to parts of the North American coast.

CHAPTER 2 Colonization in North America, 1600–1680

2-4a The English Reformation

When interest in America revived in the late 16th century, England was rapidly becoming a Protestant kingdom. Henry VIII (1509–1547), desperate for a male heir, had cut ties with the pope in order to divorce the queen and marry Anne Boleyn. He proclaimed himself the "Only Supreme Head" of the Church of England, confiscated monastic lands, and opened the way for serious Protestant reformers. Henry's oldest daughter, Mary I (1553–1558), reimposed Catholicism, burned hundreds of Protestants at the stake, and drove thousands into exile. Many of them became Calvinists. However, Elizabeth I, the daughter of Henry VIII and Anne Boleyn, accepted Protestantism, and the exiles returned. The Church of England became Calvinist in doctrine and theology but remained largely Catholic in structure, liturgy, and ritual. By the time of Elizabeth's death, England's Catholics were a tiny, fitfully persecuted minority, but they had powerful allies abroad, especially in Spain.

Some Protestants demanded the eradication of Catholic vestiges and the replacement of the Anglican Book of Common Prayer with sermons and psalms as the dominant mode of worship. These Puritans, also called **Non-Separatists**, insisted they were loyal to the true Church of England and resisted any relaxation of Calvinist rigor. They would play a major role in English expansion overseas. More extreme Protestants, called **Separatists**, denied that the Church of England was a true church and began to set up independent congregations of their own. Some of them would found the small colony of Plymouth.

2-4b From Plundering to Colonization

In the mid-16th century, England was a rather backward country of some 3 million people, but its population was growing rapidly. The country's chief export was woolen cloth, which found ready markets in continental Europe, fueling the growth of sheep farms. Increasingly, people and sheep competed for the same land. When farms were enclosed for sheep pasture, laborers were set adrift and often faced bleak prospects, creating the impression that England was overpopulated. Thousands headed for London, lifting the city's population from 50,000 in 1500 to 375,000 by 1650. As England's population and wealth grew, so too did its ambitions. English merchants and policymakers wanted their country to stake a claim in the contest for American riches. Sir Francis Drake, Sir Walter Raleigh, and other English "sea dogs" tried to break into Spain and Portugal's American markets, plundered Spanish colonies and treasure fleets, and explored America's Pacific side—often with Queen Elizabeth's approval. Although such exploits could be highly profitable, they could not sustain permanent colonization.

The English had two models for successful colonization. The conquistador model, based on coerced exploitation of native populations, had yielded Spain massive profits and possessions with moderate investments. Many English policy advocates urged the Court to follow the Spanish example in order to challenge Spanish preeminence in the Americas. The most prominent of them was Richard Hakluyt, who published accounts of England's overseas exploits and offered advice on how to make future colonization efforts more successful.

Another colonization model was closer at hand in Ireland, which the English Court had claimed for centuries. In the mid-16th century, the English tried to impose their agriculture, language, local government, legal system, aristocracy, and religion upon the Irish, who responded by becoming more intensely Roman Catholic than ever. England's colonization efforts in Ireland took the form of war, terror, and ethnic replacement with Protestants. A few decades later, English conquistadors would carry that colonization model across the Atlantic into their dealings with Native Americans. The English formed their preconceptions about American Indians largely from contact with the Irish, who, claimed one Elizabethan, are "more uncivil, more uncleanly, more barbarous and more brutish in their customs and demeanors, than in any part of the world that is known."

One such conquistador was Sir Humphrey Gilbert, a well-educated humanist and a veteran of the Irish wars, who proposed that England grab control of the Newfoundland fisheries, a nursery of seamen and naval power. In 1583, he took a fleet across the Atlantic north to claim the region. The crews of 22 Spanish and Portuguese fishing vessels and 18 French and English ships listened in wonder as he read his royal patent to them, divided up the land among them, assigned them rents, and established the Church of England for this mostly Catholic group. He then sailed away to explore more of the American coast. His own ship went under during a storm. Another ambitious English conquistador, Sir Walter Raleigh, Gilbert's half-brother, received a patent from Queen Elizabeth to colonize North America in more southern latitudes. In 1587, after a failed attempt two years earlier, Raleigh sent a large expedition to Roanoke Island, off the coast of North Carolina. The expedition included a few women, a sign that the English envisioned a permanent colony. When John White, the colony's governor, sailed back to England for more supplies, his return to Roanoke was delayed by the assault of the Spanish armada on England. By the time he reached Roanoke in 1590, the settlers had vanished, leaving a cryptic message—"CROATOAN"—carved on a tree (see Map 2.2). The colonists may have settled among the Chesapeake nation of Indians near the entrance to Chesapeake Bay. Sketchy evidence suggests that the Powhatans, the region's most powerful Indians, destroyed the Chesapeakes, along with any English living with them, in spring 1607, just as the first Jamestown settlers were arriving in the bay.

The Spanish Armada touched off a war that lasted until 1604 and strained the resources of England. The loss of the Armada, first to nimbler English ships in the English Channel and then to fierce storms off the Irish coast, crippled Spain, which had already begun to weaken due to a declining population and decreasing tax revenues. Sensing an opening, London became intensely involved in American affairs by launching **privateering** fleets against Spain. Even though London merchants remained more interested in trade with India, the Mediterranean, and Muscovy than in North American projects, the city's growing involvement with Atlantic privateering marked a significant shift: England had turned toward the Atlantic.

▲ **MAP 2.2 Roanoke Colony, 1584–1590** Roanoke marked the first English attempt to plant a permanent colony in North America.

Q *What advantages and dangers did Roanoke colony's location have?*

Q *What may have prompted the local Indians to destroy the colony?*

2-4c The Swarming of the English

In the 17th century, more than 700,000 people crossed the Atlantic to the English colonies in North America and the Caribbean. Most European migrants were single young men who arrived as servants. At first even some Africans were treated as servants, not slaves.

The Europeans who settled in New England or the Hudson or Delaware valleys were the most fortunate. Because Puritans and Quakers migrated as families into healthy regions, their population expanded at a rate far beyond anything known in Europe. The descendants of this small, idealistic minority soon became a substantial part of the total population, and they played a role in American history far out of proportion to their original numbers. As Table 2.1 shows, the New England and Middle Atlantic colonies together attracted only 5.4 percent of the immigrants, but by 1700 they contained 37 percent of all the newcomers' descendants in the English colonies and 55 percent of the Europeans' offspring.

2-5 The Chesapeake and West Indian Colonies

Q *Why did the English, crossing the Atlantic at roughly the same time, create such radically different societies in the Chesapeake, the West Indies, and New England?*

In 1606, King James I of England (1603–1625) chartered the Virginia Company with authority to colonize North America between the 34th and 45th parallels. A **joint-stock company** of numerous small investors, the Virginia Company had two branches: the Plymouth Company, which received jurisdiction over the northern portion of the grant, and the London Company, which received the southern portion (see Map 2.3). In 1607, the Plymouth Company established a settlement at Sagadahoc on the coast of Maine, but the settlers abandoned the venture within a year, having failed to open trade with the region's Abenaki Indians. In that same year, the London Company sent out three ships with 104 colonists, who landed at a defensible peninsula on what they called the James River. They built a fort and other crude buildings and named their settlement Jamestown. Investors hoped to find gold or silver, a northwest passage to Asia, a cure for syphilis, or other valuable products for sale in Europe. The settlers expected to persuade local Indians to work for them, much as Spain had done. If the Indians proved hostile, the settlers were told to form alliances with more distant Indians and subdue those who resisted. Company officials did not realize that a chief named Powhatan ruled more than 30 villages across a vast domain, **Tsenacommacah** ("our land"), below the **fall line**. He had no rival within striking distance. The company's other expectations proved equally skewed.

2-5a The Jamestown Disaster

The colony was a deathtrap. Every summer, the river became contaminated around Jamestown and sent out killing waves of dysentery and typhoid fever. Before long, malaria also set in. Only 38 colonists survived the first year. The survivors owed their good fortune to the resourcefulness of Captain John Smith, a soldier and adventurer who outmaneuvered the other leaders of the colony. When his explorations uncovered neither gold or silver nor any quick route to Asia, he concentrated on sheer survival. He visited Powhatan's village, hoping to awe the chief and convince him to sell corn. For his part, Powhatan sought to embrace Jamestown as a new tributary village for his confederacy. He staged a ritual performance in which Smith was symbolically clubbed to death and then reawakened as Powhatan's kin. The chief's ten-year-old daughter, Pocahontas, played a role in the ritual as a giver of life. The event was probably carefully scripted, something that Smith missed.

For a while, friendly relations prevailed between the settlers and the Powhatans, and Virginia's prospects seemed bright. A new royal charter extended its boundaries to the Pacific, and the London Company sent in more than 700 new settlers. But an intense drought failed the crops, and the colonists starved again. They survived by eating horses, rats, cats, and the leather of their boots. Some resorted to cannibalism, and many pushed into native villages, demanding and stealing corn, taking hostages, and killing Indians. Smith, who had been wounded in an explosion, sailed back to England. Only 60 colonists survived the winter of 1609–1610.

At this low point, a new governor arrived with 300 new soldier-settlers, who set out to establish English power in the region. Open warfare with Indians broke out. Powhatan's warriors picked off any settlers who strayed far from Jamestown. The English retaliated by slaughtering whole villages and destroying crops, as they had in Ireland. The war finally ended after the English captured Pocahontas and used her as a hostage to negotiate peace. She converted to Christianity and married John Rolfe, a widower. In 1614, Powhatan accepted the colonists' peace offer. Demoralized, he passed on leadership of the confederacy to his brother Opechancanough.

Despite the Indian war, the colony's prospects improved. The governors imposed martial law on the settlers and sent some of them to healthier locations, such as Henrico, 50 miles upstream. Through Rolfe's efforts, the colony began to produce a cash crop. He imported from the West Indies a mild, sweet-scented strain of tobacco, which swiftly took over English markets. The king, who had insisted no one could build a colony "upon smoke," was proved wrong, and soon the settlers were growing tobacco in the streets of Jamestown.

2-5b Reorganization, Reform, and Crisis

The London Company adopted an ambitious reform program for the colony. It encouraged economic diversification, such as glass-blowing, the planting of grapevines, and the raising of silkworms. English common law replaced martial law. The settlers were allowed to elect their own assembly, the **House of Burgesses**, to meet with the governor and his council and make local laws. Finally, the most popular reform permitted settlers to own land. Under this **headright** system, a colonist received

Table 2.1 THE PATTERN OF SETTLEMENT IN THE ENGLISH COLONIES TO 1700

Region	Immigrants (or Settlers) (in thousands)				Population in 1700 (in thousands)			
	Europeans		Africans		European Americans		African Americans	
West Indies	220	(29.6%)	316	(42.5%)	33	(8.3%)	115	(28.8%)
South	135	(18.1%)	30	(4.0%)	82	(20.5%)	22	(5.5%)
Mid-Atlantic	20	(2.7%)	2	(0.3%)	51	(12.8%)	3	(0.8%)
New England	20	(2.7%)	1	(0.1%)	91	(22.8%)	2	(0.5%)
Total	395	(53.1%)	349	(46.9%)	257	(64.4%)	142	(35.6%)

to more than £150 for every surviving settler, at a time when skilled English craftsmen were lucky to earn £50 per year. Such extravagance guaranteed that future colonies would be organized in different ways.

2-5c Tobacco, Servants, and Survival

During the two decades following Opechancanough's 1622 attack, Virginia proved that it could survive. Despite an appalling death rate, about a thousand new settlers came each year, raising the population above 8,000 by 1640. The export of tobacco financed the importation of indentured servants, even after oversupply plummeted the price of tobacco in the 1630s. Most servants were young men who agreed to work for a term of years in exchange for the cost of passage, plus bed and board during their years of service, and modest freedom dues when their terms expired. Those signing indentures in England usually had valuable skills and negotiated terms of four or five years. Those men arriving without an indenture, most of whom were younger and less skilled, were sold by the ship captain to a planter. Those older than age 19 served five years, whereas those younger than 19 served until age 24. The system turned servants into freemen, who then hoped to prosper on their own. Most former servants became tenants for several years while they tried to save enough to buy their own land.

Better tobacco prices enabled many to succeed between 1640 and 1660, but those who imported the servants were always in a stronger economic position, collecting the headright of 50 acres for each one. When tobacco prices fell again after 1660, upward mobility became even more difficult. Political offices usually went to the richest 15 percent of the settlers, and eventually their descendants monopolized the posts of justice

2.7 Regal State Illustration of Powhatan with tobacco pipe enthroned in his lodge, from vignette embellishing Smith's map of Virginia, first published in 1612.

Q What does the image tell us about how the English understood Powhatan as a chief?

50 acres for each person whose passage to Virginia he financed. By 1623, the company had shipped 4,000 settlers to Virginia, but the economic diversification program failed. Only tobacco found a market. Corn still provided most of the food. Instead of growing silkworms and grapes, Virginians raised Indian crops with Indian methods, which meant using hoes instead of plows.

The flood of newcomers strained the food supply and soured relations with the Indians. In March 1622, Opechancanough launched an attack to wipe out the colony. Without a last-minute warning from a friendly Indian, Jamestown might not have survived. Still, 347 settlers were killed that day, and most of the outlying settlements were destroyed. Newcomers who arrived in subsequent months had nowhere to go, and with food again scarce, hundreds died over the winter.

Back in London, several stockholders withdrew their capital and asked the king to intervene. In 1624, the king declared the London Company bankrupt and assumed direct control of Virginia, making it the first royal colony, with a governor and council appointed by the Crown. The London Company had invested some £200,000 in the enterprise, equal

2.8 Pocahontas After her conversion, Pocahontas went to England, where she was widely celebrated. The inscription around the portrait says "Matoaka [one of her Indian names] alias Rebecka [her baptismal name] daughter of the powerful Prince Powhatan, Emperor of Virginia."

2.9 The Opechancanough Massacre of 1622 This famous event, as portrayed in an engraving from the workshop of Theodor de Bry, depicts the warriors as treacherous, bloodthirsty savages and the settlers as innocent victims.

Q *Images like this one were highly popular across Europe. Why?*

of the peace (who presided over county courts), the pool from which the members of the House of Burgesses were normally chosen. Virginia, a prospering colony with a long history of local self-government, was becoming a class-based society.

2-5d The Collapse of Tsenacommacah

Because tobacco plants quickly wore out the soil, the settlers pushed steadily up the James, York, and Potomac rivers, attacking Powhatan villages, converting native fields into plantations, and fencing off hunting grounds into headrights. Pigs and cattle crowded Indian lands and diseases ravaged Indian communities. In 1644, Opechancanough made a desperate bid to push back the settlers. His warriors killed more than 400 colonists, but soon lost the upper hand. English militia subjugated Powhatan villages and captured the chief. Nearly 100 years old, Opechancanough was shot in captivity. Two years later, the remaining Powhatans became subjects of the king of England. Indians continued to occupy small pockets of land in Virginia, but Tsenacommacah as a political entity was no more.

2-5e Maryland

Maryland arose from the social and religious vision of Sir George Calvert, baron of Baltimore, and his son Cecilius, who both became Catholics and looked to America as a refuge for persecuted English and Irish Catholics. The colony was named after Henrietta Maria, the French Catholic queen of Charles I (1629–1649). The Maryland charter of 1632 made Baltimore "lord proprietor" of the colony. The most sweeping delegation of power that the Crown could make, it came close to making Baltimore king within Maryland. After 1630, most new colonial projects were **proprietary colonies**, often with the Maryland charter as a model. Many of them embodied the distinctive social ideals of their founders (see Map 2.4).

Like Champlain, the Calverts believed that Catholics and Protestants could live in harmony in a single colony. Cecilius Calvert, second lord of Baltimore, extended religious tolerance to all Maryland's Christians, but he also expected servants, who were mostly Protestants, to continue to serve Catholic gentlemen even after their indentures expired. This turned the gentlemen into manor lords, with the power to preside over feudal courts that were nearly obsolete in England. However, the conditions for Catholics improved in England during the reign of Charles I, which meant that fewer of them immigrated to Maryland. A small minority in a largely Protestant colony, Maryland's Catholic elite failed to preserve the manorial system. Protestant servants acquired their own land, and the Maryland assembly, the House of Delegates, became more forceful than Virginia's House of Burgesses in demanding the liberties of Englishmen. Like Virginia, Maryland became a rural colony of independent-minded tobacco planters, who strove to better their futures by raising their crop for Atlantic markets. Religion provided the biggest difference between the two colonies. Virginia was determinedly Anglican, while Maryland had no established church.

2-5f Chesapeake Family Life

At first, European men outnumbered women in Virginia by at least 5 to 1. Among new immigrant servants as late as the 1690s, the ratio was still 5 to 2. Population became self-sustaining about 1680, when live births finally began to outnumber deaths. Among adults, this transition was felt after 1700. Until then, most prominent people were immigrants.

Life expectancy improved as the colonists planted orchards to provide wholesome cider to drink, but it still remained much lower than in England, where those who reached puberty could expect to live into their 50s. Chesapeake immigrants had survived childhood diseases in Europe, but men at age 20 typically lived only to about 45, with 70 percent dead by age 50. Women died at even younger ages, especially in areas

▲ **MAP 2.3 Virginia Company Charter, 1606** This charter gave the Plymouth Company jurisdiction over what would become New England and New York, and the London Company jurisdiction over most of what became Virginia and North Carolina. They shared jurisdiction over the intervening area. The inset map shows Virginia's revised sea-to-sea boundaries, laid out in the 1609 charter.

Q *What motivated the king of England to grant such a vast domain to the Virginia Company?*

Q *How could the English justify sea-to-sea charters?*

▲ **MAP 2.4 Virginia and Maryland, circa 1675** Nearly 70 years after the founding of Jamestown, settlement remained confined to the tidewater and the eastern shore.

Q What made the Chesapeake Bay such a desirable destination for English settlers?

Q Why did the settlements remain confined to the shore and the tidewater?

ravaged by malaria, a dangerous disease during pregnancy. In those places, women rarely lived to age 40. For many, marriage became unattainable. About 70 percent of the men never married or, if they did, fathered no children. Most men had to wait years after completing their service before they could marry. Because women could not marry until they had fulfilled their indentures, most spent a good part of their childbearing years unwed. Despite severe legal penalties, about one-fifth of the women had illegitimate children and roughly one-third were pregnant on their wedding day. Virtually all women married, most as soon as they could, usually to a landowner. In short, upward mobility for women exceeded that for men.

In a typical Chesapeake marriage, the groom was in his 30s and the bride eight or ten years younger. Although men outlived women, this age gap meant that the husband usually died before his wife, who then quickly remarried. In one Virginia county, three-fourths of all children lost a parent, and one-third lost both. Native-born settlers married at a much earlier age than immigrants; women were often in their middle to late teens when they wed. Orphans were a major community problem.

2-5 The Chesapeake and West Indian Colonies

Stepparents were common because surviving spouses with property usually remarried. Few lived long enough to become grandparents. By the time the oldest child in a household was 20, the husband and wife, because of successive remarriages, might not even be that child's blood relatives. Under these circumstances, family loyalties tended to focus on other kin—uncles, aunts, cousins, older stepbrothers or stepsisters—thus contributing to the value that Virginia and Maryland placed on hospitality. Only a small number of men could reach the patriarchal ideal of heading one's own household. Because fathers died young, even the office-holding elite that took shape after 1650 had difficulty passing on its status to its sons. Only toward the end of the 17th century were the men holding office likely to be descended from fathers of comparable distinction.

2-5g The West Indies and the Transition to Slavery

In the 17th century, far more Englishmen went to the West Indies than to the Chesapeake. Between 1624 and 1640, they settled the Leeward Islands (St. Christopher, Nevis, Montserrat, and Antigua) and Barbados, tiny islands covering just over 400 square miles. In the 1650s, England seized Jamaica from Spain, increasing this total by a factor of 10. At first, English planters grew tobacco, using the labor of indentured servants, but beginning around 1645 in Barbados, sugar replaced tobacco, with dramatic social consequences. The Dutch, then being driven from Brazil by the Portuguese, provided some of the capital for this transition, showed the English how to raise sugar, introduced them to slave labor on a massive scale, and for a time dominated the exportation and marketing of the crop. The French built small island colonies in the eastern Caribbean (see Map 2.5).

Sugar became so valuable that planters imported most of their food from North America rather than divert land and labor from the cash crop. Sugar required a heavy investment in slaves and mills, and large planters with many slaves soon dominated the islands. Ex-servants found little employment, and most of them left after their terms expired. Many joined the buccaneers or moved to the mainland. Their exodus hastened the transition to slavery. In 1660, Europeans outnumbered slaves in the English islands by 33,000 to 22,000. By 1700, the white population had stagnated, but the number of slaves had increased sixfold. Planters appropriated about 80 percent of their slaves' labor for their own profit, an unprecedented rate of exploitation. They often worked slaves to death and then bought others to replace them. Of the 316,000 Africans imported before 1700, only 115,000 remained alive in that year.

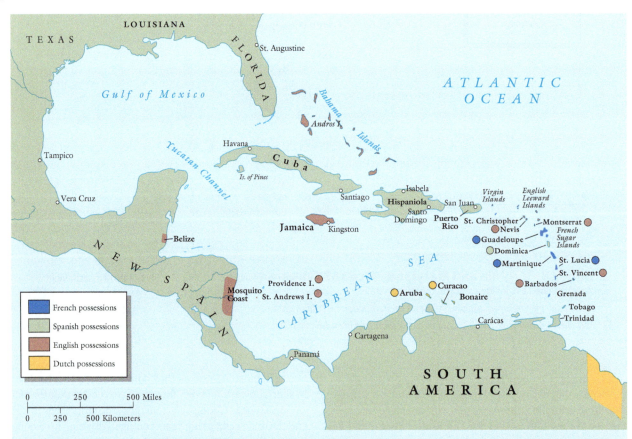

▲ **MAP 2.5 Principal West Indian Colonies in the 17th Century** Spain retained control of the large islands of Cuba, Hispaniola, and Puerto Rico, while its English, French, and Dutch rivals settled the smaller but fertile islands east of Puerto Rico and south of Cuba.

Q How can we explain the fact that four European empires managed to simultaneously hold colonies in the Caribbean in the 17th century?

Q Which of the four empires was best positioned to exploit the Caribbean resources, and why?

2.10 Slaves on a Sugar Plantation in Antigua Sugar was an even more demanding crop than tobacco, partly because workers could easily cut themselves on the sharp edges of the cane stalks, and because planters tried to compel workers to toil almost around the clock at harvest time so that the cane could be crushed in a mill and the juice boiled before it could spoil. A weary slave could easily lose fingers or an arm while trying to feed the mill.

Q *Is the painting idealized and romanticized? How and why?*

Observers were depressed by the moral climate on the islands, where underworked and overfed planters arrogantly dominated their overworked and underfed slaves. Yet, the islands generated enormous wealth for the British Empire, far more than the mainland colonies. Around 1700, the islands sent sugar worth £710,000 per year to England at a time when Chesapeake planters were getting only £230,000 for their tobacco.

2-5h The Rise of Slavery in North America

Africans reached Virginia in 1619 when, as John Rolfe reported, a Dutch ship "sold us twenty Negars." Their status was ambiguous for decades after slavery had been sharply defined in the West Indies. In the Chesapeake, many of the first Africans were Creoles with a great deal of intercultural experience around the Atlantic world and were in a stronger position to negotiate with their masters than later comers would be. Some Africans were treated as servants and won their freedom after several years.

Because the English had no experience with slavery at home, a rigid caste system took time to crystallize. When Hugh Davis was whipped in 1630 "for abusing himself to the dishonor of God and shame of Christians, by defiling his body in lying with a negro," his offense may have been sodomy rather than miscegenation. The record is unclear. The case of Elizabeth Key, a mulatto, a Christian, and the bastard daughter of Thomas Key, shows similar ambiguity. In 1655, when she claimed her freedom, her new owner fought to keep her enslaved. William Greensted, who had fathered two children by her, sued on her behalf, won, and then married her. He had probably fallen in love with her.

In the late 17th century, the caste structure of the Chesapeake colonies began to consolidate. Fewer indentured servants reached the Chesapeake from England, as the Delaware Valley and the expanding English army and navy competed more successfully for the same young men. Slaves, many of them imported from Barbados, took their place. Some of the emerging great planters deliberately chose to replace indentured servants with enslaved Africans. In Virginia, a series of laws in the 1660s began to institutionalize slavery by solidifying the blurred and shifting lines between freedom and unfreedom and servitude and slavery. Most importantly, the laws stipulated that the children of slaves inherited the status of their mother, which reversed the common-law practice and meant that a mulatto child of a slave woman inherited the mother's status of unfreedom. Virginia was turning from temporary servitude toward lifelong and hereditary slavery.

2-6 The New England Colonies

Q *How did religious concerns shape the colonization of New England?*

In New England, unlike the Chesapeake colonies, settlers reproduced the mixed economy of old England, with minor variations. Their quarrel with England was over religion, not economics. They came to America, they insisted, to worship as God commanded, not as the Church of England required.

2-6a The Pilgrims and Plymouth

The Pilgrims were Separatists who left England for the Netherlands between 1607 and 1609, convinced that the Church of England was no true daughter of the Reformation. They hoped to worship freely in the Netherlands. After a decade there, they became disillusioned by Dutch religious pluralism, which prompted a minority of the congregation to seek religious fulfillment in America. In 1620, the *Mayflower* sailed for Virginia with 102 passengers, roughly one-third of them Pilgrims, but the ship was blown off course in late 1620, landing first on Cape Cod and then on the mainland well north of the charter boundaries of Virginia, at a place they named Plymouth. Before landing, the passengers agreed to the Mayflower Compact, which bound them all to obey the decisions of the majority, a sound precaution in a colony with uncertain legal status.

Short on supplies, the colonists suffered keenly during the first winter. Half of them died, including the governor and all but three of the married women. William Bradford became governor, and he would be reelected annually for all but five years until his death in 1656.

The settlers fared much better when spring came. During the previous three years, the Indian communities of the area had been ravaged by diseases spread by European traders. As much as 90 percent of the region's Indians may have died. The much-diminished Wampanoags sought an alliance with the settlers, hoping to recruit their support against rival Narragansetts. Mediated by Samoset and Squanto, Patuxet Indians who spoke broken English, the settlers met with a powerful Wampanoag **sachem** (or chief), Massasoit. Massasoit promised to regulate the relations between the Indians and the colonists, believing that the arrangement had bound the newcomers to him as tributary dependents. The English, in turn, believed that Massasoit had submitted his people under English sovereignty. Despite such misunderstandings, relative peace prevailed for several years, allowing the Plymouth Bay colony to survive. By 1630, the settlers numbered about 300. They founded several new towns and sold their surplus crops to the colonists flooding into Massachusetts Bay.

2-6b Massachusetts Bay

In 1629, several English Puritans obtained a charter for the Massachusetts Bay Company, a typical joint-stock corporation except for one feature: The charter did not specify where the company was to be located. Led by John Winthrop, the Puritans decided to carry the charter to New England, beyond the gaze of Charles I, who had become impatient with Puritan demands for reforming the Church of England. Charles expected obedience from the Puritans, who came to realize that church reform would have better prospects across the Atlantic. Rather than using the charter to organize a business corporation in England, they used it to found a colony of pure Christianity in New England, far away from state control. Puritan colonists came from the broad middle range of English society, and most of them owned property. When they sold it to go to America, they probably liquidated far more capital than the London Company had invested in the Chesapeake Bay. A godly haven was expensive to build.

An advance party that sailed in 1629 took over a fishing village on the coast and renamed it Salem. The next year, more than 1,000 colonists arrived. In small groups, they scattered around Massachusetts Bay, founding towns and appointing a minister and a magistrate for each. Church and state were closely bound from the start. The local congregation was the first institution to take shape, and from it evolved the town meeting. The colonists planted corn and English grains, but one-third of them perished during the first winter. Then conditions rapidly improved, as they had at Plymouth a decade earlier. About 13,000 settlers came to Massachusetts by 1641, most as families—a unique event in Atlantic empires to that time. They raised sheep, produced woolen textiles, and embarked on active shipbuilding. The colony began to prosper after 1650, when Boston merchants opened up West Indian markets for New England grain, lumber, and fish.

The very existence of colonies committed to free labor was odd. To sustain free labor, towns severely restricted inward migration, thus guaranteeing a home market to their own craftsmen and other laborers. But towns also imposed strict discipline upon the settlers: New England magistrates whipped more freemen than any other English colonies. And to prosper, the New England colonies had to trade with more typical colonies, the societies elsewhere in the hemisphere that raised tobacco and sugar with unfree labor.

2-6c Covenant Theology

Puritans embraced what they called covenant theology. According to this system, God had made two biblical covenants with humans: the covenant of works and the covenant of grace. In the covenant of works, God had promised Adam that if he kept God's law he would never die, but Adam disobeyed, was expelled from the Garden of Eden, and died. All of Adam's descendants remain under the same covenant, but because of his fall can never be capable of keeping the law; they *deserve* damnation. But God was merciful and answered sin with the covenant of grace. God will save his chosen people; everyone else will be damned. Even though the covenant of works can no longer bring eternal life, it remains in force and establishes the strict moral standards that every Christian must strive to follow, before and after conversion. A Christian's inability to

What They Said

English Colonists and Huron Indians Enter New Worlds

Europeans and Native Americans both encountered a "new world" in the Americas from the 16th century onward. Europeans had discovered an entire hemisphere that seemed drastically different from Europe. Native Americans found their lifeways so fundamentally transformed by European colonialism that the Americas became a new and often alien world for them. That much was common to both, but what exactly was new to each could be strikingly different. The two documents here illuminate these complexities. The first, an excerpt from William Bradford's history of the Plymouth colony, describes the Pilgrims' views of the landscape after their landing. The second is a French Jesuit's description of Huron Indians' reaction to a smallpox epidemic. Both documents are alive with anxiety, but what are its causes and consequences? What role does knowledge—or its lack—play in both cases? How do the colonists and Indians try to cope in their respective new worlds?

▶ William Bradford, 1620

It is recorded in scripture as a mercie to the apostle & his shipwraked company, that the barbarians shewed them no smale kindness in refreshing them, but these savage barbarians, when they mette with them (as after will appeare) were readier to fill their sids full of arrows then otherwise. And for the season it was winter, and they that know the winters of the cuntrie, know them to be sharp & violent, & subjecte to cruell & feirce stormes, deangerous to travill to known places, much more to serch an unknown coast. Besids, what could they see but a hideous & desolate wildernes, full of wild beasts & willd men? and what multituds ther might be of them they knew not. Nether could they, as it were, goe up to the tope of Pisgah, to vew from this willdernes a more goodly cuntrie to feed their hops; for which way soever they turnd their eys (save upward to the heavens) they could have litle solace or content in respecte of any outward objects. For sumer being done, all things stand upon them with a wetherbeaten face; and the whole countrie, full of woods & thickets, represented a wild & savage heiw. If they looked behind them, ther was the mighty ocean which they had passed, and was now as a maine barr & goulfe to separate them from all the civill parts of the world.... What could now sustaine them but the spirite of God & his grace? May not & ought not the children of these fathers rightly say: *Our faithers were Englishmen which came over this great ocean, and were ready to perish in this willdernes....*

▶ Jérôme Lalemant, 1640

They observed, with some sort of reason, that, since our arrival in these lands, those who had been the nearest to us, had happened to be the most ruined by the diseases, and that the whole villages of those who had received us now appeared utterly exterminated; and certainly, they said, the same would be the fate of all the others if the course of this misfortune were not stopped by the massacre of those who were the cause of it. This was a common opinion, not only in private conversation but in the general councils held on this account, where the plurality of the votes went for our death, — there being only a few elders, who thought they greatly obliged us by resolving upon banishment.

What powerfully confirmed this false imagination was that, at the same time, they saw us dispersed throughout the country, — seeking all sorts of ways to enter the cabins, instructing and baptizing those most ill with a care which they had never seen. No doubt, they said, it must needs be that we had a secret understanding with the disease (for they believe that it is a demon), since we alone were all full of life and health, although we constantly breathed nothing but a totally infected air, — staying whole days close by the side of the most foul-smelling patients, for whom every one felt horror; no doubt we carried the trouble with us, since, wherever we set foot, either death or disease followed us. In consequence of all these sayings, many had us in abomination; they expelled us from their cabins, and did not allow us to approach their sick, and especially children: not even to lay eyes on them, — in a word, we were dreaded as the greatest sorcerers on earth.

Wherein truly it must be acknowledged that these poor people are in some sense excusable. For it has happened very often, and has been remarked more than a hundred times, that where we were most welcome, where we baptized most people, there it was in fact where they died the most; and, on the contrary, in the cabins to which we were denied entrance, although they were sometimes sick to extremity, at the end of a few days one saw every person prosperously cured. We shall see in heaven the secret, but ever adorable, judgments of God therein.

Sources: (top) William Bradford, "Of Plimoth Plantation" (Boston: Wright and Potter, 1900), pp. 95–126. (bottom) Reuben Gold Thwaites, ed., *The Jesuit Relations and Allied Documents: Travels and Explorations of the Jesuit Missionaries in New France 1610–1791*, Vol. XIX (Cleveland, The Burrows Brothers Company Publishers, 1899), 91–93.

keep the law usually triggered the conversion experience by demonstrating that only faith, not works, could save.

At this level, covenant theology merely restated Calvinist orthodoxy, but the Puritans gave it a novel social dimension by pairing each personal covenant with a communal counterpart. Each congregation organized itself into a church, a community of the elect. The founders of each church, after satisfying one another of their own conversions, agreed that within their church the Gospel would be properly preached and discipline would be strictly maintained. God, in turn, promised to bestow saving grace within that church—not to everyone, but presumably to most of the children of the elect. This communal covenant determined not who was saved or damned, but the rise and fall of nations or peoples. As a people, New Englanders agreed to obey the law, and God promised to prosper them. If magistrates enforced God's law and the people supported these efforts, God would not punish the whole community for the misdeeds of individuals. But if sinners escaped public account, God's anger would be terrible toward his chosen people of New England. God gave them much and demanded much in return. In England, the government had refused to assume a godly role. Puritans fleeing to America hoped to escape the divine wrath that threatened England and to create in America the kind of churches that God demanded.

2-6d Puritan Family Life

In rural areas, New Englanders soon observed a remarkable fact. After the first winter, deaths were rare. The place was undeniably healthy, and families grew rapidly as unprecedented numbers of children reached maturity. The settlers had left most European diseases behind and had encountered no new ones in the bracing climate. For the founders and their children, life expectancy far exceeded the European norm. More than one-fifth of the men who founded Andover lived past age 80. Infant mortality fell, and few mothers died in childbirth. Because people lived so long, New England families became intensely patriarchal. Many fathers refused to grant land titles to their sons before their own deaths. In the early years, settlers often moved, looking for the richest soil, the best neighbors, and the most inspiring minister. By the mid-1640s, most of them had found what they sought. Migration into or out of country towns became much lower than in England, and the New England town settled into a tight community that slowly became an intricate web of cousins. Once the settlers had formed a typical farming town, they grew reluctant to admit "strangers" to their midst. New Englanders largely avoided slavery, not out of sympathy for Africans or hatred of the institution, but to keep outsiders from contaminating their religion.

2-6e Conversion, Dissent, and Expansion

The vital force behind Puritanism was the quest for conversion. Probably because of John Cotton's stirring sermons in Boston, the settlers crossed an invisible boundary in the mid-1630s. As Cotton's converts described their religious experiences, their neighbors turned from analyzing the legitimacy of their own conversions to assessing the validity of someone else's. Churches began to impose tests for regeneracy, and the standards of acceptance escalated rapidly.

The conversion experience was deeply ambiguous to a Puritan. Anyone who found no inner trace of saving grace was damned. It began with the discovery that one could not keep God's law because all people were sinners. It progressed through despair to hope, which always arose from passages of scripture that spoke to that person's condition. A "saint" at last found reason to believe that God had saved him or her. The whole process involved a painful balance between assurance and doubt. A saint was sure of salvation, but never too sure.

This quest for conversion generated dissent and new colonies. In the mid-1630s, Reverend Thomas Hooker, alarmed by Cotton's preaching, led his congregation west from Massachusetts, where a new colony emerged along the Connecticut River. In 1639, an affluent group planted the New Haven Colony on Long Island Sound. Their spiritual leader, Reverend John Davenport, imposed the strictest requirements for church membership in New England. While the founders of Connecticut Colony feared that Massachusetts was becoming too severe in certifying church membership, the New Haveners worried that the Bay colony was too lenient.

The residents of most towns agreed on the kind of worship they preferred, but some settlers, such as Roger Williams and **Anne Hutchinson**, made greater demands. Williams was a Separatist who refused to worship with anyone who did

2.11 Portrait of Robert Gibbs (1670) New Englanders did not provide distinctive garments for small boys and girls. They wore the same clothes.

Q *What does the image reveal about childhood in 17th-century New England?*

CHAPTER 2 Colonization in North America, 1600–1680

not explicitly repudiate the Church of England. Nearly all Massachusetts Puritans were Non-Separatists who claimed only to be reforming the Anglican Church. In 1636, after Williams challenged the king's right as a Christian to grant Indian lands to anyone at all, the colony banished him. He fled to Narragansett Bay with a few disciples and founded Providence. He developed eloquent arguments for religious liberty and the complete separation of church and state.

Anne Hutchinson, an admirer of John Cotton, claimed that virtually all other ministers were preaching only the covenant of works, not the covenant of grace, and were leading their people to hell. In Boston, she won a large following, many of them women. At her trial there, she claimed to have received direct messages from God (the Antinomian heresy). By forcefully defending her beliefs, Hutchinson also challenged the patriarchal Puritan gender order. She was banished in 1638 and fled with followers to Narragansett Bay, where they founded Newport and Portsmouth. These towns united with Providence to form the colony of Rhode Island and accepted both the religious liberty and the separation of church and state that Williams advocated.

This territorial expansion was fast, mostly unplanned, and locally driven. None of the new Puritan colonies—Connecticut, New Haven, and Rhode Island—sprang into existence with royal charters (see Map 2.6). The expansion stemmed not only from religious idealism, but also from a need for more land to accommodate a steady stream of transatlantic migration. Puritans spread to interior New England with their fields and fences, disturbing deer and other wildlife and disrupting native hunting economies. Pushed into poor lands, the Pequot Indians forged trade relations with the Dutch along the Hudson River to secure weapons and military support. In 1637, the Puritans launched a war against the Pequots, attacking them with their Narragansett and Mohegan allies. In May, New Englanders faced a choice of two Pequot villages to attack—one held by warriors, the other inhabited by women, children, and elderly. They chose the latter, set it on fire, and with their Narragansett and Mohegan allies shot anyone who tried to flee. More than 400 died. Many of the surviving Pequots were sold into slavery in the West Indies.

Fearful of renewed Indian wars, the factious New England colonies tightened their binds. Massachusetts, Plymouth, Connecticut, and New Haven formed a defensive alliance, the New England Confederation (the religiously unorthodox Rhode Island was not invited to join). The confederation nurtured ties with the Mohegans, who had clashed with the Narragansetts over the vacated Pequot lands, hoping to gain access to new lands through a native proxy.

2-6f *Puritan Indian Missions*

The Puritans coveted the Indians' lands, but they also coveted their souls. Building the perfect Christian community in the New World required, in the minds of some Puritans, extending God's grace to the natives. Serious efforts to convert Indians to Protestantism began in the 1640s on Martha's Vineyard under Thomas Mayhew, Sr., and Thomas Mayhew, Jr. The Mayhews worked with local sachems and challenged only the powwaws (tribal medicine men) in their efforts to spread Christianity. They encouraged Indian men to teach the settlers how to hunt whales, an activity that made them a vital part of the settlers' economy without threatening their identity as men. John Eliot, pastor of the Roxbury church, focused his efforts on the Massachusett Indians. He translated the Bible into the Massachusett language and gave sermons in that language. In contrast to the Mayhews, he attacked the authority of the sachems as well as the powwaws, challenged the traditional tribal structure, and insisted on turning Indian men into farmers, a female role in these native societies.

Both methods—Eliot's assertive approach and the Mayhews' more measured one—brought results among the New England Indians who struggled to explain the success of English colonization and their own weakened condition. By the 1670s, a string of 14 "praying towns" extended from Massachusetts to Connecticut, and more than 2,000 Indians were in various stages of conversion. Yet, only a few natives would achieve the kind of conversion experience that Puritans required for full membership in a church. Few Indians shared the Puritan sense of sin. They could not grasp why their best deeds should stink in the nostrils of the Lord. The praying towns provided the beleaguered Indians some means to cope with the consequences of colonialism—disease, death, land loss, alcoholism—but they also caused fear and resentment, further deepening the chasm between the natives and the newcomers.

2-6g *Congregations, Towns, and Colony Governments*

By the mid-17th century, life in the New England colonies began to fall into distinctive and broadly similar patterns. Congregations abandoned the Anglican Book of Common Prayer, vestments, incense, church courts, and the need to be ordained by a bishop. The sermon became the dominant rite, and each congregation chose and ordained its own minister. No singing was permitted, except of psalms. A 1648 synod issued the Cambridge Platform, which defined "Congregationalist" worship and church organization.

By then the town had become something distinct from the congregation. Town meetings decided who got how much land. It was distributed broadly but never equally. In Springfield, at one extreme, the Pynchon family controlled most of the land and most of the labor as well. In other towns, such as Dedham, the distribution was much more equitable. In some villages, town meetings occurred often, made most of the decisions, and left only the details to a board of elected "selectmen." In others, the selectmen did most of the governing. Usually, all adult males participated in local decisions, but Massachusetts and New Haven restricted the vote for colony-wide offices to only those men who were full church members, a decision that greatly narrowed the electorate.

Massachusetts had a bicameral legislature by the 1640s. Voters in each town chose representatives who met as the Chamber of Deputies, or lower house. Voters also elected the governor and the magistrates, or upper house. Massachusetts defined its legal system in the "Body of Liberties" of 1641 (which may actually be history's first bill of rights) and in a

▲ **MAP 2.6 New England in the 1640s** The five Puritan colonies spread over the Atlantic coast and nearby islands, the shores and islands of Narragansett Bay, both sides of Long Island Sound, and much of the Connecticut Valley. Although New Hampshire and Maine (not named as such on this map) were not founded by Puritans, Massachusetts extended its government over those settlers during the English civil wars. The inset map shows the principal military campaign of the Pequot War.

Q *Why did New England not become the domain of a single colony?*
Q *What made the New England settlers vulnerable to Indian attacks?*

comprehensive law code of 1648 that was widely imitated in other colonies. Massachusetts sharply reduced the number of capital offenses under English law and listed them in the order of the Ten Commandments. Unlike England, Massachusetts seldom executed anyone for a crime against property. Other distinctive features of the legal system included an explicit recognition of the liberties of women, children, servants, foreigners, and even "the Bruite Creature," or animals; a serious effort to ban professional lawyers; and the swift punishment of crime.

New England also transformed the traditional English jury system. New Haven abolished juries altogether because the Bible does not mention them, but the other colonies vastly expanded the role of civil (noncriminal) juries, using them even to decide appeals, something that never happened in England. Except in capital trials, however, the criminal jury—a fixture of English justice—almost disappeared in New England. The punishment of sin involved fidelity to the covenant and was too important to leave to 12 ordinary men. This system worked

2.12 The Puritan Massacre of the Pequot Indians, 1637 The massacre took place at what is now Mystic, Connecticut. Most of the victims were women and children. The Indians shown in the outer circle were Narragansett allies of the settlers and were appalled by the carnage.

well because even sinners shared its values. Most offenders appeared in court and accepted their punishments. Acquittals were rare, almost unheard of in New Haven. Yet, hardly anyone ran away to avoid trial or punishment.

2-6h Infant Baptism and New Dissent

Although most of the founders of the New England colonies became church members during the fervor of the 1630s, their children had trouble achieving conversion. They had never lived as part of a persecuted minority in England, nor had they experienced the joy of joining with other holy refugees in founding their own church. They had to find God on their own and then persuade their elders—who were on guard because leniency had let Williams, Hutchinson, and other deviants through—that their conversions were authentic. Most failed. They grew up, married, and requested baptism for their children. The Cambridge Platform declared that only "saints" (the converted) and their children could be baptized, which excluded increasing numbers from the church's full embrace. By the mid-17th century, this problem was becoming acute.

Dissenters offered two answers, and the ministers a third. Some colonists became Baptists, who argued that only converted adults (and no children) should receive baptism. Quakers, who arrived in New England in the 1650s, taught that salvation was available to all those who would allow their Inner Light, God's presence within a person, to shine forth—a blasphemous notion to Puritans, who believed in predestination. The clergy's answer to the lack of conversions became known as the Half-Way Covenant. Parents who had been baptized but had not experienced conversion could bring their children before the church, "own the covenant with God," and have their children baptized. Aging church members resisted the Half-Way Covenant, but as the founders died off in the 1670s and 1680s, it took hold and soon led to something like universal baptism.

Yet, dissent and tension persisted. The orthodox colonies were divided over whether to persecute or to ignore their Baptist and Quaker minorities. Ministers preached "jeremiads," shrill warnings against any backsliding from the standards of the founding generation. The new partial church members could have their children baptized but could not accept communion or vote.

2-7 From Civil War to the First Restoration Colonies

Q *In what ways did the Restoration colonies differ from those founded earlier in the Chesapeake and New England?*

England's first American colonies had emerged during a period of overall stability in the mother country. In the 1640s, however, England fell apart. Tensions mounted during the reign of Charles I, who, like Spanish and French monarchs, aspired to build a centralized realm of religious uniformity and personal rule. After governing without Parliament from 1629 to 1640, Charles I tried to impose the Anglican Book of Common Prayer upon Presbyterian Scotland. The Scots revolted and invaded England. Charles had to summon Parliament, which in 1642 rose against the authoritarian king. Parliament won the military struggle.

In 1649, it executed the king, abolished the House of Lords, and proclaimed England a commonwealth (or republic). In 1653, the army named its most successful general, Oliver Cromwell, lord protector of England. When the protectorate collapsed after Cromwell's death in 1658, part of the army invited Charles II to return from exile and accept the throne, but with limitations to his authority. By then the Church of England had nearly disintegrated. The new Restoration government worked hard to restore the old order. It brought back the House of Lords and reestablished the Church of England. The English state, denying any right of dissent, persecuted both Catholics and Protestant dissenters: Presbyterians, Congregationalists, Baptists, and Quakers. This persecution would drive thousands of Quakers to the Delaware Valley in the 1670s.

The disorder of the English civil wars spread into the American colonies as well. In Maryland, Protestants overthrew Lord Baltimore's regime, but the Puritan-dominated parliament sided with him. To appease Maryland's Protestant majority, Baltimore responded with the Toleration Act of 1649, which granted the freedom of worship to all Christians. In the West Indies, the colonists took advantage of the collapse of royal power by demanding and receiving elective assemblies. The new assemblies of Barbados and the Leeward Islands diverted their trade from England to the Dutch, who took over much of the English West Indies and Chesapeake sugar and tobacco trade.

If the Restoration reestablished much of the old order in England, it ushered in a new era in the colonies. The Crown took control of the governments of Barbados, Jamaica, and the Leeward Islands and imposed restrictions on their recently granted assemblies. The Crown insisted that it had created and granted the constitutional structure for each colony, a view that few settlers accepted, believing that they had an inherent right to constitutional rule. Charles II envisioned England as a centralized imperial state embodied in the person of the monarch and he saw the colonies as a means to fulfill his vision. He bestowed vast landholdings in the North American mainland on the noblemen who had supported the Stuart cause during the civil wars. The king owed the loyal elite something, and a colonial charter cost him nothing. New colonies, moreover, would yield the state much-needed revenue through trade and taxes. During the Restoration era (1660–1688), six new colonies were founded, doubling the number of England's mainland colonies.

Most of the new colonies shared certain common features and also differed in some respects from earlier settlements. All were proprietary in form, which empowered the organizers to pursue daring social experiments. Except for Pennsylvania, the Restoration colonies were all founded by men with big ideas and small purses. The proprietors tried to attract settlers from the older colonies because importing them from Europe was expensive. The most readily available prospects were servants completing their indentures in the West Indies and being driven out by the sugar revolution. Many went to Carolina. The most prized settlers, however, were New Englanders. Proprietors distrusted both their piety and their politics, but New Englanders had built the most thriving colonies in North America. However, few of them would go farther south than New Jersey.

The Restoration colonies made it easy for settlers to acquire land, and they competed with one another by offering newcomers strong guarantees of civil and political liberties. They all promised either toleration or full religious liberty, at least for Christians. Whereas Virginia and New England (except Rhode Island) were still homogeneous societies, the Restoration colonies attracted a mix of religious and ethnic groups. They all found it difficult to create political stability out of this diversity.

2-7a *Carolina, Harrington, and the Aristocratic Ideal*

In 1663, eight courtiers obtained a charter by which they became the board of proprietors for a colony to be founded south of Virginia. Calling their province Carolina in honor of the king, they tried to colonize the region in the 1660s but achieved no success until the following decade. Most of the settlers came from two sources. Former servants from Virginia and Maryland, many in debt, hoped that they could claim land around Albemarle Sound in what eventually became North Carolina. Other former servants came from Barbados. They settled what would become South Carolina.

To the proprietors in England, these scattered settlements made up a single colony called Carolina. With the help of the philosopher John Locke, they drafted the Fundamental Constitutions of Carolina, an incredibly complex plan for organizing a colony. The document drew on the work of Commonwealth England's most prominent republican thinker, James Harrington, author of *Oceana* (1656). He aspired to design a republic that could endure—unlike ancient Athens or Rome, which had finally become despotic states. Harrington argued that widespread ownership of land was the best guarantee against absolute government. He also proposed several other republican devices, such as frequent rotation of officeholders (called "term limits" today), the secret ballot, and a bicameral legislature, with the smaller, upper house proposing laws and the larger one approving or rejecting them. Harrington had greater impact on colonial governments than any other thinker of his time.

The Carolina proprietors had set out to create in a distant land a model aristocratic society founded on an elaborate distribution of privileges and responsibilities. The Fundamental Constitutions proposed a government that was far more complex than any colony could sustain. For example, England had three supreme courts; Carolina would have eight. The document envisioned a class of lowly whites, "leetmen," who would live on small tracts and serve the great landlords. The document accepted slavery. "Every Freeman of Carolina shall have absolute Power and Authority over his Negro Slaves," declared Article 110. Carolina presented its organizers with unanticipated obstacles to these aristocratic goals. The proprietors assumed that landownership would be the key to everything else, including wealth and status, but many settlers prospered in other ways. The ex-servants from overcrowded Barbados who settled in Carolina resisted the hierarchical Fundamental Constitutions. They were also disappointed in the prospects of sugar cultivation in Carolina and instead began to raise cattle and hogs, letting them run free on open land. Some of their African slaves were probably America's first cowboys. In the Albemarle region, settlers from Virginia moved in to exploit the thick forests to produce masts, turpentine, tar, and pitch for sale for English shipbuilders. They channeled the bulk of their commerce through Virginia's ports. The settlers also traded with the Indians, usually for deerskins, often acquired from the Cherokees and Creeks west of the Appalachians. As in New France and New Netherland, the Indian trade sustained a genuine city, Charleston, founded in 1670. Charleston traders sold their Indian clients guns, clothing, and liquor, stirring competition among different groups. The Westos and Yamasees won favored status by offering an alluring commodity: Indian slaves, captured from Spanish Florida and the interior. The Indian slave trade would become the colony's biggest business and it would profoundly shape the geopolitics of the Southeast.

2-7b New York: An Experiment in Absolutism

In 1664, James, Duke of York, obtained a charter from his royal brother for a colony between the Delaware and Connecticut rivers. Charles II claimed that New Netherland was rightfully English territory because it was included in the Virginia charter of 1606 (see Map 2.7). James sent a fleet to Manhattan, and the English settlers on Long Island rose to support his claim. Reluctantly, Stuyvesant surrendered without resistance. The English renamed the province New York. New Amsterdam became New York City, and Fort Orange became Albany. The Dutch ceded New Netherland with few regrets, never having been able to turn a profit with it. New York took over all of Long Island. It also inherited New Netherland's role as mediator between the settlers and the Iroquois Confederacy. In effect, the Duke of York's autocratic colony assumed most of the burdens of this relationship while unintentionally conferring most of the benefits on the Quakers who would begin to settle the Delaware Valley a decade later. The shield provided by New York and the Iroquois would make the Quaker experiment in pacifism a viable option.

Although English soldiers abused many Dutch civilians, official policy toward the Dutch was conciliatory. Those who chose to leave could take their property with them. Those who stayed retained their property and were assured of religious toleration. Most stayed. Except in New York City and the small Dutch portion of Long Island, Dutch settlers still lived under Dutch law. Dutch inheritance practices, which were far more generous to women than English law, survived in New York well into the 18th century. Against the hopes of England's merchants, New York continued to trade with Amsterdam. The Duke boldly tried to do in New York what he and the king did not dare attempt in England—to govern without an elective assembly. A 1665 legal code, the Duke's Laws, shifted power to the governor and his council, upsetting English settlers far more that the Dutch, who had no experience with representative government. This made it difficult to attract English colonists, a problem that became aggravated when the Duke of York granted the area west of the lower Hudson River as a separate colony of New Jersey to two Carolina proprietors, Sir George Carteret and Baron John Berkeley. New Jersey granted settlers the right to elect an assembly, which made that colony far more attractive to English settlers than New York. The creation of New Jersey also slowed the flow of Dutch settlers across the Hudson and thus helped to keep New York Dutch.

The transition from a Dutch to an English colony did not go smoothly. James expected his English invaders to assimilate the conquered Dutch, but the reverse was more common for a generation or so. Most Englishmen who settled in New York after the conquest married Dutch women (few unmarried English women were available) and sent their children to the Dutch Reformed Church. In effect, the Dutch were assimilating the English. Nor did the Dutch give up their loyalty to the Netherlands. When the Netherlands recaptured the colony in 1672 during an Anglo-Dutch War, the Dutch settlers refused to assist New York's war effort. New York City became New Orange after William III of Nassau, the military leader of the Dutch Republic. The Dutch again concluded that the colony was not worth what it cost and ceded it permanently to England in 1674. The new governor, Major Edmund Andros, established an autocratic rule that alienated the colony's English and Dutch settlers alike. He arrested prominent Dutch merchants who, threatened with the confiscation of their property, relented and swore an oath of loyalty to England. He also helped secure bilingual ministers for the Dutch Reformist pulpits, which caused alarm among ordinary Dutch Protestants. New York's English merchants harbored their own grievances. They resented the Dutch elite's staying power and insisted that the colony had to become more English and less autocratic to attract newcomers. The merchants refused to pay duties not accepted by an elective assembly, and the court of assize, New York's circuit court that had been under the governor's control, supported the tax strike. English towns on Long Island joined the demands for an elective assembly, an urgent matter now that William Penn's much freer Quaker colony on the Delaware threatened to drain away New York's English population.

The Duke finally relented and conceded an assembly. In 1683, it adopted a Charter of Liberties that proclaimed government by consent. It also imposed English law on the Dutch parts of the province. However, New York remained in the shadow of Philadelphia, which drew far more immigrants and absorbed a growing share of the Atlantic trade.

2-8 Brotherly Love: The Quakers and America

Q How did Pennsylvania's policy toward the Native Americans differ from the Indian policies of New England and the Chesapeake colonies? What explains those differences?

The most fascinating social experiment of the Restoration era took place in the Delaware Valley, where Quakers led another family-based, religiously motivated migration of more than 10,000 people between 1675 and 1690. Founded by George Fox during England's civil wars, the Society of

▲ **MAP 2.7 The Duke of York's Colonial Charter** This map shows the boundary of New York as set forth in the charter of 1664, the compromise boundary the first English governor negotiated with Connecticut, and the principal manors created in the 17th century.

Q *How was Charles II able to grant such a massive colonial charter to his brother James, Duke of York?*

Q *What threats and challenges did New York face during its early years?*

Friends expanded dramatically in the ensuing years as it went through a heroic phase of missionaries and martyrs, including four who were executed in Massachusetts. After the Restoration, persecution in England finally prompted Quakers to seek refuge in America. Like the Puritans in New England, the Roman Catholic Calverts in Maryland, and the aristocratic proprietors in Carolina, the Quakers saw America as a haven for a kind of ideal society that could no longer be achieved in Europe.

2-8a Quaker Beliefs

Quakers were radically different from other Christians. They insisted that God, in the form of the Inner Light, is present in all people, who can become good—even perfect—if only they will let that light shine forth. They took literally Jesus' advice to "Turn the other cheek." They became pacifists, enraging Catholics and most other Protestants, nearly all of whom had found ways to justify war. Quakers also obeyed Jesus' command to "swear not."

They denounced oaths as sinful. Again, other Christians reacted with horror because their judicial systems rested on oaths.

Although orderly and peaceful, Quakers struck others as dangerous radicals whose beliefs would bring anarchy. For instance, slavery made the Friends uncomfortable, although they did not embrace abolitionism until a century later (see Chapter 5). Also, in what they called "the Lamb's war" against human pride, Quakers refused to doff their hats to social superiors. Hats symbolized the social hierarchy of Europe. Every man knew his place so long as he understood whom to doff to, and who should doff to him. And Quakers refused to accept or to confer titles. They called everyone "thee" or "thou," familiar terms used by superiors when addressing inferiors, especially servants.

The implications of Quaker beliefs appalled other Christians. The Inner Light seemed to obliterate predestination, original sin, maybe even the Trinity. Quakers had no sacraments, not even an organized clergy. They denounced Protestant ministers as "hireling priests." Quakers also held distinctive views about revelation. If God speaks directly to Friends, that Word must be as inspired as anything in the Bible. Quakers compiled books of their "sufferings," which they thought were the equal of the Acts of the Apostles in the New Testament, a claim that seemed blasphemous to others.

While allowing each member to follow the Light in some unique way, Quakers found ways to deal with discord. The heart of Quaker worship was the "weekly meeting" of the local congregation. There was no sermon or liturgy. People spoke whenever the Light inspired them. The few men and women who spoke often and with great effect became recognized as **public Friends**, the closest the Quakers came to having a clergy. Public Friends occupied special, elevated seats in some meetinghouses, and many went on missionary tours in Europe or America. The weekly meetings within a region sent representatives to a "monthly meeting," which resolved questions of policy and discipline. The monthly meetings sent delegates to the "yearly meeting" in London. At every level, decisions had to be unanimous. There is only one Inner Light, and it must convey the same message to every believer. This insistence on unanimity provided strong safeguards against schism.

2.13 Quaker Meeting House in Philadelphia, early 18th century Hooded women are seen seated in rows opposite men in a Quaker meeting house.

Q *In what ways does the image capture some of the central Quaker beliefs and practices?*

Q *Why might have those practices been repugnant to other denominations?*

2-8 Brotherly Love: The Quakers and America

2-8b Quaker Families

Quakers transformed the traditional family as well. Women enjoyed almost full equality, and some of them, such as Mary Dyer, became exceptional preachers, even martyrs. Women held their own formal meetings and made important decisions about discipline and betrothals. Quaker reforms also affected children, whom most Protestants saw as tiny sinners whose wills must be broken by severe discipline. Quakers, who did not worry about original sin, saw children as innocents in whom the Light would shine if only they could be protected from worldly corruption. In America, Quakers created affectionate families, built larger houses than non-Quakers with equivalent resources, and worked hard to acquire land for all of their children. Earlier than other Christians, they began to limit family size to give more love to the children they did have. Once the missionary impulse faded, they seldom associated with non-Quakers. To marry an outsider meant expulsion from the Society, a fate more likely to befall poor Friends than rich ones.

2-8c West New Jersey

In 1674, the New Jersey proprietors split their holding into two colonies. Sir George Carteret claimed what he now called East New Jersey, a province near New York City with half a dozen towns populated by Baptist, Quaker, Puritan, and Dutch Reformed settlers. Lord Berkeley claimed West New Jersey. Soon, Quakers bought all of West New Jersey and parts of East New Jersey, positioning themselves between Maryland and New York. West New Jersey Quakers launched an unprecedented political experiment—the most radical in America before the Revolution—by envisioning a religiously tolerant society of godly people, who would live in harmony without internal conflict or lawyers, keep the government close to the people, and make land easily available. But as

2.14 Mr. and Mrs. Thomas Mifflin, Oil Painting by John Singleton Copley (1773) Traditional family portraits emphasized the patriarch's superiority. Quakers stressed the equality of husbands and wives.

2.15 Penn's Treaty with the Indians, by Benjamin West This 1771 painting celebrates William Penn's efforts, nearly a century earlier, to establish peaceful relations with the Delaware Indians.

Q How does the painting idealize the relations between the Quakers and the Indians?

Q What Christian motives can you find in the painting?

non-Quaker immigration increased, the system broke down. Quaker rule collapsed, and the Crown took over the colony in 1702.

2-8d Pennsylvania

By then, Quaker attention had already shifted to the west bank of the Delaware River. There, William Penn launched a much larger, if rather more cautious, "holy experiment" in brotherly love. The son of a Commonwealth admiral, Penn grew up surrounded by privilege. He knew well both Charles II and the Duke of York, attended Oxford, went on the grand tour of Europe, and began to manage his father's Irish estates. Then something happened that embarrassed his family. "Mr. William Pen," reported a neighbor in December 1667, "is a Quaker again, or some very melancholy thing." Penn often traveled to the continent on behalf of the Society of Friends, winning converts and recruiting settlers in the Netherlands and Germany.

A gentleman and a Quaker, Penn was no ordinary colonizer. In 1681, using his contacts at court, he secured a royal charter for a proprietary colony, Pennsylvania. More thought went into planning Pennsylvania than any other colony. Twenty drafts survive of Penn's constitution for the province, which, like Carolina's first constitution, was inspired by the ideas of James Harrington. But as in Carolina, lofty ideas for a perfect government proved too complex for a new society of transatlantic migrants who were more concerned with mere survival in a new environment. Many of the first settlers had to live in caves and dugouts along river valleys and fend off aggravated Indians. Yet, Penn's ideas of representative government, religious liberty, and ready availability of land through a **quitrent** system of annual fees survived to shape Pennsylvania's future.

In England, persecution had kept Quaker antiauthoritarianism in check. In the colony, these attitudes soon became public. Penn envisioned that Pennsylvania would rely on tightly regulated trade with England, but the colony's transatlantic commerce was soon eclipsed by a trade with the Caribbean colonies, which was dominated by Quakers from Barbados, Jamaica, New York, and Boston. These wealthy men became the opposition faction in the colony, demanding more land and resisting Penn's quitrents. The legislature became divided. Pennsylvania became a haven for all religions, but its politics remained turbulent into the 1720s.

Despite these controversies, Pennsylvania quickly became an economic success, well established in the Caribbean trade as an exporter of wheat and flour. Philadelphia along the Delaware quickly grew into a major Atlantic port city. Quaker families thrived, and the colony's policy of religious liberty attracted thousands of outsiders. Quakers from other English colonies flocked in, as too did German pacifists, who shared the ideals of the Society of Friends. But among the immigrants were also Anglicans and Presbyterians who warned that the Quakers were unfit to rule—anywhere.

Pennsylvania owed its success to its Atlantic and Caribbean connections that provided a steady inflow of goods and people. But Pennsylvania also owed its success to its creative and, among English colonies, unique Indian policy. Unlike any other colonists, the Quakers entered America unarmed. Egalitarian-minded pacifists, they wanted to treat Native Americans fairly and integrate them into their "peaceful kingdom." The Delawares, an ethnically diverse native society of farmers and hunters, controlled the lands around the Delaware River. Penn recognized the Delawares' sovereignty over their territory and negotiated treaties with payments for land transactions. Although there were clashes between Indians and settlers over land, for a few decades a mutual accommodation was possible on Pennsylvania's borderlands. Native refugees from near and distant war zones gravitated to the region. With its diverse colonial and native population, the mid-Atlantic had become North America's most heterogeneous region.

Conclusion

In the 16th century, France, the Netherlands, and England all challenged Spanish power in Europe and across the ocean. After 1600, all three founded their own colonies in North America and the Caribbean. New France became a land of missionaries and traders and fashioned close ties of cooperation with most nearby Indians. New Netherland also was founded to participate in the fur trade. Both colonies slowly acquired an agricultural base.

The English, by contrast, desired the land itself. They founded colonies of settlement and did not seek to incorporate Indians into their political, legal, and social communities. English colonialism posed a direct challenge to indigenous power and sovereignty across the eastern seaboard, except in the Delaware Valley, where Quakers maintained relative peace. England's southern mainland and Caribbean colonies produced staple crops for sale in Europe, first with the labor of indentured servants and then with enslaved Africans. The Puritan and Quaker colonies became smaller versions of England's mixed economy, with an emphasis on family farms. Maintaining the fervor of the founders was a problem for both. After conquering New Netherland, England controlled the Atlantic coastline from Maine to South Carolina.

Yet, in the late 17th century, the European presence and power in North America were still limited. Three colonial empires—Spain, France, and England—possessed viable outposts on the continent, but those outposts were confined to the margins. All three empires claimed vast portions of the continent in legal documents and on maps, but on the ground Native Americans controlled most of its shores and all of its vast interior. New France along the St. Lawrence Valley and the Spanish settlements in Florida and along the Rio Grande Valley were small enclaves bounded by powerful independent native societies. The more populous English colonies were expanding on the Atlantic lowlands and up its major river valleys, but this expansion unfolded without a centralized imperial plan, and it fragmented England's colonial realm as much as it extended it. Rivalries and disputes among England's North American colonies were rife throughout the 17th century. Moreover, the western frontiers of the English colonies brushed against native societies that were determined to protect their lands and lifestyles. Overseas colonialism had become entrenched in North America, but the continent's future remained undetermined. No one people yet had a decisive advantage.

CHAPTER REVIEW

Review

1. How did Europe's political and religious landscape change in the 16th century?
2. What were the main similarities and differences between French and Spanish colonial projects in North America?
3. What key motivations drove Dutch colonialism in North America?
4. What kinds of ambitions and historical developments committed England to overseas colonization?
5. Why did the English, crossing the Atlantic at roughly the same time, create such radically different societies in the Chesapeake, the West Indies, and New England?
6. How did religious concerns shape the colonization of New England?
7. In what ways did the Restoration colonies differ from those founded earlier in the Chesapeake and New England?
8. How did Pennsylvania's policy toward the Native Americans differ from the Indian policies of New England and the Chesapeake colonies? What explains those differences?

Critical Thinking

1. Does the splintering of New England into multiple colonies, each with a somewhat different vision of the Puritan mission, indicate that religious uniformity could be maintained only under the strong government of a single state?
2. In the 17th century, Quakers came closer than any other settler group to affirming equality as a positive value. Does their experience in England and America suggest how difficult it might be to persuade an entire society to embrace that value?

Identifications

Review your understanding of the following key terms, people, and events for this chapter (terms in bold in text are included in the Glossary).

predestination, p. 38
Huguenots, p. 38
Pedro Menéndez de Avilés, p. 38
coureurs de bois, p. 39
mourning wars, p. 40
intendant, p. 41
patroonship, p. 44
Yankees, p. 44
Non-Separatists, p. 45
Separatists, p. 45
privateer, p. 45
joint-stock company, p. 46
Tsenacommacah, p. 47
fall line, p. 47
House of Burgesses, p. 47
headright, p. 47
proprietary colonies, p. 49
sachem, p. 54
Anne Hutchinson, p. 56
public Friends, p. 63
quitrent, p. 65

Suggested Readings

W. J. Eccles, *The French in North America, 1500–1783*, rev. ed. (1998) is a concise and authoritative survey. **Bruce Trigger**, *The Children of Aataentsic: A History of the Huron People to 1660* (1976), and **Daniel Richter**, *The Ordeal of the Longhouse: The Peoples of the Iroquois League in the Era of European Colonization* (1992) detail the fates of Huron and Iroquois Confederacies. For the Dutch republic and overseas empire, see **C. R. Boxer**, *The Dutch Seaborne Empire, 1600–1800* (1965) and **Jonathan I. Israel**, *The Dutch Republic: Its Rise, Greatness, and Fall, 1477–1806* (1995). **Karen O. Kupperman**, *Indians and English: Facing Off in Early America* (2000) is an effort to keep Indians and the settlers of early Virginia and New England within a common focus. **J. H. Elliott**, *Empires of the Atlantic World: Britain and Spain in America, 1492–1830* (2006) offers a penetrating comparison of the two empires. **Colin G. Calloway**, *New Worlds for All: Indians, Europeans, and the Remaking of Early America* (1997), and **Daniel K. Richter**, *Facing East from Indian Country: A Native History of Early America* (2001) reexamine early America from a native perspective.

Edmund S. Morgan's *American Slavery, American Freedom: The Ordeal of Colonial Virginia* (1975) is a classic study of class struggle and the rise of chattel slavery in Virginia. **Kathleen M. Brown's** *Good Wives, Nasty Wenches, and Anxious Patriarchs: Gender, Race, and Power in Colonial Virginia* (1996) is essential for understanding gender and race relations in colonial Virginia. **David Hall**, *Days of Wonder, Days of Judgment: Popular Religious Belief in Early New England* (1989) offers a fascinating view into the beliefs and mindset of 17th-century New England colonists. **Daniel Vickers**, *Farmers and Fishermen: Two Centuries of Work in Essex County, Massachusetts, 1630–1850* (1994) is an outstanding introduction to the New England economy. For the West Indies, **Richard S. Dunn**, *Sugar and Slaves: The Rise of the Planter Class in the English West Indies, 1624–1713* (1972) remains indispensable. For the Restoration colonies, see especially **Peter H. Wood**, *Black Majority: Negroes in Colonial South Carolina from 1670 through the Stono Rebellion* (1974); and **Alan Gallay**, *The Indian Slave Trade: The Rise of the English Empire in the American South, 1670–1717* (2002). **Evan Haefeli's** *New Netherland and the Dutch Origins of American Religious Liberty* (2012) traces Dutch influences in American religious and cultural life.

 MINDTAP is a fully online personalized learning experience built upon Cengage Learning content. MindTap® combines student learning tools—readings, multimedia, activities, and assessments—into a singular Learning Path that guides students through the course and helps students develop the critical thinking, analysis, and communication skills that are essential to academic and professional success.

3 Empires, Indians, and the Struggle for Power in North America, 1670–1720

3-1 Indians, Settlers, Upheaval: The Cataclysmic 1670s and 1680s

Learning Objective: Describe the factors that led to mounting tensions and the eruption of violent conflicts between Indians and Europeans in different parts of North America in the 1670s and 1680s.

The Pueblo Revolt
Metacom's War
Virginia's Indian War
Bacon's Rebellion
New France Besieged

3-2 Converging Empires: Spain and France in North America

Learning Objective: Trace how negotiation, conciliation, and alliance-making shaped France's and Spain's Indian policies.

Spanish New Mexico
French and Indians on the Middle Ground
French Canada in Transition
French Illinois, French Louisiana, and Spanish Texas

3-3 The Rise of England's Atlantic Empire

Learning Objective: Define the Glorious Revolution and describe how it changed England's North American colonies.

The Foundations of Empire: Mercantilism and the Navigation Acts
Crisis in England and the Expansion of Royal Authority
The Dominion of New England
The Glorious Revolution in England and America
The Salem Witch Trials
The New Imperial Order

3-4 An Empire of Settlement: The Growth of British America

Learning Objective: Identify the ways in which the colonial household was an effective engine of British expansion. Examine whether the British colonial household gave an advantage over Britain's imperial rivals in North America. Give examples of the limits that Indians imposed on the European colonies in the 18th century.

The Atlantic Prism and the Spectrum of Settlement
The Engine of British Expansion: The Colonial Household
The Voluntaristic Ethic, Public Life, and War
Spanish and French Counterpoints
Queen Anne's War and the Yamasee War
The Colonial Rim and the Indigenous Interior

3.1 *The Kingfisher Engaging the Barbary Pirates on 22 May, 1681,* **by Willem van de Velde the Younger** By the end of the 17th century, England had become the greatest naval power in the world, a position that it would maintain until overtaken by the United States in the Second World War.

THE HALF-CENTURY BETWEEN 1670 AND 1720 was a

period of intensifying imperial rivalry and accelerating colonization in North America. The small and scattered European colonies transformed into imperial realms with expanding spheres of influence, and their growing ambitions provoked violent native resistance and bitter imperial wars that destabilized large parts of the continent. The turmoil triggered internal reforms that only accelerated imperial expansion. By the 1720s, Spain, France, and Britain had entrenched themselves in North America, each possessing its distinctive vision for empire.

Everyday life in North America also changed dramatically. As the European presence magnified, more and more native societies had to either relocate or learn to live with the newcomers. Relatively few in number, the French and Spaniards built societies that offered multiple places for Native Americans and Africans. In English America, most changes emanated from the mother country, which emerged in the 18th century as the dominant Atlantic power, survived a revolution that disposed a king, and adopted a unique constitution that rested on parliamentary supremacy and responsible government under the Crown. By 1700, England and the colonies had begun to converge around the newly defined principles of English constitutionalism. The colonies formed a spectrum of settlement with contrasting economies, social relationships, and institutions, which daunted the English government. Yet by 1700, England had created a system of regulation that respected colonial liberties while asserting imperial power. ■

3-1 Indians, Settlers, Upheaval: The Cataclysmic 1670s and 1680s

Q *Why did violence erupt between Indians and Europeans in different parts of North America in roughly the same period?*

In 1670, after three generations of sustained colonization, Europeans possessed scattered settlements on North America's eastern seaboard and along a few of its major rivers. No sharp boundaries separated Indian lands from colonial settlements. Boston, the largest city north of Mexico, was only 15 miles from an Indian village. The English settlements on the James, Susquehannock, Hudson, and Connecticut rivers and the Spanish settlements along the upper Rio Grande Valley amounted to little more than narrow ribbons in Indian worlds. New France along the St. Lawrence Valley brushed against the powerful and expanding Iroquois confederacy. In the event of war, nearly every European settlement was open to attack.

With time, the commercial possibilities of North America had become much clearer. The French mastered the fur trade because they controlled the St. Lawrence system, the critical all-water route from the Atlantic to the interior. South Carolinians went around the southern extreme of the Appalachians. The Spaniards sought to expand their commercial reach to the interior from bases in New Mexico and Florida. All of them needed Indian trading partners.

In some ways, America had become as much a new world for Indians as it had for colonists. European cloth, muskets, hatchets, knives, and pots appealed to Indians and spread far into the interior, and many Indians who used them gradually abandoned traditional skills and became increasingly dependent on European goods. They became consumers whose economies and societies depended on imported commodities. Drunkenness, a by-product of European trade, became a major, if intermittent, social problem. Aggressive proselytism disrupted existing social hierarchies in Indian societies and created deep internal conflicts. Diseases spread from European outposts into Indian lands, devastating many coastal societies. The increasing death toll magnified the depleted Indians' need for captives, greatly increasing the intensity of wars among native societies. In the 1670s and 1680s, almost simultaneously in different parts of the continent, the mounting tensions erupted into violent revolts and war.

CHRONOLOGY

1673	Dutch retake New York for 15 months
1675	Lords of Trade established • Metacom's War breaks out in New England
1676	Bacon's Rebellion begins in Virginia
1680	Pueblo Revolt in New Mexico
1683	New France invades Iroquoia
1684	Massachusetts charter revoked
1685	Louis XIV revokes Edict of Nantes
1686	Dominion of New England established
1688–1689	Glorious Revolution in England
1689	Anglo-French wars begin • Glorious Revolution spreads to Massachusetts, New York, and Maryland
1691	Leisler executed in New York
1692	Nineteen people hanged for witchcraft in Salem • Spaniards retake New Mexico
1696	Parliament passes comprehensive Navigation Act • Board of Trade replaces Lords of Trade
1699	French establish Louisiana • Woolens Act passed
1701	Iroquois make peace with New France
1702–1704	Carolina slavers destroy Florida missions
1707	Anglo-Scottish union creates kingdom of Great Britain
1713–1714	Britain and France make peace • George I ascends British throne
1715	Yamasee War devastates South Carolina
1716–1720	Spain establishes missions and military forts in Texas
1722	New Orleans becomes the capital of Louisiana

3-1a The Pueblo Revolt

In the late 17th century, the Spanish missions of North America entered a period of crisis. Franciscan zeal began to slacken, and fewer priests took the trouble to master Indian languages, insisting instead that the Indians learn Spanish. For all of their good intentions, the missionaries regarded Indians as children and savage inferiors and often whipped or shackled them for minor infractions. Disease also took its toll. Indian population loss led to pressing labor demands by missionaries and *encomenderos*, holders of tributary native labor. Despite strong prohibitions, settlers enslaved Indians in Florida and New Mexico.

The greatest challenge to the Spanish arose in New Mexico, where the Pueblo population had fallen from 80,000 in 1598 to 17,000 in 1679. A prolonged drought, together with Apache and Navajo attacks, prompted many Pueblos to abandon Christianity and resume their old forms of worship. The Spanish responded by whipping 47 medicine men for sorcery and by hanging three of them in 1675. A fourth committed suicide. Popé, a San Juan Pueblo medicine man, was one of those whipped for his beliefs. He moved north to Taos Pueblo, where he organized the most successful Indian revolt in American history. In 1680, in a carefully timed uprising, the Pueblos killed 200 of the 1,000 Spaniards in New Mexico and destroyed or raided every Spanish building in the province. They desecrated every church and killed 21 of New Mexico's 40 priests (see Map. 3.1). "Now," they declared, "the God of the Spaniards, who was their father, is dead," but the Pueblos' own god, whom they obeyed, "[had] never died." Spanish survivors fled from Santa Fe down the Rio Grande to El Paso.

Popé lost his influence when traditional Pueblo rites failed to end the drought or stop the attacks of hostile Indians. Many also struggled with Popé's extreme vision for a Spanish-free Pueblo world, which involved annulling Franciscan-sanctioned marriages and rejecting the new crops the Spanish had introduced. When the Spanish returned in 1692, the Pueblos were badly divided. Most villages yielded without much resistance, and Spain accepted their submission, but Santa Fe held out until December 1693. When it fell, the Spanish executed 70 men and gave 400 women and children to the returning settlers as their slaves. The Spanish failed to bring the Hopi Indians in the west under their rule, but New Mexico's core area along the upper Rio Grande Valley they once again controlled.

However, the Spaniards soon realized that restoring the old colonial order in New Mexico would be difficult. During their 12-year absence, the region had changed profoundly. Pueblo rebels had confiscated the horse herds of the fleeing Spaniards, and most of the animals had spread among the neighboring native societies through trading and raiding. In the Great Plains, the Apaches developed a dynamic culture of horseback hunting and warfare and expanded their settlements at the expense of other native groups. In the Great Basin north of New Mexico, the Ute Indians staged mounted raids into Pueblo villages, taking horses and captives with their new allies, the Comanches, recent

▲ **MAP 3.1 Pueblo Rebellion, 1680**

Q *How does the map help in understanding why the Pueblo Indians succeeded in driving the Spanish colonists out of their homelands in 1680?*

Q *What clues does the map offer to explain the eventual failure of the Pueblo Revolt?*

What They Said

Why Did the Pueblo Indians Revolt against the Spaniards in 1680?

The Pueblo Revolt of 1680 was the most successful indigenous rebellion against European colonialism in North America, and it shocked the Spanish imperial administration to the core. Desperate to understand what had happened, the Spaniards interrogated numerous captured Pueblo Indians, asking them to divulge what they knew about the causes, goals, and organization of the revolt.

▶ Declaration of Josephe, Spanish-speaking Indian

…he said that he … has heard it generally stated that while they were besieging the villa the rebellious traitors burned the church and shouted in loud voices, "Now the God of the Spaniards, who was their father, is dead, and Santa Maria, who was their mother, and the saints, who were pieces of rotten wood," saying that only their god lived… . The captains and chiefs ordered that the names of Jesus and of Mary should nowhere be uttered, and that they should discard their baptismal names, and abandon the wives whom God had given them in matrimony, and take the ones that they pleased. He saw that as soon as the remaining Spaniards had left, they ordered all the estufas erected, which are their houses of idolatry, and danced throughout the kingdom the dance of the cazina, making many masks for it in the image of the devil.

▶ Declaration of Lucas, Píro Indian

…he said that of everything contained in the question he knows only that the temples and images, crosses and rosaries were burned generally by all the Indians of the districts, and he also heard it said that each one was to live according to such law as he wished, forsaking that of the Spaniards, which was not good, and that these commands came from the jurisdictions above here; he does not know who gave them nor does he understand the languages, or any other except his own, which is Pira.

▶ Declaration of Pedro Naranjo of the Queres Nation

…in the past years, at the summons of an Indian named Popé who is said to have communication with the devil, it happened that in an estufa of the pueblo of Los Taos there appeared to the said Popé three figures of Indians who never came out of the estufa. They gave the said Popé to understand that they were going underground to the lake of Copala. He saw these figures emit fire from all the extremities of their bodies, and that one of them was called Caudi, another Tilini, and the other Tleume; and these three beings spoke to the said Popé, who was in hiding from the secretary, Francisco Xavier, who wished to punish him as a sorcerer… .

…he stated that the said Indian, Popé, came down in person and with him El Saca and El Chato from the pueblo of Los Taos … and he ordered in all the pueblos through which he passed that they instantly break up and burn the images of the holy Christ, the Virgin Mary and the other saints, the crosses, and everything pertaining to Christianity… . They did this, and also many other things which he does not recall, given to understand that this mandate had come from the Caydi [Caudi] and the other two who emitted fire from their extremities in the said estufa of Taos, and that they thereby returned to the state of their antiquity, as when they came from the lake of Copala; that this was the better life and the one they desired, because the God of the Spaniards was worth nothing and theirs was very strong, the Spaniard's God being rotten wood. These things were observed and obeyed by all except some who, moved by the zeal of Christians, opposed it, and such persons the said Popé caused to be killed immediately. He saw to it that they at once erected and rebuilt their houses of idolatry which they call estufas, and made very ugly masks in imitation of the devil in order to dance the dance of the cacina; and he said likewise that the devil had given them to understand that living thus in accordance with the law of their ancestors, they would harvest a great deal of maize, many beans, a great abundance of cotton, calabashes, and very large watermelons and cantaloupes; and that they could erect their houses and enjoy abundant health and leisure… . Following what has already been stated, in order to terrorize them further and cause them to observe the diabolical commands, there came to them a pronouncement from the three demons already described, and from El Popé, to the effect that he who might still keep in his heart a regard for the priests, the governor, and the Spaniards would be known from his unclean face and clothes, and would be punished. And he stated that the said four persons stopped at nothing to have their commands obeyed.

Q *What do the three declarations excerpted above reveal about Pueblo motives? Could such declarations allow the Spaniards to construct a coherent and conclusive picture of the rebellion and its causes? What kind of difficulties do these documents pose to a historian who seeks to understand the revolt from an indigenous perspective?*

Sources: (top) "Declaration of Josephe, Spanish-speaking Indian," in Charles W. Hackett, ed. *Revolt of the Pueblo Indians of New Mexico and Otermin's Attempted Reconquest, 1680–1682* (Albuquerque: University of New Mexico Press, 1942), 2: 238–240. (middle) "Declaration of Lucas, Piro Indian," in Charles W. Hackett, ed. *Revolt of the Pueblo Indians of New Mexico and Otermin's Attempted Reconquest, 1680–1682* (Albuquerque: University of New Mexico Press, 1942), 2: 243–274. (bottom) "Declaration of Pedro Naranjo of the Queres Nation," in Charles W. Hackett, ed. *Revolt of the Pueblo Indians of New Mexico and Otermin's Attempted Reconquest, 1680–1682* (Albuquerque: University of New Mexico Press, 1942), 2: 245–248.

migrants from the north. Powerful equestrian Indians were converging around New Mexico, and the future of the Spanish colonial venture seemed far from certain.

3-1b Metacom's War

In 1675, five years before the Pueblo Revolt began, violence erupted between Indians and English settlers in New England. As in New Mexico, the conflict had been brewing for years. Indians and colonists clashed over borders and proper ways of using the land. The colonists' growing settlements shrank the Indians' land base, and their free-running hogs and cows wrecked the Indians' cornfields. The settlers wanted clear pastures and fenced farms, while Indians needed extensive forests for hunting. English efforts to convert Indians and bring them into praying towns only increased the tension. Many New England families had also become heavily involved in Indian slave trade, sending captured Native Americans—men, women, and children—to sugar plantations in the Caribbean on the ships that coursed through Boston and other New England ports.

The pressure of English colonialism was particularly hard on the Wampanoags, whose lands around the Narragansett Bay were invaded by colonists from Plymouth, Rhode Island, and Massachusetts. Led by Metacom (the English called him King Philip), the Wampanoags began to prepare for war. Metacom was a sachem and the son of Massasoit, who had maintained an alliance with the Pilgrims from the 1620s through the 1650s. English missionaries tried repeatedly to convert the influential sachem, but Metacom became convinced that accommodation with the colonists would weaken and destroy his people. With only 1,000 Wampanoags left and half of them living in praying towns, Metacom denounced the English. "If I be a praying sachem," he declared, "I shall be a poor and weak one, and easily be trod upon by others."

War broke out after Plymouth executed three Wampanoags for murdering John Sassamon, a Harvard-educated Indian preacher who may have been spying on Metacom. The fighting began in the frontier town of Swansea in June 1675 after settlers killed an Indian they found looting an abandoned house. When the Indians demanded satisfaction, the settlers laughed in their faces. The Indians took revenge, and the violence escalated into war (see Map 3.2).

The settlers, recalling their easy triumph over the Pequots a generation earlier (see Chapter 2), were confident of victory. But since then, the Indians had acquired flintlock muskets. They had built forges to make musket balls and repair their weapons. They had become marksmen with the smoothbore musket by firing several smaller bullets, instead of a single shot, with each charge. Settlers, who seldom hunted, were often armed with older firelocks and were terrible shots. In the tradition of European armies, they discharged volleys without aiming. To the shock of the colonists, Metacom won several engagements against Plymouth militia, usually by ambushing the noisy intruders. He then moved northwest to the upper Connecticut Valley, where local Indians, after being ordered to disarm, joined him instead. Together they burned five towns in three months.

Massachusetts and Connecticut joined the fray. As winter approached, rather than attack Metacom's Wampanoags, they went after the Narragansetts, who had welcomed some Wampanoag refugees while trying to remain neutral. Many prominent settlers dreamed of acquiring their fertile lands. In the Great Swamp Fight of December 1675, a Puritan army, with the aid of Indian guides, attacked an unfinished Narragansett fort during a blizzard and massacred hundreds of Indians, most of them women and children, but not before Indian snipers picked off a high percentage of the officers. The surviving warriors joined Metacom's confederacy and showed that they too could use terror. They torched more towns. During the war, about 2,000 settlers were killed and two dozen towns, more than half of New England's colonial settlements, were destroyed. The colonists abandoned the interior and retreated to the coast.

Terrified settlers demanded the annihilation of all nearby Indians, even Christian converts. The Massachusetts government, shocked to realize that it could not win the war without Indian allies, did what it could to protect the **praying Indians**. The magistrates evacuated them to a bleak island in Boston Harbor and broke up an attempt to massacre them. Despite a miserable winter, many agreed to fight Metacom in the spring campaign. The struggle against the colonists turned into a civil war among the Indians.

The war nearly tore New England apart. Increase Mather, a prominent Boston minister, saw the conflict as God's judgment on a sinful people and warned that no victory would come until New England repented and reformed. Many settlers agreed, interpreting the war and its unprecedented cruelty as a sign of moral corruption, the New Englanders' degeneration from civilization into savagery. By slaughtering Indians for their savage cruelty, the colonists feared that they had become savages themselves. Quakers saw the war as divine punishment for their persecution by the Puritans. The settlers finally turned the tide in 1676. Governor Andros of New York persuaded the powerful Mohawks to attack Metacom's winter camp and disperse his people, who by then were short of gunpowder. The New Englanders, working closely with Mohegan and Christian Indian allies, adopted Indian tactics to attack Metacom's war parties and killed hundreds of Indians, including Metacom. A total of 5,000 Indians died, and hundreds of survivors were sold into slavery in the West Indies. Some of those enslaved had not been party to the conflict and had requested asylum from it. The settlers put Metacom's severed head on display in Plymouth to mark the end of a war that, in proportion to population, has proved the most fatal in American history.

▲ **MAP 3.2 New England in Metacom's War, 1675–1676** This map locates Indian villages and New England towns, and it indicates which towns were destroyed, damaged, or unscathed during the war.

Q What does the map reveal about the causes of Metacom's War?

Q What does the map reveal about New England's society and economy?

3-1c Virginia's Indian War

In Virginia, Governor Sir William Berkeley, who had defeated Opechancanough 30 years earlier, rejoiced in the New Englanders' woes. Metacom's War was the least they deserved for the way the Puritans had dismantled England and executed Charles I during the civil wars. Then Virginia began to have its own troubles.

In 1675, the Doegs, Algonquian-speaking people who had fled Virginia to seek safety in the Potomac Valley, demanded payment of an old debt from a Virginia planter. When he refused, they ran off some of his livestock. After his overseer killed one of the Doegs, the others fled but later returned to ambush and kill the man. The county militia mustered and followed the Doegs across the Potomac into Maryland. At a fork in the trail, the militia split into two parties. Each party found a group of Indians in a shack a few hundred yards up the path it was following. Both parties fired at point-blank range, killing 11 at one cabin and 14 at the other. One of the bands was indeed Doeg, but the other was not: "Susquehannock friends," blurted one Indian as he fled.

The Susquehannocks were a strong Iroquoian-speaking people with firearms. They had moved south to escape Iroquois attacks, and Maryland had invited them to occupy lands north of the Potomac, hoping to build a buffer of loyal Indians against the Five Nations. Berkeley, eager to avoid war, sent John Washington (ancestor of George) with Virginia militia to investigate the killings and, if possible, to set things right. But Washington preferred vengeance. His Virginia militia joined with a Maryland force, and together they besieged a formidable Susquehannock fort on the north bank of the Potomac, too strong to take without artillery. When the Indians sent out five or six sachems to negotiate, the militia murdered them and then laid siege to the fort for six weeks. The Indians, short of provisions, finally broke out one night with all of their people, killing several militiamen. After hurling taunts of defiance

THE KING PHILIP WAR — A RAID ON THE SETTLERS.

3.2 Engraving from *The Providence Plantations for 250 Years*, 1886 A depiction of a Native American raid on the settlers in New England during King Philip's War.

Q *Engravings like this became wildly popular in New England after the Metacom's War. Why?*

and promises of vengeance, they disappeared into the forest. In January 1676 they killed 36 Virginians. The colonists began to panic.

Berkeley favored a defensive strategy against the Indians; most settlers wanted to attack. In March 1676, the governor summoned a special session of the Virginia legislature to approve the creation of a string of forts above the fall line of the major rivers, with companies of "rangers" to patrol the stretches between them. Berkeley also hoped to maintain a distinction between the clearly hostile Susquehannocks and other Indians who might still be neutral or friendly. Frontier settlers, mostly former servants frustrated by low tobacco prices and unable to acquire tidewater lands because speculators had bought them up, demanded war against all Indians. Finally, to avoid further provocation, Berkeley restricted the fur trade to a few close associates. To the men excluded from that circle, his actions looked like favoritism. To settlers in frontier counties, whose access to new lands was blocked by Indians and who now had to pay higher taxes, Berkeley's strategy seemed intolerable.

Colonists denounced the building of any more forts and demanded an offensive campaign waged by unpaid volunteers, who would take their rewards by plundering and enslaving Indians. In April, the frontiersmen found a reckless leader in Nathaniel Bacon, a young newcomer to the colony with a scandalous past and £1,800 to invest. Using his political connections (he was the governor's cousin by marriage), he managed an appointment to the council soon after his arrival in the colony in 1674. Bacon, the owner of a trading post in Henrico County at the falls of the James River (now Richmond), was one of those excluded from the Indian trade under Berkeley's new rules.

3-1d *Bacon's Rebellion*

Against Berkeley's orders, Bacon led his men south in search of the elusive Susquehannocks. After several days, the weary force reached a village of friendly Occaneechees, who offered them shelter, announced that they knew where to find a Susquehannock camp, and volunteered to attack it. They surprised and defeated the Susquehannocks and returned with their captives to celebrate the victory with Bacon. But after the Occaneechees fell asleep, Bacon's men massacred them, seized their furs and prisoners, and then boasted of their prowess as Indian killers.

By then Berkeley had outlawed Bacon, dissolved the legislature, and called the first general election since 1661. The old assembly had recently imposed a property requirement for voting, but Berkeley suspended it and asked the burgesses to bring their grievances to the June assembly for redress. "How miserable that man is," he complained, "that Governes a People where six parts of seaven at least are Poore Endebted Discontented and Armed."

To show their resentment against elite planters, voters elected a fair number of burgesses who were not justices of the peace; since midcentury, justices of the peace had dominated the House of Burgesses and other political offices (see Chapter 2). The voters of Henrico elected Bacon to the assembly. Berkeley had Bacon arrested when he reached Jamestown, and made Bacon kneel before him and the council and apologize for his disobedience. Berkeley pardoned Bacon and restored him to his seat on the council. By then, even Governor Berkeley had abandoned the effort to distinguish between hostile and friendly Indians, but he still favored a defensive war. While the burgesses were passing laws to reform the county courts, the vestries, and the tax system, Bacon slipped away to Henrico, summoned his followers again, and marched on Jamestown. At gunpoint, he forced Berkeley to commission him as general of volunteers and compelled the legislature to authorize another expedition against the Indians.

Berkeley retreated downriver to Gloucester County and mustered its militia, but they refused to follow him against Bacon. They would fight only Indians. Mortified, Berkeley fled to the eastern shore, the only part of the colony that was safe from Indian attack and thus still loyal to him. Bacon hastened to Jamestown, summoned a meeting of planters at the governor's Green Spring mansion, made them swear an oath of loyalty to him, and ordered the confiscation of the estates of Berkeley's major supporters, who were men in the process of becoming great planters. Meanwhile, Berkeley raised his own force on the eastern shore by promising the men an exemption from taxes for 21 years and the right to plunder Bacon's supporters.

Beyond New England, few Indians killed other Indians in 1676. Virginia settlers fought one another during this civil

3.3 Crude Housing for Settlers in North America When the first settlers came to North America, their living quarters were anything but luxurious. The crude housing shown in this modern reconstruction of Jamestown remained typical of Virginia and Maryland throughout the 17th century.

Q *Why did the first settlers not build larger and more comfortable homes for themselves?*

war, and royal government collapsed under the strain. During that summer, hundreds of settlers tried to make their fortunes by plundering Indians, other colonists, or both. Fueled by simmering class resentments, Bacon's Rebellion was the largest colonial upheaval before 1775 (see Map 3.3).

Bacon never did kill a hostile Indian. While he was slaughtering and enslaving the unresisting Pamunkeys along the frontier, Berkeley assembled a small fleet and retook Jamestown in August. Bacon rushed east and laid siege to Jamestown, exhibiting his Indian captives along the way as a demonstration of his ability to protect the colonists against the natives. He captured the wives of prominent Berkeley supporters and forced them to stand in the line of fire as he dug his trenches closer to the capital. After suffering only a few casualties, the governor's men grew discouraged and in early September the whole force returned to the eastern shore. Bacon burned Jamestown to the ground. He also boasted of his ability to hold off an English army, unite Virginia with Maryland, and win Dutch support for setting up an independent Chesapeake republic.

Instead, Bacon died of dysentery in October, and Berkeley soon regained control of Virginia. Using the ships of the London tobacco fleet, he overpowered the plantations that Bacon had fortified. Then, in January 1677, a force of 1,000 redcoats arrived, too late to help but in time to strain the colony's depleted resources. Ignoring royal orders to show clemency, Berkeley hanged 23 of the rebels. A new assembly repudiated the reforms of 1676, and in many counties the governor's men used their control of the courts to continue plundering the Baconians through confiscations and fines.

The rebellion had brought a festering class conflict to the surface, awakening Virginians to the need of social reform. In its aftermath many of the emerging great planters deliberately chose to replace their indentured servants with enslaved Africans whom they could dominate without legal restraint. Virginia's whites became increasingly fixated on racial difference. New legislation outlawed marriages between blacks and whites, forbade planters from freeing slaves unless they paid for their transportation beyond the colony, and prohibited free blacks from voting, bearing arms, or employing white servants. Skin color became the primary marker of identity, and dark skin became associated with slavery. As the colony gradually developed its system of racial slavery, class tensions among its white settlers diminished. Finding a bond in their shared sense of racial superiority, the commoners and the elite disregarded the vast distinctions of wealth and power among themselves and united in an alliance based on racial solidarity and white supremacy.

3-1e New France Besieged

Like Spain and England, France faced a serious crisis in the late 17th century. New France had established peace with the powerful **Iroquois League** in the 1660s, which had given the colony a much-needed respite from war. The peace allowed the fur trade, New France's economic engine, to flourish, but it collapsed in the early 1680s. Epidemics had devastated the Iroquois, reigniting their mourning wars against neighboring Indians, many of whom were allied with the French (see Chapter 2). In the 1670s, the Iroquois had also established an alliance, the **Covenant Chain of Peace**, with New York, which pulled them away from the French orbit. New York's autocratic governor, Edmond Andros, urged the Iroquois to push the French out of the Great Lakes. Armed by New York, the Iroquois attacked French traders, and soon open warfare raged across the Iroquois-French borderlands. Both sides suffered enormous losses. The Five Nations raided St. Lawrence settlements, attacked Montreal, and forced the French to abandon all their forts in the western Great Lakes. The French and their Indian allies retaliated by burning Iroquois villages and their food caches. They opened

▲ **MAP 3.3 Bacon's Rebellion in Virginia, 1676** Settlement had just reached the fall line by the 1670s. The map also shows Bacon's two military campaigns, against the Occaneechees and the Pamunkeys.

Q *What clues does the map offer to explain the causes of Bacon's Rebellion?*

Q *What factors led to the failure of Bacon's Rebellion?*

3.4 Henry Latrobe's Sketch of Green Spring, the Home of Governor Sir William Berkeley, at the Time of Bacon's Rebellion Green Spring was one of the first great houses built in Virginia. Latrobe made this drawing in the 1790s.

3-1 Indians, Settlers, Upheaval: The Cataclysmic 1670s and 1680s

Iroquois graves to steal burial items, depriving Iroquois lands of their spiritual power. The Iroquois lost one-fourth of their population of 8,000.

While fighting the English-allied Iroquois in the south and the west, the French faced another threat from the north. In 1670, the English Crown chartered the Hudson's Bay Company, which soon established trading posts on James Bay, challenging France's monopoly on the Canadian fur trade. The French launched attacks on the English posts, and New France became entangled in warfare on multiple fronts. Unlike in New England and Virginia where the violence soon exhausted itself, in New France the crisis persisted.

3-2 Converging Empires: Spain and France in North America

Q *How did negotiation, conciliation, and alliance-making shape France's and Spain's Indian policies?*

The wars and crises of the 1670s and 1680s shocked the Spanish, French, and English colonists. Settlers and colonial administrators responded to the upheavals with systematic violence, seeking to punish and vanquish the enemies who threatened their existence. Bloodshed washed over Virginia, New England, New Mexico, and New France. But the chaos also triggered critical self-reflection and reforms. In the late 17th century, Spain, France, and England implemented new policies and practices that secured their battered realms and reinvigorated their imperial projects. By the early 18th century, all three were expanding again, each claiming an ever-greater portion of the continent and its resources.

Spanish, French, and English colonists shared the desire to expand their holdings, but they employed increasingly divergent strategies to achieve their goals. The English maintained alliances with powerful native confederacies like the Iroquois, but, growing rapidly in number, began to rely increasingly on raw force in their dealings with Indians. Lacking England's demographic power, the Spaniards and French attempted to expand their spheres *through* Indians, by keeping as many native societies as possible in their orbit. Both tried coercing and dictating to Indians, but soon realized that diplomacy and mediation brought more enduring results. While England's North American realm was turning into a settler empire—self-sufficient, land-hungry, and intolerant of native presence—Spain and France built negotiated empires that offered distinctive places for native peoples.

3-2a Spanish New Mexico

By the mid-1690s, Spain had reestablished colonial rule in New Mexico. The Pueblo Revolt had been suppressed, the Franciscans were rebuilding destroyed missions, and soldiers reasserted Spanish control over the Pueblo communities. The Spaniards were determined to turn New Mexico into a robust colony that would anchor Spanish power in western North America. But the presence of powerful horse-riding native societies on New Mexico's borders made the Spanish position precarious. Horse and captive raids by the Apaches, Utes, and Comanches threatened the colony from without, while the prospect of another Pueblo uprising threatened it from within. In 1696, the Pueblos revolted again. Although the Spaniards rapidly suppressed the uprising, they realized that their old strategies were no longer feasible.

The Spanish colonists adopted a more conciliatory policy toward the Pueblos. The settlers accepted smaller landholdings and reduced their demands on Pueblo labor. Officers implemented new laws that protected the Pueblos against colonial exploitation and secured their landholdings. Franciscans adopted a more pragmatic attitude toward religious indoctrination and allowed previously prohibited Pueblo ceremonies. To appease the priests, Pueblos accepted Catholic sacraments but performed their traditional rituals in underground *kivas*. The Spaniards and Pueblos remained distinct peoples within a colonial society that was based on unequal access to power, but gradually the social distance between them narrowed. They forged kinship relationships through the Catholic institution of godparenthood, and intermarriages became more common. Mixed Spanish-Pueblo settlements emerged along the upper Rio Grande Valley, and cultural blending deepened.

Such accommodations did not erase political antagonisms and cultural differences between the Spaniards and the Pueblos, but they did help to sustain a viable multicultural society in the upper Rio Grande Valley. The Pueblos never launched another major revolt against the Spaniards, and the two groups combined forces against Ute, Comanche, and Navajo raiders. New Mexico mounted punitive expeditions against native raiders and formed diplomatic ties with the plains Apaches, who were pressured by the Comanche-Ute coalition. Spanish officials invited Apache groups to relocate near New Mexico, hoping to turn them into a bulwark against the expanding nomads. Desperate to secure Spanish support, many Apaches pledged to accept Christianity and build permanent villages on New Mexico's borderlands.

3-2b French and Indians on the Middle Ground

New France was also undergoing transformation. In the 1680s, New France was in a perilous situation, fighting the English-allied Iroquois in the south and west, and the English Hudson's Bay Company in the north. More a financial liability than an asset to the French Crown, the colony received limited support from the mother country, and seemed to be dissipating. Yet, only a generation later, France's North American empire was secure and expanding. It boasted a vast interior fur trade system and its territorial claims arched from the St. Lawrence Valley across the Great Lakes basin down the Mississippi Valley to the Gulf Coast.

The French success was grounded in a new Indian policy that gradually took shape in the late 17th century in the Great Lakes region (see Map 3.4). There the Iroquois expansion made possible an unusual accommodation between the colonists and the Indians. The survival of the Iroquois Five Nations depended on their ability to assimilate captives seized from other nations through incessant warfare. Iroquois raiders, armed with English muskets, terrorized western Indians and carried away thousands of captives. The Iroquois wars depopulated nearly all of what is now the state of Ohio and much of the Ontario peninsula. The Indians around lakes Erie and Huron either fled west to escape these horrors or were absorbed by the Iroquois. The refugees, mostly Algonquian-speaking nations, founded new communities farther west. Most of these villages contained families from several different nations, and village loyalties gradually supplanted older political or ethnic loyalties. When refugees disagreed with one another, the collapse of traditional political structures made it difficult to resolve conflicts. Over time, French officials, soldiers, and missionaries began to mediate.

French policymakers were eager to bring these Indians into an alliance network that would shield the fragile New France against the Iroquois and contain the English east of the Appalachians. They began by easing tensions among the Great Lakes Indians, while supplying them with firearms, metal utensils, and other European goods. Threatened by common enemies, the French and the Indians recognized their mutual dependency and the necessity of adapting to each other's expectations. Little by little, they crafted an alliance that rested on creative compromises that transformed the Great Lakes basin into a middle ground where the two peoples accommodated one another in ways that benefited both.

French officials who gave orders rather than listened only alienated the Indians, who were accustomed to making decisions by consensus. Vastly outnumbered, the French knew that they could not impose their will on the Indians. The

▲ **MAP 3.4 French Middle Ground in North America, circa 1700** French power in North America rested mostly on the arrangements French governors worked out with refugee Algonquian Indians trying to resist Iroquois raids in the Great Lakes region.

Q *Why did a middle ground emerge in the western Great Lakes region?*

Q *What factors allowed France to claim and maintain presence in the Great Lakes region for over a century against demographically superior English colonies?*

governor of New France became a version of a traditional Indian chief. Algonquians called him **Onontio** ("Great Mountain"), the supreme alliance chief who won cooperation through persuasion and generosity. Gift exchanges became central to the middle ground diplomacy, the French customarily showing more generosity as an acknowledgment of their dependency on the Algonquians' military support. Cultural differences between the two peoples did not disappear, but both learned to negotiate around them. For example, the murders of French traders by Indians required careful balancing between two legal traditions. The French demanded the perpetrator to be identified, tried, and executed; the Indians wanted to appease the victim's kin by "covering" the death with presents or by "raising the dead" with a slave who took the victim's vacated social place. The solution of the middle ground was a cultural hybrid that allowed both sides to maintain face. Indians surrendered murderers to French authorities, who condemned them to death, only to quietly allow them to escape to freedom. Both sides detested such compromises but, desperate for support, accepted them nonetheless. By doing so, they sustained their alliance and held the interior.

Backed by their Indian allies, the French gained an upper hand in their struggles with the English and the Iroquois. They blocked English competition from James Bay and used their Indian allies to thwart English expansion in the south. During King William's War (1689–1697), the allied French and Indians raided across the English frontier, devastating most of coastal Maine and parts of New Hampshire. Throughout the 1690s, the French–Indian coalition also kept inflicting heavy losses on the Iroquois. By 1701, the Five Nations were exhausted. They negotiated a peace treaty known as the Grand Settlement with the French and some 30 native groups in Montreal. The Iroquois agreed to remain neutral in any war between France and England. They stopped their raids in the Great Lakes region, and the English pledged to protect their hunting rights in the west. France's Indian allies, supported by a new French fort erected at Detroit in 1701, began returning to the fertile lands around lakes Erie and Huron. By the 1710s, the interior fur trade was thriving again, supplying Indians with much-needed manufactured goods and sustaining France's expanding inland empire.

3-2c *French Canada in Transition*

The lucrative fur trade kept the cost-conscious French government committed to the North American imperial project. Supported by the Crown and protected by Indian allies, the French population along the St. Lawrence Valley grew, through natural increase, from about 10,000 in the 1680s to over 30,000 in the 1720s. A nearly continuous belt of small farms lined both banks of the valley for over 150 miles. Each farm was an elongated rectangle about 165 yards wide with an access to the river through which the habitants shipped their farming products to the growing cities of Quebec, Trois-Rivières, and Montreal, the center of the western fur trade. The population was intensely Catholic, and a seminary (now Laval University) in Quebec served its spiritual needs.

New France attracted few non-French immigrants and remained for a long time ethnically homogenous. It was in many ways as French as New England was English. This started to change with the creation of the Great Lakes middle ground, which alerted French policymakers to the value of captives and slaves in Indian diplomacy. France's western allies brought captives taken from enemy Indians for sale or offered them as ceremonial gifts that cemented bonds between allies. Louis XIV had expressly forbidden the enslavement of Indians, but the command became a dead letter and was officially rescinded in 1709. By the 1720s, up to 5 percent of New France's population consisted of Indian slaves, who labored as field hands, domestic servants, dock loaders, and millers. Some women became wives and concubines of the settlers. As in Spanish New Mexico and Florida, the incorporated Indians were exposed to intense religious indoctrination. Arriving from distant interior places—many were Apaches from the Great Plains—the captive-slaves were highly vulnerable to European microbes and died in vast numbers. Few survived in bondage longer than a decade.

3-2d *French Illinois, French Louisiana, and Spanish Texas*

In the 17th century, French and Spanish colonial projects had unfolded on the opposite sides of the continent and in isolation from each another; in the early 18th century, they began to converge in the heart of the continent (see Map 3.5). The convergence began when the French discovered the Mississippi River. The French dreamt about a water passage across North America to Asia into the 1670s, only to learn that the Mississippi River flowed into the Gulf of Mexico, not the Pacific. Their ambitions turned from the west to the south. In 1682, René-Robert Cavelier, *sieur* de La Salle, traveled down the Mississippi to its mouth, claimed possession of the entire area for France, and called it Louisiana for Louis XIV. When La Salle returned to the Gulf two years later, he overshot the mouth of the Mississippi, landed in Texas, and wandered around for three years in search of the great river until his exasperated men murdered him.

The Mississippi Valley became a magnet for the French. Around 1700, several disgruntled Frenchmen established a new settlement around the town of Kaskaskia in what became the Illinois Country near the confluence of the Mississippi and Ohio rivers. The habitants rejected seigneurs, feudal dues, and tithes, which had become established in the St. Lawrence Valley. Most prospered as wheat farmers and married Christian Indian women from the Great Lakes missions. By the mid-18th century, the Illinois settlements contained some 3,000 residents.

Another French settlement emerged downriver on the Gulf Coast. In 1699, a Crown-sponsored expedition led by Pierre le Moyne d'Iberville landed with 80 men at Biloxi, built a fort, and began trading with the Indians. Soon, he moved his headquarters to Mobile, closer to the more populous nations of the interior, especially the Choctaws, who were looking

3.5 La Salle and Father Hennepin on the Mississippi After La Salle and his party traveled down the Mississippi to its mouth, he claimed possession of the entire area for France. Father Louis Hennepin made this drawing in about 1683.

Q How could Hennepin's drawing reinforce France's right to claim the Mississippi Valley and the lands around it?

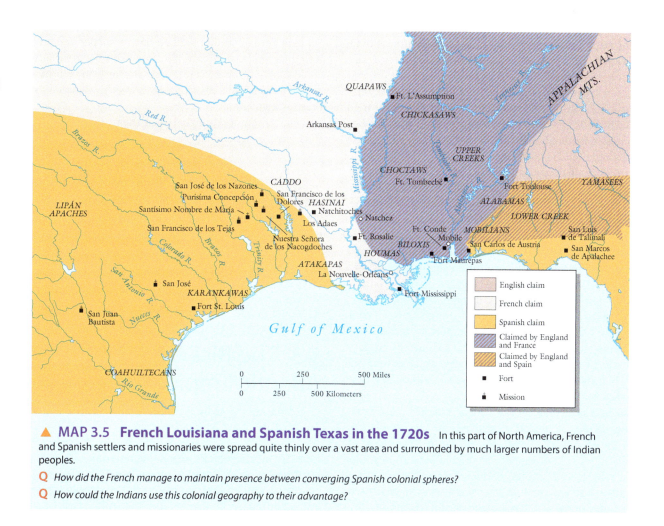

▲ **MAP 3.5   French Louisiana and Spanish Texas in the 1720s**   In this part of North America, French and Spanish settlers and missionaries were spread quite thinly over a vast area and surrounded by much larger numbers of Indian peoples.

Q How did the French manage to maintain presence between converging Spanish colonial spheres?

Q How could the Indians use this colonial geography to their advantage?

3-2 Converging Empires: Spain and France in North America

for allies against the English. The Choctaws could still field 5,000 warriors but had suffered heavy losses from slaving raids organized by South Carolinians and carried out mostly by that colony's Chickasaw and Creek allies. About 1,800 Choctaws had been killed and 500 enslaved during the preceding decade.

Using the Choctaws as an anchor, the French integrated themselves into the southern Indian trade system, which had been oriented toward English Carolina and Virginia. West of the lower Mississippi Valley, the French established ties with the powerful Osages and Caddos, who controlled access to the hide, food, and slave trades of the Great Plains. A thick exchange network emerged around French Louisiana. As in the Great Lakes, this frontier exchange economy was based on close, face-to-face interactions between the French and several, often competing native societies. This fluid and multiethnic exchange system allowed the French to carve out a colonial niche in the midst of powerful indigenous societies. Although European diseases had been ravaging the area since the 16th century, the Indians around the lower Mississippi Valley still numbered about 70,000. In 1708, the French settlers numbered fewer than 300, including 80 Indian slaves. They were lucky to survive at all.

French ventures into the lower Mississippi Valley galvanized the Spaniards, who correctly saw French settlements as a potential threat to their mines in northern Mexico and their shipping lines on the Gulf. French ministers specifically planned Louisiana as a springboard for an invasion into northern New Spain. In 1690, alarmed by rumors of La Salle's expedition, Spain sent missionaries into eastern Texas; they brought smallpox with them. Their explanation that the epidemic was God's "holy will" did not mollify the Tejas Indians, who soon banished them. In 1698, the Spaniards tried to make inroads by sea and built a garrison in Pensacola Bay to establish a foothold on the Gulf Coast between the Florida missions and French Louisiana.

In 1716, Spain tried again in Texas by sending missionaries and soldiers among the powerful Caddos, who lived in several populous agricultural villages east of the Mississippi and north of the Gulf Coast. Before its disintegration, the Caddos had been linked to the Cahokia-centric trading and ceremonial network (see Chapter 1), but now their villages had become commercial and cultural centers in their own right. Their widely dispersed local villages united into three confederacies, commanding a vast domain. The Caddo society was matrilineal—it traced descent through the maternal line—and women organized the all-important agricultural work. Male chiefs, caddis, led the local villages, and each confederacy was headed by a xinesí, a paramount religious leader, but all elite men depended on the guidance of the female heads of households.

The Spaniards struggled to understand the Caddo world, and the Caddos struggled to understand the newcomers. Unlike the French, the Spaniards did not seek to establish trade or marry Indian women. Instead of kinship ties, they offered religious education. Franciscan priests, who lived in celibacy, baffled the Caddos, who expected visitors to travel with women, which signaled peaceful intentions. The Spaniards did build two forts and six missions in east Texas among the Caddos, but the Franciscans won few converts. The forts suffered frequent depredations by Indians carrying French muskets, and eventually the soldiers and priests fled west to the San Antonio River, which became the nucleus of Spanish Texas. By 1720, a small colony with ranches, missions, and a presidio (military garrison) had risen along the river. In response, France bolstered its hold on the Gulf Coast. It created the Company of the Indies, which shipped 7,000 settlers and 2,000 African slaves to Louisiana and founded New Orleans, which became the capital in 1722. Settlers died in staggering numbers in the humid subtropical climate where mosquitoes and yellow fever thrived, but the colony persisted.

Policymakers had envisioned Spanish Texas and French Louisiana as imperial outposts that would transform critical parts of North America into Spanish and French spaces, but both projects evolved into something quite different. The low mid-continent became a complex world marked by imperial rivalries, colonial compromises, and flexible allegiances. In Louisiana, a growing black population carved out a distinct place in the frontier exchange economy that sustained the colony. Although most of them were slaves, the Africans enjoyed considerable economic autonomy in the colony. Laboring as herders, hunters, woodcutters, and boatmen, they moved freely around Louisiana and marketed their garden products in frequent small transactions. Many sold their labor as militiamen, eventually winning their freedom. In Spanish Texas, seminomadic Indians incorporated missions into their seasonal migrations as resource depots where they could subsist on Spanish resources during lean months; come spring, they left the missions, ignoring the objections of the Franciscan priests.

On the borderlands between them, the Spaniards and the French competed for the loyalties of the Caddos and other native groups, who traded with both, keeping their options open. But the Spaniards and the French also cooperated in unexpected ways. To prevent smuggling, the Spanish Crown refused to open a seaport on the Gulf Coast, which left Texas isolated from the empire's supply lines. Los Adaes, the easternmost settlement and the capital of Spanish Texas, was established to contain French encroachments, but it became dependent on the nearby French town of Natchitoches for food. Here, imperial visions and colonial realities were becoming startlingly disconnected.

3-3 The Rise of England's Atlantic Empire

Q *What was the Glorious Revolution and how did it change England's North American colonies?*

Like Spain and France, England redefined its goals and position in North America in the late 17th and early 18th centuries. While Spanish and French realms were expanding and colliding in the interior and the Gulf Coast, England's fragmented and divided mainland colonies began to coalesce into a coherent, centrally governed Atlantic empire. This was a long and convoluted process that was rooted in rapidly changing conditions in the mother country.

In the late 17th century, as England gradually recovered from the chaos of its civil wars, the Stuart monarchs and Parliament realized that the overseas colonies were slipping out of their control. The Caribbean colonies were under royal administration, but they were trading much of their sugar to Dutch merchants who dominated the world's oceanic trade. The Chesapeake colonies were doing the same with their tobacco. Alarmed, England turned toward the Atlantic once again. In a sense, it now first realized just how important colonies were to its prosperity, power, and prestige.

3-3a The Foundations of Empire: Mercantilism and the Navigation Acts

During the 17th century, most European powers followed a set of policies now usually called **mercantilism**. According to mercantilist theory, power derived ultimately from the wealth of a country. The world's wealth, however, was thought to be finite, which meant that each nation should organize itself in a way that allowed it to carve out the largest possible slice of the global wealth. Competing for the fixed pool of riches, nations were thought to be either growing richer or poorer, and to augment their power, they had to expropriate the resources of their rivals. The key means to achieve this was a positive **balance of trade** with other nations; a healthy nation imported less than it exported, and most of its exports were luxuries. Colonies were considered essential, for they provided the mother country with raw materials and bought its manufactured commodities. Clearly, a nation had to control the commerce of its colonies, but mercantilists disagreed over the best ways to promote growth. The Dutch favored virtual free trade within Europe, whereas England came to prefer stronger state regulation of the domestic and imperial economy.

In line with mercantilist principles, the English Parliament passed three Navigation Acts between 1651 and 1673. Primarily aimed at removing the Dutch from England's colonial markets and dislodging the Netherlands from its dominant position in world trade, the acts established three major regulations: All colonial trade was to be carried on English ships; **enumerated commodities**, of which sugar and tobacco were most important, could be shipped from the colony of origin only to England or to another colony, the intent being to give England a monopoly over the export of major staples from every English colony to Europe and the rest of the world; and products from Europe and Asia had to land and be levied in England before they could be delivered to colonies.

England intended nothing less than a revolution in Atlantic trade. In 1675, the Crown created a new agency, the Lords of Trade, to enforce the Navigation Acts and administer the colonies. Custom officers were sent to the colonies to collect duties and vice-royalty courts, tribunals without juries, were established to prosecute violators. Gradually, England dislodged the Dutch and established hegemony over its Atlantic trade. By the early 18th century, the Royal Navy was the largest in the Atlantic world, and nearly all British colonial trade was carried on English ships. Colonial commerce accounted for a rapidly growing share of Britain's overseas trade. Sugar, tobacco, and other staple crops all passed through Britain on their way to their ultimate destination. Nearly all of the manufactured goods consumed in the colonies were made in Britain.

The Navigation Acts reordered England's Atlantic trade, but they also redefined England's relationship with its overseas colonies: Tobacco- and sugar-producing colonies in the Chesapeake and the Caribbean found their market outlets and profits diminished. Beneath the surface of tightly regulated trade, smuggling persisted, sustaining long-standing traditions of colonial freedom from imperial supervision. Building an empire would take time.

3-3b Crisis in England and the Expansion of Royal Authority

England's tightening control of its American colonies sprang from mercantilist thinking, but it also reflected autocratic aspirations of the Stuart monarchs, who hoped to rule without parliamentary restrictions. In 1676, when Bacon's Rebellion caused both Virginia's tobacco production and England's customs revenues to plummet, King Charles II was obliged to ask Parliament for more money. Headed by a growing opposition that was soon named the **Whigs**, Parliament demanded an amendment to royal succession. Charles II had no legitimate children, which made his brother James, duke of York, heir to the throne. James had become a Catholic, and the Whigs, terrified by the prospect of a Catholic king, demanded his exclusion from the throne in favor of his Protestant daughters by his first marriage. Charles, after getting secret financial support from King Louis XIV of France, dissolved Parliament in 1681 and ruled without it until he died in 1685.

The prolonged struggles between the Stuart court and the Whig opposition had a profound impact on the colonies. Supported by the **Tories**, Stuart followers who favored legitimate succession, the monarchy set out to reinforce royal power, both in England and in the colonies. Although the Navigation Acts now regulated their Atlantic commerce, the colonies enjoyed considerable freedom from direct imperial control. Local autonomy, embodied in representative assemblies, had become an expected part of colonial life. Most colonists believed that they had an inherent right to government by consent. Stuart reforms challenged that autonomy head-on. The Stuarts issued strict instructions to royal governors and they imposed new revenue acts on Virginia, New York, and Jamaica, England's key sugar colony in the Caribbean. The acts obliged the colonies to pay for their own government in exchange for the right to have elected assemblies.

The Stuarts deplored the eclectic nature of the colonial system. In the late 1670s, there was only one royal colony, Virginia,

3.6 Gillis van Schendel, *Tobacco* (1628) This scene from an Amsterdam public house associates tobacco with dissipation. Note the man in the lower right throwing up on the floor and the animal above him enjoying a pipe while dancing with humans. Because no Dutch colony adopted tobacco as a staple crop, the source of tobacco could have been Virginia, in violation of English trade policy.

on the mainland. Only Virginia had royally appointed governors, who could veto laws passed by its representative assembly. New England colonies were corporate colonies, where legislatures or property-holding men elected all officials, including governors. The rest of the mainland colonies were proprietary in form, chartered by the king to individuals or groups who held full governing rights. The Lords of the Trade viewed all New England and proprietary colonies with deep suspicion. Seen from London, they were dangerously autonomous entities that engaged in smuggling, violated the Navigation Acts, and practiced religious policies that contradicted English laws. The Stuarts aspired to a more uniform and centralized administration of the colonies. The possibility of authoritarian rule suddenly emerged in English America.

3-3c The Dominion of New England

Charles II died and his brother became King James II in early 1685. James II focused on New England in his endeavor to assert royal authority in America. Absolutist New York now became the king's model for reorganizing New England. James disallowed the New York Charter of Liberties of 1683 that proclaimed government by consent (see Chapter 2) and sent Sir Edmund Andros, the autocratic governor of New York from 1674 to 1680, to Massachusetts to take over a new sprawling administrative domain called the Dominion of New England. All colonies north of Pennsylvania lost their charters as New Hampshire, Plymouth, Rhode Island, Connecticut, New York, and both Jerseys were lumped together in the Dominion. Andros disbanded elected assemblies and governed the supercolony through an appointive council and a superior court that rode the circuit, dispensing justice. He imposed religious toleration and tied voting rights to property rather than church membership, trying to dissolve the close relationship between the church and the state that characterized the Puritan order.

At first, Andros won support from merchants who had been excluded from politics by the Puritan requirement that they be full church members, but his rigorous enforcement of the Navigation Acts soon alienated them too. When he tried to compel New England farmers to take out new land titles that included annual quitrents (land taxes), he enraged the whole countryside. His suppression of a tax revolt in Essex County, Massachusetts, started many people thinking more highly of their rights as Englishmen than of their peculiar liberties as Puritans. By 1688, government by consent seemed more valuable than ever.

3.7 A London Coffeehouse The first coffeehouses dated from the 1650s, and by the 18th century merchants routinely met in such specialized establishments as the Virginia Coffeehouse or the New England Coffeehouse to transact their colonial business. England's rapidly growing consumption of coffee, tea, and chocolate stimulated most of the demand for sugar, which in turn sustained the Atlantic slave trade.

Q How and why did coffeehouses emerge as popular places of political debate from the 17th century onward?

3-3d The Glorious Revolution in England and America

The Dominion of New England was the most drastic of the Stuart experiments in imperial reform. It was also the last. In 1688, the birth of a son to James II raised the prospect of a Catholic *dynasty* in England. A cadre of Whig and Tory leaders swallowed their mutual hatred and invited William of Orange, the *stadholder* (governor) of the Netherlands, to England. William, the husband of the king's older Protestant daughter Mary by the king's first marriage, had become the most prominent Protestant soldier in Europe during a long war against Louis XIV. William landed in England with 21,000 soldiers, forcing James II to flee to France. Parliament elected William and Mary to the throne, completing an elite-engineered bloodless coup against "popery" and arbitrary power. The Glorious Revolution preserved the institution of the monarchy, but profoundly changed its character. It secured Protestant succession to the throne, reaffirmed Parliament's right to control taxation and legislation, and confirmed English liberties and the rule of law.

The Glorious Revolution reverberated across English North America, revealing deep fractures within colonial societies. The Boston militia overthrew Andros, and all New England colonies reestablished their old governments. In New York City, most of the active rebels were Dutch Calvinists, and their leader, Jacob Leisler, took over the government. Fearing conquest by Catholics from New France, Leisler acted like a Dutch *stadholder* in a nominally English colony. He jailed many of his English opponents without a trial, only to be outmaneuvered by powerful groups in England who persuaded the Dutch king of England to destroy Leisler. William appointed a new governor, Henry Sloughter, who arrested Leisler and his son-in-law, tried both for treason, and had them hanged, drawn (disemboweled), and quartered. A new assembly restored a modified version of the abolished Charter of Liberties of 1683, this time denying toleration to Catholics. Bitter struggles between Leislerians and Anti-Leislerians raged for decades in New York.

In Maryland, Protestant rebels overthrew the Catholic government of Lord Baltimore, who had refused to proclaim William and Mary even after all the other colonies had done so. The proprietary charter of Lord Baltimore and the Calvert family was withdrawn, and the Protestants set up a new government. The Calverts regained their proprietary power in 1715 when they converted to Anglicanism, and Maryland remained under Protestant control. The Protestant majority established the Church of England as Maryland's official church and barred Catholics from voting and holding public office. The colony's experiment in religious toleration was over.

Massachusetts also was transformed. Unlike other New England colonies, Massachusetts failed to restore its original charter. A new charter, issued in 1691, retained traces of the dissolved Dominion of New England. Massachusetts remained a royal colony and absorbed Plymouth and Maine. The colony's traditional town meetings survived and the General Court continued to control land distribution, but its governors and justices were now appointed in London. In accordance with English law, Massachusetts was required to grant toleration to other Protestant denominations, which the Puritan clergy deemed as heretic. Rather than church membership, voting rights were now based on property qualifications, and Puritan "saints" lost their control over the colony's politics. Liberty and property had triumphed over godliness. John Winthrop's vision of a "city upon a hill" had been replaced by a different kind of order emanating out of London.

3-3e The Salem Witch Trials

A year later, Massachusetts was gripped by a witchcraft crisis. Witchcraft accusations arose in Salem Village (modern Danvers) among a group of girls that included a young daughter and a niece of the local minister, Samuel Parris. They then spread to older girls, some of whom had been orphaned during the Indian wars. The girls howled, barked, and stretched themselves into frightful contortions. At first, Parris treated the outbursts as cases of demonic possession, but after weeks of prayer sessions brought no improvement, he accepted a diagnosis of witchcraft. With adult encouragement, the girls accused many village residents of witchcraft, mostly people who did not approve of Parris. The number of the accused escalated sharply, and the crisis spread far beyond the village after 14-year-old Abigail Hobbs confessed in April that she had made a compact with the devil in Maine at age 10 just before the outbreak of the Indian war that had since devastated northern New England. Altogether about 150 people were accused in Essex County and beyond. Satan, supported by Indian warriors on the frontier and by witches within the colony, seemed determined to destroy Massachusetts.

The trials began in Salem Town in June. The court, which included judges badly compromised by their willing service to the Andros regime, hung 19 people, pressed one man to death because he refused to stand trial, and allowed several other people to die in jail. All of those executed insisted on their innocence. Of 50 who confessed, none was hanged. Many of the victims were grandmothers, several quite conspicuous for their piety. One was a former minister at Salem Village who had become a Baptist. The governor finally halted the trials after someone accused his wife of witchcraft. By then, public support for the trials was collapsing. The Salem witch trials provided a bitter finale to the era of political uncertainty that had afflicted Massachusetts during the Stuarts' imperial reforms. Along with the new charter of 1691, the trials brought the Puritan era to a close.

3.8a (left) and 3.8b (right) Calvinism on Its Deathbed and Le Roy de France Louis XIV's persecution of the Huguenots led his supporters to hope that France would soon be rid of all Protestants. Le Roy de France, a Dutch Protestant response to the persecution, depicts Louis, the "Sun King," as death.

3-3f The New Imperial Order

The Glorious Revolution killed ambitions for unrestricted governing power and absolute rule in English America and guaranteed that royal colonies would have representative governments. Royal colonies became the norm, and by 1730 there were seven of them: Virginia, New York, Massachusetts, New Hampshire, New Jersey, North Carolina, and South Carolina. The monarch administered these colonies through governors, but both Crown and colonists now took it for granted that royal colonies would have representative governments. The monarch would appoint governors and (except in Massachusetts) their councils, but settlers would elect an assembly to vote on taxes and local laws. Connecticut and Rhode Island continued to elect their governors, retaining their corporate form of government. Maryland and Pennsylvania (along with Delaware, which became a separate colony under the Penn proprietorship in 1704) were the only surviving proprietary provinces on the mainland, and their proprietors were usually careful to abide by London's imperial regulations and representatives.

Such careful compromises between the Crown and the colonies were fraught with tension, however, for the Glorious Revolution had a complex legacy in English America. The consolidation of royal power under King William established the principle of limited constitutional monarchy in England, which in turn allowed for greater self-governance in the colonies. But the Glorious Revolution also emboldened England to tighten its hold on the colonies. Enjoying internal stability at long last under King William, England grew stronger and more confident, which reignited the vision of a more integrated, wealth-producing empire. Underneath the liberal reforms of the Glorious Revolution, the process of imperial centralization began by the Stuarts thus continued.

In 1696, then, England passed two major pieces of commercial legislation that aimed to consolidate its imperial system. First, Parliament passed a new, comprehensive Navigation Act that plugged several loopholes in earlier laws and extended to America the English system of vice-admiralty courts, which dispensed quick justice without juries. When the new courts settled routine maritime disputes or condemned enemy merchant ships captured by colonial privateers, their services were welcomed, but when the courts tried to assume jurisdiction over the Navigation Acts, they aroused controversy. Sometimes the common-law courts intervened and took over these cases. William also replaced the Lords of Trade in 1696 with a new agency, the Board of Trade. Its powers were almost purely advisory. It corresponded with governors and other officials in the colonies, listened to lobbyists in England, and made policy recommendations to appropriate governmental bodies. The board tried to collect information on complex questions and offer helpful advice. It was, in short, an early attempt at government by experts. John Locke, England's foremost philosopher and an able economist, was one of the board's first members. Together with the new Navigation Act, the Board of Trade helped create a secure and thriving commercial zone that connected England to its American colonies.

Another difficult problem was resolved in 1707 when England and Scotland agreed to merge their separate parliaments and become the single kingdom of Great Britain. At a stroke, the Act of Union placed Scotland inside the Navigation Act system, legalized Scottish participation in the tobacco trade, and opened numerous colonial offices to ambitious Scots. By the mid-18th century, Scotland owed its growing prosperity to its colonial trade.

The transformations that took place between 1689 and 1707 defined the structure of the British Empire until the American Revolution. Although Parliament claimed full power over the colonies, in practice it seldom regulated anything except Atlantic commerce. By the early 18th century, London was the center of a secure transatlantic empire united around commerce and Protestantism and against Catholicism and arbitrary power. Crown officials pulled back from Stuart autocracy and allowed the colonies considerable freedom in their internal affairs. The empire had stumbled into a system of de facto federalism, an arrangement that no one could quite explain or justify. Parliament exercised only limited powers, and the colonies controlled the rest. What seemed an arrangement of convenience in London soon acquired overtones of right in America, the right to consent to all taxes and local laws. Yet, the colonists were committed to England and the Atlantic empire. "It is no little blessing of God," Cotton Mather wrote in 1700, "that we are part of the English nation." A few years earlier, Mather had struggled, and failed, to preserve Puritan rule in New England, but the consolidation of England's imperial power compelled the colonists to align with the distant mother country.

The relationship, moreover, was starting to yield unforeseen benefits. A wildly unstable nation for a half-century, England emerged by the early 18th century as the most stable and dynamic among European powers. The key to England's success, nearly everyone agreed, lay in its "mixed and balanced" constitution. Government by the king, the House of Lords, and the House of Commons mirrored society itself—the monarchy, aristocracy, and commonality—and literally embodied all three in its structure. Each checked the power of the others, and as long as each placed the public good ahead of its own interests, English liberty would be secure. The prospect that corrupt Crown ministers could manipulate and undermine the House of Commons fueled anxiety and endless debates during the 18th century, but the English on both sides of the Atlantic believed that they were the freest people in history. The English empire, they believed, would be an empire of liberty.

It would also be, they realized, an empire of unprecedented prosperity and power. From the 1690s on, England raised larger fleets and armies than it had ever mobilized before. To support them, the kingdom created for the first time a **funded national debt**, in which the state agreed to pay the interest due to its creditors ahead of all other obligations.

History Through Film: Three Sovereigns for Sarah (1986)

Directed by Philip Leacock.
Starring Vanessa Redgrave (Sarah Cloyse), Phyllis Thaxter (Rebecca Nurse), and Kim Hunter (Mary Easty).

This film, originally a PBS American Playhouse miniseries, is the most powerful and effective dramatization ever made of the Salem witch trials of 1692. The three principal actresses were all previous Academy Award winners. When this series appeared, British director Philip Leacock was perhaps best known in the United States for *The War Lover* (1962) and *The Daughters of Joshua Cabe* (1972).

The screenplay by Victor Pisano, who also produced the film, concentrates on the three Towne sisters: Sarah Cloyse (Vanessa Redgrave), Rebecca Nurse (Phyllis Thaxter), and Mary Easty (Kim Hunter). Rebecca Nurse's ordeal became a major turning point in the Salem tragedy. Hers was one of the early trials, and at first the jury acquitted her, only to be urged by the judges to reconsider the verdict. They did, and she was hanged. After this reversal, no one else was acquitted. Mary Easty, after she too had been convicted, sent a petition to the magistrates, one of the most eloquent documents ever written in colonial America. As a committed Christian, she accepted her own death, but she urged the judges to reconsider their procedures because she knew that she was innocent, and so must be many of the other condemned witches. She was hanged. Of the three sisters, only Sarah Cloyse survived the trials. The film focuses on Cloyse's lifelong efforts to vindicate the reputations of her older sisters. Vanessa Redgrave's portrayal of her suffering and her resistance to the whole appalling affair is one of the most compelling performances of her acting career.

3.9 The witch crisis of 1692 began in the parsonage of Reverend Samuel Parris (shown above), then spread throughout Salem Village and to other towns, mostly in Essex County.

Samuel Parris, c.1685 (oil on card), American School, (17th century) / © Massachusetts Historical Society, Boston, MA, USA / The Bridgeman Art Library

The screenplay, by concentrating on the three sisters and their families, brings home the human tragedy that the trials became. This emphasis forced Pisano to leave out other important victims. For example, the Reverend George Burroughs, the only minister executed in the trials (or in any New England colony in the 17th century, for that matter), is not even mentioned. In addition, Pisano never explains that Sarah Cloyse survived because the grand jury refused to indict her. Grand juries were exempt from explaining their decisions to anyone else, and so we do not know why she became an exception, but evidently the jurors believed that she was too dedicated a Christian woman to sell her soul to the devil. Finally, the screenplay attributes the onset of the crisis to fortune telling in the Samuel Parris household by Tituba, an Indian slave from South America who reached the village via Barbados. Guilt for indulging in this occult activity presumably triggered the seizures of the afflicted girls. Several historians have demolished this interpretation since the film appeared. We do not know what provoked the girls' fits.

Three Sovereigns for Sarah is a compelling, relentless drama. It romanticizes nothing and makes clear, unlike some Hollywood depictions of these events, that nothing about the trials was sexy. The accusation scenes, dominated by girls, convey the madness of the whole affair. Most of those accused and executed were grandmothers. When they are turned off the ladder, their bodies bounce as the nooses take hold. This film is a cinematic triumph. ■

This simple device gave Britain enormous borrowing power. The government created the Bank of England to facilitate its own finances, and the London Stock Exchange emerged. Parliament levied a heavy land tax on the gentry and excises on ordinary people to meet wartime expenses. Together, debt, bank, stock market, and new sources of revenue added up to a financial revolution that enabled England to outspend France, despite having only one-fourth of France's population. Sustained by taxes and loans, the English state was able to organize large-scale military campaigns to protect its interests in Europe and across the Atlantic. If in the 17th century the colonists had often sought distance from England and its control, they now began to look to it for protection.

3-4 An Empire of Settlement: The Growth of British America

Q Why was the colonial household such an engine of British expansion? Did it give Britain an advantage over its imperial rivals in North America? What limits did Indians impose on the European colonies in the 18th century?

By 1700, when 250,000 settlers and slaves were already living in England's mainland colonies, the population was doubling every 25 years. New France matched that pace, but with only

14,000 people in 1700, it could not close the gap. The population of Spanish New Mexico was beginning to grow, but Spanish Texas had only a few hundred settlers, and Florida's mission belt was rapidly declining. In the struggle for empire, a growing population became England's greatest asset. If Spain and France were building North American empires on trade, missions, and Indian diplomacy, England was building one on settlement.

3-4a The Atlantic Prism and the Spectrum of Settlement

In 1700, English America was an amalgam of two connected but distinctive parts. Facing east from the Atlantic coast, it was part of a vast transoceanic commercial empire that linked it to England's ports, merchants, government, and culture. Facing west from the coast, English America was a sprawling empire of settlers, who were growing explosively in number and pushing their frontiers inland. If the colonies' Atlantic linkages had become increasingly structured in the late 17th century, giving them a measure of unity, the colonies themselves were anything but (see Map 3.6).

America had divided the English. Moving across the Atlantic for a range of religious, political, and economic reasons, the colonists had sorted themselves out along a vast arc from the cold North to the subtropical Caribbean. If we imagine England as a source of white light, and the Atlantic as a prism refracting that light, English America becomes a spectrum of settlement, with each color merging imperceptibly into the shade next to it. Each province had much in common with its neighbors but shared few traits with more distant colonies (see Table 3.1).

The most pronounced differences involved life expectancy, the sex ratio (the ratio of men to women in any society), and family structure. At one extreme were buccaneers, the all-male, multiethnic societies in the Caribbean that lived only for plunder. In the sugar colonies, European men often died by age 40, and slaves even sooner. Despite the appalling death rate in the sugar and tobacco colonies, most young men remained optimistic and upbeat, as they looked forward to challenging the world and making their fortunes. Female settlers were scarce in the islands at first; families hardly existed. Even when the sex ratio became more equal, couples had few children. Life expectancy in early Carolina was slightly better than in the islands, slightly lower than in the Chesapeake colonies. In Virginia and Maryland, men who survived childhood diseases lived to an average age of about 45 years during the last half of the 17th century, still less than in England, where life expectancy exceeded 50. Then, as natural increase replaced immigration as the main source of population growth after 1680, women became more numerous, married much earlier, and raised larger families.

The northern colonies were much healthier. In the Delaware and Hudson valleys, a man who reached adulthood could expect to live past 60. On Long Island in the 1680s, one woman claimed that she had more than 300 living descendants. New England was one of the healthiest places in the world. Because the sex ratio rapidly approached equality and because the economy permitted couples to marry perhaps two years earlier than in England, population exploded.

These demographic differences had major consequences. For example, the Caribbean and southern colonies were youthful societies in which men with good connections could expect to achieve high office while in their 30s, or even 20s. By contrast, the New England colonies gradually became dominated by grandfathers. A man rarely became even a selectman by age 40.

The degree of racial and ethnic mixture also varied from region to region, along with economic priorities. The West Indies already had a large slave majority by 1700, when English settlers were still a clear majority in the southern mainland colonies, but African slaves became a majority in Carolina in the 1710s. They would comprise 40 percent of Virginia's population by the 1730s. Africans were less numerous in the Delaware and Hudson valleys, although slavery became deeply entrenched in New York City and parts of northern New Jersey. Most colonies had large numbers of Indians living among the settlers. In the southern colonies, most Indians were slaves, seized from the interior by English and native slave raiders. In the northern colonies, most Indians were nominally free people who had stayed behind as their nations retreated or dissolved in the face of expanding settlements. They struggled to blend in by dressing, speaking, farming, and drinking like the colonists, while quietly trying to preserve their customs and identities. In the Middle Atlantic region, settlers from all over northwestern Europe were creating a new ethnic mosaic. English colonists were probably always a minority, outnumbered at first by the Dutch, and later by Germans, Scots, and Irish. New England was in every sense the most English of the colonies. The farther south one went, the more diverse the population—the farther north, the more uniform (see Map 3.7).

Slavery and staple crops went together. Slave societies raised sugar, rice, or tobacco for sale in Europe. General farming and family labor also went together. By 1700, the mid-Atlantic was the wheat belt of North America and commercially oriented. New Englanders farmed primarily for local consumption, but many coastal towns exported fish, livestock, and lumber to the West Indies. Patterns of ecological change reflected the different regional economies. New Englanders cut timber for sale at such a rate that it created climatic change: moister air, drier hillsides, and more winds. The numbers of several species of birds and mammals declined drastically, reducing the region's biodiversity. In the south, intensive tobacco cultivation depleted the soil of minerals and nutrients, causing crop failures and forcing the settlers to rotate tobacco with corn, wheat, and other crops.

Cultural patterns also varied among the colonies. Settlers lived in local and regional communities that followed their distinctive forms of civic life and worship. The intensity of religious observance differed immensely across the spectrum of settlement, ranging from irreverence and indifference in the West Indies to intense piety in Pennsylvania and New England. Literacy followed a similar pattern. Colonists everywhere tried to prevent slaves from learning to read, and low literacy

▲ **MAP 3.6 Government and Religion in the British Colonies, 1720** This map shows which colonies were royal, proprietary, or corporate in structure; where Anglican or Congregational churches were established by law; where the Quakers or the Dutch Reformed church predominated; and where numerous sects competed for the loyalties of the settlers.

Q *In what ways were the British colonies united and divided in the early 17th century?*

Q *In what ways was religion shaped by English colonialism in 17th-century North America?*

prevailed wherever slavery predominated. Chesapeake settlers provided almost no formal schooling for their children before the 1690s. Massachusetts founded Harvard College in 1636, and in 1642 required every town to have a writing school, and larger towns to support a Latin grammar school. Along the spectrum, piety, literacy, and education grew stronger from south to north. Public support for the clergy, and hence the proportion of ministers, followed the same pattern. Both were much greater in the north.

3-4b The Engine of British Expansion: The Colonial Household

Diverse as they were, the English colonies shared a key characteristic: They were all growing rapidly in number. The engine of that expansion was the colonial household. Ordinary northern farmers and southern great planters shared something in common that distinguished their households from those in England. With few exceptions, colonial families

3.10 George III (1760–1820) Going into His Palace by a Side Entrance In court culture, even everyday events, such as the king entering or leaving his palace by a side gate, had to display the honor, splendor, and hierarchy surrounding the monarch.

rejected the English customs of entail and primogeniture. **Entail** prohibited a landowner, or his heir, from dividing up his landed estate (i.e., selling part of it) during his lifetime. **Primogeniture** obliged him to leave all of his land to his eldest surviving son. Primogeniture and entail became more common in the 18th-century colonies than they had been before, but they never came to structure social relations the way they did in England. A Virginia planter, for example, might entail his home estate (the site of his big house) and bequeath it to his oldest son, but he would also leave land and slaves, and sometimes whole plantations, to his other sons. The primacy of the eldest son was far more sentimental than structural. The patriarchs of colonial households tried to pass on their status to all of their sons and to provide dowries that would enable all of their daughters to marry men of equal status. Until 1750 or so, these goals were usually realistic. For younger sons, then, the colonies presented unique opportunities. They could marry earlier (especially in regions with relatively balanced sex ratios) and have more children than their counterparts in Europe. Benjamin Franklin's *Autobiography*, colonial America's greatest success story, boasted that he was "the youngest Son of the youngest Son for 5 Generations back." Some women were able to acquire property, usually by inheritance from a deceased husband, particularly in the Chesapeake colonies during the long period when men greatly outnumbered women. Single women who crossed the Atlantic as servants

Table 3.1 THE SPECTRUM OF SETTLEMENT: DEMOGRAPHY, ETHNICITY, ECONOMY, 1650–1700

Category	West Indies	Lower South	Chesapeake	Mid-Atlantic	New England
Life expectancy for men, at age 20	40	42	45	60+	Late 60s
Family size	Below replacement rate	About two children	Rising after 1680	Very large	Very large
Race and ethnicity	Black majority by circa 1670s	Black majority by circa 1710	Growing black minority	Ethnic mix, N.W. Europe, English a minority	Almost all English
Economy	Sugar	Rice	Tobacco	Furs, farms	Farms, fishing, shipbuilding

▲ **MAP 3.7 Area of English Settlement by 1700** This map differentiates the areas settled before 1660 from those settled between 1660 and 1700, or roughly the Restoration era.

Q *What factors explain the growth of English settlements in the late 18th century?*

Q *How did the Appalachian Mountains shape the history of English colonization in North America?*

were desperate people who had hit bottom in England. Those who survived in the colonies enjoyed a fantastic chance at upward mobility. By marrying landowners, many won a respectability that was never available to them in England.

English households had become Americanized in the colonies during the earliest years of settlement, as soon as Virginia and Plymouth made land available to nearly all male settlers. By the mid-18th century, the question was whether that system could survive the pressures of a rising population. Social change began to drive households toward English practices. Only expansion onto new lands might enable colonial households to provide equal opportunity for all sons, but probably not for all daughters.

Colonial households were patriarchal. The father protected and cared for his family and hoped to be loved and revered by his wife and children but insisted on being obeyed. A man's local standing depended on his success as a master at home. A mature male was expected to be the master of others. In New England and Pennsylvania, most householders probably thought they were the rough equals of other householders. Above all, a patriarch strove to perpetuate his household into the next generation and to preserve his own independence, or autonomy. Of course, complete independence was impossible. Every household owed small debts or favors to its neighbors, but these temporary obligations seldom compromised a family's standing in the community.

Farmers tried to grow an agricultural surplus, if only as a hedge against drought, storms, and other unpredictable events. Farmers marketed their surplus and used the proceeds to pay taxes or their ministers' salaries and to buy British imports. These arrangements sometimes placed families in short-term debt to merchants, but most farmers and artisans avoided long-term debt. Settlers accepted temporary dependency among freemen—of sons on their parents, indentured servants on their masters, or apprentices and journeymen on master craftsmen. Sons often worked as laborers on local farms, as sailors, or as journeymen craftsmen, provided that such dependence was temporary. A man who became permanently dependent on others lost the respect of his community.

3-4c The Voluntaristic Ethic, Public Life, and War

Householders carried their quest for independence into public life. In entering politics and in waging war, their autonomy became an ethic of voluntarism. Few freemen could be coerced into doing something of which they disapproved. Local officials serving without pay frequently ignored orders contrary to their own interests or the interests of their community. Colonists waged wars with short-term volunteers for whom terror against Indian women and children was often the tactic of choice. While Europe was moving toward professional armies and limited wars, the colonists demanded quick and total victories.

Most young men accepted military service only if it suited their future plans. They would serve only under officers they knew, and then for only a single campaign. Few reenlisted. To the exasperation of professional British soldiers, provincials, like Indians, regarded blind obedience to commands as slavery. They did not enlist in order to become soldiers for life. After serving, they used their bonus and their pay, and often the promise of a land grant, to speed their way to becoming householders themselves. Military service, for those who survived, could lead to landownership and an earlier marriage.

3-4d Spanish and French Counterpoints

British households—independent, patriarchal, sizable, and often geographically mobile—did not have equivalents elsewhere in North America. In Spanish America, a substantial settler society emerged only in New Mexico, whereas Florida and California were essentially missionary enterprises. As in British America, New Mexico's colonial families were patriarchal and often large, but they were not self-reliant or mobile in the way the British households were. The centralized and urban-oriented Spanish imperial system discouraged the dispersal of population in the countryside—and beyond effective Crown control. Moreover, many Spanish men had both Spanish and native wives, and such intimate ties bound the families to local communities. Finally, the rise of powerful Indian societies around New Mexico made any attempts to extend Spanish settlements into the interior dangerous and virtually impossible. As a result, Spain's settlement frontier never moved far beyond the Rio Grande Valley.

Households in French North America mirrored their British counterparts in some respects; they too were patriarchal and growing. In New France and Louisiana, however, reliance on river transportation and the presence of powerful native societies nearby placed strong constraints on household mobility. This was particularly the case in the St. Lawrence Valley, where the British threat, the seigneurial system, and a centralized imperial administration helped keep the settlers fixed in place. A typical St. Lawrence household had an established relationship with a seigneur through annual charges and obligations, was loyal to the Crown and the governor-general, relied on its local parish as a source for spiritual and social guidance, and provided men to militia companies that protected a shared riverine world against British and Indian attacks. Individual Frenchmen pushed deep into the interior, whereas French families had deep roots in particular places and tended to stay put.

3-4e Queen Anne's War and the Yamasee War

The land appetite of the colonial household rather than royal officials drove the expansion of British North America. In the early 18th century, more and more families pushed farther west, looking for cheap land and new economic opportunities. Sons of growing families sought unclaimed farmland and the patriarchal independence it conveyed. Life in the frontier was hard—most farmsteads were far from roads, and isolated—but diminishing prospects in the old communities lured settlers westward. Crown-sponsored exploration and royal charters had launched England's North American empire; locally driven settlement would build it.

The expansion of English settlement did not go unchallenged. The French in the north, the Spaniards in the south, and native peoples across the western frontier monitored the growing English ambitions with alarm (see Map 3.8). When another war broke out in Europe (War of the Spanish Succession) in 1702, English colonists clashed with France, Spain, and Indians from Massachusetts to Florida in a series of conflicts that came to be known as Queen Anne's War.

In 1704, the French and Indians destroyed Deerfield, Massachusetts, in a winter attack and marched most of its people into captivity in Canada. Hundreds of New Englanders from Deerfield and other towns spent months or even years as captives. One of them was Eunice Williams, young daughter of John Williams, the pastor of Deerfield. Refusing to return to New England when the town's captives were released, she remained in Canada, became a Catholic, and married an Indian. Another New England woman who refused to return was Esther Wheelwright, daughter of a prominent Maine family. Captured by the Abenakis, she was taken to New France, where she also refused repatriation, converted to Catholicism, became a nun

(Esther Marie Joseph de L'Enfant Jésus), and finally emerged as mother superior of the Ursuline order in Canada—surely an unlikely career for a Puritan girl.

As the war dragged on, New Englanders twice failed to take Port Royal in Acadia, but a combined British and colonial force finally succeeded in 1710, renaming the colony Nova Scotia. An effort to subdue Quebec the following year met with disaster when many of the British ships ran aground in a treacherous stretch of the St. Lawrence River.

Farther south, the imperial struggle was grimmer and even more tragic (see Map 3.9). The Franciscan missions of Florida were already in decline, but Carolina slavers still targeted mission Indians. Between 1702 and 1704, James Moore, the governor of Carolina, devastated Florida with a large force of Indian allies. The invaders failed to take the Spanish fort of St. Augustine, but wrecked missions, dragged 4,000 women and children into slavery, and drove 9,000 Indians from their homes. Other raiders—British, Creeks, and Yamasees—followed, destroying the remaining Spanish missions in Florida. By the mid-1710s, much of Florida was nearly empty of Indians, and the Spanish presence in the region was confined to St. Augustine and two Gulf Coast outposts, San Marcos and Pensacola.

▲ **MAP 3.8 Northeastern Theater of War, 1689–1713** For a quarter of a century, starting with King William's War, the colonies north of the Quaker settlements in the Delaware Valley were locked in a brutal and costly struggle against the French and Indians to their north and west.

Q *Why did the Franco-English wars become so protracted in the Northeast?*

Q *What kind of dangers and opportunities did the colonial wars between England and France introduce to the Indians?*

3.11 Portrait of Esther Wheelwright Esther Wheelwright (1696–1780), an English Puritan who was captured by the French and Indians during Queen Anne's War, converted to Catholicism and became Sister Esther Marie Joseph de L'Enfant Jésus and eventually mother superior of the Ursuline nuns in the province of Quebec.

Q *What can Esther Wheelwright's life and career teach us about race, gender, identity, and belonging in early 18th-century North America?*

Carolina's greed for Indian slaves and other abuses finally alienated the colony's strongest Indian allies, the Yamasees. Traders frequently abused Indian women, including some of high status, an offense almost unknown within Indian communities. Moreover, the chaos and destruction of the ongoing wars among the British, Spaniards, and their Indian allies undermined the Yamasees' ability to bring slaves and deerskins to Carolina markets, threatening to leave them impoverished and isolated. In 1707, to resolve disputes between traders and Indians, Carolina created the office of Indian agent, which was held first by John Wright and then Thomas Nairne. They belonged to rival factions of Indian traders, and their controversies paralyzed the colony's government. In late 1714, Wright's bloc filed so many lawsuits against Nairne that for six months he could not leave Charleston to address Yamasee grievances. When the exasperated Indians threatened war, the government sent both Nairne and Wright to resolve the crisis in April 1715. Nairne brought a message of peace; Wright privately threatened war, which would most likely lead to enslavement. Appalled and angered, the Yamasees killed both men and all the other traders who had just arrived to collect their debts. Throughout the Southeast, most Indian nations trading with Carolina followed the Yamasees' example, killing nearly all of the colony's experienced traders and launching attacks that almost wrecked the colony. The loose native coalition disintegrated soon, however, allowing South Carolina to organize itself for a counteroffensive. The Yamasees were thrust back and nearly destroyed. Carolina made peace with most of the Indians, and the Yamasees fled as refugees to Florida.

The Yamasee War profoundly changed the Southeast. Carolina split into two separate colonies with their own governments, and both South and North Carolina became royal colonies in 1729, when the disillusioned proprietors sold their interests to the Crown. South and North Carolina also diverged economically and socially. North Carolina's economy continued to revolve around the naval stores industry and small farms, while South Carolina developed a profitable plantation economy. The turmoil of the Yamasee War forced Carolinians to abandon the Indian slave trade that had supported their colonial project for four decades by providing bodies for the lucrative Caribbean slave trade. South Carolina shifted increasingly to rice cultivation and African slavery, deepening its links to the Caribbean colonies that supplied it with slaves. Rice became the colony's mainstay, produced by African slaves who dried tidewater swamps and provided the planters with the technical knowledge of West African rice cultivation. The Yamasee War thus marked the birth of a new economic regime of African slavery and cash crops that would dominate the South until the Civil War. By the 1730s, two-thirds of South Carolina's 30,000 people were African slaves, most toiling on rice plantations.

▲ **MAP 3.9 Southeastern Theater of War, 1702–1713** In this theater, the English and their Indian allies did most of the attacking, destroyed Spain's Florida missions, and enslaved thousands. Spain and France tried to attack Charleston, South Carolina, but their 1706 expedition failed after it was ravaged by disease.

Q Why did the American Southeast become a setting for protracted and intensive wars in the early 18th century?

Q How did war shape the history of the Southeast?

3.12 South Carolina Colonists Enslaving an Indian The colony enslaved thousands of Indians from 1680 through 1715, a practice that was finally abandoned after the Yamasee War nearly destroyed the colony.

3-4f The Colonial Rim and the Indigenous Interior

The wars and their chaotic violence halted the movement of British settlers onto new lands in New England and the Carolinas in the early 18th century. In the wars' aftermath, Maine had only four towns left, while South Carolina struggled to adjust to the rice economy that forced settlers to live in humid, swampy lowlands where malaria, yellow fever, and smallpox were rampant. By 1720, after half a century of existence, South Carolina still had only 5,200 settlers (and 11,800 slaves). In Pennsylvania, Maryland, and Virginia—colonies that had not been deeply involved in the wars—the expansive thrust continued.

Queen Anne's War and the Yamasee War removed some of the major causes of animosity among the rival North American powers, ushering in a "Long Peace" that lasted into the early 1740s. The Yamasee War had ended the highly destabilizing Indian slave trade in the Southeast, while in the Northeast the 1701 Grand Settlement and the ensuing Iroquois neutrality stabilized relations among the French, English, and native nations. Imperial claims over the continent seemed

Interpreting the Visual Past

A Native American Representation of the Colonial Southeast

In 1721, the chiefs of the Catawba confederation gave Francis Nicholson, the governor of South Carolina, a present: a skin map of the Southeast, drawn by a Nasaw Indian mapmaker (the Nasaws were members of the Catawba confederation). At first sight, the map is a straightforward depiction of polities in space. The map names 11 Catawba villages: Casuie, Charra, Nasaw, Nustie, Saxippaha, Succa, Suttirie, Wasmisa, Waterie, Wiapie, and Youchine. It also includes two other native groups, the Cherokees and Chickasaws, and two colonial polities, Virginia and Charles Town (later Charleston), the capital of South Carolina. Looked at closely, however, the map accrues complexity. Its geographical proportions seem strange; it does not conform to such European cartographic conventions as cardinal directions. The mapmaker seems to be more concerned with the relations among different societies than their actual geographical position and proportions. The map is also selective, leaving out many groups such as the powerful Creek and Choctaw confederations. Polities are depicted differently—native ones with circles, British ones with squares, and all in different sizes—but they are connected with a complex web of pathways. There are also three animate entities—two humans and a deer—that may convey symbolic meaning. A caption identifies the smaller human figure as "An Indian a Hunting."

Q *Study carefully what kinds of things this map emphasizes and how it depicts space and the relationships among different societies. Consider each item separately, but also think about how it contributes to the mapmaker's overall message. For example, how does the deer-hunting, musket-carrying Indian embody the interactions between native and colonial societies in the Southeast? And what is the symbol in the lower left corner? Why might the native mapmaker have thought it important to include it?*

Q *The map was probably meant to serve as a social manual that would educate the British on how to behave on the frontier. How do you think the Catawbas expected the British to see and treat native societies?*

Figure 3.1 **Nasaw Map of the Southeast, 1721.**

to have reached a rough balance. France claimed a massive, triangle-shaped domain that extended from the Mississippi Delta northeastward to Newfoundland and northwestward to the Canadian plains. Spain clung to its Florida bases, but focused increasingly on fortifying its defensive outposts in the Southwest. Britain disputed France's vast claims in the interior, but since its settlements were still confined east of the Appalachians, the issue was yet pressing.

The tidy blocks and lines on European maps concealed a more complex reality, however. In 1720, the Indians still controlled more than 90 percent of the continent and most of the lands claimed by France, Spain, and Britain. In fact, beyond shores and key interior places, Europeans knew very little of North America's geography, and everywhere native nations contested European pretensions of dominance with their presence, borders, and power. French and Spanish outposts were like small islands in oceans of Indians. French Louisiana was deeply dependent on the trade and military support of the many small and large native nations around it. "We can do nothing by ourselves," Louisiana's frustrated French governor would complain as late as 1750, after half a century of colonization. In New Mexico and Texas, the Apaches, Comanches, and other horse-mounted societies raided with virtual impunity the missions and villages that were supposed to denote Spain's imperial authority in the region.

Despite their overwhelming numbers, the British too had to acknowledge the native presence on their western frontiers. The still-powerful Iroquois employed careful play-off politics to check France and Britain's meddling and territorial aspirations, threatening to side with one empire to restrain the other. The Creeks, Cherokees, and Choctaws did the same in the Southeast, pitting the British colonies against French Louisiana and Spain's Florida bases. Less populous and weaker nations relied on smaller-scale political maneuvering to contain European ambitions. They cultivated personal ties with colonial leaders and used cultural brokers to enhance mutual understanding and preserve peaceful relations. Groups like the Catawbas, a small, multiethnic confederation living in the North Carolina Piedmont, mixed deft diplomacy, persuasion, and closely regulated trade to preserve their autonomy and land base. They called the British "nothings," people who lacked kinship ties with native peoples and should therefore rely on the Catawbas to survive. The Catawbas managed to retain a fraction of their ancient homelands, on which they live to this day.

Conclusion

Although much of North America was still under native control in the early 18th century, Spain, France, and Britain had entrenched themselves on the continent. The three imperial powers wanted roughly similar things in North America—territory, prosperity, freedom, opportunities to serve their god better—and they held roughly similar views of the land and its peoples, pronouncing them both wild and in need of improvement. If challenged by natives who refused to submit, the three powers were quick to use violence, as the suppression of a series of Indian rebellions in the 1670s and 1680s demonstrated. But there were also differences, which became increasingly pronounced in the late 17th and early 18th centuries as rivalries over dominance in North America intensified.

Few in number and unable to subdue the Indians, the Spaniards and French both found it necessary to mediate and coexist with native peoples in order to extend their imperial reach. Their settlements remained concentrated along river valleys—Spain's in the upper Rio Grande, France's in the St. Lawrence and the Mississippi—and both strove to expand their spheres of influence into the interior through Indian alliances. By the early 18th century, France was becoming dominant, having erected a sprawling commercial inland empire built on creative Indian diplomacy. Spain's influence in Florida was faltering, and its outposts in the Southwest were surrounded by expanding independent Indians. The Spanish Empire adopted an increasingly defensive stance in North America and began to treat New Mexico and Texas as buffers that would shield the empire's crucial silver-mining districts in northern Mexico against foreign encroachments.

While Spain and France were jockeying for position in the interior, a different kind of empire emerged in the east: The disparate English colonies coalesced into a flourishing, Atlantic-spanning British Empire. The British saw their enterprise as a modern empire of commerce, constitutional liberalism, and Protestantism, which it was. Outsiders—Indians, Africans, and Catholics—saw it as an aggressive settler empire and a vicious racial regime. Increasingly, they also deemed it overwhelming. By 1720, with more than 400,000 settlers in the mainland colonies, the British Empire started to appear uncontainable.

Such ascendancy would have been difficult to imagine half a century earlier, when English America had been a collection of diverse, disagreeing, and autonomous colonies. From the 1670s onward, however, the English government found ways to regulate colonial trade, mostly for the mutual benefit of England and the colonies. Once the Crown gave up its claims to absolute power, both sides discovered much on which they could agree.

Political values in England and the colonies began to converge during and after the Glorious Revolution. Englishmen throughout the empire insisted that the right to property was sacred, that without it liberty could never be secure. They celebrated liberty under law, government by consent, and the toleration of all Protestants. They barred Catholics from succession to the throne and loaded them with severe disabilities of other kinds. In an empire dedicated to "liberty, property, and no popery," Catholics became big losers.

So did Indians and Africans. Racism directed against Indians mostly welled up from below, taking root among ordinary settlers who competed with Indians for land and other resources, and then bore the brunt of Indian reprisals. Colonial elites tried, often ineffectually, to contain this popular rage at Indians that nearly tore apart both New England and Virginia in 1675–1676. By contrast, racism directed against enslaved Africans was typically imposed from above and increasingly enforced by law. Ordinary settlers and Africans knew one another by name, made love, sometimes even married, stole hogs together, ran away together, and even fought together under Nathaniel Bacon's leadership. Class, more than race, separated people from one another. This changed during the late 17th and early 18th centuries when Chesapeake planters replaced indentured servitude with African slavery, brushed aside inequalities among themselves, and erected a new regime of racial slavery and white supremacy.

By the 18th century, the British colonists, despite or perhaps even because of their growing racism, had come to believe they were the freest people on earth. They attributed this fortune to their widespread ownership of land and to the English constitutional principles they had incorporated into their own governments. When George I became king in 1714, they proudly proclaimed their loyalty to the Hanoverian dynasty, which guaranteed a Protestant succession to the British throne. In their minds, the British Empire had become the world's last bastion of liberty.

CHAPTER REVIEW

Review

1. Why did violence erupt between Indians and Europeans in different parts of North America in roughly the same period?
2. How did negotiation, conciliation, and alliance-making shape France's and Spain's Indian policies?
3. What was the Glorious Revolution and how did it change England's North American colonies?
4. Why was the colonial household such an engine of British expansion? Did it give Britain an advantage over its imperial rivals in North America? What limits did Indians impose on the European colonies in the 18th century?

Critical Thinking

1. From the Restoration era to the American Revolution, most Englishmen and colonists understood politics as a perpetual struggle between power and liberty, one in which victory had almost always gone to power. How then was the English empire able to increase both its power and its commitment to liberty over that period?
2. Discuss the changing forms of racism and the role they played in the English colonies between their founding and the Yamasee War.
3. What enabled sparsely settled New France to resist British expansion for more than half a century, whereas Spanish Florida seemed almost helpless against a similar threat?

Identifications

Review your understanding of the following key terms, people, and events for this chapter (terms in bold in text are included in the Glossary).

praying Indians, p. 73
Iroquois League, p. 76
Covenant Chain of Peace, p. 76
Onontio, p. 80
mercantilism, p. 83
balance of trade, p. 83
enumerated commodities, p. 83
Whigs, p. 83
Tories, p. 83
funded national debt, p. 87
entail, p. 91
primogeniture, p. 91

Suggested Readings

Jill Lepore's *The Name of War: King Philip's War and the Origins of American Identity* (1998); **Andrew L. Knaut's** *The Pueblo Revolt of 1680* (1995); and **Wilcomb Washburn's**, *The Governor and the Rebel: A History of Bacon's Rebellion in Virginia* (1957) are all essential to understanding the crisis of the 1670s and 1680s. For the transition to slavery after Bacon's Rebellion, see **Anthony S. Parent, Jr.,** *Foul Means: The Formation of a Slave Society in Virginia, 1660–1740* (2003). For a superb study of Native Americans in the English backcountry, see **James H. Merrell,** *The Indians' New World: The Catawbas and Their Neighbors from European Contact through the Era of Removal* (1989).

Ian K. Steele, *The English Atlantic, 1675–1740: An Exploration of Communication and Community* (1986) is a careful, imaginative, and original analysis of the tumultuous period. For the Dominion of New England and the Glorious Revolution in the colonies, see **Richard R. Johnson,** *Adjustment to Empire: The New England Colonies, 1675–1715* (1981); and **John M. Murrin,** "The Menacing Shadow of Louis XIV and the Rage of Jacob Leisler: The Constitutional Ordeal of Seventeenth-Century New York," in **Stephen L. Schechter and Richard B. Bernstein, eds.,** *New York and the Union: Contributions to the American Constitutional Experience* (1990), pp. 29–71. The best study of Salem witchcraft, which is also a superb introduction to the Indian wars in northern New England, is **Mary Beth Norton,** *In the Devil's Snare: The Salem Witchcraft Crisis of 1692* (2002).

For the French and Spanish colonies and their relations with Native Americans in these critical decades, see especially **Richard White,** *The Middle Ground: Indians, Empires, and Republics in the Great Lakes Region, 1650–1815* (1991); **Ramón Gutiérrez,** *When Jesus Came, the Corn Mothers Went Away: Marriage, Sexuality, and Power in New Mexico, 1500–1846* (1991); **Daniel H. Usner, Jr.,** *Indians, Settlers, & Slaves in a Frontier Exchange Economy: The Lower Mississippi Valley before 1783* (1992); **Alan Gallay,** *The Indian Slave Trade: The Rise of the English Empire in the American South, 1670–1717* (2002); **Juliana Barr,** *Peace Came in the Form of a Woman:*

Indians and Spaniards in the Texas Borderlands (2007); **Ned Blackhawk**, *Violence over the Land: Indian and Empires in the early American West* (2007); **Michael Witgen**, *An Infinity of Nations: How the Native New World Shaped Early North America* (2012); and **Brett Rushforth**, *The Bonds of Alliance: Indigenous and Atlantic Slaveries in New France* (2012). For a ground-breaking study of New England's involvement in Indian slave trade, see **Wendy Warren**, *New England Bound: Slavery and Colonization in Early America* (2016).

On the householder economy in English North America, see **Laurel Thatcher Ulrich's** *Good Wives: Images and Reality in the Lives of Women in Northern New England* (1982), and **Mary M. Schweitzer**, *Custom and Contract: Household, Government, and the Economy in Colonial Pennsylvania* (1987).

> **MINDTAP** is a fully online personalized learning experience built upon Cengage Learning content. MindTap® combines student learning tools—readings, multimedia, activities, and assessments—into a singular Learning Path that guides students through the course and helps students develop the critical thinking, analysis, and communication skills that are essential to academic and professional success.

4 Provincial America and the Struggle for a Continent, 1720–1763

4-1 Expansion versus Anglicization
Learning Objective: Identify the ways that American colonists attempted to imitate British society in the 18th century.

Threats to Householder Autonomy
Anglicizing the Role of Women

4-2 Expansion, Immigration, and Regional Differentiation
Learning Objective: List the principal differences between the populations and economies of the three major colonial regions, the South, the mid-Atlantic, and New England.

Emergence of the Old South
The Mid-Atlantic Colonies: The "Best Poor Man's Country"
The Backcountry
New England: A Faltering Economy and Paper Money

4-3 Anglicizing Provincial America
Learning Objective: Define the Enlightenment and explain how it shaped the 18th-century colonies.

The World of Print
The Enlightenment in America
Women and the Consumer Revolution
Georgia: The Failure of an Enlightenment Utopia

4-4 The Great Awakening
Learning Objective: Describe the Great Awakening and how it changed religion in the American colonies in the 18th century.

Origins of the Revivals
Whitefield Launches the Transatlantic Revival
Disruptions
Long-Term Consequences of the Revivals
New Colleges
The Denominational Realignment

4-5 Political Culture in the Colonies
Learning Objective: Analyze why Britain's "Country" values prevailed in most southern colonies while "Court" politics took hold in most northern provinces.

The Rise of the Assembly and the Governor
Court and Country Politics

4-6 The Renewal of Imperial Conflict
Learning Objective: Detail how Indians and African slaves took advantage of opportunities presented by a new round of European wars starting in 1739.

Challenges to French Power
The Danger of Slave Revolts and War with Spain
France versus Britain: King George's War
The Impending Storm

4-7 The War for North America
Learning Objective: Explain what made the War for North America (1754–1763) so much more decisive than the three earlier Anglo-French wars.

The Albany Congress and the Onset of War
Britain's Years of Defeat
A World War
Imperial Tensions: From Loudoun to Pitt
The Years of British Victory
The Peace of Paris

4.1 George Washington in the Uniform of a Colonel of the Virginia Regiment Charles Willson Peale's 1772 portrait is the earliest recorded image of Washington. It is telling that, amidst the American revolutionary crisis, he chose to be painted in the uniform that he wore as a provincial officer in the French and Indian War more than a decade earlier. Like other American colonists, Washington took great pride in his British identity by the mid-18th century.

THE BRITISH COLONISTS, who thought they were the freest people on earth, faced a growing dilemma in the 18th century. To maintain the opportunity that settlers had come to expect, the colonies had to expand onto new lands. But provincial society also emulated the cultural values of Great Britain—its architecture, polite learning, religion, and politics. Relentless expansion made this commitment difficult because new settlements were not genteel. The two goals often worked at cross-purposes. An anglicized province would become more hierarchical than the colonies had been so far and might not even try to provide a rough equality of opportunity. The settlers hoped to sustain both goals, an effort that brought renewed conflict with their neighbors—the Indians, the Spanish, and the French.

When the British again went to war against Spain and France after 1739, the settlers joined in the struggle and declared that liberty itself was at stake. Less fortunate people among them disagreed. Slaves in the southern colonies saw Spain, not Britain, as their hope for liberty. In the eastern woodlands, most Indians identified France, not Britain, as the one possible ally that might remain committed to their survival and independence. ■

4-1 Expansion versus Anglicization

Q *In what ways did American colonists attempt to imitate British society in the 18th century?*

In the 18th century, as the British colonists sought to emulate their homeland, many of the institutions and material goods they had left behind in the 17th century began to reappear, a process known to historians today as **anglicization**. After 1740, for example, imports of British goods grew spectacularly. The gentry, merchants, and professionals dressed in the latest London fashions and embraced the capital's standards of taste and elegance. Southern planters erected "big houses," such as Mount Vernon, built by Lawrence Washington and bequeathed to his half-brother George. In Boston, on Beacon Hill, the merchant Thomas Hancock erected a stylish residence that later passed to his nephew John. Newspapers and learned professions based on English models proliferated after 1700, and colonial seaports began to resemble Bristol and other provincial ports in England.

But the population of British North America doubled every 25 years. Each generation required as many new colleges, ministers, lawyers, physicians, craftsmen, printers, sailors, and unskilled laborers as all the preceding generations combined. Without them, standards of "civility" would decline. Colonial institutions had to grow to meet these needs. As the 18th century progressed, the colonies became the scene of a contest between the unrelenting pace of raw expansion and these newer, anglicizing tendencies.

The southern colonies, which looked to England to satisfy their needs for skilled talent, could no longer attract as many people as they needed. In 1700, for example, Oxford and Cambridge universities in England had managed to meet the colonies' demand for Anglican clergymen, most of whom went to the southern provinces. By 1750, the colonial demand far exceeded what stagnant Oxford and Cambridge could supply, and the colonies were also importing Scottish and Irish clergy. Before long, those sources also proved inadequate. By contrast, northern colonies trained their own ministers, lawyers, and doctors in their own colleges, as well as their own skilled craftsmen through apprenticeships. Although still colonies, they were becoming America's first modernizing societies. They learned to do for themselves what Britain did for the southern colonies.

Much of this change occurred during prolonged periods of warfare. By midcentury, the wars were becoming a titanic struggle for control of the North American continent. Indians gradually realized that they would be the ultimate victims of British victory. Constant expansion for the settlers meant unending retreat for them.

4-1a Threats to Householder Autonomy

As population rose, some families acquired more prestige than others. Before 1700, farmers and small planters often sat in colonial assemblies. After 1700, the assemblies grew much more slowly than the overall population. In the five colonies from New York to Maryland, their size remained almost unchanged despite enormous population growth. Those active in public life above the local level were likely to be gentlemen who performed no manual labor. They had greater wealth, a more impressive lineage, and a better education than farmers or craftsmen. But unlike members of Parliament, few of them enjoyed a patron–client relationship with the voters. In England, one or two families dominated each of the "pocket boroughs" that elected most members. In the colonies, most voters remained independent.

By midcentury, despite the high value that colonists placed on householder autonomy, patterns of dependency were beginning to emerge. In tidewater Virginia by 1760, about 80 percent of the land was entailed. That is, the landowner could not divide or sell the estate but had to bequeath it intact to his heir. Younger sons had to look west for a landed inheritance. In one Maryland county, 27 percent of the householders were tenants who worked small tracts of land without slaves, or were men who owned a slave or two but had no claim to land. Such families could not satisfy the ambitions of all their children. In Pennsylvania's Chester County, a new class of married farm laborers arose. Their employers, without granting them

CHRONOLOGY

1690	Massachusetts invents fiat money
1704	*Boston News-Letter* founded
1712	Slaves revolt in New York City
1716	Spanish begin to settle in Texas
1718	Beginning of Scots-Irish emigration to North America
1721	Boylston introduces smallpox inoculation in Boston
1730	Three hundred slaves revolt in Virginia, and 29 are hanged
1732	Georgia charter granted by Parliament
1733	Molasses Act passed
1734	Edwards launches massive religious revival in the Connecticut Valley
1735	Zenger acquitted of seditious libel in New York
1738	Spanish found Mose in Florida
1739	Slaves revolt in Stono, South Carolina
1739–1741	Whitefield launches Great Awakening
1741	New York slave conspiracy trials lead to 35 executions
1745	New England volunteers take Louisbourg
1747	Ohio Company of Virginia founded • Anti-impressment rioters in Boston resist Royal Navy
1750	Massachusetts converts from paper money to silver
1754	Washington attacks French patrol near the forks of the Ohio River • Albany Congress proposes plan for colonial union
1755	Braddock suffers disaster near Fort Duquesne • British expel Acadians from Nova Scotia
1756–1757	Loudoun antagonizes the colonies as commander in chief
1756	French take Oswego
1757	French take Fort William Henry • Pitt becomes Britain's war minister
1758	British take Fort Duquesne, Louisbourg, and Fort Frontenac • French repel British at Ticonderoga
1759	British take Ticonderoga and Crown Point • Wolfe dies taking Quebec; Montcalm also killed
1760	Montreal falls; Canada surrenders to the British
1760–1761	Cherokee War devastates South Carolina backcountry
1762	Spain enters war, loses Havana and Manila
1763	Peace of Paris ends Seven Years' War

title or lease, let them use a small patch of land on which they could build a cottage and raise some food. Called "inmates" in Chester County records (or "cottagers" in England), such people made up 25 percent of the county population. Tenants on New York manors had to accept higher rents and shorter leases after 1750. In one parish in Ipswich, Massachusetts, half the farmers had land enough for only some of their sons by 1760.

Families that could not provide for all of their children reverted toward English social norms. In Connecticut, from the 1750s to the 1770s, about 75 percent of eligible sons inherited some land, but for daughters the rate fell from 44 percent to 34 percent. When a father could not support all his sons, he favored the eldest over younger sons. The younger sons, in turn, took up a trade or headed for the frontier. To increase their resources and sustain family autonomy, many New England farmers added a craft or two to the household. The 300 families of Haverhill, Massachusetts, supported 44 workshops and 19 mills by 1767. In Northampton, more than one-third of all farming families also practiced a craft. The goal of independence continued to exercise great power, but it was under siege.

4-1b *Anglicizing the Role of Women*

The changing role of women provides a striking example of the anglicizing tendencies of the 18th century. When they married, most women received a **dowry** from their father, usually in cash or goods, not land. Under the common-law doctrine of **coverture**, the legal personality of the husband "covered" his wife, and he made all legally binding decisions. If he died first, his widow was entitled to **dower rights**, usually one-third of the estate.

Women in many, perhaps most, households had to work harder to maintain the family's status—at the spinning wheel, for example. New England women did virtually all of the region's weaving, which was a male occupation in Britain and in other colonies. Yet, women were becoming more English in other ways, thus reversing some earlier trends. Until 1700, many Chesapeake widows inherited all of their husbands' property and administered their own estates. After 1700, such arrangements were rare. In the Hudson Valley, Dutch law had been much more generous than English common law in bestowing property rights on women, but during the 18th century, English law gradually prevailed. In New England, too, as Puritan intensity waned, women suffered losses. Before 1700, courts often punished men for sexual offenses, such as fornication, and many men pleaded guilty and accepted their sentences. After 1700, almost no man would plead guilty, except to making love to his wife before their wedding day. But to avoid a small fine, some husbands humiliated their wives by denying that charge, even if their wives had already pleaded guilty after giving birth to a child that had obviously been conceived before marriage. Courts rarely convicted men of sex offenses, not even serious crimes such as rape. The European double standard of sexual behavior, which punished women for their indiscretions while tolerating male infractions, had been in some jeopardy under the Puritan regime. It now revived.

4-1 Expansion versus Anglicization

4-2 Expansion, Immigration, and Regional Differentiation

Q *What were the principal differences between the populations and economies of the three major colonial regions, the South, the mid-Atlantic, and New England?*

After 1715, settled portions of North America enjoyed their longest era of peace since their founding. Until midcentury, people poured into these areas, usually without provoking the strong Indian nations of the interior. As the colonies expanded, they evolved into distinct regions, but only New Englanders acquired a self-conscious sense of regional identity before independence.

Renewed immigration, particularly of unfree migrants, drove much of the postwar expansion. After 1730, the flow became enormous. In that year, about 630,000 settlers and slaves lived in the mainland colonies. By 1775, another 248,000 Africans and 284,000 Europeans had landed, including 50,000 British convicts, shipped mostly to Maryland and Virginia, where they served long indentures. All told, by the onset of the American Revolutionary War in 1775, approximately three-fourths of all immigrants to the 13 mainland colonies arrived as slaves, servants, convicts, or in some other unfree status. During this period, the African slave trade to North America reached its peak. European migration decisively outweighed the influx of slaves only after 1763.

4-2a Emergence of the Old South

The forced migration of enslaved Africans to North America grew out of the larger Atlantic slave trade. Between 1519 and 1867, the dates of the first and last known transatlantic slave voyages directly from Africa, Europeans enslaved and carried upwards of 12.5 million Africans to the Western Hemisphere. (More than 1 million slaves perished during the **Middle Passage** across the Atlantic Ocean.) During the colonial era, the vast majority of slaves—about 90 percent—were taken to Brazil or the West Indies, both sugar-producing regions. Although each of Britain's 13 mainland colonies had slavery, only the southern colonies bore some resemblance to the slave societies of Brazil and the Caribbean sugar islands.

Almost 90 percent of the slaves in British North America went to the southern colonies. At least 84,000 went to Charleston, 70,000 to Virginia, and 25,000 to Maryland. One-eighth of the slaves went to northern colonies. About 80 percent of the slaves arrived from Africa on overcrowded, stinking British-owned vessels. Most of the rest came, a few at a time, from the West Indies on smaller New England ships.

This massive influx created the Old South, a society consisting of wealthy slaveholding planters, a much larger class of small planters, and tens of thousands of slaves. By 1720, slaves made up 70 percent of South Carolina's population. By 1740, they were 40 percent of Virginia's and 30 percent of Maryland's. (In comparison, slaves comprised 90 percent of Jamaica's population.) Slaves did most of the manual labor in the southern colonies, and their arrival transformed the social structure. In 1700, most members of Virginia's House of Burgesses were small planters who raised tobacco with a few indentured servants and perhaps a slave or two. After 1730, the typical burgess was a great planter who owned at least 20 slaves. And by 1750, the rice planters of South Carolina were richer than any other group in British North America. Tobacco and rice planters had few contacts with each other, except in North Carolina, where they did not get along. They did not yet think of themselves as "southerners."

The life of slaves in the upper South (Maryland, Virginia, and the Albemarle region of North Carolina) differed considerably from that of slaves in the lower South (from Cape Fear in North Carolina through South Carolina and eventually Georgia). Chesapeake tobacco planters organized their enslaved labor into a **gang system**, groups of slaves closely supervised and disciplined by a white overseer. Weather permitting, owners kept their slaves in the fields all day. To make their plantations more self-sufficient, they also trained perhaps 10 percent of them as skilled artisans. The planters, who saw themselves as benevolent paternalists, encouraged family life among their slaves, who by the 1720s were achieving a rate of reproduction almost equal to that of the settlers. Slaveholders justified brutal whippings as fatherly corrections of members of their household.

Paternalism even extended to religion. In the 1720s, for the first time on any significant scale, many Virginia planters began to urge their slaves to convert to Christianity. At first, only adults who had a good command of the catechism, which they had to memorize because literacy for them was illegal, were accepted into the church, but by the 1730s, growing numbers of infants were baptized. These efforts expanded despite a massive slave uprising. A rumor spread that the British government had promised freedom to any slave who converted but that the colony was suppressing the news. In September 1730, about 300 slaves tried to escape through the Great Dismal Swamp. The planters hired Indians to track them, crushed the rebels, and hanged 29 of them. Yet, the conversions continued to gain momentum, mostly, it seems, because planters hoped that Christianized slaves would be more dutiful.

South Carolina planters also began with paternalistic goals, but the rice swamps and mosquitoes defeated them. Whites supervising slave gangs in rice fields usually caught malaria. Although seldom fatal, malaria left its victims vulnerable to other diseases that often did kill them. Many planters relocated their big houses to higher ground, at a safe distance from the fields. With few exceptions, they made no efforts to Christianize their laborers.

Africans fared much better than whites in marshy rice fields. (Modern medicine has shown that many Africans possess a **sickle cell** in their blood that protects against malaria, but it can expose their children to a deadly form of inherited anemia.) As the ability of Africans to resist malaria became evident, Carolina planters seldom ventured into the rice fields and became less paternalistic than their Virginia counterparts except toward their household servants. After midcentury, many chose to spend their summers in Charleston or in

4.2a (top left), 4.2b (bottom left), and 4.2c (right) **Britain's African Slave Trade at Its Peak** **(a)** African middlemen on the coast launched expeditions ever deeper into the interior to capture slaves, preferably young men, usually yoked together in a coffle, and marched often hundreds of miles to ships going to America. Many died along the way. **(b)** The captives were packed aboard slave ships, often so tightly that they could scarcely move and had to inhale the stench and humiliation of their own human waste. The most famous illustration of such a ship, the *Brooks* of Liverpool, was published by antislavery advocates in London in 1789 and gave a tremendous boost to what became Britain's abolitionist movement. **(c)** Cruel Instruments of Restraint. Aboard ship, the captives' wrists (top) and ankles (bottom) were shackled. The thumbscrew (middle, left) was used to torture rebellious slaves, and the speculum oris (middle, right) to force open the mouths of slaves who refused to eat. Slaves who died were dumped at sea. Some living slaves who jumped overboard to escape their fate in America were eaten by sharks, which had learned to follow slave ships.

Q *How did the cruel methods and tools of the slave trade and Middle Passage begin to define enslaved Africans as property and not people even before they reached the western hemisphere?*

homes on high ground in the interior. Some even sailed off to Newport, Rhode Island.

This situation altered work patterns. To get local manufactures, planters relied on white artisans in Charleston, many of whom bought or leased slaves, who then did most of the actual work. To produce rice, planters devised the **task system**. Slaves had to finish certain assignments each day, but then their time was their own. They used this free time to raise crops, hunt, or fish, activities that enabled them to create their own largely invisible economy.

Thus, while many Chesapeake slaves were becoming skilled artisans, South Carolina's plantation slaves were heading in the other direction. Before rice became the colony's staple, they had performed numerous tasks, but the huge profits from rice now condemned nearly all of them to extremely unpleasant labor in the marshes, although it, in turn, freed them from direct oversight by their masters. Rice culture produced low rates of African reproduction. Yet, slaves preferred it to gang labor. It gave them more control over their own lives.

The task system also slowed assimilation into the British world. African words and customs survived longer in South Carolina than in the Chesapeake colonies. Newly imported slaves spoke **Gullah**, originally a pidgin language (that is, a simple second language that enabled people from different cultures to communicate). Gullah began with phrases common to many West African languages, gradually added English words, and became the natural language of later generations.

South Carolina's enslaved population failed to grow by natural increase until perhaps the 1770s, a half-century later than in the tobacco colonies. Even South Carolina planters had difficulty replacing themselves before 1760. But by the Revolution, the American South was becoming the world's only self-sustaining slave society. Nowhere else could colonies with staple crops reproduce their enslaved labor force without continuous imports from Africa.

Slavery required brute force to sustain everywhere it took hold. Slaves convicted of arson were often burned at the stake, an unthinkable punishment for a white person. Whippings were frequent, with the master or overseer setting the number of stripes. In South Carolina, one overseer killed five slaves in two or three years before 1712. When one slave fell asleep and lost a parcel of rice in the river, the overseer chained him, whipped him twice a day, refused to give him food, and confined him at night in a "hellish Machine contrived by him into the Shape of a Coffin where [he] could not stir." The victim finally killed himself.

If such extreme cruelty was rare, random acts of violence were common and, from a slave's perspective, unpredictable. In Virginia, William Byrd II was one of the most refined settlers in the colony. His diary reveals that when he and his wife Lucy disagreed, the slaves could suffer. "My wife and I had a terrible quarrel about whipping Eugene while Mr. Mumford was there but she had a mind to show her authority before company but I would not suffer it, which she took very ill." This time Eugene was spared, but slaves were not always so lucky. On another occasion, "My wife caused Prue to be whipped violently notwithstanding I desired not, which provoked me to have Anaka whipped likewise who had deserved it much more, on which my wife flew into such a passion she hoped she would be revenged of me." This time both slaves were whipped. House servants must have dreaded days that Byrd spent in Williamsburg, leaving Lucy in charge of the plantation.

The southern colonies prospered in the 18th century by exchanging their staple crops for British imports. By midcentury, much of this trade had been taken over by Scots. Glasgow became the leading tobacco port of the Atlantic. Tobacco profits remained precarious before 1730 but then improved in later decades, partly because Virginia guaranteed a high-quality leaf by passing an inspection law in 1730 (Maryland followed suit in 1747), and partly because a tobacco contract between Britain and France brought lucrative revenues to both governments and opened up a vast continental market for Chesapeake planters. By 1770, more than 90 percent of their tobacco was reexported to Europe from Britain.

Other exports and new crafts also contributed to rising prosperity. South Carolina continued to export provisions to the sugar islands and deerskins to Britain. Indigo, used as a dye by the British textile industry, received a cash bounty from Parliament and emerged at midcentury as a second staple crop, pioneered by a woman planter, Eliza Lucas Pinckney. North Carolina, where the population increased fivefold between 1720 and 1760 and more than doubled again by 1775, sold naval stores (pitch, resin, turpentine) to British shipbuilders. Many Chesapeake planters turned to wheat as a second cash crop. It required mills to grind it into flour, barrels in which to pack it, and ships to carry it away. It did for the Chesapeake what tobacco had failed to do: It created cities. Norfolk and Baltimore had nearly 10,000 people by 1775, and smaller cities, such as Alexandria and Georgetown, also thrived. Shipbuilding, linked to the export of wheat, became a major Chesapeake industry.

4-2b The Mid-Atlantic Colonies: The "Best Poor Man's Country"

The mid-Atlantic colonies had been pluralistic societies from the start. Immigration added to this ethnic and religious diversity after 1700. The region had the most prosperous family farms in America and, by 1760, the two largest cities, Philadelphia and New York. Pennsylvania outpaced New York in the competition for immigrants. In the 1680s and 1690s, New York governors had granted some political supporters enormous manorial estates in the Hudson Valley that discouraged immigration. As late as 1750, the small colony of New Jersey had as many settlers as New York but fewer slaves. Pennsylvania's growth exploded, driven by both natural increase and the surge of immigration. The 12th of 13 colonies to be founded, Pennsylvania was the second most populous by 1770, surpassed only by Virginia.

After 1720, Ireland and Germany replaced England as the main source of voluntary immigrants. About 70 percent of Ireland's emigrants came from Ulster. They were Presbyterians whose forebears had come to Ireland from Scotland in the 17th century. (Historians now call them the Scots-Irish, a term seldom used at the time.) Most left Ireland to avoid an increase in rents and to enjoy greater trading privileges than Parliament had allowed them. Most Ulster immigrants headed for the Delaware Valley. Maybe 30 percent of Irish immigrants came from southern Ireland. Most were Catholics, but perhaps one-fourth were Anglicans. Roughly 80,000 Catholic and Protestant Irish reached the Delaware Valley before 1776.

Nearly 85,000 free and unfree immigrants were Germans. Many arrived as **redemptioners**, a new form of indentured service attractive to married couples because it allowed families to find and bind themselves to the same master. After completing their service, most streamed into the interior of Pennsylvania, where by 1750 Germans outnumbered the original English and Welsh settlers. Others moved on to the southern backcountry with the Irish.

These colonies grew excellent wheat and built their own ships to carry it abroad. At first, New York flour outsold

Pennsylvania's, but Pennsylvania gained the edge in the 1720s after it instituted a system of public inspection and quality control. When Europe's population surged after 1740, the middle colonies shipped flour across the Atlantic. Around 1760, both Philadelphia and New York City overtook Boston's stagnant population of 15,000. Philadelphia, with 32,000 people, was the largest city in British North America by 1775.

4-2c The Backcountry

Many Scots-Irish, and some Germans, pushed west into the mountains and up the river valleys into the interior parts of Virginia and the Carolinas. In South Carolina, about 100 miles of pine barrens separated these backcountry settlements from the coastal plantations. Most English-speaking colonists were immigrants from Ulster, northern England, or lowland Scotland, who brought their folkways with them and soon gave the region its own distinctive culture. Although most of them farmed, many hunted or raised cattle. Unlike the coastal settlements, the backcountry had no newspapers, few clergymen or other professionals, and little elegance. South Carolina's backcountry had almost no government. A visiting Anglican clergyman bemoaned "the abandon'd Morals and profligate Principles" of the settlers. Refined easterners found the backcountry frightening. Clannish and violent, backcountry settlers drank heavily and hated Indians. By the 1750s, the situation grew tense in Pennsylvania, where the Quaker assembly insisted on handling differences with the Indians through peaceful negotiations. Once war broke out, most backcountry men demanded their extermination. Virginia and South Carolina faced similar tensions.

4-2d New England: A Faltering Economy and Paper Money

New England, a land of farmers, fishermen, lumberjacks, shipwrights, and merchants, still considered itself more pious than the rest of the British Empire, but the region faced serious problems. Few immigrants went there. In fact, since about 1660, more people had been leaving the region, mostly for New York and New Jersey, than had been arriving.

New England's relative isolation in the 17th century began to have negative consequences after 1700. Life expectancy declined as diseases from Europe, especially smallpox and diphtheria, invaded the region. The first settlers had left them behind, but lack of exposure in childhood made later generations vulnerable. When smallpox threatened to devastate Boston in 1721, Zabdiel Boylston, a self-taught doctor who drew on Muslim examples, began inoculating people with the disease, believing that healthy ones would survive the injection and become immune. Although the city's leading physicians opposed the experiment as too risky, it worked and soon became a regular feature of public health in many colonies. Even so, a diphtheria epidemic in the 1730s and high military losses after 1740 took their toll. New England's rate of population growth fell behind that of other regions.

After peace returned in 1713, New England's economy weakened. The region had prospered in the 17th century, mostly by exporting cod, grain, cattle, and barrel staves to the West Indies. But after 1700, declining wheat yields left the Yankees struggling to feed themselves, much less others. They compensated by opening new markets in the lucrative French sugar islands, sending fish and forest products to the islands in exchange for molasses, which they used as a sweetener (cheaper than sugar) or distilled into rum. British West Indian planters, alarmed by the flood of French molasses, urged Parliament to stamp out New England's trade with the French islands. Parliament passed the Molasses Act of 1733, which placed a prohibitive duty on all foreign molasses. Strictly enforced, the act would have strangled New England trade; instead, bribery and smuggling kept the molasses flowing.

Shipbuilding gave New England most of its leverage in the Atlantic economy. Yankees built more ships than all of the other colonies combined. New England ships earned enough from freight in most years to offset trade losses, but Boston merchants often had to scramble to pay for their imports. New England ran unfavorable balances with nearly every trading partner, especially England. Yankees imported many British products but produced little that Britain cared to buy. Whale oil, used in lamps, was an exception. A thriving whaling industry emerged on the island of Nantucket, but trade with the mid-Atlantic and Chesapeake colonies was not profitable. Settlers there eagerly bought rum and a few slaves from Yankee vessels that stopped on their way back from the West Indies. Newport became deeply involved in slave trading along the African coast. That traffic never supplied a large percentage of North America's slaves, but it contributed greatly to Newport's growth.

New England's experience with paper money illustrates these economic difficulties. In response to a military emergency in 1690, Massachusetts invented **fiat money**—that is, paper money backed, not by silver or gold, but only by the government's promise to accept it in payment of taxes. This system worked well enough to prompt most other colonies to do likewise, but serious depreciation set in after the Treaty of Utrecht in 1713.

The declining value of money touched off a fierce debate that raged from 1714 until 1750. Creditors and members of Parliament attacked paper money as fraudulent: Only gold and silver, they claimed, had real value. Defenders retorted that, in most other colonies, paper was holding its value. The problem, they insisted, lay with the New England economy, which could not generate enough exports to pay for the region's imports. The elimination of paper, they warned, would only deepen the region's problems. War disrupted shipping in the 1740s, and military expenditures sent New England currency to a new low. In 1748, Parliament agreed to reimburse Massachusetts for these expenses, but at an earlier exchange rate. Governor William Shirley and House Speaker Thomas Hutchinson, an outspoken opponent of paper money, persuaded a skeptical legislature to use the grant to retire all paper and convert to silver money.

That decision was a drastic example of anglicization. Although fiat money was the colony's invention, Massachusetts repudiated its offspring in 1750 in favor of

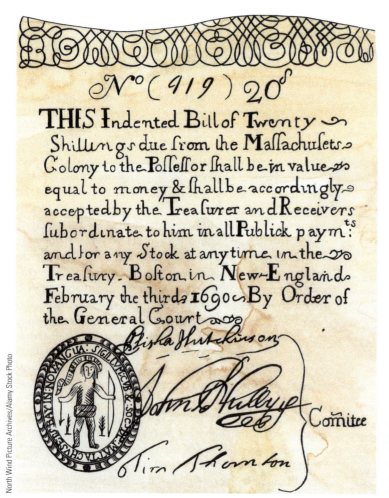

4.3 First American Paper Money, Massachusetts (1690) Facing daunting military costs during King William's War, Massachusetts issued the first paper money in the western world in 1690. Other colonies soon followed suit, creating a challenge for Parliament that lasted until American independence.

British methods of public finance. But as Hutchinson's critics had warned, silver gravitated to Boston and then to London to pay for imports. Lacking sufficient currency, New England's economy fell into a deep recession in 1750. It did not revive until the next French war.

4-3 Anglicizing Provincial America

Q *What was the Enlightenment and how did it shape the 18th-century colonies?*

Forms of production had made American colonial regions diverse. They became more alike through what they imported from Britain. Although each region exported its own distinctive products, patterns of consumption became quite similar throughout the colonies. In the mid-1740s, the mainland colonies and the West Indies consumed almost identical amounts of British imports. A decade later, the mainland provinces had forged ahead by a margin of 2 to 1. Their ability to consume ever-larger quantities of British goods was making the mainland colonies more valuable than the sugar islands to the empire. The mainland also welcomed English revivalists and absorbed much of Britain's intellectual and political culture.

4-3a The World of Print

Few 17th-century American settlers owned books and, except in New England, even fewer engaged in the intellectual debates of the day. For most of the century, only Massachusetts had printing presses, first in Cambridge to serve Harvard College, the clergy, and the government, and then in Boston beginning in 1674. For the next century, Boston remained the print capital of North America. In the 1680s, William Bradford became Philadelphia's first printer, but he soon moved to New York. By 1740, Boston had eight printers; Philadelphia and New York had two apiece. No other community had more than one.

Not surprisingly, Boston also led the way in newspaper publishing. John Campbell, the city's postmaster, established the *Boston News-Letter* in 1704. By the early 1720s, two more papers had opened in Boston. Philadelphia and New York City had each acquired one. The *South Carolina Gazette* was founded in Charleston in 1732 and the *Virginia Gazette* in Williamsburg in 1736. Benjamin Franklin took charge of the *Pennsylvania Gazette* in 1729, and **John Peter Zenger** launched the controversial *New York Weekly Journal* in 1733 and won a major victory for freedom of the press when a jury acquitted him of seditious libel, the common-law crime of criticizing government officials.

Newspapers helped spread the **Enlightenment**—a broad intellectual movement that applied reason to a wide range

4.4 An 18th-Century Printing Press This printing press resembles the one that James Franklin brought to Boston from London in 1717. Benjamin, his younger brother and apprentice, used the press to learn the trade of a printer.

Q *Despite its clear connection to the Enlightenment, why was printing still considered an artisanal (ungenteel) craft in the 18th century?*

of human affairs—from Europe to North America. Colonial papers were weeklies that devoted their space to European matters. Before midcentury, they rarely reported local news because they assumed their readers already knew it. At first, they merely reprinted items from the *London Gazette*. Beginning in the 1720s, however, the *New England Courant*, under James Franklin, began to reprint Richard Steele's essays from the *Spectator;* Joseph Addison's pieces from the *Tatler;* and the angry, polemical writings, mostly aimed at religious bigotry and political and financial corruption, of "Cato," a pen name used jointly by John Trenchard and Thomas Gordon. *Cato's Letters* became immensely popular among colonists.

Benjamin Franklin personified the Enlightenment values that the newspapers were spreading. As a boy, although raised in Puritan Boston, he skipped church on Sundays to read Addison and Steele and to perfect his prose style. As a young printer with his brother's *New England Courant* in the 1720s, he helped publish the writings of John Checkley, an Anglican apologist whom the courts twice prosecuted in vain attempts to silence him. Franklin joined the Church of England after moving to Philadelphia. After 1729, he made his *Pennsylvania Gazette* the best edited and most widely read paper in America.

Franklin always sought ways to improve society. In 1727, he helped found the Junto, a workingman's debating society that met weekly to discuss literary and philosophical questions. It later evolved into the American Philosophical Society, which still thrives near Independence Hall. He was also a founder of North America's first Masonic lodge in 1730, the Library Company of Philadelphia a year later, the Union Fire Company in 1736, the Philadelphia Hospital in 1751, and an academy that became the College of Philadelphia (now the University of Pennsylvania) in the 1750s. But his greatest fame arose from his ingenious electrical experiments. He also invented the Franklin stove (much more efficient than a fireplace) and the lightning rod. He became the most celebrated North American in the world.

4-3b The Enlightenment in America

Aside from a common emphasis on rational thought, the Enlightenment varied among European nations. The English Enlightenment, which rejected a wrathful God and exalted man's capacity for knowledge and social improvement, had the greatest impact in America. It grew out of the rational and benevolent piety favored by Low Church (or latitudinarian) Anglicans in Restoration England. They disliked rigid doctrine, scoffed at conversion experiences, attacked superstition, and rejected all "fanaticism," whether that of High Church Laudians, who had brought on England's great crisis of

1640–1642, or that of the Puritans, who had executed Charles I. High Church men, a small group after 1689, still stood for orthodoxy, ritual, and liturgy.

Enlightened writers celebrated Sir Isaac Newton's laws of motion as one of the greatest intellectual achievements of all time, joined the philosopher John Locke in looking for ways to improve society, and began to suspect that moderns had surpassed the ancients in learning and wisdom. John Tillotson, archbishop of Canterbury until his death in 1694, embodied this "polite and Catholick [that is, universal] spirit." He preached morality rather than dogma and had a way of defending the doctrine of eternal damnation that left his listeners wondering how a merciful God could possibly have ordained such a cruel punishment.

Enlightened ideas won an elite constituency in the mainland colonies even before newspapers began circulating these new views. Tillotson had a huge impact on America. His sermons appeared in numerous southern libraries and made a deep impression on tutors at Harvard College, including John Leverett, Jr. After Leverett became Harvard's president in 1708, Tillotson's ideas became entrenched in the curriculum. For the rest of the century, most Harvard-trained ministers, although still nominal Calvinists, embraced latitudinarian piety. They stressed the similarities, not the differences, between Congregationalists and Anglicans and favored broad religious toleration. After 1800, most Harvard-educated ministers became Unitarians who no longer believed in hell or the divinity of Jesus.

In 1701, largely in reaction against this trend at Harvard, a new college was founded as a bastion of orthodoxy and finally settled in New Haven, Connecticut. It was named Yale College in honor of a wealthy English benefactor, Elihu Yale, who gave his library to the school. Ironically, these Anglican books helped to convert the Yale faculty to the rational religion of the English Enlightenment that the institution had been founded in protest against. In 1722, the entire faculty, except for 19-year-old Jonathan Edwards, converted to the Church of England and sailed for England to be ordained by the bishop of London. Their leader, Timothy Cutler, became the principal Anglican spokesman in Boston.

The rise of the legal and medical professions further spread Enlightenment ideas. Early colonists despised lawyers as men who took advantage of the misery of others and who deliberately stirred up discord. By the mid-18th century, however, lawyers emerged, particularly in New England, as a new learned elite.

Medicine also became an enlightened profession, with Philadelphia setting the pace. William Shippen

4.5 **Robert Feke's Portrait of Benjamin Franklin as a Gentleman** This portrait, painted at about the time that Franklin retired as a printer in 1747, announced his coming out as a gentleman. Note the wig and ruffled cuffs, indicating that Franklin would no longer be working with his hands.

earned degrees at Princeton and Edinburgh, the best medical school in the world at the time, before returning to Philadelphia in 1762, where he became the first American to lecture on medicine, publish a treatise on chemistry, and dissect human cadavers, a practice that shocked the unenlightened. His student, John Morgan, became the first professor of medicine in North America when the College of Philadelphia established a medical faculty a few years later. Benjamin Rush, who also studied at Princeton and Edinburgh, brought the latest Scottish techniques to the newly founded Philadelphia Hospital. He too became an enlightened reformer, attacking slavery and alcohol and supporting the American Revolution.

4-3c Women and the Consumer Revolution

By the 1730s and 1740s, consumption of British products joined learning as a key measure of refinement and social class in the American colonies. The period witnessed the birth of an Anglo-American **consumer society**. Small manufacturing concerns scattered throughout England produced huge quantities of consumer goods, including cloth, ceramics, glassware, paper, and cutlery, which colonists purchased at a dizzying pace. Each succeeding generation of colonial Americans owned more British imports than the previous generation. By one measure, the American market for imported goods rose 120 percent between 1750 and 1773.

The explosion in British goods contributed to the process of anglicization in the American colonies. Items manufactured in England quickly replaced locally made goods, resulting in a more homogenous British material culture in America. In 1751 Benjamin Franklin boasted, "A vast Demand is growing for British Manufacturers, a glorious market wholly in the Power of Britain."

The emerging consumer society provided new opportunities for colonial American women, particularly in port cities. Women participated in a commercial urban economy in which they enjoyed broad influence through their consumption patterns. The exercise of choice in the marketplace could be liberating at a time when other public venues, particularly politics, remained closed to their participation.

Products related to tea and clothing became especially feminized by the mid-18th century. Imported from South Asia by English merchants, tea began to appear in the homes of wealthier American colonists in the early 1700s. By the 1740s, taking tea had become a common afternoon practice for refined ladies and gentlemen. The ritual provided women with a social space where they exercised a measure of control due in part to their mastery of the pots, cups, saucers, spoons, strainers, and sugar tongs that made up a proper tea service. A New York newspaper declared the young men of the city "utterly ignorant in the Ceremony of the Tea-Table" and advised employing a knowledgeable woman "to teach them the Laws, Rules, Customs, Phrases and Names of the Tea Utensils."

By midcentury, colonial women also embraced clothing fashions imported from London. The expanded production and availability of cloth made purchasing fabric preferable to investing the time and energy necessary to create homespun. Women learned of the latest fashions from British periodical literature, such as the *Spectator*, as well as from advertisements by merchants and shopkeepers in American newspapers. Events such as balls and tea parties served as arenas for women to display the newest fashions as evidence of their social distinction.

For their part, colonial men did not escape the lure of British fashion. In 1759, the Reverend Jonathan Boucher relocated from the north of England to Port Royal, Virginia, a small tobacco community on the Rappahannock River. The move left him feeling underdressed. "I'm noth'g amongst the Lace and Lac'd fellows that are here," Boucher reported. Wigs, increasingly of a shorter length, helped to define masculine gentility in the colonies. As with other products, male colonists desired the most authentically British wigs available—those made with English human hair.

4-3d Georgia: The Failure of an Enlightenment Utopia

In the 1730s, Anglican humanitarianism and the Enlightenment belief in the possibility of social improvement converged in Britain to provide support for the founding of Georgia. The sponsors of this project hoped to create a society that could make productive use of England's "worthy" poor (but not the lazy or criminal poor). They also intended to shield South Carolina's slave society from Spanish Florida by populating Georgia with disciplined, armed freemen. Appalled by what cheap English gin was doing to the sobriety and industry of England's working people, Georgia's sponsors prohibited hard liquor as well as slavery. Slaves would make Georgia just like South Carolina, with all of that colony's vulnerabilities.

A distinguished group of trustees set themselves up as a nonprofit corporation and announced that they would give land away, not sell it. Led by James Oglethorpe, they got a 20-year charter from Parliament in 1732, raised money from Anglican friends, and launched the colony on land claimed by both Spain and Britain. They interviewed many prospective settlers to distinguish the worthy poor from the unworthy. They engaged silk and wine experts to produce staples that no English colony had yet made profitable, and recruited Scottish Highlanders as soldiers.

In 1733, the first settlers laid out Savannah, a town with spacious streets. Within 10 years, 1,800 charity cases and just over 1,000 self-supporting colonists reached Georgia. The trustees refused to consult the settlers on what might be good for Georgia. As refined men, they believed they knew what the colony needed. They created no elective assembly, nor did they give the British government much chance to supervise them. Because, under its charter, Georgia's laws had to be approved by the British Privy Council, the trustees passed only three "laws" during their 20 years of rule. One laid out the land system, and the others prohibited slavery and hard liquor.

Interpreting the Visual Past — A Display of Consumer Goods

This portrait by an unknown artist shows a young girl, Susanna Truax, of Dutch descent, at home in Albany, New York. Truax, only four at the time of the portrait in 1730, displays several of the material goods that had started to flood into the colonies from Britain. She wears a bright, striped dress, typical of the fabric then sought after by American consumers. On the table sit a teapot, sugar cubes, and a cup and saucer, while Truax holds a lump of sugar in her spoon. Apparently at ease with the consumer revolution of the mid-18th century, Truax lived until 1805, long enough to witness a few more revolutions.

Q *The portrait in colonial America offered an opportunity to display one's possessions and social status. What can we learn about the standing of Truax's family from the painting? Why might a girl so young have been placed with material goods normally associated with adults?*

Q *How does the portrait illustrate the process of anglicization in the colonies? Does it matter that Truax belonged to a Dutch family? What does her ancestry tell us about the competing forces of cultural diversity and consolidation in the 18th century?*

4.6 Artist Unknown, Susanna Truax, 1730.

They governed through "regulations" instead of laws. An elective assembly, they promised, would come once Georgia's character had been firmly set.

The land system never worked as intended. The trustees gave 50 acres to every male settler whose passage was paid for out of charitable funds. Those who paid their own way could claim up to 500 acres. Ordinary farmers did poorly; they could not support a family on 50 acres of the sandy soil around Savannah. Because the trustees envisioned every landowner as a soldier, women could not inherit land, nor could landowners sell their plots.

The settlers could not grow grapes or persuade the sickly worms that survived the Atlantic crossing to make silk out of mulberry leaves. They clamored for rum, smuggled it into the colony when they could, and insisted that Georgia would never thrive without slaves. By the mid-1740s, enough people had died or left to reduce the population by more than half, and by 1752, it had fallen below the 2,800 who had first settled the colony. Between 1750 and 1752, the trustees dropped their ban on alcohol, allowed the importation of slaves, called an elective assembly (only to consult, not legislate), and finally surrendered their charter. The establishment of royal government in 1752 gave Georgia an elective assembly with full powers of legislation, and the colony became what it was never meant to be, a smaller version of South Carolina, producing rice and indigo with slave labor. By then, ironically, it had done more to spread religious revivalism than to vindicate Enlightenment ideals.

4-4 The Great Awakening

Q What was the Great Awakening and how did it change religion in the American colonies in the 18th century?

Between the mid-1730s and the early 1740s, an immense religious revival swept across the Protestant world. Within the British Empire, it affected some areas more intensely than others. England, Scotland, Ulster, New England, the mid-Atlantic colonies, and, for a time, South Carolina responded warmly to emotional calls for a spiritual rebirth. Southern Ireland, the West Indies, and the Chesapeake colonies remained on the margins until Virginia and Maryland were drawn into a later phase of the movement in the 1760s and 1770s. This "Great Awakening" shattered some denominational loyalties in the colonies and enabled the Methodists and the Baptists to surge ahead of all Protestant rivals after 1780.

4-4a Origins of the Revivals

Some of the earliest revivals originated in the colonies. Around 1720, Theodorus Jacobus Frelinghuysen of the Dutch Reformed Church sparked several of them in New Brunswick, New Jersey. Gilbert Tennent, the local Presbyterian pastor, watched and learned. Tennent was a younger son of William Tennent, Sr., an Anglican-turned-Presbyterian minister who had moved from Ulster to America. At Neshaminy, Pennsylvania, he set up his Log College, where he trained his sons and other young men as **evangelical** preachers. Evangelicals were committed to spreading the teachings of the Bible in an emotional style that resulted in conversion experiences among their listeners. The Tennent family dominated the **Presbytery** (a regional body) of New Brunswick, used it to ordain ministers, and sent them off to congregations that requested one, even in other presbyteries. These intrusions angered the Philadelphia **Synod**, the overall governing body of the Presbyterian Church in the colonies (see Figure 4.1). Most of its ministers emphasized orthodoxy over a personal conversion experience. In a 1740 sermon, *The Dangers of an Unconverted Ministry,* Gilbert Tennent warned that those preachers were leading their people to hell. His attack split the church. In 1741, the outnumbered revivalists withdrew and founded their own Synod of New York.

In New England, Solomon Stoddard of Northampton, between the 1670s and his death in 1729, presided over six revivals. Jonathan Edwards, his grandson and successor, touched off a revival in 1734 and 1735 that rocked dozens of Connecticut Valley towns. Edwards's *A Faithful Narrative of the Surprising Work of God* (1737) explained what a **revival** was—an emotional response to God's Word that brought sudden conversions to scores of people. He described these conversions in acute detail and won admirers even in Britain.

In England, John Wesley and George Whitefield set the pace. At worldly Oxford University, Wesley and his brother Charles founded the Holy Club, a High Church society whose members fasted until they could barely walk. These methodical practices prompted scoffers to call them "Methodists." In 1735, Wesley went to Georgia as a missionary, but the settlers rejected his ascetic piety. In 1737, on the return voyage to England, some Moravians convinced him that, for all his zeal, he had never grasped the central Protestant message, justification by faith alone. Some months later, he was deeply moved by Edwards's *Faithful Narrative.* Soon Wesley found his life's mission, the conversion of sinners, and it launched him on an extraordinary preaching career for the next half-century.

George Whitefield, a talented amateur actor in his youth, joined the Holy Club at Oxford and became an Anglican minister. He followed Wesley to Georgia, founded an orphanage, then returned to England and preached all over the kingdom to raise money for it. He had the power to move masses of people through a single sermon, and he too began to preach the "new birth"—the necessity of a conversion experience. When many pastors banned him from their pulpits, he began preaching in open fields to anyone who would listen. Newspapers reported the controversy, and soon his admirers told the press where he would be on any given day. Colonial newspapers, keenly sensitive to the English press, followed his career.

4-4b Whitefield Launches the Transatlantic Revival

In 1739, Whitefield made his second trip to America, and thousands flocked to hear him preach. After landing in Delaware, he preached his way northward through Philadelphia, New Jersey, and New York City, and then headed south through the Chesapeake colonies and into South Carolina. In September 1740, he sailed to Newport and for two months toured New England. During his travels, he met Benjamin Franklin, Gilbert Tennent, and Jonathan Edwards. In the cities he sometimes attracted as many as 30,000 people, twice Boston's population. His voice was so musical, claimed one observer, that he could seduce a crowd just by the way he pronounced "Mesopotamia." Using his acting skills, he imitated Christ on the cross, shedding "pious tears" for poor sinners. Or he became God at the Last Judgment, thundering: "Depart from me ye accursed into everlasting fire!" When he wept, so did his audience. When he condemned them, they fell to the ground in agony.

Although Whitefield wore the surplice of an Anglican minister and carried the *Book of Common Prayer* when he preached, Anglican ministers distrusted him. In Charleston and New York City, the official spokesmen for the bishop of London denounced him, but Presbyterians, Congregationalists, and Baptists embraced him, at least until some of them began

Fig. 4.1 **The Synod of Philadelphia by 1738** The chart shows the organization of the Presbyterian Church in the colonies. In actuality, some presbyteries had more churches than others. Arrows indicate descending lines of authority.

to fear that he was doing more harm than good. To many he embodied the old Non-Separatist ideal that all English Protestants were somehow members of the same church.

4-4c Disruptions

After Whitefield departed, other preachers tried to assume his role, but they aroused fierce controversy. In South Carolina, Hugh Bryan, a wealthy planter, began preaching the evangelical message to his slaves. In 1742, when memories of a major slave revolt were still fresh (see later section), he denounced slavery as a sin and warned that God would pour out his wrath on the colony unless it repented. Proclaiming himself an American Moses, he tried to part the waters of the Savannah River and lead the slaves to freedom in Georgia. He almost drowned and had to be rescued. He then confessed publicly that he had been deluded. Bryan discredited evangelicalism among the planters of the lower South for another generation, but he and his family continued to convert their own slaves. African American evangelical piety, including some of the first black preachers, took root from these efforts.

Whitefield's successors also disrupted New England. Gilbert Tennent, who lacked Whitefield's musical voice and Oxford diction, spoke with a Scottish burr and specialized in "Holy Laughter," the scornful peals of a triumphant God as sinners tumble into hell. He abandoned the usual garb of a minister for a robe and sandals and let his hair grow long, thereby proclaiming himself a new John the Baptist heralding the Second Coming of Christ.

James Davenport succeeded Tennent. He denounced unregenerate ministers by name. He liked to preach by eerie candlelight, roaring damnation at his listeners, even grabbing Satan and wrestling him back to hell. He advised admirers to drink rat poison rather than listen to another lifeless sermon. In 1743, he established the Shepherd's Tent in New London to train awakened preachers. This outdoor school abandoned the classical curriculum of colleges and insisted only on a valid conversion experience. He organized a book burning, in which titles by Increase Mather and other New England dignitaries went up in flames, and he threw his britches on the fire, declaring them a mark of human vanity. A grand jury, asked to indict him, proclaimed him mad instead. He too repented, and the Shepherd's Tent collapsed.

4-4d Long-Term Consequences of the Revivals

The revivals had dramatic consequences. Amid the enthusiasm of Whitefield's tour, more men than usual joined a church, but after another year or two, men became hard to convert. The number of women church members soared, however, until by 1800 they often formed a majority of 3 or 4 to 1 in evangelical churches, and in some congregations they acquired an informal veto over the choice of the minister. Partly in reaction to the revivals, thousands of men became **Freemasons**, often instead of joining a church. They very nearly turned these voluntary associations into a religion of manliness, complete with mysterious rituals that extolled sobriety, industry, brotherhood, benevolence, and citizenship. The movement peaked during the American Revolution and for a few decades after it.

The revivals shattered the unity of New England's Congregational Church. Evangelicals seceded from dozens of congregations to form their own "Separate" churches. Many of those that survived went Baptist by the 1760s, thereby gaining protection under the toleration statutes of the New England colonies. In the middle colonies, the revivals strengthened denominational loyalties and energized the clergy. In the 1730s, most people in the region, particularly in New Jersey and Pennsylvania, had never joined a church. The revivals prompted many of them to become **New Side** (evangelical) Presbyterians, **Old Side** (antirevival) Presbyterians, or nonevangelical Anglicans. Similar cleavages ran through the German population. The southern colonies were less affected, although evangelical Presbyterians made modest gains in the Virginia piedmont after 1740. Finally, in the 1760s, the Baptists began to win thousands of converts in Virginia,

4.7 William Hogarth's *Credulity, Superstition, and Fanaticism* (1762) Opponents of the revivals condemned their excessive emotionalism.

Q *How does the artist use various forms of exaggeration in the church scene to register his opposition to religious revivalism?*

as did the Methodists after 1776. Their numbers surpassed the Baptists' within a few decades.

The revivals created new cosmopolitan links with Britain and between colonies. Whitefield ran the most efficient publicity machine in the Atlantic world. In London, Glasgow, and Boston, periodicals called *The Christian History* carried news of revivals occurring all over the empire. For years, London evangelicals held regular "Letter Days" at which they read accounts of revivals in progress. When fervor declined in New England, Edwards organized a Concert of Prayer with his Scottish correspondents, setting regular times for them all to beseech the Lord to pour out his grace once more. As Anglicans split into Methodists and Latitudinarians, Congregationalists into pro-revival **New Lights** and antirevival **Old Lights**, and Presbyterians into comparable New Side and Old Side synods, evangelicals discovered that they had more in common with revivalists in other denominations than with antirevivalists in their own.

4-4e New Colleges

The Great Awakening created several new colleges. In 1740, North America had only three: Harvard, William and Mary, and Yale. Although Yale eventually embraced the revivals, all three opposed them at first. In 1746, middle colony evangelicals, eager to show their commitment to classical learning after the fiasco of the Shepherd's Tent, founded the College of New Jersey (now Princeton University). It graduated its first class in 1748 and settled in Princeton in 1756. Unlike the older colleges, it drew students from all 13 colonies and sent its graduates throughout America, especially to the middle and southern colonies. It also reshaped the Presbyterian Church. When Presbyterians healed their schism and reunited in 1758, the New Siders set the terms. Outnumbered in 1741, they held a large majority of ministers by 1758. Through control of Princeton, their numbers had increased rapidly. The Old Side, still dependent on the University of Glasgow in Scotland, could barely replace those who died.

New Light Baptists founded the College of Rhode Island (now Brown University) in the 1760s. Dutch Reformed revivalists set up Queens College (now Rutgers University) in New Jersey. Eleazer Wheelock opened an evangelical school for Indians in Lebanon, Connecticut. After his first graduate, Samson Occum, raised £12,000 for the school in England, Wheelock moved to New Hampshire and used most of the money to found Dartmouth College instead, although Dartmouth occasionally admitted an Indian. By 1790, Dartmouth was turning out more graduates, and far more ministers, than any other American college.

In the 1750s, Anglicans countered with two new colleges of their own: the College of Philadelphia (now the University of Pennsylvania), which had Old Side Presbyterian support, and King's College in New York (now Columbia University). Their undergraduate programs remained small, however, and few of their students chose a ministerial career. In the competition for student loyalties, nonevangelicals could not yet compete effectively with revivalists.

4-4f The Denominational Realignment

The revivals transformed American religious life. In 1700, the three strongest denominations had been the Congregationalists in New England, the Quakers in the Delaware Valley, and the Anglicans in the South. By 1800, all three had lost ground to newcomers: the Methodists, who grew at an astonishing rate as heirs of the collapsing Church of England during and after the Revolution; the Baptists, who leaped into second place; and the Presbyterians. Methodists and Baptists, who did not expect their preachers to attend college, recruited them from a much broader segment of the population than their rivals could tap. Although they never created their own Shepherd's Tent, they embraced similar principles, demanding only a conversion experience, integrity, knowledge of the Bible, and a talent for preaching.

Anti-revivalist denominations, especially Anglicans and Quakers, suffered heavy losses. New Light Congregationalists made few gains because, when their people left the established churches of New England to move west, they usually joined a Presbyterian church, which gave them a support structure that isolated congregations in a pluralistic society could not sustain.

What They Said

The Controversy over Religious Revivals

The feud between New Lights and Old Lights in New England sparked a public debate between the revivalist minister Jonathan Edwards and the antirevivalist clergyman Charles Chauncy in the early 1740s. A man of the Enlightenment, Chauncy attacked the revivals as frauds because of their emotional excess. Edwards agreed that no emotional response, however intense, could itself prove the presence of God in a person's soul. Yet, he insisted that intense feeling must always accompany the reception of divine grace. In effect, Edwards countered Chauncy's emotional defense of reason with his own rational defense of emotion.

▶ Charles Chauncy

…that *Terror* so many have been the Subjects of; Expressing itself in *strange Effects* upon the *Body*, such as *swooning away* and *falling to the Ground*, where Persons have lain, for a Time, speechless and motionless; bitter *Shriekings* and *Screamings*; *Convulsion-like Tremblings* and *Agitations, Strugglings,* and *Tumblings* which, in some Instances, have been attended with Indecencies I shan't mention … I am not against the *Preaching of Terror*; but whenever this is done, it ought to be in a Way that may enlighten the Mind, as well as to alarm the Passions: And I am greatly mistaken, if this has been the Practice, among some Sort of Preachers, so much as it ought to be. And to this it may be owing, that Religion, of late, has been *more a Commotion in the Passions* than a *Change* in the *Temper* of the *Mind*.

▶ Jonathan Edwards

Now if such things are enthusiasm, and the fruits of a distempered brain, let my brain be evermore possessed of that happy distemper! If this be distraction, I pray God that the world of mankind may be all seized with this benign, meek, beneficent, beatifical, glorious distraction! …there is that uniformity observable, that it is easy to be seen that in general it is the same spirit from whence the work in all parts of the land has originated. And what notions have they of religion, that reject what has been described, as not true religion!

As there is the clearest evidence, from those things that have been observed, that this is the work of God; so it is evident that it is a very great and wonderful and exceeding glorious work of God. This is certain, that it is a great and wonderful event, a strange revolution, an unexpected, surprising overturning of things, suddenly brought to pass; such as never has been seen in New England, and scarce ever has been heard of in any land.

Q How did Chauncy use vivid descriptive language to discredit the religious revivals? What was his explanation for the physical manifestations of religious conversion displayed during the Great Awakening?

Q How did Edwards use the Enlightenment principle of logical reasoning to counter the argument that the revivals were not authentic? Are there points of agreement between him and Chauncy?

Sources: (top) From a sermon/pamphlet by Charles Chauncy, *Seasonable Thoughts on the State of Religion in New-England, a Treatise in Five Parts* (Boston: Printed by Rogers and Fowle, for Samuel Eliot in Cornhill, 1743), 76–77, 109. Accessed via Google Books. https://goo.gl/fTr2EK; (bottom) From sermon/pamphlet by Jonathan Edwards, *Edwards on Revivals: Containing a Faithful Narrative of the Surprising Work of God in the Conversion of Many Hundred Souls in Northhampton, Massachusetts, A.D. 1735: Also Thoughts on the Revival of Religion in New England, 1742, and the Way in which It Ought to be Acknowledged and Promoted* (New York: Dunning & Spalding, 1832), 174–177.

4-5 Political Culture in the Colonies

Q Why did Britain's "Country" values prevail in most southern colonies while "Court" politics took hold in most northern provinces?

In politics as in other activities, the colonies became more like Britain in the 18th century. A quarter-century of warfare after 1689 convinced the settlers that they needed Britain's protection and strengthened their admiration for its parliamentary system. Colonists agreed that they were free because they were British—and Protestants—who also had mixed constitutions that united monarchy, aristocracy, and democracy in almost perfect balance. In the colonies, the governor stood for monarchy; the council, or upper house, for aristocracy (the House of Lords in Britain); and the assembly for democracy (the House of Commons).

By the 1720s, the Crown appointed the governor for every colony except Connecticut and Rhode Island, which kept the power granted by their 17th-century charters to select their own governors. The two New England colonies, along with

CHAPTER 4 Provincial America and the Struggle for a Continent, 1720–1763

their neighbor Massachusetts, also elected their councils (although Massachusetts did so indirectly, through its assembly). The Crown appointed the council in every other colony. In all 13 colonies, once the Crown took over Georgia, the settlers elected the assembly.

As with the structure, the style of colonial politics increasingly resembled that of Britain. Since the Glorious Revolution of 1688, the dominant pattern of politics in England had pitted the Court, or ruling government, against the Country, or party out of power. Court statesmen favored policies that strengthened central ministerial control, particularly in the waging of war. The Country opposition stood for liberty by denouncing patronage and institutions such as standing armies as engines of corruption. The colonies reproduced the dynamic, yet with an important twist. Whereas the Country party, by definition, never came into power in Britain, Country principles, especially in the southern colonies, often came to dominate politics in British North America.

4-5a The Rise of the Assembly and the Governor

The rise of the assembly was a major political trend of the era. The right to vote in the colonies was more widely shared than in England, where two-thirds of adult males were disfranchised. By contrast, something like three-fourths of free adult white men in the colonies became potential voters for assembly representatives by some point in their adult lives. The frequency of elections varied—from every seven years in New York (by the 1740s) and Virginia, as well as in Britain, to at least once a year in five colonies. As the century advanced, legislatures sat longer and passed more laws. The lower house—the assembly—began to initiate most major bills. It made most of its gains at the expense of the council, not the governor.

Every royal colony except New York and Georgia already had an assembly with a strong sense of its own privileges when the first royal governor arrived, yet governors also grew more powerful. Because the governor's instructions usually challenged some existing practices, clashes occurred. The first royal governors never got all of their demands, but they often won concessions and became more adept over the years. In royal colonies, between 1730 and 1765, most governors learned that their success depended less on their prerogatives (royal powers embodied in their commissions) than on their ability to win the assembly's cooperation through persuasion or patronage.

Early in the century, conflicts between governor and assembly tended to be legalistic. Each cited technical precedents to justify the governor's prerogatives or the assembly's privileges. Later on, when conflict spilled over into pamphlets and newspapers, it often pitted an aggrieved minority (unable to win a majority in the assembly) against both governor and assembly. These contests were ideological. The opposition accused the governor of corrupting the assembly, and he in turn denounced his critics as a "faction." Everyone condemned factions, embryonic political parties, as self-interested and destructive. Hardly anyone claimed to be a party member; the other side was the faction.

4-5b Court and Country Politics

The joint rise of the assembly and the governor produced different political cultures in the southern and northern colonies (see Table 4.1). In most southern colonies, the "Country" principles of the British opposition became the common assumptions of public life, acceptable to both governor and assembly, typically after a failed attempt by a governor to impose the "Court" alternative. In Britain, despite vociferous protests from the Country opposition, ruling governments built legislative majorities through **placemen**, members of Parliament who received financial inducements and often owed their seats to supporting the government. Yet, when Virginia's Governor Alexander Spotswood (served 1710–1722) used patronage to fill the assembly with his own placemen, the voters turned nearly all of them out at the next election. Then, just as Spotswood had learned that he could not dominate the house through patronage, so the assembly discovered that it could not coerce a governor who controlled a permanent revenue from the Crown.

4.8 The Governor's Palace at Williamsburg, Virginia
The governor's palace was finished during the term of Governor Alexander Spotswood (1710–1722) and restored in the 20th century. For Spotswood, the palace was an extension of royal might and splendor across the ocean. He set a standard of elegance that many planters imitated when they built their own great houses in the second quarter of the 18th century.

Q *How did the governor's palace express through architecture the principles of anglicization and the Enlightenment?*

■ Table 4.1 THE SPECTRUM OF COLONIAL POLITICS

Constitutional Type	Successful	Unsuccessful
Northern "Court"	New York, circa 1710–1728 New Hampshire after 1741 Massachusetts after 1741 New Jersey after 1750	New York after 1728 Pennsylvania (successful in peace, ineffective in war)
Southern "Country"	Virginia after 1720 South Carolina after 1730 Georgia after 1752	Maryland North Carolina

Connecticut and Rhode Island never really belonged to either system.

Accordingly, Virginia and South Carolina cultivated a **politics of harmony**, a system of ritualized mutual flattery. Governors found that they could accomplish more through persuasion than through patronage, and the assemblies openly showed their appreciation. The planters of Virginia and South Carolina concluded that their societies embodied almost exactly what British opposition writers had been demanding. Factions disappeared, allowing the governor and the assembly to pursue the "common good" in an atmosphere free of rancor or corruption. Georgia adopted similar practices in the 1750s.

This system worked because the planters were doing what Britain wanted them to do: growing staple crops and shipping them to Britain or other destinations allowed by Parliament. Both sides could agree on measures that would make this process more efficient, such as the Virginia Tobacco Inspection Act of 1730. In Virginia, public controversy all but ceased. Between 1720 and 1765, particularly during the able administration of Sir William Gooch (1727–1749), the governor and House of Burgesses engaged in only one public quarrel, an unparalleled record of political harmony. South Carolina's politics became almost as placid from the 1730s into the 1760s, but harmony there masked serious social problems that were beginning to emerge in the unrepresented backcountry. By contrast, the politics of harmony never took hold in Maryland, where the lord proprietor always tried to seduce assemblymen with his lavish patronage, nor in factional North Carolina, where the tobacco and rice planters in some years paralyzed the government with their fierce wrangling, while disgusting the growing backcountry in the process.

The northern colonies never produced a politics of harmony. Instead, with many economic interests and ethnic and religious groups to satisfy, northern colonial governors often resorted to a Court-style politics to control and offset the multiple factions. The long ministry of Sir Robert Walpole (1721–1742), recognized by some as Britain's first prime minister, provided a model for savvy colonial governors when using patronage for rewarding some groups and disciplining others. William Shirley, governor of Massachusetts from 1741 to 1756, used judicial and militia appointments and war contracts to sustain a majority in the assembly. Like Walpole, he was a master of Court politics. In New Hampshire, Benning Wentworth created a political machine that rewarded just about every assemblyman from the 1750s to 1767. Ineffective oppositions in both colonies accused their governor of corrupting the assembly, but Shirley and Wentworth each claimed that his actions were essential to his colony's needs. Both governors remained in control.

The opposition, although seldom able to implement its demands at the provincial level, was important nonetheless. It kept settlers alert to any infringements on their liberties, and it usually dominated the Boston town meeting from 1720 on. Boston artisans engaged in ritualized mob activities with a sharp political edge. Every year on November 5, Guy Fawkes Day, a North End mob and a South End mob bloodied each other for the privilege of burning, on Beacon Hill, effigies of the pope, the devil, and the Stuart pretender to the British throne. These men were raucously celebrating liberty, property, and no popery—the British constitution, as they understood it. The violence made many wealthy merchants nervous, and by 1765 some of them would become its victims.

In both north and south, colonists embraced Country political ideals with more enthusiasm than British subjects in England ever had. In particular, colonists absorbed the warnings of the British opposition—that men in power nearly always tried to destroy liberty and that corruption was power's most dangerous weapon. By 1776, that view would justify independence and the repudiation of a "corrupt" king and Parliament.

4-6 The Renewal of Imperial Conflict

 How did Indians and African slaves take advantage of opportunities presented by a new round of European wars starting in 1739?

A new era of imperial war began in 1739 and continued, with only a brief interruption, until 1763. The British colonies, New Spain, New France, and the Indians of the Eastern Woodlands all became involved in a war to determine who would dominate North America.

4-6a *Challenges to French Power*

By the second quarter of the 18th century, the French colonial project in North America remained land rich but settlement poor. Although France claimed more territory than Britain, it had far fewer white colonists and continued to depend on

118 CHAPTER 4 Provincial America and the Struggle for a Continent, 1720–1763

Indian alliances for military strength. The French hold on the interior also began to weaken, both north and south. Indians returned to the Ohio Valley, mostly to trade with pacifist Pennsylvania or with Fort Oswego, a new British post on Lake Ontario. Compared with the French, the British were often clumsy in their dealings with Indians, but they had one advantage: cheaper trade goods. Many Indians created what the French disparagingly called **republics**, villages outside the French alliance system that were eager for British trade. The chiefs at Venango, Logstown, and other republics accepted people from all tribes—Delawares from the east, Shawnees from the south and east, Mingoes (Iroquois who had left their homeland) from the north, and other Algonquian peoples of the Great Lakes region to the west. Because inhabitants of each new village had blood relatives among all of the nearby nations, the chiefs welcomed colonial traders and hoped that none of their Indian neighbors would endanger their own relatives by attacking these communities.

Sometimes the French system of mediation broke down. For instance, an arrogant French officer decided to take over the lands of the Natchez Indians (the last of the Mississippian mound builders) and ordered them to leave. While pretending to comply, the Natchez planned a counterstroke and on November 28, 1729, killed every French male in the vicinity. In the war that followed, the French and their Choctaw allies destroyed the Natchez as a distinct people, although some refugees found homes among the Chickasaws or the Creeks.

In 1730, the French barely averted a massive slave uprising in New Orleans. To stir up hatred between Indians and Africans, they turned over some of the African leaders of the revolt to the Choctaws to be burned alive. Unable to afford enough gifts to sustain alliances with both Choctaws and Chickasaws, they encouraged hostilities between the two nations. This policy seriously damaged the French. Instead of weakening the pro-British Chickasaws, it touched off a civil war among the Choctaws, and France lost both influence and prestige.

4-6b The Danger of Slave Revolts and War with Spain

In the immediate term, the Spanish presence in Florida proved more troublesome to the British, particularly in South Carolina. In the 16th century, Francis Drake had proclaimed himself a liberator when he attacked St. Augustine and promised freedom to Indians and Africans who, he assumed, were groaning under Spanish tyranny (see Chapter 3). By the 1730s, these roles had been reversed. On several occasions after 1680, Spanish Florida had promised freedom to any slaves who escaped from Carolina and were willing to accept Catholicism. In 1738, the governor established, just north of St. Augustine, a new town, Gracia Real de Santa Teresa de Mose (or Mose for short, pronounced "Moe-shah"), and made it the first community of free blacks in what is now the United States. The very existence of Mose acted as a magnet for Carolina slaves.

In 1739, Florida's governor offered liberty to any slaves from the British colonies who could make their way to Florida. This manifesto, and rumors about Mose, touched off the Stono Rebellion in South Carolina, the most violent slave revolt in the history of the 13 colonies. Some of the rebellion's leaders were Catholics from the African Kingdom of the Kongo, where Portuguese missionaries had made numerous converts since the 16th century.

On September 9, 1739, 20 slaves attacked a store at Stono (south of Charleston), killed the owner, seized weapons, and moved on to assault other houses and win new recruits. Heading toward Florida, they killed another 25 settlers that day. At the Edisto River, they stopped, raised banners, and shouted "Liberty!" hoping to begin a general uprising. There the militia caught them and killed about two-thirds of the growing force. In the weeks that followed, the settlers killed another 60. No rebels reached Florida, but, as the founders of Georgia had foreseen, South Carolina was indeed vulnerable in any conflict with Spain.

4.9 *Savages of Several Nations, New Orleans, 1735* This painting by Alexandre de Batz depicts a multiethnic Indian village near New Orleans. The woman at lower left was a Fox Indian who had been captured and enslaved. The African boy was an adoptee.

4-6 The Renewal of Imperial Conflict

At that moment, the War of Jenkins's Ear broke out between Britain and Spain, derisively named for a ship captain and smuggler who had displayed his severed ear to Parliament as proof of Spanish cruelty. The war cost Britain dearly because Spanish defenses held everywhere. Some 3,000 men from the 13 colonies, eager for plunder, joined expeditions in 1741 and 1742 against the seaport of Cartagena in New Granada (now Colombia), and against Cuba and Panama (see Map 4.1). All were British disasters. Most of the men died of disease; only 10 percent of the volunteers returned home. But one survivor, Lawrence Washington, so admired the British naval commander, Edward Vernon, that he named his Virginia plantation after him. Britain also experienced a surge of patriotic fervor from the war. Both "God Save the King" and "Rule Britannia" were written during the struggle.

Georgia was supposed to protect South Carolina. General Oglethorpe, its governor, retaliated against the Spanish by invading Florida in 1740. He dispersed the black residents of Mose and occupied the site, but the Spaniards mauled his garrison in a surprise counterattack (see Map 4.2). Oglethorpe retreated without taking St. Augustine and returned to Georgia with disturbing reports. Spain, he said, was sending blacks into the British colonies to start slave uprisings, and Spanish priests in disguise were mingling with the black conspirators. This news set off panics in the rice and tobacco colonies, but it had its biggest impact in New York City.

Back in 1712, a slave revolt had shaken New York. After setting fire to a barn one night, slaves had shot 15 settlers who rushed to put out the blaze, killing nine. Twenty-one slaves were executed, some after gruesome tortures. By 1741, New York City's 2,000 slaves were the largest concentration of blacks in British North America outside of Charleston. On March 18, Fort George burned down in what was probably an accident,
but when a series of other suspicious fires broke out, the settlers grew nervous. New York's racial tensions combined with the supposed threat of Spanish Catholics, evident in Oglethorpe's warning, led to widespread fears of a "popish plot" to murder the city's whites and free the slaves. The number of individuals accused in the conspiracy escalated throughout the spring. The New York conspiracy trials, which proceeded from May into August of 1741, reminded one observer that the testimony of several girls in the Salem witch trials of 1692 had led to 19 hangings. The toll in New York was worse. Four whites and 18 slaves were hanged, 13 slaves were burned alive, and 70 banished to the West Indies. The judges spoke pompously about the sacred rights of Englishmen, again in danger from popish conspirators, and grew enraged at any African who dared to imperil what the colony would not let him share.

In 1742, King Philip V of Spain nearly accomplished what Oglethorpe and the New York judges dreaded. He sent 36 ships and 2,000 soldiers from Cuba with orders to devastate Georgia and South Carolina, "sacking and burning all the towns, posts, plantations, and settlements" and freeing the slaves. Although the invaders probably outnumbered the entire population of Georgia, Oglethorpe carried out an ingenious bluff to mask the weakness of his forces. The Spanish departed in haste, leaving British North America as a safe haven once more for liberty, property, no popery—and slavery.

4-6c France versus Britain: King George's War

In 1744, when France joined Spain in the war against Britain, the main action shifted to the north. After the French laid siege to Annapolis Royal, the capital of Nova Scotia, Governor Shirley of Massachusetts intervened to save the small garrison, and the French withdrew. Shirley then planned a rash attack on Louisbourg, the French fortress on Cape Breton Island. The Massachusetts governor, with a force of untrained Yankees and timely assistance from the British navy, subdued the mightiest fortress in America.

After that nothing went right. Hundreds of volunteers died before regular troops arrived to garrison Louisbourg. Plans to attack Quebec by sea in 1746 and 1747 came to nothing because no British fleet appeared. French and Indian raiders assaulted the weakly defended frontier. Bristol County farmers rioted against high taxes, and four towns in western Massachusetts seceded to join Connecticut.

When the Royal Navy finally docked at Boston in late 1747, its commander, Admiral Charles Knowles, sent bands of men known as **press gangs** on merchant ships in the harbor and ashore to force anyone they could seize into serving with the fleet. Angry locals descended on the sailors, took some officers hostage, and controlled the streets of Boston for three days. The Knowles Riot, as it has become known, signified the largest protest against imperial officials in the colonies between the Glorious Revolution of 1688 and the Stamp Act Riots of 1765 (see Chapter 5). Knowles soon relented and released all of the Massachusetts men he had impressed. (The rioters let him keep outsiders.) After the disturbance, the strongest defender

▲ **MAP 4.1 Caribbean Theater of War, 1739–1742** Spanish defenses held up remarkably well against repeated and very costly British attacks.

Q In terms of geography, what made attacks on coastal defenses so difficult?

Q Given that Britain lost most battles in the War of Jenkins's Ear, what might have contributed to the surge of British nationalism in the war?

▲ MAP 4.2 **Southeastern Theater of War, 1739–1742** Florida's defenders repelled a British attack led by James Oglethorpe, and then Oglethorpe turned back a much larger Spanish invasion of Georgia.

Q *How did Spanish Florida pose a threat to Britain's southern colonies on multiple levels?*

Q *In geopolitical terms, Georgia was created as a buffer to protect South Carolina from Britain's enemies. How did the plan work in the fighting of the late 1730s and early 1740s?*

of Boston's crowd action was the young Samuel Adams, fresh out of Harvard, where his master's thesis explored when it was legitimate to resist civil government.

Ultimately, to offset losses in Europe, Britain returned Louisbourg to France under the peace settlement that ended the war in 1748. Enormous sacrifices gained Yankees nothing except pride.

4-6d The Impending Storm

The war drove back the frontiers of British settlement, but the colonies had promised postwar land grants to many volunteers for their service. Thus, peace touched off a frenzy of expansion that alarmed Indians and French alike. The British, aware that their hold on Nova Scotia was feeble, sent four regiments of redcoats and recruited 2,500 Protestants from the continent of Europe to populate the colony. In 1749, they founded Halifax as the new capital of Nova Scotia.

In the 13 colonies, settlers eagerly pressed on to new lands. Yankees swarmed into Maine and New Hampshire and west into the middle colonies, creating serious tensions. By refusing to pay rent to the manor lords of the Hudson Valley, they sparked a tenant revolt in 1753 that was subdued only with difficulty. A year later, Connecticut's delegation to the Albany Congress (see next section) bribed Iroquois chiefs to acquire title to all of northern Pennsylvania, which Connecticut claimed on the basis of its sea-to-sea charter of 1663. Various controversies with the Mohawks west of Albany so infuriated Chief Hendrik that he bluntly told the governor of New York in 1753, "The Covenant Chain is broken between you and us [the Iroquois League]. So brother you are not to hear of me any more, and Brother we desire to hear no more of you." New York, Pennsylvania, and Virginia competed for trade with the new Indian republics between Lake Erie and the Ohio River. Expansion pitted colony against colony, as well as settler against Indian, and British against French. Virginians, whom the Indians called "long knives," were particularly aggressive. Citing their own 1609 sea-to-sea charter (see Map 2.3, p. 50), they organized the Ohio Company of Virginia in 1747 to settle the Ohio Valley and established their first outpost where the Monongahela and Allegheny rivers converge to form the Ohio River (the site of modern Pittsburgh). The company hired George Washington as a surveyor. Farther south, encroachments upon the Cherokees nearly provoked war with South Carolina in 1750.

4.10 Portrait of Chief Hendrik of the Mohawks
Hendrik's ultimatum to New York in 1753 precipitated the summoning of the Albany Congress a year later. This print shows him in British military clothing.

Q *In his dress and presentation, how did Hendrik integrate anglicized and indigenous cultural forms?*

The French began to panic. The fall of Louisbourg had interrupted the flow of French trade goods to the Ohio Country for several years, and the men who had long been conducting Indian diplomacy had either died or left office by the late 1740s. Authoritarian newcomers from France replaced them and began giving orders to western Indians instead of negotiating with them. But the French did make some constructive moves. They repaired Louisbourg and built Fort Beauséjour on the neck connecting mainland Canada to Nova Scotia. In 1755, they erected Fort Carillon (Ticonderoga to the British) on Lake Champlain to protect Crown Point (see Map 4.3).

The French clearly intended to prevent British settlement west of the Alleghenies. Marquis Duquesne sent 2,000 Canadians, with almost no Indian support, to erect a line of posts from Lake Erie to Fort Duquesne (now Pittsburgh). Duquesne thought this policy so beneficial to the Indians that it needed no explanation. Yet, the Mingoes warned him not to build a fort in their territory, and a delegation of Delawares and Shawnees asked the Virginians if they would be willing to expel the French from the Ohio Country and then go back home.

The Indians did not like the response. In 1753, Virginia sent Washington to the Ohio Country to warn Duquesne to withdraw, and a small Virginia force further threatened Indian control of the territory by beginning to build its own fort at the forks of the Ohio. Duquesne ignored Washington, advanced toward the Ohio, expelled the Virginians, took over their site, and finished building what now became Fort Duquesne. Virginia sent Washington back to the Ohio in 1754. On May 28, after discovering a French patrol nearby, he launched an attack. That order set off a world war.

4-7 The War for North America

Q *What made the War for North America (1754–1763) so much more decisive than the three earlier Anglo-French wars?*

In spring 1754, both New France and Virginia expected a limited clash at the forks of the Ohio River. Neither anticipated the titanic struggle that encounter would set off, nor did the French and British governments, which hoped to limit any conflict to a few strategic points in North America. New Englanders, however, saw an apocalyptic struggle in the making between "Protestant freedom" and "popish slavery,"

▲ MAP 4.3 **France versus Britain in North America by 1755** North of the Ohio River, much of North America was becoming a series of fortresses along the frontiers separating New France from the British colonies.

Q *Where did the North American empires of Britain and France converge?*

Q *In their emerging military strategy, how did the French compensate for their relatively small number of white settlers?*

with the North American continent as the battleground. "The continent is not wide enough for us both," declared one preacher, "and they [the French] intend to have the whole." Thus began the French and Indian War, pitting France against Britain for the control of North America.

4-7a The Albany Congress and the Onset of War

Britain, fearful that the Six Nations (the Tuscaroras had joined the original Five Nations by the 1720s) might side with New France, ordered New York to host an intercolonial congress at Albany to redress Iroquois grievances. The governor invited every colony as far south as Virginia, except nonroyal Connecticut and Rhode Island. Virginia and New Jersey declined to attend. Governor Shirley of Massachusetts, on his own initiative, invited Connecticut and Rhode Island to participate, and the Massachusetts legislature asked its delegates to work for a plan of intercolonial union.

In Philadelphia, Benjamin Franklin too was thinking about colonial union. On May 9, 1754, his *Pennsylvania Gazette* printed one of the first political cartoons in American history, with the caption "JOIN, or DIE." A month later, he drafted his "Short Hints towards a Scheme for Uniting the Northern Colonies," which he presented to the **Albany Congress** in June. His plan called for a "President General" to be appointed by the Crown as commander in chief and to administer the laws of the union, and for a "Grand Council" to be elected for three-year terms by the lower houses of each colony. To take effect, the plan would require approval by the Crown and each colonial legislature, and presentation to Parliament for its consent. The Albany Congress adopted an amended version of Franklin's proposal.

Shirley and Franklin were far ahead of public opinion. Newspapers ignored the Albany Plan. Every colony rejected it, most with little debate, some unanimously. The voting was close only in Massachusetts, which had borne the heaviest burden in the earlier French wars. As Franklin later explained, the colonies feared that the president general might become too powerful. But they also distrusted each other. Despite the French threat, they were not ready to put aside their differences and unite. They did not yet see themselves as "Americans."

4.11 Benjamin Franklin's Snake Cartoon One of the first newspaper cartoons in colonial America, this device appeared in the *Pennsylvania Gazette* in May 1754. The cartoon called for colonial union on the eve of the Albany Congress and drew on the folk legend that a snake, cut into pieces, could revive and live if it somehow joined its severed parts together before sundown.

Q Why was it so difficult to convince the various British colonies to cooperate in the face of the clear French and Indian threat?

4-7b Britain's Years of Defeat

After news arrived that Washington had surrendered his small force to the French at Great Meadows in July 1754, Britain decided that the colonies were incapable of uniting in their own defense. Instead, London sent redcoats to Virginia in 1755—two regiments, commanded by General Edward Braddock.

At a meeting called by Braddock at Alexandria, Virginia, Governor Shirley persuaded him to accept a much bolder plan for battling the French than what London had authorized. Instead of a single expedition aimed at one fort, to be followed by others if time permitted, the campaign of 1755 became four distinct offensives designed to crush the outer defenses of New France and leave it open to British invasion (see Map 4.4). Braddock was so impressed with Shirley that he named him second in command of the British army in North America, not bad for an English lawyer with no military training who had arrived in Boston almost penniless 25 years earlier.

Braddock and Shirley tried to make maximum use of both redcoats and provincials. The redcoats were disciplined, long-term professional soldiers trained to fight other professional armies. Irregular war in the forests of North America made them uneasy. Provincials, by contrast, were recruited by individual colonies. They were volunteers, often quite young, who enlisted for a single campaign. The Americans knew little about military drill, expected to serve under the officers who had recruited them, and sometimes disobeyed orders that they disliked. They admired the courage of the redcoats but were shocked by their irreverent speech, which included too much swearing for Yankee tastes, and by the brutal discipline that professional soldiers had to endure. Yet, thousands of colonists, mostly immigrants, enlisted in the British army, providing up to 40 percent of its strength in North America by 1760.

Under the plan, Nova Scotia's redcoats, together with New England provincials, would assault Fort Beauséjour, where the Acadian peninsula joins mainland Canada. New England and New York provincials under William Johnson, an Irish immigrant who had influence with the Mohawks, would attack Crown Point. Shirley, commissioned as a British colonel, would lead two regiments of redcoats (recently recruited in New England) to Niagara and cut off New France from the western Indians. Braddock would take Fort Duquesne.

Instead, Braddock erred in his Indian strategy and marched to disaster. The western Delawares asked him whether their villages and hunting rights would be secure under the British. "No Savage," he sneered, "Should Inherit the Land." The chiefs responded, "That if they might not have Liberty To Live on the Land they would not Fight for it." He "did not need their Help," Braddock retorted. It took him several months to hack a road through the forest wide enough for his artillery. Taking care to prevent ambushes at two fords of the Monongahela, he crossed that stream on July 9 and pushed on, confident that he had overcome all obstacles.

Fort Duquesne's commander could muster only 72 French, 146 Canadians, and 637 Indians against 1,400 British regulars and 450 Virginia provincials. The French ran into the British vanguard a few miles southeast of the fort. They clashed along a narrow path with thick forest and brush on either side. The French and Indians took cover on the British flanks. Braddock's rear elements rushed toward the sound of the guns where, massed together, the British formed a gigantic bull's eye. The French and Indians poured round after round into them; the British fired wild volleys into the trees. The British lost 977 killed or wounded, and their artillery. Braddock was killed. Only 39 French and Indians were killed or wounded. The redcoats finally broke and ran. Washington, who had fought as a Virginia volunteer on Braddock's staff, reported that, for the rest of the year, offensive operations would be impossible. Braddock's road through the wilderness became a highway for the enemy. For the first time in their history, Pennsylvania's settlers faced the horrors of a frontier war.

In Nova Scotia, Fort Beauséjour fell on June 17, 1755. Then the commanders did something to indicate that this war would not be a conventional, limited struggle. When the Acadians refused to take an oath that might have obliged them to bear arms against other Frenchmen, the British and Yankees responded with an 18th-century version of ethnic cleansing. They rounded up between 6,000 and 7,000 Acadians, forced them aboard ships, and expelled them from the province, to be scattered among the 13 colonies, none of which was prepared for the influx. A second roundup in 1759 caught most of the families that had evaded the first one. The officers who organized these expulsions insisted that they had found a humane way of compelling French Catholics to assimilate with the Protestant majority. Reasoning also that the Acadians were not British subjects because they had not taken the oath, and that only British subjects could own land in a British colony, the government of Nova Scotia confiscated the land the Acadians had farmed for generations

▲ **MAP 4.4 British Offenses, 1755** The British launched four major offenses against the French: in Nova Scotia, at Lake George, at Fort Oswego, and at the Forks of the Ohio River, where Edward Braddock led his men to disaster.

Q Why did the British have such difficulty translating their population and military advantages to military success early in the French and Indian War?

Q Could the British have employed a different, more effective military strategy at the outset of the war?

and redistributed it to Protestant settlers, mostly from New England. About 3,000 Acadian refugees, after spending miserable years as unwanted Catholic exiles in a Protestant world, finally made it to French Louisiana, where their descendants became known as Cajuns. Others went to France, and some even made their way back to Nova Scotia or what later became New Brunswick. Few remained in the 13 colonies.

In the major northern theater of war in 1755, Johnson led his provincials against Crown Point. The French commander, Jean-Armand, Baron Dieskau, hoping to repeat the French success against Braddock, attacked a body of provincials on September 8 and drove it back in panic to its base camp at Fort William Henry near Lake George. French regulars assailed the fort but were driven off with heavy losses in a six-hour struggle. Colonial newspapers proclaimed the battle a great victory because the provincials had not only held the field but had also wounded and captured Dieskau. Johnson probably could have taken poorly defended Crown Point, but he too had been wounded and was content to hold Fort William Henry and nearby Fort Edward at the headwaters of the Hudson.

Farther west, Shirley's Niagara campaign reached Oswego on Lake Ontario and then stopped for the winter, checked by the French at Fort Frontenac on the lake's northern shore. Heavy snows soon cut off Oswego. Malnutrition and disease ravaged the garrison.

4-7c A World War

With the death of Braddock and the capture of Dieskau, military amateurs took over both armies: Shirley in the British colonies and Governor-General Pierre de Rigaud de Vaudreuil in New France. Vaudreuil, a Canadian, understood his colony's weakness without Indian support. The white population of the 13 colonies outnumbered that of New France by 13 to 1; Massachusetts alone had nearly three times as many settlers as New France. Vaudreuil also knew that if the redcoats and the British colonies concentrated their resources in a few critical places, they might well overwhelm New France. Thus, Vaudreuil sought allies among the Indians and sought to

History Through Film: *The War That Made America* (2006)

A four-hour documentary that aired on PBS in January 2006. Written, produced, and directed by Eric Stange and Ben Loeterman.

This ambitious documentary uses actual locations, historical reenactments, and a narrator to explore the French and Indian War in North America. The narrator is Graham Greene, an Academy Award nominee and Oneida Indian whose ancestors fought in the war. The narrative emphasizes the different roles and expectations of the British army, the settlers in the British colonies, the French army, and many of the Indian nations that fought in the conflict, mostly in an effort to guarantee that they could survive on their own native lands.

The writers begin the story with the prewar struggle between Virginia and New France for control of the Forks of the Ohio River (modern Pittsburgh), which both sides recognize as the gateway to the Great West. We watch a youthful and inexperienced George Washington, well played by Larry Nehring, open hostilities in 1754 by firing on a French patrol without realizing that it is a diplomatic mission carrying a message to the governor of Virginia. To Washington's horror, his most important Indian ally, known to the English as the Half King, then murders the patrol's commanding officer, probably to make the breach between the French and the Virginians unbridgeable and to increase the chief's local prestige. The French retaliate by attacking Washington's force at improvised Fort Necessity. Washington has to surrender to the murdered commander's brother, but because he could not read French, he does not realize that in the document he has to sign, he takes full responsibility for the killing.

Viewers then witness General Edward Braddock's disastrous defeat in 1755, the ravaging of the frontiers of Pennsylvania and Virginia, the serious quarrels between Lord Loudoun (the new British commander) and the colonists, the resurgence of British power under the leadership of William Pitt, and the fall of New France after defeats at Quebec and Montreal. Pontiac's War of 1763–1764 and the atrocities committed by the Paxton Boys get major attention. The final episode argues that Britain's victory left the army and the home government so arrogant and confident of their power that they alienated the North American colonists. Ironically, Greene tells us, the unintended consequences of the struggle prove far more important than the intended ones. The victory lessened Britain's power in America by provoking a revolution that led to the creation of the United States of America under the leadership of George Washington, whose highest ambition 20 years before independence had been to acquire a commission in the regular British army.

Not all viewers will accept the documentary's premise that the French and Indian War was the most important conflict ever fought on North American soil, but they will have to take that argument seriously. ■

4.12 In July 1755, a combined French and Indian force killed British General Edward Braddock and soundly defeated his army at the Battle of the Monongahela, events depicted in *The War That Made America*.

engage British settlers, most of whom had little redcoat support, along a broad front. A horrible frontier war ensued.

As long as Vaudreuil was in charge, New France kept winning. Indian attacks devastated frontier settlements, especially in Pennsylvania, a pacifist colony without a militia or any forts when the war began. Even so, the French government decided that New France needed a professional general and sent Louis-Joseph, Marquis de Montcalm, in 1756. Shocked and repelled by the brutality of frontier warfare, Montcalm tried to turn the conflict into a traditional European struggle of sieges and battles in which the advantage (as Vaudreuil well understood) would pass to the British. Nevertheless, Montcalm won several major successes. Oswego fell in summer 1756. When Fort William Henry surrendered to him a year later, he promised the garrison the honors of war, which meant that it could keep its property and march unmolested to Fort Edward. But France's Indian allies considered this agreement a betrayal of their customs. They killed or carried off 308 of the 2,400 prisoners, an event that colonial newspapers called the Massacre of Fort William Henry. Most of those killed were trying to save their property, which the Indians considered their rightful plunder. Montcalm lost heavily at Fort William Henry. He was never again able to raise sizable bodies of western Indians, and because the British blamed him for the "massacre," they refused to grant the honors of war to any French force for the rest of the conflict.

Meanwhile, Braddock's defeat, combined with the British loss of Minorca in the Mediterranean, convinced London that the struggle with France could not be limited to a few outposts. Britain declared war in 1756, and the French and Indian War in the colonies merged with a general European struggle—the Seven Years' War (1756–1763)—involving France, Austria, and Russia against Prussia, which was heavily subsidized by Britain. Although religion had little to do with the war in Europe, the Seven Years' War aligned coalitions of Protestant states against Catholic states in a way not seen for a century. To many colonial clergymen, a Protestant victory might herald the onset of the Millennium. The conflict spread even to India, where British forces expelled the French from nearly the whole subcontinent.

Reluctant to antagonize Britain, Spain remained neutral for most of the war, a choice with huge implications in North America. In the previous war, Spain had been able to turn the slaves of South Carolina against their masters and create unrest even in New York. Spanish hostilities early in the war would have opened another theater of conflict. Instead, Spain's neutrality permitted Britain to concentrate an overwhelming force against New France.

4-7d Imperial Tensions: From Loudoun to Pitt

When London realized in 1755 that the amateur Shirley had taken command of the British army in North America, it dispatched an irascible Scot, John Campbell, earl of Loudoun, to replace him. Loudoun had a special talent for infuriating provincials. Colonial units did not care to serve under his command and sometimes bluntly rejected his orders. Provincials believed they had a contractual relationship with *their* officers; they had never agreed to serve under Loudoun's professionals. They refused to serve beyond their term of enlistment, which expired on November 1 or December 1 of each year. When ordered to stay longer, many of them defiantly marched home.

Many British officers despised the provincials. "The Americans are in general the dirtiest most contemptible cowardly dogs that you can conceive," snarled General James Wolfe. "They fall down dead in their own dirt and desert by battalions, officers and all." General John Forbes was usually more positive, but he too once suggested "shooting dead a Dozen of their cowardly Officers at the Head of the Line." Some British officers held more favorable opinions. Horatio Gates, Richard Montgomery, Hugh Mercer, and Arthur St. Clair all remained in America after the war and became generals in the American army during the Revolution. In the House of Commons in 1765, Colonel Isaac Barré praised the courage of America's "Sons of Liberty"—a label soon adopted by men resisting Britain's postwar policies.

As the new commander in chief, Loudoun faced other problems: the quartering (or housing) of British soldiers, the relative rank of British and provincial officers, military discipline, revenue, and smuggling. He tried to impose authoritarian solutions on them all. When he sent redcoats into a city, he demanded that the assembly pay to quarter them, or else he would take over buildings by force. He tried to make any British senior captain superior in rank to any provincial officer, a rule that angered such experienced New England officers as General John Winslow and his six colonels. Loudoun ordered New England troops to serve directly under British officers and to accept the harsh discipline of the British army, an arrangement that, New Englanders insisted, violated their enlistment terms. They refused to cooperate. If a colonial assembly refused to vote adequate supplies, Loudoun urged Parliament to tax the colonies directly.

In 1757, William Pitt came to power as Britain's war minister and found workable solutions using voluntaristic principles to the problems that had defeated Loudoun's authoritarian methods. Pitt understood that consent worked better than coercion in the colonies. Colonial assemblies built barracks to house British soldiers. Pitt declared that every provincial officer would rank immediately behind the equivalent British rank but above all lesser officers, British or provincial. He then promoted every British lieutenant colonel to the rank of "colonel in America only." That decision left only about 30 British majors vulnerable to being ordered about by a provincial colonel, but few of them had independent commands anyway. Provincial units under the command of their own officers cooperated with the British army, and the officers began to impose something close to British discipline on them, including hundreds of lashes for routine offenses. Quite a few men began to reenlist.

Rather than impose a parliamentary tax, Pitt set aside £200,000 beginning in 1758 (later reduced to £133,000)

4.13 "The English Lion Dismember'd" (1756) This striking cartoon reflects British consternation during the first half of the Seven Years' War. France had just taken the Mediterranean island of Minorca from the British.

and told the colonies that they could claim a share of it in proportion to their contribution to the war effort. In effect, he gave the colonies incentive to compete voluntarily in support of the war. The subsidies covered something less than half of the cost of fielding 20,000 provincials each year from 1758 to 1760, and rather smaller numbers in 1761 and 1762 as operations shifted to the Caribbean. By then, Canada, Martinique, and Guadeloupe, as well as Spanish Havana, were all in British hands.

Pitt had no patience with military failure. After Loudoun failed to attack Louisbourg in 1757, Pitt replaced him with James Abercrombie. He also put Jeffrey Amherst in charge of a new Louisbourg expedition, with James Wolfe as one of his brigadiers. By 1758, the British Empire had put together a military force capable of overwhelming New France and knew how to use it. Cooperation between redcoats and provincials became devastatingly effective.

4-7e The Years of British Victory

By 1758, the Royal Navy had cut off reinforcements and supplies to Canada. Britain had sent a large navy and more than 30 regiments to North America. Combined with 20,000 provincials, thousands of bateau men rowing supplies into the interior, and swarms of **privateers** (private ships with government authorization to take enemy prizes) preying on French commerce, Britain had mustered perhaps 60,000 men in North America and nearby waters. Most of them now closed in on the 75,000 people of New France. Montcalm, who was running out of goods for the Indian trade, refused to encourage more Indian attacks on the frontier and prepared to defend the approaches to Canada at Forts Duquesne, Niagara, Frontenac, Ticonderoga, Crown Point, and Louisbourg.

Spurred on by Quaker mediators, the British and colonial governments came to terms with the western Indians in 1758, arranging an uneasy peace mostly by promising not to seize their lands after the war. Few settlers or officials had yet noticed a new trend that was emerging during the conflict. Before the 1750s, Indian nations had often waged terrible wars against one another. Now, however, few Indians in the northeastern woodlands were willing to attack others. In 1755, for example, some Senecas fought with New France and some Mohawks with the British, but they carefully avoided confronting each other. This Iroquois sense of solidarity was spreading. Iroquois and western Algonquians, once deadly enemies, saw real advantages in cooperation. A pan-Indian identity was beginning to emerge.

Peace with the western Indians in 1758 permitted the British to revive the grand military plan of 1755, except that this time the overall goal was the conquest of New France (see Map 4.5). Amherst and Wolfe, with 9,000 regulars and 500 provincials, besieged Louisbourg, and it fell in September, enabling Nova Scotia to annex Cape Breton Island. Colonel John Bradstreet's 3,000 provincials advanced to Lake Ontario, took Fort Frontenac, and began building a fleet. This victory cut off the French in the Ohio Valley from their supplies. A powerful force of regulars under John Forbes and provincials under Washington marched west, this time through Pennsylvania, to attack Fort Duquesne, but the French blew up the fort and retreated north just before they arrived. The British erected Fort Pitt on the ruins.

The only British defeat in 1758 occurred in northern New York when Abercrombie ordered a costly frontal assault against a heavily fortified position at Ticonderoga (Carillon). When Pitt heard the news, he sacked Abercrombie, put Amherst in charge of the New York theater of war, and left Wolfe at Louisbourg to plan an attack up the St. Lawrence River against Quebec.

In 1759, while the provincials on Lake Ontario took Niagara, Amherst spent the summer cautiously reducing Ticonderoga and Crown Point. (Pitt expected him to

▲ MAP 4.5 **Conquest of Canada, 1758–1760** In three campaigns, the British, with strong colonial support, first subdued the outer defenses of New France, then took Quebec in 1759 and Montreal in 1760.

Q Compare this map with Map 4.4, which details the British offensive of 1755. What similarities and differences do you notice? What made the offensive of 1758–1760 more successful?

Q Dating to the seventeenth century, the Saint Lawrence River Valley had signified the heart of New France. How did the British finally manage to conquer the region?

reach Montreal.) The most dramatic campaign occurred farther east. In June, Wolfe ascended the St. Lawrence with 8,000 redcoats and colonial rangers and laid siege to Quebec, defended by Montcalm with 16,000 regulars, Canadian militia, and Indians. When an attack below the city failed, Wolfe mounted howitzers on high ground across the river from Quebec and began reducing the city to rubble. Frustrated by the French refusal to come out and fight, he turned loose his American rangers ("the worst soldiers in the universe," he boasted), who burned more than 1,400 farms. Anyone who resisted was shot and scalped. Still the French held out.

By September, both Wolfe and Montcalm realized that the British fleet would soon have to depart or risk being frozen in during the long winter. Wolfe made a last desperate effort, preferring to die rather than fail. His men silently sailed up the river, climbed a formidable cliff above the city in darkness, and on the morning of September 13, 1759, deployed on the Plains of Abraham behind Quebec. Montcalm panicked. Instead of using his artillery to defend the walls from inside (Wolfe's force had been able to drag only two small guns with them), he marched out of Quebec onto the plains. Both generals now got what they craved most, a set piece but brief European battle. Wolfe and Montcalm were mortally wounded, but the British swept the field and took Quebec. Montreal fell in 1760, and Canada surrendered.

Only later, in January 1762, after France had been defeated, did Spain finally enter the war. British forces quickly took Havana and even Manila in the distant Philippines. France and Spain sued for peace.

4.14 Death of General Wolfe (1771) Benjamin West, who was born in Pennsylvania, taught himself to paint, opened a studio in Philadelphia, and then went to Europe. He studied the great Italian masters for several years and then settled in London, where he became the first American artist to have an enormous impact. Contemporary heroes had been displayed in classical attire, but West used their actual uniforms. George III was so impressed that he made West the history painter to the royal court.

Q *Although sentiment and nationalism are usually more associated with the 19th century than the 18th century, how does West use each sensation to produce feeling in the painting?*

4-7f The Peace of Paris

In 1763, the Peace of Paris ended the war. Britain returned Martinique and Guadeloupe to France. France gave Britain several minor West Indian islands and all of North America east of the Mississippi, except New Orleans. In exchange for Havana, Spain ceded Florida to the British and agreed to pay a large ransom for Manila. To compensate its Spanish ally, France gave New Orleans and Louisiana west of the Mississippi to Spain. Most Spanish and African occupants of Florida withdrew to other parts of the Spanish Empire, but nearly all of the French settlers remained in Canada, the Illinois Country, and what was now Spanish Louisiana.

British colonists were jubilant. The age of warfare and frontier carnage seemed over at last. Britain and the colonies could now develop their vast resources in an imperial partnership that would bring unprecedented prosperity. But western Indians angrily rejected the peace settlement. No one had conquered them, and they denied the right of France to surrender their lands to Great Britain. They began to plan their own war of liberation.

Conclusion

Between 1713 and 1754, expansion and renewed immigration pushed North American settlement ever farther into the interior (see Map 4.6). With a population that doubled every 25 years, many householders could no longer give all of their sons and daughters the level of economic success that they were enjoying. By midcentury, many family members took up a trade or looked westward for what their fathers could not provide. Women worked harder just to sustain opportunity for their households. Many families had to favor sons over daughters and the eldest son over his younger brothers, reluctantly following practices used in England.

The colonies anglicized in other ways as well. Newspapers and the learned professions spread the Enlightenment to the colonies. Male and female colonists rapidly consumed British goods. English revivalists, especially George Whitefield, had a huge impact in North America. Northern colonies borrowed Court politics from Walpole's Britain, while most southern colonies favored politics as envisioned by Britain's Country opposition. Both considered themselves the freest people on earth. When imperial rivalries again led to war after 1739, the colonists discovered that African slaves associated Spain with liberty, while most Eastern Woodland Indians still looked to New France for support. The threat of internal upheaval kept King George's War indecisive in the 1740s. Taking advantage of Spain's neutral position when Britain and France went to war in 1755, the British Empire concentrated its resources and conquered New France.

The French and Indian War left behind vivid memories. Provincials admired the courage of the redcoats and the victories they won but hated their brutal discipline and arrogant officers. British officials greatly exaggerated what military force alone could accomplish and underestimated colonial contributions to the imperial cause. The concord and prosperity that were supposed to follow the empire's great triumph yielded instead to bitter strife.

▲ **MAP 4.6 Growth of Population to 1760** Between 1700 and 1760, the population of the British colonies had increased by more than a factor of six, from 250,000 to almost 1.6 million. Settlement had filled the piedmont in most areas and was beginning to cross the Appalachian watershed into the Ohio Valley.

Q *What factors contributed to the greater population growth and territorial expansion in the mid-Atlantic and southern regions compared to the north?*

Q *From a British imperialistic perspective, what were the advantages and disadvantages of America's prodigious population growth?*

CHAPTER REVIEW

Review

1. In what ways did American colonists attempt to imitate British society in the 18th century?
2. What were the principal differences between the populations and economies of the three major colonial regions, the South, the mid-Atlantic, and New England?
3. What was the Enlightenment and how did it shape the 18th-century colonies?
4. What was the Great Awakening and how did it change religion in the American colonies in the 18th century?
5. Why did Britain's "Country" values prevail in most southern colonies while "Court" politics took hold in most northern provinces?
6. How did Indians and African slaves take advantage of opportunities presented by a new round of European wars starting in 1739?
7. What made the War for North America (1754–1763) so much more decisive than the three earlier Anglo-French wars?

Critical Thinking

1. "How is it that we hear the loudest yelps for liberty among the drivers of Negroes?" asked Dr. Samuel Johnson, a towering literary figure in 18th-century England, on the eve of the Revolutionary War. Thomas Jefferson, George Washington, Patrick Henry, James Madison, and many other prominent spokesmen for the American cause owned dozens, even hundreds, of slaves. Is there any way that being a large slaveholder might have increased a planter's commitment to liberty as it had come to be understood in England and the colonies by that time? Did Johnson have a point?
2. The Duc de Choiseul, who negotiated the Treaty of Paris that ended the Seven Years' War in 1763, and the Comte de Vergennes, who negotiated the Franco-American alliance of 1778, both claimed that France's decision to cede Canada to Great Britain in 1763 was a master stroke of French policy because, with no enemy to fear on their borders, the colonies would no longer need British protection and would soon move toward complete independence. By contrast, the leaders of colonial resistance after 1763 always insisted that Britain's postwar policies provoked both the resistance and independence. Who was right?

Identifications

Review your understanding of the following key terms, people, and events for this chapter (terms in bold in text are included in the Glossary).

anglicization, p. 102
dowry, p. 103
coverture, p. 103
dower rights, p. 103
Middle Passage, p. 104
gang system, p. 104
sickle cell, p. 104
task system, p. 105
Gullah, p. 106
redemptioners, p. 106
fiat money, p. 107
John Peter Zenger, p. 108
Enlightenment, p. 108
consumer society, p. 111
evangelical, p. 113
Presbytery, p. 113
Synod, p. 113
revival, p. 113
Freemasons, p. 114
New Side, p. 114
Old Side, p. 114
New Lights, p. 115
Old Lights, p. 115
placemen, p. 117
politics of harmony, p. 118
republics, p. 119
press gangs, p. 120
Albany Congress, p. 123
privateers, p. 128

Suggested Readings

The most important study of immigration in the 18th century is **Marianne S. Wokeck, *Trade in Strangers: The Beginnings of Mass Migration to North America*** (1999). The ***Trans-Atlantic Slave Trade Database***, available at www.slavevoyages.org, provides updated figures on the Atlantic slave trade and information on every documented slave ship voyage in the early modern Atlantic world. For the nature of slave life in colonial North America, see **Philip D. Morgan's *Slave Counterpoint: Black Culture in the Eighteenth-Century Chesapeake & Lowcountry*** (1998). For gentility and the Enlightenment, excellent studies include **Richard L. Bushman, *The Refinement of America: Persons, Houses, Cities*** (1992); and **Ned Landsman, *From Colonials to Provincials: Thought and Culture in America, 1680–1760*** (1998). **Jennifer L. Anderson, *Mahogany: The Costs of Luxury in Early America*** (2012) explores the human and environmental impact of an important luxury good. For women and the consumer revolution, see **Zara Anishanslin, *Portrait of a Woman in Silk: Hidden Histories of the British Atlantic World*** (2016). **Mark A. Noll, *The Rise of Evangelical Religion: The Age of Edwards, Whitefield, and the Wesleys*** (2003), provides a comprehensive overview of the Great Awakening. **Richard R. Beeman's *Varieties of Political Experience in Eighteenth-Century America*** (2004); and

Brendan McConville's *The King's Three Faces: The Rise & Fall of Royal America, 1688–1776* (2006), are ambitious studies of politics in the British colonies.

For the renewal of imperial conflict after 1739, see **Jill Lepore**, *New York Burning: Liberty, Slavery, and Conspiracy in Eighteenth-Century Manhattan* (2005); **Denver Brunsman**, *The Evil Necessity: British Naval Impressment in the Eighteenth-Century Atlantic World* (2013); **Fred Anderson**, *Crucible of War: The Seven Years War and the Fate of Empire in British North America, 1754–1766* (2000); **Timothy J. Shannon**, *Indians and Colonists at the Crossroads of Empire: The Albany Congress of 1754* (2000); and **Christopher Hodson**, *The Acadian Diaspora: An Eighteenth-Century History* (2012).

MINDTAP is a fully online personalized learning experience built upon Cengage Learning content. MindTap® combines student learning tools—readings, multimedia, activities, and assessments—into a singular Learning Path that guides students through the course and helps students develop the critical thinking, analysis, and communication skills that are essential to academic and professional success.

5 Reform, Resistance, Revolution, 1763–1776

5-1 Imperial Reform
➤ *Learning Objective:* Describe how Britain's victory in the Seven Years' War led to controversial imperial reforms for its American colonies.

Impetus for Reform
Indian Policy and Pontiac's War
The Sugar Act
The Currency Act and the Quartering Act
The Stamp Act

5-2 The Stamp Act Crisis
➤ *Learning Objective:* Explain how Parliament resolved the Stamp Act crisis without fully surrendering its right to tax the American colonies.

Nullification
Repeal

5-3 The Townshend Crisis
➤ *Learning Objective:* Identify what made the resolution of the Townshend crisis less satisfying for American colonists than the end to the Stamp Act crisis.

The Townshend Program
Resistance: The Politics of Escalation
The Wilkes Crisis
The Boston Massacre
Partial Repeal
Disaffection

5-4 Internal Cleavages: The Contagion of Liberty
➤ *Learning Objective:* Trace how the British imperial crisis helped to expose tensions within American society among the following groups: patriots and loyalists (and loyal colonies); artisans and gentlemen; tenants and landlords; settlers and proprietors; women and men; and slaves and masters.

Divided Loyalties
Urban and Rural Discontent
Slaves and Women

5-5 The Last Imperial Crisis
➤ *Learning Objective:* Analyze why the colonists started a revolution after the Tea Act lowered the price of tea.

The Tea Crisis
Britain's Response: The Coercive Acts
The Radical Explosion
The First Continental Congress
Toward War

5-6 The Improvised War
➤ *Learning Objective:* Detail how the onset of war with Britain influenced America's decision to declare independence and the language in the Declaration of Independence.

The Second Continental Congress
War and Legitimacy, 1775–1776
Independence

5.1 **Engagement at the North Bridge in Concord, April 19, 1775**
This 1775 painting by Ralph Earl is quite accurate in its details. It shows the first American military victory in the war when the militia drove the British back from Concord Bridge and eventually through Lexington and all the way to Boston.

BRITAIN LEFT AN ARMY IN NORTH AMERICA after 1763 and taxed the colonies to pay part of its cost. The colonists agreed that they should contribute to their own defense but insisted that taxation without representation violated their rights as Englishmen. Three successive crises, provoked by parliamentary taxation, shattered Britain's North American empire by 1776.

In the Stamp Act crisis, the colonists first petitioned Parliament for a redress of grievances. When that effort failed, they nullified the Stamp Act and continued their resistance until Parliament repealed the tax in 1766. The settlers joyfully celebrated their victory. In the Townshend crisis of 1767–1770, Parliament imposed new taxes on certain imported goods. The colonists petitioned and resisted simultaneously, mostly through an intercolonial nonimportation movement. The British sent troops to Boston. After several violent confrontations, the soldiers withdrew, while Parliament modified but did not repeal the Townshend Revenue Act. The duty on tea remained. Repeal of the other duties broke the back of the nonimportation movement. Nobody celebrated. The Tea Act of 1773 launched the third crisis, and it quickly escalated. Boston destroyed British tea without bothering to petition first. When Parliament responded with the

Coercive Acts of 1774, the colonists created the Continental Congress to organize further resistance. Neither side dared back down, and the confrontation careened toward military violence. War broke out in April 1775. Fifteen months later, the colonies declared their independence. ■

5-1 Imperial Reform

Q How did Britain's victory in the Seven Years' War lead to controversial imperial reforms for its American colonies?

In 1760, George III (1760–1820) inherited the British throne at the age of 22. The king's pronouncements on behalf of religion and virtue at first won him many admirers in North America, but the political coalition leading Britain to victory over France fell apart. The king's new ministers set out to reform the empire.

5-1a Impetus for Reform

At the start of his reign, George feared that the Seven Years' War would bankrupt Britain. He had cause for concern. By the Treaty of Paris in 1763, Britain's national debt had nearly doubled from its prewar levels and stood at more than £130 million. Interest alone absorbed more than half of annual revenues, and Britain was already one of the most heavily taxed societies in the world.

Adding to the challenge, the war was not a one-time cost. The sheer scale of Britain's victory required more revenue just to police its new conquests. In April 1763, George Grenville became first lord of the treasury and the king's leading minister. Grenville pursued a policy of leaving 20 battalions (about 7,000) men in America, mostly in Canada and Florida, with small garrisons scattered throughout Indian territory. Because the colonists would receive the benefit of this protection, Grenville argued, they ought to pay a reasonable portion of the cost, and eventually all of it. He never asked the settlers to contribute anything to Britain's national debt or to urgent domestic needs, but he insisted that they contribute to their own defense.

The king's **Proclamation of 1763** further outlined Britain's approach to governing its expanded American empire. The measure set up governments in Canada, Florida, and other conquered colonies, and it created the so-called Proclamation Line along the Appalachian watershed to regulate the pace of western expansion (see Map 5.1). No settlements could be planted west of that line unless Britain first purchased the land from the Indians. Settlers would be encouraged to move instead to Nova Scotia, northern New England, Georgia, or Florida.

For colonists, many of whom had fought against France to open western lands to settlement, Britain's initial policies after the Seven Years' War were troubling. A more skillful approach to reforming the empire might have built on the voluntaristic measures that William Pitt had used to win the war. Instead, Grenville reverted to the demands for coercive reforms that had crisscrossed the Atlantic during Britain's years of defeat from 1755 to 1757. In his mind, Britain had won the war, not with the cooperation of the colonies, but despite their obstruction. London, he believed, had to act quickly to establish its authority before the colonies, with their astonishing rate of growth, slipped completely out of control. In effect, he set in motion a self-fulfilling prophecy in which the British government brought about precisely what it was trying to prevent. Nearly every step it took undermined the colonies' loyalty to Britain.

5-1b Indian Policy and Pontiac's War

Initially, at least, events on the ground seemed to support Grenville's reasoning that Britain needed a residual force to keep the peace in North America. In 1760, upon the British defeat of the French, General Jeffery Amherst had made a fateful decision to stop distributing Indian gifts. His contempt for Indian customs deprived the government of most of its leverage with natives just when their ability to unite had become stronger than ever.

In 1761, Neolin, a western Delaware, reported a vision in which God commanded Indians to return to their ancestral ways. Neolin's call for an end to Indian dependence on European goods, especially rum, resonated with his followers, who were dismayed by the British decision to end gifts. He stopped short of condemning the French still living in the Great Lakes region. Many of his followers even hoped that their fierce resolve would attract the support of King Louis XV of France (1715–1774), restore the friendly relations of the past, and halt British expansion.

With unprecedented unity, the Indians struck in 1763. **Pontiac's War**, named for an Ottawa chief and follower of Neolin, combined Seneca, Mingo, Delaware, Shawnee,

CHRONOLOGY

1759–1761	Cherokee War devastates South Carolina backcountry
1760	George III becomes king of Great Britain
1763	Grenville ministry takes power • Wilkes publishes *North Briton* No. 45 • Pontiac's War begins • King issues Proclamation of 1763
1764	Parliament passes Currency Act and Sugar Act
1765	Parliament passes Quartering Act • Stamp Act passed and nullified • Rockingham replaces Grenville as prime minister
1766	Parliament repeals Stamp Act, passes Declaratory Act and Revenue Act of 1766 • Chatham (Pitt) ministry takes power
1767	Parliament passes New York Restraining Act and Townshend Revenue Act
1768	Massachusetts assembly dispatches Circular Letter • Wilkes elected to Parliament • Massacre of St. George's Fields in England • Massachusetts refuses to rescind Circular Letter • *Liberty* riot in Boston • Assemblies supporting Circular Letter are dissolved • Redcoats sent to Boston
1769	Nonimportation becomes effective • Regulators achieve major goals in South Carolina
1770	North becomes prime minister • Boston Massacre • Townshend Revenue Act partially repealed • Nonimportation collapses
1771	North Carolina regulators defeated at Alamance Creek
1772–1773	*Gaspée* affair • Twelve colonies create committees of correspondence
1773	Tea Act passed • Boston Tea Party • Wheatley's poetry published
1774	American Quakers prohibit slaveholding • Parliament passes Coercive Acts and Quebec Act • First Continental Congress convenes
1775	Revolutionary War begins at Lexington and Concord • Second Continental Congress creates Continental army • Olive Branch Petition fails • George III issues Proclamation of Rebellion
1775–1776	Americans invade Canada
1776	Paine publishes *Common Sense* • British evacuate Boston • Continental Congress approves Declaration of Independence

Wyandot, Miami, Ottawa, and other warriors. They attacked 13 British posts in the West. Between May 16 and June 20, all of the forts fell except Niagara, Pitt, Detroit, and a tiny outpost on Green Bay that the Indians did not bother to attack. For months, the Indians kept Detroit and Pitt under close siege, something Indians were supposed to be incapable of doing. They hoped to drive British settlers back to the eastern seaboard.

Enraged by these successes, Amherst ordered Colonel Henry Bouquet, commander at Fort Pitt, to distribute smallpox-infested blankets among the western nations, contributing to a lethal epidemic in 1763 and 1764. "You will do well to try to Inoculate the Indians by means of Blankets," he wrote to Bouquet, "as well as to Try Every other Method that can serve to Extirpate this Execrable Race." In 1764, British and provincial forces ended resistance, restored peace, and compelled the Indians to return their hundreds of captives, many of whom preferred to stay. The British then reluctantly accepted the role that the French had played in the Great Lakes region by distributing gifts and mediating differences. On that question, the Indians won an important victory.

Still, Britain's reversal on gifts and other imperial reforms failed to keep the peace between settlers and Indians. Perhaps sensing the Indians' growing unity, many settlers began to assume that all Indians must be the enemies of all whites. In December 1763, the Scots-Irish of Paxton Township, Pennsylvania, murdered six unarmed Christian Indians—two old men, three women, and a child—at nearby Conestoga. Two weeks later, the "Paxton Boys" slaughtered 14 more Christian Indians who had been brought to Lancaster for protection. After Governor John Penn removed 140 Moravian mission Indians to Philadelphia for safety, the Paxton Boys marched on the capital, determined to kill them all.

Denouncing the Paxton Boys as "Christian white Savages," Benjamin Franklin led a delegation from the assembly that met the marchers at Germantown and persuaded them to go home after they presented a list of their grievances. The Moravian Indians had been spared. But efforts to bring the murderers to justice failed, and Pennsylvania and Virginia frontiersmen virtually declared an open season on Indians that continued for years. Settlers in Augusta County, Virginia, slaughtered nine Shawnees in 1765. Frederick Stump murdered 10 more in Pennsylvania in 1768 but could not be convicted in his frontier county. Such atrocities kept western Indians smoldering. London had hoped that its officials would bring evenhanded justice to the frontier. Indians had won real benefits from Britain's postwar policies, such as protection from land speculators, but otherwise they found no good option between Amherst's smallpox blankets and the murderous rage of the Paxton Boys.

5-1c *The Sugar Act*

In a step that settlers found ominous, Grenville's Sugar Act of 1764 proclaimed it "just and necessary, that a revenue be raised … in America for defraying the expenses of defending, protecting, and securing" the colonies. The act placed duties on Madeira wine, coffee, and other products, but Grenville expected the greatest revenue to come from the molasses duty of three pence per gallon. The Molasses Act of 1733 had been designed to keep French molasses out of North America by

▲ MAP 5.1 **Pontiac's War and the Proclamation Line of 1763** Britain claimed possession of North America east of the Mississippi only to face an extraordinary challenge from the Indians of the interior, who wiped out eight garrisons but could not take Detroit, Niagara, or Fort Pitt.

Q Why did Pontiac and his coalition target former French forts that had only become British as a result of the Seven Years' War?

Q How did Pontiac's War reinforce the logic of Britain's imperial reforms, such as the Proclamation of 1763?

imposing a prohibitive duty of six pence per gallon. Instead, by paying a bribe of about a penny per gallon, merchants got French molasses certified as British. By 1760, more than 90 percent of all molasses imported into New England came from the French islands. Planters in the British islands gave up, lost interest in New England markets, and turned their molasses into quality rum for sale in Britain and Ireland. Nobody, in short, had any interest in stopping the trade in French molasses. New England merchants said they were willing to pay a duty of one penny (the current cost of bribes), but Grenville insisted on three. He hoped to raise £100,000 per year from the molasses duty, although in public he seldom put the figure above £40,000.

The Sugar Act also launched Grenville's war against smugglers. It vastly increased the amount of paperwork required of ship captains and permitted seizures of ships for what owners considered to be mere technicalities. In effect, Grenville tried to make it more profitable for customs officers to hound the merchants than to accept bribes from them. The Sugar Act encouraged them to prosecute violators in vice-admiralty courts, which did not use juries, rather than in common-law courts, which did. Prosecutors were virtually immune from any suit for damages, even when the merchant won an acquittal, so long as the judge certified "probable cause" for the seizure.

5-1d The Currency Act and the Quartering Act

Grenville passed several other imperial measures. The Currency Act of 1764 responded to wartime protests of London merchants against Virginia's paper money, which had lost almost 15 percent of its value between 1759 and 1764. The act forbade the colonies to issue any paper money as legal tender. The money question was urgent because the Sugar Act (and, later, the Stamp Act) required that all duties be paid in specie (silver or gold). Supporters of those taxes argued that the new duties would keep the specie in America to pay the army, but the colonists replied that the drain of specie from some colonies would put impossible constraints on trade. Boston and Newport, for instance, would pay most of the molasses tax, but specie collected there would follow the army to Quebec, New York, the Great Lakes, and Florida. Grenville saw "America" as a single region in which specie would circulate to the benefit of all. The colonists knew better. As of 1765, "America" existed only in British minds, not yet in colonial hearts.

Another reform measure was the Quartering Act of 1765, requested by Sir Thomas Gage, Amherst's successor as army commander. Gage asked for parliamentary authority to quarter soldiers in private homes, if necessary, when on the march and away from their barracks. Parliament ordered colonial assemblies to vote specific supplies, such as beer and candles, for the troops, which the assemblies were willingly doing already. But it also required the army to quarter its soldiers only in public buildings, such as taverns (which existed in large numbers only in cities) and not in private homes. The Quartering Act solved no problems, but it created several new ones.

5-1e The Stamp Act

In early 1764, when Parliament passed the Sugar Act, Grenville announced that a stamp tax on legal documents and on publications might also be needed. No one in the House of Commons, he declared, doubted Parliament's right to impose such a tax. Because Parliament had never levied a direct tax on the colonies, however, he also knew that he must persuade the settlers that a stamp tax would not be a constitutional innovation. This measure, his supporters insisted, did not violate the principle of no taxation without representation. The colonists were no different from the large nonvoting majority of subjects within Great Britain. They all shared **virtual representation** in Parliament. Each member of Parliament represented the entire empire, not just his constituency. Grenville also denied that there was any legal difference between external taxes (port duties, such as that on molasses) and internal (or inland) taxes, such as the proposed stamp tax.

Grenville put off passage of the Stamp Act while he collected more complete information about legal forms in the colonies. He also indicated that, if the colonies could devise a revenue plan better than a stamp tax, he would listen. His offer created confusion and became a public relations disaster for the government. All 13 colonial assemblies drafted petitions objecting to the Stamp Act as a form of taxation without representation. Most of them also attacked the duties imposed by the Sugar Act because they went beyond the regulation of trade. With few exceptions, they too rejected the distinction between internal and external taxes. Both, they declared, violated the British constitution. While agreeing that they ought to contribute to their own defense, they urged the government to return to the traditional method of requisitions, in which the Crown asked a colony for a specific sum, and the assembly decided how (or whether) to raise it. Colonists feared that taxation by Parliament might tempt Britain to rule them without consulting their assemblies.

As these petitions reached London, Parliament refused to receive them, citing a standing rule that prohibited petitions against money bills and declaring that any challenge to Parliament's right to pass such a tax was inadmissible. To Grenville, requisitions were not a better idea. They had often been tried, had never worked efficiently, and never would. He rejected the petitions with a clear conscience. But to the colonists, he seemed to have acted in bad faith all along. He had asked their advice and had then refused even to consider it.

The Stamp Act passed in February 1765, to go into effect on November 1. All contracts, licenses, commissions, and most other legal documents would be void unless they were executed on officially stamped paper. Law courts would not recognize any document that lacked the proper stamp, and the colonists would quietly, if grudgingly, accept Parliament's power to tax them. The act would almost enforce itself. A stamp duty was also put on all newspapers and pamphlets, a requirement likely to anger every printer in the colonies. Playing cards and dice were also taxed.

When the Stamp Act became law, most colonial leaders resigned themselves to a situation that seemed beyond their power to change. Daniel Dulany, a Maryland lawyer who did more than any other colonist to refute the argument for virtual representation, drew a line short of overt resistance. "I am upon a Question of *Propriety* not of Power," he wrote; "...at the same Time that I invalidate the Claim upon which [the Stamp Act] is founded, I may very consistently recommend a Submission to the Law, whilst it endures." But ordinary settlers recognized that direct action, and nothing else, might prevent implementation of the act.

5.2 This is the Place to Affix the Stamp This haunting image appeared in a Philadelphia newspaper in October 1765, reflecting deep colonial anger at the Stamp Act. A skull and crossbones replaced the symbol of the Crown that appeared on official stamps required by the act.

5-2 The Stamp Act Crisis

Q *How did Parliament resolve the Stamp Act crisis without fully surrendering its right to tax the American colonies?*

Resistance to the Stamp Act began in spring 1765 and continued for nearly a year, until it was repealed. Patrick Henry, a newcomer to the Virginia House of Burgesses, launched the first wave by introducing five resolutions on May 30 and 31. His resolves passed by margins ranging between 22 to 17 and 20 to 19; one was rescinded and expunged from the record the next day. Henry had two more in his pocket that he decided not to introduce. But over the summer, the *Newport Mercury* printed six of Henry's seven resolutions, and the *Maryland Gazette* published all of them. Neither paper reported that some of the seven had not passed. To other colonies, Virginia seemed to have taken a far more radical position than it actually had. The last resolve printed in the *Maryland Gazette* claimed that anyone defending Parliament's right to tax Virginia "shall be Deemed, an Enemy to this his Majesty's Colony."

In their fall or winter sessions, eight colonial legislatures passed new resolutions condemning the Stamp Act. Nine colonies sent delegates to the Stamp Act Congress, which met in New York in October. It passed resolutions affirming colonial loyalty to the king and "all due subordination" to Parliament but condemned the Stamp Act and Sugar Act. By 1765, nearly all colonial spokesmen agreed that the Stamp Act was unconstitutional, that colonial representation in Parliament (urged by a few writers) was impractical because of the distance and the huge expense, and thus that the Stamp Act had to be repealed. They accepted the idea of virtual representation *within* the colonies—their assemblies, they said, represented both voters and nonvoters in each colony—but the colonists ridiculed the argument when it was applied across the Atlantic. A disfranchised Englishman who acquired sufficient property could become a voter, pointed out Daniel Dulany, in a pamphlet that was widely admired, even in Britain. But, Dulany explained, no colonist, no matter how wealthy he became, could vote for a member of Parliament. Members of Parliament paid the taxes that they levied on others within Britain, but they would never pay any tax imposed on the colonies.

5-2a Nullification

No matter how eloquent, resolutions and pamphlets alone could not defeat the Stamp Act. Street violence might, however, and Boston showed the way, led by men calling themselves Sons of Liberty. On August 14, the town awoke to find an effigy of Andrew Oliver, the stamp distributor,

140 CHAPTER 5 Reform, Resistance, Revolution, 1763–1776

hanging on what became the town's Liberty Tree (a gallows for hanging enemies of the people). The sheriff dared not remove the effigy. After dark, a crowd of men roamed the streets, shouted defiance at the governor and council, demolished a new building Oliver was erecting that "they called the Stamp Office," beheaded and burned Oliver's effigy, and finally invaded Oliver's home, "declaring they would kill Him." He had already fled to a neighbor's home. Thoroughly cowed, he resigned.

On August 26, another crowd all but demolished the elegant mansion of Lt. Governor Thomas Hutchinson. Most Bostonians believed that, in letters to British friends, he had defended and even helped to draft the Stamp Act. In fact, he had opposed it. Shocked by the destruction of property, the militia finally appeared to police the streets, but when Governor Francis Bernard tried to arrest those responsible for the first riot, he got nowhere. Bostonians deplored the events of August 26 but approved those of August 14. No one was punished for either event, although the whole city knew that Ebenezer McIntosh, a shoemaker and an organizer of the annual Pope's Day (Guy Fawkes Day) processions, led both riots.

Everywhere except in Georgia, the stamp master was forced to resign before the law took effect on November 1. With no one to distribute stamps, the act could not be implemented. Merchants adopted **nonimportation agreements** (boycotts of British goods) to pressure the British into repeal. In other cities the Sons of Liberty followed Boston's lead and took control of the streets. After November 1, they agitated to open the ports and courts, which had closed down rather than operate without stamps. Neither the courts nor the customs officers had any stamps to use because nobody dared distribute them. As winter gave way to spring, most ports and some courts resumed business. Only Newport matched Boston's level of violence, but in New York City a clash between the Sons of Liberty and the British garrison grew ugly and almost escalated into an armed encounter. Violent resistance worked. The Stamp Act was nullified—even in Georgia, eventually.

5-2b *Repeal*

The next move was up to Britain. For reasons that had nothing to do with the colonies, the king dismissed Grenville in summer 1765 and replaced his ministry with a narrow coalition organized primarily by William Augustus, duke of Cumberland, the king's uncle. An untested young nobleman, Charles Watson-Wentworth, Marquess of Rockingham, took over the treasury. This "Old Whig" ministry had to deal with the riots in America. Cumberland—the man who had sent Braddock to America in the winter of 1754–1755—may have favored a similar use of force in late 1765. If so, he never had a chance to issue the order. On October 31, minutes before an emergency cabinet meeting to address the American crisis, he died of a heart attack, leaving Rockingham in charge of the government. At first, Rockingham favored amending the Stamp Act, but by December he had decided on repeal. To win over the other ministers, the king, and Parliament, he would need great skill.

To Rockingham, the only alternative to repeal seemed to be a ruinous civil war in America, but as the king's chief minister, he could hardly tell Parliament that the world's greatest empire must yield to unruly mobs. He needed a better reason for repeal. Even before the first American nonimportation agreements reached London on December 12 (New York City's) and December 26 (Philadelphia's), he began to mobilize British merchants and manufacturers who traded with America. They petitioned Parliament to repeal the Stamp Act. They condemned the Grenville program as an economic disaster, and their arguments gave Rockingham the leverage he needed.

He won the concurrence of the other ministers only by promising to support a Declaratory Act affirming Parliament's sovereignty over the colonies. Rockingham still faced resistance from the king, who favored "modification" rather than repeal. George III appeared willing to repeal all of the stamp duties except those on dice and playing cards, the two levies most difficult to enforce. Only Grenville, however, was ready to use the army to enforce even an amended Stamp Act. Rockingham brought the king around by threatening to resign, which would have forced the king to bring back Grenville, whom he hated. Many pro-American witnesses appeared before Parliament to urge repeal, including Benjamin Franklin, who gave a masterful performance. Slowly, Rockingham put together his majority.

Three pieces of legislation ended the crisis. The first, the Declaratory Act, affirmed that Parliament had "full power and authority to make laws and statutes of sufficient force and validity to bind the colonies and people of America … in all cases whatsoever." Rockingham resisted pressure to insert the word "taxes" along with "laws and statutes." That omission permitted the colonists, who drew a sharp distinction between legislation (which, they conceded, Parliament had a right to pass) and taxation (which it could not), to interpret the act as an affirmation of their position, while nearly everyone in Britain read precisely the opposite meaning into the phrase "laws and statutes." Old Whigs hoped that Parliament would never again insist on its sovereign power over America. Like the royal veto of an act of Parliament, that power existed, explained Edmund Burke; and like the veto, which had not been used for almost 60 years, it should never again be invoked. The colonists agreed. They read the Declaratory Act as a face-saving gesture that made repeal of the Stamp Act possible.

The second measure repealed the Stamp Act as "greatly detrimental to the commercial interests" of the empire. The third, which modern historians call the Revenue Act of 1766 even though its preamble described it as a regulation of trade, reduced the duty on molasses from three pence per gallon to one penny, but imposed it on all molasses, British or foreign, imported into the mainland colonies. Although the act was more favorable to the molasses trade than any other

5.3a (top) and 5.3b (bottom) **Du Simitière, *Boston Affairs* (1765) and *Boston Affairs* (1767)** Boston's Pope's Day processions into 1765 had raucously applauded the king's role as protector of Europe's Protestants, but in 1767 they sided with the political opposition in England, especially John Wilkes.

Q How did colonists adapt existing forms of public celebrations and protests to oppose Britain's imperial reforms in the 1760s?

measure yet passed by Parliament, it clearly was also a revenue measure, and it generated more income for the empire than any other colonial tax. Few colonists attacked it for violating the principle of no taxation without representation. In Britain, it seemed that the colonists objected only to internal taxes but would accept external duties.

Against the advice of British friends, the colonists greeted repeal with wild celebrations. Over the next decade, many communities observed March 18 as the anniversary of the Stamp Act's repeal. Neither side fully appreciated the misunderstandings that had made repeal possible or their significance. In the course of the struggle, both sides, British and colonial, had rejected the distinction between internal and external taxes. They could find no legal or philosophical basis for condemning the one while approving the other. Hardly anyone except Franklin noticed in 1766 that the difference was quite real and that the crisis had in fact been resolved according to that distinction. Parliament had tried to extend its authority over the internal affairs of the colonies and had failed, but it continued to collect port duties in the colonies, some to regulate trade, others for revenue. No one could justify this division of authority, but the external–internal cleavage marked, even defined, the power axis of the empire, the boundary between what Parliament could do on its own and what, internally, only the Crown could do, and then only with the consent of the colonists.

Another misunderstanding was equally grave. Only the riots had created a crisis severe enough to push Parliament into repeal. Both sides, however, preferred to believe that economic pressure had been decisive. For the colonies, this conviction set the pattern of resistance for the next two imperial crises.

5-3 The Townshend Crisis

Q *What made the resolution of the Townshend crisis less satisfying for American colonists than the end to the Stamp Act crisis?*

The good will created by repeal did not last. In 1766, the king again replaced his ministry. This time he persuaded William Pitt to form a government. Pitt's ministry, which included many former supporters of Grenville, faced serious opposition within Parliament. Pitt compounded that problem by accepting a peerage as Earl of Chatham, a decision that removed his compelling oratory from the House of Commons and left Charles Townshend, the chancellor of the exchequer (treasury), as his spokesman in that chamber. A witty, extemporaneous speaker, Townshend had betrayed every leader he ever served. The only consistent policy in his political career had been his hard-line attitude toward the colonies.

5-3a The Townshend Program

Chatham learned that he could not control the House of Commons from his position in the House of Lords. During the Christmas recess of 1766–1767, he saw the extent of his failure and began to slip into an acute depression that lasted more than two years. He refused to communicate with other ministers or even with the king. The colonists, who admired him more than any other Englishman of the day, expected sympathy from his administration. Instead, they got Townshend, who took charge of colonial policy in spring 1767.

The Townshend Revenue Act of 1767 imposed new duties in colonial ports on certain imports that colonists could legally buy only from Britain: tea, paper, glass, red and white lead, and painter's colors. But Townshend also removed more duties on tea within Britain than he could offset with the new revenue to be collected in the colonies. Revenue, clearly, was not his main object. The statute's preamble stated his real goal: to use the new American revenues to pay the salaries of governors and judges in the colonies, thereby freeing them from dependence on the assemblies. This devious strategy aroused suspicions of conspiracy in the colonies. Even sober provincials began to fear that, in the bowels of the British government, men were plotting against their liberties.

Other measures gave appellate powers to the vice-admiralty courts in Boston, Philadelphia, and Charleston and created a separate American Board of Customs Commissioners to enforce the trade and revenue laws in the colonies. The board was placed in Boston, where resistance to the Stamp Act had been fiercest, rather than in Philadelphia, which had been rather quiet in 1765 and would have been a much more convenient location. Townshend was eager for confrontation.

The British army also began to withdraw from nearly all frontier posts and concentrate near the coast. Although the primary motive was to save money, the implications were striking. An army in America to guard the frontier, partially supported by the colonists, was one thing, but an army far distant from the frontier presumably existed to police the colonists. Why should they pay costs to enforce policies that would deprive them of their liberties?

Townshend ridiculed the distinction between internal and external taxes, which he attributed to Chatham and the colonists, but he declared that he would honor it anyway. After winning approval for his program, he died suddenly in September 1767 and passed on to others the dilemmas he had created. Frederick, Lord North, replaced him as chancellor of the exchequer. Chatham resigned, and the Duke of Grafton became prime minister.

5-3b Resistance: The Politics of Escalation

The external–internal distinction perplexed the colonists. Since 1765, they had objected to all taxes for revenue, but in 1766, they had accepted the penny duty on molasses with few complaints. Defeating the Townshend Revenue Act would prove tougher than nullifying the Stamp Act. Parliament had never been able to impose its will on the internal affairs of the colonies, as the Stamp Act fiasco demonstrated, but it did control the seas. Goods subject to duties might arrive on any of hundreds of ships from Britain each year, but screening the cargo of every vessel threatened to impose an enormous, perhaps impossible burden on the Sons of Liberty. General nonimportation would be easier to implement, but British trade played a bigger role in the colonial economy than North American trade did in Britain's. To hurt Britain a little, the colonies would have to harm themselves a lot.

The colonists divided over strategies of resistance. The radical *Boston Gazette* called for complete nonimportation of all British goods. The merchants' paper, the *Boston Evening Post,* disagreed. In October, the Boston town meeting

Interpreting the Visual Past

A British Cartoon of the Stamp Act Repeal

"The Repeal or the Funeral of Miss Americ-Stamp." This London cartoon, published on March 18, 1766, the day Parliament repealed the Stamp Act, became one of the most popular satirical prints of the 18th century. The print's artist, Benjamin Wilson, had close ties to the Marquess of Rockingham, who orchestrated the repeal. The main focus is a funeral procession of the Stamp Act's supporters carrying the act to a burial vault. George Grenville has the dubious honor of holding the coffin (note the child size, as the act "died" at just over four months old). The text above the vault indicates that it holds other taxes and legislation "which tended to alienate the Affections of Englishmen to their Country."

In the background, three ships, labeled "Conway," "Rockingham," and "Grafton" after the parliamentary leaders responsible for the repeal of the Stamp Act, prepare to carry the large unshipped cargoes destined for America that have accumulated on the dock. Stamps just returned from America are also stacked on the wharf.

Q *The cartoon sacrifices subtlety (note the action of the dog toward the Stamp Act's supporters) to deliver a clear political message. How might the scene have been different had Wilson tried to incorporate the other key components of the repeal, the Declaratory Act and the Revenue Act of 1766?*

Q *Despite the somber tone of the cartoon, how does it express optimism about the future relationship between Britain and its American colonies?*

Q *How might the cartoon have reinforced Americans' perception that their nonimportation agreements had forced the British to repeal the Stamp Act?*

5.4 Benjamin Wilson, "The Repeal or the Funeral of Miss Americ-Stamp," 1766.

encouraged greater use of home manufactures and urged voluntary nonconsumption of British goods, but no organized resistance developed and the Townshend duties became operative in November 1767 with little opposition. A month later, John Dickinson, a Philadelphia lawyer, tried to rouse his fellow colonists through 12 urgent letters printed in nearly every colonial newspaper. These *Letters from a Farmer in Pennsylvania* denied the distinction between internal and external taxes, insisted that all parliamentary taxes for revenue violated the colonists' rights, and speculated darkly about Townshend's motives.

Massachusetts again set the pace of resistance. In February 1768, its assembly petitioned the king, not Parliament, against the new measures. Without waiting for a reply, it also sent a Circular Letter to the other assemblies, urging them to pursue "constitutional measures" of resistance against the Quartering Act, the new taxes, and the use of Townshend revenues to pay the salaries of governors and judges. The implication was that, because Britain responded only to resistance, the colonies had better work together. By the spring of 1768, nonimportation also finally began to take hold in Boston and New York, although Philadelphia held out until early 1769.

The British ministry got the point. Wills Hill, earl of Hillsborough and secretary of state for the American colonies (an office created in 1768), responded so sharply that he turned tepid opposition into serious resistance. He ordered the Massachusetts assembly to rescind the Circular Letter and instructed all governors to dissolve any assembly that accepted it. In June 1768, the Massachusetts House voted 92 to 17 not to rescind. Most other assemblies had shown little interest in the Townshend program, particularly in the southern colonies, where governors already had fixed salaries. Even so, they bristled at being told what they could or could not debate. They took up the Circular Letter or began to draft their own. One by one, their assemblies were dissolved until government by consent seemed in serious peril.

The next escalation again came from Boston. On March 18, 1768, the town's celebration of the anniversary of the Stamp Act's repeal grew so raucous that the governor and the new American Board of Customs Commissioners asked Hillsborough for troops. He ordered General Gage, based in New York, to send two regiments from Nova Scotia to Boston. On June 10, before Gage could respond, a riot broke out in Boston after customs collectors seized John Hancock's sloop *Liberty* for having smuggled Madeira wine (taxed under the Sugar Act) on its *previous* voyage. By waiting until the ship had a new cargo, informers and customs officials could split larger shares when the sloop was condemned. Terrified by the fury of the popular response, the commissioners fled to Castle William in Boston Harbor and again petitioned Hillsborough for troops. He sent two more regiments from Ireland.

In early October 1768, the British fleet entered Boston Harbor in battle array and landed 1,000 soldiers, sent by Gage from Nova Scotia. The regiments from Ireland joined them later. To warn the public against the dangers posed by a standing army in time of peace, the patriots compiled a "Journal of the Times," describing how British soldiers were undermining public order in Boston—clashing with the town watch, endangering the virtue of young women, disturbing church services, and picking fights. The "journal" always appeared first as a newspaper column in some other city, usually New York. Only later was it reprinted in Boston, after memories of any specific incident had grown hazy.

Though detested, Britain's initial experiment in military coercion managed to halt violence against customs officers in Boston for several months. London was satisfied enough to withdraw half the soldiers in summer 1769. As Boston calmed, the town started winning sympathy among the southern colonies, which had not been deeply involved in resistance to the Townshend duties. Virginia, Maryland, and South Carolina each adopted nonimportation agreements. In the Chesapeake, the movement had more support among planters than among tobacco merchants, who were mostly Scots loyal to their parent firms. No enforcement mechanism was ever put in place. Charleston, however, took nonimportation seriously. Up and down the continent, the feeble resistance of mid-1768 became formidable in 1769.

5-3c The Wilkes Crisis

John Wilkes, a member of Parliament and a radical opposition journalist, had fled into exile in 1763 and had been outlawed for publishing an attack on the king in his newspaper, *The North Briton* No. 45. In 1768, just as the Townshend crisis was brewing, George III dissolved Parliament and issued writs for the usual septennial elections. Wilkes returned from France and won a seat for the English county of Middlesex. He then received a one-year sentence in King's Bench Prison. Hundreds of supporters gathered to chant "Wilkes and Liberty!" or even "No Wilkes? No King!" On May 10, 1768, as the new Parliament convened, Wilkites just outside the prison clashed with soldiers who fired into the crowd, killing six and wounding 15. Wilkes denounced "the massacre of St. George's Fields." The House of Commons expelled Wilkes and ordered a new election, but the voters chose him again. Two more expulsions and two more elections took place the next year, until April 1769 when, after Wilkes won again by 1,143 votes to 296, the House voted to seat the loser. Wilkes had created a constitutional crisis. His adherents founded "the Society of Gentlemen Supporters of the Bill of Rights," which raised money to pay off his huge debts and organized a national campaign on his behalf. About one-fourth of the voters of the entire kingdom signed petitions demanding a new general election. Wilkites called for a reduction of royal patronage and major reforms of the electoral system. They also began the regular publication of parliamentary debates and sympathized openly with North American protests. Colonial Sons of Liberty applauded Wilkes. If he lost, they warned, their own liberties would be in danger. Boston even printed a parody of the Apostles' Creed. It began: "I believe in Wilkes, the firm patriot, maker of number 45. Who was born for our good. Suffered under arbitrary power. Was banished and imprisoned." It ended with a hope for "the resurrection of liberty, and the life of universal freedom forever. Amen." In 1769, South Carolina's assembly borrowed £1,500 sterling from the colony's treasurer and donated it to Wilkes. When the assembly passed an appropriation to cover the gift, the council rejected the bill. Because neither side would yield, the assembly voted no taxes after 1769 and passed no laws after 1771. Royal government broke down over the Wilkes question.

The Townshend crisis and the Wilkite movement became an explosive combination. Many colonists began to question the British government's commitment to liberty. That a conspiracy existed to destroy British and colonial liberty began to seem quite plausible.

5-3d The Boston Massacre

By late 1769, the redcoats had intimidated Boston for nearly a year. The Sons of Liberty finally reciprocated. The town watch clashed with the army's guard posts because the watch, when challenged by the redcoats' call "Who goes there?" refused to give the required answer: "Friends." Under English common law, soldiers could not fire on civilians without an order from

5.5 Paul Revere's Engraving of the British Army Landing in Boston, 1768 The navy approached the city in battle array, a sight familiar to veterans of the French wars. To emphasize the peaceful, Christian character of Boston, Revere exaggerated the height of the church steeples.

Q How does the engraving by Revere, which is presented as a factual representation, actually make a political argument?

a civil magistrate, except in self-defense when their lives were in danger. By the fall of 1769, no magistrate dared issue such a command. Clashes between soldiers and civilians grew frequent, and justices of the peace singled out the soldiers for punishment.

By 1770, the soldiers often felt under siege. The Sons of Liberty also freely intimidated merchants who violated nonimportation. They nearly lynched Ebenezer Richardson, a customs informer who fired a musket from his home into a stone-throwing crowd and killed an 11-year-old boy. The lad's funeral on February 26, 1770, became an enormous display of public mourning. And although Richardson was convicted of murder, George III pardoned him.

After the funeral, tensions between soldiers and citizens reached a fatal climax. Off-duty soldiers often supplemented their meager wages with part-time employment, a practice that angered local artisans, who resented competition in the city's depressed economy. On Friday, March 2, 1770, three soldiers visited John Hancock's wharf. "Soldier, will you work?" asked Samuel Gray, a rope maker. "Yes," replied one. "Then go and clean my shit house," sneered Gray. After an ugly brawl, won by the workers despite reinforcements for the redcoats, Gray's employer persuaded their colonel to confine his men to barracks. Peace prevailed through the Puritan Sabbath that ran from Saturday night to sunrise on Monday, but everyone expected trouble on Monday, March 5.

After dark on Monday, fire bells began ringing throughout the town, and civilians and soldiers clashed at several places. A crowd hurling snowballs and rocks closed in on the lone sentinel guarding the hated customs house that stored the king's revenue. The guard called for help. Eight soldiers, including two who had been in the wharf brawl, rushed to his aid and loaded their weapons. Captain Thomas Preston took command and ordered the soldiers to drive the attackers slowly back with fixed bayonets. The crowd taunted the soldiers, daring them to fire. One soldier apparently slipped, discharging his musket into the air as he fell. The others then fired into the crowd, killing five and wounding six. One of the victims was Samuel Gray; another was Crispus Attucks, a man of African and Indian ancestry.

With the whole town turning out, the soldiers were withdrawn to Castle William. Preston and six of his men stood trial for murder and were defended, brilliantly, by two radical patriot lawyers, John Adams and Josiah Quincy, Jr., who believed that every accused person deserved to have a proper defense. Preston and four of the soldiers were acquitted. The other two were convicted only of manslaughter, which permitted them to plead a legal technicality called "benefit of clergy." They were branded on the thumb and released. The **Boston Massacre**, as the Sons of Liberty called this encounter, became the colonial counterpart to the Massacre of St. George's Fields in England. It marked the failure of Britain's first attempt at military coercion.

History Through Film: *John Adams* (2008)

A seven-part miniseries that aired on HBO in the spring of 2008. Directed by Tom Hooper. Starring Paul Giamatti (John Adams), Laura Linney (Abigail Adams), Stephen Dillane (Thomas Jefferson), David Morse (George Washington), Tom Wilkinson (Benjamin Franklin).

Based on David McCullough's Pulitzer Prize–winning biography, *John Adams* traces the political career of its title character (Paul Giamatti) in seven episodes, each approximately an hour. The net effect delivers to Adams something that the vainglorious Massachusetts lawyer and politician could have only dreamed of: a starring role in the founding of the United States, from the movement for independence in the 1770s through his work in President George Washington's administration as vice president and his own presidency in the 1790s to his busy retirement in the early 1800s.

The first episode, "Join or Die," centers on Adams's legal defense of the British soldiers accused of murdering five colonists on March 5, 1770, in the Boston Massacre (for background, see the text in this section). Adams agreed to defend the soldiers and their commanding officer, Captain Thomas Preston (Ritchie Coster), on the principle that all men deserve a fair trial. After Adams's successful defense in the trial, the last part of the episode compresses time to depict the deteriorating relations between Britain and America due to the Tea Act of 1773 and the Coercive Acts of 1774. The episode ends with Adams riding to Philadelphia (purposefully on his own horse rather than in an ornate carriage) to represent Massachusetts in the First Continental Congress.

Unfortunately, the episode is riddled with historical errors, starting in its first scenes. From home, Adams responds to ringing church bells, usually an indication of fire, to discover a scene of confusion on King Street with crowds running, Captain Preston yelling at his men not to fire, and freshly wounded men and boys dying in the snow. Actually, Adams was at a friend's house in South Boston and missed the whole commotion. "When We arrived We saw nothing," Adams wrote in his autobiography. The episode never introduces Adams's legal partner, Josiah Quincy, Jr., and it combines the prosecution of Preston and his men into one trial when they were actually separate. Adams's key witness, Richard Palmes (John Bedford Lloyd), was not a disheveled rope maker, as the film suggests, but a prominent merchant. Finally, the program exaggerates Adams's legal achievement by having the jury declare all the soldiers "not guilty." In fact, two of Preston's men were found guilty of the lesser charge of manslaughter.

The end of "Join or Die" includes a chilling portrayal of the tarring and feathering of a British customs official around the time of the Boston Tea Party in December 1773. John Hancock (Justin Theroux) orders the punishment and John Adams's cousin, Samuel Adams (Danny Huston), approves, to the dismay of John. The problem is that the incident never took place. Moreover, Hancock and Samuel Adams were never documented at any tarring and feathering, which happened infrequently. Similar errors persist throughout the remaining six episodes of *John Adams*.

Why bother then to watch the miniseries? *John Adams* is visually stunning, with some of the most ambitious sets of colonial and early national America ever realized (much of it was filmed in Colonial Williamsburg, Virginia). The first episode invites viewers to feel the bustle of the Boston waterfront, complete with teams of maritime workers and towering ships' masts. In addition, the series features a realistic, engaging portrayal of the storied marriage of John and Abigail Adams (Laura Linney, who, like Giamatti, won an Emmy Award for her role). As in real life, Abigail serves as John's moral anchor. She warns him before his closing statement in the Boston Massacre trial to avoid his cardinal sin of vanity. "Vanity?" asks John. To which Abigail replies, "You have overburdened your argument with ostentatious erudition."

Adams would go on to remind the Boston jury that "facts are stubborn things" (which he truly said). We must take the same message to heart when viewing *John Adams*. The series forces us both to appreciate the wonder of early America and to take in our history, regardless of the medium, with a critical eye.

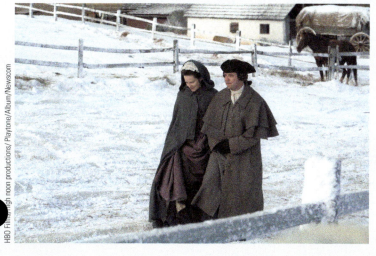

5.6 *John Adams* includes a convincing portrayal of the storied marriage between John and Abigail Adams.

5-3e Partial Repeal

The day of the massacre marked a turning point in Britain too, for on March 5, Lord North asked Parliament to repeal the Townshend duties, except the one on tea. North wanted all of them repealed, but the cabinet had rejected complete repeal by a 5-to-4 margin. As with the Stamp Act, Britain had three choices: enforcement, repeal, or modification. Force having failed, North chose the middle ground that had been rejected in 1766—modification. He claimed to be retaining only a preamble without a statute, a vestige of the Townshend Revenue Act, while repealing the substance. In fact, he did the opposite. Tea provided nearly three-fourths of the revenue under the act. North kept the substance but gave up the shadow.

This news reached the colonies just after nonimportation had achieved its greatest success in 1769 (see Table 5.1). The colonies reduced imports by about one-third from what they had been in 1768, but the impact on Britain was slight, partly because Britain had found a lucrative market for textiles by selling new uniforms to the huge Russian army. North had hoped that partial repeal, although it would not placate all of the colonists, would at least divide them. It did. Most merchants favored renewed importation of everything but tea, while the Sons of Liberty, most of whom were artisans, still supported broad nonimportation to sustain increased demand for their own manufactures.

Resistance collapsed first in Newport, where smuggling had always been the preferred method of challenging British authority. It spread to New York City, where the boycott on imports had been most effective. Soon Philadelphia caved in, followed by Boston in October 1770. By contrast, nonimportation had not caused a ripple in the import trade of the Chesapeake colonies. North's repeal was followed by an orgy of importation of British goods, setting record highs everywhere.

5-3f Disaffection

Repeal in 1770 lacked the impact that it had in 1766. There was no public rejoicing, not even when Lord North's government (he had replaced Grafton as prime minister in January 1770) took further steps to reduce tensions. The Quartering Act expired quietly in 1770, some of the more objectionable features of the vice-admiralty courts were softened, and the Currency Act of 1764 was repealed in stages between 1770 and 1773, as even London began to recognize that it was harming trade. Yet, North failed to restore confidence in the justice and decency of the British government. To a degree now difficult to appreciate, the empire ran on trust, or voluntarism, what people at the time called "affection." Its opposite, disaffection, had a more literal and dangerous meaning to them than it does today.

That fear sometimes broke through the surface calm between 1770 and 1773. Rhode Islanders had often clashed with customs officers and had even fired on the king's ships once or twice without stirring much interest in other colonies. Then in 1772, a predatory customs vessel, the *Gaspée*, ran aground near Providence while pursuing some peaceful coastal ships. After dark, men with blackened faces boarded the *Gaspée*, wounded its captain, and burned the ship. Britain sent a panel of dignitaries to the colony with instructions to send the perpetrators to England for trial. The inquiry failed because no one would talk.

Twelve colonial assemblies considered this threat so ominous that they created permanent **committees of correspondence** to keep in touch with each other and *anticipate* new threats to their liberties. Even colonial moderates now believed that British officials were conspiring to destroy liberty in America. When Governor Hutchinson announced in 1773 that, under the Townshend Act, Massachusetts Superior Court justices would receive their salaries from the imperial treasury, Boston created its own committee of correspondence and urged other towns to do the same. Boston's role in the "patriot" cause had grown dramatically since the convention of 1768, and such Bostonians as John Adams had become major spokesmen for colonial resistance. A plot to destroy their liberties now seemed plausible to many colonials. Hutchinson, amused at first, grew alarmed when most towns of any size followed Boston's lead. That there was a plot to destroy their liberties seemed obvious to them.

The Boston Massacre trials and the *Gaspée* affair convinced London that it was pointless to prosecute individuals for politically motivated crimes. Whole

Table 5.1 EXPORTS IN £000 STERLING FROM ENGLAND AND SCOTLAND TO THE AMERICAN COLONIES, 1766–1775

Colony	1766	1767	1768	1769	1770	1771	1772	1773	1774	1775
New England	419	416	431	224	417	1,436*	844	543	577	85.0
New York	333	424	491	76	480	655*	349	296	460	1.5
Pennsylvania	334	383	442	205	140	747*	526	436	646	1.4
Chesapeake†	520	653	670	715	997*	1,224*	1,016	589	690	1.9
Lower South‡	376	292	357	385*	228	515*	1,016	448	471	130.5
Totals	1,982	2,168	2,391	1,605	2,262	4,577*	3,310	2,312	2,844	220.3

Average total exports, 1766–1768 = £2,180; 1769 = 73.6% of that average, or 67.1% of 1768 exports; 1770 = 103.8% of that average, or 94.6% of 1768 exports.
*These totals surpassed all previous highs.
†Chesapeake = Maryland and Virginia.
‡Lower South = Carolinas and Georgia.

communities would have to be punished. That choice brought the government to the edge of a precipice. Was the empire held together by law and consent, or only by force? The use of force against entire communities could lead to outright war, and war is not and cannot be a system of justice. The spread of committees of correspondence within Massachusetts and throughout the colonies suggested that settlers who had been unable to unite against New France at Albany in 1754 now deemed unity against Britain essential to their liberties. By 1773, several New England newspapers were calling on the colonies to create a formal union.

In effect, the Townshend crisis never ended. With the tea duty standing as a symbol of Parliament's right to tax the colonies without their consent, genuine imperial harmony was becoming impossible. North's decision to retain the tea tax in 1770 did not guarantee that armed resistance would break out five years later, but it severely narrowed the ground on which any compromise could be built. The price of miscalculation had grown enormously.

5-4 Internal Cleavages: The Contagion of Liberty

Q *How did the British imperial crisis help to expose tensions within American society among the following groups: patriots and loyalists (and loyal colonies); artisans and gentlemen; tenants and landlords; settlers and proprietors; women and men; and slaves and masters?*

In his reply to his wife Abigail Adams's call to "Remember the Ladies" at the Second Continental Congress (see following sections), John Adams claimed to but laugh. "We have been told that our Struggle has loosened the bands of Government everywhere," he acknowledged. "That Children and Apprentices were disobedient—that schools and Colledges were grown turbulent—that Indians slighted their Guardians and Negroes grew insolent to their Masters." Indeed, American resistance to British imperial policies in the 1760s and 1770s opened new divisions and exposed existing cleavages in colonial American society. The imperial crisis encouraged a wide range of groups—including slaves, women, artisans, tenants, and even those who remained loyal to the Crown—to conceive of liberty in new ways.

5-4a Divided Loyalties

The imperial crisis divided Americans most obviously according to political allegiance. After American independence, it became common to characterize **loyalists**, those who remained committed to the king and to the British Empire, as backward, cowardly, and conservative to a fault. For the radical Thomas Paine, loyalists operated according to a "servile, slavish, self-interested fear" that kept them in Britain's corner. The early historian of the American Revolution Mercy Otis Warren called loyalists "Blockheads."

Despite these stereotypes, loyalism was far from a marginal position. Between one-fifth and one-third of all Americans remained loyal to the Crown during the imperial crisis (still others were disaffected and avoided choosing a side, unless forced).

The terms "loyalist" and "patriot" (describing an American revolutionary) did not apply until the Revolutionary War, but the divisions were already becoming apparent by the late 1760s. The Townshend crisis was a far more accurate predictor of future behavior than response to the Stamp Act had been. Nearly everyone had denounced the Stamp Act, including such future loyalists as Daniel Dulany. By contrast, most merchants and lawyers who resisted nonimportation in 1768 became loyalists by 1775. Artisans, merchants, and lawyers who supported the boycotts, especially those who favored continuing them past 1770, became patriots.

In other respects, few differences distinguished the supporters and opponents of American resistance to British policies. The two sides shared a common appreciation for British liberties and the rule of law. Many loyalists also resented London's efforts to tax the American colonies. Still, for some, particularly in official government positions, the cost of supporting resistance proved too high. For others, a cautious cast of mind or temperament impeded radical action. The longtime Massachusetts colonial official Thomas Hutchinson fit both cases. "My Temper Does Not Incline to Enthusiasm," he once stated. For a generation, Hutchinson had been the most reliable public opponent of British navy press gangs in Boston and had privately opposed the Stamp Act. Yet, in June 1774, upon being relieved of his duties as Massachusetts governor, he sailed for England, never to return. In London, Hutchinson connected with other American-born British subjects exiled from their home. The group included the celebrated artists Benjamin West and John Singleton Copley, who reported in August that he "dined with Gov'r Hutchinson, and I think there was 12 of us altoge[the]r, all Bostonians, and we had Choice Salt Fish for Dinner."

Besides high colonial officials, northern Anglican clergymen constituted the most loyal group to the Crown. From 1760, the Massachusetts native Jacob Bailey served as an Anglican missionary on the Maine frontier. A Harvard classmate of John Adams, Bailey faced increasing pressure in the 1760s and 1770s to violate his sacred oath to the king, the head of his church, in favor of supporting the American resistance movement. Bailey endured numerous public threats and the slaughter of his livestock before fleeing to Nova Scotia in 1779. The war would turn other religious groups, most notably Quakers and German pietists in Pennsylvania, into de facto loyalists for abiding by their spiritual belief in pacifism and refusing to take sides in the imperial conflict.

The tactics of American resistance produced further divisions in the colonial population. The Sons of Liberty censured those who did not support resistance as "Tories," after the one of Britain's two traditional parties most associated with monarchism. As nonimportation emerged as a leading tactic for resisting British policies, committees formed in the colonies to monitor consumption behavior. Individuals signaled their political allegiance by the beverages they drank and the garments they wore. The consequences of violating nonimportation agreements ranged from forced confessions and apologies to acts of violence and public humiliation, such as tarring and feathering.

The aggressive efforts to enforce compliance often backfired. Sixteen-year-old Kezia Coffin, a member of a wealthy whaling family in Nantucket, Massachusetts, denounced the American rebels in her diary: "It is Liberty which they pretend they are fighting for yet don't allow others liberty to think as they please." The loyalism of Coffin's family concerned her cousins Benjamin Franklin and his sister Jane Mecom. The break with Britain proved especially personal for Franklin. He disowned his son William, the colonial governor of New Jersey, for remaining loyal to the British Crown.

As with families, the imperial crisis divided entire British colonies and Atlantic regions from one another. By the early 1770s, Britain had 26 imperial units in the Western Hemisphere; half would remain loyal. Events during the Stamp Act crisis of 1765–1766 and Townshend crisis of 1767–1770 anticipated this divergence within the British Atlantic community. Leaders of the American resistance hoped for support in British Canada, particularly Nova Scotia. Despite an influx of New England settlers and some street protests against the Stamp Act, the Nova Scotia assembly never objected to the British taxes. London-based business interests and the Royal Navy's primary North American base at Halifax dominated the colony's politics.

Nova Scotia joined Quebec, Florida, Bermuda, Grenada, Barbados, Jamaica, and Georgia (briefly) as British colonial territories where the Stamp Act went into effect. As the two largest, most populous, and most lucrative Caribbean colonies, Jamaica and Barbados also represented the most disappointing losses for the American resistance movement. The British West Indies as a whole paid 78 percent of total stamp revenues before the law's repeal. With their large slave populations (and fear of slave rebellions) and close political and economic ties to Britain, the sugar islands objected to what the Barbados assembly called the "violent spirit" of American protests. The response opened a rift in the formerly close relationship between the mainland colonies and the West Indies. Upon learning of the Barbadian position, John Dickinson defended colonial resistance in declaring, "I am a North-American." By the First Continental Congress in 1774, American leaders still held out some hope (in vain) of Canadian participation, but did not bother to court the West Indian colonies.

5-4b Urban and Rural Discontent

Patriot leaders also faced challenges from within their own ranks. Urban artisans, who had mobilized to resist Britain in 1765 and 1769, demanded more power. In Boston, where the economy had been faltering since the 1740s while taxes remained high, Britain's policies bore hard on the town and gave an angry edge to its protests. Boston's radical artisans set the pace of resistance in every imperial crisis. In New York City, Philadelphia, and Charleston, artisans began to play a much more assertive role in public affairs.

Tensions increased in the countryside as well as in the cities. Three processes intensified discontent in rural areas: a revival of old proprietary claims, massive foreign immigration, and settlement of the backcountry.

Between about 1730 and 1750, the men who owned 17th-century proprietary charters or manorial patents finally began to see prospects for huge profits by enforcing these old legal claims. Taken together, the claims of New York's manor lords, the East Jersey proprietors, and the Penn (Pennsylvania), Baltimore (Maryland), Fairfax (Virginia), and Granville (North Carolina) families blanketed the colonies from New York to North Carolina. They were the biggest winners in America's **feudal revival**, the use of old charters to pry income from the settlers (see Map 5.2).

In the charged atmosphere created by the imperial crisis, the attempt to raise land rents and leases produced unrest in several rural areas. Some of the largest disturbances took place on the great estates of the Hudson Valley in New York. As leases became more restrictive and as Yankees swarmed into New York, discontent increased. In 1753, the proprietor of Livingston Manor had difficulty putting down Yankee rioters, and tension spread throughout the Hudson Valley over the next decade.

In 1766, several thousand angry farmers, inspired by the Stamp Act riots, took to the fields and the roads to protest the terms of their leases. They threatened to kill the lord of Livingston Manor or to pull down the New York City mansions of absentee landlords. Supported by some of the city's most prominent Sons of Liberty, the colony called in redcoats to suppress the riots. New York's experience exposed the difficulties of uniting urban and rural radicals in a common cause. But when New York landlords tried to make good their claims to the upper Connecticut Valley, the settlers defied them, set up their own government, and, after a long struggle, ultimately became the independent state of Vermont.

Massive immigration from Europe, mostly through Philadelphia, and the settlement of the backcountry added to rural social tensions. Most immigrants were Scottish or Scots-Irish Presbyterians, Lutherans, or German Reformed Protestants. They were dissenters from the prevailing faith in the colonies they entered, whether it was the Quaker religion in Pennsylvania or the Church of England from Maryland to Georgia. They angered Indians by squatting on their land and, often, by murdering those in their way—behavior that the Paxton Boys' 1763 uprising attempted to justify. In the Carolina backcountry, the newcomers provoked the Cherokee War of 1759–1761, which brutalized and demoralized the whole region.

After the Cherokee War, bands of outlaws, men dislocated by the war, began roaming the countryside, plundering the more prosperous farmers and often raping their wives and daughters. As the violence peaked between 1765 and 1767, the more respectable settlers organized themselves as "regulators" (a later generation would call them "vigilantes") to impose order in the absence of organized government. South Carolina claimed jurisdiction over the backcountry, but the colony's law courts were in Charleston, more than 100 miles to the east.

▲ MAP 5.2 **Feudal Revival: Great Estates of Late Colonial America** On the eve of the Revolution, more than half of the land between the Hudson Valley and North Carolina was claimed by men who had inherited or acquired various kinds of 17th-century charters or patents.

Q Although they were generally separate from Britain's imperial reforms of the 1760s and 1770s, how did the attempts by proprietors and other large landowners to raise rents resemble official British policies?

Q How did the feudal revival, in which a small number of people held vast amounts of land, clash with the spirit of the emerging American Revolution?

Even though most white settlers now lived in the backcountry, they elected only two of the 48 members of South Carolina's assembly. They had no local government.

The regulators in South Carolina soon caused as many disturbances as they put down. By 1769, civil war was only averted when the governor promised to create a circuit court system for the colony that would finally bring government to the backcountry. Violence ebbed, but tensions remained severe.

In the North Carolina backcountry, a separate regulator movement emerged to address abuses and corruption in the colony's government. The backcountry contained over half the colony's population but elected only 17 of 78 assemblymen. By 1770, after first trying to work within the assembly, the regulators openly challenged the authority of the colonial government. In early 1771, North Carolina governor William Tryon responded by marching 1,000 militiamen westward. They defeated a force of more than 2,000 poorly armed regulators at the battle of Alamance Creek. Seven regulators were hanged, and many fled the colony. North Carolina entered the Revolution as a bitterly divided society.

5-4c Slaves and Women

In Charleston, South Carolina, in 1765, the Sons of Liberty marched through the streets chanting "Liberty and No Stamps." To their amazement, slaves organized a parade of their own, shouting, "Liberty! Liberty!" Merchant Henry Laurens tried to convince himself that they probably did not understand the meaning of the word.

Around the middle of the 18th century, slavery came under serious attack for the first time. An antislavery movement arose on both sides of the Atlantic and attracted both future patriots and loyalists. In the 1740s and 1750s, Benjamin Lay, John Woolman, and Anthony Benezet urged fellow Quakers to free their slaves. In the 1750s, the Quaker Yearly Meeting placed the slave trade off-limits and finally, in 1774, forbade slaveholding altogether. Any Friend not complying by 1779 would be disowned. Britain's Methodist leader, John Wesley, in most other respects a social conservative, also attacked slavery, as did several colonial disciples of Jonathan Edwards. A few decades after the Great Awakening, many evangelicals were beginning to agree with South Carolina's Hugh Bryan in 1742, that slavery was a sin.

By the 1760s, supporters of slavery found that they now had to defend the institution. Hardly anyone had bothered to do so earlier, because a social hierarchy seemed necessary and inevitable, and slavery simply marked the bottom extreme. As equal rights became a popular topic, however, some suggested that *all* people could claim these rights, and slavery came under attack. In Scotland, Adam Smith, the most original economist of the age, praised African slaves for their "magnanimity," which, he claimed, "the soul of the sordid master is scarce capable of conceiving." Arthur Lee, a Virginian, defended the character of his fellow planters against Smith's charge but discovered that he could not justify slavery, "always the deadly enemy to virtue and science." Patrick Henry agreed. Slavery, he wrote, "is as repugnant to humanity as it is inconsistent with the Bible and destructive of liberty." He did keep slaves, but only because of "the general inconvenience of living without them. I will not, I cannot justify it." Granville Sharp, an early abolitionist, brought the Somerset case before the Court of King's Bench in 1771 and compelled Chief Justice William Murray, baron Mansfield, to declare slavery incompatible with the "free air" of England. That reluctant decision enabled many of England's 10,000 or 15,000 blacks to claim their freedom.

New Englanders began to head in similar directions. Two women, Sarah Osborn and **Phillis Wheatley**, played leading roles in the movement. Osborn, an English immigrant to Newport, Rhode Island, and a widow, opened a school in 1744 to support her family. A friend of revivalist George Whitefield, she also taught women and blacks and began holding evening religious meetings, which turned into a big local revival. At one point in the 1760s, about one-sixth of Newport's Africans were attending her school. That made them the most literate African population in the colonies, even though they were living in the colonial city with the highest percentage of its merchants deeply involved in the African slave trade. Osborn's students supported abolition of the slave trade and, later, of slavery itself.

In 1761, an eight-year-old girl who would become known as Phillis Wheatley arrived in Boston from Africa and was purchased by wealthy John Wheatley as a servant for his wife, Susannah, who treated her more like a daughter than a slave and taught her to read and write. In 1767, Phillis published her first poem in Boston, and she visited London as a celebrity in 1773 after a volume of her poetry was published there. Her poems deplored slavery but rejoiced in the Christianization of Africans. Some of them supported the patriot cause against Britain, but she withheld those from the London edition.

Soon many of Boston's blacks sensed an opportunity for emancipation. On several occasions in 1773 and 1774, they petitioned the legislature or the governor for freedom, arguing that, although they had never forfeited their natural rights, they were being "held in slavery in the bowels of a free and Christian Country." When the legislature passed a bill on their behalf, Governor Hutchinson vetoed it. Boston slaves made it clear to Hutchinson's successor General Gage that they would serve him as a loyal militia in exchange for their freedom. In short, they offered allegiance to whichever side supported their emancipation. Many patriots began to rally to their cause. "If we would look for Liberty ourselves," the town of Medfield declared in 1773, "…we ought not to continue to enslave others but immediately set about some effectual method to prevent it for the future."

The patriots could look to another group of allies as well. Many women became indispensable to the broader resistance movement. Although they could not vote or hold office, nonimportation, without their willing support, would have been not just a failure, but a fiasco. In thousands of households, women joined the intense discussions about liberty and agreed to make homespun clothing to take the place of imported British textiles. Moreover, women made a disproportionate sacrifice by giving up tea, which they mostly consumed, while men kept drinking rum (which escaped the first rounds of nonimportation).

5.7 Phillis Wheatley Portrait of Phillis Wheatley by Scipio Moorhead, a black artist, appeared opposite the title page of her collected poems, published in 1773.

Freedom's ferment made a heady wine. After 1773, further challenges to British power would continue to trigger enormous social changes within the colonies.

5-5 The Last Imperial Crisis

Q *Why did the colonists start a revolution after the Tea Act lowered the price of tea?*

The surface calm between 1770 and 1773 ended when Lord North moved to save the East India Company, Britain's largest corporation, from bankruptcy. It was being undersold in southeastern England and the colonies by low-priced, smuggled Dutch tea, which left the company's warehouses bulging with millions of unsold pounds of its own. North's main concern was the company, not colonial resistance to Townshend's tea duty. He failed on both fronts, creating a colonial crisis too big for Britain to handle without solving the company's problems.

5-5a *The Tea Crisis*

Lord North tried to rescue the company by empowering it to undersell its Dutch rivals. Franklin, in London as a colonial agent, reminded North that he could achieve that goal, for sound economic reasons, by repealing the Townshend duty in the colonies. North rejected that idea. The settlers would hardly revolt if he somehow managed to give them cheap tea! His Tea Act of 1773 repealed import duties on tea in England but retained the Townshend duty in the colonies. In both places, legal tea would be cheaper than anyone else's. The company would be saved, and the settlers, to get cheap tea, would accept Parliament's power to tax them.

Another aspect of the Tea Act antagonized most merchants in the colonies. The company sold tea to all comers at public auctions in London, but the Tea Act gave it a monopoly on the shipping and distribution of tea in the colonies. Only company ships could carry it, and a few consignees in each port would have the exclusive right to sell it. The combined dangers of taxation and monopoly again forged the coalition of artisans and merchants that had helped defeat the Stamp Act by 1766 and resist the Townshend Act by 1769. Patriots saw the Tea Act as a Trojan horse that would destroy liberty by seducing the settlers into accepting parliamentary sovereignty. North also unintentionally gave a tremendous advantage to those determined to resist the Tea Act. He had devised an oceanic, or external, measure that the colonists could actually nullify despite British control of the seas. No one would have to police the entire waterfront, looking for tea importers. The patriots had only to wait for the specially chartered tea ships and prevent their cargoes from landing.

5.8 "The Bostonians Paying the Excise-Man, or Tarring and Feathering" This London cartoon of 1774 satirized the Sons of Liberty.

Q *How does the cartoon use powerful imagery to remove America from the moral high ground in the imperial crisis?*

Direct threats usually did the job. Most tea ships quickly departed—except in Boston. There, Governor Hutchinson, whose sons were the local tea consignees, decided to face down the radicals. He refused to grant clearance papers to three tea ships that, under the law, had to pay the Townshend duty within 21 days of arrival or face seizure. Hutchinson meant to force them to land the tea and pay the duty. This deadline led to urgent mass meetings for several weeks and, finally, a major crisis. Convinced that they had no other way to block the landing of the tea, the radicals organized the **Boston Tea Party**. Disguised as Indians, they threw 342 chests of tea, worth about £11,000 sterling (the equivalent of more than $1 million in current dollars), into Boston Harbor on the night of December 16, 1773.

5-5b Britain's Response: The Coercive Acts

This willful destruction of private property shocked both Britain and America. Convinced that severe punishment was essential to British credibility, Parliament passed four **Coercive Acts** during spring 1774. The Boston Port Act closed the city's port until the town paid for the tea. A new Quartering Act allowed the army to quarter soldiers among civilians, if necessary. In response to the Boston Massacre trials, the Administration of Justice Act permitted a British soldier or official, charged with a crime while carrying out his duties, to be tried in another colony or in England. Most controversial of all was the Massachusetts Government Act. It modified the Massachusetts charter of 1691, made its elected council appointive, and restricted town meetings. In effect, it made Massachusetts like other royal colonies. Before it passed, the king named General Gage, already the commander of the British army in North America, as the new governor of Massachusetts, with the understanding that he could use military force against civilians.

Parliament passed a fifth law, unrelated to the Coercive Acts but significant nonetheless. The Quebec Act established French civil law and the Roman Catholic Church in the Province of Quebec, provided for trial by jury in criminal but not in civil cases, gave legislative but not taxing power to an appointive governor and council, and extended Quebec's administrative boundaries to the area between the Great Lakes and the Ohio River, saving the legitimate charter claims of other colonies. Historians now regard the act as a farsighted measure that gave French Catholics the toleration that the empire had denied to Acadians 20 years earlier, but settlers from New England to Georgia were appalled. Instead of leniency and toleration, they saw a deliberate revival of the power of New

5.9 "The Able Doctor, or America Swallowing the Bitter Draught" This 1774 engraving by Paul Revere used "The Bostonians Paying the Excise-Man" as a model but turned it into a patriot statement. In Revere's version, the British are forcing tea down the throat of America (represented by a ravished lady, Liberty). The British are also imposing martial law in Boston.

France and the Catholic Church on their northern border, now bolstered by Britain's naval and military might. The Quebec Act intensified the fear that evil ministers in London were conspiring to destroy British and colonial liberties. Many colonists suspected that the autocratic government of Quebec might become a model for restructuring their own provinces. Settlers lumped the Quebec Act with the Coercive Acts and coined their own name for all of them—the Intolerable Acts.

5-5c The Radical Explosion

The interval between passage of the Port Act in March and the Massachusetts Government Act in May permits us to compare the response that each provoked. The Port Act was quite enforceable and immune to nullification by the colonists. It led to the summoning of the First Continental Congress and another round of nonimportation; but the colonists *did* nullify the Government Act. This resistance led to war. The redcoats marching to Concord on April 19, 1775 were trying to enforce that act against settlers who absolutely refused to obey it.

Gage took over as governor of Massachusetts in May 1774, before passage of the Massachusetts Government Act. In June, he closed the ports of Boston and Charlestown, just north of Boston. The navy gave him that power. While Boston split over the proper response, a mass meeting in New York City rejected immediate nonimportation in favor of an intercolonial congress. Philadelphia followed New York's lead. In both cities, cautious merchants hoped that a congress might postpone or prevent radical measures of resistance.

North assumed that the Coercive Acts would isolate Boston from the rest of the province, Massachusetts from the rest of New England, and New England from the other colonies, a goal that Britain would pursue through 1777. Instead, contributions began pouring in from all of the colonies to help Boston survive. The Stamp Act crisis and the Townshend crisis had been largely urban affairs. The Intolerable Acts politicized the countryside on a scale never seen before. When royal governors outside Massachusetts dismissed their assemblies to prevent them from joining the resistance movement, colonists elected **provincial congresses**, or conventions, to organize resistance. These bodies were larger than the legal assemblies they displaced, and they mobilized far more people. As the congresses took hold, royal government began to collapse almost everywhere. Numerous calls for a continental congress made the movement irresistible. By June, it was also obvious that any congress would adopt nonimportation. Except for some details, that issue had been settled, even before the congress met, by mandates that the delegates brought with them.

Yet, Gage remained optimistic well into the summer. Then news of the Massachusetts Government Act arrived on August 6. Gage's authority disintegrated when he tried to enforce the act, which marked the most dramatic attempt yet made by Parliament to control any colony's internal affairs. The councilors that Gage appointed to the new upper house either resigned their seats or fled to Boston to seek the army's protection. The Superior Court could not hold its sessions, even in Boston under the guns of the army, because jurors refused to take an oath under the new act. At the county level (the real center of royal power in the colony), popular conventions closed the courts and took charge of law enforcement in August and September. Gage began to realize that none of his major objectives was achievable.

Before this explosion of radical activity, Gage had called for a new General Court to meet in Salem in October. Many towns sent representatives, but others followed the lead of the Worcester County Convention, which urged all towns to elect delegates to a provincial congress in Concord, 17 miles inland, out of range of the navy. Although Gage revoked his call for a General Court, about 90 representatives met at Salem anyway. When Gage refused to recognize them, they adjourned to Concord in early October and joined the 200 delegates already gathered there as the Massachusetts Provincial Congress. That body became the de facto government of the colony and adopted the radical demands of the Suffolk Convention (representing Boston and its hinterland), which included a purge of unreliable militia officers, the creation of a special force of armed "minutemen" able to respond rapidly to any crisis, and the payment of taxes to the congress in Concord, not to Gage in Boston. The Provincial Congress collected military stores at Concord and created an executive arm, the Committee of Public Safety.

5.10 "The Alternative of Williams-burg" (1775)
Published in London, this cartoon highlights the violence and intimidation faced by loyalists. A Virginia loyalist is forced to sign a patriot document by a mob of club-wielding "liberty men." On the left, a man is led toward a gallows in the background from which hangs a sack of feathers and a barrel of tar.

North assumed that Gage's army would uphold the new Massachusetts government. Instead, Gage's government survived only where the army could protect it. Thoroughly frustrated, he wrote North on October 30 that "a small Force rather encourages Resistance than terrifys." Gage then stunned London by asking for 20,000 redcoats, nearly as many as had been needed to conquer Canada.

5-5d The First Continental Congress

Into 1774, colonial patriots had looked to John Wilkes in London for leadership. At the **First Continental Congress**, they began relying on themselves. Twelve colonies (all but Georgia) sent delegates. In September 1774, they met at Philadelphia's Carpenters' Hall, a center of artisan strength. They scarcely even debated nonimportation. The southern colonies insisted, and the New Englanders agreed, that nonimportation finally be extended to molasses, which still generated revenue under the penny duty of 1766. The delegates were almost unanimous in adopting nonexportation if Britain did not redress colonial grievances by September 1775. Nonexportation was much more radical than nonimportation because it raised the threat of repudiating debts to British merchants, which colonial exports normally paid for.

Joseph Galloway, a Pennsylvania loyalist, submitted a plan of imperial union that would have required all laws affecting the colonies to be passed by both Parliament and an intercolonial congress, but his proposal was tabled by a vote of six colonies to five. The Congress spent three weeks trying to define colonial rights. Everyone insisted that the Coercive Acts, the Quebec Act, and all surviving revenue acts had to be repealed, and that all infringements on trial by jury had to be rejected. The delegates generally agreed on what would break the impasse, but they had trouble finding the precise language for their demands. They finally accepted the new principle of no *legislation* without consent—but added a saving clause that affirmed colonial assent to existing acts of Parliament that *only* regulated their trade.

Congress petitioned the king, not Parliament, because patriots no longer recognized it as a legitimate legislature for the colonies. Congress explained its position in separate addresses to the people of the 13 colonies, the people of Quebec, and the people of Great Britain. It took two other radical steps: It agreed to meet again in May 1775 if the British response was inadequate, and it created **the Association**—with citizen committees in every community—to enforce its trade sanctions against Britain. Most towns and counties heartily embraced the idea, and perhaps 7,000 men served on such committees during the winter of 1774–1775. In approving the Association, Congress began to act as a central government for the United Colonies.

5-5e Toward War

The news from Boston and Philadelphia shook the North ministry. "The New England Governments are in a State of Rebellion," George III wrote North, "blows must decide whether they are to be subject to this Country or independent." Although Franklin kept assuring the British that Congress meant exactly what it said, both North and the opposition assumed that conciliation could be achieved on lesser terms. Edmund Burke, out of office since 1766, urged a return to pre-1763 understandings without explaining how to restore the loyalty that had made them workable. "A great empire and little minds go ill together," he cautioned in an eloquent speech urging conciliation. Lord Chatham (William Pitt) introduced a bill to prohibit Parliament from taxing the colonies, to recognize Congress, and even to ask it to provide revenue for North American defense and to help pay down the national debt. When a government spokesman challenged him, Chatham retorted that his plan, if implemented, "must annihilate your power … and at once reduce you to that state of insignificance for which God and nature designed you." Neither plan passed.

The initiative lay with Lord North, who still hoped for a peaceful solution, but in January 1775, he made war inevitable. He ordered Gage to send troops to Concord, destroy the arms stored there, and arrest John Hancock and Samuel Adams. Only after sending this dispatch did he introduce his own Conciliatory Proposition. Parliament pledged that it would tax no colony that paid its share for imperial defense and gave proper salaries to its royal officials, but Britain would use force against delinquent colonies. To assure hard-liners that he was not turning soft, he introduced his New England Restraining Act on the same day. It barred Yankees from the Atlantic fisheries and prohibited commerce between New England and any place except Britain and the British West Indies, precisely the trade routes that Congress was blocking through nonimportation. Both sides were now committed to economic sanctions.

North's orders to Gage arrived before his Conciliatory Proposition reached America, and Gage obeyed. He hoped to surprise Concord with a predawn march, but Boston radicals knew about the expedition almost as soon as the orders were written. They had already made careful preparations to alert the whole countryside. Their informant, in all likelihood, was Gage's wife, Margaret Kemble Gage, a New Jerseyan by birth. At 2:00 a.m. on the night of April 18–19, about 700 elite troops began their march toward Concord. Paul Revere, a Boston silversmith who had done as much as anyone to create the information network that he now set in motion, galloped west with the news that "The redcoats are coming!" When he was captured past Lexington by a British patrol, Dr. Samuel Prescott, who was returning from a lady friend's house at the awkward hour of 1:00 a.m., managed to get the message through to Concord. As the British approached Lexington Green at dawn, they found 60 or 70 minutemen drawn up to face them. The outnumbered militia began to withdraw. Then somebody—probably a colonial bystander but possibly a British soldier—fired the first shot in what became the Battle of Lexington. The British line fired, killing eight and wounding nine. From every direction, like angry hornets, the countryside surged toward them. Secrecy had become pointless, and the British broke out their regimental fifes and drums. Cheered by the tunes, they marched to Concord and into another world war.

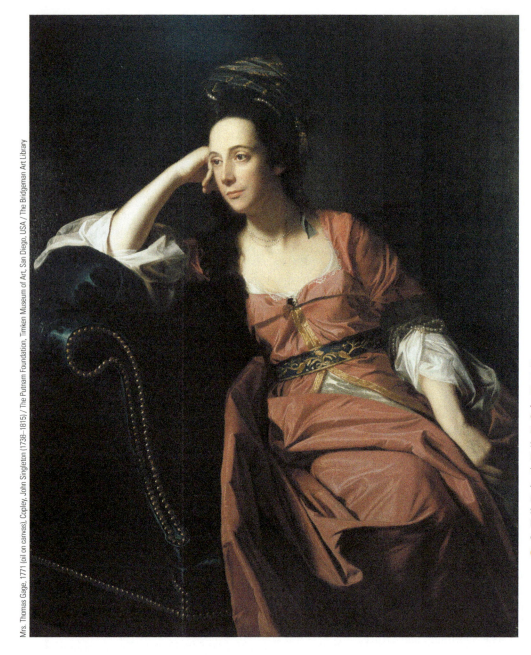

5.11 John Singleton Copley's 1771 Portrait of Margaret Kemble Gage, the New Jersey Woman Who Married General Sir Thomas Gage Pro-American in her sympathies, she was, in all probability, the highest-ranking informant that the Sons of Liberty ever acquired. Although no surviving document proves her involvement, Gage shipped her to England after Lexington and Concord, and the couple never again cohabited.

Q *How did the possible intelligence supplied by Margaret Kemble Gage to the patriot side both resemble and expand upon the actions of other women in the American resistance movement?*

5-6 The Improvised War

Q *How did the onset of war with Britain influence America's decision to declare independence and the language in the Declaration of Independence?*

In April 1775, neither side had a plan for winning a major war. Gage sent soldiers to enforce acts of Parliament. The militia fought for a political regime that Parliament was determined to change. They drove the British from Concord Bridge and pursued them all the way to Boston. Suffering only 95 casualties, they inflicted 273 on the British. Had a relief force not met the battered British survivors near Lexington, all of them might have been lost (see Map 5.3).

Even though no adequate command or supply structure existed, the colonists besieged Boston. After two months, Gage finally declared that all settlers bearing arms, and those who aided them, were rebels and traitors. He offered to pardon anyone who returned to his allegiance, except John Hancock and Samuel Adams. Instead of complying, the besiegers escalated the struggle two days later. They fortified the high ground on Breed's Hill (next to Bunker Hill) near Charlestown and overlooking Boston. The British sent 2,400 men, one-fifth of the garrison, to take the hills on June 17. Merely by seizing Charlestown Neck, a smaller force could have cut off the Yankee militia at low risk to itself. Instead, to prove that civilians had no chance against a regular army, General William Howe launched three frontal

CHAPTER 5 Reform, Resistance, Revolution, 1763–1776

attacks. Secure behind their defenses, the settlers shot more than 1,000 of the attackers, killing 92 officers (about one-sixth of those lost in the entire war), before they ran out of ammunition and withdrew. The defenders suffered about 370 casualties, nearly all during the retreat. A few more such victories, reflected one officer, and no one would be left alive to carry the news to London.

Well into 1776, both sides fought an improvised war. In May 1775, Vermont and Massachusetts militia took Fort Ticonderoga on Lake Champlain and seized the artillery and gunpowder that would be used months later to end the siege of Boston. Crown Point also fell. With nearly all of their forces in Boston, the British were too weak to defend other positions or to intervene in the short Indian conflict—Lord Dunmore's War—that broke out in the upper Ohio Valley in 1774. The collapse of royal government meant that the rebels now controlled the militia and most of the royal powder houses.

The militia became the key to political allegiance. Compulsory service with the militia politicized many waverers, who decided that they really were patriots only when a redcoat shot at them or when they drove a loyalist into exile. The militia kept the countryside committed to the Revolution wherever the British army was too weak to overwhelm them.

5-6a The Second Continental Congress

When the **Second Continental Congress** met in May 1775, it inherited the war. For months it pursued conflicting strategies of resistance and conciliation. It voted to turn the undisciplined men besieging Boston into a Continental army. As in earlier wars, the soldiers were volunteers willing to serve for only a few months, or a single campaign. In the absence of royal authority, they elected their officers, who tried to win obedience through persuasion, not command. Supplying them with food and munitions became a huge problem.

5.12 The Battle of Lexington, April 19, 1775 Ralph Earl's painting, which was engraved by Amos Doolittle in 1775, accurately portrays the opening shots of the Revolutionary War. The British are firing a volley into the Lexington militia, who are trying to leave the field without offering resistance. In fact, the first British soldiers who fired did so without orders, possibly in response to a shot from a colonial bystander. The militia was indeed trying to withdraw.

Q *How did the image reflect the differences in experience and training between the British regulars and the American militia?*

Most of the men were Yankees who would have preferred to serve under their own officers, but Congress realized that a successful war effort would have to engage the other colonies as well. On June 15, at the urging of John Adams of Massachusetts, Congress made George Washington of Virginia commanding general. When Washington took charge of the Continental army, he was appalled at the poor discipline among the soldiers and their casual familiarity with their officers. He insisted that officers behave with dignity and instill obedience. As the months passed, most of them won his respect. At year's end, however, nearly all of the men went home, and Washington had to train a new army for 1776. But enthusiasm for the cause remained strong, and fresh volunteers soon filled his camp.

In June 1775, Congress authorized an invasion of Canada to win over the French before they could side with the British and attack New York or New England. Two forces moved northward. One, under General Richard Montgomery, took Montreal. The other, commanded by Colonel Benedict Arnold, advanced on Quebec through the Maine forests and laid siege to the city, where Montgomery joined Arnold in December. With enlistments about to expire, they decided to assault the city, partly to get maximum service out of their men and partly to inspire some to reenlist. Their attack in a blizzard on December 31 was a disaster. Nearly half of the 900 men still with them were killed, wounded, or captured. Montgomery was killed and Arnold wounded. Both were hailed as American heroes.

The colonial objective in this fighting was still to restore government by consent under the Crown. After rejecting Lord North's Conciliatory Proposition out of hand, Congress approved an Olive Branch Petition to George III on July 5, 1775, in the hope of ending the bloodshed. Moderates, led by Dickinson, strongly favored the measure. The petition affirmed the colonists' loyalty to the Crown, did not even mention "rights," and implored the king to take the initiative in devising "a happy and permanent reconciliation." Another document written mostly by Virginia's Thomas Jefferson, "The Declaration of the Causes and Necessities of Taking Up Arms," set forth the colonies' grievances and justified their armed resistance. "We have counted the cost of this contest," Jefferson proclaimed, "and find nothing so dreadful as voluntary slavery." Like the Olive Branch, the declaration assured the British people "that we mean not to dissolve that Union which has so long and so happily subsisted between us." It reached London along with news of Bunker (Breed's) Hill. George III replied with a formal proclamation of rebellion on August 23. Predictably, the king's refusal to receive this moderate petition strengthened colonial radicals.

Congress began to function increasingly like a government, but with few exceptions, it assumed royal rather than parliamentary powers, which were taken over by the individual colonies. Congress did not tax or regulate trade, beyond encouraging nonimportation. It passed no laws. It took command of the Continental army, printed paper money, opened diplomatic relations with Indian nations, took over the postal service, and decided which government was legitimate in individual colonies—all functions previously performed by the Crown. In short, Congress thought of itself as a temporary plural executive for the continent, not as a legislature.

5-6b *War and Legitimacy, 1775–1776*

Into 1776, the British reacted with fitful displays of violence and grim threats of turning slaves and Indians against the settlers. When the weak British forces could neither restore order nor make good on their threats, they conciliated no one, enraged thousands, and undermined British claims to legitimacy. The navy burned Falmouth (now Portland), Maine, in October 1775. On November 7, John Murray, Earl of Dunmore and governor of Virginia, offered freedom to any slaves of rebel planters who would join his 200 redcoats. About 800 mustered under his banner only to fall victim to smallpox after the Virginia militia defeated them in a single action. **Dunmore's Proclamation**, as it became known, had a more immediate political influence, as the prospect of a mass slave emancipation pushed planters in Virginia and neighboring southern colonies toward independence.

In a separate action, Dunmore bombarded Norfolk, setting several buildings ablaze. The patriots, who considered Norfolk a loyalist bastion, burned the rest of the city and then blamed Dunmore for its destruction. Overall, his campaign undermined whatever loyalist sentiment survived among Virginia planters beyond Norfolk.

British efforts suffered other disasters in Boston and the Carolinas. The greatest colonial victory came at Boston, where most of the British army lay virtually imprisoned. On March 17, 1776, after Washington fortified Dorchester Heights south of the city and brought heavy artillery (from Ticonderoga) to bear on it, the British pulled out and sailed for Nova Scotia. A loyalist uprising by Highland Scots in North Carolina was crushed at Moore's Creek Bridge on February 27, and a British naval expedition sent to take Charleston was repulsed with heavy losses in June. Cherokee attacks against Virginia failed in 1776 because they occurred after Dunmore had left and did not fit into any larger general strategy. Before spring turned to summer, patriot forces had won control of the territory of all 13 colonies. Except in East and West Florida, Quebec, and Nova Scotia, the British had been driven from the continent.

5-6c *Independence*

Dismissal by George III of the Olive Branch Petition left moderates no option but to yield or fight. In late 1775, Congress created a committee to correspond with foreign powers. By early 1776, delegates from New England, Virginia, and Georgia already favored independence, but they knew that unless they won over all 13 colonies, the British would be able to divide them. The British attack on Charleston in June nudged the Carolinas toward independence.

Resistance to independence came mostly from the mid-Atlantic colonies, from New York through Maryland. Elsewhere, provincial congresses had supplanted the colonial assemblies in 1774 and 1775. In the middle colonies, however, both assemblies and congresses met and competed for the loyalties of the people. None of the five legal assemblies in the mid-Atlantic region ever repudiated the Crown. All of them had to be overthrown along with royal (or proprietary) government itself. The last royal governor to be driven from his post was New Jersey's William Franklin (Benjamin's son), who was arrested on June 19, 1776, to prevent him from summoning a new session of the regular assembly.

In the struggle for middle colony loyalties, Thomas Paine's pamphlet *Common Sense* became a huge success. Published in Philadelphia in January 1776, it sold more than 100,000 copies within a few months and reached more people than any other colonial tract ever had. Paine, a recent immigrant from England, wasted no reverence on Britain's mixed and balanced constitution. To him, George III was "the Pharaoh of England" and "the Royal Brute of Great Britain." Paine attacked monarchy and aristocracy as degenerate institutions and urged Americans to unite under a simple republican government of their own. "Reconciliation and ruin are nearly related," he insisted. "There is something very absurd, in supposing a Continent to be perpetually governed by an island."

The British continued to alienate the colonists. The king named Lord George Germain, a hard-liner, as secretary of state for the American colonies, and thus as war minister. Germain tried to hire 20,000 Russian mercenaries, who, smirked one British official, would make "charming visitors at New York and civilize that part of America wonderfully." When that effort failed, the British bought the services of 17,000 soldiers from Hesse and other north German states.

▲ **MAP 5.3 Lexington, Concord, and Boston, 1775** The British march to Lexington and Concord on April 19, 1775, touched off the Revolutionary War. The colonists drove the redcoats back to Boston and then besieged the city for 11 months until the British withdrew.

Q *How did the geography of the Massachusetts countryside and the improvised nature of the opening battles of the American Revolutionary War tend to favor the patriot side and its militia forces?*

Q *How might the outcome of the opening battles of the Revolutionary War gone differently had the Americans declared independence before the war started?*

What They Said

Contrasting Views of American Independence

In January 1776, with war continuing between Britain and its American colonies, the idea of American independence gained currency for the first time. In a remarkable coincidence, on January 9, the same day that Thomas Paine's pamphlet *Common Sense* calling for independence was first published, an anonymous loyalist writing under the name "Junius" argued against independence in a letter printed in the *New-Hampshire Gazette*. Whereas Paine's pamphlet helped to ignite a revolution, Junius's letter ultimately failed in its attempt to keep New Hampshire's rebellious assembly (known as the Provincial Congress) from supporting independence. On January 9, however, this outcome was far from clear. These two works, published on the same day, indicate the wide spectrum of political views that existed in America on the eve of independence.

▶ Junius, "To the Congress at Exeter"

We began the Controversy on this Principle, to seek *Redress of Grievances*: since, we have lost Sight of the Object, and are in Quest of what will terminate most certainly in our Ruin, & Destruction: I mean INDEPENDENCY upon Great Britain; a Step that the Public are exceedingly averse to; but the Public in general are ignorant of the Design & Tendency of the Conduct of their Representatives....

[W]e depend wholly on ourselves—that is a Continent of 1000 Miles Sea Coast defending themselves without one Ship of War against 310 Battle Ships compleatly manned and fitted. A Country that can pay but 30 Thousand Men, at War with a Nation that has paid, and can pay 150 thousand. A Country of three Millions of Inhabitants, fighting with a Nation of 15 Millions. A Country that can raise but 1 Mil[lion] in Specie. A Country without Arms, without Ammunition, without Trade, contending with a Nation that enjoys the whole in the fullest Latitude.

▶ Thomas Paine, *Common Sense*

Every thing that is right or natural pleads for separation. The blood of the slain, the weeping voice of nature cries, 'TIS TIME TO PART. Even the distance at which the Almighty hath placed England and America, is a strong and natural proof, that the authority of the one, over the other, was never the design of Heaven....

It is not in numbers, but in unity, that our great strength lies; yet our present numbers are sufficient to repel the force of all the world.... Youth is the seed time of good habits, as well in nations as in individuals. It might be difficult, if not impossible, to form the Continent into one government half a century hence. The vast variety of interests, occasioned by an increase of trade and population would create confusion. Colony would be against colony. Each being able might scorn each other's assistance: and while the proud and foolish gloried in their little distinctions, the wise would lament, that the union had not been formed before. Wherefore, the *present time* is the *true time* for establishing it.

Q *What fears did Junius have about a broader military conflict between Britain and America?*

Q *How does Paine use reason to overcome objections to independence? Do any of his arguments answer the fears expressed by Junius?*

Q *Regardless of the merits of their respective arguments, how do the works of Junius and Paine highlight the importance of events on the battlefield in shaping public opinion about independence?*

Sources: (top) Junius, "To the Congress at Exeter," *The New-Hampshire Gazette, and Historical Chronicle*, January 9, 1776, page 1; Library of Congress microfilm no. sv97017977; (bottom) Thomas Paine, *Common Sense*, originally published Philadelphia, 1776. Au. cited: Dover Thrift Edition, Mineola, New York, 1997, pp. 22, 25, 34, & 40.

(The colonists called them all **Hessians**.) To Jefferson, this action was "the last stab to [the] agonizing affection" that had once bound together the people of Britain and North America. Disturbing (but false) rumors suggested that Britain and France were about to sign a "partition treaty," dividing the eastern half of North America between them. Many congressmen concluded, some of them sadly, that only independence could counter these dangers by engaging Britain's European enemies on America's side. As long as conciliation was the goal, France would not participate, because American success would mean restoring the British Empire to its former glory. But Louis XVI (1774–1793) might well help the colonies win their independence if that meant crippling Britain.

From April to June, about 90 communities issued calls for independence. Most of them looked no further back than 1775 to justify their demand. The king had placed the colonists outside his protection, was waging war against them, and had hired foreigners to kill them. Self-defense demanded a permanent separation.

Congress finally broke the stalemate. On May 15, 1776, it voted to suppress "every kind of authority" under the British Crown, thus giving radicals an opportunity to seize power in Pennsylvania and New Jersey. Moderates still controlled New York, Delaware, and Maryland, but they reluctantly accepted independence as inevitable. In early June, Congress named a committee of five, including Jefferson, John Adams, and Franklin, to prepare a declaration that would vindicate America's decision to the whole world once independence had actually been decided upon.

On July 2, with the necessary votes in place, Congress passed Richard Henry Lee's resolution "that these United colonies are, and of right, ought to be, Free and Independent States; … and that all political connexion between them, and the state of Great Britain, is, and ought to be, totally dissolved." Two days later, 12 colonies, with New York abstaining for the time being, unanimously approved Jefferson's Declaration of Independence, as amended by Congress. "We hold these truths to be self-evident, that all men are created equal, that they are endowed by their Creator with certain unalienable Rights, that among these are Life, Liberty, and the pursuit of Happiness," Congress proclaimed in what is perhaps the most famous statement ever made in American public life. Whenever "any Form of Government becomes destructive of these ends, it is the Right of the People to alter or to abolish it, and to institute new Government, laying its foundation on such principles … as to them shall seem most likely to effect their Safety and Happiness."

Years later, Jefferson claimed that the Declaration "was intended to be an expression of the American mind." Rather than a product of any single philosophical tradition, it is a masterpiece of intellectual synthesis. Jefferson drew on several Enlightenment influences, including the natural rights theories of John Locke, the English opposition tradition, the moral sense philosophy of leading Scottish thinkers, and the universalist message of French *philosophes*. In turn, the Declaration itself became embraced as an Enlightenment text that contributed immediately to the law of nations, particularly for defining statehood, independence, and the recognition of new states.

After its opening rhetorical flourishes, the longest section of the Declaration listed 27 grievances indicting George III as a tyrant. The charges were crucial for justifying political separation from Britain and for enlisting support—both at home and abroad—for the American cause. As with the dozens of community declarations that preceded it, the Declaration emphasized the war as the key reason for independence. The indictment against the king builds to the final five most severe charges, all of which highlight war crimes committed by George III. The 27th and last grievance blames him for exciting "domestic insurrections amongst us," a veiled reference to Dunmore's Proclamation offering freedom to slaves who left their masters for the British war effort.

As if on cue, during the three days that Congress spent proclaiming American independence, the first ships of the largest armada yet sent across the Atlantic began landing British soldiers on Staten Island. Americans celebrated the creation of their new republic at the very moment that they faced a military challenge more ominous than any they had ever confronted before.

Conclusion

Between 1763 and 1776, Britain and the colonies became trapped in a series of self-fulfilling prophecies. Britain feared that without major reforms to guarantee Parliament's control of the empire, the colonies would drift toward independence. Colonial resistance to the new policies convinced the British that a movement for independence was already under way, a perception that led to sterner measures. Until a few months before it happened, nearly all colonists denied that they desired independence, but they began to fear that the British government was determined to deprive them of their rights as Englishmen. Britain's policy drove them toward a closer union with one another and finally provoked armed resistance. With the onset of war, both sides felt vindicated. The thousands of redcoats heading toward America did not bode well for colonial liberties. When the colonists did leave the empire, British ministers believed that their predictions had finally come true.

Both sides were wrong. The British had no systematic plan to destroy liberty in North America, and until the winter of 1775–1776, hardly any colonists favored independence. But the three imperial crises undermined mutual confidence and brought about what no one had desired in 1765, or even 1774—an independent American nation. Unable to govern North America, Britain now faced the grim task of conquering it instead.

CHAPTER REVIEW

Review

1. How did Britain's victory in the Seven Years' War lead to controversial imperial reforms for its American colonies?
2. How did Parliament resolve the Stamp Act crisis without fully surrendering its right to tax the American colonies?
3. What made the resolution of the Townshend crisis less satisfying for American colonists than the end to the Stamp Act crisis?
4. How did the British imperial crisis help to expose tensions within American society among the following groups: patriots and loyalists (and loyal colonies); artisans and gentlemen; tenants and landlords; settlers and proprietors; women and men; and slaves and masters?
5. Why did the colonists start a revolution after the Tea Act *lowered* the price of tea?
6. How did the onset of war with Britain influence America's decision to declare independence and the language in the Declaration of Independence?

Critical Thinking

1. The colonists insisted that the right to property was essential to the preservation of liberty. Taxation without representation was unconstitutional precisely because it deprived them of their property without their consent. How then could they find it appropriate and legitimate to resist British policies by destroying the property of stamp distributors, Thomas Hutchinson, and the East India Company?
2. In 1775, Lord North promised that Parliament would not tax any colony that paid its share of the costs of imperial defense and gave adequate salaries to its civil officers, but Congress rejected the proposal out of hand. Had George Grenville offered something of the kind between 1763 and 1765, might Britain have averted the Revolution? Specifically, if he had praised New Englanders and Virginians for their vigorous cooperation with the empire during the French and Indian War while censuring colonies such as Maryland and North Carolina for their lack of cooperation, would Boston have rioted and Patrick Henry have urged resistance?

Identifications

Review your understanding of the following key terms, people, and events for this chapter (terms in bold in text are included in the Glossary).

Proclamation of 1763, p. 136
Pontiac's War, p. 136
virtual representation, p. 139
nonimportation agreements, p. 141
Boston Massacre, p. 146
committees of correspondence, p. 148
loyalists, p. 149
feudal revival, p. 150
Phillis Wheatley, p. 152
Boston Tea Party, p. 155
Coercive Acts, p. 155
provincial congress, p. 156
First Continental Congress, p. 157
(the) Association, p. 157
Second Continental Congress, p. 159
Dunmore's Proclamation, p. 160
Hessians, p. 163

Suggested Readings

The best one-volume narrative history of the coming of the Revolution remains **Merrill Jensen's** *The Founding of a Nation: A History of the American Revolution, 1763–1776* (1968). **Bernard Bailyn's** *The Ideological Origins of the American Revolution* (1967) is necessary for understanding the ideological context for American protests. **Alan Taylor's** *American Revolutions: A Continental History, 1750–1804* (2016) is an ambitious attempt to explain the Revolution from the perspective of multiple groups and geographical vantages.

On the three imperial crises, **Edmund S. Morgan** and **Helen M. Morgan's** *The Stamp Act Crisis, Prologue to Revolution*, 3rd ed. (1953, 1995) has lost none of its saliency. **Pauline Maier's** *From Resistance to Revolution: Colonial Radicals and the Development of American Opposition to Britain, 1765–1776* (1972); **Richard D. Brown's** *Revolutionary Politics in Massachusetts: The Boston Committee of Correspondence and the Towns* (1970); and **Eric Hinderaker, Boston's Massacre** (2017) are all excellent on the process of disaffection. Important studies of America's internal tensions and urban protests include **Gary B. Nash's** *The Urban Crucible: Social Change, Political Consciousness, and the Origins of the American Revolution* (1979); and **Benjamin L. Carp's** *Rebels Rising: Cities and the American Revolution* (2007).

For engaging treatments of the imperial crisis from the British perspective, see **S. Max Edelson**, *The New Map of Empire: How Britain Imagined America before Independence* (2017); and **Eliga H. Gould**, *The Persistence of Empire: British Political Culture in the Age of the American Revolution* (2000).

David Hackett Fischer's *Paul Revere's Ride* (1994) and **Woody Holton's** *Forced Founders: Indians, Debtors, Slaves and the Making of the American Revolution in Virginia* (1999) trace the opening of the improvised war in Massachusetts and Virginia, respectively. **Pauline Maier's** *American Scripture: Making the Declaration of Independence* (1997) uses 90 local declarations of independence issued in spring 1776 to give context to Jefferson's famous text. Inversely, **David Armitage's** *The Declaration of Independence: A Global History* (2009) explores the broad global influences and impact of the document.

> **MINDTAP** is a fully online personalized learning experience built upon Cengage Learning content. MindTap® combines student learning tools—readings, multimedia, activities, and assessments—into a singular Learning Path that guides students through the course and helps students develop the critical thinking, analysis, and communication skills that are essential to academic and professional success.

6 The Revolutionary Republic, 1776–1789

6-1 Hearts and Minds: The Northern War, 1776–1777
▶ *Learning Objective:* Explain how the British decision to allow Washington's army to escape New York in August 1776 came back to haunt them in the battles of Trenton and Princeton.

The British Offensive
The Trenton-Princeton Campaign

6-2 The Campaigns of 1777 and Foreign Intervention
▶ *Learning Objective:* Identify what led France to intervene on the American side in the war.

The Loss of Philadelphia
Saratoga
French Intervention
Spanish Expansion and Intervention

6-3 The Crisis of the Revolution, 1778–1783
▶ *Learning Objective:* List the different considerations that drove loyalists, African Americans, and Indians to join the British war effort.

Loyalists, Black and White
The Indian Struggle for Unity and Survival
Violence and Attrition
Mutiny and Reform

6-4 The British Offensive in the South
▶ *Learning Objective:* Determine the factors that contributed to American victory in the south after the initial success of Britain's southern campaign.

Britain's Southern Strategy
The Partisan War
From the Ravaging of Virginia to Yorktown and Peace

6-5 A Revolutionary Society
▶ *Learning Objective:* Analyze the social changes that came about in the United States either directly or indirectly as a result of the American Revolution.

Religious Transformations
The First Emancipation
The Challenge to Patriarchy
Western Expansion, Discontent, and Conflict with Indians
The Northwest Ordinance

6-6 American Constitutionalism
▶ *Learning Objective:* Detail ways that state constitutions advanced American constitutional thinking during the revolutionary era.

John Adams and the Separation of Powers
Early State Constitutions
Massachusetts Redefines Constitutionalism
Articles of Confederation

6-7 The Constitution: A More Perfect Union
▶ *Learning Objective:* Examine how conditions in the United States in the 1780s influenced the outcome of the Constitution.

Commerce, Debt, and Shays's Rebellion
Cosmopolitans versus Localists
The Philadelphia Convention
Ratification

6.1 *The Surrender of Lord Cornwallis* This painting by John Trumbull, completed in 1820, celebrates the American victory over the British in the last major battle of the Revolutionary War, at Yorktown, Virginia, in October 1781. Claiming illness, the British commanding officer, General Lord Cornwallis, did not attend the ceremony, sending in his place General Charles O'Hara. General George Washington followed suit, directing his second-in-command, General Benjamin Lincoln, to accept the symbolic sword of surrender from O'Hara. Washington, to the right, looks on with his American forces, while their French allies observe to the left.

THE REVOLUTIONARY WAR killed a higher percentage of Americans who fought in it than any other American conflict except the Civil War. It too was a civil war. People were more likely to fight neighbors during the Revolution than they were between 1861 and 1865, when the geographical line separating the two sides would be much sharper. Twice, in 1776 and 1780, the British might have won, but in both campaigns the Americans somehow rallied. They won only by bringing in France as an ally. France brought in Spain.

During the war, Americans began to think, more than before, in crude racial categories. Ideas about racial inferiority clashed sharply with claims of universal rights and human equality. As whites, blacks, and Indians redefined their differences, they often resorted to racial stereotypes. Most Indians and enslaved Africans hoped that Britain would win the war.

Even as the war raged and the economy disintegrated, Americans drafted state constitutions and eloquent bills of rights that reached far beyond the racism many of them felt. They knew they were attempting something daring—the creation of a stable, enduring republic. Some European monarchies were 1,000 years old. No republic had lasted that long. Educated people knew a great deal about the city-states of classical Greece and about republican Rome—how they had called forth the noblest sentiments of patriotism for a time and then decayed into despotisms. Still, once Americans broke with Britain, they warmly embraced republicanism and never looked back. They were able to build viable republican governments because they grasped the voluntaristic dynamics of their society. They knew they had to restructure their governments through persuasive means. The use of force against armed fellow citizens would be self-defeating.

The war demonstrated how weak Congress was, even after ratification of the Articles of Confederation in 1781. Congress could not pay its bills. It could not expel the British from their western military posts or defeat the Indians of the Ohio Country. Yet in the Northwest Ordinance of 1787, Congress announced plans to create new states and admit them to the Union as equals of the original 13. Also in 1787, the Philadelphia Convention drafted a new Constitution for the United States. After ratification by 11 states, it went into effect in April 1789. The federal system it created became the most distinctive achievement of the revolutionary generation. ■

6-1 Hearts and Minds: The Northern War, 1776–1777

Q *How did the British decision to allow Washington's army to escape New York in August 1776 come back to haunt them in the battles of Trenton and Princeton?*

The price of patriotism escalated once independence became America's goal. The men ruling Britain believed the loss of the colonies would be fatal to British power. As a result, Britain raised more soldiers and larger fleets than ever before and more than doubled its national debt. Americans, too confident after their early successes, staggered initially under the onslaught before later recovering.

6-1a The British Offensive

The first setback came in Canada. In May 1776, when a fresh British force sailed up the St. Lawrence River, the Americans, weakened by smallpox, had to retreat. By July, Sir Guy Carleton drove them back into northern New York, to Fort Ticonderoga on Lake Champlain. Both sides built ships to control that strategic waterway. Largely through Benedict Arnold's efforts, the Americans held, and Carleton returned to Canada for the winter.

Farther south, Richard, Viscount Howe, admiral of the British fleet, and his brother General William Howe prepared an awesome striking force on Staten Island. They also acted as peace commissioners, with power to restore whole colonies to the king's peace and to pardon individual rebels. They hoped to avoid using their huge army, but when they wrote George Washington to open negotiations, he refused to accept the letter because it did not address him as "General." To do so would have recognized the legitimacy of his appointment. Unable to negotiate, the Howes had to fight.

Washington had moved his army from Boston to New York City, where he had about 19,000 men to face more than 30,000 redcoats and Hessians. Early successes had kept morale high among American forces and helped sustain the *rage militaire* (warlike enthusiasm) that had prompted thousands to volunteer in 1775 and 1776, including 4,000 veterans of 1775 who reenlisted for 1776. Although some men served in the Continental army and others with state militia units, the difference between them was still minimal. Neither had formal military training, and the men in both served only for short terms.

Washington was reluctant to abandon any large city. Against conventional military wisdom, he divided his inferior force and sent half of it from Manhattan to Long Island. Most of the men dug in on Brooklyn Heights, just two miles from lower Manhattan, and waited for a frontal attack. The British

CHRONOLOGY

1769	Spanish found San Diego
1775	Settlement of Kentucky begins
1776	Virginia becomes first state to adopt a permanent constitution and bill of rights • British forces land on Staten Island • Declaration of Independence • Pennsylvania constitution creates unicameral legislature • British win battle of Long Island; New York City falls • Washington wins at Trenton
1777	Washington wins at Princeton • Howe takes Philadelphia • Burgoyne surrenders at Saratoga • Congress completes Articles of Confederation
1778	Franco-American alliance
1779	Indians form alliances from the Gulf to the Great Lakes • Spain declares war on Britain • Continental dollar collapses
1780	Massachusetts constitution approved • Pennsylvania adopts gradual emancipation • British take Charleston, overrun South Carolina • Gordon riots in London • Arnold's treason exposed • Americans win at King's Mountain
1781	Continental army mutinies • Americans win at Cowpens • Congress creates executive departments • Articles of Confederation ratified • Cornwallis surrenders at Yorktown
1782	Americans massacre 100 unarmed Indians at Gnadenhutten
1783	Peace of Paris recognizes American independence
1785	Congress passes Land Ordinance
1786	Virginia passes Statute for Religious Freedom • Annapolis Convention
1786–1787	Shays's Rebellion in Massachusetts
1787	Northwest Ordinance • Philadelphia Convention drafts federal Constitution
1787–1788	Eleven states ratify the Constitution
1789	First federal Congress sends Bill of Rights to the states for ratification
1799	New York adopts gradual emancipation
1804	New Jersey adopts gradual emancipation

invaded Long Island, a loyalist stronghold, and on August 27, 1776, sent a force around the American left flank through unguarded Jamaica Pass. While Hessians feinted a frontal assault, the flanking force crushed the American left and rear and sent the survivors reeling.

The Howes did nothing to prevent the evacuation of the rest of the American army to Manhattan, which occurred under the cover of a fierce nor'easter storm. Instead, on September 11 the British opened informal talks with several members of Congress on Staten Island. The talks collapsed when the Americans insisted that the British recognize their independence before discussing other issues. Washington evacuated lower Manhattan. The British took New York City, much of which was destroyed on September 21 by fire, most likely set by Americans. The Howes then appealed directly to the people to lay down their arms and return to British allegiance within 60 days in exchange for a full pardon. In southern New York State, several thousand complied.

In October, the Howes drove Washington's remaining forces from Manhattan and Westchester. Although the brothers could have destroyed Washington's army on Long Island or Manhattan, they probably knew what they were doing. British victories and the American reliance on short-term volunteers were destroying Washington's army. British success seemed to prove that no American force could stand before a properly organized British army. But to capture Washington's entire army would have been a political embarrassment, leading to massive treason trials, executions, and great bitterness. Instead, Britain's impressive victories demoralized Americans and encouraged them to go home, many taking their muskets with them. In September, 27,000 Americans stood fit for duty in the northern theater (including the Canadian border); by December, only 6,000 remained, most of whom intended to leave when their enlistments expired on December 31.

The Howes' strategy nearly worked. In December, British forces swept across New Jersey as far south as Burlington. They captured Charles Lee, next in command after Washington, and Richard Stockton, a signer of the Declaration of Independence. Several thousand New Jersey residents, including Stockton, took the king's oath. To seal off Long Island Sound from both ends, the Howes also captured Newport, Rhode Island. Many observers thought the war was all but over as sad remnants of the Continental army crossed the Delaware River into Pennsylvania, confiscating all boats along the way so that the British could not follow them. One general believed that the time had come to "bargain away the Bubble of Independency for British Liberty well secured." Even Jefferson began to think about terms on which a restoration of the monarchy might be acceptable.

6-1b The Trenton-Princeton Campaign

Washington knew he had to do something dramatic to restore morale and encourage his soldiers to reenlist. In mid-December, the New Jersey militia, which had been silent for weeks, showed him how by harassing British outposts and patrols in the Delaware Valley, pushing the Hessian garrison at Trenton toward exhaustion. On Christmas night 1776, Washington crossed the ice-choked Delaware and marched south, surprising the Trenton garrison at dawn, which was nearly blinded by another nor'easter (see Map 6.1). At small cost to the attackers, nearly 1,000 Hessians surrendered.

The British sent their most energetic general, Charles, Earl Cornwallis, south with 8,000 men to "bag the fox"—Washington and the 5,000 Continentals and militia still with him. Cornwallis caught him at Trenton near sunset on January 2 but decided to wait until dawn before attacking. British patrols watched the Delaware to prevent another escape across the river, but Washington tried nothing of the kind. With his campfires burning, he muffled the wheels of his wagons and guns and stole around the British left flank, heading north. At dawn, he met a British regiment beginning its march from Princeton to Trenton. In the Battle of Princeton, the Americans, with a 5-to-1 edge in numbers, mauled yet another garrison.

Washington's two quick victories had an enormous impact on the war, although they inspired few reenlistments. The Howes, who had seemed to possess a firm grasp of revolutionary warfare, blundered in not hounding Washington's remnant of an army to its destruction after Princeton, if that was still possible. As the British departed, the New Jersey militia returned, asking who had sworn oaths to the king. Those who had taken the oath now groveled, as the price of acceptance, or fled to British lines. The Howes had encouraged loyalists to expose themselves and then abandoned them to the king's enemies. Together, the British and Hessians had lost the hearts and minds of the settlers. In 1777, few would be willing to declare for the Crown. The Revolution survived.

6-2 The Campaigns of 1777 and Foreign Intervention

Q *What led France to intervene on the American side in the war?*

Britain's thoughtful strategy of 1776 gave way to incoherence in 1777. The Howes again had a plan for winning the war, but it required 20,000 reinforcements that did not exist. Instead, Lord George Germain, Britain's war minister, ordered the Howes to take Philadelphia. He also sent John Burgoyne, a poet and playwright as well as a general, to Canada with orders to march his army south and link up with the garrison of New York City, commanded by Sir Henry Clinton.

The British aimed to control the Hudson River and isolate New England, where they still believed the rebellion to be strongest. Yet, without a firm commitment from the Howes to send men to support Burgoyne's march, the campaign made little sense. Instead, the Howes kept their forces together, rejected an overland march to Philadelphia as too risky, and decided to invade by sea—decisions that allowed Washington to shift men north to oppose Burgoyne.

6-2a The Loss of Philadelphia

After Trenton and Princeton, Washington demanded stricter discipline and longer terms of enlistment. Congress responded by raising the number of lashes a soldier could receive from 39 to 100 and by promising a cash bonus to anyone enlisting for three years, and a land bounty to anyone serving for the duration. Congress never came close to raising the 75,000 men it hoped for, but these new policies did create a solid foundation for a more experienced army. Longer terms made military training a real possibility, which in turn made the Continentals much more professional than the militia.

The Continental army acquired its own distinctive character. The men who signed up were often poor. About half of the New Jersey Line came from families that were not on the tax rolls. Some recruits were British deserters. Short-term militiamen, by contrast, usually held a secure place in their communities and were more likely than the Continentals to be church members. As the 1777 recruits came in, the two northern armies, swelled by militia, grew to about 28,000 men fit for duty—17,000 in northern New York and 11,000 under Washington.

In July 1777, the Howes sailed south from New York with 13,000 men. After his experience in New York, Washington was wary of being trapped in a city. Instead of trying to hold Philadelphia, he took up strong positions at Brandywine Creek along the British marching route but left open a line of retreat. On September 11, Howe again outmaneuvered him, drove in his right flank, and forced him to retreat. Congress fled to Lancaster. The British occupied Philadelphia on September 26.

After failing to destroy a British outpost at Germantown, Washington headed west to Valley Forge, where the army endured a miserable winter. There, Frederick Wilhelm, Baron von Steuben, a Prussian serving with the Continental army who would soon become a major general, devised a drill manual for Americans based on Prussian standards. (Known informally as the "blue book," the manual influences drill and ceremony in the U.S. Army to this day.) Through Steuben's efforts, the Continentals became far more soldierly. Other European volunteers also helped. From France came the Marquis de Lafayette and Johann, Baron de Kalb. The Poles sent Thaddeus Kosciuszko (a talented engineer) and Casimir, Count Pulaski. De Kalb and Pulaski were killed in American service. By the last years of the war, perhaps one-fifth of all Continental officers were professional soldiers from Europe, who gave the American officer corps an aristocratic tone that sometimes alarmed civilians.

6-2b Saratoga

In northern New York, Fort Ticonderoga fell to Burgoyne on June 2, 1777, but little went right for the British after that. Without support from the Howes, Burgoyne's army of 7,800, advancing from Ticonderoga toward Albany, was overwhelmed in the upper Hudson Valley. As his supply line to Canada grew longer, American militia swarmed behind him to cut it. By the time Burgoyne's surviving soldiers reached the Hudson and started toward Albany, the Americans under Horatio Gates outnumbered them 3 to 1. The British got as far as Bemis Heights, 30 miles north of Albany, but failed to break through in two costly battles, with Benedict Arnold distinguishing himself. Burgoyne retreated 10 miles to **Saratoga**, where he surrendered his entire army on October 17.

▲ **MAP 6.1 Revolutionary War in the Northern States** This map shows the campaigns in New York and New Jersey in 1776–1777, in northern New York and around Philadelphia in 1777, and at Monmouth, New Jersey, in 1778. The inset shows Washington's Trenton and Princeton campaigns after Christmas 1776.

Q *In a typical European conflict, Britain would have been the victor after winning major battles and occupying large American seaports, including New York and Philadelphia. Why was this not the case in the American Revolutionary War?*

Q *How did George Washington adjust his strategy after suffering a major defeat at New York in the summer of 1776?*

6-2c French Intervention

If Trenton and Princeton restored American morale, Saratoga won French hearts and minds. Since May 1776, Louis XVI had authorized secret aid to the American rebels. A French dramatist, Pierre-Augustin Caron de Beaumarchais, author of *The Barber of Seville* (1775) and later *The Marriage of Figaro* (1784), set up a fake firm to smuggle supplies through Britain's weak blockade of the American coast. (The British navy had committed most of its ships to transport and supply the army.) Without this aid, the Americans could not have continued the war.

In December 1776, Benjamin Franklin arrived in France as an agent of Congress. Although the French court could not officially receive him without risking a declaration of war

6-2 The Campaigns of 1777 and Foreign Intervention

6.2 Benjamin Franklin as Noble Savage, 1777 Franklin charmed the French court and polite society by playing the role of an American rustic. His diplomatic skill helped to secure France as an ally in the war against Britain.

Q *How did Franklin's appearance help to define the new American character?*

by Britain, the 70-year-old Franklin took Parisian society by storm. He adopted simple clothes, replaced his wig with a fur cap, and played to perfection the role of an innocent man of nature that French philosophes associated with Pennsylvania. Through Beaumarchais, he kept the supplies flowing and organized privateering raids on British commerce, which the French court claimed it could not stop.

The fall of Philadelphia alarmed Foreign Minister Charles Gravier, Comte de Vergennes. He feared that Congress might give up unless France entered the war. But Burgoyne's defeat at Saratoga convinced Louis that the Americans could win and that intervention was a good risk. Franklin and Vergennes signed two treaties in February 1778. One, a commercial agreement, granted Americans generous trading terms with France. In the other, France made a perpetual alliance with the United States, recognized American independence, agreed to fight until Britain conceded independence, and disavowed all territorial ambitions on the North American continent. Americans could not have hoped for more. Vergennes also brought Spain into the war a year later.

Franklin's treaties stunned London. Lord North proposed a plan of conciliation that conceded virtually everything but independence and sent a distinguished group of commissioners under Frederick Howard, Earl of Carlisle, to present it to Congress and block the French alliance. In 1775, such terms would have resolved the imperial crisis, but in June 1778, Congress, recognizing them as signs of British desperation, rejected them out of hand.

The war now transformed into a global conflict. George III declared war on France, recalled the Howe brothers, and ordered General Clinton to abandon Philadelphia. Fearing a French invasion of the British Isles while most of the Royal Navy was in American waters, the British redeployed their forces on a global scale. They stood on the defensive in America through most of 1778 and 1779 and even evacuated Newport, but loyalists, based in New York City or Long Island, often raided Connecticut and New Jersey.

6-2d Spanish Expansion and Intervention

Like France, Spain was eager to avenge old defeats against Britain. The Spanish king, Charles III (1759–1788), had endured the loss of Florida shortly after ascending the throne but had received Louisiana from France in compensation. Spanish rule there did not begin well. In 1769, Spain suppressed a small revolt against its restrictions on trade, but in later years, when its trade policy became more favorable, Louisiana enjoyed a level of prosperity it had never known before. The province attracted 2,000 immigrants from the Canary Islands, perhaps 3,000 Acadian refugees, and other French settlers from the Illinois Country.

Spaniards also moved into California, partly in response to the migration of Russian hunters into Alaska. Spain founded San Diego in 1769. In the next few years, Spaniards explored the Pacific coastline as far north as southern Alaska, set up an outpost at San Francisco Bay, and built a series of Franciscan missions under Junípero Serra. With little danger from other Europeans, Spain sent relatively few soldiers to California. In fact, its California frontier embodied many aspects of the earlier Florida missions. For the last time in the history of North America, missionaries set the tone for a whole province. As in Florida earlier, Indians died in appalling numbers from European diseases, and many bristled under the severe discipline of the missions.

Charles III saw the danger of one imperial power urging the subjects of another to revolt and never made an alliance with the United States, but in 1779 he joined France's war against Britain, hoping to retake Gibraltar and stabilize Spain's North American borders. Britain held Gibraltar, but Spain took West Florida. In 1783, Britain ceded East Florida as well, giving Spain, for the first time in a century, control of the entire coastline of the Gulf of Mexico. The treaty did not specify the northern boundary for Spanish West Florida, which resulted in a prolonged and bitter dispute between the United States and Spain. The Americans insisted that the boundary ran along the 31st parallel, while the Spanish claimed the east flank of the Mississippi River all the way up to the Ohio and Tennessee rivers.

History Through Film: Hamilton's America (2016)

Documentary that aired for the PBS series Great Performances *in the fall of 2016. Directed by Alex Horwitz. Starring Lin-Manuel Miranda, Thomas Kail, Alex Lacamoire, Ron Chernow, Leslie Odom, Jr., Christopher Jackson, Phillipa Soo, Barack Obama, George W. Bush.*

Arguably the most celebrated American cultural phenomenon of the early 21st century, the musical *Hamilton* has introduced a new generation to the American founders through rap lyrics and multiethnic casting. *Hamilton's America* provides a behind-the-scenes look at the musical, while also telling the biography of the musical's creator, Lin-Manuel Miranda, and its protagonist, Alexander Hamilton, America's first treasury secretary.

The documentary follows Miranda with footage dating to 2008, when he first started penning the opening number to the musical (then envisioned as *The Hamilton Mixtape*), shortly after returning from a vacation during which he read historian Ron Chernow's biography *Alexander Hamilton*. In 2009, Miranda performed the song before President Barack Obama and First Lady Michelle Obama at the White House Evening of Poetry, Music and the Spoken Word. The performance went viral, providing momentum for Miranda and his principle collaborators, musician Alex Lacamoire and director Thomas Kail, to complete the full musical. In early 2015, it debuted to rave reviews off Broadway at the Public Theater before soon moving to the Richard Rogers Theater on Broadway. *Hamilton's America* carries the story through the 2016 Tony Awards, in which *Hamilton* received a record-setting 16 nominations, winning 11 (including best musical), and Miranda's triumphant return to the White House to perform again, this time with his full cast, and to interview President Obama.

With *Hamilton*, Miranda accomplished something improbable in the eyes of most historians: transform Hamilton, "the ten-dollar Founding Father," from a conservative icon to a liberal hero. The musical emphasizes Hamilton's humble origins as a penniless, orphaned immigrant from the Caribbean who came to America to help found a country that was, like him, "young, scrappy, and hungry." The show's biggest applause line comes from a scene at the Battle of Yorktown at the close of the Revolutionary War in which Hamilton and the French aristocrat and general, the Marquis de Lafayette, declare: "Immigrants: We get the job done." The show further sells Hamilton to a contemporary audience by stressing his antislavery views in contrast to the slaveholding of his rival Thomas Jefferson.

Despite its popularity, the revisionism of *Hamilton* has not escaped criticism. Historians point out, immigrant or not, Hamilton became one of the most elitist founders and a fervent critic of democracy, arguing at the Constitutional Convention that the president and senators should serve for life. Moreover, while Miranda may have cast black and Latino actors as the founders, he includes few actual nonwhite characters in his story. The musical's celebratory tone is representative of "Founders Chic," a genre defined by uncritical salutes to the genius of the founders.

The documentary format of *Hamilton's America* allows for more nuance. The musical's actors visit historic and contemporary sites associated with their historical subjects. Miranda's trip to Wall Street and the New York Stock Exchange, as well as an interview with Senator Elizabeth Warren, provides the opportunity to explore Hamilton's mixed legacy of American financial success and economic inequality. The actor Christopher Jackson, who played George Washington in the musical's original production, makes a moving visit to Mount Vernon, Washington's estate, and discusses the challenge as an African American of playing a white slaveholder. The program even complicates common perceptions of Aaron Burr, who killed Hamilton in a duel and serves as the musical's chief villain. As a result, even without seeing *Hamilton* on stage, viewers of the documentary will engage deeply with the musical's parting question about how history is made and the past is remembered: "Who lives, who dies, who tells your story?" ■

6.3 Lin-Manuel Miranda as Alexander Hamilton in the musical *Hamilton*. In the background, Aaron Burr (to the left, Leslie Odom, Jr.) and George Washington (to the right, Christopher Jackson), applaud the musical's hero.

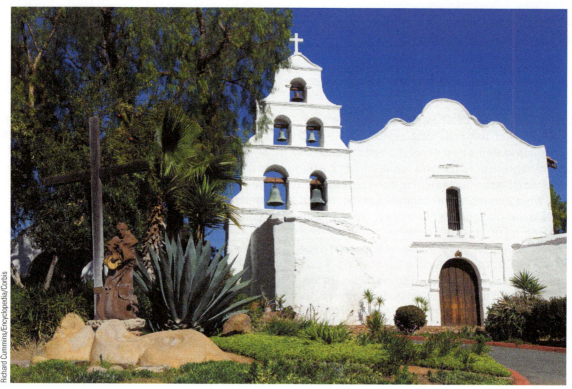

6.4 San Diego de Alcala This mission, the first California mission established by Spain, was founded on July 16, 1769.

6-3 The Crisis of the Revolution, 1778–1783

Q *What different considerations drove loyalists, African Americans, and Indians to join the British war effort?*

Americans expected a quick victory under the French alliance. Instead, the struggle turned into a grim war of attrition, testing which side would first exhaust its resources or lose the will to fight. The longer the war dragged on, the more it split each of America's broad cultural groups: whites, African Americans, and Indians. At times, America's revolutionaries even turned on one another.

The British sought to capitalize on American disunity. Loyalists became much more important to the British war effort, both as a source of manpower and as a major justification for continuing the war. The British also welcomed increasing numbers of Indians and African Americans to their side. Even as the imperial conflict between Britain and America turned into a global war, American society fractured into civil war and discord.

6-3a Loyalists, Black and White

Loyalists continued to embrace English ideas of liberty. They thought that creating a new American union was a far riskier venture than remaining part of the British Empire. Still, many waited until the fighting reached their door before deciding which soldiers to join. The British, in turn, were slow to take advantage of the loyalists. At first, British officers regarded loyalist military potential with the same disdain that they bestowed on the patriots. But after Saratoga, loyalists, who stood to lose everything in an American victory, showed that they could be impressive soldiers.

As much as a third of the white population chose the British side, and another third or more remained neutral or disaffected at different junctures of the war. 19,000 men joined one of some 40-odd loyalist military units, mostly after 1778, when Britain grew desperate for soldiers. Unlike most patriots, loyalists served long terms, even for the duration. They could not go home unless they won. By 1780, the number of loyalists under arms may have exceeded the number of Continentals by almost 2 to 1. American states retaliated by banishing prominent loyalists under pain of death and by confiscating their property.

When given the choice, most slaves south of New England also sided with Britain. In New England, they sensed that they could gain freedom by joining the rebels; many volunteered for service. Elsewhere, although some fought for the Revolution, they realized that their best chance of emancipation lay with the British army. During the war, at least 50,000 and as many as 100,000 slaves fled their owners amidst the commotion of the conflict; of that total, the British evacuated about 20,000 at the end of the war.

The decision to flee carried risks. In South Carolina during Clinton's 1776 invasion, hundreds reached the Sea Islands to join the British, only to face their owners' wrath when the British failed to rescue them. Some approached British units only to be treated as contraband (property). They faced possible resale. But most slaves who reached British lines won their freedom, even though the British army never became an instrument of systematic emancipation. When the British withdrew after the war, blacks went with them, many to Jamaica, some to Nova Scotia, others to London. In the 1780s, the British created a colony for former slaves at Sierra Leone in West Africa. A few even ended up in Australia.

The war, in short, created an enormous stream of refugees, black and white. In addition to 20,000 former slaves, some 60,000 to 70,000 colonists left for other parts of the British Empire. The American Revolution created 30 refugees for every 1,000 people, compared with 5 per 1,000 created by the French Revolution in the 1790s. About 35,000 settlers found their way to the Maritime Provinces. Another 6,000 to 10,000 fled to Quebec, settled upriver from the older French population, and in 1791 became the new province of Upper Canada (later Ontario).

After 1783, loyalist refugees helped to reinvigorate the British Empire. In Canada, low taxes and a generous land policy, which required an oath of allegiance to George III, attracted thousands of loyalist immigrants from the United States (known as "late loyalists" because they fled after the Revolutionary War). By the War of 1812, four-fifths of Upper Canada's 100,000 people were American-born. Although only one-fifth of them could be traced to the loyalist emigration, these settlers supported Britain in that war. In a real sense, the American Revolution laid the foundation for two new nations—the United States and Canada—and competition between them for settlers and their loyalties continued long after the fighting stopped.

6-3b The Indian Struggle for Unity and Survival

As the war persisted, Indians also increasingly joined the British. Most Indians saw that an American victory would threaten their survival as a people on their ancestral lands. They supported Britain in the hope that a British victory might stem the flood of western expansion, and they achieved a level of unity without precedent in their history (see Map 6.2).

At first, most Indians tried to remain neutral. The British were rebuffed when they asked the Iroquois to fight against the colonists. Delawares and Shawnees, defeated in Dunmore's War in 1774, also stood neutral. Only the Cherokees took up arms in 1776. Short on British supplies, they took heavy losses before making peace and accepting neutrality—although a splinter group, the Chickamaugas, continued to resist. In the Deep South, only the Catawbas—by now much reduced in number—fought on the American side.

Burgoyne's invasion brought the Iroquois into the war. Mohawks in the east and Senecas in the west sided with Britain under the leadership of **Joseph Brant**, a literate, educated Mohawk and a Freemason. His sister, Mary Brant, emerged as a skillful diplomat in the alliance between the Iroquois and the loyalists. A minority of Oneidas and Tuscaroras fought with the Americans. Most were becoming Christians under a patriot Presbyterian missionary, Samuel Kirkland. Despite severe strains during the Revolution, the Iroquois League did not dissolve until after the war, when those who fought for Britain migrated to Canada.

A minority of Shawnees, led by Cornstalk, and of Delawares, led by White Eyes and Killbuck, desired friendly relations with the Americans. They provided intelligence to American forces and served as wilderness guides, but they refused to fight other Indians and did their best to preserve peace along the frontier. Christian Moravian Indians in the Ohio Country took a similar stance. The reluctance of Indians to kill other Indians, already becoming evident during the Seven Years' War, grew even more obvious during the Revolution. Loyalists and patriots were far more willing than Indians to kill one another.

Frontier racism, already conspicuous in Pontiac's War, intensified and made Indian neutrality all but impossible. Backcountry settlers from Carolina through New York refused to accept the neutrals on their own terms. Indian warriors, especially young men influenced by nativist prophets, increasingly believed that the Great Spirit had created whites, Indians, and blacks as separate peoples who ought to remain apart. Their militancy further enraged the settlers. White hunters, disdained by easterners as "near savages," secured their identity as "whites" (a fairly new term) by killing Indians.

Hatred of Indians grew so extreme that it threatened to undercut the American war effort. In 1777, American militia murdered Cornstalk, and in 1778 militiamen killed White Eyes. Four years later, Americans massacred 100 unarmed Moravian mission Indians at Gnadenhutten, Ohio. Nearly all of them were women and children who knelt in prayer as, one by one, their skulls were crushed with mallets. This atrocity brutalized Indians as well as settlers. Until then, most Indians had refrained from the ritual torture of prisoners, but after Gnadenhutten they resumed the custom—selectively. They burned alive any known leaders of the massacre whom they captured.

Faced with hatred, Indians united to protect their lands. They won the frontier war north of the Ohio River. The Iroquois ravaged the Wyoming Valley of Pennsylvania in 1778. When an American army devastated Iroquoia in 1779 and committed many atrocities along the way, the Indians fell back on the British post at Niagara and continued the struggle. In 1779, nearly all Indians, from the Creeks on the Gulf Coast to the nations of the Great Lakes, exchanged emissaries and planned an all-out war along the frontier. George Rogers Clark of Virginia thwarted their offensive with a daring winter raid in which he captured Vincennes and cut off the western nations from British supplies, but the Indians regrouped, and by 1782 drove the Virginia "long knives" out of the Ohio Country.

6-3c Violence and Attrition

The escalating costs of war, both human and financial, ravaged Britain and the United States. After 1778, George III's determination to continue the war bitterly divided his kingdom. Much of the British public doubted that the war could be won. Trade was disrupted, thousands of ships were lost to privateers, taxes and the national debt soared, military recruits became harder to find, and a French invasion became a serious threat. Political dissent rose and included widespread demand for the reduction of royal patronage and for electoral reforms. By several measures, the American Revolutionary War was one of the least popular wars in British history.

6.5 **Joseph Brant, Portrait by Gilbert Stuart (1786)** Brant, a Mohawk and a Freemason, was one of Britain's most effective commanders of loyalist and Indian forces. After the war, he led most of the Six Nations to Canada for resettlement.

Desperate for men, the British army had been quietly recruiting Irish Catholics, and North supported a modest degree of toleration for English and Scottish Catholics. This leniency produced a surge of Protestant violence culminating in the Gordon riots, named for an eccentric agitator, Lord George Gordon. For a week in June 1780, crowds roared through London, smashing Catholic chapels attached to foreign embassies, liberating prisoners from city jails, and finally attacking the Bank of England. The army, supported by Lord Mayor John Wilkes, put down the rioters. This spectacular violence discredited the reformers and gave North one more chance to win the war.

In America, shocking acts of violence became commonplace. In May 1777, a British-Hessian unit in New Jersey ambushed a Continental Army patrol and hacked to death an American officer, William Martin, and several of his men, apparently in retaliation for an earlier American attack. Martin's body was so badly mutilated that Washington had it delivered in a makeshift coffin to the nearby British headquarters of General Cornwallis with a cover letter complaining that the officer was "unnecessarily murdered with the most aggravated circumstances of barbarity." Cornwallis responded matter-of-factly, "When a man is kill'd in that manner [with sabers], his body must of course be mangled."

Prisoners of war suffered perhaps the harshest treatment in the war. From 1776 to 1783, British forces occupying New York City converted abandoned or decommissioned warships anchored just off shore into floating prisons. The most notorious of these ships, the *Jersey*, exposed American prisoners to inhuman crowding, poor ventilation, and severe want of food and clothing. In total, about 18,000 men languished on British prison ships during the war, and at least 8,500 died—a nearly 50 percent mortality rate. A former prisoner, the writer Philip Freneau accused the British of purposefully killing Americans in his narrative poem "The British Prison-Ship" (1781): "ungenerous Britons, you/Conspire to murder those you can't subdue." By the end of the war, Congress sponsored squalid and brutal prisons of its own, but they never equaled the mortality rates on the British prison vessels.

Over time, the twin forces of violence and attrition impacted America's full population. Indian raids reduced harvests, and military levies kept thousands of men away from productive work. Loyalist raids into Connecticut and New Jersey wore down the defenders and destroyed a great deal of property. A 1779 raid on Virginia carried off or destroyed property worth £2 million. Merchants lost most of their European and West Indian markets, although a few of them made huge profits through blockade running or

▲ MAP 6.2 **War on the Frontier, 1777–1782** Indian unity strengthened during the Revolution beyond what had been achieved in Pontiac's War.

Q *Given Indian unity and strength in the trans-Appalachian West during the Revolutionary War, should the British Proclamation Line of 1763 be determined a success?*

Q *Would Native Americans have experienced a different long-term fate had Britain defeated America and stopped independence?*

privateering. Average household income plunged by more than 40 percent. Even major American triumphs came at a high price. Burgoyne's surrender left Americans with the burden of feeding his army for the rest of the war. Provisioning a French fleet in American waters, and later a French army, put huge strains on American resources.

These heavy demands led to the collapse of the Continental dollar in 1779–1780. Congress had been printing money to pay its bills, using the Spanish dollar as its basic monetary unit. With French support bolstering American credit, this practice worked reasonably well into 1778. The money depreciated, but without causing widespread dissatisfaction. As the war

6.6 Nineteenth-Century Representation of British Prison Ship in New York Harbor The British regarded American prisoners as loathsome traitors and treated them accordingly. Far more Americans died as POWs than in combat. Thousands died on hulks or prison ships in the harbor.

ground on, though, the value of Continental money fell to less than a penny on the dollar in 1779. Congress agreed to stop the printing presses and to rely instead on requisitions from the states and on foreign and domestic loans, but without paper money it could not even pay the army. Congress and the army had to requisition supplies directly from farmers in exchange for certificates geared to an inflation rate of 40 to 1, well below its true rate. Many farmers, rather than lose money on their crops, simply cut back production. William Beadle, a Connecticut shopkeeper, tried to fight inflation by accepting Continental money at face value until he saw the consequences. Rather than leave his wife and children impoverished, he slit their throats and shot himself.

6-3d Mutiny and Reform

America's national government, consisting solely of Congress, struggled to meet the war's many challenges. The makeshift structure of Congress remained largely unchanged since the First Continental Congress in 1774, with each state having one vote. The formal expression of this arrangement, the Articles of Confederation, was not ratified by the states until March 1, 1781, only months before the major fighting of the war ended. The Articles did not change the most glaring weakness of the national government, the inability to tax.

Congress might have limped through the war without any significant reforms, except for one dire threat: Continental soldiers—unpaid, ill clothed, and often poorly fed—grew mutinous. As Continentals became more professional through frequent drill, they also became more contemptuous of civilians. The winter of 1779–1780, the worst of the century, marked a low point in morale among the main force of Continentals snowed in with Washington at Morristown, New Jersey. Many deserted. In May 1780, two Connecticut regiments of the Continental Line, without food for three days, threatened to go home, raising the danger that the whole army might dissolve. Their officers barely managed to restore control. On paper, Washington had 16,000 men. His real strength was 3,600 and not even enough horses to move his artillery.

6.7 John Trumbull, "American Prisoners" Conditions on British prison ships almost reached the horrors of the Middle Passage from Africa but lasted longer.

Q *What, if any, risks did the British incur by treating American prisoners so poorly?*

Discontent again erupted in the army on New Year's Day 1781. Insisting that their three-year enlistments had expired, 1,500 men of the Pennsylvania Line got drunk, killed three officers, and marched out of their winter quarters at Morristown. General Clinton sent agents from New York to promise these men a pardon and their back pay if they defected to the British, but instead the mutineers marched south toward Princeton and turned Clinton's agents over to Pennsylvania authorities, who then executed the agents. Congress, reassured, negotiated with the soldiers. More than half of them accepted discharges, and those who reenlisted got furloughs and bonuses. Encouraged by this treatment, 200 New Jersey soldiers at Pompton also mutinied, but Washington used New England units to disarm them and executed two of the leaders.

Congress saw these outbursts as calls for national reforms. While armed partisans were making the war more radical, politics became more conservative, moving toward the creation of European state forms, such as executive departments and a bank. Congress abandoned its cumbersome committee system and created executive departments of foreign affairs, finance, war, and marine. Robert Morris, a Philadelphia merchant, became secretary of finance, helped organize the Bank of North America (the first in America), and made certain that the Continental army was clothed and well fed, although it still was not paid. Congress began to requisition more revenue from the states to support its reforms, but efforts to amend the Articles of Confederation to allow for a direct national tax failed. The reforms of 1781 were barely sufficient to keep a smaller army in the field for the rest of the war.

6-4 The British Offensive in the South

Q *After the initial success of Britain's southern campaign, what factors contributed to American victory in the south?*

In 1780, the British attacked in the Deep South with great success. The Revolution entered its most critical phase and nearly collapsed. "I have almost ceased to hope," Washington confessed. In December 1778, a small British amphibious force had taken Savannah and had held it through 1779. The British even restored royal government with an elective assembly in Georgia between 1780 and 1782. By early 1780, they were ready to launch a major offensive. General Clinton had finally devised a strategy for winning the war (see Map 6.3).

6-4a Britain's Southern Strategy

Much of Clinton's New York army would sail to Charleston, take it, and dispatch loyalists to pacify the countryside. Clinton's plan reflected a change of thinking in London since France entered the war. Rather than snuff out the American rebellion in the north, where it was strongest, the British would concentrate on the south, where it was weakest. The strategy would capitalize on the Deep South as the likeliest recruiting ground for armed loyalists. Having pacified the region, Clinton would then attempt to destroy Washington's army and consolidate Britain's gains in the north and south.

6.8 Gadsden Flag Americans experimented with many different flags during the Revolution. One of the most popular motifs was a snake paired with the motto "Don't tread on me!" as in this flag designed by the South Carolina soldier and statesman Christopher Gadsden.

Clinton's invasion of South Carolina began with awesome successes. While the British navy sealed off Charleston from the sea, an army of 10,000 closed off the land approaches to the city and forced Benjamin Lincoln and 5,000 defenders to surrender on May 12, 1780. Loyalists under Banastre Tarleton caught the 350 remaining Continentals at the Waxhaws near the North Carolina border on May 29 and, in what became infamous as "Tarleton's quarter," killed them all. This calculated brutality was designed to terrorize civilians into submission. It worked for a time, but Thomas Sumter began to retaliate after loyalists burned his plantation. His mounted raiders attacked British outposts and terrorized loyalists. At Hanging Rock on August 6, Sumter's 800 men scattered 500 loyalists, killing or wounding nearly half of them. All participants on both sides were colonists. Civil war consumed the Deep South.

Confident of British control of South Carolina, Clinton left Cornwallis in command of 8,300 men and sailed north to confront Washington. Yet to Clinton's dismay, New Jersey militia and the state's regiments of the Continental Line blocked British advances in June 1780. The stout defense forced the British to withdraw to New York. With Washington's army intact, Clinton ignored the French when they took Newport.

The British commander also failed in his attempt to take over the American base at West Point. For months, Clinton had negotiated secretly with a disgruntled Benedict Arnold (he had won little recognition for his heroics in the Saratoga campaign) for the surrender of West Point, which would have opened the Hudson to British ships as far north as Albany. But in September 1780 the Americans captured Clinton's agent, John André, with documents detailing the treason. André was hanged, and Arnold fled to British lines and became a general in the British army.

The developments in the north forced the British to pin all their hopes on the southern campaign. Despite Sumter's harassment, Cornwallis's conquest of the Carolinas proceeded rapidly. Congress scraped together 900 tough Maryland and Delaware Continentals, put Horatio Gates, the victor at Saratoga, in command, and sent them south against Cornwallis. Bolstered by 2,000 Virginia and North Carolina militia, Gates rashly offered battle at Camden on August 16,

6.9 Banastre Tarleton (1782) During the British southern campaign of 1780 and 1781, Tarleton gained notoriety for his ruthless treatment of Americans while commanding a unit of loyalist soldiers popularly known as "Tarleton's Raiders."

even though many of his men suffered from diarrhea after eating half-baked bread. The militia, who lacked bayonets, fled in panic at the first British charge. The exposed Continentals fought bravely but were crushed.

Two days after Camden, Tarleton surprised Sumter's camp at Fishing Creek, near the Waxhaws, killing 150 men and wounding 300. In four months, the British had destroyed all of the Continental forces in the Deep South, mauled Sumter's partisans, and opened North Carolina to invasion. These victories seemed to fulfill Cornwallis's boast that he would strip "three stripes … from the detestable thirteen." He unleashed his loyalists to pacify South Carolina and marched confidently on to "liberate" North Carolina.

6-4b The Partisan War

But resistance continued. In the west, frontier riflemen, led by Daniel Morgan and enraged by Britain's support for Indians, crossed the Blue Ridge 1,800 strong to challenge Patrick Ferguson's loyalists at King's Mountain near the North Carolina border. On October 7, 1780, Morgan lost only 88 men as his marksmen picked off many defenders. He overwhelmed

6.10 "The Present State of Great Britain" (1779), Probably by James Gillray The war is going badly for weary John Bull (England). America, the Indian, is stealing liberty; the Dutch are lifting Britain's purse; and the French are attacking. Only a surly Scot is defending John Bull, and he may lose his dagger.

Q *How does the cartoon reflect Britain's global challenges in the second half of the Revolutionary War?*

the loyalists, killing 160 men, including Ferguson, and capturing 860. They shot many prisoners and hanged a dozen, their answer to "Tarleton's quarter." This victory, the first major British setback in the Deep South, stung Cornwallis, who halted his drive into North Carolina.

In October 1780, Congress sent General **Nathanael Greene**, a Rhode Islander, to the Carolinas with a small Continental force. After Sumter withdrew to nurse a wound, Francis Marion took his place. A much abler leader, Marion (who became known as the Swamp Fox) operated from remote bases in the marshy low country. Greene's prospects still seemed desperate. The ugliness of the partisan war—the mutilation of corpses, killing of prisoners, and wanton destruction of property—and the condition of his soldiers appalled him. Yet Greene and Marion devised a masterful strategy of partisan warfare that finally wore out the British.

In the face of a greatly superior enemy, Greene ignored a maxim of war and split up his force of 1,800 Continentals. He sent 300 men east to bolster Marion and ordered Daniel Morgan and 300 riflemen west to threaten the British outpost of Ninety-Six. Cornwallis, worried that after King's Mountain, Morgan might raise the entire backcountry against the British, divided his own army. He sent Tarleton with a mixed force of 1,100 British and loyalists after Morgan, who decided to stand with his back to a river at Cowpens, where a loyalist kept cattle. Including militia, Morgan had 1,040 men.

Tarleton attacked at Cowpens on January 17, 1781. In another unorthodox move, Morgan sent his militia out front as skirmishers. He ordered them to fire two rounds and then redeploy in his rear. Relieved of their fear of a bayonet charge, they obeyed. As they pulled back, the British rushed forward into the Continentals, who also retreated at first, then wheeled and fired a lethal volley. After Morgan's cavalry charged into the British left flank, the militia returned to the fray. Although Tarleton escaped, Morgan annihilated his army.

As Morgan rejoined Greene, Cornwallis staked everything on his ability to find Greene and crush him, precisely what he had failed to do to Washington after Trenton and Princeton. But Greene proved elusive and lured Cornwallis into a march of exhaustion into North Carolina. In March 1781, nearly three months after the last major engagement at Cowpens, Greene judged that Cornwallis was so weak that the Americans could offer battle at Guilford Court House. With militia he outnumbered Cornwallis 4,400 to 1,900. On March 15, even though the British retained possession of the battlefield, they lost one-quarter of their force and the strategic initiative. Cornwallis retreated to Wilmington to refit.

Throughout the southern campaign, the British had confronted an enemy far deadlier than the Americans—mosquitoes. Malaria, the mosquito-borne disease that American colonists had long known, ravaged Cornwallis's army. In April 1781, with another hot disease season looming, Cornwallis explained to Clinton that he would have to get "to the upper parts of the Country, where alone I can hope to preserve the troops from fatal sickness, which has so nearly ruined the Army last autumn." Cornwallis decided to march north to Virginia in search of healthier conditions and better battlefield results.

▲ **MAP 6.3 War in the Lower South, 1780–1781** British victories in 1780 nearly restored Georgia and South Carolina to the Crown, but after Guilford Court House in March 1781, the Americans regained the advantage throughout the region.
Q Why did Britain struggle to maintain territory that it gained during the war?
Q Had Britain pursued its southern strategy earlier in the war, might the outcome have been different?

Instead of following him, Greene returned to South Carolina, where he and Marion took the surviving British outposts one by one. After the British evacuated Ninety-Six on July 1, 1781, they held only Savannah and Charleston in the Deep South. Against heavy odds, Greene had reclaimed the region for the Revolution.

6-4c From the Ravaging of Virginia to Yorktown and Peace

Both Cornwallis and Washington believed that events in Virginia would decide the war. When a large British force

Interpreting the Visual Past — A French View of Yorktown

An unknown artist completed this hand-colored copper engraving after news of the American-French allied victory at Yorktown reached Paris in the fall of 1781. Without the benefit of witnessing the event, the artist made several factual errors. The coloring of the American and French uniforms in the foreground is inexact, and imaginary mountains dot the countryside. Most fancifully, European-style castles in the background are meant to represent the settlement at Yorktown.

Still, the image is valuable for providing a rare French perspective on the Revolutionary War. Note especially the prominent place of the French naval fleet in the engraving. The artist used imagination to suggest what historians now accept as fact: Without French assistance, it is doubtful that America could have won its independence.

Q Compare the French image with the painting of Yorktown by the American artist John Trumbull at the opening of this chapter. What differences do you notice?

Q Trumbull's version of the British surrender at Yorktown has more accurate details. Yet, like the artist of the French engraving, Trumbull was not present at Yorktown. Moreover, he completed his painting nearly 40 years later. Does this information change your interpretation of the two works? Does the French engraving have any claim to providing a more honest account of Yorktown?

6.11 French Engraving of the Battle of Yorktown, 1781.

raided the state in late 1780, Governor Thomas Jefferson called up enough militia to keep the British bottled up in Portsmouth, while he continued to ship men and supplies to Greene in the Carolinas. Thereafter, the state's ability to raise men and supplies almost collapsed.

In January 1781, Clinton sent Arnold by sea from New York with 1,600 men, mostly loyalists. They sailed up the James and gutted the new capital of Richmond. When Jefferson called out the militia, few responded. Most Virginia freemen had already done service, if only as short-term militia, thousands in response to the 1780 raid. Cornwallis took command in April, and Arnold departed for New York. But the raids continued into summer, sweeping as far west as Charlottesville, where Tarleton, who had recruited a new legion since Cowpens, scattered the Virginia legislature and almost captured Jefferson. Many of Jefferson's slaves greeted the British as liberators. Washington sent Lafayette with 1,200 northern Continentals to contain the damage. On Clinton's orders, Cornwallis withdrew to **Yorktown**—a small settlement on a peninsula surrounded by the James and York rivers and Chesapeake Bay—to await reinforcements from the Royal Navy (see Map 6.4).

6-4 The British Offensive in the South

▲ **MAP 6.4 Virginia and the Yorktown Campaign** After the British ravaged much of Virginia, Washington and a French fleet and army were able to trap Lord Cornwallis at Yorktown, force his surrender, and guarantee American independence.

Q *Count the number of factors that came together to ensure American success at Yorktown. Was one factor more important than any other, or would you rate them equally?*

Q *What was the logic of Cornwallis setting up camp on a peninsula at Yorktown even though it left him open to being trapped?*

At last, Washington saw an opportunity to launch a major strike. He learned that a powerful French fleet under Francois, Comte de Grasse, with 3,000 soldiers would sail from Saint-Domingue for Chesapeake Bay on August 13. Cooperating closely with the French army commander, Jean Baptiste Donatien, Comte de Rochambeau, Washington sprang his trap. Rochambeau led his 5,000 soldiers from Newport to the outskirts of New York, where they joined Washington's 5,000 Continentals.

After feinting an attack to freeze Clinton in place, Washington led the combined French and American armies 400 miles south to tidewater Virginia, where they linked up with Lafayette's Americans and the other French army brought by de Grasse. Once de Grasse's fleet beat off a British relief force at the Battle of the Capes on September 5, Washington cut off all retreat routes and besieged Yorktown. On October 19, 1781, Cornwallis surrendered his army of 8,000 men. Many escaped slaves died during the siege, most from smallpox, but planters hovered nearby to reclaim survivors.

Yorktown brought down the British government in March 1782. Lord North resigned, and George III even drafted an abdication message but never released it. The new ministry, committed to American independence as the price of peace, continued to fight the French in the Caribbean and the Spanish at Gibraltar, but the British evacuated Savannah and Charleston to concentrate their remaining forces in New York City.

184 CHAPTER 6 The Revolutionary Republic, 1776–1789

The Treaty of Paris ended the war in 1783. The American diplomatic commission of John Jay, John Adams, and Benjamin Franklin won British recognition of territory east of the Mississippi, with the river (absent New Orleans) marking the western boundary of the new republic. New Englanders retained the right to fish off Newfoundland. The treaty recognized the validity of prewar transatlantic debts, and Congress promised to urge the states to restore confiscated loyalist property.

These terms gave American diplomats almost everything they could have desired. Western Indians, by contrast, were appalled to learn that the treaty gave their lands to the United States. They had not been conquered, whatever European diplomats might say. Their war for survival continued with few breaks into 1795.

Congress still faced ominous problems. In March 1783, many Continental officers threatened a coup d'état unless Congress granted them generous pensions. Washington, confronting them at their encampment at Newburgh, New York, fumbled for his glasses and remarked, "I have grown gray in your service, and now find myself growing blind." Tears filled the eyes of his comrades in arms, and the threat of a coup vanished.

In Philadelphia two months later, unpaid Pennsylvania soldiers marched on the statehouse, where both Congress and the state's executive council sat. Ignoring Congress, they demanded that Pennsylvania redress their grievances. Congress felt insulted and left the city for Princeton, where it reconvened in Nassau Hall. Its archives and administrative departments remained in Philadelphia. "I confess I have great apprehensions for the union of the states," wrote Charles Thomson, secretary to Congress since 1774. The British threat, Thomson knew, had created the American Union.

He feared that the Union would dissolve with the return of peace. Congress moved on from Princeton to Annapolis and eventually settled in New York, but the Union's survival remained uncertain.

6-5 A Revolutionary Society

Q *What social changes came about in the United States either directly or indirectly as a result of the American Revolution?*

Independence transformed America. The biggest winners were free householders, who gained enormous benefits from the democratization of politics and the chance to colonize the West. Besides loyalists, the biggest losers were Indians, determined to resist settler expansion. Many slaves won freedom, and women struggled for greater dignity. Both succeeded only when their goals proved compatible with the ambitions of white householders.

6-5a Religious Transformations

Independence left the Anglican Church vulnerable, if only because George III was its "supreme head." Although most Anglican clergymen supported the Revolution or remained neutral, an aggressive loyalist minority stirred the wrath of patriots. Religious dissenters disestablished the Anglican Church in every southern state. They deprived it of its tax support and other privileges, such as the sole right to perform marriages. In 1786, Virginia passed Jefferson's Statute for Religious Freedom, which declared that efforts to use coercion

6.12 Interior of Touro Synagogue in Newport, Rhode Island The synagogue shown here presents the best surviving example of Jewish artistic taste in 18th-century America.

in matters of religion "tend only to beget habits of hypocrisy and meanness." In Virginia, church attendance and the support of ministers became voluntary activities.

Other states moved more slowly. In New England, Congregational churches supported the Revolution and were less vulnerable to attack. Ministers' salaries continued to be paid out of public taxes, although lawful dissenters, such as Baptists, could insist that their church taxes go to their own clergy. The Congregational Church exercised other public or quasi-public functions, especially on thanksgiving, fast, and election days. Disestablishment did not become complete until 1818 in Connecticut and 1833 in Massachusetts.

Although most states still restricted the holding of office to Christians or Protestants, many people were coming to regard the coercion of anyone's conscience as morally wrong. Jews and Catholics both gained from the new atmosphere of tolerance. When Britain recognized the Catholic Church in the Quebec Act of 1774, most Protestants had shuddered with dread, but in 1790, when John Carroll of Maryland became the first Roman Catholic bishop in the United States, hardly anyone protested. Before independence, an Anglican bishop had become an explosive issue, but in the 1780s, the Church of England reorganized itself as the Protestant Episcopal Church and began to consecrate its own bishops. Both Episcopalians and Presbyterians paid homage to republican values by adopting written constitutions.

6-5b The First Emancipation

The Revolution freed tens of thousands of slaves, but it also gave new vitality to slavery in the region that people were beginning to call "the South." Within a generation, slavery was abolished in the emerging "North." Race became a defining factor in both regions. In the South, most blacks remained slaves. In the North, they became free but not equal. The independent householder and his voluntaristic ethic remained almost a white monopoly.

Many slaves freed themselves. The British army enabled more than half the slaves of Georgia and a significant fraction in South Carolina to choose freedom. A similar process was under way in Virginia in 1781, only to be cut short at Yorktown. Hundreds of New England slaves won freedom through military service. Many revealed what they were fighting for in the surnames they chose. Jeffrey Liberty, Cuff Liberty, Dick Freeman, and Jube Freeman served in one Connecticut regiment. After the Massachusetts bill of rights proclaimed that all people were "born free and equal," Elizabeth (Bett) Freeman sued her master in 1781 and won her liberty. Thereafter, most of the slaves in Massachusetts and New Hampshire simply walked away from their masters.

Elsewhere, legislative action was necessary. Pennsylvania led the way in 1780 with the modern world's first **gradual emancipation** statute. Rather than emancipate, or free, slaves immediately, it declared that children born to slaves after a given date would become free at age 28. The slaves, not masters or taxpayers, thus bore the costs of their own emancipation. This requirement left them unable to compete on equal terms with free white men, who usually entered adult life with inherited property. Some masters shipped their slaves south shortly before emancipation, and some whites kidnapped freedmen and carried them south. The Pennsylvania Abolition Society existed largely to fight these abuses. By 1800, Philadelphia had America's largest community of free blacks, with their own churches and other voluntary societies.

The Pennsylvania pattern took hold, with variations, in most other northern states until all of them had made provision for emancipation. Where slaves constituted more than 10 percent of the population, as in southern New York and northeastern New Jersey, slaveholders' resistance delayed legislation for years. New York yielded in 1799, New Jersey in 1804.

In the upper South, many Methodists and Baptists opposed slavery in the 1780s, only to retreat in later years. Maryland and Virginia authorized the **manumission**, or freeing, of individual slaves by their owners. By 1810, more than one-fifth of Maryland's slaves had been freed, as had 10,000 of Virginia's 300,000 slaves, including more than 123 freed under Washington's will after he died in 1799. But slaves were essential to the plantation economy and were usually their masters' most valuable asset. In the South, emancipation would have amounted to a social revolution and the impoverishment of the planter class. Planters supported such humane reforms as the Christianization of their slaves, but they resisted emancipation, especially with the rise of cotton as a new cash crop after the war. Cut off from British textiles during the war, South Carolina slaves insisted on growing cotton as a substitute. Their owners saw the huge potential of that crop which, in effect, condemned the children and grandchildren of those slaves to indefinite bondage.

Maryland and Virginia, where population growth among the slaves exceeded what the tobacco economy could absorb, banned the Atlantic slave trade, as had all other states outside the Deep South. Georgia and South Carolina, to make good their losses during the war and to meet the demand for cotton after 1790, reopened the Atlantic slave trade. South Carolina imported almost 60,000 more Africans before Congress prohibited that traffic in 1808.

6-5c The Challenge to Patriarchy

Nothing as dramatic as emancipation altered relations between the sexes. With the men away fighting, many women were left in charge of the household, sometimes with interesting consequences. "I hope you will not consider yourself as commander in chief of your own house," Lucy Knox warned her soldier husband, Henry, in 1777, "but be convinced … that there is such a thing as equal command." Although some women acquired new authority, nearly all of them had to work harder to keep their households functioning. The war cut them off from most European consumer goods. Household manufactures, largely the task of women, filled the gap. Women accepted these duties without demanding broader legal or political rights, but soaring food prices made many of them assertive. In numerous food riots, women tried to force merchants to lower prices or stop hoarding grain.

Attitudes toward marriage were also changing. The common-law rule of coverture still denied wives any legal personality, but a few persuaded state governments not to impoverish them by confiscating the property of their loyalist husbands. Many writers insisted that good marriages rested on mutual affection, not on property settlements. In portraits of wealthy northeastern families, husbands and wives were beginning to appear as equals. Parents were urged to respect the personalities of their children and to avoid severe discipline. Traditional reverence for the elderly was yielding to an idealization of youth and energy.

In 1780, to relieve the sufferings of Continental soldiers, Esther de Berdt Reed organized the Philadelphia Ladies Association, the first women's society in American history to take on a public role. Although few women yet demanded equal political rights, the New Jersey Constitution of 1776 let them vote if they headed a household (usually as a widow) and paid taxes. This right was revoked in 1807.

Especially in the Northeast, more women learned to read and write. Philosophers, clergymen, and even popular writers were beginning to treat women as morally superior to men, a sharp reversal of earlier teachings. The first female academies were founded in the 1790s. By 1830, nearly all native-born women in the Northeast had become literate. The ideal of the "**republican wife**" and the "**republican mother**" took hold, giving wives and mothers an expanding educational role within the family. They encouraged diligence in their husbands and patriotism in their sons. The novel became a major cultural form in the United States. Its main audience was female, as were many of the authors. Novels cast women as central characters and warned young women to beware of suitors motivated only by greed or lust.

6-5d Western Expansion, Discontent, and Conflict with Indians

Westward expansion continued during the Revolutionary War. With 30 axmen, Daniel Boone, a North Carolina hunter, hacked out the Wilderness Road from Cumberland Gap to the

6.13 **Liberty and Washington (c. 1800)** This example of folk art shows how women came to personify liberty in the early American republic. While placing a laurel on a bust of George Washington, the female figure stomps on a crown that represents monarchy.

Kentucky bluegrass country in early 1775. The first settlers called Kentucky "the best poor man's country" and claimed it should belong to those who tilled its soil, not to speculators in the Transylvania Company, which claimed ownership. Few Indians lived in Kentucky, but it was the favorite hunting ground of the Shawnees and other nations. Their raids often prevented settlers from planting crops. Instead they hunted and put up log cabins against the inside walls of large rectangular stockades, 10 feet high and built from oak logs. At each corner, a blockhouse with a protruding second story permitted the defenders to fire along the outside walls. Three of these "Kentucky stations" were built—at Boonesborough, St. Asaph, and Harrodsburg (see Map 6.2).

Because of the constant danger, settlement grew slowly at first. Kentucky lived up to its old Indian reputation as the "dark and bloody ground." Only a few thousand settlers stuck it out until the war ended, when they were joined by swarms of newcomers. Speculators and absentees were already trying to claim the best bluegrass land. The Federal Census of 1790 listed 74,000 settlers and slaves in Kentucky and about half that many in Tennessee, where the Cherokees had ceded a large tract after their defeat in 1776. Those settlers thrived

▲ **MAP 6.5 Western Land Claims during the Revolution** One of the most difficult questions that Congress faced was the competing western land claims of several states. After Virginia ceded its claims north of the Ohio to Congress, other states followed suit, creating the national domain and what soon became the Northwest Territory.

Q How did the creation of the Northwest Territory end the possibility that the United States would formally establish new colonies in western lands?

Q What assumption did the Northwest Territory make about Native American claims to land west of the Mississippi River?

both because few Indians lived there and because British and Spanish raiders found it hard to reach them.

To the south and north of this bulge, settlement was much riskier. After the war, Spain supplied arms and trade goods to Creeks, Cherokees, Choctaws, and Chickasaws who were willing to resist Georgia's attempt to settle its western lands. North of the Ohio River, Britain refused to withdraw its garrisons and traders from Niagara, Detroit, and a few other posts, even though, according to the Treaty of Paris, those forts now lay within the boundaries of the United States. To justify their refusal, the British cited Congress's failure to honor treaty obligations to loyalists and British creditors. When small groups of Indians sold large tracts of land to Georgia, Pennsylvania, and New York, as well as to Congress, the Indian nations repudiated those sales and, supported by either Spain or Britain, continued to resist.

During the Revolutionary War, Americans had recruited soldiers with promises of land after the war, and now they needed Indian lands to fulfill these pledges. The Indian nations that supported the United States suffered the most. In the 1780s, after Joseph Brant led most of the Iroquois north to Canada, New York confiscated much of the land of the friendly Iroquois who stayed. South Carolina dispossessed the Catawbas of most of their lands. The states had a harder time seizing the land of hostile Indians who had Spanish or British aid.

Secessionist movements arose in the 1780s when neither Congress nor eastern state governments seemed able to solve western problems. Some Tennessee settlers seceded from North Carolina to maintain, briefly, a separate state of Franklin. Separatist sentiment also ran strong in Kentucky. Settlers in western Pennsylvania thought of setting up on their own after Spain closed the Mississippi to American traffic in 1784. When Congress refused to accept Vermont's independence from New York, even the radical Green Mountain Boys sounded out Canadian officials about readmission to the British Empire as a separate province.

6-5e The Northwest Ordinance

After Virginia ceded its land claims north of the Ohio River to Congress in 1781, other states followed suit. Jefferson offered a resolution in 1784 that would have created 10 or more new states in this Northwest Territory. In the Land Ordinance of 1785, Congress authorized the survey of the Northwest Territory and its division into townships six miles square, each composed of 36 "sections" of 640 acres. Surveyed land would be sold at auction starting at a dollar per acre. Alternate townships would be sold in sections or as a whole, to satisfy settlers and speculators, respectively.

In July 1787, while the Constitutional Convention met in Philadelphia, Congress (in New York) returned to the problems of the Northwest Territory and passed the **Northwest Ordinance** (see Map 6.5). It authorized the creation of from 3 to 5 states, to be admitted to the Union as equals of the original 13. The ordinance thus rejected colonialism among white people except as a temporary phase through which a "territory" would pass on its way to statehood. Congress would appoint a governor and a council to rule until population reached 5,000. At that point, the settlers could elect an assembly empowered to pass laws, although the governor (modeled on earlier royal governors) had an absolute veto. When population reached 60,000, the settlers could adopt their own constitution and petition Congress for statehood. The ordinance protected civil liberties, provided for public education, and prohibited slavery in the territory.

Southern delegates all voted for the Northwest Ordinance despite its antislavery clause. The clause may have been part of a larger Compromise of 1787, involving both the ordinance and the clauses on slavery in the federal Constitution. The Philadelphia Convention permitted states to count three-fifths of their slaves for purposes of representation and direct taxation. The antislavery concession to northerners in the ordinance was made at the same time that southern states won this concession in Philadelphia. Several congressmen were also delegates to the Constitutional Convention and traveled back and forth between the two cities while these decisions were being made. They may have struck a deal.

6-6 American Constitutionalism

Q In what ways did state constitutions advance American constitutional thinking during the revolutionary era?

Another major preoccupation of Americans both during and following the Revolutionary War centered on a basic question: Having disposed of British authority, how would they create new governments? The first wave of constitutionalism focused on the states. In 1776, the prospect of independence touched off intense debate among Americans about how best to reconstitute authority. They agreed that every state needed a written constitution to limit the powers of government in terms more explicit than the precedents, statutes, and customs that made up Britain's unwritten constitution. That constitution had resulted in parliamentary sovereignty, the idea that Parliament held **sovereign power** (or ultimate control) over Britain and its overseas empire. Americans disagreed and instead maintained that their individual colonial (and later state) assemblies were sovereign within their respective borders. In essence, the American reply to Britain's sovereign Parliament was 13 sovereign state legislatures. After 1776, Americans moved from embracing state sovereignty and the European notion that sovereignty must be lodged in government toward ever-fuller expressions of **popular sovereignty**—the theory that all power must be derived from the people. This learning process at the state level would have profound influence on the U.S. Constitution.

6-6a John Adams and the Separation of Powers

No one influenced the development of state constitutions more than John Adams. By the spring of 1776, when he wrote

Thoughts on Government, Adams was already moving away from the British notion of a "mixed and balanced" constitution, in which government by King, Lords, and Commons embodied the distinct social orders of British society. He was groping toward quite a different notion, the **separation of powers**. Government, he affirmed, should be divided into three branches—an executive armed with veto power, a legislature, and a judiciary independent of both. The legislature, he insisted, must be bicameral, so that each house could expose the failings of the other. **Unicameral legislatures** (those with a single legislative body), which Thomas Paine advocated and Georgia, Pennsylvania, and Vermont all adopted, risked having one interest dominate the government.

Governments exist to promote the happiness of the people, Adams declared. Happiness depends on "virtue," both public and private. **Public virtue** meant "patriotism," the willingness of citizens to value the common good above their personal interests and even to die for their country. The form of government that rests entirely on virtue, Adams argued, is a republic. Americans must elect legislatures that would mirror society. Britain had put the nobility in one house and the commoners in another, but in America, everyone was a commoner. America had no social orders. A free government did not embody distinctly social orders to be stable. It could uphold republican values through virtue and by being properly balanced within itself.

6-6b Early State Constitutions

In June 1776, Virginia became the first state to adopt a permanent, republican constitution. The provincial congress (called a "convention" in Virginia), which had assumed full legislative powers, affirmed "that the legislative and executive powers ... should be separate and distinct from the judiciary," but then wrote a constitution that made the legislature supreme. It chose the governor, the governor's council, and all judges above the level of justice of the peace. The governor had no veto and hardly any patronage. The lower house faced annual elections, but members of the upper house served four-year terms.

George Mason drafted a declaration of rights that the Virginia delegates passed before approving the constitution, on the theory that the people should define their rights before empowering the government. The convention's amended text affirmed human equality but, unlike Mason's original version, was carefully worded to exclude enslaved people. Mason upheld the right to life, liberty, property, and the pursuit of happiness, condemned hereditary privilege, called for rotation in office, provided guarantees for trial by jury and due process, and extolled religious liberty. Legally, Virginia's bill of rights was merely a statute, with no more authority than any other law, but it was eloquent, and many states copied it.

Other states adopted variations of the Virginia model. Because America had no aristocracy, uncertainty about the proper makeup of the upper house was widespread. Some states imposed higher property qualifications on "senators" than on "representatives." In three states, the lower house elected the upper house, but most states created separate election districts for senators. Most states also increased the number of representatives in the lower house. Inland counties, which were underrepresented in most colonial assemblies, became better represented, and men of moderate wealth won a majority of seats in most states, displacing the rich, who had won most late colonial elections. Most states also stripped the governor of patronage and of such royal prerogatives as the power to dissolve the legislature. At this stage, only New York empowered the governor—in conjunction with a Council of Revision—to veto bills.

Pennsylvania crafted the most radical state constitution. In June 1776, radicals overthrew the British colonial government, rejected the leadership of both the old Quaker and Proprietary parties, and elected artisans to office in Philadelphia and ordinary farmers in rural areas. The radicals summoned a special convention whose only task was to write a constitution. That document established a unicameral assembly and a plural executive of 12 men, one of whom would preside and thus be called "president." All freemen who paid taxes, and their adult sons living at home, could vote. Elections were annual, voting was by secret ballot, legislative sessions were open to the public, and no representative could serve for more than four years out of any seven. All bills were to be offered to the public for discussion before passage. Only at the next legislative session could they be passed into law, except in emergencies.

The Pennsylvania constitution, however revolutionary, generated intense conflict. Many residents condemned it as illegitimate because such a small group had produced the constitution. In 1790, it was replaced with a new state constitution that created a bicameral legislature and an elective governor with a veto that could be overridden.

6-6c Massachusetts Redefines Constitutionalism

Pennsylvania's experience exposed the dangers of resting sovereignty solely in the government. Another bitter struggle occurred in Massachusetts. After four years of intense debate, Massachusetts found a way to lodge sovereignty with the people and not with government—that is, a way to distinguish a constitution from simple laws. This achievement became the hallmark of American constitutionalism.

The breakthrough did not come easily. After the British withdrew from Boston in March 1776, the General Court (still the name for the assembly) reformed. But rather than follow the old system in which most towns elected a single representative, the legislature reapportioned its representatives in proportion to population. The new system rewarded the older, populous eastern towns like Boston at the expense of lightly settled western towns. In response, the western Massachusetts counties exploded in protest.

In fall 1776, the General Court responded to growing unrest by asking the towns to authorize it to draft a constitution. By a 2-to-1 margin, the voters agreed, a result that

▲ **MAP 6.6 Advance of Settlement to 1790** Between 1760 and 1790, America's population grew from nearly 1.6 million to almost 4 million. The area of settlement was spreading west of Pittsburgh and into much of Kentucky and parts of Tennessee.

Q *Until 1790, most population growth still took place within existing states. What were the political implications of these population increases, particularly in western areas, at the state level?*

Q *How did America's population growth and advancing settlement help to drive national policies in the 1780s?*

reflected growing *distrust* of the legislature. The legislature drafted a constitution over the next year and then, in an unusual precaution, asked the towns to ratify it. The voters rejected it by the stunning margin of 5 to 1. Many voters, angry about a particular clause, condemned the entire document. Chastened, the General Court urged the towns to postpone the question until after the war. Rural Berkshire County threatened to secede from the state unless the legislature called a constitutional convention. These farmers insisted that they were now in a "state of nature," subject to no legitimate government. They might even join another state that had a proper constitution. With Vermont already seceding from New York, theirs was no idle threat.

The General Court gave in, and a convention met in Boston in December 1779. John Adams drafted a constitution that the convention used as its starting point. A constitution now had to be drafted by a convention that was elected for that specific purpose, and then ratified by the people. The people would then be the source of all legitimate authority.

Since 1776, Adams's thoughts on the separation of powers and bicameralism had matured. Like the Virginia constitution, the Adams draft began with a bill of rights. Both houses would be elected annually. The House of Representatives would be chosen by the towns, as reapportioned in 1776. Senators would be elected by counties and apportioned according to property values, not population. The people would elect the governor, who would have a veto that two-thirds of both houses could override. Property qualifications rose as a man's civic duties increased. For purposes of ratification only, all free adult males were eligible to vote. Everyone (that is, all free men) would have a chance to consent to the basic social compact. Men had to vote on each article separately, not on the whole document.

During spring 1780, town meetings began the ratification process. The convention tallied the results and declared that the constitution had received the required two-thirds majority. The new constitution, although often amended, is still in force today, making it the world's oldest written constitution. Starting with New Hampshire in 1784, other states adopted the Massachusetts model. Its separate constitutional convention, followed by a popular ratifying process, represented the purest embodiment of popular sovereignty and one of the greatest legacies of the revolutionary era.

6-6d Articles of Confederation

While passionately debating their state constitutions, few Americans gave serious thought to how the larger American nation ought to be governed. In summer 1776, Congress began discussing the American union and whether to continue voting by state. Delegates from large states favored representation according to population, but no census existed to give precise numbers, and the small states insisted on being treated as equals.

In an early draft of the Articles of Confederation, John Dickinson rejected proportional representation in favor of state equality. He also enumerated the powers of Congress, which did not include levying taxes or regulating trade. To raise money, Congress would have to print it or requisition specific amounts from the states. In the final version of the Articles, requisitions would be based on each state's free population. Some members of Congress urged that each slave be counted as three-fifths of a person for the purpose of apportioning requisitions, but this amendment was never ratified.

In 1777, Thomas Burke of North Carolina introduced a resolution that eventually became part of the Articles of Confederation: "Each state retains its sovereignty, freedom and independence, and every power, jurisdiction, and right, which is not by this confederation expressly delegated to the United States in Congress assembled." Acceptance of Burke's resolution, with only Virginia dissenting, ensured that the Articles would contain a firm commitment to state sovereignty.

By March 1781, when the states finally ratified the Articles, Congress had become a weak institution. In 1776, the states had looked to Congress to confer legitimacy on their governments, especially in the middle states, but as the states adopted their own constitutions, their legitimacy, based on the people, became stronger than that of Congress. Fittingly, establishing the process for admitting new states (through the Land Ordinance of 1785 and the Northwest Ordinance of 1787) signified the most important accomplishment of the national government under the Articles of Confederation.

6-7 The Constitution: A More Perfect Union

 How did conditions in the United States in the 1780s influence the outcome of the Constitution?

The 1780s were difficult times. The economy failed to rebound, debtors fought creditors, and state politics became bitter and contentious. Out of this ferment arose the demand to amend or even replace the Articles of Confederation.

6-7a Commerce, Debt, and Shays's Rebellion

After the Revolutionary War, the American economy entered a deep depression marked by a large trade deficit and rampant debt. In 1784, British merchants flooded American markets with exports worth £3.7 million, the greatest volume since 1771, but Americans could not pay for them. Exports to Britain that year were £750,000—less than 40 percent of the £1.9 million of 1774, the last year of peace. When Britain invoked the Navigation Acts to close the British West Indies to American ships (but not to American goods), indirect returns through this once-profitable channel also faltered. Trade with France closed some of the gap, but because the French could not offer the long-term credit that the British had provided, it remained disappointing. Exports rose to almost £900,000 by 1785, still far below prewar levels.

Individuals suffered in the postwar economy. Private debts became a huge social problem that the states, buried under their own war debts, could not easily mitigate. Merchants, dunned by British creditors, sued their customers, many of whom could not even pay their taxes. Farmers, many faced with the loss of their crops and even their farms, resisted foreclosures and looked to their states for relief.

About half of the states issued paper money in the 1780s, and many passed **stay laws** to postpone the date on which a debt would come due. Massachusetts rejected both options and raised taxes to new heights. In 1786, many farmers in Hampshire County took matters into their own hands. Crowds gathered to prevent the courts from conducting business, much as patriots had done against the British in 1774. Governor James Bowdoin insisted that acts of resistance once appropriate against a tyrannical monarch were unacceptable in a government elected by the people. But in early 1787, the protestors, loosely organized under a Continental army veteran, Captain Daniel Shays, threatened the federal arsenal at Springfield. An army of volunteers under Benjamin Lincoln marched west with artillery and scattered the protestors. Yet Shaysites won enough seats in the May assembly elections to pass a stay law. In Massachusetts, **Shays's Rebellion** converted into nationalists many gentlemen and artisans who until then had opposed strengthening the central government.

6-7b *Cosmopolitans versus Localists*

The tensions racking Massachusetts surfaced elsewhere as well. Angry debtors in other states closed law courts or even besieged the legislature. State politics reflected a persistent rift between "cosmopolitan" and "localist" coalitions (see Map 6.6). Merchants, professional men, urban artisans, commercial farmers, southern planters, and former Continental army officers made up the cosmopolitan bloc. They favored aggressive trade policies, hard money, payment of public debts, good salaries for executive officials and judges, and leniency to returning loyalists. Localists were farmers, rural artisans, and militia veterans who distrusted those policies. They demanded paper money, debtor relief, and generous salaries for representatives so that ordinary men could afford to serve. In most states, localists used these issues to control legislatures.

Congress also faced severe fiscal problems. Between October 1781 and February 1786, it requisitioned $15.7 million from the states but received only $2.4 million. Its annual income had fallen to $400,000 at a time when interest on its debt neared $2.5 million and the principal on the foreign debt was about to come due. Requisitions were beginning to seem as inefficient as George Grenville had predicted when he proposed the Stamp Act.

Foreign relations took an ominous turn. Without British protection, American ships that entered the Mediterranean risked capture by Barbary pirates and the enslavement of their crews. In 1786, Foreign Secretary John Jay negotiated a treaty with Don Diego de Gardoqui, Spanish minister to the United States. It offered northern merchants trading privileges with Spanish colonies in exchange for closure of the Mississippi River to American traffic for 25 years. Seven northern states voted for the treaty, but all five southern states in Congress rejected these terms, thus defeating the treaty, which needed nine votes for ratification under the Articles of Confederation. Angry talk of disbanding the Union filled Congress. Delegates began haggling over which state would join what union after a breakup. The quarrel became public in early 1787 when a Boston newspaper called for dissolution of the Union.

By the mid-1780s, many cosmopolitans were becoming nationalists eager to strengthen the Union. Many of them had served long, frustrating years in the army or in Congress, unable to carry out measures that they considered vital to the Confederation. In 1785, some of them tried to see what could be done outside Congress. To resolve disputes about navigation rights on the Potomac River, Washington invited Virginia and Maryland delegates to a conference at Mount Vernon,

6.14 Daniel Shays and Job Shattuck Veterans of the Revolutionary War, Shays and Shattuck helped to lead the farmers' revolt in western Massachusetts known as Shays's Rebellion. This woodcut from a Boston almanac in 1787 exaggerates the organization of the uprising by giving the men uniforms, a flag, and artillery.

Q How did the image both overestimate and underestimate the potential power of Shays's Rebellion?

where they drafted an agreement acceptable to both states and to Congress. Prompted by James Madison, the Virginia legislature urged all states to participate in a convention at Annapolis to explore ways to improve American trade.

Four states, including Maryland, ignored the call, and the New Englanders had not yet arrived when, in September 1786, the delegates from the four middle states and Virginia accepted a report drafted by Alexander Hamilton of New York. It asked all of the states to send delegates to a convention at Philadelphia the next May "to devise such further provisions as shall appear to them necessary to render the constitution of the Federal Government adequate to the exigencies of the Union." Seven states responded positively before Congress endorsed the convention on February 21, 1787, and five accepted later. Rhode Island refused to participate. Madison used the winter months to study the defects of classical and European confederacies and to draft his own plan for a stronger union.

6-7c The Philadelphia Convention

The convention opened in May 1787 with a plan similar to the Virginia constitution of 1776. It proposed an almost sovereign Parliament for the United States. By September, the delegates had produced a document much closer to the Massachusetts constitution of 1780, with a clear separation of powers. The delegates, in four months of secret sessions, repeated the constitutional learning process that had taken four years at the state level after 1776.

Most Virginia and Pennsylvania delegates, who arrived early, formed a nationalist bloc. With Washington presiding, Governor Edmund Randolph proposed the **Virginia Plan** (also known as the "large state" plan). Drafted by Madison, it proposed a bicameral legislature, with representation in both houses apportioned according to population. The legislature would choose the executive and the judiciary. It would possess all powers currently lodged in Congress and the power "to legislate in all cases to which the separate States are incompetent." It could "negate all laws passed by the several States, contravening in [its] opinion … the articles of Union." Remarkably, the plan did not include specific powers to tax or regulate trade, although Madison intended to add them later on. His plan also required ratification by state conventions, not by state legislatures. Within two weeks, the delegates agreed on three-year terms for members of the lower house and seven-year terms for the upper house. The legislature would choose the executive for a single term of seven years.

In mid-June, delegates from the small states struck back. William Paterson proposed the **New Jersey Plan**, which kept the system under the Articles with each state having one vote. The plan also gave the existing Congress power to levy import duties and a stamp tax (as in Grenville's imperial reforms of 1764 and 1765), to regulate trade, and to use force to collect delinquent requisitions from the states (as in North's Conciliatory Proposition of 1775). In another alternative, perhaps designed to terrify the small states into accepting the Virginia Plan, Hamilton suggested a government in which both the senate and the executive would serve "on good behavior"—that is, for life! To him, the British constitution still seemed the best in the world, but he never formally proposed his plan. No other New York delegate would have supported it.

All of the options before the convention at that point seemed counterrevolutionary. Madison's Parliament for America, Paterson's emulation of Grenville and North, and Hamilton's enthusiasm for the British Empire all challenged in major ways the principles of 1776. But as the summer progressed, the delegates asked themselves what the voters would or would not accept and relearned the hard lessons of popular sovereignty that the state constitutions had taught. The result was a federal Constitution that was, in its own way, revolutionary.

Before the Constitution took its final shape, however, the debate grew as hot as the summer weather. The small states warned that their voters would never accept a constitution that let the large states swallow them. The large states insisted on proportional representation in both houses. "The Large States dare not dissolve the Confederation," retorted Delaware's Gunning Bedford in the most inflammatory outburst of the convention. "If they do, the small ones will find some foreign ally of more honor and good faith, who will take them by the hand and do them justice." Then the Connecticut delegates announced that they would be happy with proportional representation in one house and state equality in the other.

In July, the delegates accepted this **Connecticut Compromise** and then completed the document by September. They finally realized that they were creating a government of laws, to be enforced on individuals through federal courts, and were not propping up a system of congressional resolutions to be carried out (or ignored) by the states. Terms for representatives were reduced to two years, and terms for senators to six, with each state legislature choosing two senators. The president would serve four years, could be reelected, and would be chosen by an **Electoral College** (an idea borrowed from the system for choosing state senators in Maryland's 1776 state constitution). Each state received as many electors as it had congressmen and senators combined, and the states were free to decide how to choose their electors. Each elector had to vote for two candidates for president, of whom one had to be from another state. This provision reflected a fear that localist impulses might block a majority for anyone. Washington would surely be the first president, but there was no obvious choice after him.

In other provisions, free and slave states agreed to count only three-fifths of the slaves in apportioning both representation and direct taxes. The enumeration of congressional powers became lengthy and explicit and included taxation, the regulation of foreign and interstate commerce, and the catchall "necessary and proper" clause. Madison's negative on state laws yielded to the gentler "supreme law of the land" clause. Over George Mason's last-minute objection, the delegates refused to include a bill of rights.

What They Said

Virginians Debate the Constitution

The Constitution has served as the framework of the United States government for more than 225 years, making it difficult today to conceive of any alternative. Yet, when first proposed, the Constitution faced passionate opposition in many states. Nowhere was ratification more contentious than in Virginia. For most of June 1788, the Virginia Ratifying Convention met and debated in Richmond. Supporters of the Constitution, such as James Madison and John Marshall, faced off against their neighbors and fellow revolutionaries, including Patrick Henry, George Mason, and James Monroe.

Below are excerpts of speeches from the debate by Henry and Madison. For Anti-Federalists like Henry, the proposed new government threatened liberty on at least two levels, by not protecting individual liberties and by removing sovereignty from the states. Henry argued that the true design of the Constitution was to create "consolidated" government—that is, a purely centralized governing authority. In response, Madison claimed that the Constitution provided for federal, or shared, authority between the national and state governments. Ultimately, Madison's argument carried the day, but just barely. On June 25, the Virginia convention ratified the Constitution by a vote of 89 to 79.

▶ Patrick Henry

Mr. Chairman, the public mind, as well as my own, is extremely uneasy at the proposed change of government…. A year ago, the minds of our citizens were at perfect repose. Before the meeting of the late Federal Constitution at Philadelphia, a general peace and a universal tranquillity prevailed in this country; but since that period, they are exceedingly uneasy and disquieted….

I would make this inquiry of those worthy characters who composed a part of the late Federal Constitution. I am sure they were full impressed with the necessity of forming a great consolidated government, instead of a confederation. That this is a consolidated government is demonstrably clear; and the danger of such a government is, to my mind, very striking…. Who authorized them to speak the language of, *We, the People*, instead of, *We, the States*? States are the characteristics and the soul of a confederation. If the States be not the agents of this compact, it must be one great consolidated National Government, of the people of all the States…. The people gave them no power to use their name. That they exceeded their power is perfectly clear.

▶ James Madison

He [Henry] informs us that the people of this country are at perfect repose, that every man enjoys the fruits of his labor peaceably and securely, and that everything is in perfect tranquillity and safety. I wish sincerely, sir, this were true. If this be their happy situation, why has every State acknowledged the contrary?

The principal question is, whether it be a federal or consolidated government…. I conceived myself that it is of a mixed nature; it is in a manner unprecedented. We cannot find one express example in the experience of the world: it stands by itself. In some respects it is a government of a federal nature; in others it is of a consolidated nature. Even if we attend to the manner in which the Constitution is investigated, ratified, and made the act of the people of America, I can say, notwithstanding what the honorable gentleman has alleged, that this government is not completely consolidated, nor is it entirely federal. Who are parties to it? The people—but not the people as composing one great body; but the people as composing thirteen sovereignties…. Should all the States adopt it, it will be then a government established by the Thirteen States of America.

Q How did Henry and Madison interpret conditions under the Articles of Confederation differently?

Q Are you surprised that Henry valued the power of the states more than that of the people? How might Virginia's long colonial experience and Britain's imperial reforms of the 1760s and 1770s help to explain his veneration for state sovereignty?

Q How did Madison attempt to minimize his differences with Henry and other Anti-Federalists? Do you think his rhetoric was effective?

Sources: (top) From speech delivered by Patrick Henry, June 1788. From *Debates and other Proceedings of the Convention of Virginia, Convened at Richmond, on Monday the 2nd day of June 1788, for the purpose of deliberating on the Constitution recommended by the Grand Federal Convention*, 3 vols. (Petersburg, VA., 1788-1789). Reprinted in Samuel Eliot Morison, ed., *Sources and Documents Illustrating the American Revolution, 1764–1788, and the Formation of the Federal Constitution*, 1st ed. (New York: Oxford University Press, 1923) pp. 307–310; (bottom) From speech delivered by James Madison, June 1788. From *Debates and other Proceedings of the Convention of Virginia, Convened at Richmond, on Monday the 2nd day of June 1788, for the purpose of deliberating on the Constitution recommended by the Grand Federal Convention*, 3 vols. (Petersburg, VA., 1788–1789). Reprinted in Samuel Eliot Morison, ed., *Sources and Documents Illustrating the American Revolution, 1764–1788, and the Formation of the Federal Constitution*, 1st ed. (New York: Oxford University Press, 1923) pp. 332, 333 & 337.

With little debate, the convention approved a revolutionary proposal for ratifying the Constitution. This clause called for special conventions in each state and declared that the Constitution would go into force as soon as any nine states had accepted it, even though the Articles of Confederation required unanimous approval for all amendments. The delegates understood that they were proposing an illegal but peaceful overthrow of the existing legal order—that is, a revolution. They hoped that once nine or more states accepted the Constitution, the others would follow their example after the new government got under way and would make ratification unanimous. At that point, their revolution would become both peaceful and legal. The Constitution would then rest on popular sovereignty in a way that the Articles never had. The **Federalists**, as supporters of the Constitution now called themselves, were willing to risk destroying the Union in order to save and strengthen it, but they knew that they would have to use persuasion, not force, to win approval.

6-7d Ratification

Back home, Federalist delegates made a powerful case for the Constitution in newspapers, most of which favored a stronger central government. Most Anti-Federalists, or opponents of the Constitution, were localists with few interstate contacts and limited access to the press. Federalists gave them little time to organize. The first ratifying conventions met in December. Delaware ratified unanimously on December 7, Pennsylvania by a 46-to-23 vote five days later, and New Jersey unanimously on December 18. Georgia ratified unanimously on January 2, and then Connecticut approved by a lopsided margin.

Except in Pennsylvania, these victories were in small states. Ironically, although the Constitution was mostly a "large state" document, small states embraced it while large states hesitated. Small states, once they had equality in the senate, saw advantages in a strong central government. Under the Articles, for example, New Jerseyans had to pay duties to neighboring states on foreign goods imported through New York City or Philadelphia. Under the Constitution, import duties would go to the federal government, a clear gain for every small state but Rhode Island, which stood to lose revenue at both Providence and Newport.

Pennsylvania was the only large state with a solid majority for ratification. But Anti-Federalists there demanded a federal bill of rights and major changes in the structure of the new government. Large states could think of going it alone; small states could not—except Rhode Island, with its two cities and its long history of defying its neighbors.

The first hotly contested state was Massachusetts, which set a pattern for struggles in other divided states. Federalists there won by a slim margin (187 to 168) in February 1788. They blocked Anti-Federalist attempts to make ratification conditional on the adoption of specific amendments. Instead, they won their slim majority by promising to support a bill of rights by constitutional amendment *after* ratification.

The Rhode Island legislature voted overwhelmingly against summoning a ratifying convention. Maryland and South Carolina ratified easily in April and May, bringing the total to eight of the nine states required. Then conventions met almost simultaneously in New Hampshire, Virginia, New York, and North Carolina. In each, a majority at first opposed ratification.

As resistance stiffened, the ratification controversy turned into the first great debate about the American Union, over what kind of national government the United States ought to have. Anti-Federalists argued that the new government would be too remote from the people to be trusted with the broad powers specified in the Constitution. They warned that in a House of Representatives divided into districts of 30,000 people (twice the size of Boston), only very prominent men would be elected. The absence of a bill of rights also troubled them.

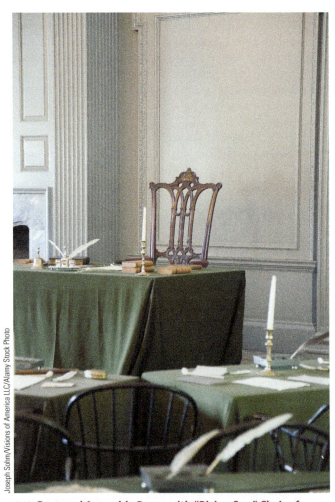

6.15 Restored Assembly Room with "Rising Sun" Chair of George Washington, Independence Hall, Philadelphia Washington sat in this chair in his role as president of the Constitutional Convention in 1787. Benjamin Franklin confessed that during the difficult days of the Convention he could not tell whether the sun on the chair's back was rising or setting. By the end of the Convention, however, Franklin was confident that the sun, like America, was rising.

During the struggle over ratification, Hamilton, Madison, and Jay wrote a series of 85 essays, published first in New York newspapers, and then widely reprinted elsewhere. They defended the Constitution almost clause by clause. Signing themselves "Publius," they later published the collected essays as *The Federalist Papers*, the most comprehensive body of political thought produced by the revolutionary generation. In *Federalist, no. 10*, Madison challenged 2,000 years of received wisdom when he argued that a large republic would be more stable than a small one. Small republics were unstable, he insisted, because majority factions could easily gain power within them, crush the rights of minorities, and ignore the common good. But in a huge republic as diverse as the United States, factions would seldom be able to forge a majority. "Publius" hoped that the new government would draw on the talents of the wisest and best-educated citizens. To those who accused him of trying to erect an American aristocracy, he noted that the Constitution forbade titles and hereditary rule.

Federalists won a narrow majority (57 to 46) in New Hampshire on June 21, and Madison guided Virginia to ratification (89 to 79) five days later (see the "What They Said" feature). New York approved, by 30 votes to 27, one month later, bringing 11 states into the Union, enough to launch the new government. North Carolina rejected the Constitution in July 1788 but finally ratified in November 1789 after the first Congress had drafted the Bill of Rights and sent it to the states. Rhode Island, after refusing seven times to call a ratifying convention, finally summoned one that ratified by a vote of only 34 to 32 in May 1790. The Bill of Rights was ratified a year later.

Conclusion

Americans survived the most devastating war they had yet fought and won independence, but only with massive aid from France. Most Indians and blacks, free to do so, sided with Britain. During the struggle, white Americans affirmed liberty and equality for themselves in their new state constitutions and bills of rights, but they rarely applied these values to blacks or Indians, even though every northern state adopted either immediate or gradual emancipation. The discontent of the postwar years created the Federalist coalition, which drafted and ratified a new national Constitution to replace the Articles of Confederation. Federalists endowed the new central government with more power than Parliament had ever successfully exercised over the colonies but insisted that the Constitution was fully compatible with the liberty and equality proclaimed during the Revolution. Nothing resembling American federalism had ever been tried before. Under this new system, sovereignty was removed from government and bestowed on the people, who then empowered separate levels of government through their state and federal constitutions. As the Great Seal of the United States proclaimed, it was a *novus ordo seclorum*, a new order for the ages.

CHAPTER REVIEW

Review

1. How did the British decision to allow Washington's army to escape New York in August 1776 come back to haunt them in the battles of Trenton and Princeton?
2. What led France to intervene on the American side in the war?
3. What different considerations drove loyalists, African Americans, and Indians to join the British war effort?
4. After the initial success of Britain's southern campaign, what factors contributed to American victory in the south?
5. What social changes came about in the United States either directly or indirectly as a result of the American Revolution?
6. In what ways did state constitutions advance American constitutional thinking during the revolutionary era?
7. How did conditions in the United States in the 1780s influence the outcome of the Constitution?

Critical Thinking

1. Americans today often forget that, among other things, the American Revolution was a war. How did the war affect the character of the Revolution? Had the war not turned so bitter or continued for so long, is it possible that American society might have developed differently? If so, how?
2. For the past century, American historians have passionately debated whether the federal Constitution fulfilled or undermined the revolutionary principles of 1776. Which side do you support?

Identifications

Review your understanding of the following key terms, people, and events for this chapter (terms in bold in text are included in the Glossary).

Saratoga, p. 170
Joseph Brant, p. 175

Nathanael Greene, p. 181
Yorktown, p. 183
gradual emancipation, p. 186
manumission, p. 186
republican wife/mother, p. 187
Northwest Ordinance, p. 189
sovereign power, p. 189
popular sovereignty, p. 189
separation of powers, p. 190
unicameral legislature, p. 190
public virtue, p. 190
stay laws, p. 193
Shays's Rebellion, p. 193
Virginia Plan, p. 194
New Jersey Plan, p. 194
Connecticut Compromise, p. 194
Electoral College, p. 194
Federalists, p. 196

Suggested Reading

John Ferling's *Almost a Victory: The American Victory in the War of Independence* (2007) is the best single volume on the war. **Holger Hoock's** *Scars of Independence: America's Violent Birth* (2017) emphasizes violence in reframing the American Revolution. The essays in **John Shy's** *A People Numerous and Armed: Reflections on the Military Struggle for American Independence*, rev. ed. (1990), have had a tremendous influence on other historians. **David Hackett Fischer's** *Washington's Crossing* (2004) introduces important insights on Trenton and Princeton. **Andrew Jackson O'Shaughnessy**, *The Men Who Lost America: British Leadership, the American Revolution, and the Fate of Empire* (2014), tells the war from the British perspective. **J.R. McNeil's** chapter on Yorktown in *Mosquito Empires: Ecology and War in the Greater Caribbean, 1620–1914* (2010) has changed how scholars understand Cornwallis's defeat.

Maya Jasanoff's *Liberty's Exiles: American Loyalists in the Revolutionary World* (2011) has quickly become the standard work on loyalists. For the war's impact on slavery, see **Cassandra Pybus**, *Epic Journeys of Freedom: Runaway Slaves of the American Revolution and their Global Quest for Liberty* (2006), and **Simon Schama**, *Rough Crossings: Britain, the Slaves, and the American Revolution* (2006). For the Indian experience, see **Colin G. Calloway**, *The American Revolution in Indian Country: Crisis and Diversity in Native American Communities* (1995). **Rosemarie Zagarri's** *Revolutionary Backlash: Women and Politics in the Early American Republic* (2007) analyzes what women gained from the Revolution.

The single most important book on emerging American constitutionalism remains **Gordon S. Wood**, *The Creation of the American Republic, 1776–1787* (1969). The most recent thorough study of the Philadelphia Convention is **Richard Beeman**, *Plain, Honest Men: The Making of the American Constitution* (2009). **Saul Cornell** provides a thoughtful approach to *The Other Founders: Anti-Federalism and the Dissenting Tradition in America* (1999). **Woody Holton's** *Unruly Americans and the Origins of the Constitution* (2008) also highlights opponents of the Constitution.

MINDTAP is a fully online personalized learning experience built upon Cengage Learning content. MindTap® combines student learning tools—readings, multimedia, activities, and assessments—into a singular Learning Path that guides students through the course and helps students develop the critical thinking, analysis, and communication skills that are essential to academic and professional success.

7 Completing the Revolution, 1789–1815

7-1 Establishing the National Government
▶ *Learning Objective:* Explain the Federalist plan for organizing the national government and its finances.

The "Republican Court"
The First Congress
Hamiltonian Economics: The National Debt
Hamiltonian Economics: The Bank and the Excise
The Rise of Jeffersonian Opposition

7-2 The American Republic in a Changing World
▶ *Learning Objective:* Identify the principal foreign and internal threats to the newly independent United States in the late 18th century.

New Spain and the Bourbon Reforms
Americans and the French Revolution
Citizen Genêt
Western Troubles
The Collapse of the Miami Confederacy
The Jay Treaty
The Election of 1796
Troubles with France, 1796–1800
The Crisis at Home, 1798–1800
Election of 1800

7-3 The Jeffersonians in Power
▶ *Learning Objective:* List the principal reforms of the national government during Thomas Jefferson's administration.

The Republican Program
The Jeffersonians and the Courts
Justice Marshall's Court
Louisiana
Lewis and Clark

7-4 The Republic and the Napoleonic Wars, 1803–1815
▶ *Learning Objective:* Analyze the place of the United States within the changing international politics between 1803 and 1815.

The Dilemmas of Neutrality
Trouble on the High Seas
Embargo
The Road to War
The War Hawk Congress, 1811–1812
American Strategy in 1812
The Rise of Tecumseh
The War with Canada, 1812–1813
Tecumseh's Last Stand
The British Offensive, 1814
The Hartford Convention
The Treaty of Ghent

7.1 **View of the City of New Orleans, Celebrating the Louisiana Purchase, 1803** The early United States grew rapidly both in population and size, nearly doubling with the Louisiana Purchase in 1803. The image here captures the dynamism of the new nation that now stretched from the Mississippi River to the Rocky Mountains. At the same time, white settlers would use slave labor in much of this new western territory, and New Orleans would become a leading departure point in the domestic slave trade.

ALMOST BY ACCLAMATION, George Washington became the first president under the Constitution. Washington and his closest advisers (they would soon call themselves Federalists) believed that the balance between power and liberty had tipped toward anarchy after the Revolution. "Local mischiefs," they said, had nearly destroyed the union of the states that had made independence possible. Federalists wanted the Constitution to counter democratic excesses. They were determined to make the national government powerful enough to command respect abroad and to impose order at home. For the most part, they succeeded, but in the process, they aroused a determined opposition that feared the Federalists' consolidation of central power at the expense of the states and the citizenry. These self-styled Democratic Republicans (led almost from the beginning by Thomas Jefferson) were as firmly tied to revolutionary ideals of limited government and a citizenry of independent farmers as the Federalists were to visions of an orderly commercial republic with a powerful national state. The fight between Federalists and Democratic Republicans echoed the revolutionary contest between liberty and power—conducted this time against an ominous backdrop of international intrigue and war between France (which entered a republican revolution of its own in 1789) and Britain. Only when this Age of Democratic Revolution ended in 1815 could Americans survey the kind of society and government that their own Revolution had made. ■

7-1 Establishing the National Government

Q *What was the Federalist plan for organizing the national government and its finances?*

George Washington left Mount Vernon for the temporary capital in New York City in April 1789. The way was lined with the grateful citizens of the new republic. Militia companies and local dignitaries escorted him from town to town, crowds cheered, church bells marked his progress, and lines of girls in white dresses waved demurely as he passed. At Newark Bay, he boarded a flower-bedecked barge and, surrounded by scores of boats, crossed to New York City. He arrived on April 23 and was inaugurated seven days later.

7-1a The "Republican Court"

Reporting for work, President Washington found the new government embroiled in its first controversy—an argument over the dignity that would attach to his own office. Vice President John Adams had asked the Senate to create a title of honor for the president. Adams and others wanted a title that would reflect the power of the new executive. They rejected "His Excellency" because that was the term used for ambassadors, colonial governors, and other minor officials. Among the other titles they considered were "His Highness," "His Mightiness," "His Elective Highness," "His Most Benign Highness," "His Majesty," and "His Highness, the President of the United States, and Protector of Their Liberties." The Senate debated the question for a full month, and then gave up when it became clear that the more democratic House of Representatives disliked titles. They settled on the literal description in the Constitution of "President of the United States of America," which later became expressed informally as "Mr. President." A senator from Pennsylvania expressed relief that the "silly business" was over. Thomas Jefferson pronounced the whole affair "the most superlatively ridiculous thing I ever heard of."

Jefferson would learn, however, that much was at stake in the argument over titles. The Constitution provided a blueprint for the republic. George Washington's administration would translate the blueprint into a working state. It mattered very much how citizens addressed their president, for that was part of the huge constellation of laws, customs, and forms of etiquette that would give the new government either a republican or a courtly tone. Many Federalists wanted to bolster presidential power against the localism and democracy that, they believed, had nearly killed the republic in the 1780s. Washington's stately inaugural tour, the high salaries paid to executive appointees, the endless round of formal balls and presidential dinners, the public celebration of the president's birthday (an English royal custom), the appearance of Washington's profile on some of the nation's coins—all dramatized the power and grandeur of the new government, particularly of its executive. When Jefferson became secretary of state and attended official social functions, he often found that aristocratic sentiments prevailed, "unless there chanced to be some [democrat] from the legislative Houses." Thus, the battle over presidential titles was not "silly business." It was a revealing episode in the argument over how questions of power and liberty that Americans had debated since the 1760s would finally be answered.

7-1b The First Congress

Leadership of the First Congress fell to James Madison, the Virginia congressman who had helped write the Constitution. Under his guidance, Congress strengthened the new national government at every turn. First it passed a **tariff**, or tax, on imports, which would be the government's chief source of income. Next, it turned to amendments to the Constitution demanded by the state ratifying conventions.

Madison proposed 19 constitutional amendments to the House. The 10 that survived congressional scrutiny and ratification by the states became the **Bill of Rights**. They reflected fears that were raised by a generation of struggle with centralized power. The First Amendment guaranteed the freedoms of speech, press, and religion against federal interference. The Second and Third Amendments, prompted by old fears of a standing army, guaranteed the continuation of a militia of armed citizens and stated the specific conditions under which soldiers could be quartered in citizens' households. The Fourth through Eighth Amendments defined a citizen's rights in court and when under arrest—rights that had been central to the Revolution's list of grievances. The Ninth Amendment stated that the enumeration of specific rights in the first eight amendments did not imply a denial of other rights. Finally, the Tenth Amendment stated that powers not assigned to the national government by the Constitution remained with the states and the citizenry, though the intentional omission of the word "expressly" left room for argument.

Madison, a committed nationalist, had performed skillfully. Many doubters at the ratifying conventions had called for amendments that would weaken the national government. By channeling their fears into the area of civil liberties, Madison soothed popular fears while preserving governmental power.

To fill out the framework of government outlined in the Constitution, Congress created the executive departments of war, state, and treasury and guaranteed that the president would appoint the heads of those departments (and their assistants), thus removing them from congressional control. Congress next created the federal courts, which were demanded by but not specified in the Constitution. The Judiciary Act of 1789 established a Supreme Court with six members, along with 13 district courts and three **circuit courts** of appeal. The act allowed certain cases to be appealed from state courts to these federal circuit courts presided over by traveling Supreme Court justices, thus dramatizing

CHRONOLOGY

1789	George Washington inaugurated as first president of the United States • Judiciary Act establishes the Supreme Court and federal circuit courts
1790	Hamilton delivers his Report on Public Credit to Congress • Congress drafts the Bill of Rights
1794	Federalists' excise tax triggers Whiskey Rebellion • The Battle of Fallen Timbers
1796	Jay's Treaty and Pinckney's Treaty ratified
1798	XYZ Affair results in undeclared war with France • Alien and Sedition Acts passed by Congress
1801	Thomas Jefferson inaugurated as third president of the United States
1803	United States purchases Louisiana Territory from France • *Marbury v. Madison* establishes the doctrine of judicial review
1804–1806	Lewis and Clark explore the Louisiana Purchase and the Columbia River basin
1807	*Chesapeake-Leopard* Affair ignites anti-British sentiment • Congress passes Embargo Act
1810	Henry Clay elected Speaker of the House
1812	War with England begins
1813	The Battle of the Thames
1814	Federalists convene the Hartford Convention • Treaty of Ghent ends the War of 1812
1815	American victory at the Battle of New Orleans

7.2 George Washington in 1796, Near the End of His Presidency
The artist captured the formal dignity of the first president and surrounded him with gold, red velvet, a presidential throne, and other emblems of kingly power.

Q *What republican features of the painting help to balance its monarchical character?*

federal power. As James Madison and other members of the intensely nationalist First Congress surveyed their handiwork, they could congratulate themselves on having strengthened national authority at every opportunity.

7-1c Hamiltonian Economics: The National Debt

Washington filled posts in his cabinet with familiar faces. As secretary of war, he chose Henry Knox, an old comrade from the Revolution. The State Department went to his fellow Virginian, Thomas Jefferson. He chose Alexander Hamilton of New York, his trusted aide-de-camp during the Revolution, to head the Department of the Treasury.

Hamilton was the most single-minded nationalist in the new government. He was a brilliant economic thinker, an admirer of the British system of centralized government and finance, and a supremely arrogant and ambitious man. More than any other cabinet member, and perhaps even more than Washington (he later referred to Washington's presidency as "my administration"), Hamilton directed the making of a national government.

In 1789, Congress asked Secretary of the Treasury Hamilton to report on the public debt. The debt fell into three categories, Hamilton reported. The first was the $11 million owed to foreigners—primarily debts to France incurred during the Revolution. The second and third—roughly $24 million each—were debts owed by the national and state governments to American citizens who had supplied food, arms, and other resources to the revolutionary cause. Congress agreed that both justice and the credibility of the new government dictated that the foreign debts be paid in full, but the domestic debts raised troublesome questions. Those debts consisted of notes issued during the Revolution to soldiers, and to merchants, farmers, and others who had helped the war effort. Over the years, speculators had purchased many of these notes at a fraction of their face value; when word spread that the Constitution would create a government likely to pay its debts, speculators and their agents fanned out across the countryside, buying all the notes they could find. By 1790, the government debt was concentrated in the hands of businessmen and speculators—most of them northeasterners—who had bought notes at prices only 10 percent to 30 percent of their original value. Full payment would bring them enormous windfall profits.

The Revolutionary War debt of the individual states was another source of contention. Nationalists, with Hamilton at their head, wanted to assume the states' debts as part of a national debt. The states' debts also had been bought up by speculators, and they posed another problem as well: Many states, including all of the southern states with the exception of South Carolina, had paid off most of their notes in the 1780s; the other states still had significant outstanding debts. If the federal government assumed the states' debts, money would flow out of the southern, middle, and western states into the Northeast, whose citizens would hold fully four-fifths of the combined national debt.

That is precisely what Hamilton proposed in his Report on Public Credit, issued in January 1790. He urged Congress to assume the states' debts and combine them with the federal government's foreign and domestic debts into a consolidated national debt. He agreed that the foreign debt should be paid promptly, a move that would announce to the international community that the government of the United States would pay its bills. But he insisted that debts owed to Americans be a permanent, tax-supported fixture of government. Under his plan, the government would issue securities to its creditors and would pay an annual rate of interest of 4 percent. A permanent debt would encourage wealthy financiers to invest in government securities, thus allying them with the national state. Servicing the debt would also require a significant enlargement of the federal civil service, national financial institutions, and federal taxes. The national debt, in short, was at the center of Alexander Hamilton's plan for a powerful national state.

7-1d Hamiltonian Economics: The Bank and the Excise

As part of that plan, Hamilton asked Congress to charter a Bank of the United States. The government would store its funds in the bank and would supervise its operations, but directors representing private stockholders would control the bank. The Bank of the United States would print and back the national currency and would regulate other banks. Hamilton's proposal also made stock in the bank payable in government securities, thus (1) adding to the value of the securities, (2) giving the bank a powerful interest in the fiscal stability of the government, and (3) binding the holders of the securities even closer to the national government. Those who looked closely saw that Hamilton's Bank of the United States was a carbon copy of the Bank of England.

To fund the national debt, Hamilton called for a federal **excise tax** (a tax on goods) on wines, coffee, tea, and spirits. The tax on spirits would fall most heavily on the whiskey produced in abundance on the frontier. Its purpose, stated openly by Hamilton, was not only to produce revenue but also to establish the government's power to create an internal tax and to collect it in the most remote regions of the republic.

Passed in April 1791, the national bank and the federal excise measures completed Hamilton's organization of government finances. Taken separately, the consolidated government debt, the national bank, and the federal excise tax ably solved discrete problems of government finance. Taken together, however, they constituted a full-scale replica of the treasury-driven government of Britain.

7-1e The Rise of Jeffersonian Opposition

In 1789, nearly every federal officeholder wanted to make the new government work. In particular, Alexander Hamilton at Treasury and James Madison in the House of Representatives expected to continue the political partnership that had helped them write the Constitution and get it ratified. Yet, in the debate over the national debt, Madison led congressional opposition to Hamilton. In 1792, Thomas Jefferson joined the opposition, insisting that Hamilton's schemes would dismantle the Revolution. Within a few short years, the consensus of 1789 had degenerated into an angry argument over what sort of government would finally result from the American Revolution.

Hamilton's proposal for a national debt provided the last major compromise between the two sides. Madison and other southerners opposed the debt because they did not want northern speculators to reap fortunes from notes bought at rock-bottom prices from soldiers, widows, and orphans. He branded Hamilton's plan "public plunder." But at the urging of Jefferson, Madison and the congressional opposition compromised with Hamilton. In exchange for accepting his proposals on the debt, they won his promise to locate the permanent capital of the United States at a site on the Potomac River (which would become Washington, D.C.). The compromise went to the heart of American revolutionary republicanism. Hamilton intended to tie northeastern commercial interests to the federal government. If New York or Philadelphia became the permanent capital, political and economic power might be concentrated there as it was in Paris and London—court cities in which power, wealth, and every kind of excellence were in league against the countryside. The compromise would distance the commercial power of the cities from the federal government and would put an end to the "republican court" that had formed around President Washington.

Hamilton's proposed Bank of the United States split the nation's political elites and their followers into permanent factions, Hamilton's Federalists and Jefferson and Madison's Democratic Republicans, or Republicans for short (not to be confused with the modern Republican Party founded in the 1850s; see Chapter 14). Jefferson argued that Congress had no constitutional right to charter a bank, and that allowing Congress to do so would revive the popular fears of centralized despotism that had nearly defeated ratification of the Constitution. Hamilton responded with the first

What They Said

Washington, Jefferson, and the Image of the President

For American politics in the 1790s, style was substance. George Washington surrounded the office of the presidency with formality, which became characteristic of Federalist style. Below is a description of President Washington at a formal reception near the end of his presidency by the Massachusetts writer and public official William Sullivan, who at the time was a young lawyer.

More democratic members of the new government, including Secretary of State Thomas Jefferson, considered the Federalist style reminiscent of European court society. When he became president in 1801, Jefferson introduced a less formal tone for his administration. In 1804, Sir John Augustus Foster took over his duties as Secretary of the British Legation in Washington. He described President Thomas Jefferson's unassuming Democratic Republican style at an official government function.

▶ Description of George Washington

On entering, he [the visitor] saw the tall manly figure of Washington clad in black velvet; his hair in full dress, powdered and gathered behind in a large silk bag; yellow gloves on his hands; holding a cocked hat with cockade in it, and the edges adorned with a black feather about an inch deep. He wore knee and shoe buckles; and a long sword, with a finely wrought and polished steel hilt, which appeared at the left hip; the coat worn over the sword, so that the hilt, and the part below the folds of the coat behind, were in view. The scabbard was white polished leather.

He stood always in front of the fire-place, with his face towards the door of entrance…. He received his visitor with a dignified bow, while his hands were so disposed of as to indicate, that the salutation was not to be accompanied with shaking hands. This ceremony never occurred in these visits, even with his most near friends.

▶ Description of Thomas Jefferson

Having mentioned Mr. Jefferson, it may be interesting to the reader to have the following description of his person as he appeared to me on my arrival in the United States in the year 1804. He was a tall man with a very red freckled face and grey neglected hair; his manners goodnatured, frank and rather friendly though he had somewhat of a cynical expression of countenance. He wore a blue coat, a thick grey-coloured hairy waistcoat, with a red under-waistcoat lapped over it, green velveteen breeches with pearl buttons, yarn stockings, and slippers down at the heels; his appearance being very much like that of a tall large-boned farmer. He said he washed his feet as often as he did his hands in order to keep off cold, and appeared to think himself unique in so doing.

Q How did the public presentation of Washington and Jefferson differ? How did their images relate to what the two men wanted to accomplish as president of the United States?

Q Why do you think Washington avoided shaking hands with his guests? Why do you think Jefferson felt free to talk about washing his feet?

Sources: (top) William Sullivan, *The Public Men of the Revolution* (Philadelphia: Carey and Hart, 1847), p. 120; (bottom) *The Quarterly Review* Vol. LXVIII (London: John Murray, 1841), p. 24.

---

argument for expanded federal power under the clause in the Constitution empowering Congress "to make all laws which shall be necessary and proper" to the performance of its duties. President Washington and a majority in Congress sided with Hamilton.

Jefferson's strict constructionism (his insistence that the government had no powers beyond those specified in the Constitution) revealed his fears of the de facto constitution that Hamilton was making. Jefferson argued that the federal bank was unconstitutional, that a federal excise tax was certain to arouse public opposition, and that funding the debt would reward speculators and penalize ordinary citizens. More important, Jefferson argued, Hamilton used government securities and stock in the Bank of the United States to buy the loyalty not only of merchants and speculators but also of members of Congress. "The ultimate object of all this," insisted Jefferson, "is to prepare the way for a change, from the present republican form of government, to that of a monarchy, of which the English constitution is to be the model."

7.3 Portrait of Alexander Hamilton by John Trumbull, 1804 Washington's brilliant, ambitious, and slippery secretary of the treasury, he almost single-handedly designed the fiscal structure of the new United States.

For their part, Hamilton and his Federalist supporters insisted that centralization of power and a strong executive were necessary to the survival of the republic. The alternative was a return to the localism and public disorder of the 1780s and, ultimately, the failure of the Revolution. The argument drew its urgency from the understanding of both Hamilton and his detractors that the United States was a weak republic in a world governed by kings and aristocrats, and that republics had a long history of failure. They all knew that Americans might yet lose their Revolution. As both sides began to mobilize popular support, events in Europe came to make that fear all too real. The combination of external threats and internal discord placed the American republican experiment in jeopardy.

7-2 The American Republic in a Changing World

Q *What were the principal foreign and internal threats to the newly independent United States in the late 18th century?*

The American Revolution and the creation of the United States dominate the historical accounts of late 18th-century North America. The year 1776 is a hinge around which the history of the continent—indeed, the hemisphere—seems to turn. Yet, the rise of the United States was only one of many sweeping developments that shaped American history during this period. The Spaniards reorganized their colonial system and forged a transcontinental empire in North America. The French remained a powerful presence in the Caribbean, the British strove to turn Canada into a seat of imperial resurgence, and both harbored ambitions to reclaim their lost North American empires. The Native Americans, who still controlled most of the continent, continued to live according to their own traditions and challenged European pretensions to continental dominance.

7-2a New Spain and the Bourbon Reforms

In the mid-18th century, Spain and its American empire were in a spiraling crisis. A declining population, fiscal inefficiency, and the ascendancy of its rivals had relegated the once formidable empire to a secondary status. To reverse the trend, Spain's Bourbon kings, who had held the Spanish Crown since 1700, implemented sweeping reforms to restore the empire to its former glory. Aspiring to build a more secular and modern Spain, they reorganized the justice system, reformed taxation, simplified the top-heavy mercantilist bureaucracy, and limited the Church's role in the government. The reforms had far-reaching consequences in North America, where the Bourbons meant to thwart the rising might of the newly independent United States.

The late 18th century witnessed a resurgence of Spanish power and influence in North America. Spain had claimed an unbroken, transcontinental zone across the lower continent since 1783, when Britain ceded East and West Florida to it (see Chapter 6). In the following decades, the Bourbon Court made a concerted effort to turn those claims into an imperial realm. In California, Franciscan missionaries built 21 missions on the coastal lowlands, bringing tens of thousands of Indians into the Catholic fold—and into a colonial regime of religious indoctrination, coerced labor, and social surveillance. The Indians were incorporated into mission communities in which they were exposed to new marital and sexual norms, new foods, and new lethal microbes. The result was a demographic and cultural catastrophe. The mission Indians "fatten, sicken, and die," one Franciscan noted. The Indian population of coastal California collapsed roughly by half in a generation, but the missions survived, entrenching Spanish power in California. In 1821, some 3,200 Hispanics—missionaries, soldiers, colonists—lived there, frustrating competing colonization efforts. Russian trappers and traders, advancing down the Pacific coast, established a foothold in northern California but failed to push farther south. British merchants as well operated along the Pacific coast, and a 1795 treaty between Spain and Britain established the Pacific Northwest as a free zone. California, however, remained beyond Britain's reach.

Spanish administrators also managed to secure New Mexico and Texas, which in the early 18th century had been exposed to devastating raids by the equestrian Apaches and Comanches (see Chapter 3). A sprawling, continent-wide smallpox epidemic ravaged the powerful Comanches in the early 1780s, opening the door for Spanish diplomats. Spanish New Mexico and Texas formed alliances with the temporarily weakened Comanches, and the new allies launched a joint war against the Apaches. By 1800, most Apaches had retreated in the mountains and desert shrublands south and west of the Rio Grande, where many of them moved into Spanish-monitored "peace establishments," which foreshadowed the 19th-century Indian reservations in the United States.

Spain's main ambition, however, was to contain the United States in Louisiana (which it had won from France in 1762) and in the Floridas. Again, the Spaniards relied on Indian diplomacy. The Spanish Crown considered Louisiana primarily as a buffer colony and made little effort to change its French and African character (see Chapter 3). Instead, they focused on building a network of loyal Indians—Chickasaws, Choctaws, Creeks, and Cherokees—who would block the westward-pushing American settlers. The strategy was a striking success, allowing Spain to operate far above its demographic weight. The Gulf of Mexico, with Spain in control of its northern shore, was essentially a "Spanish lake." Moreover, by sponsoring an anti-U.S. Indian alliance system on both sides of the Mississippi Valley, the Spaniards blocked the Americans from the great river, cutting off Ohio and other booming western territories from ocean access. Through the 1780s and 1790s, American settlers in the trans-Appalachian West felt oppressed and victimized by Spain. Increasingly, they blamed the Federalist elite for their blight, accusing it of disinterest in western affairs.

7-2b Americans and the French Revolution

At the same time, shifts in transatlantic geopolitics also imperiled the new republic. Late in 1792, French revolutionaries rejected monarchy and proclaimed the French Republic. They beheaded Louis XVI in January 1793. Eleven days later, the French, who were already at war with Austria and Prussia, declared war on conservative Britain, thus launching a war that, with periodic outbreaks of peace, would embroil the Atlantic world until the defeat of France in 1815.

Americans could not have escaped involvement even if they wanted to. Treaties signed in 1778 allied the United States with France, although Federalists and Jeffersonians would argue whether those treaties applied to the French Republic that had killed the king who made them. Americans had overwhelmingly supported the French Revolution of 1789 and had applauded the progress of French republicanism during its first three years. Their gratitude for French help during the American Revolution and hopes for international republicanism faced severe tests in 1793, when the French Republic began to execute thousands of aristocrats, priests, and other "counterrevolutionaries," and when the French threatened the sovereignty of nations by declaring a war of all peoples against all monarchies. The argument between Jeffersonian republicanism and Hamiltonian centralization was no longer a squabble within the U.S. government. National politics was now caught up and subsumed within the struggle over international republicanism.

As Britain and France went to war in 1793, President Washington declared American neutrality, thereby abrogating the 1778 treaties with the French. Washington and most of his advisers realized that the United States was in no condition to fight a war. They also wanted to stay on good terms with Britain. Ninety percent of American imports came from Britain, and 90 percent of the federal revenue came from customs duties on those imports. Thus, both the nation's commerce and the financial health of the government depended on good relations with Britain. Moreover, Federalists genuinely sympathized with the British in the war with France. They regarded the United States as a "perfected" England and viewed Britain as the defender of hierarchical society and ordered liberty against the homicidal anarchy of the French.

Jefferson and his friends saw things differently. They applauded the French for carrying on the republican revolution Americans had begun in 1776, and they had no affection for the monarchical politics of the Federalists or for Americans' continued neocolonial dependence on British trade. Although the Jeffersonians agreed that the United States should stay out of the war, they sympathized as openly with the French as the Federalists did with the British. Common people formed Democratic-Republican societies to raise toasts, organize parades, and otherwise celebrate the spread of republican ideas throughout the Atlantic world.

7-2c Citizen Genêt

Throughout the war years from 1793 to 1815, both Britain and France, by intervening freely in the internal affairs of the United States, made American isolationism impossible.

In April 1793, the French sent Citizen Edmond Genêt as minister to the United States. Genêt's ruling Girondists were the revolutionary faction that had declared the war on all monarchies; they ordered Genêt to enlist American aid with or without the Washington administration's consent. After the president's proclamation of neutrality, Genêt openly commissioned American privateers to harass British shipping and enlisted Americans in intrigues against the Spanish outpost of New Orleans. Genêt then opened France's Caribbean colonies to American shipping, providing American shippers a choice between French free trade and British mercantilism. Genêt's mission ended abruptly in summer 1793, when Robespierre and the infamous Terror drove the Girondists from power.

The British answered Genêt's free-trade declaration with a promise to seize any ship trading with French colonies in the Caribbean. Under these Orders in Council, the British seized 250 American ships. Royal Navy press gangs also searched American ships for British sailors who had deserted or who had switched to safer, better-paying work in the American merchant marine. Under British law, the Royal Navy could impress any British seafaring subject into service during wartime. Inevitably, American sailors were also impressed into the British navy in a contemptuous and infuriating assault on American sovereignty. Meanwhile, the British, operating from Canada and from their still-garrisoned forts in the Northwest, began promising military aid to the Indians north of the Ohio River. Thus, while the French ignored the neutrality of the United States, the British engaged in both overt and covert acts of war.

7-2d Western Troubles

The problems with France and on the high seas were accompanied by an intensified threat from British and Indian forces in the west, as well as from settlers in that region. The situation came to a head in summer and fall 1794. The Shawnee and their allies plotted with the British and talked of driving all settlers out of their territory. At the same time, frontier whites, sometimes with the encouragement of English and Spanish officials, grew increasingly contemptuous of a national government that could neither pacify the Indians nor guarantee their free use of the Mississippi River. President Washington heard that 2,000 Kentuckians were armed and ready to attack New Orleans—a move that would have started a war between the United States and Spain. Settlers in Georgia were making unauthorized forays against the Creeks, and settlers up and down the frontier refused to pay the Federalists' excise tax on whiskey—a direct challenge to federal authority known as the **Whiskey Rebellion**. In western Pennsylvania, mobs tarred and feathered excise officers and burned the property of distillers who paid the tax. In July 1794, near Pittsburgh, 500 militiamen marched on the house of the unpopular federal excise collector General John Neville. Neville, his family, and a few federal soldiers fought the militiamen, killing two and wounding six before they abandoned the house to be looted and burned. Two weeks later, 6,000 "Whiskey Rebels" met at Braddock's Field near Pittsburgh, threatening to attack the town. Sectional tensions between eastern elites and western settlers threatened to dismantle the infant republic.

Faced with serious international and domestic threats to his new government, Washington determined to defeat the Indians and the Whiskey Rebels by force, thus securing American control of the Northwest. He sent General "Mad Anthony" Wayne against the northwestern Indians. Wayne's decisive victory at Fallen Timbers in August 1794—fought almost in the shadow of a British fort—ended the Indian–British challenge in the Northwest for many years. In September, Washington ordered 12,000 federalized militiamen from eastern Pennsylvania, Maryland, Virginia, and New Jersey to quell the Whiskey Rebellion. The president promised amnesty to rebels who pledged to support the government and prison terms to those who did not. As the army marched west from Carlisle, they found defiant liberty poles but no armed resistance. Arriving at Pittsburgh, the army arrested 20 suspected rebels—none of them leaders—and marched them back to Philadelphia for trial. In the end, only two "rebels," both of them feebleminded, were convicted. President Washington pardoned them, and the Whiskey Rebellion was over.

7-2e The Collapse of the Miami Confederacy

Although the territories of many of the woodland Indians were still intact in 1790, they were in serious trouble. The Iroquois had been restricted to reservations in New York and Pennsylvania, and many had fled to Canada. In the Northwest, a multitribal Miami Confederacy led by Blue Jacket and Little Turtle—with the help of the British, who still occupied seven forts within what was formally the United States—continued to trade furs and to impede white settlement. Skirmishes with settlers, however, brought reprisals, and the Indians now faced not only hostile pioneers but the U.S. Army as well. In the Ohio Country, punitive expeditions led by General Josiah Harmar and General Arthur St. Clair failed in 1790 and 1791—the second ending in an Indian victory in which 630 soldiers died.

7.4 Washington Reviewing the Western Army at Fort Cumberland, Maryland In fall 1794, in his effort to suppress the Whiskey Rebellion, Washington became the first and last sitting president to lead troops in the field. After reviewing the militiamen at Fort Cumberland and at Bedford, Pennsylvania, the president left the army in charge of subordinates, including Alexander Hamilton, to march to Pittsburgh.

In 1794, the U.S. finally succeeded in defeating the Miami Confederacy with General Wayne's victory at Fallen Timbers, near present-day Toledo. The Treaty of Greenville forced the Native Americans to cede two-thirds of what are now Ohio and southeastern Indiana (see Map 7.1). As compensation, the U.S. government agreed to dispense annuity payments, which soon became a standard practice in treaty negotiations between the United States and Indians. The government also began to distribute cattle, pigs, and hoes, hoping to transform the Indians from hunters and warriors into farmers. This practice rapidly evolved into a sweeping "civilization" program that would frame U.S. Indian policy for well over a century.

Following their victory at Fallen Timbers, whites filtered into what remained of Indian lands. In 1796, President Washington threw up his hands and announced that "I believe scarcely any thing, short of a Chinese Wall, or a line of troops, will restrain Land Jobbers and the encroachment of settlers upon the Indian Territory." Five years later, Governor William Henry Harrison of the Indiana Territory admitted that frontier whites "consider the murdering of the Indians in the highest degree meritorious."

7-2f The Jay Treaty

While he sent armies against Indians and frontiersmen, President Washington capitulated to the British on the high seas. In 1794, he sent John Jay, chief justice of the Supreme Court, to negotiate the conflicts between the United States and Britain. Armed with news of Wayne's victory, Jay extracted a promise from the British to remove their troops from American territory in the Northwest. On every other point of dispute, however, he agreed to British terms. Jay's Treaty made no mention of British navy impresses or other violations of American maritime rights, nor did it refer to the old issue of British payment for slaves carried off during the Revolution. The treaty did allow small American ships back into the West Indies, but only on terms that the Senate would reject. In short, Jay's Treaty granted British trade a most-favored-nation status in exchange for the agreement of the British to abandon their northwestern forts. Given the power of Britain, it was the best that Americans could expect. Washington, obliged to choose between an unpopular treaty and an unwinnable war, passed Jay's Treaty on to the Senate, which, in June 1795, ratified it by a bare two-thirds majority.

During the fight over Jay's Treaty, dissension within the government was first aired in public. The seaport cities and much of the Northeast reacted favorably to the treaty. It ruled out war with England and cemented an Anglo-American trade relationship that strengthened both Hamilton's national state and the established commercial interests that supported it. The South, on the other hand, saw Jay's Treaty as a blatant sign of the designs of Britain and the Federalists to subvert republicanism in both France and the United States. The Virginia legislature branded the treaty as unconstitutional,

▲ **MAP 7.1 The West, 1790–1796** In 1790, the United States "owned" nearly all of its present territory east of the Mississippi River, but white Americans remained concentrated east of the Appalachians (see Map 8.1 on page 228) and independent Indian peoples controlled the rest of the country, their territorial sovereignty recognized by the treaties they had formed with the U.S. government. The Battle of Fallen Timbers and the resultant Treaty of Greenville pushed white settlement across Ohio and into Indiana, but the Indians of the Northwest remained intact, determined, and in touch with the British in Canada. Native Americans also controlled nearly the entire Southwest, and Florida and the Gulf Coast—including all outlets from the interior to the Caribbean—remained in Spanish hands. The American West was very far from secure in the 1790s.

Q What was the primary obstacle to western settlement in the early 1790s?

Q Why was the Battle of Fallen Timbers in 1794 so integral to the future expansion of the United States?

and Republican congressmen demanded to see all documents relating to Jay's negotiations. Washington responded by telling them that their request could be legitimate only if the House was planning to initiate **impeachment** proceedings, thus tying approval of the treaty to his enormous personal prestige.

Meanwhile, on March 3, 1796, Washington released the details of a treaty that Thomas Pinckney had negotiated with Spain. In this treaty, Spain recognized American neutrality and set the border between the United States and Spanish Florida on American terms. Most important, Pinckney's Treaty ended Spanish claims to the Ohio Valley and gave Americans the unrestricted right to navigate the Mississippi River and to transship produce at the Spanish port of New Orleans. Combined with the victory at Fallen Timbers, the British promise to abandon their posts in the Northwest, and Washington's personal popularity, Pinckney's Treaty helped turn the tide in favor of the unpopular Jay's Treaty. Dissension in the trans-Appalachian West abated. With a diminishing number of hotheads willing to oppose Washington, western representatives joined the Northeast and growing numbers of southerners to ratify Jay's Treaty. Spain and its native allies now faced an increasingly united and expansionist republic on their borders.

7-2g The Election of 1796

George Washington refused to run for reelection in 1796, thus setting a two-term limit observed by every president until Franklin Roosevelt (see Chapter 25). Washington could be proud of his accomplishments. He had presided over the creation of a national government. He had secured American control over the western settlements by ending British, Spanish, and Indian military threats and by securing free use of the Mississippi River for western produce. Those policies, together with the federal invasion of western Pennsylvania, had made it evident that the government could control its most distant regions. Washington had also avoided war with Britain, although not without overlooking assaults on American sovereignty. As he was about to leave government, he wrote, with substantial help from Hamilton, his Farewell Address. In it he warned against "permanent alliances with any portion of the foreign world." America, he said, should act independently in international affairs—an ideal that many felt had been betrayed in Jay's Treaty. Washington also warned against internal political divisions.

Washington's retirement opened the way to the very competition for public office that he warned against. In 1796, Americans experienced their first contested presidential election. The Federalists chose as their candidate John Adams of Massachusetts, who had served as vice president. The Democratic Republicans nominated Thomas Jefferson. According to the gentlemanly custom of the day, the candidates did not campaign in person, but friends of the candidates, the newspaper editors who enjoyed their patronage, and even European governments ensured that the election would be hotly contested.

Adams won a close election. The distribution of electoral votes revealed the sectional bases of Federalist and Republican support: Adams received only 2 electoral votes south of the Potomac, and Jefferson received only 18 (all but 5 of them in Pennsylvania) north of the Potomac. Behind the outcome, there was considerable intrigue. Alexander Hamilton, who had retired from the Treasury in 1795, knew that he could not manipulate the independent and almost perversely upright John Adams. So, he secretly instructed South Carolina's Federalist electors to withhold their votes from Adams. That would have given the presidency to Adams's running mate, Thomas Pinckney. (Before the ratification of the Twelfth Amendment in 1804, the candidate with a majority of the electoral votes became president, and the second-place candidate became vice president.) Like some of Hamilton's other schemes, this one backfired. New England electors heard of the plan and angrily withheld their votes from Pinckney. As a result, Adams was elected president and his opponent Thomas Jefferson became vice president. Adams took office with a justifiable mistrust of many members of his own party and with the head of the opposition party as his second in command. It was not an auspicious beginning.

7-2h Troubles with France, 1796–1800

As Adams entered office, an international crisis was already in full swing. France, regarding Jay's Treaty as an Anglo-American alliance, broke off relations with the United States. The French hinted that they intended to overthrow the reactionary government of the United States but would postpone taking action in the hope that a friendlier Thomas Jefferson would replace "old man Washington" in 1797. When the election went to John Adams, the French gave up on the United States and set about denying Britain its new de facto ally. In 1797, the French ordered that American ships carrying "so much as a handkerchief" made in England be confiscated without compensation; in the same vein, they announced that American seamen serving in the British navy (most of whom were impressed and had no choice) would be summarily hanged if captured.

President Adams wanted to protect American commerce from French depredations, but he knew that the United States might not survive a war with France. He also knew that French grievances (including Jay's Treaty and the abrogation of the French-American treaties of 1778) were legitimate. He decided to send a mission to France, made up of three respected statesmen: Charles Cotesworth Pinckney of South Carolina, John Marshall of Virginia, and Elbridge Gerry of Massachusetts. When the delegates reached Paris, however, they were left cooling their heels in the outer offices of the Directory—the revolutionary committee of five that had replaced France's beheaded king. At last, three French officials (the correspondence identified them only as "X, Y, and Z," and the incident later became known as the **XYZ Affair**) discreetly hinted that France would receive them if they paid a bribe of $250,000, arranged for the United States to loan $12 million to the French government, and apologized for unpleasant remarks that John Adams had made about France. The delegates refused, saying "No, not a sixpence," and returned home. There a journalist transformed their remark into "Millions for defense, but not one cent for tribute."

President Adams asked Congress to prepare for war, and the French responded by seizing more American ships. Thus began, in April 1798, an undeclared war between France and the United States in the Caribbean, known today as the Quasi War. While the French navy dealt with the British in the north Atlantic, French privateers inflicted costly blows on American shipping. But after nearly a year of fighting, with the British providing powder and shot for American guns, the U.S. Navy chased the French privateers out of the Caribbean. Fearful of losing their American possessions entirely, French policymakers began to seek for a foothold in the North American mainland.

7-2i The Crisis at Home, 1798–1800

The troubles with France precipitated a crisis at home. Disclosure of the XYZ correspondence, together with the Quasi War in the Caribbean, produced a surge of public hostility toward the French and their Republican friends in the United States. Many Federalists, led by Alexander Hamilton, wanted to use the crisis to destroy their political opponents.

Without consulting President Adams, the Federalist-dominated Congress passed several wartime measures. The first was a federal property tax—graduated, spread equally between sections of the country, and justified by military necessity, but a direct federal tax nonetheless. Congress then passed four laws known as the **Alien and Sedition Acts**. The first three were directed at immigrants: They extended the naturalization period to become citizens from 5 to 14 years and empowered the president to detain enemy aliens during wartime and to deport those he deemed dangerous to the United States. The fourth law—the Sedition Act—set jail terms and fines for persons who advocated disobedience to federal law or who wrote, printed, or spoke "false, scandalous, and malicious" statements against "the government of the United States, or the President of the United States [note that Vice President Jefferson was not included], with intent to defame... or to bring them or either of them, into contempt or disrepute."

President Adams never used the powers granted under the Alien Acts, but the Sedition Act resulted in the prosecution of 14 Republicans, most of them journalists. William Duane, editor of the Philadelphia *Aurora* newspaper, was indicted when he and two Irish friends circulated a petition against the Alien Act on the grounds of a Catholic church. Another prominent Republican went to jail for statements made in a private letter. Matthew Lyon, a scurrilous Republican congressman from Vermont, had brawled with a Federalist representative in the House chamber; he went to jail for his criticisms of President Adams, Federalist militarism, and what he called the "ridiculous pomp" of the national administration.

Republicans charged that the Alien and Sedition Acts violated the First Amendment, and they turned to the states for help. Southern states, which had provided only 4 of the 44 congressional votes for the Sedition Act, took the lead. Jefferson provided the Kentucky legislature with draft resolutions, and Madison did the same for the Virginia legislature. These so-called **Virginia and Kentucky Resolves** restated the constitutional fundamentalism that had guided Republican opposition from the beginning. Jefferson's Kentucky Resolves reminded Congress that the Alien and Sedition Acts gave the national government powers not mentioned in the Constitution and that the Tenth Amendment reserved such powers to the states. He also argued that the Constitution was a "compact" between sovereign states and that state legislatures could "nullify" federal laws they deemed unconstitutional, thus anticipating constitutional theories that states'-rights southerners would use after 1830.

Federalists took another ominous step when President Adams asked Congress to create a military prepared for war. Adams wanted a stronger navy, both because the undeclared war with France was being fought on the ocean and because he agreed with other Federalists that America's future as a commercial nation required a respectable navy. Hamilton and his followers, who were becoming known as "**High Federalists**" for their strident views, preferred a standing army. At the urging of Washington and against his own judgment, Adams appointed Hamilton inspector general. As such, Hamilton would be the de facto commander of the U.S. Army. Congress authorized a 20,000-man army, and Hamilton proceeded to raise it. Congress also provided for a much larger army to be called up in the event of a declaration of war. When Hamilton expanded the officer corps in anticipation of such an army, he excluded Republicans and commissioned only his political friends. High Federalists wanted a standing army to enforce the Alien and Sedition Acts and to put down an impending rebellion in the South. Beyond that, there was little need for such a force. The war was being fought at sea, and most Americans believed that the citizen militia could hold off any land invasion until an army was raised. The Republicans, President Adams, and many other Federalists now became convinced that Hamilton and his High Federalists were determined to destroy their political opponents, enter into an alliance with Britain, and impose Hamilton's statist designs by force.

Adams was angry. First the Hamiltonians had tried to rob him of the presidency. Then they had passed the Alien and Sedition Acts, the direct tax, and plans for a standing army without consulting him. None of this would have been possible if not for the crisis with France.

Adams, who had resisted calls for a declaration of war, began looking for ways to declare peace. He opened negotiations with France and stalled the creation of Hamilton's army while the talks took place. In the agreement that followed, the French canceled the obligations that the United States had assumed under the treaties of 1778. But they refused to pay reparations for attacks on American shipping since 1793—the very point over which many Federalists had wanted war. Peace with France cut the ground from under the militaristic High Federalists. Hamilton would campaign against Adams in 1800, damaging the president's chances for reelection.

7-2j The Election of 1800

Thomas Jefferson and his Democratic Republicans approached the election of 1800 better organized and more determined than they had four years earlier. Moreover, events in the months preceding the election worked in their favor. The Alien and Sedition Acts, the direct tax of 1798, and the Federalist military buildup were never popular. Taken together, these events gave credence to the Republicans' allegation that the Federalists were using the crisis with France to consolidate their power, destroy liberty and the opposition, and overthrow the American republic. The Federalists countered by warning that the election of Jefferson and his radical allies would release the worst horrors of the French Revolution onto the streets of American towns. Each side believed that its defeat in 1800 would mean the end of the republic.

The Democratic Republicans were strong in the South and weak in the Northeast. Jefferson knew that he had to win New York, the state that had cost him the 1796 election. Jefferson's running mate, the New Yorker **Aaron Burr**, arranged a truce between New York's Republican factions and chose candidates for the state legislature who were both locally respected and committed to Jefferson. The strategy succeeded. The Republicans carried New York City and won a slight majority in the legislature. New York's electoral votes belonged to Jefferson. Jefferson and Burr won the election with 73 votes each. Adams had 65 votes, and his running mate Charles Cotesworth Pinckney had 64 (see Map 7.2). (In order to distinguish between their presidential and vice-presidential candidates—and thus thwart yet another of Hamilton's attempts to rig the election—the Federalists of Rhode Island had withheld 1 vote from Pinckney.) Jefferson and Burr had tied, though everyone knew that Jefferson was the presidential candidate. But under the Constitution, a lame-duck Federalist Congress decided the outcome. Federalists supported Burr to keep Jefferson from becoming president, prompting talk of civil war in Republican strongholds.

After six quarrelsome days and 35 ballots on which most Federalist congressmen voted for Burr (whose part in these proceedings has never been fully uncovered), a compromise was reached: Many Federalists abandoned Burr but turned in blank ballots and thus avoided voting for the hated (but victorious) Jefferson. With that, the "Revolution of 1800" had won its first round.

7-3 The Jeffersonians in Power

 What were the principal reforms of the national government during Thomas Jefferson's administration?

On the first Tuesday of March 1801, Thomas Jefferson left his rooms at Conrad and McMunn's boardinghouse in Washington and walked up Pennsylvania Avenue. Jefferson received military salutes along the way, but he forbade the pomp and ceremony that had ushered Washington into office. Accompanied by a few friends and a company of artillery from the Maryland militia (and not by Hamilton's regulars), Jefferson walked (no carriages) up the street and into the unfinished Capitol building. The central tower and the wing that would house Congress were only half completed. Jefferson joined Vice President Burr, other members of the government, and a few foreign diplomats in the newly finished Senate chamber.

7-3a The Republican Program

Jefferson took the oath of office from Chief Justice John Marshall, a distant relative and political opponent from Virginia. Then, in a small voice that was almost inaudible to those at a distance, he delivered his inaugural address. Referring to the political discord that had brought him into office, he began with a

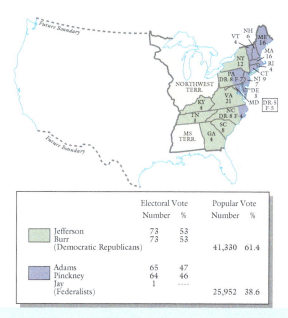

▲ **MAP 7.2 Presidential Election, 1800** The electoral votes in 1800 split along starkly sectional lines. The South voted for Jefferson, New England voted for Adams, and the election was decided by close contests in Pennsylvania and New York.

Q *Why was New York so crucial to Jefferson's winning coalition of states?*

Q *What conclusions could be drawn about the future of the Federalist Party based on this electoral map?*

plea for unity, insisting that "every difference of opinion is not a difference of principle. We have called by different names brethren of the same principle. We are all Republicans, we are all Federalists." Jefferson did not mean that he and his opponents should forget their ideological differences. He meant only to invite moderate Federalists into a broad Republican coalition in which there was no room for the statist designs of Alexander Hamilton and his High Federalist friends.

Jefferson went on to outline the kind of government a republic should have. A "wise and frugal" government would respect the powers of the states and preserve the liberties ensured by the Bill of Rights. It would be small, and it would pay its debts without incurring new ones, thus ending the need for taxation and cutting the ground from beneath the burgeoning Federalist state. It would rely for defense on "a disciplined militia" that would fight invaders while regulars were being trained, thus eliminating Hamilton's standing army. It would protect republican liberties from enemies at home and from the nations of Europe. And, Jefferson promised, it would ensure "the encouragement of agriculture, and of commerce as its handmaiden." Beyond the fostering of an agrarian republic and the maintenance of limited government, Jefferson promised little. Blessed with peace abroad and the defeat of the High Federalists at home, he believed that the United States could at last enter into its experiment with truly republican government.

The simplicity of Jefferson's inauguration set the social tone of his administration. The new president reduced the number and grandeur of formal balls, levees, and dinners. He sent his annual messages to Congress to be read by a clerk, rather than delivering them in person in the manner of English kings and Federalist presidents. He refused to ride about Washington in a carriage, preferring to carry out his errands on horseback. Abandoning grand banquets, Jefferson entertained senators and congressmen at small dinners, which were served at a round table without formal seating, thus ending the fine-tuned hierarchy of the Federalists' old arrangements. Jefferson presided over the meals without wearing a wig and dressed in old homespun clothes and a pair of worn bedroom slippers. The casualness (slovenliness, said some of his critics) did not extend to what was served at dinner, however. The food was prepared by expert chefs and accompanied by fine wines, and it was followed by brilliant conversation perfected by Jefferson while he was a diplomat and a visitor to the salons of Paris.

Jefferson's first order of business was to reduce the size and expense of government. The Federalists, despite their big government dispositions, had left a surprisingly small federal establishment. Jefferson found only 316 employees who were subject to presidential appointment and removal. Those employees, together with 700 clerks and assistants and 3,000 post office workers, made up the entire federal civil service. Jefferson reduced the diplomatic corps and replaced officeholders who were incompetent, corrupt, or avowedly antirepublican. Even so, the rate of turnover was only about 50 percent during his first term. The replacements were not the violent revolutionaries that Federalists had warned against but Republican gentlemen who matched the social status of the departing Federalists. Jefferson altered the politics of the civil service, but he left its size and shape intact.

Jefferson made more substantial cuts in the military. The Federalists had built a sizable army and navy to prepare for war and, if necessary, to put down opposition at home. Legislation passed in March 1802 reduced the army to two regiments of infantry and one of artillery—a total of 3,350 officers and men, most of whom were assigned to western posts far from the centers of white population. Similar cutbacks reduced the navy. The goal, Jefferson explained, was to rely mainly on the militia for national defense but to maintain a small, well-trained professional army as well. (The same legislation that reduced the army created the military academy at West Point.) At Jefferson's urging, Congress also abolished the direct tax of 1798 and repealed the parts of the Alien and Sedition Acts that had not already expired. Jefferson personally pardoned the 10 victims of those acts who were still in jail and repaid their fines with interest.

Thus, with a few strokes, Jefferson dismantled the repressive apparatus of the Federalist state. By reducing government expenditures, he reduced the government's debt and the army of civil servants and papermen gathered around it. During Jefferson's administration, the national debt fell from $80 million to $57 million, and the government built up a treasury surplus, even after paying $15 million in cash for the **Louisiana Purchase** (discussed later in this chapter). Although some doubted the wisdom of such stringent economy, no one questioned Jefferson's frugality.

7.5 Portrait of Jefferson by Rembrandt Peale, 1805 A self-consciously plain President Jefferson posed for this portrait in January 1805, near the end of his first term. He wears an unadorned fur-collared coat, is surrounded by no emblems of office, and gazes calmly and directly at the viewer.

7-3b The Jeffersonians and the Courts

Jefferson next turned his attention to the federal courts. The Constitution had created the Supreme Court but had left the creation of lesser federal courts to Congress. The First Congress had created circuit courts presided over by the justices of the Supreme Court. Only Federalists served on the Supreme Court under Washington and Adams, and Federalists on the circuit courts had extended federal authority into the hinterland—a fact that prosecutions under the Alien and Sedition Acts had made abundantly clear. Jeffersonian mistrust of the federal courts intensified when the lame-duck Federalist Congress passed a Judiciary Act early in 1801. The act reduced the number of associate justices of the Supreme Court from six to five when the next vacancy occurred, thus reducing Jefferson's chances of appointing a new member to the Court. The Judiciary Act also took Supreme Court justices off circuit and created a new system of circuit courts. This allowed Adams to appoint 16 new judges, along with marshals, federal attorneys, clerks, and justices of the peace. Adams worked until nine o'clock on his last night in office signing commissions for these "**midnight judges**." All of them were staunch Federalists. Coupled with President Adams's appointment of Federalist John Marshall as chief justice in January, the Judiciary Act ensured long-term Federalist domination of the federal courts.

Republicans disagreed on what to do about the Federalists' packing of the courts. Some distrusted the whole idea of an independent judiciary and wanted judges elected by popular vote. Jefferson and most in his party wanted the courts shielded from democratic control, but they deeply resented the Federalist "midnight judges" created by the Judiciary Act of 1801. Jefferson replaced the new federal marshals and attorneys with Republicans and dismissed some of the federal justices of the peace, but judges were appointed for life and could be removed only through impeachment. The Jeffersonians hit on a simple solution: They got rid of the new judges by abolishing their jobs. Early in 1802, with some of Jefferson's supporters questioning the constitutionality of what they were doing, Congress repealed the Judiciary Act of 1801 and thus did away with the midnight appointees.

With the federal courts scaled back to their original size, Republicans in Congress went after High Federalists who were still acting as judges. As a first test of impeachment, they chose John Pickering, a federal attorney with the circuit court of New Hampshire. Pickering was a highly partisan Federalist and a notorious alcoholic. The Federalists who had appointed him had long considered him an embarrassment. The House drew up articles of impeachment, and the senate removed Pickering by a strict party vote.

On the same day, Congress went after bigger game: It voted to impeach Supreme Court Justice Samuel Chase.

7.6 A Federalist Attack upon Jefferson From the beginning, Federalists branded Jefferson as a friend to a French Revolution that had promised liberty and equality, then degenerated into violence and dictatorship. Here Jefferson worships at the altar of Gallic Despotism in a political cartoon.

Q *What is the symbolism of the eagle holding the Constitution in the cartoon?*

He hated the Jeffersonians, but his faults did not add up to the "high crimes and misdemeanors" that are the constitutional grounds for impeachment. Moderate Republicans doubted the wisdom of impeaching Chase. Their uneasiness grew when John Randolph took over the prosecution. Randolph led a radical states'-rights faction of the Republican Congress. As Randolph led the prosecution of Samuel Chase, he lectured in his high-pitched voice that Jefferson was double-crossing southern Republicans in an effort to win support in the Northeast. (There was some truth to the accusation: Jefferson envisioned a national Republican coalition, sometimes at the expense of radical states'-rights southerners.) Most Republican senators sided with Jefferson. With Jefferson's approval, many Republicans in the Senate joined the Federalists in voting to acquit Samuel Chase, thus isolating and humiliating Randolph and his states'-rights friends.

7-3c Justice Marshall's Court

Chief Justice John Marshall probably cheered the acquittal of Justice Chase because it was clear that Marshall was next on the list. Secretary of state under John Adams, Marshall was committed to Federalist ideas of national power, as he demonstrated with his decision in the case of **Marbury v. Madison**. William Marbury was one of the justices of the peace whom Jefferson had eliminated in his first few days in office. He sued Jefferson's secretary of state, James Madison, for his commission. Although Marbury never got his job, Marshall used the case to hand down important rulings that laid the basis for the practice of **judicial review**—the Supreme Court's power to rule on the constitutionality of acts of Congress. In arguing that Congress could not alter the jurisdiction of the Supreme Court, Marshall stated that the Constitution is "fundamental and paramount law" and that it is "emphatically the province and duty of the judicial department to say what law is."

Some Republicans saw Marshall's ruling as an attempt to arrogate power to the Court, but Jefferson and other moderates noted that Marshall was less interested in the power of the judiciary than in its independence. Ultimately, they decided they trusted Marshall more than they trusted the radicals in their own party. With the acquittal of Justice Chase, Jeffersonian attacks on the federal courts ceased.

Justice Marshall confirmed his independence in the treason trial of former vice president Aaron Burr in 1807. Following his failed attempt at the presidency in 1801, Burr's relations with northern Federalists so declined that he killed Alexander Hamilton in a duel in 1804. The disgraced Burr headed west and organized a cloudy conspiracy that may have involved (according to varying testimonies) an invasion of Mexico or Florida or the secession of Louisiana. President Jefferson ordered his arrest. Burr was tried for treason at Richmond, Virginia, with the chief justice, who was riding circuit, on the bench. Kings had frequently used the charge of treason to silence dissent. Marshall stopped what he and other Federalists considered Jefferson's attempt to do the same thing by limiting the definition of treason to overt acts of war against the United States or to adhering to the republic's foreign enemies—and by requiring two witnesses to an overt act of treason. Under these guidelines, Burr went free. At the same time, the United States had formally separated internal dissent from treason.

7-3d Louisiana

It was Jefferson's good fortune that Europe remained at peace and stayed out of American affairs for the early part of his first term. The one development that posed an international threat to the United States turned into a grand triumph: the purchase of the Louisiana Territory from France (see Map 7.3).

By 1801, half a million Americans lived west of the Appalachians, and Republicans saw westward expansion as the best hope for the survival of the republic. Social inequality and the erosion of yeoman independence would almost inevitably take root in the East, but in the vast lands west of the mountains, the republic could renew itself for many generations to come. To serve that purpose, however, the West needed ready access to markets through the river system that emptied into the Gulf of Mexico at New Orleans. "There is on the globe," wrote President Jefferson, "one single spot, the possessor of which is our natural and habitual enemy. It is New Orleans."

In 1801, under Pinckney's Treaty, Spain allowed Americans to transship produce from the interior via the Mississippi River and New Orleans. The year before, however, Spain had secretly ceded the Louisiana Territory (roughly, all the land west of the Mississippi drained by the Missouri and Arkansas rivers) to France, having concluded that the United States' westward thrust could not be stalled. Napoleon Bonaparte had plans for a new French empire in America with the sugar island of Hispaniola (present-day Haiti and the Dominican Republic) at its center, and with mainland colonies feeding the islands and thus making the empire self-sufficient. Late in 1802, the Spanish, who had retained control of New Orleans, closed the port to American commerce, creating rumors that they would soon transfer the city to France, which would have threatened the very existence of American settlements west of the Appalachians. President Jefferson sent a delegation to Paris early in 1803 with authorization to buy New Orleans for the United States.

By the time the delegates reached Paris, events had dissolved French plans for a new American empire. The slaves of Saint-Domingue (the French colony on Hispaniola) had revolted and had defeated French attempts to regain control of the island. At the same time, another war between Britain and France seemed imminent. Napoleon—reputedly chanting, "Damn sugar, damn coffee, damn colonies"—decided to bail out of America and concentrate his resources in Europe. He astonished Jefferson's delegation by offering to sell not only New Orleans but the whole Louisiana Territory—which would double the size of the United States—for the bargain price of $15 million.

Jefferson, who had criticized Federalists when they violated the letter of the Constitution, faced a dilemma: The

7.7 **John Marshall** A Virginian and distant relative of Thomas Jefferson, John Marshall became chief justice of the Supreme Court in the last months of John Adams's administration. He used the Court as a conservative, centralizing force until his death in 1835.

president lacked the constitutional power to buy territory, but the chance to buy Louisiana was too good to refuse. It would ensure Americans access to the rivers of the interior; it would eliminate a serious foreign threat on America's western border; and it would give American farmers enough land to sustain the agrarian republic for a long time to come. Swallowing his constitutional scruples (and at the same time half-heartedly asking for a constitutional amendment to legalize the purchase), Jefferson told the American delegates to buy Louisiana. Republican senators quickly ratified the Louisiana treaty over Federalist objections that the purchase would encourage rapid settlement and add to backcountry barbarism and Republican strength. For his part, Jefferson was certain that the republic had gained the means of renewing itself through time. As he claimed in his second inaugural address, he had bought a great "empire of liberty."

7-3e Lewis and Clark

The Americans knew almost nothing about the land they had bought. Only a few French trappers and traders had traveled the plains between the Mississippi and the Rocky Mountains, and no white person had seen the territory drained by the Columbia River. In 1804, Jefferson sent an expedition under Meriwether Lewis, his private secretary, and William Clark, brother of the Indian fighter George Rogers Clark, to explore the new land. To prepare for the expedition, Lewis studied astronomy, zoology, and botany; Clark was already an accomplished mapmaker. The two explorers kept meticulous journals about one of the epic adventures in American history.

In May 1804, Lewis and Clark and 41 companions boarded a keelboat and two large canoes at the village of St. Louis. They poled and paddled 1,600 miles up the Missouri River, passing through rolling plains dotted by the farm villages of the Pawnee, Oto, Missouri, Crow, Omaha, Hidatsa, and Mandan peoples. The villages of the lower Missouri had been cut off from the western buffalo herds and reduced to dependence by mounted Sioux warriors, who had begun to establish their hegemony over the northern plains.

Lewis and Clark traveled through Sioux territory and stopped for the winter at the heavily fortified Mandan villages at the big bend of the Missouri River in Dakota Country. In the spring they hired Toussaint Charbonneau, a French fur trader, to guide them to the Pacific. Charbonneau was useless, but his wife, a teenaged Shoshone girl named Sacajawea, was an indispensable guide, interpreter, and diplomat. With her help, Lewis and Clark navigated the upper Missouri, crossed the

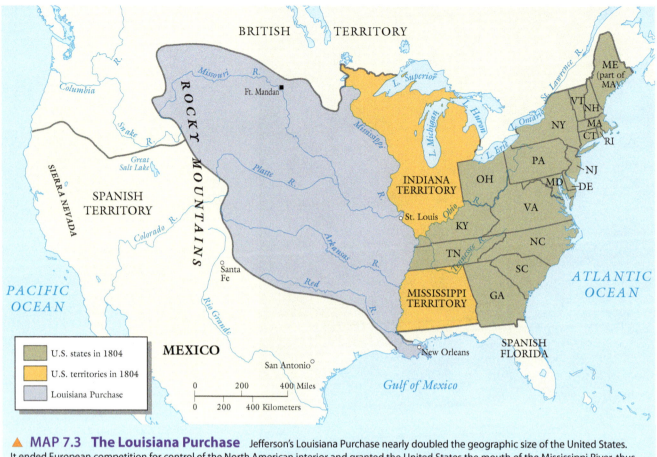

▲ **MAP 7.3 The Louisiana Purchase** Jefferson's Louisiana Purchase nearly doubled the geographic size of the United States. It ended European competition for control of the North American interior and granted the United States the mouth of the Mississippi River, thus strengthening white settlements between the Appalachians and the Mississippi and increasing American control over those settlements.

Q Why did the Jefferson administration place so much emphasis on acquiring New Orleans?

Q How did the physical geography within the Louisiana Purchase help to determine how the Lewis and Clark expedition would explore and map the territory?

Rockies to the Snake River, and followed that stream to the Columbia River. They reached the Pacific in November 1805 and spent the winter at what is now Astoria, Oregon. Retracing their steps the following spring and summer, they returned to St. Louis in September 1806. They brought with them many volumes of drawings and notes, along with assurances that the Louisiana Purchase had been worth many, many times its price.

As Jefferson stood for reelection in 1804, he could look back on an astonishingly successful first term. He had dismantled the government's power to coerce its citizens, and he had begun to wipe out the national debt. The Louisiana Purchase had doubled the size of the republic at remarkably little cost. Moreover, by eliminating France from North America, it had strengthened the argument for reducing the military and the debts and taxes that went with it. Jefferson was more certain than ever that the republic could preserve itself through peaceful expansion. The "wise and frugal" government he had promised in 1801 was becoming a reality.

The combination of international peace, territorial expansion, and inexpensive, unobtrusive government left the Federalists without an issue in the 1804 election. They nominated Charles Cotesworth Pinckney of South Carolina as their presidential candidate and then watched Jefferson capture the electoral votes of every state but Delaware and Connecticut. As he began his second term in 1805, Jefferson could assume that he had ended the Federalist threat to the republic.

7-4 The Republic and the Napoleonic Wars, 1803–1815

Q *What was the place of the United States within the changing international politics between 1803 and 1815?*

In spring 1803, a few weeks after closing the deal for Louisiana, Napoleon declared war on Britain. This 11-year war, like the wars of the 1790s, dominated the national politics of the United States. Most Americans wanted to remain neutral. Few Republicans supported Bonaparte as they had supported the French revolutionaries of 1789, and none but the most rabid Federalists wanted to intervene on the side of Britain. Neither France nor Britain, however, would permit American neutrality.

7-4a The Dilemmas of Neutrality

At the beginning, both Britain and France, whose rural economies were disrupted by war, encouraged the Americans to resume their role as neutral carriers and suppliers of food. For a time, Americans made huge profits. Between 1803 and 1807, U.S. exports—mostly foodstuffs and plantation staples—rose from $66.5 million to $102.2 million. Reexports—goods produced in the British, Spanish, and French islands of the Caribbean, picked up by American vessels, and then reloaded in American ports onto American ships bound for Europe—rose even faster, from $13.5 million to $58.4 million.

In 1805, the Royal Navy under Admiral Lord Horatio Nelson destroyed the French and Spanish fleets at the Battle of Trafalgar. Later that year, Napoleon's armies won a decisive victory over Austria and Russia at the Battle of Austerlitz and won effective control of Europe. The war reached a stalemate: Napoleon's army occupied Europe, and the British navy controlled the seas.

Britain decided to use its naval supremacy to blockade Europe and starve the French into submission. The Essex Decision of 1805 empowered the Royal Navy to seize American ships engaged in the reexport trade with France. Then Britain blockaded long stretches of the European coast. Napoleon responded with the Berlin Decree, outlawing all trade with the British Isles. The British answered with an Order in Council, which demanded that neutral ships trading with Europe stop first for inspection and licensing in a British port. Napoleon responded with the Milan Decree, which stated that any vessel that obeyed the British decrees or allowed itself to be searched by the Royal Navy was subject to seizure by France. Beginning in 1805 and ending with the Milan Decree in December 1807, the barrage of European decrees and counter-decrees meant that one or the other of the warring powers would outlaw virtually all American commerce with Europe.

7-4b Trouble on the High Seas

Given British naval supremacy, France had few opportunities to harass American shipping. The Royal Navy, on the other hand, maintained a loose blockade of the North American coast and stopped and searched American ships as they left the major seaports. Hundreds of ships were seized, along with their cargoes and crews. Many British sailors, including legions of deserters from the Royal Navy, continued to hide in the American merchant marine, where they avoided the danger, low pay, bad food, and draconian discipline of the British navy. British ships commandeered those men. They also took British subjects who had taken out U.S. citizenship (an act the British did not recognize) and native-born Americans, particularly those who still bore a cultural resemblance to the British in their dress, speech, and manners. An estimated 10,000 American citizens were impressed into the Royal Navy between 1793 and 1812, more than 6,000 of them after the resumption of the Anglo-French wars in 1803. American diplomats and newspapers protested the practice by using the menacing term "**impressment**," as opposed to the more common British terms "press" or "impress," to describe the systematic violation of U.S. sovereignty.

The kidnapping of American sailors enraged Americans and brought the country close to war in summer 1807. In June, the American naval frigate *Chesapeake* signed on four English deserters from the British navy, along with some Americans who had joined the British navy, and then deserted. Some of the deserters spotted their old officers from HMS *Leopard* in Norfolk, Virginia, and taunted them on the streets. The *Leopard* left port and resumed its patrol of the American coast. On June 21, the *Leopard* caught the *Chesapeake* off Hampton Roads and demanded the return of the British deserters. When the American captain refused, the British fired on the *Chesapeake*, killing three Americans and wounding 18. The British then boarded the *Chesapeake*, seized the four deserters, and later hanged one of them.

The *Chesapeake* affair set off huge anti-British demonstrations in the seaport towns and angry cries for war throughout the country. President Jefferson responded by barring British ships from American ports and American territorial waters and by ordering state governors to prepare to call up as many as 100,000 militiamen. The United States in 1807 stood at the brink of full-scale war with the most powerful nation in the world.

7-4c Embargo

Jefferson wanted to avoid war, which would inevitably bring high taxes, government debt, a bloated military and civil service, and the repression of dissent—precisely the evils that Jefferson had vowed to eliminate. Worse, war carried the danger of defeat and thus the possible failure of the United States.

Jefferson had one more card to play: He could suspend trade with Europe altogether and thus keep American ships out of harm's way. Jefferson assumed that U.S. farm products and the U.S. market for imported goods were crucial to the European economies. He could use trade as a means of "peaceable coercion" to enforce respect for American neutral rights and keep the country out of war. Convinced that America's yeoman republic could survive without European luxuries more easily than Europe could survive without American food, Jefferson decided to give "peaceable coercion" a serious test. Late in 1807, he asked Congress to suspend all U.S. trade with foreign countries.

Congress passed the **Embargo Act** on December 22. Within a few months, it was clear that it would not work. The British found other markets and other sources of food. The embargo most hurt American commerce. Its 1807 exports of $108 million dropped to $22 million in 1808. The economy slowed in every section of the country, but it ground to a halt in the cities of the Northeast. While much of the oceangoing merchant fleet rotted at anchor, unemployed sailors, dockworkers, and other maritime workers and their families sank to levels of economic despair seldom seen in British North America. Federalists accused Jefferson of plotting an end to commerce and a reversion to rural barbarism, and they often took the lead in trying to subvert the embargo through smuggling and other means.

Interpreting the Visual Past

Capturing the World: The Illustrations of the Journals of Lewis and Clark

President Thomas Jefferson had several goals for the Lewis and Clark expedition, ranging from geographical discovery to the establishment of trade with Native Americans and the consolidation of U.S. sovereignty over the newly acquired lands. He also instructed the team to observe and record the region's indigenous habitants, flora, fauna, minerals, soil, topography, and climate. As the expedition's naturalist, Lewis drew several detailed illustrations of animals, including this one of the eulachon (*Thaleichthys pacificus*), a small migratory ocean fish that lives along the Pacific coast. The drawings are interesting in their own right as artifacts of one of the most influential expeditions in American history, but a historian might want to probe their broader political and cultural implications. A straightforward drawing of a fish can prompt questions that illuminate an entire society and epoch.

Q What do drawings like this one suggest about early 19th-century American views of nature and the environment? How was the Lewis and Clark expedition as a scientific endeavor a product of its time?

Q How did the geopolitical, commercial, and scientific goals of the expedition support one another? In what ways can describing, naming, and classifying nature be a political act?

7.8 Meriwether Lewis, Drawing of an Eulachon from the Journals of the Lewis and Clark Expedition, 1806.

The Federalists gained ground in the elections of 1808. James Madison, Jefferson's old ally and chosen successor, was elected president with 122 electoral votes to 47 for his Federalist opponent, Charles Cotesworth Pinckney. Although Republicans retained control of both houses of Congress, Federalists made significant gains in Congress and won control of several state legislatures. Federalist opposition to the embargo, and to the supposed southern, agrarian stranglehold on national power, was gaining ground.

7-4d The Road to War

When President Madison took office in spring 1809, it was clear that the embargo had failed. It created misery in the seaport cities, choked off the imports that provided 90 percent of federal revenue, and revived Federalist opposition to Republican dominance. Early in 1809, Congress passed the Non-Intercourse Act, which retained the ban on trade with Britain and France but reopened trade with other nations. It also gave President Madison the power to reopen trade with either Britain or France once one of the countries agreed to respect American rights. Neither complied, and the Non-Intercourse Act proved nearly as ineffective as the embargo.

In 1810, Congress passed Macon's Bill No. 2, a complex piece of legislation that rescinded the ban on trade with France and Britain but also authorized the president to reimpose the Non-Intercourse Act on either belligerent if the other agreed to end its restrictions on U.S. trade. Napoleon decided to test the Americans. In September 1810, the French promised, with vague conditions, that France would repeal the Berlin and Milan Decrees. Although the proposal was a clear attempt to lead the United States into conflict with Great Britain, Madison saw no choice but to go along with it. He accepted the French promise and proclaimed in November 1810 that the British had three months to follow suit.

In the end, Madison's proclamation led to war. The French repealed only those sections of the Berlin and Milan Decrees that applied to the neutral rights of the United States. The British refused to revoke their Orders in Council and told the Americans to withdraw their restrictions on British trade until the French had repealed theirs. The United States would either have to obey British orders (thus making American exports and the American merchant marine a part of the British war effort—a neocolonial situation that was utterly repugnant to most Americans) or go to war. When Congress reconvened in November 1811, it voted military measures in preparation for war with Great Britain.

7-4e The War Hawk Congress, 1811–1812

Republicans controlled both houses of Congress in 1811–1812; they made up 75 percent of the House and 82 percent of the Senate, but they were a divided majority. The Federalist minority was united in opposition to Madison. The Federalists were often joined by northeastern Republicans who followed the pro-British, Federalist line on international trade, and by Republicans who wanted a more powerful military than other Republicans would allow. Also opposed to Madison were the self-styled Old Republicans of the South, led by John Randolph. It was a deeply divided Congress that met the war crisis.

In this confused situation, a group of talented young congressmen took control. Nearly all of them were Republicans from the South or the West: Richard M. Johnson and Henry Clay of Kentucky, John C. Calhoun and William Lowndes of South Carolina, George M. Troup of Georgia, Peter B. Porter from the Niagara district of New York, and others. Called the **War Hawks**, these ardent nationalists wanted to declare war on England to protect U.S. rights. Through their organizational, oratorical, and intellectual power, they won control of Congress. Henry Clay, only 34 years old and serving his first term in Congress, was elected Speaker of the House. More vigorous than his predecessors, Clay controlled debate, packed key committees, worked tirelessly behind the scenes, and imposed order on his fellow congressmen.

In the winter and spring of 1811–1812, the War Hawks led Congress into a declaration of war. In November they voted military preparations, and in April they enacted a 90-day embargo—not to coerce the British but to return American ships safely to port before war began. On June 1, Madison sent a war message to Congress. This was to be the first war declared under the Constitution, and the president stayed out of congressional territory by not asking explicitly for a declaration of war. He did, however, present a list of British crimes that could be interpreted in no other way: (1) the enforcement of the Orders in Council, even within the territorial waters of the United States; (2) the impressment of American seamen; (3) the use of spies and provocateurs within the United States; and (4) the wielding of "a malicious influence over the Indians of the Northwest Territory."

Congress declared war on June 18. The vote was far from unanimous: 79 to 49 in the House of Representatives, 19 to 13 in the Senate. All 30 Federalists voted against the declaration, as did one in five Republicans, nearly all of them from the Northeast. Thus, the war was declared by the Democratic

7.9 Henry Clay This portrait of Henry Clay was engraved at about the time the brilliant first-term congressman from Kentucky, as Speaker of the House, helped his fellow War Hawks steer the United States into the War of 1812.

Republican Party, more particularly by the Republicans of the South and the West. The Northeast, whose commercial rights were supposedly the issue at stake, opposed the declaration.

7-4f American Strategy in 1812

The War Hawks declared a war to defend the sovereignty, the western territory, and the maritime rights of the United States. The war they planned and fought, however, bore the stamp of southern and western Republicanism. Federalists and many northeastern Republicans expected a naval war. After all, the British had committed their atrocities on the ocean, and some, remembering U.S. naval successes against France in the Quasi War of 1798–1800, predicted similar successes against Great Britain. Yet, when Madison asked Congress to prepare for war, the War Hawks led a majority that strengthened the U.S. Army and left the navy weak. Reasoning that no U.S. naval force could challenge British control of the seas, they prepared instead for a land invasion of British Canada.

The decision to invade Canada led the Federalists, along with many of Randolph's Old Republicans, to accuse Madison and the congressional majority of planning a war of territorial aggression. Some members of Congress did want to annex Canada to the United States, but most saw the decision to invade Canada as a matter of strategy. Lightly garrisoned and with a population of only half a million (many of them French, and most of the others American émigrés of doubtful loyalties), Canada seemed the easiest and most logical place in which to damage the British. It was also from bases in Canada that the British armed the Indians of the Northwest, and western Republicans were determined to end that threat decisively. Indeed, many Republicans saw Canada as a counterrevolutionary monarchist regime that was posed to roll back American republicanism and pull the United States back into Britain's imperial fold. Finally, Canada was a valuable colony of Britain. The American embargoes, coupled with Napoleon's control of Europe, had impaired Britain's ability to supply its plantation colonies in the West Indies, and Canadian farmers had begun to fill the gap. Thus, Canada was both valuable and vulnerable, and American policymakers reasoned that they could take it and hold it hostage while demanding that the British back down on other issues. Although U.S. military strategy focused on Canada, maritime rights and national honor, along with the British-fed Indian threat west of the Appalachians, were the central issues in 1812.

7-4g The Rise of Tecumseh

Native peoples east of the Mississippi River recognized alliances with Britain as a final chance to hold back American settlers. Northwestern Indians had lost much of their land at the Battle of Fallen Timbers and the Treaty of Greenville. Relegated to smaller territory but still dependent on the European fur trade, they fell into competition with settlers and other Indians for the diminishing supply of game. The Creeks, Choctaws, and other nations of the Southeast faced the same problem: Even when they chased settlers out of their territory, the settlers managed to kill or scare off the deer and other wildlife, thus ruining the old hunting grounds. When the Shawnee sent hunting parties farther west, they met irate western Indians. The Choctaws also sent hunters across the Mississippi, where they found both new sources of furs and angry warriors of the Osage and other peoples of Louisiana and Arkansas. The Indians of the interior now realized that the days of the fur trade, on which they depended for survival, were numbered.

Faced with shrinking territories, the disappearance of wildlife, and diminished opportunities to be traditional hunters and warriors, many Indian societies sank into despair. Epidemics of European diseases (smallpox, influenza, measles) attacked peoples who were increasingly sedentary and vulnerable. Old internal frictions grew nastier. In the Southeast, full-blooded Indians came into conflict with mixed-blood Indians, who often no longer spoke the native language and who wanted their people to adopt white ways. Murder and clan revenge plagued native communities, and depression and suicide became more common. The use of alcohol, which had been a scourge on Indian societies for two centuries, increased. Indian males spent more time in their villages and less on the hunt, and by most accounts they drank more and grew more violent when they drank.

Out of this cultural wreckage emerged visionary leaders who spoke of a regenerated native society and the expulsion of all whites from the old tribal lands. The prophet who came closest to military success was Tenskwatawa, a Shawnee who had failed as a warrior and medicine man. He went into a deep trance in 1805 and awoke with a prophetic vision not unlike Neolin's in the early 1760s (see Chapter 5). First, all Indians must stop drinking and fighting among themselves. They must also return to their traditional food, clothing, tools, and hairstyles, and must extinguish all of their fires and start new ones without using European tools. All who opposed the new order (including local chiefs, medicine men, shamans, and witches) must be put down by force. When all of that had been done, God (a monotheistic, punishing God borrowed from the Christians) would restore the world that Indians had known before the whites came over the mountains.

Tenskwatawa's message soon found its way to the Delawares (who attacked the Christians among their people as witches) and other native peoples of the Northeast. Several native leaders who had embraced the United States' civilization program were executed. When converts flooded into the prophet's home village, he moved to Prophetstown (Tippecanoe) in what is now Indiana. There, with the help of his brother Tecumseh, he created an army estimated by the whites at anywhere between 650 and 3,000. Tecumseh, who took control of the movement, announced to the whites that he was the sole chief of all the Indians north of the Ohio River. Land cessions by anyone else would be invalid. Tenskwatawa's prophecy and Tecumseh's leadership had united the Indians of the Northwest in an unprecedented stand against white encroachment.

Tecumseh's confederacy posed a threat to the United States. A second war with England was looming, and Tecumseh was receiving supplies and encouragement from the British in Canada. He was also planning to visit the southern Indians in an attempt to bring them into his confederacy. The prospect of unified resistance by the western tribes in league with the British jeopardized every settler west of the Appalachians. In 1811, William Henry Harrison led an army toward Prophetstown. With Tecumseh away in the South, Tenskwatawa ordered a risky attack on Harrison's army and was beaten at the Battle of Tippecanoe. But Tecumseh's confederacy remained a formidable opponent of the United States.

7-4h The War with Canada, 1812–1813

The United States attacked Canada in 1812, with disastrous results (see Map 7.4). The plan was to invade Upper Canada (Ontario) from the Northwest, thus cutting off the Shawnee, Potawatomi, and other pro-British Indian tribes from their British support. When General William Hull, governor of Michigan Territory, took a poorly supplied, badly led army of militiamen and volunteers into Canada from a base in Detroit, he found that the British had outguessed him. The area was crawling with British troops and their Indian allies. With detachments of his army overrun and his supply lines cut, he retreated to the garrison at Detroit. Under siege, he heard that Indian forces had captured the garrison at Fort Dearborn (Chicago) and sacked Fort Mackinac in northern Michigan Territory. British general Isaac Brock, who knew that Hull was afraid of Indians, sent a note into the fort telling him, "the numerous body of Indians who have attached themselves to my troops, will be beyond my controul the moment the contest commences." Without consulting his officers, Hull surrendered his army of 2,000 to the smaller British force. Hull was later court-martialed for cowardice, but the damage was done: The British and Indians transformed the American invasion of Upper Canada into a British occupation of much of the Northwest—the largest surrender of U.S. territory in history.

The invasion of Canada from the east went no better. In October a U.S. force of 6,000 faced 2,000 British and Indians across the Niagara River separating Ontario from western New York. The U.S. regular army crossed the river, surprised the British, and established a toehold at Queenston Heights. While the British prepared a counterattack, New York militiamen refused to cross the river to reinforce the regulars. Ohio militiamen had behaved the same way when Hull invaded Canada, and similar problems had arisen with the New York militia near Lake Champlain. Throughout the war, citizen-soldiers proved that Jefferson's confidence in the militia could not be extended to the invasion of other countries. The British regrouped and slaughtered the outnumbered, exhausted U.S. regulars at Queenston Heights.

As winter set in, it was clear that Canada would not fall as easily as the Americans had assumed. The invasion, which U.S. commanders had thought would knife through an apathetic Canadian population, had the opposite effect: The attacks by the United States turned the ragtag assortment of American loyalist émigrés discharged British soldiers, and American-born settlers into a self-consciously British Canadian people.

7-4i Tecumseh's Last Stand

Tecumseh's confederacy, bruised but not broken in the Battle of Tippecanoe, allied itself with the British in 1812. On a trip to the southern tribes, Tecumseh found the traditionalist wing of the Creeks—led by medicine men who called themselves Red Sticks—willing to join him. The augmented confederacy provided stiff resistance to the United States throughout the war. The Red Sticks chased settlers from much of Tennessee. They then attacked a group of settlers who had taken refuge in a stockade surrounding the house of an Alabama trader named George Mims. In what whites called the Massacre at Fort Mims, the Red Sticks (reputedly in collusion with the black slaves within the fort) killed at least 247 men, women, and children. In the Northwest, Tecumseh's warriors, fighting alongside the British, spread terror throughout the white settlements.

A wiser U.S. Army returned to Canada in 1813. It raided and burned the Canadian capital at York (Toronto) in April, and then fought inconclusively throughout the summer. An autumn offensive toward Montreal failed, but the Americans had better luck on Lake Erie. The barrier of Niagara Falls kept Britain's saltwater navy out of the upper Great Lakes, and on Lake Erie, the British and Americans engaged in a frenzied shipbuilding contest throughout the first year of the war. The Americans won. In September 1813, Commodore Oliver Hazard Perry destroyed the British fleet off the American anchorage at Put-in-Bay, after which he reported triumphantly to General William Henry Harrison: "We have met the enemy and they are ours."

Control of Lake Erie enabled the United States to cut off supplies to the British in the Northwest, and Harrison's army retook the area and continued on into Canada. On October 5, Harrison caught up with a force of British and Indians at the Thames River and beat them badly. In the course of that battle, Richard M. Johnson, a War Hawk congressman acting as commander of the Kentucky militia, was credited with killing Tecumseh. Proud militiamen returned to Kentucky with pieces of hair and clothing and even swatches of skin torn from Tecumseh's corpse. Their officers reaped huge political rewards: The Battle of the Thames would produce a president of the United States (Harrison), a vice president (Johnson), three governors of Kentucky, three lieutenant governors, four U.S. senators, and about 20 congressmen—telling evidence of how seriously the settlers of the interior had taken Tecumseh.

The following spring, General Andrew Jackson's Tennessee militia, aided by Choctaw, Creek, and Cherokee allies, attacked and slaughtered the Red Sticks, who had fortified themselves at Horseshoe Bend in Alabama. Jackson enforced a treaty on the Creeks, who ceded 22 million acres of land in the Mississippi Territory. With the Battle of the Thames and the Battle of Horseshoe Bend, the military power of the Indian peoples east of the Mississippi River was broken.

7-4j The British Offensive, 1814

The British defeated Napoleon in April 1814, thus ending the war in Europe. They then turned their attention to the American war and went on the offensive. They had already blockaded

▲ **MAP 7.4 War of 1812** Early in the war, Americans chose to fight the British in Canada, with costly and inconclusive results. Later, the British determined to blockade the whole coast of the United States and, late in the war, to raid important coastal towns. The results were equally inconclusive: Both sides could inflict serious damage, but neither could conquer the other. The one clear military outcome—one that the Americans were determined to accomplish—was the destruction of Indian resistance east of the Mississippi.

Q What options did the Americans have for attacking the British in the War of 1812?

Q Despite the United States having a far greater population in North America, what important tactical advantage did the British establish in the war?

much of the American coast from Georgia to Maine. During summer 1814, they raided Chesapeake Bay and marched on Washington, D.C. They chased the army and politicians out of town and burned down the Capitol building and the president's mansion. In September, the British attacked Baltimore, but could not blast their way past the determined garrison that commanded the harbor from Fort McHenry. This was the battle that inspired Francis Scott Key to write the lyrics of "The Star-Spangled Banner," which was set to the tune of an old English drinking song ("To Anacreon in Heaven," music by John

Stafford Smith). It became the national anthem in the 1930s. When a British offensive on Lake Champlain stalled during the autumn, the war reached a stalemate: Britain had turned back the invasion of Canada and had blockaded the American coast, but neither side could take and hold the other's territory.

The British now shifted their attention to the Gulf Coast, particularly to New Orleans, a city of vital importance to U.S. trans-Appalachian trade and communications. Peace negotiations had begun in August, and the British wanted to capture and hold New Orleans as a bargaining chip. A large British force landed eight miles south of New Orleans. There they met an American army made up of U.S. regulars, Kentucky and Tennessee militiamen, clerks, workingmen, free blacks from the city, and about a thousand French pirates—all under the command of Andrew Jackson of Tennessee. Throughout late December and early January, unaware that a peace treaty had been signed on December 24, the armies exchanged artillery barrages and the British probed and attacked American lines. On January 8, they launched a frontal assault. A formation of 6,000 British soldiers marched across open ground toward 4,000 Americans concealed behind breastworks. With the first American volley, it was clear that the British had made a mistake. Veterans of the bloodiest battles of the Napoleonic wars swore that they had never seen such withering fire; soldiers in the front ranks who were not cut down threw themselves to the ground and surrendered when the shooting stopped. The charge lasted half an hour. At the end, 2,000 British soldiers lay dead or wounded. American casualties numbered only 70. Fought nearly two weeks after the peace treaty, the Battle of New Orleans had no effect on the outcome of the war or on the peace terms, but it salved the injured pride of

7.10 **Death of Tecumseh** The Battle of the Thames relieved the Northwest of the British and Indian threat. Through prints like this, Richard M. Johnson gained the reputation for killing Tecumseh.

7-4 The Republic and the Napoleonic Wars, 1803–1815

Americans, fostered a potent and unifying patriotism, and made a national hero and a political power of Andrew Jackson.

7-4k The Hartford Convention

While most of the nation celebrated Jackson's victory, events in Federalist New England went differently. New Englanders had disliked Republican trade policies, and their congressmen had voted overwhelmingly against going to war. The New England states seldom met their quotas of militiamen for the war effort, and some Federalist leaders had openly urged resistance to the war. The British had encouraged that resistance by not extending their naval blockade to the New England coast, and throughout the first two years of the war, New England merchants and farmers had traded freely with the enemy. In 1814, after the Royal Navy had extended its blockade northward and had begun to raid the towns of coastal Maine, some Federalists talked openly about seceding and making a separate peace with Britain.

In an attempt to undercut the secessionists, moderate Federalists called a convention at Hartford to air the region's grievances. The Hartford Convention, which met in late December 1814, proposed amendments to the Constitution that indicated New England's position as a self-conscious minority within the Union. First, the convention delegates wanted the "three-fifths" clause, which led to overrepresentation of the South in Congress, and the Electoral College (see Chapter 6) stricken from the Constitution. They also wanted to deny naturalized citizens—who were strongly Republican—the right to hold office. They wanted to make it more difficult for new states, all of which sided with the Republicans and their southern leadership, to enter the Union. Finally, they wanted to require a two-thirds majority of both houses for a declaration of war—a requirement that would have prevented the War of 1812.

Leaders of the Hartford Convention, satisfied that they had headed off the secessionists, took their proposals to Washington in mid-January. They arrived to find the capital celebrating news of the peace treaty and Jackson's victory at New Orleans. When they aired their sectional complaints, they were branded as traitors. Although Federalists continued for a few years to wield power in southern New England, the Hartford debacle ruined any chance of a nationwide Federalist resurgence after the war. Andrew Jackson had stolen control of American history from New England. He would do so again in the years ahead.

7-4l The Treaty of Ghent

Britain's defeat of Napoleon had spurred British and American efforts to end a war that neither wanted. In August 1814, they opened peace talks in the Belgian city of Ghent. Perhaps waiting for the results of their 1814 offensive, the British opened with proposals that the Americans were certain to reject. They demanded the right to navigate the Mississippi. Moreover, they wanted territorial concessions and the creation of the permanent, independent Indian buffer state in the Northwest that they had promised their Indian allies. The Americans ignored these proposals and talked instead about impressment and maritime rights. As the autumn wore on and the war reached stalemate, both sides began to compromise. The British knew that the Americans would grant concessions in the interior only if they were thoroughly defeated, an outcome that British commanders thought impossible. For their part, the Americans realized that British maritime depredations were by-products of the struggle with Napoleonic France. Faced with peace in Europe and a senseless military stalemate in North America, negotiators on both sides began to withdraw their demands. The Treaty of Ghent, signed on Christmas Eve

7.11 The Taking of the City of Washington (1814) The United States suffered one of its greatest military embarrassments in 1814, when the British raided Washington, D.C., brushed off the opposition, and burned most government buildings, including the president's house and the Capitol building.

Q *Are there any clues that this print was produced in London rather than in America?*

History Through Film

Master and Commander: The Far Side of the World (2003)

Directed by Peter Weir.
Starring Russell Crowe (Capt. Jack Aubrey), Paul Bettany (Dr. Stephen Maturin), James D'Arcy (1st Lt. Tom Pullings), Max Pirkis (Blakeney, midshipman), Billy Boyd (Barrett Bonden, coxswain).

Peter Weir directed this epic historical drama based on the acclaimed Aubrey-Maturin sea novel series by Patrick O'Brian. The year is 1805. As Britain and France duel for global supremacy during the Napoleonic Wars, British navy captain "Lucky" Jack Aubrey (Russell Crowe) receives orders off the northern coast of Brazil to "intercept French Privateer Acheron en route to Pacific intent on carrying the war into those waters . . . Sink, Burn or take her a Prize." The film's action follows Aubrey's frigate, HMS *Surprise*, south in pursuit of Acheron around Cape Horn and into the Pacific. Aubrey's close friend, the naval surgeon Stephen Maturin (Paul Bettany), joins him throughout this adventure to "the far side of the world."

The film borrows scenes and dialogue from more than a dozen of the twenty novels in O'Brian's series. The movie title comes from the first book in the series, *Master and Commander*, and refers to an officer rank in the British navy that Aubrey received upon getting his first ship command in 1800 (by 1805, he has been promoted to post-captain). The subtitle comes from the tenth novel, *The Far Side of the World*, from which the film also gets its plot, with a crucial difference: The enemy in the novel is not a French privateer but an American navy frigate, USS *Norfolk*, during the War of 1812. The film's producers changed the villain, worrying that American audiences would not cheer the sinking of the Stars and Stripes, especially so close to the terrorist attacks of September 11 (the film was released in 2003).

The decision kept the War of 1812 from providing the backdrop for at least one truly great film. Yet, the war still has an indirect influence on the movie. In *The Far Side of the World*, O'Brian based the fictional *Norfolk* on the actual American frigate USS *Essex*. Commanded by Captain David Porter, *Essex* wreaked havoc on Britain's Pacific whaling fleet in 1813, before being decimated by the British navy off the coast of Valparaiso, Chile, in 1814. In the film, *Acheron's* French captain (Thierry Segall) channels Porter's mischievous spirit. Moreover, as a 44-gun "super frigate" with a heavy, reinforced hull, *Acheron* overmatches the 28-gun *Surprise*, much like USS *Constitution* (nicknamed "Old Ironsides") and other oversized American frigates dominated their British counterparts in the War of 1812. If *Acheron* seems like *Constitution* in French sheathing, it is no accident. The film's special-effects team created computer models of the French privateer based on digital images of "Old Ironsides."

Regardless of Britain's enemy, the *Master and Commander* film, like the book series, provides insight into how the Royal Navy became the supreme fighting force of its time, on sea or land. The wooden world of a sailing vessel reproduced the social hierarchy and inequities of British society. It required teams of skilled seafarers, many of them pressed into service, to keep a British naval vessel afloat. At the same time, the navy produced real-life Aubreys, officers who used shipboard discipline, skilled leadership, and superior seamanship to keep their large, diverse crews working in unison. Through the magic of cinema, viewers appreciate how these men braved storms, tedium, and the horrific violence of naval warfare.

Master and Commander delights with other historical details and references. Without physically appearing, Britain's greatest naval hero, Admiral Nelson, has a presence in the film, both through Aubrey's firsthand accounts and as an inspiration to the young midshipman Blakeney (Max Pirkis). Like Nelson, Blakeney loses his arm in battle. By incorporating the Galapagos Islands from O'Brian's storyline, Weir also makes clever allusions to Charles Darwin. Maturin, a naturalist as well as a physician, collects many of the same specimens that Darwin later used to conceive of the idea of evolution through natural selection. Maturin is denied the achievement because he has to abandon his discoveries in the name of duty.

Weir and Crowe had aspirations of turning *Master and Commander* into a series, but its box office returns did not justify a sequel. Instead, another maritime saga released in 2003, *Pirates of the Caribbean*, based on the Disneyland theme park attraction, would become a franchise. This is unfortunate. Not simply the lesser of two evils (or "lesser of two weevils," as Jack Aubrey might say), *Master and Commander* is the finest film on the Age of Sail ever made. ∎

7.12 Russell Crowe stars as the fictional British navy captain Jack Aubrey in *Master and Commander: The Far Side of the World*.

7-4 The Republic and the Napoleonic Wars, 1803–1815

7.13 ***A View of the Bombardment of Fort McHenry* by J. Bower, 1816** The British attack on Baltimore depended upon getting past Fort McHenry, which guarded the approach to the harbor. The Americans strengthened the garrison and blocked the narrow inlet with sunken ships. British ships fired as many as 1,800 exploding shells at the fort, to no avail. Baltimore's Francis Scott Key was aboard a British vessel (he was trying to negotiate the release of a prisoner). He witnessed the bombardment and wrote a poem entitled "The Defense of Fort McHenry," which eventually became the national anthem.

1814, simply ended the war. The border between Canada and the United States remained where it had been in 1812; Indians south of that border—defeated and without allies—were left to the mercy of the United States; and British maritime violations were not mentioned. The makers of the treaty stopped a war that neither side could win, trusting that a period of peace would resolve the problems created by two decades of world war.

Conclusion

In 1816, Thomas Jefferson was in retirement at Monticello, satisfied that he had defended liberty against the Federalists' love of power. The High Federalists' attempt to consolidate power, militarize government, and jail their opposition had failed. Their direct taxes were repealed. Their debt and their national bank remained in place, but only under the watchful eyes of true republicans. And their attempt to ally the United States with the antirepublican designs of Britain had ended in what many called the Second War of American Independence. American independence was truly won, and Jefferson's vision of a union of independent republican states seemed to have been realized.

Yet, for all his successes, Jefferson saw that he must sacrifice some of his longest-held dreams. Jefferson's republican ideal was grounded in farmer-citizens whose vision was local and who wanted nothing more from government than protection of their property and rights. Jefferson's imagined yeomen traded farm surpluses for European manufactured goods—a system that encouraged rural prosperity, prevented the growth of cities and factories (the much-feared nurseries of corruption and dependence), and thus sustained the landed independence on which republican citizenship rested. Westward expansion, Jefferson had believed, would ensure the yeoman republic for generations to come. By 1816, that dream was ended. The British and French had "cover[ed] the earth and sea with robberies and piracies," disrupting America's vital export economy whenever it suited their whims. Arguing as Hamilton had argued in 1790, Jefferson insisted, "we must now place the manufacturer by the side of the agriculturalist."

CHAPTER REVIEW

Review

1. What was the Federalist plan for organizing the national government and its finances?
2. What were the principal foreign and internal threats to the newly independent United States in the late 18th century?
3. What were the principal reforms of the national government during Thomas Jefferson's administration?
4. What was the place of the United States within the changing international politics between 1803 and 1815?

Critical Thinking

1. In the 1790s, Federalists and Democratic Republicans argued about the nature of the new national government. On what specific issues was this argument conducted? Was there a larger argument underlying these specifics?
2. Thomas Jefferson had a vision of the American republic and of the role of the national government within it. In what ways did his presidency succeed in realizing that vision? In what ways did it fail?

Identifications

Review your understanding of the following key terms, people, and events for this chapter (terms in bold in text are included in the Glossary).

tariff, p. 202
Bill of Rights, p. 202
circuit court, p. 202
excise tax, p. 204
Whiskey Rebellion, p. 208
impeachment, p. 211
XYZ Affair, p. 211
Alien and Sedition Acts, p. 212
Virginia and Kentucky Resolves, p. 212
High Federalists, p. 212
Aaron Burr, p. 213
Louisiana Purchase, p. 214
midnight judges, p. 215
Marbury v. Madison, p. 216
judicial review, p. 216
impressment, p. 219
Embargo Act, p. 219
War Hawks, p. 221

Suggested Readings

Stanley Elkins and Eric McKitrick, *The Age of Federalism: The Early American Republic, 1788–1800* (1993); and **Gordon S. Wood**, *Empire of Liberty: A History of the American Republic, 1789–1815* (2009) are definitive surveys of these years. For the politics of the founding generation, see **Stuart Leibiger**, *Founding Friendship: George Washington, James Madison, and the Creation of the American Republic* (1999); **Joanne B. Freeman**, *Affairs of Honor: National Politics in the New Republic* (2001); and **James Roger Sharp**, *American Politics in the Early Republic: The New Nation in Crisis* (1993). **Lance Banning**, *The Jeffersonian Persuasion: Evolution of a Party Ideology* (1980); **Drew R. McCoy**, *The Elusive Republic: Political Economy in Jeffersonian America* (1980); and **Annette Gordon-Reed and Peter S. Onuf**, *"Most Blessed of Patriarchs": Thomas Jefferson and the Empire of the Imagination* (2016) are insightful studies of Jeffersonianism.

Alan Taylor's *The Civil War of 1812: American Citizens, British Subjects, Irish Rebels, and Indian Allies* (2010) offers a penetrating look into the complex divisions, anxieties, and ambitions behind the War of 1812. For other perspectives on the crises leading to the war, see **R. David Edmunds**, *Tecumseh and the Quest for Indian Leadership* (2006); **Francis D. Cogliano**, *Emperor of Liberty: Thomas Jefferson's Foreign Policy* (2014); and **Paul A. Gilje**, *Free Trade and Sailors' Rights in the War of 1812* (2013). For an effective survey of the war, see **Donald R. Hickey**, *The War of 1812: A Forgotten Conflict* (1989). **Nicole Eustace's** *1812: War and the Passions of Patriotism* (2012) explores the American patriotic legacy of the conflict, while **Troy Bickham**, *The Weight of Vengeance: The United States, the British Empire, and the War of 1812* (2012) details its implications for Britain and Canada.

 MINDTAP is a fully online personalized learning experience built upon Cengage Learning content. MindTap® combines student learning tools—readings, multimedia, activities, and assessments—into a singular Learning Path that guides students through the course and helps students develop the critical thinking, analysis, and communication skills that are essential to academic and professional success.

8 Northern Transformations, 1790–1850

8-1 Postcolonial Society, 1790–1815
Learning Objective: Determine the nature of the northern agricultural economy and of agricultural society in the years 1790 to 1815.

Farms
Neighbors
Standards of Living
Inheritance
The Seaport Cities

8-2 The Northwest: From Backcountry to Frontier
Learning Objective: Detail how eastern opinion of the Northwest and of its settlers changed between 1790 and 1820.

The Backcountry, 1790–1815
Settlement

8-3 Transportation Revolution, 1815–1850
Learning Objective: List improvements in transportation that channeled commerce within and between regions.

Transportation in 1815
Internal Improvements
Time, Money, and New Markets

8-4 Northeastern Farms, 1815–1850
Learning Objective: Analyze how northern farm families experienced the transition into commercial agriculture between 1815 and 1850.

The New England Livestock Economy
New Farm Households
The Landscape of Privacy

8-5 The Northwest in Transition
Learning Objective: Describe how northern and southern settlers flooding into the Northwest after 1815 viewed the new market economy differently.

Southern Settlers
Northern Farmers

8-6 The Beginnings of the Industrial Revolution
Learning Objective: Explain why America's first factories started in the northern countryside.

Factory Towns: The Rhode Island System
Factory Towns: The Waltham-Lowell System
Cities
Metropolitan Industrialization

8.1 **A Bird's-Eye View of New York City, 1850** After 1825, prints and lithographs such as this were printed in New York and sent through the new channels of trade to help decorate parlor walls throughout the North and West. This one depicts New York City. The ships surrounding Manhattan Island are testimony to New York's dominance of both coastal and international trade. But maritime occupations were far outnumbered by men and women who manufactured goods and did the paperwork for an expanding market that was transforming the North.

IN 1790, AMERICAN SOCIETY approximated Jefferson's ideal: The United States was a nation of farmers who provided for themselves and sent surpluses overseas to be traded for manufactured goods. To put it in a less bucolic way, Americans remained on the colonial periphery of North Atlantic capitalism. They sent timber, cured fish, wheat, tobacco, rice, and money to Europe (primarily Britain), and Europe (again, Britain was the big player) sent manufactured goods—along with bills for shipping, insurance, banking, and tariff duties—back to America. In the 25 years following adoption of the Constitution, this old relationship fed significant economic growth in the United States, as European wars increased the demand for American produce and American shipping. Americans sent growing mountains of food and raw materials overseas, and they decorated their homes with comforts and small luxuries produced in British factories.

Beginning in the 1790s and accelerating dramatically with the peace of 1815, northern farmers changed that relationship: By 1830, the primary engine of northern economic development was no longer the North Atlantic trade; it was the self-sustained internal development of the northern United States. Northeastern businessmen noted that rural markets were expanding, that imports were unreliable, and that a crowded countryside produced people eager to work for wages.

They began to invest in factories. New factory towns, together with the old seaports and new inland towns that served a commercializing agriculture, provided the country's first significant domestic market for food. Governments of the northern states built roads and canals that linked farmers to distant markets, and farmers turned to cash-crop agriculture and bought necessary goods (and paid mortgages and crop loans) with the money they made. By 1830, a large and growing portion of New England, the mid-Atlantic, and the Northwest had transcended colonial economics to become an interdependent, self-sustaining market society.

The pioneering sociologist Max Weber made a distinction between capitalism and the *spirit* of capitalism. Economic exchange and the desire for profit, Weber noted, have existed in all societies. Only a few, however, have organized capitalism into an everyday culture. Historians have coined the term "**Market Revolution**" to describe the transformation of the North from a society with markets to a market society—a society in which the market was implicated in the ways in which northerners saw the world and dealt with it. This chapter describes that revolution in the North up to 1850. The succeeding chapter describes the very different patterns of change in the South in the same years. ■

8-1 Postcolonial Society, 1790–1815

Q *What was the nature of the northern agricultural economy and of agricultural society in the years 1790 to 1815?*

In 1782, J. Hector St. John de Crèvecoeur, a French soldier who had settled in rural New York, explained America's agrarian republic through the words of a fictionalized farmer. First of all, he said, the American farmer owns his own land and bases his claim to dignity and citizenship on that fact. Second, according to the farmer, landownership endows the American farmer with the powers and responsibilities of fatherhood. "Often when I plant my low ground," he said, "I place my little boy on a chair which screws to the beam of the plough—its motion and that of the horses please him; he is perfectly happy and begins to chat. As I lean over the handle, various are the thoughts which crowd into my mind. I am now doing for him, I say, what my father did for me; may God enable him to live that he may perform the same operations for the same purposes when I am worn out and old!"

8-1a *Farms*

Crèvecoeur's farmer, musing on liberty and property, working the ancestral fields with his male heir strapped to the plough, was concerned with proprietorship and fatherhood, not with making money. He shared those concerns with most northern farmers. Their first concern was to provide food and common comforts for their households. Their second was to achieve long-term security and the ability to pass their farms on to their sons. The goal was to create what rural folks called a "**competence**": the ability to live up to neighborhood standards of material decency while protecting the long-term independence of the household. Farmers thought of themselves first as fathers, neighbors, and stewards of family resources, and they avoided financial risk. Weather, bad crop years, pests, and unexpected injuries or deaths provided enough of that without adding the uncertainties of cash-crop agriculture and international commodity prices.

In this situation, most farmers played it safe. They raised a variety of animals and plants and did not concentrate on a single cash crop. Most farms in New England and the middle states were divided into corn and grain fields, pasturage for

CHRONOLOGY

1790	Samuel Slater builds his first Arkwright spinning mill at Pawtucket, Rhode Island
1791	Vermont enters the union as the 14th state
1793	Beginning of Anglo-French War • Ohio enters the union as the 17th state
1807	Robert Fulton launches first steamboat
1812	Second war with Britain begins
1813	Boston Associates erect their first textile mill at Waltham, Massachusetts
1815	War of 1812 ends
1818	National Road completed to Ohio River at Wheeling, Virginia
1822	President Monroe vetoes National Road reparations bill
1825	New York completes the Erie Canal between Buffalo and Albany
1828	Baltimore and Ohio Railroad (America's first) completed
1835	Main Line Canal connects Philadelphia and Pittsburgh

animals, woodlands for fuel, a vegetable garden, with perhaps a dairy cow. The multifarious configurations of these farms provided a hedge against the uncertainties of rural life. Farm families ate most of what they grew, bartered much of the rest within their neighborhoods, and gambled surpluses on long-distance trade.

West Indian and European markets for American meat, grain, and corn had been growing since the mid-18th century. They expanded dramatically between 1793 and 1815, when war disrupted farming in Europe. Many northern farmers, particularly in the mid-Atlantic states, expanded production to take advantage of these overseas markets (see Map 8.1). The prosperity and aspirations of hundreds of thousands of farmers rose, and their houses were sprinkled with tokens of comfort and gentility. The same markets, however, sustained traditions of household independence and neighborly cooperation. Farmers continued to provide for their families from their own farms and neighborhoods, and they risked little by increasing their surpluses and sending them overseas. They profited from world markets without becoming dependent on them.

Production for overseas markets after 1790 did, however, alter relationships within farm families—usually in ways that reinforced the independence of the household and the power of its male head. Farm labor in post-revolutionary America was carefully divided by sex. Men worked in the fields, and production for markets both intensified that labor and made it more exclusively male. In the grain fields of the middle states, for instance, the long-handled scythe was replacing the sickle as the principal harvest tool. Women could use the sickle efficiently, but because of its length and weight, men were better able to wield the scythe. At the same time, farmers completed the substitution of ploughs for hoes as the principal cultivating tools—not only because ploughs worked better, but also because rural Americans had developed a prejudice against women working in the fields, and ploughs were male tools. By the early 19th century, visitors to the long-settled farming areas (with the exception of some mid-Atlantic German communities) seldom saw women in the fields. In his travels throughout France, Thomas Jefferson spoke harshly of peasant communities where he saw women doing field labor.

At the same time, household responsibilities multiplied and fell more exclusively to women. Farm women's labor and ingenuity helped create a more varied and nutritious rural diet in these years. Bread and salted meat were still the staples. The bread was the old mix of Indian corn and coarse wheat ("Rye and Injun," the farmers called it), with crust so thick that it was used as a scoop for soups and stews. Though improved brines and pickling techniques augmented the supply of salt meat, farmers' palates doubtless told them it was the same old salt meat.

But by the 1790s, improved winter feeding for cattle and better techniques for making and storing butter and cheese kept dairy products on the tables of the more prosperous farm families throughout the year. Chickens became more common, and farmwomen began to fence and manure their kitchen gardens, planting them with potatoes, turnips, cabbages, squashes, beans, and other vegetables that could be stored in the root cellars that were becoming standard features of farmhouses.

8-1b *Neighbors*

Rural communities were far more than accumulations of independent farm-owning households. The struggle to maintain household independence involved most farm families in elaborate networks of neighborly cooperation, and long-term, give-and-take relationships with neighbors were essential economic and social assets. Few farmers possessed the tools, the labor, and the food they would have needed to be truly self-sufficient. They regularly worked for one another, borrowed oxen and plows, and swapped one kind of food crop for another. Women traded ashes, herbs, butter and eggs, vegetables, seedlings, baby chicks, goose feathers, and the products of their spinning wheels and looms. The regular exchange of such goods and services was crucial to the workings of rural neighborhoods. Some undertakings—house and barn raisings and husking bees, for example—brought the whole neighborhood together, transforming a necessary chore into a pleasant social event. The gossip, drinking, and dancing that took place on such occasions were fun. They were also—like the exchanges of goods and labor—social rituals that strengthened the neighborly relations within which farmers created a livelihood and passed it on to their sons.

Few of these neighborhood transactions involved money. In 1790, no paper money had yet been issued by the states or the federal government, and the widespread use of Spanish, English, and French coins testified to the shortage of specie. In New England, farmers kept careful accounts of neighborhood debts. In the South and West, farmers used a **"changing system"** in which they simply remembered what

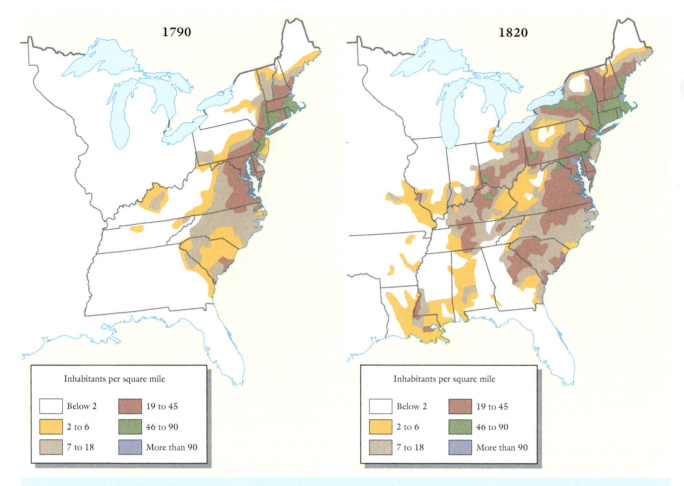

▲ **MAP 8.1 Population Density, 1790–1820** The population of the United States nearly doubled between 1790 and 1820, growing from 5.2 million to 9.6 million persons. In the South, an overwhelmingly rural population spread rapidly across space. The population of the Northeast and mid-Atlantic also occupied new territory over these years, but the rise of seaport towns and intensely commercialized (and often overcrowded) farming areas was turning the North into a much more densely settled region.

Q How did different economic ideologies in the North and South affect the pace of economic development and population density?

Q What other factors might have encouraged more sprawling development in the South and West?

they owed; they regarded the New England practice as a sign of Yankee greed and lack of character. Yet, farmers everywhere relied more on barter than on cash.

Country storekeepers and village merchants handled relationships between farmers and long-distance markets, and they were as much a part of their neighborhoods as of the wider world. In most areas, farmers brought produce—often a mixed batch of grain, vegetables, ashes, goose down, and so on—to the storekeeper, who arranged its shipment to a seaport town. Some paid cash for produce, but most simply credited the farmer's account. Farmers also bought store goods on credit, and when bad crop years or bad luck made them unable to pay, storekeepers tended to wait for payment without charging interest.

In many instances, the store was incorporated into the relations of local exchange. Hudson River merchants paid the same prices for local goods that were to be sold locally over long periods of time—a price that reflected their relative value within the local barter economy. When sent to New York City, the prices of the same goods rose and fell with their value on international markets. Storekeepers also played a role in local networks of debt, for it was common for farmers to bring their grain, ashes, butter, and eggs to the store, and to have them credited to the accounts of neighbors to whom they were in debt, thus turning the storekeeper into a broker within the complicated web of neighborhood obligations.

8-1c Standards of Living

In 1790, most farmhouses in the older rural areas were small, one-story structures, and few farmers bothered to keep their surroundings clean or attractive. They repaired their fences only when they became too dilapidated to function. They rarely planted trees or shrubs, and housewives threw out garbage for chickens and pigs that foraged near the house.

Inside, there were few rooms and many people. Beds stood in every room, and few family members slept alone. Growing up in Bethel, Connecticut, the future show-business entrepreneur P. T. Barnum shared a bed with his brother and an Irish servant. Guests shared beds in New England taverns

8.2 Venerate the Plough This image, celebrating America's independent yeoman farmer, was engraved for the *Columbian Magazine* and used for a medal of the Philadelphia Society for the Promotion of Agriculture starting in 1786.

Q What features of the image reinforce the perception of agriculture as a virtuous pursuit?

until the 1820s. The hearth remained the source of heat and light in most farmhouses. Between 1790 and 1810, over half the households in central Massachusetts, an old and relatively prosperous area, owned only one or two candlesticks, suggesting that one of the great disparities between wealthy families and their less affluent neighbors was that the wealthy could light their houses at night. Another disparity was in the outward appearance of houses.

Increased income from foreign markets did result in improvement. Farmers bought traditional necessities such as salt and pepper, gunpowder, tools, and coffee and tea, but these were now supplemented with an increasingly alluring array of little luxuries such as crockery, flatware, finished cloth, mirrors, clocks and watches, wallpaper, and the occasional book. At mealtimes, only the poorest families continued to eat with their fingers or with spoons from a common bowl. By 1800, individual place settings with knives and forks and china plates, along with individual chairs instead of benches, had become common in rural America.

8-1d Inheritance

Northern farmers between 1790 and 1815 were remarkably like Jefferson's yeoman-citizen ideal: prosperous, independent, living in rough equality with neighbors who shared the same status. Yet, even as rural Americans acted out that vision, its social base was disintegrating. Overcrowding and the growth of markets caused the price of good farmland to rise sharply throughout the older settlements. Most young men could expect to inherit only a few acres of exhausted land, or to move to wilderness land. Failing that, they could expect to quit farming altogether. Crèvecoeur's baby boy—who in fact ended up living in Boston—was in a more precarious position than his seat on his father's plough might have indicated.

In revolutionary America, fathers had been judged by their ability to support and govern their households, to serve as good neighbors, and to pass land on to their sons. After the war, fewer farm fathers were able to do that. Those in the old settlements had small farms and large families, which made it impossible for them to provide a competence for all of their offspring. Fathers felt that they had failed as fathers, and their sons, with no prospect of an adequate inheritance, were obliged to leave home. Most fathers tried to provide for all of their heirs (generally by leaving land to their sons and personal property to their daughters). Few left all of their land to one son, and many stated in their wills that the sons to whom they left the land must share barns and cider mills—even houses— on farms that could be subdivided no further. Such provisions indicated a social system that had reached the end of the line.

Outside New England, farm **tenancy** was on the increase. In parts of Pennsylvania and other areas, farmers often bought farms when they became available in the neighborhood, rented them to tenants to augment the household income, and gave them to their sons when they reached adulthood. The sons of poorer farmers often rented a farm in the hope of saving enough money to buy it. Some fathers bought tracts of unimproved land in the backcountry —sometimes on speculation, more often to provide their sons with land they could make into a farm. Others paid to have their sons educated, or arranged an apprenticeship to provide them with an avenue of escape from a crowded countryside. As a result, more and more young men left home. The populations of the old farming communities grew older and more female, while the populations of the rising frontier settlements and seaport cities became younger and more male. The young men who stayed home often had nothing to look forward to but a lifetime as tenants or hired hands.

8-1e The Seaport Cities

When the first federal census takers made their rounds in 1790, they found 94 percent of Americans living on farms and in rural villages. The remaining 6 percent lived in 24 towns with a population of more than 2,500 (a census definition of "urban" that included many communities that were, by modern standards, very small). Only five places had populations over 10,000: Boston (18,038), New York (33,131), Philadelphia (42,444), Baltimore (13,503), and Charleston (16,359). All five were seaports, which is testimony to the key role of international commerce in the economy of the early republic.

The little streams of produce that left farm neighborhoods joined with others on the rivers and the coastal shipping lanes, and they piled up as a significant national surplus on the docks of the seaport towns. When war broke out between Britain and France in 1793, the overseas demand for American foodstuffs, and thus the production of American farms, increased. The warring European powers also needed shipping to carry products from the Caribbean islands to Europe. America's

8.3 The Dining Room of Dr. Whitbridge, a Rhode Island Country Doctor, circa 1815
It is a comfortable, neatly furnished room, but with little decoration. The doctor must sit near the fire in layered clothing to ward off the morning chill.

saltwater merchants, free from the old colonial restrictions, responded by building one of the great merchant fleets in the world, and American overseas trade entered a period of unprecedented growth. Ocean trade during these years was risky and uneven, subject to the tides of war and the strategies of the belligerents. But by 1815, wartime commerce had transformed the seaports and the institutions of American business. New York City had become the nation's largest city, with a population that grew to 96,373 in 1810. Philadelphia's population had risen to 53,722 by 1810; Boston's to 34,322; and Baltimore's to 46,555. Economic growth in the years 1790 to 1815 was most palpably concentrated in these cities.

Seaport merchants in these years amassed the private fortunes and built the financial infrastructure that would soon take up the task of commercializing and industrializing the northern United States. Old merchants like the Brown brothers of Providence and Elias Hasket Darby of Salem grew richer, and newcomers like the immigrant John Jacob Astor of New York City built huge personal fortunes. To manage those fortunes, new institutions emerged. Docking and warehousing facilities improved dramatically. Bookkeepers were replaced by accountants, who were familiar with the new double-entry system of accounting, and insurance and banking companies were formed to handle the risks and rewards of wartime commerce.

The cities prospered in these years. The main thoroughfares and a few of the side streets were paved with cobblestones and lined with fine shops and townhouses. But in other parts of the cities, visitors learned that the boom was creating poverty as well as wealth. There had been poor people and depressed neighborhoods in the 18th-century seaports, but not on the scale that prevailed between 1790 and 1820. A few steps off the handsome avenues were narrow streets crowded with ragged children, browsing dogs and pigs, with garbage and waste filling the open sewers.

The slums were evidence that money created by commerce was being distributed in undemocratic ways. Per capita wealth in New York rose 60 percent between 1790 and 1825, but the wealthiest 4 percent of the population owned over half of that wealth. The wages of skilled and unskilled labor rose in these years, but the increase in seasonal and temporary employment, together with the recurring interruptions of foreign commerce, cut deeply into the security and prosperity of ordinary women and men. Added to the old insecurities of sickness, fire, accident, aging, and any number of personal misfortunes, these ate up the gains made by laborers, sailors, and most artisans and their families.

Meanwhile, the status of artisans in the big cities was undergoing change. In 1790, artisans were the self-proclaimed "middling classes" of the towns. They demanded and usually received the respect of their fellow citizens. Skilled manual workers constituted about half the male workforce of the seaport cities, and their respectability and usefulness, together with the role they had played in the Revolution, had earned them an honorable status.

That status rested in large part on their independence. In 1790, most artisan workshops were household operations with at most one or two apprentices and hired **journeymen**—wage earners who looked forward to owning their own shops one day. Most master craftsmen lived modestly (on the borderline of poverty in many cases) and aspired only to support their household in security and decency, and to do so by performing useful work. They identified their way of life with republican virtue. Jefferson proclaimed them "the yeomen of the cities."

The patriarchal base of that republicanism, however, was eroding. With the growth of the maritime economy, the nature of construction work, shipbuilding, the clothing trades, and other specialized crafts changed. Artisans were being replaced by cheaper labor and undercut by subcontracted "slop work" performed by semiskilled rural outworkers. Perhaps one in five master craftsmen entered the newly emerging business class. The others took work as laborers or wage-earning craftsmen. By 1815, most young craftsmen in the seaports could not hope to own their own shops. The world of artisans like Paul Revere, Benjamin Franklin, and Thomas Paine was passing out of existence. Wage labor was taking its place.

History Through Film: A Midwife's Tale (1998)

Directed by Richard D. Rodgers (PBS).

The historian Laurel Thatcher Ulrich's *A Midwife's Tale* won the Pulitzer Prize for history and biography in 1991. Shortly thereafter, the Public Broadcasting System (PBS) turned the book into a documentary movie—a close and imaginative analysis of the diary of Martha Ballard, a Maine farmwoman and midwife of the late 18th and early 19th centuries. Events are acted out on screen, and period modes of dress, housing, gardening, washing, coffin making, spinning and weaving, and other details are reconstructed with labored accuracy.

The viewer hears the sounds of footfalls, horses, handlooms, and dishes, but the only human sounds are an occasional cough, exclamation, or drinking song. The principal narrative is carried by an actress who reads passages from the diary, and Thatcher occasionally breaks in to explain her own experiences with the diary and its interpretation. The result is a documentary film that knows the difference between dramatizing history and making it up. It also dramatizes the ways in which a skilled and sensitive historian goes about her work.

Martha Ballard was a midwife in a town on the Kennebec River. She began keeping a daily diary at the age of 50 in 1785, and continued until 1812. Most of the film is about her daily life: delivering babies, nursing the sick, helping neighbors, keeping house, raising and supervising the labor of her daughters and niece, gardening, and tending cattle and turkeys. In both the book and the film, the busyness of an ordinary woman's days—and a sense of her possibilities and limits—in the early republic come through in exhausting detail. The dailiness of her life is interrupted only occasionally by an event: a fire at her husband's sawmill, an epidemic of scarlet fever, a parade organized to honor the death of George Washington, the rape of a minister's wife by his enemies (including the local judge, who is set free), and a neighbor's inexplicable murder of his wife and six children.

There is also the process of getting old. At the beginning, Martha Ballard is the busy wife in a well-run household. As she ages and her children leave to set up households of their own, Ballard hires local girls who—perhaps because an increasingly democratic culture has made them less subservient than Ballard would like, perhaps because Ballard is growing old and impatient, perhaps both—tend to be surly. Her husband, a surveyor who works for merchants speculating in local land, is attacked twice in the woods by squatters and spends a year and a half in debtor's jail—not for his own debts but because, as tax collector, he failed to collect enough. While the husband is in jail and his aging wife struggles to keep the house going, their son moves his own family into the house and Martha is moved into a single room and is made to feel unwanted—a poignant and unsentimental case of the strained relations between generations that historians have discovered in the early republic.

A Midwife's Tale is a modest film that comes as close as a thorough and imaginative historian and a good filmmaker can to recreating the texture of lived experience in the northeastern countryside at the beginning of the 19th century. Students who enjoy the movie should go immediately to the book. ■

8.4 The midwife and farm woman Martha Ballard (portrayed by Kaiulani Lee) writes in her diary, the primary source for the book and film, *A Midwife's Tale*.

8.5 Procession of Victuallers, 1815
The frequent and festive parades in the seaport cities included militia companies, political officials, clergymen, and artisans organized by trade. In this Philadelphia parade celebrating the end of the War of 1812, the victuallers, preceded by militia cavalrymen, carry a penned steer and a craft flag high atop a wagon, while butchers in top hats and clean aprons ride below. Behind them, shipbuilders drag a ship through the streets.

Q *How did the organization of the parade communicate the place of artisans within early northeastern urban society?*

8-2 The Northwest: From Backcountry to Frontier

Q *How did eastern opinion of the Northwest and its settlers change between 1790 and 1820?*

The United States was a huge country in 1790, at least on paper. In the treaty that ended the War of Independence in 1783, the British ignored Indian claims and ceded all of the land from the Atlantic Ocean to the Mississippi River to the new republic, with the exceptions of Spanish Florida and New Orleans. The states then surrendered their individual claims to the federal government, and in 1790 George Washington became president of a nation that stretched nearly 1,500 miles inland. Still, most white Americans lived on thin strips of settlement on the Atlantic coast and along the few navigable rivers that emptied into the Atlantic. Some were pushing their way into the wilds of Maine and northern Vermont, and in New York others set up communities as far west as the Mohawk Valley. Pittsburgh was a struggling new settlement, and two outposts had been established on the Ohio River: at Marietta and at what would become Cincinnati.

8-2a *The Backcountry, 1790–1815*

To easterners, the backcountry whites, who were displacing the Indians, seemed no different from the defeated aborigines. In fact, in accommodating themselves to a borderless forest used by both Indians and whites, many settlers—like many Indians—had melded Indian and white ways. To clear the land, backcountry farmers simply girdled the trees and left them to die and fall down by themselves. They plowed the land by navigating between the stumps. To easterners' minds, the worst offense was that women often worked the fields, particularly while their men, as did Indians, spent long periods away on hunting trips for food game and animal skins for trade. The arch-pioneer Daniel Boone, for instance, braided his hair, dressed himself in Indian leggings, and, with only his dogs for company, disappeared for months at a time on "long hunts." When easterners began to "civilize" his neighborhood, Boone moved farther west.

Eastern visitors were appalled not only by the poverty, lice, and filth of frontier life but also by the drunkenness and violence of the frontiersmen. Americans everywhere drank heavily in the early years of the 19th century, but everyone agreed that westerners drank more and were more violent when drunk than men anywhere else. Stories arose of half-legendary heroes such as Davy Crockett of Tennessee, who wrestled bears and alligators and had a recipe for Indian stew, and Mike Fink, a Pennsylvania boatman who brawled and drank his way along the rivers of the interior until he was shot and killed in a drunken episode that none of the participants could clearly remember. Samuel Holden Parsons, a New Englander serving as a judge in the Northwest Territory, called the frontiersmen "our white savages." Massachusetts conservative Timothy Pickering branded them "the least worthy subjects of the United States. They are little less savage than the Indians."

8-2b *Settlement*

After 1789, settlers of the backcountry made two demands of the new national government: protection from Indians and a guarantee of the right to navigate the Ohio and Mississippi rivers. The Indians were pushed back in the 1790s and removed as a threat in the War of 1812; in 1803, Jefferson's Louisiana Purchase ended the European presence on the rivers and at the crucial chokepoint at New Orleans. Over these years, the pace of settlement quickened. In 1790, only 10,000 settlers lived west of the Appalachians—about one American in 40. By 1800, the number of settlers had risen to nearly 1 million. By 1820, 2 million Americans were westerners—one in five.

The new settlers bought land from speculators who had acquired tracts under the Northwest Ordinance in the Northwest; from English, Dutch, and American land companies in western New York; and from land dealers in western areas of the Southeast and in northern New England. They built frame

8.6 Colonel Crockett 1839 The frontiersman Davy Crockett, pictured here as a colonel in the Tennessee militia, helped to cement the reputation of the early American backcountry as wild, dangerous, and uncivilized.

Q *Although Crockett was clearly white, how did race factor into the eastern critique of western frontiersmen?*

houses surrounded by cleared fields, planted marketable crops, and settled into the struggle to make farms out of the wilderness and to meet mortgage payments along the way. Ohio entered the union in 1803, followed by Indiana (1816) and Illinois (1818). As time passed, the term *backcountry*, which easterners had used to refer to the wilderness and the dangerous misfits who lived in it, fell into disuse. By 1820, the term **frontier** had replaced it. The new western settlements no longer represented the backwash of American civilization. They were its cutting edge.

8-3 Transportation Revolution, 1815–1850

Q *How did improvements in transportation channel commerce within and between regions?*

After 1815, dramatic **internal improvements** in transportation—more and better roads, canals, and railroads—tied old communities together and penetrated previously isolated neighborhoods and transformed them. Most of these projects were the work of state governments. Together, the improvements produced a **transportation revolution** that made the transition to a market society physically possible by drastically reducing the cost of shipping surplus crops and goods (see Map 8.2).

8-3a *Transportation in 1815*

In 1815, the United States was a rural nation stretching from the old settlements on the Atlantic coast to the trans-Appalachian west, with transportation facilities that ranged from primitive to nonexistent. Americans despaired of communicating, to say nothing of doing business on a national scale. In 1816, a Senate committee reported that $9 would move a ton of goods across the 3,000-mile expanse of the North Atlantic. The same $9 would move the same ton of goods only 30 miles inland. A year later, the cost of transporting wheat from the new settlement of Buffalo to New York City was three times higher than the selling price of wheat in New York. Farming for profit made sense only for farmers near urban markets or with easy river access to the coast.

Transporting goods into the western settlements was even more difficult. Keelboatmen like Mike Fink could navigate upstream—using eddies and back currents, sailing when the wind was right, but usually poling their boats against the current. Skilled crews averaged only 15 miles a day, and the trip from New Orleans to Louisville took three to four months. Looking for better routes, some merchants dragged finished goods across Pennsylvania and into the West at Pittsburgh, but transport costs made these goods prohibitively expensive. Consequently, the trans-Appalachian settlements—home to one in five Americans by 1820—remained marginal to the market economy.

8-3b Internal Improvements

In 1816, Congress resumed construction of the **National Road** (first authorized in 1802) that linked the Potomac River with the Ohio River at Wheeling, Virginia (now West Virginia)—an attempt to link west and east through the Chesapeake. The smooth, crushed-rock thoroughfare reached Wheeling in 1818. At about the same time, Pennsylvania extended the Lancaster Turnpike to make it run from Philadelphia to the Ohio River at Pittsburgh. These ambitious roads into the West, however, had limited effects. The National Road made it easier for settlers and a few merchants' wagons to reach the West, but the cost of moving bulky farm produce over the road remained high. Eastbound traffic on the National Road consisted largely of cattle and pigs, which carried themselves to market. Farmers continued to float their corn, cotton, wheat, salt pork, and whiskey south by riverboat and from there to eastern markets.

It was the steamboat that first made commercial agriculture feasible in the Northwest. Tinkerers and mechanics had been experimenting with steam-powered boats for a generation or more when an entrepreneur named **Robert Fulton** launched the first commercial steamboat, the *Clermont*, on an upriver trip from New York City to Albany in 1807. Over the next few years, Americans developed flat-bottomed steamboats that could navigate rivers even at low water. The first steamboat reached Louisville from New Orleans in 1815. Two years later, with 17 steamboats already working western rivers, the *Washington* made the New Orleans–Louisville run in 25 days, a feat that convinced westerners that two-way river trade was possible. By 1820, 69 steamboats were operating on western rivers. The 60,000 tons of produce that farmers and planters had shipped out of the interior in 1810 grew to 500,000 tons in 1840. The steamboat had transformed the interior from an isolated frontier into a busy commercial region that traded farm and plantation products for manufactured goods.

In the East, state governments created rivers where nature had made none. In 1817, Governor DeWitt Clinton, after failing to get federal support, talked the New York legislature into building a canal linking the Hudson River to Lake Erie, thus opening a continuous water route between the Northwest and New York City. The **Erie Canal** was a visionary feat of engineering. Designed by self-taught engineers and built by gangs of Irish immigrants, local farm boys, and convict laborers, it stretched 364 miles from Albany to Buffalo. Although "Clinton's Ditch" passed through carefully chosen level ground, it required a complex system of 83 locks, and it passed over 18 rivers on stone aqueducts. Construction began in 1819, and the canal reached Buffalo in 1825. It was clear even before then that the canal would repay New York State's investment of $7.5 million many times over, and that it would transform the territory that it served.

The Erie Canal would direct the trade of the whole Great Lakes watershed into New York City, but its first and most powerful effects were on western New York, which had been a raw frontier accessible to the East only over a notoriously bad state road. By 1830, the New York corridor of the Erie Canal, settled largely from hill-country New England, was one of the world's great grain-growing regions, dotted with market towns and new cities like Syracuse, Rochester, and Buffalo.

The Erie Canal was an immense success, and legislators and entrepreneurs in other states joined a canal boom that lasted for 20 years. When construction began on the Erie Canal, there were fewer than 100 miles of canal in the United States. By 1840, there were 3,300 miles, nearly all of them in the Northeast and Northwest. Northwestern states, Ohio in particular, built ambitious canal systems that linked isolated areas to the Great Lakes and thus to the Erie Canal. Northeastern states followed suit. A canal between Worcester and Providence linked the farms of central Massachusetts with Narragansett Bay. Another canal linked the coal mines of northeastern Pennsylvania with the Hudson River at Kingston, New York. In 1835, Pennsylvania completed a canal from Philadelphia to Pittsburgh.

The canal boom was followed quickly by a boom in railroads. The first of them connected burgeoning cities to rivers and canals. The Baltimore and Ohio Railroad, for example, linked Baltimore to the rivers of the West. Although the approximately 3,000 miles of railroads built between the late 1820s and 1840 helped the market positions of some cities, they did not constitute a national or even a regional rail network. A national system developed with the 5,000 miles of track laid in the 1840s and with the flurry of railroad building that by 1860 gave the United States a rail network of 30,000 miles—a continuous, integrated system that created numerous links between the East and the Northwest and threatened to put canals out of business (see Maps 8.3 and 8.4). In fact, the New York Central, which paralleled the Erie Canal, rendered that canal obsolete. Other railroads, particularly in the northwestern states, replaced canal and river transport almost completely, even though water transport remained cheaper. By 1860, few farmers in the North and West lived more than 20 road miles from railroads, canals, or rivers that could deliver their produce to regional, national, and international markets.

8-3c Time, Money, and New Markets

The transportation revolution brought a dramatic reduction in the time and money that it took to move heavy goods. Turnpikes cut the cost of wagon transport, but goods traveled most cheaply on water. In 1816, freight rates on the Ohio–Mississippi system had been 1.3 cents per ton-mile for downriver travel and 5.8 cents for upriver travel. Steamboats cut both costs to a bit more than a third of a cent. The Erie Canal and the Ohio canals reduced the distance between East and West and carried goods at about one cent per ton-mile. By 1830, farmers in the Northwest and western New York could grow wheat and sell it at a profit on the New York market.

Interpreting the Visual Past

Transportation before the Market Revolution

The Russian artist Pavel Petrovich Svinin completed this watercolor painting, *Travel by Stage Coach near Trenton, New Jersey*, between 1811 and 1813, when he traveled up and down the East Coast sketching and taking notes. It captures the state of transportation in America before the Market Revolution. The coach is small and open to the weather, the passengers are crowded and uncomfortable (one of them has lost his hat), and the road is a dirt path with a steep incline—difficult when going uphill, dangerous when going down. The driver, like many of the people who worked with horses, is black.

Q Considering that Trenton was one of the most developed parts of the country in the early 1810s, what does this image tell us about the state of early American transportation? Despite the obvious drawbacks, what advantages are apparent compared to travel in other, less developed parts of the country?

Q Reflect on how a historian might use this painting as evidence. What does it show about the relationship between transportation and the Market Revolution? What does the painting illustrate about early American social relations?

8.7 Pavel Petrovich Svinin, *Travel by Stage Coach near Trenton, New Jersey*, 1811–1813.

Improvements in speed were nearly as dramatic. The overland trip from Cincinnati to New York in 1815 (by keelboat upriver to Pittsburgh, then by wagon the rest of the way) had taken a minimum of 52 days. Steamboats traveled from Cincinnati to New Orleans, and then passed goods on to coasting ships that finished the trip to New York City in a total of 28 days. By 1840, the Ohio canal system enabled Cincinnati to send goods north through Ohio, across Lake Erie, over the Erie Canal, and down the Hudson to New York City—an all-water route that reduced costs and made the trip in 18 days. Similar improvements occurred in the densely settled and increasingly urbanized Northeast. By 1840, travel time between the big northeastern cities had been reduced from one-fourth to one-eleventh of what it had been in 1790. These improvements in speed and economy made a northern market economy possible.

Improved transportation helped to bring together previously isolated markets—the final step of the Market Revolution.

Foreign trade, which had driven American economic growth up until 1815, continued to expand. The value of American exports in 1815 had stood at $52.6 million, while imports totaled $113 million. Both rose dramatically in the years of the Market Revolution: Exports (now consisting more of southern cotton than of northern food crops) continued to increase, and the flow of imported manufactured goods increased as well. Yet, foreign trade now accounted for a smaller proportion of American—particularly northern—market activity. Before 1815, Americans had exported about 15 percent of their total national product. By 1830, exports accounted for only 6 percent of a vastly increased national production. The reason for this shift was that after 1815, the United States developed self-sustaining domestic markets for farm produce and manufactured goods. The great engine of economic growth in the North and West was not the old colonial relationship with Europe but a self-sustaining domestic market.

8-3 Transportation Revolution, 1815–1850

8.8 The Erie Canal at Lockport, New York, in 1839 The canal stretched for 364 miles between Albany and Buffalo, linking New York City to the Great Lakes through the Hudson River. It required complex engineering, including locks (pictured here), which raised or lowered boats to navigate water at different elevation levels.

Until 1840, the Market Revolution produced greater results within regions than between them. The farmers of New England traded food for finished goods from Boston, Lynn, Lowell, and other towns in what was becoming an urban, industrial region. Philadelphia traded manufactures for food from the farmers of the Delaware Valley. The Erie Canal created a huge potential for interregional trade, but until 1839 most of its westbound tonnage originated in western New York. In the West, market-oriented farmers fed such rapidly growing cities as Rochester, Pittsburgh, and Cincinnati, which in turn supplied the farmers with locally manufactured farm tools, furniture, shoes, and other goods. Thus, although the Market Revolution was initially more a regional than an interregional phenomenon, it was clear to anyone who looked at a map that the New England, mid-Atlantic, and Northwestern states were on their way to becoming an integrated market society—one that did not include southern plantations that grew for export (see Chapter 9).

8-4 Northeastern Farms, 1815–1850

Q *How did northern farm families experience the transition into commercial agriculture between 1815 and 1850?*

In the old farming communities of the Northeast, the transformations of the early 19th century sent many young people off to cities and factory towns and others to the West. Those who remained at home engaged in new forms of agriculture on a transformed rural landscape, while their cousins in the Northwest turned a wilderness into cash-producing farms. In both regions, farmers abandoned the old mixed, safety-first agriculture and began to raise a single crop intended for distant markets. That decision committed them to buying things that their forebears had grown or made, participating as both producers and consumers in a new market economy.

8-4a The New England Livestock Economy

New Englanders who tried to grow grain on their rocky, worn-out soil could not compete with the farmers of western New York and the Northwest. At the same time, however, the new factories and growing cities of the Northeast provided Yankee farmers with a market for meat and other perishables. Beef became the great New England cash crop. Dairy products were not far behind, and the proximity to city markets encouraged the spread of poultry and egg farms, fruit orchards, and truck gardens. The burgeoning shoe industry bought leather from the farmers, and woolen mills created a demand for wool, and thus for great flocks of New England sheep. As a result, millions of trees were stripped from the New England landscape to make way for pastureland.

The rise of livestock specialization reduced the amount of land under cultivation. Early in the century, New Englanders still tilled their few acres in the old three-year rotation: corn the first year, rye the second, fallow the third. By the 1820s and 1830s, as farmers raised more livestock and less grain, the land that remained in cultivation was farmed more intensively. Farmers saved manure and ashes for fertilizer, plowed more deeply and systematically, and tended their crops more carefully. These improved techniques, along with cash from the sale of their livestock and the availability of food at stores, encouraged Yankee farmers to allocate less and less land to the growing of food crops. In Concord, Massachusetts—the hometown of the agrarian republic—the portion of town land in tillage dropped from 20 to 7 percent between 1771 and 1850.

The transition to livestock-raising transformed woodlands into open pastures. As farmers leveled the forests, they

▲ **MAP 8.2 Rivers, Roads, and Canals, 1825–1860** In the second quarter of the 19th century, transportation projects linked the North and Northwest into an integrated economic and social system. There were fewer improvements in the South: Farm produce traveled down navigable rivers from bottomland plantations to river and seaport towns, thence to New York for shipment overseas. Southern legislatures and entrepreneurs saw little use for further improvements.

Q *Compare this map with Map 8.1. How did new transportation networks linking the North and Northwest help to make possible greater population density in northeastern cities?*

Q *What might have been some of the social, economic, and political consequences of the relative isolation of southern communities?*

sold the wood to fuel-hungry cities. It was a lucrative, although short-term, market. In the 1820s, manufacturers began marketing cast-iron stoves that heated houses more cheaply and more efficiently than open hearths, and canals brought cheap Pennsylvania anthracite to the Northeast. The shift came too late to prevent massive deforestation. In 1790, in the central Massachusetts town of Petersham, forest covered 85 percent of the town lands. By 1830, the creation of pastureland through commercial woodcutting had reduced the forested area to 30 percent. (By 1850, woods covered only 10 percent of the town, the pasturelands were overgrazed and ruined, and the landscape was dotted with abandoned farms.)

With the shift to specialized market agriculture, New England farmers became customers for necessities that their forebears had produced themselves or had acquired through barter. The turning point came in the 1820s. Farm families heated their houses with coal dug by Pennsylvania miners. They wore cotton cloth made by the factory women at Lowell. New Hampshire farm girls made straw hats for them, and the craftsmen of Lynn made their shoes. By 1830

8-4 Northeastern Farms, 1815–1850   **243**

8.9 View of the First American Railway Train The first locomotives were simply steam engines mounted on wheeled platforms, and the first coaches were stagecoaches on metal wheels. Within a few years, both engines and coaches had taken on their familiar 19th-century designs.

Q What can the passengers and their dress tell us about early railway travel in America?

or so, many farmers were even buying food. The Erie Canal and the western grain belt sent flour from Rochester into eastern neighborhoods where grain was no longer grown. Many farmers found it easier to produce specialized crops for market, and to buy butter, cheese, eggs, and vegetables at country stores.

As a result, spinning wheels and handlooms disappeared from the farmhouses of New England. Farm families that bought the new cast-iron stoves enjoyed pies and bread baked from western white flour; the old "Rye and Injun" disappeared. All of these things cost money and committed farm families to increasing their cash incomes. Standards of living rose dramatically. At the same time, northeastern farmers depended on markets in ways that their fathers and grandfathers would have considered dangerous not only to family welfare but to the welfare of the republic itself.

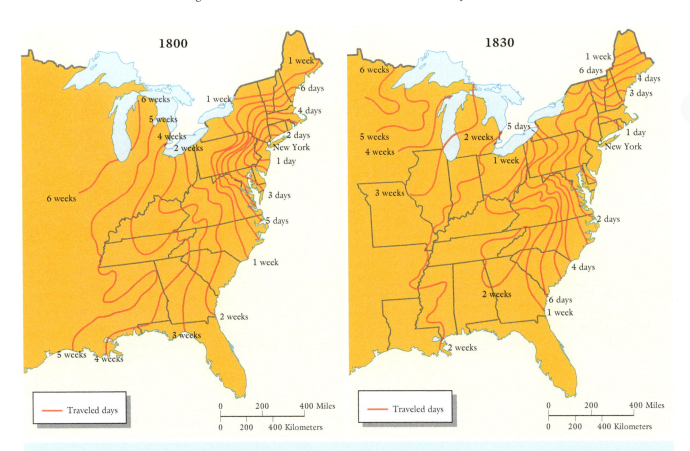

▲ **MAP 8.3 Time Required to Travel from New York City, 1800 and 1830** These maps illustrate the increasing ease of travel in the first third of the 19th century. In general, travelers could cover nearly twice as much territory in a day in 1830 as in 1800, although in both cases travel became more difficult as one left the densely settled East.

Q Which areas had the most dramatic change in travel time between 1800 and 1830? Which areas had the least change?

Q How did the factor of travel time influence major economic decisions and trends?

CHAPTER 8 Northern Transformations, 1790–1850

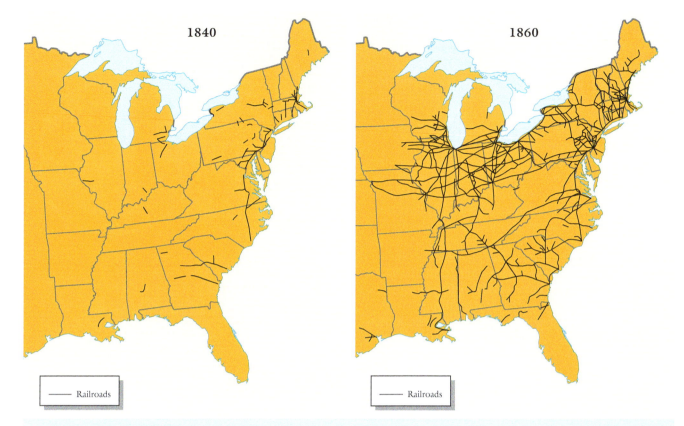

▲ **MAP 8.4 Railroads in the United States, 1840 and 1860** In these 20 years, both the North and South built railway systems. Northerners built rail lines that integrated the market economies of the Midwest and the East—both within sections and between them. For the most part, southern railroads linked the plantation belt with the ocean. Revealingly, only a few lines connected the North and South.

Q Compare these maps with Map 8.2. Why did the pattern of railroad development so closely follow existing transportation networks created by canals and roads?

Q Why did railroads run from East to West but not from North to South? What might have been some of the social and political consequences of this pattern?

8-4b New Farm Households

The Market Revolution had an equally dramatic impact on the relations within households. For one thing, Americans began to limit the size of their families. White women who married in 1800 had given birth to an average of 6.4 children. Those who married between 1800 and 1849 averaged 4.9 children. The decline was most pronounced in the North, particularly in commercialized areas.

Rural birthrates remained at 18th-century levels in the southern uplands, in the poorest and most isolated communities of the North, and on the frontier. (As New Yorker Washington Irving passed through the Northwest in the 1830s, he noted in his journal: "Illinois—famous for children and dogs—in house with nineteen children and thirty-seven dogs.") These communities practiced the old labor-intensive agriculture and relied on the labor of large families. For farmers who used newer techniques or switched to livestock or grain, large families made less sense. Moreover, large broods hampered the ability of future-minded parents to provide for their children and conflicted with new notions of privacy and domesticity that were taking shape among an emerging rural **middle class**—a social group that, like its urban counterpart, defined itself against poorer laborers and those who did not adapt to the new market society.

Before 1815, farmwives had labored in the house, the barnyard, and the garden while their husbands and sons worked in the fields. With the Market Revolution came a sharper distinction between male work that was part of the cash economy and female work that was not. Even such traditional women's tasks as dairying, vegetable gardening, and poultry raising became men's work once they became cash-producing specialties. A Pennsylvanian who lived among businesslike New Englanders in the Northwest was appalled at such tampering with hallowed gender roles and wrote the Yankees off as "a shrewd, selfish, enterprising, cow-milking set of men."

At the same time, new kinds of women's work emerged within households. Though there were fewer children to care for, the culture began to demand forms of child rearing that were more intensive, individualized, and mother-centered. Store-bought white flour, butter, and eggs and the new iron stoves eased the burdens of food preparation, but they also created demands for pies, cakes, and other fancy foods that earlier generations had only dreamed of. And while farm women no longer spun and wove their own cloth, the availability of manufactured cloth created the expectation that their families would dress more neatly and with greater variety than they had in the past, and women spent more time sewing, washing, and ironing. Similar expectations demanded greater personal and domestic cleanliness and taste, and farm women worked at planting flower beds; cleaning and maintaining prized furniture, mirrors, rugs, and ceramics; and scrubbing floors and children. The market and housework grew hand in hand: Among the first mass-produced commodities in the United States was the household broom.

Housework was tied to new notions of privacy, decency, and domestic comfort. Before 1820, farmers cared little about how their houses looked, often tossing trash and garbage out the door for pigs and chickens that foraged near the house. In the 1820s and 1830s, as farmers began to grow cash crops and adopt middle-class ways, they began to plant shade trees and to keep their yards free of trash. They painted their houses and sometimes their fences and outbuildings, arranged their woodpiles into neat stacks, surrounded their houses with flowers and ornamental shrubs, and tried to hide their privies from view. The new sense of refinement extended into other aspects of country life. The practice of chewing (and spitting) tobacco was gradually banned in churches and meeting halls, and in 1823 the minister in Shrewsbury, Massachusetts, ordered dogs out of the meetinghouse.

Inside, prosperous farmhouses took on an air of privacy and comfort. As separate kitchens and iron stoves replaced open hearths, many families used a set of matched dishes for individual place settings. The availability of finished cloth also permitted the regular use of tablecloths, napkins, doilies, curtains, bedspreads, and quilts. Oil lamps replaced homemade candles, and the more prosperous families began to decorate their homes with wallpaper and upholstered furniture. Farm couples moved their beds away from the hearth and (along with the children's beds that had been scattered throughout the house) put them into spaces designated as bedrooms. They took washstands and basins out of the kitchen and put them into the bedroom, thus making sleeping, bathing, and sex more private than they had been in the past. At the center of this new house stood the farmwife, apart from the bustling world of commerce but decorating and caring for the amenities that commerce bought, and demanding that men respect the new domestic world that commerce had made possible.

8-4c The Landscape of Privacy

By 1830, the Market Revolution was transforming the rural landscape of the North. The forests had been reduced, the swamps had been drained, and most of the streams and rivers were interrupted by mill dams. Bears, panthers, and wolves had disappeared, along with the beaver and many of the fish. Now there were extensive pastures where English cattle and sheep browsed on English grasses dotted with English wildflowers like buttercups, daisies, and dandelions. Next to the pastures were neatly cultivated croplands that were regularly fertilized and seldom allowed to lie fallow. And at the center stood painted houses and outbuildings surrounded by flowers and shrubs and vegetable gardens. Many towns,

8.10 A Soap Advertisement from the 1850s The rigors of "Old Washing Day" lead the mother in this advertisement to abuse the children and house pets, while her husband leaves the house. With American Cream Soap, domestic bliss returns: The children and cats are happy, the husband returns, and the wife has time to sew.

Q *Consider the advertisement in relation to advertising today. What, if anything, has changed in the use of psychology to influence consumer behavior?*

particularly in New England, had planted shade trees along the country roads, completing a rural landscape of straight lines and human cultivation—a landscape that looked both settled and comfortable, and that made it easy to think of nature as a commodity to be altered and controlled.

Within that landscape, old practices and old forms of neighborliness fell into disuse. Neighbors continued to exchange goods and labor and to contract debts that might be left unpaid for years, but debts were more likely to be owed to profit-minded storekeepers and creditors, and even debts between neighbors were often paid in cash. Traditionally, storekeepers had allowed farmers to bring in produce and have it credited to a neighbor/creditor's account—a practice that made the storekeeper an agent of neighborhood bartering. In 1830, half of all the stores in rural New England still carried accounts of this sort, but storekeepers increasingly demanded cash payment or charged lower prices to those who paid cash.

The farm newspapers that appeared in these years urged farmers to keep careful records of the amount of fertilizer used, labor costs, and per-acre yields, and discouraged them from relying on the old system of neighboring. Neighborly rituals like parties, husking bees, and barn raisings—with their drinking and socializing—were scorned as inefficient and morally suspect wastes of time. *The Farmer's Almanac* of 1833 warned New England farmers: "If you love fun, frolic, and waste and slovenliness more than economy and profit, then make a husking."

8.11 McCormick Reaper This advertisement, for a farm machinery company in Ohio, illustrates how mechanized agriculture helped to revolutionize the American economy. Patented in the 1830s, the McCormick reaper used a wheel frame pulled by horses to reap (cut) crops at harvest. Two young men look on, holding respectively a sickle and a scythe, the instruments displaced by the new technology.

By 1830, the efficient northern farmer concentrated on producing commodities that could be marketed outside the neighborhood, and used his cash income to buy material comforts for his family, pay debts, and provide a cash inheritance for his children. Maintaining economic independence in the North now required unprecedented levels of dependence on the outside world.

8-5 The Northwest in Transition

 How did northern and southern settlers flooding into the Northwest after 1815 view the new market economy differently?

One reason the Market Revolution in the Northeast went as smoothly as it did was that young people with little hope of inheriting land in the old settlements moved to towns and cities or to the new farmlands of the Northwest. Between 1815 and 1840—precisely the years in which northeastern agriculture became a cash-crop business—migrants from the older areas transformed the Northwest Territory into a working agricultural landscape. The region became the meeting ground of market-conscious northerners and southerners still more accustomed to older forms of subsistence farming and neighbor-to-neighbor exchange.

8-5a Southern Settlers

In the Northwest until the 1820s, most settlers were yeomen from Kentucky and Tennessee, usually a generation removed from Virginia, the Carolinas, and western Maryland. They moved along the Ohio and up the Muskingum, Miami, Scioto, Wabash, and Illinois rivers to set up farms in the southern and central counties of Ohio, Indiana, and Illinois. When southerners moved north of the Ohio River into territory that banned slavery, they often did so saying that slavery blocked opportunities for poor whites. The Methodist preacher Peter Cartwright left Kentucky thinking, "I would get entirely clear of the evil of slavery," and "could raise my children to work where work was not thought a degradation." Similar hopes drew thousands of other southern yeomen north of the Ohio.

But even those who rejected slavery seldom rejected southern folkways. Like their kinfolk in Kentucky and Tennessee, the farmers of southern and central Ohio, Indiana, and Illinois remained tied to the river trade and to a mode of agriculture that favored free-ranging livestock over cultivated fields. The typical farmer fenced in a few acres of corn and left the rest of his land in woods to be roamed by hogs known as "razorbacks" and "land sharks." These animals were thin and tough (they seldom grew to over 200 pounds), and they could run long distances, leap fences, and fend for themselves in the woods. They were notoriously fierce: More settlers were injured by their own hogs than by wild animals. When it was time to gather the hogs for slaughter, many settlers played it safe and hunted them with guns.

The southern-born pioneers of the Northwest, like their cousins across the Ohio River, depended more on their families and neighbors than on distant markets. Newcomers found that they could neither rent tools from their southern neighbors nor present them with "gifts" during hard times. Southerners insisted on repaying debts in kind and on lending tools rather than renting them, thus engaging outsiders in the elaborate network of "neighboring" through which transplanted southerners made their livings. As late as the 1840s, in the bustling town of Springfield, Illinois, barter was the preferred system of exchange. "In no part of the world," said a Scotsman in southern Illinois, "is good neighborship found in greater perfection than in the western territory."

8-5b Northern Farmers

In the 1820s, with improved transportation and with the wars with Indians and Canadians at an end, northeastern migrants entered the Northwest. They settled near the Great Lakes, filling the new lands of Michigan and the northern counties of the older northwestern states. Most of them were New Englanders who had spent a generation in western New York (such settlers accounted for three-fourths of the early population of Michigan). The rest came directly from New England. Arriving in the Northwest along the market's busiest arteries, they practiced an intensive, market-oriented agriculture. They penned their cattle and hogs and fattened them up, making them bigger and worth more than those farther south. They planted their land in grain and transformed the region—beginning with western New York's Genesee County in the 1820s and rolling through the Northwest—into one of the world's great wheat-producing regions. In 1820, the Northwest had exported only 12 percent of its agricultural produce. By 1840, that figure had risen to 27 percent, and it stood much higher among northern-born grain farmers.

The new settlers were notably receptive to improvements in farming techniques. While there were plenty of southern proponents of progress and plenty of backward northerners, the line between new and old agricultural ways separated northern grain farmers from southern settlers. In breaking new land, for instance, southerners still used the old shovel plow, which dug a shallow furrow and skipped over roots. Northerners preferred newer, more expensive cast-iron plows, which cut cleanly through oak roots four inches thick. By the 1830s, the efficient, expensive grain cradle had replaced the age-old sickle as the principal harvest tool in northwestern wheat fields. Instead of threshing their grain by driving cattle and horses over it, farmers bought new horse-powered and treadmill threshers and used hand-cranked fanning mills to speed the process of cleaning the grain.

Most agricultural improvements were tailored to grain and dairy farming and were taken up most avidly by the northern farmers. Others rejected them as expensive and unnatural. They thought that cast-iron plows poisoned the soil and that fanning mills made a "wind contrary to nater," and thus offended God. John Chapman, an eccentric Yankee who earned the nickname "Johnny Appleseed" by planting apple tree cuttings in southern Ohio and Indiana before the settlers arrived, planted only low-yield, common trees. He regarded grafting, which farmers farther north and east were using to improve the quality of their apples, as "against nature." Southerners scoffed at the Yankee fondness for mechanical improvements, the systematic breeding of animals and plants, careful bookkeeping, and farm techniques learned from books. "I reckon," said one, "I know as much about farming as the printers do."

8-6 The Beginnings of the Industrial Revolution

 Why did America's first factories start in the northern countryside?

In the 50 years following 1820, American cities grew faster than ever before or since. The old seaports—New York City in particular—grew rapidly in these years, but the fastest growth was in new cities that served commercial agriculture and in factory towns that produced for a largely rural domestic market. Even in the seaports, growth derived more from commerce with the hinterland than from international trade. Paradoxically, the Market Revolution in the countryside had produced the beginnings of industry and the greatest period of urban growth in U.S. history.

8-6a *Factory Towns: The Rhode Island System*

Jeffersonians held that the United States must always remain rural. Americans, they insisted, could expand into the West, trade their farm surpluses for European finished goods, and thus avoid creating cities with their dependent social classes. Proponents of domestic manufactures argued that Americans could enjoy the benefits of factory production without the troublesome blight of industrial cities. They assured Americans that abundant waterpower—particularly the fast-running streams of the Northeast—would enable Americans to build their factories in the countryside. Such a decentralized factory system would provide employment for country women and children and thus subsidize the independence of struggling farmers. It was on those premises that the first American factories were built.

The American textile industry originated in industrial espionage. The key to the mass production of cotton and woolen textiles was a water-powered machine that spun yarn and thread. The machine had been invented and patented by the Englishman Richard Arkwright in 1769, and the British government forbade the machinery and the people who worked with it to leave the country. Scores of textile workers, however, defied the law and made their way to North America. One of them was Samuel Slater, who had served an apprenticeship under Jedediah Strutt, a partner of Arkwright who had improved on the original machine. Working from memory while employed by Moses Brown, a Providence merchant, Slater built the first Arkwright spinning mill in America at Pawtucket, Rhode Island, in 1790.

Slater's first mill was a small frame building tucked among the town's houses and craftsmen's shops. Although its capacity was limited to the spinning of cotton yarn, it provided work for children in the mill and for women who wove yarn into cloth in their homes. Thus this first mill satisfied American requirements: It did not require the creation of a factory town, and it supplemented the household incomes of farmers and artisans. As his business grew and he advertised for widows with children, however, Slater was greeted by families headed by landless, impoverished men. Slater's use of children from these families prompted respectable farmers and craftsmen to pull their children out of Slater's growing complex of mills. More poor families arrived to take their places, and during the first years of the 19th century, Pawtucket became a disorderly mill town.

Soon Slater and other mill owners built factory villages in the countryside where they could exert better control over their operations and their workers. The practice became known as the **Rhode Island System** (or "family" system). At Slatersville, Rhode Island, Oxford, Massachusetts, and other locations in southern New England, mill owners built whole villages surrounded by company-owned farmland that they rented to the husbands and fathers of their mill workers. The workplace was closely supervised, and drinking and other troublesome practices were forbidden in the villages. Fathers and older sons worked either on rented farms or as laborers at the mills. By the late 1820s, Slater and most of the other owners were getting rid of the outworkers and were buying power looms, thus transforming the villages into self-contained factory towns that turned raw cotton into finished cloth, but at great cost to old forms of household independence. When President Andrew Jackson visited Pawtucket in 1829, he remarked to Samuel Slater, "I understand you taught us how to spin, so as to rival Great Britain in her manufactures; you set all these thousands of spindles to work, which I have been delighted in viewing, and which have made so many happy, by a lucrative employment." "Yes sir," replied Slater. "I suppose that I gave out the psalm and they have been singing to the tune ever since."

CHAPTER 8 Northern Transformations, 1790–1850

8.12 Pawtucket in 1817 Here is America's first textile milling town. It is set beside a waterfall that provides power for the mills. A bridge runs directly over the brink of the falls, and men and boys fish and play in the pool below them.

Q *Consider how factories violated the Jeffersonian ideal of yeoman farming. How might have this pastoral scene helped to ease the transition from agriculture to industrialization?*

8-6b Factory Towns: The Waltham-Lowell System

A second act of industrial espionage was committed by a Boston merchant named Francis Cabot Lowell. Touring English factory districts in 1811, Lowell asked questions and made secret drawings of the machines. He also experienced a genteel distaste for the squalor of the English textile towns. Returning home, Lowell joined with wealthy friends to form the Boston Manufacturing Company—soon known as the Boston Associates. In 1813, they built their first mill at Waltham, Massachusetts, and then expanded into Lowell, Lawrence, and other new towns near Boston during the 1820s.

The company built mills according to the **Waltham-Lowell System**, which differed from the early Rhode Island mills in two ways: (1) They were heavily capitalized and as fully mechanized as possible, turning raw cotton into finished cloth with little need for skilled workers; and (2) their workers were young, single women recruited from the farms of northern New England—farms that were switching to livestock raising, and thus had little need for the labor of daughters. The company provided boardinghouses for them and enforced rules of conduct both on and off the job. The young women, soon to become known as **Lowell mill girls**, worked steadily, never drank, seldom stayed out late, and attended church faithfully. They dressed neatly—often stylishly—and read newspapers and attended lectures. They impressed visitors, particularly those who had seen factory workers in other places, as a dignified and self-respecting workforce.

The brick mills and prim boardinghouses set within landscaped towns and occupied by the sober, well-behaved Lowell girls signified the Boston Associates' desire to build a profitable textile industry without creating a permanent working class. According to the plan, the young farm women would work for a few years in a carefully controlled environment, send their wages back to their families, and return home to live as country housewives. They did in fact form an efficient, decorous workforce, but the decorum was imposed less by the owners than by the women themselves. In order to protect their own reputations, they punished transgressions and shunned fellow workers who misbehaved. Nor did most of the Lowell women send their wages home or, as was popularly believed, use them to pay for their brothers' college educations. Some saved their money to use as dowries that their fathers could not afford. More, however, spent their wages on themselves, particularly on clothes and books.

The owners of the factories expected that the young women's sojourn would reinforce their own paternalism and that of the girls' fathers. Instead, it produced a self-respecting sisterhood of wage-earning women. Twice in the 1830s, the women of Lowell went on strike, proclaiming that they were not wage slaves but "the daughters of freemen." The women survived as a labor force into the late 1840s, when new waves of immigrants, particularly from Ireland, displaced them from northern factories (see Chapter 10). By then, the majority of Lowell mill girls had become housewives, but not on the terms their mothers had known. One in three of them married Lowell men and became city dwellers. Those who returned home remained unmarried longer than their sisters who had stayed on the farm, and then married men about their own age who worked at something other than farming. Thus the Boston Associates kept their promise to produce cotton cloth profitably without creating a permanent working class, but they did not succeed in shuttling young women between rural and urban paternalism and back again. Wage labor, the ultimate degradation for agrarian-republican men, opened a road to independence for thousands of young women.

8-6c Cities

The Market Revolution hit American cities—the old seaports as well as the new marketing and manufacturing towns—with particular force. Here there was little concern for creating a classless industrial society: Vastly wealthy men of finance, a new middle class that bought and sold an ever-growing variety of consumer goods, and the impoverished women and men who made those goods lived together in communities that unabashedly recognized the reality of social class.

The richest men were seaport merchants who had survived and prospered during the world wars that ended in 1815. They carried on as importers and exporters, took control of banks and insurance companies, and made great fortunes in urban real estate. Those in Boston constituted an urbane and responsible cluster of old Protestant families known as the **Boston Brahmins**. The elite class of Philadelphia was less unified and perhaps less responsible, and that of New York even

8-6 The Beginnings of the Industrial Revolution

8.13 Lowell Mill Girls Early cotton textile factories in New England employed young farm women as wage laborers, a role customarily filled by men in Europe.

Q *How did the appearance of the Lowell mill girls attempt to counter the stereotype of wage labor as demeaning and potentially corrupting?*

less. These families continued in international commerce, profiting mainly from cotton exports and from a vastly expanded range of imports. They speculated in urban real estate, and they sometimes invested in manufacturing ventures.

Below the old mercantile elite (or, in the case of the new cities of the interior, at the top of society) stood a growing middle class of wholesale and retail merchants, small manufacturers, and an army of lawyers, salesmen, auctioneers, clerks, bookkeepers, and accountants who handled the paperwork for a new market society. At the head of this new middle class were the wholesale merchants of the seaports who bought hardware, crockery, and other commodities from importers (and increasingly from American manufacturers) and then sold them in smaller lots to storekeepers from the interior. The greatest concentration of wholesale firms was on Pearl Street in New York City. Slightly below them were the large processors of farm products, including the meat packers of Cincinnati and the flour millers of Rochester, and large merchants and real estate dealers in the new inland cities.

Another step down were specialized retail merchants who dealt in books, furniture, crockery, and other consumer goods. Alongside the merchants stood master craftsmen who had become manufacturers. With their workers busy in backrooms or in household workshops, they now called themselves shoe dealers and merchant tailors. At the bottom of this new commercial world were hordes of clerks, most of them young men who hoped to rise in the world. Many of them—one study puts the figure at between 25 percent and 38 percent—did move up in society. Both in numbers and in the nature of the work, this white-collar army formed a new class created by the Market Revolution, particularly by the emergence of a huge consumer market in the countryside.

In the 1820s and 1830s, the commercial classes transformed the look and feel of American cities. As retailing and manufacturing became separate activities (even in firms that did both), the merchants, salesmen, and clerks now worked in quiet offices on downtown business streets. The seaport merchants built counting rooms and decorated their warehouses in the "new counting house style." Both in the seaports and the new towns of the interior, impressive brick-and-glass storefronts appeared on the main streets. Perhaps the most telling monuments of the new business society were the handsome retail arcades that began going up in the 1820s. Boston's Quincy Market (1825), a two-story arcade on Philadelphia's Chestnut Street (1827), and Rochester's four-story Reynolds Arcade (1828) provided consumers with comfortable, gracious spaces in which to shop.

8-6d Metropolitan Industrialization

While businessmen were developing a new middle-class ethos, and their families were flocking to the new retail stores to buy emblems of their status, the people who made the consumer goods were growing more numerous and disappearing from view. With the exception of textiles and a few other commodities, few goods were made in mechanized factories before the 1850s. Most of the clothes and shoes, brooms, hats, books, furniture, candy, and other goods available in country stores and city shops were made by hand. City merchants and master craftsmen met the growing demand by hiring more workers. The largest handicrafts—shoemaking, tailoring, and the building trades—were divided into skilled and semiskilled segments and farmed out to subcontractors who could turn a profit only by cutting labor costs. The result was the creation of an urban working class, not only in the big seaports and factory towns but in scores of milling and manufacturing towns throughout the North and West as well.

The rise of New York City's ready-made clothing trade provides an example. In 1815, wealthy Americans wore tailor-made clothing. Everyone else wore clothes sewn by women at home. In the 1820s, the availability of cheap manufactured cloth and an expanding pool of cheap—largely female—labor, along with the creation of the southern and western markets, transformed New York City into the center of a national market in ready-made clothes. The first big market was in "Negro cottons"—graceless shirts, pants, and sack dresses in which southern planters clothed their slaves. Within a few years, New York manufacturers were sending dungarees and hickory shirts to western farmers and supplying inexpensive clothing to urban workers. By the 1830s, many New York tailoring houses, including the storied Brooks Brothers, offered fancier ready-made clothes to the new middle class.

High rents and costly real estate, together with the absence of waterpower, prohibited locating large factories in cities, but the nature of the clothing trade and the availability of cheap labor gave rise to a system of subcontracting that transformed

What They Said

The Lowell Mill Girls

A distinctive feature of the early Industrial Revolution in America was that women, not men, supplied the majority of factory labor. The use of young farm women in the Waltham-Lowell factory system responded to both a demographic challenge—a shortage of young working men because of new opportunities in western areas—and the Jeffersonian ideological bias against wage labor as a demeaning, corrupting influence.

As the following documents suggest, however, the use of women in factories did not silence all critics of wage labor. In 1840, the New England intellectual Orestes Brownson applied old fears about the moral depravity of wages to the Lowell mill girls, who he claimed would be so tarnished by their experience that they would never marry. In fact, after finishing their stint in the textile mills, most Lowell women did marry and many entered public life as reformers, including the author of the other document selection, Lucy Larcom. A successful poet, Larcom wrote a memoir of her childhood in the 1880s that upheld the dignity of the work by her and other Lowell girls against critics like Brownson.

▶ Orestes Brownson

We pass through our manufacturing villages; most of them appear neat and flourishing. The operatives are well dressed, and we are told, well paid. They are said to be healthy, contented, and happy. This is the fair side of the picture; the side exhibited to distinguished visitors. There is a dark side, moral as well as physical. Of the common operatives, few, if any, by their wages, acquire a competence … the great many mass wear out their health, spirits, and morals, without becoming one whit better off than when they commenced labor. The bills of mortality in these factory villages are not striking, we admit, for the poor girls when they can toil no longer go home to die. The average life, working life we mean, of the girls that come to Lowell, for instance, from Maine, New Hampshire, and Vermont, we have been assured, is only about three years. What becomes of them then? Few of them ever marry; fewer still ever return to their native places with reputations unimpaired. "She has worked in a Factory," is almost enough to damn to infamy the most worthy and virtuous girl.

▶ Lucy Larcom

I do not believe that any Lowell mill-girl was ever absurd enough to wish to be known as a "factory-lady," although most of them knew that "factory-girl" did not represent a high type of womanhood in the Old World. But they themselves belonged to the New World, not to the Old; and they were making their own traditions, to hand down to their Republican descendants,—one of which was and is that honest work has no need to assert itself or to humble itself in a nation like ours, but simply to take its place as one of the foundation stones of the Republic.

The young women who worked at Lowell had the advantage of living in a community where character alone commanded respect. They never, at their work or away from it, heard themselves contemptuously spoken of on account of their occupation, except by the ignorant or weak-minded, whose comments they were of course too sensible to heed.

Q What does Brownson seem to most oppose: wage labor, or the notion of working women—or both? How might his critique have been different if only men had worked in early factories?

Q How does Larcom respond to the charge that work, especially by women, violated republican principles?

Q Although Larcom claims that the Lowell mill girls were largely immune from outside criticism, what evidence suggests that Brownson won at least a partial victory in the debate about the probity of working women?

Sources: (top) Orestes A. Brownson, "The Laboring Classes," an Article from the Boston *Quarterly Review* (Boston: Benjamin H. Greene, 1840), p. 11; (bottom) Lucy Larcom, *A New England Girlhood, Outlined from Memory* (Boston: Houghton Mifflin Company, 1889), pp. 201–202.

8.14 Charles Oakford's Hat Store in Philadelphia, circa 1855 Such specialized retail establishments (unlike the craftsmen's shops that preceded them) hid the process of manufacturing from customers' view.

needlework into the first "sweated" trade in America. Merchants kept a few skilled male tailors to take care of the custom trade and to cut cloth into patterned pieces for ready-made clothing. The pieces were sent out, often by way of subcontractors, to needleworkers who sewed them together in a process known as the **putting-out system**, or cottage industry, because the work was done in homes or small workshops. Male tailors continued to do the finishing work on men's suits, but most of the work—on cheap goods destined for the countryside—was done by women who worked for piece rates that ranged from 75 cents to $1.50 per week. Along with clothing, women in garrets and tenements manufactured the items with which the middle class decorated itself and its homes: embroidery, doilies, artificial flowers, fringe, tassels, fancy-bound books, and parasols. All provided work for ill-paid legions of female workers in the putting-out system.

Other trades followed similar patterns. For example, northeastern shoes were made in uniform sizes and sent in barrels all over the country. Like tailoring, shoemaking was divided into skilled operations and time-consuming unskilled tasks. Men performed the skilled work of cutting and shaping the uppers. The drudgery of sewing the pieces together went to low-paid women. In the shops of Lynn, Massachusetts, in the shoemakers' boardinghouses in Rochester and other new manufacturing cities of the interior, and in the cellars and garrets of New York City, skilled shoemakers performed the most difficult work for taskmasters who passed the work along to subcontractors who controlled poorly paid, unskilled workers. Skilled craftsmen could earn as much as $2 per day making custom boots and shoes. Men shaping uppers in boardinghouses earned a little more than half of that. Women binders could work a full week and earn as little as 50 cents. In this as in other trades, wage rates and gendered tasks reflected the old family division of labor, which was based on the assumption that female workers lived with an income-earning husband or father. In fact, increasing numbers of them were young women living alone or older women who had been widowed, divorced, or abandoned—often with small children.

In their shops and counting rooms, the new middle class entertained notions of gentility based on the distinction between manual and nonmanual work. Lowly clerks and wealthy merchants prided themselves on the fact that they worked with their heads and not their hands. They fancied that their entrepreneurial and managerial skills were making the Market Revolution happen, while manual workers simply performed tasks thought up by the middle class. The old distinction between proprietorship and dependence, which had placed master craftsmen and independent tradesmen, along with farm-owning yeomen, among the respectable "middling sort," disappeared. The men and women of an emerging working class struggled to find dignity and a sense of public worth in a society that hid them from view and defined them as "hands."

Conclusion

In the first half of the 19th century, northern society became based in buying and selling. The Northeast—New York City in particular—sloughed off its old colonial status and moved from the periphery to the industrial and financial core of the world market economy. Britain was the first country to make this industrial transition, yet it deemphasized agriculture, drew its populations into cities, and relied on the export of manufactured goods as its principal source of income. The American North, on the other hand, built factories and commercial farms at the same time and as parts of the same process. The market for American manufactures was in the American countryside. (Industrial exports from the United States were insignificant until the end of the 19th century.) The principal market for American food was in American towns and cities, and even on farms whose proprietors were too busy with staple crops to grow the old array of food. The result was a massive commercialization of the northwestern, mid-Atlantic, and New England states and the beginnings of their integration into a unified northern capitalist democracy.

CHAPTER REVIEW

Review

1. What was the nature of the northern agricultural economy and of agricultural society in the years 1790 to 1820?
2. How did eastern opinion of the Northwest and its settlers change between 1790 and 1820?
3. How did improvements in transportation channel commerce within and between regions?
4. How did northern farm families experience the transition into commercial agriculture between 1815 and 1850?
5. How did northern and southern settlers flooding into the Northwest after 1815 view the new market economy differently?
6. Why did America's first factories start in the northern countryside?

Critical Thinking

1. The economic changes associated with the Market Revolution did not take hold until the 1820s. Why? What were the constraints upon growth before then, and how did those constraints help shape earlier economic development?
2. How did America's new market economy impact women? To what extent did the experience of women differ according to their social class? Even as the economic lives of women changed, sometimes dramatically, why did attitudes about them remain mostly unchanged?

Identifications

Review your understanding of the following key terms, people, and events for this chapter (terms in bold in text are included in the Glossary).

Market Revolution, p. 232
competence, p. 232
changing system, p. 233
tenancy, p. 235
journeyman, p. 236
frontier, p. 239
internal improvements, p. 239
transportation revolution, p. 239
National Road, p. 240
Robert Fulton, p. 240
Erie Canal, p. 240
middle class, p. 245
Rhode Island System, p. 248
Waltham-Lowell System, p. 249
Lowell mill girls, p. 249
Boston Brahmins, p. 249
putting-out system, p. 252

Suggested Readings

For the Market Revolution, see **Charles Sellers**, *The Market Revolution: Jacksonian America, 1815–1846* (1994); and **John L. Larson**, *The Market Revolution in America: Liberty, Ambition, and the Eclipse of the Common Good* (2010). **Christopher Clark's** *Social Change in America: From the Revolution through the Civil War* (2006) surveys social development in these years. An essential treatment of social and cultural results of transportation improvement is **Carol Sheriff**, *The Artificial River: The Erie Canal and the Paradox of Progress* (1997). Studies of rural society include **Christopher Clark**, *The Roots of Rural Capitalism: Western Massachusetts, 1780–1860* (1990); **Laurel Thatcher Ulrich**, *A Midwife's Tale: The Life of Martha Ballard, Based on Her Diary, 1785–1812* (1990); **Martin Bruegel**, *Farm, Shop, Landing: The Rise of a Market Society in the Hudson Valley, 1780–1860* (2002); and **Carolyn Merchant**, *Ecological Revolutions: Nature, Gender, and Science in New England* (1989).

David R. Meyer's *The Roots of American Industrialization* (2003) surveys urban-industrial development. Specialized studies include **Thomas Dublin**, *Women at Work: The Transformation of Work and Community in Lowell, Massachusetts, 1810–1860* (1979); **Michael Zakim**, *Ready-Made Democracy: A History of Men's Dress in the American Republic, 1760–1860* (2003); and **Brian P. Luskey**, *On the Make: Clerks and the Quest for Capital in Nineteenth-Century America* (2011). For the emergence of social-economic classes, see **Sean Wilentz**, *Chants Democratic: New York City and the Rise of the American Working Class* (1984); **Christine Stansell**, *City of Women: Sex and Class in New York, 1789–1860* (1986); and **Richard Stott**, *Workers in the Metropolis: Class, Ethnicity and Youth in Antebellum New York City* (1990).

 MINDTAP is a fully online personalized learning experience built upon Cengage Learning content. MindTap® combines student learning tools—readings, multimedia, activities, and assessments—into a singular Learning Path that guides students through the course and helps students develop the critical thinking, analysis, and communication skills that are essential to academic and professional success.

9 The Old South, 1790–1850

9-1 Old Farms: The Southeast
▶ **Learning Objective:** List the principal differences between the slave economies of the Chesapeake and the South Carolina–Georgia lowcountry.

The Chesapeake, 1790–1820
Flirting with Emancipation
The Lowcountry, 1790–1820

9-2 New Farms: The Rise of the Deep South
▶ **Learning Objective:** Describe the ways that the economy and society of the Cotton Belt differed from that of older plantation regions.

Slavery and Capitalism
The Interstate Slave Trade
Cotton and Slave Labor
Mastery as a Way of Life

9-3 The Southern Yeomanry
▶ **Learning Objective:** Assess how southern yeoman farmers differed from planters who presided over much larger plantations.

Yeomen and Planters
Yeoman Neighborhoods

9-4 Slave Culture
▶ **Learning Objective:** Identify the prominent features of the cultural life that slaves made for themselves within the limits of slavery.

Slave Families and the Slave Trade
Slave Theology
Religion and Revolt
Gabriel's Rebellion
Denmark Vesey
Nat Turner

9-5 A Southern Market Revolution?
▶ **Learning Objective:** Determine the nature and limits of the Market Revolution in the South.

9.1 *The Old Plantation* In the late 18th century, the South Carolina slaveholder John Rose most likely painted this scene of slaves dancing and playing musical instruments. The painting offers a rare glimpse into early plantation life and shows that, within the considerable oppression of slavery, individual slaves managed to keep their own cultural ways.

THE SOUTHERN STATES experienced a parallel Market Revolution, but it was transacted on southern terms. From the 1790s onward, international markets and technological innovation encouraged planters to grow cotton. Cotton became the great southern cash crop, and the plantation spread across an expanding Deep South. The planters sent mountains of cotton (along with tobacco from the Upper South, rice from the Georgia–Carolina coast, and sugar from Louisiana) to Britain. They made a lot of money, and they bought a lot of nice things. Other southerners, however, were not as fortunate. Enslaved workers experienced longer hours and tighter discipline than in the past. They lost their families and friends to a soulless interstate slave trade, and they watched their masters' commitment to slavery harden into an unmovable political axiom. In addition, most white farmers moved to the edges of the commercial economy. They continued in the old-style mixed agriculture, and traded relatively little beyond their neighborhoods. In the North, country people became the great consumer market that drove regional economic development. In the South, slaves and most whites bought little, and what they bought was made outside of the region.

The South experienced stupendous economic growth between 1790 and 1850, but most southern investment and entrepreneurial talent went into producing plantation staples for export, an activity that produced wealth for the planters, but that strengthened the South's neocolonial dependence upon Britain and, increasingly, the northeastern United States. It put the South in the peculiar position of helping to fuel the capitalist transformation of the North and Europe while not realizing the full commercial benefits of the economic changes. ■

9-1 Old Farms: The Southeast

Q *What were the principal differences between the slave economies of the Chesapeake and the South Carolina–Georgia lowcountry?*

In 1790, the planters of Virginia and South Carolina were among the richest men in the new republic. But international markets for their tobacco and rice were declining, and they faced uncertain futures.

9-1a The Chesapeake, 1790–1820

In 1790, the future of plantation agriculture in the Chesapeake (the states of Virginia, Maryland, and Delaware) was precarious. The market for tobacco, its principal crop, had been falling since before the Revolution, and it continued to decline after 1790. Tobacco also depleted the soil, and by the late 18th century, tidewater farms and plantations were giving out. As lands west of the Appalachians opened to settlement, white tenants, laborers, and small farmers left the Chesapeake in droves. Many of them moved to Kentucky, Tennessee, or the western reaches of Virginia. Many others found new homes in nonslave states north of the Ohio River. Faced with declining opportunities within the slave societies of the Chesapeake, thousands of the poorer whites voted with their feet.

With tobacco profits falling, many Chesapeake planters were switching to wheat, corn, and livestock. They did it on a large scale. In many parts of the region, the old tobacco lands gave way to grain fields and pastures, and by 1830, Richmond rivaled Rochester, New York, as the nation's leading flour-milling center. It was a sensible move, but it left the Chesapeake with a huge investment in slaves who were less and less necessary. Grazing animals and raising wheat required less labor than tobacco. Enslaved workers planted individual tobacco plants and then pruned, weeded, and picked worms off of them by hand. At harvest time they picked the leaves one at a time, then hung them to cure, packed them, and shipped them off to market. In sharp contrast, grain and livestock took care of themselves through most of the year. Planters with large numbers of slaves had to think up new uses for them. Some divided their land into small plots and rented both the plots and their slaves to white tenant farmers; others, particularly in Maryland, recruited tenants from the growing ranks of free blacks; still others hired out their slaves as artisans and urban laborers.

The increasing diversification of the Chesapeake economy assigned new chores to slave women and men. Wheat cultivation, for example, meant a switch from the hoes used for tobacco to the plow and grain cradle, both of which called for the upper-body strength of adult men. The grain economy also required carts, wagons, mills, and good roads, and thus created a need for greater numbers of slave artisans, who were nearly all men. Many of these artisans were hired out to urban employers and lived as a semifree caste in cities and towns. In the new economy of the Chesapeake, male slaves did the plowing, mowing, sowing, ditching, and carting and performed most of the tasks requiring artisanal skills. All of this work demanded high levels of training and could be performed by someone working either alone or in a small group with little need for supervision.

Slave women were left with the lesser tasks. Contrary to legend, few slave women in the Chesapeake worked as domestic servants in the planters' houses. Some were assigned to such chores as cloth manufacture, sewing, candle molding, and the preparation of salt meat, but most female slaves still did farmwork—hoeing, weeding, spreading manure, cleaning stables—that was monotonous, unskilled, and closely supervised. This new division of labor was clearly evident during the wheat harvest. On George Washington's farm, for example, male slaves, often working beside temporary white laborers, moved in a broad line as they mowed the grain. Following them came a gang of children and women on their hands and knees binding wheat

CHRONOLOGY

1791–1803	Slave revolt in French colony of Saint-Domingue (Haiti)
1792	Kentucky enters the union as the 15th state
1793	Eli Whitney invents the cotton gin
1796	Tennessee enters the union as the 16th state
1800	Gabriel's Rebellion in Virginia
1803	Jefferson purchases the Louisiana Territory from France
1804	Haiti becomes an independent republic
1808	International slave trade ends
1812	Second war with Britain begins
1817	Mississippi enters the union
1819	Alabama enters the union • Adams-Onis Treaty conveys Florida and the Gulf Coast to the United States
1822	Denmark Vesey's slave conspiracy in South Carolina
1831	Nat Turner's rebellion in Virginia

into shocks. Thomas Jefferson, who had been startled to see French women working in the fields, abandoned his concern for female delicacy when his own slaves were involved. At the grain harvest, he instructed his overseers to organize "gangs of half men and half women."

9-1b *Flirting with Emancipation*

Neither new crops nor new employments, however, erased the growing fact that Chesapeake proprietors needed less slave labor than they had in the past—or the parallel fact that their slaves reproduced at a higher rate than almost any other Americans. Nothing, it seemed, could employ the great mass of enslaved people or repay the planters' huge investment in them. In this situation, some Chesapeake planters (who had, after all, fought a revolution in the name of natural rights) began to manumit their slaves. The farmers of Maryland and Delaware in particular set their slaves free. By 1810, 76 percent of Delaware blacks and 23 percent of Maryland blacks were free. (In 1790, these figures had stood at 31 percent and 7 percent, respectively.) Virginia's economic and cultural commitment to the plantation was stronger, but even in the Old Dominion there was a movement to manumit slaves. George Washington stated that he wished "to liberate a certain species of property," and manumitted his slaves by will. Robert Carter, reputedly the largest slaveholder in Virginia, also freed his slaves, as did many others. The free black population of Virginia stood at 3,000 in 1782, when the state passed a law permitting manumission. The number of free blacks rose to 12,766 in 1790, to 20,124 in 1800, and to 30,570 in 1810. These were impressive numbers, but the birthrate of Virginia slaves erased them. Between 1780 and 1810, the slave population of the state rose from 250,000 to 400,000.

Emancipation moved slowly in Virginia for several reasons. First, few Virginia planters could afford to free their slaves without compensation. Second, white Virginians feared the social consequences of black freedom. Thomas Jefferson, for instance, owned 175 slaves when he penned the phrase that "all men are created equal." He lived off their labor, sold them to pay his debts, gave them away as gifts, sold them away from their families as a punishment, and kept one of them, a woman named Sally Hemings, as a mistress and fathered several children by her. Through it all he insisted that slavery was wrong. He could not imagine emancipation, however, without sending freed slaves far from Virginia. A society of free blacks and whites, Jefferson insisted, would end in disaster with "the extermination of the one or the other race."

9-1c *The Lowcountry, 1790–1820*

The other center of plantation slavery in 1790 was lowcountry South Carolina and Georgia. Here the principal crop was rice, which, along with other American foodstuffs, enjoyed a rise in international demand during the European wars between 1793 and 1815. But lowcountry planters faced increasing competition from rice farmers in India, Java, Burma, and Europe. The rice coast—one of the great sources of American wealth in the 18th century—remained profitable, but it was losing relative position to faster-growing regions. The planters of the lowcountry, like those in Virginia, remained wealthy men. Their long-term future, however, was in doubt.

9.2 Blacks Working on the James River, 1798–1799 In the Chesapeake, enslaved and free black watermen provided transportation in a region that had poor roads and good rivers. They performed skilled, often hazardous work, and they lived for days and weeks at a time without white supervision.

Q How did the diversification of the Chesapeake economy make this and other new kinds of work possible for free and enslaved black men?

Thousands of slaves in this region had either run away or been carried off by the British in the Revolution, and planters knew that the African slave trade was scheduled to end in 1808 (the earliest date allowed by the Constitution). Lowcountry planters, unlike their Chesapeake counterparts, could not imagine emancipating their slaves. They rushed to import as many Africans as they could in the time remaining. From 1783 to 1808, between 100,000 and 190,000 captive people were brought directly from Africa to the United States, nearly all of them to Charleston and Savannah. It was the busiest period in the history of the slave trade in North America.

In the plantation counties of coastal South Carolina and Georgia, slaves made up 80 percent of the population, and more than 90 percent in many parishes. Farms and slave labor forces were big, and rice cultivation demanded intensive labor, often performed by workers who stood knee-deep in water. The work and the hot, sticky climate encouraged deadly summer diseases, which kept white owners and overseers out of the fields. Many of the wealthiest planters built homes in Charleston and Savannah and hired others to manage their plantations. Both they and planters who stayed on their farms organized enslaved workers according to the task system, as they had since the early 18th century (see Chapter 4). Each morning the owner or manager assigned a specific task to each slave. When the task was done, the rest of the day belonged to the slave. Slaves who did not finish their task were punished, and when too many slaves finished early, the owners assigned heavier tasks. In the 18th century, each slave had been expected to tend three to four acres of rice each day. In the early 19th century, with the growth of a competitive rice market, the assignment was raised to five acres.

Slaves under the task system won the right to cultivate land as **private fields**, not the little garden plots common in the Chesapeake but farms of up to five acres on which they grew produce and raised livestock for market. There was a lively trade in slave-produced goods, and eventually slaves in the lowcountry not only produced and exchanged property but also passed it on to their children. The owners tolerated such activity because slaves on the task system worked hard, required minimal supervision, produced much of their own food, and made money for their owners. The rice planters in South Carolina and Georgia were among the richest men in the United States.

9-2 New Farms: The Rise of the Deep South

Q *In what ways did the economy and society of the Cotton Belt differ from that of older plantation regions?*

While the old centers of slavery and southern power stagnated or declined, planters discovered a new and promising cash crop. British textile factories had been buying raw cotton since the mid-18th century. Southern planters knew they could sell all of the cotton they could grow. But long-staple cotton, the only variety that could be profitably grown, was a delicate plant that thrived only on the Sea Islands off the coasts of Georgia and South Carolina. The short-staple variety was hardier, but its sticky seeds had to be removed by hand before the cotton could be milled. It took a full day for an adult slave to clean a single pound of short-staple cotton—an expenditure of labor that took the profit out of cotton. In 1790, the United States produced only 3,000 bales of cotton, nearly all of it on the long-staple plantations of the Sea Islands.

Scores of tinkerers tried to devise a mechanical cotton-cleaner, but it was **Eli Whitney**, a Connecticut Yankee who had come south to work as a tutor, who made a model of a **cotton gin** (a southern contraction of "engine") that combed the seeds from the fiber with metal pins fitted into rollers. Working with Whitney's machine, a slave could clean 50 pounds of short-staple cotton in a day. Others quickly developed improved models, and amid a storm of patent disputes and litigation, cotton became the great southern cash crop and contributed to the development of global capitalism.

9-2a *Slavery and Capitalism*

Along with the profitability of short-staple cotton, it was the national government that made possible the southern **Cotton Belt**—a region specializing in cotton production that stretched south from South Carolina into Florida and west to eastern Texas by the mid-19th century (see Map 9.1). Planters did not take their money and slaves into the interior until the government had ended Indian resistance in the War of 1812. Jefferson's Louisiana Purchase of 1803 had secured free navigation of the Mississippi Valley, and the United States gained Florida and the Gulf Coast under the Adams-Onis Treaty of 1819. Given military security and access to markets, the greater South was safe for slavery.

Planters and their slaves had moved into upland South Carolina and Georgia in the 1790s, transforming a sparsely settled farm country into the first great short-staple cotton region. With the end of war in 1815, the plantation rolled west into a Cotton Belt that stretched beyond the Mississippi River. By 1834, the new states of Alabama, Mississippi, and Louisiana grew more than half of a vastly increased U.S. cotton crop. In 1810, the South produced 178,000 bales of ginned cotton, more than 59 times the 3,000 bales it had produced in 1790. With the opening of new cotton lands, production jumped to 334,000 bales in 1820 and to 1,350,000 bales in 1840. In these years, cotton made up from one-half to two-thirds of the value of all U.S. exports. The South produced three-fourths of the world supply of cotton—a commodity that, more than any other, was the raw material of industrialization in Britain and Europe and, increasingly, in the northeastern United States. Cotton, in short, was a very big business.

Without the labor of enslaved African Americans, cotton could not have become the world's most widely traded commodity and fueled the Industrial Revolution. Indeed, though a premodern institution, slavery was integral to the development of American and global

9.3 **Cotton Gin** With the turn of a handle, Eli Whitney's cotton gin eased the removal of seeds from short-staple cotton. But, far from eliminating the need for slave labor, the 1793 invention created a new task for enslaved workers and led to the expansion of cotton plantations in the Deep South.

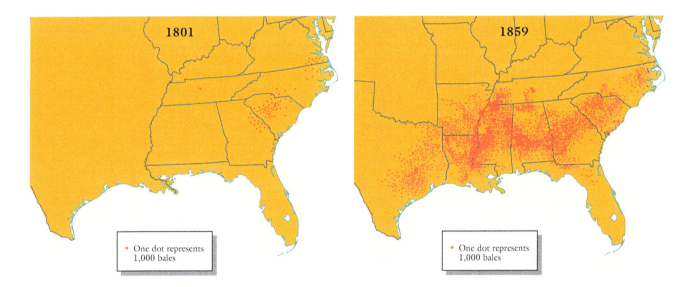

▲ MAP 9.1 **Cotton Production, 1801 and 1859** Short-staple cotton thrived wherever there was fertile soil, heat and humidity, low altitude, and a long growing season. As a result, a great belt of cotton and slavery took shape in the Lower South, from the midlands of South Carolina through eastern Texas.

Q *Aside from climate, what other factors came together in the first half of the 19th century to support such rapid expansion of cotton production in the Lower South?*

Q *What were the economic costs for the South in placing so much emphasis in producing a single commodity?*

9-2 New Farms: The Rise of the Deep South

capitalism. The U.S. was unique among all other industrializing nations in that it both grew and manufactured its own cotton. The work of slaves represented the first step in what emerged as the most dynamic and far-reaching production complex in human history to that point. Creating and maintaining the Cotton Belt involved banks that capitalized on the slave trade, insurance companies that underwrote the trade, riverboat operators who transported cotton and slaves, cotton traders in New Orleans known as "factors," textile mills in Britain and the northern U.S., merchant houses in New York and Liverpool, and slave traders who secured the labor necessary to keep the cotton flowing. In New Orleans alone, there were about twenty separate establishments whose sole business was the buying and selling of enslaved people.

The Deep South also required massive flows of capital to make the Cotton Belt possible. In the 1820s and into the early 1830s, the Second Bank of the United States and its affiliate state branches lent southern borrowers, mostly elite planters, millions of dollars. This money helped to fuel the ongoing cycle of land and slavery expansion: The more land and slave purchases planters could finance, the more cotton they could produce; the more cotton, the more profits and ability to repay debts before starting the cycle anew. Planters could only borrow such high amounts because they owned the biggest pool of collateral in the United States in the form of enslaved African Americans. By the Civil War, America's nearly four million slaves were worth more than $3 billion, or about 20 percent of all the wealth owned by U.S. citizens.

Over time, southerners developed more complex global financial innovations to meet the insatiable demand for land, slaves, and cotton. In 1827, the Louisiana state legislature chartered the Consolidated Association of the Planters of Louisiana (C.A.P.L.). The organization pioneered efforts at using slaves as collateral to raise capital overseas to then reinvest in more slaves and land in the Cotton Belt. The C.A.P.L. did this by selling bonds—backed by slaves—on the financial markets of the Western world. Banks like Baring Brothers of London, which had helped to finance the U.S. purchase of Louisiana in 1803, sold the bonds to investors in London, Hamburg, Amsterdam, Paris, Philadelphia, Boston, New York, and other financial centers. After President Andrew Jackson vetoed the recharter of the Second Bank of the United States in 1832 (see Chapter 11), several southern states filled the lending vacuum by replicating the C.A.P.L. innovations to raise global capital in their own banks. In the mid-1830s, a visitor to former Chickasaw Indian land in northeastern Mississippi observed: "People here are run mad with speculation. They do business in ... a kind of phrenzy. [Gold] is scarce, but credit is plenty."

9-2b The Interstate Slave Trade

With the international slave trade abolished in 1808, the source of slaves for the Cotton Belt was the old seaboard states—states with a huge population of slaves and a shrinking need for them. As early as the 1790s, the Chesapeake states of Virginia, Delaware, and Maryland were net exporters of slaves. Those states sent 40,000 to 50,000 enslaved workers south and west in that decade. The number rose to 120,000 in the 1810s. The slave families and slave communities of the Chesapeake lost 1 in 12 of their members in the 1790s, 1 in 10 between 1800 and 1810, and 1 in 5 between 1810 and 1820. In the 1820s, South Carolina and Kentucky joined the slave-exporting states, and 150,000 slaves left their homes and crossed state lines. In total, around 1 million slaves were moved from the older slave states westward by 1860. The trade in slaves reordered the human geography of the South. In 1790, Virginia and Maryland had held 56 percent of all American slaves. By 1860, they held only 15 percent (see Map 9.2).

Masters or masters' sons carried as many as 30 percent of enslaved migrants to the new lands of the Cotton Belt. These slaves made new plantations and new lives surrounded by some of the people they had known at home. But most were sold and resold as individuals in the **interstate slave trade**. Soon after the Revolution, men known as "Georgia Traders" appeared in the Upper South, buying slaves on speculation and selling them farther south. By 1820, the slave trade had become an organized business with sophisticated financing, sellers who had an accurate knowledge of slave prices in various southern markets, a well-traveled shipping route between Norfolk and New Orleans, and systems of slave pens and safe houses along the roads of the interior. With the exception of the plantation itself, the domestic slave trade was the biggest and most modern business in the South. The centrality of that trade advertised the nature of southern economic development: While northerners exchanged wheat, furniture, books, and shoes with each other, southerners exchanged slaves.

Most slaves moved into the Cotton Belt with other slaves who were strangers, under the temporary ownership of traders who knew them only as merchandise. Those who were transported by ship experienced some of the horrors of the old Middle Passage from Africa: cramped quarters, minimal food, discipline at the hands of nervous white crewmen, and the odd murder or casual rape. Those who walked west from the old plantations along the Cotton Belt experienced their own share of terrors. The journey could take as long as seven weeks, and traders organized it with military precision.

9-2c Cotton and Slave Labor

The cotton plantations operated more efficiently than the old estates on the Chesapeake and in the lowcountry. First, cotton planters exerted a more disciplined and direct control over their enslaved workers. Masters on the seaboard had hired their slaves out, given them time and land with which to grow their own food, and worked them by the task system or under slave overseers—all of which reduced the costs of supervising and providing for slaves. On the cotton frontier, good land and slave labor were too valuable to be worked

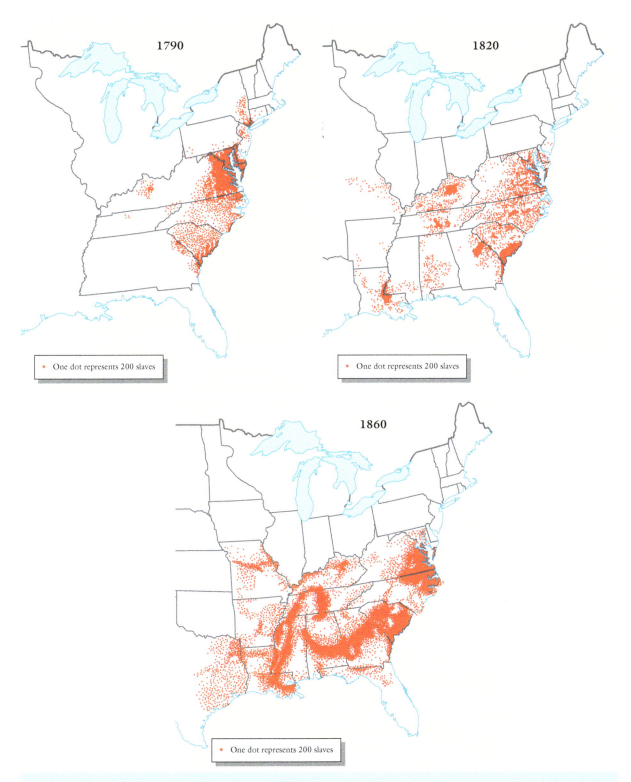

▲ **MAP 9.2 Distribution of Slave Population, 1790, 1820, and 1860** In 1790, slaves were concentrated in the Chesapeake and in the South Carolina and Georgia low country. Over the next 70 years, Chesapeake planters put thousands of slaves into the interstate trade, which sold them into the Cotton Belt stretching from the interior of the Carolinas to eastern Texas.

Q *How did economic and demographic conditions in the Chesapeake make possible the interstate slave trade?*

Q *How does the interstate slave trade challenge popular conceptions of western expansion as a march of democracy and liberty?*

9-2 New Farms: The Rise of the Deep South

9.4 Price, Birch & Co., Alexandria, Virginia From this location, marked openly with the sign "Dealers in Slaves," thousands of slaves were kept in squalid pens before being auctioned or transported, most often to New Orleans, where they were sold within the interstate slave trade.

in casual ways, and new farms had to become profitable in a short time. Enslaved men and women who had grown up with the relatively loose work routines of the lowcountry and the Chesapeake now performed the backbreaking labor of turning forests into farms. (They had to "whittle a plantation right out of the woods," recalled one slave.) Slaves worked in gangs, usually under white owners or overseers. Clearing trees, rolling logs, pulling stumps, clearing and burning brush, and building cabins, fences, and outbuildings was hard labor. The planters preferred crews of young men for these tasks, but such slaves were expensive, and everyone was put to work. A teenage boy sold from the Chesapeake to Mississippi saw women clearing brush from new land, and remarked that "such work was not done by women slaves in Virginia." Another slave recalled that her mother drove a two-horse plow "when she warn't cleanin' new ground or diggin' ditches." The labor of making new farms lasted from dawn to dusk, and enslaved men and women worked under the eyes of owners who knew that they must turn the forest into cash-producing farms or go broke.

Once established, these southern plantations were among the most intensely commercialized farms in the world. Many of them grew nothing but cotton, buying food from their neighbors or from merchants who sold corn meal and salt pork in bulk. Others grew supplementary crops and produced their own food. But nearly all of the plantation owners, from the proudest grandee to the ambitious farmer with a few slaves, organized labor in ways that maximized production and reinforced the dominance of the white men who owned the farms.

Slaves from the Chesapeake and the rice coast experienced cotton cultivation as a difficult step down. Cotton required a long growing season and a lot of attention, but it did not demand much skill. Early in the spring, the land was cleared and ploughed, and gangs of slaves walked the furrows dropping seeds. During the growing season, black laborers constantly thinned the plants and cleared the fields of weeds, "chopping" the fields with hoes in the hot, humid Deep South summer. The cotton ripened unevenly. In a harvest season that could last long past Christmas, pickers swept through the fields selecting only the ripe bolls, then repeated the task until the full crop was harvested. Slaves in the diversifying Chesapeake had made barrels and crates, boats, wagons, barns, and storage sheds; slaves on the rice coast farther south had built complex systems of dikes and levees and had mastered the science of moving and controlling large amounts of water. In the Cotton Belt, they gave up those skills and went to work with axes, hoes, and their hands. (Tobacco and sugar, the other western plantation crops, were no less labor intensive.)

The work was relentless. Planters in the East had found it economical to allow slaves to work at varied tasks, at irregular times, or under the tasking system. They gave slaves only part of their food (often cornmeal and nothing else), then provided time and land with which slaves grew their own vegetables and raised chickens and pigs. Planters on the cotton frontier did away with all that. Only a few Cotton Belt planters retained the task system, and these were looked upon as eccentrics by their neighbors, who worked their slaves in gangs from dawn to dusk six days a week. Cotton land was too valuable to permit large slave gardens. It made more sense to keep the slaves constantly at cotton cultivation and to supply them with all of their food. It was a more efficient and productive way of growing cotton. It was also a way of reducing the slaves' customary privileges within

9.5 Going to Tennessee The Pennsylvanian Lewis Miller met with this group of slaves near Staunton, Virginia, in 1853. They were being sent from their old farms in Virginia to the slave markets of Tennessee and from there to the cotton fields of the newer southern states. In the years after 1820, hundreds of thousands of Upper South slaves suffered this migration.

Q *In what ways did the interstate slave trade resemble the Middle Passage? How were the two forced migrations different?*

slavery, and of enforcing the master's role as the giver and taker of all things. Even slaves who grew their own food did so in white-supervised fields and not in family plots. In order to create "a perfect dependence," an Alabama planter insisted that "my Negroes have no time whatever."

The masters set harsher working conditions and longer hours than slaves had known in their old homes. Slaves could not hope to reinstitute the task system, the family gardens and little farms, the varied tasks, or the uneven hours of labor that they had known on the coast. Yet, slaves were able to force some concessions from their masters. Gardens reappeared in many new slave quarters, and some slaves found that they could hold masters to agreed-upon standards of time and work. Masters who demanded extra hours of labor on Sunday found the work particularly slow going. In the 1840s, a Mississippi planter noted that slaves had adapted to the long hours, close supervision, and pace of work under the gang system, but would perform the new customary workload and nothing more: "All of them know what their duty is upon a plantation, and that they are generally willing to do, and nothing more." When asked to work harder or longer "they will not submit to it, but become turbulent and impatient of control, and all the whips in Christendom cannot drive them to perform more than they think they ought to do, or have been in the long habit of doing."

On the whole, the exploitation of slave labor after 1820 became more rigorous, with a humane veneer. Planters imposed a new and more total control over their slaves, but they clothed it within a larger attempt to make North American slavery paternalistic and humane, and to portray themselves as gentlemen and not as heartless slave drivers. Food and clothing seem to have improved, and individual cabins for slave families became standard. State laws often forbade the more brutal forms of discipline, and they uniformly demanded that slaves be given Sunday off.

By some measures, material standards rose. Slaves suffered greater infant mortality than whites, but those who survived infancy lived out "normal" life spans. Brazil, Cuba, and other slave societies had to import Africans to make up for the deaths of slaves, but the slave population of the southern states increased threefold—from 657,000 to 1,981,000—between 1790 and 1830. With the importation of new Africans banned after 1808 (and with runaways outnumbering new Africans who were smuggled into the country), the increase was due entirely to the fact that—alone among the slave societies of the Western Hemisphere—the American slave population was healthy enough to reproduce itself.

Material conditions on the plantations sprang from both planter self-interest and an attempt to exert a kindly, paternal control over slaves, whom planters often called "our people" or "our family, black and white." But humane treatment came at a high price. At the same time that they granted slaves protection from the worst kinds of brutality, Cotton Belt states enacted slave codes that defined slaves as persons without rights. The Louisiana code of 1824, for instance, stated that "[The slave] is incapable of making any kind of contract... . They can transmit nothing by succession... . The slave is incapable of exercising any public office, or private trust... . He cannot be a party in any civil action... . Slaves cannot marry without the consent of their masters, and their marriages do not produce any of the civil effects which result from such contract." It was the exact opposite of the rights enjoyed by the white men who owned the plantations, controlled the slaves, and wrote the laws.

9-2d Mastery as a Way of Life

Plantation masters, both the old southeastern nabobs and the cotton planters of newer regions, were the acknowledged economic, social, cultural, and political elite of the South. Their authority rested on economic power and on their connections—often family relationships—with each other. But they dressed their power in gentility and an aura of mastery, a visible "right to rule" that few others, North or South, could match. That power and authority were tied intimately to the ownership of slaves. When assessing a planter's standing, contemporaries seldom added up his acreage or his money. Instead, they counted slaves. In the most common calculation, the ownership of 20 slaves separated planters from yeoman farmers.

It was a good enough measure, for the planter class made itself out of slaves. Slave labor bought the carpets, chandeliers, fine clothes, English chivalric novels, and racehorses with which planters displayed their social mastery. Just as important, slaves enabled planters and their ladies to distinguish themselves as gentlefolk who did not work. An observer of one plantation mistress noted that "She has a faithful nurse (Negro) to whose care she abandons her babes entirely, only when she has a fancy to caress them does she see them. Eight children and cannot lay to their charge the loss of a single night's rest." The ownership of slaves transformed a harried housewife into a lady.

Southern farmers without slaves tended to sire very large families and to keep their children in the fields. The women worked outdoors as well. Southerners who owned slaves had fewer children, sent them to school, and moved their wives indoors. The skin of farmwomen was weathered, cracked, and darkened by the sun; plantation mistresses were less exhausted, and their skin was smoother and literally whiter.

The opposite of gentility was the South Carolina farmer who, according to a neighbor, "used to work [his daughters] in the fields like Negroes." According to northern visitors, this association of labor with slavery encouraged laziness among southern whites and robbed work of the dignity it enjoyed in other parts of the country. Most southern white yeoman farmers would have disagreed, but the association of black labor, white leisure, and white gentility was central to the plantation regime.

The exercise of mastery by plantation owners extended to patriarchal control over their own families. Among southern white men, wealth generally counted for less than did maintaining one's personal and family honor and thus winning membership in the democracy of honorable males. Children learned early that their first duty was to their family's reputation. As John Horry Dent, an Alabama slaveholder and bad amateur poet, put it:

> Honor and shame from all conditions rise;
> Act well your part and there the honor lies.

In particular, women and girls who misbehaved—with transgressions ranging from simple gossip to poor housekeeping to adultery—damaged not only their own reputations but also the honor of the fathers or husbands who could not control them. Such a charge could mean social death in a rural community made up of patriarchal households and watchful neighbors. Mastery and honor came to define the South's identity.

9-3 The Southern Yeomanry

Q *How did southern yeoman farmers differ from planters who presided over much larger plantations?*

Some southern boosters advertised cotton as a "democratic" crop that could be cultivated at a profit by almost any southern farmer, but that is not how it worked. Cotton, like other

9.6 Olivier Plantation in 1861
The artist Marie Adrien Persac portrayed this southern Louisiana plantation as a site of white gentility, not of slavery and sugar production. The smoking chimneys of the processing plant at right tell us that work is going on. But the fields, the slave quarters, and the slaves themselves are hidden from view.

Q *What role did the ideology of southern gentility, as portrayed in this image, play in perpetuating slavery?*

Interpreting the Visual Past — A View of Slavery as Benevolent

Here is a representation of plantation society by a northern apologist for slavery, Edward Williams Clay, in 1841. The white family is genteel: a well-dressed, relaxed, and subdued father and mother, two well-dressed and well-behaved children, and a well-bred dog. In the text to the right, the master/father assures us that he has inherited his slaves (he does not buy or sell them) and that he is devoting his fortune to their welfare and happiness.

For their part, the slaves are content. They live in whitewashed houses, they are nicely dressed, they play and dance, and healthy, contented old folks look on with pleasure. The wording to the left voices the slaves' devotion to their master: "God Bless you massa! you feed and clothe us. When we are sick you nurse us, and when too old to work, you provide for us!"

Q *How is slavery portrayed in this picture? What is missing? Aside from the text, how do the postures and facial expressions of whites and blacks advance a particular interpretation of slavery?*

Q *The print advances a view of slavery more common to the South than to the North. Are you surprised that a northern artist completed the print and that it was first printed in New York? What does this tell us about northern society by the early 1840s and how some Americans, in the North and South, understood slavery?*

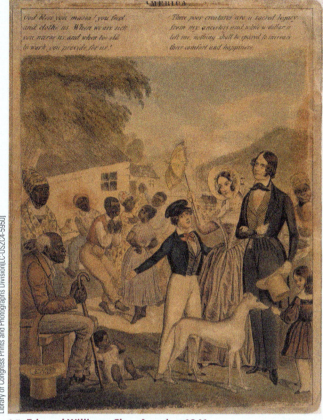

9.7 **Edward Williams Clay, *America*, 1841.**

plantation crops, rewarded economies of scale: Planters with big farms and many slaves operated more efficiently and more profitably than farmers with fewer resources. The wealthier planter families bought up good cotton land with ready access to markets. They also bought up the majority of slaves. Only 30 percent to 35 percent of southern white families owned at least one slave in 1830, and that percentage dropped as time passed. On the eve of the Civil War, only one white family in four owned a slave. Among the minority of southerners who were slave owners, half owned fewer than five, and less than 5 percent owned 20 or more slaves—the roughly agreed-upon number that separated planters from yeoman farmers. Cotton, it turned out, was not democratic. Among southern whites it produced not only an unequal distribution of wealth but a dual economy: plantations at the commercial center and a marginally commercial yeomanry on the fringes.

9-3a Yeomen and Planters

As land prices and local taxes rose in the plantation counties, many of the poorer whites moved out. Those who stayed subsisted on poor, hilly land far from navigable rivers. They tended to be commercial farmers, growing a few bales of cotton with family labor and perhaps a slave or two. Many of them were poor relatives of prosperous plantation owners. They voted the great planters into office and used their cotton gins and tapped into their marketing networks. Some of them worked as overseers for their wealthy neighbors, sold them food, and served on local slave patrols. Economic disparities between planters and farmers in the plantation belt continued to widen, but the farmers remained tied to the cotton economy and its economic and social imperatives.

Most yeomen, however, lived away from the plantations in neighborhoods with few slaves and limited commercial activities. Large numbers of them moved into nonslave territory north of the Ohio River, but most stayed in the South: in the upcountry and the eastern slopes of the Appalachians from the Chesapeake through Georgia, the western slopes of the mountains in Kentucky and Tennessee, the pine-covered hill country of northern Mississippi and Alabama, and in swampy, hilly, heavily wooded lands throughout the southern states. All of these areas were unsuitable for plantation crops. Here the farmers built a yeoman society that retained many of the characteristics of the 18th-century countryside, North and South. But while northern farmers commercialized in the 19th century, their southern cousins continued in a

9.8 A Map of the Burial Ground in Farmville, Virginia In 1840, a lawyer sketched the map of a graveyard in slaveholding country near the Appomattox River to make a point in a court case. It was a map of the living as well: rich whites at the top, poor whites in the middle, blacks at the bottom, yet all occupying the same ground.

parts of the upcountry South preferred raising livestock to growing cotton or tobacco. They planted cornfields and let their pigs run loose in the woods and on unfenced private land. In late summer and fall, they rounded up the animals and sold them to drovers who herded them cross-country and sold them to flatland merchants and planters. Thus, these hill-country yeomen lived off a market with which they had little firsthand experience. It was a way of life that sustained some of the most fiercely independent neighborhoods in the country.

A larger group of southern yeomen practiced mixed farming for household subsistence and neighborhood exchange, with the surplus sent to market. Most of them owned their own land. The settlement of new lands in the old backcountry and the southwestern states reversed the 18th-century drift toward white tenancy. Few of these farmers kept slaves. In the counties of upland Georgia, for instance, between seven and nine out of 10 households were without slaves. These farmers practiced a mixed agriculture that was complicated by the nature of southern cash crops. Northern yeomen before 1815 had grown grain and livestock with which they fed their families and traded with neighbors. Whatever was left over, they sent to market. But cotton, like tobacco and other southern cash crops, was not a food. It was useful only as a market crop. Most middling and poor southern farmers played it safe: They put their improved land into corn and sweet potatoes, and set pigs and cattle loose to browse the remaining land. The more substantial and ambitious of them cultivated a few acres of cotton. They grew more cotton as transportation made markets more accessible, but few southern yeomen became wholly dependent on the market. With the income from a few bales of cotton, they could pay their debts and taxes and buy coffee, tea, sugar, tobacco, cloth, and shoes. But they continued to enter and leave the market at will, and to retain the ability to subsist within their neighborhoods. In the yeoman neighborhoods of the southern states, the economic and social practices of the 18th century were alive and well.

9-3b Yeoman Neighborhoods

The way of life in most southern farm neighborhoods discouraged businesslike farming and individual ambition. Because few farms were self-sufficient, farmers routinely traded labor and goods with each other. In the plantation counties, such cooperation tended to reinforce the power of planters, who put some of their resources at the disposal of their poorer neighbors. In the upcountry, cooperation reinforced neighborliness. As one upland Georgian remarked, "Borrowing ... was neighboring." Debts contracted within the network of kin and neighbors were generally paid in kind or in labor, and creditors often allowed their neighbors' debts to go unpaid for years.

Among southern neighborly restraints on entrepreneurialism, none was more distinctive than the region's attitude toward fences. Northerners never tired of

household- and neighborhood-centered agriculture until the Civil War and beyond.

Many southern farmers stayed outside the market almost entirely. The mountaineers of the southern Appalachians sent a trickle of livestock and timber out of their neighborhoods, but the mountains remained largely outside the market until the coming of big-business coal mines in the late 19th century. Moreover, farmers in large comparing their neatly fenced farms with the dilapidated or absent fences of the South. In the capitalist North, well-maintained fences were a sign of ambitious, hardworking farmers. The poorly maintained fences of the South, they said, were a sign of laziness. Actually, the scarcity of fences in most southern neighborhoods was the result of local custom and state law. Georgia, for instance, required farmers to fence their planted fields but not the rest of their land. In country neighborhoods where families fished and hunted for food, and where livestock roamed freely, fences conflicted with a local economy that required neighborhood use of privately owned land. In this sense, the northerners were right: The absence of fences in the South reflected neighborhood constraints on the private use of private property, and thus on individual acquisitiveness and ambition. Such constraints, however, were necessary to the subsistence of families and neighborhoods as they were organized in the upland South.

Southern farmers marketed their cotton and food surpluses at country stores, and again the patterns of the 18th and early 19th centuries persisted. Northern stores, particularly in the more commercializing regions, were stocking their shelves with a wider variety of imported and domestic goods to serve farm families that no longer produced for themselves and that had money to spend. Southern yeomen, on the other hand, bought very little. A relatively prosperous backwoods farmer in South Carolina recalled that "My farm gave me and my whole family a good living on the produce of it, and left me, one year after another, one hundred and fifty silver dollars, *for I never spent more than ten dollars a year,* which was for salt, nails and the like. Nothing to wear, eat or drink was purchased, as my farm provided all."

Families such as these continued to live without carpets or curtains, to eat homegrown food from wooden or pewter plates, and to wear everyday cloth spun and woven by the women of the family, although many who could afford it wore clothing fashioned from machine-made cloth on Sunday. And like the rest of their transactions, yeomen seldom bought items or settled debts in cash. The store of Leach Carrigan and Samuel Carrigan in South Carolina, for instance, traded 85 percent of its merchandise for cotton. While the northern countryside and the lowland plantation districts functioned in businesslike ways, the old barter economy—and the forms of family independence and neighborly cooperation on which it rested—persisted in the southern upcountry.

Unlike the plantations, the farm neighborhoods of the South were places in which white people worked. Most farmers relied solely on family labor. They sired many children and put them to work at an early age. Farmwives often labored in the fields, particularly at peak times. Even those who were spared from fieldwork took up heavy burdens. A southern yeoman remembered that his mother worked "in the house sutch as cooking carding spinning and weaving and washing. Thare [were] 14 in the family," and "she did not have any servant to help her." Poor whites occupied a social space in the South at odds with the planter class above them, yet enjoyed rights and privileges unknown to the slaves below them.

9-4 Slave Culture

 What were prominent features of the cultural life that slaves made for themselves within the limits of slavery?

In 1790, slaves in the Chesapeake had lived for generations in the same neighborhoods—old communities filled with kinfolk, ancestral graveyards, family gardens, and familiarity with each other and with local whites. They had made a distinctively African American way of life within the boundaries of slavery. Slaves along the South Carolina–Georgia rice coast, living and working in large groups under minimal white supervision, had made their own African American ways. In the early decades of the 19th century, hundreds of thousands of these people were torn from their communities and sold into the cotton states. It began a period of cultural destruction and reconstruction equaled only by the process of enslavement itself. We can view that process intimately by looking into the most vital of slave institutions: the slave family and slave religion.

9-4a *Slave Families and the Slave Trade*

In law, in the census, and in the minds of planters, slaves were members of a plantation household over which the owner exercised absolute authority as owner, paternal protector, and lawgiver. Yet, both slaveholders and slaves knew that slaves could not be treated like farm animals or little children. Wise masters learned that the success of a plantation depended less on terror and draconian discipline (though whippings—and worse—were common) than on the accommodations by which slaves traded labor and obedience for privileges and some measure of autonomy within the bonds of slavery. These privileges included holidays, garden plots, friendships and social gatherings both on and off the plantation, hunting and fishing rights, the right to trade slave-made goods, and—most vitally—the right to make their own families. These hard-won privileges provided some of the ground on which slaves in the old plantation states had made their own lives within slavery. The domestic slave trade and movement onto the cotton frontier cut that ground from beneath them. Slaves learned painfully that they were not members of families or communities—either the masters' or their own. They were property, and they could be bought and sold.

The most precious privilege on Chesapeake plantations had been the right to live in families. As early as the revolutionary era, most Chesapeake slaves lived in units consisting of a mother, a father, and their small children. On Charles Carroll's Maryland farms in 1773, for example, 325 of the 400 slaves lived in such families. At Thomas Jefferson's Monticello, most slave marriages were for life, and small children almost always lived with both parents. The most common exceptions were fathers who had married away from their own plantations and who visited "broad wives" and children during their off hours. Owners encouraged stable marriages because they made farms more peaceful and productive and because they flattered the owners' own religious and paternalistic sensibilities. For their part, slaves demanded families as part of the price of their labor.

Yet, slave families had always been vulnerable. Many slaveholders coerced sex from female slaves. Some kept slaves as mistresses. The planters tended, however, to keep these liaisons within bounds. While the slave community seldom punished sex before marriage, it took adultery seriously. Slaveholders knew that violations of married slave women could be enormously disruptive and strongly discouraged them. Slave sales also threatened families, but most sales before 1800 or so took place within neighborhoods, damaging slave families and communities without destroying them. The most serious threat was the death or bankruptcy of the slaveholder, which led to the division of property among heirs. Yet even these events, in comparison to what came later, tended to keep slaves in the same extended neighborhood.

This all changed with the growth of the Cotton Belt and the interstate slave trade. Masters in the seaboard states claimed (often truthfully) that they tried to keep slave families together and that they sold slaves to traders only out of dire necessity or as a means of getting rid of troublesome individuals. The latter category could be used as a threat. One slave remembered: "Slaves usually got scared when it became clear that Negro-Trader [John] White was in the community. The owners used White's name as a threat to scare the slaves when they had violated some rule." "If a man did anything out of the way," recalled another slave, "he was in more danger of being sold than being whipped."

Chesapeake planters and slaves knew, however, that the slave trade was more than a means of settling debts or punishing individuals. It had become an important source of income. The children of slaves in the exporting states could expect to be sold into long-distance markets when they came of age. The systematic selling of teenaged and young adult slaves, who commanded the highest prices, became a standard way in which Chesapeake gentlemen maintained their status. John Randolph of Roanoke, one of the great planter-politicians of Virginia, routinely translated younger members of his "plantation family" into cash. In 1823, he traveled to New York to see the great match race between the northern horse American Eclipse and the southern horse Henry. In a moment of pride and exuberance, he shouted from the grandstand that he would bet "a year's crop of negroes" on the southern champion.

Professional slave traders made no effort to hide their willingness to break slave families. Neither did the frontier planters who bought slaves from the older states. One planter insisted that "it is better to buy *none in families,* but *to select only choice, first rate, young hands from 14 to 25 years of age* (buying no children or aged negroes)." Seaboard planters, trying to convince themselves and anyone who would listen that they were responsible paternalists, made a sharp division between the plantation "family" and the well-known horrors of the domestic slave trade, but the slaves knew better. A Virginia slave woman had this to say of the planter who had sold her daughters: "he was a mean dirty slave trader."

Separated from their kinfolk and communities, Cotton Belt slaves began the old process of negotiation with their masters, and they reconstructed families. Cotton planters preferred young men for the labor of clearing the land, but they soon began importing nearly equal numbers of women, encouraging marriage, and providing cabins for slave families. Families made for greater peace and quiet on the plantations,

9.9 Five Generations of a Slave Family on a South Carolina Sea Island Plantation, 1862 Complex family ties such as those of the family shown here were among the most hard-won and vulnerable cultural accomplishments of enslaved blacks.

Q *Nearly all successful human societies place some value on the family unit defined broadly, but what particular conditions and threats made enslaved African Americans particularly cherish families?*

and they were a good long-term investment in the production of new slaves. The slaves grasped the opportunity. From the 1820s, 51 percent of rural Louisiana slaves lived in families composed of two parents and their children. That figure was smaller than it had been on the old farms, but in view of what the slaves had been through, it was surprisingly large.

Slaveholders who encouraged slave marriages—perhaps even solemnizing them with a religious ceremony—knew that marriage implied a form of self-ownership that conflicted with the slaves' status as property. Some conducted ceremonies in which couples "married" by jumping over a broomstick. Others had the preacher omit the phrases "let no man put asunder" and "till death do you part" from the ceremony. Slaves knew that such ceremonies had no legal force. A Virginia slave remarked, "We slaves knowed that them words wasn't bindin'. Don't mean nothin' lessen you say, 'What God has jined, caint no man pull asunder.' But dey never would say dat. Jus' say 'Now you married.'" A South Carolina slave preacher routinely ended the ceremony with "Till death or buckra [whites] part you."

Slaves built their sense of family and kinship around such uncertainties. Because separation from father or mother was common, children spread their affection among adult relatives, treating grandparents, aunts, and uncles almost as though they were parents. In fact, slaves often referred to all of their adult relatives as "parents." They also called nonrelatives "brother," "sister," "aunt," and "uncle," thus extending a sense of kinship to the slave community at large. Slaves chose as surnames for themselves the names of former owners, Anglicized versions of African names, or names that simply sounded good. They rarely chose the name of their current owner. Families tended to use the same given names over and over, naming boys after their father or grandfather, perhaps to preserve the memory of fathers who might be taken away. They seldom named girls after their mothers, however. Unlike southern whites, slaves never married a first cousin, even though many members of their community were close relatives. Slaves practiced these customs consistently, often without the knowledge of slaveholders.

9-4b Slave Theology

Until the mid-18th century, neither enslaved Africans nor their masters showed much interest in Christianizing slaves. That changed with the rise of evangelical Christianity in the South (see Chapter 10). Blacks participated in the revivals of the southern Great Awakening, and the number of Christian slaves increased steadily in the second half of the 18th century. In the slave communities of the Upper South, as well as the burgeoning free and semifree black populations in the towns, the evangelical revivals of the late 18th and early 19th centuries appealed powerfully to African Americans, who sensed that the bonds of slavery were loosening. By 1820, most blacks in the Chesapeake considered themselves Christians. They would take their religion with them when they went farther south.

Between the Revolution and 1820, Chesapeake slaves embraced Christianity and began to turn it into a religion of their own. Slaves attended camp meetings, listened to **itinerant preachers** (those who usually lacked their own parish and therefore traveled from place to place), and joined the Baptist and Methodist congregations of the southern revival. The revivalists, in turn, welcomed slaves and free blacks to their meetings and sometimes recruited them as preachers. Evangelical preaching, singing, and spiritual exercises were much more attractive than the cold, high-toned lectures of the Anglicans. So were the humility and suffering of evangelical whites, most of whom were poor men and outsiders. Finally, the slaves gloried in the evangelicals' assault on the slaveholders' culture and in the antislavery sentiments of many white evangelicals. The result was a huge increase in the number of African American Christians. Methodists, who counted converts more carefully than some others, claimed 20,000 black members in 1800—one in three American Methodists.

The integrated congregations, however, did not last. There were exceptions, but most congregations were in fact internally segregated, with blacks sitting in the back of the church or upstairs in the gallery, and with only whites serving in positions of authority. Blacks, with both positive and negative encouragement from whites, organized independent churches in Baltimore, Wilmington, Richmond, Norfolk, and the scattered villages that had risen to serve the Chesapeake's new mixed economy. Even Charleston boasted an independent Methodist conference made up of 4,000 slaves and free blacks in 1815. By 1820, roughly 700 independent black churches operated in the United States. There had been none at all 30 years earlier. And on the plantations, slaves met informally—sometimes with the masters' permission, sometimes without it—to preach and pray.

Slaves understood and used the message of Christianity in their own ways. The biblical notion that slavery could be punishment for sin and the white southern notion that God intended blacks to be slaves never took root among enslaved Christians. Hannah Scott, a slave in Arkansas, remarked on what she heard a white preacher say: "But all he say is 'bedience to de white folks, and we hears 'nough of dat without him telling us." One slave asked a white preacher, "Is us slaves gonna be free in heaven?" The preacher had no answer. As one maid boldly told her mistress, "God never made us to be slaves for white people."

Another way in which slave religion differed from what was preached to them by whites was in the practice of conjuring, folk magic, root medicine, and other occult knowledge, most of it passed down from West Africa. Such practices provided help in areas in which Christianity was useless. They could reputedly cure illnesses, make people fall in love, ensure a good day's fishing, or bring harm to one's enemies. Sometimes African magic was in competition with plantation Christianity. Just as often, however, slaves combined the two. For instance, slaves sometimes determined the guilt or innocence of a person accused of stealing by hanging a Bible by a thread, then watching the way it turned. The form was West African; the Bible was not.

What They Said

The Treatment of Slave Families

The separation of families constituted one of the principal tragedies of slavery. In 1852, a slave mother, Maria Perkins, was caught up in the domestic slave trade. She wrote from Charlottesville, Virginia, to her husband about the sale of their son, Albert. At the same time, George Fitzhugh, also in Virginia, was a leading defender of slavery. In his view, the institution protected slaves, especially compared to the condition of northern workers, by adopting them as members of a slave master's own family.

▶ Maria Perkins

Charlottesville, Oct 8th, 1852

Dear Husband I write you a letter to let you know of my distress my master has sold albert to a trader on Monday court day and myself and other child is for sale also and I want you to let [me] hear from you very soon before next cort if you can I don't know when I don't want you to wait till Christmas I want you to tell dr Hamelton and your master if either will buy me they can attend to it know and then I can go afterwards. I don't want a trader to get me they asked me if I had got any person to buy me and I told them no they took me to the court houste too they never put me up a man buy the name of brady bought albert and is gone I don't know where they say he lives in Scottesville my things is in several places some is in staunton and if I should be sold I don't know what will become of them I don't expect to meet with the luck to get that way till I am quite heartsick nothing more I am and ever will be your kind wife Maria Perkins.

▶ George Fitzhugh

The slaves are all well fed, well clad, have plenty of fuel, and are happy. They have no dread of the future–no fear of want. A state of dependence is the only condition in which reciprocal affection can exist among human beings–the only situation in which the war of competition ceases, and peace, amity and good will arise. A state of independence always begets more or less of jealous rivalry and hostility. A man loves his children because they are weak, helpless and dependent; he loves his wife for similar reasons. When his children grow up and assert their independence, he is apt to transfer his affection to his grand-children. He ceases to love his wife when she becomes masculine or rebellious; but slaves are always dependent, never the rivals of their master. Hence, though men are often found at variance with wife or children, we never saw one who did not like his slaves, and rarely a slave who was not devoted to his master.

Q *Slaves uniformly feared the unpredictability and destructiveness of the domestic slave trade. Within Perkins's brief letter, how many social and personal injuries can you count?*

Q *How does the experience of the Perkins family counter the benign depiction of slavery presented by Fitzhugh?*

Q *Given Fitzhugh's patriarchal definition of family, which depended on the unequal status of women and children, is it possible that he and other slave masters truly viewed slaves as members of their families? Put another way, were slaves simply at the bottom of a larger patriarchal structure on plantations?*

Sources: (top) From a letter written in 1852 by Maria Perkins, a slave mother, reproduced in Ulrich B. Phillips, *Life and Labor in the Old South* (Boston: Little, Brown, and Company, 1929), p. 212; (bottom) From George Fitzhugh, *Sociology for the South, or the Failure of Free Society* (Richmond: A. Morris, 1854), pp. 246–247.

While Christianity could not cure sick babies or identify thieves, it gave slaves something more important: a sense that they were a historical people with a role to play in God's cosmic drama. In slave Christianity, Moses the liberator (and not the slaveholders' Abraham) stood beside Jesus. The slaves' appropriation of the book of Exodus denied the smug assumption of the whites that they were God's chosen people who had escaped the bondage of despotic Europe to enter the promised land of America. To the slaves, America was Egypt, they were the chosen people, and the slaveholders were Pharaoh. Thomas Wentworth Higginson, a Boston abolitionist who went south during the Civil War to lead a Union regiment of freed South Carolina slaves, wrote that his men knew the Old Testament books of Moses and the New Testament book of Revelation. "All that lies between," he said, "even the life of Jesus, they hardly cared to read or to hear." He found their minds "a vast bewildered chaos of Jewish history and biography; and most of the events of the past, down to the period of the American Revolution, they instinctively attribute to Moses."

The slaves' religious songs, which became known as spirituals, told of God's people, their travails, and their ultimate deliverance. In songs and sermons, the figures

9.10 Slave Cabins on a Plantation in Northern Florida Consisting of one room and set exactly 12 feet apart, this was minimal housing indeed. Yet, it provided slaves with a place to live in families and the rudimentary sense of proprietorship exercised by these black workers sitting in front of their "own" houses.

9.11 A Secret Slave Prayer Meeting Many masters encouraged or overlooked the religious life that slaves made for themselves. But others opposed it. Their slaves often met in secret, praying and singing in a whisper, far enough from whites so that their meetings could not be heard.

Q *For slaveholders, what were the potential risks of allowing slaves to pursue their own spiritual and religious practices?*

of Jesus and Moses were often blurred, and it was not always clear whether deliverance—accompanied by divine retribution—would take place in this world or the next. But deliverance always meant an end to black slavery, often with a reversal of relations between slaves and masters. "The idea of a revolution in the conditions of the whites and blacks," said the escaped slave Charles Ball, "is the cornerstone of the religion of the latter."

retribution and deliverance into their own hands. Each time, they were armed with some mix of republican equalitarianism and evangelical Christianity.

9-4c Religion and Revolt

In comparison with slaves in Cuba, Jamaica, Brazil, and other New World plantation societies, North American slaves seldom went into organized, armed revolt. The environment of the United States was unfriendly to such events. American plantations were relatively small and dispersed, and the southern white population was large, vigilant, and very well armed. Whites also enjoyed—until the cataclysm of the Civil War—internal political stability. There were thus few situations in which slaves could hope to win their freedom by violent means. Thousands of slaves demonstrated their hatred of the system by running away. Others fought masters or overseers, sabotaged equipment and animals, stole from planters, and found other ways to oppose slavery, but most knew that open revolt was suicide.

Christianity convinced slaves that history was headed toward an apocalypse that would result in divine justice and their own deliverance. It thus contained the possibility of revolt. But slave preachers seldom indulged in prophecy and almost never told their congregations to become actively engaged in God's divine plan, for they knew that open resistance was hopeless. Slave Christians believed that God hated slavery and would end it, but that their role was to have faith in God, to take care of one another, to preserve their identity as a people, and to await deliverance. Only occasionally did slaves take

9-4d Gabriel's Rebellion

Masters who talked of liberty, natural rights, and equality before God sometimes worried that slaves might imagine that such language could apply to them. The long slave revolt in the French Caribbean colony of Saint-Domingue, which resulted in the independent black republic of Haiti in 1804, gave American slave masters reason to fear. Southern slaves from the 1790s onward whispered of natural rights and imagined themselves as part of a larger democratic revolution. In 1800, a conservative Virginia white complained: "Liberty and Equality has been infused into the minds of the negroes." A South Carolina congressman agreed that "this newfangled French philosophy of liberty and equality" was stirring up the slaves. Even Thomas Jefferson, who applauded the spread of French republicanism, conceded, "the West Indies appears to have given considerable impulse to the minds of the slaves … in the United States."

This covert republic of the slaves sometimes came into the open. In Richmond in 1800, a slave blacksmith named Gabriel hatched a conspiracy, which became known as **Gabriel's Rebellion**, to overthrow Virginia's slave regime. Gabriel had been hired out to Richmond employers for most of his adult life; he was shaped less by plantation slavery than by the democratic, loosely interracial underworld of urban artisans. In the late 1790s, the repressive acts of the

Federalist national government and the angry responses of the Jeffersonian opposition (see Chapter 7), along with the news from Haiti, drove the democratic sensibilities of that world to new heights.

Gabriel, working with his brother and other hired-out slave artisans, planned his revolt with meticulous attention to detail. Working at religious meetings, barbecues, and the grog shops of Richmond, they recruited soldiers among slave artisans, adding plantation slaves only at the last moment. Gabriel planned to march an army of 1,000 men on Richmond in three columns. The outside columns would set diversionary fires in the warehouse district and prevent the militia from entering the town. The center would seize Capitol Square, including the treasury, the arsenal, and Governor James Monroe.

Although his army would be made up of slaves, and although his victory would end slavery in Virginia, Gabriel hoped to make a republican revolution, not a slave revolt. His chosen enemies were the Richmond "merchants" who had controlled his labor. Gabriel expected "the poor white people" and "the most redoubtable republicans" to join him. He in fact had the shadowy support of two Frenchmen, and rumors indicated that other whites were involved, although never at levels that matched the delusions of the conspirators or of worried whites. Gabriel planned to kill anyone who opposed him, but he would spare Quakers, Methodists, and Frenchmen, for they were "friendly to liberty." Unlike earlier slave insurgents, Gabriel did not plot violent retribution or a return to or reconstruction of West Africa. He was an American revolutionary, and he dreamed of a truly democratic republic for Virginia. His army would march into Richmond under the banner "Death or Liberty."

Gabriel recruited at least 150 soldiers who agreed to gather near Richmond on August 30, 1800. The leaders expected 500 to 600 more to join them as they marched upon the town. On the appointed day, however, it rained heavily, washing out bridges and making roads impassable. Rebels could not reach the meeting point, and amid white terror and black betrayals, Gabriel and his henchmen were hunted down, tried, and sentenced to death. In all, the state hanged 27 supposed conspirators, while others were sold and transported out of Virginia. The condemned carried their republican dreams to their graves. When asked to explain the revolt, one condemned man replied in terms that could only have disturbed the white republicans of Virginia: "I have nothing more to offer than what General Washington would have had to offer, had he been taken by the British and put to trial by them. I have adventured my life in endeavoring to obtain the liberty of my countrymen, and am a willing sacrifice in their cause."

9-4e Denmark Vesey

A second major slave conspiracy may not have been a conspiracy at all. In 1822, **Denmark Vesey**, a free black of Charleston, South Carolina (he had won a lottery and bought himself), stood trial for plotting rebellion. Vesey was a leading member of an African Methodist congregation that had seceded from the white Methodists and had been independent from 1817 to 1821. Vesey and some of the other members read widely in political tracts, including the antislavery arguments in the Missouri debates (see Chapter 11). They also read the Bible, and talked openly of their delivery out of Egypt. According to testimony coerced from slaves who wanted to avoid prosecution themselves, Vesey and his coconspirators planned the destruction of Charleston in 1822. A few dozen Charleston blacks would take the state armory, the story went, then arm rural slaves who would rise up to help them. They would kill the whites and commandeer ships in the harbor and make their getaway to black-controlled Haiti.

We cannot know how much of that was true. But Charleston's white authorities pulled the story out of terrified blacks, believed it, and hanged Vesey and 35 other accused conspirators—22 of them on one day. For many years afterwards, frightened whites "knew" that most of the conspirators (estimates ranged from 600 to 9,000) remained at large and lived among them.

9-4f Nat Turner

There is no doubt that the revolt in Southampton County, Virginia, in August 1831 was real. It was led by **Nat Turner**, a Baptist lay preacher, not a republican visionary like Gabriel or Denmark Vesey. Turner was, he told his captors, a Christian prophet and an instrument of God's wrath. Around 1830, he received visions of the final battle in Revelation, recast as a war between white and black spirits. He saw Christ crucified against the night sky, and the next morning he saw Christ's blood in a cornfield. Convinced by a solar eclipse in February 1831 that the time had come, Turner began telling other slaves about his visions, recruited his force, and launched his bloody revolt. Turner and his followers hacked to death 55 white men, women, and children before they were stopped. In the aftermath, Virginia executed at least 40 blacks, including Turner, who managed to hide in the woods for two months. White mobs also responded to the revolt by killing dozens more blacks in Virginia.

The revolts of Gabriel, Turner, and Vesey, along with scores of more limited conspiracies, deeply troubled southern whites. Slaveholders were committed to a paternalism that was increasingly tied to the South's attempt to make slavery both domestic and Christian. For their part, slaves recognized that they could receive decent treatment and pockets of autonomy in return for outward docility. Gabriel, Vesey, and Turner opened wide cracks in that mutual charade. During the Turner revolt, slaves whose masters had been murdered joined the rebels without a second thought. A plantation mistress who survived by hiding in a closet listened to the murders of her husband and children, and then heard her house servants arguing over possession of her clothes. A Charleston grandee named Elias Horry, upon finding that his coachman was among the Vesey conspirators, asked him, "What were your

9.12 Nat Turner This contemporary woodcut depicts scenes from Nat Turner's rebellion. In this bloodiest of all North American slave revolts, 55 whites, most of them women and children, were hacked to death.

intentions?" The formerly docile slave replied that he had intended "to kill you, rip open your belly, and throw your guts in your face."

9-5 A Southern Market Revolution?

Q *What were the nature and limits of the Market Revolution in the South?*

The South experienced explosive economic growth between 1790 and 1860 that constituted a Market Revolution, but in different ways and with different results than in the North. The plantation was a profitable business, and it was big. In 1860 the cash value of the southern slave population was $3 billion. That was more than the value of investments in banking, railroads, and manufacturing combined. The annual rate of return on the larger plantations stood at 10 percent—higher than that of factories or banks.

Southern expansion, however, had its limits. Economic growth was concentrated on the largest farms, and prosperity and change did not reach far beyond those farms. Planters invested their profits in more slaves and more land. The result was a lack of diversification and an increasing concentration of resources in the hands of the planter class. The South was a poor market for manufactured goods, outside of finery purchased by the larger planters. Most white farmers relied on the production of their households and neighbors, and they remained marginal to the market economy. They bought finished goods from the outside, but at a far lower rate than their northern counterparts. Slaves wore shoes and cheap cloth made in the Northeast and bought by their masters. Overall, the South continued to export its plantation staples and to pay outsiders for shipping, financial services, and finished goods. In contrast, the commercialization of northern farms created a rural demand for credit, banking facilities, farm tools, clothing, and other consumer goods and services—most of them provided by other northerners—and thus made a Market Revolution that included most northern families. In the South, economic growth produced more cotton and more slavery and comparatively little else.

Not that the South neglected technological change and agricultural improvement. Southerners developed the early cotton gin into big milling machines. They also improved steamboat design, making flat-bottomed boats that could travel far up shallow rivers. They also developed, among others, a machine with a huge wooden screw powered by horses or mules to press ginned cotton into tight bales for shipping. Jordan Goree, a slave craftsman in Huntsville, Texas, won a reputation for being able to carve whole trees into perfect screws for these machines. There were, however, few such innovations, and they had to do with the processing and shipping of cotton. Despite the experiments of a few gentleman-planters, there were almost no improvements in the *cultivation* of cotton aside from the ever crueller treatment of slaves. The truth is that cotton was a labor-intensive crop that discouraged innovation. Moreover, slaves often resisted "progress." They sabotaged tools and draft animals, scattered

History Through Film: 12 Years a Slave (2013)

Directed by Steve McQueen.
Starring Chiwetel Ejiofor (Solomon Northup), Lupita Nyong'o (Patsey), Michael Fassbender (Edwin Epps), Brad Pitt (Bass).

Upon its release in 2013, *12 Years a Slave* was instantly hailed by critics and historians as the most accurate, powerful film depiction of slavery ever made, helping it to win the Academy Award for Best Picture. Unlike other films that explore the issues of race, slavery, and freedom in 19th-century America, including such strong productions as *Amistad* (1997) and *Glory* (1989), *12 Years* is told entirely from the slave's perspective. There are no scenes between whites without slaves present. The effect is to immerse the viewer in the horrific world of American slavery before the Civil War, when the interstate slave trade meant that no person with dark skin could rest easy, regardless of his or her whereabouts or legal status.

The film follows the true story of Solomon Northup (played brilliantly by Chiwetel Ejiofor), a free black violinist and family man in Saratoga, New York. In 1841, Northup accepts a job playing violin in a circus with a pair of white men traveling to Washington, D.C. After enjoying a night out with the men, Northup wakes up drugged and shackled in a slave pen in the shadow of the Capitol Building. He is beaten senseless and shipped south to New Orleans, where he is forced to adopt the name and persona of a slave, "Platt," as he is passed from master to master in Louisiana.

12 Years hews closely to Northup's own narrative written and published in 1853, the subtitle of which summarizes his saga: "Narrative of Solomon Northup, a Citizen of New-York, Kidnapped in Washington City in 1841, and Rescued in 1853, From a Cotton Plantation Near the Red River, in Louisiana." With few exceptions, director Steve McQueen found no need to deviate from Northup's narrative (something that mars an earlier film adaptation, *Solomon Northup's Odyssey*, made for public television in 1984 by the pioneering African American photographer Gordon Parks). As the noted abolitionist and escaped slave Frederick Douglass commented on Northup's story, "its truth is stranger than fiction."

The majority of the film centers on Northup's enslavement on different plantations in the Louisiana Cotton Belt. He quickly learns the mix of violence and negotiation that characterized slavery in the American South. Depending on his master, Northup can win small rewards, including a new fiddle, yet he also faces and witnesses constant acts of cruelty. The experience of women, both slaves and slave mistresses, gets special attention. An enslaved mother, Eliza (Adepero Oduye), never recovers from the tragedy of being torn from her two children. Another slave woman, Patsey (Lupita Nyong'o, in an Academy Award-winning performance), must confront the sexual advances of a sadistic slave master, Edwin Epps (Michael Fassbender), and the malicious jealousy of his wife, Mary (Sarah Paulson).

Ultimately, *12 Years* triumphs most by capturing the hopelessness of slavery without denying the agency, or free will, of individual slaves. Northup faces dehumanizing circumstances, but he never surrenders his humanity. Whether plotting an escape or making the calculated decision to comply with his masters, Northup retains some control over his actions (sadly, the same is not always true for the female slaves, particularly Patsey). His resilience finally pays off when a journeyman Canadian carpenter, Bass (Brad Pitt), helps to set in motion his release.

But there is no happy ending. Although Northup reunites with his wife and children, his brothers and sisters on the plantation remain trapped in slavery and his abductors escape punishment (Northup brought his kidnappers to trial, but they went free on legal technicalities). If the audience feels uncomfortable watching *12 Years*, that is the point. American viewers are also left to consider why the most redeeming white character was Canadian and why it took a British director (McQueen) and a largely international, non-American cast to bring this most American of stories fully to light.

9.13 *12 Years a Slave*, released to critical acclaim in 2013, tells the true story of Solomon Northup, a free black man who was kidnapped and sold into slavery before the Civil War.

---

manure in haphazard ways, and passively resisted innovations that would have added to their drudgery. The cotton fields continued to be cultivated by enslaved people working with clumsy, mule-drawn plows that barely scratched the soil, by women wielding heavy hoes, and by gangs who harvested the crop by hand.

Southern state governments spent comparatively little on internal improvements—there was no southern transportation revolution. A Virginia canal linked the flour mills at Richmond with inland grain fields, and another would connect Chesapeake Bay with the National Road, thus realizing—too late—Washington's and Jefferson's dreams of a thoroughfare between the Chesapeake and the Ohio Valley. But planters built their farms on alluvial land with access to the South's magnificent system of navigable rivers. They had little interest in expensive, state-supported internal improvements that their own neighborhoods did not need. Upcountry whites, particularly in the Upper South, sometimes campaigned for roads and canals, but they seldom got such measures through planter-dominated legislatures.

Nor did the South build cities, much less a regional *system* of cities. In 1800, about 82 percent of the southern workforce and about 70 percent of the northern workforce were employed in agriculture. By 1860, only 40 percent of the northern workforce was so employed. In the South, the proportion had risen to 84 percent. The old northern seaports grew dramatically in the early 19th century, and they extended their sway over systems of satellite cities. New York, which became America's great city in the first third of the 19th century, exercised commercial and cultural power over the old capital at Albany, as well as new Erie Canal cities such as Utica, Syracuse, Rochester, and Buffalo. Between 1800 and 1840, the urban population of New York State rose from 12.7 percent to 19.4 percent, despite the settlement of huge tracts of new agricultural land. In Massachusetts, the urban population rose from 15.4 percent to 37.9 percent in these years. By 1840, every northeastern and mid-Atlantic state with the exceptions of Maine and Vermont had at least 10 percent of its people living in cities. No southern state urbanized at that level. Virginia, at 6.9 percent, had the largest urban population of any of the future Confederate states.

Commercial and manufacturing cities sprouted up throughout the interior of the North. The few southern cities were located on the periphery of the region and served as transportation depots for plantation crops. River cities like Louisville, Memphis, and St. Louis were little more than stopping places for steamboats. The great seaports of New Orleans, Charleston, and Baltimore had in the past shipped plantation staples directly to British and European markets. But as the 19th century progressed, they sent more and more of their goods by coasting vessel to New York City to be shipped to foreign ports. In turn, Europe's manufactured goods were funneled into New York, and then sold off to the southern (and northern) countryside. The commercial metropolis of the southern United States was becoming less London and more New York. What had *not* changed was the colonial status of the South.

Thus while the North and the Northwest developed towns and cities throughout their regions, southern cities continued to be few and to perform the colonial functions of 18th-century seaport towns. Southern businessmen turned to New York City for credit, insurance, coastal and export shipping, and finished goods. *De Bow's Review,* the principal business journal of the South, reported that South Carolina storekeepers who bought goods from Charleston wholesalers claimed they had bought them directly from New York City, for it was well known that New York provided better goods at lower prices than any supplier in the South. De Bow testified to the superior skill and diversification of the North when, after trying several New Orleans sources, he awarded the publishing contract for his *Review* to a northern printer. That was not surprising in any case, because De Bow received three-fourths of his income from northern advertisers.

Conclusion

On the eve of the Civil War, James H. Hammond, a slaveholding senator from South Carolina, asked, "What would happen if no cotton was furnished for three years…. England would topple headlong and carry the whole civilized world with her save the south. No, you dare not make war on cotton. No power on earth dares to make war on cotton. Cotton is king." Hammond was arguing, as Jefferson had argued in 1807, that farmers at the fringes of the world market economy could coerce the commercial-industrial center. He was wrong. The commitment to cotton and slavery had isolated the South politically. It had also deepened the South's dependence on the world's financial and industrial centers. Ironically, slavery and cotton, each critical to the growth of global capitalism, left the South itself with uneven market and industrial development. The North transformed its role as a part of the old colonial periphery (the suppliers of food and raw materials) into a part of the core (the suppliers of manufactured goods and financing) of the world market economy, while the South continued to export plantation staples in exchange for imported goods. In the process, the South worked itself deeper and deeper into dependence, now as much upon the American Northeast as upon the old colonial rulers in London.

CHAPTER REVIEW

Review

1. What were the principal differences between the slave economies of the Chesapeake and the South Carolina–Georgia lowcountry?
2. In what ways did the economy and society of the Cotton Belt differ from that of older plantation regions?
3. How did southern yeoman farmers differ from planters who presided over much larger plantations?
4. What were prominent features of the cultural life that slaves made for themselves within the limits of slavery?
5. What were the nature and limits of the Market Revolution in the South?

Critical Thinking

1. The central institutions of slave culture were the family and religion. Some have argued that these institutions helped slaves accommodate to slavery, whereas others have argued that they helped them resist it, and still others have argued that they did both. What is your position on this question?
2. Historians have long debated how to characterize the southern economy and society. Some contend that it was stridently capitalist, while others argue that this is impossible because the southern economy depended on slavery, a primitive, pre-capital form of labor. Where do you stand in this debate? Does it matter whether the South was capitalist or not? Why or why not?

Identifications

Review your understanding of the following key terms, people, and events for this chapter (terms in bold in text are included in the Glossary).

private fields, p. 258
Eli Whitney, p. 258
cotton gin, p. 258
Cotton Belt, p. 258
interstate slave trade, p. 260
itinerant preachers, p. 269
Gabriel's Rebellion, p. 271
Denmark Vesey, p. 272
Nat Turner, p. 272

Suggested Readings

In recent years, several works have transformed our understanding of the Deep South and its place in the national and global economy. For leading examples, see **Walter Johnson**, *River of Dark Dreams: Slavery and Empire in the Cotton Kingdom* (2013); **Edward E. Baptist**, *The Half Has Never Been Told: Slavery and the Making of American Capitalism* (2014); and **Sven Beckert**, *Empire of Cotton: A Global History* (2014). On planter culture, see **Bertram Wyatt-Brown**, *Honor and Violence in the Old South* (1986); **Kenneth S. Greenberg**, *Honor & Slavery* (1997); and **Elizabeth Fox Genovese and Eugene D. Genovese**, *The Mind of the Master Class: History and Faith in the Southern Slaveholders' Worldview* (2005). **Walter Johnson**'s *Soul by Soul: Life Inside the Antebellum Slave Market* (1999) brilliantly undermines the myth of slaveholder paternalism. For the domestic slave trade, see also **Steven Deyle**, *Carry Me Back: The Domestic Slave Trade in American Life* (2005); and **Adam Rothman**, *Slave Country: American Expansion and the Origins of the Deep South* (2005).

On the southern yeomanry, see **Stephanie McCurry**, *Masters of Small Worlds: Yeoman Households, Gender Relations, & the Political Culture of the South Carolina Lowcountry* (1995); and **Steven Hahn**, *The Roots of Southern Populism: Yeoman Farmers and the Transformation of the Georgia Upcountry, 1850–1890* (1983). Two classic works on slave culture are **Eugene D. Genovese**, *Roll, Jordan, Roll: The World the Slaves Made* (1974); and **Lawrence W. Levine**, *Black Culture and Black Consciousness: Afro-American Folk Thought from Slavery to Freedom* (1977). **Charles Joyner**, *Down by the Riverside: A South Carolina Slave Community* (1986); **Mark M. Smith**, *Mastered by the Clock: Time, Slavery and Freedom in the American South* (1986); and **Albert J. Raboteau**, *Canaan Land: A Religious History of African Americans* (2001) are also essential.

 MINDTAP is a fully online personalized learning experience built upon Cengage Learning content. MindTap® combines student learning tools—readings, multimedia, activities, and assessments—into a singular Learning Path that guides students through the course and helps students develop the critical thinking, analysis, and communication skills that are essential to academic and professional success.

10 Toward an American Culture, 1815–1850

10-1 The Democratization of Culture
Learning Objective: Analyze in what ways literacy and print helped to democratize American culture.

A Revolution in Print

10-2 The Northern Middle Class
Learning Objective: Describe the central cultural maxims of the emerging northern middle class.

A New Middle Class
The Evangelical Base
Domesticity

10-3 The Plain People of the North
Learning Objective: Identify the alternatives to middle-class culture within the North.

The Rise of Democratic Sects
The Providential Worldview
Family and Society
The Emergence of Mormonism

10-4 A New Popular Culture
Learning Objective: The amusements of common folk were varied, but they exhibited a few common themes. Trace those themes.

Blood Sports
Boxing
An American Theater
Minstrelsy
Novels and the Penny Press

10-5 Family, Church, and Neighborhood: The White South
Learning Objective: Describe the specific ways in which evangelical Protestantism acted as a conservative force within southern culture.

The Beginnings of the Bible Belt
Slavery and Southern Evangelicals
Gender, Power, and the Evangelicals
Religious Conservatism
Pro-Slavery Christianity
The Mission to the Slaves

10-6 Race
Learning Objective: Consider the ways in which the racial order of the North changed in the first half of the 19th century.

Free Blacks
The Beginnings of Modern Racism

10-7 Citizenship
Learning Objective: Describe how American voting rights changed between the adoption of the Constitution and the Civil War.

10.1 P.T. Barnum and Tom Thumb, circa 1850 Here is Phineas Taylor Barnum, America's greatest showman, together with the sprightly midget Tom Thumb, his first hugely successful attraction. The photograph conveys the combination of chicanery, farce, strangeness, and straight-faced respectability that made Barnum (but not Tom Thumb) a rich man.

AMERICANS AFTER 1815 experienced wave after wave of social and cultural change. Territorial expansion, the growth of the market, and the spread of plantation slavery broke old social patterns. Americans in these years reinvented family life. They created American forms of popular literature and art. They flocked to evangelical churches that expanded and remade American religious life. They began, in short, to make a distinctively American culture.

The emerging American culture was more or less uniformly republican, capitalist, and Protestant. But different kinds of Americans made different cultures out of the revolutionary inheritance, market expansion, and revival religion. Southern farmers and their northern cousins thought differently about fatherhood and the proper way to make a family. Northeastern businessmen and southern planters agreed that economic progress was indeed progress, but they differed radically on its moral implications. Slaveholders, factory hands, rich and poor farmers, and middle-class women all heard the same Bible stories and learned different lessons. The result, visible from the 1830s onward, was an American national culture that was (and is) less an accepted body of rules than an ongoing conversation. This chapter identifies the varying ways in which Americans thought about four of the hot spots in that conversation: family life and personal identity, the Christian inheritance, the question of race, and the nature of republican citizenship. ■

10-1 The Democratization of Culture

Q *In what ways did literacy and print help to democratize American culture?*

The weakening of traditional authority created spaces that Americans filled in their own ways. Important pillars of old cultures remained: The Bible and revolutionary ideas of liberty and equality were fundamental. But the transportation network that carried wheat and cotton out of rural neighborhoods brought new things in: furniture and ways of arranging it, new clothing styles, new forms of entertainment, new information, new aspirations. In part, Americans made new ways of thinking and living as consumers of these cultural goods.

Among the items reaching Americans was information—newspapers, books, magazines, business communications, personal letters, and travelers who carried news. The information circulated among a public that was remarkably literate and well informed. The literacy rate in the preindustrial United States was among the highest ever recorded. In 1790, approximately 85 percent of adult men in New England and 60 percent of those in Pennsylvania and the Chesapeake could read and write. The literacy rate among women was lower—about 45 percent in New England—but on the rise. By 1820, all but the poorest white Americans, particularly in the North, could read and write. The United States, more than perhaps any other country, was a nation of readers.

10-1a A Revolution in Print

The rise of a reading public was accompanied by a print revolution: Enterprising men (and a few women) learned how to make their livings by providing cheap Bibles and English novels, almanacs, newspapers, and other printed matter. People were encouraged to read by their republican governments. The states provided schools, and the national government helped the flow of print in ways that were unprecedented.

The governments of Great Britain and the European powers tried to control the circulation of information; they established few post offices, taxed newspapers, monitored what was said in the newspapers and even in the mail, and prosecuted people who said the wrong things in print. There were attempts to do such things in America. The Stamp Tax of 1765 had included a tax on newspapers, and in 1798 Federalists had jailed editors with whom they disagreed. Americans defeated both of these attempts. The First Amendment guaranteed freedom of the press, and the U.S. government (with that brief Federalist exception) did not interfere with newspapers. Just the opposite: Newspapers enjoyed discounted postal rates and circulated far beyond their points of publication. A law of 1792 allowed newspapers to mail copies to each other without cost, and the editors of country weeklies cut national and international news from the New York, Baltimore, and Philadelphia papers, combined it with local advertising and legal notices, and provided their readers with cheap sources of information that were remarkably uniform throughout the North and West and much of the South. In effect, then, government directly and knowingly subsidized the rise of a democratic and national reading public.

Newspapers were the most widely distributed form of print in the new republic. In 1790, 106 newspapers were being published in the United States. In 1835, 1,258 were in publication, 90 of which were dailies. In the latter year, the number of newspapers per capita in the United States was two to three times greater than in Great Britain. Though only about one household in 10 subscribed to a newspaper, the democratic public knew what was in them, for the papers were passed from hand to hand, read aloud in groups, and made available at taverns and public houses.

CHRONOLOGY

1825	Charles Grandison Finney begins religious revival meetings in upstate New York
1830	Joseph Smith founds the Church of Jesus Christ of Latter-Day Saints
1831	First minstrel show is presented
1843	William Miller's Adventists expect the world to end
1845	George Lippard's lurid novel *The Quaker City* becomes a best seller
1849	Astor Place theater riot in New York City leaves 20 dead
1852	Harriet Beecher Stowe publishes *Uncle Tom's Cabin*

Improvements in distribution and printing technology encouraged other forms of popular literature as well. The emerging evangelical crusade made innovative use of print. Sunday school tracts, temperance pamphlets, and other religious materials were printed in New York and distributed efficiently and cheaply through the mails, while the American Bible Society devised a realistic plan to provide every household in America with a free Bible. Newspapers were men's reading, but the religious tracts tended to find their way into the hands of women. Women also were the principal readers of novels, a new form of reading matter that Thomas Jefferson and other authorities denounced as frivolous and aberrant. Novels were seen as dangerous not only because they contained questionable subject matter but also because girls and women read them silently and in private. Printed matter provided information and opinion for the men who exercised power and conducted the public life of democracy, but it could also provide sustenance for the spirits and imaginations of Americans who were excluded from power and the public.

The increase in literacy and in printed matter accelerated both the market and democratic individualism. Books and newspapers were scarce in the 18th century, and most Americans had experienced the written word only as it was read aloud by fathers, ministers, or teachers. After 1790, private, silent reading of new kinds of texts became common. No longer were adult male authorities the sole interpreters of the world for families and neighborhoods. The new print culture encouraged Americans to read, think, and interpret information for themselves.

10-2 The Northern Middle Class

  What were the central cultural maxims of the emerging northern middle class?

"The most valuable class in any community," declared the poet-journalist Walt Whitman in 1858, "is the **middle class**." At that time, the term *middle class* (and the social group that it described) had been in use no more than 30 or 40 years.

The Market Revolution had created new towns and cities and transformed the old ones, and it had turned the rural North into a landscape of family-owned commercial farms. Those who claimed the title "middle class" were largely the new kinds of proprietors made in that transformation—city and country merchants, master craftsmen who had turned themselves into manufacturers, and the mass of market-oriented farmers. They lived at the centers of the new marketing and communications networks, and they developed a self-conscious middle-class identity that was remarkably uniform throughout the North.

10-2a *A New Middle Class*

New England played a disproportionate role in the making of middle-class culture. The region was the first center of factory production, and southern New England farms were thoroughly commercialized by the 1830s. Yankee migrants dominated the commercial heartland of western New York and the northern regions of the Northwest. Even in the seaport cities (New York's Pearl Street wholesale houses are a prime example), businessmen from New England were often at the center of economic innovation. This Yankee middle class invented cultural forms that became the core of an emerging business civilization. Liberty for them meant self-ownership and the freedom of action and ambition. Equality meant equality of opportunity. They upheld the autonomous and morally accountable individual against the claims of traditional neighborhoods and traditional families. They devised an intensely private, mother-centered domestic life. Most of all they adhered to a reformed Yankee Protestantism whose moral imperatives became the foundation of American middle-class culture.

10-2b *The Evangelical Base*

Religion helped to define the new middle-class culture. From the 1790s, a series of intense religious revivals took place on the western frontier. By the mid-1820s and 1830s, these revivals, together known as the **Second Great Awakening**, reached the emerging middle class of the North and continued in areas throughout the country into the 1850s. The evangelist Charles Grandison Finney, who led his first revival in 1825, was most responsible for bringing the awakening to the northern middle class. So fiery were the revivals in and around Finney's base of Rochester, New York, and other towns along the Erie Canal that people began to call the area the "Burned-Over District." The revivals had much in common with the First Great Awakening of the 1730s and 1740s (see Chapter 4). Transplanted New Englanders, the heirs of what was left of Yankee Calvinism, composed much of Finney's audience and would have easily recognized his vivid warnings of hell for the sinful and unconverted.

Yet, the message of the Second Great Awakening also differed from the First in significant ways. Finney and other preachers reached beyond the traditional Puritan themes of original sin, innate sinfulness, and predestination. Those living through the economic changes associated with the Market Revolution had witnessed firsthand the ability of humans to

10.2 Charles Finney The evangelist, pictured here at the height of his preaching power in the 1830s, was remarkably successful at organizing the new middle-class culture into a millennial crusade.

audience. At the same time, middle-class evangelicals retained the Puritans' Old Testament sense of cosmic history. They enlisted personal holiness in a fight to the finish between the forces of good and evil in this world. Building on these imperatives, the entrepreneurial families of the East and Northwest constructed an American middle-class culture after 1825. It was based, paradoxically, on an intensely private and emotionally loaded family life and an aggressively reformist stance toward the world at large.

10-2c Domesticity

The message of the Second Great Awakening had application in both the home and workplace, where qualities such as industry, sobriety, and self-discipline (all freely chosen moral behaviors) led to success in the new market culture. At the same time, the Yankee middle class made crucial distinctions between the home and the world—distinctions that grew from the disintegration of the old patriarchal household economy.

Men in cities and towns now went off to work, leaving wives and children to spend the day at home. Even commercializing farmers made a distinction between (male) work that was oriented toward markets and (female) work that was tied to household maintenance (see Chapter 8). The new middle-class evangelicalism encouraged this division of domestic labor. The public world of politics and economic exchange, said the preachers, was the proper sphere of men; women, on the other hand, were to exercise new kinds of moral influence within households. As one evangelical put it, "Each has a distinct sphere of duty—the husband to go out into the world—the wife to superintend the house-hold. ... Man profits from connection with the world, but women never; their constituents [sic] of mind are different. The one is raised and exalted by mingled association. The purity of the other is maintained in silence and seclusion."

The result was a feminization of domestic life. In the old yeoman-artisan republic, fathers were God's delegated authorities on earth, assigned the task of governing women, children, and other underlings. Middle-class evangelicals raised new spiritual possibilities for women and children. Mothers replaced fathers as the principal rearers of children, and they enlisted the doctrines of free agency and individual moral responsibility in that task. Middle-class mothers raised their children with love and reason, not fear. They sought to develop the children's conscience and their capacity to love, to teach them to make good moral choices, and to help them to prepare for conversion and a lifetime of Christian service.

Middle-class mothers could take up these tasks because they could concentrate their efforts on household duties and because they had fewer children than their mothers or grandmothers had had. In Utica, New York, for example, women who entered their childbearing years in the 1830s averaged only 3.6 births apiece; those who had started families only 10 years earlier averaged 5.1 births. Housewives also spaced their pregnancies differently. Unlike their forebears, who gave birth to a child about once every two years throughout their childbearing years, Utica's middle-class housewives had their children at

shape their environment. And as middle-class Christians improved the material and social worlds, the doctrines of human inability and natural depravity, along with faith in divine providence, made less sense.

To such an audience, Finney preached the organizing principle of northern middle-class evangelicalism: "God," he insisted, "has made man a moral free agent." Neither the social order, the troubles of this world, nor the spiritual state of individuals was divinely ordained. People would make themselves and the world better by choosing right over wrong—though they would choose right only after submitting their rebellious wills to the will of God. It was a religion that valued individual holiness over a permanent and sacred social order. It made the spiritual nature of individuals a matter of prayer, submission, and choice. Thus, it gave Christians the means—through the spread of revivals—to bring on the thousand-year reign of Christianity that they believed would precede the Second Coming of Christ. As Charles Finney told his Rochester audience, "If [Christians] were united all over the world the Millennium might be brought about in three months."

Yankee evangelists had been moving toward Finney's formulation since the turn of the 19th century. Like Finney, they borrowed revival techniques from the Methodists (weeklong meetings in which women prayed in public, and an "**anxious bench**"—a space reserved in meetings for the most likely converts), but toned them down for their own more "respectable" five-year intervals, which meant that they could give each child close attention. As a result, households were quieter and less crowded; children learned from their mothers how to govern themselves and seldom experienced the rigors of patriarchal family government. Thus, mothers assumed responsibility for nurturing the children who would be carriers of the new middle-class culture, and male authorities recognized the importance of that job. Edward Kirk, a minister in Albany, insisted that "the hopes of human society are to be found in the character, in the views, and in the conduct of mothers."

Middle-class women and girls became a huge market for new forms of popular literature. There were cookbooks, etiquette books, manuals on housekeeping, sermons, and sentimental novels, many of them written and most of them read by women. The works of popular religious writers such as Lydia Sigourney, Lydia Maria Child, and Timothy Shay Arthur found their way into thousands of middle-class homes. **Sarah Josepha Hale**, whose *Godey's Lady's Book* was the first mass-circulation magazine for women, acted as an arbiter of taste not only in furniture, clothing, and food but also in sentiments and ideas. Upon reviewing the sentimental literature read in middle-class homes, Nathaniel Hawthorne was not the only "serious" writer to deplore a literary marketplace dominated by "a damned mob of scribbling women."

Hawthorne certainly had economic reason for complaint. Sentimental novels written by women outsold by wide margins his *Scarlet Letter* and *House of Seven Gables*; Ralph Waldo Emerson's essays; Henry David Thoreau's *Walden*; Herman Melville's *Moby Dick*; Walt Whitman's *Leaves of Grass*; and other works of the American Renaissance of the 1850s. Susan Warner's *The Wide, Wide World* broke all sales records when it appeared in 1850. Harriet Beecher Stowe's *Uncle Tom's Cabin* (1852) broke the records set by Warner. In 1854, Maria Cummins's *The Lamplighter* (the direct target of Hawthorne's lament about scribbling women) took its place as the third of the monster best sellers of the early 1850s.

These sentimental novels upheld the new middle-class domesticity. They sacralized the middle-class home and the trials and triumphs of Christian women. In sentimental **domestic fiction**, women assume the role of evangelical ministers, demonstrating Christian living by precept, example, and moral persuasion. Female moral influence, wielded by women who had given themselves to God, is at war with the male world of politics and the marketplace—areas of power, greed, and moral compromise. Although few sentimental writers shared the views of the feminist Margaret Fuller, they would have agreed with her on the place of religion in women's lives. "I wish women to live first for God's sake," she wrote. "Then she will not make an imperfect man her God, and thus sink to idolatry."

Popular sentimental novels were not, as Hawthorne and his friends believed, frivolous fairy tales into which house-wives retreated from the real world. They were subversive depictions of a higher spiritual reality that would move the feminine ethos of the Christian home to the center of civilization. That vision drove an organized public assault on irreligion, drunkenness, prostitution, slavery, and other practices and institutions that substituted passion and force for Christian love (see Chapter 12), an assault that tried to "domesticate" the world and shape it in the image of the middle-class evangelical home.

10-3 The Plain People of the North

Q *Within the North, what were the alternatives to middle-class culture?*

From the 1830s onward, northern middle-class reformers proposed their religious and domestic values as a national culture for the United States. Even in their own region, however, most people rejected their cultural leadership. The

10.3 **"The Polka Fashions" from *Godey's Lady's Book*, 1845** The popular magazine acted as an arbiter of taste in nearly all things for women, including formal dancing attire.

Q *What were the distinguishing features of upper-class women's fashion in the 1840s?*

plain folk of the North were a varied lot: settlers in the lower Northwest who remained culturally southern; hill-country northerners who had experienced little of what their middle-class cousins called "progress"; refugees from the countryside who had taken up urban wage labor; and increasing thousands of Irish and German immigrants. They did share a cultural conservatism—often grounded in the traditional, father-centered family—that rejected sentimentalism and reformist religion out of hand. As often as not, that conservatism was grounded in religious values that were very different from those of the new middle class.

10-3a The Rise of Democratic Sects

During the American revolutionary era, state constitutions withdrew government support from religion, and the First Amendment to the U.S. Constitution clearly prescribed the separation of church and the national state. Reduced to their own sources of support, the established churches—Congregationalism in New England, the Church of England (renamed Episcopalianism) in the South and much of the mid-Atlantic—went into decline. In 1780, nearly all of the 750 Congregational churches in the United States were in New England. In the next 40 years, although the nation's population rose from 4 million to 10 million, the number of Congregational churches rose only to 1,100. Ordinary women and men were leaving the churches that had dominated the religious life of colonial America, sometimes ridiculing the learned clergy as they departed. To many elites in the former established churches, it seemed that the republic was plunging into atheism.

They were wrong. The collapse of the established churches, the social dislocations of the post-revolutionary years, and the increasingly antiauthoritarian, democratic sensibilities of ordinary northerners provided fertile ground for the growth of new democratic sects. These were the years of camp meeting revivalism, years in which Methodists and Baptists grew from small, half-organized sects into the great popular denominations they have been ever since (see Map 10.1). They were also years in which fiercely independent dropouts from older churches were putting together a loosely organized movement that would become the Disciples of Christ. At the same time, ragged, half-educated preachers were spreading the Universalist and Freewill Baptist messages in upcountry New England, while in western New York young **Joseph Smith** was receiving the visions that would lead to Mormonism.

The result was, first of all, a vast increase in the variety of choices on the northern religious landscape, but within that welter of new churches, the fastest-growing sects shared a roughly uniform democratic style. First, they renounced the need for an educated, formally authorized clergy. Religion was now a matter of the heart and not the head. **Crisis conversion** (understood in most churches as spiritual transformation that resulted from direct experience of the Holy Ghost) was a necessary credential for preachers; a college degree was not. The new preachers substituted emotionalism and storytelling for Episcopal ritual and Congregational theological lectures. Stories attracted listeners, and they were harder for the learned clergy to refute. The new churches also held up the Bible as the one source of religious knowledge, thus undercutting all theological knowledge and placing every literate Christian on a level with the best-educated minister. These tendencies often ended in **Restorationism**—the belief that all theological and institutional changes since the end of biblical times were man-made mistakes, and that religious organizations must restore themselves to the purity and simplicity of the church of the Apostles. In sum, this loose democratic creed rejected learning and tradition and raised up the priesthood of all believers.

Baptists and Methodists were by far the most successful at preaching to the new democratic audience. The United States had only 50 Methodist churches in 1783; by 1820 it had 2,700. Over those same years, the number of Baptist churches rose from 400 to 2,700. Together, in 1820, these two denominations outnumbered Episcopalians and Congregationalists by three to one, almost a reversal of their relative standings 40 years earlier. Baptists based much of their appeal on localism and congregational democracy. Methodist success, on the other hand, entailed skillful national organization. Bishop Francis Asbury, the head of the church in its fastest-growing years, built an episcopal bureaucracy that seeded churches throughout the republic and sent **circuit-riding preachers** to places that had none. These early Methodist missions were grounded in self-sacrifice to the point of martyrdom. Asbury demanded much of his itinerant preachers, and until 1810, he strongly suggested that they remain celibate. "To marry," he said, "is to locate." Asbury also knew that married circuit riders would leave many widows and orphans behind, for hundreds of them worked themselves to death. Of the men who served as Methodist itinerants before 1819, at least 60 percent died before the age of 40.

From seaport cities to frontier settlements, few Americans escaped the sound of Methodist preaching in the early 19th century. The Methodist preachers were common men who spoke plainly, listened carefully to others, and carried hymnbooks with simple tunes that anyone could sing. They also, particularly in the early years, shared traditional folk beliefs with their humble flocks. Some of the early circuit riders relied heavily on dreams; some could predict the future; many visited heaven and hell and returned with full descriptions.

In the end, however, it was the hopefulness and simplicity of the Methodist message that attracted ordinary Americans. Even more than Finney (a Presbyterian), the Methodists rejected the old terrors of Calvinist determinism and taught that although salvation comes only through God, men and women can open themselves to divine grace and thus play a decisive role in their own salvation. They also taught that a godly life is a gradual, lifetime growth in grace, thus allowing for repentance for minor, and sometimes even major, lapses of faith and behavior. By granting responsibility (one might say sovereignty) to the individual believer, the Methodists established their democratic credentials and drew hundreds of thousands of Americans into their fold.

▲ MAP 10.1 **Growth of American Methodism, 1775–1850** This is a county-by-county map of the rise of American Methodism from the Revolution through the eve of the Civil War. In 1775, Methodism was almost nonexistent in British North America. By 1850, the Methodists were the largest Protestant denomination in the United States. They were truly a national faith: There were Methodist churches in almost every county in the country.

Q What factors help explain the growth of American Methodism?
Q How can we explain the regional variations in American Methodism in 1850?

10-3b The Providential Worldview

Northern plain folk favored churches as doctrinally varied as the people themselves. These ranged from the voluntaristic "free grace" doctrines of the Methodists to the iron-bound Calvinism of most Baptists, from the fine-tuned hierarchy of the Mormons to the near-anarchy of the Disciples of Christ. They included the most popular faiths (Baptists and Methodists came to contain two-thirds of America's professing Protestants), as well as such smaller sects as Hicksite Quakers, Universalists, Adventists, Moravians, and Freewill Baptists. Yet for all their diversity, these churches had important points in common. Most shared an evangelical emphasis on individual experience over churchly authority. Most favored democratic, local control of religious life and distrusted outside organization and religious professionalism. They also rejected middle-class optimism and reformism, even as several of the groups emerged in the same Burned-Over District of upstate New York as Finney and other preachers of the Second Great Awakening.

The most pervasive strain was a belief in providence—the conviction that human history is part of God's vast and unknowable plan, and that all events are willed or allowed by God. Middle-class evangelicals spoke of providence, too, but they seemed to assume that God's plan was manifest in the progress of market society and middle-class religion. Humbler evangelicals held to the older notion that providence is immediate, mysterious, and unknowable. They believed that the events of everyday life are parts of a vast blueprint that exists only in the mind of God—and not in the vain aspirations of women and men. When making plans, they added the caveat "the Lord willing," and they learned to accept misfortune with fortitude. They responded to epidemics, bad crop years, aches and pains, illness, and early death by praying for the strength to endure.

Such providentialism lent itself to millennial thinking. Middle-class evangelicals were **postmillennialists**. They believed that Christ's Second Coming would occur at the end of 1,000 years of social perfection brought about by the missionary conversion of the world. Ordinary Baptists, Methodists, and Disciples of Christ, however, were **premillennialists**. They assumed that the millennium would arrive with world-destroying violence, followed by 1,000 years of Christ's rule on earth. Some northern evangelicals boldly predicted the fiery end of the world. Prophets rose and fell, and thousands of people looked for signs of the approaching millennium in thunderstorms, shooting stars, eclipses, economic panics and depressions, and—especially—in hints that God had placed in the Bible.

One avid student of those hints was William Miller, a Vermont Baptist who, after years of systematic study, concluded that God would destroy the world during the year following March 1843. Miller publicized his predictions throughout the 1830s, and near the end of the decade the **Millerites** (as his followers were called) accumulated thousands of believers—most of them conservative Baptists, Methodists, and Disciples in hill-country New England and in poor neighborhoods in New York, Ohio, and Michigan. As the end approached, the believers read the Bible, prayed, and attended meeting after meeting. A publicist named Henry Jones reported that a shower of meat and blood had fallen on Jersey City, and newspapers published stories alleging that the Millerites were insane and sexually licentious. Some, the press reported, were sewing "ascension robes" in which they would rise straight to heaven without passing through death.

When the end of the year—March 23, 1844—came and went, most of the believers quietly returned to their churches.

10.5 Prophetic Chart A fixture at Millerite Adventist meetings, prophetic charts such as the one shown here displayed the succession of biblical kingdoms and the prophecies of Daniel and John. Millerites revised their charts when the world failed to end in 1843.

A committed remnant, however, kept the faith, and by the 1860s founded the Seventh-Day Adventist Church. The Millerite movement was a reminder that hundreds of thousands of northern Protestants continued to believe that the God of the Old Testament governed everything from bee stings to the course of human history, and that one day he would destroy the world in fire and blood.

10-3c *Family and Society*

Baptists, Methodists, Disciples of Christ, and the smaller popular sects evangelized primarily among persons who had been bypassed or hurt by the Market Revolution. Many had been reduced to dependent, wage-earning status. Others had become market farmers or urban storekeepers or master workmen; few had become rich. Their churches taught them that the temptations of market society were at the center of the world they must reject.

Often their rhetoric turned to criticism of market society, its institutions, and its centers of power. The Quaker schismatic Elias Hicks, a Long Island farmer who fought the

10.4 Joseph Smith, 1842 Smith founded the Mormon Church in 1830 and attracted thousands of followers before being killed in Carthage, Illinois, in 1844.

worldliness and pride of wealthy urban Quakers, listed the following among the mistakes of the early 19th century: railroads, the Erie Canal, fancy food and other luxuries, banks and the credit system, the city of Philadelphia, and the study of chemistry. The Baptist millenarian William Miller expressed his hatred of banks, insurance companies, stock jobbing, chartered monopolies, personal greed, and the city of New York. In short, what the evangelical middle class identified as the march of progress, poorer and more conservative evangelicals often condemned as a descent into worldliness that would almost certainly provoke God's wrath.

Members of the popular sects often held to the patriarchal family form in which they had been raised, and with which both the Market Revolution and middle-class domesticity seemed at war. Hundreds of thousands of northern Protestants considered the erosion of domestic patriarchy a profound cultural loss and not, as it seemed to the middle class, an avenue to personal liberation. Their cultural conservatism was apparent in their efforts to sustain the father-centered family of the old rural North or to revive it in new forms.

For some, religious conversion came at a point of crisis in the traditional family. William Miller, for example, had a strict Calvinist upbringing in a family in which his father, an uncle, and his grandfather were all Baptist ministers. As a young man he rejected his family, set about making money, and became a deist—actions that deeply wounded his parents. When his father died, Miller was stricken with guilt. He moved back to his hometown, took up his family duties, became a leader of the Baptist church, and (after reading a sermon entitled "Parental Duties") began the years of Bible study that resulted in his world-ending prophecies. Alexander Campbell, one of the founders of the Disciples of Christ, dramatized his filial piety when he debated the freethinking socialist Robert Owen before a large audience in the Methodist meetinghouse in Cincinnati in 1828. He insisted that his white-haired father (a Scots Presbyterian minister) stand in the pulpit above the debaters.

10-3d The Emergence of Mormonism

Over the long term, the most successful religious group to emerge from the Burned-Over District was the Church of Jesus Christ of Latter-Day Saints (also known as the Mormon Church). In 1827, according to the group's founder and prophet, Joseph Smith, the Angel Moroni led him to golden plates near his family's farm outside Palmyra, New York. Smith translated the plates into *The Book of Mormon*, which, together with the Old and New Testaments, became the basis of a new faith. *The Book of Mormon* tells the story of a light-skinned people, descendants of the Hebrews, who had sailed to North America long before Columbus. They had an epic, violent history and a covenanted relationship with God, and Jesus had visited them following his crucifixion and resurrection.

In 1830, Smith printed 5,000 copies of *The Book of Mormon* and founded the Mormon Church. Like other religious groups of the era, its organization countered the weakening of patriarchal authority and other social disruptions connected to the Market Revolution. The church was ruled, not by professional clergy, but by an elaborate lay hierarchy of adult males. On top sat the father of Joseph Smith, who was appointed Patriarch of the Church. Below him were Joseph Smith and his brother Hyrum, who were called First and Second Elders. The hierarchy descended through a succession of male authorities that finally reached the fathers of households. Smith claimed that this hierarchy restored the ancient priesthood that had disappeared over the 18 centuries of greed and error that he labeled the Great Apostasy of the Christian churches.

The Mormon Church grew rapidly, claiming 8,000 members by the mid-1830s. But its inclusiveness and new theology aroused suspicion and intense hostility among mainstream Protestant denominations. The Mormons faced persecution that drove them from western New York to Ohio, Missouri, Illinois, and ultimately Utah (see Chapter 13).

10-4 A New Popular Culture

 The amusements of common folk were varied, but they exhibited a few common themes. What were those themes?

Not all of the northern plain folk spent their time in church. Particularly in cities and towns, they became both producers and consumers of a nonreligious (sometimes irreligious) commercial popular culture. The sports and shows attended by northern plain folk, like the churches they attended, were often grounded in an antisentimental view of the world and in traditional forms of patriarchy and masculinity.

10-4a Blood Sports

Urban working-class neighborhoods were particularly fertile ground for popular amusements. Young workingmen formed a bachelor subculture that contrasted with the piety and self-restraint of the middle class. They organized volunteer fire companies and militia units that spent more time drinking and fighting rival groups than drilling or putting out fires. Gathering at firehouses, saloons, and street corners, they drank, joked, boasted, and nurtured notions of manliness based on physical prowess and coolness under pressure.

They also engaged in such "**blood sports**" as cock fighting, ratting, and dog fighting, even though many states had laws forbidding such activities. Such contests grew increasingly popular during the 1850s and often were staged by saloonkeepers doubling as sports impresarios. One of the best known was Kit Burns of New York City, who ran Sportsman Hall, a saloon frequented by prizefighters, criminals, and their hangers-on. Behind the saloon was a space—reached through a narrow doorway that could be defended against the police—with animal pits and a small amphitheater that seated 250 but that regularly held 400 yelling spectators. Although workingmen dominated the audiences, a few members of the old aristocracy who rejected middle-class ways also attended these

History Through Film: Gangs of New York (2002)

Directed by Martin Scorsese.
Starring Leonardo DiCaprio (Amsterdam Vallon), Daniel Day-Lewis (Bill "The Butcher" Cutting), and Cameron Diaz (Jenny Everdeane).

This is Martin Scorsese's movie about the Five Points of New York—a dangerous neighborhood that was home to the working-class world that sustained the new forms of urban popular culture. The film is an operatic tragedy about an Irish boy (Leonardo DiCaprio) whose father, the leader of a gang called the Dead Rabbits, is killed by a nativist chieftain (Daniel Day-Lewis) in a gang fight. He grows up in an orphanage and returns to the neighborhood to take revenge. He becomes part of the criminal entourage of his father's killer, falls in love with a beautiful and talented female thief (Cameron Diaz) who was raised (and used) by the same gang boss, and bides his time—tortured all the while by the prospect of killing a second father figure. In the end, the Irish boy resurrects his father's gang and challenges the nativists to a battle for control of the Five Points. The battle coincides with the Draft Riots of 1863, and the film ends (as it began) in a horrendous bloodbath. The Irish thug kills the nativist thug and the film ends with U2 singing "We Who Built America."

For those who can stomach close-up fights with clubs and hatchets, it is a good enough melodrama. Unhappily, Scorsese casts his story against real history and gets much of it wrong. The film takes pains to "reconstruct" Manhattan's Five Points, but our first view of the neighborhood is taken from a painting of a Brooklyn street made 50 years earlier. The oppressive noise and overcrowding that contemporary visitors describe are obliterated by a large public space at the center of the Points—historically nonexistent, but a fine field for the gang fights that begin and end the movie. Scorsese does cast the nativist leader as a butcher, a trade that was in fact dominated by nonimmigrant workers who were at the center of street gangs, prizefighting, and other low activities. He also reconstructs a theatrical performance—complete with actors in blackface—that rings true. But he puts his characters into too many fictional places. Historically, the gangs were headquartered at saloons, firehouses, and stables. Scorsese's operatic sensibilities, however, move the Dead Rabbits into catacombs beneath the Old Brewery—complete with torchlight, a crude armory, and an untidy pyramid of skulls. The nativists, on the other hand, prefer an Asian motif, holding their get-togethers in an ornate Chinese theater and social house that lends an air of orientalist extravaganza to a neighborhood that knew nothing of such things. The catalog of crimes against history could go on and on: The Dead Rabbits did not follow the cross into battle (Irish street gangs were not particularly religious), Irish priests did not look like Peter the Hermit, and Leonardo DiCaprio does not have a convincing Irish accent.

The "reformers" who minister to the Five Points receive equally silly treatment. Chief among the reformers are the aristocratic Schermerhorns. In fact, most Five Points missionaries were middle-class evangelicals who had little to do with the Schermerhorns or the other old families of New York. The movie reformers hold a dance for the neighborhood; in fact, the evangelicals hated dancing and parties. The reformers also attend a public hanging, cheering as four innocent men are put to death. But New York had outlawed public executions a generation earlier; felons were now hanged within prison walls before small invited audiences. Even if public hangings had persisted, reformers would not have attended them (they had stopped going to such spectacles soon after 1815), and had they been dragged out of their parlors to witness an execution, they would not have cheered. There is also an appearance by P. T. Barnum. Barnum had made his museum the premier middle-class entertainment spot in New York by eschewing low theater, cockfights, and other raucous and violent shows. Yet, the movie has Barnum sponsoring a bare-knuckle prizefight—an act that would have cost him his reputation and his livelihood. The climactic riot includes another Barnum fabrication: Barnum's museum is set on fire; his menagerie escapes, and a terrified elephant romps through the burning streets. It almost certainly did not happen, but even the most fact-bound historian must bow to Scorsese's artistic license on that one. ■

10.6 Daniel Day-Lewis (playing Bill "The Butcher" Cutting) and his Five Points gang.

events. In 1861, for instance, 250 spectators paid as much as $3 each to witness a fight between roosters belonging to the prizefighter John Morrissey and Mr. Genet, president of the New York City board of aldermen. A newspaper estimated bets on the event at $50,000.

10-4b Boxing

Prizefighting emerged from the same subterranean culture that sustained cockfights and other blood sports. This sport, imported from Britain, called for an enclosed ring, clear rules, cornermen, a referee, and a paying audience. Boxing's popularity rose during the 1840s and 1850s, a time of increasing immigration and violence in poor city neighborhoods. Many of the fighters had close ties with ethnic-based saloons, militia units, fire companies, and street gangs such as New York's (Irish) Dead Rabbits and (native) Bowery B'hoys, and many labored at occupations with a peculiarly ethnic base. Some of the best American-born fighters were New York City butchers—a licensed, privileged trade from which cheap immigrant labor was systematically excluded. Butchers usually finished work by 10 a.m. They could then spend the rest of the day idling at a firehouse or a bar and often were prominent figures in neighborhood gangs. A prizefight between an American-born butcher and an Irish day laborer would attract a spirited audience that understood its class and ethnic meaning.

10-4c An American Theater

In the 18th and early 19th centuries, all American theaters were in the large seaport cities. Those who attended were members of the urban elite, and nearly all of the plays, managers, and actors were English. After 1815, new theaters sprang up not only in New York and Philadelphia but also in dozens of other new towns, while traveling troupes carried theatrical performances to the smallest hamlets. The new theaters catered to male, largely plebeian audiences. Before 1830, the poorer theatergoers—nearly all of them men—occupied the cheap balcony seats (with the exception of the second balcony, which was reserved for prostitutes); artisans and other workingmen filled benches in the ground-floor area known as "the pit"; wealthier and more genteel patrons sat in the boxes. Those sitting in the pit and balcony joined in the performance: They ate and drank, talked, and shouted encouragement and threats to the actors. The genteel New Yorker Washington Irving lamented the "discharge of apples, nuts, and gingerbread" flying out of the balconies.

10.7a (left) and 10.7b (right) Prizefighters The Irishman James "Yankee" Sullivan (left) and the nativeborn Tom Hyer (right) were immensely popular heroes of Irish and native workingmen, as well as of the street gangs and political factions of their respective ethnic groups.

Q *What explains the rapid rise of boxing as a popular sport in the mid-19th-century United States?*

What They Said

A Fatal Prizefight, 1842

In 1842, in Hastings, New York, the English boxer Chris Lilly beat the Irishman Tom McCoy to death in a 119-round prizefight. A crowd of more than 2,000 attended the contest. The respectable press denounced the fight as an affront to humanity and civilization. A sportswriter, while he regretted that the fight had not been stopped, admired the male beauty of the losing fighter and the bravery and dignity with which he died. Following are three editorials.

The Sun (Baltimore), 17 September 1842

In connection with [prize-fighting] we now present … a terrible illustration of the consequences of this imbruting and pernicious vice; a detail of scenes enacted in a civilized country, calculated to summon the blush of shame to the cheek of manhood for such voluntary degradation of our race. It will be seen that in a matter of "sport"—to gratify the devilish taste of a certain class of the community—and for a purse of a few dollars, a wretched man has been beaten to death—in the presence of a crowd of spectators bearing the human form…. As a civilized people, we shudder at the contemplation of the scenes familiar to the old Gladiatorial arena, but in comparison with those witnessed the other day in New York, and in view of "the enlightened age in which we live," the former are elevated in their character and become a virtue in our eyes. Let us earnestly hope, that while we import the virtues, many of the foibles, and some of the vices of the old world, we may be able to avoid the diabolical iniquity and savage barbarity of its blood-stained "ring."

Public Ledger (Philadelphia), 15 September 1842

Beauties of the Ring—A Foul Murder—; A foul murder was committed in New York on Tuesday, which, for brutality and shocking barbarity, exceeds the most atrocious act of the kind recently recorded. It was the more atrocious from the fact that it was committed in the presence of thousands, who stood coolly looking on, enjoying the sport and encouraging it by approbative cries. That such an act should be committed in the presence of thousands of pleased spectators, in the nineteenth century, shows that we have begun too soon to boast of our civilization—that there still exists a low brutality of feeling in a large portion of the public, which could not be exceeded in the most debased condition of any former age, or among the most abject of its people.

Excerpts from the Sportswriter's Account

If Lilly's appearance was fine, *McCoy's* was beautiful. His skin had a warmer glow than the former's; his form was more elegantly proportioned, and his air and style more graceful and manlike. His swelling breast curved out like a cuirass; his shoulders were deep, with a bold curved blade, and the muscular development of the arms large and finely brought out. His head was rather large and long, yet it indicated courage and a love for strife, and the manner in which it was set betokened strength.

*Round 28*th—Lilly cool as a cucumber, and wary as an Indian—McCoy, on the contrary, too free, and too ready to fight…. McCoy, game as a pebble, and fearless as a lion, rushed wildly in, caught two or three more before he could clinch, and then was badly thrown.

Round 103d. McCoy suffering very much, scarcely able to breathe, and spitting [blood] from his mouth…. He came up bravely (the noble boy!), without the slightest indication of a desire to shrink, got in a good body blow, but in the close was badly thrown.

*Round 120*th—[McCoy] was led slowly to the mark, and took his position—a dying man—but as erect, as dignified, as game as ever. Lilly was also much fatigued, and enduring considerable suffering from the heavy body blows he had received.

Q *The newspapers condemned prizefighting in the name of civilization, religion, and a proper sense of manhood. Look closely at the language that they applied to the boxing community. How did they characterize those people and what they did? How did that characterization buttress their own conceptions of "civilization?"*

Q *The sportswriter described the aesthetics of the male body and the bravery, dignity, and sense of honor with which the doomed fighter conducted himself. In what fundamental ways did this description conflict with the world that the editorialists were making and defending?*

Sources: (top) *The Sun* (Baltimore newspaper), 17 September 1842; (middle) *Public Ledger* (Philadelphia newspaper), 15 September 1842; (bottom) *The American Fistiana: Containing a History of Prize Fighting in the United States, with all the Principal Battles for the Last Forty Years* (New York: H. Johnson, 1849), pp. 15–21.

As time passed, rowdyism turned into violence. Working-class theatergoers protested the elegant speech, gentlemanly bearing, and understated performances of the English actors, which happened to match the speech, manners, and bearing of the American urban elite. Protests were directed not only at the English actors but also at the ladies and gentlemen in the orchestra who were seen as adherents of an aristocratic English culture unsuitable in a democratic republic.

The first theater riot occurred in 1817, when the English actor Charles Incledon refused a New York audience's demand that he stop what he was doing and sing "Black-Eyed Susan." Such assaults grew more common even though separate theaters began to offer separate kinds of performances for rich and poor. The violence culminated in the rivalry between the American actor Edwin Forrest and the English actor William Charles Macready in the 1840s (see "Interpreting the Visual Past").

Playhouses that catered to working-class audiences continued to feature Shakespearean tragedies (*Richard III*, played broadly and with a lot of swordplay, was the favorite), but they soon shared the stage with works written in the American vernacular. The stage "Yankee," rustic but shrewd, appeared at this time, and so did Mose the Bowery B'hoy, a New York volunteer fireman who performed feats of derring-do. Both frequently appeared in opposition to well-dressed characters with English accents. The Yankee outsmarted them; Mose beat them up.

10-4d Minstrelsy

The most popular form of theater was the blackface **minstrel show**. These shows were blatantly racist, and they were the preferred entertainment of workingmen in northern cities from 1840 to 1880. The first minstrel show was presented in 1831 when a white showman named Thomas Rice blacked his face and "jumped Jim Crow," imitating a black shuffle-dance he had seen on the Cincinnati docks.

Minstrel shows developed a form that every theatergoer knew by heart. The shows lasted an hour and a half and were presented in three sections. The first consisted of songs and dances performed in a walkaround, in which the audience was encouraged to clap and sing along. This was followed by a longer middle section in which the company sat in a row with a character named Tambo at one end and a character named Bones at the other (named for the tambourine and bones, the instruments they played), with an interlocutor in the middle. The Tambo character, often called Uncle Ned, was a simple-minded plantation slave dressed in plain clothing. The Bones character, usually called Zip Coon, was a dandified, oversexed free black dressed in top hat and tails. The interlocutor was the straight man—fashionably dressed, slightly pretentious, with an English accent. This middle portion of the show consisted of a conversation among the three, which included pointed political satire, skits ridiculing the wealthy and the educated, and sexual jokes that bordered on obscenity. The third section featured songs, dances, and jokes, most of them familiar enough so that the audience could sing along and laugh at the right places.

The minstrel shows introduced African American song and dance—in toned-down, Europeanized form—to audiences who would not have permitted black performers on the stage. They also reinforced racial stereotypes that were near the center of American popular culture. Finally, hiding behind black masks, minstrel performers dealt broadly with aspects of social and political life that other performers avoided.

10.8 Jim Crow Thomas D. Rice wearing the costume of his character "Jim Crow," in 1833.

Q *What contemporary racial stereotypes was Thomas Rice channeling and reinforcing?*

Q *Why did minstrelsy shows appeal to white audiences in the North?*

10-4e Novels and the Penny Press

Few of the commodities made widely available by the Market Revolution were more ubiquitous than newspapers and inexpensive books. Improvements in printing and papermaking enabled entrepreneurs to sell daily newspapers for a penny. Cheap "story papers" became available in the 1830s, "yellowback" fiction in the 1840s, and dime novels from the 1850s onward. Although these offerings were distributed throughout the North and the West, they found their first and largest audience among city workers.

Interpreting the Visual Past

The Actors' War: Forrest and Macready

Edwin Forrest was America's great native-born actor. He was a democratic-nationalist hero, with a voice (according to the democratic press) like the roar of Niagara Falls and a body "carved out of the American forest." He played Shakespeare as American melodrama filled with bombast and physicality. Forrest's great international rival was the British actor William Charles Macready. Macready was engaged, both as an actor and a theater manager, in a campaign to rescue the theater from democracy. He insisted that acting demanded study and formal training, and that plays be performed with fidelity to the text (Shakespeare the way Shakespeare wrote it) before knowledgeable audiences that rewarded the best actors and the best plays. Macready condemned Forrest's extravagant acting style and his working-class audiences as the opposite of high culture and good taste. Their rivalry began during Forrest's tour of Great Britain in 1846, and culminated in Macready's visit to America three years later. Macready was hissed in Boston and showered with rotten potatoes in New York, and he had to dodge a sheep carcass that was thrown onto the stage in Cincinnati. The attacks on Macready came to a head when he played the elite Astor Place Opera House in New York. Handbills told American democrats to descend on the "English Aristocratic Opera House," and the militia was called out to protect Macready, the theater, and its genteel audience. The result was the worst theater riot in American history, which left 20 dead.

These pictures portray Forrest and Macready as Shakespeare's Macbeth. They are similar, but the differences are telling. Macready stands beneath a vast sky in an open countryside. His body is composed, his toes are properly pointed, and he gazes meaningfully into the heavens. Forrest, on the other hand, stands before a gothic/melodramatic backdrop that features a witch's cauldron, threatening rocks, and broken trees. His body is less elegant and more powerful than Macready's, he stares forcefully off-stage, and his weapon is bigger than Macready's. Macready is prepared for a classical performance. Forrest is ready for physical melodrama.

Q Look closely at these pictures. Find as many differences in dress, demeanor, and surroundings as you can. What do these differences say to you about these two men?

Q Edwin Forrest was often hailed as a model of a new kind of American manhood. What were the components of that model, and how do they relate to the themes of this chapter?

10.9a (left) and 10.9b (right) Augustus Robin, *Edwin Forrest as Macbeth*, mid 19th century (left). Thomas Sherratt, *William Charles Macready as Macbeth*, mid 19th century (right).

10.10a (left) and 10.10b (right) Yellow-Back Novels Here are two pulp fiction hits of the 1840s: an erotic novel about the "amorous and lively" Mary Ann Temple (left) and a crime story about robberies and murders committed by the "Female Land Pirate" (right)—not the kinds of women encountered in middle-class sentimental fiction.

Q *What social and cultural developments explain the wide popularity of such sensational novels as* Mary Ann Temple *and* The Female Land Pirate?

Mass-audience newspapers were heavily spiced with sensationalism. The *Philadelphia Gazette* in late summer 1829, for instance, treated its eager readers to the following: "Female Child with Two Heads," "Bats," "Another Shark," "More Stabbing," "Fishes Travelling on Land," "Dreadful Steam Boat Disaster," "Raffling for Babies," "Combat with a Bear," "Lake Serpent," "Atrocious Murder," and much more. Henry David Thoreau commented on the "startling and monstrous events as fill the daily papers," while his friend Ralph Waldo Emerson reported that Americans were "reading all day murders & railroad accidents." These sensational stories portrayed a haunted, often demonic nature that regularly produced monstrosities and ruined the works of humankind, as well as a human nature that, despite appearances, was often deceptive and depraved.

Working-class readers discovered a similarly untrustworthy world in cheap fiction. George Lippard's *The Quaker City* (1845) sold more than 200,000 copies in six years, making it the best-selling American book before the sentimental blockbusters of the 1850s. *The Quaker City* was a fictional exposé of the hypocrisy, lust, and cruelty of Philadelphia's outwardly genteel and Christian elite. Lippard and other adventure writers (whose works accounted for 60 percent of all American fiction titles published between 1831 and 1860) indulged in a pornography of violence that included cannibalism, blood drinking, and murder by every imaginable means. They also dealt with sex in unprecedentedly explicit ways, introducing readers not only to seduction and rape but also to transvestitism, child pornography, necrophilia, miscegenation, group sex, homosexuality, and—perhaps most shocking of all—women with criminal minds and insatiable sexual appetites. The scenes of gore and sexual depravity were presented voyeuristically—as self-righteous exposés of the perversions of the rich and powerful and stories of the Founders' Republic trampled upon by a vicious elite that pretended virtue but lived only for its appetites.

Popular fictions—like most popular plays and much of what went on in blood sports, the prize ring, and the penny press—were melodramatic contests between good and evil. Evil was described in terms reminiscent of original sin: It provided the background of all human action, and heroes met a demonic world with courage and guile without hoping to change it. Melodramatic heroes frequently acknowledged evil in themselves while claiming moral superiority over the hypocrites and frauds that governed the world. A murderer in Ned Buntline's *G'hals of New York* (1850) remarks, "There isn't no *real* witue [virtue] and honesty nowhere, 'cept among the perfessional dishonest." By contrast, in middle-class sentimental novels, the universe was benign; good could be nurtured, and evil could be defeated and transformed. Harriet Beecher Stowe's slave driver Simon Legree—the best-known villain in American literature—is evil not because of a natural disposition toward evil, but because he had been deprived of a mother's love during childhood. The world, in Stowe's view, could be nurtured into being good. Most northern plain folk (whether they favored church or popular entertainments) did not want to fix an imperfect and often chaotic world. They wanted only to live decently and bravely within it.

10-5 Family, Church, and Neighborhood: The White South

 In what specific ways did evangelical Protestantism act as a conservative force within southern culture?

The southern states experienced cultural transformations of a more conservative nature—transformations grounded in persistent localism, in the father-centered family, and in the pervasive influence of a traditionalist evangelical Christianity.

10-5a *The Beginnings of the Bible Belt*

In the first third of the 19th century, evangelical Protestantism and revivalism of the Second Great Awakening transformed the South into what it has been ever since: the Bible Belt. That transformation began when poor and middling whites found spiritual alternatives to the culture of the gentry—to their formalistic Episcopalianism, their love of luxury and display, and their enjoyment of money and power. Early southern Baptists and Methodists demanded a crisis conversion followed by a life of piety and a rejection of what they called "the world." To no small degree, the world was the economic, cultural, and political world controlled by the planters. James McGready, who preached in rural North Carolina in the 1790s, openly condemned the gentry: "The world is in all their thoughts day and night. All their talk is of corn and tobacco, of land and stock. The price of merchandise and negroes are inexhaustible themes of conversation. But for them, the name of Jesus has no charms; it is rarely mentioned unless to be profaned." This was dangerous talk, as McGready learned when young rakes rode their horses through one of his outdoor meetings, tipped over the benches, set the altar on fire, and threatened to kill McGready.

Southern Baptists, Methodists, and Presbyterians spread their message during the awakening through the **camp meeting**, and this too was subversive of southern social distinctions. Though its origins stretched back into the 18th century, the first full-blown camp meeting took place at Cane Ridge, Kentucky, in 1801. Here the annual "Holy Feast," a three-day communion service of Scots-Irish Presbyterians, was transformed into an outdoor revival at which hundreds experienced conversion under Presbyterian, Methodist, and Baptist preaching. Estimates of the crowd at Cane Ridge ranged from 10,000 to 20,000 persons. Some converts fainted, others jerked uncontrollably, and a few barked like dogs, all of them visibly taken by the Holy Spirit. These exercises fell upon women and men, whites and blacks, rich and poor, momentarily blurring social hierarchy in moments of profound and very public religious ecstasy. A witness to a later camp meeting recounted that "to see a bold and courageous Kentuckian (undaunted by the horrors of war) turn pale and tremble at the reproof of a weak woman, a little boy, or a poor African; to see him sink down in deep remorse, roll and toss, and gnash his teeth, till black in the face, entreat the prayers of those he came to devour ... who can say the change was not supernatural?" Southern white men, even when under religious conviction, sometimes resisted this loss of mastery and self-control. One preacher remembered a "fine, strong, good-looking young man" who felt himself giving in to camp meeting preaching. He "found no relief until he drew a large pistole out of his pocket, with which he intended to defend himself if any one should offer to speak to him on the subject of religion."

The early southern evangelicals irritated and angered the elite and white men generally, for they seemed to question not only worldliness but also the white male dominance that held the southern world together. The conversion of wives and children (not to mention slaves) could trouble southern families; the conversion of white men could render them "womanish." The governors of southern farms and southern families, however, had little to worry about. The Baptists, Methodists, and Presbyterians of the South, though they never stopped railing against greed and pride, found that they could conquer the South and live comfortably with a system of fixed hierarchy and God-given social roles—with slavery and father-dominated families in particular.

10-5b *Slavery and Southern Evangelicals*

Slavery became a major case in point. For a brief period after the Revolution, evangelicals joined with an elite minority of slaveholders to oppose slavery. Methodists and Baptists preached to slaves as well as to whites, and Bishop Francis Asbury, the principal architect of American Methodism, admired John Wesley's statement that slavery was against "all the laws of Justice, Mercy, and Truth." In 1780, a conference of Methodist preachers ordered circuit riders to free their slaves and advised all Methodists to do the same. In 1784, the Methodists declared that they would excommunicate members who failed to free their slaves within two years. Many lay Methodists took the order seriously. On the Delmarva Peninsula (Delaware and the Eastern Shore of Maryland and Virginia), for instance, Methodist converts freed thousands of slaves in the late 18th century.

The period of greatest evangelical growth, however, came during the years in which the South committed irrevocably to plantation slavery. As increasing numbers of both slaves and slave owners came within the evangelical fold, the southern churches had to rethink their position on human bondage. The Methodists never carried out their threat to excommunicate slaveholders, and in 1816 confessed, "little can be done to abolish the practice so contrary to moral justice." Similarly, the Baptists and Presbyterians never translated their antislavery rhetoric into action. By 1820, evangelicals were coming to terms with slavery. Instead of demanding freedom for slaves, they suggested, as the Methodist James O'Kelly put it, that slave owners treat slaves as "dear brethren in Christ." After 1830, with much of the planter elite converted to evangelicalism, this would evolve into a full-scale effort to Christianize the institution of slavery.

10-5c Gender, Power, and the Evangelicals

Southern white men, yeomen as well as planters, distrusted the early evangelicals for more than their views on slavery. The preachers seemed even more grievously mistaken about white manhood and the integrity of white families. Southerners were localistic and culturally conservative. They distrusted outsiders and defended rural neighborhoods grounded in the sovereignty of fathers.

The early evangelicals threatened southern patriarchy. They preached individual salvation to women, children, and slaves—often hinting that the "family" of believers could replace blood ties. Churches sometimes intervened in family disputes or disciplined family members in ways that subverted patriarchal control. Perhaps worse, many of the preachers failed to act out the standards of southern manhood in their own lives. James McGready and other camp meeting preachers often faced hecklers and rowdies and quietly took their beatings, which violated the southern notions of male honor.

As they had with slavery, southern evangelicals came to terms with the notions of manhood and the father-centered families of the South. The preachers learned to assert traditional forms of manhood. Their fathers and often themselves, they said, had fought the British and Indians heroically. They revealed that they had often been great drinkers, gamblers, fighters, and fornicators before submitting to God, and they also began fighting back when attacked. Peter Cartwright, who conquered much of Kentucky and southern Illinois for Methodism, walked on many occasions out of the pulpit to confront hecklers, and punched more than a few of them. The preachers also made it clear that they would pose no threat to the authority of fathers. They discouraged the excesses of female and juvenile piety. At the same time, church disciplinary cases involving adultery, wife beating, private drunkenness, and other offenses committed within families became more and more rare.

10-5d Religious Conservatism

More fundamentally, evangelicals upheld the southern world of fixed hierarchy and God-given social roles, and their churches reinforced localistic neighborhoods and the patriarchal family. Some southern communities began when a whole congregation moved onto new land. Others were settled by the chain migration of brothers and cousins, and subsequent revivals spread through family networks. Rural isolation limited most households to their own company during the week, but on Sundays church meetings united the neighborhood's cluster

10.11 Colonel and Mrs. Whiteside Colonel and Mrs. James Whiteside are pictured at home in their mansion on the heights above Chattanooga, Tennessee, with their infant son and their slaves. The colonel, Bible in hand, looks directly at his wife, while she looks shyly and indirectly back at him.

Q *What does this carefully constructed painting reveal about the southern genteel ideal?*

of extended families into a community of believers. In most neighborhoods, social connections seldom extended beyond that. The word "church" referred ultimately to the worldwide community of Christians, and the war between the "church" and the "world" referred to a cosmic history that would end in millennial fire. But in the day-to-day understandings of southern evangelicals, the church was the local congregation and the world was local sins and local sinners. Churches disciplined members for such worldly practices as drinking, gambling, dancing, swearing, fornication, and adultery.

Southern evangelicalism rested on the sovereignty of God, a conviction of human imperfection, and an acceptance of disappointment and pain as part of God's grand and unknowable design. When the young son of a planter family died, his mother was certain that he died because his parents had loved him more than God: "But God took him for he saw he was our idol." Francis Pickens of South Carolina lost his wife and child, and wrote, "I had almost forgot there was a God, and now I stand the scattered... and blasted monument of his just wrath." It was a far cry from the middle-class North's sentimentalism and the romantic, redemptive deaths of children in sentimental fiction.

Within this flawed and dangerous world, patriarchal social relations were crucial to Christian living. Southerners revered the patriarch and slaveholder Abraham more than any other figure in the Bible, and John C. Calhoun would proclaim "Hebrew Theocracy" the best government ever experienced by humankind. The father must—like Abraham—govern and protect his household, the mother must assist the father, and the women, children, and slaves must faithfully act out the duties of their stations. Eternal salvation was possible for everyone, but the saved lived out their godliness by striving to be good mothers, good fathers, good slaves. By the same token, a Christian never questioned his or her God-given social role.

10-5e Pro-Slavery Christianity

In revolutionary and early national America, white southerners had been the most radical of republicans. Jeffersonian planter-politicians led the fights for equal rights and the absolute separation of church and state, and southern evangelicals were the early republic's staunchest opponents of slavery. By 1830, however, the South was an increasingly conscious minority within a democratic and capitalist nation. The northern middle classes proclaimed a link between material and moral progress, identifying both with individual autonomy and universal rights. A radical northern minority was agitating for the immediate abolition of slavery (Chapter 12).

Southerners met this challenge with an "intellectual blockade" against outside publications and ideas and with a moral and religious defense of slavery. The Bible provided plenty of ammunition. Southerners preached that the Chosen People of the Old Testament had been patriarchs and slaveholders, and that Jesus had lived in a society that sanctioned slavery and never criticized the institution. Some ministers claimed that blacks were the descendants of Ham and thus deserved enslavement. The most common religious argument, however, was that slavery had given millions of heathen Africans the priceless opportunity to become Christians and to live in a Christian society. Thornton Stringfellow, a Virginia Baptist minister, insisted that "their condition... is now better than that of any equal number of laborers on earth, and is daily improving."

Like their northern counterparts, southern clergymen applauded the material improvements of the age, but they insisted that moral improvement occurred only when people embraced the timeless truths of the Bible. The South Carolinian William F. Hutson put it simply: "In religion and morals, we doubt all improvements, not known to certain fishermen who lived eighteen hundred years ago." Northern notions of progress through individual liberation, equal rights, and universal Christian love were wrongheaded and dangerous. The Presbyterian John Adger asserted that relations of dominance and submission (and not "barbarism and personal savage independence") were utterly necessary to both social and individual fulfillment, and that the distribution of rights and responsibilities was unequal and God-given. "The rights of the father are natural, but they belong only to the fathers. Rights of property are natural, but they belong only to those who have property," and such natural rights were coupled with the awesome duties of fatherhood and proprietorship. In the end, southern pro-slavery intellectuals rejected Jefferson's "self-evident" equality of man; Edmund Ruffin, for instance, branded that passage of the Declaration of Independence as "indefensible" as well as "false and foolish."

10-5f The Mission to the Slaves

By the 1820s, southern evangelicalism had long since abandoned its hostility toward slavery, and slaveholders commonly attended camp meetings and revivals. These prosperous converts faced conflicting duties. Their churches taught them that slaves had immortal souls and that planters were responsible for their spiritual welfare. A planter on his deathbed told his children that humane treatment and religious instruction for slaves was the duty of slave owners; if these were neglected, "we will have to answer for the loss of their souls." After Nat Turner's bloody slave revolt in 1831 (Chapter 9), missions to the slaves took on new urgency: If the churches were to create a Christian society in the South, that society would have to include the slaves. The result after 1830 was a concerted attempt to Christianize the slaves.

To this end, Charles Colcock Jones, a Presbyterian minister from Georgia, wrote manuals on how to preach to slaves. He taught that no necessary connection linked social position and spiritual worth: There were good and bad slaveholders and good and bad slaves. He also taught, preaching from the Epistles of Paul ("Servants, obey your masters"), that slaves must accept the master's authority as God's, and that obedience was their prime religious virtue. Jones warned white preachers never to become personally involved with their slave listeners—to pay no attention to their quarrels, their complaints about their master or about their fellow slaves, or about working conditions on the plantation. "We separate entirely their religious from their civil condition," he said, "and contend that one may be attended to without interfering with the other." The catechism Jones prepared for slaves included the question, "What did God make you for?" The answer was, "To make a crop."

The evangelical mission to the slaves was not as completely self-serving as it may seem. For to accept one's worldly station, to be obedient and dutiful within that station, and to seek salvation outside of this world were precisely what the planters demanded of themselves and their own families. An important goal of plantation missions was to create safe and profitable plantations. Yet that goal was to be achieved by Christianizing both slaveholders and slaves—a lesson that some slaveholders learned when they were expelled from their churches for mistreating their slaves. As for the slaves, we have seen that they listened selectively to what white missionaries preached, and turned evangelical Christianity into a religion of their own (see Chapter 9). This continued throughout the Second Great Awakening, which drew thousands of slaves into Methodist and Baptist churches. The slaves responded to the awakening's democratizing message even as they continued to adapt Christianity to African practices, often organizing their own services beyond white oversight.

10-6 Race

 In what ways did the racial order of the North change in the first half of the 19th century?

Americans in the first half of the 19th century revised the racial order as well as the religious and domestic order of their society. White Americans had long assumed that Africans belonged at the bottom of society, but they assumed that others belonged there as well. In a colonial world in which many whites were indentured servants, tenants, apprentices, and workers who lived in their employers' homes, where increasing numbers of blacks were formally free and many others were hired out as semifree, few Americans made rigid distinctions concerning the "natural" independence of whites and the "natural" dependence of blacks. (All Americans, after all, were colonial dependents of the British king.) The language of colonial social division separated gentlemen from the "middling sort," and relegated the propertyless and dependent to the "lower orders" or the "lower sort." While the better-off whites were far from color blind, they wrote off poverty, disorder, drunkenness, and rioting as the work not of blacks but of an undifferentiated substratum of "Negroes, sailors, servants, and boys."

Modern racism—the notion that blacks were a separate and hopelessly inferior order of humankind—emerged from developments in the early 19th century: national independence and the crucial new distinction between Americans who were citizens and those who were not, the recommitment to slavery in the South, and the making of what would be called "free labor" in the North. Whites who faced lifetimes of wage labor and dependence struggled to make dignity out of that situation. At the same time, freed slaves entered the bottom of a newly defined "free labor" society and tried to do the same. With plenty of help from the wealthy and powerful, whites succeeded in making white democracy out of the rubble of the old patriarchal republic. In the process, they defined nonwhites as constitutionally incapable of self-discipline, personal independence, and political participation.

10-6a Free Blacks

There had been sizable pockets of slavery in the northern colonies, but revolutionary idealism, coupled with the growing belief that slavery was inefficient, led one northern state after another to abolish it. Vermont, where there were almost no slaves, outlawed slavery in its revolutionary constitution. By 1804, every northern state had taken some action, usually by passing laws that mandated gradual emancipation. The first of such laws, and the model for others, was passed in Pennsylvania in 1780. This law freed slaves born after 1780 when they reached their 28th birthday. Slaves born before 1780 would remain slaves, and slave children would remain slaves through their prime working years. By 1830, only a handful of aging blacks remained slaves in the North.

Gradual emancipation did not stop at the Mason-Dixon Line. We have seen (Chapter 9) that thousands of Chesapeake slaveholders freed their slaves in the decades following the Revolution. Virginia seriously considered abolishing slavery outright. In 1832, a Virginia constitutional convention argued the question of immediate emancipation by state law. With the western counties supporting abolition (but insisting that freed blacks be transported from the state) and some of the eastern, slaveholding counties threatening to secede from the state if abolition won, the convention rejected emancipation by a vote of 73–58. In the Deep South, where slavery was a big and growing business, whites did not talk about emancipation. They assumed that slavery was permanent, and that the only proper status for blacks was bondage and submission to whites.

From Virginia on north, the rising population of free blacks gravitated to the cities and towns. Despite the flood of white immigrants from Europe and the American countryside, African Americans constituted a sizable minority in the rapidly expanding cities. New York City's black population, 10.5 percent in 1800, was still 8.8 percent in 1820. Philadelphia, the haven of thousands of southern refugees, was 10.3 percent African American in 1800, 11.9 percent in 1820.

Blacks in the seaports tended to take stable, low-paying jobs. A few became successful (occasionally wealthy) entrepreneurs, while some others practiced skilled trades. Many took jobs as waiters or porters in hotels, as merchant seamen, as barbers, and as servants in wealthy families. Others worked as dockworkers and laborers. Still others became dealers in used clothing, or draymen with their own carts and horses, or food vendors in the streets and in basement shops. (In New York, oysters were a black monopoly.) As never before, free black faces and voices became parts of the landscape and soundscape of cities and towns—hawking buttermilk, hot corn, and oysters, talking and laughing in the streets, jostling their way through

10.12 Portrait of a Sailor, c. 1800 In the early 19th century, free African Americans in the North found new opportunities in a variety of occupations, including sailing. By 1820, about 20 percent of all American seamen were black

city crowds. More than a few whites were disturbed. The New York journalist Mordecai Noah, like many other elite whites, had expected freed slaves to be grateful and deferential to their former masters, but "instead of thankfulness for their redemption, they have become impudent and offensive beyond all precedent."

African Americans with money established businesses and institutions of their own. At one end were black-owned gambling houses, saloons, brothels, oyster cellars, and dance halls, which often served a mixed clientele. At the other end were institutions built by self-consciously "respectable" free blacks. Most prominent among these were churches, which sprang up wherever African Americans lived. In Philadelphia, black preachers Richard Allen and Absalom Jones rebelled against segregated seating in St. George's Methodist Church and, in 1794, founded two separate black congregations. The African Methodist Episcopal Church grew from Allen's church, and established itself as a national denomination in 1816. Sustained by the evangelical fervor of the Second Great Awakening, black evangelical churches proliferated in the North, promoting a liberating faith and the abolition of slavery. The membership of the African Methodist Episcopal Church reached 20,000 by the 1850s. Schools and relief societies, usually associated with churches, also grew quickly. Black Masonic lodges attracted hundreds of members. Many of the churches and social organizations took names that proudly called up the blacks' African origins. In Philadelphia, for instance, there were African Methodists, Abyssinian Baptists, the Daughters of Ethiopia, the African Dorcas Society—to name only a few. Not only their names and activities but their presence as black-owned buildings filled with respectable former slaves caught the attention of their white and black neighbors. It was from this matrix of black businesses and institutions that black abolitionists—David Walker in Boston, Frederick Douglass in New Bedford and Rochester, the itinerant Sojourner Truth, and many others—would emerge to demand abolition of slavery and equal rights for black citizens.

10-6b The Beginnings of Modern Racism

In post-revolutionary America, the most important social and political distinction was not between black and white or rich and poor. It was between the heads of independent households and the women, slaves, servants, apprentices, and others who were their dependents. Wage labor and tenancy reduced the number of northern whites who were, by traditional measures, independent. They fought that threat in a number of ways: Their skills and labor, they said, constituted a kind of property; their manhood conferred judgment and strength and thus independence. These were assertions of worth and independence that had little to do with the ownership of property. In ways that were sometimes subtle but just as often brutal, they often made those assertions at the expense of African Americans. Along with the value of their labor and their manhood, white men discovered the decisive value of white skin.

Whites in the early 19th century began refusing to work alongside blacks, and some of the earliest and most decisive racist assaults came when whites asserted their control over some occupations and relegated blacks to others. They chased blacks out of skilled jobs by pressuring employers to discriminate, and often by outright violence. As a result, African Americans disappeared from the skilled trades, while many unskilled and semiskilled blacks lost their jobs on the docks and in warehouses. In 1834, a Philadelphian reported that "colored persons, when engaged in their usual occupations, were repeatedly assailed and maltreated, usually on the [waterfront]. Parties of white men have insisted that no blacks shall be employed in certain departments of labor." And as their old jobs disappeared, blacks were systematically excluded from the new jobs that were opening up in factories.

Even whites who remained in positions of personal dependence (servants, waiters, and other jobs that were coming to be defined as "black" work) refused the signs and language of servility. White servants refused to wear livery, which became the uniform of black servants of the rich. Whites also refused to be called "servants." As early as 1807, when an English visitor asked a New England servant for her master, the woman replied that she had no master. "I am Mr.___'s *help*," she said. "I'd have you know, *man*, that I am no *sarvant*; none but *negars* are *sarvants*." There was trouble off the job as well. As early as the 1790s, whites had disrupted African American church meetings, and they frequently attacked black celebrations of northern emancipation and Haitian independence. Black neighborhoods and institutions came under increasing attack. In the late 1820s and early 1830s, every northern city experienced antiblack rioting. In 1829, white mobs destroyed black homes and businesses in Cincinnati. Hundreds of blacks fled that city for Canada; many others sought refuge in slaveholding Kentucky. Between 1828 and 1849 in Philadelphia, simmering racial tensions between blacks and working-class whites erupted into five sprawling race riots that wrecked black churches, businesses, and homes.

Above all, white populists pronounced blacks unfit to be citizens of the republic. Federalists and other upper-class whites had often supported various forms of black suffrage; less-privileged whites opposed it. The insistence that blacks were incapable of citizenship reinforced an equally natural white male political capacity. The most vicious racist assaults were often carried out beneath symbols of the revolutionary republic. Antiblack mobs in Baltimore, Cincinnati, and Toledo called themselves Minute Men and Sons of Liberty. Philadelphia blacks who gathered to hear the reading of the Declaration of Independence on the Fourth of July were attacked for "defiling the government." The more respectable and powerful whites had long been worried about the mixed-race underclass of the cities and towns. Now, as the disorder that they expected of the lower orders took the form of race riots, the authorities responded. But rather than protect the jobs, churches, schools, businesses, friends, and political rights of African Americans from criminal attack, they determined to stop the trouble by removing black people—from employment, from public festivities, from their already-limited citizenship, and, ultimately, from the United States. Cities either excluded black children from public schools or set up segregated schools. In 1845, when Massachusetts passed a law declaring that all children had the right to attend neighborhood schools, the Boston School Committee blithely ruled that the law did not apply to blacks. Blacks were also excluded from white churches or sat in segregated pews. Even the Quakers seated blacks and whites separately.

10-7 Citizenship

Q *How did American voting rights change between the adoption of the Constitution and the Civil War?*

The transition from republic to democracy—and the relation of that transition to the decline of patriarchy and efforts to shore up white manhood—took on legal, institutional shape in a redefinition of republican citizenship. The revolutionary constitutions of most states retained colonial freehold (property) qualifications for voting. In the yeoman societies of the late 18th century, freehold qualifications granted the vote to between one-half and three-quarters of adult white men. Many of the disfranchised were dependent sons who expected to inherit citizenship along with land. Some states dropped the freehold clause and gave the vote to all adult men who paid taxes, but with little effect on the voting population. Both the freehold and taxpaying qualifications tended to give political rights to heads of households, granting active citizenship to independent fathers and not to their dependents. Arthur St. Clair, the territorial governor of Ohio, argued for retention of the Northwest Ordinance's 50-acre freehold qualification for voting in territorial elections in set-piece republican language: "I do not count independence and wealth always together," he said, "but I pronounce poverty and dependence inseparable." When Nathaniel Macon, a respected old revolutionary from North Carolina, saw that his state would abolish property qualifications in 1802, he suggested that the suffrage be limited to married men. Like St. Clair's proposition, it was an attempt to maintain the old distinction between citizen-householders and disfranchised dependents.

Between 1790 and 1820, citizenship grounded in fatherhood and proprietorship gave way to a democratic insistence on equal rights for all white men. There were several reasons for that development. First, the proportion of adult white men who could not meet property qualifications multiplied at an alarming rate. In the new towns and cities, artisans and laborers and even many merchants and professionals did not own real estate. And in the West, new farms were often valued below property qualifications. This became particularly troublesome after the War of 1812, when a large proportion of veterans could not vote. In Shenandoah County, Virginia,

10.13 "The People" from John Latrobe, *The Juvenile National Calendar* (1824) Here is a page from a children's book published in 1824. It depicts The People engaged in democratic politics. Some are shouting, shoving, and turning politics into raucous play. Others, in more genteel postures, look on with amusement and disdain. All are white men. In democratic America, children learn that The People include "each of the men who are aged twenty-one." There are no women or nonwhites in the picture. They are not part of The People.

for instance, 700 of 1,000 men at a militia muster could not vote. In 1829, the "Non-Freeholders of the City of Richmond" petitioned for the right to vote, arguing that the ownership of property did not make a man "wiser and better." "Virtue" and "intelligence," they insisted, were "not among the products of the soil." Even the aging Thomas Jefferson had come to believe, by 1824, that property restrictions violated "the principal of equal political rights."

In the early 19th century, state after state extended the vote to all adult white men. In 1790, only Vermont granted the vote to all free men. Kentucky entered the Union in 1792 without property or taxpaying qualifications. Tennessee followed with a freehold qualification, but only for newcomers who had resided in their counties for less than six months. The federal government dropped the 50-acre freehold qualification in the territories in 1812. Of the eight territories that became states between 1796 and 1821, none kept a property qualification, only three maintained a taxpaying qualification, and five explicitly granted the vote to all white men. In the same years, one eastern state after another widened the franchise. By 1840, only Rhode Island retained a propertied electorate, primarily because Yankee farmers in that state wanted to retain power in a society made up increasingly of urban, immigrant wage earners. (When Rhode Island finally reformed the franchise in 1843, the new law included a freehold requirement that applied only to the foreign-born, and explicitly withheld the franchise from blacks.) With that exception, the white men of every state held the vote.

Suffrage reform gave political rights to propertyless men, and thus took a long step away from the Founders' republic and toward mass democracy. At the same time, however, reformers explicitly restricted the vote to those who were white and male. New Jersey's revolutionary constitution, for instance, had granted the vote to "persons" who met a freehold qualification. This loophole enfranchised property-holding widows, many of whom exercised their rights. A law of 1807 abolished property restrictions and gave the vote to all white men. The same law ended female voting. The question of woman suffrage would not be considered again until women raised it in 1848. It would not be settled until well into the 20th century.

New restrictions also applied to blacks. The revolutionary constitutions of Massachusetts, New Hampshire, Vermont, and Maine—northeastern states with tiny black minorities—granted the vote to free blacks. New York and North Carolina laws gave the vote to "all men" who met the qualifications, and propertied African Americans (a tiny but symbolically crucial minority) routinely exercised the vote. Post-revolutionary laws that extended voting rights to all white men often specifically excluded or severely restricted votes for blacks. Free blacks lost the suffrage in New York, New Jersey, Pennsylvania, Connecticut, Maryland, Tennessee, and North Carolina—all states in which they had previously voted. By 1840, fully 93 percent of blacks in the North lived in states that either banned or severely restricted their right to vote, and the restrictions were explicitly about race. A delegate to the New York constitutional convention of 1821, noting the movement of freed slaves into New York City, argued against allowing them to vote: "The whole host of Africans that now deluge our city (already too impertinent to be borne), would be placed upon an equal with the citizens." At the Tennessee convention that eliminated property and residence requirements for whites while it stripped the vote from free blacks in 1834, delegate G. W. L. Marr declared: "We the People" meant "we the free white people of the United States and the free white people only." The convention declared blacks "outside the social compact." A year later, Nathaniel Macon told a North Carolina convention that in 1776, free blacks had been "no part of the then political family."

Thus, the "universal" suffrage of which many Americans boasted was far from universal. New laws dissolved the ties between political rights and property, and thus saved the citizenship of thousands who were becoming propertyless tenants and wage earners. The same laws that gave the vote to all white men, however, explicitly barred other Americans from political participation. Faced with the disintegration of Jefferson's republic of proprietor-patriarchs, the wielders of power had chosen to blur the emerging distinctions of social class while they hardened the boundaries of sex and race. In 1790, citizenship had belonged to men who were fathers and farm owners. Forty years later, the citizenry was made up of those who were (the phrase came into use at this time) "free, white, and twenty-one." Much more explicitly and completely than had been the case at the founding, America in 1830 was a white man's republic.

Conclusion

By the second quarter of the 19th century, Americans had made a patchwork of regional, class, and ethnic cultures. The new middle classes of the North and West compounded their Protestant and republican inheritance with a new entrepreneurial faith in progress. The result was a way of life grounded in the self-made and morally accountable individual and the sentimentalized (often feminized) domestic unit.

Most Americans, however, did not live and think like the middle class. The poorer urban dwellers and farmers of the North remained grimly loyal to the unsentimental, male-dominated families of their fathers and grandfathers, to new and old religious sects that preached human depravity and the mysterious workings of providence, and to the suspicion that perfidy and disorder lurked behind the smiling moral order of market economics and middle-class culture.

In the South, most white farmers persisted in a neighborhood-based, intensely evangelical, and socially conservative way of life; when asked their opinions, they often talked like classic Jeffersonian yeomen. Southern planters, although they shared in the northern elite's belief in material progress and the magic of the market, were bound by family values, a system of slave labor, and a code of honor that was strikingly at variance with middle-class faith in an orderly universe and perfectible individuals. And we have seen (Chapter 9) that slaves in these years continued to make cultural forms of their own. Despite their exclusion from the white world of liberty and equality, they tied their aspirations to the family, to an evangelical Protestant God, and to the individual and collective dignity that republics promise to their citizens.

CHAPTER REVIEW

Review

1. In what ways did literacy and print help to democratize American culture?
2. What were the central cultural maxims of the emerging northern middle class?
3. Within the North, what were the alternatives to middle-class culture?
4. The amusements of common folk were varied, but they exhibited a few common themes. What were those themes?
5. In what specific ways did evangelical Protestantism act as a conservative force within southern culture?
6. In what ways did the racial order of the North change in the first half of the 19th century?
7. How did American voting rights change between the adoption of the Constitution and the Civil War?

Critical Thinking

1. Compare and contrast the domestic lives and family values of the northern middle class and the southern planter elite.
2. Compare and contrast the racial orders of the North and South in 1850. How do you explain the similarities and differences?

Identifications

Review your understanding of the following key terms, people, and events for this chapter (terms in bold in text are included in the Glossary).

middle class, p. 281
Second Great Awakening, p. 281
anxious bench, p. 282
Sarah Josepha Hale, p. 283
domestic fiction, p. 283
Joseph Smith, p. 284
crisis conversion, p. 284
Restorationism, p. 284
circuit-riding preachers, p. 284
postmillennialists, p. 285
premillennialists, p. 286
Millerites, p. 286
blood sports, p. 287
minstrel show, p. 291
camp meeting, p. 294

Suggested Readings

Daniel Walker Howe's *What Hath God Wrought: The Transformation of America, 1815–1848* (2007) emphasizes the communications revolution as an important catalyst for social changes during the era. **Stuart M. Blumin**, *The Emergence of the Middle Class: Social Experience in the American City, 1760–1900* (1989) is a thorough study of work and material life among the urban middle class. Studies that treat middle-class religion, family, and sentimental culture include **Paul E. Johnson**, *A Shopkeeper's Millennium: Society and Revivals in Rochester, New York, 1815–1837* (1978); **Mary P. Ryan**, *Cradle of the Middle Class: The Family in Oneida County, New York, 1790–1865* (1981); and **Jane Tompkins**, *Sensational Designs: The Cultural Work of American Fiction, 1790–1860* (1985). **Nathan O. Hatch**, *The Democratization of American Christianity* (1989) is a good introduction to plain-folk religion in these years. **Paul C. Gutjahr**'s *The Book of Mormon: A Biography* (2012) provides a balanced history and analysis of the influential book.

Studies of popular literature and entertainments include **Elliott J. Gorn**, *The Manly Art: Bare-Knuckle Prize Fighting in America* (1986); **Eric Lott**, *Love & Theft: Blackface Minstrelsy and the American Working Class* (1993); and **David S. Reynolds**, *Beneath the American Renaissance: The Subversive Imagination in the Age of Emerson and Melville* (1988). Essential books on the culture of southern whites are cited in the Suggested Readings for Chapter 9. Students should also consult **Christine Leigh Heyerman**, *Southern Cross: The Beginnings of the Bible Belt* (1997); **Elizabeth Fox Genovese and Eugene D. Genovese**, *Slavery in White and Black: Class and Race in the Southern Slaveholders' New World Order* (2008); and **Lacy K. Ford**, *Deliver Us from Evil: The Slavery Question in the Old South* (2009). On the racial order of the North, see **David R. Roediger**, *The Wages of Whiteness: Race and the Making of the American Working Class* (revised edition, 2007); and **John Wood Sweet**, *Bodies Politic: Negotiating Race in the American North, 1730–1830* (2007).

 MINDTAP is a fully online personalized learning experience built upon Cengage Learning content. MindTap® combines student learning tools—readings, multimedia, activities, and assessments—into a singular Learning Path that guides students through the course and helps students develop the critical thinking, analysis, and communication skills that are essential to academic and professional success.

11 Whigs and Democrats, 1815–1840

11-1 The American System
Learning Objective: Identify the components of the "American System" and find out what the American system promised to accomplish.

National Republicans
Commerce and the Law

11-2 1819
Learning Objective: Trace the political issues that were raised by the Missouri controversy and the Panic of 1819.

The Argument over Missouri
The Missouri Compromise
The Panic of 1819

11-3 Republican Revival
Learning Objective: Describe the events and political motives that contributed to the republican revival that formed around Andrew Jackson.

Martin Van Buren Leads the Way
The Election of 1824
"A Corrupt Bargain"
Jacksonian Melodrama

11-4 Adams versus Jackson
Learning Objective: Identify the principal events of the John Quincy Adams administration, and examine how they contributed to his defeat in 1828.

Nationalism in an International Arena
Nationalism at Home
The Birth of the Democratic Party
The Election of 1828
A People's Inauguration
The Spoils System

11-5 Jacksonian Democracy and the South
Learning Objective: Describe how Jacksonian Democrats dealt with the widening differences between the North and South.

Southerners and Indians
Indian Removal
Southerners and the Tariff
Nullification
The "Petticoat Wars"
The Fall of Calhoun
Petitions, the Gag Rule, and the Southern Mails

11-6 Jacksonian Democracy and the Market Revolution
Learning Objective: Analyze how Democrats and Whigs in the national government argued questions raised by economic development.

The Second Bank of the United States
The Bank War
The Beginnings of the Whig Party

11-7 The Second American Party System
Learning Objective: Describe what was peculiar about the Second Party System.

"Martin Van Ruin"
The Election of 1840

11.1 Jackson as Democracy Incarnate
Andrew Jackson struck a romantic military pose for this portrait painted in 1820. Posing as the embodiment of democracy and as an extravagantly melodramatic hero, Jackson imposed himself on his times as few Americans have done.

NATIONAL POLITICAL LEADERS from the 1820s until the outbreak of the Civil War faced two persistent problems. First, economic development and territorial expansion made new demands on government—demands that involved federal participation in state and local affairs. Second, a deepening rift between slave and free states rendered such involvement contested and dangerous.

The Whig Party proposed the **American System** as the answer to both questions. The national government, said the Whigs, should subsidize roads and canals, foster industry with protective tariffs, and maintain a national bank to control credit and currency. The result would be a peaceful, prosperous, and truly national market society. If the South, the West, and the Northeast profited by doing business with each other, the argument went, sectional jealousies would quiet down. Jacksonian Democrats, on the other hand, argued that the American System was unconstitutional, that it violated the rights of states and localities, and that it taxed honest citizens to benefit corrupt and wealthy insiders. Most dangerous of all, argued the Democrats, Whigs would create an activist, interventionist national government that would anger the slaveholding South. To counter both threats, the Jacksonians resurrected Thomas Jefferson's rhetoric of states' rights and inactive, inexpensive government—all of it deeply inflected in the code of white male equality, domestic patriarchy, and racial slavery. ■

11-1 The American System

Q *What were the components of the "American System"? What did the American System promise to accomplish?*

President James Madison delivered his annual message to the Fourteenth Congress in December 1815. He asked for legislation to create a new national bank, a tariff to protect American manufacturers, and congressional support for canals and roads. Congress agreed. Made up overwhelmingly of Jeffersonian Republicans and led by the young southern and western nationalists who had favored the war with Britain, this Congress reversed many of the positions taken by Jefferson's old party. It chartered a national bank, enacted a protective tariff, and debated a national system of roads and canals at federal expense. Most prewar Republicans had viewed such programs as heresy. But by 1815, the Republican majority in Congress accepted them as orthodox and necessary. Secretary of the Treasury Albert Gallatin explained: "The War has renewed and reinstated the national feelings which the Revolution had given and which were daily lessened. The people have now more general objects of attachment with which their pride and political opinions are connected. They are more American."

Even as they convinced themselves that they had won the war, Republicans were painfully aware of the weaknesses that the war had displayed. Put simply, the United States had been unable to coordinate a national fiscal and military effort: Bad roads, local jealousies, and a bankrupt treasury had nearly lost the war. In addition, the war and the years leading up to it convinced many Republicans, including Jefferson and Madison, that the export economy rendered the United States dangerously dependent on Europe (and especially Great Britain). Finally, many of the younger Republicans in Congress were interested less in ideological purity than in bringing commerce into new regions. The nation, they said, must abandon Jefferson's export-oriented agrarianism and encourage prosperity and national independence through subsidies to commerce, manufactures, and internal improvements.

11-1a *National Republicans*

Henry Clay of Kentucky, retaining his power in the postwar Congress, headed the drive for protective tariffs, the bank, and internal improvements. He called his program the "American System," arguing that it would foster national economic growth and harmony between geographic sections, thus a happy and prosperous republic.

In 1816, Congress chartered a Second Bank of the United States, headquartered in Philadelphia and empowered to establish branches wherever it saw fit. The government agreed to deposit its funds in the Bank; to accept the Bank's notes as payment for government land, taxes, and other transactions; and to buy one-fifth of the Bank's stock. The Bank of the United States was more powerful than the one that had been rejected (by one vote) by a Republican Congress in 1811. The fiscal horrors of the War of 1812, however, had convinced most representatives to support a national currency and centralized control of money and credit. The alternative was to allow state banks—which had increased in number from 88 to 208 between 1813 and 1815—to issue the unregulated and grossly inflated notes that had weakened the war effort and promised to throw the anticipated postwar boom into chaos.

With no discussion of the constitutionality of what it was doing, Congress chartered the Bank of the United States as the sole banking institution empowered to do business throughout the country. Notes issued by the Bank would be the first semblance of a national currency (they would soon constitute from one-tenth to one-third of the value of notes in circulation). Moreover, the Bank could regulate the currency by demanding that state bank notes used in transactions with the federal government be redeemable in gold. In 1816, the Bank set up shop in Philadelphia's Carpenter's Hall, and in 1824, it moved around the corner to a Greek Revival edifice modeled after the Parthenon—a marble embodiment of the republican conservatism that directors of the Bank of the United States promised as their fiscal stance. From that vantage point they would fight (with a few huge lapses)

CHRONOLOGY

1816	Congress charters a Second Bank of the United States and the first avowedly protective tariff • *Dartmouth College v. Woodward* defines a private charter as a contract that cannot be altered by a state legislature
1819	Controversy arises over Missouri's admission to the Union as a slave state • Panic of 1819 marks the first failure of the national market economy
1820	Missouri Compromise adopted
1823	Monroe Doctrine written by Secretary of State John Quincy Adams
1824	*Gibbons v. Ogden* asserts federal control of interstate commerce
1824–1825	Adams wins the presidency over Andrew Jackson • Adams appoints Henry Clay as secretary of state • Jacksonians charge a "Corrupt Bargain" between Adams and Clay
1827	Cherokees in Georgia declare themselves a republic
1828	Jackson defeats Adams for the presidency • "Tariff of Abominations" passed by Congress • John C. Calhoun's *Exposition and Protest* presents doctrine of nullification
1830	Congress passes the Indian Removal Act
1832	Jackson reelected over Henry Clay • *Worcester v. Georgia* exempts the Cherokees from Georgia law • Jackson vetoes recharter of the Bank of the United States
1833	Force Bill and Tariff of 1833 end the nullification crisis
1834	Whig Party formed in opposition to Jacksonians
1835	Treaty of New Echota
1836	Congress adopts "gag rule" to table antislavery petitions • Van Buren elected president
1837	Financial panic ushers in a severe economic depression
1838	U.S. Army marches the remaining Cherokees to Indian Territory
1840	Whig William Henry Harrison defeats Van Buren for presidency

a running battle with state banks and local interests in an effort to impose fiscal discipline and centralized control over an exploding market economy.

The same Congress drew up the nation's first overtly protective tariff in 1816. Shut off from British imports during the war, the Americans had built their first factories, almost entirely in southern New England and the mid-Atlantic. The British planned to flood the postwar market with cheap goods and kill American manufactures, and Congress determined to stop them. Shepherded through the House by Clay and his fellow nationalist John C. Calhoun of South Carolina, the Tariff of 1816 raised import duties an average of 25 percent, protecting American manufactures at the expense of consumers and foreign trade. Again, wartime difficulties and wartime nationalism had paved the way: Since Americans could not depend on imported manufactures, Congress saw domestic manufactures as a patriotic necessity and a spur to commerce between the sections. The Northeast and the West supported the tariff, and it had enough southern support to ensure its passage. Tariffs would rise and fall between 1816 and the Civil War, but the principle of protectionism would persist.

Many of the Founders had seen a national transportation system as essential to the prosperity and safety of the union. George Washington had urged roads and canals linking the Atlantic states with the interior—providing western farmers with the civilizing benefits of commerce and securing their loyalty to the United States. Thomas Jefferson shared Washington's views and, like his fellow Virginian, he favored improvements that would link the Potomac River with the Ohio. In 1802, President Jefferson signed a bill that began construction of the Cumberland Road (often called the National Road) from Cumberland, Maryland, to the Ohio River at Wheeling.

These early dreams and projects served the postcolonial economy: They would deliver farm produce to the coast and then to international markets; the coastal towns would receive imported goods and ship them back into the countryside. As early as 1770, George Washington had dreamed of making the Potomac River a busy "Channel of Commerce between Great Britain" and the farmers of the interior. Others dreamed of other routes and rivers, but nearly all proponents of transportation into the West shared the great assumption of Washington's early vision: The export economy would remain dominant; the United States would be an independent, unified, and prosperous economic colony of the Old World.

Henry Clay's American System grew into a new vision: a national transportation network that would make the United States economically independent of Europe and interdependent within itself. The Bank of the United States would supply fiscal stability and a uniform, trustworthy currency. The tariff would encourage northeasterners to build factories and citizens in other parts of the country to buy what American manufacturers made, and farmers would enjoy expanded domestic markets. The West would sell food to the cities and to the plantation South, and the South would supply the burgeoning textile industry with cotton. The system would not deny international trade, but it would make the United States an economically integrated and independent nation.

Bills for transportation projects, however, did not get through Congress. Internal improvements were subject to local ambitions: Canals and roads that helped one place hurt another. Some areas—southern New England and eastern Pennsylvania are examples—had already built good roads and did not want to subsidize the competition. There were also objections based on old Republican ideals. Roads and canals were big public works projects with scores of contractors and subcontractors—all dependent on government subsidies, with the potential for becoming a system of corruption that was impossible to stop. Finally, federally sponsored improvements, however beneficial, were constitutionally doubtful. In the Constitutional Convention, Benjamin Franklin had proposed that the power to build roads and cut canals within the

11.2 The Second Bank of the United States Located in downtown Philadelphia and modeled on the Parthenon in classical Athens, the new bank building was intended to be both republican and awesome. It was from here that gentleman-directors attempted to impose their kind of order on the exploding monetary and credit systems of the 1820s and 1830s.

states be written into the Constitution, and his proposal had been voted down. National support for internal improvements could be justified only by the "necessary and proper" and "general welfare" clauses. The Republicans could charter a Second Bank of the United States because Hamilton's bank had established the precedent. Roads and canals—extensive local projects at national expense—would stretch those clauses much further, worrying many Republicans (most of them southern) that future legislatures would justify whatever struck them as necessary and proper at any given time.

When Congress agreed to complete the National Road—the one federal internal improvement already under way—President Madison and his Republican successor James Monroe vetoed the bills, refusing to support further internal improvements without a constitutional amendment. In 1822, Monroe even vetoed a bill authorizing repairs on the National Road, stating once again that the Constitution did not empower the federal government to build roads within the states. As a result, the financing and construction of roads and canals fell to the states, overwhelmingly the *northern* states. Henry Clay watched his vision of transportation as a nationalizing force turn into northern regionalization and southern isolation, a dangerous trend that continued throughout his long political life.

11-1b Commerce and the Law

The courts after 1815 played an important nationalizing and commercializing role. John Marshall, who presided over the Supreme Court from 1801 to 1835, took the lead. From the beginning he saw the Court as a conservative hedge against the excesses of provincial democratic legislatures. His early decisions protected the independence of the courts and their right to review legislation (see Chapter 7). From 1816 onward, his decisions encouraged business and strengthened the national government at the expense of the states. His most important decisions protected the sanctity of contracts and corporate charters against state legislatures. In ***Dartmouth College v. Woodward*** (1819), he overturned New Hampshire's decision to turn the college into a public institution by upholding its original corporate charter from 1769. With this, corporate charters acquired the legal status of contracts, beyond the reach of democratic politics, which helped protect business corporations operating under charters granted by state governments.

Two weeks after deciding the *Dartmouth* case, Marshall handed down the majority decision in ***McCulloch v. Maryland***. The Maryland legislature, nurturing old Jeffersonian doubts about the constitutionality of the Bank of the United States, had attempted to tax the Bank's Baltimore branch, which in fact was a corrupt and ruinous institution (see later section). The Bank had challenged the legislature's right to do so, and the Court decided in favor of the Bank. Marshall stated, first, that the Constitution granted the federal government "implied powers" that included chartering the Bank, and he denied Maryland's right to tax the Bank or any other federal agency: "The power to tax," he said, "involves the power to destroy." It was Marshall's most explicit blow against Jeffersonian strict construction. Americans, he said, "did not design to make their government dependent on the states." And yet there were many, particularly in Marshall's native South, who remained certain that that was precisely what the Founders had intended.

In *Gibbons v. Ogden* (1824), the Marshall Court broke a state-granted steamship monopoly in New York Harbor. The monopoly, Marshall argued, interfered with federal jurisdiction over interstate commerce. Like the *Dartmouth* case and *McCulloch v. Maryland*, this decision empowered the national government in relation to the states, and like them, it encouraged private entrepreneurs. As surely as congressmen who supported the American System, John Marshall's Supreme Court assumed a natural and beneficial link between federal power and market society.

Meanwhile, the state courts were working on quieter but equally profound transformations of American law. In the early republic, state courts had often viewed property not only as a private possession but also as part of a neighborhood. Thus, when a miller built a dam that flooded upriver farms or impaired the fishery, the courts might make him take those interests into account, often in ways that reduced the business uses of his property. By 1830, New England courts routinely granted the owners of industrial mill sites unrestricted water rights, even when the exercise of those rights inflicted damage on their neighbors. In the courts of northern and western states, what was coming to be called "progress" demanded legal protection for the business uses of private property, even when such uses conflicted with old common-law restraints.

11-2 1819

Q *What enduring political issues were raised by the Missouri controversy and the Panic of 1819?*

Many traditionalist Jeffersonians disliked these developments, but they could not stop them. That changed in 1819. First, the debate that surrounded Missouri's admission as a slave state revealed the centrality and vulnerability of slavery within the national Union. Second, a severe financial collapse led many Americans to doubt the Market Revolution's compatibility with the Jeffersonian republic. By 1820, politicians were determined to reconstruct the limited-government, states'-rights coalition that had elected Thomas Jefferson.

11-2a The Argument over Missouri

Early in 1819, slaveholding Missouri applied for admission to the Union as the first new state to be carved out of the Louisiana Purchase. New York congressman James Tallmadge, Jr., quickly proposed two amendments to the Missouri statehood bill. The first would bar additional slaves from being brought into Missouri (16 percent of Missouri's people were already slaves). The second would emancipate Missouri slaves born after admission when they reached their 25th birthday. Put simply, the **Tallmadge Amendments** would admit Missouri only if Missouri agreed to become a free state.

The congressional debates on the Missouri question had little to do with humanitarian objections to slavery and everything to do with political power. Rufus King of New York, an old Federalist who led the northerners in the Senate, insisted that he opposed the admission of a new slave state "solely in its bearing and effects upon great political interests, and upon the just and equal rights of the freemen of the nation." Northerners had long chafed at the added representation in Congress and in the Electoral College that the "three-fifths" rule granted to the slave states (see Chapter 6). The rule had, in fact, added significantly to southern power: In 1790, the South, with 40 percent of the white population, controlled 47 percent of the votes in Congress—enough to decide close votes both in Congress and in presidential elections. Federalists pointed out that of the 12 additional electoral votes the three-fifths rule gave to the South, 10 had gone to Thomas Jefferson in 1800 and had given him the election. Without the bogus votes provided by slavery, they argued, Virginia's stranglehold on the presidency would have been broken with Washington's departure in 1796.

11.3 Henry Clay Clay was the most consistent and eloquent spokesman for the American System. His supposed participation in the "Corrupt Bargain" of 1825 severely hurt his chances of becoming president.

Q *In what ways does the painting portray Clay as a champion of the American System?*

In 1819, the North held a majority in the House of Representatives. The South, thanks to the recent admissions of Alabama and southern-oriented Illinois, controlled a bare majority in the Senate. The Tallmadge Amendments passed in the House of Representatives by a starkly sectional vote, then went on to the Senate. There, a unanimous South defeated the Tallmadge Amendments with the help of the two Illinois senators and three northerners. Deadlocked between a Senate in favor of admitting Missouri as a slave state and a House dead set against it, Congress broke off one of the angriest sessions in its history and went home.

11-2b The Missouri Compromise

The new Congress that convened in the winter of 1819–1820 passed the legislative package that became known as the **Missouri Compromise** (see Map 11.1). Massachusetts offered its northern counties as the new free state of Maine, thus neutralizing fears that the South would gain votes in the Senate with the admission of Missouri. Senator Jesse Thomas of Illinois proposed the so-called Thomas Proviso: If the North would admit Missouri as a slave state, the South would agree to outlaw slavery in territories above 36° 30'N latitude—a line extending from the southern border of Missouri to Spanish (within a year, Mexican) territory. That line would open Arkansas Territory (present-day Arkansas and Oklahoma) to slavery and would ban slavery from the remainder of the Louisiana Territory—land that would subsequently become all or part of nine states.

Congress admitted Maine with little debate, but the Thomas Proviso met northern opposition. Finally, a joint Senate-House committee decided to separate the two bills. With half of the southern representatives and nearly all of the northerners supporting it, the Thomas Proviso passed. Congress next took up the admission of Missouri. With the votes of a solid South and 14 compromise-minded northerners,

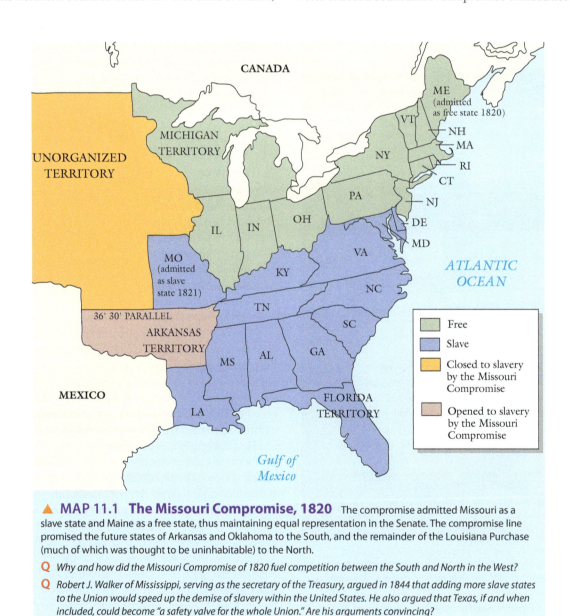

▲ **MAP 11.1 The Missouri Compromise, 1820** The compromise admitted Missouri as a slave state and Maine as a free state, thus maintaining equal representation in the Senate. The compromise line promised the future states of Arkansas and Oklahoma to the South, and the remainder of the Louisiana Purchase (much of which was thought to be uninhabitable) to the North.

Q Why and how did the Missouri Compromise of 1820 fuel competition between the South and North in the West?

Q Robert J. Walker of Mississippi, serving as the secretary of the Treasury, argued in 1844 that adding more slave states to the Union would speed up the demise of slavery within the United States. He also argued that Texas, if and when included, could become "a safety valve for the whole Union." Are his arguments convincing?

Missouri entered the Union as a slave state. President James Monroe applauded the "patriotic devotion" of the northern representatives "who preferr'd the sacrifice of themselves at home" to endangering the Union. His words were prophetic: Nearly all of the 14 were voted out of office in the next election.

The Missouri crisis brought the South's commitment to slavery and the North's resentment of southern political power into collision. While northerners vowed to relinquish no more territory to slavery, southerners talked openly of disunion and civil war. A Georgia politician announced that the Missouri debates had lit a fire that "seas of blood can only extinguish." President Monroe's secretary of state, John Quincy Adams, saw the debates as an omen: Northerners would unanimously oppose the extension of slavery whenever the question came to a vote. Viewing the crisis from Monticello, the aging Thomas Jefferson was distraught: "A geographical line, coinciding with a marked principle, moral and political, once conceived and held up to the angry passions of men, will never be obliterated; every new irritation will mark it deeper and deeper… . This momentous question, like a fire-bell in the night, awakened and filled me with terror. I considered it at once the knell of the Union." The Missouri question underlined a basic fact of American national politics: If politicians argued about slavery, they would split along North–South lines and the Union would be endangered.

11-2c The Panic of 1819

Politicians debated the Missouri question against a darkening backdrop of economic depression. The origins of the Panic of 1819 were international and numerous. European agriculture was recovering from the Napoleonic wars, thereby reducing the demand for American foodstuffs, while revolutionary wars in Latin America cut off the supply of precious metals, the base of the international money supply. American bankers and businessmen met the situation by expanding credit and issuing banknotes that were mere dreams of real money, thereby creating an inflationary bubble. When the price of cotton collapsed in 1819, the bubble burst.

The president of the Second Bank of the United States, Langdon Cheves of South Carolina, responded to the crisis by curtailing credit and demanding that state banknotes received by the Bank of the United States be redeemed in specie (silver and gold). By doing so, Cheves rescued the Bank from the paper economy created by state-chartered banks, but at huge expense: When the state banks were forced to redeem their notes in specie, they demanded payment from their own borrowers, and the national money and credit system collapsed.

The depression that followed the Panic of 1819 was the first failure of the market economy. Local ups and downs had occurred since the 1790s, but this collapse was nationwide. Employers who could not meet their debts went out of business, and hundreds of thousands of workers lost their jobs. In Philadelphia, unemployment reached 75 percent. A tent city of the unemployed sprang up on the outskirts of Baltimore. Other cities and towns were hit as hard, and the situation was no better in the countryside. Thomas Jefferson reported that farms in his neighborhood were selling for what had earlier been a year's rent.

Faced with a collapse that none could control and that few understood, many Americans directed their resentment onto the Bank of the United States. John Jacob Astor, a New York merchant and reputedly the richest man in America, admitted that "there has been too much Speculation and too much assumption of Power on the Part of the Bank Directors which has caused [sic] the institution to become unpopular." William Gouge, who would become the Jacksonian Democrats' favorite economist, put it more bluntly: When the Bank demanded that state banknotes be redeemed in specie, he said, "the Bank was saved and the people were ruined." By the end of 1819, the Bank of the United States had won the name that it would carry to its death in the 1830s: the Monster.

11-3 Republican Revival

 What were the events and political motives that contributed to the republican revival that formed around Andrew Jackson?

The crises during 1819 and 1820 prompted demands for a return to Jeffersonian principles. President Monroe's happily proclaimed Era of Good Feelings—a new era of partyless politics created by the collapse of Federalism—was, according to worried Republicans, a disaster. Without opposition, Jefferson's dominant Republican Party had lost its way. The nationalist Congress of 1816 had enacted much of the Federalist program under the name of Republicanism. The result, said the old Republicans, was an aggressive government that helped bring on the Panic of 1819. At the same time, the collapse of Republican Party unity in Congress had allowed the Missouri question to divide Congress along dangerous sectional lines. By 1820, many Republicans were calling for a Jeffersonian revival that would limit government power and guarantee southern rights within the Union.

11-3a Martin Van Buren Leads the Way

The busiest and the most astute of those Republicans was Martin Van Buren of New York. An immensely talented man without family connections (his father was a Hudson Valley tavern keeper) or formal education, Van Buren built his political career out of a commitment to Jeffersonian principles, personal charm, and party discipline. He and his colleagues in New York had begun to invent the modern political party. The Founders had denounced parties, claiming that republics rested on civic virtue, not competition. Van Buren's New York experience, however, along with his reading of national politics, told him that disciplined political parties were necessary democratic tools. Van Buren insisted that competition and party divisions were inevitable and good, but that they must be made to serve the republic. He wrote: "We must always have party distinctions, and the old ones are the best… If the old ones are suppressed, geographical differences founded on local instincts or what is worse, prejudices between free & slave holding states will inevitably take their place." Van Buren claimed that the one-party politics of the Era of Good Feelings had allowed privileged insiders to create a big national state and to reorganize politics along sectional lines. Arriving in Washington in the aftermath of the Missouri debates and the Panic of 1819, he hoped to apply his new politics to what he perceived as a dangerous turning point in national public life.

Working with like-minded politicians, Van Buren reconstructed the coalition of northern and southern agriculturalists that had elected Thomas Jefferson. The result was the Democratic Party and, ultimately, a national two-party system that persisted until the eve of the Civil War.

11-3b The Election of 1824

With the approach of the 1824 presidential election, Van Buren and his friends supported William H. Crawford, Monroe's secretary of war and a staunch Georgia Republican. The Van Burenites controlled the Republican **congressional caucus**, the body that traditionally chose the party's presidential candidates. The public distrusted the caucus as undemocratic because it represented the only party in government and thus could dictate the choice of a president. Van Buren, however, continued to regard it as a necessary tool of party discipline. With most congressmen fearing their constituents, only a minority showed up for the caucus vote. They dutifully nominated Crawford.

With Republican Party unity broken, the list of sectional candidates grew. John Quincy Adams was the son of a Federalist president, successful secretary of state under Monroe, and one of the northeastern Federalist converts to Republicanism who, according to people like Van Buren and Crawford, had blunted the republican thrust of Jefferson's old party. Adams entered the contest as New England's favorite son. Henry Clay of Kentucky, chief proponent of the American System, expected to carry the West. John C. Calhoun of South Carolina announced his candidacy, but when he saw the swarm of candidates, he dropped out and put himself up as the sole candidate for vice president.

The wild card was Andrew Jackson of Tennessee, who in 1824 was known only as a military hero—scourge of the southern Indians and victor over the British at New Orleans (see Chapter 7). He was also a frontier nabob with a reputation for violence: He had killed a rival in a duel, had engaged in a shootout in a Nashville tavern, and had reputedly stolen his wife from her estranged husband. According to Jackson's detractors, such impetuosity marked his public life as well. As commander of U.S. military forces in the South in 1818, Jackson had led an unauthorized invasion of Spanish Florida, claiming that it was a hideout for Seminole warriors who raided into the United States and a sanctuary for runaway Georgia slaves. During the action, he had occupied Spanish forts, summarily executed Seminoles, and hanged two British subjects. Secretary of State John Quincy Adams had belatedly approved the raid, knowing that the show of American force would

11.4 John Quincy Adams Adams enjoyed a remarkably productive career as Monroe's secretary of state, then rode into the presidency in the conflicted and controversial election of 1824. The intelligence and erudition that the picture projects had served him well as a diplomat. As president, they marked him as aloof, aristocratic, and incapable of governing a democratic nation.

encourage the Spanish to sell Florida to the United States. After serving briefly as the governor of newly acquired Florida in 1821, Jackson retired from public life. It was a short retirement because only two years later Tennessee voters elected him to the U.S. Senate. In 1824, eastern politicians knew Jackson only as a "military chieftain," "the Napoleon of the woods," a frontier hothead, and, possibly, a robber-bridegroom.

Jackson may have been all of those things, but he was immensely popular, particularly in the new states of the South and West. In the election of 1824, in the 16 states that chose presidential electors by popular vote (six states still left the choice to their legislatures), Jackson polled 152,901 votes to Adams's 114,023 and Clay's 47,217. Crawford, who suffered a crippling stroke during the campaign, won 46,979 votes. Jackson's support was not only larger but also more nearly national than that of his opponents. Adams carried only his native New England and a portion of New York. Clay's meager support was limited to the Northwest, and Crawford's to the Southeast and to the portions of New York that Van Buren was able to deliver. Jackson carried 84 percent of the votes of his own Southwest, won victories in Pennsylvania, New Jersey, North Carolina, Indiana, and Illinois, and ran a close second in several other states (see Map 11.2).

11-3c "A Corrupt Bargain"

Jackson assumed that he had won the election: He had received 42 percent of the popular vote to his nearest rival's 33 percent, and he was clearly the nation's choice, but his 99 electoral votes were 32 shy of the plurality demanded by the Constitution. And so, acting under the Twelfth Amendment, the House of Representatives selected a president from among the top three candidates. As the candidate with the fewest electoral votes, Henry Clay was eliminated, but he remained Speaker of the House and had enough support to throw the election to either Jackson or Adams. Years later, Jackson told a dinner guest that Clay had offered to support him in exchange for Clay's appointment as secretary of state—an office that traditionally led to the presidency. When Jackson turned him down, according to Jacksonian legend, Clay went to Adams and made the same offer. Adams accepted what became known as the **"Corrupt Bargain"** in January 1825. During the House vote, Clay's supporters, joined by several old Federalists, switched to Adams, giving him a one-vote victory. The new president appointed Henry Clay as his secretary of state.

Reaction to the alleged Corrupt Bargain dominated the Adams administration and created a rhetoric of intrigue and

11.5 "The Symptoms of a Locked Jaw" In 1827, Henry Clay published a rebuttal of Jacksonian charges that he had participated in a Corrupt Bargain to deliver the presidency to John Quincy Adams. Here, a pro-Clay cartoonist displays Clay as a tailor in the act of sewing Andrew Jackson's mouth shut. Neither the rebuttal nor the cartoon worked: The long-term suspicions of the bargain with Adams ruined Clay's chances to become president.

betrayal that nourished a rising democratic movement. After the vote in the House of Representatives, Jackson declared, "The rights of the people have been bartered for promises of office." He continued, "So you see, the *Judas* of the West has closed the contract and will receive the thirty pieces of silver. His end will be the same." Others in Washington agreed, denouncing the Clay-Adams union as "unnatural & preposterous" and "monstrous." The charge of corruption would follow Clay for the rest of his political life.

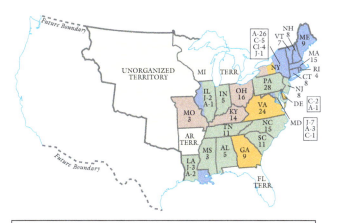

	Electoral Vote		Popular Vote	
	Number	%	Number	%
Jackson (Democratic Republican)	99	37.9	152,901	42.3
J. Q. Adams (Democratic Republican)	84	32.2	114,023	31.6
Crawford (Democratic Republican)	41	15.7	46,979	13
Clay (Democratic Republican)	37	14.2	47,217	13.1

▲ **MAP 11.2 Presidential Election, 1824**
Voting in the four-cornered contest of 1824 was starkly sectional. John Quincy Adams carried his native New England, while Crawford and Clay carried only a few states in their own sections. Only Andrew Jackson enjoyed national support: He carried states in every section but New England, and he ran a strong second in many of the states that were awarded to other candidates.

Q *In what ways did the election of 1824 pave the way for modern American politics?*

Q *Was Andrew Jackson's claim that he was robbed of presidency justified?*

11-3d Jacksonian Melodrama

Andrew Jackson regarded the intrigues that robbed him of the presidency in 1825 as the culmination of a long train of corruption that the nation had suffered over the previous decade. Although his campaign had made only vague policy statements, he had firm ideas of what had gone wrong with the republic, and he made his views known in what he called "memorandums." (This was the kind of gaffe that appalled his educated eastern opponents and pleased nearly everyone else.)

A frontier planter with a deep distrust of banks, Jackson claimed that self-serving miscreants in the Bank of the United States brought on the Panic of 1819. The national debt, he insisted, was another source of corruption. It must be paid off and never allowed to recur. The federal government under

James Monroe was filled with swindlers, and in the name of a vague nationalism they were taking power for themselves and scheming against the liberties of the people. The politicians had been bought off, said Jackson, and had attempted—through "King Caucus"—to select a president by backstairs deals rather than by popular election. Finally, in 1825, they had stolen the presidency outright.

Like hundreds of thousands of other Americans, Jackson sensed that something had gone wrong with the republic—that selfishness and intrigue had corrupted the government. In the language of revolutionary republicanism, which Jackson had learned as a boy in the Carolina backwoods and would speak throughout his life, a corrupt power once again threatened to snuff out liberty.

In his memorandums, Jackson set against the designs of that power the classic republican safeguard: a virtuous citizenry. Unlike most of his revolutionary forebears, however, he believed that government should follow the will of popular majorities. An aroused public, he said, was the republic's best hope: "My fervent prayers are that our republican government may be perpetual, and the people alone by their virtue, and independent exercise of their free suffrage can make it perpetual."

More completely than any of his rivals, Jackson had captured the rhetoric of the revolutionary republic. And, with his fixation on secrecy, corruption, and intrigues, he transformed both that rhetoric and his own biography into popular melodrama. Finally, with a political alchemy that his rivals never understood, Jackson submerged old notions of republican citizenship into a firm faith in majoritarian democracy: Individuals might become selfish and corrupt, he believed, but a democratic majority was, by its very nature, opposed to corruption and governmental excess. Thus, the republic was safe only when governed by the will of the majority. The Corrupt Bargain of 1825 had made that clear: Either the people or political schemers would rule.

11-4 Adams versus Jackson

 What were the principal events of the John Quincy Adams administration, and how did they contribute to his defeat in 1828?

While Jackson plotted revenge, John Quincy Adams assumed the duties of the presidency. He was well prepared. The son of a Federalist president, he had been an extraordinarily successful secretary of state under Monroe, guiding American diplomacy in the postwar world.

11-4a *Nationalism in an International Arena*

In the Rush-Bagot Treaty of 1817 and the British-American Convention of 1818, Secretary of State John Quincy Adams helped pacify the Great Lakes, restore American fishing rights off the coast of Canada, and draw the U.S.-Canadian boundary west to the Rocky Mountains—actions that transformed the Canadian-American frontier from a battleground into the peaceful border that it has been ever since. He pacified the southern border as well. In 1819, following Jackson's raid into Florida, the Adams-Onís Treaty procured Florida for the United States and defined the U.S.-Spanish border west of the Mississippi in ways that gave the Americans claims to the Pacific Northwest.

Trickier problems had arisen when Spanish colonies in the Americas declared their independence. Spain could not prevent this, and the powers of Europe, victorious over Napoleon and determined to roll back the republican revolution, talked openly of helping Spain or of annexing South American territory for themselves. Both the Americans and the British opposed such a move, and the British proposed a joint statement outlawing the interference of any outside power (including themselves) in Latin America. Adams had thought it better for the United States to make its own policy than to "come in as cock-boat in the wake of the British man-of-war." In 1823, he wrote what became known as the **Monroe Doctrine**. Propounded at the same time that the United States recognized the new Latin American republics, it declared American opposition to any European attempt at colonization in the New World without (as the British had wanted) denying the right of the United States to annex new territory. Although the international community knew that the British navy, and not the Monroe Doctrine, kept the European powers out of the Americas, Adams had announced that the United States was determined to become the preeminent power in the Western Hemisphere.

11-4b *Nationalism at Home*

As president, Adams translated his fervent nationalism into domestic policy. In his first annual message to Congress, he outlined an ambitious program for national development under the auspices of the federal government: roads, canals, a national university, a national astronomical observatory ("lighthouses of the skies"), and other costly initiatives:

> The spirit of improvement is abroad upon the earth.... While foreign nations less blessed with ... freedom ... than ourselves are advancing with gigantic strides in the career of public improvement, were we to slumber in indolence or fold up our arms and proclaim to the world that we are palsied by the will of our constituents, would it not ... doom ourselves to perpetual inferiority?

Congressmen could not believe their ears. Here was a president who had received only one in three votes and who had entered office accused of intrigues against the democratic will. And yet at the first opportunity he told Congress to pass an ambitious program and not to be "palsied" by the will of the electorate. Hostile politicians and journalists never tired of joking about Adams's "lighthouses of the skies." More lasting, however, was the connection they drew between federal public works projects and high taxes, intrusive government, the denial of democratic majorities, and expanded opportunities for corruption, secret deals, and special favors. Even members of Congress who favored Adams's program were afraid to vote for it. Congress never acted on the president's proposals, and the Adams administration emerged as little more than a long prelude to the election of 1828.

11-4c The Birth of the Democratic Party

As early as 1825, it was clear that the election of 1828 would pit Adams against Andrew Jackson. Van Buren and like-minded Republicans, with their candidate Crawford hopelessly incapacitated, switched their allegiance to Jackson. They wanted Jackson elected, however, not only as a popular hero but as head of a disciplined and committed Democratic Party that would continue the states'-rights, limited-government positions of the old Jeffersonian Republicans.

The new Democratic Party linked white democracy with the defense of southern slavery. Van Buren began preparations for 1828 with a visit to John C. Calhoun of South Carolina. Calhoun was moving along the road from postwar nationalism to states'-rights conservatism. He also wanted to stay on as vice president and thus keep his presidential hopes alive. After convincing Calhoun to support Jackson, Van Buren embarked on reviving the alliance of "the planters of the South and the plain Republicans of the North" that had elected Jefferson. Thus, a new Democratic Party, committed to states' rights and minimal government and dependent on the votes of both slaveholding and nonslaveholding states, would ensure white democracy, the continuation of slavery, and the preservation of the Union. The alternative, Van Buren argued, was an expensive and invasive national state (Adams's "lighthouses of the skies"), the isolation of the slaveholding South, and mortal danger to the republic.

11-4d The Election of 1828

The presidential campaign of 1828 was an exercise in slander rather than a debate on public issues. Adhering to custom, neither Adams nor Jackson campaigned directly, but their henchmen viciously personalized the campaign. Jacksonians hammered away at the Corrupt Bargain of 1825, while the Adams forces attacked Jackson's character. They reminded voters of his duels and tavern brawls and circulated a "coffin handbill" describing Jackson's execution of militiamen during the Creek War. The most egregious slander centered on Andrew Jackson's marriage. In 1790, Jackson had married Rachel Donelson, probably aware that she was estranged but not divorced from a man named Robards. Branding the marriage an "abduction," the Adams team screamed that Jackson had "torn from a husband the wife of his bosom," and had lived with her in a state of "open and notorious lewdness." They branded Rachel Jackson (now a deeply pious plantation housewife) an "American Jezebel," a "profligate woman," and a "convicted adulteress" whose ungoverned passions made her unfit to be First Lady of a "Christian nation."

The Adams strategy backfired. Many voters did agree that only a man who strictly obeyed the law was fit to be president and that Jackson's "passionate" nature disqualified him. But others criticized Adams for making Jackson's private life a public issue and claimed that his rigid legalism left no room for privacy or for local notions of justice. Whatever the legality of their marriage, Andrew and Rachel Jackson had lived as models of fidelity for nearly 40 years. Their neighbors had long ago forgiven whatever transgressions they may have committed. Thus, Jackson's supporters accused the Adams campaign of a gross violation of privacy and defended Jackson's marriage—and his duels, brawls, executions, and unauthorized military forays—as a triumph of what was honorable and just over what was narrowly legal. The attempt to brand Jackson as a lawless man, in fact, enhanced his image as a melodramatic hero who battled shrewd, unscrupulous, legalistic enemies by drawing on his natural nobility and force of will.

The campaign caught the public imagination. Voter turnout was double what it had been in 1824, totaling 56.3 percent. Jackson won with 56 percent of the popular vote (a landslide unmatched until the 20th century) and with a margin of 178 to 83 in electoral votes. Adams carried New England, Delaware, and most of Maryland, and took 16 of New York's 36 electoral votes. Jackson carried every other state (see Map 11.3). It was a clear triumph of democracy over genteel statesmanship, of limited government over expansive nationalism, and of the South and the West over New England. Just as clearly, it was a victory of popular melodrama over old forms of cultural gentility.

11.6 Rachel Donelson Jackson as a Mature Plantation Mistress
Andrew Jackson supposedly wore this miniature portrait of his beloved Rachel over his heart after her death in 1828.

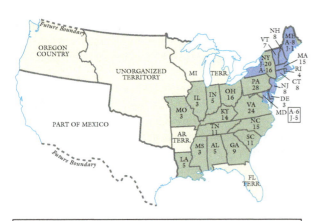

▲ **MAP 11.3 Presidential Election, 1828**
The 1828 presidential contest was a clear result of the organizing efforts that were building a national Democratic Party under the name of Andrew Jackson. Jackson picked up all of the states that had gone for Crawford or Clay in 1824, leaving only New England and small portions of the mid-Atlantic for John Quincy Adams.

Q *In what ways were Martin Van Buren's efforts critical to Jackson's victory?*

Q *How do changes in voting participation explain Jackson's victory?*

11-4e A People's Inauguration

Newspapers estimated that from 15,000 to 30,000 citizens came to Washington to witness Jackson's inauguration on March 4, 1829. They were "like the inundation of the northern barbarians into Rome," remarked Senator Daniel Webster. Many had traveled as much as 500 miles, and "they really seem to think that the country is rescued from some dreadful danger." As members of the Washington establishment watched uneasily, the crowd filled the open spaces and the streets near the east portico of the Capitol Building, where Jackson was to deliver his inaugural address.

Jackson arrived at the Capitol in mourning. In December, his wife Rachel had gone to Nashville to shop and had stopped to rest in a newspaper office. There, for the first time, she read the accusations that had been made against her. She fainted on the spot. Although she had been in poor health, no one would ever convince Jackson that her death in January was not caused by his political enemies. He assumed the presidency wearing a black suit and black tie, a black armband, and a black hatband that trailed down his neck in what was called a weeper.

Jackson's inaugural address was vague. He promised "proper respect" for states' rights, a reform of the civil service, and the retirement of the national debt through "a strict and faithful economy." Beyond that, he said little, although he took every opportunity to flatter the popular majority. He had been elected "by the choice of a free people" (and not by King Caucus or Corrupt Bargains), and he pledged "the zealous dedication of my humble abilities to their service and their good." He finished—as he often finished an important statement—by reminding Americans that a benign providence looked over them. He then looked up to a roar of applause.

The crowd followed Jackson from the Capitol to the White House, invading the mansion, muddying the carpets, tipping things over, breaking dishes, and standing in dirty boots on upholstered chairs. Jackson had to retreat to avoid being crushed. The White House staff lured much of the crowd outside by moving the punch bowls and liquor to the lawn. A wealthy Washington matron who had admired the well-behaved crowd at the inaugural address exclaimed, "What a scene did we witness! *The Majesty of the People* had disappeared, and a rabble, a mob, of boys, negros, women, children, scrambling, fighting, romping. What a pity, what a pity." A Democratic newspaper reported more favorably: "General Jackson is *their own* President.... He was greeted by them with an enthusiasm which bespoke him the Hero of a popular triumph."

11-4f The Spoils System

Jackson had begun to assemble his administration months before he took office. Martin Van Buren, who had mobilized much of the support Jackson gained between 1824 and 1828, was the new secretary of state—positioned to succeed Jackson as president. He became Jackson's most valued adviser. Other appointments were less promising, for Jackson filled cabinet posts with old friends and political supporters who, in many cases, proved unfit for their jobs. A critic looked at Jackson's cabinet and pronounced it—with the exception of Van Buren—"the Millennium of the Minnows."

Others were more concerned about what Jackson would do to the civil service than about whom he named to his cabinet. During the campaign, Jackson had vowed to fire corrupt officeholders—a term he applied to grafters, incompetents, long-term officeholders who considered their jobs personal property, and those who supported John Quincy Adams. Opponents soon complained that Jackson was replacing able public servants with political hacks who had been promised government posts in return for political support. They soon had convincing evidence: Samuel Swarthout, whom Jackson had appointed collector of the Port of New York (an office that handled $15 million in tariff revenue annually), stole $1.2 million and took off for Europe. Jackson insisted that he merely intended to end the long tenures that, he said, turned the civil service into "support of the few at the expense of the many," but the furor over his **"spoils system"** raged on. Jackson removed about 1 in 10 executive appointees during his eight years in office, and his replacements were most decidedly *political* appointees. Acting out of his own need for personal loyalty and on the advice of Van Buren and other architects of the Democratic Party, Jackson filled vacancies—down to postmasters in the smallest towns—with Democrats who had worked for his election.

In resorting to patronage to build the party, Jackson gave his opponents an important issue. Revolutionary republicans feared a government of lackeys dependent on a powerful executive,

11.7 The President's Levee Robert Cruikshank drew Jackson's inaugural reception with men and women of all classes, children, dogs, and bucking horses celebrating the Old General's victory. Cruikshank subtitled his lithograph "All Creation Going to the White House."

Q What does the picture reveal about how citizens saw and related to the institution of presidency in the 1830s?

and congressional opponents argued that Jackson was using appointments to "convert the entire body of those in office into corrupt and supple instruments of power." "A standing army," railed Henry Clay in the Senate, "has been, in all free countries, a just object of jealousy and suspicion. But is not a corps of one hundred thousand dependents upon government, actuated by one spirit, obeying one will, and aiming at one end, more dangerous than a standing army?" It became an anti-Jacksonian axiom that Jackson had made the federal civil service an arm of the Democratic Party and of despotic executive power.

returning to republican fundamentals. Although southerners expected Jackson to look after southern interests, disagreement arose within the administration about how those interests should be protected. Some sided with Vice President Calhoun, who argued that states had the right to veto federal legislation and in extreme cases to secede from the Union. Others agreed with Secretary of State Van Buren that the Union was inviolable and that the South's best safeguard was in a political party committed to states' rights within the Union. The differences were fought out in the contest between Calhoun and Van Buren for the right to succeed Jackson as president, a contest that shaped every major issue of Jackson's first term.

11-5 Jacksonian Democracy and the South

Q At the national level, how did Jacksonian Democrats and their rivals deal with widening differences between the North and South?

Andrew Jackson was a national figure, but his base of support was in the South, where he won 8 of every 10 votes in 1828. Southerners had grown wary of an activist government in which they were in the minority. They looked to Jackson not only as a military hero but also as a Tennessee planter who talked about

11-5a *Southerners and Indians*

When Jackson entered office, a final crisis between frontier whites and the native peoples of the Eastern Woodlands was under way. Many earlier policymakers had believed that the American agrarian republic could assimilate Native Americans through civilization programs that transformed tribespeople into yeoman farmers who would voluntarily give up their hunting grounds for white settlement (see Chapter 7). But Indians' continuing resistance and white Americans' deep-seated beliefs in native savagery frustrated such scenarios.

In 1818, President James Monroe declared that "experience has clearly demonstrated that independent Savage communities cannot long exist within the limits of a civilized population…. it seems indispensable that their independence as communities should cease, and that the control of the United States over them should be complete and undisputed." The architects of the new American nation claimed sovereignty over Indian-occupied territories east of the Mississippi River and imagined westward expansion as a legitimate, indeed providential, undertaking that turned undeveloped native lands into flourishing, privately owned farms. By the 1820s, few Indians remained east of the Appalachians. The Iroquois of New York were penned into tiny reservations, and the tribes of the Great Lakes region were broken and scattered.

Yet, in the early 1820s, more than 120,000 Indians still lived between the Appalachians and the Mississippi River. Cherokees, Creeks, Choctaws, Chickasaws, and Seminoles in the South comprised half of them, living on their ancestral lands with tenure guaranteed by federal treaties that, at least implicitly, recognized them as sovereign peoples. Congress had appropriated funds for schools, tools, seeds, and training to help these populous peoples make the transition to farming. Some government officials assumed that the tribes would eventually trade their old lands and use their farming skills on new land west of the Mississippi. In contrast, many southern Indians embraced the United States' civilization program as a means to build stronger governments and economies and ultimately protect their lands as sovereign nations. They became **Civilized Tribes** with schools, roads, mills, individual property rights, cotton plantations, and large numbers of black slaves. The lives of their propertied, slaveholding elite families did not differ much from those of their wealthy white neighbors in Georgia, Alabama, and Mississippi.

Southern whites resented federal Indian policy as an affront to both white democracy and states' rights. The poorer farmers coveted the Indians' land, and states'-rights southerners denied the federal government's authority to make treaties or to recognize sovereign peoples within their states. Resistance centered in Georgia, where Governor George Troup brought native lands under the state's jurisdiction and then turned them over to poor whites by way of lotteries, thus tying states' rights to white hunger for Indian land. At one point, Troup sent state surveyors onto Creek territory before federal purchase from the Indians was complete, telling President Adams that if he resisted state authority he would be considered a "public enemy."

The Cherokees in Georgia pressed the issue in 1827 by declaring themselves a republic with its own written constitution, legislature, courts, police, and appointed principal leader—a sovereign indigenous nation within the state of Georgia. The Georgia legislature promptly declared Cherokee law null and void, extended Georgia's authority into Cherokee country, and began surveying the lands for sale. Hinting at the old connection between state sovereignty and the protection of slavery, Governor Troup warned that the federal "jurisdiction claimed over one portion of our population may very soon be asserted over *another*." Alabama and Mississippi quickly followed Georgia's lead by extending state authority over Indian lands and denying federal jurisdiction.

11-5b Indian Removal

President Jackson agreed that the federal government lacked the authority to recognize native sovereignty within a state and declared that he could not protect the Cherokees and the other Civilized Tribes from state governments. Instead, he offered to remove them to federal land west of the Mississippi, where they would be under the authority of the benevolent federal government. Congress made that offer official in the **Indian Removal Act** of 1830.

The Cherokees, with the help of New England missionaries, had taken their claims of sovereignty to court in the late 1820s. In 1831, John Marshall's Supreme Court ruled in *Cherokee Nation v. Georgia* that the Cherokees could not sue Georgia because they were not a foreign nation but a "domestic dependent nation"—a dependent of the federal government, and not of the state of Georgia. In a consequential formulation, Marshall noted that the relationship between the tribes and the United States "resembles that of a ward to his guardian." Cherokees understood the decision as an affirmation of their sovereignty and initiated another federal court case against Georgia. The Court's decision in *Worcester v. Georgia* (1832) declared that Georgia's extension of state law over Cherokee land was unconstitutional. Marshall's ruling, which was strongly motivated by his desire to assert the precedence of federal power over states' power in Indian affairs, was a victory for the Cherokees—although, as it turned out, a hollow one. President Jackson ignored the decision, reportedly telling a congressman, "John Marshall has made his decision: Now let him enforce it!"

The prolonged struggles with Georgia and the rapid economic and social changes among the Cherokees had split their nation into traditionalists who persistently opposed removal and those who favored accommodation with the whites. In 1835, a small minority group signed a Treaty of New Echota with the U.S. government, hoping to secure tolerable terms for the removal that seemed inevitable to its members. The vast majority of the Cherokees denounced the treaty, but to no avail. In 1838, Jackson's successor, Martin Van Buren, sent the army to march the 15,000 remaining Cherokees to a new Indian Territory in today's Oklahoma. At least four thousand of them died along this Trail of Tears of exposure, disease, starvation, and white depredation. Their suffering continued in the West. The Cherokees had brought their pre-existing internal divisions and disputes to Indian Territory, where bloodshed and instability plagued their lives for decades. They also clashed with the Comanches, Osages, and other powerful Plains Indians, who resented the newcomers on their borders. The Cherokee removal was but one of many cases of ethnic cleansing in the early 19th-century United States. Numerous native groups were moved to the West from Ohio, Michigan, Wisconsin, Illinois, and across the South, where westward-pushing settlers demanded more land for farms and plantations. In total, some 80,000 Native Americans were removed from the eastern United States during the 1820s and 1830s. Some, like the Seminoles in the Florida Everglades and Black Hawk's Sauks, Fox, and Kickapoos, fought back, but eventually they too had to go.

What They Said

President Andrew Jackson and the Cherokee Nation Debate Indian Removal

First introduced by Thomas Jefferson as an idea in 1803, the removal of eastern Indians west of the Mississippi River became one of the most contested issues in the early republic. The first selection below is Andrew Jackson's second State of the Union address on December 6, 1830, in which the president discusses the recently passed Indian Removal Act. The second is a memorial of the Cherokee Nation to the U.S. Congress.

▶ Andrew Jackson, State of the Union Address, December 6, 1830

What good man would prefer a country covered with forests and ranged by a few thousand savages to our extensive Republic, studded with cities, towns, and prosperous farms, embellished with all the improvements which art can devise or industry execute, occupied by more than 12,000,000 happy people, and filled with all the blessings of liberty, civilization, and religion?

…to better their condition in an unknown land our forefathers left all that was dear in earthly objects. Our children by thousands yearly leave the land of their birth to seek new homes in distant regions. Does Humanity weep at these painful separations from every thing, animate and inanimate, with which the young heart has become entwined? Far from it. It is rather a source of joy that our country affords scope where our young population may range unconstrained in body or in mind, developing the power and faculties of man in their highest perfection.

…can it be cruel in this Government when, by events which it can not control, the Indian is made discontented in his ancient home to purchase his lands, to give him a new and extensive territory, to pay the expense of his removal, and support him a year in his new abode? How many thousands of our own people would gladly embrace the opportunity of removing to the West on such conditions! If the offers made to the Indians were extended to them, they would be hailed with gratitude and joy.

And is it supposed that the wandering savage has a stronger attachment to his home than the settled, civilized Christian? Is it more afflicting to him to leave the graves of his fathers than it is to our brothers and children? Rightly considered, the policy of the General Government toward the red man is not only liberal, but generous. He is unwilling to submit to the laws of the States and mingle with their population. To save him from this alternative, or perhaps utter annihilation, the General Government kindly offers him a new home, and proposes to pay the whole expense of his removal and settlement.

▶ Memorial of the Cherokee Nation, 1830

We are aware that some persons suppose it will be for our advantage to remove beyond the Mississippi. We think otherwise. Our people universally think otherwise. Thinking that it would be fatal to their interests, they have almost to a man sent their memorial to Congress, deprecating the necessity of a removal….

We wish to remain on the land of our fathers. We have a perfect and original right to remain without interruption or molestation. The treaties with us, and laws of the United States made in pursuance of treaties, guaranty our residence and our privileges, and secure us against intruders. Our only request is, that these treaties may be fulfilled, and these laws executed.

But if we are compelled to leave our country, we see nothing but ruin before us. The country west of the Arkansas territory is unknown to us. From what we can learn of it, we have no prepossessions in its favor. All the inviting parts of it, as we believe, are preoccupied by various Indian nations, to which it has been assigned. They would regard us as intruders…

…the far greater part of that region is, beyond all controversy, badly supplied with wood and water; and no Indian tribe can live as agriculturists without these articles. All our neighbors … would speak a language totally different from ours, and practice different customs. The original possessors of that region are now wandering savages lurking for prey in the neighborhood…. Were the country to which we are urged much better than it is represented to be … still it is not the land of our birth, nor of our affections. It contains neither the scenes of our childhood, nor the graves of our fathers.

…there is not a man within our limits so ignorant as not to know that he has a right to live on the land of his fathers, in the possession of his immemorial privileges, and that this right has been acknowledged by the United States; nor is there a man so degraded as not to feel a keen sense of injury, on being deprived of his right and driven into exile….

Q *What sorts of similarities can you detect in the tone and style of the two documents? How does each use notions of law, history, and civilization to bolster its case? How does each depict Native Americans' relationship to land? By 1830, the Cherokees had developed a deep understanding of the United States and its ambitions, legal system, and self-understanding. They had interacted with its political agents, traders, and missionaries for more than three generations, and many of them were literate mixed-bloods (people with both white and Indian ancestry) who knew the American value system intimately. How effective, do you think, was the Cherokee Nation's memorial in soliciting a sympathetic emotional response among the American audience?*

Sources: (top) *Andrew Jackson*, State of the Union Address, December 6, 1830; (bottom) *Memorial of the Cherokee Nation*, 1830.

11.8 Trail of Tears In 1838, the U.S. Army marched some 15,000 Cherokee men, women, and children, along with their animals and whatever they could carry, out of their home territory and into Oklahoma. At least 4,000—most of them old or very young—died during the march.

Q *Does the painting commemorate the suffering of Cherokees under forced relocation or sanitize the history of Indian Removal?*

Indian removal also had profound political consequences in the United States. It violated Supreme Court decisions and thus strengthened Jackson's reputation as an enemy of the rule of law and a friend of local, "democratic" solutions. At the same time, it reaffirmed the link between racism and white democracy in the South and announced Jackson's commitment to state sovereignty and limited federal authority.

11-5c Southerners and the Tariff

In 1828, a Democratic Congress passed a tariff, hoping to win votes for Jackson in the upcoming presidential election. Assured of support in the South, they fished for votes in the mid-Atlantic states and the Northwest by protecting raw wool, flax, molasses, hemp, and distilled spirits. The result was a patchwork tariff that pleased northern and western farmers but that worried the South and violated Jackson's own ideas of what a "judicious" tariff should be. Protective tariffs hurt the South by diminishing exports of cotton and other staples and by raising the price of manufactured goods. More ominous, they demonstrated the power of other sections to write laws that helped them and hurt the outnumbered South. Calling the new bill a **"Tariff of Abominations,"** the legislature of one southern state after another denounced it as unconstitutional, unjust, and oppressive.

South Carolina, guided by Vice President Calhoun, led the opposition to the Tariff of 1828. During the War of 1812 and the ensuing Era of Good Feelings, Calhoun's South Carolina—confident of its future and deeply engaged in international markets for its rice and cotton—had favored the economic nationalism of the American System. Then the Missouri debates and the Denmark Vesey slave conspiracy of 1822 (see Chapter 9) sent South Carolinians looking for ways to safeguard slavery. Their fears grew more intense when federal courts shot down a state law forbidding black merchant seamen from moving about freely while their ships were docked at Charleston. Carolinians were disturbed too by persistent talk of gradual emancipation—at a time when their own commitment to slavery was growing stronger. Finally, southerners noted that in the congressional logrolling that made the Tariff of 1828, many western representatives had abandoned their old Jeffersonian alliance with the South to trade favors with the Northeast.

With the growth in the Northeast of urban markets for western produce, the American System's promise of interdependence among regions was beginning to work, but in ways that united the northern states against the export-oriented South. The Tariff of 1828 was the last straw: It benefited the city and commercial food producers at the expense of the plantation, and it demonstrated that the South could do nothing to block the passage of such laws.

11-5d Nullification

As early as 1827, Calhoun concluded that southern states could protect themselves from national majorities only if they possessed the power to veto federal legislation within their boundaries. In 1828, in his anonymously published essay *Exposition and Protest*, he argued that the Constitution was a contract between sovereign states and that the states (not the federal courts) could decide the constitutionality of federal laws. A state convention (like the conventions that had ratified the Constitution) could nullify any federal law within state borders. "Constitutional government and the government of a majority," Calhoun argued, "are utterly incompatible." *Exposition and Protest* echoed the Virginia and Kentucky Resolves of 1798 and 1799 and anticipated the secessionist arguments of 1861: The Union was a voluntary compact between sovereign states, states were the ultimate judges of the validity of federal law, and states could break the compact if they wished.

Nullification was extreme, and Calhoun and his friends tried to avoid using it. They knew that President Jackson was a states'-rights slaveholder who disliked the Tariff of 1828, and they assumed that Vice President Calhoun would succeed to the presidency and would protect southern interests. They were wrong on both counts. Jackson favored states' rights, but only within a perpetual and inviolable union. A tariff was ultimately a matter of foreign policy, clearly within the jurisdiction of the federal government. To allow a state to veto a tariff would be to deny the legal existence of the United States.

Jackson revealed his views at a celebration of Jefferson's birthday on April 13, 1830. Calhoun's southern friends dominated the speechmaking, and Jackson listened quietly as speaker after speaker defended the extreme states'-rights position. After the formal speeches were over, the president rose to propose an after-dinner toast. "Our Federal Union: *It must be preserved*," he said. Isaac Hill, a New Hampshire Democrat and a supporter of Van Buren, reported, "an order to arrest Calhoun where he sat would not have come with more blinding, staggering force." Dumbstruck, the southerners looked to Calhoun, who as vice president was to propose the second toast. Shaken by Jackson's unqualified defense of the Union, Calhoun offered this toast: "The Union. Next to our liberties the most dear." They were strong words, but they had little meaning after Jackson's affirmation of the Union. A few days later, a South Carolina congressman on his way home asked the president if he had any message for him to take back. "Yes, I have," replied Jackson. "Please give my compliments to my friends in your state, and say to them, that if a single drop of blood shall be shed there in opposition to the laws of the United States, I will hang the first man I can lay my hand on engaged in such treasonable conduct, upon the first tree I can reach."

Having reaffirmed the Union and rejected nullification, Jackson asked Congress to reduce the tariff rates in the hope that he could isolate the nullifiers from southerners who simply hated the tariff. The resulting Tariff of 1832 lowered the rates on many items but still affirmed the principle of protectionism. That, along with Boston abolitionist William Lloyd Garrison's declaration of war on slavery in 1831, followed by Nat Turner's bloody slave uprising in Virginia that same year (see Chapter 9), led the whites of South Carolina and Georgia to intensify their distrust of outside authority and their insistence on the right to govern their own neighborhoods. South Carolina, now with Calhoun's open leadership and support, called a state convention that nullified the Tariffs of 1828 and 1832.

In Washington, President Jackson raged that nullification (not to mention the right of secession that followed logically from it) was illegal. Insisting that "disunion ... is *treason*," he asked Congress for a Force Bill empowering him to personally lead a federal army into South Carolina. At the same time, however, he supported the rapid reduction of tariffs. When Democratic attempts at reduction bogged down, Henry Clay, who was now back in the Senate, took on the tricky legislative task of rescuing his beloved protective tariff while quieting southern fears. The result was the Compromise Tariff of 1833, which, by lowering tariffs over the course of several years, gave southern planters the relief they demanded while maintaining moderate protectionism and allowing northern manufacturers time to adjust to the lower rates. Congress also passed the Force Bill. Jackson signed both into law on March 2, 1833.

With that, the nullification crisis came to a quiet end. No other southern state had joined South Carolina in nullifying the tariff, although some states had made vague pledges of support in the event that Jackson led his army to Charleston. The Compromise Tariff of 1833 isolated the South Carolina nullifiers. Deprived of their issue and most of their support, they declared victory and disbanded their convention, but not before nullifying the Force Bill. Jackson chose to overlook that last defiant gesture because he had accomplished what he wanted: He had asserted a perpetual Union, and he had protected southern interests within it.

11-5e The "Petticoat Wars"

The spoils system, Indian removal, nullification, and other heated questions of Jackson's first term were fought out against a backdrop of gossip, intrigue, and angry division within the inner circles of Jackson's government. The talk centered on Peggy O'Neal Timberlake, a Washington tavern keeper's daughter who, in January 1829, had married John Henry Eaton, Jackson's old friend and his soon-to-be secretary of war. Eaton was middle-aged; his bride was 29, pretty, flirtatious, and, according to Washington gossip, "frivolous, wayward, [and] passionate." Knowing that his marriage might cause trouble for the new administration, Eaton had asked for and received Jackson's blessing—and, by strong implication, his protection.

The marriage of John and Peggy Eaton came at a turning point in the history of both Washington society and elite sexual mores. Until the 1820s, most officeholders had left their families at home. They took lodgings at taverns and boardinghouses and lived in a bachelor world of shirtsleeves, tobacco, card playing, and occasional liaisons with local women. But in the 1820s, the boardinghouse world was giving way to high society. Cabinet members, senators, congressmen, and other officials moved into Washington houses, and their wives presided over the round of dinner parties through which much

11.9 President Andrew Jackson's Celestial Cabinet, 1836 This lithograph cartoon satirizes Andrew Jackson's cabinet meeting on the uproar over Peggy Eaton.

Q *What do the controversies around Peggy Eaton reveal about American values, morals, and politics of the time?*

Q *What does the controversy tell us about women's status and agency in society?*

of the government's business was done. As in other wealthy families, political wives imposed new forms of gentility and politeness on these affairs, and they assumed the responsibility of drawing up the guest lists. Many of them determined to exclude Peggy Eaton from polite society.

The shunning of Peggy Eaton split the Jackson administration in two. Jackson was committed to protecting her. He had met his own beloved Rachel while boarding at her father's Nashville tavern, and their grand romance (as well as the gossip that surrounded it) was a striking parallel to the affair of John and Peggy Eaton. That, coupled with Jackson's honor-bound agreement to the Eaton marriage, ensured that he would protect the Eatons to the bitter end. Always suspicious of intrigues, Jackson labeled the "dark and sly insinuations" about Peggy Eaton part of a "conspiracy" against his presidency. Before long, his suspicions centered on Vice President Calhoun, whose wife, Floride Bonneau Calhoun, a powerful Washington matron, was a leader of the assault on Peggy Eaton. Sensing that Jackson was losing his patience with Calhoun, fellow Democrats, soon after the Jefferson birthday banquet in spring 1830, showed Jackson a letter from William H. Crawford revealing that while serving in Monroe's cabinet, Calhoun, contrary to his protestations, had favored censuring Jackson for his unauthorized invasion of Florida in 1818. An open break with Calhoun became inevitable.

11-5f The Fall of Calhoun

Jackson resolved the Peggy Eaton controversy, as he would resolve nullification, in ways that favored Van Buren in his contest with Calhoun. He pointedly made Peggy Eaton the official hostess at the White House. Then, in spring 1831, Van Buren gave Jackson a free hand to reconstruct his tangled administration. He offered to resign his cabinet post and engineered the resignations of nearly all other members of the cabinet, thus allowing Jackson to remake his administration without firing anyone. Many of those who left were southern supporters of Calhoun. Jackson replaced them with a mixed cabinet that included political allies of Van Buren. Also at this time, President Jackson began to consult with an informal Kitchen Cabinet that included journalists Amos Kendall and Francis Preston Blair, along with Van Buren and a few others. The Peggy Eaton controversy and the resulting shakeup in the administration were contributing mightily to the success of Van Buren's southern strategy.

Van Buren's victory over Calhoun came to a quick conclusion. As part of his cabinet reorganization, Jackson appointed Van Buren minister to Great Britain—an important post that would temporarily remove him from the heat of Washington politics. Vice President Calhoun, sitting as president of the Senate, rigged the confirmation so that he cast the deciding vote against Van Buren's appointment—a petty act that turned out to be his last exercise of national power. Jackson replaced Calhoun with Van Buren as the vice presidential candidate in 1832 and let it be known that he wanted Van Buren to succeed him as president.

11-5g Petitions, the Gag Rule, and the Southern Mails

The Democratic Party's rigid party discipline and its commitment to slavery and states' rights antagonized many northerners and evangelical Protestants who advocated abolition, energetic government, and social and moral reforms. The antagonism came to a head in 1835, when abolitionists launched a "postal campaign," flooding the mail—in the North and South—with antislavery tracts that condemned slavery in the federal territories, the interstate slave trade, and the admission of new slave states. The southerners and most northerners considered such tactics incendiary.

Some Jacksonians, including Jackson, wanted to stop the postal campaign with a federal censorship law. Calhoun and other southerners, however, argued that the states had the right to censor mail crossing their borders. Knowing that state censorship of the mail was unconstitutional and that federal censorship of the mail would be a political disaster, Jackson's administration devised an informal solution. Without changing the law, the general postmaster simply looked the other way as local postmasters removed abolitionist materials from the mail. Calhoun and his supporters continued to demand state censorship, but the Democrats had no intention of relinquishing federal control over the federal mail. They made it clear, however, that no abolitionist literature would reach the South as long as Democrats controlled the U.S. Post Office.

The Democrats dealt in similar ways with antislavery petitions to Congress. With their postal campaign disabled, abolitionists began to bombard Congress with petitions to abolish slavery and the slave trade in the District of Columbia (where Congress had undisputed authority) and to deny the slaveholding Republic of Texas admission to the Union. Pressured by irritated pro-slavery representatives to resolve the matter, Congress conceived an unusual procedure: It simply voted at each session to table the petitions without reading them, thus acknowledging that they had been received but sidestepping any debate on them. This procedure, which became known as the **"gag rule,"** was passed by the support of southern representatives and the vast majority of northern Democrats. Increasingly, abolitionists sent their petitions to ex-president John Quincy Adams, who had returned to Washington as a congressman from Massachusetts. Adams spoke forcefully against slavery and the violations of civil liberties in Congress, evading the gag rule, which was rescinded in 1844, after eight years in effect. Thus, the Jacksonians answered the question that had arisen with the Missouri debates: how to protect the slaveholding South within the federal Union. Whereas Calhoun and other southern radicals found the answer in nullification and other forms of state sovereignty, Jackson and the Democratic coalition insisted that the Union was inviolable and that any attempt to dissolve it would be met with force. At the same time, a disciplined Democratic Party uniting northern and southern agrarians into a states'-rights, limited-government majority could guarantee southern rights within the Union. This answer to the southern question stayed in place until the breakup of the Democratic Party on the eve of the Civil War.

11-6 Jacksonian Democracy and the Market Revolution

Q *How did Democrats and Whigs in the national government argue questions raised by economic development?*

Jacksonian Democrats cherished the simplicity of Jefferson's agrarian republic. They assumed power at the height of the Market Revolution, and they spent much of the 1830s and 1840s trying to reconcile the market and the republic. Like the Jeffersonians before them, Democrats welcomed commerce as long as it served the liberty and rough equality of white men, but paper currency and the dependence on credit that came with the Market Revolution posed problems. The so-called paper economy separated wealth from "real work" and encouraged an unrepublican spirit of luxury and greed. Worst of all, the new paper economy required government-granted privileges that the Jacksonians, still speaking the language of revolutionary republicanism, branded "corruption." For the same reasons, the protective tariffs and government-sponsored roads and canals of the American System were unacceptable. The Jackson presidency aimed to curtail government involvement in the economy, to end special privilege, and thus to rescue the republic from the Money Power.

Jackson's policies met with growing opposition, which coalesced into a new party, the Whigs, in 1834. The Whigs favored an activist central government that would encourage orderly economic development through the American System of protective tariffs, a federally subsidized transportation network, and a national bank. This system, they argued, would encourage national prosperity. At the same time, it would create a truly national market economy that would soften sectional divisions. Jacksonian rhetoric about the Money Power and the Old Republic, they argued, was little more than the demagoguery of unqualified, self-seeking politicians.

11-6a The Second Bank of the United States

The argument between Jacksonians and their detractors came to focus on the Second Bank of the United States that Congress had chartered in 1816. The national government deposited its revenue in the bank, thus giving it an enormous capital base. The government deposits also included state banknotes that had been used to pay customs duties or to buy public land; the Bank of the United States had the power to demand redemption of these notes in specie, thus discouraging state banks from issuing inflationary notes that they could not back up. The bank also issued notes of its own, which served as the beginnings of a national paper currency. Thus, with powers granted under its federal charter, the Bank of the United States exercised central control over the nation's monetary and credit systems.

Most members of the business community valued the Bank of the United States because it promised a stable, uniform paper currency and competent, centralized control over the banking system. But millions of Americans resented and distrusted the national bank, citing its role in the Panic of 1819 as evidence of the dangers posed by privileged, powerful institutions. President Jackson agreed with the latter opinion. A southwestern agrarian who had lost money in an early speculation, he was leery of paper money, banks, and the credit system. He insisted that both the bank and paper money were unconstitutional and that the only safe, natural, republican currencies were gold and silver. Above all, Jackson saw the Bank of the United States as a government-sponsored concentration of power that threatened American liberty.

History Through Film *Amistad* (1997)

Directed by Steven Spielberg.
Starring Matthew McConaughey (Roger Baldwin), Morgan Freeman (Theodore Joadson), Anthony Hopkins (John Quincy Adams), Djimon Hounsou (Cinque).

In 1839, an American cruiser seized the Cuban slave ship *Amistad* off the shore of Long Island. The ship carried 41 Africans who had revolted, killed the captain and crew, and commandeered the ship—along with two Spanish slave dealers who bargained for their lives by promising to sail the ship east to Africa, then steered for North America. The Africans were imprisoned at New Haven and tried for piracy and murder in federal court. The government of Spain demanded their return, and southern leaders pressured President Van Buren for a "friendly" decision. The legal case centered on whether the Africans were Cuban slaves or kidnapped Africans. (The international slave trade was by then illegal.) The New Haven court acquitted them, the federal government appealed the case, and the Supreme Court freed them again. The Africans were returned to Sierra Leone.

The Africans spend most of the movie in a dark jail or in court, and the film centers on them and their experiences with two groups of Americans: the abolitionists who are trying to free them, and the political and legal officials who want to hang them—largely to keep their own political system intact. Spielberg's abolitionists are Lewis Tappan, a black activist (Morgan Freeman), an obscure young white lawyer (Matthew McConaughey), and, in the grand finale, congressman and former president John Quincy Adams (played wonderfully by Anthony Hopkins). In the historical case, the defense was handled by veteran abolitionists or by persons who had been working with abolitionists for a long time. Spielberg shaped this group to tell his own story, beginning with reluctant and confused reformers and politicians who, along with the audience, gradually realize the moral imperatives of the case.

11.10 *Amistad* (1997) tells the story of 41 Africans who stage a revolt on the slave ship carrying them to Cuba and the trial that follows.

In one of the film's more powerful sequences, the Africans' leader, Cinque (Djimon Hounsou), through a translator, tells his story to the lawyer: his village life in Sierra Leone (the one scene filmed in bright sunlight), his capture by Africans, his transportation to the slave fort of Lomboko, the horrors of the passage on the Portuguese slaver *Tecora*, the slave market in Havana, and the bloody revolt on the *Amistad*—all of it portrayed wrenchingly on the screen. The Africans' story continues in jail, as they study pictures in a Bible and try to figure out the American legal, political, and moral system. In court, they finally cut through the mumbo jumbo by standing and chanting "Give Us Free!"

In a fictive interview on the eve of the Supreme Court case, Cinque tells Adams that he is optimistic because he has called on the spirits of his ancestors to join him in court. This moment, he says, is the whole reason for their having existed at all. Adams, whose own father had helped lead the Revolution, speaks for his and Cinque's ancestors before the Supreme Court: To the prosecution's argument that the Africans are pirates and murderers and to southern arguments that slavery is a natural state, he answers that America is founded on the "self-evident truth" that one's natural state is freedom. It is a fine Hollywood courtroom speech: Adams has honored his ancestors, the justices and the audience see the moral rightness of his case, and the Africans are returned to Sierra Leone. (In a subscript, Spielberg tells us that Cinque returns to a village that had been destroyed in civil war, but the final ironic note is overwhelmed by the moral triumphalism of the rest of the movie.) ■

11-6b The Bank War

The charter of the Bank of the United States ran through 1836, but Senators Henry Clay and Daniel Webster encouraged Nicholas Biddle, the Bank's brilliant, aristocratic president, to apply for recharter in 1832. Clay planned to oppose Jackson in the presidential election later that year, and he knew that Jackson hated the bank. He and his friends hoped to provoke the hot-tempered Jackson into a response they could use against him in the election. The Bank applied for recharter in January 1832, and Congress passed the bill in early July and sent it on to the president. Jackson understood the early request for recharter as a political ploy. On July 4, Van Buren visited the White House and found Jackson sick in bed; Jackson took Van Buren's hand and said, "The bank, Mr. Van Buren, is trying to kill me, *but I will kill it!*" Jackson vetoed the bill.

Jackson's Bank Veto Message was a manifesto of Jacksonian democracy. It combined Jeffersonian verities with appeals to the public's prejudice and declared that the bank was "unauthorized by the Constitution, subversive of the rights of the states, and dangerous to the liberties of the people." Its charter, Jackson complained, bestowed special privilege on the bank and its stockholders, who were almost all northeastern businessmen or, worse, British investors. Having made most of its loans to southerners and westerners, the bank was a huge monster that sucked resources out of the agrarian South and West and poured them into the pockets of northeastern gentlemen and their English friends. The Bank Veto Message was a long, rambling attack that, in the opinion of the Bank's supporters, demonstrated Jackson's unfitness for office. "It has all the fury of a chained panther biting the bars of its cage," said Nicholas Biddle. "It really is," he concluded, "a manifesto of anarchy." So certain were they that the public shared their views that Clay's supporters distributed Jackson's Bank Veto Message as *anti*-Jackson propaganda during the 1832 campaign. They were wrong. Most voters shared Jackson's attachment to a society of virtuous, independent producers and to pristine republican government. They also agreed that the republic was being subverted by parasites, who grew rich by manipulating credit, prices, paper money, and government-bestowed privileges. Jackson portrayed himself as both the protector of the Old Republic and a melodramatic hero contending with illegitimate, aristocratic, privileged, secretive powers. With the bank and Jackson's veto as the principal issues, Jackson won reelection by a landslide in 1832 (see Map 11.4).

Jackson began his second term determined to kill the Bank of the United States before Congress could reverse his veto. The bank would be able to operate under its old charter until 1836, but Jackson hurried its death by withdrawing government deposits as they were needed and by depositing new government revenues in carefully selected state banks—soon to be called "Pet Banks" by the opposition. By law, the decision to remove the deposits had to be made by the secretary of the treasury. Two successive treasury secretaries refused to do so; Jackson removed both from office and appointed Roger B. Taney, a loyal Democrat who promptly withdrew the deposits. Without the deposits, the Second Bank withered away.

11-6c The Beginnings of the Whig Party

Conflict over deposit removal and related questions of presidential power united anti-Jacksonians—most of them committed advocates of the American System—into the Whig Party. The name of the party, as everyone who understood the language of the republic knew, stood for legislative opposition to a power-mad executive. Jackson, argued the Whigs, had transformed himself from the limited executive described in the Constitution into King Andrew I. They listed the spoils systems and frequent vetoes of congressional legislation as his principal offenses. While earlier presidents had exercised the veto only nine times, Jackson alone used it 12 times during his two terms.

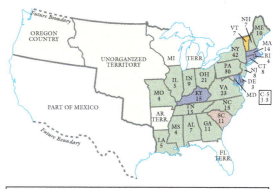

▲ **MAP 11.4 Presidential Election, 1832**
The election of 1832 was a landslide victory for Andrew Jackson. The National Republican Henry Clay carried only his native Kentucky, along with Delaware and southern New England. A defeated and resentful South Carolina ran its own candidate. Jackson, on the other hand, won in the regions in which he had been strong in 1828 and added support in New York and northern New England.

Q *In what ways did the debates over the national bank shape the outcome of the election of 1832?*

Q *Was Andrew Jackson's 1832 campaign an anti-establishment campaign?*

According to his critics, the president used his veto power in particular to restrain the growth of the markets, the American System, and federal spending. The bank veto conveyed the same position, and the withdrawal of the government deposits brought the question of "executive usurpation" to a head, causing uneasiness even among the president's supporters,

Henry Clay, who had watched as Jackson denied one component after another of his American System, joined with Daniel Webster to lead the old National Republican coalition (the name that anti-Jacksonians had assumed since 1824) into the new Whig Party. They were joined by southerners (including Calhoun) who resented Jackson's treatment of the South Carolina nullifiers and Biddle's bank, and who distrusted his assurances on slavery. Jackson's war on the Bank of the United States chased lukewarm supporters into the opposition, enabling Democrats to point to an increasingly sharp division between the Money Power and the Old Republic.

The dismantling of the Second Bank of the United States had left a federal surplus of $5 million (produced by tariff proceeds and sales of public lands) without a depository. Jackson wanted to prevent the surplus money from being redistributed to the states, fearing that it would bolster the hated paper economy and encourage Congress to keep land prices and tariff rates high. Whigs, who by now despaired of ever creating a

Interpreting the Visual Past: King Andrew the First

This widely distributed opposition cartoon depicts President Andrew Jackson as "King Andrew the First." It was a powerful cartoon, for Americans knew that their nation had begun in opposition to monarchy, and to a royal government that usurped power and encroached upon liberty. Jackson's opponents called themselves Whigs, in honor of the parliamentary faction that had opposed royal power in Britain. In fact, Jackson favored a small, inactive national government and used (abused, said his critics) presidential power to limit the powers of the government in Washington, largely by vetoing bills passed by the Whig legislatures that he faced throughout his presidency.

In the cartoon, King Andrew holds his scepter in one hand and a vetoed bill in the other. Internal improvements, the Bank of the United States, and the Constitution lie in ruins at his feet. The small print lists his crimes in detail: He had appointed federal officials that Whigs did not like, he had ignored Supreme Court decisions (on Indian removal in particular), and he had vetoed a lot of legislation—all of it in violation of "the will of the people."

Q Andrew Jackson has traditionally been known as a "powerful" president. What was the nature of his power, and to what ends did he use it?

Q The cartoon refers repeatedly to "the People." In the language and context of the cartoon, who were they?

11.11 "King Andrew the First", circa 1833.

federally subsidized, coordinated transportation system, picked up the idea of redistribution. With help from the like-minded Democrats, they passed the Deposit Act of 1836, which increased the number of banks receiving federal deposits (thus removing power from Jackson's Pet Banks) and distributed the federal surplus to the states to be spent on roads, canals, and other internal improvements. Jackson, who distrusted state-chartered banks as much as he distrusted the Bank of the United States, planned to veto the bill, but faced an overwhelming congressional coalition of Whigs and Democrats. He demanded a provision limiting the state banks' right to print banknotes. With that provision, he reluctantly signed the Deposit Act.

Jackson and many members of his administration had deep fiscal and moral concerns about the inflationary boom that accompanied the rapid growth of commerce, credit, roads, canals, new farms, and the other manifestations of the Market Revolution in the 1830s. After insisting that his hard-money, anti-inflationary provision be added to the Deposit Act, Jackson issued a **Specie Circular** in 1836. This provided that speculators could only buy large parcels of public land with silver and gold coins, while settlers could continue to buy farm-sized plots with banknotes. Henceforth, speculators would have to bring wagonloads of coins from eastern banks to frontier land offices. With this provision, Jackson hoped to curtail speculation and to reverse the flow of specie out of the South and West. The Specie Circular was Jackson's final assault on the paper economy. It repeated familiar themes: It favored hard currency over paper, settlers over speculators, and the South and West over the Northeast.

11-7 The Second American Party System

Q *What was peculiarly national about the Second Party System?*

In his farewell address in 1837, Jackson spoke once again of the incompatibility between the republic and the Money Power. He warned against a revival of the Bank of the United States and against all banks, paper money, the spirit of speculation, and every aspect of the "paper system." That system encouraged greed and luxury, which were at odds with republican virtue, he said. Worse, it thrived on special privilege, creating a world in which insiders meeting in "secret conclaves" could buy and sell elections. The solution, as always, was a society of small producers, a vigilant democratic electorate, and a chaste republican government that granted no special privileges.

11-7a "Martin Van Ruin"

Sitting beside Jackson as he delivered his farewell address was his chosen successor, Martin Van Buren. In the election of 1836, the Whigs had acknowledged that Henry Clay, the leader of their party, could not win a national election. Instead, they ran three sectional candidates: Daniel Webster in the Northeast, the old Indian fighter William Henry Harrison in the West, and Hugh Lawson White of Tennessee, a turncoat Jacksonian, in the South. With this ploy, the Whigs hoped to deprive Van Buren of a majority and throw the election into the Whig-controlled House of Representatives.

The strategy failed. Van Buren had engineered a national Democratic Party that could avert the dangers of sectionalism, and he questioned the patriotism of the Whigs and their sectional candidates, asserting, "True republicans can never lend their aid and influence in creating geographical parties." That, along with his association with Jackson's popular presidency, won him the election. Van Buren carried 15 of the 26 states and received 170 electoral votes against 124 for his combined opposition. His popular plurality, however, was less than 51 percent (see Map 11.5).

Van Buren had barely taken office when the inflationary boom of the mid-1830s collapsed. Economic historians ascribe the Panic of 1837 and the ensuing depression largely to events outside the country. The Bank of England, concerned over the flow of British gold to American speculators, cut off credit to firms that did business in the United States. As a result, British demand for American cotton fell sharply, and the price of cotton dropped by half. With much of the speculative boom tied to cotton grown in the South, the economy collapsed. The first business failures came in March 1837, just as Van Buren took office. By May, New York banks, unable to accommodate

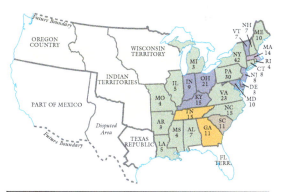

▲ **MAP 11.5 Presidential Election, 1836**
In 1836, the Whigs tried to beat the Democrats' national organization with an array of sectional candidates, hoping to throw the election into the House of Representatives. The strategy failed. Martin Van Buren, with significant support in every section of the country, defeated the three Whig candidates combined.

Q *Is it fair to say that the Whigs lost the election of 1836 rather than the Democrats winning it?*

Q *In what ways was the election of 1832 different from previous elections?*

people who were demanding hard coin for their notes, suspended specie payments. Other banks followed suit, and soon banks all over the country went out of business. The financial and export sectors of the economy suffered most. In the seaport cities, one firm after another closed its doors, and about one-third of the workforce was unemployed. For those who kept their jobs, wages declined by 30 to 50 percent. It was the deepest, most widespread, and longest economic depression Americans had ever faced.

Whigs blamed the depression on Jackson's hard-money policies, particularly his destruction of the Bank of the United States and his Specie Circular. With economic distress the main issue, Whigs scored huge gains in the midterm elections of 1838, even winning control of Van Buren's New York with a campaign that castigated the president as "Martin Van Ruin." Democrats blamed the crash on speculation, luxury, and Whig paper money. Whigs demanded a new national bank, but Van Buren proposed the complete divorce of government from the banking system. Under his plan, the federal government would simply hold and dispense its money without depositing it in banks. He also required that customs and land purchases be paid in gold and silver coins or in notes from specie-paying banks, a provision that allowed government to regulate state banknotes without resorting to a central bank. Van Buren asked Congress to set up the Independent Treasury in 1837, and Congress spent the rest of Van Buren's time in office arguing about it. The **Independent Treasury Bill** finally passed in 1840, completing the Jacksonian separation of bank and state.

11-7b The Election of 1840

Whigs were confident that they could take the presidency away from Van Buren in 1840. Trying to offend as few voters as possible, they passed over their best-known leaders, Senators Henry Clay and Daniel Webster, and nominated William Henry Harrison of Ohio as their presidential candidate. Harrison was the hero of the Battle of Tippecanoe (see Chapter 7) and a westerner whose Virginia origins made him palatable in the South. He was also a proven vote-getter: As the Whigs' "western" candidate in 1836, he had carried seven states scattered across the Northwest, the mid-Atlantic, New England, and the Upper South. Best of all, he was a military hero who had expressed few opinions on national issues and who had no political record to defend. As his running mate, the Whigs chose John Tyler, a states'-rights Virginian who had joined the Whigs out of hatred for Jackson. To promote this baldly pragmatic ticket, the Whigs came up with a catchy slogan: "Tippecanoe and Tyler Too." One wealthy New York City Whig admitted that the slogan (and the ticket) had "rhyme, but no reason in it."

Early in the campaign, a Democratic journalist, commenting on Harrison's political inexperience and alleged unfitness for the presidency, wrote, "Give [Harrison] a barrel of hard cider, and settle a pension of two thousand a year on him, and my word for it, he will sit out the remainder of his days in his log cabin." Whigs, who had been trying to shake their elitist image, seized on the statement and launched what was known as the Log Cabin Campaign. The log cabin, the cider barrel, and Harrison's folksiness and heroism constituted the entire Whig campaign, while Van Buren was pictured as living in luxury at the public's expense. The Whigs conjured up an image of a nattily dressed President "Van Ruin" sitting on silk chairs and dining on gold and silver dishes while farmers and workingmen struggled to make ends meet. Whig doggerel contrasted Harrison the hero with Van Buren the professional politician:

> The knapsack pillow'd Harry's head
> The hard ground eas'd his toils;
> while Martin on his downy bed
> Could dream of naught but spoils.

Democrats howled that Whigs were peddling lies and refusing to discuss issues, but they knew they had been beaten at their own game. Harrison won only a narrow majority of the popular vote, but a landslide of 234 to 60 votes in the Electoral College (see Map 11.6).

The election of 1840 signaled the completion of the Second Party System—the most fully national alignment of parties in U.S. history. Andrew Jackson had won in 1828 with Jefferson's old southern and western agrarian constituency; in 1832, he had carried his old voters and had won added support in the mid-Atlantic states and in northern New England. In 1836, Whigs capitalized

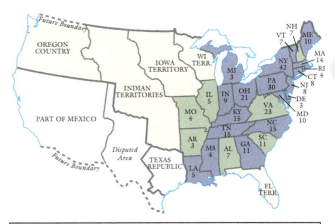

▲ **MAP 11.6 Presidential Election, 1840** In 1840, the Whigs united under William Henry Harrison, the one Whig candidate who had won national support four years earlier. Borrowing campaign tactics from the Democrats and inventing many of their own, Whigs campaigned hard in every state. The result was a Whig victory and a truly national two-party system.

Q Why did Harrison win the election of 1840?

Q It what ways did the election of 1840 break new ground in American politics?

11.12 The Times This Whig cartoon from the 1840 campaign blames the Panic of 1837 on the Democrats. The factories are closed, the bank has suspended specie payments, and sailors and craftsmen are out of work, but the sheriff, the prison, the pawnbroker, and the liquor store are doing a booming business.

on southern resentment of Jackson's defeat of nullification and on southern mistrust of the New Yorker Van Buren. They broke the Democratic hold on the South, carrying Kentucky, Georgia, South Carolina, and even Jackson's Tennessee. Jackson had won 8 in 10 southern votes; Van Buren carried barely half. The election of 1840 completed the transition: Harrison and Van Buren contested the election in nearly every state and they received nearly equal levels of support in the slave and free states. Van Buren's dream of a national party system that transcended sectional differences was realized. Ironically, the final pieces fell into place in an election that cost him the presidency.

The election of 1840 also witnessed the high-water mark of voter turnout. Whig and Democratic organizations focused on presidential elections, and prospective voters met a quadrennial avalanche of oratory, door-to-door canvassing, torchlight parades, and party propaganda. Neither Democrats nor Whigs could take any state in the Union for granted. (In 1828, winning candidates carried individual states by an average of 36 percent; by 1840, that figure had dropped to 11 percent.) Whigs and Democrats maintained organizations and contested elections in nearly every neighborhood in the country, and the result was increased popular interest in politics. In 1824, about one in four adult white men had voted in the presidential election. Jackson's vengeful campaign of 1828 lifted the turnout to 56.3 percent, and it stayed at about that level in 1832 and 1836. The campaign of 1840 brought out 78 percent of eligible voters, and the turnout remained at that high level for the rest of the 19th century.

In every part of the country, Whigs presented themselves as the party of active government and economic progress. They promised good roads, public schools, stable currency, and social harmony. In the North, the wealthiest men were Whigs (8 in 10 of the merchant elites in New York and Boston, for example). But the Whig Party received its core northern support among the market farmers, local merchants, and manufacturers created by the new market economy and the fires of middle-class revivals—supporters not only of Whig nationalism but of roads and canals and a wide array of reforms in their own neighborhoods. In the South, Whigs ran well in plantation districts and in county-seat towns—the centers of southern wealth, commerce, and gentility. Many southern leaders came to dislike Jackson, and they took their personal followings into the Whig Party. Whigs also won votes in areas—eastern Tennessee and western North Carolina are examples—where farmers *wanted* to be brought into the flow of commerce. Put very simply, Whigs tended to be persons who were or wanted to be beneficiaries of the Market Revolution, and who embraced its attendant social and cultural transformations. They saw themselves as "improvers."

The Democrats, on the other hand, posed as defenders of the common (white) man and the Old Republic. They tended to be persons who had been hurt or bypassed by the Market Revolution; who belonged to conservative, otherworldly churches; and who distrusted Whigs who talked about progress, big government, and social homogeneity. In the South, Democrats were strong in districts with small farms, few slaves, and limited market activity. The northern Democrats were a coalition of small farmers, working people, and small businessmen, along with cultural minorities (Irish immigrants, for instance, were almost unanimously Democratic). North and South, Democrats were localists. They argued for the limited national government that since Jefferson's day had been a bulwark of the revolutionary republic, of white male democracy, and of chattel slavery.

Conclusion

Thus, the party system answered the questions of slavery and economic development that had helped bring it into being. Nationally, Democrats stopped the American System. They dismantled the Bank of the United States, refused federal support for roads and canals, and revised the tariff in ways that mollified the export-oriented South. As a result, the stupendous growth of the American economy between 1830 and 1860 became a question of state and local—not national—government action. Neither the national commercial society envisioned by the Whigs nor the return to Jeffersonian agrarianism favored by many Democrats came into being. Instead, the United States experienced an almost inadvertent experiment in laissez-faire capitalism, with results that reflected the aims of the most ambitious states. Trade and transportation networks linked the North and mid-Atlantic and isolated the export economy of the South—a result that few politicians had intended. Regarding the political problems surrounding slavery, the two-party system did what Van Buren had hoped it would do: Because both Whigs and Democrats needed both northern and southern support, they focused national political debates on economic development and stayed away from the questions of sectionalism and slavery. It worked that way until the party system disintegrated on the eve of the Civil War.

CHAPTER REVIEW

Review

1. What were the components of the "American System"? What did the American System promise to accomplish?
2. What enduring political issues were raised by the Missouri controversy and the Panic of 1819?
3. What were the events and political motives that contributed to the republican revival that formed around Andrew Jackson?
4. What were the principal events of the John Quincy Adams administration, and how did they contribute to his defeat in 1828?
5. At the national level, how did Jacksonian Democrats and their rivals deal with widening differences between North and South?
6. How did Democrats and Whigs in the national government argue questions raised by economic development?
7. What was peculiarly national about the Second Party System?

Critical Thinking

1. Jacksonian Democrats represented themselves as a revival of Jeffersonian democracy. In what ways was that representation accurate? In what ways was it not?
2. Whigs claimed to be the party of economic progress. Yet, unlike modern pro-growth politicians, they demanded a powerful, interventionist national government. How did they argue that position?

Identifications

Review your understanding of the following key terms, people, and events for this chapter (terms in bold in text are included in the Glossary).

American System, p. 303
Dartmouth College v. Woodward, p. 306
McCulloch v. Maryland, p. 306
Tallmadge Amendments, p. 307
Missouri Compromise, p. 308
congressional caucus, p. 310
"Corrupt Bargain," p. 311
Monroe Doctrine, p. 312
"spoils system," p. 314
Civilized Tribes, p. 316
Indian Removal Act, p. 316
"Tariff of Abominations," p. 318
nullification, p. 319
"gag rule," p. 321
Specie Circular, p. 325
Independent Treasury Bill, p. 326

Suggested Readings

Sean Wilentz, *The Rise of American Democracy: Jefferson to Lincoln (2006)* is a comprehensive political history. **Harry L. Watson**, *Liberty and Power: The Politics of Jacksonian America* (1990) is an excellent shorter synthesis. **Mathew**

Mason, *Slavery & Politics in the Early American Republic* (2006) and **Don E. Fehrenbacher**, *The Slaveholding Republic: An Account of the United States Government's Relations to Slavery* (2001) document the centrality of slavery through all these years. On southern Indians and the Indian removal, see **Claudio Saunt**, *A New Order of Things: Property, Power, and the Transformation of the Creek Indians, 1733–1816* (1999) and **Theda Perdue and Michael Green**, *The Cherokee Removal: A Brief History with Documents* (2005). On specific issues, see **John Lauritz Larson**, *Internal Improvement: National Public Works and the Promise of Popular Government in the Early United States* (2001); **A.F.C. Wallace**, *The Long, Bitter Trail: Andrew Jackson and the Indians* (1993); **R. Kent Newmeyer**, *The Supreme Court under Marshall and Taney* (1968); **Morton J. Horwitz**, *The Transformation of American Law, 1780–1860* (1977); **Robert Pierce Forbes**, *The Missouri Compromise and Its Aftermath: Slavery and the Meaning of America* (2007); **William W. Freehling**, *Prelude to Civil War: The Nullification Controversy in South Carolina, 1816–1836* (1965); **Richard E. Ellis**, *The Union at Risk: Jacksonian Democracy, States' Rights and the Nullification Crisis* (1987); and **Catherine Allgor**, *Parlor Politics: In Which the Ladies of Washington Help Build a City and a Government* (2000). **Steve Inskeep**, *Jacksonland: President Andrew Jackson, Cherokee Chief John Ross, and a Great American Land Grab* (2015), is an incisive and highly readable study of President Jackson and the Indian Removal. For Indian Removal as ethnic cleansing, see **Gary Clayton Anderson**, *Ethnic Cleansing: The Crime That Should Haunt America* (2014).

MINDTAP is a fully online personalized learning experience built upon Cengage Learning content. MindTap® combines student learning tools—readings, multimedia, activities, and assessments—into a singular Learning Path that guides students through the course and helps students develop the critical thinking, analysis, and communication skills that are essential to academic and professional success.

12 Antebellum Reform, 1820–1860

12-1 The Politics of Progress
Learning Objective: Identify Whig and Democratic conceptions of the duties and limits of government.

Markets and Governments
Banks, Roads, Canals

12-2 The Politics of Social Reform: Schools and Asylums
Learning Objective: Identify Whig and Democratic positions on the issues of public schools, prisons, and asylums.

Public Schools
Ethnicity, Religion, and the Schools
Prisons
Asylums

12-3 The Politics of Alcohol
Learning Objective: Trace the history of alcohol as a social and political question from the 1820s through the 1840s. Identify which Americans favored temperance and which opposed it.

The Alcoholic Republic
Temperance Movement
The Origins of Prohibition
The Washingtonians
Ethnicity and Alcohol
The South and Social Reform

12-4 The Politics of Slavery and Race
Learning Objective: Determine how Whigs and Democrats differed on questions of slavery and race.

Democratic Racism
Antislavery before 1830
Abolitionists
Agitation

12-5 The Politics of Gender and Sex
Learning Objective: Trace how Democrats and Whigs differed on questions of gender and sex. Based on what you know about the political cultures of the two parties, explain those differences.

Moral Reform
Women's Rights

12.1 **Harriet Beecher Stowe** Harriet Beecher Stowe was a daughter of Rev. Lyman Beecher, an evangelist who helped start the temperance movement in the United States. Her sister, Catharine Beecher, was a prominent reformer of housekeeping and domestic life. Her brother, Henry Ward Beecher, was an ardent antislavery advocate and a nationally famous preacher, and her husband, Calvin Stowe, designed the public school system for the state of Ohio. Harriet wrote *Uncle Tom's Cabin*, a huge best seller and the most powerful of antislavery tracts. She filled her book with the well-documented horrors of slavery, but she grounded it in the reform culture in which she grew up and which she helped to shape. Stowe and her family and coworkers wanted more than the end of slavery and alcohol abuse. They wanted to shape America in the image of northern evangelicalism and the middle-class home.

BETWEEN 1820 AND 1845, Thomas Jefferson's agrarian republic became Andrew Jackson's mass democracy. Politicians who built the Whig and Democratic parties participated in the economic and social transformations of those years. They were also consumers and producers of the new forms of popular culture. In making their political appeals, they tapped skillfully into the national patchwork of aspiration, fear, and resentment. John Quincy Adams, Henry Clay, and their National Republican and Whig allies envisioned smooth-running, government-sponsored transportation and financial systems. Such visions echoed the faith in cosmic order, material progress, and moral improvement that had become cultural axioms for the more prosperous and cosmopolitan Americans. Democrats, on the other hand, defended Jefferson's republic of limited government and white liberty and equality. They portrayed a haunted political universe in which trickery, deceit, and special privilege—the old signs of encroaching power—lurked behind the promises of the Whigs.

Whigs and Democrats constructed their coalitions largely at the neighborhood and state levels. Their arguments for and against state-supported internal improvements and state-chartered banks and corporations mirrored the national debate, and thus strengthened and nationalized party loyalties. Local cultural battles—arguments over alcohol, sexual morality, education, crime, and much more—also sharpened Democratic and Whig attitudes.

In the North, the churchgoing middle class provided the Whig Party with a political culture, a reform-oriented social agenda, and most of its electoral support. Whig evangelicals believed that with God's help they could improve the world by improving the individuals within it, and they enlisted the Whig Party in that campaign. On a variety of issues, including prostitution, temperance, public education, and state-supported insane asylums and penitentiaries, Whigs used government to improve individual morality and discipline. Democrats argued that attempts to legislate morality were anti-republican and wrong. Questions of social reform provoked the angriest differences between Democrats and Whigs, particularly in the North. Not all reform movements, however, strengthened the party system. When some whiggish northerners insisted upon women's rights and the immediate emancipation of all slaves, they attacked the foundations of the white republic and the party system, opening important questions that the political parties wanted to ignore. ■

12-1 The Politics of Progress

Q *What were Whig and Democratic conceptions of the duties and limits of government?*

Whigs assumed that both markets and government were agents of progress. Democrats, locally as well as nationally, preached that markets were good and governments were necessary, but that collaboration between the two produced corruption.

12-1a Markets and Governments

Whigs praised the new market economy as more than a means of producing national wealth. The market was, they insisted, an engine of social and moral progress. Markets created opportunities, and individuals who developed good work habits and moral discipline would prosper. Thus, the market would discourage laziness and ignorance and encourage social harmony, good manners, and disciplined ambition. At the same time, it would fill American homes with comfortable furniture and moral housewives. William H. Seward, the Whig governor of New York, supported transportation projects because they broke down neighborhood isolation and hastened the emergence of a market society, with "all the consequent advantages of morality, piety, and knowledge." The market, in short, produced moral progress.

Whigs believed that Americans enjoyed a harmony of class interests and an equality of opportunity that every virtuous person would recognize and that only the

CHRONOLOGY

1819	New York State builds the first prison under the Auburn system
1826	Reformers found the American Society for the Promotion of Temperance
1831	William Lloyd Garrison begins publication of the antislavery *Liberator* • New York Magdalen Society publishes its first annual report
1883	Abolitionists found the American Anti-Slavery Society
1840	Working-class drinkers found the Washington Temperance Society
1848	First Women's Rights Convention held in Seneca Falls, New York
1851	Maine becomes the first of 17 states to enact statewide prohibition
1860	New York enacts the Married Women's Property Act

resentful, the mean-spirited, and the unworthy would doubt. (Almost as much as the Democrats, Whigs excluded racial minorities from the "Americans.") To poor farmers and city workers who believed that the Market Revolution undermined traditional forms of independence, Whigs promised social mobility within a new system of interdependence, but only to deserving individuals. Pointing to self-made Whigs such as Daniel Webster and Abraham Lincoln, Whigs promised national prosperity in a world that rewarded virtue.

As they did nationally, Whigs at the state and local levels wanted government to subsidize economic development and the moral improvement that would come along with it. Government should build roads, establish public schools, and create and oversee a stable, reliable currency. It should also foster virtue. "The government," remarked a New York City Whig in 1848, "is not merely a machine for making wars and punishing felons, but is bound to do all that is within its power to promote the welfare of the People." *The American Review*, a Whig periodical, went further: "Forms of government are instituted for the protection and fostering of virtue, and are valuable only as they accomplish this."

Democrats saw things differently. Few of them condemned market society, but they argued forcefully against activist government, high taxes, and government partnerships with private interests. In contrast to Whig optimism, they tended to view human nature through a grim combination of classical republicanism and gothic romance and saw government not as a tool of progress but as a potential evil—a concentration of power in the hands of imperfect, self-interested men. The only safe course was to limit its power. In 1837, the *United States Magazine and Democratic Review* declared: "The best government is that which governs least," and went on to denounce the "natural imperfection, both in wisdom and judgment and purity of purpose, of all human legislation, exposed constantly to the pressure of partial interest; interests which, at the same time that they are essentially selfish and tyrannical, are ever vigilant, persevering, and subtle in all the arts of deception and corruption." It was a lot like what Democrats saw in stage melodramas, read in cheap fiction, and heard in their conservative churches. Most of all, Democrats insisted that Whig governments would create privilege and inequality. Corporate charters, banks, and subsidies to turnpike, canal, and railroad companies, they said, benefited insiders and transformed republican government into an engine of corruption and inequality.

Jackson himself acknowledged that varying levels of talent and energy (not to mention inheritance and social connections) create inequalities of power and wealth. He and other Democrats never talked of economic leveling. But they constantly accused Whigs of using government to make the rich richer. The granting of government privileges, warned one Democrat, was sure "to break up that social equality which is the legitimate foundation of our institutions, and the destruction of which would render our boasted freedom a mere phantom." By contrast, the government favored by the Whigs would enrich a favored few. Democrats demanded limited government that was deaf to the demands of special interests. Neither government nor the market, they said, should be allowed to subvert the democracy of white men on which the republic rested.

12-1b Banks, Roads, Canals

Andrew Jackson's national administration destroyed the Bank of the United States (see Chapter 11). As a result, regulation of banking, credit, and currency fell to the state governments. Banks emerged as a central political issue in nearly every state, particularly after the widespread bank failures following the crash of 1837. Whigs defended banks as agents of economic progress, arguing that they provided credit for roads and canals, loans to businessmen and commercial farmers, and the banknotes that served as the chief medium of exchange. Democrats branded banks as government-protected agents of inequality dominated by insiders who controlled artificial concentrations of money, who enjoyed chartered privileges, and who issued banknotes and expanded or contracted credit to suit their own advantage.

In state legislatures, Whigs defended what had become a roughly standard system of private banks chartered by state governments. They had the right to circulate banknotes and had **limited liability** to protect directors and stockholders from debts incurred by the bank. Many Democrats proposed abolishing all banks—"a set of swindling machines," said one western Democrat. Others proposed reforms, demanding, for example, a high ratio of specie reserves to banknotes as a guard against inflationary paper money. Democrats also wanted to hold bank directors and stockholders responsible for corporate debts and bankruptcies. Some proposed banning corporate charters altogether.

By these and other means, Democrats in the states protected currency and credit from the government favoritism, dishonesty, and elitism that, they argued, enriched Whig insiders and impoverished honest Democrats. Whigs responded that corporate privileges and immunities and an abundant, elastic currency were keys to economic development, and they fought Democrats every step of the way.

Democrats in Congress and the White House blocked federally funded roads and canals (see Chapter 11). In response, the states launched the transportation revolution themselves, either by taking direct action or by chartering private corporations to do the work. State legislatures everywhere debated the wisdom of direct state action, of corporate privileges, of subsidies to canals and railroads, and of government debt. Predictably, Whigs favored direct action by state governments. Democrats often supported internal improvements, but they opposed "partial" legislation that would benefit part of a state at the expense of the rest. They also opposed projects that would lead to higher taxes and put state governments into debt. They made the same argument in every state: Beneath Whig plans for extensive improvements lay schemes to create special privilege, inequality, debt, and corruption—all at the expense of a hoodwinked people.

The argument about government and economic development in the states mirrored the national debate. Whigs wanted to use government and the market to make an economically and morally progressive—albeit hierarchical—republic. Democrats viewed both government and the new institutions of market society with suspicion and vowed not to subvert the equal rights and rough equality of condition that were, in their view, the preconditions of republican citizenship. In language that echoed their Jeffersonian forebears, Jacksonian Democrats demanded that the market remain subservient to the republic. These state-level debates helped to cement party loyalties and make them national. Whig and Democratic arguments about banks and internal improvement were essentially the same in every state. In arguing their cases in Alabama or Pennsylvania, legislators and voters strengthened their identities as Democrats or Whigs and their ties with like-minded people throughout the republic. Thus, these state-level fights bolstered a national two-party system that did its best to ignore regional differences.

12-2 The Politics of Social Reform: Schools and Asylums

 What were Whig and Democratic positions on the issues of public schools, prisons, and asylums?

The establishment of public schools and institutions for criminals and the insane worked the same way. Whigs and Democrats agreed that such state-supported institutions had become necessary. But Whigs wanted them to improve the character and morals of their inmates, and were willing to spend money for that purpose. Democrats wanted to educate children and incarcerate criminals and the insane, but they wanted to do it cheaply. The debates over state-run institutions, in short, gave Americans another opportunity to behave like Democrats and Whigs.

12-2a Public Schools

During the second quarter of the 19th century, local and state governments built systems of tax-supported public schools, known as **common schools**. Before that time, most children learned reading, writing, and arithmetic at home, in poorly staffed town schools, in private schools, or in charity schools run by churches or other benevolent organizations. Despite the lack of any system of education, most children learned to read and write. That was, however, more likely among boys than among girls, among whites than among blacks, and among northeasterners than among westerners or southerners.

By the 1830s, Whigs and Democrats agreed that providing common schools was a proper function of government, and Democrats often agreed with Whigs that schools could equalize opportunity. Massachusetts Democrat Robert Rantoul, for example, believed that rich and poor children should "be brought equally and together up to the starting point at the public expense; after that we must shift for ourselves." More radical Democrats, however, wanted public schooling that would erase snobbery. Marcus Morton, Democratic governor of Massachusetts, wrote that it was the job of the common schools to democratize children "before the pride of family or wealth, or other adventitious distinction has taken a deep root in the young heart."

The reformers who created the most advanced, expensive, and centralized state school systems were Whigs: Horace Mann of Massachusetts, Henry Barnard of Connecticut, Calvin Stowe (husband of Harriet Beecher) of Ohio, and others. These reformers talked more about character building and Whig Protestant culture than about the three R's. They wanted schools that would downplay class divisions, but they were interested less in democratizing wealthy children than in civilizing the poor. Calvin H. Wiley, the Whig superintendent of schools in North Carolina, promised that proper schools would make Americans "homogeneous ... intelligent, eminently republican, sober, calculating, moral and conservative." William Seward, the Whig governor of New York, insisted that "education tends to produce equality, not by leveling all to the condition of the base, but by elevating all to the association of the wise and good."

The schools taught a basic Whig axiom: that social questions could be reduced to questions of individual character. A textbook entitled *The Thinker, A Moral Reader* (1855) told children to "remember that all the ignorance, degradation, and misery in the world, is the result of indolence and vice." To teach that lesson, the schools had children read from the King James Bible and recite prayers acceptable to all of the Protestant sects. Such texts reaffirmed a common Protestant morality while avoiding divisive doctrinal matters. Until the arrival of significant numbers of Catholic immigrants in the 1840s and 1850s, few parents complained about Protestant religious instruction in the public schools.

12.2 The Eureka Schoolhouse in Springfield, Vermont Mandated by state law and supported by local taxes, such one-room schools taught generations of American children the three R's.

Political arguments centered less on curriculum than on organization. Whigs wanted state-level centralization and proposed state superintendents and state boards of education, **normal schools** (state teachers' colleges), texts chosen at the state level, and uniform school terms. They also (often with the help of economy-minded Democrats) recruited young women as teachers. In addition to fostering civility and Protestant morality in the schools, these women were a source of cheap labor. Salaries for female teachers in the northern states ranged from 40 percent to 60 percent lower than the salaries of their male coworkers. Largely as a result, the proportion of women among Massachusetts teachers rose from 56 percent in 1834 to 78 percent in 1860.

Democrats objected to the Whigs' insistence on centralization as elitist, intrusive, and expensive. They gave power to individual school districts, thus enabling local school committees to shape the curriculum, the length of the school year, and the choice of teachers and texts to local needs and preferences. Centralization, they argued, would create a metropolitan educational culture that served the purposes of the rich but ignored the preferences of farmers and working people. It was standard Democratic social policy: inexpensive government and local control. Henry Barnard, Connecticut's superintendent of schools, denounced his Democratic opponents as "ignorant demagogues" and "a set of blockheads."

12-2b Ethnicity, Religion, and the Schools

The argument between Whig centralism and Democratic parsimony dominated the debate over public education until the children of Irish and German immigrants entered schools by the thousands in the mid-1840s. Most immigrant families were poor and relied on their children to work and supplement the family income. Consequently, their children's attendance at school was irregular at best. Moreover, most immigrants were Catholics. The Irish regarded Protestant prayers and the King James Bible as heresies and as hated tools of British oppression. Some of the textbooks were worse. Olney's *Practical System of Modern Geography*, a standard textbook, declared that "the Irish in general are quick of apprehension, active, brave and hospitable; but passionate, ignorant, vain, and superstitious." A nun in Connecticut complained that Irish children in the public schools "see their parents looked upon as an inferior race." Whigs, joined by many native-born Democrats, saw Catholic complaints as popish assaults on the Protestantism that they insisted was at the heart of American republicanism.

Some school districts, particularly in the rural areas to which many Scandinavian and German immigrants found their way, created foreign-language schools and provided bilingual instruction. In other places, state support for church-run charity schools persisted. New York City supported both Catholic and Protestant schools until 1825. So did Lowell, Massachusetts; Hartford and Middletown, Connecticut; and Milwaukee, Wisconsin, at various times from the 1830s through the 1860s. New Jersey provided state support to Catholic as well as other church schools until 1866. In northeastern cities, however, where immigrant Catholics often formed militant local majorities, such demands led to violence and to organized nativist (anti-immigrant) politics. In 1844, the Native American Party, with the endorsement of the Whigs, won the New York City elections. That same year in Philadelphia, riots that pitted avowedly Whig Protestants against Catholic immigrants, ostensibly over the issue of Bible reading in schools, killed 13 people. Such conflicts would severely damage the northern Democratic coalition in the 1850s.

12-2c Prisons

From the 1820s onward, state governments built institutions to house orphans, the dependent poor, the insane, and criminals. The Market Revolution increased the numbers of

Prisoners at the State Prison at Auburn.

12.3 Auburn Prison Inmates at New York's Auburn Prison were forbidden to speak and were marched in lockstep between workshops, dining halls, and their cells.

12.4 The Whipping Post and Pillory at New Castle, Delaware
Delaware was a slave state that continued to inflict public, corporal punishment on lawbreakers. One criminal is tied to the post, while another, up above, is held in a pillory.

Q *Punishment in early and mid-19th-century United States was often a public spectacle. Why? What clues does the painting offer as to the contemporary thinking and sensibilities?*

such persons and made them more visible, more anonymous, and more separated from family and community resources. Americans in the 18th century (and many in the 19th century as well) had assumed that poverty, crime, insanity, and other social ills were among God's ways of punishing sin and testing the human capacity for both suffering and charity. By the 1820s, however, reformers were arguing that deviance was the result of childhood deprivation. "Normal" people, they argued, learned discipline and respect for work, property, laws, and other people from their parents. Deviants were the products of brutal, often drunken households devoid of parental love and discipline. The cure was to place them in a controlled setting, teach them work and discipline, and turn them into useful citizens.

In state legislatures, Whigs favored putting deviants into institutions for rehabilitation. Democrats, although they agreed that the states should incarcerate criminals and deviants, regarded attempts at rehabilitation as wrongheaded and expensive. They favored institutions that isolated the insane, warehoused the dependent poor, and punished criminals. Most state systems were a compromise between the two positions.

Pennsylvania built prisons at Pittsburgh (1826) and Philadelphia (1829) that put solitary prisoners into cells to contemplate their misdeeds and to plot a new life. The results of such solitary confinement included few reformations and numerous attempts at suicide. Only New Jersey imitated the Pennsylvania system. Far more common were institutions based on the model developed in New York at Auburn (1819) and Sing Sing (1825). In the **Auburn system**, prisoners slept in solitary cells and marched in military formation to meals and workshops. They were forbidden to speak to one another at any time. The rule of silence, it was believed, encouraged both discipline and contemplation. The French writer Alexis de Tocqueville, visiting a New York prison in 1830, remarked that "the silence within these vast walls ... is that of death... . There were a thousand living beings, and yet it was a vast desert solitude."

The Auburn system was designed both to reform criminals and to reduce expenses, for the prisons sold workshop products to the outside. Between these two goals, Whigs favored rehabilitation. Democrats favored profit-making workshops, and thus lower operating costs and lower taxes. Robert Wiltse, named by the Democrats to run Sing Sing prison in the 1830s, used harsh punishments (including flogging and starving), sparse meals, and forced labor to punish criminals and make the prison pay for itself. In 1839, William Seward, as the newly elected Whig governor of New York, fired Wiltse and appointed administrators who substituted privileges and rewards for punishment and emphasized rehabilitation over profit making. They provided religious instruction; they improved food and working conditions; and they cut back on the use of flogging. When Democrats took back the statehouse in the 1842 elections, they discovered that the Whigs' brief experiment in kindness had produced a $50,000 deficit, so they swiftly reinstated the old regime.

12-2d Asylums

The leading advocate of humane treatment of the insane was **Dorothea Dix**, a Boston humanitarian who was shocked by the incarceration and abuse of the insane in common jails. She traveled throughout the country, urging citizens to pressure their state legislatures into building asylums committed to what reformers called "moral treatment." The asylums were to be clean and pleasant places, preferably outside the cities, and the inmates were to be treated humanely. Attendants were not to beat inmates or tie them up, although they could use cold showers as a form of discipline. Dix and other reformers wanted the asylums to be safe, nurturing environments in which the insane could be made well.

By 1860, the legislatures of 28 of the 33 states had established state-run insane asylums. Whig legislators, with minimal support from Democrats, approved appropriations for the more expensive and humane moral treatment facilities. Occasionally, however, Dorothea Dix won Democratic support as well. In North Carolina, she befriended the wife of a powerful Democratic legislator as the woman lay on her deathbed. The dying woman convinced her husband to support building an asylum. His impassioned speech won the approval of the lower house for a state asylum to be named Dix Hill. In the North Carolina senate, however, the proposal won the votes of 91 percent of the Whigs and only 14 percent of the Democrats—a partisan division that held in state after state.

12-3 The Politics of Alcohol

Q *Trace the history of alcohol as a social and political question from the 1820s through the 1840s. Which Americans favored temperance? Which opposed it?*

Central to party formation in the North was the fight between evangelical Whigs who demanded that government regulate public (and often private) morality and Democrats who feared both big government and the Whig cultural agenda. The most persistent issue in that argument was the question of alcohol—so much so that in many places the temperance question defined the differences between Democrats and Whigs.

12.5 Barroom Dancing, circa 1820 Inns, taverns, saloons, and bars were important public places in 19th-century United States, fostering a particular kind of public sphere.

Q *Based on the painting, what are some of the defining features of that sphere?*

12-3a The Alcoholic Republic

The years 1790 to 1830 witnessed a dramatic rise in alcohol consumption. Americans had been drinking alcohol since the time of the first settlements. (The Puritan flagship *Arabella* had carried three times as much beer as water.) But drinking, like all other "normal" behaviors, took place within a structure of paternal authority. Americans tippled every day in the course of their ordinary activities: at family meals and around the fireside, at work, and at barn raisings, militia musters, dances, court days (even judges and juries passed the bottle), weddings, funerals, corn huskings—even at the ordinations of ministers. Under such circumstances, drinking—even drunkenness—seldom posed a threat to authority or to the social order.

That old pattern of communal drinking persisted into the 19th century, but during the 50 years following the Revolution, it gradually gave way to a new pattern. Farmers, particularly those in newly settled areas, regularly produced a surplus of grain that they turned into whiskey. In Washington County in western Pennsylvania, for example, 1 family in 10 operated a distillery in the 1790s. Whiskey was safer than water and milk, which were often tainted, and it was cheaper than coffee or tea. It was also cheaper than imported rum, so Americans embraced whiskey as their national drink and consumed extraordinary quantities of it. Per capita consumption of pure alcohol in all its forms increased from three to nearly four gallons annually between 1790 and 1830, and most of the increase was in the form of cheap and potent whiskey. By 1830, per capita consumption of distilled spirits was more than five gallons per year—the highest it has ever been, and three times what it is in the United States today. The United States had become, as one historian has said, an "alcoholic republic."

The nation's growing thirst was driven not by conviviality or neighborliness but by a desire to get drunk. Most Americans drank regularly, although with wide variations. Men drank far more than women, the poor and the rich drank more than the emerging middle class, city dwellers drank more than farmers, westerners drank more than easterners, and southerners drank a bit more than northerners. Throughout the nation, the heaviest drinking took place among the increasing numbers of young men who lived away from their families and outside the old social controls: soldiers and sailors, boatmen and other transport workers, lumberjacks, schoolmasters, journeyman craftsmen, college students. Among such men, the controlled tippling of the 18th century gave way to the binge and to solitary drinking. By the 1820s, American physicians were learning to diagnose delirium tremens—the trembling and the paranoid delusions brought on by withdrawal from physical addiction to alcohol. By that decade, social reformers branded alcohol as a threat to individual well-being, domestic peace, public order, and the republic itself.

12-3b Temperance Movement

Drinking had been a part of social life since the beginnings of English settlement, but the withering of authority during the Market Revolution led to increased consumption, increased public drunkenness, and a perceived increase in alcohol-fed violence and social problems. After repeated false starts, the temperance crusade began in earnest in 1826, when northeastern evangelicals founded the American Society for the Promotion of Temperance, soon renamed the **American Temperance Society**. The movement's manifesto was Lyman Beecher's *Six Sermons on the Nature, Occasions, Signs, Evils, and Remedy of Intemperance* (1826). Addressing the churchgoing middle class, Beecher declared alcohol an addictive drug and warned that even moderate drinkers risked becoming hopeless drunkards. Thus, temperance, like other evangelical reforms, was presented as a contest between self-control and slavery to one's appetites. By encouraging total abstinence, reformers hoped to stop the creation of new drunkards while the old ones died out. Even though Beecher pinned his hopes on self-discipline, he wanted middle-class abstainers to spread reform through both example and coercion. As middle-class evangelicals eliminated alcohol from their own lives, they also ceased to offer it to their guests, buy or sell it, or provide it to their employees, and they encouraged their friends to do the same.

Beecher's crusade gathered strength in the middle-class revivals of the 1820s and 1830s. Charles Grandison Finney (see Chapter 10), in his revival at Rochester, made total abstinence a condition of conversion. Many other ministers and churches followed suit, and by the mid-1830s, the evangelical middle class had largely disengaged from alcohol and the people who drank it. Following a temperance lecture by Finney's coworker Theodore Dwight Weld, Rochester grocers Elijah and Albert Smith rolled their stock of whiskey out on the sidewalk, smashed the barrels, and let the liquor spill into the street. Other Rochester merchants threw their liquor into the Erie Canal or sold it off at cost. Hundreds of evangelical businessmen pledged that they would refuse to rent to merchants who sold liquor, sell grain to distillers, or enter a store that sold alcohol. Many of them made abstinence a condition of employment, placing ads that carried the line "None But Temperate Men Need Apply." Abstinence and opposition to the use of distilled spirits (people continued to argue about wine and beer) had become a badge of middle-class respectability.

Among themselves, the reformers achieved considerable success. By 1835, the American Temperance Society claimed 1.5 million members and estimated that 2 million Americans had renounced ardent spirits (whiskey, rum, and other distilled liquors); 250,000 had formally pledged to completely abstain from alcohol. The society further estimated that 4,000 distilleries had gone out of business, and that many of the survivors had cut back their production. Many politicians stopped buying drinks to win votes. The Kentucky Whig Henry Clay, once known for keeping late hours, began to serve only cold water when he entertained, and in 1833 members of Congress formed the American Congressional Temperance Society. The U.S. Army put an end to the age-old liquor ration in 1832, and increasing numbers of militia officers stopped supplying their men with whiskey. The annual consumption of alcohol, which had reached an all-time high in the 1820s, dropped by more than half in the 1830s (from 3.9 gallons of pure alcohol per adult in 1830 to 1.8 gallons in 1840).

12.6 "Death on the Striped Pig," 1839 This cartoon, portraying the Massachusetts tavern keepers' famous striped pig. In the upper-left corner, the devil says, "Go it, Stripes. You are the best servant I ever sent into the field."

Q What or who does the striped pig represent?

Q What is the cartoon's message?

12.7 "The Drunkard's Progress" This popular print describes the drunkard's progression from social drinking to alcoholism, isolation, crime, and death by suicide. His desolate wife and daughter and his burning house are at bottom.

12-3 The Politics of Alcohol 339

12-3c The Origins of Prohibition

In the middle 1830s, Whigs made temperance a political issue. Realizing that voluntary abstinence would not end drunkenness, Whig evangelicals drafted coercive, prohibitionist legislation. First, they attacked the licenses granting grocery stores and taverns the right to sell liquor by the drink and to permit it to be consumed on the premises. The licenses were important sources of revenue for local governments. They also gave local authorities the power to cancel the licenses of troublesome establishments. Militant temperance advocates, usually in association with local Whigs, demanded that the authorities use that power to outlaw all public drinking places. In communities throughout the North, the licensing issue, always freighted with divisions over religion and social class, became the issue around which local parties organized. The question first reached the state level in Massachusetts, when in 1838 a Whig legislature passed the Fifteen-Gallon Law, which decreed that merchants could sell ardent spirits only in quantities of 15 gallons or more, thus outlawing every public drinking place in the state. In 1839, Massachusetts voters sent enough Democrats to the legislature to rescind the law.

The Whig attempt to cancel tavern licenses proved unenforceable because proprietors simply operated without licenses or found ways to get around the laws. While the Massachusetts Fifteen-Gallon Law was in effect, one Boston tavern keeper painted stripes on a pig and charged patrons an admission fee of six cents (the old price of a drink) to view the "exhibition." He then provided customers—who paid over and over to see the pig—with a "complimentary" glass of whiskey.

Leading Democrats agreed with Whigs that Americans drank too much, but whereas Whigs insisted that regulating morality was a proper function of government, Democrats warned that coercive government intrusion into areas of private choice would violate republican liberties. In many communities, alcohol became the defining difference between Democrats and Whigs. In 1834, for instance, a Whig campaign worker ventured into a poor neighborhood in Rochester and asked a woman how her husband planned to vote. "Why, he has always been Jackson," she said, "and I don't think he's joined the Cold Water."

12-3d The Washingtonians

Not all temperance movements sprang from organized political and evangelical action. One evening in 1840—in the depths of a devastating economic depression—six craftsmen were drinking at Chase's Tavern in Baltimore. More or less as a joke, they sent one of their number to a nearby temperance lecture. He came back a teetotaler and converted the others. They then drew up a total abstinence pledge and promised to devote themselves to the reform of other drinkers. Within months, from this beginning a national movement had emerged, called the **Washington Temperance Society**. With a core membership of men who had opposed temperance in the 1830s, the Washingtonians differed from older temperance societies in several ways. First, they identified themselves as members of the laboring classes. Second, they were separated from the churches. Although many of them were churchgoers (usually Methodist or Baptist), many were not, and the Washingtonians avoided religious controversy by avoiding religion. Third, the Washingtonians—at least those who called themselves True Washingtonians—rejected recourse to politics and legislation and concentrated instead on the conversion of drinkers through compassion and persuasion. Finally, they welcomed "hopeless" drunkards—who accounted for about 10 percent of the membership—and hailed them as heroes when they sobered up.

Whig reformers welcomed the Washingtonians at first, but they soon had second thoughts. The nonreligious character of the movement disturbed those who saw temperance as an arm of evangelical reform. Previous advocates of temperance had assumed that sobriety would be accompanied by evangelical decorum. Instead, the meetings, picnics, and parades held by the Washingtonians were continuous with a popular culture that Whig evangelicals opposed. While the temperance regulars read pamphlets and listened to lectures by clergymen, lawyers, and doctors, the Washingtonians enjoyed raucous sing-alongs, comedy routines, barnyard imitations, dramatic skits, and even full-dress minstrel shows geared to temperance themes. Meetings featured experience speeches by reformed drunkards. Speaking extemporaneously, they omitted none of the horrors of an alcoholic life—attempts at suicide, friendships betrayed, fathers and mothers desolated, wives beaten and abandoned, children dead of starvation. Although Washingtonians had given up alcohol, their melodramatic tales, street parades, songbooks, and minstrel shows—even when presented with a Methodist or Baptist accent—were not the temperance reformation that Lyman Beecher and the Whigs had had in mind.

Nowhere did the Washingtonians differ more sharply from the temperance regulars than in their visions of the reformed life. The Whig reformers tied abstinence to individual ambition and middle-class domesticity. They expected men who quit drinking to withdraw from the male drinking world and to retreat into the comfort of the newly feminized middle-class family. Washingtonians, on the other hand, translated traditional male sociability into sober forms. Moreover, they called former drinkers back to the responsibilities of traditional fatherhood. Their experience stories began with the hurt drunkards had caused their wives and children and ended with their transformation into dependable providers and authoritative fathers. While the Whig temperance regulars tried to extend the ethos of individual ambition and the new middle-class domesticity into society at large, Washingtonians sought to rescue the self-respect and moral authority of working-class fathers.

The Washington Temperance Society collapsed toward the end of the 1840s, but its legacy survived. Among former drinkers in the North, it had introduced a new sense of domestic responsibility and a healthy fear of drunkenness.

Consumption of pure alcohol dropped from 1.8 to 1.0 gallons annually in the 1840s. Along the way, the Washingtonians and related groups created a self-consciously respectable native Protestant working class in American cities.

12-3e Ethnicity and Alcohol

In the 1840s and 1850s, millions of Irish and German immigrants poured into neighborhoods recently stirred by working-class revivals and temperance agitation. The newcomers had their own time-honored relations to alcohol. The Germans introduced lager beer to the United States, thus providing a wholesome alternative for Americans who wished to give up spirits without joining the teetotalers. The Germans also built old-country beer halls in American cities, complete with sausage counters, oompah bands, group singing, and other family attractions. For their part, the Irish reaffirmed their love of whiskey—a love forged in colonial oppression and in a culture that accepted trouble with resignation—a love that legitimized levels of male drunkenness and violence that Americans, particularly the temperance forces, found appalling. Differences in immigrant drinking were given architectural expression. German beer halls provided seating arrangements for whole families. Irish bars, on the other hand, provided a bar but no tables or chairs. If a drinker had to sit down, they reasoned, it was time for him to go home.

In the 1850s, native resentment of Catholic immigrants drove thousands of Baptist and Methodist "respectables" out of the Democratic coalition and into nativist Whig majorities that—beginning with Maine in 1851—established legal prohibition in several northern and mid-Atlantic states. Many of these Democrats became part of the North's Republican majority on the eve of the Civil War.

12-3f The South and Social Reform

On economic issues, southern state legislatures divided along the same lines as northern legislatures: Whigs wanted government participation in the economy, Democrats did not. On social questions, however, southern Whigs and Democrats both opposed moralizing legislation. The South was a rural, conservative region of father-dominated households. Southern voters, Whigs as well as Democrats, perceived attempts at "social improvement" as intrusive, wrongheaded assaults on the autonomy of neighborhoods and families.

The southern states enacted school laws and drew up blueprints for state school systems, but the white South had little need for schools to enforce a common culture. Moreover, the South had less money and less faith in government. Consequently, southern schools tended to be locally controlled, to be infused with southern evangelical culture, and to have a limited curriculum and a short school year. In 1860, northern children attended school for an average of more than 50 days a year; white children in the South attended school for an average of 10 days annually.

By 1860, every slave state except Florida and the Carolinas had built prisons modeled on the Auburn system. Southern prisons, however, stressed punishment and profits over rehabilitation. Some southern Whigs favored northern-style reforms, but they knew that voters would reject them. Popular votes in Alabama in 1834 and in North Carolina in 1846 brought in resounding defeats for proposals to build or reform penitentiaries in those states. While northern evangelicals preached that criminals could be reformed, southern preachers demanded Old Testament vengeance, arguing that hanging, whipping, and branding were inexpensive, more effective than mere incarceration, and sanctioned by the Bible. Other southerners, defending the code of honor, charged that victims and their relatives would be denied vengeance if criminals were hidden away in prisons. Some southern prisons leased convict labor (and sometimes whole prisons) to private entrepreneurs, and the dream of reforming criminals was never taken seriously in the South.

The South did participate in temperance. By the 1820s, Baptists and Methodists had made deep inroads into southern society. Southern ministers preached against alcohol, while churchgoing women discouraged their husbands, sons, and suitors from drinking. (An Alabama man complained that "the women our way seem determined to deprive us of all of our privileges; if I offer to take a drink of whiskey as I used to do, my wife tells me of the *Temperance Society*, and says its mean, and low, and sinful.") Many southern men either stopped or reduced their drinking, and the South contributed its share to the national drop in alcohol consumption. During the 1840s, the Washington Temperance Society and other voluntary temperance groups won a solid footing in southern cities and county-seat towns, with leaders who included Whigs and Democrats alike. But legal prohibition, which became dominant in the North, got nowhere in the South. In the 1850s, while 17 northern legislatures passed statewide prohibition, the only slave state to follow was tiny, northern-oriented Delaware.

At bottom, southern resistance to social reform stemmed from a conservative, Bible-based acceptance of suffering and human imperfection and a commitment to the power and independence of white men who headed families—"families" that included their slaves as well as their wives and children. Any proposal that sounded like social tinkering or the invasion of paternal rights was doomed to failure. Moreover, many reforms—public schools, Sunday schools, reform-oriented prisons, prohibition, humane asylums—were seen as the work of well-funded missionaries from the Northeast who wanted to shape society in their own image. The Virginian John Randolph spoke for many southerners when he warned against the Yankees' "meddling, obtrusive, intrusive, restless, self-dissatisfied spirit," exhibited in "Sunday schools, Missionary Societies, subscriptions to Colonization Societies—taking care of the Sandwich Islanders, free negroes, and God knows who." The southern distrust of reform was powerfully reinforced after 1830, when northern reformers began to call for the abolition of slavery and equality of the sexes—reforms that most white southerners found unthinkable.

12-4 The Politics of Slavery and Race

Q *How did Whigs and Democrats differ on questions of slavery and race?*

Most whites in antebellum America believed in "natural" differences based on sex and race. God, they said, had given women and men and whites and blacks different mental, emotional, and physical capacities. Because humankind (female and nonwhite more than others) was innately sinful and prone to disorder, God ordained a fixed social hierarchy in which white men exercised power over others. Slaves and free blacks accepted their subordinate status only as a fact of life, not as something that was natural and just. Some women also opposed patriarchy, but before 1830, hierarchy based on sex and race was seldom questioned in public, particularly by persons who were in a position to change it.

In the antebellum years, as southerners and most northerners stiffened their defense of white supremacy (see Chapter 10), a radical minority of Whig evangelicals began to envision a world based on Christian love and individual worth and accomplishment, not "natural" differences. They also questioned the more virulent forms of racism. While conservative Christians insisted that relations based on dominance and submission were the lot of a sinful humankind, reformers argued that such relations interposed human power, too often in the form of brute force, between God and the individual spirit. They called for a world that substituted spiritual freedom and Christian love for every form of worldly domination. The result was a community of uncompromising radical reformers who attacked slavery as America's great national sin. In doing so, they assaulted the white republic and the core compromise of the American political system.

12-4a Democratic Racism

Whigs and Democrats both wanted to keep slavery and race out of politics, and neither encouraged the aspirations of slaves or free blacks. But it was the Democrats who incorporated racism into their political agenda. Minstrel shows, for example, often reflected the Democratic line on current events, and Democratic cartoonists featured minstrelsy's bug-eyed, woolly-haired caricatures of blacks. By the time of the Civil War, Democrats mobilized voters almost solely with threats of "amalgamation" and "Negro rule." Meanwhile, educated Democrats learned to think in racist terms. Among most scientists, biological determinism replaced historical and environmental explanations of racial differences; many argued that whites and blacks were separate species. Democrats welcomed that "discovery." John Van Evrie, a New York doctor and Democratic pamphleteer, declared that "it is a palpable and unavoidable fact that Negroes are a different species," and that the story of Adam and Eve referred only to the origin of *white* people. In 1850, the *Democratic Review* confided, "Few or none now seriously adhere to the theory of the unity of the races. The whole state of the science at this moment seems to indicate that there are several distinct races of men on the earth, with entirely different capacities, physical and mental."

As whites came to perceive racial differences as God-given and immutable, they changed the nature of those differences as well. In the 18th and early 19th centuries, whites had stereotyped blacks as ignorant and prone to drunkenness and thievery, but they had also maintained a parallel stereotype of blacks as loyal and self-sacrificing servants. From the 1820s onward, racists continued to regard blacks as incompetent, but they found it harder to distinguish mere carelessness from dishonesty. Now they saw blacks as treacherous, shrewd, and secretive—individuals who only *pretended* to feel loyalty to white families and affection for the white children they took care of, while awaiting the chance to steal from them or poison them. The writer Herman Melville, a lifelong Democrat who shared little of his compatriots' racism but who helped codify their fascination with duplicity and deceit, dramatized these fears in *Benito Cereno*, a novel about slaves who commandeer a sailing ship and its captain and crew, then (with knives secretly at the throats of their captives) act out a servile charade for unsuspecting visitors who come aboard.

12-4b Antislavery before 1830

Before 1830, few whites opposed slavery politically. Quakers had condemned both the slave trade and slavery in the 1750s, and Methodists and some Baptists had done the same late in the century. Washington, Jefferson, and other Chesapeake gentlemen doubted the wisdom, if not the morality, of holding slaves. New England Federalists had condemned slavery in the course of condemning southern Jeffersonians. But there were too few Quakers to make a difference, and the movement to free slaves in the Upper South and the antislavery sentiments of southern evangelicals both died out early in the 19th century. Southerners and most northerners—when they bothered to think about it at all—tended to accept slavery as an unchangeable institution that they had inherited, an institution grounded, ultimately, in human (read "black") depravity and God's unknowable plan. The New England and mid-Atlantic states freed (and then shunned) their slaves but seldom argued that the South should do the same.

The biggest organization that addressed questions of slavery and race before 1830 was the **American Colonization Society**, founded in 1816. This elite organization of white men never attacked slavery. The rising population of free blacks was their principal concern. "The rapid increase of the black population in some parts of our country," said a Boston colonizationist in 1822, "is becoming every year more serious." Their answer was to colonize free blacks (but not slaves) in Liberia, on the west coast of Africa. The society held its first meeting in the chamber of the House of Representatives, with Bushrod Washington, stepson of George Washington, as president. Early members included Henry Clay, John Taylor of Caroline,

Andrew Jackson, and other political leaders of the West, the middle states, and the Upper South. Blacks, they said, would continue to suffer from white prejudice and their own deficiencies as long as they stayed in the United States. They would exercise freedom and learn Christian and republican ways only if exported to Liberia. Among the favored fundraising sites for the ACS were July 4 celebrations—festivities from which blacks were excluded.

Free blacks had agitated against slavery and legal racism for many years, demanding both abolition and equal rights. While a few sailed to Liberia, most insisted that colonization was not an offer of freedom but an attempt to round up black people and make them disappear. The black abolitionist James Forten spoke for many when he insisted that colonization "originated more immediately from prejudice than from philanthropy." Opposition to colonization created an immediatist, confrontational black antislavery movement—a movement that decisively shaped the later abolition crusade.

12-4c Abolitionists

Few white Americans actively opposed slavery before 1830, but the writing was on the wall. Emancipation in the North constituted an implicit condemnation of slavery in the South. So did events outside the United States. Toussaint L'Ouverture's successful slave revolution in Saint-Domingue threatened slavery everywhere (see Chapter 7). Mexico, Peru, Chile, Gran Colombia (present-day Colombia, Venezuela, Ecuador, and Panama), and other new republics carved out of the Spanish mainland empire emancipated their slaves. The British, whose navy could enforce their dictates at sea, outlawed the Atlantic slave trade in 1808, and the United States followed suit. The most powerful blow came in 1830, when the British Parliament emancipated the slaves of Jamaica, Bermuda, and other Caribbean islands ruled by Britain.

Historians usually date American **abolitionism** from 1831, when the veteran reformer **William Lloyd Garrison** published the first issue of the *Liberator* in Boston. Garrison condemned slavery not simply as a social problem or a bad idea but as America's great national sin. He demanded immediate emancipation and equal citizenship for African Americans. "I am in earnest," he declared in his first editorial. "I will not equivocate—I will not excuse—I will not retreat a single inch—and I will be heard!" Garrison opposed discrimination as well as slavery, thus coupling southern slavery with the national question of race. From the beginning, he enjoyed the support and influence of northern free blacks. In its first year fully three-fourths of the *Liberator*'s subscribers and one-fifth of its writers were black, and when Garrison and his coworkers formed the New England Anti-Slavery Society in 1832 blacks made up one-fourth of the membership. Black orators such as Frederick Douglass and Sojourner Truth became stars of a well-organized abolitionist lecture circuit, and the heartfelt autobiographies of escaped slaves (many of them "as told to" white abolitionists) were mainstays of abolitionist literature, steering the movement away from the legalism of the colonizationists and toward personal, emotional appeals. When the wealthy abolitionist Gerrit Smith harbored the fugitive slave Harriet Powell on his estate, he invited his friends to meet her. He told Powell to "make good abolitionists of them by telling them the story of your life."

Abolitionists proposed not only emancipation but also racial equality. Assuming that God had created blacks and whites as members of one human family, they opposed the "scientific" racism spouted by Democrats and many Whigs. Moderates and latecomers to the movement spoke of inherent racial characteristics, but still tended to view blacks in benign (if condescending) ways. Harriet Beecher Stowe, for instance, portrayed blacks as simple, innocent, loving people who possessed a capacity for sentiment and emotionalism that most whites had lost. In 1852, Horace Mann told an audience

12.8 The Resurrection of Henry Box Brown One of the most resourceful of escaped slaves was Henry Brown of Richmond. Distraught at the sale of his wife and children, in 1849 he paid a white storekeeper to ship him as "dry goods" to James Miller McKim, a well-known abolitionist in Philadelphia. Brown was nailed into a small shipping crate and, after moving by two freight wagons, two trains, and a steamboat on which he was packed upside down, he arrived at McKim's house in free territory. He became a hero to abolitionists, who renamed him "Box" Brown. Afraid of recapture, he moved to England.

Interpreting the Visual Past

An Abolitionist View of Southern Society

This provocative woodcut appeared in the *Anti-Slavery Almanac for 1840* (Boston, 1839). At the center, a southern mob lynches slaves and their abolitionist allies. Surrounding the hanging tree are men (there are no women in the picture) engaged in other activities that northern reformers insisted grew from the brutality and despotism of southern society. Men duel with pistols and knives, others engage in a no-holds-barred wrestling match, others gamble and get drunk, and still others cheer for (and bet on) cockfights and horse races. At one corner of the picture, a white man tortures a slave by drawing a cat's claws down his back. At the other corner, a white master whips a slave child. The enemy here is not simply slavery but the debauchery and unbridled passions that abolitionists associated with it.

Q *Compare this with the photo on page 258. Both pictures are extreme overstatements, but they overstate their cases in different ways. Why do you think a southern apologist and a northern abolitionist chose these specific ways to portray the same society? Why do white women and children appear in the southern picture? Why are they absent in the abolitionist portrayal? Why is the southern picture set in a domestic environment? Why are all traces of family life absent from the abolitionist portrayal?*

12.9 Anti-Slavery Almanac for 1840, "The peculiar Domestic Institutions of our Southern brethren," Boston, 1839.

of blacks in Ohio that "in intellect, the blacks are inferior to the whites, while in sentiment and affections, the whites are inferior to the blacks." Radical abolitionists, however, remained committed to racial equality. Lydia Maria Child of New York City declared, "In the United States, colored persons have scarcely any chance to rise. But if colored persons are well treated, and have the same inducements to industry as others, they [will] work as well and behave as well." The abolitionists backed up their equalitarian rhetoric with successful campaigns against segregation in Boston's schools and public transportation, and against legal bans on miscegenation. Most of their fellow citizens disliked the abolitionists—not only because their attack upon slavery threatened the Union and the party system that held it together, but because their integrated movement and their anti-racist campaigns undermined the white republic.

The radicalized abolitionists were a combination of old and new reformers. Some of them—Wendell Phillips, Thomas Wentworth Higginson, Theodore Parker—were cultivated Bostonians who opposed slavery as an affront to reason and humanity. Others were Quakers—the poet John Greenleaf Whittier, the lay minister Lucretia Mott, and many more—who added their antislavery experience and convictions to the cause. Abolitionists found their greatest support, however, in southern New England, western New York, northern Ohio, and among the new middle classes of the cities—ground that Yankee settlement, the Market Revolution, and Finneyite revivals had turned into the heartland of the northern Whig Party.

It was also the center of the new evangelical domesticity, and of the questioning of traditional roles for women and men. Women from evangelical families participated in church affairs and in the temperance movement, and the more radical of them moved into abolitionism. The American Colonization Society and other early antislavery societies were largely elite and entirely male and they made male arguments: Slavery, they said, was economically and socially irrational and dangerous. Abolitionists, on the other hand, enrolled blacks, women, and white men who questioned the old rigidities of gender and race. They attacked slavery on moral grounds, and their appeals were unabashedly emotional. Abolitionist speeches, pamphlets, and escaped-slave narratives attacked slavery less for its supposed irrationality as a labor system than for what it did to slaves. The crucial argument, repeated over and over, was that slavery crushed the family, and particularly the sentimental relation between mothers and small children.

This argument reached its culmination in Harriet Beecher Stowe's *Uncle Tom's Cabin*, which was first published in installments in an antislavery newspaper. When published as a book in 1852, it became the most powerful antislavery tract, in part because it successfully dramatized the moral and political imperatives of the northern middle class. At its core, **Uncle Tom's Cabin** indicts slavery as a system of absolute power at odds with domesticity and Christian love. The novel reverses the power relations of this world: In it, the home, and particularly the kitchen, is the ultimate locus of good, whereas law, politics, and the marketplace—the whole realm of white men—are moved to the periphery and defined as unfeeling destroyers. Based solidly in revival Christianity, the novel lambasts the rational calculation, greed, and power-hunger of the "real world" that was made and governed by white men and upholds the domestic space filled with women, slaves, and children who gain spiritual power through submission to Christ. The two most telling scenes—the deaths of the Christian slave Uncle Tom and the perfect child Eva St. Claire—reenact the crucifixion of Jesus. Uncle Tom prays for his tormentors as he is beaten to death, and little Eva extracts promises of Christian behavior from her deathbed. Both are powerless, submissive characters who die in order to redeem a fallen humankind. Their deaths are thus Christian triumphs that convert the powerful and hasten the millennial day when the world will be governed by a feminized Christian love and not by male power.

12-4d Agitation

Antislavery, unlike other reforms, was a radical attack on one of the nation's central institutions, and the movement attracted a minority even among middle-class evangelicals. Both Lyman Beecher and Charles Finney opposed the abolitionists in the 1830s, arguing that emancipation would come about sooner or later through the religious conversion of slave owners; antislavery agitation and the denunciation of slaveholders, they argued, would divide Christians, slow the revival movement, and thus actually delay emancipation. Finney warned his abolitionist friend Theodore Dwight Weld that the logical end of antislavery was civil war. Other opponents, including some within the antislavery ranks, were outraged that blacks and whites and men and women met, organized, and socialized together, and that women and blacks delivered speeches to mixed audiences. When the American Antislavery Society held an organizing convention in Philadelphia in 1833, the city's hotels, churches, and meeting halls refused to admit its members, and the police announced that they could not protect "the amalgamationist conclave." Most of the delegates boarded in black households, and they met in a black-owned hall next door to Philadelphia's oldest black church.

Radical abolitionists knew that they were a small, despised minority, and that government and most citizens wanted to ignore the question of slavery. The abolitionists staged a series of campaigns to force government and the public to face the South's "peculiar institution." In 1835, the society launched its **Postal Campaign** and then deluged Congress with petitions to curtail slavery (see Chapter 11). Two-thirds of the signers of these petitions were women, prompting a Mississippi senator to declare that there would be less trouble "if the ladies and Sunday school children would let us alone."

From the beginnings of antislavery agitation, the public response was often violent. Riots aimed at blacks and their white friends exploded in nearly every northern city. Mobs destroyed black neighborhoods in New York and Philadelphia. A mob surrounded a convention of the Boston Female Anti-slavery Society in 1835, forced the women to leave, then went looking for Garrison. Garrison was roughed up, but then he escaped the mob by going

12.10 Woman and a Sister For many years, the British antislavery forces had used the iconic image of a male slave, kneeling and holding up his chains, with the words "Am I not a man and a brother?" American abolitionists used that image as well, but added a similar image of a supplicant female slave, underlining the participation of women and the emerging centrality of women's issues in the American antislavery movement.

into police custody, where he was charged with disturbing the peace. In July 1834, a New York City mob sacked the house of the white abolitionist merchant Lewis Tappan; moved on to the Reverend Charles Finney's Chatham Street Chapel, where abolitionists were said to be meeting, and finished the evening by attacking a British (and thus supposedly aristocratic) actor at the Bowery theater. The manager saved his theater by waving two American flags and ordering an American actor to perform popular minstrel routines for the mob. Democracy and working-class aspirations—not to mention local authorities—were in league with racism.

Southern whites had fewer free blacks or abolitionists to attack, but they found their own ways to respond. A crowd in Charleston rushed the post office, removed anti-slavery literature that was held there, and made a bonfire at the center of town. A committee in Mississippi invited Garrison and other antislavery leaders to come south and be hanged. In Congress, southerners and their northern friends forced President Jackson to permit southern postal workers to censor the mails. They also forced Democrats and southern Whigs to adopt the gag rule, abridging the right of petition to avoid discussion of slavery in Congress (see Chapter 11).

In these ways, abolitionists demonstrated the complicity of the party system (and the Democrats in particular) in the institution of slavery. They brought the slavery question to public attention and tied it to questions of civil liberties in the North and political power nationally. They thus threw light on the compromises with slavery that made the United States possible, and they undermined the white republic at its foundations. Moreover, they did all that with an active, public membership that included prominent women and blacks. The abolitionists were a dangerous minority indeed.

12-5 The Politics of Gender and Sex

Q *How did Democrats and Whigs differ on questions of gender and sex? Knowing what you know about the political cultures of the two parties, how do you explain those differences?*

Whigs valued a reformed masculinity that was lived out in the sentimentalized homes of the northern business classes or in the Christian gentility of the Whig plantation and farm. Jacksonian voters defended domestic patriarchy. Whereas most were unimaginative paternalists, Democrats often made heroes of men whose flamboyant, rakish lives directly challenged Whig domesticity. Whigs denounced Andrew Jackson for allegedly stealing his wife from her lawful husband; Democrats often admired him for the same reason. Richard M. Johnson of Kentucky, who was vice president under Martin Van Buren, openly kept a mulatto mistress and had two daughters by her; with his pistols always at hand, he accompanied her around Washington, D.C. "Prince" John Van Buren, the president's son and a prominent New York Democrat, met a "dark-eyed, well-formed Italian lady," who called herself Amerigo Vespucci and claimed to be a direct descendant of the man for whom America was named. She became young Van Buren's "fancy lady," remaining with him until he lost her in a high-stakes card game.

Whigs made Democratic contempt for sentimental domesticity a political issue. William Crane, a Michigan Whig, claimed that Democrats "despised no man for his sins," and went on to say that "brothel-haunters flocked to this party, because here in all political circles, and political movements, they were treated as nobility." Much of the Whig cultural agenda (and much of Democratic hatred of that agenda) was rooted in contests between Whig and Democratic masculine styles.

12-5a Moral Reform

Sexual self-control became a badge of middle-class status. Men supposedly had the greatest difficulty taming their appetites. The old image—beginning with Eve and including Delilah and Jezebel and other dangerous women of the Old Testament—of woman as seductress persisted in the more traditionalist churches and in the pulp fiction from which middle-class mothers tried to protect their sons (see Chapter 10). Whig evangelicals, on the other hand, believed that women were naturally free of desire and that only men were subject to the animal passions. "What terrible temptations lie in the way of your sex," wrote Harriet Beecher Stowe to her husband. "Tho I did love you with an almost insane love before I married you, I never knew yet or felt the pulsation which showed me that I could be tempted in that way. I loved you as I now love God." The middle-class ideal combined female purity and male self-control. For the most part, it was a private reform, contained within the home. Sometimes, however, evangelical domesticity produced moral crusades to impose that ethos on the world at large. Many of these crusades were led by women from Whig families.

In 1828, a band of Sunday school teachers, most of them women, initiated an informal mission to prostitutes that grew into the **New York Magdalen Society**. Taking a novel approach to an age-old question, the society argued that prostitution was created by brutal fathers and husbands who abandoned their young daughters or wives, by dandies who seduced them and turned them into prostitutes, and by lustful men who bought their services. Prostitution, in other words, was not the result of the innate sinfulness of prostitutes; it was the result of the brutality and lust of men. The solution was to separate prostitutes from bad male power, pray with them, and convert them to middle-class morality.

The Magdalen Society's *First Annual Report* (1831) inveighed against male lust and printed shocking life histories of prostitutes. Some men, however, read it as pornography. Others used it as a guidebook to the seamier side of New York City. The wealthy male evangelicals who had bankrolled the Magdalen Society withdrew their support, and the organization fell apart. Thereupon many of the women reformers set up the Female Moral Reform Society, with a House of Industry in which prostitutes were taught morality and household skills to prepare them for new lives as domestic servants in pious middle-class homes. This effort also failed, largely because few prostitutes were interested in domestic service or evangelical religion. That fact became distressingly clear when in 1836 the society was obliged to close its House of Industry after the residents had taken it over during the caretaker's absence.

The Female Moral Reform Society was more successful with members of its own class. Its newspaper, the *Advocate of Moral Reform*, circulated throughout the evangelical North, eventually reaching 555 auxiliary societies with 20,000 readers. Now evangelical women fought prostitution by publishing the names of customers. They campaigned against pornography, obscenity, lewdness, and seduction and taught their sons to be pure, even when it meant dragging them out of brothels. Occasionally, they prosecuted men who took advantage of servant girls. They also publicized the names of adulterers, and they had seducers brought into court. In the process, women reformers fought the sexual double standard and assumed the power to define what was respectable and what was not.

12-5b Women's Rights

From the late 1820s onward, middle-class women in the North assumed roles that would have been unthinkable to their mothers and grandmothers. Evangelical domesticity made loving mothers (and not stern fathers) the principal rearers of children. Housewives saw themselves as missionaries to their families, influencing the moral choices their children and husbands made. In that role, women became arbiters of fashion, diet, and sexual behavior. Many joined the temperance movement and moral reform societies, where they became public reformers while posing as mothers protecting their sons from rum sellers and seducers. They gained a sense of spiritual empowerment that led some to question their own subordinate status within a system of gendered social roles. Lydia Maria Child, a writer of sentimental fiction and manuals on household economy as well as a leading abolitionist and moral reformer, proclaimed, "Those who urged women to become missionaries and form tract societies … have changed the household utensil to a living, energetic being, and they have no spell to turn it into a broom again."

Nearly all early feminists, like Child, were veterans of the antislavery crusade. Abolitionists, following the perfectionist implications of Whig evangelicalism to their logical ends, called for absolute human equality and a near-anarchist rejection of impersonal institutions and prescribed social roles. It became clear to some female abolitionists that the critique of slavery (a root-and-branch denunciation of patriarchy and prescribed hierarchy) applied as well to inequality based on sex.

Radical female abolitionists reached the conclusion that they were human beings first and women second. In 1837, **Sarah Grimke** announced, "The Lord Jesus defines the duties of his followers in his Sermon on the Mount … without any reference to sex or condition … never even referring to the distinction now so strenuously insisted upon between masculine and feminine virtues… . Men and women are CREATED EQUAL! They are both moral and accountable beings, and whatever is right for a man to do is right for woman."

Such talk—and worse, the fact that women were delivering such speeches in public—aroused opposition even among abolitionists. In 1840, the American Antislavery Society sent a delegation to an international convention in London—with women delegates and the woman abolitionist Abbey Kelley on the business committee. The convention voted to exclude women, and the Americans came home angry and divided. Garrison and the radicals supported full rights for women and published their speeches and writings in the *Liberator*. Others wished to win public favor for antislavery issues and argued that the woman question was at best a distraction. The result was a split in the antislavery crusade, largely over the question of women's rights, and intensification of the feminist movement.

Beginning about 1840, women lobbied state legislatures against the common-law custom that women and children were under the protection and authority of their husbands and fathers, and thus had limited rights to property and over themselves. The reformers won significant changes in the laws governing women's rights to own and inherit property, to keep the wages of their own labor, and to retain custody of children in cases of divorce. Fourteen northern states passed such legislation, culminating in New York's wide-ranging Married Women's Property Act in 1860.

The first Woman's Rights Convention met in Seneca Falls, New York, in 1848. The busiest organizer of the convention was **Elizabeth Cady Stanton**, wife of the abolitionist Henry B. Stanton and an attendee at the London convention of 1840. Stanton was a lukewarm abolitionist, but the argument over women in the movement drove her into full-time feminism. Along with other feminist abolitionists, she organized the **Seneca Falls Convention**. The only male delegate was the black abolitionist Frederick Douglass. Sojourner Truth, another prominent black opponent of slavery, also attended. Nearly all of the other delegates were white women abolitionists. Both as abolitionists and as feminists, they based their demands for equality not only on legal and moral arguments but also on the spirit of republican institutions. The principal formal document issued by the convention, a Declaration of Sentiments and Resolutions based on the Declaration of Independence, denounced "the repeated injuries and usurpations on the part of man toward woman."

Most of those "injuries and usurpations" were political. The central issue was the right to vote. Lucretia Mott and other Quaker delegates, along with many Garrisonian abolitionists, did not want a *political* movement. ("Lizzy," Mott chided Stanton, "thee will make us ridiculous.") But Stanton believed

History Through Film: Not for Ourselves Alone (1999)

Directed by Ken Burns (PBS).

In 1999, Ken Burns made a documentary film on the women's rights movement. Part One tells the story from about 1840 through the Civil War. It is vintage Ken Burns: old photographs scanned to give them the appearance of movies, period documents read over the pictures by actors (in this case, Sally Kellerman), modern-day experts speaking with authority, the same period music that Burns used in *The Civil War* and his other forays into the 19th century, and the same undercurrent of sentimentality. The film focuses on the collaboration and friendship between Susan B. Anthony and Elizabeth Cady Stanton, and through that medium and within its limits, it tells its story well.

Elizabeth Cady Stanton was descended, on her mother's side, from one of the great landholding families of colonial New York. Her father was a prosperous lawyer and judge. Young Elizabeth hungered for education, but no American college admitted women. She enrolled at Emma Willard's Female Seminary in Troy, New York, and shared her family's interest in the temperance and antislavery movements. She met lawyer and well-known antislavery speaker Henry B. Stanton through her cousin, wealthy abolitionist Gerrit Smith, and married Stanton in 1840. (Elizabeth excised the word "obey" from the ceremony.) The Stantons honeymooned at an antislavery convention in London that year. Organizers of the convention segregated women and men and forbade the women to speak. Stanton realized—as legions of women would realize—that the logic of antislavery applied to women as well as slaves, and that rights reform that was less than universal was badly flawed. The Stantons took up housekeeping in Boston, then moved to Seneca Falls in western New York. Henry Stanton was frequently away on lecture tours, and Elizabeth stayed at home, had babies, and grew weary of housework.

In 1848, after a visit with her friend and fellow activist Lucretia Mott, she helped organize the first Woman's Rights Convention in Seneca Falls. She authored the declaration demanding civil and legal equality for women, including the demand (truly shocking to contemporaries) that women be allowed to vote. Shortly after the Seneca Falls Convention, Stanton met Susan B. Anthony, another veteran reformer. Anthony, a Quaker, had been born into much humbler circumstances than Stanton, remained unmarried, and often upbraided other women reformers for marrying and having children. The differences between Stanton and Anthony added up to a lifelong collaboration: The educated and housebound Stanton wrote the manifestos, and the brave and unencumbered Anthony took them into lecture halls and the state legislature. They and their coworkers won some battles (in the area of women's property rights in particular), but could do little more than publicize their radical demands for the legal reform of marriage and for civil and political equality. This limitation became painfully clear during the Civil War, when their fellow reformers told Stanton and Anthony to delay women's rights while slaves were freed and given the same rights for which the women's movement had fought. At the close of Part One, women's civil and legal equality remain far from realization.

Not For Ourselves Alone tells a familiar story clearly and entertainingly. Along the way, it portrays a friendship between women within the antebellum reform community and (intermittently) throws light on the workings of a reform culture that enlisted much of the zeal and intellect of the antebellum North. ∎

12.11 *Not For Ourselves Alone* focuses on the long friendship between Elizabeth Cady Stanton and Susan B. Anthony to tell the story of the early women's rights movement.

What They Said

Making Fun of Women's Rights

In 1848, delegates to the first women's rights convention issued a Declaration of Sentiments modeled on the Declaration of Independence. Here is their list of demands (as reported in the *New York Herald*, 30 July 1848):

> The history of mankind is a history of repeated injuries and usurpations on the part of man toward woman, having in direct object the establishment of an absolute tyranny over her. To prove this, let fact be submitted to a candid world.
>
> He has never permitted her to exercise her … right to the elective franchise.
>
> He has compelled her to submit to laws in the formation of which she has had no voice.
>
> …having deprived her of this first right of citizens, the elective franchise, thereby leaving her without representation in the halls of legislation, he has oppressed her on all sides.
>
> He has made her, if married, in the eyes of the law, civilly dead.
>
> He has taken from her all right in property, even to the wages she earns.
>
> …in the covenant of marriage, she is compelled to promise obedience to her husband—he becoming, to all intents and purposes, her master—the law giving him power to deprive her of her liberty, and to administer chastisement.
>
> …he has monopolized nearly all the means of profitable employment, and from those she is permitted to follow, she receives but a paltry remuneration.
>
> He closes against her all the avenues to wealth and distinction which he considers most honorable to himself. As a teacher of theology, medicine or law, she is not known.
>
> He has denied her the facilities for obtaining a thorough education—all colleges being closed against her.
>
> …he has created a false public sentiment by giving to the world a different code of morals for men and women, by which moral delinquencies which exclude woman from society are not only tolerated but deemed of little account in men.
>
> He has usurped the prerogative of Jehovah himself, claiming it as his right to assign for her a sphere of action, when that belongs to her conscience and her God.

In 1856, the New York legislature received petitions making the same complaints and demanding the same rights. Here is the legislature's response (as reported in the *Plattsburgh Republican*, 29 March 1856):

> Judge Foote, of Ontario, the learned chairman of the Assembly Judiciary Committee, last week made a report on "Women's Rights" that set the whole House in roars of laughter…. [The committee has] left the subject pretty much to the married gentlemen. They have considered it with the aid of the … experience married life has given them. Thus, aided they are enabled to state, that ladies always have the best piece, and choicest titbit at table—They have the best seat in the cars, carriages and sleighs; the warmest place in winter and the coolest place in summer. They have their choice on which side of the bed they will lie…. A lady's dress costs three times as much as that of a gentleman; and at the present time, with the prevailing fashion, one lady occupies three times as much space in the world as a gentleman. It has thus appeared to the married gentlemen of our committee … that if there is any inequality or oppression in the case, the gentlemen are the sufferers. They, however, have presented no petitions for redress, having doubtless made up their minds to yield to an inevitable destiny.
>
> On the whole, the committee have concluded to recommend no measure, except, that as they have observed several instances in which husband and wife have both signed the same petition. In such case, they would recommend the party to apply for a law authorizing them to change dresses, so that the husband may wear the petty coats, and, the wife the breeches, and thus indicate to their neighbors, and the public the true relation in which they stand to each other.

Q Why did the women use the Declaration of Independence as a model, and why did they begin their list of demands with the rights of citizenship?

Q At this time the idea of political, legal, and civil equality between women and men was, for the great majority of Americans, unthinkable. This was grounded in the cultural axiom that there were separate spheres of activity prescribed for the sexes by nature and God. Can you explain the antics of the legislature in terms of that cultural axiom?

Q How would the women of Seneca Falls have responded to the legislature's statements?

Sources: (top) *New York Herald*, 30 July 1848; (bottom) *Plattsburgh Republican*, 29 March 1856.

12.12 Elizabeth Cady Stanton with Two of Her Three Sons
Suffragist, social activist, and abolitionist, Stanton wrote, "The prejudice against color, of which we hear so much, is no stronger than that against sex. It is produced by the same cause, and manifested very much the same way. The negro's skin and the woman's sex are *prima facie* evidence that they were intended to be in subjection to the white Saxon man."

Q *Why did Stanton juxtapose racial slavery and women's status and abolitionist and suffragist movements?*

rights," she said, "involving in their last results equality everywhere, roused all the antagonism of a dominant power, against the self-assertion of a class hitherto subservient."

Conclusion

By the 1830s, most citizens firmly identified with either the Whig or Democratic Party, so much so that party affiliation was a big part of personal identity. In the states and neighborhoods, Whigs embraced commerce and activist government, arguing that both would foster prosperity, social harmony, and moral progress. Faith in progress and improvement led northern and western Whigs, primarily the more radical evangelicals among them, to imagine that liberty and equality might apply to women and blacks as well as white men. The Democratic response to this was grounded in a defense of white patriarchy and the Old Republic. Like the Whigs, they did not doubt the value of commerce. But they worried that the market and its infrastructure of banking, credit, and paper money—all of it subsidized by government—forced inequality upon the white male citizenry and corrupted the republic. Democrats also looked with angry disbelief at attempts of Whigs (and rebellious members of Whig families) to govern private and public behavior, and sometimes even to attack the "natural" and fundamental distinctions of sex and race.

Whigs reformulated the revolutionary legacy of liberty and equality, moving away from classical notions of citizenship and toward liberty of conscience and equality of opportunity within a market-driven democracy. They often attempted to civilize that new world by using government power to encourage commerce, social interdependence, cultural homogeneity, and moral uplift. Democrats trusted none of that. Theirs was a Jeffersonian formulation grounded in a fierce defense of the liberty and equality of white men, and in a minimal, inexpensive, decentralized government that protected the liberties of those men without threatening their independence or their power over their households and within their neighborhoods. That was the fundamental political argument in the United States from the 1820s to the 1850s, and, for all its noise and uproar, it underwrote a party system that was outwardly stable and safe. But with the rise of antislavery and the acquisition of new territory, the political system was forced to address questions that the parties could not control.

that political rights—voting in particular—were crucial. Voting was central to the "democratic" pattern that granted liberty and equality to white men regardless of class and excluded Americans who were not white and male. Thus, female participation in politics was a direct challenge to a male-ordained women's place. A distraught New York legislator agreed: "It is well known that the object of these unsexed women is to overthrow the most sacred of our institutions... . Are we to put the stamp of truth upon the libel here set forth, that men and women, in the matrimonial relation, are to be equal?" Later, Elizabeth Cady Stanton recalled such reactions: "Political

CHAPTER REVIEW

Review

1. What were Whig and Democratic conceptions of the duties and limits of government?
2. What were Whig and Democratic positions on the issues of public schools, prisons, and asylums?
3. Trace the history of alcohol as a social and political question from the 1820s through the 1840s. Which Americans favored temperance? Which opposed it?

4. How did Whigs and Democrats differ on questions of slavery and race?
5. How did Democrats and Whigs differ on questions of gender and sex? Knowing what you know about the political cultures of the two parties, how do you explain those differences?

Critical Thinking

1. Choose a position either defending or attacking this statement: "Differences between Whigs and Democrats on economic policy, social reform, race, and gender boil down to differences in Whig and Democratic conceptions of white manhood."
2. What were the goals and assumptions that drove the movements for public schools, humane prisons and asylums, and temperance? Were those primarily Democratic or Whig assumptions?

Identifications

Review your understanding of the following key terms, people, and events for this chapter (terms in bold in text are included in the Glossary).

limited liability, p. 333
common schools, p. 334
normal schools, p. 335
Auburn system, p. 336
Dorothea Dix, p. 337
American Temperance Society, p. 338
Washington Temperance Society, p. 340
American Colonization Society, p. 342
abolitionism, p. 343
William Lloyd Garrison, p. 343
Uncle Tom's Cabin, p. 345
Postal Campaign, p. 345
New York Magdalen Society, p. 346
Sarah Grimke, p. 347
Elizabeth Cady Stanton, p. 347
Seneca Falls Convention, p. 347

Suggested Readings

On state-level internal improvements, see **John Majewski**, *A House Divided: Economic Development in Pennsylvania and Virginia before the Civil War* (2000). An entertaining introduction to money and banking is **Stephen Mihm**, *A Nation of Counterfeiters: Capitalists, Con Men, and the Making of the United States* (2007). **Carl F. Kaestle**, *Pillars of the Republic: Common Schools and American Society, 1780–1860* (1983), surveys the politics of schools. Influential studies of prisons and asylums include **David J. Rothman**, *The Discovery of the Asylum: Social Order and Disorder in the New Republic* (1971); **Michael Meranze**, *Laboratories of Virtue: Punishment, Revolution, and Authority in Philadelphia, 1760–1835* (1996); and **Thomas J. Brown**, *Dorothea Dix: New England Reformer* (1998). Drinking and temperance are the subjects of **W. J. Rorabaugh**, *The Alcoholic Republic: An American Tradition* (1979). **Christine Sismondo's** *America Walks into a Bar: A Spirited History of Taverns and Saloons, Speakeasies and Grog Shops* (2011) traces the centrality of bars and taverns in American social and political life. The literature on reform movements is synthesized in **Steven Mintz**, *Moralists & Modernizers: America's Pre-Civil War Reformers* (1995), which can be supplemented by **Bruce Dorsey**, *Reforming Men & Women: Gender in the Antebellum City* (2002) and **Richard S. Newman**, *The Transformation of American Abolitionism: Fighting Slavery in the Early Republic* (2002). See also **Robert H. Abzug**, *Cosmos Crumbling: American Reform and the Religious Imagination* (1994); **John W. Quist**, *Restless Visionaries: The Social Roots of Antebellum Reform in Alabama and Michigan* (1998); **Lori D. Ginzberg**, *Women and the Work of Benevolence: Morality, Politics, and Class in the 19th-Century United States* (1990); and **Ginzberg**, *Elizabeth Cady Stanton: An American Life* (2009). The cultural and moral underpinnings of reform are a subtext of **Karen Halttunen's** subtle and important *Murder Most Foul: The Killer and the American Gothic Imagination* (1998). **Sally G. McMillen's** *Seneca Falls and the Origins of the Women's Rights Movement* (2008) is an incisive and accessible study of the Seneca Falls convention, and **Jean H. Baker's** *Sisters: The Lives of America Suffragists* (2005) traces the rise of women's rights movement through the lives and experiences of individual women.

MINDTAP is a fully online personalized learning experience built upon Cengage Learning content. MindTap® combines student learning tools—readings, multimedia, activities, and assessments—into a singular Learning Path that guides students through the course and helps students develop the critical thinking, analysis, and communication skills that are essential to academic and professional success.

13 Manifest Destiny: An Empire for Liberty—or Slavery? 1845–1860

13-1 Growth as the American Way
Learning Objective: *Explain why many Americans thought westward expansion was their "manifest destiny."*

Manifest Destiny and Slavery
The Expansionist Impulse
New Mexico and California
The Oregon and California Trails
The Mormon Migration
The Republic of Texas
The Annexation Controversy
Acquisition of Texas and Oregon

13-2 The Mexican War
Learning Objective: *Discuss the causes and consequences of the Mexican War.*

Military Campaigns of 1846
Military Campaigns of 1847
Antiwar Sentiment
The Wilmot Proviso

13-3 The Election of 1848
Learning Objective: *Explain how the issue of slavery affected the election of 1848.*

The Free Soil Party
The Gold Rush and California Statehood

13-4 The Compromise of 1850
Learning Objective: *Identify and explain the importance of the separate measures that made up the Compromise of 1850.*

The Senate Debates
Passage of the Compromise
The Fugitive Slave Law
The Slave-Catchers
Uncle Tom's Cabin

13-5 Filibustering
Learning Objective: *Discuss the relationship between filibustering and the expansion of slavery.*

Cuba
The Gray-Eyed Man of Destiny

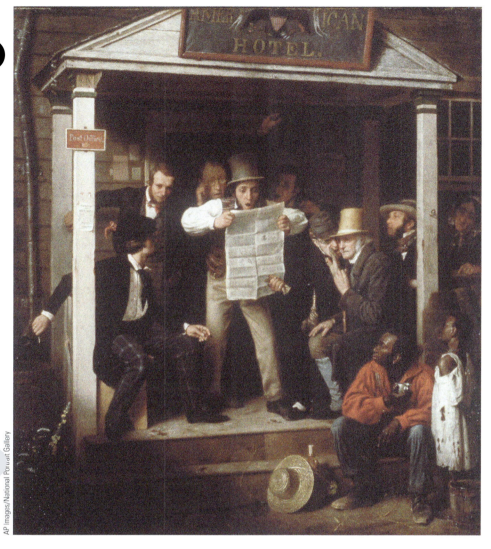

13.1 *War News from Mexico*
Richard Caton Woodville's 1848 painting captures the excitement felt by some Americans as they read newspaper accounts of the Mexican War (1846–1848). But notice that the African American man and child, dressed in rags, are not part of the celebratory group gathered on the porch of the allegorical "American Hotel," although they appear interested in the war news. The painting reminds us that an underlying question of the Mexican War was whether slavery would be extended into new territory; it also reminds us that African Americans were not equal members of the American nation. At the far right we can see that an old woman peers out the window to see what is going on; she, too, is not part of the main group at the heart of the painting—just as women were not yet voting citizens of the American republic. The strong narrative thrust of Woodville's painting marks it as one of many "genre paintings" that in the 1830s, 1840s, and 1850s depicted ordinary Americans and often told allegorical stories of daily life and politics.

THE UNITED STATES became a transcontinental nation between 1845 and 1848, increasing in size by 50 percent. Through annexation, negotiation, and war, the United States gained more than 1 million square miles, with western migration and settlement playing an important role in making this territorial acquisition desirable. Many Americans enthusiastically supported expansionism and celebrated the creation of an American empire. But expansionism aroused opposition as well. On both sides of the debate, the nation's politicians and citizens worried over an increasingly fraught question: Was this new empire for liberty—or for slavery? The acquisition of vast new stretches of land reopened the issue of slavery's expansion and planted the bitter seeds of civil war. ■

CHRONOLOGY

1844	Senate rejects Texas annexation • James K. Polk elected president
1845	Congress annexes Texas • Mexico spurns U.S. bid to buy California and New Mexico
1846	United States declares war on Mexico • United States and Britain settle Oregon boundary dispute • United States occupies California and New Mexico • House passes Wilmot Proviso • U.S. forces under Zachary Taylor capture Monterrey, Mexico
1847	Americans win Battle of Buena Vista • U.S. Army under Winfield Scott lands at Veracruz • Mexico City falls
1848	Treaty of Guadalupe Hidalgo ends Mexican War, fixes Rio Grande as border, cedes New Mexico and California to United States • Gold discovered in California • Spain spurns Polk's offer of $100 million for Cuba • Zachary Taylor elected president
1849	John C. Calhoun pens "Address of the Southern Delegates" • California seeks admission as a free state
1850	Taylor dies; Millard Fillmore becomes president • Bitter sectional debate culminates in Compromise of 1850 • Fugitive Slave Law empowers federal commissioners to recover escaped slaves
1851	Fugitive Slave Law provokes rescues and violent conflict in North • American filibusters executed in Cuba
1852	*Uncle Tom's Cabin* becomes best seller • Franklin Pierce elected president
1854	Anthony Burns returned from Boston to slavery • William Walker's filibusters invade Nicaragua • Pierce tries to buy Cuba • Ostend Manifesto issued
1856	William Walker legalizes slavery in Nicaragua
1860	William Walker executed in Honduras

13-1 Growth as the American Way

 What impulses lay behind the "Manifest Destiny" of America's westward expansion?

By 1850, older Americans had seen the area of the United States quadruple in their lifetime. Since the Louisiana Purchase of 1803, the American population had also quadrupled. Many Americans in 1850 considered this evidence of God's beneficence to this virtuous republic. During the 1840s, a group of expansionists affiliated with the Democratic Party began to call themselves the **Young America movement**. They proclaimed that it was the **Manifest Destiny** of the United States "to overspread and to possess the whole of the continent which Providence has given us for the development of the great experiment of liberty," as John L. O'Sullivan, editor of the *Democratic Review*, wrote in 1845.

For Native Americans, however, Manifest Destiny was a story of defeat and contraction. By 1850, the diseases and guns first introduced by whites had reduced the Indian population north of the Rio Grande to fewer than half a million, a fraction of the population of two or three centuries earlier. The relentless westward march of white settlements had pushed all but a few thousand Indians beyond the Mississippi. In the 1840s, the U.S. government decided to create a "permanent Indian frontier" at about the 95th meridian (roughly the western borders of Iowa, Missouri, and Arkansas). But white emigrants were already violating that frontier on the overland trails to the Pacific, and settlers were pressing against the borders of Indian Territory. In little more than a decade, the idea of "one big reservation" in the West would give way to the policy of forcing Indians onto small reservations. The government "negotiated" with Indian chiefs for vast cessions of land in return for annuity payments that were often extracted by shrewd or corrupt traders. Many Indians perished of disease, malnutrition, and alcohol—first introduced by whites—and in futile efforts to break out of the reservations and regain their land.

13-1a Manifest Destiny and Slavery

By 1846, the empire for liberty that Thomas Jefferson had envisioned for the Louisiana Purchase seemed more an empire for slavery. Territorial acquisitions since 1803 had brought into the republic the slave states of Louisiana, Missouri, Arkansas, Florida, Texas, and parts of Alabama and Mississippi. Only Iowa, admitted in 1846, had joined the ranks of the free states.

Although the division between slavery and freedom in the rest of the Louisiana Purchase had supposedly been settled by the Compromise of 1820, the expansion of slavery into new territories instead became an explosive issue (see Map 13.1). The issue first arose with the annexation of Texas, which helped provoke war with Mexico in 1846—a war that many antislavery northerners considered an ugly effort to expand slavery.

13-1b The Expansionist Impulse

Many Americans of European descent saw their future in the West. In the 1840s, newspaper editor Horace Greeley urged, "Go west, young man." And to the West they went in unprecedented numbers, driven in part by the depression of 1837–1843 that prompted thousands to search for cheap land and better opportunity.

An earlier wave of migration had populated the region between the Appalachians and the Missouri River, bringing a new state into the Union on an average of every three years. Reports from explorers, fur traders, missionaries, and sailors filtered back from California and the Pacific Northwest, describing the bounteous resources and benign climates of those wondrous regions. Guidebooks rolled off the presses describing the boundless prospects that awaited settlers who

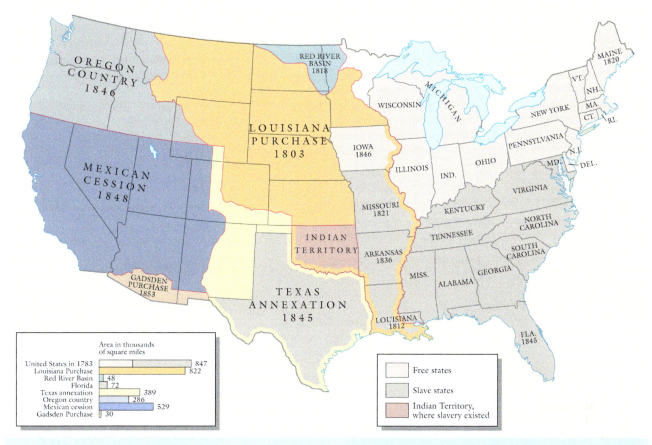

▲ **MAP 13.1 Free and Slave States and Territories, 1848** This map illustrates the larger number of slave than free states entering the Union from the territories acquired from France (Louisiana Purchase) and Spain (Florida). It also shows the huge amount of new territory added by the acquisition of Texas and the Southwest from Mexico and the settlement of the Oregon boundary in the 1840s.

Q How does this map reveal the critical importance of the territory that would become the states of Kansas and Nebraska in the controversy over the expansion of slavery?

Q Does this map reveal that slavery threatened to become a national phenomenon?

would turn "those wild forests, trackless plains, untrodden valleys" into "one grand scene of continuous improvements, universal enterprise, and unparalleled commerce."

13-1c New Mexico and California

By the time Mexico won its independence from Spain in 1821, some 80,000 Mexicans lived in portions of the region west of the 98th meridian. Three-fourths of them had settled in the Rio Grande Valley of New Mexico and most of the rest in California. Centuries earlier, the Spaniards had introduced horses, cattle, and sheep to the New World. These animals became the economic mainstay of Hispanic society along New Spain's northern frontier. Later, Anglo-Americans would adopt Hispanic ranching methods to invade and subdue the lands of the arid western plains. Spanish words still describe the tools of the trade and the land: *bronco, mustang, lasso, rodeo, stampede, canyon, arroyo, mesa*.

Colonial society on New Spain's northern frontier had centered on the **missions** and the ***presidios***. Intended to Christianize Indians, the missions also became an instrument to exploit their labor, while the presidios (military posts) protected the settlers from hostile Indians. By the late 18th century, the mission system had fallen into decline, and 15 years after Mexican independence in 1821, it collapsed entirely. The presidios, underfunded and understaffed, also declined, so that the defense of Mexico's far northern provinces increasingly fell to the residents. But by the 1830s, many residents of New Mexico and California were more interested in bringing American traders in than in keeping American settlers out. A flourishing trade over the Santa Fe Trail from Independence, Missouri, brought American manufactured goods to Santa Fe, New Mexico (and points south), in exchange for Mexican horses, mules, beaver pelts, and silver (see Map 13.2). New England ships carried American goods all the way around the horn of South America to San Francisco and other California ports in exchange for tallow and hides produced by *californio* ranchers. This trade linked the economies of New Mexico and California more closely to the United States than to the Mexican heartland.

Interpreting the Visual Past — Manifest Destiny

John Gast's 1872 painting, *American Progress*, offers a detailed allegory of Manifest Destiny: It is meant to teach viewers the meanings of western expansion. Visual allegories of nationhood in the 19th century often centered around female figures as embodiments of civilization: At the center of this painting is the figure of American Progress (Columbia), with the star of empire on her forehead. Precariously clad in a diaphanous gown, she strides westward, with coils of telegraph wire draped over her right arm, and a clearly labeled "School Book" in her right hand: She is bringing both technology and education to the West. The figures on the ground also tell a careful story of progress, involving not only different technologies but also different types of settlers. Ultimately, the painting offers a benevolent view of what was often a violent process of conquering territory.

Q What stories does this painting tell regarding technologies of white civilization such as the railroad?

Q How does the painting organize a visual narrative of settlement moving from east to west? Does it represent such settlement as inevitable? Why or why not?

Q How does the painting view Native Americans? How do they respond to "American Progress"?

13.2 **John Gast, *American Progress*, 1872.**

13-1d The Oregon and California Trails

At the depth of the economic depression in 1842 and 1843, Oregon fever swept the Mississippi Valley. Thousands of farm families sold their land, packed their worldly goods in covered wagons along with supplies for five or six months on the trail, hitched up their oxen, and headed out from Independence or St. Joseph, Missouri, for the trek of almost 2,000 miles to the river valleys of Oregon or California. From 1840 to 1869, an estimated 50,000 emigrants made the trek to Oregon (see Map 13.2).

Adult men outnumbered women by more than 2 to 1 on the western trails before the gold rush. Many women

▲ **MAP 13.2 Overland Trails, 1846** The Santa Fe Trail was mainly a route for trade between the United States and the Mexican province (before 1848) of New Mexico. The other three trails carried hundreds of thousands of Americans to new homes in the West.

Q Why didn't migrants stop and settle in the territories they passed through?

Q Whose land did white settlers pass through on these Overland Trails?

were reluctant emigrants, and their diaries testified to their unhappiness: "What had possessed my husband, anyway, that he should have thought of bringing us away out through this God-forsaken country?" wrote one woman. She was sorry she had ever consented "to take this wild goose chase." For some families it did turn out to be a wild goose chase, but for many of those who stayed the course and settled in the far West, it was a success story in which women were critical in transforming settlements into communities.

On the way west, migrants passed through regions claimed by three nations—the United States, Mexico, and Britain—and they settled on land owned by Mexico (California) or claimed jointly by the United States and Britain (Oregon, which then stretched north to the border of Russian Alaska). But no matter who claimed it, the land was inhabited mostly by Indians. Few emigrants thought about settling down along the way, for this vast reach of arid plains, forbidding mountains, and burning wastelands was then known as the **Great American Desert**. Whites considered it suitable only for Indians and a disappearing breed of fur trappers. But one group did find its new home at the edge of the Great Salt Lake.

13-1e The Mormon Migration

Subjected to persecution that drove them from their original home in western New York to Ohio, Missouri, and eventually to Illinois, the **Mormons** established Nauvoo, Illinois, a thriving community of 15,000 souls, based on collective economic effort and theocratic discipline imposed by their founder and prophet, Joseph Smith. But the people of Illinois proved no more hospitable to the Mormons than the sect's previous neighbors. Smith provoked hostility with his insistence that God spoke through him, his autocratic suppression of dissent, and his assertion that the Mormons were the only true Christians and would inherit the

13.3 The Alamo Site of the Battle of the Alamo in 1836, the Alamo Mission is today Texas's most visited historic landmark.

earth. When a dissident faction of Mormons published Smith's latest revelation, which sanctioned polygamy, he ordered their printing press destroyed. The county sheriff arrested him, and in June 1844, a mob broke into the jail and killed him.

Smith's martyrdom prompted yet another exodus. His successor, Brigham Young, led the Mormons on the long trek westward. A man of iron will and administrative genius, Young organized the migration down to the last detail. Arriving with the advance guard of Mormon pioneers at a pass overlooking the Great Salt Lake Basin on July 24, 1847, Young, who was ill with tick fever, struggled from his wagon and stared at the barren desert and mountains surrounding the lake. "This is the right place," he declared. Here the Mormons could create their Zion undisturbed.

They built a flourishing community, making the desert bloom with grain and vegetables irrigated by water they ingeniously diverted from mountain streams. Young reigned as leader of the church, and from 1850 to 1857 as governor of the newly created Utah Territory.

Zion, however, did not remain undisturbed. Relations with the government in Washington, D.C., and with territorial officials were never smooth, especially after Young's proclamation in 1852 authorizing polygamy. When conflict between the Mormons and the U.S. Army broke out in 1857, Young surrendered his civil authority and made an uneasy peace with the government.

13-1f *The Republic of Texas*

As the Mormons were starting west, a crisis between Mexico and the United States was coming to a boil. The United States had renounced any claim to Texas in a treaty with Spain negotiated in 1819. By the time the treaty was ratified in 1821, Mexico had won its independence from Spain. The new Republic of Mexico, seeking to develop its northern borderlands in Texas, gave Stephen F. Austin, a Missouri businessman, a large land grant to settle 300 American families there. Despite their pledge to become Roman Catholics and Mexican citizens, these immigrants and many who followed remained Protestants and Americans at heart. They also brought in slaves, in defiance of a recent Mexican law abolishing slavery. Despite Mexican efforts to ban any further immigration, 30,000 Americans lived in Texas by 1835, outnumbering Mexicans 6 to 1.

American settlers, concentrated in east Texas, initially had little contact with Mexican ***tejanos*** (Texans), whose settlements were farther south and west. But political events in Mexico City in 1835 had repercussions on the northern frontier. A new conservative national government seemed intent on consolidating its authority over the northern territories. In response, Anglo-American settlers and *tejanos* forged a political alliance to protest any further loss of autonomy in their province. When the Mexican government responded militarily, many Texans—both Anglo and Mexican—fought back. In March 1836, delegates from across Texas met at a village appropriately called Washington. They declared Texas an independent republic and adopted a constitution based on the U.S. model.

The American Revolution had lasted seven years; it took the Texans less than seven months to win and consolidate their independence. Mexican general Antonio López de Santa Anna led the Mexican army that captured the **Alamo** (a former mission converted to a fort) in San Antonio on March 6, 1836, killing all 187 of its defenders, including the legendary Americans Davy Crockett and Jim Bowie. Rallying to the cry "Remember the Alamo!" Texans swarmed to the revolutionary army commanded by Sam Houston. When the Mexican army slaughtered another force of more than 300 men after they had surrendered at Goliad on March 19, the Texans became further inflamed. A month later, Houston's army, aided by volunteers from southern U.S. states, routed a larger Mexican force on the San Jacinto River (near present-day Houston) and captured Santa Anna. Under duress, he signed a treaty granting Texas its independence. The Mexican congress later repudiated the treaty but could not muster enough strength to reestablish its authority north of the Nueces River. The victorious Texans elected Sam Houston president of their new republic and petitioned for annexation to the United States.

13-1g *The Annexation Controversy*

President Andrew Jackson, wary of provoking war with Mexico or quarrels with antislavery northerners, rebuffed the annexationists. So did his successor, Martin Van Buren. Although disappointed, the Texans turned their energies to building their republic. The British government encouraged the Texans, in the hope that they would stand as a buffer against further U.S. expansion. Texas leaders made friendly responses to some of the British overtures, probably in the hope of provoking American annexationists to take action. They did.

Vice President John Tyler had unexpectedly become president after the death of President William Henry Harrison from pneumonia in 1841, only weeks after his inauguration as the first Whig president. Tyler was nominally a Whig—but he soon broke with the Whig Party that had elected him. A states-rights Virginian who sought to create a new coalition to reelect him in 1844, Tyler seized on the annexation of Texas as "the only matter that will take sufficient hold of the feelings of the South to rally it on a southern candidate."

Tyler's secretary of state, John C. Calhoun, negotiated a treaty of annexation with the eager Texans, but then he made a mistake: He released to the press his letter informing the British minister to the United States that, together with other reasons, Americans wanted to annex Texas in order to protect slavery. This seemed to confirm abolitionist charges that annexation was a pro-slavery plot. Northern senators of both parties defeated the treaty in June 1844.

By then, Texas had become the main issue in the forthcoming presidential election. Whig candidate Henry Clay had come out against annexation, as had the leading contender for the Democratic nomination, former president Martin Van Buren. Van Buren's stand ran counter to the rising tide of Manifest Destiny sentiment within the Democratic Party. It also angered southern Democrats, who were determined to have Texas. Through eight ballots at the Democratic National Convention, they blocked Van Buren's nomination; on the ninth, the southerners broke the stalemate by nominating one of their own, James K. Polk of Tennessee. Polk's nomination undercut President Tyler's forlorn hope of being reelected on the Texas issue, so he bowed out of the race.

Polk ran on a platform that called for not only the annexation of Texas but also the acquisition of all of Oregon up to 50°40′ (the Alaskan border) (see Map 13.3). That demand was aimed at voters in the western free states, who believed that bringing Oregon into the Union would balance the expansion of slavery into Texas. Polk was more than comfortable with this platform. In fact, he wanted not only Texas and Oregon, but California and New Mexico as well.

Texas fever swept the South during the campaign. So powerful was the issue that Clay began to waver, stating that he would support annexation if it could be done without starting a war with Mexico. This concession won him a few southern votes but angered northern antislavery Whigs. Many of them voted for James G. Birney, candidate of the Liberty Party, which opposed adding any more slave territory. Birney probably took enough Whig votes from Clay in New York to give Polk victory there and in the Electoral College.

13-1h Acquisition of Texas and Oregon

Although the election was extremely close (Polk won only a plurality of 49.5 percent of the popular vote), Democrats regarded it as a mandate for annexation. Congress passed a joint resolution of annexation in March 1845, and Texas became the 15th slave state. Backed now by the United States, Texans claimed a southern and western border beyond the

▲ **MAP 13.3 Settlement of the Oregon Boundary Dispute, 1846** Before the 1840s, the only white residents of the Oregon Country were fur traders and missionaries. Migration of Americans over the Oregon Trail created pressures to make all of Oregon part of the United States, but President Polk was not willing to go to war for the boundary of 50°40′.

Q What does this map show about British and American tensions in the 19th century?

Q Why wasn't President Polk willing to go to war over the disputed area of the map?

Nueces River all the way to the Rio Grande, which nearly tripled the area that Mexico had formerly defined as Texas. Mexico responded by breaking off diplomatic relations with the United States.

Meanwhile, Polk lost no time in addressing his promise to annex Oregon. "Our title to the country of the Oregon is 'clear and unquestionable,'" he said in his inaugural address. The problem was to persuade Britain to recognize the title. Both countries had jointly "occupied" Oregon since 1818, overseeing the fur trade carried on by British and American companies. Chanting the slogan "Fifty-four forty or fight!" many Americans in 1845 demanded all of Oregon, as pledged in the Democratic platform. But Polk proved unwilling to fight for 50°40′. So far, Americans had settled only in the region south of the Columbia River, at roughly the 46th parallel. In June 1846, Polk accepted a compromise treaty that split the Oregon country between the United States and Britain at the 49th parallel. Several Democratic senators from the Old Northwest accused Polk of betrayal and voted against the treaty. They had supported Texas to the Rio Grande, and they had expected Polk to support Oregon to 50°40′. A sectional breach had opened in the Democratic Party that would soon grow wider.

History Through Film — *The Alamo* (1960)

Directed by John Wayne.
Starring John Wayne (Davy Crockett), Richard Widmark (Jim Bowie), Laurence Harvey (William Travis).

The legendary actor John Wayne worked a decade to obtain backing for an epic film about the heroic but doomed defense of the Alamo. When the movie was finally released in 1960, Wayne not only played the lead role as Davy Crockett, but he was also the producer and director. Out of his depth in this last role, he received advice from the director of Wayne's best movies, John Ford, which helped overcome some but not all of the awkward, sentimental scenes in the film.

Three hours long, *The Alamo* begins with General Sam Houston, commander of the Texas revolutionary army, ordering Colonel William Travis to delay the Mexican regulars commanded by Santa Anna at the Alamo long enough for Houston to organize his ragtag volunteers in east Texas into an effective fighting force. Colonel Jim Bowie, a rival of Travis for command of the garrison, considers the Alamo (a mission converted into a fort) a trap and wants to pull out, because the Mexican army outnumbers the Texans 20 to 1.

Right away, Hollywood departs from historical reality. Houston had actually ordered Bowie to blow up the Alamo and retreat to join him, but Bowie and Travis agreed to stay and fight, supported by Davy Crockett and his fellow Tennessee volunteers who had come to Texas looking for excitement. The tension between Travis and Bowie (with Crockett as a mediator) was real and is vividly portrayed, if sometimes overdramatized, in the film, but the tension concerned their relative authority, not strategy.

In wide-screen splendor, the film depicts the approach of the Mexican army, the artillery duels between the garrison and the Mexicans, and the infantry assaults that finally overpower the garrison after 13 days of resistance, killing them to the last man, sparing only the wife and child of a Texas lieutenant. The combat footage in the final attack is spectacular. Mexican artillery bombards the Alamo; infantrymen move forward, taking heavy casualties, swarm over the wall, and overwhelm the doomed defenders. Bowie is wounded early in the fight and sent to an improvised hospital in the chapel, where he dies fighting from his bed. Travis is killed at the gate after dispatching several Mexicans with his sword. Crockett fights with fury until he is impaled by a Mexican lancer, but lives long enough to throw a torch into the powder magazine, blowing up the fort and hundreds of Mexicans.

In reality, none of it happened this way. Bowie had gone to bed with typhoid fever early in the siege; Travis was killed early in the final assault with a bullet through his head; and Crockett, along with a few others, surrendered but were executed on Santa Anna's orders. For Hollywood, and perhaps for most Americans, however, history is less important than legend. The Alamo became a heroic legend, a rallying cry for Texans in 1836, and a powerful symbol ever since. The film version dramatizes the legend better than an accurate version could have done.

The movie also reflects the cold-war mentality of the 1950s and Wayne's own full-blooded anti-communist stance. Crockett's windy speeches about freedom and individual rights evoke the 1950s rhetoric of "better dead than red." Ironically, the Texans were fighting for an independent republic with slavery, in defiance of Mexico's recent abolition of the institution—an issue that the film virtually ignores.

Although *The Alamo* might have carried more punch if it had been edited down to two hours, it nevertheless is visually powerful. It received seven Academy Award nominations, including one for Best Picture, but received only one Oscar—for sound. ■

13.4 John Wayne in a Poster Advertising *The Alamo*.

13-2 The Mexican War

Q *What were the causes and consequences of the Mexican War?*

Having avoided a war with Britain, Polk provoked one with Mexico. In 1845, he sent a special envoy to Mexico City with an offer to buy California and New Mexico for $30 million. To help Mexico make the right response, he ordered federal troops to the disputed border area between Mexico and Texas, dispatched a naval squadron to patrol the Gulf Coast of Mexico, and instructed the American consul at Monterey (the Mexican capital of California) to stir up annexation sentiment among settlers there. These strong-arm tactics provoked a political revolt in Mexico City that brought a militant anti-American regime to power.

Polk responded in January 1846 by ordering 4,000 soldiers under General Zachary Taylor to advance all the way to the Rio Grande. Recognizing that he could achieve his goals only through armed conflict, Polk waited for news from Texas that would justify a declaration of war. Finally, on May 9, 1846, word arrived that two weeks earlier Mexican troops had crossed the Rio Grande and attacked an American patrol, killing 11 soldiers. Polk had what he wanted and sent a war message to Congress on May 11. Most Whigs opposed war with Mexico, but in the end, not wanting to be branded unpatriotic, all but a handful of them voted for what they called "Mr. Polk's War."

The United States went to war with a tiny regular army of fewer than 8,000 men, supplemented by 60,000 volunteers in state regiments, and an efficient navy that quickly established domination of the sea-lanes. Mexican soldiers outnumbered American in most of the battles, but the Americans had higher morale, better leadership, better weapons (especially artillery), and the backing of a more determined, stable government and a far stronger economy. The U.S. forces won every battle—and the war—in a fashion that humiliated Mexico and left a legacy of national hostility and border violence.

13.5 **American Forces in Saltillo, Mexico** This posed photograph of General John E. Wool and his staff, members of Zachary Taylor's army on its march southward from Monterrey through Saltillo in November 1846, is the earliest known photograph of an American military force. Photography had recently been invented, and pictures such as this one were extremely rare before the 1850s.

13-2a *Military Campaigns of 1846*

The Mexican War's first phase was carried out by Zachary Taylor, whose 4,000 regulars routed numerically superior Mexican forces on the Rio Grande in early May, even before Congress had declared war. Those victories made "Old Rough and Ready" Taylor a hero, a reputation he rode to the presidency two years later. Reinforced by several thousand volunteers, Taylor pursued the retreating Mexicans 100 miles south of the Rio Grande to the heavily fortified Mexican city of Monterrey, and took the city after four days of fighting in September 1846. Mexican resistance in the area crumbled, and Taylor's force settled down as an army of occupation.

Meanwhile, the second phase of American strategy had gone forward in New Mexico and California. In June 1846, General Stephen Watts Kearny led an army of 1,500 tough frontiersmen and regulars west from Fort Leavenworth toward Santa Fe. Kearny's army occupied Santa Fe on August 18 without firing a shot. With closer economic ties to the United States than to their own country, which taxed them well but governed them poorly, many New Mexicans seemed willing to accept American rule.

After receiving reinforcements, Kearny sent part of his army into the Mexican province of Chihuahua. In the most extraordinary campaign of the war, these troops marched 1,500 miles, foraging supplies along the way; fought and beat two much larger enemy forces; and finally linked up with Zachary Taylor's army near Monterrey in spring 1847 (see Map 13.4).

Kearny led another contingent across deserts and mountains to California. Events there had anticipated his arrival. In June 1846, a group of American settlers backed by Captain John C. Frémont, a renowned western explorer with the army topographical corps, captured Sonoma and raised the flag of an independent California, displaying the silhouette of a grizzly bear. This "bear-flag revolt" paved the way for the conquest of California by the *americanos*. The U.S. Pacific Fleet seized California's ports and the capital at Monterey; sailors from the fleet and volunteer soldiers under Frémont subdued Mexican resistance. Kearny's weary and battered force arrived in December 1846, barely in time to help with the mopping up.

13-2b *Military Campaigns of 1847*

The Mexican government refused to admit that the war was lost. Early in 1847, Santa Anna raised new levies and marched north to attack Taylor's army near Monterrey. Taylor, 62 years old, was still rough but not as ready to withstand a counteroffensive as he had been a few weeks earlier. After capturing Monterrey in September 1846, he had let the defeated Mexican army go and had granted an eight-week armistice in the hope that it would allow time for peace negotiations. Angry at Taylor's presumption in making such a decision and suspicious of the general's political ambitions, Polk canceled the armistice and named General-in-Chief Winfield Scott to command the third phase of the war. A large, punctilious man, Scott acquired the nickname "Old Fuss and Feathers" for a military professionalism that contrasted with the homespun manner of "Rough and Ready" Zach Taylor. Scott decided to invade Mexico from a beachhead at Veracruz and in January 1847 ordered the transfer of more than half of Taylor's troops to his own expeditionary force (see Map 13.4).

Left with fewer than 5,000 men, most of them untried volunteers, Taylor complained bitterly of political intrigue and military favoritism. Nevertheless, he marched out to meet Santa Anna's army of 18,000. In a two-day battle on

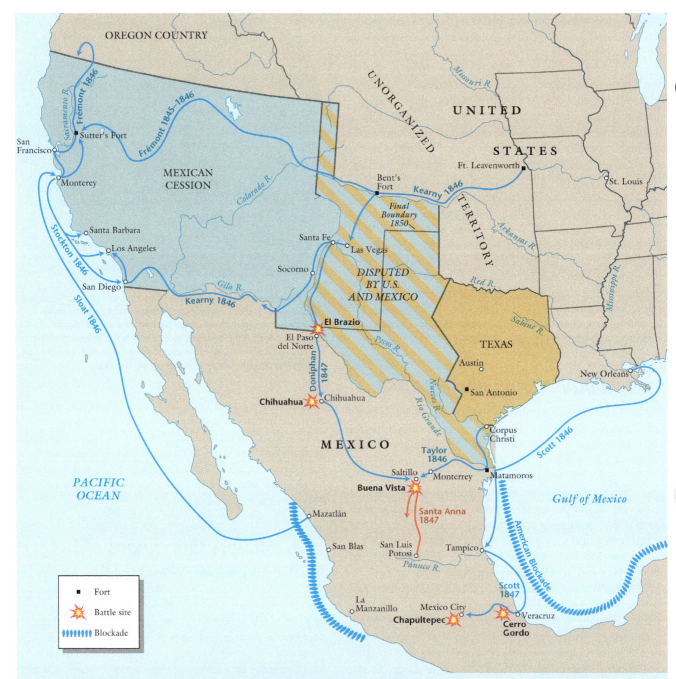

▲ **MAP 13.4 Principal Campaigns of the Mexican War, 1846–1847** This map provides a graphic illustration of the vast territory over which the Mexican War was fought; the distance from Veracruz to San Francisco is 2,500 miles.

Q *Does this map show that the Mexican War was primarily a land war or a naval war?*

Q *What strategies for winning the war does this map reveal?*

February 22 and 23 at Buena Vista, Taylor's force inflicted twice as many casualties as they suffered in a fierce struggle highlighted by the brilliant counterattack of a Mississippi regiment commanded by Jefferson Davis. The bloodied Mexican army retreated toward the capital. When news of the victory reached the East, Taylor's popularity soared to new heights. If Polk had wanted to quash a political rival by taking away most of his troops—as Taylor believed—he had achieved just the opposite.

But it was General Scott who actually won the war. With a combined army–navy force, he took the coastal fortress at Veracruz in March 1847. Over the next five months, his army, which never totaled more than 14,000 men, marched and fought its way over more than 200 miles of mountains and plains to Mexico City. Scott's outnumbered forces captured Mexico City on September 14, after fierce hand-to-hand combat in the battles of Contreras, Churubusco, Molino del Rey, and Chapultepec.

13-2c Antiwar Sentiment

The war had enthusiastic support in the South and West and among Democrats, but Whigs and many people in the Northeast, especially in New England, considered it "a wicked and disgraceful war." Democrats and Whigs had different notions of progress. Democrats believed in expanding American institutions over *space*—in particular, the space occupied by Mexicans and Indians. Whigs, on the other hand, believed in improving American institutions over *time*. "Opposed to the instinct of boundless acquisition stands that of Internal Improvement," said Horace Greeley. "A nation cannot simultaneously devote its energies to the absorption of others' territories and the improvement of its own."

Antislavery people raised their eyebrows when they heard Manifest Destiny rhetoric about "extending the blessings of American liberty" to benighted regions. They suspected that the real reason was the desire to extend slavery. Hosea Biglow, the rustic Yankee philosopher created by the abolitionist poet James Russell Lowell, observed:

> They jest want this Californy
> So's to lug new slave-states in
> To abuse ye an' to scorn ye,
> And to plunder ye like sin

13-2d The Wilmot Proviso

The slavery issue overshadowed all others in the debate over the Mexican War. President Polk could not understand the reason for the fuss. "There is no probability," he wrote in his diary, "that any territory will ever be acquired from Mexico in which slavery would ever exist." But other Americans were less sure. Many southerners hoped that slavery would spread into the fertile lowlands of Mexican territory. Many northerners feared that it might. The issue came to a head early in the war. On August 8, 1846, Pennsylvania Democratic congressman David Wilmot offered an amendment to an army appropriations bill: "...that, as an express and fundamental condition of the acquisition of any territory from the Republic of Mexico ... neither slavery nor involuntary servitude shall ever exist in any part of said territory."

This famous **Wilmot Proviso** framed the national debate over slavery for the next 15 years. The House passed the amendment. Nearly all northern Democrats joined all northern Whigs in the majority, while southern Democrats and southern Whigs voted almost unanimously against it. In the Senate, greater southern strength defeated the proviso. This outcome marked an ominous wrenching of the party division between Whigs and Democrats into a *sectional* division between free and slave states. It was a sign that the two-party system might not successfully contain the convulsive question of slavery expansion.

Several factors underlay the split of northern Democrats from their own president on this issue. Ever since southern Democrats had blocked Van Buren's nomination in 1844, resentment had been growing in the party's northern wing. Polk's acceptance of 49° latitude for Oregon's northern boundary exacerbated this feeling. "Our rights to Oregon have been shamefully compromised," fumed an Ohio Democrat. "The administration is Southern, Southern, Southern! ... Since the South have fixed boundaries for free territory, let the North fix boundaries for slave territories." The reduced rates

13.6 Runaway Slave Advertisement, 1847 This 1847 advertisement by a slave owner near St. Louis, Missouri reveals the desperate attempt of a family of five slaves–a husband, wife, and three children–to free themselves by escaping north. The slave owner assumes that they are on their way to Chicago, located in a "free state."

Q *Under federal law, would this family be safe from slave catchers once they arrived there?*

of the Walker tariff in 1846 (sponsored by Robert J. Walker of Mississippi, Polk's secretary of the treasury) dismayed Democrats from Pennsylvania's industrial districts. Polk further angered Democrats from the Old Northwest by vetoing a rivers and harbors bill that would have provided federal aid for transportation improvements in their districts. The Wilmot Proviso was in part the product of these pent-up frustrations over what northerners were increasingly calling "the slave power." "The time has come," said a Democratic congressman in 1846, "when the Northern Democracy should make a stand. Every thing has taken a Southern shape and been controlled by Southern caprice for years.... We must satisfy the Northern people ... that we are not to extend the institution of slavery as a result of this war."

The slavery issue hung like the sword of Damocles over Polk's efforts to negotiate peace with Mexico. Polk also came under pressure from expansionist Democrats who, excited by military victory, wanted more Mexican territory, perhaps even "all Mexico." Polk had sent diplomat Nicholas Trist with Scott's army to negotiate the terms of Mexican surrender. Authorized to pay Mexico $15 million for California, New Mexico, and a Texas border on the Rio Grande, Trist worked out such a treaty. In the meantime, though, Polk had succumbed to the "all Mexico" clamor. He ordered Trist back to Washington, intending to replace him with someone who would exact greater concessions from Mexico. Trist ignored the recall, signed the **Treaty of Guadalupe Hidalgo** on February 2, 1848, and sent it to Washington. Although angered by Trist's defiance, Polk nonetheless decided to end the controversy by submitting the treaty to the Senate, which approved it on March 10 by a vote of 38 to 14. Half the opposition came from Democrats who wanted more Mexican territory and half from Whigs who wanted none. As it was, the treaty sheared off half of Mexico and increased the size of the United States by one-fourth.

13-3 The Election of 1848

Q *How did the question of slavery affect the election of 1848?*

The treaty did nothing to settle the question of slavery in the new territory, however. Mexico had abolished the institution two decades earlier; would the United States reintroduce it? Many Americans looked to the election of 1848 to decide the matter. Four positions on the issue emerged, each identified with a candidate for the presidential nomination.

The Wilmot Proviso represented the position of those determined to bar slavery from all territories. The Liberty Party endorsed the proviso and nominated Senator John P. Hale of New Hampshire for president. Southern Democrat John C. Calhoun formulated the "southern-rights" position. Directly challenging the Wilmot Proviso, Calhoun introduced resolutions in the Senate in February 1847 affirming the right of slave owners to take their human property into any territory. The Constitution protected the right of property, Calhoun pointed out; Congress could no more prevent a settler from taking his slaves to California than it could prevent him from taking his horses there.

Although most southerners agreed with Calhoun, the Democratic Party sought a middle ground. The Polk administration endorsed the idea of extending the old Missouri Compromise line of 36°30′ to the Pacific. This would have excluded slavery from present-day Washington, Oregon, Idaho, Utah, Nevada, and the northern half of California, but would have allowed it in present-day New Mexico, Arizona, and southern California. Secretary of State James Buchanan, also a candidate for the Democratic presidential nomination (Polk did not seek renomination), embraced this position.

Another compromise position became known as **"popular sovereignty."** Identified with Senator Lewis Cass of Michigan, yet another contender for the Democratic nomination, this concept proposed to let the settlers of each territory decide for themselves whether to permit slavery. This solution contained a crucial ambiguity: It did not specify *at what stage* the settlers of a territory could decide on slavery. Most northern Democrats assumed that a territorial legislature would make that decision as soon as it was organized. Most southerners assumed that the decision would not be made until the settlers had drawn up a state constitution. That would normally happen only after several years as a territory, during which time slavery might well have taken deep enough root to be implanted in the state constitution. So long as neither assumption was tested, each faction could support popular sovereignty.

The Democratic convention nominated Cass for president, thereby seeming to endorse popular sovereignty. In an attempt to maintain party unity, however, the platform made no mention of the matter. The attempt was not entirely successful: Two Alabama delegates walked out when the convention refused to endorse Calhoun's southern-rights position, and an antislavery faction from New York walked out when it failed to win a credentials fight.

The Whig convention tried to avoid a similar schism by adopting no platform at all, but the slavery issue would not die. In the eyes of many antislavery delegates who styled themselves **Conscience Whigs**, the party made itself ridiculous by nominating Zachary Taylor for president. Desperate for victory, the Whigs chose a hero from a war that most of them had opposed. But the fact that Taylor was also a large slaveholder who owned several plantations in Louisiana and Mississippi was too much for the Conscience Whigs. They bolted from the party and formed a coalition with the Liberty Party and antislavery Democrats.

13-3a *The Free Soil Party*

These **Free-Soilers** met in convention in August 1848 and nominated former president Martin Van Buren. The meeting resembled a religious camp meeting more than a political gathering. Speakers proclaimed slavery "a great moral, social, and political evil—a relic of barbarism which must necessarily be swept away in the progress of Christian civilization." The convention did not say how that would be done, but it did adopt a platform calling for "no more Slave States and no more Slave Territories."

The campaign was marked by the futile efforts of both major parties to bury the slavery issue. Free Soil pressure compelled both northern Democrats and Whigs to take a stand against slavery in the territories. Whigs pointed to their earlier support of the Wilmot Proviso, while Democrats said popular sovereignty would keep the territories free. In the South, though, the two parties presented other faces. There, the Democrats pointed with pride to their expansionist record that had brought to the nation hundreds of thousands of square miles of territory—into which slavery might expand. But Taylor proved the strongest candidate in the South because he was a southerner and a slaveholder. "Will the people of [the South] vote for a Southern President or a Northern one?" asked southern newspapers. "We prefer Old Zack with his sugar and cotton plantations and four hundred negroes to all their compromises."

Taylor carried 8 of the 15 slave states and increased the Whig vote in the South by 10 percent over 1844, while the Democratic vote declined by 4 percent. Although he did less well in the North, he carried New York and enough other states to win the election. The Free-Soilers won no electoral votes but polled 14 percent of the popular vote in the North. They also elected nine congressmen along with two senators who would be heard from in the future: Salmon P. Chase of Ohio, architect of the Free Soil coalition in 1848, and Charles Sumner of Massachusetts, leader of the Conscience Whigs.

13-3b The Gold Rush and California Statehood

In 1848, workers building a sawmill on the American River near Sacramento discovered flecks of gold in the riverbed. The word gradually leaked out, reaching the East in August 1848, where a public that had been surfeited with tall tales out of the West greeted this news with skepticism. But in December, Polk's final message to Congress confirmed the "extraordinary" discoveries of gold. Two days later, a tea caddy containing 320 ounces of pure gold from California arrived in Washington. Now all doubts disappeared. By spring 1849, 100,000 gold-seekers were poised to take off by foot on the overland trail or by ship—either around Cape Horn or to the isthmus of Central America, where, after a land crossing, they could board another ship to take them up the Pacific Coast. Eighty thousand actually made it that first year (5,000 succumbed to a cholera epidemic).

San Francisco became a boomtown and a new center of Pacific trade, with ships arriving filled with cargos of wheat, coffee, sugar, rice, and other commodities from Chile, Australia, China, and Alaska. Men and women (outnumbered 10 to 1 by men) rushed to California from Chile, Mexico, Peru, France, Belgium, and China. African Americans and Miwok Indians also worked as miners—although they were quickly pushed aside by land-hungry Anglo-Americans, who in 1850 instituted discriminatory laws that not only privileged whites but forced the expulsion of Mexicans—many of whom were American citizens under the Treaty of Guadalupe Hidalgo. While a few miners struck it rich, most instead earned a bare pittance—and soon raced off to new gold rushes in British Columbia, Colorado, and Nevada.

The population increase meant that the political organization of California could not be postponed: Miners needed law and order; settlers needed courts, land and water laws, mail service, and other amenities of established government. In New Mexico, the 60,000 former Mexican citizens, now Americans, also needed a governmental structure for their new allegiance. Nor could the growing Mormon community at Salt Lake be ignored.

Still, the slavery question paralyzed Congress. In December 1848, lame-duck president Polk recommended extension of the Missouri Compromise 36°30′ line to the Pacific. The Whig-controlled House defied him, reaffirmed the Wilmot Proviso, drafted a bill to organize California as a free territory, and debated abolishing the slave trade and even slavery itself in the District of Columbia. Fistfights flared in Congress; southerners declared that they would secede if any of those measures became law; the Democratic Senate quashed all the bills. A southern caucus asked Calhoun to draft an address setting forth its position. He eagerly complied, producing in January 1849 a document that breathed fire against "unconstitutional" northern efforts to keep slavery out of the territories. Calhoun reminded southerners that their "property, prosperity, equality, liberty, and safety" were at stake and prophesied secession if the South did not prevail.

But Calhoun's firebomb fizzled. Only two-fifths of the southern congressmen and senators signed it. Southern Whigs wanted nothing to do with it. They looked forward to good times in the Taylor administration and opposed rocking the boat.

They were in for a rude shock. Taylor viewed matters as a nationalist, not as a southerner. He proposed to admit California and New Mexico (the latter comprising present-day New Mexico, Arizona, Nevada, Utah, and part of Colorado) immediately as *states*, skipping the territorial stage.

From the South came cries of outrage. Immediate admission would bring in two more free states because slavery had not existed under Mexican law, and most of the 49ers were Free Soil in sentiment. With the administration's support, Californians held a convention in October 1849, drew up a constitution excluding slavery, and applied to Congress for admission as a state. Taylor's end run would tip the existing balance of 15 slave and 15 free states in favor of the North, probably forever. The South would lose its de facto veto in the Senate. "For the first time," said freshman senator Jefferson Davis of Mississippi, "we are about permanently to destroy the balance of power between the sections." Davis insisted that slave labor was suitable to mining and that slavery should be permitted in California. Southerners vowed never to "consent to be thus degraded and enslaved" by such a "monstrous trick and injustice" as admission of California as a free state.

13.7 The California Gold Rush Prospectors for gold in the foothills of California's Sierra Nevada came from all over the world, including China. This photograph shows American-born and Chinese miners near Auburn, California, a year or two after the initial gold rush of 1849. It illustrates the original technology of separating gravel from gold by panning or by washing the gravel away in a sluice box, leaving the heavier gold flakes behind.

13-4 The Compromise of 1850

Q *What issues were at stake in the congressional debates that led to the Compromise of 1850? How successfully did the compromise resolve these issues?*

California and New Mexico became the focal points of a cluster of slavery issues that faced the Congress of 1849–1850. An earlier Supreme Court decision (*Prigg v. Pennsylvania*, 1842) had relieved state officials of any obligation to enforce the return of **fugitive slaves** who had escaped into free states, declaring that this was a federal responsibility. Southerners therefore demanded a strong national fugitive slave law (in utter disregard of their oft-stated commitment to states' rights); antislavery northerners, on the other hand, were calling for an end to the disgraceful buying and selling of slaves in the national capital; and in the Southwest, a shooting war threatened to break out between Texas and New Mexico. Having won the Rio Grande as their southern border with Mexico, Texans insisted that the river must also mark their western border with New Mexico. (That would have given Texas more than half of the present state of New Mexico.)

This dispute also involved slavery because the terms of Texas's annexation authorized the state to split into as many as five states, and the territory it carved out of New Mexico would create the potential for still another slave state.

These problems produced both a crisis and an opportunity. The crisis lay in the threat to break up the Union. Southern states agreed to meet at Nashville in June 1850 "to devise and adopt some mode of resistance to northern aggression." Few doubted that the mode would be secession unless Congress met southern demands at least halfway, but Congress got off to an unpromising start. Sectional disputes prevented either major party from commanding a majority in electing a Speaker of the House. Through three weeks and 62 ballots, the contest went on while tempers shortened. Northerners and southerners shouted insults at each other, fistfights broke out, and a Mississippian drew a revolver during one heated debate. Southern warnings of secession became a litany: "If, by your legislation, you seek to drive us from the territories of California and New Mexico," thundered Robert Toombs of Georgia, "*I am for disunion.*" On the 63rd ballot, the exhausted legislators finally elected Howell Cobb of Georgia as Speaker by a plurality rather than a majority.

13-4a The Senate Debates

As he had in 1820 and 1833, Henry Clay hoped to turn the crisis into an opportunity. Seventy-two years old, a veteran of 30 years in Congress, three times an unsuccessful candidate for president, Clay was the most respected and still the most magnetic figure in the Senate. A nationalist from the border state of Kentucky, he hoped to unite North and South in a compromise. On January 29, 1850, he presented eight proposals to the Senate and supported them with an eloquent speech, the first of many to be heard in that body during what turned out to be the most famous congressional debate in U.S. history. Clay grouped the first six of his proposals into three pairs, each pair offering one concession to the North and one to the South. The first pair would admit California as a free state but would organize the rest of the Mexican cession without restrictions against slavery. The second would settle the Texas boundary dispute in favor of New Mexico but would compensate Texas to enable the state to pay off bonds it had sold when it was an independent republic. (Many holders of the Texas bonds were southerners.) The third pair of proposals would abolish the slave trade in the District of Columbia but would guarantee the continued existence of slavery there unless both Maryland and Virginia consented to abolition. Of Clay's final two proposals, one affirmed that Congress had no jurisdiction over the interstate slave trade; the other called for a strong national fugitive slave law.

At the end of a long, grueling bargaining process, the final shape of the **Compromise of 1850** closely resembled Clay's package. The public face of this process featured set speeches in the Senate, the most notable of which were those of John C. Calhoun, Daniel Webster, and William H. Seward, a rising star of the new generation. Each spoke for one of the three principal viewpoints on the issues.

On March 4, Calhoun, suffering from consumption (he would die within a month), sat shrouded in flannel as a colleague read his speech to a rapt audience. Unless northerners returned fugitive slaves in good faith, Calhoun warned, unless they consented to the expansion of slavery into the territories, the South might not remain in the Union.

Webster's speech three days later was both a reply to Calhoun and an appeal to the North for compromise. "I wish to speak today, not as a Massachusetts man, nor as a Northern man, but as an American," he said. "I speak to-day for the preservation of the Union. Hear me for my cause." Although Webster had voted for the Wilmot Proviso, he now urged Yankees not to insist upon it. Nature would exclude slavery from New Mexico. He even endorsed a fugitive slave law.

On March 11, Seward expressed the antislavery position. Both slavery and compromise were "radically wrong and essentially vicious," he said. In reply to Calhoun's arguments for the constitutional protection of slavery in the territories, he invoked the law of God in whose sight all persons were equal. Instead of legislating the expansion of slavery or the return of fugitive slaves, he said, the country should be considering how to bring slavery peacefully to an end, for "you cannot roll back the tide of social progress."

13-4b Passage of the Compromise

While these speeches were being delivered, committee members worked ceaselessly behind the scenes to fashion compromise legislation. But in reaching for a compromise, Clay chose what turned out to be the wrong tactic. He lumped most of his proposals together in a single bill, hoping that supporters of any given part of the compromise would vote for the whole in order to win the part they liked. Instead, most senators and representatives voted against the package in order to defeat the parts they disliked. President Taylor continued to insist on the immediate admission of California (and New Mexico, when it was ready) with no quid pro quo for the South. Exhausted and discouraged, Clay fled Washington's summer heat, leaving a young senator from Illinois, Stephen A. Douglas, to lead the forces of compromise.

Another rising star of the new generation, Douglas reversed Clay's tactics. Starting with a core of supporters made up of Democrats from the Old Northwest and Whigs from the upper South, he built a majority for each part of the compromise by submitting it separately and adding its supporters to his core: northerners for a free California, southerners for a fugitive slave law, and so on. This effort benefited from Taylor's sudden death on July 9 (of gastroenteritis, after consuming large quantities of iced milk and cherries on a hot Fourth of July). The new president, Millard Fillmore, was a conservative Whig from New York who gave his support to the compromise. One after another, in August and September, the separate measures became law: the admission of California as a free state; the organization of the rest of the Mexican cession into the two territories of New Mexico and Utah without restrictions against slavery; the settlement of the Texas–New Mexico border dispute in favor of New Mexico and the compensation of Texas with $10 million; the abolition of the slave trade in the District of Columbia and the guarantee of slavery there; and the passage of a new fugitive slave law. When it was over, most Americans breathed a sigh of relief, and President Fillmore christened the Compromise of 1850 "a final settlement" of all sectional problems. Calhounites in the South and antislavery activists in the North branded the compromise a betrayal of principle, but for the time being they seemed to be in a minority.

The compromise produced consequences different from what many anticipated. California came in as the 16th free state, but its senators during the 1850s were in fact conservative Democrats who voted with the South on most issues. California law even allowed slave owners to keep their slaves while sojourning in the state. The territorial legislatures of Utah and New Mexico legalized slavery, but few slaves were brought there. And the fugitive slave law generated more trouble and controversy than all the other parts of this final settlement combined.

13-4c The Fugitive Slave Law

The Constitution required that a slave who escaped into a free state must be returned to his or her owner, but it failed to specify how that should be done. Under a 1793 law, slave owners

What They Said

The Senate Debates the Compromise of 1850

Two of the most notable Senate speeches during the debates over the Compromise of 1850 were delivered by Daniel Webster and William H. Seward. Many of Webster's former antislavery admirers repudiated him after his much-anticipated speech. Seward, by contrast, was catapulted into renown because of what became known as his "higher law" speech. In these selections Webster and Seward reveal their differences regarding a fugitive slave law as part of the compromise.

▶ Daniel Webster

But I will state ... one complaint of the South, which has in my opinion just foundation; and that is, that there has been found at the North, among individuals and among the Legislatures of the North, a disinclination to perform, fully, their constitutional duties, in regard to the return of persons bound to service, who have escaped into the free States. In that respect, it is my judgement that the South is right, and the North is wrong. Every member of every northern Legislature is bound, by oath, like every other officer in the country, to support the Constitution of the United States; and this article of the Constitution, which says to these States, they shall deliver up fugitives from service, is as binding in honor and conscience as any other article. No man fulfills his duty in any Legislature who sets himself to find excuses, evasions, escapes from the constitutional obligation...

I say that the South has been injured in this respect, and has a right to complain. Then, sir, there are those abolition societies, of which I am unwilling to speak, but in regard to which I have very clear notions and opinions. I do not think them useful. I think their operations for the last twenty years have produced nothing good or valuable ... I cannot but see what mischiefs their interference with the South has produced. And is it not plain to every man?

▶ William H. Seward

We deem the principle of the law for the recapture of fugitives ... unjust, unconstitutional, and immoral ... Your Constitution and laws convert hospitality to the refugee, from the most degrading oppression on earth, into a crime, but all mankind except you esteem that hospitality a virtue. The right of extradition of a fugitive from justice, is not admitted by the law of nature and of nations, but rests in voluntary compacts...

I know that there are laws of various sorts which regulate the conduct of men. There are constitutions and statutes, codes mercantile and codes civil; but when we are legislating for States, especially when we are founding States, all these laws must be brought to the standard of the laws of God, and must be tried by that standard, and must stand or fall by it...

The Constitution regulates our stewardship; the Constitution devotes the domain to union, to justice, to defence, to welfare, and to liberty.

But there is a higher law than the Constitution, which regulates our authority over the domain, and devotes it to the same noble purposes. The territory is a part—no inconsiderable part—of the common heritage of mankind, bestowed upon them by the Creator of the Universe. We are his stewards, and must so discharge our trust so as to secure, in the highest attainable degree, their happiness.... .

Q How do Webster's and Seward's views of the Constitution differ? How does Webster justify returning fugitive slaves to slavery? On what grounds does Seward justify not enforcing a fugitive slave law?

Sources: (top) Daniel Webster's congressional speech March 7, 1850. From *Appendix* to the Congressional Globe, 31st Congress, 1st Session, vol. XXII, pt. 1 (1850), 269, 274–276; (bottom) William H. Seward's congressional speech March 11, 1850. From *Appendix* to the Congressional Globe, 31st Congress, 1st Session, vol. XXII, pt. 1 (1850), 262, 263, 265, 266, 268.

---

could take their recaptured property before any state or federal court to prove ownership. This procedure worked well enough so long as officials in free states were willing to cooperate. But as the antislavery movement gained momentum in the 1830s, some officials proved uncooperative. And professional slave-catchers sometimes went too far—kidnapping free blacks, forging false affidavits to "prove" they were slaves, and selling them south into bondage. Several northern states responded by passing antikidnapping laws that gave alleged fugitives the right of trial by jury. The laws also prescribed criminal penalties for kidnapping. The U.S. Supreme Court declared Pennsylvania's anti-kidnapping law unconstitutional. But the Court also ruled that enforcing the Constitution's fugitive slave clause was entirely a federal responsibility, thereby absolving the states of any need to cooperate in enforcing it. Nine northern states thereupon passed **personal liberty laws** prohibiting the use of state facilities (courts, jails, police or sheriffs, and so on) in the recapture of fugitives.

Fugitive slaves vividly dramatized the poignancy and cruelties of bondage. A man or woman risking all for freedom was not an abstract issue but a real human being whose plight invited sympathy and help. Consequently, many northerners who were not necessarily opposed to slavery in the South nonetheless felt outrage at the idea of fugitives being seized in a land of freedom and returned to slavery. The **"underground railroad"** that helped spirit slaves out of bondage took on legendary status. Stories of secret chambers where fugitives were hidden, dramatic trips at night between stations on the underground, and clever or heroic measures to foil pursuing bloodhounds exaggerated the legend.

Probably fewer than 1,000 of a total 3 million slaves actually escaped to freedom each year. But to southerners the return of those fugitives—like the question of the legality of slavery in California or New Mexico—was a matter of *honor* and *rights*. "Although the loss of property is felt," said Senator James Mason of Virginia, sponsor of the Fugitive Slave Act, "the loss of honor is felt still more." The fugitive slave law, said another southern politician, was "the only measure of the Compromise [of 1850] calculated to secure the rights of the South." Southerners therefore regarded obedience to the fugitive slave law as a test of the North's good faith in carrying out the compromise.

The provisions of that law were extraordinary. It created federal commissioners who could issue warrants for arrests of fugitives and before whom a slaveholder would bring a captured fugitive to prove ownership. All the slaveholder needed for proof was an affidavit from a slave-state court or the testimony of white witnesses. The fugitive had no right to testify on his or her own behalf. The commissioner received a fee of $10 if he found the owner's claim valid, but only $5 if he let the fugitive go. (The difference was supposedly justified by the larger amount of paperwork required to return the fugitive to slavery.) The federal treasury would pay all costs of enforcement. The commissioner could call on federal marshals to apprehend fugitives, and the marshals in turn could deputize any citizen to help. A citizen who refused could be fined up to $1,000, and anyone who harbored a fugitive or obstructed his or her capture would be subject to imprisonment.

13-4d *The Slave-Catchers*

Abolitionists denounced the law as draconian, immoral, and unconstitutional. They vowed to resist it. Opportunities soon came, as slave owners sent agents north to recapture fugitives, some of whom had escaped years earlier (the act set no statute of limitations). In February 1851, slave-catchers arrested a black man living with his family in Indiana and returned him to an owner who said he had run away 19 years before. A Maryland man tried to claim ownership of a Philadelphia woman who he said had escaped 22 years earlier; he also wanted her six children, all of whom were born in Philadelphia. In this case, the commissioner disallowed his claim to both mother and children, but statistics show that the law was rigged in favor of the claimants. In the first 15 months of its operation, 84 fugitives were returned to slavery and only 5 were released. (For the entire decade of the 1850s, the ratio was 332 to 11.)

Two of the most famous of these fugitive slaves were William and Ellen Craft, whose successful struggle for liberty inspired other slaves and abolitionists on both sides of the Atlantic. Both born in slavery, William and Ellen were married in Georgia in 1846. Unwilling to give birth to children who might be sold away from her, Ellen plotted with her husband to escape to the North. Light enough to pass for white (she was the daughter of her master and his light-skinned concubine), Ellen sewed herself a pair of trousers and posed as a deaf-mute invalid young man traveling to Philadelphia for medical treatment attended by "his" slave William. After some close calls, they made it to Philadelphia at the end of 1848 and moved on to Boston in 1849.

After passage of the Fugitive Slave Law in 1850, however, two agents from Georgia appeared in Boston to recapture the Crafts. Local abolitionists spirited them away to Canada and then to England, where the Crafts lived for the next 19 years and had five children.

Unable to protect their freedom through legal means, many other blacks, with the support of white allies, also resorted to flight and resistance. Thousands of northern blacks fled to Canada—3,000 in the last three months of 1850 alone. In February 1851, slave-catchers arrested a fugitive who had taken the name Shadrach when he escaped from Virginia a year earlier. They rushed him to the federal courthouse, where a few deputy marshals held him, pending a hearing. But a group of black men broke into the courtroom, overpowered the deputies, and spirited Shadrach out of the country to Canada. This was too much for the Fillmore administration. In April 1851, another fugitive, Thomas Sims, was arrested in Boston, and the president sent 250 soldiers to help 300 armed deputies enforce the law and return Sims to slavery.

Continued rescues and escapes kept matters at a fever pitch for the rest of the decade. In the fall of 1851, a Maryland slave owner and his son accompanied federal marshals to Christiana, Pennsylvania, a Quaker village, where two of the man's slaves had taken refuge. The hunters ran into a fusillade of gunfire from a house where a dozen black men were protecting the fugitives. When the shooting stopped, the slave owner was dead and his son was seriously wounded. Three of the blacks fled to Canada. This time Fillmore sent in the marines. They helped marshals arrest 30 black men and half a dozen whites who were indicted for treason. But the U.S. attorney dropped charges after a jury acquitted the first defendant, a Quaker.

Two of the most famous fugitive slave cases of the 1850s ended in tragedy. In spring 1854, federal marshals in Boston arrested a Virginia fugitive, Anthony Burns. Angry abolitionists poured into Boston to save him. Some of them tried to attack the federal courthouse, where a deputy was killed in an exchange of gunfire. But the new president, Franklin Pierce, was determined not to back down. "Incur any expense," he wired the district attorney in Boston, "to enforce the law." After every legal move to free Burns had failed, Pierce sent federal troops. While thousands of angry Yankees lined the streets under American flags hanging upside down to signify the loss of liberty in the cradle of the Revolution, 200 marines and soldiers marched this lone black man back into bondage.

Two years later, Margaret Garner escaped from Kentucky to Ohio with her husband and four children. When a posse of marshals and deputies caught up with them, Margaret seized a kitchen knife and tried to kill her children and herself rather than return to slavery. She managed to cut her three-year-old daughter's throat before she was overpowered. After complicated legal maneuvers, the federal commissioner remanded the fugitives to their Kentucky owner. He promptly sold them down the river to Arkansas, and, in a steamboat accident along the way, one of Margaret Garner's sons drowned in the Mississippi.

Such events had a profound impact on public emotions. Most northerners were not abolitionists, and few of them regarded black people as equals, but millions of them moved closer to an antislavery—or perhaps it would be more accurate to say anti-southern—position in response to the shock of seeing armed slave-catchers on their streets. "When it was all over," agreed two previously conservative Whigs in Boston after the Anthony Burns affair, "I put my face in my hands and wept I could do nothing less…. We went to bed one night old-fashioned, conservative, compromise Union Whigs and waked up stark mad Abolitionists."

Several northern states passed new personal liberty laws in defiance of the South. Although those laws did not make it impossible to recover fugitives, they made it so difficult, expensive, and time consuming that many slave owners gave up trying. The failure of the North to honor the Fugitive Slave Law, part of the Compromise of 1850, was one of the South's bitter grievances in the 1850s. Several southern states cited it as one of their reasons for seceding in 1861.

13-4e *Uncle Tom's Cabin*

A novel inspired by the plight of fugitive slaves further intensified public sentiment. Harriet Beecher Stowe was a member of a prominent New England family of clergymen and writers, and was herself a short story writer. In the 1840s, while living in Cincinnati with her husband, a minister, she became acquainted with fugitive slaves who had escaped across the Ohio River. Outraged by the Fugitive Slave Act of 1850, in 1851 she began to write a new piece of fiction—managing to write a chapter a week after she had put her children to bed.

Uncle Tom's Cabin became a runaway best seller, and was eventually translated into 20 languages. The novel's powerful central theme was the tragedy of the breakup of families by slavery—dramatized in scenes that would become an important part of American popular culture, such as the slave Eliza's escape across the ice-choked Ohio River to save her son from a slave trader. Throughout the novel Stowe spoke directly to white women readers, asking them to imagine being torn from their own children. Yet, it was not just women who responded to her calls to end slavery: Men, too, wrote of being deeply affected by the tragic story she told.

Although banned in some parts of the South, *Uncle Tom's Cabin* found a wide but hostile readership there. Pro-slavery authors rushed into print with more than a dozen novels challenging Stowe's themes, but all of them together made nothing like the impact of *Uncle Tom's Cabin*. The book helped shape a whole generation's view of slavery.

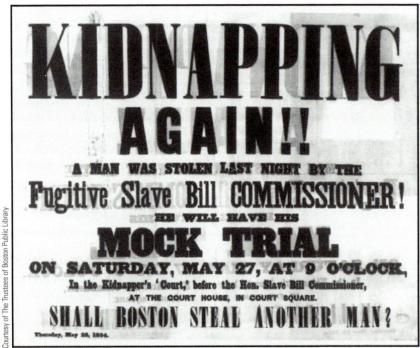

13.8 Kidnapping Again! This is a typical poster printed by abolitionist opponents of the Fugitive Slave Law. It was intended to rally the citizens of Boston against the recapture and reenslavement of Anthony Burns, a fugitive slave from Virginia seized in Boston in May 1854.

Q *How does this poster attempt to arouse the reader's outrage?*

13.9 **Harriet Tubman** Born into slavery in Maryland around 1822, Harriet Tubman escaped to freedom in 1849, settling at first in Philadelphia. Despite the many dangers she faced, Tubman returned to the South over and over in the years before the Civil War, helping her own relatives as well as dozens of other slaves to escape north. Wanted posters throughout the upper South described this "Moses," as Tubman was called, but she eluded capture. During the Civil War the intrepid Tubman worked for the Union army as a nurse and cook, as well as a scout and spy in Confederate territory. Tubman was also active in the woman suffrage movement late in the century. Working by necessity in secret before the Civil War, today Tubman is remembered, along with Frederick Douglass, as one of the most prominent abolitionists of the 19th century.

13-5 Filibustering

Q *How was filibustering related to demands for the expansion of slavery?*

If the prospects for slavery in New Mexico appeared unpromising, southerners could contemplate a closer region where slavery already existed—Cuba. Enjoying an economic boom based on slave-grown sugar, this Spanish colony only 90 miles from American shores had nearly 400,000 slaves in 1850—more than any American state except Virginia. President Polk, his appetite for territory not yet sated by the acquisition of Texas, Oregon, and half of Mexico, offered Spain $100 million for Cuba in 1848. The Spanish foreign minister spurned the offer, stating that he would rather see the island sunk in the sea than sold.

13-5a *Cuba*

If money did not work, revolution might. Cuban planters, restive under Spanish rule, intrigued with American expansionists in the hope of fomenting an uprising on the island. Their leader was Narciso López, a Venezuelan-born Cuban soldier of fortune. In 1849, López recruited several hundred American adventurers for the first **"filibustering"** expedition against Cuba (from the Spanish *filibustero*, a freebooter or pirate). When President Taylor ordered the navy to prevent López's ships from leaving New York, López shifted his operations to the friendlier environs of New Orleans, where he raised a new force of filibusters, many of them Mexican War veterans. Port officials in New Orleans looked the other way when the expedition sailed in May 1850, but Spanish troops

13.10 Harriet Beecher Stowe and Family Harriet Beecher Stowe, the author of *Uncle Tom's Cabin*, was part of a large and influential family. In this formal 1850 photograph, Stowe is seated on the far right in the first row; her father, Lyman Beecher, one of the most prominent ministers in American history, is seated in the middle of the row. Left of Lyman Beecher is Harriet Beecher Stowe's sister Catherine Beecher, famous both as an educator and for her books on household management that expounded the national importance of women in their domestic roles. In the back row, on the right, stands Stowe's brother Henry Ward Beecher, widely regarded as the most inspiring preacher of the post–Civil War era. While Harriet's father Lyman had been a stern, Calvinist-inspired minister demanding individual repentance during numerous religious revivals before the Civil War, his son Henry instead emphasized the importance of the heart and individual responsibility in his own preaching. We can see that same emphasis on the central importance of emotion and "right feeling" in Harriet Beecher Stowe's abolitionist writings.

Q What does this formal photograph reveal about middle-class family relationships in the mid-19th century?

drove the filibusters into the sea after they had established a beachhead in Cuba.

Undaunted, López escaped and returned to a hero's welcome in the South, where he raised men and money for a third try in 1851. This time, William Crittenden of Kentucky, nephew of the U.S. attorney general, commanded the 420 Americans in the expedition, but the invasion ended in fiasco and tragedy. Spanish soldiers suppressed a local uprising timed to coincide with the invasion and then defeated the filibusters, killing 200 and capturing the rest. López was garroted in the public square of Havana. Then 50 American prisoners, including Crittenden, were lined up and executed by firing squad.

These events dampened southerners' enthusiasm for Cuba, but only for a time. "Cuba must be ours," declared Jefferson Davis, in order to "increase the number of slave-holding constituencies." In 1852, the Democrats nominated Franklin Pierce of New Hampshire for president. Although a Yankee, Pierce had a reputation as a "doughface"—a northern man with southern principles. Southern Democrats were delighted with his nomination. Pierce was "as reliable as Calhoun himself," wrote one, while another said that "a nomination so favorable to the South had not been anticipated." Especially gratifying was Pierce's support for annexing Cuba, which he made one of the top priorities of his new administration after winning a landslide victory over a demoralized Whig Party weakened by schism between its northern and southern wings.

Pierce covertly encouraged a new filibustering expedition to Cuba. This one was to be led by former governor John Quitman of Mississippi. While Quitman was recruiting hundreds of volunteers, southerners in Congress introduced a resolution to suspend the neutrality law that prohibited American interference in the internal affairs of other countries. But at the last moment Pierce backed off, fearful of political damage in the North if his administration became openly identified with filibustering. The Quitman expedition never sailed.

Pierce again tried to buy Cuba, instructing the American minister in Madrid to offer Spain $130 million. The minister was Pierre Soulé, a flamboyant Louisianan who managed to alienate most Spaniards by his clumsy intriguing. Soulé's crowning act came in October 1854 at a meeting with the American ministers to Britain and France in Ostend, Belgium. He persuaded them to sign what came to be known as the Ostend Manifesto. "Cuba is as necessary to the North American republic as any of its present ... family of states," declared this document. If Spain persisted in refusing to sell, then "by every law, human and divine, we shall be justified in wresting it from Spain."

This "manifesto of the brigands," as antislavery Americans called it, caused an international uproar. The administration repudiated the Ostend Manifesto and recalled Soulé. Nevertheless, acquisition of Cuba remained an objective of the Democratic Party. The issue played a role in both the 1860 presidential election and the secession controversy during 1860 and 1861. Meanwhile, American filibustering shifted its focus 750 miles south of Havana to Nicaragua. There, the most remarkable of the *filibusteros*, William Walker, had proclaimed himself president and restored the institution of slavery.

13-5b The Gray-Eyed Man of Destiny

A native of Tennessee and a brilliant, restless man, Walker had earned a medical degree from the University of Pennsylvania and studied and practiced law in New Orleans before joining the 1849 rush to California. Weighing less than 120 pounds, Walker seemed an unlikely fighter or leader of men, but he fought three duels, and his luminous eyes, which seemed to transfix his fellows, won him the sobriquet "gray-eyed man of destiny."

Walker found his true calling in filibustering. At the time, numerous raids were taking place back and forth across the border with Mexico, some of them staged to seize more of that country for the United States. In 1853, Walker led a ragged "army" of footloose 49ers into Baja California and Sonora and declared the region an independent republic. Exhaustion and desertion depleted his troops, however, and the Mexicans drove the survivors back to California.

Walker decided to try again, with another goal. Many southerners eyed Nicaragua's potential for growing cotton, sugar, coffee, and other crops. The unstable Nicaraguan government offered a tempting target. In 1854, Walker signed a contract with rebel leaders in the civil war of the moment. The following spring, he led an advance guard of filibusters to Nicaragua and proclaimed himself commander-in-chief of the rebel forces. At the head of 2,000 American volunteers, he gained control of the country and named himself president in 1856. The Pierce administration extended diplomatic recognition to Walker's regime.

The other Central American republics soon formed an alliance to invade Nicaragua and overthrow Walker. To win greater support from the southern states, Walker issued a decree in September 1856 reinstituting slavery in Nicaragua. A convention of southern economic promoters meeting in Savannah praised Walker's efforts "to introduce civilization in the States of Central America, and to develop these rich and productive regions by slave labor." Boatloads of new recruits arrived in Nicaragua from New Orleans, but in spring 1857, they succumbed to disease and to the Central American armies.

Walker escaped to New Orleans, where he was welcomed as a hero. He had no trouble recruiting men for another attempt, but the navy stopped him in November 1857. Southern congressmen condemned the naval commander and encouraged Walker to try again. He did, in December 1858, after a New Orleans jury refused to convict him of violating the neutrality law. On this third expedition, Walker's ship struck a reef and sank. Undaunted, he tried yet again. He wrote a book to raise funds for another invasion of Nicaragua, urging "the hearts of Southern youth to answer the call of honor... . The true field for the expansion of slavery is in tropical America." A few more southern youths answered the call, but they were stopped in Honduras. There, on September 12, 1860, the gray-eyed man met his destiny before a firing squad.

Conclusion

Within the three-year period from 1845 to 1848, the annexation of Texas, the settlement of the Oregon boundary dispute with Britain, and the acquisition by force of New Mexico and California from Mexico added 1,150,000 square miles to the United States. This expansion was America's "Manifest Destiny," according to Senator Stephen A. Douglas of Illinois. He further proclaimed:

> Increase, and multiply, and expand, is the law of this nation's existence. You cannot limit this great republic by mere boundary lines. Any one of you gentlemen might as well say to a son twelve years old that he is big enough, and must not grow any larger, and in order to prevent his growth put a hoop around him and keep him to his present size. Either the hoop must burst and be rent asunder, or the child must die. So it would be with this great nation.

But other Americans feared that the country could not absorb such rapid growth without strains that might break it apart. At the outbreak of the war with Mexico, Ralph Waldo Emerson predicted that "the United States will conquer Mexico, but it will be as the man swallows the arsenic, which brings him down in turn. Mexico will poison us." Emerson proved correct. The poison was the reopening of the question of slavery's expansion, which had supposedly been settled by the Missouri Compromise in 1820. The admission of Texas as a huge new slave state and the possibility that more slave states might be carved out of the territory acquired from Mexico provoked northern congressmen to pass the Wilmot Proviso. Southerners bristled at this attempt to prevent the further expansion of slavery. Threats of secession and civil war poisoned the atmosphere in 1849 and 1850.

The Compromise of 1850 defused the crisis and appeared to settle the issue once again, but events would soon prove that this compromise had merely postponed the crisis. The fugitive slave issue and filibustering expeditions to acquire more slave territory kept sectional controversies smoldering. In 1854, the Kansas-Nebraska Act would cause them to burst into a hotter flame than ever.

CHAPTER REVIEW

Review

1. What impulses lay behind the "Manifest Destiny" of America's westward expansion?
2. What were the causes and consequences of the Mexican War?
3. How did the question of slavery affect the election of 1848?
4. What issues were at stake in the congressional debates that led to the Compromise of 1850? How successfully did the compromise resolve these issues?
5. How was filibustering related to demands for the expansion of slavery?

Critical Thinking

1. Between 1803 and 1845, the territorial size of the United States increased by only 5 percent (with the acquisition of Florida in 1819). Yet, in the three years from 1845 to 1848, the size of the United States mushroomed by another 50 percent. How do you explain this remarkable phenomenon?
2. Why was the issue of slavery in the territories so important and controversial in the 1840s and 1850s when slavery already existed in half of the states?

Identifications

Review your understanding of the following key terms, people, and events for this chapter (terms in bold in text are included in the Glossary).

Young America movement, p. 354
Manifest Destiny, p. 354
missions, p. 355
presidios, p. 355
Great American Desert, p. 357
Mormons, p. 357
tejanos, p. 358
Alamo, p. 358
Wilmot Proviso, p. 363
Treaty of Guadalupe Hidalgo, p. 364
popular sovereignty, p. 364
Conscience Whigs, p. 364
Free-Soilers, p. 364
fugitive slaves, p. 366
Compromise of 1850, p. 367
personal liberty laws, p. 369
underground railroad, p. 369
filibustering, p. 371

Suggested Readings

On Manifest Destiny and filibustering, see **Amy S. Greenberg**, *Manifest Manhood and the Antebellum American Empire* (2005). For an excellent account of the history of the West, see **Robert V. Hine** and **John Mack Faragher**, *The American West: An Interpretive History* (2000). On the rise of a Native American empire that resisted European colonization, see **Pekka Hämäläinen**, *The Comanche Empire* (2009). The political polarization produced by the controversy over the annexation of Texas is clearly laid out by **Joel H. Silbey**,

Storm over Texas: The Annexation Controversy and the Road to Civil War (2005). For the Mexican War, see **Amy Greenberg**, *A Wicked War: Polk, Clay, Lincoln and the 1846 U.S. Invasion of Mexico* (2012). On the gold rush, see **Malcolm J. Rohrbough**, *Days of Gold: The California Gold Rush and the American Nation* (1997); **Susan Lee Johnson**, *Roaring Camp: The Social World of The California Gold Rush* (2000); and **David Igler**, *The Great Ocean: Pacific Worlds from Captain Cook to the Gold Rush* (2013). For the conflict provoked by the issue of slavery's expansion into territory acquired from Mexico, a classic is **David M. Potter**, *The Impending Crisis 1848–1861* (1976); see also **Michael A. Morrison**, *Slavery and the American West: The Eclipse of Manifest Destiny and the Coming of the Civil War* (1997); and **Leonard D. Richards**, *The Slave Power: The Free North and Southern Domination, 1780–1860* (2000). The partisan roots of sectional conflict are emphasized in **Michael F. Holt**, *The Fate of Their Country: Politicians, Slavery Extension, and the Coming of the Civil War* (2004). On filibustering, see **Robert E. May**, *Manifest Destiny's Underworld: Filibustering in Antebellum America* (2004).

> **MINDTAP** is a fully online personalized learning experience built upon Cengage Learning content. MindTap® combines student learning tools—readings, multimedia, activities, and assessments—into a singular Learning Path that guides students through the course and helps students develop the critical thinking, analysis, and communication skills that are essential to academic and professional success.

14 The Gathering Tempest, 1853–1860

14-1 Kansas and the Rise of the Republican Party
Learning Objective: *Explain the causes of the demise of the Whig Party in the 1850s as well as the appeal of the Republican Party that replaced it.*

- The Kansas-Nebraska Act
- Death of the Whig Party

14-2 Immigration and Nativism
Learning Objective: *Define nativism and discuss its relationship to the issue of slavery.*

- Immigrants in Politics
- The Rise of the Know-Nothings
- The Decline of Nativism

14-3 Violent Conflict in the 1850s
Learning Objective: *Discuss the causes of violence in Kansas in the 1850s.*

- Bleeding Kansas
- The Caning of Sumner

14-4 The Election of 1856
Learning Objective: *Explain how the issue of slavery affected the election of 1856.*

- The Dred Scott Case
- The Lecompton Constitution

14-5 The Economy in the 1850s
Learning Objective: *Summarize the differences between economic development in the North and the South during the 1840s and 1850s.*

- "The American System of Manufactures"
- The Southern Economy
- The Sovereignty of King Cotton
- Labor Conditions in the North
- The Panic of 1857
- Sectionalism and the Panic
- The Free-Labor Ideology
- *The Impending Crisis*
- Southern Nonslaveholders

14-6 The Lincoln-Douglas Debates
Learning Objective: *Identify the major issues of the Lincoln-Douglas debates.*

- The Freeport Doctrine
- John Brown at Harpers Ferry

14.1 Stump Speaking George Caleb Bingham's 1853–1854 genre painting *Stump Speaking* captures the cultural importance of politics in American life in the pre–Civil War era. Here a diverse rural audience listens to an open-air speaker. We can see plainly dressed men and women sitting on the ground and listening intently, a bored child, and well-fed and well-dressed gentlemen seated on chairs. The standing man in the foreground, wearing hat and coat, seems about to interrupt the speaker—or perhaps is just listening especially closely. This portrait of political engagement reminds us that oratory was a central part of the practice of politics in mid-19th-century America.

THE WOUNDS caused by the 1850 battle over slavery in the territories had barely healed when they were reopened. This time the strife concerned the question of slavery in the Louisiana Purchase territory, an issue presumably settled 34 years earlier by the Missouri Compromise of 1820.

The Compromise of 1820 had admitted Missouri as a slave state but had banned slavery from the rest of the Purchase north of 36°30". To obtain southern support for the organization of Kansas and Nebraska as territories, Senator Stephen Douglas consented to the repeal of this provision. Northern outrage at this repudiation of a "sacred contract" killed the Whig Party and gave birth to the antislavery Republican Party. In 1857, the Supreme Court added insult to injury with the **Dred Scott** decision, which denied Congress the power to restrict slavery from the territories. The ominous reorientation of national politics along sectional lines was accompanied by a bloody civil war in Kansas and a raid on the federal arsenal at **Harpers Ferry**, Virginia, by **John Brown** and his followers. ■

CHRONOLOGY

1852	Plenary Council of Catholic Church seeks tax support for parochial schools
1853	American Party ("Know-Nothings") emerges
1854	Crimean War begins • Congress passes Kansas-Nebraska Act • Republican Party organized • Antebellum immigration reaches peak
1855	Ethnic riots in several cities • "Border ruffian" legislature in Kansas legalizes slavery
1856	Civil war in Kansas • Preston Brooks canes Charles Sumner on Senate floor • Crimean War ends • Buchanan wins three-way presidential election
1857	Supreme Court issues Dred Scott decision • Lecompton constitution written in Kansas • Congress enacts lower tariff • Panic of 1857 • Helper's *Impending Crisis* published
1858	Kansas voters reject Lecompton constitution • Lincoln-Douglas debates
1859	Congress defeats federal slave code for territories • John Brown's raid at Harpers Ferry
1860	Shoemakers' strike in New England • Buchanan vetoes Homestead Act

14-1 Kansas and the Rise of the Republican Party

Q *Why did the Whig Party die, and why did the Republican Party emerge as the new majority party in the North?*

By 1853, land-hungry settlers had pushed up the Missouri River to its confluence with the Kansas and Platte rivers, and entrepreneurs were talking about a railroad across the continent to San Francisco. But settlement west of Missouri and land surveys for a railroad required the organization of this region as a territory. Accordingly, in 1853 the House passed a bill creating the Nebraska Territory, embracing the area north of Indian Territory (present-day Oklahoma) up to the Canadian border. But the House bill ran into trouble in the Senate. Under the Missouri Compromise, slavery would be excluded from the new territory. Having lost California, the pro-slavery forces were determined to salvage something from Nebraska. Missourians were particularly adamant, because a free Nebraska would leave them almost surrounded on three sides by free soil.

The sponsor of the Senate bill was Stephen A. Douglas, chairman of the Senate Committee on Territories. Only 5 feet 4 inches tall, Douglas had earned the nickname Little Giant for his parliamentary skill, which he had demonstrated most dramatically in helping pass the Compromise of 1850 through Congress. In Douglas's opinion, the application of popular sovereignty to the slavery question in New Mexico and Utah had been the centerpiece of the compromise. The initial draft of his Nebraska bill merely repeated the language used for those territories, specifying that when any portion of the Nebraska Territory came in as a state, it could do so "with or without slavery, as its constitution may provide."

This was not good enough for southern congressmen, who insisted on an explicit repeal of the Missouri Compromise. Sighing that this would "raise a hell of a storm," Douglas nevertheless agreed. He further agreed to divide the area in question into two territories: Kansas west of Missouri and Nebraska west of Iowa and Minnesota. To many northerners this looked suspiciously like a scheme to mark Kansas out for slavery and Nebraska for freedom.

14-1a The Kansas-Nebraska Act

The **Kansas-Nebraska Act** did "raise a hell of a storm." Contemporaries and historians have speculated endlessly on Douglas's motives. Some thought he wanted to win southern support for the presidential nomination in 1856. Perhaps, but he risked losing northern support. Others point out that Douglas's real estate holdings in Illinois would have increased in value if a transcontinental railroad were to traverse the Nebraska Territory and that southern opposition could block this route. The most likely reason, however, was Douglas's passionate belief in Manifest Destiny, in filling up the continent with American settlers and institutions. For this, he was willing to pay the South's price for support of his Kansas-Nebraska bill. But he failed to recognize the depth of northern opposition to the "slave power" and to the expansion of slavery. Douglas had no firm moral convictions about slavery. He said that he cared not whether the settlers voted slavery up or down; the important thing was to give them a chance to vote.

But many Americans did care. They regarded the expansion of slavery as a national question, and one that was too important to be left to territorial voters. One of them was an old acquaintance of Douglas, **Abraham Lincoln**. An antislavery Whig who had served four terms in the Illinois legislature and one term in Congress, Lincoln was propelled back into politics by the shock of the Kansas-Nebraska bill. He acknowledged the constitutional right to hold slave property in the states where it already existed, but he believed slavery was "an unqualified evil to the negro, the white man, and to the state.... There can be no moral right in connection with one man's making a slave of another." Lincoln admitted he did not know how to bring this deeply entrenched institution to an end. He understood that race prejudice was a powerful obstacle to emancipation. Still, he believed that the country must face up to the problem. It must stop any further expansion of slavery as the first step on the long road to its "ultimate extinction."

Lincoln excoriated Douglas's "care not" attitude toward whether slavery was voted up or down. He branded Douglas's assertion that slavery would never be imported into Kansas because of the region's supposedly unsuitable climate a "LULLABY argument." The climate of eastern Kansas was similar to that of the Missouri River valley in Missouri, where slaves were busily raising hemp and tobacco. Missouri slaveholders were already poised to take their slaves into the

14.2 Abraham Lincoln Nominated to oppose Stephen A. Douglas's reelection to the Senate from Illinois in 1858, Abraham Lincoln was not yet a national figure. But his status would change dramatically with the Lincoln-Douglas debates of 1858, which focused on the issue of slavery. Lincoln's eloquence in this series of debates propelled him into national prominence.

Kansas River valley. "Climate will not ... keep slavery out of these territories," said Lincoln. "Nothing in *nature* will." Many of the Founding Fathers had looked forward to the day when slavery would no longer exist in republican America. Instead, the United States had become the world's largest slaveholding society, and Douglas's bill would permit slavery to expand even further. In a political speech at Peoria, Illinois, in October 1854, Lincoln insisted:

> The monstrous injustice of slavery deprives our republican example of its just influence in the world—enables the enemies of free institutions, with plausibility, to taunt us as hypocrites... . Let us re-adopt the Declaration of Independence, and with it, the practices, and policy, which harmonize with it... . If we do this, we shall not only have saved the Union; but we shall have so saved it, as to make, and to keep it, forever worthy of the saving.

With these eloquent words, Lincoln gave voice to the feelings rising up against the Kansas-Nebraska bill. Abolitionists, Free-Soilers, northern Whigs, and even many northern Democrats held impassioned meetings to form anti-Nebraska coalitions, but they could not stop passage of the bill. It cleared the Senate easily, supported by a solid South and 15 of the 20 northern Democrats. In the House, it passed by a vote of 113 to 100.

14-1b Death of the Whig Party

These proceedings completed the destruction of the Whigs as a national party. Southern Whigs had been disappearing ever since Zachary Taylor had "betrayed" them on the issue of a free California. After the presidential election of 1852, few Whigs remained in the cotton South. In that year, the Whig Party nominated General Winfield Scott for president. Although he was a Virginian, Scott, like Taylor, took a national rather than a southern view. He was the candidate of the northern Whigs in the national convention, which nominated him on the 53rd ballot after a bitter contest between the northern and southern wings of the party. A mass exodus of southern Whigs into the Democratic Party enabled Franklin Pierce to carry all but two slave states in the election. The unanimous vote of northern Whigs in Congress against the Kansas-Nebraska bill was the final straw. The Whig Party never recovered its influence in the South.

Whig strength seemed to be on its last legs in the North as well. Antislavery Whig leaders, such as William H. Seward and Lincoln, hoped to channel the flood of anti-Nebraska sentiment through the Whig Party, an effort akin to containing Niagara Falls. Free-Soilers and antislavery Democrats spurned the Whig label. Political coalitions arose spontaneously in the North under various names: anti-Nebraska, Fusion, People's, Independent. The name that caught on evoked memories of America's first fight for freedom in 1776: Republican. The first use of this name seems to have occurred at an anti-Nebraska rally in a Congregational church at Ripon, Wisconsin, in May 1854. Soon, most of the congressional candidates fielded by anti-Nebraska coalitions ran their campaigns under the Republican banner.

The 1854 elections were disastrous for northern Democrats. One-fourth of Democratic voters deserted the party. The Democrats lost control of the House of Representatives when 66 of 91 incumbent free-state Democratic congressmen went down to defeat. Combined with the increase in the number of Democratic congressmen from the South, where the party had picked up the pieces of the shattered Whig organization, this rout brought the party under southern domination more than ever.

But who would pick up the pieces of old parties in the North? The new Republican Party hoped to do so, but it suffered a shock in urban areas of the Northeast. Hostility toward immigrants created a tidal wave of **nativism** that threatened to swamp the anti-Nebraska movement. "Nearly everybody appears to have gone deranged on Nativism," reported a Pennsylvania Democrat, while a Whig in upstate New York warned that his district was "very badly infected with Know-nothingism." Described as a "tornado," a "hurricane," a "freak of political insanity," the **Know-Nothings** won landslide victories in Massachusetts and Delaware, polled an estimated 40 percent of the vote in Pennsylvania, and did well elsewhere in the Northeast and border states. Who were these mysterious Know-Nothings? What did they stand for?

14.3 Stephen A. Douglas The Little Giant began his meteoric rise to leadership of the Democratic Party with his successful effort to have the Compromise of 1850 enacted by Congress. Having forestalled sectional schism in 1850, he drove a wedge more deeply than ever between North and South with the Kansas-Nebraska bill of 1854. Six years later, Douglas became a victim of sectional schism when the Democratic Party split into northern and southern factions and thereby ruined his chance of winning the presidency.

Q Why did Douglas sponsor a bill in 1854 that he knew would "raise a hell of a storm"?

14-2 Immigration and Nativism

Q *What were the origins of nativism? How did this movement relate to the slavery issue?*

During the early 19th century, immigration was less pronounced than in most other periods of U.S. history. The volume of immigration (the number of new immigrants in proportion to the whole population) was little more than 1 percent in the 1820s, increasing to 4 percent in the 1830s. Three-quarters of the newcomers were Protestants, mainly from Britain. Most of them were skilled workers, farmers, or members of white-collar occupations.

In the 1840s, a combination of factors abruptly quadrupled the volume of immigration and changed its ethnic and occupational makeup. The pressure of expanding population on limited land in Germany and successive failures of the potato crop in Ireland impelled millions of German and Irish peasants to emigrate (see Figure 14.1). A majority came to the United States, where recovery from the depression of the early 1840s brought an economic boom and an insatiable demand for labor. During the decade after 1845, 3 million immigrants entered the United States—15 percent of the total American population in 1845, the highest proportional volume of immigration in American history. Many of them, especially the Irish, joined the unskilled and semiskilled labor force in the rapidly growing eastern cities.

Most of the new arrivals were Roman Catholics. Anti-Catholicism had centuries-deep roots in Anglo-American Protestantism. Fear of the pope and of the Roman Church as autocratic and anti-republican was never far below the surface of American political culture, and scurrilous anti-Catholic literature circulated during the 1830s. Several ethnic riots between Protestant and Catholic workers over the years culminated in pitched battles and numerous deaths in Philadelphia in 1844. In several eastern cities nativist political parties sprang up in the early 1840s with the intent of curbing the political rights of immigrants.

Nativism appeared to subside with the revival of prosperity after 1844, but the decline was temporary. Established Americans perceived more recent arrivals as responsible for an increase of crime and poverty in the cities. They also viewed immigrant culture with suspicion. The social and political life of both the Irish and the Germans revolved around taverns and beer parlors at a time when the temperance crusade had sharply curtailed drinking among native-born Protestants (see Chapter 12).

14-2a *Immigrants in Politics*

The growing political power of immigrants became a bone of contention. Most of the immigrants became Democrats, because that party welcomed or at least tolerated them and many Whigs did not. Foreign-born voters leaned toward the pro-slavery wing of the Democratic Party, even though seven-eighths of them settled in free states. Mostly working-class and poor, they rubbed shoulders against the small northern black population; Irish American mobs sometimes attacked black neighborhoods and rioted against black workers. They supported the Democratic Party as the best means of keeping blacks in slavery and out of the North. These attitudes sparked hostility toward immigrants among many antislavery people.

Attitudes toward immigrants had political repercussions. Two of the hottest issues in state and local politics during the early 1850s were temperance and schools. The temperance crusaders had grown confident and aggressive enough to go into politics. The drunkenness and rowdiness they associated with Irish immigrants became one of their particular targets. Beginning with Maine in 1851, 12 states had enacted prohibition laws by 1855. Although several of the laws were soon weakened by the courts or repealed by legislatures, they exacerbated ethnic tensions.

So too did battles over public schools versus parochial schools. Catholics resented the Protestant domination of public

14.4 Birth of the Republican Party The Kansas-Nebraska Act galvanized antislavery northerners of all parties into new anti-Nebraska organizations opposed to the repeal of the Missouri Compromise's ban on slavery in Louisiana Purchase territories north of 36°30". Appealing to the "spirit of '76," these organizations coalesced into the Republican Party, which held its first convention at Pittsburgh on Washington's birthday in 1856 to organize a national party in preparation for the presidential nominating convention later that year.

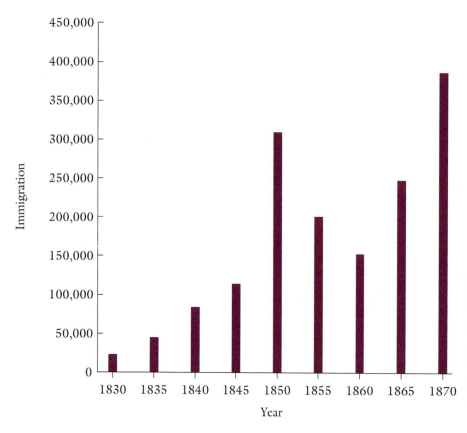

Figure 14.1 **Immigration to the United States** Revolution in Germany and potato famine in Ireland were significant factors behind the dramatic rise in immigration to the United States between 1845 and 1850. Another surge in immigration occurred after the Civil War ended in 1865.

Source: Data from *Historical Statistics of the United States, Millennial Online Addition*, "U.S. Immigrants and Emigrants: 1820–1998" [Table Ad1-2].

education and the reading of the King James Bible in schools. The Catholic Church began to build parochial schools for the faithful, and in 1852, the first Plenary Council of American bishops decided to seek tax support for these schools or tax relief for Catholic parents who sent their children to them. This effort set off heated election contests in numerous northern cities and states. Anti-Catholic "free school" tickets won most of these elections on a platform of defending public schools against the "bold effort" of this "despotic faith" to "uproot the tree of Liberty."

14-2b The Rise of the Know-Nothings

It was in this context that the Know-Nothings (their formal name was the American Party) burst onto the political scene. This party was the result of the merger in 1852 of two secret fraternal societies that limited their membership to native-born Protestants: the Order of the Star-Spangled Banner and the Order of United Americans. Recruiting mainly young men in skilled blue-collar and lower white-collar occupations, the merged order had a membership of 1 million or more by 1854. The order supported temperance and opposed tax support for parochial schools. Members wanted public office restricted to native-born men and sought to lengthen the naturalization period before immigrants could become citizens. Members were also pledged to secrecy; if asked about the order, they were to reply, "I know nothing."

This was the tornado that swept through the Northeast in the 1854 elections. Although the American Party drew voters from both major parties, it cut more heavily into the Whig constituency. Northern Whigs who had not already gone over to the Republicans flocked to the Know-Nothings.

When the dust of the 1854 elections settled, it was clear that those who opposed the Democrats would control the next House of Representatives. But who would control the opposition—antislavery Republicans or nativist Americans?

Some northern voters adhered to both political faiths. But many Republicans warned against flirting with religious bigotry. In a letter to a friend, Abraham Lincoln asked:

> How can any one who abhors the oppression of negroes, be in favor of degrading classes of white people? ... As a nation, we began by declaring that "all men are created equal." We now practically read it "all men are created equal, except negroes." When the Know Nothings get control, it will read "all men are created equal, except negroes, and foreigners, and Catholics." When it comes to this I should prefer emigrating to some country where they make no pretense of loving liberty—to Russia, for instance, where despotism can be taken pure, and without the base alloy of hypocrisy.

14-2c The Decline of Nativism

In 1855, Republican leaders maneuvered skillfully to divert the energies of northern Know-Nothings from their crusade against the pope to a crusade against the slave power. Two developments helped them. The first was turmoil in Kansas, which convinced many northerners that the slave power was a greater threat than the pope. The second was an increase of nativist sentiment in the South. The American Party won elections in Maryland,

14.5 "Forcing Slavery Down the Throat of a Freesoiler" This striking 1856 political cartoon shows a Freesoiler bound against his will to the Democratic Platform. Four of the small figures are prominent Democrats, including Stephen Douglas, who are attempting to force the Freesoiler to swallow the issue of slavery.

Q How would you interpret the portrayal of the fifth small figure here, the African American man?

Q Is this antislavery image also pro-black?

Kentucky, and Tennessee and polled at least 45 percent of the votes in five other southern states. Violence in several southern cities with large immigrant populations revealed a significant streak of nativism in the South.

These developments had important implications at the national level. Southern Know-Nothings were pro-slavery, whereas many of their Yankee counterparts were antislavery. Just as the national Whig Party had floundered on the slavery issue, so did the American Party during 1855 and 1856. At the party's first national council in June 1855, most of the northern delegates walked out when southerners and northern conservatives joined forces to pass a resolution endorsing the Kansas-Nebraska Act. A similar scene occurred at an American Party convention in 1856. By that time, most northern members of the party had, in effect, become Republicans.

Nativism faded. The volume of immigration suddenly dropped by more than half in 1855 and stayed low for the next several years. Ethnic tensions eased, and cultural issues such as temperance and schools receded. But there was no easing of the conflict between North and South over the extension of slavery. That conflict led to civil war—and the war seemed already to have begun in the territory of Kansas.

14-3 Violent Conflict in the 1850s

Q *How was violence in Kansas related to the issue of slavery?*

When it became clear that southerners had enough votes to pass the Kansas-Nebraska Act, the stage was set for conflict. At first, Missouri settlers in Kansas posted the stronger numbers. As the year 1854 progressed, however, settlers from the North came pouring in. Alarmed by this influx, bands of Missourians, labeled **"border ruffians"** by the Republican press, rode into Kansas prepared to vote as many times as necessary to install a pro-slavery government. In fall 1854, they cast at least 1,700 illegal ballots and sent a pro-slavery territorial delegate to Congress.

When the time came for the election of a territorial legislature the following spring, David Rice Atchison led a contingent of border ruffians to Kansas for the election. "There are eleven hundred coming over from Platte County to vote," he told his followers, "and if that ain't enough, we can send five thousand—enough to kill every God-damned abolitionist in the Territory."

His count was accurate. Nearly 5,000 came and voted illegally to elect a pro-slavery territorial legislature. The territorial governor pleaded with President Pierce to nullify the election, but Pierce listened to Atchison and removed the governor. Meanwhile, the new territorial legislature legalized slavery and adopted a slave code that even authorized the death penalty for helping a slave to escape.

Members of the so-called Free State Party, outraged by these proceedings, had no intention of obeying laws enacted by this "bogus legislature." By fall 1855, they constituted a majority of bona fide settlers in Kansas. They called a convention, adopted a free-state constitution, and elected their own legislature and governor. By January 1856, two territorial governments in Kansas stood with their hands at each other's throats.

14-3a *Bleeding Kansas*

Kansas now became the leading issue in national politics (see Map 14.1). The Democratic Senate and President Pierce recognized the pro-slavery legislature meeting in the town of

Lecompton, while the Republican House of Representatives recognized the antislavery legislature in the town of Lawrence. Southerners saw the struggle as crucial to their future. "The admission of Kansas into the Union as a slave state is now a point of honor," wrote Congressman Preston Brooks of South Carolina. "The fate of the South is to be decided with the Kansas issue." On the other side, Charles Sumner of Massachusetts gave a well-publicized speech in the Senate on May 19 and 20 entitled "The Crime against Kansas." "Murderous robbers from Missouri," charged Sumner, "from the drunken spew and vomit of an uneasy civilization" had committed the "rape of a virgin territory, compelling it to the hateful embrace of slavery." Among the southern senators Sumner singled out for special condemnation and ridicule was a cousin of Congressman Brooks, Andrew Butler of South Carolina. Butler was a "Don Quixote," said Sumner, "who had chosen a mistress to whom he has made his vows … the harlot, Slavery."

14-3b The Caning of Sumner

Sumner's speech incensed southerners, none more than Preston Brooks, who decided to avenge his cousin. Two days after the speech, Brooks walked into the Senate chamber and began beating Sumner with a heavy cane. His legs trapped beneath the desk that was bolted to the floor, Sumner wrenched the desk loose as he stood up to try to defend himself, whereupon Brooks clubbed him so ferociously that Sumner slumped forward, bloody and unconscious.

News of the incident sent a thrill of pride through the South and a rush of rage through the North. Charleston newspapers praised Brooks for "standing forth so nobly in defense of … the honor of South Carolinians." Brooks resigned from Congress after censure by the House and was unanimously reelected. From all over the South came gifts of new canes, some inscribed with such mottoes as "Hit Him Again" and "Use Knock-Down Arguments." But in the North, the Republicans gained thousands of voters as a result of the affair. It seemed to prove their contentions about "the barbarism of slavery." "Has it come to this," asked the poet William Cullen Bryant, editor of the *New York Evening Post*, "that we must speak with bated breath in the presence of our Southern masters? … Are we to be chastised as they chastise their slaves?" A veteran New York politician reported that he had "never before seen anything at all like the present state of deep, determined, & desperate feelings of hatred, & hostility to the further extension of slavery, & its political power."

Republicans were soon able to add "Bleeding Kansas" to "Bleeding Sumner" in their repertoire of winning issues. Even as Sumner was delivering his speech in Washington, an "army" of pro-slavery Missourians, complete with artillery, marched on the free-state capital of Lawrence, Kansas. On May 21, they shelled and sacked the town, burning several buildings.

14.6 Free-State Men Ready to Defend Lawrence, Kansas, in 1856 After pro-slavery forces sacked the free-state capital of Lawrence in 1856, northern settlers decided they needed more firepower to defend themselves. Somehow they got hold of a six-pound howitzer. This cannon did not fire a shot in anger during the Kansas troubles, but its existence may have deterred the "border ruffians."

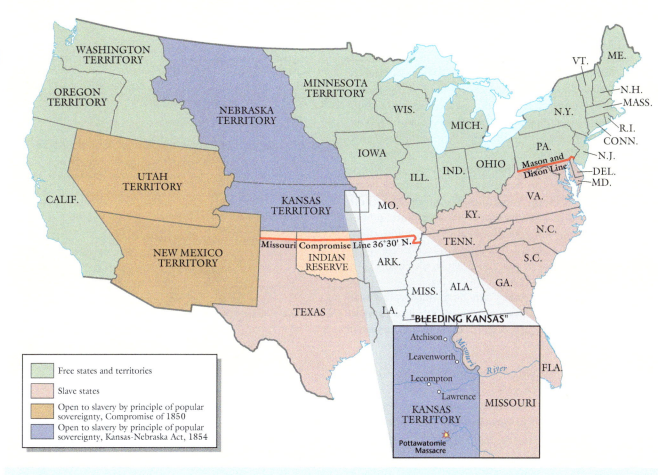

▲ **MAP 14.1 Kansas-Nebraska and the Slavery Issue** On the main map, note how much territory was opened to slavery on the principle of popular sovereignty by the Compromise of 1850 and the Kansas-Nebraska Act. The enlarged inset map shows how close together were the centers of Free Soil and pro-slavery forces in Lawrence and Lecompton, respectively.

Q Why did Southerners believe that the "fate of the South" was to be decided with the Kansas issue?

Q Why was Nebraska Territory less hotly contested?

A rival force of free-state men arrived too late to intercept them. One of the free-state "captains" was John Brown, an abolitionist zealot who considered himself anointed by the Lord to avenge the sins of slaveholders. When he learned of the murder of several free-state settlers and the sack of Lawrence, he "went crazy—crazy," according to one of his followers. We must "fight fire with fire," Brown declared. "Something must be done to show these barbarians that we, too, have rights." Leading four of his sons and three other men to a pro-slavery settlement at Pottawatomie Creek on the night of May 24–25, 1856, Brown dragged five men from their cabins and split open their heads with broadswords.

Brown's murderous act set off a veritable civil war in Kansas. One of Brown's sons was among the estimated 200 men killed in bushwhacker raids. Not until President Pierce sent a tough new territorial governor and 1,300 federal troops to Kansas in September 1856 did the violence subside—just in time to save the Democrats from possible defeat in the presidential election.

14-4 The Election of 1856

 What role did the issue of slavery play in the election of 1856?

By 1856, the Republicans had become the largest party in the North. They were also the first truly sectional party in American history, for they had little prospect of carrying a single county in the slave states. At their first national convention, the Republicans wrote a platform that focused mainly on that "relic of barbarism," slavery. The platform also incorporated the old Whig program of federal aid to internal improvements, including a railroad to California. For its presidential nominee, the party steered away from its most prominent leaders, who were identified with the old parties,

Interpreting the Visual Past: The Caning of Sumner

On May 22, 1856, pro-slavery congressman Preston Brooks of South Carolina beat Senator Charles Sumner of Massachusetts with a heavy cane on the floor of the Senate. Brooks injured Sumner so severely that he was not able to return to the Senate for over three years. The caning of Sumner was the worst of several instances of North-South violence or threatened violence on the floor of Congress in the 1850s, presaging the violence on the battlefields of the 1860s.

This political cartoon depicts that notorious violence, making its pro-northern sympathies graphically clear both in its caption and its visualization of the attack on Sumner. At a Sumner rally in New York shortly after the caning, Henry Ward Beecher had asserted that "the symbol of the North is the pen; the symbol of the South is the bludgeon." The caption picks up on that theme, offering ironic commentary on a thuggish "Southern chivalry" wielding "clubs" rather than argument in the Senate. But as with any political cartoon, its full impact depends not just on words but also on a powerful image.

Q How does the artist visually emphasize his pro-northern position? What choices has he made in positioning the bodies of the two men here? How does he visually emphasize the viciousness of the attack? Why does the fallen Sumner hold a quill in one hand and a scroll with the word "Kansas" on it in the other?

Q The artist has hidden the face of Brooks. Is this an effective artistic choice? Why or why not?

Q Why does the artist show cartoon figures in the background smiling at the violence? What message does he convey?

14.7 **Lithograph Depicting The Caning of Charles Sumner, 1856.**

and turned instead to John C. Frémont. This "Pathfinder of the West" had a dashing image as an explorer and for his role in the acquisition of California. With little political experience, he had few political enemies, and his antislavery credentials were satisfactory.

The Democrats chose as their candidate James Buchanan, a veteran of 30 years in various public offices. The Democratic platform endorsed popular sovereignty and condemned the Republicans as a "sectional party" that incited "treason and armed resistance in the Territories."

This would be a three-party election because the American Party was still in the field. Having become mainly a way station for former southern Whigs, the party nominated ex-Whig Millard Fillmore. The three-party campaign sifted out into a pair of two-party contests: Democrats versus Americans in the South and Democrats versus Republicans in the North. Fillmore, despite a good showing of 44 percent of the popular vote in the South, carried only Maryland. Considering Buchanan colorless but safe, the rest of the South gave him three-fourths of the electoral votes he needed for victory (see Table 14.1).

The real excitement in this election showed itself in the North. For many Republicans, the campaign was a moral cause, an evangelical crusade against the sin of slavery. Republican "Wide Awake" clubs marched in torchlight parades chanting "Free Soil, Free Speech, Free Men, Frémont!" A veteran politician in Indiana marveled: "Men, Women & Children all seemed to be out, with a kind of fervor I have never witnessed before in six Pres. Elections in which I have taken an active part." The turnout of eligible voters in the North was a remarkable 83 percent. One awestruck journalist, anticipating a Republican victory, wrote that "the process now going on in the United States is a *Revolution*."

Not quite. Although the Republicans swept New England and the upper parts of New York State and the Old Northwest—both settled by New Englanders, where evangelical and antislavery reform movements had taken hold—the contest in the lower North was close. Buchanan needed only to carry Pennsylvania and either Indiana or Illinois to win the presidency, and the campaign focused on those states. The immigrant and working-class voters of the eastern cities and the rural voters of the lower Midwest, descendants of upland southerners who had settled there, were antiblack and anti-abolitionist in sentiment. They were ripe for Democratic propaganda that accused Republicans of favoring racial equality. "**Black Republicans**," declared an Ohio Democratic newspaper, intended to "turn loose ... millions of negroes, to elbow you in the workshops, and compete with you in fields of honest labor." A Democrat in Pennsylvania told voters that "the one aim" of the Republicans was "to elevate the African race in this country to complete equality of political and economic condition with the whiteman." Indiana Democrats organized parades with young girls in white dresses carrying banners inscribed: "Fathers, save us from nigger husbands."

Table 14.1 POPULAR AND ELECTORAL VOTES IN THE 1856 PRESIDENTIAL ELECTION

Candidate	Free States		Slave States		Total	
	Popular	Electoral	Popular	Electoral	Popular	Electoral
Buchanan (Democrat)	1,227,000	62	607,000	112	1,833,000	174
Frémont (Republican)	1,338,000	114	0	0	1,338,000	114
Fillmore (American)	396,000	0	476,000	8	872,000	8

The Republicans in these areas denied that they favored racial equality. They insisted that the main reason for keeping slavery out of the territories was to enable white farmers and workers to make a living there without competition from black labor. But their denials were in vain. Support for the Republican Party by prominent black leaders, including Frederick Douglass, convinced hundreds of thousands of voters that the Black Republicans were racial egalitarians. For the next two decades, that sentiment would be one of the most potent weapons in the Democratic arsenal.

The charge that a Republican victory would destroy the Union was even more effective. Buchanan set the tone in his instructions to Democratic Party leaders: "The Black Republicans must be … boldly assailed as disunionists, and the charge must be re-iterated again and again." It was. And southerners helped the cause by threatening to secede if Frémont won. Fears of disruption caused many conservative ex-Whigs in the North to support Buchanan, who carried Pennsylvania, New Jersey, Indiana, Illinois, and California and won the presidency (see Map 14.2).

But southerners did not intend to let Buchanan forget that he owed his election mainly to the South. "Mr. Buchanan and the Northern Democracy are dependent on the South," wrote a Virginian after the election. "If we can succeed in Kansas … and add a little more slave territory, we may yet live free men under the Stars and Stripes."

14-4a *The Dred Scott Case*

The South took the offensive at the outset of the Buchanan administration. Its instrument was the Supreme Court, which had a majority of five justices from slave states, led by Chief Justice Roger B. Taney of Maryland. Those justices saw the Dred Scott case as an opportunity to settle once and for all the question of slavery in the territories.

Dred Scott was a slave whose owner, an army surgeon, had kept him at military posts in Illinois and in Wisconsin Territory for several years before taking him back to Missouri. After the owner's death, Scott sued for his freedom on the grounds of his prolonged stay in the Wisconsin Territory, where slavery had been outlawed by the Missouri Compromise. The case worked its way up from Missouri courts through a federal circuit court to the U.S. Supreme Court. There it attracted attention as a test case of Congress's power to prohibit slavery in the territories.

The southern Supreme Court justices decided to declare that the Missouri Compromise ban on slavery in the territories was unconstitutional. To avoid the appearance of a purely sectional decision, they sought the concurrence of a northern Democratic justice, Robert Grier of Pennsylvania. President-elect Buchanan played an improper role by pressing his fellow Pennsylvanian to go along with the southern majority. Having obtained Justice Grier's concurrence, Chief Justice Taney issued the Court's ruling stating that Congress lacked the power to keep slavery out of a territory, because slaves were property and the Constitution protects the right of property. For good measure, Taney also wrote that the circuit court should not have accepted the Scott case in the first place because black men were not citizens of the United States and therefore had no standing in its courts. The two non-Democratic northern justices dissented vigorously. They stated that blacks were legal citizens in several northern states and were therefore citizens of the United States. To buttress their opinion that Congress could prohibit slavery in the territories, they cited Congress's constitutional power to make "all needful rules and regulations" for the territories. Modern scholars agree with the dissenters. In 1857, however, Taney had a majority, and his ruling became law.

Republicans denounced Taney's decision as a "gross perversion" of the Constitution. Several Republican state legislatures resolved that the ruling was "not binding in law and conscience." They looked forward to the election of a Republican president who could "reconstitute" the Court and secure a reversal of the decision. "The remedy," said the *Chicago Tribune*, "is the ballot box.… . Let the next President be Republican, and 1860 will mark an era kindred with that of 1776."

14-4b *The Lecompton Constitution*

Instead of settling the slavery controversy, the Dred Scott decision intensified it. Meanwhile, pro-slavery advocates, having won legalization of slavery in the territories, moved to ensure that it would remain legal when Kansas became a state. That required deft maneuvering, because legitimate antislavery settlers outnumbered pro-slavery settlers by more than two to one. In 1857, the pro-slavery legislature (elected by the fraudulent votes of border ruffians two years earlier) called for a constitutional convention at Lecompton to prepare Kansas for statehood. Because the election for delegates was rigged, Free Soil voters refused to participate. One-fifth of the

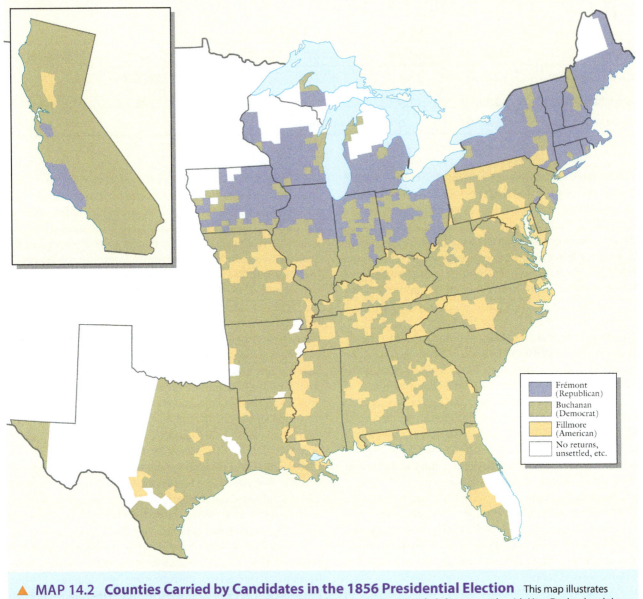

▲ **MAP 14.2 Counties Carried by Candidates in the 1856 Presidential Election** This map illustrates the sharp geographical division of the vote in 1856. The pattern of Republican counties coincided almost exactly with New England and the portions of other states settled by New England migrants during the two preceding generations.

Q What were the reasons for Buchanan's popularity in the mid-Atlantic states?

Q How would you explain the differing support for Buchanan and Fillmore in the South?

registered voters thereupon elected convention delegates, who met at Lecompton and wrote a state constitution that made slavery legal.

Then a nagging problem arose. Buchanan had promised that the Lecompton constitution would be presented to voters in a fair referendum. The problem was how to pass the pro-slavery constitution, given the antislavery majority of voters. The convention came up with an ingenious solution. Instead of a referendum on the whole constitution, it would allow the voters to choose between a constitution "with slavery" and one "with no slavery." The catch was that the constitution "with no slavery" guaranteed slave owners' "inviolable" right of property in the 200 slaves already in

Kansas and their progeny. It also did nothing to prevent future smuggling of slaves across the 200-mile border with Missouri. Once in Kansas, they, too, would become "inviolable" property.

Free-state voters branded the referendum a farce and boycotted it. One-quarter of the eligible voters went to the polls in December 1857 and approved the constitution "with slavery." Meanwhile, in a fair election policed by federal troops, the antislavery party won control of the new territorial legislature and promptly submitted both constitutions to a referendum that was boycotted by pro-slavery voters. This time, 70 percent of the eligible voters went to the polls and overwhelmingly rejected both constitutions.

Which referendum would the federal government recognize? That question proved even more divisive than the Kansas-Nebraska debate four years earlier. President Buchanan faced a dilemma. He had promised a fair referendum. But southerners, who dominated both the Democratic Party and the administration, threatened secession if Kansas was not admitted to statehood under the Lecompton constitution "with slavery." "If Kansas is *driven out of the Union for being a Slave State*," thundered Senator James Hammond of South Carolina, "can any Slave State remain in it with honor?" Buchanan caved in. He explained to a shocked northern Democrat that if he did not accept the Lecompton constitution, southern states would "secede from the Union or take up arms against us." Buchanan sent the Lecompton constitution to Congress with a message recommending statehood. Kansas, said the president, "is at this moment as much a slave state as Georgia or South Carolina."

What would Stephen Douglas do? If he endorsed the Lecompton constitution, he would undoubtedly be defeated in his bid for reelection to the Senate in 1858. And he regarded the Lecompton constitution as a travesty of popular sovereignty. He broke with the administration on the issue. He could not vote to "force this constitution down the throats of the people of Kansas," he told the Senate, "in opposition to their wishes and in violation of our pledges."

The fight in Congress was long and bitter. The South and the administration had the votes they needed in the Senate and won handily there, but the Democratic majority in the House was so small that the defection of even a few northern Democrats would defeat the Lecompton constitution. The House debate at one point got out of hand, and a wild fistfight erupted between Republicans and southern Democrats. "There were some fifty middle-aged and elderly gentlemen pitching into each other," wrote a bemused reporter, "most of them incapable, from want of wind and muscle, from doing each other any serious harm."

When the vote was finally taken, two dozen northern Democrats defected, providing enough votes to defeat Lecompton. Both sides then accepted a compromise proposal to resubmit the constitution to Kansas voters, who decisively rejected it. This meant that while Kansas would not come in as a slave state, neither would it come in as a free state for some time yet. Nevertheless, the Lecompton debate had split the Democratic Party, leaving a legacy of undying enmity between southerners and Douglas. The election of a Republican president in 1860 was now all but assured.

14-5 The Economy in the 1850s

Q *How did economic developments in the 1840s and 1850s widen the breach between North and South?*

Beginning in the mid-1840s, the American economy enjoyed a dozen years of unprecedented growth and prosperity, particularly for the railroads. The number of miles in operation quintupled. Railroad construction provided employment for many immigrants and spurred growth in industries that produced rails, rolling stock, and other railroad equipment. Most railroad construction took place in the Old Northwest, linking the region more closely to the Northeast and continuing the reorientation of transportation networks from a north-south river pattern to an east-west canal and rail pattern. By the mid-1850s, the east-west rail and water routes carried more than twice as much freight tonnage as the north-south river routes (see Map 14.3). This closer binding of the western and eastern states reinforced the effect of slavery in creating a self-conscious "North" and "South."

Although the Old Northwest remained predominantly agricultural, rapid expansion of railroads there laid the basis for its industrialization. During the 1850s, industrial output in the free states west of Pennsylvania grew at twice the rate of Northeast industrial output and three times the rate in the South. The Northwest urban growth rate tripled that of the Northeast and quadrupled that of the South. Chicago became the terminus for 15 rail lines in the 1850s, during which its population grew by 375 percent. In 1847, two companies that contributed to the rapid growth of agriculture during this era built their plants in Illinois: the McCormick reaper works at Chicago and the John Deere steel-plow works at Moline.

Economic expansion considerably outstripped even the prodigious pace of population increase. While the number of Americans grew by 44 percent during these 12 years (1844–1856), the value of both exports and imports increased by 200 percent; mined coal tonnage by 270 percent; banking capital, industrial capital, and industrial output by approximately 100 percent; farmland value by 100 percent; and cotton, wheat, and corn harvests by about 70 percent. These advances meant a significant increase of per capita production and income, although the distance between rich and poor was widening—a phenomenon that has characterized all capitalist economies during stages of rapid industrial growth.

By the later 1850s, the United States had forged ahead of most other countries to become the second-biggest industrial producer in the world, behind only Britain. But the country was still in the early stages of industrial development. Agricultural product processing and raw materials still played the dominant role. By 1860, the four leading industries, measured by value added in manufacturing, were cotton textiles, lumber products, boots and shoes, and flour milling. Iron and machinery, industries typical of a more mature manufacturing economy, ranked sixth and seventh.

14-5a *"The American System of Manufactures"*

The United States had pioneered in one crucial feature of modern industry: the mass production of **interchangeable parts**. This revolutionary concept had begun with the manufacture of firearms earlier in the 19th century and had spread to many products by the 1850s. High wages and

14.8 Bridge of the Milwaukee and Chicago Railroad at Racine, Wisconsin By the 1850s, Chicago had become the hub for a dozen or more railroads that tied the fast-growing Midwest to the older South and East. This illustration shows the railroad bridge over the Root River between Chicago and Milwaukee.

a shortage of the skilled craftsmen who had traditionally fashioned guns, furniture, locks, watches, and other products had compelled American entrepreneurs to seek alternative methods. "Yankee ingenuity," already world-famous, came up with an answer: special-purpose machine tools that would cut and shape an endless number of parts that could be fitted together to make whole guns, locks, clocks, and sewing machines in mass quantities. These products were less elegant and less durable than products made by skilled craftsmen, but they were also less expensive and thus more widely available to the "middling classes."

Such American-made products were the hit of the first World's Fair, the Crystal Palace Exhibition at London in 1851. British manufacturers were so impressed by Yankee techniques, which they dubbed "the American system of manufactures," that they sent two commissions to the United States to study them. The British also invited Samuel Colt of Connecticut, inventor of the famous six-shooting revolver, to set up a factory in England stocked with machinery from Connecticut. In testimony before a parliamentary committee in 1854, Colt summed up the American system of manufactures in a single sentence: "There is nothing that cannot be produced by machinery." Although the British had a half-century head start over Americans in the Industrial Revolution, Colt's testimony expressed a philosophy that would enable the United States to surpass Britain as the leading industrial nation by 1880.

The British industrial commissions cited the American educational system as an important reason for the country's technological proficiency. "Educated up to a far higher standard than those of a much superior grade in the Old World," reported the 1854 commission, "every [American] workman seems to be continually devising some new thing to assist him in his work, and there is a strong desire ... to be 'posted up' in every new improvement." By contrast, the British workman, trained by long apprenticeship "in the trade," rather than in school, lacked "the ductility of mind and the readiness of apprehension for a new thing" and was therefore "unwilling to change the methods he has been used to."

Whether this British commission was right in its belief that American schooling encouraged the "adaptative versatility" of Yankee workers, it was certainly true that public education and literacy were more widespread in the United States than in Europe. Almost 95 percent of adults in the free states were literate in 1860, compared with 65 percent in England and 55 percent in France. The standardization and expansion of public school systems that had begun earlier in New England had spread to the mid-Atlantic states and into the Old Northwest by the 1850s. Nearly all children received a few years of schooling, and most completed at least six or seven years.

This improvement in education coincided with the feminization of the teaching profession, which opened up new career opportunities for young women. By the 1850s, nearly three-quarters of the public school teachers in New England were women (who worked for lower salaries than male teachers), a trend that was spreading to the mid-Atlantic states and the Old Northwest as well.

14-5b *The Southern Economy*

In the South, 80 percent of the free population and only 10 percent of the slaves were literate. This was one of several differences between North and South that antislavery people pointed to as evidence of the backward, repressive, and pernicious nature of a slave society.

Still, the South shared in the economy's rapid growth following recovery from the depression of 1837–1843. Cotton prices and production both doubled between 1845 and 1855. Similar increases in price and output emerged in tobacco and sugar. The price of slaves also doubled during this decade. Southern crops provided three-fifths of all U.S. exports, with cotton alone supplying more than half.

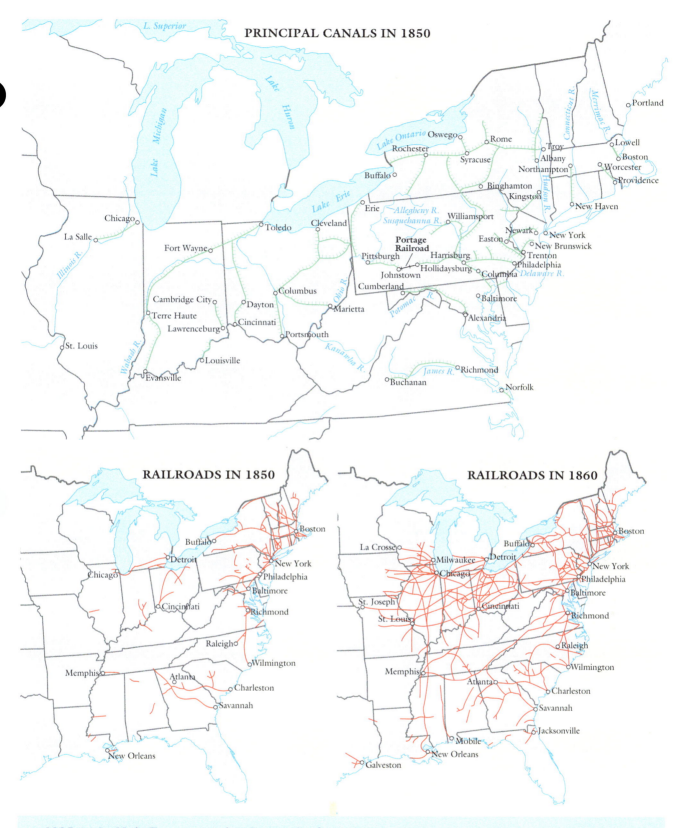

▲ MAP 14.3 **Main Transportation Routes in the 1850s** These maps illustrate how the transportation networks by natural waterways (rivers and the Atlantic coastal waters) oriented commerce north and south while the canals and railroads linked east and west. By 1860, railroads tied the midwestern states economically to the Northeast.

Q Why was railroad development so different in North and South?
Q How important were transportation networks to patterns of settlement?

14-5 The Economy in the 1850s

14.9 Colt Arms Plant in Hartford, Connecticut Samuel Colt's factory for manufacturing firearms was a showpiece for the American system of manufactures in the 1850s. All of the processes for production of the famous Colt revolver were housed under one roof, with power-driven machinery cutting the metal and shaping the interchangeable parts. Hand filing was necessary, however, for a perfect fit of the parts, because the tolerances of machine tools were not yet as finely calibrated as they later became.

14.10 The Country School This famous painting by Winslow Homer portrays the typical one-room rural schoolhouse in which millions of American children learned the "three R's" (reading, 'riting, and 'rithmetic) in the 19th century. By the 1850s, teaching elementary school was a profession increasingly dominated by women, an important change from earlier generations.

But a growing number of southerners deplored the fact that the **colonial economy** of the South was so dependent on the export of agricultural products and the import of manufactured goods. Northern or British firms owned the ships that carried southern cotton; Yankees or Englishmen provided most of the financial and commercial services. In the years of rising sectional tensions around 1850, many southerners began calling for economic independence from the North. How could they obtain their rights, they asked, if they were "financially more enslaved than our negroes?" Yankees "abuse and denounce slavery and slaveholders," declared a southern newspaper in 1851, yet "we purchase all our luxuries and necessaries from the North.... Our slaves are clothed with Northern manufactured goods and work with Northern hoes, ploughs, and other implements.... The slaveholder dresses in Northern goods ... and on Northern-made paper, with a Northern pen, with Northern ink, he resolves and re-resolves in regard to his rights."

Southerners must "throw off this humiliating dependence," declared James D. B. De Bow, the young champion of economic diversification in the South. In 1846, De Bow had founded in New Orleans a periodical eventually known as *De Bow's Review*. Proclaiming on its cover that "Commerce is King," the *Review* set out to make this slogan a southern reality. De Bow took the lead in organizing annual commercial conventions that met in various southern cities during the 1850s. In its early years, this movement encouraged southerners to invest in shipping lines, railroads, textile mills ("bring the spindles to the cotton"), and other enterprises. "Give us factories, machine shops, work shops," declared southern proponents of King Commerce, "and we shall be able ere long to assert our rights."

Economic diversification in the South did make headway during the 1850s. The slave states quadrupled their railroad mileage, increased the amount of capital invested in manufacturing by 77 percent, and boosted their output of cotton textiles by 44 percent. But northern industry was growing even faster. In 1860, the North had five times more industrial output per capita than the South, and it had three times the railroad capital and mileage per capita and per thousand square miles. Southerners had a larger percentage of their capital invested in land and slaves in 1860 than they had had 10 years earlier. Some 80 percent of the South's labor force worked in agriculture—the same as 60 years earlier. By contrast, while farming remained, at 40 percent, the largest single occupation in the North, the northern economy developed a strong manufacturing and commercial sector whose combined labor force almost equaled that of agriculture by 1860.

14-5c The Sovereignty of King Cotton

A good many southerners preferred to keep it that way. "That the North does our trading and manufacturing mostly is true," wrote an Alabama planter in 1858. "We are willing that they should. Ours is an agricultural people, and God grant that we may continue so. It is the freest, happiest, most independent, and with us, the most powerful condition on earth." In the later 1850s, the drive for economic diversification in the South lost steam. King Cotton reasserted its primacy over King Commerce as cotton output *and* prices continued to rise, suffusing the South in a glow of prosperity. "Our Cotton is the most wonderful talisman on earth," declared a planter. "By its power we are transmuting whatever we choose into whatever we want." In a speech that became famous, James Hammond of South Carolina told his fellow senators in 1858 that "the slaveholding South is now the controlling power of the world…. No power on earth dares to make war on cotton. Cotton *is* king."

Even the commercial conventions in the South seem to have embraced this gospel. By the later 1850s, one of the main goals of these conventions was to reopen the African slave trade, prohibited by law since 1808. The conventions also lobbied for the annexation of Cuba, which would bring a productive agricultural economy and 400,000 more slaves into the United States.

Nowhere in the South, said defenders of slavery, did one see such "scenes of beggary, squalid poverty, and wretchedness" as one could find in any northern city. Slaves, they insisted, enjoyed a higher standard of living than white "wage slaves" in northern factories. Slaves never suffered from unemployment or wage cuts, they received free medical care, and they were taken care of in old age.

This argument reached its fullest development in the writings of George Fitzhugh, a Virginia farmer-lawyer whose newspaper articles were gathered into two books published in 1854 and 1857, *Sociology for the South and Cannibals All*. Free-labor capitalism, said Fitzhugh, was a competition in which the strong exploited and starved the weak. Slavery, by contrast, was a paternal institution that guaranteed protection of the workers. "Capital exercises a more perfect compulsion over free laborers than human masters over slaves," wrote Fitzhugh, "for free laborers must at all times work or starve, and slaves are supported whether they work or not…. What a glorious thing is slavery, when want, misfortune, old age, debility, and sickness overtake [the slave]."

14-5d Labor Conditions in the North

How true was this portrait of poverty and starvation among northern workers? Some northern labor leaders did complain that the "slavery" of the wage system gave "bosses" control over the hours, conditions, and compensation of labor. But there is no evidence that a northern workingman ever offered to change places with a southern slave. Average per capita income was about 40 percent higher in the North than in the South. Although that average masked large disparities between rich and poor—even between the middle class and the poor—those disparities were no greater, and probably smaller, in the North than in the South.

To be sure, substantial numbers of recent immigrants, day laborers, and young single women in large northern cities lived on the edge of poverty—or slipped over the edge. Many women seamstresses, shoe binders, milliners, and the like, who worked 60 or 70 hours per week in the outwork system, earned less than a living wage. Some of them resorted to prostitution in order to survive. The widespread adoption of the newly invented sewing machine in the 1850s did nothing to make life easier for seamstresses; it only lowered their per-unit piecework wages and forced them to turn out more shirts and trousers than before. Many urban working-class families could not survive on the wages of an unskilled or semiskilled man. Women had to take in laundry, boarders, or outwork, and one or more children also had to work. Much employment was seasonal or intermittent, leaving workers without wages for long periods, especially during the winter. The poverty, overcrowding, and disease in the tenement districts of a few large cities—especially New York City—seemed to lend substance to pro-slavery claims that slaves were better off.

But they were not—even apart from the psychological contrast between being free and being a slave. New York City's poverty, although highly concentrated and visible, was exceptional. In the North, only one-fourth of the people lived in cities or towns of more than 2,500 people. Wages and opportunities for workers were greater in the North than anywhere else in the world, including the South. That was why 4 million immigrants came to the United States from 1845 to 1860 and why seven-eighths of them settled in free states. It was also why twice as many white residents of slave states migrated to free states than vice versa.

14.11a (top) and 14.10b (bottom) Southern Portraits of Slavery and Free Labor Romanticized images of happy, well-fed slaves enjoying their work picking cotton were common in pro-slavery literature (top). Such images were often contrasted with the supposed harshness of life in northern tenement districts, as in this illustration of a communal pump that has run dry on a hot summer day in an immigrant neighborhood on New York's Lower East Side (bottom).

14-5e The Panic of 1857

In fall 1857, the relative prosperity of the North was interrupted by a financial panic that caused a short-lived but intense depression. When the Crimean War in Europe (1854–1856) cut off Russian grain from the European market, U.S. exports had mushroomed to meet the deficiency. After the Crimean War ended, U.S. grain exports slumped. The sharp rise in interest rates in Britain and France, caused by the war, spread to U.S. financial markets in 1857 and dried up sources of credit. Meanwhile, the economic boom of the preceding years had caused the American economy to overheat: Land prices had soared, railroads had built beyond the capacity of earnings to service their debts, and banks had made too many risky loans.

This speculative house of cards came crashing down in September 1857. The failure of one banking house sent a wave of panic through the financial community. Banks suspended specie payments, businesses failed, railroads went bankrupt, construction halted, and factories shut down. Hundreds of thousands of workers were laid off, and others went on part-time schedules or took wage cuts, just as the cold winter months were arriving. The specter of class conflict similar to the European revolutions of 1848 haunted the public. Unemployed workers in several northern cities marched in parades carrying banners demanding work or bread. A mob broke into the shops of flour merchants in New York City. On November 10, a crowd gathered on Wall Street and threatened to break into the U.S. customs house and sub-treasury vaults, where $20 million was stored. Soldiers and marines had to be called out to disperse the mob.

But the country got through the winter with little violence. No one was killed in the demonstrations—in contrast to the dozens who had been killed in ethnic riots a few years earlier and the hundreds killed in the guerrilla war in Kansas. Class conflict turned out to be the least threatening of the various discords that endangered society in the 1850s. Charity and public works helped tide the poor over the winter, and the panic inspired a vigorous religious revival. Spontaneous prayer meetings arose in many northern cities, bringing together bankers and seamstresses, brokers and street sweepers. They asked God's forgiveness for the greed and materialism that, in a self-flagellating mood, they believed had caused the panic.

The depression was short-lived. By early 1858, banks had resumed specie payments; the stock market rebounded in the spring; factories reopened; railroad construction resumed; and by spring 1859, recovery was complete. The modest labor union activities of the 1850s revived after the depression, as workers in some industries went on strike to bring wages back to pre-panic levels. In February 1860, the shoemakers of Lynn, Massachusetts, began the largest strike in U.S. history up to that time, eventually involving 20,000 workers in the New England shoe industry. Despite the organization of several national unions of skilled workers during the 1850s, however, less than 1 percent of the labor force was unionized in 1860.

14-5f *Sectionalism and the Panic*

The Panic of 1857 intensified sectional animosities. The South largely escaped the depression. Its export-driven economy seemed insulated from domestic downturns. After a brief dip, cotton and tobacco prices returned to high levels and production continued to increase: The cotton crop set new records in 1858 and 1859 (see Map 14.4). Southern boasts about the superiority of the region's economic and labor systems took on added bravado. "Who can doubt, that has looked at recent events, that cotton is supreme?" asked Senator James Hammond in March 1858. "When thousands of the strongest commercial houses in the world were coming down," he told Yankees, "what brought you up? ... We have poured in upon you one million six hundred thousand bales of cotton... . We have sold it for $65,000,000, and saved you."

Northerners were not grateful. In fact, many blamed southern congressmen for blocking measures, especially higher tariffs, that would have eased the effects of the depression and helped not only manufacturers but also unemployed workers. In each session of Congress from 1858 through 1860, a combination of southerners and about half of the northern Democrats blocked Republican efforts to raise tariffs. In the words of one bitter Pennsylvania Republican, this was proof that Congress remained "shamelessly prostituted, in a base subserviency to the Slave Power."

Three other measures acquired additional significance after the Panic of 1857. Republicans supported each of them as a means to promote economic health and to aid farmers and workers, but southerners perceived all of them as aimed at helping *northern* farmers and workers and used their power to defeat them. One was a homestead act to grant 160 acres of public land to each farmer who settled and worked the land. Believing that this bill "would prove a most efficient ally for Abolition by encouraging and stimulating the settlement of free farms with Yankees," southern senators defeated it after the House had passed it in 1859. The following year both houses passed the Homestead Act, but Buchanan vetoed it and southern senators blocked an effort to pass it over his veto. A similar fate befell bills for land grants to a transcontinental railroad and for building agricultural and mechanical colleges to educate farmers and workers. In the Old Northwest, where these measures were popular, Republican prospects for 1860 were enhanced by southern and Democratic opposition to them.

14-5g *Free-Labor Ideology*

By the later 1850s, the Republican antislavery argument had become a finely honed philosophy that historians have labeled a **free-labor ideology**. It held that all work in a free society was honorable, but that slavery degraded the calling of manual labor by equating it with bondage. Slaves worked inefficiently, by compulsion; free men were stimulated to work hard and efficiently by the desire to get ahead. Social mobility was central to the free-labor ideology. Free workers who practiced the virtues of industry, thrift, self-discipline, and sobriety could move up the ladder of success. "I am not ashamed to confess," Abraham Lincoln told a working-class audience in 1860, "that twenty-five years ago I was a hired laborer, mauling rails, at work on a flat-boat—just what might happen to any poor man's son!" But in the free states, said Lincoln, a man knows that "he can better his condition... . The free labor system opens the way for all—gives hope to all, and energy, and progress, and improvement of condition to all."

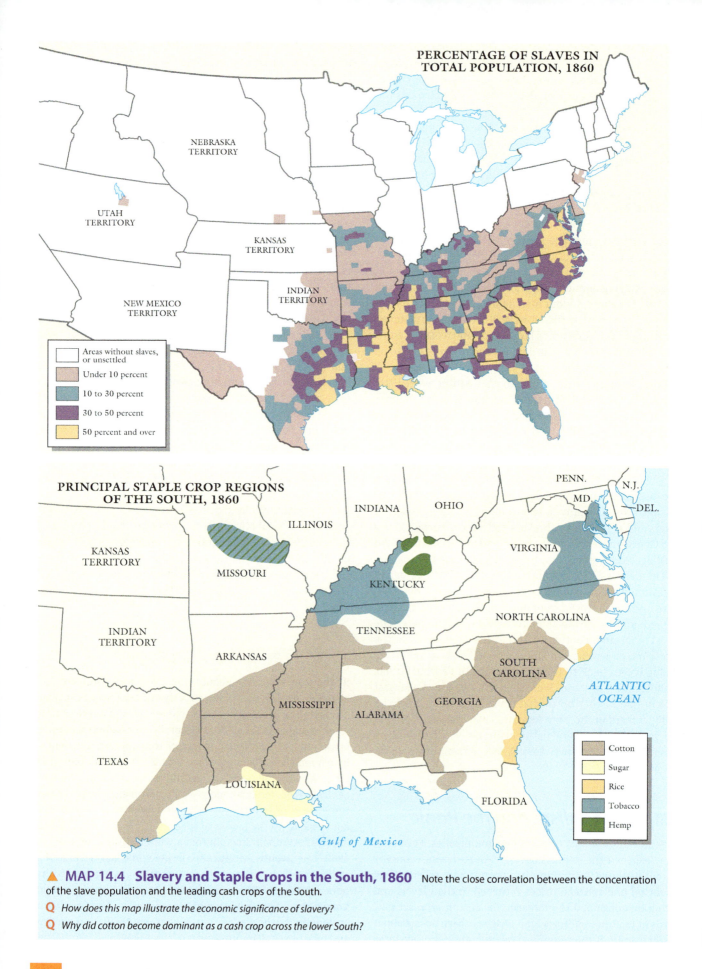

▲ MAP 14.4 **Slavery and Staple Crops in the South, 1860** Note the close correlation between the concentration of the slave population and the leading cash crops of the South.

Q How does this map illustrate the economic significance of slavery?
Q Why did cotton become dominant as a cash crop across the lower South?

14.12 The Panic on Wall Street This October 1857 *Harper's Weekly* cartoon pictures the consternation among New York investors and financiers when banks and businesses crashed in autumn 1857, leading to a short but sharp recession in 1857 and 1858. Notice the frantic men in the background pounding on the doors of a failed bank, while in the foreground one man looks at us and smirks, having likely made a profit from others' disasters.

Q *What attitude towards the 1857 Panic does this cartoon reveal?*

Lincoln drew a rosy picture of northern reality, for large numbers of workers in the North had little hope of advancing beyond the status of wage laborer. Still, he expressed a belief that was widely shared in the antebellum North. "There is not a working boy of average ability in the New England states, at least," observed a visiting British industrialist in 1854, "who has not an idea of some mechanical invention or improvement in manufactures, by which, in good time, he hopes to better his condition, or rise to fortune and social distinction." Americans could point to numerous examples of men who had achieved dramatic upward mobility. Belief in this "American dream" was most strongly held by Protestant farmers, skilled workers, and white-collar workers who had some real hope of getting ahead. These men tended to support the Republican Party and its goal of excluding slavery from the territories.

For slavery was the antithesis of upward mobility. Bondsmen were "fatally fixed in that condition for life," as Lincoln noted. Slaves could not hope to move up the ladder of success, nor could free men who lived in a society where they had to compete with slave labor. "Slavery withers and blights all it touches," declared an Iowa Republican. "It is a curse upon the poor, free, laboring white men." In the United States, social mobility often depended on geographic mobility. The main reason so many families moved into new territories was to make a new start, to get ahead. But, declared a Republican editor, if slavery goes into the territories, "the free labor of all the states will not. If the free labor of the states goes there, the slave labor of the southern states will not, and in a few years the country will teem with an active and energetic population."

Southerners contended that free labor was prone to unrest and strikes. Of course it was, said Lincoln in a speech to a New England audience during the shoemakers' strike of 1860. "I am glad to see that a system prevails in New England under which laborers *can* strike when they want to *(Cheers)*... . I like the system which lets a man quit when he wants to, and wish it might prevail everywhere *(Tremendous applause)*." Strikes were one of the ways in which free workers could try to improve their prospects. "I want every man," said Lincoln, "to have the chance—and I believe a black man is entitled to it—in which he can better his condition." That was why Republicans were determined to contain the expansion of slavery, because if the South got its way in the territories, "free labor that can strike will give way to slave labor that cannot!"

14-5h The Impending Crisis

From the South came a maverick voice that echoed the Republicans. Hinton Rowan Helper considered himself a spokesman for the nonslaveholding whites of the South. Living in upcountry North Carolina, a region of small farms and few slaves, he had brooded for years over slavery's retarding influence on southern development. In 1857, he poured out his bitterness in a book entitled *The Impending Crisis of the South*. Using selective statistics from the 1850 census, he pictured a South mired in economic backwardness, widespread illiteracy, poverty for the masses, and great wealth for the elite. He contrasted this dismal situation with the bustling, prosperous northern economy and its near-universal literacy, neat farms, and progressive institutions. What caused this startling contrast? "Slavery lies at the root of all the shame, poverty, ignorance, tyranny, and imbecility of the South," he wrote. Slavery monopolized the best land, degraded all labor to the level of bond labor, denied schools to the poor, and impoverished all but "the lords of the lash [who] are not only absolute masters of the blacks [but] of all nonslaveholding whites, whose freedom is merely nominal, and whose unparalleled illiteracy and degradation is purposely and fiendishly perpetrated." The remedy? Nonslaveholding whites must organize and use their votes to overthrow "this entire system of oligarchical despotism."

14.13 A Southern Yeoman Farmer's Home This modest log cabin on the edge of a small clearing, with the farmer's wife drawing water from a well in the foreground, was typical of nonslaveholders' farms in the backcountry of the South. Often stigmatized as poor whites, many of these families were in fact comfortable by the standards of the day. They did not feel the sense of oppression by the planter class that Hinton Rowan Helper believed they should feel.

No southern publisher dared touch this book. Helper lugged his bulky manuscript to New York City, where a printer brought it out in summer 1857. *The Impending Crisis* was virtually banned in the South, and few southern whites read it, but it made a huge impact in the North. Republicans welcomed it as confirmation of all they had been saying about the evils of slavery and the virtues of free labor. The Republican Party subsidized an abridged edition and distributed thousands of copies as campaign documents. During the late 1850s, a war of books (Helper's *Impending Crisis* versus Fitzhugh's *Cannibals All*) exacerbated sectional tensions. Fitzhugh's book circulated freely in the North, whereas the sale or possession of Helper's book was a criminal offense in many parts of the South. Northern spokesmen did not hesitate to point out the moral: A free society could tolerate free speech and a free press, but a slave society could not.

14-5i Southern Nonslaveholders

How accurate was Helper's portrayal of southern poor whites degraded by slavery and ready to revolt against it? The touchy response of many southern leaders suggested that the planters felt uneasy about that question. After all, slaveholding families constituted less than one-third of the white population in slave states, and the proportion was declining as the price of slaves continued to rise. Open hostility to the planters' domination of society and politics was evident in the mountainous and upcountry regions of the South. These would become areas of Unionist sentiment during the Civil War and of Republican strength after it.

But Helper surely exaggerated the disaffection of most nonslaveholders in the South. Three bonds held them to the system: kinship, economic interest, and race. In the Piedmont and the low-country regions of the South, nearly half of the whites lived in slaveholding families. Many of the rest were cousins or nephews or in-laws of slaveholders in the South's extensive and tightly knit kinship network. Moreover, many young, ambitious nonslaveholders hoped to buy slaves eventually. Some of them *rented* slaves. And because slaves could be made to do the menial, unskilled labor in the South—the "mudsill" tasks, in Senator Hammond's language—white workers monopolized the more skilled, higher-paying jobs.

Even if they did not own slaves, white people owned the most important asset of all—white skin. White supremacy was an article of faith in the South (and in most of the North, for that matter). Race was a more important social distinction than class. Southern law, politics, and social ideology were based on the concept of domination by the "master race" of whites. Subordination was the Negro's fate, and slavery was the best means of subordination. Emancipation would loose a flood of free blacks on society and would undermine the foundations of white supremacy. Thus many of the poor whites in the South and immigrant workers or poorer farmers in the North supported slavery.

CHAPTER 14 The Gathering Tempest, 1853–1860

Racist themes permeated pro-slavery rhetoric. "With us," said John C. Calhoun in 1848, "the two great divisions of society are not the rich and the poor, but white and black; and all the former, the poor as well as the rich, belong to the upper class, and are respected and treated as equals." True freedom, as Americans understood it, required equality of rights and status (although not of wealth or income). Slavery ensured such freedom for all whites by putting a floor under them, a mudsill of black slaves that kept whites from falling into the mud of inequality. "Break down slavery," said a Virginia congressman, "and you would with the same blow destroy the great Democratic principle of equality among men."

14-6 The Lincoln-Douglas Debates

 What were the major issues of the Lincoln-Douglas debates?

Abraham Lincoln believed the opposite. For him, slavery and freedom were incompatible; the one must die that the other might live. This became the central theme of a memorable series of debates between Lincoln and Douglas in 1858, which came to be known as the **Lincoln-Douglas debates** and turned out to be a dress rehearsal for the presidential election of 1860.

The debates were arranged after Lincoln was nominated to oppose Douglas's reelection to the Senate. State legislatures elected U.S. senators at that time, so the campaign was technically for election by the Illinois legislature. The real issue, however, was the senatorship, and Douglas's prominence gave the contest national significance. Lincoln launched his bid with one of his most notable speeches. "'A house divided against itself cannot stand,'" he said. "I believe this government cannot endure, permanently half slave and half free... . It will become all one thing, or all the other." Under the Dred Scott decision, which Douglas had endorsed, slavery was legal in all of the territories. And what, asked Lincoln, would prevent the Supreme Court, using the same reasoning that had led it to interpret the Constitution as protecting property in slaves, from legalizing slavery in free states? (A case based on this question was then before the New York courts.) The advocates of slavery, charged Lincoln, were trying to "push it forward, till it shall become lawful in all the States." But Republicans intended to keep slavery out of the territories, thus stopping its growth and placing it "where the public mind shall rest in the belief that it is in the course of ultimate extinction."

The seven open-air debates between Douglas and Lincoln focused almost entirely on the issue of slavery. Douglas asked: Why could the country not continue to exist half slave and half free as it had for 70 years? Lincoln's talk about the "ultimate extinction" of slavery would provoke the South to secession. Douglas professed himself no friend of slavery, but if people in the southern states or in the territories wanted it, they had the right to have it. Douglas did not want black people—either slave or free—in Illinois. Lincoln's policy would not only free the slaves but would also grant them equality. "Are you in favor of conferring upon the negro the rights and privileges of citizenship?" Douglas called out to supporters in the crowd. "No, no!" they shouted back. He continued:

> Do you desire to strike out of our State Constitution that clause which keeps slaves and free negroes out of the State ... in order that when Missouri abolishes slavery she can send one hundred thousand emancipated slaves into Illinois, to become citizens and voters on an equality with yourselves? *("Never," "no.")*. ...if you desire to allow them to come into the State and settle with the white man, if you desire them to vote ... then support Mr. Lincoln and the Black Republican party, who are in favor of the citizenship of the negro. *("Never, never.")*

Douglas's demagoguery put Lincoln on the defensive. He responded with cautious denials that he favored "social and political equality" of the races. The "ultimate extinction" of slavery might take a century. It would require the voluntary cooperation of the South and would perhaps be contingent on the emigration of some freed slaves from the country. But come what may, freedom must prevail. Americans must reaffirm the principles of the Founding Fathers. In Lincoln's words, a black person was

> entitled to all the natural rights enumerated in the Declaration of Independence, the right to life, liberty and the pursuit of happiness. *(Loud cheers.)* I hold that he is as much entitled to these as the white man. I agree with Judge Douglas he is not my equal in many respects... . But in the right to eat the bread, without leave of anybody else, which his own hand earns, he is my equal and the equal of Judge Douglas, and the equal of every living man. *(Great applause.)*

Lincoln deplored Douglas's "care not" attitude about whether slavery was voted up or down. He "looks to no end of the institution of slavery," said Lincoln. By endorsing the Dred Scott decision, Lincoln claimed, Douglas looks to its "perpetuity and nationalization." Douglas was thus "eradicating the light of reason and liberty in this American people." That was the real issue in the election, insisted Lincoln:

> That is the issue that will continue in this country when these poor tongues of Judge Douglas and myself shall be silent. It is the eternal struggle between these two principles—right and wrong—throughout the world... . The one is the common right of humanity and the other the divine right of kings... . No matter in what shape it comes, whether from a king who seeks to bestride the people of his own nation and live by the fruit of their labor, or from one race of men as an apology for enslaving another race, it is the same tyrannical principle.

14.14 The Lincoln-Douglas Debates The Lincoln-Douglas contest for the Senate in 1858 produced the most famous—and fateful—political debates in American history. At stake was nothing less than the future of the nation. Thousands of people crowded into seven towns to listen to these three-hour debates that took place outdoors from August to October in weather ranging from stifling heat to cold rain.

Q *What are the similarities and differences between this portrayal of the Lincoln-Douglas Debates and George Caleb Bingham's painting* Stump Speaking *(this chapter's opening image)?*

Q *What do these idealized images reveal about the practice of politics in American life?*

14-6a The Freeport Doctrine

The popular vote for Republican and Democratic state legislators in Illinois was virtually even in 1858, but because apportionment favored the Democrats, they won a majority of seats and reelected Douglas. But Lincoln was the ultimate victor, for his performance in the debates lifted him from political obscurity, while Douglas further alienated southern Democrats. In the Freeport debate, Lincoln had asked Douglas how he reconciled his support for the Dred Scott decision with his policy of popular sovereignty, which supposedly gave residents of a territory the power to vote slavery down. Douglas replied that even though the Court had legalized slavery in the territories, the enforcement of that right would depend on the people who lived there. This was a popular answer in the North, but it gave added impetus to southern demands for congressional passage of a federal slave code in territories such as Kansas, where the Free-Soil majority had by 1859 made slavery virtually null. In the next two sessions of Congress after the 1858 elections, southern Democrats, led by **Jefferson Davis**, tried to pass a federal slave code for all territories. Douglas and northern Democrats joined with Republicans to defeat it. Consequently, southern hostility toward Douglas mounted as the presidential election of 1860 approached.

History Through Film: *Abe Lincoln in Illinois* (1940)

Directed by John Cromwell.
Starring Raymond Massey (Abraham Lincoln), Gene Lockhard (Stephen Douglas), Ruth Gordon (Mary Todd Lincoln).

Raymond Massey's portrayal of Abraham Lincoln in Robert Sherwood's Broadway play, which opened in 1938 and was made into a movie in 1940, launched this Canadian-born actor as the image and voice of Lincoln on stage, screen, and radio for a generation. More people saw or heard Massey as Lincoln than ever saw or heard the real Lincoln. Perhaps that was appropriate because Sherwood's Lincoln spoke more to the generation of the Second World War than to the generation of the Civil War.

In one of the film's most dramatic scenes of the Lincoln-Douglas debates, Massey/Lincoln delivers a speech against slavery that applied equally to fascist totalitarianism and defended democracy in language resonant with the four freedoms that the Allies fought for in the Second World War. In an interview, Massey said, "If you substitute the word *dictatorship* for the word *slavery* throughout Sherwood's script, it becomes electric for our time." In the final scene, as Lincoln departs from Springfield to take up the burdens of the presidency, Massey's Lincoln sees beyond the challenge of disunion to the challenge to democracy in a world at war.

14.15 Raymond Massey as the 23-year-old Abraham Lincoln just elected captain of a New Salem militia company in the Black Hawk War of 1832.

Sherwood skillfully wove together Lincoln's words with his own script to portray Lincoln's growth from the gawky youth of 1831 to the champion of freedom and democracy in 1861. Sherwood took many liberties, but what scriptwriter does not? He combined bits and pieces of several Lincoln speeches into one; he invented incidents and wrenched chronology in some of the 12 scenes from these 30 years of Lincoln's life.

Perhaps the film's sharpest departure from reality is the tension it depicts between "politics," which is bad, and "democracy," which is good. Sherwood's Lincoln doesn't want to play the dirty game of politics; early in the film, the homespun youth declares: "I don't want to be no politician." It is Mary Todd Lincoln who is ambitious for her husband and pushes a reluctant Abraham toward his destiny. The real Lincoln loved the game of politics and played it masterfully. He was also as ambitious in his own right as Mary was for him; Lincoln's law partner William Herndon said that Abraham's ambition was "a little engine that knew no rest." Sherwood's Lincoln who transcends politics to become a great statesman could not have existed without the real Lincoln, the ambitious politician. ■

14-6b John Brown at Harpers Ferry

Southern tempers were already frayed at the start of the 1859–1860 session of Congress because of what had happened at **Harpers Ferry**, Virginia, in the previous October. After his exploits in Kansas, John Brown had disappeared from public view. But he had not been idle. Like the Old Testament warriors he admired, Brown intended to carry his war against slavery into Babylon—the South. His favorite New Testament passage was Hebrews 9:22: "Without shedding of blood there is no remission of sin." Brown worked up a plan to capture the federal arsenal at Harpers Ferry, arm slaves with the muskets he seized there, and move southward along the Appalachian Mountains, attracting more slaves to his army along the way until the "whole accursed system of bondage" collapsed.

Brown recruited 5 black men and 17 whites, including three of his sons, for this reckless scheme. He also had the secret support of a half-dozen Massachusetts and New York abolitionists, who had helped him to raise funds. On the night of October 16, 1859, Brown led his men across the Potomac River and occupied the sleeping town of Harpers Ferry without resistance. Few slaves flocked to his banner, but the next day, state militia units poured into town and drove Brown's band into the fire-engine house. At dawn on October 18, a company of U.S. Marines commanded by Colonel Robert E. Lee and Lieutenant J. E. B. Stuart stormed the engine house and captured the surviving members of Brown's party. Four townsmen, one marine, and ten of Brown's men (including two of his sons) were killed; not a single slave was liberated.

John Brown's raid lasted 36 hours, but its repercussions resounded for years. Brown and six of his followers were promptly tried by the state of Virginia, convicted, and hanged. This scarcely ended matters. The raid sent a wave of revulsion and alarm through the South. Although no slaves had risen in revolt, it revived fears of slave insurrection that were never far beneath the surface of southern consciousness. Exaggerated reports of Brown's network of abolitionist supporters confirmed southern suspicions that a widespread northern conspiracy was afoot, determined to destroy their society. Although Republican leaders denied any connection with Brown and disavowed his actions, few southerners believed them. Had not Lincoln talked of the extinction of slavery? And had not William H. Seward, who was expected to be the next Republican presidential nominee, given a campaign speech in 1858 in which he predicted an irrepressible conflict between the free and slave societies?

Many northerners, impressed by Brown's dignified bearing and eloquence during his trial, considered him a martyr to freedom. In his final statement to the court, Brown said:

> I see a book kissed, which I suppose to be the Bible, which teaches me that all things whatsoever I would that men should do to me, I should do even so to them. It teaches me, further, to remember them that are in bonds as bound with them. I endeavored to act up to that instruction… . Now, if it is deemed necessary that I should forfeit my life for the furtherance of the ends of justice, and mingle my blood further with the blood of my children and with the blood of millions in this slave country whose rights are disregarded by wicked, cruel, and unjust enactments, I say, let it be done.

On the day of Brown's execution, bells tolled in hundreds of northern towns, guns fired salutes, and ministers preached sermons of commemoration. "The death of no man in America has ever produced so profound a sensation," commented one northerner. Ralph Waldo Emerson declared that Brown had made "the gallows as glorious as the cross."

This outpouring of northern sympathy for Brown shocked and enraged southerners and weakened the already frayed threads of the Union. "The Harper's Ferry invasion has advanced the cause of disunion more than any event that has happened since the formation of the government," observed a Richmond, Virginia, newspaper. "I have always been a fervid Union man," wrote a North Carolinian, but "the endorsement of the Harper's Ferry outrage … has shaken my fidelity… . I am willing to take the chances of every possible evil that may arise from disunion, sooner than submit any longer to Northern insolence."

14.16 The Last Moments of John Brown This famous 1882–1884 painting of John Brown by Thomas Hovenden reminds us that the memory of Brown's 1859 attack on Harpers Ferry resonated deeply in American culture. Here, a sentimental portrait of Brown portrays him about to kiss a baby, while the soldiers who will escort him to his death are positioned as an honor guard. Depicting Brown as a gentle hero and martyr to the cause of antislavery, this genre painting avoids grappling with the ferocity and violence of Brown's actions, whether in Kansas or at Harpers Ferry.

Q How would you explain the importance of John Brown in American political history?

Something approaching a reign of terror now gripped the South. Every Yankee seemed to be another John Brown; every slave who acted suspiciously seemed to be an insurrectionist. Hundreds of northerners were run out of the South in 1860, some wearing a coat of tar and feathers. Several "incendiaries," both white and black, were lynched. "Defend yourselves!" Senator Robert Toombs cried out to the southern people. "The enemy is at your door … meet him at the doorsill, and drive him from the temple of liberty, or pull down its pillars and involve him in a common ruin."

Conclusion

Few decades in American history witnessed a greater disjunction between economic well-being and political upheaval than the 1850s. Despite the recession following the Panic of 1857, the total output of the American economy grew by 62 percent during the decade. Railroad mileage more than

What They Said

Reactions to John Brown

The October 1859 attack on Harpers Ferry by John Brown electrified the nation and hardened sectional loyalties. These two newspaper editorials reveal the deep differences in northern and southern interpretations of Brown.

Wilmington, North Carolina, *Daily Herald*, December 5, 1859

It is useless to disguise the fact, that the entire North and Northwest are hopelessly abolitionized. We want no better evidence than that presented to us by their course in this Harper's affair. With the exception of a few papers … that have had the manliness to denounce the act as it deserved, the great majority have either sympathized with the offenders, or maintained an ominous silence.

Let us look calmly at the case: A sovereign State, in the peaceful employment of the rights guaranteed by the Constitution, has been invaded by an armed force, not foreign mercenaries, but citizens of the same Confederacy, and her people shot down in the public highways. The question is a natural one—Why is this thing done? Why is murder and rapine committed?—And who are the perpetrators? The answer is found in the fact that the State whose territory has thus been invaded, is a Southern State in which the institution of slavery exists according to the law and the gospel; and the actors in the terrible drama were but carrying out the precepts and teachings of our *Northern brethren*. The "irrepressible conflict" between the North and the South then, has already commenced; to this complexion it must come at last. It is useless to talk of the conservatism of the North. Where has there been any evidence of it? Meetings upon meetings have been held for the purpose of expressing sympathy for murderers and traitors; but none, no, not one solitary expression of horror, or disapprobation even, for the crime committed, have we yet seen from any State North of Mason & Dixon's line.

Horace Greeley, *New-York Tribune*, December 3, 1859

We are not those who say, "if slavery is wrong, then John Brown was wholly right." There are fit and unfit modes of combating a great evil; we think Brown at Harper's Ferry pursued the latter…. And, while we heartily wish every slave in the world would run away from his master tomorrow and never be retaken, we should not feel justified in entering a slave state to incite them to do so, even if we were sure to succeed in the enterprise. Of course, we regard Brown's raid as utterly mistaken and, in its direct consequences, pernicious.

But his are the errors of a fanatic, not the crimes of a felon. It were absurd to apply to him opprobrious epithets or wholesale denunciations. The essence of crime is the pursuit of selfish gratification in disregard of others' good; and that is the precise opposite of Old Brown's impulse and deed. He periled and sacrificed not merely his own life—that were, perhaps, a moderate stake—but the lives of his beloved sons, the earthly happiness of his family and theirs, to benefit a despised and downtrodden race—to deliver from bitter bondage and degradation those whom he had never seen.

Unwise, the world will pronounce him. Reckless of artificial yet palpable obligations he certainly was, but his very errors were heroic—the faults of a brave, impulsive, truthful nature, impatient of wrong, and only too conscious that "resistance to tyrants is obedience to God." Let whoever would first cast a stone ask himself whether his own noblest act was equal in grandeur and nobility to that for which John Brown pays the penalty of death on the gallows.

Q The Wilmington, North Carolina, editorial writer accuses the entire North of being "abolitionized." Is this a fair accusation? Why or why not?

Q Would southerners have been reassured by Greeley's assertion that Brown's raid was "utterly mistaken"? Why or why not? What does Greeley argue in the rest of his editorial?

Sources: (top) From an editorial in the newspaper: Wilmington, North Carolina, *Daily Herald*, December 5, 1859. (bottom) From an editorial by Horace Greeley in the newspaper *New-York Tribune*, December 3, 1859.

tripled, value added by manufacturing nearly doubled, and gross farm product grew by 40 percent. Americans were more prosperous than ever before.

Yet a profound malaise gripped the country. Riots between immigrants and nativists in the mid-1850s left more than 50 people dead. Fighting in Kansas between pro-slavery and antislavery forces killed at least 200. Fistfights broke out on the floor of Congress. A South Carolina congressman bludgeoned a Massachusetts senator to unconsciousness with a heavy cane. Representatives and senators came to congressional sessions armed with weapons as well as with violent words.

The nation proved capable of absorbing the large influx of immigrants despite the tensions and turmoil of the mid-1850s. It might also have been able to absorb the huge territorial expansion of the late 1840s had not the slavery issue been reopened in an earlier territorial acquisition, the Louisiana Purchase, by the Kansas-Nebraska Act of 1854. This legislation, followed by the Dred Scott decision in 1857, seemed to authorize the unlimited expansion of slavery. Within two years of its founding in 1854, however, the Republican Party emerged as the largest party in the North on a platform of preventing all future expansion of slavery. By 1860, the United States had reached a fateful crossroads. As Lincoln had said, it could not endure permanently half-slave and half-free. The presidential election of 1860 would decide which road America would take into the future.

CHAPTER REVIEW

Review

1. Why did the Whig Party die, and why did the Republican Party emerge as the new majority party in the North?
2. What were the origins of nativism? How did this movement relate to the slavery issue?
3. How was violence in Kansas related to the issue of slavery?
4. What role did the issue of slavery play in the election of 1856?
5. How did economic developments in the 1840s and 1850s widen the breach between North and South?
6. What were the major issues of the Lincoln-Douglas debates?

Critical Thinking

1. Why did the northern and southern economic systems develop in such different directions? Why did the effort by some southerners to escape from their "colonial" economic relationship fail?
2. One of the main points of contention in the Lincoln-Douglas debates was the question of whether the country could continue to endure half-slave and half-free. Why did Lincoln challenge Douglas's position that because the nation had so endured for 70 years, there was no reason why it could not continue to do so?

Identifications

Review your understanding of the following key terms, people, and events for this chapter (terms in bold in text are included in the Glossary).

Dred Scott, p. 377
Harpers Ferry, p. 377
John Brown, p. 377
Kansas-Nebraska Act, p. 378
Abraham Lincoln, p. 378
nativism, p. 379
Know-Nothings, p. 379
"border ruffians", p. 383
Black Republicans, p. 386
interchangeable parts, p. 389
colonial economy, p. 392
free-labor ideology, p. 395
Lincoln-Douglas debates, p. 399
Jefferson Davis, p. 400

Suggested Readings

For an overview of the 1850s, see **James M. McPherson**, *Battle Cry of Freedom: The Civil War Era* (1988). The Kansas-Nebraska Act and its political consequences are treated in **Gerald W. Wolff**, *The Kansas-Nebraska Bill: Party, Section, and the Coming of the Civil War* (1977). The conflict in Kansas is treated in **Nicole Etcheson**, *Bleeding Kansas: Contested Liberty in the Civil War Era* (2004). For the cross-cutting issue of nativism and the Know-Nothings, see **William E. Gienapp**, *The Origins of the Republican Party, 1852–1856* (1987), and **Tyler Anbinder**, *Nativism and Politics: The Know Nothing Party in the Northern United States* (1992). Two excellent studies of the role of Abraham Lincoln in the rise of the Republican Party are **Don E. Fehrenbacher**, *Prelude to Greatness: Lincoln in the 1850s* (1962), and **Kenneth Winkle**, *The Young Eagle: The Rise of Abraham Lincoln* (2003). The southern response to the growth of antislavery political sentiment in the North is the theme of **William J. Cooper, Jr.**, *The South and the Politics of Slavery 1828–1856* (1978).

The year 1857 witnessed a convergence of many crucial events; for a stimulating book that pulls together the threads of that year of crisis, see **Kenneth M. Stampp**, *America in*

1857: A Nation on the Brink (1990). For economic developments during the era, an older classic is still the best introduction: **George Rogers Taylor**, *The Transportation Revolution, 1815–1860* (1951). An important dimension of the southern economy is elucidated in **Fred Bateman and Thomas Weiss**, *A Deplorable Scarcity: The Failure of Industrialization in the Slave Economy* (1981). The political impact of the Panic of 1857 is the subject of **James L. Huston**, *The Panic of 1857 and the Coming of the Civil War* (1987). Still the best study of Republican free-labor ideology is **Eric Foner**, *Free Soil, Free Labor, Free Men: The Ideology of the Republican Party before the Civil War* (2nd ed., 1995). For southern yeoman farmers, a good study is **Stephanie McCurry**, *Masters of Small Worlds: Yeoman Households, Gender Relations, and the Political Culture of the Antebellum South Carolina Low Country* (1995). The best single study of the Dred Scott case is **Don E. Fehrenbacher**, *The Dred Scott Case: Its Significance in American Law and Politics* (1978), which was published in an abridged version with the title *Slavery, Law, and Politics: The Dred Scott Case in Historical Perspective* (1981). A thought-provoking biography of John Brown is **David S. Reynolds**, *John Brown: Abolitionist* (2005). On Harper's Ferry see also **Tony Horwitz**, *Midnight Rising: John Brown and the Raid that Sparked the Civil War* (2011).

 MINDTAP is a fully online personalized learning experience built upon Cengage Learning content. MindTap® combines student learning tools—readings, multimedia, activities, and assessments—into a singular Learning Path that guides students through the course and helps students develop the critical thinking, analysis, and communication skills that are essential to academic and professional success.

15 Secession and Civil War, 1860–1862

15-1 The Election of 1860
Learning Objective: Explain why the Republican Party chose Abraham Lincoln as its candidate in 1860.

The Republicans Nominate Lincoln
Southern Fears

15-2 The Lower South Secedes
Learning Objective: Explain why political leaders in the lower South thought secession was imperative after Lincoln's election.

Northerners Affirm the Union
Compromise Proposals
Establishment of the Confederacy

15-3 The Fort Sumter Issue
Learning Objective: Discuss the reasons why compromise efforts to forestall secession failed, and explain why war broke out at Fort Sumter.

15-4 Choosing Sides
Learning Objective: Explain why the border states remained in the Union.

The Border States
The Creation of West Virginia
Indian Territory and the Southwest

15-5 The Balance Sheet of War
Learning Objective: Summarize northern and southern advantages and disadvantages in the Civil War.

Strategy and Morale
Mobilizing for War
Weapons and Tactics
Logistics
Financing the War

15-6 Navies, the Blockade, and Foreign Relations
Learning Objective: Discuss why Confederate foreign policy failed to win diplomatic recognition from other nations.

King Cotton Diplomacy
The *Trent* Affair
The Confederate Navy
The *Monitor* and the *Virginia*

15-7 Campaigns and Battles, 1861–1862
Learning Objective: Explain how the Union's and Confederacy's respective military advantages played out in the campaigns and battles of 1861 and 1862.

The Battle of Bull Run
Naval Operations
Fort Henry and Fort Donelson
The Battle of Shiloh
The Virginia Theater
The Seven Days' Battles

15-8 Confederate Counteroffensives
Learning Objective: Identify the reasons why Confederate forces were able to launch successful counteroffensives in the summer of 1862.

The Second Battle of Bull Run

15.1 **Tent Life of the 31st Pennsylvania Infantry Regiment** This posed photograph, taken in camp near Washington, D.C. in 1861, shows us the home created by one ordinary soldier and his family in the midst of war. In the background several soldiers and an African American man watch the photographic process with interest. Many women followed their husbands to war in 1861 and 1862, when men in the Army of the Potomac spent long months in camp. But families were left behind when military campaigns began and men marched away.

AS 1860 BEGAN, THE DEMOCRATIC PARTY was one of the few national institutions left in the country. The Whig Party and the nativist American Party had been shattered by sectional antagonism in the mid-1850s. In April 1860, even the Democratic Party, at its national convention in Charleston, South Carolina, split into northern and southern camps. This virtually ensured the election of a Republican president. Such a prospect aroused deep fears among southern whites that a Republican administration might use its power to bring liberty and perhaps even equality to the slaves.

When Abraham Lincoln was elected president, the lower-South states seceded from the Union. When Lincoln refused to remove U.S. troops from **Fort Sumter**, South Carolina, the new Confederate States army opened fire on the fort. Lincoln called out the militia to suppress the insurrection. Four more slave states seceded. In 1861, the country drifted into a civil war whose immense consequences no one could foresee.

CHRONOLOGY

1860 Lincoln elected president (November 6) • South Carolina secedes (December 20) • Federal troops transfer from Fort Moultrie to Fort Sumter (December 26)

1861 Rest of lower South secedes (January–February) • Crittenden Compromise rejected (February) • Jefferson Davis inaugurated as provisional president of new Confederate States of America (February 18) • Abraham Lincoln inaugurated as president of the United States (March 4) • Fort Sumter falls; Lincoln calls out troops, proclaims blockade (April) • Four more states secede to join Confederacy (April–May) • Battle of Bull Run (Manassas) (July 21) • Battle of Wilson's Creek (August 10) • The *Trent* Affair (November–December)

1862 Union captures Forts Henry and Donelson (February 6 and 16) • Congress passes Legal Tender Act (February 25) • Battle of Pea Ridge (March 7–8) • Battle of the *Monitor* and *Merrimac* (*Virginia*) (March 9) • Battle of Glorieta Pass (March 26–28) • Battle of Shiloh (April 6–7) • Union navy captures New Orleans (April 25) • Stonewall Jackson's Shenandoah Valley campaign (May–June) • Seven Days' battles (June 25–July 1) • Second Battle of Manassas (Bull Run) (August 29–30) • Lee invades Maryland (September) • Battle of Corinth (October 3–4) • Battle of Perryville (October 8)

1863 Congress passes National Banking Act (February 25)

15-1 The Election of 1860

Q *Why did the Republican Party choose Abraham Lincoln as its candidate in 1860?*

A hotbed of southern-rights radicalism, Charleston, South Carolina, turned out to be the worst possible place for the Democrats to hold their national convention. Sectional confrontations took place inside the convention hall and on the streets. Since 1836, the Democratic Party had required a two-thirds majority of delegates for a presidential nomination, a rule that in effect gave southerners veto power. Although Stephen A. Douglas had the backing of a simple majority of the delegates, southern Democrats were determined to deny him the nomination. His opposition to the Lecompton constitution in Kansas had convinced pro-slavery southerners that they would be unable to control a Douglas administration.

The first test came in the debate on the platform. Southern delegates insisted on a plank favoring a federal slave code for the territories. Douglas could not run on a platform that contained such a plank, and if the party adopted it, Democrats were sure to lose every state in the North. By a slim majority, the convention rejected the plank and reaffirmed the 1856 platform endorsing popular sovereignty. Fifty southern delegates thereupon walked out of the convention. Even after they left, Douglas could not muster a two-thirds majority, nor could any other candidate. After 57 futile ballots, the convention adjourned to meet in Baltimore 6 weeks later to try again.

By then the party was too badly shattered to be put back together. That pleased some pro-slavery radicals. The election of a "Black Republican" president, they believed, would provide the shock necessary to mobilize a southern majority for **secession**. Two of the most prominent secessionists were William L. Yancey and Edmund Ruffin. In 1858, they founded the League of United Southerners to "fire the Southern heart ... and at the proper moment, by one organized, concerted action, we can precipitate the Cotton States into a revolution." After walking out of the Democratic convention, the eloquent Yancey inspired a huge crowd in Charleston's moonlit courthouse square to give three cheers "for an Independent Southern Republic."

In Baltimore, an even larger number of delegates from southern states walked out. They formed their own Southern Rights Democratic Party and nominated John C. Breckinridge of Kentucky (the incumbent vice president) for president on a slave-code platform. When regular Democrats nominated Douglas, the stage was set for what would become a four-party election. A coalition of former southern Whigs, who could not bring themselves to vote Democratic, and northern Whigs, who considered the Republican Party too radical, formed the Constitutional Union Party, which nominated John Bell of Tennessee for president. Bell had no chance of winning; the party's purpose was to exercise a conservative influence on a campaign that threatened to polarize the country.

15-1a The Republicans Nominate Lincoln

From the moment the Democratic Party broke apart, it became clear that 1860 could be the year when the dynamic young Republican Party elected its first president. The Republicans could expect no electoral votes from the 15 slave states. In 1856, however, they had won all but five northern states, and with only two or three of those five they could win the presidency. The crucial states were Pennsylvania, Illinois, and Indiana. Douglas might still carry them and throw the presidential election into the House, where anything could happen. Thus the Republicans had to carry at least two of the swing states to win.

As the Republican delegates poured into Chicago for their convention, their leading presidential prospect was William H. Seward of New York. An experienced politician who had served as governor and senator, Seward was by all odds the most prominent Republican, but in his long career he had made many enemies. His antinativist policies had alienated some former members of the American Party, whose support he would need to carry Pennsylvania. His "Higher Law" speech against the Compromise of 1850 and

15.2 The Inauguration of President Lincoln on March 4, 1861 Only distant photographic views survive of Abraham Lincoln's fist inauguration. Here Lincoln is just visible standing under the wood canopy in the center of the photograph as he delivers his inaugural address to a large crowd. While his face is in shadow, we can see his white shirt front. Above him, the scaffolding reminds us that the Capitol Dome was unfinished at the time.

his "Irrepressible Conflict" speech in 1858, predicting the ultimate overthrow of slavery, had given him a reputation for radicalism that might drive away voters in the vital swing states of the lower North.

Several of the delegates, uneasy about that reputation, staged a stop-Seward movement. The next candidate to the fore was Abraham Lincoln. Although he too had opposed nativism, he had done so less prominently than Seward. His "House Divided" speech had made essentially the same point as Seward's "Irrepressible Conflict" speech, but his reputation was still that of a more moderate man. He was from one of the lower-North states where the election would be close, and his rise from a poor farm boy and rail-splitter to successful lawyer and political leader perfectly reflected the free-labor theme of social mobility extolled by the Republican Party. By picking up second-choice votes from states that switched from their favorite sons, Lincoln overtook Seward and won the nomination on the third ballot. Seward accepted the outcome gracefully, and the Republicans headed into the campaign as a united, confident party.

The Republican platform appealed to many groups in the North. Its main plank pledged exclusion of slavery from the territories. Other planks called for a higher tariff (especially popular in Pennsylvania), a homestead act (popular in the Northwest), and federal aid for construction of a transcontinental railroad and for improvement of river navigation. This program was designed for a future in which the "house divided" would become a free-labor society modeled on northern capitalism. Its blend of idealism and materialism proved especially attractive to young people; a large majority of first-time voters in the North voted Republican in 1860.

15-1b *Southern Fears*

Militant enthusiasm in the North was matched by fear and rage in the South. Few people there could see any difference between Lincoln and Seward—or for that matter between Lincoln and William Lloyd Garrison. They were all Black Republicans and abolitionists. Had not Lincoln branded slavery a moral, social, and political evil? Had he not said that the Declaration of Independence applied to blacks as well as whites? Had he not expressed a hope that excluding slavery from the territories would put it on the road to ultimate extinction? To southerners, the Republican pledge not to interfere with slavery in the states was meaningless.

A Republican victory in the presidential election would put an end to the South's political control of its destiny. Two-thirds of the time from 1789 to 1860, southerners (all slaveholders) had been president of the United States. Two-thirds of the Speakers of the House and presidents pro tem of the Senate had been southerners. Southern justices had been a majority on the Supreme Court since 1791. Lincoln's election would mark an irreversible turning away from this southern ascendancy. Even southern moderates warned that the South could not remain in the Union if Lincoln won. "This Government and Black Republicanism cannot live together," said one of them.

Most whites in the South voted for Breckinridge, who carried 11 slave states (see Map 15.1). Bell won the upper-South states of Virginia, Kentucky, and Tennessee. Missouri went to Douglas—the only state he carried, although he came in second in the popular vote. Although Lincoln received less than 40 percent of the popular vote, he won every free state and swept the presidency by a substantial margin in the Electoral College (see Table 15.1).

15.3 Wide-Awake Parade in New York, October 5, 1860 The Wide-Awakes were an organization of young Republicans who roused political enthusiasm by marching in huge torchlight parades during the political campaign of 1860. A year later, many of these same men would march down the same streets in army uniforms carrying rifles instead of torches on their way to the front.

Table 15.1 VOTING IN THE 1860 ELECTION

Candidate	All States		Free States (18)		Slave States (15)	
	Popular	Electoral	Popular	Electoral	Popular	Electoral
Lincoln	1,864,735	180	1,838,347	180	26,388	0
Opposition to Lincoln	2,821,157	123	1,572,637	3	1,248,520	120
"Fusion" Tickets*	595,846	—	580,426	—	15,420	—
Douglas	979,425	12	815,857	3	163,568	9
Breckinridge	669,472	72	99,381	0	570,091	72
Bell	576,414	39	76,973	0	499,441	39

*In several states, the two Democratic parties and the Constitutional Union Party arranged a single anti-Lincoln ballot. These "fusion" tickets carried several counties but failed to win any state.

15-2 The Lower South Secedes

Q *Why did political leaders in the lower South think that Lincoln's election made secession imperative?*

Lincoln's victory provided the shock that southern fire-eaters had craved. The tension that had been building up for years suddenly exploded like a string of firecrackers, as seven states seceded one after another. According to the theory of secession, when each state ratified the Constitution and joined the Union, it authorized the national government to act as its agent in the exercise of certain functions of sovereignty, but the states had never given away their fundamental underlying sovereignty. Any state, then, by the act of its own convention, could withdraw from its "compact" with the other states and reassert its individual sovereignty. Therefore, the South Carolina legislature called for such a convention and ordered an election of delegates to consider withdrawing from the United States. On December 20, 1860, the South Carolina convention did withdraw, by a vote of 169 to 0.

The outcome was closer in other lower-South states. Unconditional unionism was rare, but many conservatives and former Whigs shrank from the drastic step of secession. At the conventions in each of the next six states to secede, some delegates tried to delay matters with vague proposals for "cooperation" among all southern states, or even with proposals to wait until after Lincoln's inauguration on March 4, 1861, to see what course he would pursue. Nonetheless, proponents of immediate secession overrode those minority factions. The conventions followed the example of South Carolina and voted to take their states out of the Union: Mississippi on January 9, 1861; Florida on the 10th; Alabama

15.4 Banner of the South Carolina Secession Convention
With its banner featuring a palmetto tree and a snake reminiscent of the American Revolution's "Don't Tread on Me" slogan, the South Carolina secession convention in 1860 looked forward to a grand new southern republic composed of all 15 slave states and built on the ruins of the old Union. Note the large South Carolina keystone of the arch and the stones of free states lying cracked and broken on the ground.

European monarchists and conservatives were already expressing smug satisfaction at "the great smashup" of the republic in North America. They predicted that other disaffected minorities would also secede and that the United States would ultimately collapse into anarchy and revolution. That was precisely what northerners and even some upper-South **Unionists** feared. "The doctrine of secession is anarchy," declared a Cincinnati newspaper. "If any minority have the right to break up the Government at pleasure, because they have not had their way, there is an end of all government." Lincoln denied that the states had ever possessed independent sovereignty before becoming part of the United States. Rather, they had been colonies or territories that never would have become part of the United States had they not accepted unconditional sovereignty of the national government. "No State, upon its own mere motion, can lawfully get out of the Union ... . They can only do so against law, and by revolution."

In that case, answered many southerners, we invoke the right of revolution to justify secession. After all, the United States was born of revolution. The secessionists maintained that they were merely following the example of their forefathers in declaring independence from a government that threatened their rights and liberties. An Alabaman asked rhetorically: "[Were not] the men of 1776, who withdrew their allegiance from George III and set up for themselves ... Secessionists?"

Northerners could scarcely deny the right of revolution: They too were heirs of 1776. But "the right of revolution, is never a legal right," said Lincoln. "At most, it is but a moral right, when exercised for a morally justifiable cause. When exercised without such a cause revolution is no right, but simply a wicked exercise of physical power." The South, in Lincoln's view, had no morally justifiable cause. In fact, the event that had precipitated secession was his very election by a constitutional majority. For southerners to cast themselves in the mold of 1776 was "a libel upon the whole character and conduct" of the Founding Fathers, said the antislavery poet and journalist William Cullen Bryant. They rebelled "to establish the rights of man ... and principles of universal liberty," whereas southerners in 1861 were rebelling to protect "a domestic despotism ... . Their motto is not liberty, but slavery."

on the 11th; Georgia on the 19th; Louisiana on the 26th; and Texas on February 1. In those six states as a whole, 20 percent of the delegates voted against secession, but most of these "went with their states" after the final votes had been tallied. Delegates from the seven seceding states met in Montgomery, Alabama, in February to create a new nation to be called the Confederate States of America.

15-2a Northerners Affirm the Union

Most people in the North considered secession unconstitutional and treasonable. In his final annual message to Congress, on December 3, 1860, President Buchanan insisted that the Union was not "a mere voluntary association of States, to be dissolved at pleasure by any one of the contracting parties." If secession were consummated, Buchanan warned, it would create a disastrous precedent that would make the United States government "a rope of sand." He continued:

> Our thirty-three States may resolve themselves into as many petty, jarring, and hostile republics ... . By such a dread catastrophe ... our example for more than eighty years would not only be lost, but it would be quoted as proof that man is unfit for self-government.

15-2b Compromise Proposals

Bryant conveniently overlooked the fact that slavery had existed in most parts of the republic founded by the revolutionaries of 1776. In any event, most people in the North agreed with Lincoln that secession was a "wicked exercise of physical power." The question was what to do about it. All kinds of compromise proposals came before Congress when it met in December 1860. To sort them out, the Senate and the House each set up a special committee. The Senate committee came up with a package of compromises sponsored by Senator John J. Crittenden of Kentucky. The Crittenden Compromise consisted of a series of proposed constitutional amendments: to guarantee slavery in the states perpetually against federal interference; to prohibit Congress from abolishing slavery in the

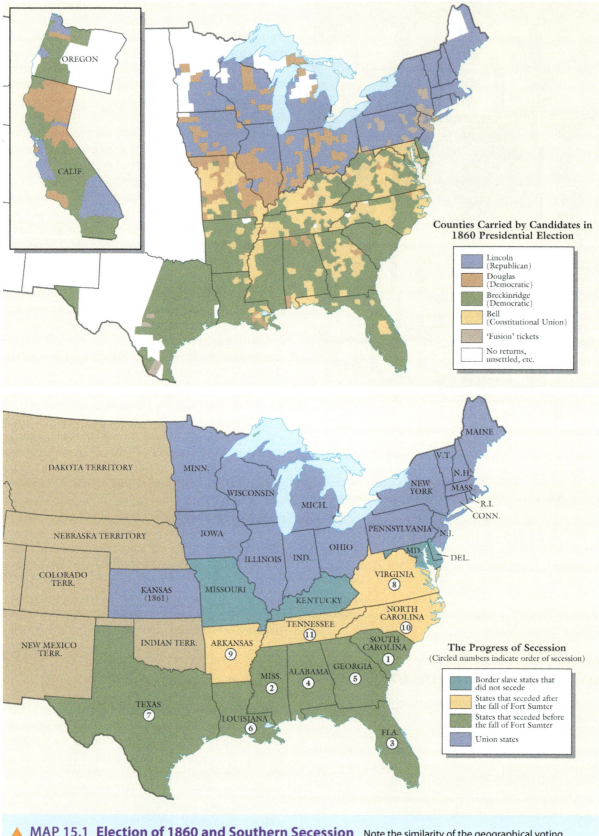

▲ **MAP 15.1 Election of 1860 and Southern Secession** Note the similarity of the geographical voting patterns in the upper map compared to Map 14.2 on p. 388.

Q *Can you explain the correlation between the vote for Breckinridge (upper map) and the first seven states to secede (lower map)?*

Q *Why didn't Douglas have more support in the South?*

District of Columbia or on any federal property (forts, arsenals, naval bases, and so on); to deny Congress the power to interfere with the interstate slave trade; to compensate slaveholders who were prevented from recovering fugitive slaves who had escaped to the North; and, most important, to protect slavery south of latitude 36° 30″ in all territories "now held *or hereafter acquired*."

Given the appetite of the South for more slave territory in the Caribbean and Central America, that italicized phrase, in the view of most Republicans, might turn the United States into "a great slavebreeding and slavetrading empire." But even though endorsement of the territorial clause in the Crittenden Compromise would require Republicans to repudiate the platform on which they had just won the election, some conservatives in the party were willing to accept it in the interest of peace and conciliation. Their votes, together with those of Democrats and upper-South Unionists whose states had not seceded, might have gotten the compromise through Congress. In any case, word came from Springfield, Illinois, where president-elect Lincoln was preparing for his inaugural trip to Washington, telling key Republican senators and congressmen to stand firm against compromise on the territorial issue. "Entertain no proposition for a compromise in regard to the *extension* of slavery," wrote Lincoln.

> We have just carried an election on principles fairly stated to the people. Now we are told in advance, the government shall be broken up, unless we surrender to those we have beaten … . If we surrender, it is the end of us. They will repeat the experiment upon us *ad libitum*. A year will not pass, till we shall have to take Cuba as a condition upon which they will stay in the Union.

Lincoln's advice was decisive. The Republicans voted against the Crittenden Compromise, which therefore failed in Congress. Most Republicans, though, went along with a proposal by Virginia for a "peace convention" of all the states to be held in Washington in February 1861. In the end, however, the peace convention produced nothing better than a modified version of the Crittenden Compromise, which suffered the same fate as the original.

Nothing that happened in Washington would have made any difference to the seven states that had seceded. No compromise could bring them back. "We spit upon every plan to compromise," said one secessionist. No power could "stem the wild torrent of passion that is carrying everything before it," wrote former U.S. senator Judah P. Benjamin of Louisiana. Secession "is a revolution [that] can no more be checked by human effort … than a prairie fire by a gardener's watering pot."

15-2c Establishment of the Confederacy

While the peace convention deliberated in Washington, the seceded states focused on a convention in Montgomery, Alabama, that drew up a constitution and established a government for the new Confederate States of America. The Confederate constitution contained clauses that guaranteed slavery in both the states and the territories, strengthened the principle of state sovereignty, and prohibited its Congress from enacting a protective (as distinguished from a revenue) tariff. It limited the president to a single 6-year term. The convention delegates constituted themselves a provisional Congress for the new nation until regular elections could be held in November 1861. For provisional president and vice president, the convention turned away from radical secessionists, such as Yancey, and elected Jefferson Davis, a moderate secessionist, and Alexander Stephens, who had originally opposed Georgia's secession but ultimately had supported it.

Davis and Stephens were two of the most able men in the South, with 25 years of service in the U.S. Congress between them. A West Point graduate, Davis had commanded a regiment in the Mexican War and had been secretary of war in the Pierce administration—a useful fund of experience if civil war became a reality. But perhaps the main reason they were elected was to present an image of moderation and respectability to the eight upper-South states that remained in the Union. The Confederacy needed those states—at least some of them—if it was to be a viable nation, especially if war came. Without the upper South, the Confederate states would have less than one-fifth of the population (and barely one-tenth of the free population) and only one-twentieth of the industrial capacity of the Union states.

Confederate leaders appealed to the upper South to join them because of the "common origin, pursuits, tastes, manners and customs [that] bind together in one brotherhood the … slaveholding states." Residents of the upper South were indeed concerned about preserving slavery, but the issue was less salient there (see Table 15.2). A strong heritage of Unionism competed with the commitment to slavery. Virginia had contributed more men to the pantheon of Founding Fathers than any other state. Tennessee took pride in being the state of Andrew Jackson, who was famous for his stern warning to John C. Calhoun: "Our Federal Union—It must be preserved." Kentucky was the home of Henry Clay, the Great Pacificator, who had put together compromises to save the Union on three occasions. These states would not leave the Union without greater cause.

15-3 The Fort Sumter Issue

Q *Why did compromise efforts to forestall secession fail, and why did war break out at Fort Sumter?*

As each state seceded, it seized the forts, arsenals, customs houses, and other federal property within its borders. Still in federal hands, however, were two remote forts in the Florida Keys, another on an island off Pensacola, and Fort Moultrie in the Charleston harbor. Moultrie quickly became a bone of contention. In December 1860, the self-proclaimed republic of South Carolina demanded its evacuation by the 84-man garrison of the U.S. Army. Moultrie was vulnerable to attack by the South Carolina militia that swarmed into the area. On the day after Christmas 1860, Major Robert Anderson, commander at Moultrie, moved his men to Fort Sumter, an uncompleted but immensely strong bastion on an artificial island in the

What They Said

Cornerstone of the Confederacy

Alexander H. Stephens of Georgia had opposed the secession of his state in January 1861. But when Georgia seceded anyway, he "went with his state," as did so many other southerners who had initially counseled against secession. Stephens was subsequently elected vice president of the Confederate States of America. On March 21, 1861, he gave an address in Savannah, Georgia, which became known as the Cornerstone Speech, in which he proclaimed slavery to be the cornerstone of the new Confederacy.

After the Civil War, however, Stephens wrote a two-volume history titled *The War Between the States*, in which he maintained that slavery was not the cornerstone of the Confederacy or the reason for secession. Instead, he argued that in seceding from the Union, southerners had defended a "great right, which lies at the foundation of the federative system"—what Stephens saw as a fundamental constitutional right of independence and state sovereignty.

▶ Alexander H. Stephens, "The Cornerstone of the Confederacy," 1861

The new Constitution [of the Confederate States] has put at rest forever all the agitating questions relating to our peculiar institution—African slavery as it exists among us—the proper status of the negro in our form of civilization. This was the immediate cause of the late rupture and present revolution.

[Thomas] Jefferson, in his forecast, had anticipated this, as the "rock upon which the old Union would split." He was right …. But whether he fully comprehended the great truth upon which that rock stood and stands, may be doubted. The prevailing ideas entertained by him and most of the leading statesmen at the time of the formation of the old Constitution were, that the enslavement of the African was in violation of the laws of nature; that it was wrong in principle, socially, morally, and politically. It was an evil they knew not well how to deal with; but the general opinion of the men of that day was, that, somehow or other, in the order of Providence, the institution would be evanescent and pass away …. Those ideas, however, were fundamentally wrong ….

Our new Government is founded upon exactly the opposite ideas; its foundations are laid, its cornerstone rests, upon the great truth that the negro is not equal to the white man; that slavery, subordination to the superior race, is his natural and moral condition. This, our new Government, is the first, in the history of the world, based upon this great physical, philosophical, and moral truth.

▶ Alexander H. Stephens, *The War Between the States*, 1868

The matter of Slavery, so-called … was of infinitely less importance to the Seceding States, than the recognition of this great principle [the right of withdrawal on the part of the seceding States]. I say Slavery, so-called, because there was with us no such thing as Slavery in the full and proper sense of that word. No people ever lived more devoted to the principles of liberty, secured by free democratic institutions, than were the people of the South. None had ever given stronger proofs of this than they had done, from the day that Virginia moved in behalf of the assailed rights of Massachusetts, in 1774, to the firing of the first gun in Charleston Harbor, in 1861. What was called Slavery amongst us, was but a legal subordination of the African to the Caucasian race. This relation was so regulated by law as to promote, according to the intent and design of the system, the best interests of both races, the Black as well as the White, the Inferior, as well as the Superior. Both had rights secured, and both had duties imposed. It was a system of reciprocal service, and mutual bonds. But even the two thousand million dollars invested in the relation thus established, between private capital and the labor of this class of population, under the system, was but as the dust in the balance, compared with the vital attributes of the rights of Independence and Sovereignty on the part of the several States.

Q *Why did Stephens deny the central importance of slavery to the seceding states in his 1868 history? How had his views changed from 1861, and why?*

Q *Did Stephens's justifications for slavery change at all between 1861 and 1868?*

Sources: (top) From speech by Alexander H. Stephens, "The Cornerstone of the Confederacy," 1861 reprinted in Alexander H. Stephens in *Public and Private with Letters and Speeches Before, During, and After the War*, ed. Henry Cleveland, Philadelphia (National Publishing Company, 1866), p. 721. (bottom) From Alexander H. Stephens, *A Constitutional View of the Late War Between the States*, (National Publishing Company, 1868).

channel leading into Charleston Bay. A Kentuckian married to a Georgian, Anderson sympathized with the South but remained loyal to the United States. He deplored the possibility of war and hoped that moving the garrison to Sumter would ease tensions by reducing the possibility of an attack. Instead, it lit a fuse that eventually set off the war.

South Carolina sent a delegation to President Buchanan to negotiate the withdrawal of the federal troops. Buchanan surprised them by saying no. He even tried to reinforce the garrison. On January 9, the unarmed merchant ship *Star of the West*, carrying 200 soldiers for Sumter, tried to enter the bay but was driven away by South Carolina artillery. Loath to start a war, Major Anderson refused to return fire with Sumter's guns. Matters then settled into an uneasy truce. The Confederate government sent General Pierre G. T. Beauregard to take command of the troops ringing Charleston Bay with their cannons pointed at Fort Sumter, and waited to see what the incoming Lincoln administration would do.

When Abraham Lincoln took the oath of office as the 16th—and, some speculated, the last—president of the United States, he knew that his inaugural address would be the most important in American history. On his words would hang the issues of union or disunion, peace or war. His goal was to keep the upper South in the Union while cooling passions in the lower South, hoping that, in time, southern loyalty to the Union would reassert itself. In his address, he demonstrated firmness in purpose to preserve the Union and forbearance in the means of doing so. He repeated his pledge not "to interfere with the institution of slavery where it exists." He assured the Confederate states, "the government will not assail *you*." His first draft had also included the phrase "unless you *first* assail it," but William H. Seward, whom Lincoln had appointed secretary of state, persuaded him to drop those words as too provocative. Lincoln's first draft had also stated his intention to use "all the powers at my disposal [to] reclaim the public property and places which have fallen." He deleted that statement as too warlike and said only that he would "hold, occupy, and possess the property, and places belonging to the government," without defining exactly what he meant or how he would do it. In his eloquent peroration, Lincoln appealed to southerners as Americans who shared with other Americans four score and five years of national history. "We are not enemies, but friends," he said.

> Though passion may have strained, it must not break, our bonds of affection. The mystic chords of memory, stretching from every battlefield and patriot grave to every living heart and hearthstone all over this broad land, will yet swell the chorus of the Union when again touched, as surely they will be, by the better angels of our nature.

Lincoln hoped to buy time with his inaugural address—time to demonstrate his peaceful intentions and to enable southern Unionists (whose numbers Republicans overestimated) to regain the upper hand. But the day after his inauguration, Lincoln learned that time was running out. A dispatch from Major Anderson informed him that provisions for the soldiers at Fort Sumter would soon be exhausted. The garrison must either be resupplied or evacuated. Any attempt to send in supplies by force would undoubtedly provoke a response from Confederate guns at Charleston. And by putting the onus of starting a war on Lincoln's shoulders, such an action would undoubtedly divide the North and unite the South, driving at least four more states into the Confederacy. Thus, most members of Lincoln's cabinet, along with the army's general-in-chief Winfield Scott, advised Lincoln to withdraw the troops from Sumter. That, however, would bestow a great moral victory on the Confederacy. It would confer legitimacy on the Confederate government and would probably lead to diplomatic recognition by foreign powers. Having pledged to "hold, occupy, and possess" national property, could Lincoln afford to abandon that policy during his first month in office?

15.5 The Bombardment of Fort Sumter, April 12, 1861 This *Harper's Weekly* illustration shows Confederate guns at Fort Johnson firing on Fort Sumter on April 13, 1861. During the war *Harper's Weekly* became immensely popular, reaching hundreds of thousands of readers, in large part because it provided detailed illustrations that satisfied Americans' intense desire to visualize the war. But this illustration is not strictly accurate: there were no Northern photographers or artists at Fort Johnson to record the bombardment, so the artists at *Harper's Weekly* simply provided a dramatic representation of their own.

The pressures from all sides caused Lincoln many sleepless nights. Finally, he hit upon a solution that evidenced the mastery that would mark his presidency. He decided to send in unarmed ships with supplies but to hold troops and warships outside the harbor with authorization to go into action only if the Confederates used force to stop the supply ships. And he would give South Carolina officials advance notice of his intention. This stroke of genius shifted the decision for war or peace to Jefferson Davis. If Confederate troops fired on the supply ships, the South would stand convicted of starting a war by attacking "a mission of humanity" bringing "food for hungry men." If Davis allowed the supplies to go in peacefully, the U.S. flag would continue to fly over Fort Sumter. The Confederacy would lose face at home and abroad, and southern Unionists would take courage.

Davis did not hesitate. He ordered General Beauregard to compel Sumter's surrender before the supply ships got there. At 4:30 a.m. on April 12, 1861, Confederate guns set off the Civil War by firing on Fort Sumter. After a 33-hour bombardment, the burning fort lowered the U.S. flag in surrender.

15-4 Choosing Sides

 Why did the border states remain in the Union?

News of the attack triggered an outburst of anger and war fever in the North. "The town is in a wild state of excitement," wrote a Philadelphia diarist. "The American flag is to be seen everywhere … . Men are enlisting as fast as possible." A New York woman wrote that the "time before Sumter" seemed like another century. "It seems as if we were never alive till now; never had a country till now."

Because the tiny U.S. Army—most of whose 16,000 soldiers were stationed at remote frontier posts—was inadequate to quell the "insurrection," Lincoln called on the states for 75,000 militia. The free states filled their quotas immediately. More than twice as many men volunteered as Lincoln had requested. Recognizing that the 90 days' service to which the militia were limited by law would be too short a time, on May 3 Lincoln issued a call for three-year volunteers. Before the war was over, more than 2 million men would serve in the Union army and navy.

The eight slave states still in the Union rejected Lincoln's call for troops. Four of them—Virginia, Arkansas, Tennessee, and North Carolina—soon seceded and joined the Confederacy. As a former Unionist in North Carolina remarked, "The division must be made on the line of slavery. The South must go with the South … . Blood is thicker than Water."

Few found the choice harder to make than **Robert E. Lee** of Virginia. One of the most promising officers in the U.S. Army, Lee believed that southern states had no legal right to secede. Still, he felt compelled to resign after the Virginia convention passed an ordinance of secession on April 17. "I must side either with or against my section," Lee told a northern friend. "I cannot raise my hand against my birthplace, my home, my children."

Most southern whites embraced war against the Yankees with more enthusiasm. When news of Sumter's surrender reached Richmond, crowds poured into the state capitol square and ran up the Confederate flag. "Everyone is in favor of secession [and] perfectly frantic with delight," wrote a participant. "I never in all my life witnessed such excitement." No one in the cheering crowds could know that before the war ended, at least 260,000 Confederate soldiers would lose their lives (along with 365,000 Union soldiers) and that the slave South they fought to defend would be utterly destroyed.

15-4a The Border States

Except for Delaware, which remained firmly in the Union, the slave states that bordered free states were sharply divided by the outbreak of war. Leaders in these states talked vaguely of neutrality, but they were to be denied that luxury.

The first blood was shed in Maryland on April 19, 1861, when a mob attacked Massachusetts troops traveling through Baltimore to Washington. The soldiers fired back, leaving 12 Baltimoreans and 4 soldiers dead. Confederate partisans burned bridges and tore down telegraph wires, cutting Washington off from the North for nearly a week until additional troops from Massachusetts and New York reopened communications and seized key points in Maryland. The troops also arrested many Confederate sympathizers. To prevent Washington from becoming surrounded by enemy territory, federal forces turned Maryland into an occupied state. Although thousands of Marylanders slipped into Virginia to join the Confederate army, a substantial majority of Maryland residents remained loyal to the Union.

Table 15.2 SLAVERY AND SECESSION

The higher the proportion of slaves and slaveholders in the population of a southern state, the greater the intensity of secessionist sentiment

	Population Who Were Slaves	White Population in Slaveholding Families
Seven states that seceded December 1860–February 1861 (South Carolina, Mississippi, Florida, Alabama, Georgia, Louisiana, Texas)	47%	38%
Four states that seceded after the firing on Fort Sumter (Virginia, Arkansas, Tennessee, North Carolina)	32%	24%
Four border slave states remaining in Union (Maryland, Delaware, Kentucky, Missouri)	14%	15%

▲ **MAP 15.2 Principal Military Campaigns of the Civil War** This map vividly illustrates the contrast between the vast distances over which the armies fought in the western theater of the war and the concentrated campaigns of the Army of the Potomac and the Army of Northern Virginia in the East.

Q *Which campaigns—west or east—were more important to the outcome of the war?*

Q *What were the relative advantages of South and North in conducting war over this vast terrain?*

The same was true of Missouri. Aggressive action by Union commander Nathaniel Lyon provoked a showdown between Unionist and pro-Confederate militia that turned into a riot in St. Louis on May 10 and 11, 1861, in which 36 people died. Lyon then led his troops in a summer campaign that drove the Confederate militia, along with the governor and pro-southern legislators, into Arkansas, where they formed a Missouri Confederate government in exile. Reinforced by Arkansas regiments, these rebel Missourians invaded their home state, and on August 10 defeated Lyon (who was killed) in the bloody battle of Wilson's Creek in the southwest corner of Missouri. The victorious Confederates marched northward all the way to the Missouri River, capturing a Union garrison at Lexington 40 miles east of Kansas City on September 20. Union forces then regrouped and drove the ragged Missouri Confederates back into Arkansas.

From then until the war's end, Unionists maintained political control of Missouri through military power. Even so, continued guerrilla attacks by Confederate "**bushwhackers**" and counterinsurgency tactics by Unionist "jayhawkers" turned large areas of the state into a no-man's-land of hit-and-run raids, arson, ambush, and murder. During these years, the famous postwar outlaws Jesse and Frank James and Cole and Jim Younger rode with the notorious rebel guerrilla chieftains William Quantrill and "Bloody Bill" Anderson. More than any other state, Missouri suffered from a civil war within the Civil War, and its bitter legacy persisted for generations.

In elections held during summer and fall 1861, Unionists gained firm control of the Kentucky and Maryland legislatures. Kentucky Confederates, like those of Missouri, formed a state government in exile. When the Confederate Congress admitted both Kentucky and Missouri to full representation, the Confederate flag acquired its 13 stars. Nevertheless, two-thirds of the white population in the four border slave states favored the Union, although some of that support was undoubtedly induced by the presence of Union troops.

15-4b The Creation of West Virginia

The war produced a fifth Union border state: West Virginia. Most of the delegates from the portion of Virginia west of the Shenandoah Valley had voted against secession. A region of mountains, small farms, and few slaves, western Virginia's economy was linked more closely to nearby Ohio and Pennsylvania than to the South. Delegates who had opposed Virginia's secession from the Union returned home determined to secede from Virginia. With the help of Union troops, who crossed the Ohio River and won a few small battles against Confederate forces in the area during summer 1861, they accomplished their goal. Through a complicated process of conventions and referendums—carried out in the midst of raids and skirmishes—they created the new state of West Virginia, which entered the Union in 1863.

15-4c Indian Territory and the Southwest

In the Indian Territory (present-day Oklahoma), the Native Americans, who had been resettled there from eastern states in the generation before the war, chose sides and carried on bloody guerrilla warfare against each other as ferocious as the bushwhacking in Missouri. The more prosperous Indians of the five "Civilized Tribes" (Cherokees, Creeks, Seminoles, Chickasaws, and Choctaws), many of them of mixed blood and some of them slaveholders, tended to side with the Confederacy. Some tribes signed treaties of alliance with the Confederate government. Aided by white and black Union regiments operating out of Kansas and Missouri, the pro-Union Indians gradually gained control of most of the Indian Territory.

In the meantime, Confederates had made their boldest bid to fulfill antebellum southern ambitions to win the Southwest. A small army composed mostly of Texans pushed up the Rio Grande Valley into New Mexico in 1861. The following February, they launched a deeper strike to capture Santa Fe. They hoped to push even farther westward and northward to gain the mineral wealth of California and Colorado gold mines, whose millions were already helping to finance the Union war effort and could do wonders for Confederate finances. A good many southerners lived in these western territories and in California.

At first, the Confederate drive up the Rio Grande went well. The Texans won a victory over the Unionist New Mexico militia and a handful of regulars at the battle of Valverde, 100 miles south of Albuquerque, on February 21, 1862. They continued up the valley, occupied Albuquerque and Santa Fe, and pushed on toward Fort Union near Santa Fe. But Colorado miners who had organized themselves into Union regiments and had carried out the greatest march of the war, over the rugged Rockies in winter, met the Texans in the battle of Glorieta Pass on March 26–28. The battle was a tactical draw, but a unit of Coloradans destroyed the Confederate wagon train, forcing the southerners into a disastrous retreat back to Texas. Of the 3,700 who had started out to win the West for the Confederacy, only 2,000 made it back. The Confederates had shot their bolt in this region; the West and Southwest remained safe for the Union.

15-5 The Balance Sheet of War

 What were northern advantages in the Civil War? What were southern advantages?

If one counts three-quarters of the border state population (including free blacks) as pro-Union, the total number of people in Union states in 1861 was 22.5 million, compared with 9 million in the Confederate states. The North's military manpower advantage was even greater because the Confederate population total included 3.7 million slaves, compared with 300,000 slaves in Union areas. At first, neither side expected to recruit blacks as soldiers. Eventually, the Union did enlist 180,000 black soldiers and 18,000 black sailors; the Confederacy did not take that step until the war was virtually over. Altogether, about 2.1 million men fought for the Union and 850,000 for the Confederacy. That was close to half of the North's male population of military age (18 to 40) and three-quarters of the comparable Confederate white population. Because the labor force of the South consisted mainly of slaves, the Confederacy was able to enlist a larger proportion of its white population. The North's economic superiority was even greater. The Union states possessed nine-tenths of the country's industrial capacity, four-fifths of its bank capital, three-fourths of its railroad mileage and rolling stock, and three-fourths of its taxable wealth.

These statistics gave pause to some southerners. In a long war that mobilized the total resources of both sides, the North's advantages might prove decisive. But in 1861, few anticipated how long and intense the war would be. Both sides expected a short and victorious conflict. Confederates seemed especially confident, partly because of their vaunted sense of martial superiority over the "bluebellied" Yankee nation of shopkeepers. Many southerners really did believe that one of their own could lick three Yankees. "Let brave men advance with flintlocks and old-fashioned bayonets, on the popinjays of Northern cities," said ex-governor Henry Wise of Virginia, now a Confederate general, and "the Yankees would break and run."

Although this turned out to be a grievous miscalculation, the South did have some reason to believe that its martial qualities were superior. A higher proportion of southerners than northerners had attended West Point and other military schools, had fought in the Mexican War, or had served as officers in the regular army. Volunteer military companies were more prevalent in the antebellum South than in the North. As a rural people, southerners were proficient in hunting, riding, and other outdoor skills useful in military operations. Moreover, the South had begun to prepare for war earlier than the North. As each state seceded, it mobilized

History Through Film: *Glory* (1989)

Directed by Edward Zwick.
Starring Matthew Broderick (Robert Gould Shaw), Denzel Washington (Trip), Morgan Freeman (Rawlins).

In 1862 some Union commanders began to organize black regiments in occupied portions of Louisiana, South Carolina, and Missouri. But despite passionate advocacy of black soldiering by Frederick Douglass and other black leaders, official enlistment of African American soldiers into the Union Army began only after Lincoln issued the Emancipation Proclamation on January 1, 1863 (see Chapter 16). *Glory* is the first feature film to treat the role of black soldiers in the Civil War. It tells the story of the 54th Massachusetts Volunteer Infantry from its organization in early 1863 through its climactic assault on Fort Wagner six months later. When the 54th moved out at dusk on July 18 to lead the attack, the idea of black combat troops still seemed a risky experiment. The *New York Tribune*, a strong supporter of black enlistment, had nevertheless observed in May 1863 that many northern whites "have no faith" that black soldiers would stand and fight southern whites who considered themselves a master race. The unflinching behavior of the regiment in the face of an overwhelming hail of lead and iron and its casualties of some 50 percent settled the matter. "Who now asks in doubt and derision 'Will the Negro fight?'" commented one abolitionist. "The answer comes to us from those graves beneath Fort Wagner's walls, which the American people will surely never forget."

Many did forget, but *Glory* revived their collective memory. Its combat scenes, climaxed by the assault on Fort Wagner, are among the most realistic and effective in any war movie. Morgan Freeman and Denzel Washington give memorable performances as a fatherly sergeant and a rebellious private who nevertheless picks up the flag when the color-bearer falls and carries it to the ramparts of Fort Wagner, where he too is killed. Matthew Broderick's portrayal of Colonel Robert Gould Shaw is less memorable because the real Shaw was more assertive and mature than Broderick's Shaw.

Except for Shaw, the principal characters in the film are fictional. There was no real Major Cabot Forbes; no tough Irish Sergeant Mulcahy; no black Sergeant John Rawlins; no brash, hardened Private Trip. A larger fiction is involved here. The movie gives the impression that most of the 54th's soldiers were former slaves. In fact, this atypical black regiment was recruited mainly in the North, so most of the men had always been free. The story that screenwriter Kevin Jarre and director Edward Zwick chose to tell is not simply about the 54th Massachusetts but about black soldiers in the Civil War. Most of the 179,000 African Americans in the Union army (and 16,000 in the navy) were slaves until a few months, even days, before they joined up. Fighting for the Union bestowed upon former slaves a new dignity, self-respect, and militancy, which helped them achieve equal citizenship and political rights—for a time—after the war.

Many of the events dramatized in *Glory* are also fictional: the incident of the racist quartermaster who initially refuses to distribute shoes to Shaw's men; the whipping Trip receives as punishment for going AWOL; Shaw's threat to expose his superior officer's corruption as a way of securing a combat assignment for the 54th; and the religious meeting the night before the assault on Fort Wagner. All of these scenes point toward a larger truth, however, most vividly portrayed symbolically in a surreal, and at first glance, irrelevant scene. During a training exercise, Shaw gallops his horse along a path flanked by stakes, each holding aloft a watermelon. Shaw slashes right and left with his sword, slicing and smashing every melon. The point becomes clear when we recall the identification of watermelons with the racist "darky" stereotype. The image of smashed melons drives home the essential message of *Glory*. ■

15-6 A scene from *Glory* showing black soldiers of the 54th Massachusetts ready to fire at the enemy.

---

militia and volunteer military companies. Not until summer 1861 would the North's greater manpower manifest itself in the form of a larger army.

15-5a Strategy and Morale

Even when fully mobilized, the North's superior resources did not guarantee success. Its military task was much more difficult than that of the South. The Confederacy had come into being in firm control of 750,000 square miles—a vast territory larger than all of Western Europe and twice as large as the 13 colonies in 1776. To win the war, Union forces would have to invade, conquer, and occupy much of that territory, cripple its people's ability to sustain a war of independence, and destroy its armies (see Map 15.2). Britain had been unable to accomplish a similar task in the war for independence, even though it enjoyed a far greater superiority of resources over the United States in 1776 than the Union enjoyed over the Confederacy in 1861. Victory does not always ride with the heaviest battalions.

To "win" the war, the Confederacy did not need to invade or conquer the Union or even to destroy its armies; it needed only to hold out long enough to convince northerners that the cost of victory was too high. Most Confederates were confident in 1861 that they were more than equal to the task. Most European military experts agreed.

The important factor of morale also seemed to favor the Confederacy. To be sure, Union soldiers fought for powerful symbols: nation, flag, Constitution. "We are fighting to maintain the best government on earth" was a common phrase in their letters and diaries. It is a "grate [sic] struggle for Union, Constitution, and law," wrote a New Jersey soldier. A Chicago newspaper declared that the South had "outraged the Constitution, set at defiance all law, and trampled under foot that flag which has been the glorious and consecrated symbol of American Liberty."

But Confederates, too, fought for nation, flag, constitution, and liberty—of whites. In addition, they fought to defend their land, homes, and families against invading "Yankee vandals," who many southern whites quite literally believed were coming to "free the negroes and force amalgamation between them and the children of the poor men of the South." An army fighting in defense of its homeland generally has the edge in morale. "We shall have the enormous advantage of fighting on our own territory and for our very existence," wrote a Confederate leader.

15-5b Mobilizing for War

More than four-fifths of the soldiers on both sides were volunteers. The Confederacy passed a conscription law in April 1862, and the Union followed suit in March 1863, but even afterward, most recruits were volunteers. In both North and South, patriotic rallies with martial music and speeches motivated local men to enlist in a company (100 men) organized by the area's leading citizens. The recruits elected their own company officers (a captain and two lieutenants), who received their commissions from the state governor. A regiment consisted of 10 infantry companies, and each regiment was commanded by a colonel, with a lieutenant colonel and a major as second and third in command—all of them appointed by the governor. Cavalry regiments were organized in a similar manner. Field artillery units were known as batteries.

Volunteer units received a state designation and number in the order of their completion—the Second Massachusetts Volunteer Infantry, the Fifth Virginia Cavalry, and so on. In most regiments, the men in each company generally came from the same town or locality. Some Union regiments were composed of men of a particular ethnic group. By the end of the war, the Union army had raised about 2,000 infantry and cavalry regiments and 700 batteries; the Confederates had organized just under half as many. As the war went on, the original thousand-man complement of a regiment was usually whittled down to half or less by disease, casualties, desertions, and detachments. The states generally preferred to organize new regiments rather than keep the old ones up to full strength.

These were citizen-soldiers, not professionals. They carried their peacetime notions of democracy and discipline into the army. That is why, in the tradition of the citizen militia, the men elected their company officers and sometimes their field officers (colonel, lieutenant colonel, and major) as well. Professional military men deplored the egalitarianism and slack discipline that resulted. Political influence often counted for more than military training in the election and appointment of officers. These civilians in uniform were extremely awkward and unmilitary at first, and some regiments suffered battlefield disasters because of inadequate training, discipline, and leadership. In time, however, raw recruits became battle-hardened veterans commanded by experienced officers.

As the two sides organized their field armies, both grouped four or more regiments into brigades and three or more brigades into divisions. By 1862, they began grouping two or more divisions into corps and two or more corps into armies. Each of these larger units was commanded by a general appointed by the president. Most of the higher-ranking generals on both sides were West Point graduates, but others were appointed because they represented an important political, regional, or (in the North) ethnic constituency whose support Lincoln or Davis wished to solidify. Some of these "political" generals, like elected regimental officers, were incompetent, but as the war went on, they too either learned their trade or were weeded out. Some outstanding generals emerged from civilian life and were promoted up the ranks during the war. In both the Union and the Confederate armies, the best officers (including generals) *led* their men by example as much as by precept; they commanded from the front, not the rear. Combat casualties were higher among officers than among privates, and highest of all among generals, who died in action at a rate 50 percent higher than enlisted men.

15-5c Weapons and Tactics

In Civil War battles, the infantry rifle was the most lethal weapon. Muskets and rifles caused 80–90 percent of the combat casualties. From 1862 on, most of these weapons were "rifled"—that is, they had spiral grooves cut in the barrel to impart a spin to the bullet. This innovation was only a decade old, dating to the perfection in the 1850s of the "minié ball" (named after French army captain Claude Minié, its principal inventor), a cone-shaped lead bullet with a base that expanded on firing to "take" the **rifling** of the barrel. This made it possible to load and fire a muzzle-loading rifle as rapidly (two or three times per minute) as the old smoothbore musket. Moreover, the rifle had greater accuracy and at least four times the effective range (400 yards or more) of the smoothbore.

Civil War infantry tactics adjusted only gradually to the greater lethal range and accuracy of the new rifle, however,

15.7 The Richmond Grays This photograph depicts a typical volunteer military unit that joined the Confederate army in 1861. Note the determined and confident appearance of these young men. By 1865, one-third of them would be dead and several others maimed for life.

for the prescribed massed formations had emerged from experience with the smoothbore musket. Close-order assaults against defenders equipped with rifles resulted in enormous casualties. The defensive power of the rifle became even greater when troops began digging into trenches. Massed frontal assaults became almost suicidal. Soldiers and their officers learned the hard way to adopt skirmishing tactics, taking advantage of cover and working around the enemy flank.

15-5 The Balance Sheet of War

Interpreting the Visual Past — The Soldier's Dream of Home

The Civil War was a home-front war, requiring the support of the civilian population at home—including women. This popular Currier & Ives print works to allay some of the uneasiness northerners on the home front might have felt as their husbands, sons, and brothers left home to become soldiers. It pictures a Union soldier asleep on the ground, with a palm tree above him to his left indicating that he is deployed in the South. Rather than portraying a soldier in battle, this image instead presents a soothing vision of an unbroken link between soldier and home. Part of an extensive visual propaganda produced during the war, it reassures viewers that men have not fundamentally changed by becoming trained killers.

Q *Think of this image as a story with several parts to be "read." Why is the soldier shown with a letter next to him on the ground? What is he dreaming, as shown in the "bubble" above him? Would this image be equally effective in your view if the soldier were shown thinking of home while awake?*

Q *How does the image allude to the violence of war? How might this scene offer comfort to those on the home front?*

15.8 **Currier & Ives, The Soldier's Dream of Home, c. 1862.**

15-5d Logistics

Wars are fought not only by men and weapons but also by the logistical apparatus that supports and supplies them. The Civil War is often called the world's first modern war because of the role played by railroads, steam-powered ships, and the telegraph, which did not exist in earlier wars fought on a similar scale (those of the French Revolution and Napoleon). Railroads and steamboats transported supplies and soldiers with unprecedented speed and efficiency; the telegraph provided rapid communication between army headquarters and field commanders.

Yet these modern forms of transport and communications were extremely vulnerable. Cavalry raiders and guerrillas could cut telegraph wires, burn railroad bridges, and tear up the tracks. Confederate cavalry became particularly skillful at sundering the supply lines of invading Union armies and thereby neutralizing forces several times larger than their own. The more deeply the Union armies penetrated into the South, the more men they had to detach to guard bridges, depots, and supply bases.

Once the campaigning armies had moved away from their railhead or wharf-side supply base, they returned to dependence on animal-powered transport. Depending on terrain, road conditions, length of supply line, and proportion of artillery and cavalry, Union armies required one horse or mule for every two or three men. Thus a large invading Union army of 100,000 men (the approximate number in Virginia from 1862 to 1865 and in Georgia in 1864) would need about 40,000 draft animals. Confederate armies, operating mostly in friendly territory closer to their bases, needed fewer. The poorly drained dirt roads typical of much of the South turned into a morass of mud in the frequently wet weather. These logistical problems did much to offset the industrial supremacy of the North, particularly during the first year of the war when bottlenecks, shortages, and inefficiency marked the logistical effort on both sides. By 1862, though, the North's economy had fully geared up for war, making the Union army the best-supplied army in history up to that time.

Confederate officials accomplished impressive feats of improvisation in creating war industries, especially munitions and gunpowder, but the southern industrial base was too slender to sustain adequate production. Particularly troublesome for the Confederacy was its inability to replace rails and rolling stock for its railroads. Although the South produced plenty of food, the railroads deteriorated to the point that food could not reach soldiers or civilians. As the war went into its third and fourth years, the northern economy grew stronger and the southern economy grew weaker.

15-5e Financing the War

One of the greatest defects of the Confederate economy was finance. The Confederate Congress, wary of dampening patriotic ardor, was slow to raise taxes. And because most capital in the South was tied up in land and slaves, little was available for buying war bonds. So, expecting a short war, the Confederate Congress authorized a limited issue of **treasury notes** in 1861, to be redeemable in **specie** (gold or silver) within two years after the end of the war. The first modest issue was followed by many more because the notes declined in value from the outset. The rate of decline increased during periods of Confederate military reverses, when people wondered whether the government would survive. By early 1863 it took eight dollars to buy what one dollar had bought two years earlier; just before the war's end, the Confederate dollar was worth one U.S. cent.

In 1863 the Confederate Congress tried to stem runaway inflation by passing a comprehensive law that taxed income, consumer purchases, and business transactions and included a "tax in kind" on agricultural products, allowing tax officials to seize 10 percent of a farmer's crops. This tax was extremely unpopular among farmers, many of whom hid their crops and livestock or refused to plant, thereby worsening the Confederacy's food shortages. The tax legislation was too little and too late to remedy the South's fiscal chaos. The Confederate government raised less than 5 percent of its revenue by taxes and less than 40 percent by loans, leaving 60 percent to be created by the printing press. That turned out to be a recipe for disaster.

In contrast, the Union government raised 66 percent of its revenue by selling war bonds, 21 percent by taxes, and only 13 percent by printing treasury notes. The Legal Tender Act authorizing these notes—the famous "greenbacks," the origin of modern paper money in the United States—passed in February 1862. Congress had enacted new taxes in 1861, including the first income tax in American history, and had authorized the sale of war bonds. By early 1862, however, these measures had not yet raised enough revenue to pay for the rapid military buildup. To avert a crisis, Congress created the greenbacks. Instead of promising to redeem them

15.9 Crossing a River This woodcut drawing portrays part of the Army of the Potomac crossing the Rapidan River in Virginia on May 4, 1864, at the beginning of what came to be called the Overland Campaign, which ended almost a year later with the surrender of the Army of Northern Virginia at Appomattox. The infantry is crossing on a pontoon bridge—planks laid over anchored boats—while supply wagons are fording the shallow river. This scene was typical of hundreds of river crossings by armies during the Civil War.

Q *What does this drawing reveal about the logistical difficulties of fighting the Civil War?*

in specie at some future date, as the South had done, Congress made them **legal tender**—that is, it required everyone to accept them as real money at face value. The North's economy suffered inflation during the war—about 80 percent over four years—but that was mild compared with the 9,000 percent inflation in the Confederacy. The greater strength and diversity of the North's economy, together with wiser fiscal legislation, accounted for the contrast.

The Union Congress also passed the National Banking Act of 1863. Before the war, the principal form of money had been notes issued by state-chartered banks. After Andrew Jackson's destruction of the Second Bank of the United States (Chapter 11), the number and variety of **banknotes** had skyrocketed until 7,000 different kinds of state banknotes were circulating in 1860. Some were virtually worthless. The National Banking Act of 1863 resulted from the desire of Republicans to resurrect the centralized banking system and create a more stable banknote currency, as well as to finance the war. Under the act, chartered national banks could issue banknotes up to 90 percent of the value of the U.S. bonds they held. This provision created a market for the bonds and, in combination with the greenbacks, replaced the glut of state banknotes with a more uniform national currency.

National banknotes would be an important form of money for the next half-century. They had two defects, however: First, because the number of notes that could be issued was tied to each bank's holdings of U.S. bonds, the volume of currency available depended on the amount of federal debt rather than on the economic needs of the country. Second, the banknotes tended to concentrate in the Northeast, where most of the large national banks were located, leaving the South and West short. The creation of the Federal Reserve System in 1913 (Chapter 21) largely remedied these defects, but Civil War legislation established the principle of a uniform national currency issued and regulated by the federal government.

15-6 Navies, the Blockade, and Foreign Relations

 Why did Confederate foreign policy fail to win diplomatic recognition from other nations?

To sustain its war effort, the Confederacy needed to import large quantities of material from abroad. To shut off these imports and the exports of cotton that paid for them, on April 19, 1861, Lincoln proclaimed a **blockade** of Confederate ports. At first, the blockade was more a policy than a reality because the navy had only a few ships on hand to enforce it. The task was formidable; the Confederate coastline stretched for 3,500 miles, with two dozen major ports and another 150 bays and coves where cargo could be landed. The U.S. Navy, which since the 1840s had been converting from sail to steam, recalled its ships from distant seas, took old sailing vessels out of mothballs, and bought or chartered merchant ships and armed them. Eventually, the navy placed several hundred warships on blockade duty. But in 1861, the blockade was so thin that 9 of every 10 vessels slipped through it on their way to or from Confederate ports.

15-6a King Cotton Diplomacy

The Confederacy, however, inadvertently contributed to the blockade's success when it adopted King Cotton diplomacy. Cotton was vital to the British economy because textiles were at the heart of British industry, and three-fourths of Britain's supply of raw cotton came from the South. If that supply was cut off, southerners reasoned, British factories would shut down, unemployed workers would starve, and Britain would face the prospect of revolution. Rather than risk such a consequence, people in the South believed that Britain (and other powers) would recognize the Confederacy's independence and then use the powerful British navy to break the blockade.

Southerners were so firmly convinced of cotton's importance to the British economy that they kept the 1861 cotton crop at home rather than try to export it through the blockade, hoping thereby to compel the British to intervene. But the strategy backfired. Bumper crops in 1859 and 1860 had piled up a surplus of cotton in British warehouses and delayed the anticipated "cotton famine" until 1862. In the end, the South's voluntary embargo of cotton cost it dearly. The Confederacy missed its chance to ship out its cotton and store it abroad, where it could be used as collateral for loans to purchase war material.

Moreover, the Confederacy's King Cotton diplomacy contradicted its own foreign policy objective: to persuade the British and French governments to refuse to recognize the legality of the blockade. Under international law, a blockade must be "physically effective" to be respected by neutral nations. Confederate diplomats claimed that the Union effort was a mere "paper blockade," yet the dearth of cotton reaching European ports as a result of the South's embargo suggested to British and French diplomats that the blockade was at least partly effective. And by 1862 it was. Slow-sailing ships with large cargo capacity rarely tried to run the blockade, and the sleek, fast, steam-powered "**blockade runners**" that became increasingly prominent had a smaller cargo capacity and charged high rates because of the growing risk of capture or sinking by the Union navy. Although most blockade runners got through, by 1862 the blockade had reduced the Confederacy's seaborne commerce enough to convince the British government to recognize it as legitimate. The blockade was also squeezing the South's economy. After lifting its cotton embargo in 1862, the Confederacy had increasing difficulty exporting enough cotton through the blockade to pay for needed imports.

Confederate foreign policy also failed to win diplomatic recognition by other nations. That recognition would have conferred international legitimacy on the Confederacy and might even have led to treaties of alliance or of foreign aid. The French emperor Napoleon III expressed sympathy for the Confederacy, as did influential groups in the British Parliament. But Prime Minister Lord Palmerston and Foreign

15.10 The Confederate Blockade Runner *Robert E. Lee* Confederate armies depended heavily on supplies brought in from abroad on blockade runners, paid for by cotton smuggled out through the Union naval cordon by these same blockade runners. The sleek, narrow-beamed ships with raked masts and smokestacks (which could be telescoped to deck level) were designed for speed and deception to elude the blockade—a feat successfully accomplished on four-fifths of their voyages during the war. One of the most successful runners was the *Robert E. Lee*, photographed here after it had run the blockade 14 times before being captured on the 15th attempt.

Q How successful was the Union blockade of Confederate ports?

Minister John Russell refused to recognize the Confederacy while it was engaged in a war it might lose, especially if recognition might jeopardize relations with the United States. The Union foreign policy team of Secretary of State Seward and Minister to England Charles Francis Adams did a superb job. Seward issued blunt warnings against recognizing the Confederacy; Adams softened them with the velvet glove of diplomacy. Other nations followed Britain's lead; by 1862, it had become clear that Britain would withhold recognition until the Confederacy had virtually won its independence, but such recognition would have come too late to help the Confederacy win.

15-6b The Trent Affair

If anything illustrated the frustrations of Confederate diplomacy, it was the *Trent* Affair. In October 1861, southern envoys James Mason and John Slidell slipped through the blockade. Mason hoped to represent the Confederacy in London and Slidell in Paris. On November 8, Captain Charles Wilkes of the U.S.S. *San Jacinto* stopped the British mail steamer *Trent* with Mason and Slidell on board, near Cuba. Wilkes arrested the two southerners, took them to Boston, and became an instant hero in the North. When the news reached England, the British government and public were outraged by Wilkes's "highhanded" action. Britain demanded an apology and the release of Mason and Slidell. The popular press on both sides of the Atlantic stirred up war fever. Soon, however, good sense prevailed and Britain softened its demands. With a philosophy of "one war at a time," the Lincoln administration released Mason and Slidell the day after Christmas 1861, declaring that Captain Wilkes had acted "without instructions." The British accepted this statement in lieu of an apology, and the crisis ended.

15-6c The Confederate Navy

Lacking the capacity to build a naval force at home, the Confederacy hoped to use British shipyards for the purpose. Through a loophole in the British neutrality law, two fast commerce raiders built in Liverpool made their way into Confederate hands in 1862. Named the *Florida* and the *Alabama*, they roamed the seas for the next two years, capturing or sinking Union merchant ships and whalers. The *Alabama* was the most feared raider. She sank 62 merchant vessels plus a Union warship before another warship, the U.S.S. *Kearsarge*, sank the *Alabama* off Cherbourg, France, on June 19, 1864. Altogether, Confederate privateers and commerce raiders destroyed or captured 257 Union merchant vessels and drove at least 700 others to foreign registry. This Confederate achievement, although spectacular, made only a tiny dent in the Union war effort, especially when compared with the 1,500 blockade runners captured or destroyed by the Union navy.

15-6d The Monitor and the Virginia

Though plagued by shortages on every hand, the Confederate navy department demonstrated great skill at innovation. Southern engineers developed "torpedoes" (mines) that sank or damaged 43 Union warships in southern bays and rivers. The South also constructed the world's first combat submarine, the *H. L. Hunley*, which sank a blockade ship off Charleston in 1864 but then went down before she could return to shore. Another important innovation was the building of ironclad "rams" to sink the blockade ships. The idea of iron armor for warships was not new—the British and French navies had prototype ironclads in 1861—but the Confederacy built the first one to see action. It was the C.S.S. *Virginia*, commonly called (even in the South) the *Merrimac* because it was rebuilt from the steam frigate U.S.S. *Merrimack*. Ready for its trial-by-combat on March 8, 1862, the *Virginia* steamed out to attack the blockade squadron at Hampton Roads. She sank one warship with her iron ram and another with her 10 guns. Other Union ships ran aground trying to escape, to be finished off (Confederates expected) the next day. Union shot and shells bounced off the *Virginia*'s armor plate. It was the worst day the U.S. Navy would have until December 7, 1941.

Panic seized Washington and the whole northeastern seaboard. In almost Hollywood fashion, however, the Union's

15.11a (top) and 15.11b (bottom) The Monitor and Merrimac The above black-and-white photograph shows the crew of the Union ironclad *Monitor* standing in front of its revolving two-gun turret. In action, the sun canopy above the turret would be taken down, and all sailors would be at their stations inside the turret or the hull, as shown in the color painting of the famed battle, on March 9, 1862, between the *Monitor* and the Confederate *Virginia* (informally called the *Merrimac* because it had been converted from the captured U.S. frigate *Merrimack*). There is no photograph of the *Virginia*, which was blown up by its crew two months later when the Confederates retreated toward Richmond because its draft was too deep to go up the James River.

Q How did the Civil War stimulate changes in the technology used to fight war?

own ironclad sailed into Hampton Roads in the nick of time and saved the rest of the fleet. This was the U.S.S. *Monitor*, completed just days earlier at the Brooklyn navy yard. Much smaller than the *Virginia*, with two 11-inch guns in a **revolving turret** (an innovation) set on a deck almost flush with the water, the *Monitor* looked like a "tin can on a shingle." It presented a small target and was capable of concentrating considerable firepower in a given direction with its revolving turret. The next day, the *Monitor* fought the *Virginia* in history's first battle between ironclads. It was a draw, but the *Virginia* limped home to Norfolk never again to menace the Union fleet. Although the Confederacy built other ironclad rams, none achieved the initial success of the *Virginia*. By the war's end, the Union navy had built or started 58 ships of the *Monitor* class, launching a new age in naval history.

15-7 Campaigns and Battles, 1861–1862

Q *How did the Union's and Confederacy's respective military advantages manifest themselves in the campaigns and battles of 1861 and 1862?*

Wars can be won only by hard fighting. Some leaders on both sides overlooked this truth. One of them was Winfield Scott, general-in-chief of the U.S. Army. Scott, a Virginian who had remained loyal to the Union, evolved a military strategy based on his conviction that a great many southerners were willing to be won back to the Union. The main elements of his strategy were a naval blockade and a combined army-navy expedition to take control of the Mississippi, thus sealing off the Confederacy on all sides and enabling the Union to "bring them to terms with less bloodshed than by any other plan." The northern press labeled Scott's strategy the Anaconda Plan, after the South American snake that squeezes its prey to death.

15-7a The Battle of Bull Run

Most northerners believed that the South could be overcome only by victory in battle. Virginia emerged as the most likely battleground, especially after the Confederate government moved its capital to Richmond in May 1861. "Forward to Richmond," clamored northern newspapers. And forward toward Richmond moved a Union army of 35,000 men in July, despite Scott's misgivings and those of the army's field commander, Irvin McDowell. McDowell believed his raw, 90-day Union militiamen were not ready to fight a real battle. They got no farther than Bull Run, a sluggish stream 25 miles southwest of Washington, where a Confederate army commanded by Beauregard had been deployed to defend a key rail junction at Manassas.

Another small Confederate army in the Shenandoah Valley under General Joseph E. Johnston had given a Union force the slip and had traveled to Manassas by rail to reinforce Beauregard. On July 21, the attacking Federals forded Bull Run and hit the rebels on the left flank, driving them back (see Map 15.3). By early afternoon, the Federals seemed to be on the verge of victory, but a Virginia brigade commanded by **Thomas J. Jackson** stood "like a stone wall," earning Jackson the nickname he carried ever after. By midafternoon, Confederate reinforcements, including one brigade just off the train from the Shenandoah Valley, had grouped for a screaming counterattack (the famed "rebel yell" was first heard here). They drove the exhausted and disorganized Yankees back across Bull Run in a retreat that turned into a rout.

Although the Battle of Manassas (or Bull Run, as northerners called it) was small by later Civil War standards, it made a profound impression on both sides. Of the 18,000 soldiers actually engaged on each side, Union casualties (killed, wounded, and captured) were about 2,800 and Confederate casualties 2,000. The victory exhilarated Confederates and confirmed their belief in their martial superiority. It also gave them a morale advantage in the Virginia theater that persisted for two years. And yet, Manassas also bred overconfidence. Some in the South thought the war was won. Northerners, by contrast, were jolted out of their expectations of a short war. A new mood of reality and grim determination gripped the North. Congress authorized the enlistment of up to 1 million three-year volunteers. Hundreds of thousands flocked to recruiting offices in the next few months. Lincoln called General **George B. McClellan** to Washington to organize the new troops into the Army of the Potomac.

An energetic, talented officer who was only 34 years old, McClellan soon won the nickname "The Young Napoleon." He had commanded the Union forces that gained control of West Virginia, and he took firm control in Washington during summer and fall 1861. He organized and trained the Army of the Potomac into a large, well-disciplined, and well-equipped fighting force. He was just what the North needed after its dispiriting defeat at Bull Run. When Scott stepped down as general-in-chief on November 1, McClellan took his place.

As winter approached, however, and McClellan did nothing to advance against the smaller Confederate army whose outposts stood only a few miles from Washington, his failings as a commander began to show. McClellan was afraid to take risks; he never learned the military lesson that no victory can be won without risking defeat. He consistently overestimated the strength of enemy forces facing him and used these faulty estimates as a reason for inaction until he could increase his own force. When Republicans in Congress and in the press began to criticize him (he was a Democrat), he accused his critics of political motives. Having built a fine fighting machine, he was afraid to start it up for fear it might break. The caution that McClellan instilled in the Army of the Potomac's officer corps persisted for more than a year after Lincoln removed him from command in November 1862.

15-7b Naval Operations

Because of McClellan, no significant action occurred in the Virginia theater after the Battle of Bull Run until spring 1862. Meanwhile, the Union navy won a series of victories over Confederate coastal forts at Hatteras Inlet on the North

▲ **MAP 15.3 Battle of Bull Run (Manassas), July 21, 1861** The key to Confederate victory in the war's first major battle was the failure of Union general Robert Patterson to prevent the Confederate troops under General Joseph Johnston (upper map) from joining those under General Pierre G. T. Beauregard via the Manassas Gap Railroad (lower map) for a counterattack that won the battle.

Q *How important was the railroad to Confederate victory at Bull Run?*

Q *Did the South or the North appear to have a greater advantage at the outset of battle?*

Carolina coast, Port Royal Sound in South Carolina, and other points along the Atlantic and Gulf coasts. These successes provided new bases from which to expand and tighten the blockade. They also provided small Union armies with takeoff points for operations along the southern coast. In February and March 1862, an expeditionary force under General Ambrose Burnside won a string of victories and occupied several crucial ports on the North Carolina sounds. Another Union force captured Fort Pulaski at the mouth of the Savannah River, cutting off that important Confederate port from the sea.

One of the Union navy's most impressive achievements was the capture in April 1862 of New Orleans, the Confederacy's largest city and principal port. Most Confederate troops in the area had been called up the Mississippi to confront a Union invasion of Tennessee, leaving only some militia, an assortment of steamboats converted into gunboats, and two strong forts flanking the river 70 miles below New Orleans. In a daring action on April 24, 1862, Union naval commander David Farragut led his fleet upriver past the forts, losing one ship but scattering or destroying the Confederate gunboats. The Union fleet compelled the surrender of New Orleans with nine-inch naval guns trained on its streets.

15-7c Fort Henry and Fort Donelson

These victories demonstrated the importance of sea power even in a civil war. Even more important were Union victories won by the combined efforts of the army and fleets of river gunboats on the Tennessee and Cumberland rivers, which flow through Tennessee and Kentucky and empty into the Ohio River just before it joins the Mississippi. The unlikely hero of these victories was Ulysses S. Grant, who had failed in several civilian occupations after resigning from the peacetime military in 1854. Grant rejoined when war broke out. His quiet efficiency and determined will won him promotion from Illinois colonel to brigadier general. When Confederate units entered Kentucky in September, Grant moved quickly to occupy the mouths of the Cumberland and Tennessee rivers.

Military strategists on both sides understood the importance of these navigable rivers as highways of invasion into the South's heartland. The Confederacy had built forts at strategic points along the rivers and had begun to convert a few steamboats into gunboats and rams to back up the forts. The Union also converted steamboats into "timberclad" gunboats and built a new class of ironclad gunboats designed for river warfare.

▲ **MAP 15.4 Kentucky–Tennessee Theater, Winter–Spring 1862** This map illustrates the importance of rivers and railroads as lines of military operations and supply. Grant and Andrew Foote advanced up the Tennessee and Cumberland rivers (moved southward), while Buell moved along the Louisville and Nashville Railroad. Confederate divisions under the overall command of General Albert Sidney Johnston used railroads to concentrate at the key junction of Corinth.

Q *How important was control of rivers to Union victory?*

Q *How important was the war in the West to the ultimate outcome of the Civil War?*

15-7 Campaigns and Battles, 1861–1862

With the help of these strange-looking but formidable craft, Grant struck in February 1862. His objectives were Forts Henry and Donelson on the Tennessee and Cumberland rivers just south of the Kentucky-Tennessee border (see Map 15.4). The gunboats knocked out Fort Henry on February 6. Fort Donelson proved a tougher nut to crack. Its guns repulsed a gunboat attack on February 14. The next day, the 17,000-man Confederate army attacked Grant's besieging army, which had been reinforced to 27,000 men. With the calm decisiveness that became his trademark, Grant directed a counterattack that penned the defenders back up in their fort. Cut off from support by either land or river, the Confederate commander asked for surrender terms on February 16. Grant's reply made him instantly famous when it was published in the North: "No terms except an immediate and unconditional surrender can be accepted. I propose to move immediately upon your works." With no choice, the 13,000 surviving Confederates surrendered (some had escaped), giving Grant the most striking victory in the war thus far.

These victories had far-reaching strategic consequences. Union gunboats now ranged all the way up the Tennessee River to northern Alabama, enabling a Union division to occupy the region, and up the Cumberland to Nashville, which became the first Confederate state capital to surrender to Union forces on February 25. Confederate military units pulled out of Kentucky and most of Tennessee and reassembled at Corinth in northern Mississippi. Jubilation spread through the North and despair through the South. By the end of March 1862, however, the Confederate commander in the western theater, Albert Sidney Johnston (not to be confused with Joseph E. Johnston in Virginia), had built up an army of 40,000 men at Corinth. His plan was to attack Grant's force of 35,000, which had established a base 20 miles away at Pittsburg Landing on the Tennessee River just north of the Mississippi-Tennessee border.

15-7d The Battle of Shiloh

On April 6, the Confederates attacked at dawn near a church called Shiloh. They caught Grant by surprise and drove his army toward the river (see Map 15.5). After a day's fighting of unprecedented intensity, with total casualties of 15,000, Grant's men brought the Confederate onslaught to a halt at dusk. One of the Confederate casualties was Johnston, who bled to death when a bullet severed an artery in his leg—the highest-ranking general on either side to be killed in the war. Beauregard, who had been transferred from Virginia to the West, took command after Johnston's death.

Some of Grant's subordinates advised retreat during the dismal night of April 6, but Grant would have none of it. Reinforced by fresh troops from a Union army commanded by General Don Carlos Buell, the Union counterattacked the next morning (April 7) and, after 9,000 more casualties to the two sides, drove the Confederates back to Corinth. Although Grant had snatched victory from the jaws of defeat, his reputation suffered a decline for a time because of the heavy Union casualties (13,000) and the suspicion that he had been caught napping the first day.

Union triumphs in the western theater continued. The combined armies of Grant and Buell, under the overall command of the top-ranking Union general in the West, Henry W. Halleck, drove the Confederates out of Corinth at the end of May. Meanwhile, the Union gunboat fleet fought its way down the Mississippi to Vicksburg, virtually wiping out the Confederate fleet in a spectacular battle at Memphis on June 6. At Vicksburg, the Union gunboats from the north connected with part of Farragut's fleet that had come up from New Orleans, taking Baton Rouge and Natchez along the way. The heavily fortified Confederate bastion at Vicksburg, however, proved too strong for Union naval firepower to subdue. Nevertheless, the dramatic succession of Union triumphs in the West from February to June, including a decisive victory at the battle of Pea Ridge in northwest Arkansas on March 7 and 8, convinced the North that the war was nearly won. "Every blow tells fearfully against the rebellion," boasted the leading northern newspaper, the New York *Tribune*. "The rebels themselves are panic-stricken, or despondent. It now requires no very far reaching prophet to predict the end of this struggle."

15-7e The Virginia Theater

But affairs in Virginia were about to take a sharp turn in favor of the Confederacy. In the western theater, the broad rivers had facilitated the Union's invasion of the South, but in Virginia a half-dozen small rivers flowing west to east provided the Confederates with natural lines of defense. McClellan persuaded a reluctant Lincoln to approve a plan to transport his army down Chesapeake Bay to the tip of the Virginia peninsula, formed by the tidal portions of the York and James rivers. That would shorten the route to Richmond and give the Union army a seaborne supply line secure from harassment by Confederate cavalry and guerrillas.

This was a good plan—in theory. But once again, McClellan's failings began to surface. A small Confederate blocking force at Yorktown held him for the entire month of April, as he cautiously dragged up siege guns to blast through defenses that his large army could have punched through in days on foot. McClellan slowly followed the retreating Confederate force up the peninsula to a new defensive line only a few miles east of Richmond. All the while he bickered with Lincoln and Secretary of War Edwin M. Stanton over the reinforcements they were withholding to protect Washington against a possible strike by Stonewall Jackson's small Confederate army in the Shenandoah Valley.

Jackson's month-long campaign in the Shenandoah (May 8–June 9), one of the most brilliant of the war, demonstrated what could be accomplished through deception, daring, and mobility. With only 17,000 men, Jackson moved by forced marches so swift that his infantry earned the nickname "Jackson's foot cavalry." Darting here and there through the valley, they marched 350 miles in the

▲ **MAP 15.5 Battle of Shiloh, April 6–7, 1862** These two maps starkly illustrate the change of fortune from the first to the second day of the battle, with Confederates driving northward the first day and then being driven back over the same ground the second day.

Q *Do you see any evidence of Union retreat after the losses of the first day of battle?*

Q *Why did Grant's reputation decline for a while after the Battle of Shiloh?*

course of one month; won four battles against three separate Union armies, whose combined numbers surpassed Jackson's by more than 2 to 1 (but which Jackson's force always outnumbered at the point of contact); and compelled Lincoln to divert to the valley some of the reinforcements McClellan demanded.

Even without those reinforcements, McClellan's army substantially outnumbered the Confederate force defending Richmond, commanded by Joseph E. Johnston. McClellan overestimated Johnston's strength at double what it was and acted accordingly. Even so, by the last week of May, McClellan's army was within six miles of Richmond (see Map 15.6). A botched Confederate counterattack on May 31 and June 1 (the battle of Seven Pines) produced no result except 6,000 Confederate and 5,000 Union casualties. One of those casualties was Johnston, who was wounded in the shoulder. Jefferson Davis named Robert E. Lee to replace him.

15-7f The Seven Days' Battles

That appointment marked a major turning point in the campaign. Lee had done little so far to earn a wartime reputation, having failed in his only field command to dislodge Union forces from control of West Virginia. His qualities as a commander began to manifest when he took over what he renamed the Army of Northern Virginia. Those qualities were boldness, a willingness to take great risks, an almost uncanny ability to read the enemy commander's mind, and a charisma that won the devotion of his men. While McClellan continued to dawdle, Lee sent his dashing cavalry commander, J. E. B. "Jeb" Stuart, to lead a reconnaissance around the Union army to discover its weak points. Lee also brought Jackson's army in from the Shenandoah Valley and launched a June 26 attack on McClellan's right flank in what became known as the Seven Days' battles (see Map 15.6). Constantly attacking, Lee's army of 90,000 drove McClellan's 100,000 away from Richmond to a new fortified base on the James River. The offensive cost the Confederates 20,000 casualties (compared with 16,000 for the Union) and turned Richmond into one vast hospital, but it reversed the momentum of the war.

15-8 Confederate Counteroffensives

Q *Why were Confederate forces able to launch successful counteroffensives in the summer of 1862?*

Northern sentiment plunged from the height of euphoria in May to the depths of despair in July. "The feeling of despondency here is very great," wrote a New Yorker, while a southerner exulted, "Lee has turned the tide, and I shall not be surprised if we have a long career of successes." The tide turned in the western theater as well, where Union conquests in the spring had brought 50,000 square miles of Confederate territory under Union control. To occupy and administer this vast area, however, drew many thousands of soldiers from combat forces, which were left depleted and deep in enemy territory and vulnerable to cavalry raids. During summer and fall 1862, the cavalry commands of Tennesseean Nathan Bedford Forrest and Kentuckian John Hunt Morgan staged repeated raids in which they burned bridges, blew up tunnels, tore up tracks, and captured supply depots and the Union garrisons trying to defend them. By August the once-formidable Union war machine in the West seemed to have broken down.

These raids paved the way for infantry counteroffensives. After recapturing some territory, Confederate forces suffered defeats at Corinth and Perryville in October. But Confederate forces in the western theater were still in better shape than they had been four months earlier.

▲ **MAP 15.6 Peninsula Campaign, April–May 1862, and Seven Days' Battles, June 25–July 1, 1862** General McClellan used Union naval control of the York and James rivers to protect his flanks in his advance up the peninsula formed by these rivers (left map). When Robert E. Lee's Army of Northern Virginia counterattacked in the Seven Days' battles (right map), McClellan was forced back to the James River at Harrison's Landing.

Q *How would you compare Lee's and McClellan's differing approaches to command?*

Q *What are the chief reasons why McClellan failed to reach Richmond during the spring and summer of 1862, despite being within six miles of the city?*

CHAPTER 15 Secession and Civil War, 1860–1862

▲ **MAP 15.7 Second Battle of Manassas (Bull Run), August 29–30, 1862** Compare this map with Map 15.3 (p. 428), the Battle of Bull Run (Manassas) on July 21, 1861. Note that some of the heaviest fighting in both battles took place around the house owned by Judith Henry. The house was destroyed and the elderly widow killed inside it in the first battle.

Q *What were the reasons behind a second Confederate victory at Bull Run?*

Q *What political and military issues were a barrier to Union victory at Second Bull Run?*

15-8 Confederate Counteroffensives

15-8a The Second Battle of Bull Run

Most attention, though, focused on Virginia. Lincoln reorganized the Union corps near Washington into the Army of Virginia under General John Pope, who had won minor successes as commander of a small army in Missouri and Tennessee. In August, Lincoln ordered the withdrawal of the Army of the Potomac from the peninsula to reinforce Pope for a drive southward from Washington. Lee quickly seized the opportunity provided by the separation of the two Union armies confronting him, by the ill will between McClellan and Pope, and by the bickering among various factions in Washington. To attack Pope before McClellan could reinforce him, Lee shifted most of his army to northern Virginia, sent Jackson's foot cavalry on a deep raid to destroy the supply base at Manassas Junction, and then brought his army back together to defeat Pope's army near Bull Run on August 29 and 30 (see Map 15.7). The demoralized Union forces retreated into the Washington defenses, where Lincoln reluctantly gave McClellan command of the two armies and told him to reorganize them into one.

Lee decided to keep up the pressure by invading Maryland. On September 4, his weary troops began splashing across the Potomac 40 miles upriver from Washington. This move presented several momentous possibilities: Maryland might be won for the Confederacy. Another victory by Lee might influence the U.S. congressional elections that fall and help Democrats gain control of Congress, and might even force the Lincoln administration to negotiate peace with the Confederacy. Successful invasion of Maryland, coming on top of other Confederate successes, might even persuade Britain and France to recognize the Confederacy. Great issues rode with the armies as Lee crossed the Potomac and McClellan cautiously moved north to meet him.

Conclusion

The election of 1860 had accomplished a national power shift of historic proportions. Southern political leaders had maintained effective control of the national government for most of the time before 1860. With Lincoln's election, the South lost control of the executive branch—and perhaps also the House. They feared that the Senate and Supreme Court would soon follow. The Republicans, southerners feared, would launch a "revolution" to cripple slavery and, as Lincoln had said in his "House Divided" speech two years earlier, place it "in course of ultimate extinction." The "revolutionary dogmas" of the Republicans, declared a South Carolina newspaper in 1860, were "active and bristling with terrible designs." Worst of all, the northern "Black Republicans" would force racial equality on the South: "Abolition preachers will be on hand to consummate the marriage of your daughters to black husbands."

Thus the South launched a preemptive counterrevolution of secession to forestall a revolution of liberty and equality they feared would be their fate if they remained in the Union. Seldom has a preemptive counterrevolution so quickly brought on the very revolution it tried to prevent. If the Confederacy had lost the war in spring 1862, as appeared likely after Union victories from February to May of that year, the South might have returned to the Union with slavery intact. Instead, successful Confederate counteroffensives in summer 1862 convinced Lincoln that the North could not win the war without striking against slavery. Another issue that rode with Lee's troops as they crossed the Potomac into Maryland in September 1862 was the fate of an emancipation proclamation Lincoln had drafted two months earlier and then put aside to await a Union victory.

CHAPTER REVIEW

Review

1. Why did the Republican Party choose Abraham Lincoln as its candidate in 1860?
2. Why did political leaders in the lower South think that Lincoln's election made secession imperative?
3. Why did compromise efforts to forestall secession fail, and why did war break out at Fort Sumter?
4. Why did the border states remain in the Union?
5. What were northern advantages in the Civil War? What were southern advantages?
6. Why did Confederate foreign policy fail to win diplomatic recognition from other nations?
7. How did the Union's and Confederacy's respective military advantages manifest themselves in the campaigns and battles of 1861 and 1862?
8. Why were Confederate forces able to launch successful counteroffensives in the summer of 1862?

Critical Thinking

1. Given the North's advantages in population and economic resources, how could the Confederacy have hoped to prevail in the war?
2. How did the factors of geography, terrain, and logistics shape the strategy and operations of each side in the war?

Identifications

Review your understanding of the following key terms, people, and events for this chapter (terms in bold in text are included in the Glossary).

Fort Sumter, p. 407
secession, p. 408
Unionists, p. 411
Robert E. Lee, p. 416
bushwhackers, p. 417
rifling, p. 420
treasury notes, p. 423
specie, p. 423
legal tender, p. 424
banknotes, p. 424
blockade, p. 424
blockade runner, p. 424
revolving turret, p. 427
Thomas J. ("Stonewall") Jackson, p. 427
George B. McClellan, p. 427

Suggested Readings

The most comprehensive one-volume study of the Civil War years is **James M. McPherson**, *Battle Cry of Freedom: The Civil War Era* (1988). For the perspective of the soldiers and sailors who fought the battles, see **Bell I. Wiley's** classic *The Life of Johnny Reb* (1943) and *The Life of Billy Yank* (1952). On the terrible costs of battle, see **Drew Gilpin Faust**, *This Republic of Suffering* (2008). For the naval war, see **James M. McPherson**, *War on the Waters: The Union and Confederate Navies, 1861–1865* (2012).

For the home front in North and South, see **Phillip Shaw Paludan**, *"A People's Contest": The Union and Civil War, 1861–1865* (1988), and **Emory Thomas**, *The Confederate Nation, 1861–1865* (1979). For women and children, see **Nina Silber**, *Daughters of the Union: Northern Women Fight the Civil War* (2005); and **George C. Rable**, *Civil Wars: Women and the Crisis of Southern Nationalism* (1989).

For the commanders in chief and their principal generals, consult **James M. McPherson**, *Tried by War: Abraham Lincoln as Commander in Chief* (2007); **William C. Cooper**, *Jefferson Davis, American* (2000); **Stephen W. Sears**, *George B. McClellan: The Young Napoleon* (1988); **Ron Chernow**, *Ulysses S. Grant* (2017); and **Emory M. Thomas**, *Robert E. Lee* (1995). A superb study of Lincoln and his cabinet is **Doris Kearns Goodwin**, *Team of Rivals: The Political Genius of Abraham Lincoln* (2005). For the guerrilla war, the most useful of several books is **Daniel E. Sutherland**, *A Savage Conflict: The Decisive Role of Guerrillas in the American Civil War* (2009). Of the many studies of diplomacy during the war, the most useful is **David P. Crook**, *The North, The South, and the Powers 1861–1865* (1974), an abridged version of which was published with the title *Diplomacy during the Civil War* (1975). On the international dimensions of the war, see **Don H. Doyle**, *The Cause of All Nations: An International History of the American Civil War* (2015).

MINDTAP is a fully online personalized learning experience built upon Cengage Learning content. MindTap® combines student learning tools—readings, multimedia, activities, and assessments—into a singular Learning Path that guides students through the course and helps students develop the critical thinking, analysis, and communication skills that are essential to academic and professional success.

16 A New Birth of Freedom, 1862–1865

16-1 Slavery and the War
Learning Objective: Explain what factors led Lincoln to issue the Emancipation Proclamation.

The "Contrabands"
The Border States
The Decision for Emancipation
New Calls for Troops
The Battle of Antietam
The Emancipation Proclamation

16-2 A Winter of Discontent
Learning Objective: Identify sources of internal dissent and dissension in both the Confederacy and the Union.

The Rise of the Copperheads
Economic Problems in the South
The Wartime Draft and Class Tensions
A Poor Man's Fight?

16-3 Blueprint for Modern America
Learning Objective: Explain how wartime legislation transformed American society. Identify how women contributed to the war effort.

Women and the War
Women as Aid Workers and Nurses

16-4 The Confederate Tide Crests and Recedes
Learning Objective: Discuss the means by which the Union achieved victory at Gettysburg.

The Battle of Chancellorsville
The Gettysburg Campaign
The Vicksburg Campaign
Chickamauga and Chattanooga

16-5 Black Men in Blue
Learning Objective: Identify how African Americans contributed to the Union war effort.

Black Soldiers in Combat
Emancipation Confirmed

16-6 The Year of Decision
Learning Objective: Explain why Lincoln thought he would not be re-elected in 1864.

Out of the Wilderness
Spotsylvania and Cold Harbor
Stalemate in Virginia
The Atlanta Campaign
Peace Overtures
The Prisoner-Exchange Controversy
The Issue of Black Soldiers in the Confederate Army

16-7 Lincoln's Reelection and the End of the Confederacy
Learning Objective: List the reasons why Lincoln instead won re-election by a wide margin in 1864.

The Capture of Atlanta
The Shenandoah Valley
From Atlanta to the Sea
The Battles of Franklin and Nashville
Fort Fisher and Sherman's March through the Carolinas
The Road to Appomattox
The Assassination of Lincoln

16.1 A Ride for Liberty This splendid painting by Eastman Johnson of a slave family escaping to Union lines during the Civil War dramatizes the experiences of thousands of slaves who thereby became "contrabands" and gained their freedom. Most of them came on foot, but this enterprising family is instead shown stealing a horse as well as themselves from their master.

Q *Most critics agree that this painting makes an argument against slavery. Why?*

ONE OF THE GREAT issues awaiting resolution as the armies moved into Maryland in September 1862 was emancipation of the slaves. The war had moved beyond the effort to restore the old Union. It now required the North to mobilize every resource that might bring victory or to destroy any enemy resource that might inflict defeat. To abolish slavery would strike at a vital Confederate resource (slave labor) and mobilize that resource for the Union along with the moral power of fighting for freedom. Slaves had already made clear their choice by escaping to Union lines by the tens of thousands. Lincoln had made up his mind to issue an emancipation proclamation and was waiting for a Union victory to give it credibility and potency.

This momentous decision would radically enlarge the scope and purpose of the Union war effort. It would also polarize northern public opinion and political parties. So long as the North fought simply for restoration of the Union, northern unity was impressive, but the events of 1862 and 1863 raised the divisive question of what kind of Union was to be restored. Would it be a Union without slavery, as abolitionists and radical Republicans hoped? Or "the Union as it was, the Constitution as it is," as Democrats desired? The answer to this question would determine not only the course of the war but also the future of the United States. ◼

16-1 Slavery and the War

Q *What factors led Lincoln to his decision to issue the Emancipation Proclamation?*

In the North, the issue of emancipation was deeply divisive. Lincoln had been elected on a platform pledged to contain the expansion of slavery, but that pledge had provoked most of the southern states to quit the Union. For the administration to take action against slavery in 1861 would be to risk the breakup of the fragile coalition Lincoln had stitched together to fight the war: Republicans, Democrats, and border-state Unionists. Spokesmen for the latter two groups served notice that, although they supported a war for the Union, they would not support a war against slavery. In July 1861, with Lincoln's endorsement, Congress passed a resolution affirming that northern war aims included no intention "of overthrowing or interfering with the rights or established institutions of the States"—in plain words, slavery—but intended only "to defend and maintain the supremacy of the Constitution and to preserve the Union."

Many northerners saw matters differently. They insisted that a rebellion sustained *by* slavery in defense *of* slavery could be suppressed only by striking *against* slavery. As Frederick Douglass stated, "War for the destruction of liberty must be met with war for the destruction of slavery."

Wars tend to develop a logic and momentum that go beyond their original purposes. When northerners discovered at Bull Run in July 1861 that they were not going to win an easy victory, many of them began to take a harder look at slavery. Slaves constituted the principal labor force in the South. They raised most of the food and fiber, built most of the military fortifications, worked on the railroads and in mines and munitions factories. Southern newspapers boasted that slavery was "a tower of strength to the Confederacy" because it enabled the South "to place in the field a force so much larger in proportion to her white population than the North." So why not convert this Confederate asset to a Union advantage by confiscating slaves as enemy property and using them to help the northern war effort?

16-1a The "Contrabands"

The slaves entered this debate in a dramatic fashion. As Union armies penetrated the South, a growing number of slaves voted for freedom with their feet. By twos and threes, by families, and eventually by scores, they escaped from their masters and came over to the Union lines. By obliging Union officers either to return them to slavery or accept them, these escaped slaves began to make the conflict a war for freedom.

Although some commanders returned escaped slaves to their masters or prevented them from entering Union camps, increasingly, most did not. When three slaves who had been working for the Confederate army escaped to General Benjamin Butler's lines near Fortress Monroe in May 1861, Butler refused to return them on the grounds that they were **contraband of war**. The phrase caught on in the North. For the rest of the war, slaves who came within Union lines were known as "contrabands"—a term that blacks disliked and that, ironically, continued to define human beings as property. On August 6, 1861, Congress passed a confiscation act that authorized the seizure of all property that was being used for Confederate military purposes, including slaves. The following March, Congress forbade the return of slaves who entered Union lines.

16-1b The Border States

The problem of slavery in the loyal border states preoccupied Lincoln. On August 30, 1861, John C. Frémont, whose political influence had won him a commission as major general and command of Union forces in Missouri, issued an order freeing the slaves of all Confederate sympathizers in Missouri. This caused such a backlash among border-state Unionists, who feared it was a prelude to a general abolition edict, that Lincoln revoked the order, lest it "alarm our Southern Union friends, and turn them against us."

In spring 1862, Lincoln tried persuasion instead of force in the border states. At his urging, Congress passed a resolution offering federal compensation to states that

CHRONOLOGY

1862 Confederacy enacts conscription (April 16) • Lincoln informs the cabinet of intention to issue Emancipation Proclamation (July 22) • Battle of Antietam (September 17) • Lincoln issues preliminary Emancipation Proclamation (September 22) • Battle of Fredericksburg (December 13) • Battle of Stones River (December 31–January 2)

1863 Lincoln issues final Emancipation Proclamation (January 1) • Union enacts conscription (March 3) • Richmond bread riot (April 2) • Battle of Chancellorsville (May 1–5) • Battle of Gettysburg (July 1–3) • Vicksburg surrenders (July 4) • Port Hudson surrenders (July 9) • New York draft riot (July 13–16) • Assault on Fort Wagner (July 18) • Battle of Chickamauga (September 19–20) • Battles of Chattanooga (November 24–25)

1864 Battle of the Wilderness (May 5–6) • Battle of Spotsylvania (May 8–19) • Fighting at Petersburg (June 15–18) leads to nine-month siege • Fall of Atlanta (September 1) • Reelection of Lincoln (November 8) • Battle of Nashville (December 15–16)

1865 Capture of Fort Fisher (January 15) • Confederates evacuate Richmond (April 2) • Lee surrenders at Appomattox (April 9) • Booth assassinates Lincoln (April 14) • Last Confederate army surrenders (June 23) • Thirteenth Amendment abolishing slavery ratified (December 6)

voluntarily abolished slavery. Three times, from March to July 1862, Lincoln urged border-state congressmen to accept the offer. He told them that the Confederate hope that their states might join the rebellion was helping to keep the war alive. Adopt the proposal for **compensated emancipation**, he pleaded, and that hope would die. The pressure for a bold antislavery policy was growing stronger, he warned them in May. Another Union general had issued an emancipation order; Lincoln had suspended it, but "you cannot," Lincoln told the border-state congressmen, "be blind to the signs of the times."

They did seem to be blind. They complained of being coerced, bickered about the amount of compensation, and wrung their hands over the prospects of economic ruin and race war, even if emancipation were to take place gradually over a 30-year period, as Lincoln had suggested. At a final meeting on July 12, Lincoln warned them, "If the war continue long … the institution in your states will be extinguished by mere friction and abrasion." Again they failed to see the light, and by a vote of 20 to 9, they rejected the proposal for compensated emancipation.

16-1c The Decision for Emancipation

That very evening, Lincoln decided to issue an emancipation proclamation in his capacity as commander in chief with power to order the seizure of enemy property. Several factors, in addition to the recalcitrance of the border states, impelled

16.2 African Americans Coming into Union Lines This photograph taken in 1862 or 1863 shows slaves fording the Rappahannock River in Virginia in order to reach freedom. Note the family groups of men, women, and children, as well as the goods that they had struggled to bring with them to their new life.

Lincoln to this fateful decision. One was a growing demand from his own party for bolder action. Another was rising sentiment in the army to "take off the kid gloves" when dealing with "traitors." Finally, Lincoln's decision reflected his sentiments about the "unqualified evil" and "monstrous injustice" of slavery.

The military situation, however, rather than his moral convictions, determined the timing and scope of Lincoln's emancipation policy. Northern hopes that the war would soon end had risen after the victories of early 1862 but had then plummeted amid the reverses of that summer.

Three courses of action seemed possible. One, favored by the so-called Peace Democrats, urged an armistice and peace negotiations to patch together some kind of Union, but that would have been tantamount to conceding Confederate victory. Republicans therefore reviled the Peace Democrats as traitorous **Copperheads**, after the poisonous snake. A second alternative was to keep on fighting—in the hope that with a few more Union victories, the rebels would lay down their arms and the Union could be restored. Such a policy would leave slavery intact. The third alternative was to mobilize all the resources of the North and to destroy all the resources of the South, including slavery—a war not to restore the old Union but to build a new one.

On July 22, a week after his meeting with the border-state representatives convinced him there could be no compromise, Lincoln notified the cabinet of his intention to issue an emancipation proclamation. It was "a military necessity, absolutely essential to the preservation of the Union," said Lincoln. "We must free the slaves or be ourselves subdued. The slaves [are] undeniably an element of strength to those who [have] their service, and we must decide whether that element should be with us or against us."

The cabinet agreed, except for Postmaster General Montgomery Blair, a resident of Maryland and a former Democrat, who warned that the border states and the Democrats would rebel against the proclamation and perhaps cost the administration the fall congressional elections as well as vital support for the war. Lincoln might have agreed two months earlier. Now he believed that the strength gained from an emancipation policy—from the slaves themselves, from the dynamic Republican segment of northern opinion, and in the eyes of foreign nations—would more than compensate for the hostility of Democrats and border-state Unionists. Lincoln did, however, accept the advice of Secretary of State Seward to delay the proclamation "until you can give it to the country supported by military success." Otherwise, Seward argued, it might be viewed "as the last measure of an exhausted government, a cry for help … our last *shriek*, on the retreat." Lincoln slipped his proclamation into a desk drawer and waited for a military victory.

16-1d New Calls for Troops

Meanwhile, Lincoln issued a call for 300,000 new three-year volunteers for the army. In July, Congress passed a militia act giving the president greater powers to mobilize the state militias into federal service and to draft men into the militia if the states failed to do so. Although not a national draft law, this was a step in that direction. In August, Lincoln called up 300,000 militia for nine months of service, in addition to the 300,000 three-year volunteers. (These calls eventually yielded 421,000 three-year volunteers and 88,000 nine-month militia.) The Peace Democrats railed against these measures and provoked antidraft riots in some localities. The government responded by arresting rioters and antiwar activists under the president's suspension of the writ of habeas corpus.[1]

Democrats denounced these "arbitrary arrests" as unconstitutional violations of civil liberties and added this issue to others on which they hoped to gain control of the next House of Representatives in the fall elections. With the decline in northern morale following the defeat at Second Bull Run, prospects for a Democratic triumph seemed bright. One more military victory by Lee's Army of Northern Virginia might crack the North's will to continue the fight. It might bring diplomatic recognition of the Confederacy by Britain and France. Lee's legions began crossing the Potomac into Maryland on September 4, 1862.

16-1e The Battle of Antietam

The Confederate invasion ran into difficulties from the start. Western Marylanders responded impassively to Lee's proclamation that he had come "to aid you in throwing off this foreign yoke" of Yankee rule. Lee split his army into five parts. Three of them, under the overall command of Stonewall Jackson, occupied the heights surrounding the Union garrison at Harpers Ferry, which lay athwart the Confederate supply route from the Shenandoah Valley (see Map 16.1). The other two remained on watch in the South Mountain passes west of Frederick. Then, on September 13, Union commander George B. McClellan had an extraordinary stroke of luck. In a field near Frederick, two of his soldiers found a copy of Lee's orders for these deployments. Wrapped around three cigars, they had apparently been dropped by a careless southern officer when the Confederate army passed through Frederick four days earlier. With this new information, McClellan planned to pounce on the separated segments of Lee's army before they could reunite.

But McClellan moved so cautiously that he lost much of his advantage. Although Union troops overwhelmed the Confederate defenders of the South Mountain passes on September 14, they advanced too slowly to save the garrison at Harpers Ferry, which surrendered 12,000 men to Jackson on September 15. Lee then managed to reunite most

---

[1] A writ of habeas corpus is an order issued by a judge to law enforcement officers requiring them to bring an arrested person before the court to be charged with a crime so that the accused can have a fair trial. The U.S. Constitution permits the suspension of this writ "in cases of rebellion or invasion," so that the government can arrest enemy agents, saboteurs, or any individual who might hinder the defense of the country, and hold such individuals without trial. Lincoln had suspended the writ, but political opponents charged him with usurping a power possessed only by Congress in order to curb freedom of speech of antiwar opponents and political critics guilty of nothing more than speaking out against the war.

Interpreting the Visual Past — Photographs of the Dead at Antietam

In October 1862, the Matthew Brady studio in New York City held an exhibition of photographs from the battlefield at Antietam. Photography as a technology came into its own during the Civil War; these photographs, taken two days after the battle, were the first images of battlefield dead most Americans had ever seen. The palpable shock many viewers felt was captured by an anonymous reviewer for the *New York Times*, who said that the photographs "bring home to us the terrible reality and earnestness of war." He commented on the "terrible fascination" that "draws one near these pictures, and makes him loth to leave them." Such photographs changed the way in which Americans saw and imagined war.

Q Why, when Americans already understood that men were killed in battle, would these photographs have brought home the "terrible reality" of war? What was it about photography as a medium of representation that changed Americans' perceptions of the human costs of war?

16.3a **Alexander Gardner, Antietam, MD. Confederate Dead by a Fence on the Hagerstown Road, September—October 1862.**

16.3b **Some of the Casualties from the Civil War Battle of Antietam, September 17, 1862.**

16-1 Slavery and the War   441

▲ **MAP 16.1 Lee's Invasion of Maryland, 1862, and the Battle of Antietam, September 17, 1862**
Both the advantages and disadvantages of Lee's defensive position in this battle are illustrated by the right-hand map. The Confederate flanks were protected by water barriers (the Potomac River on the left and Antietam Creek on the right), but the Confederates fought with their back to the Potomac and only Boteler's Ford as the single line of retreat across the river. If Burnside's attack on the Confederate right had succeeded before A. P. Hill's division arrived, Lee's forces could have been trapped north of the river.

Q What advantages and disadvantages did McClellan have at Antietam?
Q Why is Antietam considered one of the most important battles of the Civil War?

of his army near the village of Sharpsburg by September 17, when McClellan finally crossed Antietam Creek to attack. Even so, the Union forces outnumbered the Confederates by 2 to 1 (80,000 to 40,000 men), but McClellan, as usual, believed that the enemy outnumbered him. Thus, he missed several opportunities to inflict a truly crippling defeat on the Confederacy. The battle of Antietam (called Sharpsburg by the Confederates) nevertheless proved to be the single bloodiest day in American history, with more than 23,000 casualties (killed, wounded, and captured) in the two armies.

Attacking from right to left on a four-mile front, McClellan's Army of the Potomac achieved potential breakthroughs at a sunken road northeast of Sharpsburg (known ever after as Bloody Lane) and in the rolling fields southeast of town. But fearing counterattacks from phantom reserves that he was sure Lee possessed, McClellan held back 20,000 of his troops and failed to follow through. Thus, the battle ended in a draw. The battered Confederates still clung to their precarious line, with the Potomac at their back, at the end of a day in which more than 6,000 men on both sides were killed or mortally wounded— almost as many Americans as were killed or mortally wounded in combat during the entire seven years of the Revolutionary War.

Even though he received reinforcements the next day, McClellan did not renew the attack. Nor did he follow up vigorously when the Confederates finally retreated across the Potomac on the night of September 18.

16-1f The Emancipation Proclamation

Lincoln was not happy with this equivocal Union victory, despite its important consequences. Britain and France decided to withhold diplomatic recognition of the

16.4 The Emancipation Proclamation This famous contemporary painting by Francis Carpenter portrays Lincoln and his cabinet discussing the Emancipation Proclamation, which lies on the desk before Lincoln. The other members of the cabinet, from left to right, are Secretary of War Edwin M. Stanton, Secretary of the Treasury Salmon P. Chase, Secretary of the Navy Gideon Welles, Secretary of the Interior Caleb B. Smith, Secretary of State William H. Seward (seated facing Lincoln), Postmaster General Montgomery Blair, and Attorney General Edward Bates.

Confederacy. Northern Democrats failed to gain control of the House in the fall elections. And most significant of all, on September 22, Lincoln seized the occasion to issue his preliminary emancipation proclamation. It did not come as a total surprise. A month earlier, after Horace Greeley had written a strong editorial in the *New York Tribune* calling for action against slavery, Lincoln had responded with a public letter to Greeley (much as a president today might use a televised news conference). "My paramount object in this struggle," wrote Lincoln, "*is* to save the Union... . If I could save the Union without freeing *any* slave I would do it, and if I could save it by freeing *all* the slaves I would do it; and if I could save it by freeing some and leaving others alone I would also do that." Lincoln had crafted these phrases carefully to maximize public support for his anticipated proclamation. He portrayed emancipation not as an end in itself—despite his personal convictions to that effect—but only as an instrument, a *means* toward saving the Union.

Lincoln's proclamation of September 22 did not go into effect immediately. Rather, it stipulated that if any state, or part of a state, was still in rebellion on January 1, 1863, the president would proclaim the slaves therein "forever free." Confederate leaders scorned this warning, and by January 1st no southern state had returned to the Union. After hosting a New Year's Day reception at the White House, Lincoln signed the final proclamation as an "act of justice"

as well as "a fit and necessary war measure for suppressing said rebellion."

The Emancipation Proclamation exempted the border states, plus Tennessee and those portions of Louisiana and Virginia already under Union occupation because these areas were deemed not to be in rebellion, and Lincoln's constitutional authority for the proclamation derived from his power as commander in chief to confiscate enemy property. Although the proclamation did not immediately liberate slaves in areas under Confederate control, it essentially made the northern soldiers an army of liberation, however reluctant many of them were to risk their lives for that purpose. If the North won the war, slavery would die. But in the winter and spring of 1862–1863, victory was far from assured.

16-2 A Winter of Discontent

Q *What were the sources of internal dissent and dissension in the Confederacy? In the Union?*

Although Lee's retreat from Maryland suggested that the Confederate tide might be ebbing, the tide soon turned. The Union could never win the war simply by turning back Confederate invasions. Northern armies would have to invade the South, defeat its armies, and destroy its ability to fight.

Displeased by McClellan's "slows" after Antietam, Lincoln replaced him on November 7 with General Ambrose E. Burnside. An imposing man whose mutton-chop whiskers gave the anagram "sideburns" to the language, Burnside proposed to cross the Rappahannock River at Fredericksburg for a move on Richmond before bad weather forced both sides into winter quarters. Although Lee put his men into a strong defensive position on the heights behind Fredericksburg, Burnside nevertheless attacked on December 13. He was repulsed with heavy casualties that shook the morale of both the army and the public.

News from the western theater did little to dispel the gloom. The Confederates had fortified Vicksburg on bluffs commanding the Mississippi River. This bastion gave them control of an important stretch of the river and preserved transportation links between the states to the east and west. To sever those links, in November 1862 General Ulysses S. Grant launched a two-pronged drive against Vicksburg. With 40,000 men, he marched 50 miles southward from Memphis by land, while his principal subordinate William T. Sherman came down the river with 32,000 men accompanied by a gunboat fleet. But Confederate cavalry raids destroyed the railroads and supply depots in Grant's rear, forcing him to retreat to Memphis. Meanwhile, Sherman attacked the Confederates at Chickasaw Bluffs in December, with no more success than Burnside had enjoyed at Fredericksburg.

Union forces under William S. Rosecrans did score a victory by driving the Confederates to retreat at the Battle of Stones River in Tennessee, but elsewhere matters went from bad to worse. Renewing the campaign against Vicksburg, Grant bogged down in the swamps and rivers that protected that Confederate bastion on three sides. Only on the east, away from the river, did he find high ground suitable for an assault on Vicksburg's defenses. Grant's problem was to get his army across the Mississippi to that high ground. For three months, he floundered in the Mississippi-Yazoo bottomlands, while disease and exposure depleted his troops. False rumors of excessive drinking that had dogged Grant for years broke out anew, but Lincoln resisted pressures to remove him from command. "What I want," Lincoln said, "is generals who will fight battles and win victories. Grant has done this, and I propose to stand by him."

16-2a The Rise of the Copperheads

During the winter of 1863, the Copperhead faction of the Democratic Party found a ready audience for its message that the war was a failure and should be abandoned. Ohio congressman Clement L. Vallandigham, who planned to run for governor, asked northern audiences what this "wicked" war had accomplished: "Let the dead at Fredericksburg and Vicksburg answer." The Confederacy could never be conquered; the only trophies of the war were "debt, defeat, sepulchres." The solution was to "stop the fighting. Make an armistice. Withdraw your army from the seceded states." Above all, give up the unconstitutional effort to abolish slavery.

Vallandigham and other Copperhead spokesmen had a powerful effect on northern morale. Alarmed by a wave of desertions, the army commander in Ohio had Vallandigham arrested in May 1863. A military court convicted him of treason for aiding and abetting the enemy. The court's action raised serious questions of civil liberties. Was the conviction a violation of Vallandigham's First Amendment right of free speech? Could a military court try a civilian under **martial law** in a state such as Ohio where civil courts were functioning?

Lincoln was embarrassed by the swift arrest and trial of Vallandigham, which he learned about from the newspapers. To keep Vallandigham from becoming a martyr, Lincoln commuted his sentence from imprisonment to banishment—to the Confederacy! On May 15, Union cavalry escorted Vallandigham under a flag of truce to Confederate lines in Tennessee, where the southerners reluctantly accepted their uninvited guest. He soon escaped to Canada on a blockade runner. There, from exile, Vallandigham conducted his campaign for governor of Ohio—an election he lost in October 1863, after the military fortunes of the Union had improved.

16-2b Economic Problems in the South

Southerners were buoyed by their military success but were suffering from food shortages and hyperinflation. The tightening Union blockade, the weaknesses and imbalances of the Confederate economy, the escape of slaves to Union lines, and enemy occupation of some of the South's prime agricultural areas made it increasingly difficult to produce both guns and butter. Despite the conversion of hundreds of thousands of acres from cotton to food production, the deterioration of southern railroads and the priority given to army shipments made food scarce in some areas. Prices rose

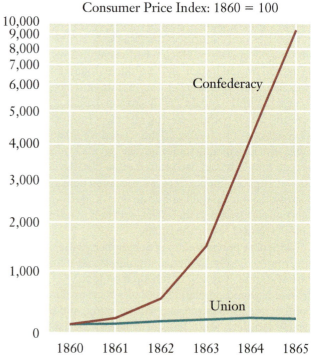

Figure 16.1 **Wartime Inflation in the Confederacy and the Union**

much faster than wages (see Figure 16.1). Even the middle class suffered, especially in Richmond, whose population had more than doubled since 1861. "The shadow of the gaunt form of famine is upon us," wrote a war department clerk in March 1863.

Poor people were worse off, especially the wives and children of nonslaveholders away in the army. By spring 1863, food supplies were virtually gone. Some women took matters into their own hands. Denouncing "speculators" who allegedly hoarded goods to drive up prices, they marched to stores, asked the price of bacon or cornmeal or salt, denounced such "extortion," and took what they wanted without paying. On April 2, 1863, a crowd of more than 1,000 women and boys looted several shops in Richmond before the militia forced them to disperse. The Confederate government subsequently released some emergency food stocks to civilians, and state and county governments aided the families of soldiers. Better crops in 1863 helped alleviate the worst shortages, but serious problems persisted.

16-2c The Wartime Draft and Class Tensions

In both South and North, the draft intensified social unrest and turned it in the direction of class conflict. In April 1862, the Confederacy enacted a draft that made all white men (with certain occupational exemptions) ages 18 to 35 liable to conscription. A drafted man could hire a substitute, but the price of substitutes soon rose beyond the means of the average southern farmer or worker, giving rise to the bitter cry that it was "a rich man's war and a poor man's fight."

The cry grew louder in October 1862 when the Confederate Congress raised the draft age to 45 and added a clause exempting one white man from the draft on every plantation with 20 or more slaves. The purpose of this "overseer exemption" was to keep up production and prevent slave uprisings. It had been prompted by the complaints of planters' wives, who had been left alone to manage the slaves after the departure of husbands, sons, and overseers for the army. The so-called **Twenty Negro Law** was regarded as blatant discrimination by nonslaveholding farm families whose men were also at the front. The law provoked widespread draft dodging and desertions.

Similar discontent greeted the enactment of a conscription law in the North. In summer 1863, some 30,000 Union soldiers would be leaving military service, along with 80,000 of the nine-month militia called into service the preceding autumn. To meet the looming shortfall of men, Congress decreed in March that all male citizens ages 20 to 45 must enroll for the draft. Not all of them would necessarily be called (administrative policy exempted married men over 35), but all would be liable.

The law was intended more to encourage volunteers to come forward than to draft men directly. The War Department set a quota for every congressional district

16.5 The Richmond Bread Riot Illustrating the economic problems of the Confederacy and the suffering of poor civilians in overcrowded cities, the bread riot in Richmond involved 1,000 women and boys who broke into shops to take food and other goods on April 2, 1863. This image from a popular northern illustrated newspaper, *Frank Leslie's Illustrated Weekly*, depicted the plight of Confederate civilians and undercut popular notions of genteel Southern womanhood propaganda.

Q *How does this illustration work as northern propaganda?*

and allowed 50 days for the quota to be met with volunteers before resorting to a draft lottery. Some districts avoided drafting anyone by offering large bounties to volunteers. The bounty system produced glaring abuses, including **bounty jumpers** who enlisted and then deserted as soon as they got their money—often to enlist again under another name somewhere else.

The drafting process was also open to abuse. Like the Confederate law, the Union law permitted hiring substitutes. To keep the price from skyrocketing as it had in the Confederacy, the law allowed a drafted man the alternative of paying a **commutation fee** of $300 that exempted him from the current draft call (but not necessarily from the next one). That provision raised the cry of "rich man's war, poor man's fight" in the North as well. The Democratic Party nurtured this sense of class resentment, and racism intensified it. Democratic newspapers told white workers, especially the large Irish American population, that the draft would force them to fight a war to free the slaves, who would then come north to take their jobs. This volatile issue sparked widespread violence when the northern draft got

THE RIOTS IN NEW YORK: DESTRUCTION OF THE COLOURED ORPHAN ASYLUM.

16.6 The Antidraft Riots The worst urban violence in American history occurred July 13–16, 1863, in New York City. Thousands of rioters attacked draft offices, homes, businesses, and individuals. Black residents of the city were among the mob's victims because they symbolized labor competition to Irish Americans, who constituted most of the rioters and who believed they would be drafted to fight a war to free the slaves. This illustration shows the burning of the Colored Orphan Asylum, a home for black orphans. More than 100 people were killed during those four days, most of them rioters shot down by police and soldiers.

Q *How does this anti-Irish illustration portray rioters in a negative light?*

under way in summer 1863. The worst riot occurred in July in New York City, where huge mobs consisting mostly of Irish Americans demolished draft offices, lynched several blacks, and destroyed huge areas of the city in four days of looting and burning.

16-2d *A Poor Man's Fight?*

The grievance that it was a rich man's war and a poor man's fight was more apparent than real. Property, excise, and income taxes to sustain the war bore proportionately more heavily on the wealthy than on the poor. In the South, wealthy property owners suffered greater damage and confiscation losses than did nonslaveholders. The war liberated 4 million slaves, the poorest class in America. Both the Union and Confederate armies fielded men from all strata of society in proportion to their percentage of the population. If anything, among those who volunteered in 1861 and 1862, the planter class was overrepresented in the Confederate army and the middle class in the Union forces because those privileged groups believed they had more at stake in the war and joined up in larger numbers during the early months of enthusiasm. Those volunteers—especially the officers—suffered the highest percentage of combat casualties.

Nor did conscription fall much more heavily on the poor than on the rich. Those who escaped the draft by decamping to the woods, the territories, or Canada were mostly poor. The Confederacy abolished substitution in December 1863 and made men who had previously sent substitutes liable to the draft. In the North, several city councils, political machines, and businesses contributed funds to pay the commutation fees of drafted men who were too poor to pay out of their own pockets. In the end, it was neither a rich man's war nor a poor man's fight. It was an American war.

16-3 Blueprint for Modern America

Q *How did wartime legislation transform American society? How did women contribute to the war effort?*

The Thirty-seventh Congress (1861–1863)—the Congress that enacted conscription, passed measures for confiscation and emancipation, and created the greenbacks and the national banking system (see Chapter 15)—also enacted three laws that, together with the war legislation, provided what one historian has called "a blueprint for modern America": the Homestead Act, the Morrill Land-Grant College Act, and the Pacific Railroad Act. For several years before the war, Republicans and some northern Democrats had tried to pass these laws to provide social benefits and to promote economic growth, only to see them defeated by southern opposition or by President Buchanan's veto. The secession of southern states, ironically, enabled Congress to pass all three laws in 1862.

The Homestead Act granted 160 acres of land to a farmer virtually free after he had lived on the land for five years and had made improvements on it. The Morrill Land-Grant College Act gave each state thousands of acres to fund the establishment of colleges to teach "agricultural and mechanical arts." The Pacific Railroad Act granted land and loans to railroad companies to spur the building of a transcontinental railroad from Omaha to Sacramento. Despite waste, corruption, and exploitation of the original Indian owners of this land, these laws helped farmers settle some of the most fertile land in the world, studded the land with state colleges, and spanned it with steel rails in a manner that altered the landscape of the western half of the country.

16.7 Union Army Hospital The Armory Square military hospital in Washington, with its clean, cheerful wards apparently decorated for the Christmas holidays, showed Union medical care at its best.

16-3a Women and the War

The war advanced many other social changes, particularly with respect to women. In factories and on farms, women replaced men who had gone off to war. Explosions in ordnance plants and arsenals killed at least 100 women, who were as surely war casualties as men killed in battle. The war accelerated the entry of women into the teaching profession, a trend that had already begun in the Northeast and now spread to other parts of the country. It also brought significant numbers of women into the civil service. During the 1850s, a few women had worked briefly in the U.S. Patent Office (including Clara Barton, who became a famous wartime nurse and founded the American Red Cross). The huge expansion of government bureaucracies after 1861 and the departure of male clerks to the army provided openings that were filled partly by women. After the war, the private sector began hiring women as clerks, bookkeepers, "typewriters" (the machine was invented in the 1870s), and telephone operators (the telephone was another postwar invention).

16-3b Women as Aid Workers and Nurses

Women's most visible impact was in the field of medicine. The outbreak of war prompted the organization of soldiers' aid societies, hospital societies, and other voluntary associations in which women played a leading role. Their most important function was to help—and sometimes to prod—the medical branches of the Union and Confederate armies to provide more efficient, humane care for sick and wounded soldiers. Dr. Elizabeth Blackwell, the first American woman to earn an MD (1849), organized a meeting of 3,000 women in New York City on April 29, 1861. They put together the Women's Central Association for Relief, which became the nucleus for the most powerful voluntary association of the war, the U.S. Sanitary Commission.

Eventually embracing 7,000 local auxiliaries, the Sanitary Commission was an essential adjunct of the Union army's medical bureau. Most of its local volunteers were women, as were most of the nurses it provided to army hospitals. Nursing was not a new profession for women, but it had lacked respect as a wartime profession. The fame won by Florence Nightingale of Britain during the Crimean War a half-dozen years earlier had begun to change that perception. As thousands of middle- and even upper-class women volunteers flocked to army hospitals, nursing began its transformation from a menial occupation to a respected profession.

The nurses had to overcome the deeply ingrained suspicions of army surgeons and the opposition of husbands and fathers who shared the cultural sentiment that the shocking, embarrassingly physical atmosphere of an army hospital was no place for a respectable woman. Many thousands of women went to work, winning grudging and then enthusiastic admiration.

16.8a (left) and 16.8b (right) Female Spies and Soldiers In addition to working in war industries and serving as army nurses, some women pursued traditionally male wartime careers as spies and soldiers. One of the most famous Confederate spies was Rose O'Neal Greenhow, a Washington widow and socialite who fed information to officials in Richmond. Federal officers arrested her in August 1861 and deported her to Richmond in spring 1862. She was photographed (left) with her daughter in the Old Capitol prison in Washington, D.C., while awaiting trial. In October 1864, she drowned in a lifeboat off Wilmington, North Carolina, after a blockade runner carrying her back from a European mission was run aground by a Union warship. The second photograph (right) shows a Union soldier who enlisted in the 95th Illinois Infantry under the name of Albert Cashier and fought through the war. A farm accident in 1911 revealed Albert Cashier to be a woman, whose real name was Jennie Hodgers. Most of the other estimated 400 women who evaded the superficial physical exams and passed as men to enlist in the Union and Confederate armies were more quickly discovered and discharged. A few, however, served long enough to be killed in action.

16-4 The Confederate Tide Crests and Recedes

Q *How did the Union army achieve a victory at Gettysburg?*

The Army of Northern Virginia and the Army of the Potomac spent the winter of 1862–1863 on opposite banks of the Rappahannock River. With the coming of spring, Union commander Joe Hooker resumed the offensive with hopes of redeeming the December disaster at Fredericksburg. On April 30, instead of charging straight across the river, Hooker crossed his men several miles upriver and came in on Lee's rear. Lee quickly faced most of his troops about and confronted the enemy in dense woods, known locally as the Wilderness, near the crossroads mansion of Chancellorsville. Nonplussed, Hooker lost the initiative.

16-4a The Battle of Chancellorsville

Even though Union forces outnumbered the Confederates by almost two to one, Lee boldly went over to the offensive. On May 2, Stonewall Jackson led 28,000 men on a stealthy march through the woods to attack the Union right flank late in the afternoon (see Map 16.2). The surprise was complete. Jackson's assault crumpled the Union flank as the sun set. Jackson then rode out to scout the terrain for a moonlight attack but was wounded on his return by jittery Confederates who mistook him and his staff for Union cavalry. Nevertheless, Lee resumed the attack the next day. In three more days of fighting that caused 12,800 Confederate and 16,800 Union casualties (the largest number for a single battle in the war so far), Lee drove the Union troops back across the Rappahannock. It was a brilliant victory.

In the North, the gloom grew deeper. Southern elation, however, was tempered by grief at the death on May 10 of Jackson, who had contracted pneumonia after amputation of his arm. Nevertheless, Lee decided to parlay his tactical victory at Chancellorsville into a strategic offensive by again invading the North. A victory on Union soil would convince northerners and foreigners alike that the Confederacy was invincible. As his army moved north in June 1863, Lee was confident of success. "There never were such men in an army before," he wrote of his troops. "They will go anywhere and do anything if properly led."

▲ **MAP 16.2 Battle of Chancellorsville, May 2–6, 1863** This map demonstrates the advantage of holding "interior lines," which enabled General Lee to shift troops back and forth to and from the Chancellorsville and Fredericksburg fronts over the course of three days while the two parts of the Union army remained separated.

Q *What other reasons for Confederate victory are visible on this map?*

Q *What effect did victory at Chancellorsville have on Confederate strategy?*

16-4b The Gettysburg Campaign

At first, all went well. The Confederates brushed aside or captured Union forces in the northern Shenandoah Valley and in Pennsylvania. Stuart's cavalry threw a scare into Washington by raiding behind Union lines into Maryland and Pennsylvania. That very success led to trouble. With Stuart's cavalry separated from the rest of the army, Lee lost the vital intelligence that the cavalry garnered as the army's eyes. By June 28, several detachments of Lee's forces were scattered about Pennsylvania, far from their base and vulnerable.

At this point, Lee learned that the Army of the Potomac was moving toward him, now under the command of George Gordon Meade. Lee immediately ordered his own army to reassemble in the vicinity of Gettysburg, an agricultural and college town at the hub of a dozen roads leading in from all directions. There, on the morning of July 1, the vanguard of the two armies met in a clash that grew into the greatest battle in American history (see Map 16.3).

As the fighting spread west and north of town, couriers pounded up the roads to summon reinforcements to both sides. The Confederates fielded more men and broke the Union lines late that afternoon, driving the survivors to a defensive position on Cemetery Hill south of town. General Richard Ewell, Jackson's successor as commander of the Confederate Second Corps, judging this position too strong to take with his own troops, chose not to press the attack as the sun went down on what he presumed would be another Confederate victory.

When the sun rose the next morning, however, the reinforced Union army was holding a superb defensive position from Culp's Hill and Cemetery Hill south to Little Round Top. Lee's principal subordinate, First Corps commander James Longstreet, advised against attack, urging instead a maneuver to the south, toward Washington, to force the Federals to attack Lee in a strong defensive position. But Lee believed his army invincible. After its victory on July 1, a move to the south might look like a retreat. Pointing to the Union lines, he said: "The enemy is there, and I am going to attack him there." Longstreet reluctantly led the attack on the Union left. Once committed, his men fought with fury. The Union troops fought back with equal fury. As the afternoon passed, peaceful areas

▲ **MAP 16.3 Battle of Gettysburg, July 1–3, 1863** On July 2 and 3, the Union army had the advantage of interior lines at Gettysburg, which enabled General Meade to shift reinforcements from his right on Culp's Hill to his left near Little Round Top over a much shorter distance than Confederate reinforcements from one flank to the other would have to travel.

Q *What are the main reasons for Union victory at Gettysburg?*

Q *How important was Union victory at Gettysburg to the outcome of the war?*

with names like Peach Orchard, Wheat Field, Devil's Den, and Little Round Top were turned into killing fields. By the end of the day, Confederate forces had made small gains at great cost, but the main Union line had held firm.

Lee was not yet ready to yield the offensive. Having attacked both Union flanks, he thought the center might be weak. On July 3, he ordered a frontal attack on Cemetery Ridge, led by a fresh division under George Pickett. After a two-hour artillery barrage, Pickett's 5,000 men and 8,000 additional troops moved forward on that sultry afternoon in a picture-book assault that forms our most enduring image of the Civil War. "Pickett's Charge" was shot to pieces; scarcely half of the men returned unwounded to their own lines. It was the final act in a three-day drama that left some 50,000 men killed, wounded, or captured: 23,000 Federals and 25,000 to 28,000 Confederates.

Lee limped back to Virginia, pursued by the Union troops. Lincoln was unhappy with Meade for not cutting off the Confederate retreat. Nevertheless, Gettysburg was a great northern victory, and it came at the same time as other important Union successes in Mississippi, Louisiana, and Tennessee.

16-4c The Vicksburg Campaign

In mid-April, Grant had begun a move that would put Vicksburg in a vise. The Union ironclad fleet ran downriver past the big guns at Vicksburg with little damage. Grant's troops marched down the Mississippi's west bank and ferried across the river 40 miles south of Vicksburg.

There they kept the Confederate defenders off balance by striking east toward Jackson instead of marching north to Vicksburg. Grant's purpose was to scatter the Confederate forces in central Mississippi and to destroy the rail network so that his rear would be secure when he turned toward Vicksburg. It was a brilliant strategy, flawlessly executed (see Map 16.4). During the first three weeks of May, Grant's troops marched 180 miles, won five battles, and trapped 32,000 Confederate troops and 3,000 civilians in Vicksburg between the Union army on land and the Union gunboats on the river.

But the Confederate army was still full of fight. Confederate soldiers threw back Union assaults against the Vicksburg trenches on May 19 and 22. Grant then settled down for a siege. Running out of supplies, the Vicksburg garrison surrendered on July 4. On July 9, the Confederate garrison at Port Hudson, 200 river miles south of Vicksburg, surrendered to a besieging Union army. Northern forces now controlled the entire length of the Mississippi River. "The Father of Waters again goes unvexed to the sea," said Lincoln. The Confederacy had been torn in two, and Lincoln knew who deserved the credit. "Grant is my man," he said, "and I am his the rest of the war."

16-4d Chickamauga and Chattanooga

Northerners had scarcely finished celebrating the twin victories of Gettysburg and Vicksburg when they learned of an important—and almost bloodless—triumph in Tennessee (see Map 16.5). On June 24, Union commander

▲ **MAP 16.4 Vicksburg Campaign, April–July 1863** This map illustrates Grant's brilliant orchestration of the campaign that involved Sherman's feint at Haynes' Bluff (top of map) on April 30 while the rest of the Union forces crossed at Bruinsburg (bottom of map) and then cleared Confederate resistance out of the way eastward to Jackson before turning west to invade Vicksburg.

Q What were Grant's chief strengths as a general?

Q How would you compare Lee and Grant as generals?

▲ **MAP 16.5 Road to Chickamauga, June–September 1863** From Murfreesboro to Chattanooga, Rosecrans's campaign of maneuver on multiple fronts forced Bragg's Army of Tennessee all the way south into Georgia in a campaign with minimal casualties before Bragg counterattacked at Chickamauga.

Q What effect did Chickamauga and Chattanooga have on Southern morale?

Q How did modes of fighting battles change over the course of the war?

William S. Rosecrans assaulted the Confederate defenses in the Cumberland foothills of east-central Tennessee. In the first week of July, the Confederates retreated all the way to Chattanooga. After a pause to resupply, Rosecrans's army advanced again in August, this time in tandem with a smaller Union army in eastern Tennessee. Again the outnumbered Confederates fell back, evacuating Knoxville on September 2 and Chattanooga on September 9. This action severed the South's only direct east-west rail link. Having sliced the Confederacy in half with the capture of Vicksburg and Port Hudson, Union forces now stood poised for a campaign into Georgia that threatened to slice it into three parts. For the Confederacy, it was a stunning reversal of the situation only four months earlier, after Chancellorsville, when the Union cause had appeared hopeless.

Confederate general Braxton Bragg reached into his bag of tricks and sent fake deserters into Union lines with tales of a Confederate retreat toward Atlanta. He then laid a trap for Rosecrans's troops as they advanced through the mountain passes south of Chattanooga. To help him spring it, Jefferson Davis approved the detachment of Longstreet with two divisions from Lee's army to reinforce Bragg. On September 19, the Confederates turned and counterattacked Rosecrans's now outnumbered army in the valley of Chickamauga Creek.

On that day and the next, in ferocious fighting that produced more casualties (35,000) than any other single battle save Gettysburg, the Confederates finally scored a victory. On September 20, after a confusion of orders left a division-size gap in the Union line, Longstreet's men broke through, sending part of the Union army reeling back to Chattanooga. Only a firm stand by corps commander George H. Thomas—a Virginian who had remained loyal to the Union—prevented a Union rout. For this feat, Thomas earned the nickname "Rock of Chickamauga." Lincoln subsequently appointed Thomas commander of the Army of the Cumberland to replace Rosecrans, who was, in Lincoln's words, "confused and stunned like a duck hit on the head" after Chickamauga.

Lincoln also sent two army corps from Virginia under Hooker and two from Vicksburg under Sherman to reinforce Thomas, whose troops in Chattanooga were under virtual siege by Bragg's forces, which held most of the surrounding heights. More important, Lincoln put Grant in overall command of the beefed-up Union forces there. When Grant arrived in late October, he welded the various northern units into a new army and opened a new supply line into Chattanooga. On November 24, Hooker's troops drove Confederate besiegers off massive Lookout Mountain.

The next day, an assault on Bragg's main line at Missionary Ridge east of Chattanooga won a smashing success against seemingly greater odds than Pickett had faced at Gettysburg. The Union troops that had been routed at Chickamauga two months earlier redeemed themselves by driving the Confederates off Missionary Ridge and 20 miles south into Georgia.

These battles climaxed a string of Union victories in the second half of 1863. The southern diarist Mary Boykin Chesnut found "gloom and unspoken despondency hang[ing] like a pall everywhere." Jefferson Davis removed the discredited Bragg from command of the Army of Tennessee and reluctantly replaced him with Joseph E. Johnston, in whom Davis had little confidence. Lincoln summoned Grant to Washington and appointed him general-in-chief of all Union armies in March 1864, signifying a relentless fight to the finish.

16-5 Black Men in Blue

Q *What contribution did African Americans make to the Union war effort?*

The events of the second half of 1863 also confirmed emancipation as a Union war aim. Northerners had not greeted the Emancipation Proclamation with great enthusiasm. Democrats and border-state Unionists continued to denounce it, and many Union soldiers resented the idea that they would now be risking their lives for black freedom. The Democratic Party had hoped to capitalize on this opposition, and on Union military failures, to win important off-year elections. Northern military victories knocked one prop out from under the Democratic platform, and the performance of black soldiers fighting for the Union knocked out another.

The enlistment of black soldiers was a logical corollary of emancipation. Proposals to recruit black soldiers, Democrats said, were part of a Republican plot to establish "the equality of the black and white races." In a way, that charge was correct. One consequence of black men fighting for the Union would be to advance the black race a long way toward equal rights. "Once let the black man get upon his person the brass letters, U.S.," said Frederick Douglass, "and a musket on his shoulder and bullets in his pocket, and there is no power on earth which can deny that he has earned the right to citizenship."

But it was pragmatism more than principle that pushed the North toward black recruitment. One purpose of emancipation was to deprive the Confederacy of black laborers and to use them for the Union. Putting some of those former laborers in uniform was a compelling idea, especially as white enlistments lagged and the North had to enact conscription in 1863. Some Union commanders in occupied portions of Louisiana, South Carolina, and Missouri began to organize black regiments in 1862. The Emancipation Proclamation legitimized this policy with its proposal to enroll able-bodied male contrabands in new black regiments, although these units would serve as labor battalions, supply troops, and garrison forces rather than as combat troops. They would be paid less than white soldiers, and their officers would be white.

16-5a Black Soldiers in Combat

Continuing pressure from abolitionists, as well as military necessity, partly eroded this discrimination. Congress enacted equal pay in 1864. Officers worked for better treatment of their men. Above all, the regiments lobbied for the right to fight as combat soldiers. Even some previously hostile white soldiers came around to the notion that black men might just as well stop enemy bullets as white men. In May and June 1863, black regiments in Louisiana fought well in an assault on Port Hudson and in defense of a Union outpost at Milliken's Bend, near Vicksburg. "The bravery of the blacks in the battle of Milliken's Bend completely revolutionized the sentiment of the army with regard to the employment of negro troops," wrote the assistant secretary of war, who had been on the spot with Grant's army.

Even more significant was the action of the 54th Massachusetts Infantry, the first black regiment raised mainly in the North. Its officers, headed by Colonel Robert Gould Shaw, came from prominent New England antislavery families. Two sons of Frederick Douglass were in the regiment—one of them as sergeant major. Shaw worked hard to win the right for the regiment to fight. On July 18, 1863, he succeeded: The 54th was assigned to lead an assault on Fort Wagner, part of the network of Confederate defenses protecting Charleston. Although the attack failed, the 54th fought courageously, suffering 50 percent casualties, including Colonel Shaw, who was killed.

16.9 Part of Company E, Fourth U.S. Colored Infantry
Organized in July 1863, most of the men were former slaves from North Carolina. The Fourth fought in several actions on the Petersburg and Richmond fronts in 1864, helping to capture part of the Petersburg defenses on June 15. Of the 166 black regiments in the Union army, the Fourth suffered the fourth-largest number of combat deaths.

The battle took place just after white mobs of draft rioters in New York had lynched blacks. Abolitionist and Republican commentators drew the moral: Black men who fought for the Union deserved more respect than white men who rioted against it. Lincoln made this point eloquently in a widely published letter to a political meeting in August 1863. When final victory was achieved, he wrote, "there will be some black men who can remember that, with silent tongue, and clenched teeth, and steady eye, and well-poised bayonet, they have helped mankind on to this great consummation; while, I fear, there will be some white ones, unable to forget that, with malignant heart, and deceitful speech, they have strove to hinder it."

16-5b Emancipation Confirmed

Lincoln's letter set the tone for Republican campaigns in state elections that fall. The party swept them all, including Ohio, where they buried Vallandigham under a 100,000-vote margin swelled by the soldier vote, which went 94 percent for his opponent. In effect, the elections were a powerful endorsement of the administration's emancipation policy. If the Emancipation Proclamation had been submitted to a referendum a year earlier, observed a newspaper editor in November 1863, "the voice of a majority would have been against it. And yet not a year has passed before it is approved by an overwhelming majority."

Emancipation would not be assured of survival until it had been christened by the Constitution. On April 8, 1864, the Senate passed the Thirteenth Amendment to abolish slavery, but Democrats in the House blocked the required two-thirds majority there. Not until after Lincoln's reelection in 1864 would the House pass the amendment, which became part of the Constitution on December 6, 1865. In the end, though, the fate of slavery depended on the outcome of the war. And despite Confederate defeats in 1863, that outcome was by no means certain. Some of the heaviest fighting lay ahead.

16-6 The Year of Decision

Q *Why did Lincoln think he would not win reelection in 1864?*

Many southerners succumbed to defeatism in the winter of 1863–1864. "I have never actually despaired of the cause," wrote a Confederate War Department official in November, but "steadfastness is yielding to a sense of hopelessness." Desertions from Confederate armies increased. Inflation galloped out of control. According to a Richmond diarist, a merchant told a poor woman in October 1863 that the price of a barrel of flour was $70: "'My God!' exclaimed she, 'how can I pay such prices? I have seven children; what shall I do?' 'I don't know, madam,' said he, coolly, 'unless you eat your children.'"

The Davis administration, like the Lincoln administration a year earlier, had to face congressional elections during a time of public discontent, for the Confederate constitution mandated such elections in odd-numbered years. Political parties had ceased to exist in the Confederacy after Democrats and former Whigs had tacitly declared a truce in 1861 to form a united front for the war effort. Many congressmen had been elected without opposition in 1861. By 1863, however, significant hostility to Davis had emerged. Although it was not channeled through any organized party, it took on partisan trappings, as an inchoate anti-Davis faction surfaced in the Confederate Congress and in the election campaign of 1863.

Some anti-administration candidates ran on a quasi-peace platform (analogous to that of the Copperheads in the North) that called for an armistice and peace negotiations. The movement left unresolved the terms of such negotiations—reunion or independence—but any peace overture from a position of weakness was tantamount to conceding defeat. The peace movement was especially strong in North Carolina, where for a time it appeared that the next governor would be elected on a peace platform (in the end, the "peace candidate" was defeated). Still, anti-administration candidates made significant gains in the 1863 Confederate elections, although they fell about 15 seats short of a majority in the House and two seats short in the Senate.

16-6a Out of the Wilderness

Shortages, inflation, political discontent, military defeat, high casualties, and the loss of thousands of slaves bent but did not break the southern spirit. As spring 1864 came on, a renewed determination infused both home front and battlefront. The Confederate armies no longer had the strength to invade the North or to win the war with a knockout blow, but they could still fight a war of attrition. If they could hold out long enough and inflict enough casualties on the Union armies, they might weaken the northern will to continue fighting.

Northerners were vulnerable to this strategy. Military success in 1863 had created a mood of confidence, and people expected a quick, decisive victory in 1864. The mood grew with Grant's appointment as general-in-chief. When Grant decided to remain in Virginia with the Army of the Potomac and to leave Sherman in command of the Union forces in northern Georgia, northerners expected these two heavyweights to floor the Confederacy with a one-two punch. Lincoln was alarmed by this euphoria. "The people are too sanguine," he told a reporter. "They expect too much at once." Disappointment might trigger despair.

Lincoln was nearly proved right. Grant's strategic plan was elegant in its simplicity. While smaller Union armies in peripheral theaters carried out auxiliary campaigns, the two principal armies in Virginia and Georgia would attack the main Confederate forces under Lee and Johnston. Convinced that in years past Union armies in various theaters had "acted independently and without concert, like a balky team, no two ever pulling together," Grant ordered simultaneous offensives on all fronts, to prevent the Confederates from shifting reinforcements to one theater from another.

History Through Film: *Lincoln* (2012)

Directed by Steven Spielberg.
Starring Daniel Day-Lewis (Abraham Lincoln), Sally Field (Mary Lincoln), David Strathairn (William H. Seward), Tommy Lee Jones (Thaddeus Stevens)

Despite its title, *Lincoln* is not a biopic, but instead tells the surprisingly gripping story of the passage of the 13th Amendment. In early 1865, as it becomes clear that the North will most likely win the Civil War in a matter of months rather than years, President Lincoln decides that he wants to make an all-out effort for passage of the 13th Amendment, in order to abolish slavery permanently from America. He meets resistance to this idea everywhere—especially from his own quarrelsome Cabinet. Why distract from the war effort? Why not wait until after the South sues for peace and the war ends? Why do this *now*? But Lincoln is clear: the Emancipation Proclamation, issued on January 1, 1863, is not enough to guarantee the *permanent* eradication of slavery. What if the next President simply overturns Lincoln's executive order for emancipation? Will slavery then return to America? No, the eradication of slavery must have a firm legal basis, Lincoln argues. It must be enshrined in the Constitution itself.

And thus begins a mad scramble to obtain enough votes in Congress to ensure the 13th Amendment's passage. Not every film can make an exciting cliffhanger out of a Congressional vote, but *Lincoln* manages this feat, in part due to the energetic direction of Steven Spielberg. In addition, the superb screenplay by the playwright Tony Kushner (*Angels in America*) brilliantly captures the horse-trading—and even corruption—involved in getting lawmakers to change their votes. Individual holdouts spring to vivid life on the screen, as they are personally cajoled and pressured by Lincoln and also by a cynical huckster hired for the task, played with gusto by a perfectly cast James Spader.

Along the way, we gain insights into the tensions in Lincoln's Cabinet, which he had composed as a "team of rivals." (The film is based in part on Doris Kearns Goodwin's excellent history *Team of Rivals: The Political Genius of Abraham Lincoln*.) We also follow the trajectory of the Radical Republican Thaddeus Stevens—played by Tommy Lee Jones—who in early 1865 would have preferred to fight for social as well as legal equality for African Americans, but is portrayed as reluctantly agreeing to postpone that larger fight out of political expediency.

Daniel Day-Lewis gives a brilliant performance, showcasing Lincoln's love of humor and off-color jokes; his canny political abilities despite his folksy style; his extraordinary intelligence, depth of knowledge, and eloquence; and his deep and abiding love of freedom and justice. The film is also good at depicting Lincoln's relationships with his family. His eldest son Robert is desperate to join the Army in the waning days of the war, chafing against his father's proscription against enlistment. The film captures both the tensions between father and son and Lincoln's tempestuous relationship with his wife Mary, played convincingly by Sally Field.

What are the faults with the film? Some viewers might object to its sentimental frame: near the opening, for instance, three earnest soldiers, fresh from the battlefield, recite the Gettysburg Address from memory to Lincoln. Is this believable for early 1865? Not really. But when the film closes with a retrospective scene of Lincoln delivering his great Second Inaugural Address, we are willing to grant the film's right to a few sentimental moments.

Critics have pointed out that the crucial story of black self-emancipation—the all-important actions of former slaves who liberated themselves from slavery by coming into Union lines, and thus *forced* the Union to deal with the issue of emancipation—receives no attention here. Obviously that important social reality deserves filmic treatment. *Lincoln* accomplishes something different: focused on the practice of politics in Washington, it ultimately makes the argument that in a democracy, we must embrace the legislative process—even if not perfect, even if exceedingly messy—as our best path forward to freedom and justice for all. ∎

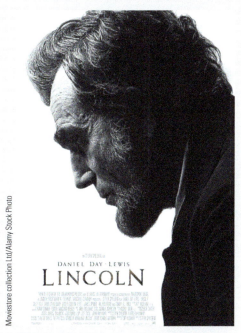

16.10 An advertising poster for the film *Lincoln* that shows the actor Daniel Day-Lewis's successful physical transformation for the role of Abraham Lincoln.

Grant's offensives began the first week of May. The heaviest fighting occurred in Virginia. When the Army of the Potomac crossed the Rapidan River, Lee attacked its flank in the thick scrub forest of the Wilderness, where Union superiority in numbers and artillery would count for little (and where Lee had defeated Hooker a year earlier at Chancellorsville). Lee's action brought on two days (May 5–6) of the most confused, frenzied fighting the war had yet seen (see Map 16.6). Hundreds of wounded men burned to death in brush fires set off by exploding shells or muzzle flashes. The battle surged back and forth, with the Confederates inflicting 18,000 casualties and suffering 12,000. Having apparently halted Grant's offensive, they claimed a victory.

16-6b Spotsylvania and Cold Harbor

But Grant did not retreat, as other Union commanders in Virginia had done. Instead, he moved toward Spotsylvania Courthouse, a key crossroads 10 miles closer to Richmond. Skillfully, Lee pulled back to cover the road junction. Repeated Union assaults during the next 12 days (May 8–19) left another 18,000 northerners and 12,000 southerners killed, wounded, or captured. The Confederates fought from an elaborate network of trenches and log breastworks they had constructed virtually overnight. Civil War soldiers had learned the advantages of trenches, which gave the defense an enormous advantage and made frontal assaults almost suicidal.

Having achieved no better than stalemate around Spotsylvania, Grant again moved south around Lee's right flank in an effort to force the outnumbered Confederates into an open fight. Lee, however, anticipated Grant's moves and confronted him from behind formidable defenses at the North Anna River, Totopotomoy Creek, and near the crossroads inn of Cold Harbor, only 10 miles northeast of Richmond. Believing the Confederates must be exhausted and demoralized by their repeated retreats, Grant decided to attack at Cold Harbor on June 3—a costly mistake. Lee's troops were ragged and hungry but far from demoralized. Their withering fire inflicted 7,000 casualties in less than an hour. "I regret this assault more than any other one I have ordered," said Grant.

▲ **MAP 16.6 Battle of the Wilderness and Spotsylvania, May 5–12, 1864** Four major battles with a total of more than 100,000 casualties to both sides were fought within a few miles of Fredericksburg between December 1862 and May 1864. Compare this map with Map 16.2. The first battle of Fredericksburg on December 13, 1862 (described p. 444), was fought in the same vicinity as the Fredericksburg fighting on May 3, 1863, shown on the Chancellorsville map.

Q *How are these battles similar or different?*

Q *How did Union and Confederate forces employ trenches to their advantage during the war?*

16-6c Stalemate in Virginia

Now Grant moved all the way across the James River to strike at Petersburg, an industrial city and rail center 20 miles south of Richmond. If Petersburg fell, the Confederates could not hold Richmond. Once more Lee's troops raced southward on the inside track and blocked Grant's troops. Four days of Union assaults (June 15–18) produced another 11,000 northern casualties but no breakthrough. Such high Union losses in just six weeks—some 65,000 killed, wounded, and captured, compared with 37,000 Confederate casualties—cost the Army of the Potomac its offensive power. Grant reluctantly settled down for a siege along the Petersburg–Richmond front that would last more than nine grueling months.

Meanwhile, other Union operations in Virginia had achieved little success. Benjamin Butler bungled an attack up the James River against Richmond and was stopped by a scraped-together army under General P. G. T. Beauregard. Jubal Early, commanding Stonewall Jackson's old corps, blocked a Union thrust up the Shenandoah Valley at Lynchburg in June. Then Early led a raid all the way to the outskirts of Washington on July 11 and 12 before being driven back to Virginia. Union cavalry under Philip Sheridan inflicted considerable damage on Confederate resources in Virginia—including the mortal wounding of Jeb Stuart in the battle of Yellow Tavern on May 11—but again failed to strike a crippling blow. In the North, frustration set in over failure to win the quick, decisive victory the public had expected in April.

16-6d The Atlanta Campaign

In Georgia, Sherman's army seemed to have accomplished more at less cost than Grant had in Virginia, but there too Union efforts had bogged down in apparent stalemate by August. The strategy and tactics of both Sherman and Johnston in Georgia contrasted with those of Grant and Lee in Virginia. Sherman forced Johnston south toward Atlanta by constantly flanking him to the Union right, generally without bloody battles (see Map 16.7). Grant constantly forced Lee back by flanking moves to the Union left, but only after bloody battles. By the end of June, Sherman had advanced 80 miles at the cost of 17,000 casualties to Johnston's 14,000—only one-third of the combined losses of Grant and Lee.

Davis grew alarmed by Johnston's apparent willingness to yield territory without a fight. Sherman again flanked the Confederate defenses (after a failed attack) at Kennesaw Mountain in early July. He crossed the Chattahoochee River and drove Johnston back to Peachtree Creek, less than five miles from Atlanta. Fearing that Johnston would abandon the city, on July 17 Davis replaced him with John Bell Hood.

A fighting general from Lee's army who had lost a leg at Chickamauga, Hood immediately prepared to counterattack against the Yankees. He did so three times, in late July. Each time, the Confederates reeled back in defeat, suffering a total of 15,000 casualties to Sherman's 6,000. At last, Hood retreated into the formidable earthworks ringing Atlanta and launched no more attacks. But his army did manage to keep Sherman's cavalry and infantry from taking the two railroads leading into Atlanta from the south. Like Grant at Petersburg, Sherman seemed to settle down for a siege.

16-6e Peace Overtures

By August, the Confederate strategy of attrition seemed to be working. Union casualties on all fronts during the preceding three months totaled a staggering 110,000—double the number for any comparable period of the war. "Who shall revive the withered hopes that bloomed at the opening of Grant's campaign?" asked the leading Democratic newspaper, the *New York World*. "STOP THE WAR!" shouted Democratic headlines. "All are tired of this damnable tragedy."

Even Republicans joined the chorus of despair. "Our bleeding, bankrupt, almost dying country longs for peace," wrote Horace Greeley of the *New York Tribune*. Greeley became involved in abortive "peace negotiations" spawned by Confederate agents in Canada. Those agents convinced Greeley that they carried peace overtures from Davis, but Lincoln was skeptical. Still, given the mood of the North in midsummer 1864, Lincoln could not reject any opportunity to stop the bloodshed. He deputized Greeley to meet with the Confederate agents in Niagara Falls on the Canadian side of the border. At almost the same time (mid-July), two other northerners met under a flag of truce with Davis in Richmond. Lincoln had carefully instructed them—and Greeley—that his conditions for peace were "restoration of the Union and abandonment of slavery."

Davis would no more accept those terms than Lincoln would accept his. Although neither of the peace contacts came to anything, the Confederates gained a propaganda victory by claiming that Lincoln's terms had been the only obstacle to peace. Northern Democrats ignored the southern refusal to accept reunion and focused on the slavery issue as the sole stumbling block. "Tens of thousands of white men must yet bite the dust to allay the negro mania of the President," ran a typical Democratic editorial. By August, even staunch Republicans were convinced that "the desire for peace" and the impression that Lincoln "is fighting not for the Union but for the abolition of slavery" made his reelection "an impossibility." Lincoln thought so, too. "I am going to be beaten," he told a friend in August, "and unless some great change takes place, *badly* beaten."

Lincoln faced enormous pressure to drop emancipation as a condition of peace, but he refused to yield. He would rather lose the election than go back on the promise he had made in the Emancipation Proclamation. Some 130,000 black soldiers and sailors were fighting for the Union. They would not do so if they thought the North intended to forsake them:

> If they stake their lives for us they must be prompted by the strongest motive ... the promise of freedom. And the promise being made, must be kept... . There have been men who proposed to me to return to slavery the[se] black warriors... . I should be damned in time & eternity for so doing. The world shall know that I will keep my faith to friends and enemies, come what will.

16.11 **Union Supply Base at City Point, Virginia** During the Union army's siege of Petersburg from June 1864 to April 1865, the army built up a huge complex of wharfs and warehouses at City Point on the James River (today's Hopewell, Virginia) where ships unloaded supplies and trains carried them to the front. Note the boxcars of the U.S. Military Rail Road shown in the photograph.

At the end of August, the Democrats nominated McClellan for president. The platform on which he ran declared, "after four years of failure to restore the Union by the experiment of war ... [we] demand that immediate efforts be made for a cessation of hostilities." Southerners were jubilant. Democratic victory on that platform, said the *Charleston Mercury*, "must lead to peace and our independence [if] for the next two months *we hold our own and prevent military success by our foes.*"

16-6f The Prisoner-Exchange Controversy

The Democratic platform also condemned the Lincoln administration's "shameful disregard" of prisoners of war in Confederate prison camps. This raised another contentious matter. By midsummer 1864, the plight of Union and Confederate captives had become one of the most bitter issues of the war. The upcoming presidential election and the generally worse conditions in southern prisons made it mainly a northern political issue.

In 1862, the Union and Confederate armed forces had signed a cartel for the exchange of prisoners captured in battle. The arrangement had worked reasonably well for a year, making large prison camps unnecessary. When the Union army began to organize regiments of former slaves, however, the Confederate government announced that if they were captured, they and their white officers would be put to death for the crime of fomenting slave insurrections. In practice, the Confederate government did not enforce this policy because Lincoln threatened retaliation on Confederate prisoners of war if it did so. But Confederate troops sometimes murdered black soldiers and their officers as they tried to

▲ **MAP 16.7 Campaign for Atlanta, May–September 1864** The main map illustrates Sherman's campaign of maneuver that forced Johnston back to Atlanta with relatively few battles. The first three inset maps show the Confederate counterattacks launched by Hood, and the fourth shows how the Union army got astride the last two railroads entering Atlanta from the south and forced Hood to evacuate the city.

Q How important was Union victory in this campaign to Lincoln's re-election?

Q What were Sherman's strengths and weaknesses as a general?

surrender—most notably at Fort Pillow, a Union garrison on the Mississippi north of Memphis, where cavalry commanded by Nathan Bedford Forrest slaughtered scores of black (and some white) prisoners on April 12, 1864.

In most cases, Confederate officers returned captured black soldiers to slavery or put them to hard labor on southern fortifications. Expressing outrage at this treatment of soldiers wearing the United States uniform, the Lincoln administration in 1863 suspended the exchange of prisoners until the Confederacy agreed to treat white and black prisoners alike. The Confederacy refused. The South would "die in the last ditch," said the Confederate exchange agent, before "giving up the right to send slaves back to slavery as property recaptured."

There matters stood as the heavy fighting of 1864 poured many thousands of captured soldiers into hastily contrived prison compounds that quickly became death camps.

Prisoners were subjected to overcrowding, poor sanitation, contaminated water, scanty rations, inadequate medical facilities, and exposure to deep-South summer heat and northern winter cold. The suffering of northern prisoners was especially acute, because the deterioration of the southern economy made it hard to feed and clothe even Confederate soldiers and civilians, let alone Yankee prisoners. Nearly 16 percent of all Union soldiers held in southern prison camps died, compared with 12 percent of Confederate soldiers in northern camps. Andersonville was the most notorious hellhole. A stockade camp of 26 acres with neither huts nor tents, designed to accommodate 15,000 prisoners, it held 33,000 in August 1864. They died at the rate of more than 100 per day. Altogether, 13,000 Union soldiers died at Andersonville.

The suffering of Union prisoners brought heavy pressure on the Lincoln administration to renew exchanges, but the Confederates would not budge on the question of exchanging

16.12 General William Tecumseh Sherman "We are not only fighting hostile armies, but a hostile people," General William Tecumseh Sherman famously said. Ahead of his time in his understanding of psychological warfare, he promised to "make war so terrible and make" the people of the South "so sick of war that generations will pass away before they would again appeal to it." Sherman's March to the Sea arguably accomplished this aim, hastening the close of war.

16.13 Burial of Union POWs at Andersonville On many days during summer 1864, at least 100 Union prisoners of war died of disease, malnutrition, or exposure at Andersonville Prison in Georgia. This scene of burial in long trenches became so commonplace as to dull the sense of horror.

black soldiers. After a series of battles on the Richmond–Petersburg front in September 1864, Lee proposed an informal exchange of prisoners. Grant agreed, on condition that black soldiers captured in the fighting be included "the same as white soldiers." Lee replied, "negroes belonging to our citizens are not considered subjects of exchange and were not included in my proposition." No exchange, then, responded Grant. The Union government was "bound to secure to all persons received into her armies the rights due to soldiers." Lincoln backed this policy. He would not sacrifice the principle of equal treatment of black prisoners, even though local Republican leaders warned that many in the North "will work and vote against the President, because they think sympathy with a few negroes, also captured, is the cause of a refusal" to exchange prisoners

16-6g The Issue of Black Soldiers in the Confederate Army

During the winter of 1864–1865, the Confederate government quietly abandoned its refusal to exchange black prisoners, and exchanges resumed. One reason for this reversal was a Confederate decision to recruit slaves to fight for the South. Two years earlier, Davis had denounced the North's arming of freed slaves as "the most execrable measure recorded in the history of guilty man." Ironically, a few black laborers and body servants with southern armies had taken up arms in the heat of battle and had unofficially fought alongside their masters against the Yankees. By February 1865, southern armies were desperate for manpower, and slaves constituted the only remaining reserve. Supported by Lee's powerful influence, Davis pressed the Confederate Congress to enact a bill for recruitment of black soldiers. The assumption that any slaves who fought for the South would have to be granted freedom generated bitter opposition to the measure. "What did we go to war for, if not to protect our property?" asked a Virginia senator. By three votes in the House and one in the Senate, the Confederate Congress finally passed the bill on March 13, 1865. Before any southern black regiments could be organized, however, the war ended.

16-7 Lincoln's Reelection and the End of the Confederacy

Q *Why, after doubting he would be re-elected, did Lincoln ultimately win reelection by a substantial margin?*

Despite Republican fears, battlefield events, rather than political controversies, had the strongest impact on U.S. voters in 1864. In effect, the election became a referendum on whether to continue fighting for unconditional victory. Within days after the Democratic national convention had declared the war a failure, the military situation changed dramatically.

16-7a The Capture of Atlanta

After a month of apparent stalemate on the Atlanta front, Sherman's army again made a large movement by the right flank to attack the last rail link into Atlanta from the south. At the battle of Jonesboro on August 31 and September 1, Sherman's men captured the railroad. Hood abandoned Atlanta to save his army. On September 3, Sherman sent a jaunty telegram to Washington: "Atlanta is ours, and fairly won."

16-7b The Shenandoah Valley

If Atlanta was not enough to brighten the prospects for Lincoln's reelection, events in Virginia's Shenandoah Valley were. After Early's raid through the valley all the way to Washington in July, Grant put Philip Sheridan in charge of a reinforced Army of the Shenandoah and told him to "go after Early and follow him to the death." Sheridan infused the same spirit into the three infantry corps of the Army of the Shenandoah that he had previously imbued in his cavalry. On September 19, they attacked Early's force near Winchester, and after a daylong battle sent the Confederates flying to the south. Sheridan pursued them, attacking again on September 22 at Fisher's Hill 20 miles south of Winchester.

16.14 Sherman's Soldiers Tearing Up the Railroad in Atlanta
One of the objectives of Sherman's march from Atlanta to the sea was to demolish the railroads so they could not transport supplies to Confederate armies. The soldiers did a thorough job. They tore up the rails and ties, made a bonfire of the ties, heated the rails in the fire, and then wrapped them around trees, creating "Sherman neckties."

Early's line collapsed, and his routed army fled 60 more miles southward.

Early's retreat enabled Sheridan to carry out the second part of his assignment in the Shenandoah Valley, which had twice served as a Confederate route of invasion and whose farms helped feed Confederate armies. Sheridan now set about destroying the valley's crops and mills so thoroughly that "crows flying over it for the balance of the season will have to carry their provender with them." Sheridan boasted that by the time he was through, "the Valley, from Winchester up to Staunton, ninety-two miles, will have little in it for man or beast."

But Jubal Early was not yet willing to give up. Reinforced by a division from Lee, on October 19 he launched a dawn attack across Cedar Creek, 15 miles south of Winchester. He caught the Yankees by surprise and drove them back in disorder. At the time of the attack, Sheridan was at Winchester, returning to his army from Washington, where he had gone to confer on future strategy. He jumped onto his horse and sped to the battlefield in a ride that became celebrated in poetry and legend. By sundown, Sheridan's charisma and tactical leadership had turned the battle from a Union defeat into another Confederate rout. The battle of Cedar Creek ended Confederate power in the valley.

Sherman's and Sheridan's victories ensured Lincoln's reelection on November 8 by a majority of 212 to 21 in the Electoral College. Soldiers played a notable role in the balloting. Every northern state except three whose legislatures were controlled by Democrats had passed laws allowing absentee voting by soldiers. Seventy-eight percent of the military vote went to Lincoln—compared with 54 percent of the civilian vote. The men who were doing the fighting had sent a clear message that they meant to finish the job.

16-7c From Atlanta to the Sea

Many southerners got the message, but not Davis. The Confederacy remained "as erect and defiant as ever," he told his Congress in November 1864. It was this last-ditch resistance that Sherman set out to break in his famous march from Atlanta to the sea.

Sherman had concluded, "We are not only fighting hostile armies, but a hostile people." Defeat of the Confederate armies was not enough to win the war; the railroads, factories, and farms that supported those armies must also be destroyed. The will of the civilians who sustained the war must be crushed. Sherman expressed more bluntly than anyone else the meaning of this strategy. He was ahead of his time in his understanding of psychological warfare. "We cannot change the hearts of those people of the South," he said, "but we can make war so terrible and make them so sick of war that generations would pass away before they would again appeal to it."

Sherman urged Grant to let him march through the heart of Georgia, living off the land and destroying all resources not needed by his army—the same policy

What They Said

The Evacuation of Atlanta: General Hood versus General Sherman on the Laws of War

Once Sherman had captured Atlanta, he ordered its citizens to evacuate the city. This famous exchange between Confederate general Hood and Sherman reveals just how swiftly the nature of warfare was changing.

> **HDQRS. ARMY OF TENNESSEE,** *OFFICE CHIEF OF STAFF,*
> *September 9, 1864*
>
> To Maj. Gen. W. T. SHERMAN, Commanding U.S. Forces in Georgia
>
> GENERAL: Your letter of yesterday's date [7th] … is received. You say therein "I deem it to be to the interest of the United States that the citizens now residing in Atlanta should remove," &c. I do not consider that I have any alternative in this matter. I therefore accept your proposition to declare a truce of two days, or such time as may be necessary to accomplish the purpose mentioned, and shall render all assistance in my power to expedite the transportation of citizens in this direction. I suggest that a staff officer be appointed by you to superintend the removal from the city to Rough and Ready, while I appoint a like officer to control their removal farther south; that a guard of 100 men be sent by either party, as you propose, to maintain order at that place, and that the removal begin on Monday next. And now, sir, permit me to say that the unprecedented measure you propose transcends, in studied and ingenious cruelty, all acts ever before brought to my attention in the dark history of war. In the name of God and humanity I protest, believing that you will find that you are expelling from their homes and firesides the wives and children of a brave people.
>
> I am, general, very respectfully, your obedient servant,
> **J. B. HOOD,** *General.*

> **HDQRS. MILITARY DIVISION OF THE MISSISSIPPI**
> *In the Field, Atlanta, Ga., September 10, 1864.*
>
> To General J. B. HOOD, *C. S. Army, Comdg. Army of Tennessee:*
>
> GENERAL: I have the honor to acknowledge the receipt of your letter of this date [9th], at the hands of Messrs. Ball and Crew, consenting to the arrangements I had proposed to facilitate the removal south of the people of Atlanta who prefer to go in that direction. I inclose you a copy of my orders, which will, I am satisfied, accomplish my purpose perfectly. You style the measure proposed "unprecedented," and appeal to the dark history of war for a parallel as an act of "studied and ingenious cruelty." It is not unprecedented, for General Johnston himself, very wisely and properly, removed the families all the way from Dalton down, and I see no reason why Atlanta should be excepted. Nor is it necessary to appeal to the dark history of war when recent and modern examples are so handy. You, yourself, burned dwelling-houses along your parapet, and I have seen to-day fifty houses that you have rendered uninhabitable because they stood in the way of your forts and men. You defended Atlanta on a line so close to town that every cannon shot and many musket shots from our line of investment that overshot their mark went into the habitations of women and children. General Hardee did the same at Jonesborough, and General Johnston did the same last summer at Jackson, Miss. I have not accused you of heartless cruelty, but merely instance these cases of very recent occurrence, and could go on and enumerate hundreds of others and challenge any fair man to judge which of us has the heart of pity for the families of a "brave people." I say that it is kindness to these families of Atlanta to remove them now at once from scenes that women and children should not be exposed to, and the "brave people" should scorn to commit their wives and children to the rude barbarians who thus, as you say, violate the laws of war, as illustrated in the pages of its dark history. In the name of common sense I ask you not to appeal to a just God in such a sacrilegious manner; you who, in the midst of peace and prosperity, have plunged a nation into war, dark and cruel war; who dared and badgered us to battle, insulted our flag, seized our arsenals and forts that were left in the honorable custody of peaceful ordnance sergeants; seized and made "prisoners of war" the very garrisons sent to protect your people against negroes and Indians long before any overt act was committed by the, to you, hated Lincoln Government; tried to force Kentucky and Missouri into rebellion, spite of themselves; falsified the vote of Louisiana, turned loose your privateers to plunder unarmed ships; expelled Union families by the thousands; burned their houses and declared by an act of your Congress the confiscation of all debts due Northern men for goods had and received. Talk thus to the marines, but not to me, who have seen these things, and who will this day make as much sacrifice for the peace and honor of the South as the best born Southerner among you. If we must be enemies, let us be men and fight it out, as we propose to do, and not deal in such hypocritical appeals to God and humanity. God will judge us in due time, and He will pronounce whether it be more humane to fight with a town full of women, and the families of "a brave people" at our back, or to remove them in time to places of safety among their own friends and people.
>
> **W. T. SHERMAN,** *Major-general, Commanding.*

Q What are the "laws of war" General Hood accuses General Sherman of violating? Is he justified in making his complaint?

Q What is Sherman's response to Hood's accusation? How effective are his arguments?

Q How had the conduct of the Civil War changed from 1861 to 1864? Why?

Sources: (top) General Hood's letter to Sherman, September 9, 1864. Author accessed at: http://www.civilwarhome.com/atlantaevacuation.htm. This website draws from the Official Records of the War, Series 1, Volume XXXIX/2 [S #78]; (bottom) General Sherman's letter to Hood, September 10, 1864. Author accessed at: http://www.civilwarhome.com/atlantaevacuation.htm. This website draws from the Official Records of the War, Series 1, Volume XXXIX/2 [S #78].

Sheridan was carrying out in the Shenandoah Valley. Grant and Lincoln were reluctant to authorize such a risky move, especially with Hood's army of 40,000 men still intact in northern Alabama. Sherman assured them that he would send George Thomas to take command of a force of 60,000 men in Tennessee, who would be more than a match for Hood. With another 60,000, Sherman could "move through Georgia, smashing things to the sea … I can make the march, and make Georgia howl!"

Lincoln and Grant finally consented. On November 16, Sherman's avengers marched out of Atlanta after burning a third of the city, including some nonmilitary property. Southward they marched 280 miles to Savannah, wrecking everything in their path that could, by any stretch of the imagination, be considered of military value.

16-7d The Battles of Franklin and Nashville

They encountered little resistance. Instead of chasing Sherman, Hood invaded Tennessee with the hope of recovering that state for the Confederacy, a disastrous campaign that virtually destroyed his army. On November 30, the Confederates attacked part of the Union force at Franklin, 20 miles south of Nashville. The slaughter claimed no fewer than 12 Confederate generals and 54 regimental commanders as casualties. Instead of retreating, Hood moved on to Nashville, where on December 15 and 16, Thomas launched an attack that almost wiped out the Army of Tennessee. Its remnants retreated to Mississippi, where Hood resigned in January 1865 (see Map 16.8).

▲ **MAP 16.8 Hood's Tennessee Campaign, October–November 1864, and Nashville, December 15–16, 1864** The battle of Nashville on December 15–16, 1864, was the most carefully planned and decisive battle of the war. After Thomas's army drove the Confederates from their first line on December 15 (solid red line), it attacked again and overran the second position (striped red line) on the 16th. The Confederate army virtually disintegrated as it retreated.

Q What led Hood to embark on this disastrous invasion of Tennessee?

Q What pressures led some Confederate soldiers to desert late in the war?

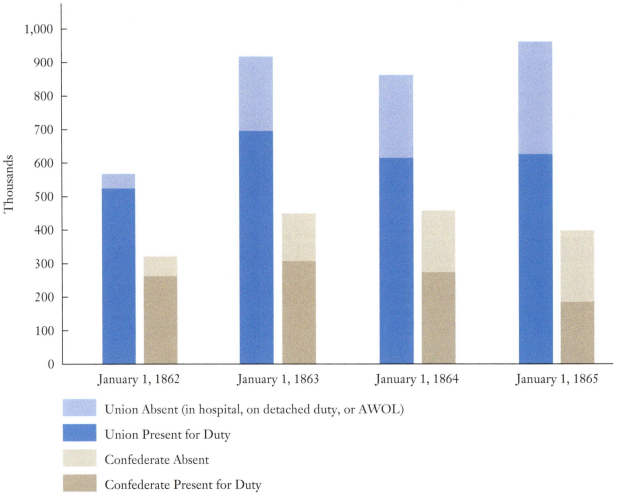

Figure 16.2 **Comparative Strength of Union and Confederate Armies**

16-7e Fort Fisher and Sherman's March through the Carolinas

Worse was yet to come for the Confederates. Lee's army in Virginia drew its dwindling supplies overland from the Carolinas and through the port of Wilmington, North Carolina, the only city still accessible to blockade runners. The big guns at massive Fort Fisher kept blockade ships at bay and protected the runners. In January 1865, though, the largest armada of the war—58 ships with 627 guns—pounded Fort Fisher for two days, disabling most of its big guns. Army troops captured the fort on January 15. That ended the blockade running, and Sherman soon put an end to supplies from the Carolinas as well.

At the end of January, Sherman's soldiers headed north from Savannah, eager to take revenge on South Carolina, which to their mind had started the war. Here, they made even less distinction between civilian and military property than they had in Georgia and left even less of Columbia standing than they had of Atlanta. Seemingly invincible, Sherman's army pushed into North Carolina and brushed aside the force that Joseph E. Johnston had assembled to stop them. The devastation left in their wake appalled Confederates.

But the war would not end until the Confederate armies surrendered, as Lincoln made clear in his second inaugural address on March 4, 1865. In the best-known words from that address, he urged a binding up of the nation's wounds "with malice toward none [and] charity for all." Even more significant, given that the conflict still raged, were these words:

> American Slavery is one of those offences which, in the providence of God ... He now wills to remove [through] this terrible war, as the woe due to those by whom the offence came ... . Fondly do we hope—fervently do we pray—that this mighty scourge of war may speedily pass away. Yet if God wills that it continue, until all the wealth piled by the bondman's two hundred and fifty years of unrequited toil shall be sunk, and until every drop of blood drawn with the lash, shall be paid by another drawn with the sword, as was said three thousand years ago, so still it must be said "the judgments of the Lord, are true and righteous altogether."

16-7f The Road to Appomattox

The Army of Northern Virginia was now the only entity that kept the Confederacy alive, but it was on the verge of disintegration. Scores of its soldiers were deserting every day (see Figure 16.2). On April 1, Sheridan's cavalry and an infantry corps smashed the right flank of Lee's line at Five Forks and cut off the last railroad into Petersburg. The next day, Grant attacked all along the line and forced Lee to abandon both Petersburg and Richmond. As the Confederate government fled its capital, its army set fire to all the military stores it could not carry. The fires spread and destroyed more of Richmond than the northern troops had destroyed of Atlanta or Columbia.

Lee's starving men limped westward, hoping to turn south and join the remnants of Johnston's army in North Carolina. Sheridan's cavalry raced ahead and cut them off at Appomattox, 90 miles from Petersburg, on April 8. When the weary Confederates tried a breakout attack the next morning, their first probe revealed solid ranks of Union infantry arrayed behind the cavalry. It was the end. "There is nothing left for me to do," said Lee, "but to go and see General Grant, and I would rather die a thousand deaths."

In an Appomattox farmhouse, the son of an Ohio tanner dictated surrender terms to a scion of one of Virginia's First Families. The terms were generous. Thirty thousand captured Confederates were allowed to go home on condition that they promise never again to take up arms against the United States.

After completing the surrender formalities on April 9, Grant introduced Lee to his staff, which included Colonel Ely Parker, a Seneca Indian. As Lee shook hands with Parker, he stared for a moment at Parker's dark features and said: "I am glad to see one real American here." Parker replied solemnly: "We are all Americans." And indeed they now were.

16-7g The Assassination of Lincoln

Wild celebrations broke out in the North at news of the fall of Richmond, followed soon by news of Appomattox. Almost overnight, the celebrations turned to mourning. On the evening of April 14, the care-worn Abraham Lincoln sought to relax by attending a comedy at Ford's Theatre. In the middle of the play, John Wilkes Booth broke into Lincoln's box and fatally shot the president in the head. A prominent actor, Booth was a native of Maryland and a frustrated, unstable egotist who hated Lincoln for what he had done to Booth's beloved South. As he jumped from Lincoln's box to the stage and escaped out a back door, he shouted Virginia's state motto at the stunned audience: "Sic semper tyrannis" ("Thus always to tyrants").

Lincoln's death in the early morning of April 15 produced an outpouring of grief throughout the North and among newly freed slaves in the South. The martyred president did not live to see the culmination of his great achievement in leading the nation to a victory that preserved its existence and abolished

16.15 The Fruits of War Several southern cities suffered enormous damage in the Civil War from Union shelling and from the fires caused by Confederate soldiers when they destroyed everything of military value before evacuating the cities. Such was true of Charleston, where a northern photographer who entered the city after it fell in February 1865 posed four black children amid the ruins to portray the symbolism of destruction and renewal.

Table 16.1 CASUALTIES IN CIVIL WAR ARMIES AND NAVIES

Confederate records are incomplete; the Confederate data listed here are therefore estimates. The actual Confederate totals were probably higher.

	Killed and Mortally Wounded in Combat	Died of Disease	Died in Prison	Miscellaneous Deaths*	Total Deaths	Wounded, Not Mortally	Total Casualties
Union	111,904	197,388	30,192	24,881	364,345	277,401	641,766
Confederate (estimated)	94,000	140,000	26,000	No Estimates	260,000	195,000	455,000
Both Armies (estimated)	205,904	337,388	56,192	24,881	624,365	472,401	1,096,766

*Accidents, drownings, causes not stated, etc.

16.16 Abraham Lincoln in 1865 This is the last photograph of Lincoln, taken on April 10, 1865, four days before his assassination. Compare this image to the photograph of Lincoln (14.2) on page 379. Four years of war had left their mark on the 56-year-old president; note the lines of strain, fatigue, and sadness in his face.

slavery. Within 11 days of Lincoln's death, his assassin was trapped and killed in a burning barn in Virginia (April 26). The remaining Confederate armies surrendered one after another (April 26, May 4, May 26, June 23), and Union cavalry captured the fleeing Jefferson Davis in Georgia (May 10). The trauma of civil war was over, but the problems of peace and reconstruction had just begun.

Conclusion

Northern victory in the Civil War resolved two fundamental questions of liberty and power left unresolved by the Revolution of 1776 and the Constitution of 1789: (1) whether this fragile republican experiment in federalism called the United States would survive as one nation; and (2) whether that nation, founded on a charter of liberty, would continue to exist as the largest slaveholding country in the world. Before 1861, the question of whether a state could secede from the Union had remained open. Eleven states did secede, but their defeat in a war that cost 625,000 lives resolved the issue (see Table 16.1). Since 1865, no state has seriously threatened secession. And in 1865, the adoption of the Thirteenth Amendment to the Constitution confirmed the supreme power of the national government to abolish slavery and ensure the liberty of all Americans.

The Civil War also accomplished a regional transfer of power from South to North. From 1800 to 1860, the slave states had used their leverage in the Jeffersonian Republican and Jacksonian Democratic parties to control national politics most of the time. A southern slaveholder was president of the United States during two-thirds of the years from 1789 to 1861. Most congressional leaders and Supreme Court justices during that period were southerners. In the 50 years after 1861, no native of a southern state was elected president, only one served as Speaker of the House and none as president pro tem of the Senate, and only 5 of the 26 Supreme Court justices appointed during that half-century were from the South. In 1860, the South's share of the national wealth was 30 percent; in 1870, it was 12 percent.

The institutions and ideology of a plantation society and a caste system that had dominated half the country before 1861 went down with a great crash in 1865—to be replaced by the institutions and ideology of free-labor capitalism. Once feared as the gravest threat to liberty, the power of the national government sustained by a large army had achieved the greatest triumph of liberty in American history. With victory and peace in 1865, the reunited nation turned its attention to the issue of equality.

CHAPTER REVIEW

Review

1. What factors led Lincoln to his decision to issue the Emancipation Proclamation?
2. What were the sources of internal dissent and dissension in the Confederacy? In the Union?
3. How did wartime legislation transform American society? How did women contribute to the war effort?
4. How did the Union army achieve a victory at Gettysburg?
5. What contribution did African Americans make to the Union war effort?
6. Why did Lincoln think he would not win reelection in 1864?
7. What factors enabled Lincoln to win reelection by a substantial margin in 1864?

Critical Thinking

1. How did a war that began, on the part of the North, with the goal of restoring a Union in which slavery existed in half of the country, become transformed into a war to give the nation a new birth of freedom?
2. In the winter of 1862–1863, northern morale was at rock bottom and the prospects for Confederate success appeared bright. Yet two years later, the Confederacy lay in ruins and its dream of independent nationhood was doomed. How and why did this happen?

Identifications

Review your understanding of the following key terms, people, and events for this chapter (terms in bold in text are included in the Glossary).

"**contraband of war**," p. 438
compensated emancipation, p. 439
Copperheads, p. 440
martial law, p. 444
Twenty Negro Law, p. 445
"**bounty jumpers**," p. 445
commutation fee, p. 445

Suggested Readings

Several studies offer important information and insights about questions of strategy and command in military operations: **Joseph G. Glatthaar**, *Partners in Command: The Relationships between Leaders in the Civil War* (1993); **Richard M. McMurry**, *Two Great Rebel Armies* (1989); **Michael C. Adams**, *Our Masters the Rebels: A Speculation on Union Military Defeat in the East, 1861–1865* (1978), reissued under the title *Fighting for Defeat* (1992); **Mark Grimsley**, *The Hard Hand of War: Union Military Policy toward Southern Civilians, 1861–1865* (1995); and **Gary W. Gallagher**, *The Confederate War* (1997).

On the path to emancipation, see **Chandra Manning**, *Troubled Refuge: Struggling for Freedom in the Civil War* (2016); **James Oakes**, *Freedom National: The Destruction of Slavery in the United States, 1861–1865* (2012); and **Ira Berlin et al., eds.**, *Slaves No More: Three Essays on Emancipation and the Civil War* (1992). Excellent studies of the Emancipation Proclamation and the Thirteenth Amendment are **Allen C. Guelzo**, *Lincoln's Emancipation Proclamation* (2004), and **Michael Vorenberg**, *Final Freedom: The Civil War, the Abolition of Slavery, and the Thirteenth Amendment* (2001). On Lincoln's changing views of slavery, see **Eric Foner**, *The Fiery Trial: Abraham Lincoln and American Slavery* (2010).

Of the many books about black soldiers in the Union army, the most useful is **Joseph T. Glatthaar**, *Forged in Battle: The Civil War Alliance of Black Soldiers and White Officers* (1990). The Confederate debate about enlisting and freeing slave soldiers is chronicled in **Bruce Levine**, *Confederate Emancipation: Southern Plans to Free and Arm Slaves During the Civil War* (2006).

For the draft riots in New York, see **Iver Bernstein**, *The New York City Draft Riots: Their Significance for American Society and Politics in the Age of the Civil War* (1990). The story of the Copperheads is told by **Jennifer L. Weber**, *Copperheads: The Rise and Fall of Lincoln's Opponents in the North* (2006). The best study of the civil liberties issue in the North is **Mark E. Neely, Jr.**, *The Fate of Liberty: Abraham Lincoln and Civil Liberties* (1990), and the same author has covered the same issue in the Confederacy in *Southern Rights: Political Prisoners and the Myth of Confederate Constitutionalism* (1999). For Civil War medicine, see **Alfred Jay Bollet**, *Civil War Medicine: Challenges and Triumphs* (2002); and **Jane E. Schultz**, *Women at the Front: Hospital Workers in Civil War America* (2004). A succinct account of the emancipation issue is **Ira Berlin, et al.**, *Slaves No More: Three Essays on Emancipation and the Civil War* (1992).

The activities of women in the U.S. Sanitary Commission, as spies, and even as soldiers are covered in **Jeanie Attie**, *Patriotic Toil: Northern Women and the Civil War* (1998); and **Elizabeth D. Leonard**, *All the Daring of a Soldier: Women of the Civil War Armies* (1999).

MINDTAP is a fully online personalized learning experience built upon Cengage Learning content. MindTap® combines student learning tools—readings, multimedia, activities, and assessments—into a singular Learning Path that guides students through the course and helps students develop the critical thinking, analysis, and communication skills that are essential to academic and professional success.

17 Reconstruction, 1863–1877

17-1 Wartime Reconstruction
Learning Objective: Discuss the plans for reconstruction considered by Lincoln during the war.

Radical Republicans and Reconstruction

17-2 Andrew Johnson and Reconstruction
Learning Objective: Examine the differing positions of Presidents Lincoln and Johnson on the issues of restoring the South to the Union and protecting the rights of freed slaves. Compare the differing positions of moderate and Radical Republicans in Congress on the same issues.

Johnson's Policy
Southern Defiance
The Black Codes
Land and Labor in the Postwar South
The Freedmen's Bureau
Land for the Landless
Churches and Schools

17-3 The Advent of Congressional Reconstruction
Learning Objective: List the major accomplishments of congressional Reconstruction.

Schism between President and Congress
The Fourteenth Amendment
The 1866 Elections
The Reconstruction Acts of 1867

17-4 The Impeachment of Andrew Johnson
Learning Objective: Explain why Andrew Johnson was impeached and then acquitted.

The Completion of Formal Reconstruction
The Fifteenth Amendment
The Election of 1868

17-5 The Grant Administration
Learning Objective: Summarize the reasons for the explosion of corruption during Grant's presidency.

Civil Service Reform
Foreign Policy Issues
Reconstruction in the South
Blacks in Office
"Carpetbaggers"
"Scalawags"
The Ku Klux Klan
The Election of 1872
The Panic of 1873

17-6 The Retreat from Reconstruction
Learning Objective: Discuss why Northerners turned away from federal involvement in Reconstruction during the 1870s.

The Mississippi Election of 1875
The Supreme Court and Reconstruction
The Election of 1876
Disputed Results
The Compromise of 1877
The End of Reconstruction

17.1 The Cotton Pickers The great American painter Winslow Homer began his career during the Civil War as a battlefront artist for *Harper's Weekly*. After the Civil War he returned to the South, painting a number of sensitive individual portraits of African Americans during Reconstruction. This 1876 painting captures the yearning of two women who, even with the end of slavery, are still picking cotton.

FROM THE BEGINNING of the Civil War, the North fought to "reconstruct" the Union. Lincoln at first attempted to restore the Union as it had existed before 1861, but once the abolition of slavery became a northern war aim, the Union could never be reconstructed on its old foundations. Instead, it must experience a "new birth of freedom," as Lincoln had said at the dedication of the military cemetery at Gettysburg.

But precisely what did "a new birth of freedom" mean? At the very least, it meant the end of slavery. The slave states would be reconstructed on a free-labor basis. But what would liberty look like for the 4 million freed slaves? Would they become citizens equal to their former masters in the eyes of the law? Would they have the right to vote? Should Confederate leaders and soldiers be punished for treason? On what terms should the Confederate states return to the Union? What would be the powers of the states and of the national government in a reconstructed Union? ■

17-1 Wartime Reconstruction

 What plans for reconstruction did Lincoln consider during the war?

Lincoln pondered these problems long and hard. At first he feared that whites in the South would never extend equal rights to the freed slaves. After all, even most northern states were denying full civil equality to the few black people within their borders. In 1862, Lincoln encouraged freedpeople to emigrate to all-black countries such as Haiti, where they would have a chance to get ahead without having to face the racism of whites. Black leaders, abolitionists, and many Republicans objected to that policy. Blacks were Americans. Why should they not have the rights of American citizens instead of being urged to leave the country?

Lincoln eventually embraced the logic and justice of that view. But in beginning the process of reconstruction, he first reached out to southern whites whose allegiance to the Confederacy was lukewarm. On December 8, 1863, Lincoln issued his Proclamation of Amnesty and Reconstruction, which offered a presidential pardon to southern whites who took an oath of allegiance to the United States and accepted the abolition of slavery. In any state where the number of white males aged 21 or older who took this oath equaled 10 percent of the number of voters in 1860, that nucleus could reestablish a state government to which Lincoln promised presidential recognition.

Because the war was still raging, this policy could be carried out only where Union troops controlled substantial portions of a Confederate state: Louisiana, Arkansas, and Tennessee in early 1864. Nevertheless, Lincoln hoped that once the process had begun in those areas, it might snowball as Union military victories convinced more and more Confederates that their cause was hopeless. But those military victories were long delayed, and in most parts of the South, reconstruction did not begin until 1865.

17-1a Radical Republicans and Reconstruction

Growing opposition within Lincoln's own party slowed the process as well. Many Republicans believed that white men who had fought against the Union should not be rewarded with restoration of their political rights while black men who had fought for the Union were denied those rights. Radical Republicans, led by Thaddeus Stevens in the House and Charles Sumner in the Senate, distrusted oaths of allegiance sworn by ex-Confederates. Rather than simply restoring the old ruling class to power, asked Sumner, why not give freed slaves the vote, to provide a genuinely loyal nucleus of supporters in the South? If the freedpeople were landless, some Radical Republicans said, provide them with land by confiscating the plantations of leading Confederates as punishment for treason.

These radical positions did not command a majority of Congress in 1864. Yet the experience of Louisiana, the first state to reorganize under Lincoln's more moderate policy, convinced even non-Radical Republicans to block Lincoln's program. Enough white men in the occupied portion of the state took the oath of allegiance to satisfy Lincoln's conditions. They adopted a new state constitution and formed a government that abolished slavery and provided a school system for blacks. But despite Lincoln's private appeal to the new government to grant literate blacks and black Union soldiers the right to vote, the reconstructed Louisiana legislature chose not to do so. It also authorized planters to enforce restrictive labor policies on black plantation workers. Louisiana's actions alienated a majority of congressional Republicans, who refused to admit representatives and senators from the "reconstructed" state.

At the same time, though, Congress failed to enact a reconstruction policy of its own. This was not for lack of trying. In fact, both houses passed the Wade-Davis reconstruction bill (named for Senator Benjamin Wade of Ohio and Representative Henry Winter Davis of Maryland) in July 1864. That bill did not **enfranchise** blacks, but it did impose such stringent loyalty requirements on southern whites that few of them could take the required oath. Lincoln therefore vetoed it.

Lincoln's action infuriated many Republicans, and the bitter squabble threatened for a time to destroy Lincoln's chances of being reelected. Union military success in fall 1864, however, reunited the Republicans behind Lincoln. The collapse of Confederate military resistance the following spring set the stage for compromise between the president and Congress on a policy for the postwar South. Two days after Appomattox, Lincoln promised that he would soon announce such a policy, which probably would have included voting rights for some blacks and stronger measures to protect their civil rights. But three days later, Lincoln was assassinated.

17-2 Andrew Johnson and Reconstruction

What were the positions of Presidents Abraham Lincoln and Andrew Johnson and of the moderate and Radical Republicans in Congress on the issues of restoring the South to the Union and protecting the rights of freed slaves?

In 1864, Republicans had adopted the name Union Party to attract the votes of War Democrats and border-state Unionists who could not bring themselves to vote Republican. For the same reason, they also nominated Andrew Johnson of Tennessee as Lincoln's running mate.

Of "poor white" heritage, Johnson had clawed his way up in the rough-and-tumble politics of east Tennessee. This region of small farms and few slaves held little love for the planters who controlled the state. Andrew Johnson denounced the planters as "stuck-up aristocrats" who had no empathy

CHRONOLOGY

1863	Lincoln issues Proclamation of Amnesty and Reconstruction
1864	Congress passes Wade-Davis bill; Lincoln kills it by pocket veto
1865	Congress establishes Freedmen's Bureau • Andrew Johnson becomes president, announces his reconstruction plan • Southern states enact Black Codes • Congress refuses to seat southern congressmen elected under Johnson's plan
1866	Congress passes civil rights bill and expands Freedmen's Bureau over Johnson's vetoes • Race riots in Memphis and New Orleans • Congress approves Fourteenth Amendment • Republicans increase congressional majority in fall elections
1867	Congress passes Reconstruction Acts over Johnson's vetoes • Congress passes Tenure of Office Act over Johnson's veto
1868	Most southern senators and representatives readmitted to Congress under congressional plan of Reconstruction • Andrew Johnson impeached but not convicted • Ulysses S. Grant elected president • Fourteenth Amendment is ratified
1870	Fifteenth Amendment is ratified
1871	Congress passes Ku Klux Klan Act
1872	Liberal Republicans defect from party • Grant wins reelection
1873	Economic depression begins with the Panic of 1873
1874	Democrats win control of House of Representatives
1875	Democrats implement Mississippi Plan • Congress passes Civil Rights Act
1876	Centennial celebration in Philadelphia • Disputed presidential election causes constitutional crisis
1877	Compromise of 1877 installs Rutherford B. Hayes as president • Hayes withdraws troops from South
1883	Supreme Court declares Civil Rights Act of 1875 unconstitutional

with the southern yeomen for whom Johnson became a self-appointed spokesman. Johnson, although a Democrat, was the only senator from a seceding state who refused to support the Confederacy. For this stance, the Republicans rewarded him with the vice presidential nomination, hoping to attract the votes of pro-war Democrats and upper-South Unionists.

Booth's bullet therefore elevated to the presidency a man who still thought of himself as primarily a Democrat and a southerner. The trouble this might cause in a party that was mostly Republican and northern was not immediately apparent, however. In fact, Johnson's enmity toward the "stuck-up aristocrats" whom he blamed for leading the South into secession prompted him to utter dire threats. "Traitors must be impoverished.... They must not only be punished, but their social power must be destroyed."

Radical Republicans liked the sound of this. Johnson seemed to promise the type of reconstruction they favored—one that would deny political power to ex-Confederates and would enfranchise blacks. They envisioned a coalition between these new black voters and the small minority of southern whites who had never supported the Confederacy. These men could be expected to vote Republican. Republican governments in southern states would guarantee freedom and would pass laws to provide civil rights and economic opportunity for freed slaves. They would also strengthen the Republican Party nationally.

17-2a Johnson's Policy

From a combination of pragmatic, partisan, and idealistic motives, therefore, Radical Republicans prepared to implement a progressive reconstruction policy. But Johnson unexpectedly refused to cooperate. Instead of calling Congress into special session, he moved ahead on his own. On May 29, 1865, Johnson issued two proclamations. The first provided a blanket **amnesty** for all but the highest-ranking Confederate officials and military officers, and those ex-Confederates with taxable property worth $20,000 or more—the "stuck-up aristocrats." The second named a provisional governor for North Carolina and directed him to call an election of delegates to frame a new state constitution. Only white men who had received amnesty and taken an oath of allegiance could vote. Similar proclamations soon followed for other former Confederate states. Johnson's policy was clear: He would exclude both blacks and upper-class whites from the reconstruction process.

Although at first many Republicans supported Johnson's policy, the radicals were dismayed. They feared that restricting the vote to whites would lead to oppression of the newly freed slaves and restoration of the old power structure in the South. They began to sense that Johnson (who had owned slaves) was as dedicated to white supremacy as any Confederate. "White men alone must govern the South," he told a Democratic senator. After a tense confrontation with a group of black men led by Frederick Douglass, who had visited the White House to urge black suffrage, Johnson told his private secretary: "I know that damned Douglass; he's just like any nigger, and he would sooner cut a white man's throat than not."

Moderate Republicans believed that black men should participate to some degree in the reconstruction process, but in 1865 they were not yet prepared to break with the president. They regarded his policy as an "experiment" that would be modified as time went on.

17-2b Southern Defiance

As it happened, none of the state conventions enfranchised a single black. Some of them even balked at ratifying the Thirteenth Amendment (which abolished slavery). Reports

17.2a (left) and 17.2b (right) Andrew Johnson and Frederick Douglass By 1866, the president and the leading black advocate for equal rights represented opposite poles in the debate about reconstruction. Johnson (left) wanted to bring the South back into the Union on the basis of white suffrage; Douglass (right) wanted black men to be granted the right to vote.

Q *How did Johnson's resistance to black voting rights become a factor in his impeachment two years later?*

from the South told of neo-Confederate violence against blacks and their white sympathizers. Johnson seemed to encourage such activities by allowing the organization of white militia units.

Then there was the matter of presidential pardons. After talking fiercely about punishing traitors, and after excluding several classes of them from his amnesty proclamation, Johnson began to issue special pardons to many ex-Confederates, restoring to them all property and political rights. Under the new state constitutions, southern voters were electing hundreds of ex-Confederates to state offices. Even more alarming to northerners, who thought they had won the war, was the election to Congress of no fewer than nine ex-Confederate congressmen, seven ex-Confederate state officials, four generals, four colonels, and even the former Confederate vice president, Alexander H. Stephens.

Somehow the aristocrats and traitors Johnson had denounced in April had taken over the reconstruction process. They did so by flattering the presidential ego. Thousands of prominent ex-Confederates applied for pardons, confessing the error of their ways and appealing for presidential mercy. Johnson reveled in his power over these once-haughty aristocrats. Johnson also received praise and support from leading northern Democrats. Although the Republicans had placed him on their presidential ticket in 1864, Johnson was after all a Democrat. That party's leaders enticed Johnson with visions of reelection as a Democrat in 1868 if he could manage to reconstruct the South in a manner that would preserve a Democratic majority there.

17-2c The Black Codes

That was just what the Republicans feared. In the fall of 1865, their concern that state governments devoted to white supremacy would reduce the freedpeople to a condition close to slavery was confirmed when some of those governments enacted "**Black Codes**."

One of the first tasks of the legislatures of the reconstructed states was to define the rights of 4 million former slaves. The option of treating them exactly like white citizens was scarcely considered. Instead, the states excluded black people from juries and the ballot box, did not permit them to testify against whites in court, banned interracial marriage, and punished blacks more severely than whites for certain crimes. Some states defined any unemployed black person as a vagrant and hired him out to a planter, forbade blacks to lease land, and provided for the apprenticing to whites of black youths.

These Black Codes aroused anger among northern Republicans, who saw them as a brazen attempt to reinstate a **quasi-slavery**. "We tell the white men of Mississippi," declared the *Chicago Tribune*, "that the men of the North will convert the State of Mississippi into a frog pond before they will allow such laws to disgrace one foot of the soil in which the bones of our soldiers sleep and over which the flag of freedom waves." And in fact, the Union army's occupation forces did suspend the implementation of Black Codes that discriminated on racial grounds.

17-2d Land and Labor in the Postwar South

The Black Codes, although discriminatory, were designed to address a genuine problem. The end of the war had left black-white relations in the South in a state of limbo. The South's economy was in a shambles. Burned-out plantations, fields growing up in weeds, and railroads without tracks, bridges, or rolling stock marked the trail of war. Nearly half of the livestock in the former Confederacy and most other tangible assets except the land had been destroyed. Law and order broke down in many areas. The war had ended early enough in the spring to allow the planting of at least some food crops. But who would cultivate them? One-quarter of the South's white farmers had been killed in the war; the slaves were slaves no more. "We have nothing left to begin anew with," lamented a South Carolina planter. "I never did a day's work in my life, and I don't know how to begin."

Despite all of this trouble, life went on. Soldiers' widows and their children plowed and planted. Slaveless planters and their wives calloused their hands for the first time. Confederate veterans drifted home and went to work. Former slave owners asked their former slaves to work the land for wages or shares of the crop, and many did so. Others refused, because for them an essential part of freedom was leaving the place where they had been in bondage.

Thus, the roads were alive with freedpeople who were on the move in summer 1865. Many of them signed on to work at farms just a few miles from their old homes. Others moved into town. Some looked for relatives who had been sold away during slavery or from whom they had been separated during the war. Some wandered aimlessly. Crime increased as people, both blacks and whites, stole food to survive, and as whites organized vigilante groups to discipline blacks and force them to work.

17-2e The Freedmen's Bureau

Into this vacuum stepped the U.S. Army and the **Freedmen's Bureau**. Tens of thousands of troops remained in the South as an occupation force until civil government could be restored. The Freedmen's Bureau (its official title was Bureau of Refugees, Freedmen, and Abandoned Lands), created by Congress in March 1865, became the principal agency for overseeing relations between former slaves and owners. Headed by the antislavery general Oliver O. Howard and staffed by army officers, the bureau established posts throughout the South to supervise free-labor wage contracts between landowners and freedpeople. The Freedmen's Bureau also issued food rations to 150,000 people daily during 1865, one-third of them to whites. Southern whites viewed the Freedmen's Bureau with hostility. Without it, however, the postwar chaos and devastation in the South would have been much greater—as some whites privately admitted. Bureau agents used their influence with freedpeople to encourage them to sign free-labor contracts and return to work.

In negotiating labor contracts, the bureau tried to establish minimum wages. Lack of money in the South, however, caused many contracts to call for **share wages**—that is, paying workers with shares of the crop. At first, landowners worked their laborers in large groups (called gangs). But many black workers resented this arrangement as reminiscent of slavery. Thus, a new system evolved, called **sharecropping**, whereby a black family worked a specific piece of land in return for a share of the crop produced on it.

17.3 The Freedmen's Bureau Created in 1865, the Freedmen's Bureau stood between freed slaves and their former masters in the postwar South, charged with the task of protecting freedpeople from injustice and repression. Staffed by officers of the Union army, the bureau symbolized the military power of the government in its efforts to keep peace in the South.

Q *How does this 1868 Harper's Weekly illustration celebrate the Freedmen's Bureau?*

17-2f Land for the Landless

Freedpeople, of course, would have preferred to own the land they farmed. Some black farmers did manage to save up enough money to buy small plots of land. Demobilized black soldiers purchased land with their bounty payments, sometimes pooling their money to buy an entire plantation on which several black families settled. Northern philanthropists helped some freedmen buy land. But most ex-slaves found the purchase of land impossible. Few of them had money, and even if they did, whites often refused to sell their land because it would mean losing a source of cheap labor and encouraging notions of black independence.

Several northern radicals proposed legislation to confiscate ex-Confederate land and redistribute it to freedpeople, but those proposals went nowhere. The most promising effort to put thousands of slaves on land of their own also failed. In January 1865, after his march through Georgia, General William T. Sherman had issued a military order setting aside thousands of acres of abandoned plantation land in the Georgia and South Carolina lowcountry for settlement by freed slaves. The army even turned over some of its surplus mules to black farmers. The expectation of **40 acres and a mule** excited freedpeople in 1865, but President Johnson's Amnesty Proclamation and his wholesale issuance of pardons restored most of this property to pardoned ex-Confederates. The same thing happened to white-owned land elsewhere in the South. Placed under the temporary care of the Freedmen's Bureau for subsequent possible distribution to freedpeople, by 1866 nearly all of this land had been restored to its former owners by order of President Johnson.

17-2g Churches and Schools

One of the success stories of Reconstruction was the founding of churches and schools by freedmen and freedwomen. Eager to move away from the control of whites, blacks founded numerous African Methodist Episcopal (AME) churches, as well as other denominations, across the South. In addition to being sites of worship, these churches became vital community centers, in which African Americans could also hone political skills. In some places churches became the sites of Republican Party convocations.

Likewise, freedmen and freedwomen were instrumental in founding schools across the South. Especially in rural areas away from towns or large plantations, black men and women had to take the initiative themselves to build schoolhouses and hire teachers. Elsewhere, the Freedmen's Bureau, hand in hand with freedpeople and Northern abolitionists, worked to set up schools.

17.4 A Black School during Reconstruction In the antebellum South, teaching slaves to read and write was forbidden. Thus, about 90 percent of the freedpeople were illiterate in 1865. One of their top priorities was education. At first, most of the teachers in the freedmen's schools established by northern missionary societies were northern white women, but as black teachers were trained, they took over the elementary schools, such as this one, photographed in the 1870s.

During the war, northern freedmen's aid societies and missionary societies founded by abolitionists had sent teachers to Union-occupied areas of the South to set up schools for freed slaves. Now, this effort was expanded. Two thousand northern teachers, three-quarters of them women, fanned out into every part of the South, working with freedpeople and the Freedmen's Bureau. As freedwomen in particular gained education as teachers, they staffed the mission schools and later the public schools established by Reconstruction state governments. By 1867 African Americans comprised one-third of the teachers in freedmen's schools, and their numbers continued to grow.

After 1870, the missionary societies concentrated more heavily on making higher education available to African Americans. Many of the traditionally black colleges in the South today were founded and supported by their efforts. This education crusade, which the black leader W. E. B. Du Bois described as "the most wonderful peace-battle of the nineteenth century," reduced the southern black illiteracy rate to 70 percent by 1880 and to 48 percent by 1900.

17-3 The Advent of Congressional Reconstruction

Q *What were the major accomplishments of congressional Reconstruction?*

Political reconstruction shaped the civil and political rights of freedpeople. By the time Congress met in December 1865, the Republican majority was determined to control the process by which former Confederate states would regain full representation. Congress refused to admit the representatives and senators elected by the former Confederate states under Johnson's reconstruction policy and set up a special committee to formulate new terms. The committee held hearings at which southern Unionists, freedpeople, and U.S. Army officers testified to abuse and terrorism in the South. Their testimony convinced Republicans of the need for stronger federal intervention to define and protect the civil rights of freedpeople. Many radicals wanted to go further and grant the ballot to black men.

Most Republicans realized that northern voters would not support such a radical policy, however. Racism was still strong in the North, where most states denied the right to vote to the few blacks living within their borders. Moderate Republicans feared that Democrats would exploit northern racism in the congressional elections of 1866 if Congress made black suffrage a cornerstone of Reconstruction. Instead, the special committee decided to draft a constitutional amendment that would encourage southern states to enfranchise blacks but would not require them to do so.

17-3a *Schism between President and Congress*

Meanwhile, Congress passed two laws to protect the economic and civil rights of freedpeople. The first extended the life of the Freedmen's Bureau and expanded its powers. The second defined freedpeople as citizens with equal legal rights and gave federal courts appellate jurisdiction to enforce those rights. To the dismay of moderates who were trying to heal the widening breach between the president and Congress, Johnson vetoed both measures. He followed this action with a speech to Democratic supporters in which he denounced Republican leaders as traitors who did not want to restore the Union except on terms that would degrade white southerners. Democratic newspapers applauded the president for vetoing bills that would "compound our race with niggers, gypsies, and baboons."

17-3b *The Fourteenth Amendment*

Johnson had thrown down the gauntlet to congressional Republicans, and they did not hesitate to take it up. With more than a two-thirds majority in both houses, they passed the Freedmen's Bureau and Civil Rights bills over the president's vetoes. Then on April 30, 1866, the special committee submitted to Congress its proposed Fourteenth Amendment to the Constitution. After lengthy debate, the amendment received the required two-thirds majority in Congress on June 13 and went to the states for ratification. Section 1 defined all native-born or naturalized persons, including blacks, as American citizens and prohibited the states from abridging the "privileges and immunities" of citizens, from depriving "any person of life, liberty, or property without due process of law," and from denying to any person "the equal protection of the laws." Section 2 gave states the option of either enfranchising black males or losing a proportionate number of congressional seats and electoral votes. Section 3 disqualified a significant number of ex-Confederates from holding federal or state office. Section 4 guaranteed the national debt and repudiated the Confederate debt. Section 5 empowered Congress to enforce the Fourteenth Amendment by "appropriate legislation." The Fourteenth Amendment had far-reaching consequences. Section 1 has become the most important provision in the Constitution for defining and enforcing civil rights.

17-4c *The 1866 Elections*

Republicans entered the 1866 congressional elections campaign with the Fourteenth Amendment as their platform. They made clear that any ex-Confederate state that ratified the amendment would be declared "reconstructed" and that its representatives and senators would be seated in Congress. Tennessee ratified the amendment, but Johnson counseled other southern legislatures to reject the amendment, which they did. Johnson then prepared for an all-out campaign to gain a friendly northern majority in the congressional elections.

Johnson began his campaign by creating a National Union Party made up of a few conservative Republicans who disagreed with their party, some border-state Unionists who

"PARDON, Columbia—'Shall I Trust These Men'?" "FRANCHISE—'And Not This Man'?"

17.5 Cartoons for Freedom One of the best political cartoonists in American history, Thomas Nast drew scores of cartoons for *Harper's Weekly* in the 1860s and 1870s advocating the use of federal power to guarantee the liberty and enforce the equal rights of freed slaves. This illustration (1865) is an eloquent graphic expression of a powerful argument for giving freedmen the right to vote: Black men who fought for the Union were more deserving of this privilege than white men who fought against it. Several of the kneeling figures are recognizable Confederate leaders: Alexander Stephens and Robert E. Lee in the foreground, Jefferson Davis to Lee's left, and John C. Breckinridge, Joseph E. Johnston, and Robert Toombs behind and to Davis's left.

Q *What other visual details does Nast's illustration include to make an argument for black male enfranchisemnt?*

supported the president, and Democrats. But many northern Democrats still carried the taint of having opposed the war effort, and most northern voters did not trust them. Further, race riots in Memphis and New Orleans, with white mobs attacking blacks, bolstered Republican arguments that national power was necessary to protect "the fruits of victory" in the South. Perhaps the biggest liability of the National Union Party was Johnson. In a whistle-stop tour through the North, he traded insults with hecklers and embarrassed his supporters by comparing himself to Christ and his Republican adversaries to Judas.

Republicans swept the election: They gained a three-to-one majority in the next Congress. Having rejected the Reconstruction terms embodied in the Fourteenth Amendment, southern Democrats now faced far more stringent terms. "They would not cooperate in rebuilding what they destroyed," wrote an exasperated moderate Republican, so "we must remove the rubbish and rebuild from the bottom. Whether they are willing or not, we must compel obedience to the Union and demand protection for its humblest citizen."

17-3d The Reconstruction Acts of 1867

In March 1867, the new Congress enacted over Johnson's vetoes two laws prescribing new procedures for the full restoration of the former Confederate states to the Union. The Reconstruction Acts of 1867 divided the 10 southern states into five military districts, directed army officers to register voters for the election of delegates to new constitutional conventions, and enfranchised males aged 21 and older (including blacks) to vote in those elections. When a state had adopted a new constitution that granted equal civil and political rights regardless of race and had ratified the Fourteenth Amendment, it would be declared reconstructed, and its newly elected congressmen would be seated.

These measures embodied a true revolution. Just a few years earlier, southern whites had been masters of 4 million slaves and part of an independent Confederate nation. Now they were shorn of political power, with their former slaves not only free but also politically empowered.

What They Said

Black Codes versus Black Politics

At first, during Reconstruction white southerners attempted to reerect a legal and racial system as close to slavery as possible. But after the passage of the Reconstruction Acts of 1867, African Americans met in conventions throughout the South to affirm a politics of freedom. These two selections trace the differences between white and black ideas of freedom after Emancipation.

From the Mississippi Black Code, November 1865

Section 2. *Be it further enacted*, that all freedmen, free Negroes, and mulattoes in this state over the age of eighteen years found on the second Monday in January 1866, or thereafter, with no lawful employment or business, or found unlawfully assembling themselves together either in the day or nighttime, and all white persons so assembling with freedmen, free Negroes, or mulattoes, or usually associating with freedmen, free Negroes, or mulattoes on terms of equality, or living in adultery or fornication with a freedwoman, free Negro, or mulatto, shall be deemed vagrants; and, on conviction thereof, shall be fined in the sum of not exceeding, in the case of a freedman, free Negro, or mulatto, $150, and a white man, $200, and imprisoned at the discretion of the court, the free Negro not exceeding ten days, and the white man not exceeding six months.

Address of the Colored Convention to the People of Alabama, 1867

As there seems to be considerable difference of opinion concerning the "legal rights of the colored man," it will not be amiss to say that we claim exactly *the same rights, privileges and immunities as are enjoyed by white men*—we ask nothing more and will be content with nothing less. *All legal distinctions between the races are now abolished. The word white* is stricken from our laws.... So long as a park or a street is a public park or street the entire public has the right to use it; so long as a car or a steamboat is a public conveyance, it must carry all who come to it, and serve all alike who pay alike. The law no longer knows white nor black, but simply men, and consequently we are entitled to ride in public conveyances, hold office, sit on juries and do everything else which we have in the past been prevented from doing solely on the ground of our color.

Q What white anxieties regarding post-emancipation society are expressed in Mississippi's Black Code?

Q How do these two documents define the legal rights of blacks differently?

Sources: (top) Mississippi Black Code, November 1865; (middle) Address of the Colored Convention to the People of Alabama, 1867. (bottom) Excerpt from U.S. Attorney General's reply to Governor Adelbert Ames' request for troops (1875).

In 1867, the emancipation and enfranchisement of black Americans seemed, as a sympathetic French journalist described it, "one of the most radical revolutions known in history."

Like most revolutions, the reconstruction process did not go smoothly. Many Southern Democrats breathed defiance and refused to cooperate. The presence of the army minimized antiblack violence, but thousands of white southerners who were eligible to vote refused to do so, hoping that their nonparticipation would delay the process long enough for northern voters to come to their senses and elect Democrats to Congress.

Blacks and their white allies organized **Union leagues** to inform and mobilize the new black voters into the Republican Party. Democrats branded southern white Republicans as "**scalawags**" and northern settlers as "**carpetbaggers**." By September 1867, the 10 states had 735,000 black voters and only 635,000 white voters registered. At least one-third of the registered white voters were Republicans.

President Johnson did everything he could to block Reconstruction. He replaced several Republican generals in command of southern military districts with Democrats. He had his attorney general issue a ruling that interpreted the Reconstruction acts narrowly, thereby forcing a special session of Congress to pass a supplementary act in July 1867. He encouraged southern whites to obstruct the registration of voters and the election of convention delegates.

Johnson's purpose was to slow the process until 1868 in the hope that northern voters would repudiate Reconstruction in the presidential election of that year, when Johnson planned to run as the Democratic candidate. Off-year state elections in fall 1867 encouraged that hope. Republicans suffered setbacks in several northern states, especially where they endorsed referendum measures to enfranchise black men.

17-3 The Advent of Congressional Reconstruction

17.6 The Burning of a Freedmen's School Because freedpeople's education symbolized black progress, whites who resented and resisted this progress sometimes attacked and burned freedmen's schools. This dramatic *Harper's Weekly* illustration shows a white mob burning a school during antiblack riots in Memphis in May 1866.

17-4 The Impeachment of Andrew Johnson

Q *Why was Andrew Johnson impeached? Why was he acquitted?*

Johnson struck even more boldly against Reconstruction after the 1867 elections. "What does Johnson mean to do?" an exasperated Republican asked another. "I am afraid his doings will make us all favor impeachment." In February 1868, Johnson removed from office Secretary of War Edwin M. Stanton, who had administered the War Department in support of the congressional Reconstruction policy. This appeared to violate the Tenure of Office Act, passed the year before over Johnson's veto, which required Senate consent for such removals. By a vote of 126 to 47 along party lines, the House impeached Johnson on February 24. The official reason for **impeachment** was that he had violated the Tenure of Office Act (which Johnson considered unconstitutional). The real reason was Johnson's stubborn defiance of Congress on Reconstruction.

Under the U.S. Constitution, impeachment by the House does not remove an official from office. It is more like a grand jury indictment that must be tried by a petit jury—in this case, the Senate, which sat as a court to try Johnson on the impeachment charges brought by the House. If convicted by a two-thirds majority of the Senate, he would be removed from office.

The impeachment trial proved long and complicated, which worked in Johnson's favor by allowing passions to cool. The Constitution specifies the grounds on which a president can be impeached and removed: "Treason, Bribery, or other high Crimes and Misdemeanors." The issue was whether Johnson was guilty of any of these acts. His able defense counsel exposed technical ambiguities in the Tenure of Office Act that raised doubts about whether Johnson had actually violated it.

Several moderate Republicans feared that the precedent of impeachment might upset the delicate balance of powers between the executive branch, Congress, and the judiciary that was an essential element of the Constitution. Behind the scenes, Johnson strengthened his case by promising to appoint the respected general John M. Schofield as secretary of war and to stop obstructing the Reconstruction acts. In the end, seven Republican senators plus all Democrats voted for acquittal on May 16, and the final tally fell one vote short of the necessary two-thirds majority.

17-4a The Completion of Formal Reconstruction

The impeachment trial's end cleared the poisonous air in Washington, and Johnson quietly served out his term. Constitutional conventions met in the South during the 1867–1868 winter and the following spring (see Map 17.1). Hostile whites described them as "Bones and Banjoes Conventions" and the Republican delegates as "ragamuffins and jailbirds." In sober fact, however, the delegates were earnest advocates of a new order, and the constitutions they wrote were among the most progressive in the nation. Three-quarters of the delegates to the 10 conventions were Republicans. About 25 percent of those Republicans were northern whites who had relocated to the South after the war; 45 percent were native southern whites who braved the social ostracism of the white majority to cast their lot with the despised Republicans; and 30 percent were blacks. Only in the South Carolina convention were blacks in the majority.

The new state constitutions enacted **universal male suffrage**, putting them ahead of most northern states on that score. Some of the constitutions disfranchised certain classes of ex-Confederates for several years, but by 1872, all such disqualifications had been removed. The constitutions mandated statewide public schools for both races for the first time in the South. Most states permitted segregated schools, but schools of any kind for blacks represented a great step forward. Most of the constitutions increased the state's responsibility for social welfare beyond anything previously known in the South.

Violence in some parts of the South marred the voting on ratification of these state constitutions. The **Ku Klux Klan**, a night-riding white terrorist organization, made its first appearance during the elections. Nevertheless, voters in seven

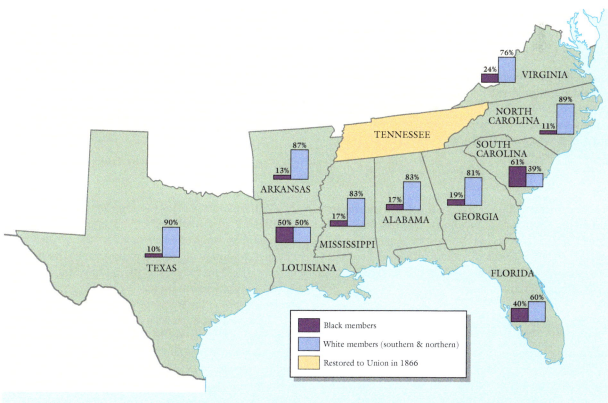

▲ **MAP 17.1 Black and White Participation in Constitutional Conventions, 1867–1868**
Although black participation in these state constitutional conventions matched the African American percentage of the population only in South Carolina and Louisiana, the very presence of any black delegates in states where slavery had prevailed three years earlier was revolutionary.

Q *How would you account for the differences among the states shown?*

Q *Why would the ratio of black and white participation in South Carolina in particular have been so different from that of neighboring Georgia and North Carolina?*

Interpreting the Visual Past

An Unholy Alliance: "This Is a White Man's Government"

This powerful allegorical cartoon by Thomas Nast, published in *Harper's Weekly* on September 5, 1868, offers a visual critique of Democrats during the 1868 elections. Nast pictures three white men, each representing a different constituency, hands clasped in an unholy alliance. On the left is an Irish American man, whose facial features are depicted in crude racist terms. His cap tells us that he is from the Five Points slum in New York City, and he carries a club labeled "A Vote" to indicate the violence he will use to ensure a white man's government. In the background we see New York's Colored Orphans Asylum in flames, as well as a black man hanged on a lamppost, to remind us that the Irish were implicated in the draft riots violence against blacks in 1863.

The central figure carries a dagger labeled "The Lost Cause" in his left hand, wears a belt buckle with the initials "CSA" (Confederate States of America), and has the initials "N.B.F" on his straw hat. He is Nathan Bedford Forrest, a founder of the Ku Klux Klan and a participant in the massacre of black soldiers at Fort Pillow (he wears a badge on the left side labeled "Fort Pillow"). The man on the right, August Belmont, is a northern financier. His badge reads "5th Avenue," and he holds a purse aloft, stuffed with banknotes, labeled "Capital for Votes." Finally, underneath the feet of the three men is a black Union veteran reaching with his left hand for a ballot box.

Q *Compare this cartoon to political cartoons by Thomas Nast elsewhere in this chapter (image 17.5 on p. 476, image 17.10 on p. 485, and image 17.11 on p. 486). Which do you find most effective visually as an argument, and why? How were political cartoons of the 1860s and 1870s different from those of today?*

17.7 Thomas Nast, "This Is a White Man's Government," 1868.

states ratified their constitutions and elected new legislatures that ratified the Fourteenth Amendment in spring 1868. That amendment became part of the U.S. Constitution the following summer, and the newly elected representatives and senators from those seven states, nearly all Republicans, took their seats in the House and the Senate.

17-4b The Fifteenth Amendment

The remaining three southern states completed the reconstruction process in 1869 and 1870. Congress required them to ratify the Fifteenth as well as the Fourteenth Amendment. The Fifteenth Amendment prohibited states from denying the right to vote on grounds of race, color, or previous condition of servitude. Its purpose was not only to prevent the reconstructed states from any future revocation of black suffrage, but also to extend equal suffrage to the border states and to the North. With final ratification of the Fifteenth Amendment in 1870, the Constitution became truly color blind for the first time in U.S. history.

But the Fifteenth Amendment still left half of the population disfranchised. Many supporters of woman suffrage were embittered by its failure to ban discrimination on the grounds of gender as well as race. The radical wing of the suffragists, led by Elizabeth Cady Stanton and Susan B. Anthony, therefore opposed the Fifteenth Amendment, causing a split in the woman suffrage movement.

This movement had shared the ideological egalitarianism of abolitionism since the Seneca Falls Convention of 1848. In 1866, male and female abolitionists formed the American Equal Rights Association (AERA) to work for both black and woman suffrage. Although some Republicans sympathized with the suffragists, they knew that no strong constituency among male voters favored granting the vote to women. Most members of the AERA thought that black enfranchisement should come first.

Stanton and Anthony refused to accept this reasoning. Why should illiterate southern blacks have the right to vote, they asked, when educated northern women remained shut out from the polls? The Fifteenth Amendment would establish "the most odious form of aristocracy the world has ever seen:

an aristocracy of sex." When a majority of delegates at the 1869 convention of the AERA voted to endorse the Fifteenth Amendment, several women led by Stanton and Anthony walked out and founded the National Woman Suffrage Association. The remaining delegates reorganized as the American Woman Suffrage Association. For the next two decades, these rival organizations, working for the same cause, remained at odds with each other.

17-4c The Election of 1868

Just as the presidential election of 1864 was a referendum on Lincoln's war policies, so the election of 1868 was a referendum on the Reconstruction policy of the Republicans. The Republican nominee was General **Ulysses S. Grant**. Although he had no political experience, Grant commanded greater authority and prestige than anyone else in the country. As general-in-chief of the army, he had opposed Johnson's Reconstruction policy in 1866 and had broken openly with the president in January 1868. That spring, Grant agreed to run for the presidency in order to preserve in peace the victory he had won in war.

The Democrats turned away from Andrew Johnson, who carried too many political liabilities. They nominated Horatio Seymour, the wartime governor of New York, bestowing on him the dubious privilege of running against Grant. Hoping to put together a majority consisting of the South plus New York and two or three other northern states, the Democrats adopted a militant platform denouncing the Reconstruction acts as "a flagrant usurpation of power ... unconstitutional, revolutionary, and void." The platform also demanded "the abolition of the Freedmen's Bureau, and all political instrumentalities designed to secure negro supremacy."

The vice presidential candidate, Frank Blair of Missouri, proclaimed that Democrats sought to "allow the white people to reorganize their own governments." The only way to achieve this bold counterrevolutionary goal was to suppress Republican voters in the South. This the Ku Klux Klan tried its best to do. In Louisiana, Georgia, Arkansas, and Tennessee, the Klan or Klan-like groups committed dozens of murders and intimidated thousands of black voters. The violence helped the Democratic cause in the South, but probably hurt it in the North, where many voters perceived the Klan as an organization of neo-Confederate paramilitary guerrillas. In fact, many Klansmen were former soldiers, and such famous Confederate generals as Nathan Bedford Forrest and John B. Gordon held high positions in the Klan.

Seymour did well in the South, carrying five former slave states and coming close in others, despite the solid Republican vote of the newly enfranchised blacks. Grant, however, swept the electoral vote 214 to 80. Seymour actually won a slight majority of the white voters nationally; without black enfranchisement, Grant would have had a minority of the popular vote.

17.8 Ulysses S. Grant as President Grant's administration has long been criticized for its rampant corruption. But his own reputation as president has risen in recent years due to a recognition of his continuing commitment to principles of justice and equality for all during Reconstruction.

17-5 The Grant Administration

Q *Why was there an explosion of corruption during Grant's presidency? Why was the Republican coalition unstable in the South?*

Grant is usually considered a failure as president. That indictment is only partly correct. Grant's inexperience and poor judgment betrayed him into several unwise appointments of officials, who were later convicted of corruption, and scandals that plagued his back-to-back administrations (1869–1877). His secretary of war was impeached for selling appointments to army posts and Indian reservations, and his attorney general and secretary of the interior resigned under suspicion of malfeasance in 1875.

Although he was an honest man, Grant was too trusting of subordinates. He appointed many former members of his military family, as well as several of his wife's relatives, to offices for which they were scarcely qualified. In an era notorious for corruption at all levels of government, many of the scandals were not Grant's fault. The Tammany Hall "Ring" of "Boss" William Marcy Tweed in New York City may have stolen more money from taxpayers than all of the federal agencies combined. It was said that the only thing the Standard Oil Company could not do with the Ohio legislature was to refine it. In Washington, one of the most widely publicized scandals, the **Credit Mobilier Affair**, concerned Congress rather than the Grant administration. Several congressmen had accepted stock in the Credit Mobilier, a construction company for the Union Pacific Railroad, which received loans and land grants from the government. In return, the company expected lax congressional supervision, thereby permitting its financial manipulations.

What accounted for this explosion of corruption in the postwar decade? During the war, expansion of government contracts and the bureaucracy had created new opportunities for the unscrupulous. Following the intense sacrifices of the war years came a relaxation of tensions and standards. Rapid postwar economic growth, led by an extraordinary rush of railroad construction, further encouraged greed and get-rich-quick schemes of the kind satirized by Mark Twain and Charles Dudley Warner in their 1873 novel *The Gilded Age*, which gave its name to the era.

17-5a *Civil Service Reform*

Some of the apparent increase in corruption during the Gilded Age was more a matter of perception. Reformers focused a harsh light into the dark corners of corruption, hitherto unilluminated because of the nation's preoccupation with war and reconstruction. Thus, reformers' publicity may have exaggerated the actual extent of corruption. In reality, during the Grant administration, several government agencies made real progress in eliminating abuses that had flourished in earlier administrations.

The chief target of civil service reform was the "**spoils system**." With the slogan "To the victor belongs the spoils," the victorious party in an election rewarded party workers with appointments as postmasters, customs collectors, and the like. The spoils system politicized the bureaucracy and staffed it with unqualified personnel who spent more time working for their party than for the government. It also plagued every incoming president (and other elected officials) with the "swarm of office seekers" that loom so large in contemporary accounts (including those of the humorist Orpheus C. Kerr, whose nom de plume was pronounced "Office Seeker").

Civil service reformers wanted to separate the bureaucracy from politics by requiring competitive examinations for the appointment of civil servants. This movement gathered steam during the 1870s and finally achieved success in 1883 with the passage of the Pendleton Civil Service Reform Act, which established the modern structure of the civil service. When Grant took office, he seemed to share the sentiments of civil service reformers; several of his cabinet officers inaugurated examinations for certain appointments and promotions in their departments. Grant also named a civil service commission headed by George William Curtis, a leading reformer and editor of *Harper's Weekly*. But many congressmen, senators, and other politicians resisted civil service reform because **patronage** greased the political machines that kept them in office. They managed to subvert reform, sometimes using Grant as an unwitting ally and thus turning many reformers against the president.

17-5b *Foreign Policy Issues*

A foreign policy controversy added to Grant's woes. The irregular procedures by which his private secretary had negotiated a treaty to annex Santo Domingo (now the Dominican Republic) alienated leading Republican senators, who defeated ratification of the treaty. Politically inexperienced, Grant acted like a general who needed only to give orders, rather than a president who must cultivate supporters. The fallout from the Santo Domingo affair widened the fissure in the Republican Party between "spoilsmen" and "reformers."

But, the Grant administration had some solid foreign policy achievements to its credit. Hamilton Fish, the able secretary of state, negotiated the Treaty of Washington in 1871 to settle the vexing *Alabama* claims. These were damage claims against Britain for the destruction of American shipping by the C.S.S. *Alabama* and other Confederate commerce raiders built in British shipyards. The treaty established an international tribunal to arbitrate the U.S. claims, resulting in the award of $15.5 million in damages to U.S. ship owners and a British expression of regret.

17-5c *Reconstruction in the South*

During Grant's two administrations, the "Southern Question" was the most intractable issue. A phrase in Grant's acceptance of the presidential nomination in 1868 had struck a responsive chord in the North: "Let us have peace." With the ratification of the Fifteenth Amendment, many people breathed a sigh of relief at the apparent resolution of "the last great point that remained to be settled of the issues of the war." It was time to deal with other matters that had been long neglected. Ever since the annexation of Texas a quarter-century earlier, the nation had known scarcely a moment's respite from sectional strife. "Let us have done with Reconstruction," pleaded the *New York Tribune* in 1870. "LET US HAVE PEACE." But there was no peace. Reconstruction was not over; it had hardly begun. State governments elected by black and white voters were in place in the South, but Democratic violence against Reconstruction and the instability of the Republican coalition that sustained it portended trouble (see Map 17.2).

17-5d Blacks in Office

About 80 percent of southern Republican voters were black. During Reconstruction there were over one hundred African American men who held statewide office, whether elected or appointed, across the South. Another eight hundred served in state legislatures. An even larger number of officeholders held local positions. By any measure, black political achievements during Reconstruction were considerable.

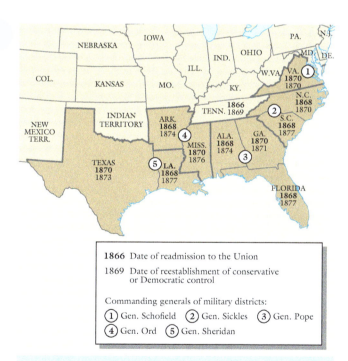

▲ **MAP 17.2 Reconstruction in the South**
The dates for each state listed on this map show how short-lived "Radical Reconstruction" was in most southern states.
Q Why would the dates of Radical Reconstruction have differed among these states?
Q What are the main reasons for the end of Radical Reconstruction?

But they were also fragile. Southern whites, who perceived the Republican Party as a symbol of conquest and humiliation, portrayed black voters and office-holders as illiterate, venal, incompetent, and corrupt. Yet most black leaders were educated and many had been free before the war. Of 14 black representatives and two black senators elected in the South between 1868 and 1876, all but three had attended secondary school and four had attended college. Several of the blacks elected to state offices were among the best-educated men of their day. Jonathan Gibbs, secretary of state in Florida from 1868 to 1872 and state superintendent of education from 1872 to 1874, was a graduate of Dartmouth College and Princeton Theological Seminary. Francis L. Cardozo, secretary of state in South Carolina for four years and treasurer for another four, was educated at the University of Glasgow and at theological schools in Edinburgh and London.

Unlike these black leaders, most black voters were former slaves who had been denied an education under the slave regime. But illiteracy did not preclude an understanding of political issues for black voters any more than it did for Irish American voters in the North, some of whom were also illiterate. Southern blacks thirsted for education. Participation in the Union League and the experience of voting were forms of education. Black churches and fraternal organizations proliferated during Reconstruction and tutored African Americans in their rights and responsibilities.

Still, the myth of black incompetence was longlasting in a racist society. The theme of "Negro rule" was also a staple of Democratic propaganda, as was the legend of the "Africanization" of southern governments during Reconstruction. These various myths were to be enshrined in folk memory, in generations of textbooks, and in film (see History Through Film: *The Birth of a Nation* (1915), page 488). In fact, however, blacks held only 15 to 20 percent of public offices, even at the height of Reconstruction in the early 1870s. No states had black governors (although the black lieutenant governor of Louisiana acted as governor for a month), and only one black man became a state supreme court justice. Nowhere except in South Carolina did blacks hold office in numbers anywhere near their proportion of the population; in that state, they constituted 52 percent of all state and federal elected officials from 1868 to 1876.

17-5e "Carpetbaggers"

Next to "Negro rule," carpetbagger corruption and scalawag rascality have been the prevailing myths of Reconstruction. Carpetbaggers did hold a disproportionate number of high political offices in southern state governments during Reconstruction. More than half of the Republican governors and nearly half of the congressmen and senators were northerners. A few did resemble the proverbial adventurer who came south with nothing but a carpetbag in which to stow the loot plundered from a helpless people. But most of the northerners were Union army officers who stayed on after the war as Freedmen's Bureau agents, teachers in black schools, or business

17.9a (top left) 17.9b (top right) and 17.9c (bottom) Three African American Members of Congress during Reconstruction Pictured clockwise are Blanche K. Bruce (top left), Robert Smalls (top right), and Robert B. Elliott (bottom). Born into slavery, Bruce and Smalls became the two most prominent blacks in Congress during the 1870s. Bruce was elected to the United States Senate from Mississippi in 1875 and served his full six-year term despite the takeover of Mississippi by white-supremacist Democrats later in 1875. Smalls gained fame when he delivered the Confederate dispatch steamer *Planter* to the Union blockade fleet outside Charleston in 1862. After working as a pilot for the navy, Smalls emerged as a leader of the South Carolina Republican Party during Reconstruction and served several terms in the House. Of West Indian descent, Elliott was born in England and immigrated to South Carolina in 1867. He was elected to the House for two terms and became an eloquent spokesman for civil rights.

investors. They hoped to rebuild southern society in the image of the free-labor North. Many were college graduates at a time when fewer than 2 percent of Americans had attended college. Most brought not empty carpetbags but considerable capital, which they invested in what they hoped would become a new South. They also invested human capital—themselves—in a drive to modernize the region's social structure and democratize its politics. But they underestimated the hostility of southern whites, most of whom regarded them as agents of an alien culture and leaders of an enemy army—as indeed they had been—in a war that for many southerners was not yet over.

17-5f "Scalawags"

Most of the native-born whites who joined the southern Republican Party came from the upcountry Unionist areas of western North Carolina and Virginia, eastern Tennessee, and elsewhere. Others were former Whigs who saw an opportunity to rebuild the South's economy in partnership with northern Republicans. Republicans, said a North Carolina scalawag, were the "party of progress, of education, of development... . Yankees and Yankee notions are just what we want in this country. We want their capital to build factories and work shops, and railroads."

But Yankees and Yankee notions were just what most southern whites did not want. Democrats saw that the southern Republican Party they abhorred was a fragile coalition of blacks and whites, Yankees and southerners, hill-country yeomen and lowcountry entrepreneurs, illiterates and college graduates. The party was weakest along the seams where these disparate elements joined, especially the racial seam. Democrats attacked that weakness with every weapon at their command, from social ostracism of white Republicans to economic intimidation of black employees and sharecroppers. The most potent Democratic weapon was violence.

17-5g The Ku Klux Klan

The generic name for the secret groups that terrorized the southern countryside was the Ku Klux Klan, but some went by other names (the Knights of the White Camelia in Louisiana, for example). Part of the Klan's purpose was social control of the black population. Sharecroppers who tried to extract better terms from landowners, or black people who were considered too "uppity," were likely to receive a midnight

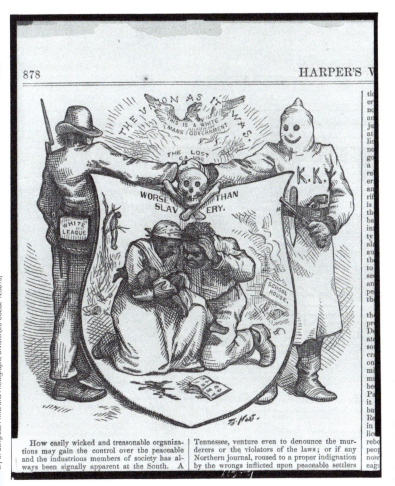

17.10 Thomas Nast, "The Union As It Was," 1874.
This Harper's Weekly cartoon shows a White Leaguer and a hooded member of the Ku Klux Klan shaking hands on the Lost Cause. Some of their violent handiwork as white supremacists is visible in the background, with a lynched body hanging from a tree on the left, while a black schoolhouse burns on the right. In the foreground an African American family tries to protect itself. The caption on the shield reads "The Lost Cause; Worse Than Slavery."

whipping—or worse—from white-sheeted Klansmen. Scores of black schools, perceived as a particular threat to white supremacy, went up in flames.

The Klan's main purpose was political: to destroy the Republican Party by terrorizing its voters and, if necessary, by murdering its leaders. No one knows how many politically motivated killings took place—certainly hundreds, probably thousands. Nearly all of the victims were Republicans; most of them were black. In one notorious incident, the Colfax Massacre in Louisiana (April 18, 1873), a clash between black militia and armed whites left three whites and nearly 100 blacks dead. Half of the blacks were killed in cold blood after they had surrendered. In some places, notably Tennessee and Arkansas, Republican militias formed to suppress and disarm the Klan, but in most areas the militias were outgunned and outmaneuvered by ex-Confederate veteran Klansmen. Some Republican governors were reluctant to use black militia against white guerrillas for fear of sparking a racial bloodbath—as happened at Colfax.

The answer seemed to be federal troops. In 1870 and 1871, Congress enacted three laws intended to enforce the Fourteenth and Fifteenth Amendments. Interference with voting rights became a federal offense, and any attempt to deprive another person of civil or political rights became a felony. The third law, passed on April 20, 1871, and popularly called the Ku Klux Klan Act, gave the president power to suspend the writ of **habeas corpus** and send in federal troops to suppress armed resistance to federal law.

Armed with these laws, the Grant administration moved against the Klan. Because Grant was sensitive to charges of "military despotism," he used his powers with restraint. He suspended the writ of habeas corpus in only nine South Carolina counties. Nevertheless, there and elsewhere federal marshals backed by troops arrested thousands of suspected Klansmen. Federal grand juries indicted more than 3,000, and several hundred defendants pleaded guilty in return for suspended sentences. To clear clogged court dockets so that the worst offenders could be tried quickly, the Justice Department dropped charges against nearly 2,000 others. About 600 Klansmen were convicted; most of them received fines or light jail sentences, but 65 went to a federal penitentiary for terms of up to five years.

17-5h The Election of 1872

These measures broke the back of the Klan in time for the 1872 presidential election. A group of dissident Republicans had emerged to challenge Grant's reelection. They believed

17.11 One of Thomas Nast's Anti-Greeley Cartoons This cartoon appeared in *Harper's Weekly* during the 1872 election campaign. It shows Greeley and Charles Sumner (whose bitterness toward President Grant caused him to support Greeley) trying to get a black man to "clasp hands across the bloody chasm" with a member of the Ku Klux Klan whose hand is dripping with the blood of the man's wife, whom he has murdered. On the Klansman's left stands a Nast caricature of an Irishman, while in the background are scenes from the New York draft riots in 1863. Nast portrays this alliance as the essence of the Liberal Republican/Democratic coalition in 1872.

that conciliation of southern whites rather than continued military intervention was the only way to achieve peace in the South. Calling themselves Liberal Republicans, these dissidents nominated Horace Greeley, the famous editor of the *New York Tribune*. Under the slogan "Anything to beat Grant," the Democratic Party also endorsed Greeley's nomination, although he had long been their antagonist. On a platform denouncing "bayonet rule" in the South, Greeley urged his fellow northerners to put the issues of the Civil War behind them and to "clasp hands across the bloody chasm which has too long divided" North and South.

This phrase would come back to haunt Greeley. Most voters in the North were still not prepared to trust Democrats or southern whites. Powerful anti-Greeley cartoons by political cartoonist Thomas Nast showed Greeley shaking the hand of a Klansman dripping with the blood of a murdered black Republican. Nast's most famous cartoon portrayed Greeley as a pirate captain bringing his craft alongside the ship of state, while Confederate leaders, armed to the teeth, hid below waiting to board it.

Grant swamped Greeley on Election Day. Republicans carried every northern state and 10 of the 16 southern and border states. Blacks in the South enjoyed more freedom in voting than they would again for a century. But this apparent triumph of Republicanism and Reconstruction would soon unravel.

17-5i *The Panic of 1873*

The U.S. economy had grown at an unprecedented pace since recovering from a mild postwar recession. The first transcontinental railroad had been completed on May 10, 1869, when a golden spike was driven at Promontory Summit, Utah Territory, linking the Union Pacific and the Central Pacific. But the building of a second transcontinental line, the Northern Pacific, precipitated a Wall Street panic in 1873 and plunged the economy into a five-year depression.

Jay Cooke's banking firm, fresh from its triumphant marketing of Union war bonds, took over the Northern Pacific in 1869. Cooke pyramided every conceivable kind of equity and loan financing to raise the money to begin laying rails west from Duluth, Minnesota. Other investment firms did the same as a fever of speculative financing gripped the country. In September 1873, the pyramid of paper collapsed. Cooke's firm was the first to go bankrupt. Like dominoes, thousands of banks and businesses also collapsed. Unemployment rose to 14 percent, and hard times set in.

17-6 The Retreat from Reconstruction

Q *Why did a majority of the northern people and their political leaders turn against continued federal involvement in southern Reconstruction in the 1870s?*

It is an axiom of American politics that the voters will punish the party in power in times of economic depression. That axiom held true in the 1870s. Democrats made large gains in the congressional elections of 1874, winning a majority in the House for the first time in 18 years.

Public opinion also began to turn against Republican policies in the South. The campaign by Liberal Republicans and Democrats against "bayonet rule" and "carpetbag corruption" that left most northern voters unmoved in 1872 found a growing audience in subsequent years. Intraparty battles among Republicans in southern states enabled Democrats to regain control of several state governments. Well-publicized corruption scandals also discredited Republican leaders. Although corruption was probably no worse in southern states than in many parts of the North, southern postwar poverty made waste and extravagance seem worse. White Democrats scored propaganda points by claiming that corruption proved the incompetence of "Negro-carpetbag" regimes.

Northerners grew increasingly weary of what seemed to be the endless turmoil of southern politics. Most of them had never had a strong commitment to racial equality, and they were growing more and more willing to let white supremacy regain sway in the South. "The truth is," confessed a northern Republican, "our people are tired out with this worn out cry of 'Southern outrages'!!! Hard times & heavy taxes make them wish the 'nigger,' 'everlasting nigger,' were in hell or Africa."

By 1875, only four southern states remained under Republican control: South Carolina, Florida, Mississippi, and Louisiana. In those states, white Democrats had revived paramilitary organizations under various names: White Leagues (Louisiana), Rifle Clubs (Mississippi), and Red Shirts (South Carolina). Unlike the Klan, these groups operated openly. In Louisiana, they fought pitched battles with Republican militias in which scores were killed. When the Grant administration sent large numbers of federal troops to Louisiana, people in both North and South cried out against military rule. The protests grew even louder when soldiers marched onto the floor of the Louisiana legislature in January 1875 and expelled several Democratic legislators after a contested election. Was this America? Republican senator Carl Schurz asked in a widely publicized speech: "If this can be done in Louisiana, how long will it be before it can be done in Massachusetts and Ohio? How long before a soldier may stalk into the national House of Representatives, and, pointing to the Speaker's mace, say 'Take away that bauble!'"

17-6a *The Mississippi Election of 1875*

The backlash against the Grant administration affected the Mississippi state election of 1875. Democrats there devised a strategy called the Mississippi Plan. The first step was to "persuade" the 10 to 15 percent of white voters still calling themselves Republicans to switch to the Democrats. Only a handful of carpetbaggers could resist the economic pressures, social ostracism, and threats that made it "too damned hot for [us] to stay out," wrote one white Republican who changed parties.

History Through Film: The Birth of a Nation (1915)

Directed by D. W. Griffith.
Starring Lillian Gish (Elsie Stoneman), Henry B. Walthall (Ben Cameron), Ralph Lewis (Austin Stoneman), George Siegmann (Silas Lynch).

Few if any films have had such a pernicious impact on historical understanding and race relations as *Birth of a Nation*. This movie popularized a version of Reconstruction that portrayed predatory carpetbaggers and stupid, brutish blacks plundering a prostrate South and lusting after white women. It perpetuated vicious stereotypes of rapacious black males. It glorified the Ku Klux Klan of the Reconstruction era, inspiring the founding of the "second Klan" in 1915, which became a powerful force in the 1920s (see Chapter 24).

The first half of the film offers a conventional Victorian romance of the Civil War. The two sons and daughter of Austin Stoneman (a malevolent Radical Republican who is a thinly disguised Thaddeus Stevens) become friends with the three sons and two daughters of the Cameron family of "Piedmont," South Carolina, through the friendship of Ben Cameron and Phil Stoneman at college. The Civil War tragically separates the families. The Stoneman and Cameron boys enlist in the Union and Confederate armies and—predictably—face each other on the battlefield. Two Camerons and one Stoneman are killed in the war, and Ben Cameron is badly wounded and captured, to be nursed back to health by—you guessed it—Elsie Stoneman. After the war, the younger Camerons and Stonemans renew their friendship. During the Stonemans' visit to South Carolina, Ben Cameron and Elsie Stoneman, and Phil Stoneman and Flora Cameron fall in love. If the story had stopped there, *Birth of a Nation* would have been just another Hollywood romance. But Austin Stoneman brings south with him Silas Lynch, an ambitious, leering mulatto demagogue who stirs up the animal passions of the ignorant black majority to demand "Equal Rights, Equal Politics, Equal Marriage." A "renegade Negro," Gus, stalks the youngest Cameron daughter, who saves herself from rape by jumping from a cliff to her death. Silas Lynch tries to force Elsie to marry him. "I will build a Black Empire," he tells the beautiful, virginal Elsie (Lillian Gish was the Hollywood beauty queen of silent films), "and you as my queen shall rule by my side."

Finally, provoked beyond endurance, white South Carolinians led by Ben Cameron organize the Ku Klux Klan to save "the Aryan race." Riding to the rescue of embattled whites in stirring scenes that anticipated the heroic actions of the cavalry against Indians in later Hollywood Westerns, the Klan executes Gus, saves Elsie, disperses black soldiers and mobs, and carries the next election for white rule by intimidating black voters. The film ends with a double marriage that unites the Camerons and Stonemans in a symbolic rebirth of a nation that joins whites of the North and South in a new union rightly based on the supremacy of "the Aryan race."

The son of a Confederate lieutenant colonel, David Wark (D. W.) Griffith was the foremost director of the silent movie era. He pioneered many precedent-setting cinematic techniques and profoundly influenced filmmaking throughout the world. *Birth of a Nation* was the first real full-length feature film, technically and artistically superior to anything before it. Apart from its place in the history of cinema, though, why should anyone today watch a movie that perpetuates such wrongheaded history and noxious racist stereotypes? Precisely because it reflects and amplifies an interpretation of Reconstruction that prevailed from the 1890s to the 1950s, and thereby shaped not only historical understanding but also contemporary behavior (as in its inspiration for the Klan of the 1920s). Although *Birth of a Nation* aroused controversy in parts of the North and was picketed by the NAACP, some 200 million people saw the film in the United States and abroad from 1915 to 1946. The story, and director Griffith, demonstrated in dramatic fashion how the South, having lost the Civil War, won the battle for how the war and especially Reconstruction would be remembered for more than half a century. ■

17.12 Ben Cameron (Henry B. Walthall) kissing the hand of Elsie Stoneman (Lillian Gish) in *Birth of a Nation*.

The second step in the Mississippi Plan was to intimidate black voters because, even with all whites voting Democratic, the party could still be defeated by the 55 percent black majority. Economic coercion against black sharecroppers and workers kept some of them away from the polls, but violence was the most effective method. Democratic "rifle clubs" showed up at Republican rallies, provoked riots, and shot down dozens of blacks in the ensuing melees. Governor Adelbert Ames—a native of Maine, a Union general who had won a medal of honor in the war, and one of the ablest of southern Republicans—called for federal troops to control the violence. Grant intended to comply, but Ohio Republicans warned him that if he sent troops to Mississippi, the Democrats would exploit the issue of "bayonet rule" to carry Ohio in that year's state elections. Grant yielded—in effect giving up Mississippi for Ohio. The U.S. attorney general replied to Ames's request for troops:

> The whole public are tired out with these annual autumnal outbreaks in the South, and the great majority are now ready to condemn any interference on the part of the government.... Preserve the peace by the forces in your own state, and let the country see that the citizens of Mississippi, who are ... largely Republican, have the courage to fight for their rights.

Governor Ames did try to organize a loyal state militia, but that proved difficult—and in any case, he was reluctant to use a black militia for fear of provoking a race war. "No matter if they are going to carry the State," said Ames with weary resignation, "let them carry it, and let us be at peace and have no more killing." The Mississippi Plan worked like a charm. In five of the state's counties with large black majorities, the Republicans polled 12, 7, 4, 2, and 0 votes, respectively. What had been a Republican majority of 30,000 in 1874 became a Democratic majority of 30,000 in 1875.

17-6b The Supreme Court and Reconstruction

Even if Grant had been willing to continue intervening in southern state elections, Congress and the courts would have constricted such efforts. The new Democratic majority in the House threatened to cut any appropriations for the Justice Department and the army intended for use in the South.

17.13 How the Mississippi Plan Worked In this *Harper's Weekly* cartoon, the black voter holds a Democratic ticket while one of the white men, described in the caption as a "Democratic reformer," holds a revolver to his head and says: "You're as free as air, ain't you? Say you are, or I'll blow your black head off!"

Q *What other intimidation techniques were used against black voters in the Mississippi state election of 1875?*

In 1876, the U.S. Supreme Court handed down two decisions that declared parts of the 1870 and 1871 laws for enforcement of the Fourteenth and Fifteenth Amendments unconstitutional. In *U.S. v. Cruikshank* and *U.S. v. Reese*, the Court ruled on cases from Louisiana and Kentucky. Both cases grew out of provisions in these laws authorizing federal officials to prosecute *individuals* (not states) for violations of the civil and voting rights of blacks. But, the Court pointed out, the Fourteenth and Fifteenth Amendments apply to actions by *states*: "No State ... deprive any person of life, liberty, or property ... nor deny to any person ... equal protection of the laws" and the right to vote "shall not be denied ... by any State." Therefore, the portions of these laws that empowered the federal government to prosecute individuals were declared unconstitutional.

The Court did not say what could be done when states were controlled by white-supremacy Democrats who had no intention of enforcing equal rights. Meanwhile, in another ruling, *Civil Rights* Cases (1883), the Court declared unconstitutional a civil rights law passed by Congress in 1875. That law banned racial discrimination in all forms of public transportation and public accommodations. If enforced, it would have effected a sweeping transformation of race relations—in the North as well as in the South. Even some of the congressmen who voted for the bill doubted its constitutionality, however, and the Justice Department had made little effort to enforce it. Several cases made their way to the Supreme Court, which in 1883 ruled the law unconstitutional—again on grounds that the Fourteenth Amendment applied only to states, not to individuals. Several states—all in the North—passed their own civil rights laws in the 1870s and 1880s, but less than 10 percent of the black population resided in those states. The mass of African Americans lived a segregated existence.

17-6c The Election of 1876

In 1876, the remaining southern Republican state governments fell victim to the passion for "reform." The mounting revelations of corruption at all levels of government ensured that reform would be the leading issue in the presidential election. In this centennial year of the birth of the United States, marked by a great exposition in Philadelphia, Americans wanted to put their best foot forward. Both major parties gave their presidential nominations to governors who had earned reform reputations in their states: Democrat Samuel J. Tilden of New York and Republican Rutherford B. Hayes of Ohio.

Democrats entered the campaign as favorites for the first time in two decades. It seemed likely that they would be able to put together an electoral majority from a "solid South" plus New York and two or three other northern states. To ensure a solid South, they looked to the lessons of the Mississippi Plan. In 1876, a new word came into use to describe Democratic techniques of intimidation: *bulldozing*. To bulldoze black voters meant to trample them down or keep them away from the polls. In South Carolina and Louisiana, the Red Shirts and the White Leagues mobilized for an all-out bulldozing effort.

The most notorious incident, the Hamburg Massacre, occurred in the village of Hamburg, South Carolina, where a battle between a black militia unit and 200 Red Shirts resulted in the capture of several militiamen, five of whom were shot "while attempting to escape." This time Grant did send in federal troops. He pronounced the Hamburg Massacre "cruel, blood-thirsty, wanton, unprovoked ... a repetition of the course that has been pursued in other Southern States."

The federal government also put several thousand deputy marshals and election supervisors on duty in the South. Although they kept an uneasy peace at the polls, they could do little to prevent assaults, threats, and economic coercion in backcountry districts, which reduced the potential Republican tally in the former Confederate states by at least 250,000 votes.

17-6d Disputed Results

When the results were in, Tilden had carried four northern states, including New York with its 35 electoral votes, and all of the former slave states except—apparently—Louisiana, South Carolina, and Florida, which produced disputed returns (see Map 17.3). Because Tilden needed only one of them to win the presidency, while Hayes needed all three, and because Tilden seemed to have carried Louisiana and Florida, it appeared initially that he had won the presidency. But frauds and irregularities reported from several bulldozed districts in the three states clouded the issue. For example, a Louisiana parish that had recorded 1,688 Republican votes in 1874 reported only 1 in 1876. Many other similar discrepancies appeared. The official returns ultimately sent to Washington gave all three states—and therefore the presidency—to Hayes, but the Democrats refused to recognize the results, and they controlled the House.

The country now faced a serious constitutional crisis. Armed Democrats threatened to march on Washington. Many people feared another civil war. The Constitution offered no clear guidance on how to deal with the matter. A count of the state electoral votes required the concurrence of both houses of Congress, but with a Democratic House and a Republican Senate, such concurrence was not forthcoming. To break the deadlock, Congress created a special electoral commission consisting of five representatives, five senators, and five Supreme Court justices split evenly between the two parties, with one member, a Supreme Court justice, supposedly an independent—but in fact a Republican.

Tilden had won a national majority of 252,000 popular votes, and the raw returns gave him a majority in the three disputed states. But an estimated 250,000 southern Republicans had been bulldozed away from the polls. In a genuinely fair and free election, the Republicans might have carried Mississippi and North Carolina as well as the three disputed states.

17-6e The Compromise of 1877

In February 1877, three months after voters had gone to the polls, the electoral commission issued its ruling. By a partisan vote of 8 to 7—with the "independent" justice voting with the Republicans—the commission awarded all of the

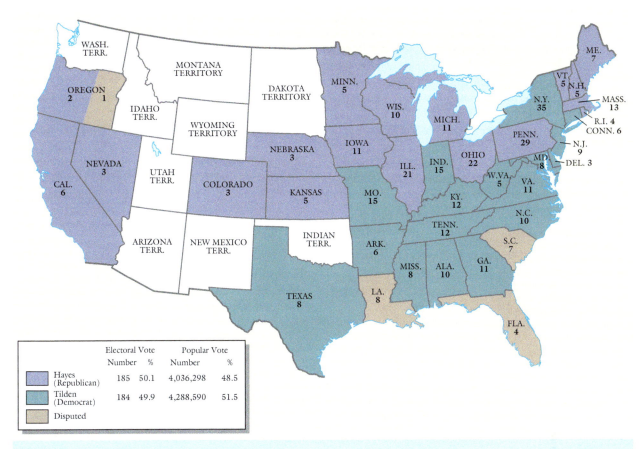

▲ **MAP 17.3 Hayes-Tilden Disputed Election of 1876** A comparison of this map with Map 17.1 on p. 479 and Map 17.2 on p. 483 shows the persistence of geographical voting patterns once Southern Democrats had overthrown most Republican state governments and effectively disfranchised many black voters.

Q Not all northern states voted for the Republican candidate, however. Why?
Q What was the process by which the disputed 1876 election was resolved?

disputed states to Hayes. The Democrats cried foul and began a **filibuster** in the House to delay the final electoral count beyond the inauguration date of March 4, to throw the election to the House of Representatives, an eventuality that threatened to bring total anarchy. But, behind the scenes, a compromise began to take shape. Both northern Republicans and Southern Democrats of Whig heritage had similar interests in liquidating the sectional rancor and in getting on with the business of economic recovery and development. To wean southern Whiggish Democrats away from a House filibuster, Hayes promised his support as president for federal appropriations to rebuild war-destroyed **levees** on the lower Mississippi and federal aid for a southern transcontinental railroad. Hayes's lieutenants also hinted at the appointment of a southerner as postmaster general, who would have a considerable amount of patronage at his disposal—the appointment of thousands of local postmasters.

Most important, southerners wanted to know what Hayes would do about Louisiana and South Carolina. Hayes signaled his intention to end "bayonet rule," which he had for some time considered a bankrupt policy. He believed that the goodwill and influence of southern moderates would offer better protection for black rights than federal troops could provide. In return for his commitment to withdraw the troops, Hayes asked for—and received—promises of fair treatment of freedpeople and respect for their constitutional rights.

17-6f The End of Reconstruction

Such promises were easier to make than to keep, as future years would reveal. In any case, the Democratic filibuster collapsed, and Hayes was inaugurated on March 4. He soon fulfilled his part of the Compromise of 1877: Ex-Confederate Democrat David Key of Tennessee became postmaster general; in 1878, the South received more federal money for internal improvements than ever before; and federal troops left the capitals of Louisiana and South Carolina. The last two Republican state governments collapsed. The old abolitionist and Radical Republican warhorses denounced Hayes's actions as a sellout of southern blacks.

But voices of protest could scarcely be heard above the sighs of relief that the crisis was over. Most Americans, including even most Republicans, wanted no more military intervention in state affairs.

Conclusion

Before the Civil War, most Americans had viewed a powerful government as a threat to individual liberties. That is why the first 10 amendments to the Constitution (the Bill of Rights) imposed strict limits on the powers of the federal government. During the Civil War and especially during Reconstruction, however, the national government had to exert an unprecedented amount of power to free the slaves and guarantee their equal rights as free citizens. That is why the Thirteenth, Fourteenth, and Fifteenth Amendments to the Constitution contained clauses stating that "Congress shall have power" to enforce these provisions for liberty and equal rights.

During the post–Civil War decade, Congress passed civil rights laws and enforcement legislation to accomplish this purpose. Federal marshals and troops patrolled the polls to protect black voters, arrested thousands of Klansmen and other violators of black civil rights, and even occupied state capitals to prevent Democratic paramilitary groups from overthrowing legitimately elected Republican state governments.

By 1875, many northerners had grown tired of or alarmed by this continued use of military power to intervene in the internal affairs of states. The Supreme Court stripped the federal government of much of its authority to enforce certain provisions of the Fourteenth and Fifteenth Amendments. Traditional fears of military power as a threat to individual liberties came to the fore again.

The withdrawal of federal troops from the South in 1877 constituted both a symbolic and a substantive end of the 12-year postwar era known as Reconstruction. Reconstruction had achieved the two great objectives inherited from the Civil War: (1) to reincorporate the former Confederate states into the Union and (2) to accomplish a transition from slavery to freedom in the South.

That transition was marred by the economic inequity of sharecropping and the social injustice of white supremacy. A third goal of Reconstruction, enforcement of the equal civil and political rights promised in the Fourteenth and Fifteenth Amendments, was betrayed by the Compromise of 1877. In subsequent decades, the freed slaves and their descendants suffered repression into segregated, second-class citizenship.

CHAPTER REVIEW

Review

1. What plans for reconstruction did Lincoln consider during the war?
2. What were the positions of Presidents Abraham Lincoln and Andrew Johnson and of moderate and Radical Republicans in Congress on the issues of restoring the South to the Union and protecting the rights of freed slaves?
3. What were the major accomplishments of congressional Reconstruction?
4. Why was Andrew Johnson impeached? Why was he acquitted?
5. Why was there an explosion of corruption during Grant's presidency? Why was the Republican coalition unstable in the South?
6. Why did a majority of the northern people and their political leaders turn against continued federal involvement in southern Reconstruction in the 1870s?

Critical Thinking

1. The two main goals of Reconstruction were to bring the former Confederate states back into the Union and to ensure the equal citizenship and rights of the former slaves. Why was the first goal more successfully achieved than the second?
2. Why have "carpetbaggers" and "scalawags" had such a bad historical image? Did they deserve it?

Identifications

Review your understanding of the following key terms, people, and events for this chapter (terms in bold in text are included in the Glossary).

enfranchise, p. 470
amnesty, p. 471
Black Codes, p. 472
quasi-slavery, p. 472
Freedmen's Bureau, p. 473
share wages, p. 473
sharecropping, p. 473
40 acres and a mule, p. 474
Union leagues, p. 477
scalawags, p. 477
carpetbaggers, p. 477
impeachment, p. 478
universal male suffrage, p. 479
Ku Klux Klan, p. 479
Ulysses S. Grant, p. 481
Credit Mobilier Affair, p. 482
spoils system, p. 482
patronage, p. 482
habeas corpus, p. 486
filibuster, p. 491
levees, p. 491

Suggested Readings

The most comprehensive history of Reconstruction remains **Eric Foner**, *Reconstruction: America's Unfinished Revolution 1863–1877* (1988). For a skillful abridgement of this book, see **Foner, A Short History of Reconstruction** (1990). An important history of black politics spanning Reconstruction is **Steven Hahn**, *A Nation Under Our Feet: Black Political Struggles in the Rural South from Slavery to the Great Migration* (2003). Incisive interpretations can be found in **Thomas J. Brown**, *Reconstruction: New Perspectives on the Postbellum United States* (2006). A classic study of the South Carolina Sea Islands as a laboratory of Reconstruction is **Willie Lee Rose**, *Rehearsal for Reconstruction: The Port Royal Experiment* (1964).

Two important studies of Andrew Johnson and his conflict with Congress over Reconstruction are **Hans L. Trefousse**, *The Radical Republicans: Lincoln's Vanguard for Racial Justice* (1969); and **Michael Les Benedict**, *The Impeachment and Trial of Andrew Johnson* (1973). Two books by **Michael Perman** connect events in the South and in Washington during Reconstruction: *Reunion without Compromise: The South and Reconstruction, 1865–1868* (1973) and *The Road to Redemption: Southern Politics 1868–1879* (1984). The emotional undertones of Reconstruction politics are analyzed in **Mark Wahlgren Summers**, *A Dangerous Stir: Fear, Paranoia, and the Making of Reconstruction* (2009). For counter-Reconstruction violence in the South, see **Hannah Rosen**, *Terror in the Heart of Freedom: Citizenship, Sexual Violence, and the Meaning of Race in the Postemancipation South* (2009); **George C. Rable**, *But There Was No Peace: The Role of Violence in the Politics of Reconstruction* (1984); **Nicholas Lemann**, *Redemption: The Last Battle of the Civil War* (2006); and **Carole Emberton**, *Beyond Redemption: Race, Violence, and the American South After the Civil War* (2013). The evolution of sharecropping and other aspects of the transition from slavery to freedom are treated in **Roger L. Ransom and Richard Sutch**, *One Kind of Freedom: The Economic Consequences of Emancipation* (1977).

Of the many books on African Americans in Reconstruction, the following are perhaps the most valuable: **Thomas Holt**, *Black over White: Negro Political Leadership in South Carolina during Reconstruction* (1977); and **Laura F. Edwards**, *Gendered Strife and Confusion: The Political Culture of Reconstruction* (1997). Both black and white churches are the subject of **Daniel Stowell**, *Rebuilding Zion: The Religious Reconstruction of the South, 1863–1877* (1998).

MINDTAP is a fully online personalized learning experience built upon Cengage Learning content. MindTap® combines student learning tools—readings, multimedia, activities, and assessments—into a singular Learning Path that guides students through the course and helps students develop the critical thinking, analysis, and communication skills that are essential to academic and professional success.

Appendix

The Declaration of Independence	A-3
The Constitution of the United States of America	A-5
Admission of States	A-13
Population of the United States	A-14
Presidential Elections	A-16
Justices of the U.S. Supreme Court	A-22

The Declaration of Independence

The Unanimous Declaration of the Thirteen United States of America

When in the Course of human events it becomes necessary for one people to dissolve the political bands which have connected them with another, and to assume among the Powers of the earth, the separate and equal station to which the Laws of Nature and of Nature's God entitle them, a decent respect to the opinions of mankind requires that they should declare the causes which impel them to the separation.

We hold these truths to be self-evident, that all men are created equal, that they are endowed by their Creator with certain unalienable Rights, that among these are Life, Liberty and the pursuit of Happiness. That to secure these rights, Governments are instituted among Men, deriving their just Powers from the consent of the governed. That whenever any Form of Government becomes destructive of these ends, it is the Right of the People to alter or to abolish it, and to institute new Government, laying its foundation on such principles and organizing its Powers in such form, as to them shall seem most likely to effect their Safety and Happiness. Prudence, indeed, will dictate that Governments long established should not be changed for light and transient causes; and accordingly all experience hath shewn, that mankind are more disposed to suffer, while evils are sufferable, than to right themselves by abolishing the forms to which they are accustomed. But when a long train of abuses and usurpations, pursuing invariably the same Object evinces a design to reduce them under absolute Despotism, it is their right, it is their duty, to throw off such Government, and to provide new Guards for their future security. Such has been the patient sufferance of these Colonies; and such is now the necessity which constrains them to alter their former Systems of Government. The history of the present King of Great Britain is a history of repeated injuries and usurpations, all having in direct object the establishment of an absolute Tyranny over these States. To prove this, let Facts be submitted to a candid world.

He has refused his Assent to Laws, the most wholesome and necessary for the public good.

He has forbidden his Governors to pass Laws of immediate and pressing importance, unless suspended in their operation till his Assent should be obtained; and when so suspended, he has utterly neglected to attend to them.

Text is reprinted from the facsimile of the engrossed copy in the National Archives. The original spelling, capitalization, and punctuation have been retained. Paragraphing has been added.

He has refused to pass other Laws for the accommodation of large districts of people, unless those people would relinquish the right of Representation in the Legislature, a right inestimable to them and formidable to tyrants only.

He has called together legislative bodies at places unusual, uncomfortable, and distant from the depository of their Public Records, for the sole Purpose of fatiguing them into compliance with his measures.

He has dissolved Representative Houses repeatedly, for opposing with manly firmness his invasions on the rights of the People.

He has refused for a long time, after such dissolutions, to cause others to be elected; whereby the Legislative Powers, incapable of Annihilation, have returned to the People at large for their exercise; the State remaining in the mean time exposed to all the dangers of invasion from without, and convulsions within.

He has endeavoured to prevent the Population of these States; for that purpose obstructing the Laws for Naturalization of Foreigners; refusing to pass others to encourage their migrations hither, and raising the conditions of new Appropriations of Lands.

He has obstructed the Administration of Justice, by refusing his Assent to Laws for establishing Judiciary Powers.

He has made Judges dependent on his Will alone, for the tenure of their offices, and the amount and payment of their salaries.

He has erected a multitude of New Offices, and sent hither swarms of Officers to harass our People, and eat out their substance.

He has kept among us, in times of peace, Standing Armies without the Consent of our legislatures.

He has affected to render the Military independent of and superior to the Civil Power.

He has combined with others to subject us to a jurisdiction foreign to our constitution, and unacknowledged by our laws; giving his Assent to their Acts of pretended Legislation: For Quartering large bodies of armed troops among us: For protecting them, by a mock Trial, from Punishment for any Murders which they should commit on the Inhabitants of these States: For cutting off our Trade with all parts of the world: For imposing Taxes on us without our Consent: For depriving us in many cases, of the benefits of Trial by Jury: For transporting us beyond Seas to be tried for pretended offences: For abolishing the free System of English Laws in a neighbouring

Province, establishing therein an Arbitrary government, and enlarging its Boundaries so as to render it at once an example and fit instrument for introducing the same absolute rule into these Colonies: For taking away our Charters, abolishing our most valuable Laws, and altering fundamentally the Forms of our Governments: For suspending our own Legislatures, and declaring themselves invested with Power to legislate for us in all cases whatsoever.

He has abdicated Government here, by declaring us out of his Protection, and waging War against us.

He has plundered our seas, ravaged our Coasts, burnt our towns, and destroyed the lives of our people.

He is at this time transporting large Armies of foreign Mercenaries to compleat the works of death, desolation and tyranny, already begun with circumstances of Cruelty and perfidy scarcely paralleled in the most barbarous ages, and totally unworthy the Head of a civilized nation.

He has constrained our fellow Citizens taken Captive on the high Seas to bear Arms against their Country, to become the executioners of their friends and Brethren, or to fall themselves by their Hands.

He has excited domestic insurrections amongst us, and has endeavoured to bring on the inhabitants of our frontiers, the merciless Indian Savages, whose known rule of warfare, is an undistinguished destruction of all ages, sexes and conditions.

In every stage of these Oppressions We have Petitioned for Redress in the most humble terms: Our repeated Petitions have been answered only by repeated injury. A Prince, whose character is thus marked by every act which may define a Tyrant, is unfit to be the ruler of a free People.

Nor have We been wanting in attentions to our British brethren. We have warned them from time to time of attempts by their legislature to extend an unwarrantable jurisdiction over us. We have reminded them of the circumstances of our emigration and settlement here. We have appealed to their native justice and magnanimity, and we have conjured them by the ties of our common kindred to disavow these usurpations, which, would inevitably interrupt our connections and correspondence. They too have been deaf to the voice of justice and of consanguinity. We must, therefore, acquiesce in the necessity, which denounces our Separation, and hold them, as we hold the rest of mankind, Enemies in War, in Peace Friends.

We, therefore, the Representatives of the United States of America, in General Congress, Assembled, appealing to the Supreme Judge of the world for the rectitude of our intentions, do, in the Name, and by Authority of the good People of these Colonies, solemnly publish and declare, That these United Colonies are, and of Right ought to be Free and Independent States; that they are Absolved from all Allegiance to the British Crown, and that all political connection between them and the State of Great Britain, is and ought to be totally dissolved; and that, as Free and Independent States, they have full Power to levy War, conclude Peace, contract Alliances, establish Commerce, and to do all other Acts and Things which Independent States may of right do. And for the support of this Declaration, with a firm reliance on the protection of divine Providence, we mutually pledge to each other our Lives, our Fortunes and our sacred Honor.

The Constitution of the United States of America

We the People of the United States, in Order to form a more perfect Union, establish Justice, insure domestic Tranquility, provide for the common defence, promote the general Welfare, and secure the Blessings of Liberty to ourselves and our Posterity, do ordain and establish this Constitution for the United States of America.

Article I

SECTION 1. All legislative Powers herein granted shall be vested in a Congress of the United States, which shall consist of a Senate and House of Representatives.

SECTION 2. The House of Representatives shall be composed of Members chosen every second Year by the People of the several States, and the Electors in each State shall have the Qualifications requisite for Electors of the most numerous Branch of the State Legislature.

No Person shall be a Representative who shall not have attained to the Age of twenty five Years, and been seven Years a Citizen of the United States, and who shall not, when elected, be an Inhabitant of that State in which he shall be chosen.

Representatives and direct Taxes[1] shall be apportioned among the several States which may be included within this Union, according to their respective Numbers, which shall be determined by adding to the whole Number of free Persons, including those bound to Service for a Term of Years, and excluding Indians not taxed, three fifths of all other Persons.[2]

The actual Enumeration shall be made within three Years after the first Meeting of the Congress of the United States, and within every subsequent Term of ten Years, in such Manner as they shall by Law direct. The Number of Representatives shall not exceed one for every thirty Thousand, but each State shall have at Least one Representative; and until such enumeration shall be made, the State of New Hampshire shall be entitled to chuse three; Massachusetts eight; Rhode Island and Providence Plantations one; Connecticut five; New York six; New Jersey four; Pennsylvania eight; Delaware one; Maryland six; Virginia ten; North Carolina five; South Carolina five; and Georgia three.

When vacancies happen in the Representation from any State, the Executive Authority thereof shall issue Writs of Election to fill such Vacancies.

The House of Representatives shall chuse their Speaker and other Officers; and shall have the sole Power of Impeachment.

SECTION 3. The Senate of the United States shall be composed of two Senators from each State, chosen by the Legislature thereof, for six Years; and each Senator shall have one Vote.[3]

Immediately after they shall be assembled in Consequence of the first Election, they shall be divided as equally as may be into three Classes. The Seats of the Senators of the first Class shall be vacated at the Expiration of the second Year, of the second Class at the Expiration of the fourth Year, and of the third Class at the Expiration of the sixth Year, so that one third may be chosen every second Year; and if Vacancies happen by Resignation, or otherwise, during the Recess of the Legislature of any State, the Executive thereof may make temporary Appointments until the next Meeting of the Legislature, which shall then fill such Vacancies.[4]

No Person shall be a Senator who shall not have attained to the Age of thirty Years, and been nine Years a Citizen of the United States, and who shall not, when elected, be an Inhabitant of that State for which he shall be chosen.

The Vice President of the United States shall be President of the Senate, but shall have no Vote, unless they be equally divided.

The Senate shall chuse their other Officers, and also a President pro tempore, in the Absence of the Vice President, or when he shall exercise the Office of President of the United States.

The Senate shall have the sole Power to try all Impeachments. When sitting for that Purpose, they shall be on Oath or Affirmation. When the President of the United States is tried, the Chief Justice shall preside: And no Person shall be convicted without the Concurrence of two thirds of the Members present.

Judgment in Cases of Impeachment shall not extend further than to removal from Office, and disqualification to hold and enjoy any Office of honor, Trust or Profit under the United States: but the Party convicted shall nevertheless be liable and subject to Indictment, Trial, Judgment and Punishment, according to Law.

Text is from the engrossed copy in the National Archives. Original spelling, capitalization, and punctuation have been retained.
1 Modified by the Sixteenth Amendment.
2 Replaced by the Fourteenth Amendment.
3 Superseded by the Seventeenth Amendment.
4 Modified by the Seventeenth Amendment.

SECTION 4. The Times, Places and Manner of holding Elections for Senators and Representatives, shall be prescribed in each State by the Legislature thereof, but the Congress may at any time by Law make or alter such Regulation, except as to the Placcs of chusing Senators.

The Congress shall assemble at least once in every Year, and such Meeting shall be on the first Monday in December, unless they shall by Law appoint a different Day.[5]

SECTION 5. Each House shall be the Judge of the Elections, Returns and Qualifications of its own Members, and a Majority of each shall constitute a Quorum to do Business; but a smaller Number may adjourn from day to day, and may be authorized to compel the Attendance of absent Members, in such Manner, and under such Penalties as each House may provide.

Each House may determine the Rules of its Proceedings, punish its Members for disorderly Behaviour, and, with the Concurrence of two thirds, expel a Member.

Each House shall keep a Journal of its Proceedings, and from time to time publish the same, excepting such Parts as may in their Judgment require Secrecy; and the Yeas and Nays of the Members of either House on any question shall, at the Desire of one fifth of those Present, be entered on the Journal.

Neither House, during the Session of Congress, shall, without the Consent of the other, adjourn for more than three days, nor to any other Place than that in which the two Houses shall be sitting.

SECTION 6. The Senators and Representatives shall receive a Compensation for their Services, to be ascertained by Law, and paid out of the Treasury of the United States. They shall in all Cases, except Treason, Felony and Breach of the Peace, be privileged from Arrest during their Attendance at the Session of their respective Houses, and in going to and returning from the same; and for any Speech or Debate in either House, they shall not be questioned in any other Place.

No Senator or Representative shall, during the Time for which he was elected, be appointed to any civil Office under the Authority of the United States, which shall have been created, or the Emoluments whereof shall have been encreased during such time; and no Person holding any Office under the United States, shall be a Member of either House during his Continuance in Office.

SECTION 7. All Bills for raising Revenue shall originate in the House of Representatives; but the Senate may propose or concur with Amendments as on other Bills.

Every Bill which shall have passed the House of Representatives and the Senate shall, before it become a Law, be presented to the President of the United States; If he approve he shall sign it, but if not he shall return it, with his Objections to that House in which it shall have originated, who shall enter the Objections at large on their Journal, and proceed to reconsider it. If after such Reconsideration two thirds of that House shall agree to pass the Bill, it shall be sent, together with the Objections, to the other House, by which it shall likewise be reconsidered, and if approved by two thirds of that House, it shall become a Law. But in all such Cases the Votes of both Houses shall be determined by yeas and Nays, and the Names of the Persons voting for and against the Bill shall be entered on the Journal of each House respectively. If any Bill shall not be returned by the President within ten Days (Sundays excepted) after it shall have been presented to him, the Same shall be a Law, in like Manner as if he had signed it, unless the Congress by their Adjournment prevent its Return, in which Case it shall not be a Law.

Every Order, Resolution, or Vote to which the Concurrence of the Senate and House of Representatives may be necessary (except on a question of Adjournment) shall be presented to the President of the United States; and before the Same shall take Effect, shall be approved by him, or being disapproved by him shall be repassed by two thirds of the Senate and House of Representatives, according to the Rules and Limitations prescribed in the Case of a Bill.

SECTION 8. The Congress shall have power To lay and collect Taxes, Duties, Imposts and Excises, to pay the Debts and provide for the common Defence and general Welfare of the United States; but all Duties, Imposts and Excises shall be uniform throughout the United States; To borrow Money on the credit of the United States; To regulate Commerce with foreign Nations, and among the several States, and with the Indian Tribes; To establish an uniform Rule of Naturalization, and uniform Laws on the subject of Bankruptcies throughout the United States; To coin Money, regulate the Value thereof, and of foreign Coin, and fix the Standard of Weights and Measures; To provide for the Punishment of counterfeiting the Securities and current Coin of the United States; To establish Post Offices and post Roads; To promote the Progress of Science and useful Arts, by securing for limited Times to Authors and Inventors the exclusive Right to their respective Writings and Discoveries; To constitute Tribunals inferior to the supreme Court; To define and punish Piracies and Felonies committed on the high Seas, and Offences against the Law of Nations;

To declare War, grant Letters of Marque and Reprisal, and make Rules concerning Captures on Land and Water; To raise and support Armies, but no Appropriation of Money to that Use shall be for a longer Term than two Years; To provide and maintain a Navy; To make Rules for the Government and Regulation of the land and naval Forces; To provide for calling forth the Militia to execute the Laws of the Union, suppress Insurrections and repel Invasions; To provide for organizing, arming, and disciplining, the Militia, and for governing such Part of them as may be employed in the Service of the United States, reserving to the States respectively, the Appointment of the Officers, and the Authority of training the Militia according to the discipline prescribed by Congress; To exercise exclusive Legislation in all Cases whatsoever, over such District (not exceeding ten Miles square) as may, by Cession of particular States, and the Acceptance of Congress, become the Seat of the Government of the United States, and to exercise like Authority over all Places purchased by the Consent of the Legislature of the State in which the Same shall be, for the Erection of Forts, Magazines, Arsenals, dock-Yards, and other needful

---

5 Superseded by the Twentieth Amendment.

Buildings;—And To make all Laws which shall be necessary and proper for carrying into Execution the foregoing Powers, and all other Powers vested by this Constitution in the Government of the United States, or in any Department or Officer thereof.

SECTION 9. The Migration or Importation of such Persons as any of the States now existing shall think proper to admit, shall not be prohibited by the Congress prior to the Year one thousand eight hundred and eight, but a Tax or duty may be imposed on such Importation, not exceeding ten dollars for each Person.

The Privilege of the Writ of Habeas Corpus shall not be suspended, unless when in Cases of Rebellion or Invasion the public Safety may require it.

No Bill of Attainder or ex post facto Law shall be passed. No Capitation, or other direct, Tax shall be laid, unless in Proportion to the Census or Enumeration herein before directed to be taken.

No Tax or Duty shall be laid on Articles exported from any State.

No Preference shall be given by any Regulation of Commerce or Revenue to the Ports of one State over those of another: nor shall Vessels bound to, or from, one State, be obliged to enter, clear, or pay Duties in another.

No Money shall be drawn from the Treasury, but in Consequence of Appropriations made by Law, and a regular Statement and Account of the Receipts and Expenditures of all public Money shall be published from time to time.

No Title of Nobility shall be granted by the United States: And no Person holding any Office of Profit or Trust under them, shall, without the Consent of the Congress, accept of any present, Emolument, Office, or Title, of any kind whatever, from any King, Prince, or foreign State.

SECTION 10. No State shall enter into any Treaty, Alliance, or Confederation; grant Letters of Marque and Reprisal; coin Money; emit Bills of Credit; make any Thing but gold and silver Coin a Tender in Payment of Debts; pass any Bill of Attainder, ex post facto Law, or Law impairing the Obligation of Contracts, or grant any Title of Nobility.

No State shall, without the Consent of the Congress, lay any Imposts or Duties on Imports or Exports, except what may be absolutely necessary for executing its inspection Laws: and the net Produce of all Duties and Imposts, laid by any State on Imports or Exports, shall be for the Use of the Treasury of the United States; and all such Laws shall be subject to the Revision and Controul of the Congress.

No State shall, without the Consent of Congress, lay any Duty of Tonnage, keep Troops, or Ships of War in time of Peace, enter into any Agreement or Compact with another State, or with a foreign Power, or engage in War, unless actually invaded, or in such imminent Danger as will not admit of delay.

Article II

SECTION 1. The executive Power shall be vested in a President of the United States of America. He shall hold his Office during the Term of four Years, and, together with the Vice President, chosen for the same Term, be elected, as follows: Each State shall appoint, in such Manner as the Legislature thereof may direct, a Number of Electors, equal to the whole Number of Senators and Representatives to which the State may be entitled in the Congress: but no Senator or Representative, or Person holding an Office of Trust or Profit under the United States, shall be appointed an Elector.

The Electors shall meet in their respective States, and vote by Ballot for two Persons, of whom one at least shall not be an Inhabitant of the same State with themselves. And they shall make a List of all the Persons voted for, and of the Number of Votes for each; which List they shall sign and certify, and transmit sealed to the Seat of the Government of the United States, directed to the President of the Senate. The President of the Senate shall, in the Presence of the Senate and House of Representatives, open all the Certificates, and the Votes shall then be counted. The Person having the greatest Number of Votes shall be the President, if such Number be a Majority of the whole Number of Electors appointed; and if there be more than one who have such Majority, and have an equal Number of Votes, then the House of Representatives shall immediately chuse by Ballot one of them for President; and if no Person have a Majority, then from the five highest on the List the said House shall in like Manner chuse the President. But in chusing the President, the Votes shall be taken by States, the Representation from each State having one Vote; A quorum for this Purpose shall consist of a Member or Members from two thirds of the States, and a Majority of all the States shall be necessary to a Choice. In every Case, after the Choice of the President, the Person having the greatest Number of Votes of the Electors shall be the Vice President. But if there should remain two or more who have equal Votes, the Senate shall chuse from them by Ballot the Vice President.[6]

The Congress may determine the Time of chusing the Electors, and the Day on which they shall give their Votes; which Day shall be the same throughout the United States.

No Person except a natural born Citizen, or a Citizen of the United States, at the time of the Adoption of this Constitution, shall be eligible to the Office of President, neither shall any Person be eligible to that Office who shall not have attained to the Age of thirty five Years, and been fourteen Years a Resident within the United States.

In Case of the Removal of the President from Office, or of his Death, Resignation, or Inability to discharge the Powers and Duties of the said Office, the Same shall devolve on the Vice President, and the Congress may by Law provide for the Case of Removal, Death, Resignation or Inability, both of the President and Vice President, declaring what Officer shall then act as President, and such Officer shall act accordingly, until the Disability be removed, or a President shall be elected.[7]

The President shall, at stated Times, receive for his Services, a Compensation, which shall neither be encreased nor diminished during the Period for which he shall have been

---

[6] Superseded by the Twelfth Amendment.
[7] Modified by the Twenty-fifth Amendment.

elected, and he shall not receive within that Period any other Emolument from the United States, or any of them.

Before he enter on the Execution of his Office, he shall take the following Oath or Affirmation:—"I do solemnly swear (or affirm) that I will faithfully execute the Office of President of the United States, and will to the best of my Ability, preserve, protect and defend the Constitution of the United States."

SECTION 2. The President shall be Commander in Chief of the Army and Navy of the United States, and of the Militia of the several States, when called into the actual Service of the United States; he may require the Opinion, in writing, of the principal Officer in each of the executive Departments, upon any Subject relating to the Duties of their respective Offices, and he shall have Power to grant Reprieves and Pardons for Offences against the United States, except in Cases of Impeachment.

He shall have Power, by and with the Advice and Consent of the Senate, to make Treaties, provided two thirds of the Senators present concur; and he shall nominate, and by and with the Advice and Consent of the Senate, shall appoint Ambassadors, other public Ministers and Consuls, Judges of the supreme Court, and all other Officers of the United States, whose Appointments are not herein otherwise provided for, and which shall be established by Law; but the Congress may by Law vest the Appointment of such inferior Officers, as they think proper, in the President alone, in the Courts of Law, or in the Heads of Departments.

The President shall have Power to fill up all Vacancies that may happen during the Recess of the Senate, by granting Commissions which shall expire at the End of their next Session.

SECTION 3. He shall from time to time give the Congress Information of the State of the Union, and recommend to their Consideration such Measures as he shall judge necessary and expedient; he may, on extraordinary Occasions, convene both Houses, or either of them, and in Case of Disagreement between them, with Respect to the Time of Adjournment, he may adjourn them to such Time as he shall think proper; he shall receive Ambassadors and other public Ministers; he shall take Care that the Laws be faithfully executed, and shall Commission all the Officers of the United States.

SECTION 4. The President, Vice President and all civil Officers of the United States, shall be removed from Office on Impeachment for, and Conviction of, Treason, Bribery, or other high Crimes and Misdemeanors.

Article III

SECTION 1. The judicial Power of the United States, shall be vested in one supreme Court, and in such inferior Courts as the Congress may from time to time ordain and establish.

The Judges, both of the supreme and inferior Courts, shall hold their Offices during good Behaviour, and shall, at stated Times, receive for their Services, a Compensation, which shall not be diminished during their Continuance in Office.

SECTION 2. The judicial Power shall extend to all Cases, in Law and Equity, arising under this Constitution, the Laws of the United States, and Treaties made, or which shall be made, under their Authority;—to all Cases affecting Ambassadors, other public Ministers and Consuls;—to all Cases of admiralty and maritime Jurisdiction;—to Controversies to which the United States shall be a Party;—to Controversies between two or more States;—between a State and Citizens of another State;[8]—between Citizens of different States,—between Citizens of the same State claiming Lands under Grants of different States, and between a State, or the Citizens thereof, and foreign States, Citizens or Subjects.

In all Cases affecting Ambassadors, other public Ministers and Consuls, and those in which a State shall be Party, the supreme Court shall have original Jurisdiction. In all the other Cases before mentioned, the supreme Court shall have appellate Jurisdiction, both as to Law and Fact, with such Exceptions, and under such Regulations as the Congress shall make.

The Trial of all Crimes, except in Cases of Impeachment, shall be by Jury; and such Trial shall be held in the State where the said Crimes shall have been committed; but when not committed within any State, the Trial shall be at such Place or Places as the Congress may by Law have directed.

SECTION 3. Treason against the United States, shall consist only in levying War against them, or in adhering to their Enemies, giving them Aid and Comfort. No Person shall be convicted of Treason unless on the Testimony of two Witnesses to the same overt Act, or on Confession in open Court.

The Congress shall have Power to declare the Punishment of Treason, but no Attainder of Treason shall work Corruption of Blood, or Forfeiture except during the Life of the Person attainted.

Article IV

SECTION 1. Full Faith and Credit shall be given in each State to the public Acts, Records, and judicial Proceedings of every other State. And the Congress may by general Laws prescribe the Manner in which such Acts, Records and Proceedings shall be proved, and the Effect thereof.

SECTION 2. The Citizens of each State shall be entitled to all Privileges and Immunities of Citizens in the several States.

A Person charged in any State with Treason, Felony, or other Crime, who shall flee from Justice, and be found in another State, shall on Demand of the executive Authority of the State from which he fled, be delivered up, to be removed to the State having Jurisdiction of the Crime.

No Person held to Service or Labour in one State, under the Laws thereof, escaping into another, shall, in Consequence of any Law or Regulation therein, be discharged from such Service or Labour, but shall be delivered up on Claim of the Party to whom such Service or Labour may be due.

SECTION 3. New States may be admitted by the Congress into this Union; but no new State shall be formed or erected within the Jurisdiction of any other State, nor any State be formed by the Junction of two or more States, or Parts of States, without the Consent of the Legislatures of the States concerned as well as of the Congress.

---

8 Modified by the Eleventh Amendment.

The Congress shall have Power to dispose of and make all needful Rules and Regulations respecting the Territory or other Property belonging to the United States; and nothing in this Constitution shall be so construed as to Prejudice any Claims of the United States, or of any particular State.

SECTION 4. The United States shall guarantee to every State in this Union a Republican Form of Government, and shall protect each of them against Invasion; and on Application of the Legislature, or of the Executive (when the Legislature cannot be convened) against domestic Violence.

Article V

The Congress, whenever two thirds of both Houses shall deem it necessary, shall propose Amendments to this Constitution, or, on the Application of the Legislatures of two thirds of the several States, shall call a Convention for proposing Amendments, which, in either Case, shall be valid to all Intents and Purposes, as Part of this Constitution, when ratified by the Legislatures of three fourths of the several States, or by Conventions in three fourths thereof, as the one or the other Mode of Ratification may be proposed by the Congress; Provided that no Amendment which may be made prior to the Year One thousand eight hundred and eight shall in any Manner affect the first and fourth Clauses in the Ninth Section of the first Article; and that no State, without its Consent, shall be deprived of its equal Suffrage in the Senate.

Article VI

All Debts contracted and Engagements entered into, before the Adoption of this Constitution, shall be as valid against the United States under this Constitution, as under the Confederation.

This Constitution, and the Laws of the United States which shall be made in Pursuance thereof; and all Treaties made, or which shall be made, under the Authority of the United States, shall be the supreme Law of the Land; and the Judges in every State shall be bound thereby, any Thing in the Constitution or Laws of any State to the Contrary notwithstanding.

The Senators and Representatives before mentioned, and the Members of the several State Legislatures, and all executive and judicial Officers, both of the United States and of the several States, shall be bound by Oath or Affirmation, to support this Constitution; but no religious Test shall ever be required as a Qualification to any Office or public Trust under the United States.

Article VII

The Ratification of the Conventions of nine States, shall be sufficient for the Establishment of this Constitution between the States so ratifying the Same.

Done in Convention by the Unanimous Consent of the States present the Seventeenth Day of September in the Year of our Lord one thousand seven hundred and Eighty seven and of the Independence of the United States of America the Twelfth. In witness whereof We have hereunto subscribed our Names,

Articles in Addition to, and Amendment of, the Constitution of the United States of America, Proposed by Congress, and Ratified by the Legislatures of the Several States, Pursuant to the Fifth Article of the Original Constitution.

Amendment I[9]

Congress shall make no law respecting an establishment of religion, or prohibiting the free exercise thereof; or abridging the freedom of speech, or of the press; or the right of the people peaceably to assemble, and to petition the Government for a redress of grievances.

Amendment II

A well regulated Militia, being necessary to the security of a free State, the right of the people to keep and bear Arms shall not be infringed.

Amendment III

No Soldier shall, in time of peace, be quartered in any house, without the consent of the Owner, nor in time of war, but in a manner to be prescribed by law.

Amendment IV

The right of the people to be secure in their persons, houses, papers, and effects, against unreasonable searches and seizures, shall not be violated, and no Warrants shall issue, but upon probable cause, supported by Oath or affirmation, and particularly describing the place to be searched, and the persons or things to be seized.

Amendment V

No person shall be held to answer for a capital or otherwise infamous crime, unless on a presentment or indictment of a Grand Jury, except in cases arising in the land or naval forces, or in the Militia, when in actual service in time of War or public danger; nor shall any person be subject for the same offence to be twice put in jeopardy of life or limb; nor shall be compelled in any criminal case to be a witness against himself, nor be deprived of life, liberty, or property, without due process of law; nor shall private property be taken for public use, without just compensation.

Amendment VI

In all criminal prosecutions, the accused shall enjoy the right to a speedy and public trial, by an impartial jury of the State and district wherein the crime shall have been committed, which district shall have been previously ascertained by law,

---

[9] The first ten amendments were passed by Congress September 25, 1789. They were ratified by three-fourths of the states December 15, 1791.

and to be informed of the nature and cause of the accusation; to be confronted with the witnesses against him; to have compulsory process for obtaining witnesses in his favor, and to have the Assistance of Counsel for his defence.

Amendment VII

In suits at common law, where the value in controversy shall exceed twenty dollars, the right of trial by jury shall be preserved, and no fact tried by a jury, shall be otherwise reexamined in any Court of the United States, than according to the rules of the common law.

Amendment VIII

Excessive bail shall not be required, nor excessive fines imposed, nor cruel and unusual punishments inflicted.

Amendment IX

The enumeration in the Constitution, of certain rights, shall not be construed to deny or disparage others retained by the people.

Amendment X

The powers not delegated to the United States by the Constitution; nor prohibited by it to the States, are reserved to the States respectively, or to the people.

Amendment XI[10]

The Judicial power of the United States shall not be construed to extend to any suit in law or equity, commenced or prosecuted against one of the United States by Citizens of another State, or by Citizens or Subjects of any Foreign State.

Amendment XII[11]

The Electors shall meet in their respective States and vote by ballot for President and Vice-President, one of whom, at least, shall not be an inhabitant of the same State with themselves; they shall name in their ballots the person voted for as President, and in distinct ballots the person voted for as VicePresident, and they shall make distinct lists of all persons voted for as President, and of all persons voted for as VicePresident, and of the number of votes for each, which lists they shall sign and certify, and transmit sealed to the seat of the government of the United States, directed to the President of the Senate;—The President of the Senate shall, in the presence of the Senate and House of Representatives, open all the certificates and the votes shall then be counted;—The person having the greatest number of votes for President, shall be the President, if such number be a majority of the whole number of Electors appointed; and if no person have such majority, then from the persons having the highest numbers not exceeding three on the list of those voted for as President, the House of Representatives shall choose immediately, by ballot, the President.

But in choosing the President, the votes shall be taken by states, the representation from each state having one vote; a quorum for this purpose shall consist of a member or members from two-thirds of the states, and a majority of all the states shall be necessary to a choice. And if the House of Representatives shall not choose a President whenever the right of choice shall devolve upon them, before the fourth day of March next following, then the Vice-President shall act as President, as in the case of the death or other constitutional disability of the President.—The person having the greatest number of votes as Vice-President, shall be the Vice-President, if such number be a majority of the whole number of Electors appointed, and if no person have a majority, then from the two highest numbers on the list, the Senate shall choose the Vice-President; a quorum for the purpose shall consist of two-thirds of the whole number of Senators, and a majority of the whole number shall be necessary to a choice. But no person constitutionally ineligible to the office of President shall be eligible to that of Vice-President of the United States.

Amendment XIII[12]

SECTION 1. Neither slavery nor involuntary servitude, except as a punishment for crime whereof the party shall have been duly convicted, shall exist within the United States, or any place subject to their jurisdiction.

SECTION 2. Congress shall have power to enforce this article by appropriate legislation.

Amendment XIV[13]

SECTION 1. All persons born or naturalized in the United States, and subject to the jurisdiction thereof, are citizens of the United States and of the State wherein they reside. No State shall make or enforce any law which shall abridge the privileges or immunities of citizens of the United States; nor shall any State deprive any person of life, liberty, or property, without due process of law; nor deny to any person within its jurisdiction the equal protection of the laws.

SECTION 2. Representatives shall be apportioned among the several States according to their respective numbers, counting the whole number of persons in each State, excluding Indians not taxed. But when the right to vote at any election for the choice of electors for President and VicePresident of the United States, Representatives in Congress, the Executive and Judicial officers of a State, or the members of the Legislature thereof, is denied to any of the male inhabitants of such State,

---

10 Passed March 4, 1794. Ratified January 23, 1795.
11 Passed December 9, 1803. Ratified June 15, 1804.
12 Passed January 31, 1865. Ratified December 6, 1865.
13 Passed June 13, 1866. Ratified July 9, 1868.

being twenty-one years of age, and citizens of the United States, or in any way abridged, except for participation in rebellion, or other crime, the basis of representation therein shall be reduced in the proportion which the number of such male citizens shall bear to the whole number of male citizens twenty-one years of age in such State.

SECTION 3. No person shall be a Senator or Representative in Congress, or elector of President and Vice-President, or hold any office, civil or military, under the United States, or under any State, who, having previously taken an oath, as a member of Congress, or as an officer of the United States, or as a member of any State legislature, or as an executive or judicial officer of any State, to support the Constitution of the United States, shall have engaged in insurrection or rebellion against the same, or given aid or comfort to the enemies thereof. But Congress may by a vote of two-thirds of each House, remove such disability.

SECTION 4. The validity of the public debt of the United States, authorized by law, including debts incurred for payment of pensions and bounties for services in suppressing insurrection or rebellion, shall not be questioned. But neither the United States nor any State shall assume or pay any debt or obligation incurred in aid of insurrection or rebellion against the United States, or any claim for the loss or emancipation of any slave; but all such debts, obligations, and claims shall be held illegal and void.

SECTION 5. The Congress shall have the power to enforce, by appropriate legislation, the provisions of this article.

Amendment XV[14]

SECTION 1. The right of citizens of the United States to vote shall not be denied or abridged by the United States or by any State on account of race, color, or previous conditions of servitude—

SECTION 2. The Congress shall have power to enforce this article by appropriate legislation.

Amendment XVI[15]

The Congress shall have power to lay and collect taxes on incomes, from whatever source derived, without apportionment among the several States, and without regard to any census or enumeration.

Amendment XVII[16]

The Senate of the United States shall be composed of two Senators from each State, elected by the people thereof, for six years; and each Senator shall have one vote. The electors in each State shall have the qualifications requisite for electors of the most numerous branch of the State legislatures.

When vacancies happen in the representation of any State in the Senate, the executive authority of such State shall issue writs of election to fill such vacancies: Provided, That the legislature of any State may empower the executive thereof to make temporary appointments until the people fill the vacancies by election as the legislature may direct.

This amendment shall not be so construed as to affect the election or term of any Senator chosen before it becomes valid as part of the Constitution.

Amendment XVIII[17]

SECTION 1. After one year from the ratification of this article the manufacture, sale, or transportation of intoxicating liquors within, the importation thereof into, or the exportation thereof from the United States and all territory subject to the jurisdiction thereof for beverage purposes is hereby prohibited.

SECTION 2. The Congress and the several States shall have concurrent power to enforce this article by appropriate legislation.

SECTION 3. This article shall be inoperative unless it shall have been ratified as an amendment to the Constitution by the legislatures of the several States, as provided in the Constitution, within seven years from the date of the submission hereof to the States by the Congress.

Amendment XIX[18]

The right of citizens of the United States to vote shall not be denied or abridged by the United States or by any State on account of sex.

Congress shall have power to enforce this article by appropriate legislation.

Amendment XX[19]

SECTION 1. The terms of the President and VicePresident shall end at noon on the 20th day of January, and the terms of Senators and Representatives at noon on the 3d day of January, of the years in which such terms would have ended if this article had not been ratified; and the terms of their successors shall then begin.

SECTION 2. The Congress shall assemble at least once in every year, and such meeting shall begin at noon on the 3d day of January, unless they shall by law appoint a different day.

SECTION 3. If, at the time fixed for the beginning of the term of the President, the President elect shall have died, the Vice-President elect shall become President. If a President shall not have been chosen before the time fixed for the beginning of his term, or if the President elect shall have failed to qualify, then the Vice-President elect shall act as President until a President shall have qualified; and the Congress may by law provide for the case wherein neither a President elect

---

14 Passed February 26, 1869. Ratified February 2, 1870.
15 Passed July 12, 1909. Ratified February 3, 1913.
16 Passed May 13, 1912. Ratified April 8, 1913.

17 Passed December 18, 1917. Ratified January 16, 1919.
18 Passed June 4, 1919. Ratified August 18, 1920.
19 Passed March 2, 1932. Ratified January 23, 1933.

nor a Vice-President elect shall have qualified, declaring who shall then act as President, or the manner in which one who is to act shall be selected, and such person shall act accordingly until a President or Vice-President shall have qualified.

SECTION 4. The Congress may by law provide for the case of the death of any of the persons from whom the House of Representatives may choose a President whenever the right of choice shall have devolved upon them, and for the case of the death of any of the persons from whom the Senate may choose a Vice-President whenever the right of choice shall have devolved upon them.

SECTION 5. Sections 1 and 2 shall take effect on the 15th day of October following the ratification of this article.

SECTION 6. This article shall be inoperative unless it shall have been ratified as an amendment to the Constitution by the legislatures of three-fourths of the several States within seven years from the date of its submission.

Amendment XXI[20]

SECTION 1. The eighteenth article of amendment to the Constitution of the United States is hereby repealed.

SECTION 2. The transportation or importation into any State, Territory, or possession of the United States for delivery or use therein of intoxicating liquors, in violation of the laws thereof, is hereby prohibited.

SECTION 3. This article shall be inoperative unless it shall have been ratified as an amendment to the Constitution by conventions in the several States, as provided in the Constitution, within seven years from the date of the submission hereof to the States by the Congress.

Amendment XXII[21]

No person shall be elected to the office of the President more than twice, and no person who has held the office of President, or acted as President, for more than two years of a term to which some other person was elected President shall be elected to the office of the President more than once.

But this Article shall not apply to any person holding the office of President when this Article was proposed by the Congress, and shall not prevent any person who may be holding the office of President, or acting as President, during the term within which this Article becomes operative from holding the office of President or acting as President during the remainder of such term.

Amendment XXIII[22]

SECTION 1. The District constituting the seat of Government of the United States shall appoint in such manner as the Congress may direct: A number of electors of President and Vice President equal to the whole number of Senators and Representatives in Congress to which the District would be entitled if it were a State, but in no event more than the least populous State; they shall be in addition to those appointed by the States, but they shall be considered, for the purposes of the election of President and Vice President, to be electors appointed by the State; and they shall meet in the District and perform such duties as provided by the twelfth article of amendment.

SECTION 2. The Congress shall have power to enforce this article by appropriate legislation.

Amendment XXIV[23]

SECTION 1. The right of citizens of the United States to vote in any primary or other election for President or Vice President, or for Senator or Representative in Congress, shall not be denied or abridged by the United States or any State by reason of failure to pay any poll tax or other tax.

SECTION 2. The Congress shall have power to enforce this article by appropriate legislation.

Amendment XXV[24]

SECTION 1. In case of the removal of the President from office or of his death or resignation, the Vice President shall become President.

SECTION 2. Whenever there is a vacancy in the office of the Vice President, the President shall nominate a Vice President who shall take office upon confirmation by a majority vote of both Houses of Congress.

SECTION 3. Whenever the President transmits to the President pro tempore of the Senate and the Speaker of the House of Representatives his written declaration that he is unable to discharge the powers and duties of his office, and until he transmits them a written declaration to the contrary, such powers and duties shall be discharged by the Vice President as Acting President.

SECTION 4. Whenever the Vice President and a majority of either the principal officers of the executive department or of such other body as Congress may by law provide, transmit to the President pro tempore of the Senate and the Speaker of the House of Representatives their written declaration that the President is unable to discharge the powers and duties of his office, the Vice President shall immediately assume the powers and duties of the office of Acting President.

Thereafter, when the President transmits to the President pro tempore of the Senate and the Speaker of the House of Representatives his written declaration that no inability exists, he shall resume the powers and duties of his office unless the Vice President and a majority of either

---

20 Passed February 20, 1933. Ratified December 5, 1933.
21 Passed March 12, 1947. Ratified March 1, 1951.
22 Passed June 16, 1960. Ratified April 3, 1961.
23 Passed August 27, 1962. Ratified January 23, 1964.
24 Passed July 6, 1965. Ratified February 11, 1967.

the principal officers of the executive department or of such other body as Congress may by law provide, transmit within four days to the President pro tempore of the Senate and the Speaker of the House of Representatives their written declaration that the President is unable to discharge the powers and duties of his office. Thereupon Congress shall decide the issue, assembling within forty-eight hours for that purpose if not in session. If the Congress, within twenty-one days after receipt of the latter written declaration, or, if Congress is not in session, within twenty-one days after Congress is required to assemble, determines by two-thirds vote of both Houses that the President is unable to discharge the powers and duties of his office, the Vice President shall continue to discharge the same as Acting President; otherwise, the President shall resume the powers and duties of his office.

Amendment XXVI[25]

SECTION 1 The right of citizens of the United States, who are eighteen years of age or older, to vote shall not be denied or abridged by the United States or by any State on account of age.

SECTION 2. The Congress shall have power to enforce this article by appropriate legislation.

Amendment XXVII[26]

No law, varying the compensation for the service of the Senators and Representatives, shall take effect, until an election of Representatives shall have intervened.

---

25 Passed March 23, 1971. Ratified July 5, 1971.
26 Passed September 25, 1789. Ratified May 7, 1992.

ADMISSION OF STATES

Order of admission	State	Date of admission	Order of admission	State	Date of admission
1	Delaware	December 7, 1787	26	Michigan	January 26, 1837
2	Pennsylvania	December 12, 1787	27	Florida	March 3, 1845
3	New Jersey	December 18, 1787	28	Texas	December 29, 1845
4	Georgia	January 2, 1788	29	Iowa	December 28, 1846
5	Connecticut	January 9, 1788	30	Wisconsin	May 29, 1848
6	Massachusetts	February 6, 1788	31	California	September 9, 1850
7	Maryland	April 28, 1788	32	Minnesota	May 11, 1858
8	South Carolina	May 23, 1788	33	Oregon	February 14, 1859
9	New Hampshire	June 21, 1788	34	Kansas	January 29, 1861
10	Virginia	June 25, 1788	35	West Virginia	June 20, 1863
11	New York	July 26, 1788	36	Nevada	October 31, 1864
12	North Carolina	November 21, 1789	37	Nebraska	March 1, 1867
13	Rhode Island	May 29, 1790	38	Colorado	August 1, 1876
14	Vermont	March 4, 1791	39	North Dakota	November 2, 1889
15	Kentucky	June 1, 1792	40	South Dakota	November 2, 1889
16	Tennessee	June 1, 1796	41	Montana	November 8, 1889
17	Ohio	March 1, 1803	42	Washington	November 11, 1889
18	Louisiana	April 30, 1812	43	Idaho	July 3, 1890
19	Indiana	December 11, 1816	44	Wyoming	July 10, 1890
20	Mississippi	December 10, 1817	45	Utah	January 4, 1896
21	Illinois	December 3, 1818	46	Oklahoma	November 16, 1907
22	Alabama	December 14, 1819	47	New Mexico	January 6, 1912
23	Maine	March 15, 1820	48	Arizona	February 14, 1912
24	Missouri	August 10, 1821	49	Alaska	January 3, 1959
25	Arkansas	June 15, 1836	50	Hawaii	August 21, 1959

POPULATION OF THE UNITED STATES

Year	Total population	Number per square mile	Year	Total population	Number per square mile	Year	Total population	Number per square mile
1790	3,929	4.5	1830	12,901	7.4	1870	39,905	13.4
1791	4,056		1831	13,321		1871	40,938	
1792	4,194		1832	13,742		1872	41,972	
1793	4,332		1833	14,162		1873	43,006	
1794	4,469		1834	14,582		1874	44,040	
1795	4,607		1835	15,003		1875	45,073	
1796	4,745		1836	15,423		1876	46,107	
1797	4,883		1837	15,843		1877	47,141	
1798	5,021		1838	16,264		1878	48,174	
1799	5,159		1839	16,684		1879	49,208	
1800	5,297	6.1	1840	17,120	9.8	1880	50,262	16.9
1801	5,486		1841	17,733		1881	51,542	
1802	5,679		1842	18,345		1882	52,821	
1803	5,872		1843	18,957		1883	54,100	
1804	5,065		1844	19,569		1884	55,379	
1805	6,258		1845	20,182		1885	56,658	
1806	6,451		1846	20,794		1886	57,938	
1807	6,644		1847	21,406		1887	59,217	
1808	6,838		1848	22,018		1888	60,496	
1809	7,031		1849	22,631		1889	61,775	
1810	7,224	4.3	1850	23,261	7.9	1890	63,056	21.2
1811	7,460		1851	24,086		1891	64,361	
1812	7,700		1852	24,911		1892	65,666	
1813	7,939		1853	25,736		1893	66,970	
1814	8,179		1854	26,561		1894	68,275	
1815	8,419		1855	27,386		1895	69,580	
1816	8,659		1856	28,212		1896	70,885	
1817	8,899		1857	29,037		1897	72,189	
1818	9,139		1858	29,862		1898	73,494	
1819	9,379		1859	30,687		1899	74,799	
1820	9,618	5.6	1860	31,513	10.6	1900	76,094	25.6
1821	9,939		1861	32,351		1901	77,585	
1822	10,268		1862	33,188		1902	79,160	
1823	10,596		1863	34,026		1903	80,632	
1824	10,924		1864	34,863		1904	82,165	
1825	11,252		1865	35,701		1905	83,820	
1826	11,580		1866	36,538		1906	85,437	
1827	11,909		1867	37,376		1907	87,000	
1828	12,237		1868	38,213		1908	88,709	
1829	12,565		1869	39,051		1909	90,492	

POPULATION OF THE UNITED STATES, CONTINUED

Year	Total population	Number per square mile	Year	Total population	Number per square mile	Year	Total population	Number per square mile
1910	92,407	31.0	1946	141,936		1982	232,520	
1911	93,868		1947	144,698		1983	234,799	
1912	95,331		1948	147,208		1984	237,001	
1913	97,227		1949	149,767		1985	239,283	
1914	99,118		1950	150,697	50.7	1986	241,596	
1915	100,549		1951	154,878		1987	234,773	
1916	101,966		1952	157,553		1988	245,051	
1917	103,414		1953	160,184		1989	247,350	
1918	104,550		1954	163,026		1990	250,122	70.3
1919	105,063		1955	165,931		1991	254,521	
1920	106,466	35.6	1956	168,903		1992	245,908	
1921	108,541		1957	171,984		1993	257,908	
1922	110,055		1958	174,882		1994	261,875	
1923	111,950		1959	177,830		1995	263,434	
1924	114,113		1960	178,464	60.1	1996	266,096	
1925	115,832		1961	183,642		1997	267,901	
1926	117,399		1962	186,504		1998	269,501	
1927	119,038		1963	189,197		1999	272,700	
1928	120,501		1964	191,833		2000	282,172	80.0
1929	121,700		1965	194,237		2001	285,082	
1930	122,775	41.2	1966	196,485		2002	287,804	
1931	124,040		1967	198,629		2003	290,326	
1932	124,840		1968	200,619		2004	293,046	
1933	125,579		1969	202,599		2005	295,753	
1934	126,374		1970	203,875	57.5[1]	2006	298,593	
1935	127,250		1971	207,045		2007	301,580	
1936	128,053		1972	208,842		2008	304,375	
1937	128,825		1973	210,396		2009	307,007	
1938	129,825		1974	211,894		2010	308,746	87.4
1939	130,880		1975	213,631		2011	311,588	
1940	131,669	44.2	1976	215,152		2012	313,914	
1941	133,894		1977	216,880		2013	316,439	
1942	135,361		1978	218,717		2014	318,563	
1943	137,250		1979	220,584		2015	320,987	
1944	138,916		1980	226,546	64.0	2016	323,128	
1945	140,468		1981	230,138		2017	325,719	

Numbers are from *Historical Statistics of the United States, Colonial Times to 1957* (1961), pp. 7, 8; *Statistical Abstract of the United States: 1974*, p. 5, Census Bureau for 1974 and 1975; *Statistical Abstract of the United States: 1988*, p. 7; https://data.worldbank.org/country/united-states data.worldbank.org for 2014-2016; and https://www.census.gov/quickfacts/fact/table/US/PST045216 for 2017.

Note: Population numbers are in thousands. Thus the number 325,719 appearing in the box alongside the year 2017 is actually 325,719,000. Numbers after 1940 represent total population including armed forces abroad, except in official census years. Density figures are for land area of continental United States.

PRESIDENTIAL ELECTIONS

Year	Number of states	Candidates[1]	Parties	Popular vote	Electoral vote	Percentage of popular vote[2]
1789	11	**George Washington**	No party designations		69	
		John Adams			34	
		Minor Candidates			35	
1792	15	**George Washington**	No party designations		132	
		John Adams			77	
		George Clinton			50	
		Minor Candidates			5	
1796	16	**John Adams**	Federalist		71	
		Thomas Jefferson	Democratic-Republican		68	
		Thomas Pinckney	Federalist		59	
		Aaron Burr	Democratic-Republican		30	
		Minor Candidates			48	
1800	16	**Thomas Jefferson**	Democratic-Republican		73	
		Aaron Burr	Democratic-Republican		73	
		John Adams	Federalist		65	
		Charles C. Pinckney	Federalist		64	
		John Jay	Federalist		1	
1804	17	**Thomas Jefferson**	Democratic-Republican		162	
		Charles C. Pinckney	Federalist		14	
1808	17	**James Madison**	Democratic-Republican		122	
		Charles C. Pinckney	Federalist		47	
		George Clinton	Democratic-Republican		6	
1812	18	**James Madison**	Democratic-Republican		128	
		DeWitt Clinton	Federalist		89	
1816	19	**James Monroe**	Democratic-Republican		183	
		Rufus King	Federalist		34	
1820	24	**James Monroe**	Democratic-Republican		231	
		John Quincy Adams	Independent Republican		1	
1824	24	**John Quincy Adams**	Democratic-Republican	108,740	84	30.5
		Andrew Jackson	Democratic-Republican	153,544	99	43.1
		William H. Crawford	Democratic-Republican	46,618	41	13.1
		Henry Clay	Democratic-Republican	47,136	37	13.2
1828	24	**Andrew Jackson**	Democratic	647,286	178	56.0
		John Quincy Adams	National Republican	508,064	83	44.0

Numbers are from *Historical Statistics of the United States, Colonial Times to 1957* (1961), pp. 682–83; the U.S. Department of Justice; and the Federal Election Commission (FEC).
[1] Before the passage of the Twelfth Amendment in 1804, the Electoral College voted for two presidential candidates; the runner-up became vice president.
[2] Candidates receiving less than 1 percent of the popular vote have been omitted. For that reason the percentage of popular vote given for any election year may not total 100 percent.

PRESIDENTIAL ELECTIONS, CONTINUED

Year	Number of states	Candidates	Parties	Popular vote	Electoral vote	Percentage of popular vote
1832	24	**Andrew Jackson**	Democratic	687,502	219	55.0
		Henry Clay	National Republican	530,189	49	42.4
		William Wirt	Anti-Masonic		7	
		John Floyd	National Republican	33,108	11	2.6
1836	26	**Martin Van Buren**	Democratic	765,483	170	50.9
		William H. Harrison	Whig		73	
		Hugh L. White	Whig	739,795	26	
		Daniel Webster	Whig		14	
		W. P. Mangum	Whig		11	
1840	26	**William H. Harrison**	Whig	1,274,624	234	53.1
		Martin Van Buren	Democratic	1,127,781	60	46.9
1844	26	**James K. Polk**	Democratic	1,338,464	170	49.6
		Henry Clay	Whig	1,300,097	105	48.1
		James G. Birney	Liberty	62,300		2.3
1848	30	**Zachary Taylor**	Whig	1,360,967	163	47.4
		Lewis Cass	Democratic	1,222,342	127	42.5
		Martin Van Buren	Free Soil	291,263		10.1
1852	31	**Franklin Pierce**	Democratic	1,601,117	254	50.9
		Winfield Scott	Whig	1,385,453	42	44.1
		John P. Hale	Free Soil	155,825		5.0
1856	31	**James Buchanan**	Democratic	1,832,955	174	45.3
		John C. Frémont	Republican	1,339,932	114	33.1
		Millard Fillmore	American	871,731	8	21.6
1860	33	**Abraham Lincoln**	Republican	1,865,593	180	39.8
		Stephen A. Douglas	Democratic	1,382,713	12	29.5
		John C. Breckinridge	Democratic	848,356	72	18.1
		John Bell	Constitutional Union	592,906	39	12.6
1864	36	**Abraham Lincoln**	Republican	2,206,938	212	55.0
		George B. McClellan	Democratic	1,803,787	21	45.0
1868	37	**Ulysses S. Grant**	Republican	3,013,421	214	52.7
		Horatio Seymour	Democratic	2,706,829	80	47.3
1872	37	**Ulysses S. Grant**	Republican	3,596,745	286	55.6
		Horace Greeley	Democratic	2,843,446	[3]	43.9
1876	38	**Rutherford B. Hayes**	Republican	4,036,572	185	48.0
		Samuel J. Tilden	Democratic	4,284,020	184	51.0

[3]Greeley died shortly after the election; the electors supporting him then divided their votes among other candidates.

(Continued)

PRESIDENTIAL ELECTIONS, CONTINUED

Year	Number of states	Candidates	Parties	Popular vote	Electoral vote	Percentage of popular vote
1880	38	**James A. Garfield**	Republican	4,453,295	214	48.5
		Winfield S. Hancock	Democratic	4,414,082	155	48.1
		James B. Weaver	Greenback-Labor	308,578		3.4
1884	38	**Grover Cleveland**	Democratic	4,879,507	219	48.5
		James G. Blaine	Republican	4,850,293	182	48.2
		Benjamin F. Butler	Greenback-Labor	175,370		1.8
		John P. St. John	Prohibition	150,369		1.5
1888	38	**Benjamin Harrison**	Republican	5,477,129	233	47.9
		Grover Cleveland	Democratic	5,537,857	168	48.6
		Clinton B. Fisk	Prohibition	249,506		2.2
		Anson J. Streeter	Union Labor	146,935		1.3
1892	44	**Grover Cleveland**	Democratic	5,555,426	277	46.1
		Benjamin Harrison	Republican	5,182,690	145	43.0
		James B. Weaver	People's	1,029,846	22	8.5
		John Bidwell	Prohibition	264,133		2.2
1896	45	**William McKinley**	Republican	7,102,246	271	51.1
		William J. Bryan	Democratic	6,492,559	176	47.7
1900	45	**William McKinley**	Republican	7,218,491	292	51.7
		William J. Bryan	Democratic; Populist	6,356,734	155	45.5
		John C. Wooley	Prohibition	208,914		1.5
1904	45	**Theodore Roosevelt**	Republican	7,628,461	336	57.4
		Alton B. Parker	Democratic	5,084,223	140	37.6
		Eugene V. Debs	Socialist	402,283		3.0
		Silas C. Swallow	Prohibition	258,536		1.9
1908	46	**William H. Taft**	Republican	7,675,320	321	51.6
		William J. Bryan	Democratic	6,412,294	162	43.1
		Eugene V. Debs	Socialist	420,793		2.8
		Eugene W. Chafin	Prohibition	253,840		1.7
1912	48	**Woodrow Wilson**	Democratic	6,296,547	435	41.9
		Theodore Roosevelt	Progressive	4,118,571	88	27.4
		William H. Taft	Republican	3,486,720	8	23.2
		Eugene V. Debs	Socialist	900,672		6.0
		Eugene W. Chafin	Prohibition	206,275		1.4
1916	48	**Woodrow Wilson**	Democratic	9,127,695	277	49.4
		Charles E. Hughes	Republican	8,533,507	254	46.2
		A. L. Benson	Socialist	585,113		3.2
		J. Frank Hanly	Prohibition	220,506		1.2

PRESIDENTIAL ELECTIONS, CONTINUED

Year	Number of states	Candidates	Parties	Popular vote	Electoral vote	Percentage of popular vote
1920	48	**Warren G. Harding**	Republican	16,143,407	404	60.4
		James N. Cox	Democratic	9,130,328	127	34.2
		Eugene V. Debs	Socialist	919,799		3.4
		P. P. Christensen	Farmer-Labor	265,411		1.0
1924	48	**Calvin Coolidge**	Republican	15,718,211	382	54.0
		John W. Davis	Democratic	8,385,283	136	28.8
		Robert M. La Follette	Progressive	4,831,289	13	16.6
1928	48	**Herbert C. Hoover**	Republican	21,391,993	444	58.2
		Alfred E. Smith	Democratic	15,016,169	87	40.9
1932	48	**Franklin D. Roosevelt**	Democratic	22,809,638	472	57.4
		Herbert C. Hoover	Republican	15,758,901	59	39.7
		Norman Thomas	Socialist	881,951		2.2
1936	48	**Franklin D. Roosevelt**	Democratic	27,752,869	523	60.8
		Alfred M. Landon	Republican	16,674,665	8	36.5
		William Lemke	Union	882,479		1.9
1940	48	**Franklin D. Roosevelt**	Democratic	27,307,819	449	54.8
		Wendell L. Willkie	Republican	22,321,018	82	44.8
1944	48	**Franklin D. Roosevelt**	Democratic	25,606,585	432	53.5
		Thomas E. Dewey	Republican	22,014,745	99	46.0
1948	48	**Harry S. Truman**	Democratic	24,105,812	303	49.5
		Thomas E. Dewey	Republican	21,970,065	189	45.1
		J. Strom Thurmond	States' Rights	1,169,063	39	2.4
		Henry A. Wallace	Progressive	1,157,172		2.4
1952	48	**Dwight D. Eisenhower**	Republican	33,936,234	442	55.1
		Adlai E. Stevenson	Democratic	27,314,992	89	44.4
1956	48	**Dwight D. Eisenhower**	Republican	35,590,472	457	57.6
		Adlai E. Stevenson	Democratic	26,022,752	73	42.1
1960	50	**John F. Kennedy**	Democratic	34,227,096	303	49.9
		Richard M. Nixon	Republican	34,108,546	219	49.6
1964	50	**Lyndon B. Johnson**	Democratic	43,126,506	486	61.1
		Barry M. Goldwater	Republican	27,176,799	52	38.5
1968	50	**Richard M. Nixon**	Republican	31,785,480	301	43.4
		Hubert H. Humphrey	Democratic	31,275,165	191	42.7
		George C. Wallace	American Independent	9,906,473	46	13.5
1972	50	**Richard M. Nixon**	Republican	47,169,911	520	60.7
		George S. McGovern	Democratic	29,170,383	17	37.5

(Continued)

PRESIDENTIAL ELECTIONS, CONTINUED

Year	Number of states	Candidates	Parties	Popular vote	Electoral vote	Percentage of popular vote
1976	50	**Jimmy Carter**	Democratic	40,827,394	297	50.0
		Gerald R. Ford	Republican	39,145,977	240	47.9
1980	50	**Ronald W. Reagan**	Republican	43,899,248	489	50.8
		Jimmy Carter	Democratic	35,481,435	49	41.0
		John B. Anderson	Independent	5,719,437		6.6
		Ed Clark	Libertarian	920,859		1.0
1984	50	**Ronald W. Reagan**	Republican	54,281,858	525	59.2
		Walter F. Mondale	Democratic	37,457,215	13	40.8
1988	50	**George H. Bush**	Republican	47,917,341	426	54
		Michael Dukakis	Democratic	41,013,030	112	46
1992	50	**William Clinton**	Democratic	44,908,254	370	43.0
		George H. Bush	Republican	39,102,343	168	37.4
		Ross Perot	Independent	19,741,065		18.9
1996	50	**William Clinton**	Democratic	45,628,667	379	49.2
		Robert Dole	Republican	37,869,435	159	40.8
		Ross Perot	Reform	7,874,283		8.5
2000	50	**George W. Bush**	Republican	50,456,062	271	47.9
		Albert Gore	Democratic	50,996,582	266	48.4
		Ralph Nader	Green	2,858,843		2.7
2004	50	**George W. Bush**	Republican	62,040,606	286	51
		John F. Kerry	Democratic	59,028,109	252	48
		Ralph Nader	Green/Independent	411,304		1
2008	50	**Barack Obama**	Democratic	66,882,230	365	53
		John McCain	Republican	58,343,671	173	46
2012	50	**Barack Obama**	Democratic	65,917,258	332	51
		Mitt Romney	Republican	60,932,235	206	47
2016	50	**Donald J. Trump**	Republican	62,984,825	304	46.1
		Hillary Clinton	Democrat	65,853,516	227	48.2
		Gary Johnson	Libertarian	4,489,221		3.3
		Jill Stein	Green	1,457,216		1.1

PRESIDENTS AND VICE PRESIDENTS

Term	President	Vice President	Term	President	Vice President
1789–1793	George Washington	John Adams	1901–1905	William McKinley (d. 1901) Theodore Roosevelt	Theodore Roosevelt
1793–1797	George Washington	John Adams	1905–1909	Theodore Roosevelt	Charles W. Fairbanks
1797–1801	John Adams	Thomas Jefferson	1909–1913	William H. Taft	James S. Sherman (d. 1912)
1801–1805	Thomas Jefferson	Aaron Burr	1913–1917	Woodrow Wilson	Thomas R. Marshall
1805–1809	Thomas Jefferson	George Clinton	1917–1921	Woodrow Wilson	Thomas R. Marshall
1809–1813	James Madison	George Clinton (d. 1812)	1921–1925	Warren G. Harding (d. 1923) Calvin Coolidge	Calvin Coolidge
1813–1817	James Madison	Elbridge Gerry (d. 1814)	1925–1929	Calvin Coolidge	Charles G. Dawes
1817–1821	James Monroe	Daniel D. Tompkins	1929–1933	Herbert Hoover	Charles Curtis
1821–1825	James Monroe	Daniel D. Tompkins	1933–1937	Franklin D. Roosevelt	John N. Garner
1825–1829	John Quincy Adams	John C. Calhoun	1937–1941	Franklin D. Roosevelt	John N. Garner
1829–1833	Andrew Jackson	John C. Calhoun (resigned 1832)	1941–1945	Franklin D. Roosevelt	Henry A. Wallace
1833–1837	Andrew Jackson	Martin Van Buren	1945–1949	Franklin D. Roosevelt (d. 1945) Harry S Truman	Harry S Truman
1837–1841	Martin Van Buren	Richard M. Johnson	1949–1953	Harry S Truman	Alben W. Barkley
1841–1845	William H. Harrison (d. 1841) John Tyler	John Tyler	1953–1957	Dwight D. Eisenhower	Richard M. Nixon
1845–1849	James K. Polk	George M. Dallas	1957–1961	Dwight D. Eisenhower	Richard M. Nixon
1849–1853	Zachary Taylor (d. 1850) Millard Fillmore (d. 1850)	Millard Fillmore	1961–1965	John F. Kennedy (d. 1963) Lyndon B. Johnson	Lyndon B. Johnson
1853–1857	Franklin Pierce	William R. D. King (d. 1853)	1965–1969	Lyndon B. Johnson	Hubert H. Humphrey, Jr. Spiro T.
1857–1861	James Buchanan	John C. Breckinridge	1969–1974	Richard M. Nixon (resigned 1974) Gerald R. Ford	Agnew (resigned 1973)
1861–1865	Abraham Lincoln	Hannibal Hamlin	1981–1985	Ronald Reagan	George H. W. Bush
1865–1869	Abraham Lincoln (d. 1865) Andrew Johnson	Andrew Johnson	1985–1989	Ronald Reagan	George H. W. Bush
1869–1873	1873 Ulysses S. Grant	Schuyler Colfax	1989–1993	George H. W. Bush	J. Danforth Quayle III
1873–1877	Ulysses S. Grant	Henry Wilson (d. 1875)	1993–1997	William Clinton	Albert Gore, Jr.
1877–1881	Rutherford B. Hayes	William A. Wheeler	1997–2001	William Clinton	Albert Gore, Jr.
1881–1885	James A. Garfield (d. 1881) Chester A. Arthur	Chester A. Arthur	2001–2005	George W. Bush	Richard Cheney
1885–1889	Grover Cleveland	Thomas A. Hendricks (d. 1885)	2005–2009	George W. Bush	Richard Cheney
1889–1893	Benjamin Harrison	Levi P. Morton	2009–2013	Barack Obama	Joseph Biden
1893–1897	Grover Cleveland	Adlai E. Stevenson	2013–2017	Barack Obama	Joseph Biden
1897–1901	William McKinley	Garret A. Hobart (d. 1899)	2017–	Donald J. Trump	Michael Pence

JUSTICES OF THE U.S. SUPREME COURT

Name	Term of service	Years of service	Appointed by	Name	Term of service	Years of service	Appointed by
John Jay	1789–1795	5	Washington	Samuel F. Miller	1862–1890	28	Lincoln
John Rutledge	1789–1791	1	Washington	David Davis	1862–1877	14	Lincoln
William Cushing	1789–1810	20	Washington	Stephen J. Field	1863–1897	34	Lincoln
James Wilson	1789–1798	8	Washington	Salmon P. Chase	1864–1873	8	Lincoln
John Blair	1789–1796	6	Washington	William Strong	1870–1880	10	Grant
Robert H. Harrison	1789–1790	—	Washington	Joseph P. Bradley	1870–1892	22	Grant
James Iredell	1790–1799	9	Washington	Ward Hunt	1873–1882	9	Grant
Thomas Johnson	1791–1793	1	Washington	Morrison R. Waite	1874–1888	14	Grant
William Paterson	1793–1806	13	Washington	John M. Harlan	1877–1911	34	Hayes
John Rutledge[1]	1795	—	Washington	William B. Woods	1880–1887	7	Hayes
Samuel Chase	1796–1811	15	Washington	Stanley Matthews	1881–1889	7	Garfield
Oliver Ellsworth	1796–1800	4	Washington	Horace Gray	1882–1902	20	Arthur
Bushrod Washington	1798–1829	31	J. Adams	Samuel Blatchford	1882–1893	11	Arthur
Alfred Moore	1799–1804	4	J. Adams	Lucius Q. C. Lamar	1888–1893	5	Cleveland
John Marshall	1801–1835	34	J. Adams	Melville W. Fuller	1888–1910	21	Cleveland
William Johnson	1804–1834	30	Jefferson	David J. Brewer	1890–1910	20	B. Harrison
H. Brockholst Livingston	1806–1823	16	Jefferson	Henry B. Brown	1890–1906	16	B. Harrison
Thomas Todd	1807–1826	18	Jefferson	George Shiras, Jr.	1892–1903	10	B. Harrison
Joseph Story	1811–1845	33	Madison	Howell E. Jackson	1893–1895	2	B. Harrison
Gabriel Duval	1811–1835	24	Madison	Edward D. White	1894–1910	16	Cleveland
Smith Thompson	1823–1843	20	Monroe	Rufus W. Peckham	1895–1909	14	Cleveland
Robert Trimble	1826–1828	2	J. Q. Adams	Joseph McKenna	1898–1925	26	McKinley
John McLean	1829–1861	32	Jackson	Oliver W. Holmes, Jr.	1902–1932	30	T. Roosevelt
Henry Baldwin	1830–1844	14	Jackson	William R. Day	1903–1922	19	T. Roosevelt
James M. Wayne	1835–1867	32	Jackson	William H. Moody	1906–1910	3	T. Roosevelt
Roger B. Taney	1836–1864	28	Jackson	Horace H. Lurton	1910–1914	4	Taft
Philip P. Barbour	1836–1841	4	Jackson	Charles E. Hughes	1910–1916	5	Taft
John Catron	1837–1865	28	Van Buren	Willis Van Devanter	1911–1937	26	Taft
John McKinley	1837–1852	15	Van Buren	Joseph R. Lamar	1911–1916	5	Taft
Peter V. Daniel	1841–1860	19	Van Buren	Edward D. White	1910–1921	11	Taft
Samuel Nelson	1845–1872	27	Tyler	Mahlon Pitney	1912–1922	10	Taft
Levi Woodbury	1845–1851	5	Polk	James C. McReynolds	1914–1941	26	Wilson
Robert C. Grier	1846–1870	23	Polk	Louis D. Brandeis	1916–1939	22	Wilson
Benjamin R. Curtis	1851–1857	6	Fillmore	John H. Clarke	1916–1922	6	Wilson
John A. Campbell	1853–1861	8	Pierce	William H. Taft	1921–1930	8	Harding
Nathan Clifford	1858–1881	23	Buchanan	George Sutherland	1922–1938	15	Harding
Noah H. Swayne	1862–1881	18	Lincoln	Pierce Butler	1922–1939	16	Harding

JUSTICES OF THE U.S. SUPREME COURT, CONTINUED

Name	Term of service	Years of service	Appointed by	Name	Term of service	Years of service	Appointed by
Edward T. Sanford	1923–1930	7	Harding	Potter Stewart	1958–1981	23	Eisenhower
Harlan F. Stone	1925–1941	16	Coolidge	Byron R. White	1962–1993	31	Kennedy
Charles E. Hughes	1930–1941	11	Hoover	Arthur J. Goldberg	1962–1965	3	Kennedy
Owen J. Roberts	1930–1945	15	Hoover	Abe Fortas	1965–1969	4	Johnson
Benjamin N. Cardozo	1932–1938	6	Hoover	Thurgood Marshall	1967–1994	24	Johnson
Hugo L. Black	1937–1971	34	F. Roosevelt	Warren E. Burger	1969–1986	18	Nixon
Stanley F. Reed	1938–1957	19	F. Roosevelt	Harry A. Blackmun	1970–1994	24	Nixon
Felix Frankfurter	1939–1962	23	F. Roosevelt	Lewis F. Powell, Jr.	1971–1987	15	Nixon
William O. Douglas	1939–1975	36	F. Roosevelt	William H. Rehnquist [2]	1971–2005	34	Nixon
Frank Murphy	1940–1949	9	F. Roosevelt	John P. Stevens III	1975–2010	35	Ford
Harlan F. Stone	1941–1946	5	F. Roosevelt	Sandra Day O'Connor	1981–2006	25	Reagan
James F. Byrnes	1941–1942	1	F. Roosevelt	Antonin Scalia	1986–2016	29	Reagan
Robert H. Jackson	1941–1954	13	F. Roosevelt	Anthony M. Kennedy	1988–2018	30	Reagan
Wiley B. Rutledge	1943–1949	6	F. Roosevelt	David Souter	1990–2009	19	G. H. W. Bush
Harold H. Burton	1945–1958	13	Truman	Clarence Thomas	1991–	—	G. H. W. Bush
Fred M. Vinson	1946–1953	7	Truman	Ruth Bader Ginsburg	1993–	—	Clinton
Tom C. Clark	1949–1967	18	Truman	Stephen G. Breyer	1994–	—	Clinton
Sherman Minton	1949–1956	7	Truman	John G. Roberts, Jr.	2005–	—	G. W. Bush
Earl Warren	1953–1969	16	Eisenhower	Samuel Anthony Alito, Jr.	2006–	—	G. W. Bush
John Marshall Harlan	1955–1971	16	Eisenhower	Sonia Sotomayor	2009–	—	Obama
William J. Brennan, Jr.	1956–1990	34	Eisenhower	Elena Kagan	2010–	—	Obama
Charles E. Whittaker	1957–1962	5	Eisenhower	Neil M. Gorsuch	2017–	—	Trump

[1] Acting chief justice; Senate refused to confirm appointment.
[2] Chief justice from 1986 on (Reagan administration).

Glossary

40 acres and a mule Largely unfulfilled hope of many former slaves that they would receive free land from the confiscated property of ex-Confederates.

abolitionism Movement begun in the North about 1830 to abolish slavery immediately and without compensation to owners.

Affordable Health Care for America Act Designed to extend healthcare to some 30 million people, expand the Medicaid system, create mechanisms for increasing competition among insurance companies, prohibit the use of pre-existing health conditions do deny coverage, and provide every American health insurance.

Agricultural Adjustment Administration (AAA) 1933 attempt to promote economic recovery by reducing supply of crops, dairy, and meat produced by American farmers.

Aguinaldo, Emilio Anti-colonial leader who fought for independence of the Philippines first from Spain and then from the United States.

Alamo Battle between Texas revolutionaries and the Mexican army at the San Antonio mission called the Alamo on March 6, 1836, in which all 187 Texans were killed.

Albany Congress An inter-colonial congress that met in Albany, New York, in June 1754. The delegates urged the Crown to assume direct control of Indian relations beyond the settled boundaries of the colonies, and they drafted a plan of confederation for the continental colonies. No colony ratified it, nor did the Crown or Parliament accept it.

Alien and Sedition Acts Four laws passed by a Federalist-controlled Congress and signed by President John Adams in 1798 during military hostilities with France. The first three laws, directed at immigrants, extended the naturalization period to become citizens from 5 to 14 years and empowered the president to detain enemy aliens during wartime and to deport those he deemed dangerous to the United States. The fourth law—the Sedition Act—set jail terms and fines for persons who advocated disobedience to federal law or publicly criticized the government.

American Colonization Society Established by elite gentlemen of the middle and upper-south states in 1816, this organization encouraged voluntary emancipation of slaves, to be followed by their emigration to the West African colony of Liberia.

American System Program proposed by Henry Clay and others to foster national economic growth and interdependence among the geographical sections. It included a protective tariff, a national bank, and internal improvements.

American Temperance Society Society established in 1826 by northeastern evangelicals that headed the crusade for alcohol temperance.

Americans with Disabilities Act (ADA) Measure that made it illegal to discriminate against people with disabilities in employment, transportation, and other key areas of public life. The law, revised in 2008, assigned enforcement responsibilities to several federal agencies.

amnesty General pardon granted to a large group of people.

Anasazi An advanced pre-Columbian cliff-dwelling culture that flourished for two centuries in what are now the states of Arizona, New Mexico, Utah, and Colorado before abandoning these sites in the late 13th century A.D.

Anderson, Marian Black opera singer who broke a color barrier in 1939 when she sang to an interracial audience of 75,000 from the steps of the Lincoln Memorial.

anglicization Process during the 18th century in which the American colonies reverted to British cultural forms, including in politics, law, fashion, religion, and consumption patterns.

anxious bench Bench at or near the front of a religious revival meeting where the most likely converts were seated.

Article X of the Covenant Addendum to the Treaty of Versailles that empowered the League of Nations to undertake military actions against aggressor nations.

(the) Association Groups created by the First Continental Congress in local committees to enforce its trade sanctions against Britain. The creation of these groups was an important sign that Congress was beginning to act as a central government.

associationalism Herbert Hoover's approach to managing the economy. Firms and organizations in each economic sector would be asked to cooperate with each other in the pursuit of efficiency, profit, and the public good.

Atlantic slave trade A European commerce that led to the enslavement of millions of people who were shipped from their African homelands to European colonies in the Americas.

Auburn system Prison system designed to reform criminals and reduce expenses through the sale of items produced in workshops. Prisoners slept in solitary cells, marched in military formation to meals and workshops, and were forbidden to speak to one another at any time.

Australian ballot (secret ballot) Practice that required citizens to vote in private rather than in public and required the government (rather than political parties) to supervise the voting process.

Aztecs The last pre-Columbian high culture in the Valley of Mexico. It was conquered by the Spaniards in 1519–1521.

baby boom generation People born between 1946 and 1964; more than 75 million babies were born in the U.S. during this time.

balance of trade The relationship between imports and exports. The difference between exports and imports is the balance between the two. A healthy nation should export more than it imports. This is known as a favorable balance of trade.

banknotes Paper money, issued by banks, that circulated as currency.

Barack Hussein Obama 44th President of the United States and the first president of African descent; voted into office in 2008 with a campaign for "hope" and "change."

Battle of Little Big Horn A battle in eastern Montana Territory on the bluffs above Little Big Horn River on June 25, 1876.

Bay of Pigs invasion Site of an ill-fated 1961 invasion of Cuba by a U.S.-trained force that attempted to overthrow the government of Fidel Castro.

Berlin Airlift American and British aircraft that provided all of the items needed in West Berlin during the Berlin Blockade.

Berlin Blockade Soviet Union cut off all highways, railroads, and water routes into West Berlin, Germany in attempt to weaken the nation.

Bill of Rights First ten amendments to the Constitution, which protect the rights of individuals from abuses by the federal government.

Black Codes Laws passed by southern states that restricted the rights and liberties of former slaves.

Black Power Mid-1960s movement that called for modifying integrationist goals in favor of gaining political and economic power for separate black-directed institutions and emphasized pride in AfricanAmerican heritage.

Black Republicans Label coined by the Democratic Party to attack the Republican Party as believers in racial equality. The Democrats used this fear to convince many whites to remain loyal to them.

blockade runner A ship designed to run through a blockade.

blockade The closing of a country's harbors by enemy ships to prevent trade and commerce, especially to prevent traffic in military supplies.

blood sports Sporting activities emphasizing bloodiness that were favored by working-class men of the cities. The most popular in the early 19th century were cockfighting, ratting, dogfights, and various types of violence between animals.

Bonus Army Army veterans who marched on Washington, D.C., in 1932 to lobby for economic relief but who were rebuffed by Hoover.

border ruffians Term used to describe proslavery Missourians who streamed into Kansas in 1854, determined to vote as many times as necessary to install a proslavery government there.

Boston Brahmins Protestant families in Boston, many of whom descended from New England's first English settlers, who constituted the city's upper class by the early 19th century.

Boston Massacre The colonial term for the confrontation between colonial protestors and British soldiers in front of the customs house on March 5, 1770. Five colonists were killed and six wounded.

Boston Tea Party In December 1773, Boston's Sons of Liberty threw 342 chests of East India Company tea into Boston harbor rather than allow them to be landed and pay the hated tea duty.

bounty jumpers Men who enlisted in the Union army to collect the bounties offered by some districts to fill military quotas; these men would enlist and then desert as soon as they got their money.

Boxers Chinese nationalist organization that instigated an uprising in 1900 to rid China of all foreign influence.

Brandt, Joseph Mohawk Indian who served as one of Britain's most effective commanders of loyalist and Indian forces in the American Revolutionary War. After the war, he led most of the Six Nations to Canada for resettlement.

Brown cases Refers to several Supreme Court cases that challenged the nation's political, social and cultural institutions by outlawing racial segregation in public schools and public facilities.

Brown, John Prominent abolitionist who fought for the antislavery cause in Kansas (1856) and led a raid to seize the Harpers Ferry arsenal in 1859.

Bryan, William Jennings A two-term Democratic congressman from Nebraska who won the party's presidential nomination in 1896 after electrifying delegates with his "Cross of Gold" speech. Bryan was twice more nominated for president (1900 and 1908); he lost all three times.

Burr, Aaron Vice President under Thomas Jefferson who killed Alexander Hamilton in a duel and eventually hatched schemes to detach parts of the west from the United States.

Bush Doctrine Denounced terrorist networks and proclaimed that the U.S. had the right to wage war against any force that endangered American as expressed in the National Security Strategy of 2002.

Bush v. Gore Court case over the 2000 election between George W. Bush and Al Gore; the courts ceased the recounting of ballots in Florida and ruled George W. Bush the 43rd President of the United States.

Bush, George H. W. Republican President (1989–1993) who directed an international coalition against Iraq in the Persian Gulf War.

Bush, George W. Republican President (2001–2009) whose two terms were defined by the September 11, 2001, attacks on the World Trade Center and the Pentagon, the resulting wars in Afghanistan and Iraq, and the financial crash of 2008. Bush did achieve tax cuts, educational reform, and medicare expansion, but much of his 'compassionate conservatism' program failed to take hold.

bushwhackers Confederate guerrilla raiders especially active in Missouri. Jayhawkers were the Union version of the same type of people. Both groups did a tremendous amount of damage with raids, arson, ambush, and murder.

Cahokia The largest city created by Mississippian mound builders. Located in Illinois near modern St. Louis, it thrived from A.D. 900 to 1250 and then declined.

Californios Spanish-speaking people whose families had resided in California for generations.

Camp David Peace Talks of 1978 President Carter negotiated a peace treaty with Menachem Begin and Anwar Sadat, leaders of Israel and Egypt.

camp meeting Outdoor revival often lasting for days; a principal means of spreading evangelical Christianity in the United States.

Capone, Al Chicago mobster who made a fortune from gambling, prostitution, and bootleg liquor during Prohibition.

caravel A new type of oceangoing vessel that could sail closer to a head wind than any other sailing ship and make speeds of from three to twelve knots per hour.

Carnegie, Andrew A Scottish immigrant who became the most efficient entrepreneur in the U.S. steel industry and earned a great fortune.

carpetbaggers Northerners who settled in the South during Reconstruction.

Carter, James Earl (Jimmy) Democratic president (1977–1981) whose single term in office was marked by inflation, fuel shortages, and a hostage crisis.

changing system Elaborate system of neighborhood debts and bartering used primarily in the South and West where little cash money was available.

Cheney, Richard (Dick) Conservative republican who served as vice president to George W. Bush.

Chicanismo Populistic pride in the Mexican American heritage that emerged in the late 1960s. Chicano, once a term of derision, became a rallying cry among activists.

Chinese Exclusion Act Suspended Chinese immigration for 10 years with the exception of a few job categories.

Chisholm Trail Trail used to get longhorn cattle from Texas to Abilene, Kansas where they were loaded into railcars and shipped to Kansas City or Chicago.

CIO The Committee (and then Congress) for Industrial Organization, founded in 1935 to organize the unskilled and semiskilled workers ignored by the AFL. The CIO reinvigorated the labor movement.

circuit court Court that meets at different places within a district.

circuit-riding preachers Methodist ministers who traveled from church to church, usually in rural areas.

City Beautiful movement A movement of urban architectural renovation.

Civil Rights Act of 1957 First civilrights act since Reconstruction, aimed at securing voting rights for African Americans in the South.

Civil Rights Act of 1964 A historic act that denied federal funding to segregated schools and barred discrimination by race and sex in employment, public accommodations, and labor unions.

Civil Rights Act of 1968 Measure that banned racial discrimination in housing and made interference with a person's civil rights a federal crime. It also stipulated that crossing state lines to incite a riot was a federal crime.

Civilized Tribes 60,000 Cherokees, Creeks, Choctaws, Chickasaws, and Seminoles who remained on their ancestral lands in the Old Southwest and were considered sovereign peoples.

Clinton, William Jefferson (Bill) Democratic president (1993–2001) whose two-term presidency witnessed rapid economic growth but also a sexual scandal that fueled an impeachment effort, which he survived.

Clovis tip A superior spear point developed before 9000 B.C. It was in use nearly everywhere in North and South America and produced such an improvement in hunting ability that it contributed to the extinction of most large mammals.

Coercive Acts Four statutes passed by Parliament in response to the Boston Tea Party, including one that closed the port of Boston until the tea was paid for, and another that overturned the Massachusetts Charter of 1691. The colonists called them the Intolerable Acts and included the Quebec Act under that label.

cold war The political, military, cultural, and economic rivalry between the United States and the Soviet Union that developed after the Second World War and lasted until the disintegration of the Soviet State after 1989.

Collier, John Activist head of the Bureau of Indian Affairs who improved U.S. policy toward Native Americans and guided the landmark Indian Reorganization Act through Congress.

colonial economy Economy based on the export of agricultural products and the import of manufactured goods; sometimes used to describe the dependence of the South on the North.

Columbian Exchange A term coined by Alfred W. Crosby to describe the exchange of plants, animals, diseases, culture, and people between the American and European continents following the Spanish discovery of the New World.

Committee on Public Information (CPI) U.S. Government agency established in 1917 to arouse support for the war and, later, to generate suspicion of war dissenters.

committees of correspondence Bodies formed on both the local and colonial levels that played an important role in exchanging ideas and information. They spread primarily anti-British material and were an important step in the first tentative unity of people in different colonies.

common schools Tax-supported public schools built by state and local governments.

Communist Party Radical group that wanted America to follow the Soviet Union's path to socialism. The CP organized some of the country's poorest workers into unions and pushed the New Deal leftward, but was never popular enough to bid for power itself.

Community Reinvestment Act of 1977 Forced banks to finance home buying in low-income neighborhoods to stimulate economic activity.

commutation fee $300 fee that could be paid by a man drafted into the Union army to exempt him from the current draft call.

compensated emancipation Idea that the federal government would offer compensation or money to states that voluntarily abolished slavery.

competence Understood in the early republic as the ability to live up to neighborhood economic standards while protecting the long-term independence of the household.

Compromise of 1850 Series of laws enacted in 1850 intended to settle all outstanding slavery issues.

congressional caucus In the early republic, the group of congressmen who traditionally chose the party's presidential candidates. By the 1820s, the American public distrusted the caucus as undemocratic because only one party contested for power. The caucus was replaced by the national nominating convention.

Connecticut Compromise Deal forged at the Constitutional Convention of 1787 by delegates from Connecticut, led by Roger Sherman, between supporters of the Virginia Plan and the New Jersey Plan. Under the compromise, one house of Congress adopted proportional representation (House of Representatives), while the other kept state equality (Senate).

conquistadores The Spanish word for conquerors.

Conscience Whigs A group of anti-slavery members of the Whig Party.

conservationist Scientific environmentalists who were concerned with making sure the nation's resources were not being wasted.

consumer society A society in which a large percentage of people buy goods and value material possessions. America first became a consumer society in the early 18th century, when British goods, including cloth, ceramics, glassware, paper, and cutlery, flooded into the colonies.

containment Label used to describe the global anticommunist nationalsecurity policies adopted by the United States to stop the expansion of communism during the late 1940s.

contraband of war Term used to describe slaves who came within the Union lines.

Contract with America 1994 Republican campaign document, largely devised by Representative Newt Gingrich, that called for overhauling the welfare system, enacting new anti-crime legislation, making it more difficult to raise federal taxes, and other measures attractive to conservative voters.

Copperheads Term used by some Republicans to describe Peace Democrats to imply that they were traitors to the Union.

Corrupt Bargain Following the election of 1824, Andrew Jackson and his supporters alleged that, in a "corrupt bargain," Henry Clay sold his support during the House vote in the disputed election of 1824 of John Quincy Adams in exchange for appointment as Secretary of State.

Cortés, Hernán Spanish conquistador who in 1519 led an expedition that defeated the Aztec empire and established Spanish imperial presence in mainland Mexico.

cosmopolitanism Ideal of American nationality developed by Randolph Bourne that encouraged creating new cultural forms from the combinations of peoples and cultures.

Cotton Belt Region stretching from South Carolina to eastern Texas and south into Florida that specialized in cotton production by the mid-19th century.

cotton gin Machine, or "engine," that used metal pins fitted into rollers to comb the seeds from short-staple cotton. Invented by Eli Whitney in 1793, it opened the way for the mass production of cotton and the expansion of slavery in the Deep South.

Coughlin, Father Charles The "radio priest" from the Midwest who alleged that the New Deal was being run by bankers. His growing antiSemitism discredited him by 1939.

counterculture Antiestablishment movement that symbolized the youthful social upheaval of the 1960s. Ridiculing traditional attitudes toward such matters as clothing, hair styles, and sexuality, the countercultureurged a more open and less regimented approach to daily life.

coureurs de bois In Canada and the northern US, a woodsman or trader of French origin.

court-packing 1937 attempt by Roosevelt to appoint one new Supreme Court justice for every sitting justice over the age of 70 and who had sat for at least 10 years. Roosevelt's purpose was to prevent conservative justices from dismantling the New Deal, but the plan died in Congress and inflamed opponents of the New Deal.

Covenant Chain of Peace An agreement negotiated by Governor Edmund Andros in 1677 that linked the colony of New York to the Iroquois Five Nations and was later expanded to include other colonies and Indian peoples.

coverture A common-law doctrine under which the legal personality of the husband covered the wife, and he made all legally binding decisions.

Credit Mobilier Affair Construction company for the Union Pacific Railroad that gave shares of stock to some congressmen in return for favors.

crisis conversion Understood in evangelical churches as a personal transformation that resulted from directly experiencing the Holy Spirit.

Cuban Missile Crisis Serious Cold War confrontation between the United States and the Soviet Union over the installation of Soviet missiles in Cuba.

Dartmouth College v. Woodward 1816 Supreme Court case that showcased one of many important decisions made by John Marshall to protect the sanctity of contracts and corporate charters against state legislatures.

Davis, Jefferson Mississippi planter and prominent leader of the Southern Democrats in the 1850s, who later served as president of the Confederacy.

Dawes Plan 1924 U.S.-backed agreement to reduce German reparation payments by more than half. The plan also called on banks to invest $200 million in the German economy.

Dawes Severalty Act 1887 legislation that called for the dissolution of Indian tribes as legal entities, offered Indians citizenship, and allotted each head of family 160 acres of farmland or 320 acres of grazing land.

Debs, Eugene Victor Leader of the Socialist Party who received almost a million votes in the election of 1912.

Denmark Vesey Leader of a slave conspiracy in and around Charleston, South Carolina, in 1822.

deregulation To reduce or remove government rules or policies; Reagan's deregulation agenda focused on the financial system.

détente An easing of tensions, particularly between the United States and the Soviet Union.

Dewey, John Philosopher who believed that American technological and industrial power could be made to serve the people and democracy.

disfranchisement Process of barring groups of adult citizens from voting.

Dix, Dorothea Boston reformer who traveled throughout the country campaigning for humane, state-supported asylums for the insane.

dollar diplomacy Diplomatic strategy formulated under President Taft that focused on expanding American investments abroad, especially in Latin America and East Asia.

Dolores Huerta and Cesar Chavez Political activists, leaders of the United Farm Workers of America, and the most influential Mexican American leaders during the 1970s.

domestic fiction Sentimental literature that centered on household and domestic themes that emphasized the toil and travails of women and children who overcame adversity through religious faith and strength of character.

domino theory Idea that if a communist movement toppled one country that surrounding nations would also fall, as if a row of dominoes, to a communist assault. Supporters of the need to preserve a non-communist government in South Vietnam often cited this cold war theory as justification for their policy choices.

Double V campaign An effort by African-American leaders to use the Second World War as the occasion for campaigns against racial discrimination at home as well as against fascism overseas.

dower rights The right of a widow to a portion of her deceased husband's estate (usually one-third of the value of the estate). It was passed to their children upon her death.

downsizing Process of cutting back in labor pools and management staffs by businesses usually due to declining profits.

dowry The cash or goods a woman received from her father when she married.

Du Bois, W. E. B. Leader of the NAACP, the editor of its newspaper, The Crisis, and an outspoken critic of Booker T. Washington and his accomodationist approach to race relations.

Dunmore's Proclamation Edict released in November 1775 by Lord Dunmore, governor of Virginia, offering freedom to slaves who left their American masters and joined British military forces. The offer, while popular with slaves, helped to push southern planters toward supporting American independence.

Earned Income Tax Credit (EITC) Assisted lower and moderate income households with children.

East Asian Co-Prosperity Sphere Proposition from Japan to China that would liberate Asian nations from Western colonialism and create a self-sufficient economic zone under Japanese leadership.

Edison, Thomas Alva Inventor of the 1800s who developed an array of devices including the phonograph, incandescent light bulb, and movie camera.

Eisenhower Doctrine Policy that stated that the United States would use armed force to respond to imminent or actual communist aggression in the Middle East.

Electoral College The group that elects the president. Each state receives as many electors as it has congressmen and senators combined and can decide how to choose its electors. Every elector votes for two candidates, one of whom has to be from another state.

Embargo Act Law passed in late 1807 and signed by President Thomas Jefferson that prohibited the movement of merchant ships and goods in and out of American ports. Enacted to punish Britain for depredations on the high seas, the act instead crippled American commerce and was revoked in 1809.

Employment Act of 1946 Called for maximum employment and declared private enterprises responsible for economic decision making.

encomienda A system of labor introduced into the Western Hemisphere by the Spanish.

It permitted the holder, or encomendero, to claim labor from Indians in a district for a stated period of time.

energy crisis OPEC raised the price of crude oil and precipitated acute worldwide shortages in 1978; gasoline became expensive and scarce.

enfranchise To grant the right to vote.

Enlightenment The new learning in science and philosophy that took hold, at least in England, between 1660 and the American Revolution. Nearly all of its spokesmen were religious moderates who were more interested in science than religious doctrine and who favored broad religious toleration.

entail A legal device that required a landowner to keep his estate intact and pass it on to his heir.

enumerated commodities A group of colonial products that had to be shipped from the colony of origin to England or another English colony. The most important commodities were sugar and tobacco.

Equal Rights Amendment (ERA) Proposed amendment to the Constitution providing that equal rights could not be abridged on account of sex. It won congressional approval in 1972 but failed to gain ratification by the states.

Erie Canal Canal linking the Hudson River at Albany with the Great Lakes at Buffalo that helped commercialize the farms of the Great Lakes watershed and channel that commerce into New York City.

Espionage, Sabotage, and Sedition Acts Laws passed in 1917 and 1918 that gave the federal government sweeping powers to silence and even imprison dissenters.

ESPN Cable network devoted entirely to sports.

evangelical A style of Christian ministry that includes much zeal and enthusiasm. Evangelical ministers emphasized personal conversion and faith rather than religious ritual.

excise tax Internal tax on goods or services.

Exodusters Name given to the 20,000 African Americans who moved to Kansas believing rumors of free land for settlers and supplies from the government in 1879.

exurbs Housing developments that expanded further away from larger cities into farmlands and small towns.

factories A term used to describe small posts established for the early slave trade along the coast of Africa or on small offshore islands.

Fair Deal Proposed in 1949 by President Truman to extend New Deal programs, enact legislation dealing with civil rights, national health care, and federal aid for education, provide funds for public housing, and support farm prices.

fall line A geographical landmark defined by the first waterfalls encountered when going upriver from the sea. These waterfalls prevented oceangoing ships from sailing further inland and thus made the fall line a significant early barrier. Land between the falls and the ocean was called the tidewater. Land above the falls but below the mountains was called the piedmont.

Family Assistance Plan (FAP) Proposed by Nixon in 1969 to replace the existing welfare policy; it called to provide every low-income family an annual income of $1,600.

Federal Reserve Act Act that brought private banks and public authority together to regulate and strengthen the nation's financial system.

Federalists Supporters of the Constitution during the ratification process. Anti-Federalists resisted ratification.

feminism Desire for complete equality between men and women.

feudal revival The reliance on old feudal charters for all of the profits that could be extracted from them. It took hold in several colonies in the mid-18th century and caused serious problems between many landowners and tenants.

fiat money Paper money backed only by the promise of the government to accept it in payment of taxes. It originated in Massachusetts after a military emergency in 1690.

filibuster Congressional delaying tactic involving lengthy speeches that prevent legislation from being enacted.

filibustering A term used to describe several groups that invaded or attempted to invade various Latin American areas to attempt to add them to the slaveholding regions of the United States. The word originated from filibustero, meaning a freebooter or pirate.

First Continental Congress This intercolonial body met in Philadelphia in September and October 1774 to organize resistance against the Coercive Acts by defining American rights, petitioning the king, and appealing to the British and American people. It created the Association, local committees in each community to enforce nonimportation.

flappers Rebellious middle-class young women who signaled their desire for independence and equality through style and personality rather than through politics.

Ford, Gerald R. A GOP member of the House of Representatives, Gerald Ford became the first person to be appointed Vice President of the United States. When Richard Nixon resigned in 1974, Ford became President.

Fort Sumter Fort in Charleston's harbor occupied by United States troops after the secession of South Carolina.

Fourteen Points Plan laid out by Woodrow Wilson in January 1918 to give concrete form to his dream of a "peace without victory" and a new world order.

free silver Idea that the government would purchase all silver offered for sale and coin it into silver dollars at the preferred ratio between silver and gold of 16 to 1.

free-labor ideology Belief that all work in a free society is honorable and that manual labor is degraded when it is equated with slavery or bondage.

Free-Soilers A term used to describe people who opposed the expansion of slavery into the territories. It came from the name of a small political party in the election of 1848.

Freedmen's Bureau Federal agency created in 1865 to supervise newly freed people. It oversaw relations between whites and blacks in the South, issued food rations, and supervised labor contracts.

freedom riders Members of interracial groups who traveled the South on buses to test a series of federal court decisions declaring segregation on buses and in waiting rooms to be unconstitutional.

Freedom Summer Summer of 1964 when nearly a thousand white volunteers went to Mississippi to aid in voter registration and other civilrights projects.

Freemasons A religion of manliness, complete with mysterious rituals that extolled sobriety, industry, brotherhood, benevolence, and citizenship.

frontier An area on the advancing edge of American civilization.

fugitive slaves Runaway slaves who escaped to a free state.

Fulton, Robert Post-2005 Supreme Court, headed by Chief Justice John Roberts, in which conservatives used their five-justice majority to issue a number of rulings that tracked the theories of legal-constitutional conservatives.

fundamentalists Religious groups that preached the necessity of fidelity to a strict moral code, individual commitment to Christ, and faith in the literal truth of the Bible.

funded national debt The state agreed to pay the interest due to its creditors before all other obligations.

Gabriel's Rebellion Carefully planned but unsuccessful rebellion of slaves in Richmond, Virginia, and the surrounding area in 1800.

gag rule Procedure in which Congress voted at each session from 1836 to 1844 to table antislavery petitions without reading them in order avoid any debate.

Gaither Report Report that encouraged President Eisenhower to increase national security and government spending in 1957.

gang system A system where planters organized their field slaves into gangs, supervised them closely, and kept them working in the fields all day. This type of labor was used on tobacco plantations.

Garrison, William Lloyd Abolitionist and publisher of the first issue of the Liberator.

Garvey, Marcus Jamaican-born black nationalist who attracted millions of African Americans in the early

Gates, Henry Lewis, Jr. Activist for the academics of African American's in the 1990s.

General William Westmoreland Recommended the "search and destroy" method in North Vietnam to incapacitate NLF and North Vietnamese forces and to allow Saigon government time to develop.

Geneva Peace Accords of 1954 Divided French Indochina into three new nations: Laos, Cambodia, and Vietnam; Vietnam was also split into two jurisdiction at the 17th parallel until an election could unify the country.

gentlemen's agreement (1907) Agreement by which the Japanese government promised to halt the immigration of its adult male laborers to the United States in return for President Theodore Roosevelt's pledge to end the discriminatory treatment of Japanese immigrant children in California's public schools.

Ghost Dance Indian ritual involving days of worship expressed in part through dance.

GI Bill Officially called the Serviceman's Readjustment Act of 1944. It provided veterans with college and job-training assistance, preferential treatment in hiring, and subsidized home loans, and was later extended to Korean War veterans in 1952.

globalization Spread of businesses throughout world.

Goldwater, Barry Republican candidate defeated by Lyndon B. Johnson in the 1964 presidential election.

Gompers, Samuel F. America's most famous trade unionist while serving as president of the AFL (1896–1924). He achieved his greatest success in organizing skilled workers.

Good Neighbor Policy Roosevelt's foreign policy initiative that formally renounced the right of the United States to intervene in Latin American affairs, leading to improved relations between the United States and Latin American countries.

Gorbachev, Mikhail Reform-minded Soviet leader whose policies helped to set the stage for the end of the Cold War in 1989-90 and the demise of the Soviet Union itself.

gradual emancipation Process in the northern states in the American revolutionary era whereby slaves gained freedom. Rather than free slaves immediately, most states set up systems in which slaves became free gradually over a number of years.

Grant, Ulysses S. General-in-chief of Union armies who led those armies to victory in the Civil War.

Great American Desert The treeless area in the plains that most Americans considered unsuitable for settlement. It generally was passed over by settlers going to the Pacific Coast areas.

Great Railroad Strike of 1877 Strike that occurred during a time of depression that caused employers to cut wages and lay off workers.

Great Recession A severe downturn in the global economy that began with the financial crash of 2008. The ensuing recovery was weak, marked by low wages and slow job creation. Wealth disparities between the rich and the poor widened, sharpening political discontent.

Great Society Series of domestic initiatives announced in 1964 by President Lyndon Johnson to "end poverty and racial injustice." They included the Voting Rights Act of 1965; the establishment of the Department of Housing and Urban Development, Head Start, and jobtraining programs; Medicare and Medicaid expansion; and various community action programs.

Great White Fleet Naval ships sent on a 45,000-mile world tour by

President Roosevelt (1907–1909) to showcase American military power.

Greene, Nathanael Mohawk Indian who served as one of Britain's most effective commanders of loyalist and Indian forces in the American Revolutionary War. After the war, he led most of the Six Nations to Canada for resettlement.

Greenwich Village Community of radical artists and writers in lower Manhattan that provided a supportive environment for various kinds of radical ideals.

Grimke, Sarah Along with her sister Angelina, this elite South Carolina woman moved north and campaigned against slavery and for temperance and women's rights.

Gulf of Tonkin Resolution Measure passed by Congress in August 1964 that provided authorization for an air war against North Vietnam after U.S. destroyers were allegedly attacked by North Vietnamese torpedoes. Johnson invoked it as authority for expanding the Vietnam War.

Gullah A language spoken by newly imported African slaves. Originally, it was a simple second language for everyone who spoke it, but it gradually evolved into modern black English.

habeas corpus Right of an individual to obtain a legal document as protection against illegal imprisonment.

hacienda A large landed estate established by wealthy Spanish colonists in the Americas for farming, ranching, manufacturing, and mining. In many parts of South America, the hacienda system survived the end of the colonial period in the early 19th century.

Hale, Sarah Josepha Editor of Godey's Ladies Book and an important arbiter of domesticity and taste for middleclass housewives.

Harlem Renaissance 1920s African-American literary and artistic awakening that sought to create works rooted in black culture instead of imitating white styles.

Harpers Ferry Site of John Brown's 1859 raid on a U.S. armory and arsenal for the manufacture and storage of military rifles.

Haymarket Bombing at an Anarchist protest meeting at Haymarket Square in Chicago on May 4 resulting in 10 deaths, 6 of them policemen.

headright A colonist received 50 acres of land for every person whose passage to America he financed, including himself. This system was introduced in Virginia.

Hessians A term used by Americans to describe the 17,000 mercenary troops hired by Britain from various German states, especially Hesse.

High Federalists A term used to describe Alexander Hamilton and some of his less-moderate supporters. They wanted the naval war with France to continue and also wanted to severely limit the rights of an opposition party.

Highway Act of 1956 Act that appropriated $25 billion for the construction of more than 40,000 miles of interstate highways over a 10-year period.

Hiroshima Japanese city destroyed by an atomic bomb on August 6, 1945.

Hitler, Adolf German fascist dictator whose aggressive policies touched off the Second World War.

Homestead (Strike) Carnegie Steel Company closed its Homestead plant planning to reopen with nonunion workers; the union went on strike refusing to leave the building, which led to a gun battle and several deaths.

Homestead Act Legislation that took effect on January 1, 1863 to provide free land for western settlers.

House of Burgesses The assembly of early Virginia that settlers were allowed to elect. Members met with the governor and his council and enacted local laws. It first met in 1619.

household deficit Difference between what U.S. households earned and what they spent.

housing bubble Refers to people who became home owners but lacked the incomes to handle a conventional mortgage.

Huguenots French Protestants who followed the beliefs of John Calvin.

Hull House First American settlement house established in Chicago in 1889 by Jane Addams and Ellen Gates Starr.

Human Genome Project Program launched in 1985 to map all genetic material in the 24 human chromosomes. It sparked ongoing debate over the potential consequences of genetic research and manipulation.

human rights policy The effort by President Jimmy Carter (1977-81) to craft a foreign policy, intended to advance both American national security and global progress, that emphasized basic political, social, and economic rights.

Hutchinson, Anne A religious radical who attracted a large following in Massachusetts, especially in Boston. She warned that nearly all of the ministers were preaching a covenant of works instead of the covenant of grace. Convicted of the Antinomian heresy after claiming that she received direct messages from God, she and her most loyal followers were banished to Rhode Island in 1638.

Immigration and Nationality Act of 1965 Law eliminating the nationalorigins quota system for immigration and substituting preferences for people with certain skills or with relatives in the United States.

Immigration and Nationality Act of 1965 Law eliminating the nationalorigins quota system for immigration and substituting preferences for people with certain skills or with relatives in the United States.

Immigration Reform and Control Act of 1986 (Simpson-Mazzoli Act) Created stricter penalties for employing undocumented workers and provided residency for people that had lived in the U.S. since 1982.

impeachment Act of charging a public official with misconduct in office.

impeachment Act of charging a public official with misconduct in office.

imperialists Those who wanted to expand their nation's world power through military prowess, economic strength, and control of foreign territory (often organized into colonies).

impressment Removal of sailors from American ships by British naval officers.

Incas The last and most extensive pre-Columbian empire in the Andes and along the Pacific coast of South America.

Independent Treasury Bill 1840 bill that permitted the federal government to hold and dispense money without depositing it in banks and required that customs and land purchases be paid in gold and silver coins or notes from specie-paying banks.

Indian Removal Act (1830) Legislation that offered the native peoples of the lower South the option of removal to federal lands west of the Mississippi. Those who did not take the offer were removed by force in 1838.

information revolution Acceleration of the speed and availability of information resulting from use of computer and satellite systems.

initiative Reform that gave voters the right to propose and pass a law independently of their state legislature.

intendant The officer who administered the system of justice in New France.

interchangeable parts Industrial technique using machine tools to cut and shape a large number of similar parts that can be fitted together with other parts to make an entire item such as a gun.

internal improvements 19th-century term for transportation facilities such as roads, canals, and railroads.

internment U.S. policy, justified on the basis of national security, of detaining about 130,000 people, including citizens, of Japanese descent and far fewer of German and Italian ancestry in special "internment camps" during the Second World War.

interstate slave trade The trade for slaves within the domestic United States, which expanded dramatically after the end of the international slave trade in 1808. By 1860, around 1 million slaves were moved westward from old slaveholding regions, particularly the Chesapeake.

Iran-contra affair Reagan administration scandal in which the U.S. secretly sold arms to Iran, a country implicated in holding American hostages, and diverted the money to finance the attempt by the contras to overthrow the Sandinista government of Nicaragua. Both transactions violated acts of Congress, which had prohibited funding the contra and selling weapons to Iran.

Iranian Revolution of January 1979 Islamic fundamentalists overthrew Iranian dictator Shah Reza Pahlavi; the rebellion led to 66 Americans taken hostage when Carter allowed the shah into the U.S. for medical assistance.

Iroquois League A confederation of five Indian nations centered around the Mohawk Valley who were very active in the fur trade. They first worked with the Dutch and then the English. They were especially successful in using adoption as a means of remaining strong.

irreconcilables Group of 14 midwestern and western senators who opposed the Treaty of Versailles.

isolationists Name given to people who were not in favor of war during World War II.

itinerant preachers Ministers who lacked their own parishes and who traveled from place to place.

Jackson, Thomas J. ("Stonewall") A native of Virginia, he emerged as one of the Confederacy's best generals in 1861–1862.

Jim Crow laws Laws passed by southern states mandating racial segregation in public facilities of all kinds.

Johnson-Reed Immigration Restriction Act of 1924 Limited immigration to the United States to 165,000 per year, shrank immigration from southern and eastern Europe to insignificance, and banned immigration from East and South Asia.

joint-stock company A form of business organization that resembled a modern corporation. Individuals invested in the company through the purchase of shares. One major difference between then and today was that each stockholder had one vote regardless of how many shares he owned. The first permanent English colonies in North America were established by joint-stock companies.

journeyman Wage-earning craftsman who completed an apprenticeship but had not yet become a master, or owner of his own business.

judicial review Supreme Court's power to rule on the constitutionality of congressional acts.

Kansas-Nebraska Act Law enacted in 1854 to organize the new territories of Kansas and Nebraska that effectively repealed the provision of the 1820 Missouri Compromise by leaving the question of slavery to the territories' settlers.

King, Martin Luther, Jr. African American clergyman who advocated nonviolent social change and shaped the civil-rights movement of the 1950s and 1960s.

Knights of Labor Secret fraternal organization founded in 1869 in Philadelphia.

Know-Nothings Adherents of nativist organizations and of the American party who wanted to restrict the political rights of immigrants.

Korean War Conflict lasting from 1950 to 1953 between communist North Korea, aided by China, and South Korea, aided by United Nations forces consisting primarily of U.S. troops.

Ku Klux Klan White terrorist organization in the South originally founded as a fraternal society in 1866.

Reborn in 1915, it achieved popularity in the 1920s through its calls for AngloSaxon purity, Protestant supremacy, and the subordination of blacks, Catholics, and Jews.

League of Women Voters (LWV) Successor to the National American Woman Suffrage Association, it promoted women's role in politics and dedicated itself to educating voters.

Lee, Robert E. U.S. army officer until his resignation to join the Confederacy as general-in-chief.

legal tender Any type of money that the government requires everyone to accept at face value.

Lend-Lease Act A 1941 act by which the United States "loaned" munitions to the Allies, hoping to avoid war by becoming an "arsenal" for the Allied cause.

levees Earthen dike or mound, usually along the banks of rivers, used to prevent flooding.

liberal Protestants Those who believed that religion had to be adapted to science and that the Bible was to be mined for its ethical values rather than for its literal meaning.

liberalism New reform movement that took shape under Franklin Roosevelt and the New Deal in the 1930s. It sought to regulate capitalism in the public interest but not the morals or behavior of private citizens.

Liberty Bonds Thirty-year government bonds with an annual interest rate of 3.5 percent sold to fund the war effort.

limited liability Liability that protected directors and stockholders of corporations from corporate debts by separating those debts from personal liabilities.

Lincoln-Douglas debates Series of seven debates between Abraham Lincoln and Stephen Douglas in their contest for election to the U.S. Senate in 1858.

Lincoln, Abraham Prominent abolitionist who fought for the antislavery cause in Kansas (1856) and led a raid to seize the Harpers Ferry arsenal in 1859.

Lindbergh, Charles A. First individual to fly solo across the Atlantic (1927) and the greatest celebrity of the 1920s.

Lodge, Henry Cabot Republican Senator from Massachusetts who led the campaign to reject the Treaty of Versailles.

Long, Huey Democratic senator and former governor of Louisiana who used the radio to attack the New Deal as too conservative. FDR regarded him as a major rival.

Lost Generation Term used by Gertrude Stein to describe U.S. writers and artists who fled to Paris in the 1920s after becoming disillusioned with America.

Louisiana Purchase Land purchased from France in 1803 that doubled the size of the United States.

Lowell mill girls Single, young farm women in New England who worked as wage laborers in mills owned by Francis Cabot Lowell's Boston Manufacturing Company, including at Lowell, Massachusetts. The company provided boardinghouses for the women and enforced strict rules of conduct.

loyalists People in the 13 colonies who remained loyal to Britain during the Revolution.

MacArthur, General Douglas Supreme commander of Allied forces in the southwest Pacific during the Second World War; leader of the occupation forces in the reconstruction of Japan; and head of United Nations forces during the Korean War.

Mahan, Alfred Thayer Influential imperialist who advocated construction of a large navy as crucial to the successful pursuit of world power.

Malcolm X Charismatic African American leader who criticized integration and urged the creation of separate black economic and cultural institutions. He became a hero to members of the Black Power movement.

Manhattan Project Major secret military operation that involved the development of the first atomic weapon.

Manifest Destiny The belief that the United States was destined to grow from the Atlantic to the Pacific and from the Arctic to the tropics. Providence supposedly intended for Americans to have this area for a great experiment in liberty.

manumission The act of freeing a slave, done at the will of the owner.

Marbury v. Madison 1803 case involving the disputed appointment of a federal justice of the peace in which Chief Justice John Marshall expanded the Supreme Court's authority to review legislation.

March on Washington for Jobs and Freedom On August 28, 1960, 200,000 people marched through Washington D.C. to the Lincoln Memorial for the rights of African Americans; Dr. Martin Luther King Jr. delivered his famous "I Have a Dream" speech on this day.

Market Revolution Term used to describe the transformation of the United States, particularly in the North, between 1815 and 1850 from a largely subsistence economy to a market society in which farmers and other business owners produced surplus goods to sell to growing regional, national, and international markets.

martial law Government by military force rather than by citizens.

mass production High-speed and high-volume production.

mass-culture critique Fear that the cultural traditions of the 1950s would be drastically altered due to the influences of art, music, and TV.

massive retaliation Assertion by the Eisenhower administration that the threat of U.S. atomic weaponry would hold Communist powers in check.

matrilineal A society that determines inheritance and roles in life based on the female or maternal line.

Mayan Indigenous people and culture of what today are southeast Mexico, Granada, and Belize.

McCarran-Walter Act Authorized the denial of immigrant status to anyone who might compromise national security by bringing dangerous ideas into the country; it also allowed the deportation of immigrants who belonged to organizations on the Attorney General's List.

McCarthy, Joseph 1946 U.S. Senator who unfairly accused numerous people of being Communists.

McCarthy, Senator Eugene Anti-war Democrat who dared to challenge Lyndon Johnson in the party's primaries and who helped prompt LBJ's decision to forgo another presidential run in 1968.

McClellan, George B. One of the most promising young officers in the U.S. army, he became the principal commander of Union armies in 1861–1862.

McCulloch v. Maryland Supreme Court case in which the Bank of the United States Baltimore branch challenged the Maryland legislature's attempt to tax the bank; lead by John Marshall, the Court decided in favor of the Bank and denied Maryland's right to tax the Bank or any other federal agency.

melting pot Term first used in the early 1900s that referred to the fusing of immigrants' culture with American culture as a continuous rebirth of the nation.

Menéndez de Avilé, Pedro The Spanish Admiral charged with Havana's protection after it was sacked by the Huguenots. Forces under Aviles' command expanded Spanish influence in the region, attacking and conquering settlements on Florida's Atlantic coast in 1565.

mercantilism An economic theory that stresses a direct relationship between a nation's wealth and its power. Mercantilist nations in the 17th century sought to increase their wealth and power through aggressive trade expansion within their colonies.

merger movement Late-19th and early 20th-century effort to integrate different enterprises into single, giant corporations able to eliminate competition, achieve economic order, and boost profits.

middle class Social group that developed in the early 19th century comprised of urban and country merchants, master craftsmen who had turned themselves into manufacturers, and market-oriented farmers—small-scale entrepreneurs who rose within market society.

middle class Social group that developed in the early 19th century comprised of urban and country merchants, master craftsmen who had turned themselves into manufacturers, and market-oriented farmers—small-scale entrepreneurs who rose within market society.

Middle Passage The forced voyage taken by enslaved Africans across the Atlantic Ocean between Africa and destinations in the Western Hemisphere. More than 1 million slaves died during the journey due to the subhuman conditions aboard slave ships.

midnight judges Federal judicial officials appointed under the Judiciary Act of 1801, in the last days of John Adams's presidency.

Midway Plaisance A section of the Columbia Exposition of 1893 that included concessions, games, the Ferris Wheel, traveling museums, and freak shows.

military–industrial complex Refers to the relationship between military, political, and economic elites committed to expanding national security capabilities.

Millerites Followers of the Baptist leader William Miller, who preached that God would destroy the world during the year following March 1843. They later formed the SeventhDay Adventist Church.

minstrel show Popular form of theater among working men of the northern cities in which white men in blackface portrayed African Americans in song and dance.

missions Outposts established by the Spanish along the northern frontier to aid in Christianizing the native peoples. They also were used to exploit these peoples' labor.

Missouri Compromise Compromise that maintained sectional balance in Congress by admitting Missouri as a slave state and Maine as a free state and by drawing a line west from the 368 309 parallel separating future slave and free states.

Monroe Doctrine Foreign policy doctrine proposed by Secretary of State John Quincy Adams in 1823 that denied the right of European powers to establish new colonies in the Americas while maintaining the United States' right to annex new territory.

Morgan, J. P. Most celebrated and powerful banker of the late 19th century.

Mormons Members of the Church of Jesus Christ of Latter-Day Saints, founded by Joseph Smith in 1830; the Book of Mormon is their Bible.

Mourning Wars An Indian war often initiated by a widow or bereaved relative who insisted that her male relatives provide captives to repair the loss.

MTV aesthetic Created a relationship between music and visual imagery.

muckrakers Investigative journalists who propelled Progressivism by exposing corruption, economic monopolies, and moral decay in American society.

Munich Conference French and British leaders met with Adolf Hitler in 1938 to avoid war.

My Lai Incident U.S. troops murdered more than 200 civilians, most of them women and children, in the small South Vietnamese village of My Lai in 1968.

narrowcasting Tactic used by TV programmers to target specific audiences with corresponding shows.

National American Women Suffrage Association (NAWSA) Organization established in 1890 to promote woman suffrage; stressed that women's special virtue made them indispensable to politics.

National Association for the Advancement of Colored People (NAACP) Organization launched in 1910 to fight racial discrimination and prejudice and to promote civil rights for blacks.

National Recovery Administration (NRA) 1933 attempt to promote economic recovery by persuading private groups of industrialists to decrease production, limit hours of work per employee, and standardize minimum wages.

National Review Magazine started in 1955 by William F. Buckley Jr. that represents conservative opinions and commentary about current events and politics.

National Road A road that attempted to link west and east through the Chesapeake by connecting the Potomac River with the Ohio River at Wheeling, Virginia in 1818.

National Security Act of 1947 Reorganized the U.S. military forces within a new Department of Defense, and established the National Security Council and the Central Intelligence Agency.

National Security Agency (NSA) Super-secret agency created in 1952 that came to enjoy broad power to monitor and archive global communications in the name of protecting national security.

National Security Strategy of 2002 Denounced terrorist networks and proclaimed that the U.S. had the right to wage war against any force that endangered Americans.

National War Labor Board (NWLB) U.S. government agency that brought together representatives of labor, industry, and the public to resolve labor disputes.

nativism Hostility of native-born Americans toward immigrants.

neoconservatives Group of intellectuals, many of whom had been anticommunist Democrats during the 1950s and 1960s, who came to emphasize hard-line foreign policies and conservative social stances.

Neolithic The period known also as the late Stone Age. Agriculture developed, and stone, rather than metal, tools were used.

Neutrality Acts Legislation that restricted loans, trade, and travel with belligerent nations in an attempt to avoid the entanglements that had brought the United States into the First World War.

New Democrat A member of the Democratic Party, such as Bill Clinton, who urged policies – such as deregulating business and financial activities, cutting federal welfare expenditures, and embracing strict crime control measures – which Democrats from the New Deal, Fair Deal, and Great Society eras had generally opposed.

New Freedom Wilson's reform program of 1912 that called for temporarily concentrating government power so as to dismantle the trusts and return America to 19thcentury conditions of competitive capitalism.

New Frontier Term used by John F. Kennedy in his 1960 campaign as a reference to what lied ahead for the country. Kennedy spoke of new social programs to rebuild rural communities, increase educational opportunities and improve urban conditions; he also promoted economic growth and more aggressive foreign policy.

New Jersey Plan Proposal by William Patterson of New Jersey at the Constitutional Convention of 1787 to maintain the existing system of representation under the Articles of Confederation in which each state had one vote in Congress. Also known as the "small state" plan.

New Left 1960s movement that sought to re-orient politics; people were urged to expand their minds and seek alternative ways of living.

New Lights Term used to describe prorevival Congregationalists.

New Look President Eisenhower's attempt to minimize the military budget by focusing on nuclear weaponry and air power.

New Nationalism Roosevelt's reform program between 1910 and 1912, which called for establishing a strong federal government to regulate corporations, stabilize the economy, protect the weak, and restore social harmony.

New Right A diverse coalition of conservatives that focused on social issues and national sovereignty; they supported the Republican party under the leadership of Ronald Reagan.

New Sides Term used to describe evangelical Presbyterians.

New Woman A term used to describe the emergence of a new style of middle-class womanhood in the late nineteenth century, as young women attended college, engaged in sports, and entered a variety of professions.

New York Magdalen Society Female established society whose mission was to separate prostitutes from male power, pray with them, and convert them to middle-class morality.

New York's 369th Regiment Black army unit recruited in Harlem that served under French command and was decorated with the Croix de Guerre for its valor.

nickelodeons Converted storefronts in working-class neighborhoods that showed early short silent films usually lasting 15 minutes, requiring little comprehension of English, and costing only a nickel to view.

Ninth and Tenth Negro Cavalries African-American army units that played a pivotal role in the Spanish-American War.

Nixon Doctrine Pledged that the U.S. would extend military assistance to anticommunist governments in Asia but would require them to supply their own combat forces.

Nixon, Richard Milhous President of the United States (1969–1974) during the final years of the Vietnam War. He resigned the presidency when he faced impeachment for the Watergate scandals.

Non-Separatists English Puritans who insisted that they were faithful members of the Church of England while demanding that it purge itself of its surviving Catholic rituals and vestments.

nonimportation agreements Agreements not to import goods from Great Britain. They were designed to put pressure on the British economy and force the repeal of unpopular parliamentary acts.

normal schools State colleges established to train teachers.

North Atlantic Treaty Organization (NATO) Established by treaty in 1949 to provide for the collective defense of noncommunist European and North American nations against possible aggression from the Soviet

Union and to encourage political, economic, and social cooperation.

Northwest Ordinance Established the Northwest Territory between the Ohio River and the Great Lakes. Adopted by the Confederation Congress in 1787, it abolished slavery in the territory and provided that it be divided into three to five states that would eventually be admitted to the Union as full equals of the original thirteen.

NSC-68 National Security Council Document number 68 (1950) that provided the rationale and comprehensive strategic vision for U.S. policy during the Cold War.

nullification Beginning in the late 1820s, John C. Calhoun and others argued that the Union was a voluntary compact between sovereign states, that states were the ultimate judges of the constitutionality of federal law, that states could nullify federal laws within their borders, and that they had the right to secede from the Union.

Office of War Information (OWI) Created in 1942 by President Roosevelt to coordinate propaganda and censorship.

Old Lights Antirevival Congregationalists.

Old Sides Antirevival Presbyterians. Olmec

Olmecs The oldest pre-Columbian high culture to appear in what is now Mexico.

Olmsted, Frederick Law Principal designer of Central Park in New York City.

Onontio An Algonquian word that means "great mountain" and that was used by Indians of the Middle Ground to designate the governor of New France.

Open Door policy The policy through which the United States sought to keep China open to American merchants and American goods in the late 19th and early 20th centuries. The policy entailed preventing European powers from establishing exclusive control over parts of China and China itself from shutting down its trade with foreign nations.

OVERLORD Massive invasion of Germany that began on June 6, 1944, known as D-Day; this event was the beginning of the end to the war in Europe.

Panama Canal An engineering marvel completed in 1914 across the new Central American nation of Panama. Connecting the Atlantic and Pacific oceans, it shortened ship travel between New York and San Francisco by 8,000 miles.

patronage The act of appointing people to government jobs or awarding them government contracts, often based on political favoritism rather than on abilities.

patroonship Vast estates along the Hudson River that were established by the Dutch. They had difficulty attracting peasant labor, and most were not successful.

Patsy Mink Equal Opportunity in Education Act Required colleges and universities to improve the financing and promotion of women's sports in 1972.

peace without victory Woodrow Wilson's 1917 pledge to work for a peace settlement that did not favor one side over the other but ensured an equality among combatants.

Pearl Harbor Japan's December 7, 1941 attack on a U.S. base in Hawaii that brought the United States into the Second World War.

Pentagon Completed in January of 1943, this five-story, five-sided building houses the United States' War Department.

people's capitalism An egalitarian capitalism in which all Americans could participate and enjoy the consumer goods that U.S. industry had made available.

Pershing, John J. Commander of the American Expeditionary Force that began landing in Europe in 1917 and that entered battle in the spring and summer of 1918.

Persian Gulf War Conflict that lasted six weeks in 1991 between the U.S. and Iraq; Bush ordered aid to Kuwait when Saddam Hussein and his armies invaded their land.

personal liberty laws Laws enacted by nine northern states to prohibit the use of state law facilities such as jails or law officers in the recapture of fugitive slaves.

placemen Appointed office holders who sat in the British Parliament. The Country party in 18th century England lobbied to ban placemen, whom they saw as a threat to the natural balance of the British system of government.

Platt Amendment Clause that the U.S. forced Cuba to insert into its constitution giving the U.S. broad control over Cuba's foreign and domestic policies.

Plessy v. Ferguson 1896 Supreme Court case that sanctioned Jim Crow laws as long as the separate facilities for black and whites were equal.

political machines Organizations that controlled local political parties and municipal governments through bribery, election fraud, and support of urban vice while providing some municipal services to the urban poor.

politics of harmony A system in which the governor and the colonial assembly worked together through persuasion rather than through patronage or bullying.

Pontiac's War A large group of Indians, including Seneca, Mingo, Delaware, Shawnee, Wyandot, Miami, Ottawa, and other warriors, joined forces in 1763, attacking 13 British posts in the West in hopes to drive British settlers back to the Eastern seaboard.

popular sovereignty The concept that settlers of each territory would decide for themselves whether to allow slavery.

popular sovereignty The concept that settlers of each territory would decide for themselves whether to allow slavery.

Postal Campaign Abolitionist tactic to force the nation to confront the slavery question by flooding the mails, both North and South, with antislavery literature. Their hope was to raise controversy within an area that was the province of the federal government.

postmillennialists Middle-class evangelicals that believed that Christ's Second Coming would occur at the end of 1,000 years of social perfection brought about by the missionary conversion of the world.

praying Indians The Christian Indians of New England.

predestination A theory that states that God has decreed, even before he created the world, who will be saved and who will be damned.

premillennialists Christians (usually ordinary Baptists, Methodists, and Disciples of Christ) who assumed that the millennium would arrive with world-destroying violence, followed by 1,000 years of Christ's rule on Earth.

Presbytery An intermediate level of organization in the Presbyterian church, above individual congregations but below the synod. One of its primary responsibilities was the ordination and placement of ministers.

presidios Military posts constructed by the Spanish to protect the settlers from hostile Indians. They also were used to keep non-Spanish settlers from the area.

press gangs Small groups within the British navy, or hired by the service, to force seamen into British naval service. Press gangs operated in the American colonies during the late 17th and 18th centuries and continued to seize U.S. citizens in the years leading to the War of 1812.

primogeniture The right, by law or custom, of the first-born to inherit the entire estate, to the exclusion of younger siblings.

private fields Farms of up to five acres on which slaves working under the task system were permitted to produce items for their own use and sale in a nearby market.

privateer Privately owned ships that were authorized by a government to attack enemy ships during times of war. The owners of the ships got to claim a portion of whatever was captured. This practice damaged any enemy country that could not dramatically increase naval protection for its merchant ships.

privateers Privately owned ships that were authorized by a government to attack enemy ships during times of war. The owners of the ships got to claim a portion of whatever was captured. This practice damaged any enemy country that could not dramatically increase naval protection for its merchant ships.

Proclamation of 1763 Issued by the Privy Council, it tried to prevent the colonists from encroaching upon Indian lands by prohibiting settlement west of the Appalachian watershed unless the government first purchased those lands by treaty.

Progressive Party Political party formed by Theodore Roosevelt in 1912 when the Republicans refused to nominate him for president. The party adopted a sweeping reform program.

Prohibition Constitutional ban on the manufacture and sale of alcohol in the United States (1920–1933).

proprietary colonies Territories with legal titles and full governing rights granted to individuals or groups by British monarchs. Several proprietary colonies were established in North America in the late 17th century; three survived until the independence of the United States.

provincial congress A type of convention elected by the colonists to organize resistance. They tended to be larger than the legal assemblies they displaced, and they played a major role in politicizing the countryside.

public Friends The men and women who spoke most frequently and effectively for the Society of Friends. They were as close as the Quakers came to having a clergy. They occupied special elevated seats in some meetinghouses.

public virtue Meant, to the revolutionary generation, patriotism and the willingness of a free and independent people to subordinate their interests to the common good and even to die for their country.

Pullman Strike 1894 Labor strike that became the first nationwide workers' strike against the railroad.

putting-out system Production system in the early Industrial Revolution in which employers "put out" materials to workers, especially women, to make finished products, such as clothing and shoes. Also known as "cottage industry" because the work was done in homes or small workshops.

quasi-slavery Position that resembled slavery, such as that created by the Black Codes.

quitrent A relic of feudalism, a quitrent was a small required annual fee attached to a piece of land. British colonial governments used it as a way of distributing land to settlers while creating a stream of revenue for themselves.

Reagan, Ronald Republican president (1981–1989) who steered domestic politics in a conservative direction and sponsored a huge military buildup.

recall Reform that gave voters the right to remove from office a public servant who had betrayed their trust.

Red Scare Widespread fear in 1919–1920 that radicals had coalesced to establish a communist government on American soil. In response, U.S. government and private citizens undertook a campaign to identify, silence, and, in some cases, imprison radicals.

redemptioners Servants with an indentured contract that allowed them to find masters after they arrived in the colonies. Many German immigrant families were redemptioners and thus were able to stay together while they served their terms.

redlining Refusal by banks and loan associations to grant loans for home buying and business expansion in neighborhoods that contained aging buildings, dense populations, and growing numbers of nonwhites.

referendum Procedure that allows the electorate to decide an issue through a direct vote.

Rehnquist, William Appointed to Chief Justice of the Supreme Court by Reagan in 1986.

republican wife/mother New status gained by women in the American Revolution that entrusted them to educating their sons and ensuring that their sons and husbands were upstanding citizens.

republics Independent Indian villages that were willing to trade with the British and remained outside the French system of Indian alliances.

Restorationism Belief that all theological and institutional changes since the end of biblical times were manmade mistakes and that religious organizations must restore themselves to the purity and simplicity of the apostolic church.

revival A series of emotional religious meetings that led to numerous public conversions.

revolving turret A low structure, often round, on a ship that moved horizontally and contained mounted guns.

Rhode Island System Factory system founded by Samuel Slater and centered on the Arkwright spinning mill at Pawtucket, Rhode Island, in the late 18th century. The system, later imitated by other mill owners, featured factory villages in the countryside where owners could exert better control over their operations and their workers.

rifling Process of cutting spiral grooves in a gun's barrel to impart a spin to the bullet. Perfected in the 1850s, it produced greater accuracy and longer range.

robber barons Industrial leaders who began to restrain their displays of wealth and make significant philanthropic contributions to the public.

Roberts Court Post-2005 Supreme Court, headed by Chief Justice John Roberts, in which conservatives used their five-justice majority to issue a number of rulings that tracked the theories of legal-constitutional conservatives.

Rockefeller, John D. Founder of the Standard Oil Company, whose aggressive practices drove many competitors out of business and made him one of the richest men in America.

Roe v. Wade Supreme Court decision in 1973 that ruled that a blanket prohibition against abortion violated a woman's right to privacy and prompted decades of political controversy.

Roosevelt Corollary 1904 corollary to the Monroe Doctrine, stating that the United States had the right to intervene in domestic affairs of hemispheric nations to quell disorder and forestall European intervention.

Roosevelt, Eleanor A politically engaged and effective First Lady, and an architect of American liberalism.

Roosevelt, Franklin Delano President from 1933 to 1945 and the creator of the New Deal.

Rough Riders Much-decorated volunteer cavalry unit organized by Theodore Roosevelt and Leonard Wood to fight in Cuba in 1898.

Russo-Japanese War Territorial conflict between imperial Japan and Russia mediated by Theodore Roosevelt at Portsmouth, New Hampshire. The peace agreement gave Korea and other territories to Japan, ensured Russia's continuing control over Siberia, and protected China's territorial integrity.

Sacco-Vanzetti Case (1920) Controversial conviction of two Italian-born anarchists accused of armed robbery and murder.

sachem An Algonquian word that means "chief."

Sand Creek massacre Attack led by Colonel John Chivington that killed 200 Cheyenne Indians that returned in peace to their Colorado reservation.

Santa María The flagship and the largest of the three ships used by Christopher Columbus during his first voyage to the Americas. The three-masted vessel ran aground off the northern coast of Haiti.

Saratoga A major turning point in the Revolutionary War. American forces prevented John Burgoyne's army from reaching Albany, cut off its retreat, and forced it to surrender in October 1777. This victory helped bring France into the war.

scalawags Term used by southern Democrats to describe southern whites who worked with the Republicans.

Scott, Dred Missouri slave who sued for freedom on grounds of prolonged residence in a free state and free territory; in 1857, the Supreme Court found against his case, declaring the Missouri Compromise unconstitutional.

secession The act of a state withdrawing from the Union. South Carolina was the first state to attempt to do this in 1860.

Second Bill of Rights 1944 Proposal by President Roosevelt advocating governmental action to ensure that Americans could enjoy a wide range of guaranteed rights, including those of regular employment, adequate food and shelter, appropriate educational opportunities, and health care.

Second Continental Congress The intercolonial body that met in Philadelphia in May 1775 a few weeks after the Battles of Lexington and Concord. It organized the Continental Army, appointed George Washington commander-in-chief, and simultaneously pursued policies of military resistance and conciliation. When conciliation failed, it chose independence in July 1776 and in 1777 drafted the Articles of Confederation, which finally went into force in March 1781.

Second Great Awakening Religious revival that spread across the United States between the 1790s and 1850s, with greatest intensity among the emerging northern middle class from the mid-1820s into the 1830s.

Seneca Falls Convention (1848) First national convention of women's rights activists.

separation of powers The theory that a free government, especially in a republic, should have three independent branches capable of checking or balancing one another: the executive, the legislative (usually bicameral), and the judicial.

Separatists One of the most extreme English Protestant groups that were followers of John Calvin. They began to separate from the Church of England and form their own congregations.

serfdom Early medieval Europe's predominant labor system, which tied peasants to their lords and the land. They were not slaves because they could not be sold from the land.

share wages Payment of workers' wages with a share of the crop rather than with cash.

sharecroppers Tenant farmers who gave up a portion of their crops, primarily as rent to the owners of the land they worked.

sharecropping Working land in return for a share of the crops produced instead of paying cash rent.

Shays's Rebellion An uprising of farmers in western Massachusetts in the winter of 1786–1787. They objected to high taxes and foreclosures for unpaid debts. Militia from eastern Massachusetts suppressed the rebels.

Sheppard-Towner Act Major social welfare program providing federal funds for prenatal and child health care, 1921–1929.

Sherman Antitrust Act of 1890 Intended to declare any form of trade restraint illegal, but proved to be useless in prosecution of corporations.

sickle cell A crescent or sickle-shaped red blood cell sometimes found in African Americans. It helped protect them from malaria but exposed some children to the dangerous and painful condition of sickle cell anemia.

sit-down strike Labor strike strategy in which workers occupied their factory but refused to do any work until the employer agreed to recognize the workers' union. This strategy succeeded against General Motors in 1937.

sit-in movement Activity that challenged legal segregation by demanding that blacks have the same access to public facilities as whites. These nonviolent demonstrations were staged at restaurants, bus and train stations, and other public places.

Sitting Bull Hunkapapa Lakota (Sioux) chief and holy man who led warriors against the U.S. Army in Montana Territory in 1876, culminating in the Battle of Little Big Horn.

slave labor Coerced involuntary work performed by people under the threat of violence or hardship. Historically, slave labor has taken many forms from chattel slavery, in which people are treated as legally owned personal property, to debt bondage where a person pledges his or her labor to pay off a loan.

Smith, Alfred E. Irish American, Democratic governor of New York who became in 1928 the first Catholic ever nominated for the presidency by a major party.

Smith, Joseph Poor New York farm boy whose visions led him to translate the Book of Mormon in late 1820s. He became the founder and the prophet of the Church of Jesus Christ of Latter-day Saints (Mormons).

Social Darwinism Set of beliefs explaining human history as an ongoing evolutionary struggle between different groups of people for survival and supremacy that was used to justify inequalities between races, classes, and nations.

social networking The process by which people socialize with one another through sites on the Internet.

Social Security Act Centerpiece of the welfare state (1935) that instituted the first federal pension system and set up funds to take care of groups (such as the disabled and unmarried mothers with children) that were unable to support themselves.

socialism Political movement that called for the transfer of industry from private to public control, and the transfer of political power from elites to the laboring masses.

soddies Houses built by Great Plains settlers made from prairie sod that was cut into blocks and stacked to form walls.

sovereign power A term used to describe supreme or final power.

Spanish Civil War Conflict between Spain's republican government and nationalist rebels led by General Francisco Franco.

specie Also called "hard money" as against paper money. In colonial times, it usually meant silver, but it could also include gold coins.

Specie Circular Provision added to the Deposit Act in 1836 that required speculators to pay in silver and gold coins when buying large parcels of public land.

spoils system A postelection practice where a victorious political party awards loyal supporters with appointive public offices.

spoils system A postelection practice where a victorious political party awards loyal supporters with appointive public offices.

Sputnik crisis Following Russia's second successful satellite launch, the possibility of nuclear weapons development forced President Eisenhower to expand military arsenal, educational resources, and research capabilities.

stagflation Condition of simultaneous economic stagnation and price inflation.

Stanton, Elizabeth Cady Feminist abolitionist who organized the Seneca Falls Convention.

staple crop A crop grown for commercial sale. It usually was produced in a colonial area and was sold in Europe. The first staple crops were sugar and tobacco.

stay laws A law that delays or postpones something. During the 1780s, many states passed stay laws to delay the due date on debts because of the serious economic problems of the times.

steel cargo containers Made shipping goods and raw materials long distances easier and less expensive.

Strategic Defense Initiative (SDI) Popularly termed "Star Wars," a proposal to develop technology for creation of a space-based defensive missile shield around the United States.

subprime mortgages Mortgages extended to homebuyers who have a poor credit history or whose financial situation suggests a high likelihood of defaulting on their housing loan.

supply-side economics Economic theory that tax reductions targeted toward investors and businesses would stimulate production and eventually create jobs.

Synod The governing body of the Presbyterian church. A synod was a meeting of Presbyterian ministers and prominent laymen to set policies for the whole church.

Taft-Hartley Act Limited a union's power to conduct boycotts, force employers to hire only union members, and to continue a strike harmful to national security; it also required union officials to sign affidavits stating that they did not belong to the Communist Party.

Tallmadge Amendments Two amendments proposed by James Tallmadge Jr. to be added to the Missouri statehood bill before Missouri's admission to the union; the first barred slaved from being brought into Missouri and the second emancipated Missouri slaves born after admission once they reached their 25th birthday.

tariff A tax on imports.

Tariff of Abominations A 1828 tariff passed by Congress to protect the manufacturers of the northern states by setting high duties on imported goods. Southern opponents denounced the tariff, arguing that it was unconstitutional and harmful to the South's agrarian interests and cotton trade.

task system A system of slave labor under which slaves had to complete specific assignments each day. After these assignments were finished, their time was their own. It was used primarily on rice plantations. Slaves often preferred this system over gang labor because it gave them more autonomy and free time.

Taylor, Frederick Winslow Chief engineer at Philadelphia's Midvale Steel Company whose goal was to make human labor mimic the efficiency of a piece of machinery.

Teapot Dome scandal Political scandal by which Secretary of Interior Albert Fall allowed oil tycoons access to government oil reserves in exchange for $400,000 in bribes.

tejanos Spanish-speaking settlers of Texas. The term comes from the Spanish word Tejas for Texas.

Temporary Assistance to Needy Families (TANF) Program that allowed each state to design its own welfare-to-work programs under general federal guidelines.

tenancy System under which farmers worked land that they did not own.

Tennessee Valley Authority (TVA) Ambitious and successful use of government resources and power to promote economic development throughout the Tennessee Valley.

Tenochtitlán The huge Aztec capital city destroyed by Cortés.

Termination and Relocation Policies designed to assimilate American Indians by terminating tribal status and relocating individuals off reservations.

Tet Offensive Surprise National Liberation Front (NLF) attack during the lunar new year holiday in early 1968 that brought high casualties to the NLF but fueled pessimism about the war's outcome in the United States.

The Medicare Prescription Drug Improvement and Modernization Act 2003 act that created Medicare Part D, a new program that would provide prescription drug benefits for Medicare recipients. The law was controversial because of its enormous cost and because the Federal government was prohibited from negotiating discounts with drug companies.

the strenuous life A phrase coined by Theodore Roosevelt to describe his ideal of a vigorous, athletic new approach to life at the turn of the century.

the surge 2007 effort by the Bush administration, and credited to General David Petraus, that temporarily helped to stabilize Iraq by the short-term deployment of additional U.S. troops and by payments to Sunni tribes in exchange for tempering their opposition to the Shitedominated government in Baghdad.

Third Reich New empire that Adolf Hitler promised the German people would bring glory and unity to the nation.

Three Mile Island Housed a nuclear power plant in Pennsylvania that experienced a major reactor malfunction in 1979; the industry stopped development following this event.

Tories A term for Irish Catholic peasants who murdered Protestant landlords. It was used to describe the followers of Charles II and became one of the names of the two major political parties in England.

transportation revolution New forms of transportation following the War of 1812, including improved roads, canals, and railroads, which made the transition to a market society physically possible by drastically reducing the cost of shipping surplus crops and goods.

treasury notes Paper money used by the Union to help finance the Civil War. One type of treasury note was known as a greenback because of its color.

Treaty of Guadalupe Hidalgo Treaty that authorized the purchase of California, New Mexico, and a Texas border on the Rio Grande from Mexico for 15 million dollars.

Triangle Shirtwaist Company New York City site of a tragic 1911 industrial fire that killed 146 workers who were unable to find their way to safety.

Triple Alliance One set of combatants in World War I, consisting of Germany, Austria-Hungary, and Italy. When Italy left the alliance, this side became known as the Central Powers.

Triple Entente One set of combatants in World War I, consisting of Britain, France, and Russia. As the war went on, this side came to be known as the Allies or Allied Powers.

Troubled Assets Relief Program (TARP) Section of the Emergency Economic Stabilization act of 2008 that authorized the Treasury Department to spread $700 billing throughout the financial system.

Truman Doctrine Policy established by President Truman in 1947 to aid Greece and Turkey in order to prevent Soviet expansionism and the spread of communism.

Trump, Donald J. Republican president who overcame long odds in the 2016 election to win the White House. Though a real estate billionaire, Trump ran as a champion of poor white Americans. He promised them that he would "make America great again."

Tsenacommacah Powhatan Indians' name for their homeland. It may be translated to mean "our land" or "densely inhabited land." Extending from the James River in the south to the Potomac River in the north and from the Eastern Shore of Virginia to the fall line, Tsenacommacah covered all of Tidewater Virginia.

Turner, Nat Baptist lay preacher whose religious visions encouraged him to lead a slave revolt in southern Virginia in 1831 in which 55 whites were killed—more than any other American slave revolt.

Turner's frontier thesis Theory developed by historian Frederick Jackson Turner, who argued that the frontier had been central to the shaping of American character and the success of the U.S. economy and democracy.

Twenty Negro Law Confederate conscription law that exempted from the draft one white man on every plantation owning 20 or more slaves. The law's purpose was to exempt overseers or owners who would ensure discipline over the slaves and keep up production but was regarded as discrimination by nonslaveholding families.

Uncle Tom's Cabin Published by Harriet Beecher Stowe in 1852, this sentimental novel told the story of the Christian slave Uncle Tom and became a best seller and the most powerful antislavery tract of the antebellum years.

underconsumptionism Theory that underconsumption, or a chronic weakness in consumer demand, had caused the depression. This theory guided the Second New Deal, leading to the passage of laws designed to stimulate consumer demand.

underground railroad A small group who helped slaves escape bondage in the South. It took on legendary status, and its role was much exaggerated.

unicameral legislature A legislature with only one chamber or house.

Union leagues Organizations that informed African American voters of, and mobilized them to, support the Republican Party.

Unionists Southerners who remained loyal to the Union during the Civil War.

United Nations (UN) An international organization of Allied powers formed in 1945 to promote peaceful political change and

Universal Declaration of Human Rights Document adopted by the United Nations in 1948 that established human rights and freedoms as cornerstones of international law.

universal male suffrage System that allowed all adult males to vote without regard to property, religious, or race qualifications or limitations.

vaqueros Mexican cowboys who rounded up cattle, branded them, and drove them to San Francisco.

Villa, Francisco ("Pancho") Favored by Woodrow Wilson to be elected Mexico's leader in 1913.

Virginia and Kentucky Resolves Resolutions authored by James Madison and Thomas Jefferson and passed by the Virginia and Kentucky legislatures in 1798 and 1799 in protest of the Alien and Sedition Acts. Jefferson's Kentucky Resolves claimed that states could nullify laws that they deemed unconstitutional, an argument that states'rights southerners would use after 1830.

Virginia Plan Drafted by James Madison for the Constitutional Convention of 1787, it proposed a bicameral legislature, with representation in both houses apportioned according to population. Also known as the "large state" plan.

virtual representation The English concept that Members of Parliament represented the entire empire, not just a local constituency and its voters. According to this theory, settlers were represented in Parliament in the same way that nonvoting subjects in Britain were represented. The colonists accepted virtual representation for nonvoting settlers within their colonies but denied that the term could describe their relationship with Parliament.

Voting Rights Act of 1965 Law that provided new federal mechanisms to help guarantee African Americans the right to vote.

Wagner Act (NLRA) Named after its sponsor Senator Robert Wagner (D-NY), this 1935 act gave every worker the right to join a union and compelled employers to bargain with unions in good faith.

Walker, Madame C. J. Black entrepreneur who built a lucrative business from the hair and skin lotions she devised and sold to black customers throughout the country.

walking cities Compact residential areas near working districts with different income and ethnic groups living in close proximity.

Waltham-Lowell System Factory system founded by Francis Cabot Lowell's Boston Manufacturing Company, which established its first mill at Waltham, Massachusetts, in 1813. The system built on the earlier Rhode Island factory model by using heavier machinery to produce finished cloth and by employing single, young farm women in New England.

War Hawks Members of the 12th Congress, most of them young nationalists from southern and western areas, who promoted war with Britain.

War Industries Board (WIB) U.S. government agency responsible for mobilizing American industry for war

Washington Temperance Society Society established in 1840 by reformed drinkers of the laboring classes who operated separate from the church and converted drinkers through compassion and persuasion.

Washington, Booker T. Founder of Tuskegee Institute and most famous for his controversial speech at the 1895 Atlanta Exposition.

Watergate Business and residential complex in Washington, D.C., that came to stand for the political espionage and cover-ups directed by the Nixon administration. The complicated web of Watergate scandals brought about Nixon's resignation in 1974.

Wells, Ida B. Anti-lynching activist who wrote and spoke in protest, gaining the attention of the North only after taking her campaign to England.

Western Federation of Miners (WFM) Association of union mine workers established in 1893 to protect their rights.

Wheatley, Phillis Eight-year-old Phillis Wheatley arrived in Boston from Africa in 1761 and was sold as a slave to wealthy John and Susannah Wheatley. Susannah taught her to read and write, and in 1767 she published her first poem in Boston. In 1773, she visited London to celebrate the publication there of a volume of her poetry, an event that made her a transatlantic sensation. On her return to Boston, the Wheatleys emancipated her.

Whigs The name of an obscure sect of Scottish religious extremists who favored the assassination of Charles and James of England. The term was used to denote one of the two leading political parties of late 17th-century England.

Whiskey Rebellion Revolt in Western Pennsylvania against the federal excise tax on whiskey.

White City Monument created for the Columbia Exposition of 1893 in Chicago.

Whitney, Eli The Connecticut-born tutor who invented the cotton gin.

Wilmot Proviso Famous proviso made by Congressman David Wilmot regarding an amendment to an army appropriations bill that framed the national debate over slavery for the next 15 years.

Wisconsin Idea Refers to a policy, first adopted in Wisconsin in the early years of the 20th century, to bring together employers, trade unionists and professionals to discuss and shape relations between industry and labor in the state; a number of other states would adopt this policy.

women's movement Took place between 1953 and 1963; women began speaking out about their political rights, race and gender discrimination, employment opportunities and equitable working environments, and the lack of public roles available to them.

Works Progress Administration (WPA) Federal relief agency established in 1935 that disbursed billions to pay for infrastructural improvements and funded a vast program of public art.

World Trade Organization (WTO) Established in 1995 to head international trade between nations.

Wounded Knee Site of a shootout between Indians and Army troops at the Pine Ridge Indian reservation in southwestern South Dakota.

XYZ Affair Incident that precipitated an undeclared war with France when three French officials (identified as X, Y, and Z) demanded that American emissaries pay a bribe before negotiating disputes between the two countries.

Yankees A Dutch word for New Englanders that originally meant something like "land pirate."

yellow journalism Newspaper stories embellished with sensational or titillating details when the true reports did not seem dramatic enough.

Yorktown The last major engagement of the Revolutionary War. Washington's army, two French armies, and a French fleet trapped Lord Cornwallis at Yorktown and forced his army to surrender in October 1781.

Young America movement A group of men affiliated with the Democratic Party in the 1840s who sought the expansion of the United States across the continent.

Zenger, John Peter Printer of the New York Weekly Journal who was acquitted in 1735 by a jury of the crime of seditious libel after his paper sharply criticized Governor William Cosby.

Zimmerman telegram Telegram from Germany's foreign secretary instructing the German minister in Mexico to ask that country's government to attack the United States in return for German assistance in regaining Mexico's "lost provinces" (Texas, New Mexico, and Arizona).

Index

Page numbers in italics refer to illustrations.

Abe Lincoln in Illinois (film), 401
Abercrombie, James, 128
abolition. *see* antislavery activity
Acadians, 124–125
Acoma Indians, 26
Adams, Abigail, 147, 149
Adams, John
    in American Revolution, 160, 163
    British soldiers defended by, 146, 147
    as colonial resistance spokesman, 148
    correspondence, 149
    films depicting, 147
    foreign policy, 212–213
    as president, 211, 212–213
    separation of powers advocated by, 189–190
    as Vice President, 202
Adams, John Quincy, 312
Adams, Samuel, 121, 157, 158
Adena Hopewell culture, 12
adobe buildings, 11
Africa
    maps, *20*
    slavery impact on, 19, 20–21
African Americans
    education, 475, 479
    free, kidnapping, 368–369
    illiteracy rate, 475
    incompetence, myth of, 483
    Irish American relations with, 381
    leaders, 483
    militia, 486, 490
    in state offices, 483
    violence against, 472, 479, 481
    voters, 479, 481, 483, 489, 490
    voting rights, 471, 472–473
African American soldiers, 419, *453*, 453–454, 458–460
African Methodist Episcopal (AME) churches, 474
African relations with whites, 97
African servants, 46, 53
African slaves
    African words and customs retained by, 106
    in Brazil, 31, 104
    cowboys, 61
    earliest, 18
    in English colonies, 66
    indentured servants replaced by, 76
    in Louisiana, 82
    migration, forced of, 104
    moral implications of, 33
    in North America, 53
    in Old South, 104
    population, 89
    racism directed against, 97
    in Revolutionary War, 167
    in South Carolina, 95
    Spain, attitude concerning, 130
    in West Indies, 52–53
afterlife, belief in, 12
Age of Democratic Revolution, 201
agriculture
    bartering and, 233–234, 246
    cotton, 255, 258–260
    diversification and, 232
    domestic market for, 232
    in English colonies, 66, 93
    equipment, 233, *235, 247,* 248
    in Europe, 17
    European market for, 231, 256
    gender and, 233, 235, 256
    independence and, 232–233, 243–244, 267
    Jeffersonian ideals of, 231, 235, 248
    livestock and, 242
    local economic networks, 233, 246, 266–267
    Market Revolution and, 231
    in Mesoamerica, 10
    in mid-Atlantic colonies, 106–107
    in North America, 10–11, *12*
    plantation life, 255, 258, 260, 262–263
    rice, 257–58
    rise of, 5
    rural diets, 233
    in South (U.S.), 393
    in South America, 6, 7
    in southwest (U.S.), 11
    in St. Lawrence Valley, 41
    surplus, 93
    tobacco, 256
aid workers, 447
Alabama, 410–411
Alamo, *358*
The Alamo (film), 360
Albany Congress, 123
Alexander Hamilton (Chernow), 173
Alexander VI, Pope, 23
Algonquins, 43
Alien Acts, 212, 213, 214, 215
America (name origin), 23
America, modern, blueprint for, 447
American Board of Customs Commissioners, 143
American colonies
    expansion *versus* Anglicization, 101, 102–103
    government, 83–84, 87–88, *90*
    independence declared by, 136
    New France separation from, *123*
    population growth, *131*
American constitutionalism, 189–190, 192
American dream, 397
American Equal Rights Association (AERA), 480–481
American independence
    birth of, 160–163
    early years, 185–189
    views concerning, 162
    winning of, 227
American-made products, 389–390
American Party, 383, 386
American Philosophical Society, 109
American Revolution
    American victory, first, *135*
    freedom and human rights message of, 33
    immigrants prior to, 104
    prelude to, 135–163
    war (*see* Revolutionary War)
    western land claims during, *188*
American seamen, impressment of, 208, 219, 221, 226
American System, 304–308, *308*
Americas
    colonization of, 3
    complex societies in, 5–10
    conquest of, 25–31
    European presence, 32–33, 34
    migration before Columbus, 5
Ames, Adelbert, 489

Amherst, Jeffrey, 128–129, 136, 137
Amistad (film), 322
Anasazi, 11–12, *13*, 14, *14*
Anderson, Robert, 413, 415
Andersonville Prison, Ga., *460*
Andes, 5, 6–7, *9*
André, John, 180
Andros, Edmund, 73, 76, 84
Andrus, Edmund, 61
Anglican Church, 185
Anglicans, 114, 115
anglicization, 102, 130
animals, domesticated, 4, 5, 33
animal species, extinction of, 4
annexation controversy, 358–359
Anthony, Susan B., 348
anti-Catholicism, 380
antidraft riots, 445–446, *446*
Antietam, Battle of, 440–442, *441, 442*
antislavery activity
    abolitionism, 343–346
    Denmark Vesey's rebellion, 272
    Gabriel's rebellion, 271–272
    literature, *331*, 345, 370
    Mexican War opposition and, 363
    Nat Turner's rebellion, 272
    posters, *370*
    Quaker involvement in, 63
    state approaches to, 297
    women's rights and, 347
Apaches, 33, 71, 78, 207
Appomatox, surrender at, 465
Arab caravans, 19
Arab ships, 19
Arkansas, 416
Arkwright, Richard, 248
Army of the Potomac, *423*, 427, 434, 442
Arnold, Benedict, 160, 168, 170, 180, 183
around the world voyage, 23
Articles of Confederation
    amending attempts, 179
    development of, 192
    ratification of, 178
art in Caribbean, *26*
Asia, imports from, 31
assembly, rise of, 117
Association, 157
astrolabe, 19
astronomy, *10*, 12
Atahualpa (Inca ruler), 26
Atchison, David Rice, 383
Atlanta campaign, 457, *459*, 460, *460*, 462
Atlantic slave trade, 19, 20–21, *85*, 104, 186

Attucks, Crispus, 146
Autobiography (Franklin), 91
autonomy. *see* independence
Aztec Codex, 30
Aztecs
    diseases, 30
    human sacrifice, *11*
    rise of, 5, 10
    Spanish encounter and conquest of, 25–26

backcountry, 107, 150, 152
Bacon, Nathaniel, 75–76, *77*, 97
Bailey, Jacob, 149
balance of trade, 83
Balboa, Vasco Nuñez de, 23
Ballard, Martha, *237*
banknotes, 424
Bank of England, 88
Bank of North America, 179
Bank of the United States, 204, 205
Baptists, 59, 113, 114–115, 186
Barbados, 52, 53, 60–61
Barbary pirates, *69*
Barnum, Phineas Taylor, 234, *279*, 288
bayonet rule, 491
beans, 10–11
Beaumarchais, Pierre-Augustin Caron de, 171, 172
beavers, *37*, 39
Beijing, China, 15–16
Benezet, Anthony, 152
Benin (city), *22*
Benin (kingdom), 21
Beringia, 4
Bering Strait, 4, 5
Berkeley, Sir William, 74, 75, 76, *77*
Bernard, Francis, 141
bicameral legislature, 190
Bill of Rights, 202, 214
bill of rights, first, 57–58
Birth of a Nation (film), 488
bison, 4
black African as slaves, 18
Black Codes, 472–473
Black Death (bubonic plague), 4, 15, 17
"Black Republicans," 386, 387, 434
Black Robe (film), 43
Blackwell, Dr. Elizabeth, 447
Blair, Frank, 481
Blair, Montgomery, 440
blockade runners, 424, *425*
Board of Trade, 87
Boleyn, Anne, 45
Bolivia, 32
book burnings, 114
Boone, Daniel, 187–188

Booth, John Wilkes, 465
"border ruffians," 383, 387
border states in Civil War, 416–418, 438–439
Boston, Mass.
    African Americans, 152
    British occupation of, 145–146, *146*
    Pope's Day procession, *142*
    port closure, 156
    as print capital, 108
    as resistance center, 150
    in Revolutionary War, *161*
    town meeting, 118, 143–144
Boston Massacre, 145–146, 147, 148, 155
Boston Tea Party, 135–136, 147, 155
bounty jumpers, 445
Bourbon kings, 206–207
Bowie, Jim, 360
Boylston, Zabdiel, 107
boys' clothing, *56*
Braddock, Edward, 124, 125, 126, *126*, 127
Bradford, William, 54, 55, 108
Bragg, Braxton, 452, 453
Brant, Joseph, 175, *176*
Brazil, 5, 31, 104
Breckinridge, John C., 408, 409
British
    Canada involvement of, 206
    Native Americans, dealings with, 136–137, 175
British America, growth of, 88–97
British Army, 135, 145–146, *146*
British Empire, 87–88, 97, 98, 136–139, 175
British goods, 148. *See also* nonimportation of British goods
British offensive (War of 1812), 223–226
British Royal Navy, 208, 209, 219, 227
Brooks, Preston, 384, *386*
Brown, Henry Box
    escape from slavery, *343*
Brown, John, 377, 385, 401–402, *402*, 403
Brownson, Orestes, 251
Brown University, 115
Bruce, Blanche K., *484*
Bryan, Hugh, 114, 152
Bryant, William Cullen, 384, 411
bubonic plague, 4, 15, 17
"buccaneer" (term), 41
buccaneers, 89
Buchanan, James, 386, 387, 388, 389, 395, 411, 415, 447
bulldozing effort, 490

I-2   INDEX

Bull Run, Battle of, 427, *428,* 438
Bull Run, Battle of, Second, *433,* 434
Burgoyne, John, 170, 172, 175, 177
burial sites, 12
Burke, Edmund, 141, 157
Burns, Anthony, 369–370, *370*
Burnside, Ambrose E., 444
Burr, Aaron, 173, 213, 216
"bushwhackers," 417
business culture, 250
Butler, Benjamin, 457
Byrd, William, 106

Cabeza de Vaca, Alvar Nuñez, 26
Cabot, John, 44
Cabral, Pedro Álvares, 31
Caddos, 82
Cahokia, Ill., 12, 13, 14, 15, *15*
Cajuns, 125
calendar system, 8, 12
Calhoun, John C., 364, 365, 372, 399
California
    statehood, 365
    U.S. acquisition of, 373
    U.S. trade with, 355
California Trail, 356–357
Calvert, Cecilius, 49
Calvin, John, 38
Calvinism, 56, *86*
Canada
    British in, 206
    foundation for, 175
    French in, 38–41, 80
    in French-Indian War, 129, *129*
    invasion of, 222, 225
    war with, 223
canals, *391*
Canary Islands, 22
capitalism, 5, 332–334, 466. *See also* Market Revolution
captives
    Aztec, 10
    in Cahokia, 13
    Iroquois, 39–40, *41*
    Muslim, 18
caravel, 19, *19*
Caribbean
    art in, *26*
    French in, 41, 206
    slavery in, 23, 31, 95
    Spain and, 23
    theater of war, *120*
    trade, 65, 66, 83
Carib Indians, 23
Carleton, Sir Guy, 168
Carlisle, Frederick Howard, Earl of, 172
Carolina (colony), 60–61, 65, 94, 95

Carolinas, march through, 464
carpetbagger corruption, 483, 485
Carroll, John, 186
Cartier, Jacques, 38
cartoons
    allegorical, *480*
    anti-Greeley, *486*
    for freedom, *476*
    Mississippi Plan, *489*
    on violent handiwork, *485*
Catawbas, 96, 97, 175, 189
Catholic Church, 30, 38, 382
Catholic missionary work, 39, *42,* 43. *See also* Spanish missions
Catholics
    anti-Catholic sentiment, 380
    English, 45, 49
    in Maryland, 49, 85
    in Quebec, 155–156
    religious tolerance benefiting, 186
    restrictions on, 97
    in Revolutionary War, 176
Central America, farm villages in, 5
Chaco Canyon, 11–12, 15
Champlain, Samuel de, 38–39, 49
Chancellorsville, Battle of, 448, *449*
Charbonneau, Toussaint, 217
Charles I, King of England, 49, 54, 59–60, 110
Charles II, King of England, 60, 61, 65, 83
Charles III, King of Spain, 172
Charleston, S.C., 180, *465*
Chase, Samuel, 215–216
Chatham, William Pitt, Earl of, 126, 127–128, 136, 143, 157
Chattanooga, Tenn., 452
Chauncy, Charles, 116
Cheng Ho, 16
Chernow, Ron, 173
Cherokees, 61, 150, 175, 188
Chesapeake colony (Jamestown, Va.). *See* Jamestown, Va.
Chichén Itzá (Mayan city), 8
Chickamauga, Tenn., 452, *452,* 453
Child, Lydia Maria, 344
China, 15–16, 17, 33
chinampas (floating gardens), 10
Choctaws, 80, 82
Christian Europe, 16–18
Christianity, 23, 26
Christian missionary work. *See also* Spanish missions
    in Canada, 39, 40
    Catholic, 39, *42,* 43
    in New England, 57
    in southwest (U.S.), 27, 71

Christian Moravian Indians, 175
Christians
    freedom of worship, 60
    slavery, beliefs concerning, 21
    societies, 34
church and state, separation of, 57
churches, freedpeople founding of, 474
Church of England, 38, 45, 54, 57, 60, 186
circuit courts of appeal, 202–203, 215
Civil Rights Cases (1883), 490
Civil War
    antiwar activists, 440
    balance sheet, 418–424
    blockade, and foreign relations, 424–427
    campaigns and battles, *417,* 427–434, 448–453, 454, 456–457, 461, 463–466
    casualties, 416, *441, 460,* 466
    class tensions, 445–446
    economic conditions during, 444–445, 454, 459
    end, 464, 465, 466
    financing, 423–424
    logistics, 422–423
    mobilization, 420
    naval operations, 424–427, 429–430
    onset of, 407
    peace movement, 454
    peace overtures, 457–458
    prisoners of war, 458–460, *460*
    strategy and morale, 419–420
    victory, 434
    weapons and tactics, 420–421
    women, 447
Clark, George Rogers, 175, 217
Clark, William, 217
class
    abolitionism, 343–346
    artisan, 236
    in cemetery, *266*
    distributive inequality, 236, 252, 265, 333
    factory system, 249
    Jeffersonian ideals of, 248
    middle class, 250, 281–282
    Peggy Eaton controversy, 319–320
    race *versus,* 398–399
    religion and, 281
    in southern U.S., 263–266, 273
    theater riots, 291–292
    urban forms of, 249–250, 252
Clay, Henry, 221, *221, 308*
Clinton, Sir Henry, 170, 172, 174, 179–180, 183, 184
clothing fashions, colonial, 111

Clovis tip, 4
Cloyse, Sarah, 88
Coercive Acts, 1774, 135–136, 147, 155–156, 157
coffeehouses, *85*
Colbert, Jean-Baptiste, 41
Colfax Massacre, 486
colonial America estates, *151*
colonial economy, 392
colonial household, 90–93
Colonial Sons of Liberty, 145
colonization
    Africa, slave trade and, 19–21
    economic aspects, 21
    English, 50–52, 56, 64, 66, 89, 90–93
    legacies of, 32
    in North America, 69
    technology advances contributing to, 33
Colt, Samuel, 390
Colt arms plant, Hartford, Conn., *392*
Columbian Exchange, 33–34
Columbia University, 115
Columbus, Christopher
    Americas, migration before, 4
    films, 32
    landing in San Salvador, 24, *24*
    overview of, 3
    ships, *19*
    voyages, 22–23, *25*
Comanches, 71, 73, 78, 207
combat submarine, world's first, 425–426
committees of correspondence, 148
Common Sense (Paine), 161, 162
communal covenant, 56
communications revolution, 17
Company of the Indies, 82
compensated emancipation, 439
Compromise of 1787, 189
Compromise of 1850, 374, *385*, 408–409
Concord, Mass., *161*
Concord Bridge, British driven from, *135*, 158
Confederacy (Confederate States of America)
    cornerstone of, 414
    counteroffensives, 432
    creation of, 411
    elections, 454
    foreign policy, 424–425
    states needed by, 413
    tide, 448–453
Confederate army
    African American soldiers in, 460
    desertions, 454
    photos, *421*
    strength, *464*
Confederate navy, 425–427
Confederate officials and military officers, amnesty for, 471, 472
Confederate soldiers, 416
Congregational Church, 114, 115
Congregational churches, 186
"Congregationalist" worship and church organization, 57
Congress. *See also* Continental Congress
    First, 202–203, 215
    War Hawk, 221–222
congressional elections, 1866, 475–476
congressional elections, 1874, 487
congressional reconstruction
    1866 congressional elections and, 475–476
    for civil rights of freedpeople, 475
    completion of, 479–480
    end of, 491
    Fourteenth Amendment, 475
    laws to protect civil rights, 475
    Reconstruction Acts of 1867, 476–477
    retreat from, 487–491
    special committee, 475
    statewide public schools, 479
    Supreme Court and, 489–490
Connecticut (colony), 57, *62*
Connecticut Compromise, 194
conquistadores, 25, 26, 28, 31
Conscience Whigs, 364
Constitution (U.S.)
    as blueprint for Republic, 202
    creation of, 168, 192–196
    debate on, 195
    Federalist goals for, 201
    ratification of, 196–197
    slavery abolished in, 454, 455, 466
    Supreme Court rulings affecting, 216
    war declared under, 221
Constitutional Convention, 1787, 189, *196*
constitutional conventions
    black and white participation in, 479, *479*
constitutionalism, 190, 192
constitutions, states ratified, 479–480
consumer culture/society
    birth of, 111
    signs of, *112*
Continental Army, 160, 170, 178–179
Continental Congress, 136, 168
Continental Congress, First, 147, 156, 157, 178
Continental Congress, Second, 159–160
Continental money, value of, 177–178
contraband of war, 438
conversion experience, 56, 59, 113
Cooke, Jay, 487
Copley, Jacob, 149
Copperheads, 440, 444, 454
corn, 5, 33–34
Cornstalk (Shawnee leader), 175
Cornwallis, Charles, Earl, 169–170, 176, 180, 181
    surrender of, *167*
    in Virginia, 182
    at Yorktown, 183
Coronado, Francisco Vasquez de, 26
corruption
    as issue in presidential election of 1876, 490
    scandals, 487
Cortés, Hernán, 25
cosmopolitans *versus* localists, 193–194
"cottagers" (term), 102–103
Cotton, John, 56, 57
cotton as king, 393, 424–425
cotton pickers (painting), *469*
Council of the Indies, 31
courts, Jeffersonians and, 215–216
Covenant Chain of Peace, 76
covenant theology, 54, 56
coverture, 103, 187
cowboys, 61
Craft, William and Ellen, 369
Credit Mobilier Affair, 482
Creek Indians, 61, 223
Crèvecoeur, J. Hector St. John de, 232, 235
Crittenden Compromise, 411, 413
Crittendon, William, 372
Crockett, Davy, 238, *239*, 360
Cromwell, Oliver, 60
Crusades, 18
Cuba, 23, 371–373
cultural patterns, colonial, 89–90
currency
    bartering and, 233–234, 246–247
    hard currency *versus* paper, 325, 333
    scarcity of, 233
    Second Bank of the United States and, 321
Currency Act, 1764, 139, 148

Da Gama, Vasco, 21
The Dangers of an Unconverted Ministry (Tennent), 113
Dartmouth College, 115
Darwin, Charles, 227
Davenport, James, 114
Davenport, John, 56
Davis, Jefferson
   African American soldier recruitment advocated by, 460
   appointments, 457
   capture of, 466
   congressional elections, 454
   Cuba, designs on, 372
   federal slave code advocated by, 400
   final resistance by, 461
   Fort Sumter surrender demanded by, 416
   Mississippi regiment commanded by, 362
   Tennessee battles overseen by, 452, 453
De Bow, James D. B., 392–393
de Bry, Theodor, 24, *24, 39, 49*
Declaration of Independence, 163, 169, 399, 409
Declaratory Act, 141
de Grasse, Francois, Comte de, 184
Delaware Indians, *65,* 66, 175
democracy, 401
Democratic filibuster, 491
Democratic Party
   black soldiers, attitude concerning, 453
   class resentments nurtured by, 445
   immigrant support for, 381
   role of national government, 304
   split in, 389, 407
Democratic Republicans, 201, 204
depression, 1837-1843, 390
De Soto, Harnando, 26
Dias, Bartolomeu, 21
Dickinson, John, 144, 150, 160
Dieskau, Jean-Armand, Baron, 125
diphtheria, 107
diseases, European. *See also* smallpox
   in Americas, 3, *30,* 30–31, 33, 54
   in California, 172, 207
   in New England, 107
   in North America, 70, 80, 222
dissection, human, 111
dissenters, religious, 56–57, 59
Dix, Dorothea, 337
Doegs, 74

domesticity. *see* home life
Dominion of New England, 84, 85, 86
Douglas, Stephen A., 373, 377, 378, *380,* 389
   slavery debates, *379,* 399, 400, *400*
Douglass, Frederick, 274, 387, 419, 438, 453, 471, *472*
dowry/dower rights, 103
Drake, Sir Francis, 45, 119
Dred Scott case, 1857, 377, 387, 399, 400, 404
drunkenness, 70
Du Bois, W. E. B., 475
Dulany, Daniel, 139, 140, 149
Dunmore's Proclamation, 160
Dunmore's War, 175
Duquesne, Marquis, 122
Dutch East India Company, 42
Dutch-English relations, 61
Dutch Reformed Church, 38
Dutch Republic
   independence, 38
   land acquired by, 42
   overseas activities of, 41
   Spain challenged by, 37
Dutch West India Company, 42, 44
dwellings
   Olmec, 8
   Anasazi, 12
   Mogollon and Hohokam, 11
   Native American, *17*
   white settlers, *76*

earth, circumference of, 22–23
East India Company, 153–154
Easty, Mary, 88
Eaton, Peggy, 319–320
economic conditions, 1950s, 389–393, 402, 404
economic depression of 1873, 487
education
   immigrants and, 335
   improvement in, 390
   religion in public schools, 334
   as social reform, 334–335
Edwards, Jonathan, 110, 113, 115, 116, 152
El Caracol, Mayan observatory, *10*
elections, 1854, 379, 383
Electoral College, 194, 226
electoral commission, 490–491
Eliot, John, 57
Elizabeth I, Queen of England, 45
Elliott, Robert B., *484*
Elmina, Fortress of, West Africa, *21*

emancipation, 186, 454
Emancipation Proclamation, 419, 434, 437–438, 439–440, 442–443, *443,* 453, 455, 457
Embargo Act, 1807, 219, 221
Emerson, Ralph Waldo, 374, 402
encomienda, 30, 31
England
   civil war, 59–60
   constitution, 87
   naval power, *69*
   Restoration, 60
   Spain challenged by, 37
English
   Dutch, dealings with, 61
   Native Americans, dealings with, 45, 47, 48, 49, *49,* 55, 78
English Atlantic empire, 82–88
English colonies, 44–66, 69–70, 73. *See also* American colonies
English Reformation, 45
English settlement, spectrum of, 89–90, 91
Enlightenment, 108, 109–111, 130, 163
entail, 91
entertainment
   animal fighting, 287, 289
   brutality in boxing, 290
   dancing, *337*
   ethnicity in boxing, 289
   male theatergoers, 289
   masculinity in, 287
   minstrelsy format, 291
   neighborhood rituals, 246
   parades, *238*
   theater riots, 291–292
enumerated commodities, 83
Ericsson, Leif, 15
Eskimos, 4
Europe (15th century), 15–24
European-Native American relations. *See also under specific European groups, e.g.:* English: Native Americans, dealings with
   coexistence, 97
   conquests, 5
   contact, first, 14–15, *24,* 25–26
   on middle ground, 78–80, 82
   new worlds, mutual, 55
   peace, 128
   racism, 97
Europeans, Americas colonized by, 3
evangelical preachers, 113
evangelicals, 115
Even the Rain (film), 32

excise tax, 204
expansionism, 353, 354–355, 373–374, 404

factories. *see also* manufacturing
    on African coast, 19
    morality and, 248–249, 251
    Rhode Island System, 248, *249*
    rural, 248
    Waltham-Lowell System, 249, 251
    women workers, 249
A Faithful Narrative of the Surprising Work of God (Edwards), 113
Fallen Timbers, Battle of, 208, 209, 222
family
    among slaves, 267–269
    intergenerational relations, 237
    midwifery, 237
    size, 245, 264
family life in English colonies, 50–52, 56, 64, 89, 90–93
farming. *see* agriculture
farm villages, 5
federalism (under British Empire), 87
Federalists, 196, 201
federal slave code, 400
federal system (U.S.), 168
felony, 486
Ferdinand of Aragon, Prince, 22
feudal revival, 150, *151*
fiat money, 107
Fifteenth Amendment, 480–481, 490
filibustering, 371–373
Fillmore, Millard, 386
financial panic of 1819, 309
financial panic of 1837, 325–326, *327*
fish, drawing of, *220*
Fitzhugh, George, 393
Florida, 410
Florida, Spanish
    boundaries of, 172
    influence, fading in, 97
    loss of, 172
    missions in, 27, *28*, 89, 94
    slaves promised freedom by, 119
    Spanish-Native American encounters in, 26
food production, 10–11
Forrest, Edwin, *292*
Forrest, Nathan Bedford, 459
Fort Beauséjour, 124
Fort Donelson, 430
Fort Duquesne, 122, 124
Fort Fisher, 464
Fort Henry, 430
Fort McHenry, bombardment of, *228*
Fort Sumter
    attack on, 407, 413, *415*
    decision regarding, 415–416
    surrender of, 416
Fort William Henry, 125, 127
Fourteenth Amendment, 475, 480, 490
Fox, George, 61
France
    American Revolution backed by, 163, 171–172
    Caribbean involvement of, 206
    Confederacy dealings with, 424–425
    defensive measures, 122
    versus Great Britain, *123*
    Great Britain, war with, 172, 207, 218–228
    land claimed by, 96
    Louisiana Territory sold by, 216
    outposts, 97
    Spain challenged by, 37
    United States, relations with, 208, 211–212, 213
    wars, 102, 120–121
Franciscans, 26–27, 30, 78, 82, 172, 207
Franklin, Battle of, 463
Franklin, Benjamin
    in American Revolution, 163
    in American Revolution prelude, 157
    on British manufacturing, 111
    colonial union advocated by, 123, *124*
    as diplomat, 137, 171–172, 185
    family, 150
    as gentleman, *110*
    in newspaper business, 108, 109
    as noble savage, *172*
    political cartoons, *124*
    as printer, *109*
    as reformer, 109
    taxation analyzed by, 143
    Townshend duty repeal advocated by, 153–154
    Whitefield, G. meeting of, 113
    writings, 91
Franklin, William, 161
free black community, first, 119
Freedmen's Bureau, 473, *473*, 475
freedpeople
    as citizens with equal legal rights, 475
    land for, 474
free labor, 54, *394*, 395, 397
free-labor capitalism, 466
free-labor societies, 37
free-labor wage contracts, 473
Freemasons, 114

Freeport doctrine, 400
Free Soil Party, 364–365, 379, *383*, 400
Free State Party, 383
free states
    immigrant migration to, 393
    and territories, *355*, 387, 393
    Union backed by, 416
Frémont, John C., 386, 387, 438
French. *See also* New France
    colonial households, 93
    fur trade, 70, 78
    Native Americans, dealings with, 38–41, 78–80, 97, 102, 118–119, 130
    power loss, 118–119
French and Indian War
    Washington, George in, *101*
French Catholics, 155–156
French-Huron alliance, 40
French-Indian War, 122–130, *125*
French Revolution, 207–208, *215*
French Revolutionary Wars, 235–236
frontier
    gender roles, 238
    racism, 175
    as term, 239
    violence in, 238
funded national debt, 87–88
furniture, Caribbean, *26*
fur trade
    in Canada, 39, 42, 78, 80
    French domination of, 70, 78–79
    in New France, 66, 76
    in New Netherland, 66
    in Virginia, 75

Gabriel's rebellion, 271–272
Gadsden flag, *180*
Gage, Margaret Kemble, 157, *158*
Gage, Sir Thomas, 139, 152, 155, 156
    in American Revolution prelude, 157
    in Revolutionary War, 158
    wife, *158*
Galloway, Joseph, 157
game, prehistoric, 4
Gangs of New York (film), 288
gang system, 104
Garner, Margaret, 370
Garrison, William Lloyd, 343, 409
Gaspie affair, 148
Gates, Horatio, 170, 180
gender
    on the frontier, 238
    income disparity, 252, 335
    literacy and, 281–283
    masculinity in religion, 295

middle-class values and, 282–283
Peggy Eaton controversy, 319–320
Seneca Falls Convention, 347
sexuality and moral reform, 346–347
southern patriarchy and, 264
threats to masculinity, 298–299
women and antislavery activity, 345, 347
women in penny press, *293*
women wage-earners, 249, 251
Genêt, Citizen Edmond, 208
George I, King of England, 98
George III, King of England
    in American Revolution, 160, 175
    in American Revolution prelude, 157
    as American Revolution's end, 184
    as Anglican Church head, 185
    ascent to throne, 136
    France, war on declared by, 172
    loyalist refugee allegiance to, 175
    painters employed by, *130*
    palace, *91*
    pardons granted by, 146
    Parliament dissolved by, 145
    revolutionaries' views concerning, 161, 163
    Stamp Act, position on, 141
Georgia
    in Civil War, 461, 463
    founding and early years, 111–113
    in Revolutionary War, 179
    secession, 411
    Spain, war with, involvement in, 120
Germain, Lord George, 161
German immigrants
    before Civil War, 380, *382*
    in mid-Atlantic colonies, 106
Germany, revolution in, *382*
Gettysburg, Battle of, 449–451, *450*, 452
Gibbs, Robert, *56*
Gilbert, Sir Humphrey, 45
Girondists, 208
global conflict, Revolutionary War as, 172
global economy, first, 3
global labor system, *33*
Glorious Revolution, 85–86, 87, 97, 120
Godey's Lady's Book, 283
Gold Rush, 365, *366*
Gooch, Sir William, 118
Goodwin, Doris Kearns, 455
Gordon riots, 176
government corruption, 311–312
governor, rise of, 117

Granada, fall of, 22, 23
Grant, Ulysses S., 481, *481*
    action against Ku Klux Klan, 486
    army, 453
    backlash against, 487
    blacks in office, 483
    carpetbagger corruption, 483, 485
    civil service reform, 482
    corruption during, 482
    foreign policy controversy, 482
    Forts Henry and Donelson victories, 429, 430
    as general in chief, 454
    on Georgia campaign, 463
    Hamburg Massacre and, 490
    on prisoners of war, 460
    reconstruction in south, 482–483
    reelection of, 486–487
    scalawags and, 485
    in Vicksburg campaign, 444, 451
    in Wilderness, 456
Gray, Samuel, 146
Great Awakening, First, 113–115, 152
Great Britain
    army, 135, 145–146, *146*
    cartoons, *181*
    Confederacy dealings with, 424
    cultural values of, 101
    formation of, 87
    France, war with, 172, 207, 218–228
    France *versus*, 123
    land claimed by, 96, 97
    navy, 208, 209, 219, 227
    political culture of, 116–118
    United States, relations with, 208
    wars, 102, 120–121
Great Plains, 4
Great Pyramid of the Sun, 10
Great Serpent Mound, Chillicothe, Ohio, *14*
Greece, classical, 167–168
Greeley, Horace, 403, 443, 457, *486*, 487
Greene, Nathanael, 181, 182
Greenland, 4, 15
Grenville, George, 136, 138, 139, 141
Grier, Robert, 387
Guanches, 22
Gullah, 106
Gutenberg, Johannes, 17

habeus corpus, 440n
haciendas, 30, 31
Hakluyt, Richard, 45
Half-Way Covenant, 59
Hamburg Massacre, 490
Hamilton (musical), 173
Hamilton, Alexander

    as Federalist, 205, 206
    killing of, 216
    manufacturing importance cited by, 228
    musicals, 173
    political involvement, 211, 212
    portraits, *206*
    as Treasury Department head, 203–204
Hamiltonian centralization, 207
Hamiltonian economics, 203–204
Hammond, James, 389, 393, 395, 398
Hancock, John, 147, 157, 158
Harper's Ferry raid, 377, 401–402
Harrington, James, 60, 65
Harrison, William Henry, 223, 358–359
Hartford Convention, 226
Harvard College, 90, 108, 110, 115
Haudenosaunee, 39
Hayes, Rutherford B., 490–491
headright system, 47–48
Helper, Hinton Rowan, 397–398
Hemings, Sally, 257
Hendrik, Mohawk Chief, 121, *122*
Hennepin, Father Louis, *81*
Henry, Patrick, 140, 152, 195
Henry VII, King of England, 44
Henry VIII, King of England, 45
Herndon, William, 401
Hessians, 161, 163, 168, 169
Higginson, Thomas Wentworth, 270, 344
High Church Laudians, 109–110
"high crimes and misdemeanors," 216
higher education, 475
High Federalists, 212, 215, 228
Hispaniola, 23
H. L. Hunley (combat submarine), 425–426
Hobbs, Abigail, 86
Hohokam, 11, *13*, 14
home life
    aesthetics of, 234–235, 246
    alcoholism and, 340
    lighting, 235
    middle-class values, 282–283
    privacy, 234, 246
Homer, Winslow, 469
Homestead Act, 395, 447
Hood, John Bell, 457, 462, 463, *463*
Hooker, Joe, 448
Hooker, Thomas, 56
horses
    as food source, 4
    Native American use of, 71, 73, 78, 207
    spread of European, 33

Horseshoe Bend, Battle of, 223
householder autonomy, threats to, 102–103
household income in Revolutionary War, 177
House of Burgesses (Va.), 47, 49, 104, 118
Houston, Sam, 360
Howe, Richard Viscount, 168, 169, 170
Howe, William, 158–159, 168, 169, 170
Hudson, Henry, 42
Hudson's Bay Company, 78
Huguenots, 38, 39, *86*
Hull, William, 223
human sacrifice, 10, *11,* 12, 23, 30
hunter-gatherers, 4, 11
Hurons, 15, 39, 40–41, 55
Hutchinson, Anne, 56, 57
Hutchinson, Thomas, 107, 108, 141, 148, 149, 152, 155

Ice Age, 4
Iceland, 15
Illinois Country, 80
immigrants
    before Columbus, 4
    in mid-Atlantic colonies, 106
    nation of, 4
    in northern cities, 393
    in politics, 381–382
    statistics, *382*
immigration
    and nativism, 380–383
    opposition to, 379, 404
    statistics, *382*
The Impending Crisis of the South (Helper), 397–398
imperial conflict, renewal of, 118–122
impressment, 219, 226
Inca Empire, 5, 7, 10, 26
indentured servants
    in Caribbean colonies, 66
    slaves replacing, 97
    in Virginia, 48, 53, 76
    in West Indies, 52, 60
independence
    in agriculture, 232–233, 248, 267
    among artisans, 236
    centralized government and, 304–305
    ethic in colonial era, 92, 93, 103
    literacy and, 281
Indians (term), 23
Indian Territory (Oklahoma), 418
industrialism, 231, 250, 252, 389–390, 404
infant baptism, 59

infant mortality, 56
infantry rifle, 420–421
inflation, wartime, *444,* 454
inheritance, rural patterns of, 235
"inmates" (term), 103
innovations, spread of, 33
interchangeable parts, 389–390
Intolerable Acts, 156
Inuits, 4, 15
Ireland, English colonization in, 45
Irish Americans, 381, 445–446
Irish Catholics, 176, 380
Irish potato famine, 380, *382*
Iroquois
    after American Revolution, 189
    attacks, 74
    attacks, end to, 41
    British, dealings with, 123
    Confederacy, 15, 39, 61, 70
    defeat of, *40*
    French, dealings with, 79, 80
    fur trade with, 42
    neutrality, 95
    power held by, 97
    reservations, 208
    in Revolutionary War, 175
    solidarity, 128
Iroquois League, 76
irrigation systems, 6, 11
Isabella of Castile, Princess, 22, 23
Islam, 16–18, *17, 18, 18*
Islamic societies, 34
Isthmus of Panama, first European crossing of, 23

Jackson, Andrew
    annexation controversy, 358
    democracy incarnate, *303*
    against government corruption, 311–312
    King Andrew the First, *324*
    in mourning, 314
    Rachel Donelson Jackson, *313*
    reputation of, 310, 313
    the South and, 315
    in War of 1812, 223, 225, 226
Jackson, Stonewall, 430–431
Jackson, Thomas J., 427
Jamaica, 23, 52, 60
James I, King of England, 46
James II, King of England, 84, 85
Jamestown, Va., 47, 48, 50–52
    Bacon, Nathaniel in, 75
    reconstruction of, *76*
    retaking of, 76
Jay, John, 185, 209
Jay Treaty, 209, 211

Jefferson, Thomas
    agricultural ideals, 231
    armed resistance supported by, 160
    artisans, 236
    description of, 205
    embargo, 219
    French Revolution backed by, 207–208, *215*
    legacy, 228
    limited government backed by, 201, 205
    Louis and Clark expedition authorized by, 220
    Louisiana Purchase authorized by, 216–217
    Northwest Territory resolution offered by, 189
    portraits, *214*
    as president, 213–215, 216, 218
    on presidential titles, 202
    religious freedom advocated by, 185–186
    in Revolutionary War, 169, 183
    Sally Hemings and, 257
    slavery and, 257
    as state department head, 203
    states' rights, 304
    as vice president, 211
    women farmers, 233, 257
    writings, 163
Jeffersonian republicanism, 204–206, 207
Jeffersonians in power, 213–218
Jesuits, 40, *42,* 43
Jews, 186
John Adams (film), 147
Johnson, Andrew, *472*
    1866 congressional elections campaign, 475–476
    enmity toward planters, 470–471
    impeachment of
        reasons of, 478
        trial process, 478–479
    progressive reconstruction policy, 471, 475
    schism with Congress, 475
    vice presidential nomination, 470, 471
Johnson, William, 124, 125
Johnston, Albert Sidney, 430, 457
Johnston, Joseph E., 427
joint-stock company, 46–47
judicial review, 216
jury system, 58–59

Kalb, Johann, Baron de, 170
Kansas, 383–384, 387, 388

Kansas-Nebraska Act, 1854, 374, 378–379, 383, *385,* 404
Kaskaskia, Ill., 80
Kentucky, 187–188, 417–418
Kentucky Resolves, 212
Kentucky-Tennessee theater (Civil War), *429*
Key, Francis Scott, 224–225
King Cotton diplomacy, 424–425
Kingdom of Jerusalem, 18
Kingfisher (ship), *69*
King George's War, 120–121, 130
King Philip (Metacom), war, 73, *75*
King William's war, 80, *94*
Knowles Riot, 120–121
Know-Nothings, 379, 382
Knox, Henry, 203
Kongo, 21
Kosciuszko, Thaddeus, 170
Ku Klux Klan (KKK), 479, 481, 485–486
Ku Klux Klan Act, 486

labor conditions in north (U.S.), 393
Lafayette, Marquis de, 170, 173
Lake Titicaca, 6
Lalemant, Jerôme, 55
land, ownership, regional attitudes toward, 267
land for freedpeople, 474
Larcom, Lucy, 251
La Salle, René-Robert Cavelier, Sieur de, 80, *81, 82*
Las Casas, Bartolomé de, 29
Latitudinarians, 115
La Venta (Olmec city), 7–8
law, national government and, 306–307
law, states' rights and, 306–307
Lawrence, Kan., *384,* 384–385
Lecompton constitution, 387–389
Lee, Charles, 169
Lee, Richard Henry, 163
Lee, Robert E.
    at Antietam, 440, 442
    Brown, J.'s raid ended by, 402
    at Five Forks, 465
    at Gettysburg, 450, 451
    Maryland, retreat from, 443
    on prisoners of war, 460
    secession supported by, 416
    in Second Battle of Bull Run, 434
    in Seven Days' battles, 431
    in Virginia, 457
    in Wilderness, 456
Leeward Islands, 52, 60
legal tender, 424
Le Moyne D'Iberville, Pierre, 80

Letters from a Farmer in Pennsylvania (Dickinson), 144
Letters from an American Farmer (Crèvecoeur), 232, 235
Leverett, John, Jr., 110
Lewis, Meriwether, 217, *220*
Lewis and Clark expedition, 1804, 217–218, 220
Lexington, Battle of, 157, *159, 161*
liberty, 97, 174, *187*
life expectancy
    in English colonies, 50–52, 56, 89
    in New England, 107
Lima, Peru, 26
Lincoln (film), 455
Lincoln, Abraham
    on African American soldiers, 454
    assassination, 465–466
    border states, dealings with, 438–439
    Civil War, 424, 434, 444, 451, 452, 453, 454, 463
    Emancipation Proclamation, 419, 434, 437–438, 439–440, 442–443, *443,* 457
    film depiction of, 401
    free-labor ideology espoused by, 395, 397
    inaugural address, 415
    inauguration, 1861, *409*
    Lincoln-Douglas debates, *379,* 399, 400, *400*
    photos, *466*
    as president, 415
    presidential election, 1860, 408–409, 434, 454
    presidential election, 1864, 457
    on prisoners of war, 460
    racial equality, views on, 399
    on revolution, 411
    slavery opposed by, 378–379, 404, 413
    South attitudes concerning, 409
    troops, call for, 416, 440
    wartime reconstruction, 470
Lincoln, Benjamin, 180
Lincoln, Mary Todd, 401
liquor, prohibition of, 111
literacy
    censorship and, 280
    in English colonies, 89–90
    gender and, 281
    media and, 280–281
    popular works, 291, 293–294
Little Ice Age, 14, 15
Locke, John, 60, 87, 110, 163
London Company, 47, 48

longhouse, *17*
Long Island, 61
López, Narciso, 371–372
Lord Dunmore's War, 1774, 159
Loudoun, John Campbell, Earl of, 127, 128
Louisbourg, fall of, 122
Louisiana, 490
    Lincoln's moderate policy toward, 470
    secession, 411
Louisiana (colony)
    blacks in, 82
    French in, 80, *81,* 82, 97
    maps, *81*
    Spanish rule of, 130, 172, 207
Louisiana Purchase, 1803, *201,* 214, 216–217, 218, *218,* 404
Louisiana Territory, *220*
Louis XIV, King of France, 41, 80, 85, *86*
Louis XV, King of France, 136
Louis XVI, King of France, 163, 171, 207
Low Church Anglicans, 109–110
loyalists, 149, *156,* 174–175
Luther, Martin, 38
Lyon, Nathaniel, 417

Macready, William Charles, *292*
Madeira Islands, 19
Madison, James
    as Congress leader, 202
    on Constitution, 195
    Hamilton, A., disagreement with, 204
    as president, 220, 221
    as secretary of state, 216
Magellan, Ferdinand, 23
maiz de ocho, 10, 12
maize, 5, 7, 10–11
malaria, 50–51, 104, 181
Mali empire, 19
mammoths, 4
Manassas, Battle of, 427, *428*
Manassas, Battle of, Second, *433,* 434
Manhattan Island, 42
Manifest Destiny, 354, 356, 373, 378
manufacturing. *see also* factories
    Amercian system of manufactures, 389–390
    clothing industry, 250, 252
    outsourcing, 252
    pre-Civil War, 404
maps, Native American, *96*
Marbury v. Madison, 216
Marco Polo, 16, 23

maritime techniques, advances in, 17–18, 19
market economy, 332–334
Market Revolution
    agricultural economy and, 231–232
    effect on gender roles, 245–246
    Jacksonian democracy and, 321
    Max Weber and, 232
    in northern U.S, 232
    psychology of, 232
    in relation to slavery, 258–260
    religion in conflict with, 286–287
    in southern U.S., 255, 273, 275
    transportation and, 241
marriage, 51–52, 187
Marshall, John, 213, 215, 216, *217*
martial law, 444
Martin, William, 176
Maryland
    in Civil War, 416, 417, 434, *442*
    as colony, 49
    maps, *51*
    Protestant takeover of, 85
Mason, George, 190
Mason, James, 425
Massachuset Indians, 57
Massachusetts, 57–58, 86, 190, 192, 193
Massachusetts Bay, 54
Massachusetts Bay Company, 54
Massachusetts Government Act, 155, 156
Massachusetts Infantry, 54th, 453
Massachusetts Provincial Congress, 156–157
Massachusetts Volunteer Infantry, 54th, 419
Massasoit (Wampanoag sachem), 54
Master and Commander: The Far Side of the World (film), 227
Mather, Cotton, 87
Mather, Increase, 73, 114
matrilineal social organization, 27
Mayans, 8, *10*, 30
Mayflower (ship), 54
Mayhew, Thomas, Jr., 57
Mayhew, Thomas, Sr., 57
McClellan, George B.
    at Antietam, 440, 442
    Army of the Potomac organized by, 427
    in presidential race, 1864, 458
    reinforcements, request for, 431
    replacement of, 444
    in Virginia, 430, 432, 434
McIntosh, Ebenezer, 141
Meade, George Gordon, 449, 451
medicine, 110–111

Mediterranean, *20*
Menéndez de Avilés, Pedro, 38
men's clothing, 111
mental health, 337
mercantilism, 83
Merrimac (ship), *426*, 426–427
Mesa Verde, Colo., 11–12
Mesoamerica, 7–8, *9*, 10
Metacom (King Philip), war, 73, 74, *74*, 75
metals, precious, 21
metalworking, 5, 17
Methodists, 113, 114–115
Mexican American War, *353*, 360–364, *362*, 418
Mexico
    conquest of, 25–26, 30
    killing epidemics in, 30
    slavery abolished in, 360
Mexico City, 26
Miami confederacy, collapse of, 208–209
mid-Atlantic colonies, 106–107
Middle Passage, 104
midnight judges, 215
A Midwife's Tale (film), 237
Mifflin, Mr. and Mrs. Thomas, *64*
migration
    urban, 231
    westward, 231, 235, 238, 247
military buildup, Federalist, 212, 213
military cuts, 214
military draft, 440, 445–446
military service, young men's attitudes concerning, 93
military techniques, advances in, 17–18
Milwaukee and Chicago Railroad bridge, Racine, Wis., *390*
Minuit, Pierre, 44
missionary societies, 475
Mississippi, 410
Mississippian culture, 12–13
Mississippi River, 226
Mississippi state election of 1875, 487, 489
Missouri, 417–418
Missouri Compromise, 1820, 374, 377, 378
mita, 31, *34*
mixed-blood Indians, 222
Moctezuma (Aztec ruler), 25
Mogollon, 11, *13*
Mohawks, 73
Mohegans, 57
Molasses Act, 1733, 107, 137–138
molasses trade, 141–142

money. *see* currency
Monitor (ship), *426*, 427
Monks Mound, Cahokia, Ill., 13
Monroe Doctrine, 312
Montcalm, Louis-Joseph, Marques de, 127, 129
Montgomery, Richard, 160
Moore, Brian, 43
Moravian Indians, 175
Morgan, Daniel, 180–181
Morgan, John, 111
Mormon migration, 357–358
Morrill Land-Grant College Act, 447
Morris, Robert, 179
Mose, Fla., 119, 120
Mott, Lucretia, 344
mound builders, 12–13, *14, 16*
Mughal Empire, 17
Muslims, 18, 19–20, 21

Nairne, Thomas, 94
Napoleon Bonaparte, 216, 218, 219, 223, 226
Napoleonic Wars, 1803-1815, 218–228
Napoleon III, French emperor, 424
Nashville, Battle of, *463*
Nast, Thomas, 476, *486*
Natchez Indians, 119
national debt (post-Revolution era), 203–204, 205, 218
National Union Party, 475–476
Native American land
    boundaries lacking for, 70
    control over, 66, 96–97
    at end of French-Indian War, 130
    at end of Revolutionary War, 185
    in Revolution era and beyond, 188–189
Native Americans
    American independence impact on, 185
    American settlement by, *6*
    British expansion impact on, 102
    British military aid to, 208, 222
    buffer state, proposed, 226
    capitalism impact on, 5
    captives, 10, 13, 39–40, *41*, 70, 93–94
    Cherokee Nation, 317
    Christianity among, 27–28, 40–41
    civil war, 73
    in Civil War, 418, 465
    colonization impact on, 69, 70, 73
    diseases, European spread among, 3, *30*, 30–31, 33, 54, 80, 172, 222
    European contact with (*see* European-Native American relations)

Indian Removal Act, 316–318
killing of, 33, 137, 175
New France, attitude concerning, 130
North America controlled by, 206
Plains Indians, 316
population decline, 30–31
in post-Revolution years, 186–187
rebellions, 97
refusal to kill other, 175
republics (multiethnic villages), 119, *119*
in Revolutionary War, 167, 175
Spanish settlement frontier limited by, 93
technological constraints, 5
trade with, 37, 61, 70, 82, 97
Trail of Tears, *318*
treatment of, 29, *39*
War of 1812, participation in, 223
wars, 71–78
Native American slaves, 29, 30, 31, 73, 78, 82, 89, 94, 95, *95*
Native American women as farmers, 5, *12*, 27, 57
nativism, 379, 380–381, 382–383, 404
Navigation Acts, 83, 84, 87, 192
Nebraska Territory, 378
Nelson, Horatio, 219, 227
neo-Confederate violence, against blacks, 472
Neolin (Delaware), 136, 222
Neolithic revolution, 5
Netherlands, 54
Neville, John, 208
New Amsterdam, *44*
New Amsterdam (city), 61
New England
    colonies, 54, 56–59, 84
    economic conditions, 107–108
    health conditions, 89
    homogenous society, 60
    maps, *58, 74*
    regional identity, 104
New England Confederation, 57
New France
    British colonies, separation from, *123*
    English, fight against, 78
    film depiction of, 43
    Iroquois confederacy bordering, 70
    and Iroquois League, 38–41, 76, 78
    maps, *42*
    middle ground, 78–80, *79*
    Native American trade with, 37, 61
    overview of, 66
    population, 88–89

New Haven (colony), 57
New Jersey
    founding of, 61
    maps, *62*
    West, 64–65
New Jersey Plan, 194
New Mexico
    as Spanish colony, 26–27, 71, 78, 89
    Spanish missions in, *28*
    U.S. acquisition of, 373
    U.S. trade with, 355
New Netherland, 37, 41–42, 44, 61, 66
New Orleans, Battle of, 225–226
New Orleans, La., *201*
New Side Presbyterians, 114
New Spain, 82, 206–207
newspapers (colonial era), 108–109
New Sweden, 44
Newton, Sir Isaac, 110
New World, *3*
New York (city)
    antidraft riots, 446, *446*
    conspiracy trials, 1741, 120
    naming of, 61
    poverty, 393
    in Revolutionary War, 169
New York (colony/state), 61, *62*, 84
New York City, 231, *231*
Niagara Falls, *37*
Nicaragua, 373
Nightingale, Florence, 447
Nina (caravel), 19, 23
non-Christian lands, division of, 23
non-Christian people, 40
non-Christian world, trade with, 17
noncombatants, African Americans as, 453
nonimportation of British goods
    agreements, 141, 145
    Boston port closure followed by, 156
    debates over, 143–144
    peak of success, 148
    resistance to, 149
    support for, 152
Non-Intercourse Act, 1809, 221
Non-Separatists, 45, 57
nonslaveholders' farms, *398*
nonslaveholding whites, southern, 397, 398–399
Norfolk, Va., 160
Norse in North America, 15, 21
north (U.S.), 393
North, Frederick, Lord
    in American Revolution prelude, 148, 156, 157
    as chancellor of exchequer, 143

    resignation, 184
    in Revolutionary War, 160, 172, 176
    tea crisis, handling of, 153–154
North America
    British army in, 135
    before Columbus, 14–15
    dominance, battles over, 97
    Spaniards in, 26–28, *27*
    war for, 122–130
North Carolina
    in Civil War, 454
    formation of, 60, 95
    provisional governor for, 471
    in Revolutionary War, 180
    in revolution prelude, 152
    secession, 416
northeastern theater of war, *94*
northern colonies
    life expectancy, 89
    political culture of, 117, 118, 130
Northern Pacific, 487
Northwest, British occupation of, 223
Northwest Ordinance, 189
Northwest Territory, *188*, 189, 208
Not for Ourselves Alone (film), 348
Nova Scotia, 94, 121, 124–125, 150
Nurse, Rebecca, 88
nurses, 447

oaths of allegiance, 470
Obama, Barack, 173
Obama, Michelle, 173
O'Brian, Patrick, 227
obsidian, weapons from, 5
Occaneechees, 75
Oglethorpe, James, 111, 120
Ohio River Valley, 12
Ohio Valley, 211
Oklahoma (Indian Territory), 418
Old Side Presbyterians, 114
Old South, 104–106
Olive Branch Petition, 160
Oliver, Andrew, 140–141
Olmecs, 7–8
Opechancanough (Powhatan's brother), 47, 48, 49, 74
Opechancanough massacre, 1622, 49
Oregon, 359, *359*, 373
Oregon Trail, 356–357
organized labor, pre–Civil War, 395
Osages, 82
Osborn, Sarah, 152
Ostend Manifesto, 372
Overland Campaign, *423*
overland trails, *357*

Pacal the Great (Mayan ruler), 8
Pacific Railroad Act, 447
pacifism
    Quaker experiment in, 61
pacifists
    German, 66
    Quakers as, 62
Paine, Thomas
    loyalists, attitude concerning, 149
    unicameral legislatures advocated by, 190
    writings, 161, 162
Palmerston, Lord, 424–425
Pamunkeys, 76
panic of 1857, 394–395, *397*, 402
pan-Indian identity, 128
paper money, 107, *108*, 139
Parker, Ely, 465
Parker, Theodore, 344
parochial schools, 381–382
Parris, Samuel, 86, 88
paternalism, 104
patriarchy, 186–187
patriots, 149, 152
patroonship, 44
"Paxton Boys," 137, 150
Peace Democrats, 440
Peace of Paris, 130
penal system, 335–337, *336*
Pendleton Civil Service Reform Act, 482
Peninsua Campaign, *432*
Penn, John, 137
Penn, William, 65, *65*
Pennsylvania
    constitution, 190
    founding and early years, 60, 65–66
    in French-Indian War, 127
    slave emancipation in, 186
Pennsylvania Infantry Regiment, 31st, *407*
Pequot Indians, 57, *59*, 73
personal covenant, 56
personal liberty laws, 369, 370
Peru, 26, 30
Petraglyph Canyon, Nev., *7*
Philadelphia, Pa., *63*, 66, 170, 172
Philadelphia Convention, 194, 196
Philadelphia Synod, 113, *114*
Philip II, King of Spain, 26, 31, 38
Philip V, King of Spain, 120
Phillips, Wendell, 344
Pickering, John, 215
Pierce, Franklin, 369–370, 372–373, 383–384, 385
Pilgrims, 54, 55
Pinckney, Charles Cotesworth, 213, 218
Pinckney, Eliza Lucas, 106

Pinckney, Thomas, 211
Pinta (caravel), 23
Pitt, William, 126, 127–128, 136, 143, 157
Pizarro, Francisco, 26
placemen, 117
plantation society, collapse of, 466
plants, domesticated, 33
pluralistic society, 42, 44
Plymouth, Mass., 45, 73
Plymouth Company, 47
Plymouth militia, 73
Pocahontas, 47, *48*
political culture, 116–118, *377*
politics of harmony, 118
politics *versus* democracy, 401
Polk, James K., 360, 361, 362, 363, 364, 365, 371
Ponce de León, Juan, 23
Pontiac's War, 1763-1764, 126, 136–137, *138*, 175
poor whites, 398
Popé (San Juan Pueblo medicine man), 71, 72
Pope, John, 434
Pope's Day procession, *142*
popular sovereignty, 189, 364
population growth, *234*, 236
Portugal
    Asian empire, 21, 31
    expansion, 18–19, 31
    independence, 31
    non-Christian lands claimed by, 23
Portuguese, 5, 19, *21*
Postwar South
    churches and schools, 474–475
    Freedmen's Bureau and, 473
    land and labor in, 473
potatoes, 7, 33–34
Powhatan, Chief, 47, *48*
Powhatan Indians, 49
praying Indians, 73
praying towns, 73
predestination, 38
Presbyterian Church, 38, *114*
Presbyterians, 106, 114, 115
Presbytery, 113
president, first, 201
president, image of, 205
presidential election, 1796, 211
presidential election, 1800, 213, *213*
presidential election, 1804, 218
presidential election, 1808, 220
presidential election, 1848, 364–365
presidential election, 1856, 385–389, *388*
presidential election, 1860, 387, 389, 399, 400, 404, 407, 408–410, *410*, 412

presidential election, 1864, 457–458, 460–461, 463–466
presidential election, 1868, 481
presidential election, 1872, 486–487
presidential election, 1876
    compromise of 1877, 490–491
    Democrats campaign, 490
    disputed results, 490
    issues in, 490
    nominations for, 490
presidential pardon to southern whites, 470
presidios, 355
press gangs, 120
Preston, Thomas, 146, 147
primogeniture, 91
Princeton, Battle of, 170
Princeton University, 115
printed books, increase in, 24
printers and printing, 108–109
printing press, 17, *109*
prisoners of war, exchanges of, 458–460
prison ships, British, 176, *178, 179*
privateers, 128
Proclamation Line of 1763, *138*
Proclamation of 1763, 136
Proclamation of Amnesty and Reconstruction, 470
Prophetstown (Tippecanoe), Ind., 222
proprietary colonies, 49
Protestant Episcopal Church, 186
The Protestant Ethic and the Spirit of Capitalism, 232
Protestant Reformation, 31, 38
Protestants, 97
Providence, R.I., 57
provincial congresses, 156
public Friends, 63
public schools, 390
public virtue, 190
Pueblo Indians
    ancestry, 12
    architecture, 12
    Christian missionary work with, 27
    revolt, *71*, 71–73, 78
    Spaniard encounter of, 26
    Spaniard relations with, 78, 82
Pulaski, Casimir, Count, 170
Puritans
    beliefs, 45
    conversion, dissent, and expansion, 56–57
    end of era, 86, 87
    family life, 56
    labor, 37
    migration, 46

Native Americans, dealings with, 57, *59*
rejection of, 109–110
sexual mores and laws, 103
pyramids, 7, 8, 10

Quakers
in American Revolution, 149
beliefs, 59, 62–63
families, 64, *64*
as free-labor society, 37
as mediators, 128
meeting houses, *63*
migration to America, 46, 61–62
Native Americans, dealings with, *65*, 66
in Pennsylvania, 65, 66
persecution, 60, 65
revivalism impact on, 115
slavery opposed by, 152
war, views on, 73
Quartering Act, 1765, 139, 144, 148, 155
quasi-slavery, 472
Quasi War of 1798-1800, 222
Quebec, 39
Quebec Act, 155–156, 157
Queen Anne's War, 93, 95
Quincy, Josiah, Jr., 146, 147
quitrent system, 65

race, American Revolution and, 167
race, class *versus*, 398–399
race relations
19th-century roots of racism, 297–299
free-black employment, 274, 297–298
reform movement and, 342
threats to masculinity, 298–299
racial equality
Republicans associated with, 387
slavery abolition associated with, 399
southern fears of, 434
Racine, Wis., bridge at, *390*
racism, 175, 399, 475
radical Republicans
on Johnson's policy, 471
on oaths of allegiance, 470
railroads, *391, 461*
Raleigh, Sir Walter, 45
Randolph, John, 221, 268
rape, 103
Raynal, Abbé, 33
reconstruction
churches and schools, 474–475
debate about, 472

in south, 482–483
southern defiance, 471–472
Reconstruction Acts of 1867, 476–477
reconstruction policy, 470
Red Sticks, 223
reform
alcoholism, *339*
Declaration of Sentiments, 349
immigration and, 283–284
prostitution, 346–347
in southern U.S., 341
temperance, 338–340
women's rights, 347–350
regional transfer of power, 466
religion
American independence impact on, 185–186
apocalyptic views in, 285–286
in British colonies, 89, 90, *90*
Christianity among slaves, 269–271
class and, 281–282, 294–295
defense of slavery, 296–297
democratic views and, 284–285
disestablishment, 284
Enlightenment influence on, 109–110
evangelicalism, 294–297
Market Revolution in conflict with, 286–287
morality and, 296
Native American before Christianity, 8, 10, 12
in Old South, 104
patriarchy in, 287, 295–296
providence in relation to progress, 285–286
segregation within, 269, 272
religious diversity, 44
religious liberty, 57, 65, 185–186
religious revivalism, 113–116, 395
religious tolerance
in Dutch Republic, 41–42
in Enlightenment era, 110
in Maryland, 49, 85
in New Jersey, 64
in New York, 61
post-Revolution, 186
in Quebec, 155–156
Renaissance, 17
representative government, 87
republic, 167–168, 190, 206
Republican militias, 486
Republican Party
elections, 1866, 476
establishment of, 204, 377, *381*
rise of, 378–379, 404
as Union Party, 470

Republican policies, public opinion against, 487
republican wife/republican mother ideal, 1878
Restoration colonies, 60
Restoration era (1660-1688), 60, 62
Revenue Act, 1766, 141–142
Revere, Paul, *146, 155,* 157
revolution, secession *versus*, 411
Revolutionary War
British offensive, 168–169, 179–185
British public opinion concerning, 175
campaigns of 1777, 170–172
cartoons, *181*
debt, 204
end, 185
foreign intervention, 171–172
French perspective on, 183
frontier, *177*
mutiny and reform, 178–179
northern war, 168–170, *171*
outbreak of, 157–161, *161,* 163
overview of, 167
prisoners of war, 176, *178, 179*
refugees, 175
southern war, 179–185, *182*
violence and attrition, 175–178
Rhode Island, 57
Richardson, Ebenezer, 146
Richmond, Va., 445, *445*
Richmond Grays, *421*
Rio Grande Valley, 78
Roanoke colony, 45, *46*
Robert E. Lee (blockade runner), *425*
Rochambeau, Jean Baptiste Donatien, Comte de, 184
Rockingham, Charles Watson-Wentworth, Marquess of, 141
Rolfe, John, 47, 53
Rome, republican, 167–168
Roosevelt, Franklin Delano, 211
Rosecranz, William S., 444, 451–452
rural areas, revolution prelude in, 150, 152
Rush, Benjamin, 111
Russell, John, 424–425
Rutgers University, 115

Sacajawea (Shoshone), 217–218
Safavid Empire, 17
Saint Domingue (*later* Haiti), 41, 216
Salem, Mass., 54
Salem witch trials, 86, 88
Saltillo, Mexico, American forces in, *361*
Samoset (Patuxet Indian), 54

INDEX I-13

San Diego, Calif., 172
San Diego de Alcala (mission), *174*
San Francisco, Calif., 365
San Lorenzo (Olmec city), 7–8
Santa María (caravel), 23
Santo Domingo affair, 482
São Tomé, 19
Saratoga, 170, 174
Sassamon, John, 73
scalawags, 485
schools
    for African Americans, 479
    country, *392*
    freedpeople founding of, 474–475
    parochial, 381–382
    public, 381–382, 390
Scotland, 59, 87
Scots-Irish immigrants, 106, 137, 150
Scott, Winfield, 379
sea travel, 19
secession
    Southern, 407, 408, 410–413, *412*, 416, 434
    threats before Civil War, 389, 399, 409
    threats post-Civil War, 466
secessionist movements, 189, 226
Second Bank of the United States
    architectural stature of, *306*
    Panic of 1819, 309
    role of national government, 305–306, 321
Second War of American Independence, 228
sectionalism, 395
Sedition Act, 212, 213, 214, 215
separation of powers, 189–190
Separatists, 45, 54, 56–57
Sepúlveda, Juan Ginés de, 29
serfdom, 31
Serra, Junipero, 172
servants
    Africans as, 46, 53
    indentured (*see* indentured servants)
settlement, land speculation, 238
settlement, spectrum of, 89–90, *91*
Seven Days' battles, 431–432, *432*
Seven Years' War (1756-1763), 127, *128*, 136, 175
Seward, William H., 368, 379, 402, 404, 415
sexual behavior, double standard of, 103
sexual offenses, 103

Seymour, Horatio, 481
sharecropping, 473
share wages, 473
Sharp, Granville, 152
Shattuck, Job, *193*
Shaw, Robert Gould, 453
Shawnees
    British, dealings with, 208
    hunting grounds, 188
    in Revolutionary War, 175
Shays, Daniel, *193*
Shays's Rebellion, 193
Shenandoah campaign, 61, 430–431
Shenandoah Valley, 4
Sherman, William T., 444, 457, *460, 461,* 462, 464
Sherwood, Robert, 401
Shiloh, Battle of, 430, 431
shipbuilding, 107
Shippen, William, 110–111
Shirley, William, 107, 118, 120, 123, 124, 125, 127
shoemakers' strike, Lynn, Mass., 1860, 395, 397
sickle cell anemia, 104
Sierra Leone, 175
silver, 26, *34,* 107, 108
Sims, Thomas, 369
slave (term origin), 18
slave-catchers, 369–370
slavery
    African culture and, *255,* 269
    in Americas, 29, 30, 31
    in Antigua, *53*
    antislavery activity, 271–273, 297
    avoidance of, 56
    in Caribbean, 23, 31
    in Carolinas, 60
    cartoons, *383*
    Christianity, 269–271
    colonization, 257, 342–343, 345
    compromise proposals, 411, 413
    cotton gin, 258
    cotton's effect on, 255, 260, 262–263, 267–268, 275
    court cases, 387
    in Crusades, 18
    declining need for, 256–257, 260
    defense of, 270, 296–297, 313, 393
    democratic views and, 271–272
    domestic slave trade, *262,* 267–269
    economic impact of, 397
    emancipation, 257, *439,* 464, 466 (*see also* Emancipation Proclamation)

    European participation in, 3, 20
    evangelical views concerning, 269
    expansionism and, 353, 354, 374, 404
    extension, opposition to, 413
    family, 267–269
    films depicting, 322
    gender roles, 256
    in Georgia, 113
    international slave trade, 258
    maps, *396*
    Missouri Compromise and, 308–309
    moral effects of, *344*
    naming practices, 269
    Native American practice of, 13
    in North America, 53
    in northern colonies, 89
    opposition to, 152
    paternalism, 263, *265,* 272
    personhood, 263
    plantation life, 255, 258, 260, 262–263, *264*
    poor white attitudes concerning, 398
    population redistribution, *261, 263*
    Portuguese participation in, 19, 21, *21,* 31
    in post-Revolution era, 189
    privileges within, 267
    prohibition of, 111 (Ga.)
    Quaker views concerning, 63
    in relation to Market Revolution, 258–260
    and secession, 416
    in southern colonies, 104–106
    southern portraits of, *394*
    striking against, 434
    task system, 258, 262
    Thomas Jefferson and, 257
    three-fifths rule and, 192, 194, 226, 307
    upward mobility contrasted with, 397
    and war, 438–440, 442–443
    westward migration and, 247, 307–309
slaves. *See also* African slaves; Native American slaves
    American independence impact on, 185, 186
    Christianity adopted by, 104, 186
    as Christians, 269–271
    emancipation of, 437–438
    family life, 267–269

invisible economy, 105
life expectancy, 89
literacy, 89–90
parades, 152
price of, 389, 398
recaptured, 459
revivalism impact on, 114
revolts, 119, 120, 216
in Revolutionary War, 174–175, 184
self-realization, 455
Spain, attitude concerning, 102
western migration of, 188
slaves, runaway
  advertisements for, *363*
  aiding, 369
  during Civil War, 437, *437*
  law and legislation, 366, 367–369
  during Revolutionary War, 174
  struggles of, 369–370
slave states and territories, *355, 385*, 393
slave trade
  Africa, colonies and, 19–21, 23, 42, *105*
  Atlantic, 19, 20–21, *85*, 104, 186
  domestic, 260, 267–269
  Indian, 61, 73, 95
  international, 258, 260
  peak, 104
Slidell, John, 425
smallpox
  Algonquins killed by, 43
  Aztecs and Incas killed by, 26, *30*
  blankets infested with, 137
  Hurons killed by, 40–41, 55
  in New England, 107
  during Revolutionary War, 160
  in Revolutionary War, 168
  Spaniard role in spreading, 82
  spread of, 4
Smalls, Robert, *484*
Smith, Adam, 152
Smith, John, 47
smoothbore musket, 421
soldiers (Civil War), 419, *422, 448*
Sons of Liberty
  Boston British occupation, response to, 146
  cartoons, *154*
  informants, *158*
  label, 127
  marches and parades, 152
  nonimportation advocated by, 148
  non-resistance supporters denounced by, 149
  Stamp Act opposed by, 140, 141
  Wilkes, J. supported by, 145
South
  Brown, J.'s raid impact on, 402
  economy, 390, 392–393, 395, 444–445, 459
  emergence of, 104–106
  in Revolutionary War, 179–185
  Unionist sentiment in, 398
South Carolina, 490
  exports, 106
  formation of, 60, 95
  population, 95
  in Revolutionary War, 180
  secession convention, 410, *411*
  slavery in, *95*, 106, 186
South Carolina convention, 479
southeast, colonial, 96, *96*
southeastern theater of war, *95, 121*
southern colonies, 89, 117, 118, 130
southern defiance, 471–472
southern Republican state governments
  fall of, 490
southern whites
  presidential pardon to, 470
Southwest (U.S.), 11–12, 96, 97, 418
sovereign power, 189
Spain
  and Caribbean, 23
  challenges to, 41, 97
  Empire, 28, 30–31, 32, *33*
  expansion, 172
  in French-Indian War, 129, 130
  versus Great Britain, 172
  land claimed by, 96
  Louisiana Territory ceded by, 216
  neutrality, 127
  non-Christian lands claimed by, 23
  outposts, 97
  power challenges, 37, 38
  reconquest of, 22
  in Revolutionary War, 172
  as slave liberator, potential, 102
  United States, relations with, 211
  wars, 102, 119–120
  world domination by, 34
Spaniards
  Americas colonized by, 5
  colonial households, 93
  expansion, 22
  Native Americans, dealings with, 10, 39, 78, 82, 97
  Pueblo revolt against, 71–73
Spanish Armada, 45

Spanish colonial households, 93
Spanish Indies, 23
Spanish missions
  in California, *174*, 207
  in crisis, 71
  destruction of, 93, 94
  Franciscan, 172
  maps, *28*
  overview of, 355
  in Texas, 82
specie, 423
spies, *448*
spoils system, 482
Spotswood, Alexander, 117
Spotsylvania, Battle of, *456*
Squanto (Patuxet Indian), 54
squash, 10–11
Stamp Act, 1765, 139, *144*, 149, 154
Stamp Act crisis, 135, 140–143, 150, 156
Stamp Act Riots, 1765, 120, 140–141
Stanton, Elizabeth Cady, 347–348, *350*
staple crops
  Caribbean production of, 66
  colony production of, 18
  slave production of, 31, 89, 106, *396*
"The Star-Spangled Banner" (Key), 224–225
state constitutions, 190
states' rights, 306–307, 313, 319
stay laws, 193
steel, 33
Stephens, Alexander H., 414
Steuben, Frederick Wilhelm, Baron von, 170
Stevens, Thaddeus, 455
Stockton, Richard, 169
Stoddard, Solomon, 113
Stones River, Battle of, 444
stone tools, 5
Stono Rebellion, 119
Stowe, Harriet Beecher, *331*, 345, 370, *372*
strict constructionalism, 205
strikes, 395, 397
Stuart, J. E. B., 402, 431, 457
stuck-up aristocrats, 470–471
Stump, Frederick, 137
Stump Speaking (painting), *377*
Stuyvesant, Pieter, 44, 61
substitutes, military, 445, 446
suffrage, 299–300
sugar, 52, *53*, 54
Sugar Act, 1764, 137–139, 140
Sumner, Charles, 384–385, *386*, 470

INDEX I-15

Supreme Court
　creation and early years, 215, 216, *217*
　Dredd Scott case, 377, 387
　and reconstruction, 489–490
　on slavery issues, 399
Susquehannocks, 74–75
Svinin, Pavel Petrovich, *241*
synagogues, *185*

Tainos (Arawaks), 23, *24*
Tallmadge Amendments, 307–308
Taney, Roger B., 387
tariff, 202
Tarleton, Benastre, 180, *180*, 181
tarring and feathering, 147, 150, *154, 156*, 208, 402
task system, 105, 106
taxation
　internal *versus* external, 142–143, 144
　resistance, 143–145
taxation without representation, 135, 139, 142
Taylor, Zachary, 365, 371, 379
tea
　cartoons, *154, 155*
　consumer culture and, 111, *112*
　taxes on, 149
Tea Act, 1773, 135, 147, 154
teaching profession, feminization of, 390
Team of Rivals (Goodwin), 455
Tecumseh (Shawnee chief), 222–223
Tejas Indians, 82
temperance, 381
Temple of the Sun (Teotihuacan), *11*
tenant farmers, 102–103
Tennent, Gilbert, 113, 114
Tennessee, 475
　Civil War in, 451–453, *463*
　secession, 416
　slavery in, 188
Tenochtitlan, 10, 25, 26
Tenskwatawa (Shawnee prophet), 222, 223
Tenure of Office Act, 478
Teotihuacan, 8, *11*
tepee, *17*
terraced agriculture, 7, *7*
Texas
　annexation of, 359, 373
　maps, *81*
　as republic, 358
　secession, 411
　slavery, 360
　Spaniards in, *81*, 82, 89
Thames, Battle of, 223
Thirteenth Amendment, 454, 455
Thoughts on Government (Adams), 189–190
"three-fifths clause," 192, 194, 226, 307
Three Sovereigns for Sarah (film), 88
Tierra del Fuego, 4
Tikal (Mayan city), 8
Tilden, Samuel J., 490
Tillotson, John, 110
Tippecanoe, Battle of, 223
Tlaxcalans, 26
tobacco
　depiction of, *84*
　in Jamestown, 47
　unfree labor production of, 54
　in Virginia, 48, 106
　in West Indies, 52
Toleration Act, 1649, 60
Toltecs, 8
tomatoes, 33–34
Tom Thumb, *279*
Tories, 83
Touro Synagogue, Newport, R.I., *185*
town meetings, 57, 86, 118, 143–144
Townshend, Charles, 143
Townshend crisis, 1767-1770, 135, 143–145, 149, 150, 156
Townshend Revenue Act, 1767, 135, 143, 148, 153–154
trade
　domestic, 231, 241–242
　French Revolutionary Wars, 235–236
　international, 231, 233, 256
　maritime, 231, 235–236
　New York City, 231
Trafalgar, Battle of, 219
transcontinental railroad, 487
transportation
　Erie Canal, 240, *242*
　federal funding of, 305–06, 312, 333–334
　market economy and, 239–242
　railroad development, 240
　steamboat development, 240
　travel time, *244*
transportation routes, *391*
Travel by Stagecoach Near Trenton, New Jersey (...), *241*
treason (defined), 216
treasury notes, 423
Treaty of Ghent, 226, 228
Treaty of Guadalupe Hidalgo, 364
Treaty of Paris, 185, 189
Treaty of Washington, 482
Trent Affair, 425
Trenton-Princeton Campaign, 169–170
Tres Zapotes (Olmec city), 7–8
Truax, Susanna, *112*
Tsenacommacah ("our land"), 47, 49
Tubman, Harriet, *371*
Tula (Toltec city), 8, 10, 13
Turner, Nat, 272
12 Years a Slave, 274
Twenty Negro Law, 445
Tyler, John, 358–359

Ulrich, Laurel Thatcher, 237
Uncle Tom's Cabin (Stowe), 345, 370, *372*
underground railroad, 369
unfree labor, 31, 54
unicameral legislatures, 190
Union army hospital, *447*
Union army strength, *464*
Unionist sentiment areas in South, 398
Union supply base, City Point, Va., *458*
Unitarians, 110
United Colonies, 157
United States
　capital, establishment of, 204
　creation of, 126, 206
　early years (post-Revolution), 185–197
　economic conditions, 192–193
　foreign policy, 207, 208, 209, 211–213
　foundation for, 175
　government, establishment of, 202–206
　growth, 354
　Indian policy, 208, 209
　maritime rights, 209, 222, 226
　Napoleonic Wars impact on, 218–228
　population, *191*
　territorial gains, 353
　trade policy, 221
universal male suffrage, 479
University of Pennsylvania, 115
upward mobility, 397
urban cultures, 7–8, 11–12, 13, 14–15
urban societies, 6–7
U.S.-Canadian border, 228
U.S. Colored Infantry, 4th, *453*
U.S. economy
　depression, 487

U.S. Sanitary Commission, 447
USS *Constitution* (ship), 227
USS *Essex* (ship), 227
U.S. v. Cruikshank, 490
U.S. v. Reese, 490
Utes, 71, 78

Vallandigham, Clement L., 444
Valley Forge, 170
Valley of Fire, Las Vegas, Nev., *7*
Valley of Mexico, 5, *10*
Van Buren, Martin, 358
Van Rensselaer, Killian, 44
Vaudreuil, Pierre de Rigaud de, 125, 127
Veracruz, Mexico, 25
Vergennes, Charles Gravier, Comte de, 172
Vermont, 150
Verrazano, Giovanni da, 38
Vesey, Denmark, 272
Vespucci, Amerigo, 23
Vicksburg campaign, 444, 451, *451*
Viking warriors, 15
Vinland, 15
violence
    against African Americans, 479, 481
    and voter intimidation, 489, 490
violent conflict, 1850s, 383–385
Virginia
    in Civil War, 457
    constitution, 190
    currency, 139
    founding and early years, 47–49
    government, 83–84
    homogenous society, 60
    Indian war, 74–75
    maps, *50, 51*
    religion in, 185–186
    in Revolutionary War, 182–185, *184*
    secession, 416
    slavery in, 53, 186
    U.S. Constitution debates in, 195
Virginia Company, 46–47
Virginia Company charter, *50*
Virginia Plan, 194
Virginia Resolves, 212
Virginia Tobacco Inspection Act, 1730, 118
virtual representation, 139, 140
voluntaristic ethic, 93

Wade-Davis reconstruction bill, 470
Walker, William, 372
Walpole, Sir Robert, 118
Wampanoags, 73

war, laws of, 462
war for North America, 122–130
War Hawks, 221, 222
War of 1812, 221–222, 223–226, *224,* 228
    conclusion of, 231
    Second Bank of the United States and, 304
War of Jenkin's Ear, 120
War of the Spanish Succession, 93
Warren, Elizabeth, 173
Warren, Mercy Otis, 149
Wars of Religion, 38
The War That Made America (film), 126
Washington, D.C., 204, 224, *226*
Washington, George
    army reviewed by, *209*
    cabinet, 203
    at Constitutional Convention, 1787, *196*
    description of, 205
    at end of Revolutionary War, 185
    foreign policy, 207, 209, 211
    in French-Indian War, 124, 126
    home, 102
    Indian policy, 208
    musical portrayals of, 173
    as president, 201, 202, *203,* 211
    in Revolutionary War, 160, *167,* 168, 169, 178, 179, 180, 181, 182, 184
    statues and busts, *187*
    as surveyor, 121
    in uniform, *101*
Washington, John, 74
Washington, Lawrence, 120
water-rights movement (Bolivia), 32
Watling's Island, Bahamas, 23
Wayne, John, 360
Weber, Max, 232
Webster, Daniel, 368
Wentworth, Benning, 118
Wesley, John, 113, 152
West (U.S.), *210*
West, Benjamin, *130,* 149
West Africans, 19, 21
western Europe, 16–17
western frontiers, 66, 97
Western Hemisphere, 24
West Indies
    colonies, *52*
    government, 60
    slavery in, 52–53, 89, 104, 150
West New Jersey (colony), 64–65
West Point military academy, 214, 418

West Virginia, 418
westward expansion
    after French-Indian War, 130
    after War of 1812, 228
    colonial era, 93
    householder autonomy and, 102, 103
    land claims during Revolution, *188*
    Louisiana Purchase role in, 216–217
    Native American preventive measures and response to, 121, 175
    in Revolution era and beyond, 187–189, *191*
Wheatley, Phyllis, 152, *153*
Wheelwright, Esther, 93–94, *94*
Whig Party, 303–304, 379
Whigs, 83
Whiskey Rebellion, 208, *209*
White Eyes (Delaware leader), 175
Whitefield, George, 113–114, 115, 130, 152
white supremacy, 76, 97, 398, 472
Whitney, Eli, 258–259
Whittier, John Greenleaf, 344
wigs, men's, 111
wigwam, *17*
Wilderness, Battle of, *456*
Wilkes, Charles, 425
Wilkes, John, 145, 157, 176
William, King, 87
William and Mary College, 115
William of Orange, 85
Williams, Eunice, 93
Williams, Roger, 56–57
Williamsburg, Va., *117*
Wilmot Proviso, 363–364, 374
Winay Wayna, terraces of, *7*
Winthrop, John, 54
Wolfe, James, 127, 128, 129, *130*
woman suffrage movement, 480
women
    American independence impact on, 185, 186–187
    anglicizing role of, 103
    and consumer revolution, 111
    education, 187
    liberty and, 149
    property rights, 91, 103
    Quakers, 64
    in resistance movement, 152
    as teachers, 390
    upward mobility, 91–92
    war work, 447, *448*
women factory workers, 251

women farmers, 5, *12,* 27, 57, 233, 257
Woolman, John, 152
working-class families, 393
world history (15th century), 15–24
world war, French-Indian War as, 125, 127
Wright, John, 94
writing systems, 8
writ of haveas corpus, 440

XYZ Affair, 211–212

Yale College, 110, 115
Yamasee War, 94–95
"Yankee ingenuity," 390
Yankees (term origin), 44
Yellow Tavern, battle of, 457
Yorktown, Battle of, *167,* 173, 183, *183,* 184, *184*

Young America movement, 354
youth, idealization of, 187
Yucatán plateau, 8

Zenger, John Peter, 108